Optimizing™ Windows NT®

Optimizing™ Windows NT®

Sean K. Daily

IDG Books Worldwide, Inc.
An International Data Group Company

Foster City, CA ◆ Chicago, IL ◆ Indianapolis, IN ◆ Southlake, TX

Optimizing™ Windows NT®
Published by IDG Books Worldwide, Inc.
An International Data Group Company
919 E. Hillsdale Blvd., Suite 400
Foster City, CA 94404
www.idgbooks.com (IDG Books Worldwide Web site)

Library of Congress Catalog Card No.: 97-074804
ISBN: 0-7645-3110-7
Printed in the United States of America
10 9 8 7 6 5 4 3 2 1
1B/RZ/RS/ZX/FC
Distributed in the United States by IDG Books Worldwide, Inc.

Distributed by Macmillan Canada for Canada; by Transworld Publishers Limited in the United Kingdom; by IDG Norge Books for Norway; by IDG Sweden Books for Sweden; by Woodslane Pty. Ltd. for Australia; by Woodslane Enterprises Ltd. for New Zealand; by Longman Singapore Publishers Ltd. for Singapore, Malaysia, Thailand, and Indonesia; by Simron Pty. Ltd. for South Africa; by Toppan Company Ltd. for Japan; by Distribuidora Cuspide for Argentina; by Livraria Cultura for Brazil; by Ediciencia S.A. for Ecuador; by Addison-Wesley Publishing Company for Korea; by Ediciones ZETA S.C.R. Ltda. for Peru; by WS Computer Publishing Corporation, Inc., for the Philippines; by Unalis Corporation for Taiwan; by Contemporanea de Ediciones for Venezuela; by Computer Book & Magazine Store for Puerto Rico; by Express Computer Distributors for the Caribbean and West Indies. Authorized Sales Agent: Anthony Rudkin Associates for the Middle East and North Africa.

For general information on IDG Books Worldwide's books in the U.S., please call our Consumer Customer Service department at 800-762-2974. For reseller information, including discounts and premium sales, please call our Reseller Customer Service department at 800-434-3422.

For information on where to purchase IDG Books Worldwide's books outside the U.S., please contact our International Sales department at 415-655-3200 or fax 415-655-3295.

For information on foreign language translations, please contact our Foreign & Subsidiary Rights department at 415-655-3021 or fax 415-655-3281.

For sales inquiries and special prices for bulk quantities, please contact our Sales department at 415-655-3200 or write to the address above.

For information on using IDG Books Worldwide's books in the classroom or for ordering examination copies, please contact our Educational Sales department at 800-434-2086 or fax 817-251-8174.

For press review copies, author interviews, or other publicity information, please contact our Public Relations department at 415-655-3000 or fax 415-655-3299.

For authorization to photocopy items for corporate, personal, or educational use, please contact Copyright Clearance Center, 222 Rosewood Drive, Danvers, MA 01923, or fax 508-750-4470.

ABOUT IDG BOOKS WORLDWIDE

Welcome to the world of IDG Books Worldwide.

IDG Books Worldwide, Inc., is a subsidiary of International Data Group, the world's largest publisher of computer-related information and the leading global provider of information services on information technology. IDG was founded more than 25 years ago and now employs more than 8,500 people worldwide. IDG publishes more than 275 computer publications in over 75 countries (see listing below). More than 60 million people read one or more IDG publications each month.

Launched in 1990, IDG Books Worldwide is today the #1 publisher of best-selling computer books in the United States. We are proud to have received eight awards from the Computer Press Association in recognition of editorial excellence and three from *Computer Currents'* First Annual Readers' Choice Awards. Our best-selling *...For Dummies®* series has more than 30 million copies in print with translations in 30 languages. IDG Books Worldwide, through a joint venture with IDG's Hi-Tech Beijing, became the first U.S. publisher to publish a computer book in the People's Republic of China. In record time, IDG Books Worldwide has become the first choice for millions of readers around the world who want to learn how to better manage their businesses.

Our mission is simple: Every one of our books is designed to bring extra value and skill-building instructions to the reader. Our books are written by experts who understand and care about our readers. The knowledge base of our editorial staff comes from years of experience in publishing, education, and journalism — experience we use to produce books for the '90s. In short, we care about books, so we attract the best people. We devote special attention to details such as audience, interior design, use of icons, and illustrations. And because we use an efficient process of authoring, editing, and desktop publishing our books electronically, we can spend more time ensuring superior content and spend less time on the technicalities of making books.

You can count on our commitment to deliver high-quality books at competitive prices on topics you want to read about. At IDG Books Worldwide, we continue in the IDG tradition of delivering quality for more than 25 years. You'll find no better book on a subject than one from IDG Books Worldwide.

John Kilcullen
CEO
IDG Books Worldwide, Inc.

Steven Berkowitz
President and Publisher
IDG Books Worldwide, Inc.

Eighth Annual Computer Press Awards 1992

Ninth Annual Computer Press Awards 1993

Tenth Annual Computer Press Awards 1994

Eleventh Annual Computer Press Awards 1995

IDG Books Worldwide, Inc., is a subsidiary of International Data Group, the world's largest publisher of computer-related information and the leading global provider of information services on information technology. International Data Group publishes over 275 computer publications in over 75 countries. Sixty million people read one or more International Data Group publications each month. International Data Group's publications include: **ARGENTINA:** Buyer's Guide, Computerworld Argentina, PC World Argentina; **AUSTRALIA:** Australian Macworld, Australian PC World, Australian Reseller News, Computerworld, IT Casebook, Network World, Publish, Webmaster; **AUSTRIA:** Computerwelt Osterreich, Networks Austria, PC Tip Austria; **BANGLADESH:** PC World Bangladesh; **BELARUS:** PC World Belarus; **BELGIUM:** Data News; **BRAZIL:** Annuário de Informática, Computerworld, Connections, Macworld, PC Player, PC World, Publish, Reseller News, Supergamepower; **BULGARIA:** Computerworld Bulgaria, Network World Bulgaria, PC & MacWorld Bulgaria; **CANADA:** CIO Canada, Client/Server World, ComputerWorld Canada, InfoWorld Canada, NetworkWorld Canada, WebWorld; **CHILE:** Computerworld Chile, PC World Chile; **COLOMBIA:** Computerworld Colombia, PC World Colombia; **COSTA RICA:** PC World Centro America; **THE CZECH AND SLOVAK REPUBLICS:** Computerworld Czechoslovakia, Macworld Czech Republic, PC World Czechoslovakia; **DENMARK:** Communications World Danmark, Computerworld Danmark, Macworld Danmark, PC World Danmark, Techworld Denmark; **DOMINICAN REPUBLIC:** PC World Republica Dominicana; **ECUADOR:** PC World Ecuador; **EGYPT:** Computerworld Middle East, PC World Middle East; **EL SALVADOR:** PC World Centro America; **FINLAND:** MikroPC, Tietoverkko, Tietoviikko; **FRANCE:** Distributique, Hebdo, Info PC, Le Monde Informatique, Macworld, Reseaux & Telecoms, WebMaster France; **GERMANY:** Computer Partner, Computerwoche, Computerwoche Extra, Computerwoche FOCUS, Global Online, Macwelt, PC Welt; **GREECE:** Amiga Computing, GamePro Greece, Multimedia World; **GUATEMALA:** PC World Centro America; **HONDURAS:** PC World Centro America; **HONG KONG:** Computerworld Hong Kong, PC World Hong Kong, Publish in Asia; **HUNGARY:** ABCD CD-ROM, Computerworld Szamitastechnika, Internetto online Magazine, PC World Hungary, PC-X Magazin Hungary; **ICELAND:** Tolvuheimur PC World Island; **INDIA:** Information Communications World, Information Systems Computerworld, PC World India, Publish in Asia; **INDONESIA:** InfoKomputer PC World, Komputek Computerworld, Publish in Asia; **IRELAND:** ComputerScope, PC Live!; **ISRAEL:** Macworld Israel, People & Computers/Computerworld; **ITALY:** Computerworld Italia, Macworld Italia, Networking Italia, PC World Italia; **JAPAN:** DTP World, Macworld Japan, Nikkei Personal Computing, OS/2 World Japan, SunWorld Japan, Windows NT World, Windows World Japan; **KENYA:** PC World East African; **KOREA:** Hi-Tech Information, Macworld Korea, PC World Korea; **MACEDONIA:** PC World Macedonia; **MALAYSIA:** Computerworld Malaysia, PC World Malaysia, Publish in Asia; **MALTA:** PC World Malta; **MEXICO:** Computerworld Mexico, PC World Mexico; **MYANMAR:** PC World Myanmar; **NETHERLANDS:** Computer! Totaal, LAN Internetworking Magazine, LAN World Buyers Guide, Macworld Netherlands, Net, WebWereld; **NEW ZEALAND:** Absolute Beginners Guide and Plain & Simple Series, Computer Buyer, Computer Industry Directory, Computerworld New Zealand, MTB, Network World, PC World New Zealand; **NICARAGUA:** PC World Centro America; **NORWAY:** Computerworld Norge, CW Rapport, Datamagasinet, Financial Rapport, Kursguide Norge, Macworld Norge, Multimediaworld Norge, PC World Ekspress Norge, PC World Nettverk, PC World Norge, PC World ProduktGuide Norge; **PAKISTAN:** Computerworld Pakistan; **PANAMA:** PC World Panama; **PEOPLE'S REPUBLIC OF CHINA:** China Computer Users, China Computerworld, China InfoWorld, China Telecom World Weekly, Computer & Communication, Electronic Design China, Electronics Today, Electronics Weekly, Game Software, PC World China, Popular Computer Week, Software Weekly, Software World, Telecom World; **PERU:** Computerworld Peru, PC World Profesional Peru, PC World SoHo Peru; **PHILIPPINES:** Click!, Computerworld Philippines, PC World Philippines, Publish in Asia; **POLAND:** Computerworld Poland, Computerworld Special Report Poland, Cyber, Macworld Poland, Networld Poland, PC World Komputer; **PORTUGAL:** Cerebro/PC World, Computerworld/Correio Informático, Dealer World Portugal, Mac*In/PC*In Portugal, Multimedia World; **PUERTO RICO:** PC World Puerto Rico; **ROMANIA:** Computerworld Romania, PC World Romania, Telecom Romania; **RUSSIA:** Computerworld Russia, Mir PK, Publish, Seti; **SINGAPORE:** Computerworld Singapore, PC World Singapore, Publish in Asia; **SLOVENIA:** Monitor; **SOUTH AFRICA:** Computing SA, Network World SA, Software World SA; **SPAIN:** Communicaciones World España, Computerworld España, Dealer World España, Macworld España, PC World España; **SRI LANKA:** Infolink PC World; **SWEDEN:** CAP&Design, Computer Sweden, Corporate Computing Sweden, Internetworld Sweden, it.branschen, Macworld Sweden, MaxiData Sweden, MikroDatorn, Nätverk & Kommunikation, PC World Sweden, PCaktiv, Windows World Sweden; **SWITZERLAND:** Computerworld Schweiz, Macworld Schweiz, PCtip; **TAIWAN:** Computerworld Taiwan, Macworld Taiwan, NEW ViSiON/Publish, PC World Taiwan, Windows World Taiwan; **THAILAND:** Publish in Asia, Thai Computerworld; **TURKEY:** Computerworld Turkiye, Macworld Turkiye, Network World Turkiye, PC World Turkiye; **UKRAINE:** Computerworld Kiev, Multimedia World Ukraine, PC World Ukraine; **UNITED KINGDOM:** Acorn User UK, Amiga Action UK, Amiga Computing UK, Apple Talk UK, Computing, Macworld, Parents and Computers UK, PC Advisor, PC Home, PSX Pro, The WEB; **UNITED STATES:** Cable in the Classroom, CIO Magazine, Computerworld, DOS World, Federal Computer Week, GamePro Magazine, InfoWorld, I-Way, Macworld, Network World, PC Games, PC World, Publish, Video Event, THE WEB Magazine, and WebMaster; online webzines: JavaWorld, NetscapeWorld, and SunWorld Online; **URUGUAY:** InfoWorld Uruguay; **VENEZUELA:** Computerworld Venezuela, PC World Venezuela; and **VIETNAM:** PC World Vietnamz. 3/24/97

Credits

ACQUISITIONS EDITOR
Anne Hamilton

DEVELOPMENT EDITORS
William Sullivan
Susannah Pfalzer

TECHNICAL EDITOR
Allen Wyatt

COPY EDITORS
Rich Adin
Carolyn Welch

PRODUCTION COORDINATOR
Tom Debolski

BOOK DESIGNERS
Jim Donohue
Kurt Krames

GRAPHICS AND PRODUCTION SPECIALISTS
Mario F. Amador
Shannon Miller
Elsie Yim

QUALITY CONTROL SPECIALISTS
Mick Arellano
Mark Schumann

ILLUSTRATOR
Joan Carol

PROOFREADER
Christine Sabooni

INDEXER
Liz Cunningham

About the Author

Sean Daily is a Microsoft Certified Systems Engineer (MCSE) and president of iNTellinet Solutions, a network consulting/integration firm and Microsoft Solutions Provider located in Santa Rosa, California. Sean is also a contributing editor to *Windows NT* magazine, author of several Windows NT books, and a frequent speaker at industry conferences and events. When not writing or consulting, he can usually be found outside pursuing one of his other passions, which include motorcycles, rollerblade hockey, snowboarding, mountain biking, and tournament paintball. He can be reached via Internet e-mail at `sean@ntsol.com` or `sean@cmez.com`.

For Stephanie and Craig

Foreword

Ever since the first computers appeared in research institutions and commercial laboratories, performance has been of paramount concern. Buying a computer system, whether you are an individual or a large corporation, is a nontrivial investment, making it necessary to try and extract the highest return on hardware and software as possible. Of course, the return on a computer's investment is measured in terms of its usability and performance, two metrics that are many times inextricably tied together.

Computer hardware is a generation old the moment it hits the market, since new releases of processors, memory, and disks are entering production every day. Even though hardware and software theoretically remain usable for decades, obsolescence makes computers worthless in far less time. While a computer doesn't change, changes in the environment that they live in makes them outdated. These changes come in the form of hardware advances, new operating systems that are designed to take advantage of new hardware, new software that is compatible only with new operating systems, and the increasing expectations of users and customers that the new hardware and software creates.

Hardware has evolved at a pace that finds comparison in no other manufacturing field. Processor speeds and disk sizes double every two years while the cost of memory continues to decrease. In 1995 a $2500 personal computer had 16MB of memory, a 2GB hard drive, and a 150MHz Pentium processor. Today, the same money will get you a 266MHz Pentium II with 32MB of memory and 6GB of disk storage. 150MHz processors have already fallen off the bottom of the low-end with the cheapest new consumer models shipping with 200MHz Pentiums with MMX technology.

As standard hardware speeds, disk capacities, and memory sizes grow, new software becomes more packed with new features as well as interface bells and whistles that always seem to require more hardware performance than are provided in the platforms that are mainstream at the time the software is released. Operating systems are no exception. In early 1995 the most popular personal computer operating system, Windows 3.11, ran well on a computer with 4MB of memory and 500MB of disk space, complete with an assortment of standard applications. Windows NT, the up-and-coming heir to the personal computer O/S throne, today requires 64MB of memory and at least 3GB of memory to shine. And the trend will continue.

What makes that 150MHz Pentium running Windows 3.11 from 1995 a dinosaur now is the increasing demands of users. Software is no longer being designed for Windows 3.11 and the solutions that worked two years ago no long meet the needs for increased capacity, connectivity, scalability, robustness, and inter-operability required today. In some sense each side in the hardware/software evolution symbiosis contributes through its advances to making the other side outdated, with user expectation and the changing roles of computers serving as an outside catalyst.

Even though computers have evolved through hundreds of generations of software and hardware in the past decades, the science of performance tuning lags far behind. Today, just as 10 years or 20 years ago, tools to measure performance are essentially the same. And, like 20 years ago, there are no general-purpose performance tuners or advisors. In fact, there are virtually no tuners or advisors that even address specific application environments, such as database or file serving.

Thus, the responsibilities of a system administrator to make use of every CPU cycle and disk revolution are no easier than they were before. In addition, administrators are not only required to ensure that applications are installed, configured, and work reliably, they must also fight the challenge to keep a computer performing at higher and higher levels in an effort to combat obsolescence – a challenge that grows as fast or faster than the computer industry evolves.

The fact that computers are also becoming more complex, with more and more types of hardware, software, and standards, means that identifying, locating, and understanding the tools and techniques available for performance monitoring and tuning are also becoming harder. For example, a new Windows NT user or administrator might be aware of the Performance Monitor utility that is included with NT's base distribution, but there is no guidance provided on how to use the tool, how to interpret its myriad objects and counters, or how to adjust system parameters or hardware configuration to remove bottlenecks.

Windows NT is a powerful and complex operating system that is being widely deployed in a range of environments unequalled in the history of operating systems. It is used for applications ranging from enterprise-level database and file servers, to departmental CPU servers, to desktop publishing, to laptop business use. No one performance tool, technique, or trick will address the different goals of these different environments.

What is needed to manage the performance of any NT system effectively is a thorough understanding of the basic NT performance issues and tuning techniques. This book serves to fill this need. In assembling tried and true methods for measuring, understanding, and enhancing performance, the chapters here will serve as a general-purpose tuning aid that will simplify your job as an NT user or administrator trying to get the most from your investment.

No person is better qualified for compiling and presenting this information than Sean Daily, who has years of experience in the area of NT performance optimization. He has written extensively on subjects related to performance in many articles published in *Windows NT* magazine, and makes his livelihood helping companies, small to large, make their NT systems perform as they should. I have confidence that every morsel of knowledge, insight, and technique you gain in these pages will make your investment in NT a more rewarding one.

Mark Russinovich, Ph.D.
September 7, 1997
Nashua, NH

Preface

Optimizing Windows NT condenses many years of research and hands-on experience with Windows NT. It's designed to serve as a comprehensive guide to maximizing NT performance for endusers and system administrators alike. This book pushes beyond the standard "dry" technical NT reference manuals and discusses various aspects of the Windows NT operating system in ways that are both informative and entertaining.

Who Should Read This Book

To get the most out of this book, you should be an intermediate to advanced NT user, and should understand basic NT concepts such as the Registry, managing services, and installing drivers. You'll find this book a particularly helpful ally if you fall into any of the following categories:

- Corporate Information Systems (IS) and network administrators responsible for the evaluation, design, implementation, and administration of Windows NT systems and networks
- Associate systems administrators responsible for basic management of Windows NT servers within their organization
- Windows NT power users who use Windows NT in government, business, or educational environments
- Graphics or CAD professionals using Windows NT systems as graphics workstations
- Windows NT users or purchasing department personnel responsible for the selection of new NT systems or upgrades
- Developers who write Windows NT–based applications

What We'll Cover

This book teaches you how to optimize and troubleshoot both Windows NT server and workstation computers by helping you understand how NT operates and where performance bottlenecks can occur. This book shows you quick ways to identify NT problems and provides methods for fixing them. You'll soon be on your way to an optimal NT environment.

Specifically, this book is designed to help you develop the following skills and knowledge:

- How to determine the proper hardware requirements for your Windows NT system(s) based on their intended use
- Understanding Windows NT's core technologies and architecture
- Understanding the different hardware technologies available on the market and which are best suited for use with Windows NT computers
- How to identify and eliminate bottlenecks in the various subsystems of Windows NT networks, servers, and desktop computers
- Understanding how different system activities affect NT's performance
- How to prepare for trouble and prevent data loss
- Awareness of third-party utility applications currently available that assist in the NT optimization process

How This Book Is Written

Most people don't read books from cover to cover (especially we computer people, come to think of it), so I've intentionally designed *Optimizing Windows NT* in a modular fashion that lets you skip around between chapters as you please. Each chapter is a self-contained entity and focuses on a different aspect of NT optimization; that way, you can read the chapters in whatever order you like. The only possible exception is Part I. Although not a requirement, I do recommend that you read the first three chapters (Part I) first, because they provide some basic information about NT's design and will help you gain a better understanding of its features and advantages. Part I also introduces you to the tools that you'll use throughout the book to implement recommended changes. After that, you can go off on whatever tangents you like, methodically eliminating those bottlenecks one at a time!

To help you explore this book, here's a summary of what to expect. I've divided *Optimizing Windows NT* into four main parts, as follows:

Part I: Getting Started with NT Optimization

Part I introduces you to Windows NT's feature set and the basic principles involved in performance optimization. Also introduced are NT's system monitoring and configuration tools. In addition, Chapter 2 provides comprehensive, component-by-component coverage of the best hardware available for your Windows NT system. This chapter lists the different choices available in each category and provides technical comparisons.

Part II: Tuning the NT Subsystems

The chapters in this part provide in-depth discussions of each of NT's major subsystems, as well as tips and techniques for increasing their performance. Here, we'll cover techniques for monitoring and optimizing NT's memory, disk, printing, and application subsystems.

Part III: Optimizing Your NT Network

Part III presents the other major component of the Windows NT operating system: networking. In this Part, we'll walk through step-by-step guidelines on how to optimize the network performance of Windows NT servers and workstations and discuss the tools you can use to monitor and manage this performance. In addition, Chapter 11 gives special coverage to the issue of optimizing Windows NT Internet servers; especially those acting as proxy and/or Web servers.

Appendixes

Optimizing Windows NT also contains several appendixes with valuable information for the reader, including summaries of useful Performance Monitor counter objects and Registry modifications discussed within the book, a comprehensive listing of the contents of the book's accompanying CD-ROM, and additional sources of Windows NT-related information.

Typographic Conventions

Optimizing Windows NT uses special typographic conventions to represent different kinds of information. For example, a certain text font indicates commands to be typed at the keyboard, another represents screen output displayed by NT, and so forth. I maintain a consistent usage throughout the book, making it easier for you to follow the information being presented. Specifically, here are the various typographical conventions this book uses:

Typestyle	Meaning
Bold	Bold typeface indicates text that you are to type using the keyboard.
Underlined	Letters are underlined when they can be used as a "hotkey" to select particular screen options such as a menu, button, or dialog box field. For example, pressing "U" would select a menu choice listed as "Underline" if it were available in a menu.
Italics	Italicized text is used whenever a term or concept appears for the first time, or when a part of the text is meant to be replaced with specific data. For example, in "\\SERVER*sharename*," *sharename* is a variable that you should replace with specific information.
`Monospaced`	Monospaced text denotes two types of text: screen output generated by Windows NT or applications, and program code listings.

Special Book Elements

Throughout *Optimizing Windows NT*, you'll see special elements within the text that provide extra information. Examples include items such as Tips, Notes, Cautions, and Sidebars, as follows, and are described using the format of the element itself.

These elements provide tips or procedures that are helpful in managing your Windows NT system.

Sidebars Are Informative

Sidebars give you information that is either an expansion of or tangential to the current topic being discussed.

Notes give you interesting or additional information about the current topic.

Cautions warn you about potential hazards or problems related to the current topic.

Cool product tips clue you in about products that enhance the functionality or usefulness of Windows NT. They contain a general description of the product in addition to information about the product's vendor.

Additional info source elements provide a pointer or recommendation to an external source of information related to the current topic, such as a Web site/Internet HTML document, book, CD-ROM, or video.

On the CD elements reference a software utility or application contained on the CD-ROM accompanying the book, in sections of the book covering topics related to that utility or application.

Cross-references point you to other places in the book that provide information related to the current topic.

Acknowledgments

"Many Bothans died to bring us this information."
— Mon Mothma, *The Return of the Jedi*

Acknowledgments — where to begin? A book of this size represents the hard work and efforts of many people other than just the author. This work contains the blood, sweat, and tears (ok, ok, so the tears were mine) of a number of highly dedicated folks. I would therefore like to acknowledge the following parties whose efforts were invaluable in making this book a reality:

Stephanie Evans, whose undying support and patience in allowing me to overturn our lives so that I could write this book are more appreciated than she'll ever know. If it weren't for her, this book wouldn't exist.

Kirk Erichsen, whose hardware knowledge is second to none, and whose dedication to squeezing every last drop of performance out of every system I find quite admirable. In addition to doing research outlines for several chapters, Kirk wrote Chapters 9 and 10 on NT networking concepts.

Bill Sullivan, Anne Hamilton, Susannah Pfalzer, and all of the graphics and production people at IDG Books Worldwide; it has been thoroughly enjoyable to work with all of them on this project.

Bill McLaren, who wrote Chapter 11 on Internet server optimization.

Eli Caul, Dane Jasper, and the rest of the SONIC crew, who provided me with the Internet bandwidth to get the job done, and with those occasional but oh-so-helpful stress-relieving Quake matches.

All of the vendors who provided the lab equipment that enabled me to test and document the various procedures described in this book. These include DeskStation Technologies (awesome Alpha machines!), Mylex Corporation (DAC-PDU960 RAID controller), Distributing Processing Technology (SmartRAID PM3334U RAID controller), Seagate Technology (Cheetah 10,000RPM SCSI drives, the fastest around), Adaptec (single and quad-channel 10/100MBps Ethernet adapters and AHA-3940U/UW SCSI adapters), Cinco Networks (NetXray network monitoring software), Logi-Soft (Virtual CD), Sunbelt Software (various NT utilities), and Granite Digital (SCSI diagnostic cables and terminators, keeping those SCSI subsystems stable!).

Various members of Windows NT-related Internet mailing lists and newsgroups who contributed their own tips and tricks, including David Cross, Ed Jay, Frank Coloccia, Marlin Gubser, Shane Zettelmier, and David Rawling.

The inventor of the café mocha, whomever you may be; my high-octane fuel of choice for late-night writing, registry hacking, and benchmarking sessions.

Contents at a Glance

Table of Contents

Appendixes

Part 1

Getting Started with NT Optimization

Chapter 1

Windows NT 101

WINDOWS NT IS A unique and powerful operating system. Right out of the box, Windows NT offers you a high degree of performance and a wealth of capabilities and features. These features can be categorized into six areas: reliability, performance, portability, compatibility, scalability, and security.

To better understand Windows NT, we'll examine these capabilities and features more closely, and find out what they mean and how they're implemented inside Windows NT.

Reliability

Windows NT is an exceptionally robust operating system that provides superior reliability. This particular aspect of NT makes it an excellent foundation for running mission-critical applications, and makes it a direct competitor to workstation-level operating systems such as UNIX. NT's reliability makes it an especially ideal client workstation and network server, because both systems need to avoid downtime. Reliability in Windows NT takes many forms, from its inherent memory protection to its native fault tolerance capabilities.

Memory protection

Windows NT prevents user applications from interfering with NT's core operating system services (known collectively as the Windows NT Executive) by running these services in a protected layer called *Kernel Mode*. To understand how and why NT's Kernel Mode is protected under NT's design, we must first understand a little about the "ring" protection model used in modern processor design. In the ring architecture model, a CPU (Central Processing Unit) defines different levels or "rings" of execution, each with its own level of privilege and protection. Both Intel and RISC-based processor designs support this design, with RISC-based CPUs supporting two rings, and Intel-based CPUs supporting four. To effectively support both RISC and Intel CPUs, Windows NT uses only two rings in its design, Rings 0 and 3. Of these, Ring 0 (also known as *supervisor mode*) is the most highly protected ring in which an application or service can run. It is physically impossible for applications running in Ring 3 to interfere with those running in Ring 0.

As we examine Windows NT's architecture more closely, we see that NT's Kernel Mode and its services operate in the processor's Ring 0, whereas user applications (running in NT's *User Mode*) run in the processor's Ring 3. This is what prevents user applications from interfering with core NT operating system services. Instead, these applications are forced to communicate with NT's low-level services using a message-passing methodology: no direct physical access of the memory space used by these services is allowed. This design makes it virtually impossible for user applications to violate the integrity of the operating system. Although this method of communication between processes provides an enormous increase in overall system reliability, it also incurs some performance penalties due to the overhead of the continual message passing between User and Kernel modes. Each transition from one mode to the other requires a processor context-switch, which in turn burns additional CPU cycles.

In addition to being isolated from the operating system itself, individual 32-bit Windows applications are also protected from one another. This is because each application running under NT is capable of running in its own private address space. This prevents one program from overwriting another's memory space accidentally, the most common cause of system lockups. NT's system architecture is depicted in Figure 1-1.

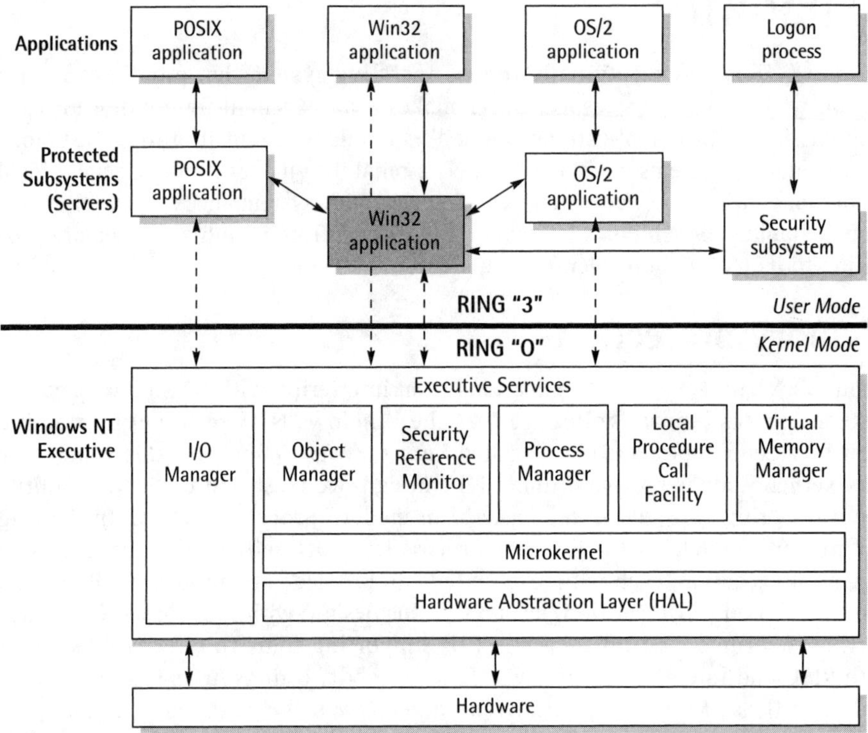

Figure 1-1: The Windows NT System Architecture.

32-bit flat memory model

As a true 32-bit operating system, Windows NT provides a *32-bit flat memory model* that allows the operating system to access 4GB (over 4 billion bytes) of memory, and individual applications up to 2GB of private address space. As mentioned earlier, this address space is also private to each application, keeping individual applications physically protected from one another in memory.

The next version of Windows NT, version 5.0, will have a 64-bit memory model that will take better advantage of the capabilities of newer 64-bit processors such as the DEC Alpha and the upcoming "Merced" Processor from Intel.

Preemptive multitasking

Windows NT uses *preemptive multitasking*, a multitasking methodology that ensures all running applications adequate access to the system's CPU(s). It also prevents individual applications from monopolizing the CPU or halting the entire system should an application become unstable or cease execution. This allows NT to continue functioning in circumstances that would bring other operating systems to a grinding halt.

Although NT offers superior reliability, a recent discovery was made that challenged the long-standing assertion that the NT O/S is impervious to User Mode applications. Dr. Mark Russinovich, a Windows NT developer and author, uncovered a flaw in NT that was exploited using a tiny application called NTCrash. When this program is run, it makes continual random calls to either of two Win32 APIs (Application Programming Interfaces), quickly causing the system to crash. After bringing the matter to Microsoft's attention, Microsoft responded by releasing Windows NT 4.0 Service Pack 2, which effectively closes the "holes" found by Dr. Russinovich (for more information, see the NT Internals web site at: `http://www.ntinternals.com/`).

Robust, transactional file system (NTFS)

Windows NT's native transactional file system (NTFS) is an advanced and extremely robust file system that provides superior reliability. As a transactional file system, NT is able to reverse incomplete or invalid write operations that occur as a result of hardware or software failure (for example, a power outage in the middle of writing a file). As a result of this design, NT is far less susceptible to corruption or damage by errant applications than other file systems.

Fault tolerance

Windows NT also includes significant *fault tolerance* features that increase its reliability. Fault tolerance refers to a system's capability to withstand various kinds of failures or malfunctions. Windows NT includes several features that help to protect the computer and its data in the event of such failures. The first is its software support (in NT Server) for several types of RAID (Redundant Array of Independent Disks), which offer data-redundancy on hard disks using technologies such as disk mirroring and duplexing (RAID Level 1), or disk striping with parity (RAID Level 5). With RAID, drive information can be recovered in the event of a failed hard disk. In addition to fault-tolerant RAID levels, NT also supports RAID 0, which offers no fault tolerance features but does provide for faster disk performance by striping data across multiple hard drives, which can be accessed more quickly than a single, larger drive.

NTFS also includes its own internal fault tolerance capabilities, by maintaining a log of filewrite operations that can be used to recover an NTFS volume's integrity in the event of power loss or other abnormal system termination. In addition to disk fault tolerance features, NT also provides fault tolerance in the form of Uninterruptible Power Supply (UPS) support. NT's UPS support enables the system to communicate with the UPS and perform such tasks as notifying users and automatically shutting down the system in the event of a power outage.

Performance

Although reliability is certainly an important feature of Windows NT, let's not forget that NT was also designed to be a high-performance operating system (after all, that's what we're here to discuss). In this section, we discuss some of NT's inherent performance-related features.

True 32

Windows NT was developed using 100% 32-bit code, which translates to better performance and an inherent speed advantage over operating systems such as Windows 95 that contain 16-bit technology. From low-level drivers to high-level applications, everything in Windows NT is 32-bit. User applications benefit from this because they are able to access a larger address space (Windows NT provides a virtual 4GB address space for every application – 2GB for the application and 2GB for the system) and are able to take advantage of Win32 API features such as multithreading.

Multitasking, multiprocessing, and multithreading

Performing multiple tasks simultaneously is an area in which Windows NT excels. As you already know, Windows NT uses a preemptive multitasking model that provides superior system stability. However, in addition to its reliability benefits, preemptive multitasking also offers performance benefits. Preemptive multitasking means that all running applications are executed in a smooth and even fashion, which translates into better overall system performance. In preemptive multitasking, the system retains control of the multitasking process, allocating CPU time to running processes as needed. After an application's allotted CPU time has expired, Windows NT automatically shifts control to the next application.

NT also offers a *symmetric multiprocessing* (SMP) feature similar to that found in the UNIX operating system that can take advantage of systems using multiple processors. This feature allows the operating system to become instantly more powerful by executing multiple processes and even individual threads of execution within a process across multiple CPUs.

Finally, in addition to its excellent multitasking capabilities, Windows NT also provides a multitasking-related feature called *multithreading.* A "thread" is defined as an individual series of processor instructions within a running process (user application or system service). Applications can be written to spawn multiple threads of execution for greater speed and efficiency.

Multithreading is like multitasking within an application. Normally, when individual tasks within an application are carried out, the program must wait for the process to complete before returning control to the user. This is the case with all 16-bit (and many 32-bit) Windows applications. When an application uses multithreading, an individual task can be embodied within a thread and executed independently of the main process. For example, a request to print a document in a word processing application might result in a separate thread of execution that runs independently of the main program.

RISC CPU support

NT was designed from the outset to support several different types of high-powered RISC (Reduced Instruction Set Computing) processors such as the PowerPC, DEC Alpha AXP, and MIPS CPUs. This allows Windows NT to run not only on Intel-based personal computers, but on high-performance workstation-level systems as well.

Presently, Windows NT supports all of the aforementioned RISC platforms in addition to the Intel x86 family of processors. Unfortunately, however, recent changes in the industry and announcements by Microsoft have shortened the lifetime for two of these platforms: the MIPS processor family and the PowerPC chip. Microsoft announced that future versions of Windows NT will not support these platforms. It should also be noted that the decision to discontinue support for MIPS and PowerPC has much to do with internal industry politics and very little to do with technical issues or limitations regarding the chips themselves.

Currently, it appears as though the future of RISC on NT seems to be solely in the hands of the DEC Alpha family of processors. Luckily, the prospects for the Alpha's future appear good—DEC is closely allied with Microsoft and has an enormous amount of development resources invested in Alpha technology. DEC recently released the newest member of the Alpha family, the Alpha 21164a, which offers a host of powerful features: 64-bit processing, execution of up to four CPU instructions simultaneously, a 128-bit or 256-bit data path, a 64-bit PCI bus (with a maximum throughput of 264MB/sec), a high-speed system bus capable of running at speeds of up to 133MHz, and CPU speeds of up to 500MHz (a future version will be faster yet). Why would you want to choose RISC over Intel's more popular CISC (Complex Instruction Set Computing) based chips such as the Pentium and Pentium Pro? In a word: power. The fastest DEC Alpha processor is able to deliver up to 50% higher performance for integer operations and up to 80% higher performance for floating point operations than the fastest Intel Pentium Pro processor.

Portability

In the past, operating systems were designed around a single hardware platform such as Intel's x86 family of processors. Unfortunately, this prevented the operating system from being capable of taking advantage of newer and more powerful hardware designs and chip types. Portability in NT means that it isn't tied to any single architecture or technology; it can be "ported" to different types of hardware without being completely rewritten. This is possible because most of Windows NT is written in C, a highly portable programming language that is easily ported between different system architectures. NT also offers other portability features, which are described below.

Meet HAL

Windows NT has a modular, layered design that prevents hardware dependence. The only hardware-specific code resides in a special low-level component of the Windows NT kernel called the *Hardware Abstraction Layer* (HAL). Fortunately, HAL comprises only a small percentage of the entire NT operating system, so developing new HALs to support additional CPU architectures is a relatively easy process. HAL operates at the lowest level, translating low-level operating system functions into instructions understandable by the specific hardware used in the system. This universal, modular design is also the reason NT enjoys such a diverse array of hardware support, from notebook PCs to multi-CPU superservers.

Installable file systems

Another portability feature of NT is its ability to support many different file systems. Currently, NT supports the FAT (File Allocation Table used in DOS, Windows 95, and OS/2 systems), NTFS (Native Transactional File System introduced with Windows NT), and CDFS (CD-ROM File System). However, because of NT's modular nature, support for additional file systems can be easily added in the future by simply creating new file system drivers and adding them to NT. This makes it relatively easy for NT to incorporate new technologies.

Although not an installable file system per se, it is also possible to have NT support the Macintosh file system by creating a Macintosh-compatible volume under Windows NT Server.

Compatibility

The key to the acceptance of any operating system is its ability to work with existing systems and applications. Therefore, Microsoft designed NT to run a wide variety of different applications and interact with a number of different foreign operating systems.

Application subsystem design

Windows NT is capable of running many different types of applications, including MS-DOS, Windows 3.x (Win16), Windows 95 and NT (Win32), POSIX, and OS/2 1.x character-mode applications. Again, the modular design of NT makes it possible to support additional APIs in the future by simply adding new subsystems. An OS/2 Presentation Manager subsystem is also available as a separate add-on product for Windows NT.

Windows-on-Windows (WOW) subsystem

Windows NT offers 16-bit Windows application support using a subsystem known as the *Windows-on-Windows 32* or WOW subsystem. WOW provides excellent Win16 compatibility by completely emulating a Windows 3.1 environment and offers the choice of running individual Windows 3.x applications in a shared or separate memory space. This support allows separate Win16 applications to communicate as seamlessly under NT as they did under Windows 3.x, using interprocess communications features such as DDE (Dynamic Data Exchange) and OLE (Object Linking and Embedding).

Interoperability with NetWare

Windows NT also provides excellent compatibility with Novell's NetWare network operating system. In Windows NT 4.0, this support is embodied in several components:

- NWLink, a NetWare compatible version of the IPX/SPX protocol.
- Client Services for Netware (CSNW), a native NCP (NetWare Core Protocol) client that enables NT to access both NetWare 3.x and 4.x servers.
- Gateway Services for NetWare (GSNW), a service that makes it possible (in NT Server only) to share NetWare file and print resources with non-NetWare clients.
- File and Print Services for NetWare (FPNW), a separate add-on product that enables a Windows NT Server to appear to NetWare clients as a NetWare 3.x server.
- Directory Service Manager for NetWare (DSMN), another add-on product that allows NetWare servers to participate in Windows NT's native Directory Services.

In addition to these components, the Windows NT Server product also offers additional NetWare-centric features, including the ability to import NetWare user accounts and login scripts and provide NetWare compatible log-ins and log-in scripts for NetWare clients via FPNW.

Interoperability with UNIX

Windows NT is able to communicate with UNIX systems through its native support of the TCP/IP (Transmission Control Protocol/Internet Protocol) suite, TCP/IP printing, and the inclusion of basic TCP/IP connectivity applications such as FTP (File Transmission Protocol) and Telnet. Third-party products are also available that allow NT and UNIX systems to share files on shared network volumes. In addition, both NT Workstation and NT Server include Internet/intranet services such as HTTP

(HyperText Transport Protocol), FTP, and Gopher servers (called Internet Information Server in NT Server and Peer Web Services in NT Workstation) to allow for cross-platform connectivity with UNIX and other TCP/IP-based systems.

Interoperability with Macintosh

Windows NT also offers significant support for Apple Macintosh computers. Both the Workstation and Server versions of NT support AppleTalk, the protocol used in Macintosh networks. Windows NT Server also allows for the creation of Macintosh name space on NTFS volumes to enable Mac/PC file sharing. Macintosh-related printing support in NT Server includes the ability for Macintosh systems to print to non-PostScript printers connected to the NT network, and PC users to send print jobs to PostScript printers on the AppleTalk network.

Scalability

Another important aspect of Windows NT is the fact that it is a *scalable* operating system. This means that it can be used on a wide range of systems, from personal computers to large systems with multiple processors. These systems may have very little, or nothing, in common other than that they can all run Windows NT. Here's a quick summary of NT's scalability features:

Multiplatform support

Due to its layered, microkernel architecture and use of the Hardware Abstraction Layer, Windows NT is essentially open-ended in its ability to support new and more powerful processors as they are developed. This allows the same operating system to be used on systems of virtually any size or power, with no effective limits.

Symmetric multiprocessor (SMP) support

Native support for Symmetric Multiprocessors is one of NT's key scalability features. SMP means that NT can scale as available hardware resources are increased, becoming instantly more efficient.

Scalable security model

Windows NT supports two different security models: the workgroup and domain models. Workgroups and domains provide very different levels of security (domains being the more secure), and together offer features to address the needs of small and large organizations alike. As a result, Windows NT can be used on networks as small as 2 computers or as large as 20,000 computers. The domain security model also offers several organizational submodels for organizations to choose from to manage users and resources across the enterprise.

Security

Some of NT's most important and touted features relate to security. Microsoft intended from the beginning for NT to be a secure operating system on which businesses and government could rely to protect their data. Windows NT's security goes far beyond that of previous personal computer operating systems, providing security on par with that of many minicomputer and mainframe systems. To accomplish this, NT offers several layers of system security.

Domain security model

Windows NT's domain security model is a sophisticated network access scheme that allows administrators to implement strict security regarding who receives access to what information and resources on the network. Special NT servers called *domain controllers* are responsible for authenticating user log on requests, and no user can gain access to network resources without first being authenticated by a domain controller. Security information on an NT system is stored in a special security database known as the SAM (Security Account Manager) database, which is continually replicated between all NT servers acting as domain controllers.

NTFS file system

Windows NT includes a special file system, NTFS, which complements NT's security design. NTFS is tightly integrated with NT's other security features, allowing administrators to utilize a variety of different access levels for users and users groups, down to the directory and file level. File level permissions means that individual files on NTFS volumes may be set with unique permissions, even different files residing in the same directory (folder).

Discretionary access control

Windows NT allows administrators and owners of system objects to have complete control over who gets what kinds of access to those objects (for example, a file or a printer). This type of security is known as *discretionary access control*, where the owner of a resource has discretion over who may access the resource and how. This level of security gives resource owners and system administrators an enormous amount of flexibility in controlling access to their data and resources.

Government C2 certification

Windows NT is a class C2-certified operating system. C2 is a strict government standard that defines the specific security features that must be present for use in U.S. government installations. These features must be met by any system wishing to obtain C2 status, and the system must pass a long and arduous testing process conducted by the government.

Audit trails

Windows NT allows for the tracking of many system events, including all security-related events that occur on a system. This process is known as *auditing.* These events are recorded in a log file, which may be examined by the system administrator. Auditing can reveal break-in attempts and other attempted security breaches and provides administrators a good record of who has accessed the system and how.

Ctrl-Alt-Del login feature

Part of NT's security is a feature designed to break "password grabbing" programs. These types of programs present a fake login screen to a user in hopes of capturing their username and password (for later use by some unauthorized party). In Windows NT, a user must press the Ctrl-Alt-Del keys before NT will present the login screen and allow the user to enter their name and password. You may know this key sequence as a system reboot or program shutdown command under MS-DOS and Windows 3.x/95, but in Windows NT, Ctrl-Alt-Del is used to "wake up" the Windows NT login manager and guarantees that the NT login screen is genuine and not a password-capture program. This works because software cannot be written to capture and process the Ctrl-Alt-Del keyboard sequence.

Is NT Self-Optimizing?

Microsoft touts Windows NT as a "highly self-optimizing" operating system. This is because NT offers self-optimization features that go well beyond all previous personal computer operating systems. With many operating systems, the ability to tune system performance requires arcane knowledge of special system startup files, settings, and system utilities. Under these operating systems (such as DOS and Windows 3.x), system performance depends heavily on these settings and can suffer greatly when they are improperly configured. One of Microsoft's design goals for Windows NT was to remove this dependence on user settings and create an operating system that automatically provides most users with a decent level of performance.

NT's self-optimizing features include the ability to dynamically allocate disk cache memory based on the available RAM in the system, dynamically modify the virtual memory/disk paging file to accommodate additional memory needs, and adjust application thread priorities as needed during operation. Don't be fooled into thinking that all of NT's performance-related settings are dynamically managed, however. It's important to understand that most of NT's performance-related settings were chosen by NT's designers as "median" values, ones that would provide the best average performance across a variety of systems, but which may or may not produce the optimal settings for your specific environment. To ensure you are getting the most from your system, it is important to understand these settings and how changing them will affect your system's operation.

Although NT's self-optimization features are impressive, this does not mean that additional optimization of NT is impossible. Actually, there's an inherent problem with this entire "self-optimizing" concept: it's virtually impossible to create one all-encompassing implementation of NT that will provide maximum performance for everyone. The problem is that computers play many different roles within an organization, including file server, database server, Internet/intranet server, user workstation, CAD system. In addition, some computers play more than one of these roles simultaneously. How then, do we tell NT exactly how our machine is being used, what applications it's running, and how to adjust itself to optimize performance?

Currently, Windows NT offers only a few basic configuration settings to define a computer's role and usage. In a perfect world, you would rank system functions in a "1-to-10" fashion in order of importance to help NT properly allocate its resources and optimize performance (or better yet, have it automatically figure this out based on the applications currently running). However, since no such "optimization scorecard" exists, the best you can do to obtain the best performance for your system is use the tips offered in this book in conjunction with some manual configuration. We also show you how to use Performance Monitor, an extremely powerful tool included with every copy of Windows NT, to identify system performance bottlenecks.

Comparing NT Workstation and NT Server

A good place to start when discussing NT optimization is with an explanation of the fundamental differences between the NT Workstation and NT Server products, and what impact these differences have on NT's performance. This is especially important because your choice of Server versus Workstation is likely to have a significant bearing on the performance of your system when handling different kinds of tasks.

Interestingly, there has been some controversy surrounding the issue of differences between NT Workstation and Server. The original controversy started when Microsoft announced during the last stages of NT 4.0's development that Windows NT Workstation 4.0 would be physically limited to a maximum of 10 simultaneous inbound TCP/IP-based network connections. An outcry from the Internet software development community quickly ensued, because this limitation would effectively force their customers to purchase Windows NT Server (which costs approximately three times as much as Workstation) to run their software. This in turn meant a higher overall product cost and a lower likelihood that customers would want to buy their products. After all, with Microsoft bundling a free Internet Information Server (IIS) with every copy of NT Server, why would anyone want to spend money on another product? Software vendors cried foul, and accused Microsoft of anticompetitive behavior (a complaint heard more and more frequently these days, I might add).

In response to the pressure put forth by the development and user communities, Microsoft removed the physical restriction from NT Workstation, but simultaneously reworded the license agreement to state that the user still could not *legally* exceed 10 inbound connections. Although many considered this reversal a victory against the Microsoft juggernaut, the victory was a relatively small one. As a result of the licensing change, it is still virtually impossible to deploy NT Workstation as an Internet server without violating the NT license agreement. Many companies who are developing Internet server software for NT continue to battle Microsoft on this issue.

The leader of this opposition is Tim O'Reilly, CEO of O'Reilly & Associates, a Sebastopol, CA, software developer and publishing company. When Microsoft justified its position by stating that there are "significant differences" between Windows NT Workstation and Server products, O'Reilly decided to take them to task. He immediately put Andrew Schulman, a senior editor at O'Reilly & Associates, to work on dissecting NT Server and Workstation to discover whether Microsoft's claim was true.

What Schulman found was that there is little or no difference between NT Workstation and Server. In fact, he discovered that by making a few well-placed changes to the NT Registry database, one could actually *convert* one product into the other. Apparently, NT references information in the Registry to determine which version it is and how it should configure itself. Furthermore, testing of NT Workstation systems converted to NT Server yielded virtually identical results to systems running "true" versions of NT Server. Even when confronted with this information, Microsoft continued to claim that the two products have important differences, and it continues to do so to this day.

The above information was garnered from several sources, some of which you may wish to consult for additional information. One location is O'Reilly & Associates' Web site at:

`http://software.ora.com/news/ms_internet_frame.html`

There is also additional information on the subject at the Windows NT Magazine Web site at:

`http://www.winntmag.com/`

When on the Windows NT magazine site, search on the keyword phrase "O'Reilly."

Although it may be tempting to try to use this trick to turn your Windows NT Workstation machine into a Server, this practice is not recommended for many reasons. The most important of these is that if the procedure is done incorrectly, NT will detect that the product is being tampered with and disable your system (believe it or not!). Doing so also violates the NT license agreement, and Microsoft Product Support definitely does not support the procedure. As a result, it's likely that you'd be on your own if you were to experience problems or require assistance with your NT installation. Finally, without the actual NT Server CD-ROM, you won't get the extra goodies that come with NT Server such as FrontPage and Network Monitor. In my opinion, these additional products (in addition to the peace of mind you'll have by not endangering your system with unsupported hacks) make the price difference between Workstation and Server worthwhile.

Aside from the extra software such as FrontPage bundled with Windows NT Server, the key differences between NT Workstation and Server, as claimed by Microsoft, are:

- The disk-cache flushing algorithm (known as the write-throttling feature) in NT Workstation and Server are different. NT Server's is tuned to handle heavier, server-like loads, whereas NT Workstation's is designed for desktop-oriented tasks.
- SRV.SYS, the server component of Windows NT, is said to be less pageable (i.e., able to be swapped to disk to recover memory) in NT Server than the one found in NT Workstation. This is because the expected load on this service under NT Server is higher, and NT attempts to enhance its performance by limiting the ability for the service to be paged from real RAM to virtual memory (disk).
- In Windows NT Workstation, the NT Virtual DOS Machine (VDM) or MS-DOS subsystem is preloaded into memory to increase application startup times for MS-DOS and 16-bit Windows applications that use it. By contrast, Windows NT Server does not preload the VDM because it is less likely that these types of applications will be run with any regularity on an NT Server.

TABLE 1-1 FEATURE DIFFERENCES BETWEEN NT WORKSTATION AND SERVER

Description of Feature	Exists in NT Workstation?	Exists in NT Server?
Dynamic Host Configuration Protocol (DHCP) for dynamic assignment and configuration of TCP/IP to network clients	No	Yes
Windows Internet Naming Service (WINS) for dynamic NetBIOS name resolution on TCP/IP networks	No	Yes
Single Network Logon (ability to act as Domain Controller)	No	Yes
Disk Fault Tolerance/RAID	No (RAID 0/Disk Striping only; no fault tolerance RAID levels)	Yes; RAID Levels 1 (Disk Mirroring) and 5 (Disk Striping with Parity)
Remote Access Server	Yes; limited to 1 concurrent RAS connection	Yes; up to 255 simultaneous RAS connections
Gateway Services for NetWare (GSNW)	No	Yes
Services for Macintosh (including Mac file and printing support)	No	Yes
Netlogon request authentication (used to run log on scripts for remote network clients)	No	Yes
Account Lockout Security Feature	No	Yes
Network Client Administrator (for creation of boot disk to perform over-the-network NT installations)	No	Yes
Domain Administration Tools (Server Manager/User Manager for Domains, etc.)	No (however, versions for NT Workstation are available on the NT Server CD-ROM)	Yes
RPL Support for diskless workstation booting	No	Yes

- Windows NT Server and Workstation are said to use a different number of system worker threads and blocking operation threads, which are used by the operating system to carry out important I/O (input/output) functions. Windows NT Server is tuned for faster performance of server-oriented applications and I/O operations, whereas NT Workstation is optimized for desktop applications.
- Windows NT Server offers a feature that allows you to tune it for either file and print server performance or application server performance, depending on its intended usage. This feature enables NT Server to achieve higher performance than NT Workstation on larger networks, because this feature doesn't exist in NT Workstation. However, even Microsoft admits that with networks of 10 users or less, the differences between NT Workstation and Server in this regard are virtually nonexistent.

Product modification issues aside, there are also other tangible differences in the features of Windows NT Workstation and Server. NT Server has a host of capabilities that are either enhanced versions of those found in NT Workstation, or not found in the NT Workstation product at all. Table 1-1 lists these features and compares how they're implemented in each of the two flavors of NT.

A final note: Sometimes the question of NT Workstation versus Server isn't only one of performance. Many server-oriented products such as the Microsoft BackOffice family of products, many network backup utilities, and other similar programs require Windows NT Server to install. These applications check to see which version they are being run on, and won't install if they don't find Windows NT Server running. Therefore, be sure to check the requirements of your software before purchasing your Windows NT software—you may not have a choice.

In real-world testing, the performance differences between NT Server and Workstation are fairly obvious even after spending only a short time with them. When using NT Workstation, desktop-oriented activities (such as running user applications or using various components of the NT Explorer interface) seem quicker and more responsive under Windows NT Workstation than under NT Server on the same system. This happens because NT Server purposefully deemphasizes local application processing in favor of server-related tasks such as file and network I/O operations. In addition, NT's caching and paging algorithms are tuned differently for the different activities Microsoft expects you'll perform with each product.

In a similar fashion, you'll also notice that a heavily taxed Windows NT Server running as a network server provides greater responsiveness for file, printer, and application requests from network clients than would a similarly configured system running NT Workstation. Although both operating systems share a common set of files, APIs, and general overall architecture, each is tuned differently for the roles they are intended to play.

Summary

In this chapter, we gave you a "crash course" on Windows NT's design, and its most important features and technologies. We discussed the benefits offered by NT "out of the box." We also investigated Microsoft's claim that NT is a completely self-optimizing operating system and discussed the limitations of this ability. In addition, we discussed the inherent differences between the Windows NT Server and Workstation products, and the role for which each was designed.

Chapter 2

Killer Hardware for Windows NT

ANY OPTIMIZATION OF A Windows NT system always begins by selecting the right hardware. If you're like me, you probably dream of constructing the "ultimate NT machine," a computer with the fastest technology that runs NT close to the speed of light. After all, if money were no object, we'd all be running Windows NT on a quad-processor 500MHz RISC system with 512MB of RAM, FibreChannel solid-state disk drives, a DVD-ROM drive, and a coprocessed OpenGL graphics adapter, with a 21-lh. monitor to top it all off (heck, I know I would!). Unfortunately, financial realities dictate that you must instead choose the fastest hardware you can afford within your budget (on the other hand, if your budget happens to allow you to purchase the system I just described, then you are truly enviable!).

Whether you're purchasing or building a new system or upgrading an existing one, this chapter will help you select the right equipment. This chapter explains the available technologies for different categories of hardware and which are best suited for use with NT. If you are interested in optimizing the hardware in your NT system, then this chapter will be close to your heart. In an industry whose technology turns over every 6 to 12 months, it's important to know what's coming down the road. Therefore, in addition to technologies already available on the market, we also discuss some up-and-coming technologies that you should be on the lookout for.

Designing Your Windows NT System

If you are building or upgrading a Windows NT computer that provides high performance, you'll need to make well-informed decisions about the hardware you purchase. A variety of factors influence the type of equipment you select, such as the size of your organization's network (if the machine will participate on a network) and whether the machine will be acting as a server or workstation. In addition, you should also consider the following factors when evaluating a product.

Performance and price/performance ratio

Because you're reading this book, product performance is an important concern for you. You'll want to make sure that the equipment you choose is not only high performance, but also offers a good price/performance ratio (many publications that review hardware use both types of criteria in their reviews). This is important because choosing the fastest product isn't always the best decision. For example, if a competitive brand offers only slightly lower performance at a significantly lower price, then the money you save may be better used on a different system component (perhaps one that makes a more significant impact on the system's overall performance).

Compatibility

The importance of verifying your equipment's compatibility with Windows NT cannot be overstated. Many unwary users have purchased a new piece of hardware only to find out (the hard way) that the product isn't supported under Windows NT. Don't be among them! Always research each product you're considering to verify that each is supported under Windows NT. In fact, you should go even further and verify that the product is also compatible with the exact version of NT you're using. Occasionally, a vendor will be slow to update their drivers for a new version of NT, and this can be almost as bad as having no NT support at all.

The definitive reference for hardware compatibility issues with Windows NT is Microsoft's Windows NT Hardware Compatibility List (HCL). When evaluating a product for use with Windows NT, always start by consulting the HCL to see if it's listed. Remember, however, that there are many NT-compatible products not listed on the HCL, and the absence of a product doesn't necessarily mean that it won't work with NT. (If a product is not listed on the HCL, your next step should be to contact the vendor directly.)

Although a copy of the Windows NT Hardware Compatibility List can be found on the Windows NT CD-ROM (it is a Windows Help file, with the filename HCL.HLP in the CD's \SUPPORT folder), new products are being added all the time. Therefore, you may periodically want to obtain a newer version copy of the Windows NT HCL, which can be found on Microsoft's Web site at: `http://www.microsoft.com/hwtest/hcl/`

Some of the important questions to ask when determining the compatibility of a product are:

- Is the product compatible with Windows NT (i.e., is it on the Windows NT Hardware Compatibility List)?
- Does the vendor support use of the product with Windows NT and/or supply drivers?
- What is the vendor's return policy should the equipment fail to work properly in your Windows NT environment?

By asking these questions ahead of time, you minimize the chance of having any "hardware nightmares" with your new equipment.

Reliability

Another important aspect of any piece of hardware is its reliability: that is, how stable is the product, and how likely is it to fail? This information can be gleaned from several sources, including the equipment's Mean-Time Between Failure (MTBF) rating, and reviews of the product in industry publications. However, the best information of all (and often the most enlightening) comes from discussing a product with others who are using it in a production environment. Obviously, this will mean finding someone who has experience with the product and is willing to share that experience. In the past, I've been very successful in finding such people in any of several places, including Usenet discussion groups, Internet mailing lists, and vendor forums on on-line services such as CompuServe and America Online.

For a list of NT-related Usenet groups and mailing lists, see Appendix B, "Other Sources of NT Information."

Support

When considering the purchase of any hardware, you should also evaluate the support available for the product. This includes the technical support and warranty (one year; three years; etc.) provided by the product vendor. Also, find out what return and repair policies are offered in the event of equipment failure, and whether on-site service is available for the product (important for larger organizations). In addition, it's a good idea to stick with companies that offer on-line support for their products, such as a World Wide Web, FTP (File Transfer Protocol), or Bulletin Board (BBS) system for driver updates and technical support information.

Processors

The key component of any computer is its microprocessor, the CPU (Central Processing Unit). These days, there are a variety of processor types to choose from, a far cry from the days of Intel's monopoly of the PC market where your choice was limited to different generations of the x86 processor. Although you may still choose an Intel processor for your Windows NT system, it's worth considering the use of RISC (Reduced Instruction Set Computing). RISC-based systems have become price-competitive with high-end Intel systems, and offer significant performance advantages over their Intel counterparts. In this section, we introduce several RISC-based processors supported by Windows NT, including Digital Alpha AXP, the PowerPC chip, and the MIPS processor family.

Choosing your CPU: how much is enough?

When selecting a CPU for your NT system, the first question you should ask is "How much is enough?" The answer depends on a variety of factors, including the role the machine will play (e.g., desktop workstation, file server, or application server) and the number of applications (or services in the case of a server) that will be running on the machine simultaneously.

Most computers today that use faster (e.g., Pentium, Pentium Pro, or RISC-based) processors don't experience significant bottlenecks at the CPU level. This is because the majority of applications run by the average user aren't *computer-bound* by nature; that is, they aren't processor intensive. Of course, there are exceptions, such as systems running complex mathematical, engineering, or CAD applications, or heavily-accessed applications servers; these types of software do tend to tax the processor and could easily cause it to become a performance bottleneck. On the other hand, your average office machine running a word processor and perhaps an e-mail application probably isn't going to bring your processor utilization anywhere close to 100 percent on a regular basis.

For additional information on monitoring CPU utilization, see Chapter 5, "Optimizing Memory and Processing."

Usually, the major bottlenecks on most computers are related to disk I/O (input/output) or RAM (Random Access Memory) limitations. The reason is that both of these subsystems (especially disks, due to their mechanical latencies) are significantly slower than the system CPU. In addition, when the system requires more RAM than is physically present in the computer, it will begin to use hard disk space as virtual memory, which further slows the system. To get an idea of how this impacts performance, keep in mind that RAM access times are measured in nanoseconds (10^{-9}, or billionths of a second) and hard disk access times are measured in milliseconds (thousandths of a second)!

As a result, the speed of the CPU is only one factor in the composite picture of your system's performance. An ultrafast processor won't do you much good if you're running *disk-bound* (disk I/O intensive) applications and have a slow disk subsystem. Remember when choosing a processor that you want one that gives you the kind of responsiveness and speed you'll be comfortable with, but that also offers a good price/performance ratio for now and for the foreseeable future. In addition, be sure to pair plenty of memory (RAM) and a fast disk subsystem with the processor to maximize the processor's capabilities.

System Bus Speed: A Key to Performance

In addition to the more recognizable attribute of processor speed (which is measured in megahertz [MHz]), there is another oft-overlooked aspect to system board performance that can make a significant difference in a computer's performance. Called the system bus speed, this is the speed at which the system/memory bus of the computer operates. Although many x86-based systems typically only support system bus speeds of up to 66MHz, there are some that support system bus speeds of 75MHz or 83MHz.

When running at these higher system bus speeds, a system's performance is practically guaranteed to improve, because the increased frequency boosts the speed of memory that is used for virtually every operation carried out by the system. Most systems derive the PCI (Peripheral Computer Interface) bus speed using a divisor of the system bus speed (often a divisor of 2; e.g., 66MHz/2 = PCI bus speed of 33MHz), which means that the performance of PCI peripherals can be improved as well.

Because CPU speed is a multiplier of this system bus speed times some multiplier (e.g., 3X, 3.5X, 4.0X, etc.), these boards can use a different multiplier to achieve the same CPU speed. For example, a board capable of running a 75MHz bus speed could run an Intel Pentium II 300MHz processor at a system bus speed of 66MHz using a CPU clock multiplier of 4.5, or at a 75MHz system bus speed using a clock multiplier of 4.0. Either would run the CPU at the rated 300MHZ speed, but the 75MHz scenario would deliver better memory and peripheral performance.

There is one strong caveat when considering the use of system bus speeds over 66MHz on systems that offer this feature: not all memory and peripherals will work at the higher speeds. Successfully using these speeds on a system motherboard usually requires the presence of high-quality 50ns (nanosecond) or 60ns memory DRAM (Dynamic RAM) memory modules or SDRAM (Synchronous DRAM) that can keep up with the increased data transfer rates, and peripherals capable of working at speeds above 33MHz. Although many peripherals will work fine at 37.5MHz or 41.5MHz PCI bus speeds, others will fail to work properly or will cause the system to hang. In addition, running certain mass controller devices (e.g., SCSI [Small Computer Standard Interface] host adapters) at these speeds can cause data corruption on attached hard disks, so be sure that the manufacturer of each device supports the higher bus speeds prior to using the peripherals in this configuration. In any case, you should be certain to do a full system and Registry backup (as discussed in Chapter 12) prior to using an existing system at system bus speeds higher than 66MHz.

Of course, it is always nice to have the fastest machine possible, since faster processors will always execute instructions more quickly. This in turn makes your applications feel snappier and more responsive (as long as excessive paging or a slow disk subsystem isn't bogging them down). Always buy the fastest processor you can afford, because even though this will not improve performance, it will extend the useful life of the machine. In the following sections, we discuss the various CPU platforms that can run Windows NT, their speeds, and compatibility issues.

In the lab used in conjunction with the writing of this book, we decided to compare the performance of a system at both 66MHz and 75MHz bus speeds using our Bench32 performance benchmarking software. We conducted a series of tests using the same basic system configuration in each iteration: an Intel Pentium II 300MHz CPU with 128MB of 50ns EDO DRAM, a Pentium II motherboard supporting a 75/83MHz bus speed (the FX83-A motherboard from Megatrends Technologies, Inc.), a Seagate Barracuda 2GB Fast/Wide SCSI hard disk, a Matrox Millenium 8MB PCI Video Card, and other miscellaneous peripheral devices. The results of the tests are shown in the following table.

PROCESSOR/SYSTEM BUS SPEED

Bench32 Test	300MHz CPU/66MHz (4.5X multiplier)	300MHz CPU/75MHz (4.0X multiplier)
Bench32 ProcessorMarks	340	376
Bench32 MemoryMarks	163	179
Bench32 DiskMarks	209	214
Bench32 VideoMarks	291	302

As you can see, running the system at the 75MHz bus speed made a significant impact on the performance of all aspects of system performance, not just memory speed. If you remember the aforestated caveats, you may be able to use a motherboard capable of running a higher system bus speed and achieve some significant performance gains in your own system.

There are several manufacturers producing x86-compatible boards capable of using higher bus speeds, including 75MHz and 83MHz. However, some manufacturers, although they provide jumper settings to enable the speeds, do not always support using the systems in these configurations (i.e., you use them at your own risk). However, due to popular demand from the user community, there are also a number of manufacturers that do support higher bus speeds (usually 75MHz, because it is more conservative) for some of their products. Listed below are a few of the Intel-compatible system board manufacturers supporting higher bus speeds on their products:

Manufacturer	Web Site URL
ASUSTek Computers, Inc.	`http://www.asus.com/` or `http://www.asustek.com.tw/`
Megatrends Corp.	`http://www.megacom.com/`
Tyan Computer Corp.	`http://www.tyan.com/`
ABIT Ltd.	`http://www.abit.com/` or `http://www.abit.com.tw/`
AIR Integration	`http://www.airwebs.com/`
AOpen	`http://www.aopen.com.tw/`

CPU support in NT

One of the primary design goals of Windows NT is the concept of *platform independence.* Whereas many operating systems are tied to a particular processor or processor family, Windows NT is capable of supporting an unlimited number of processor architectures. The magic that makes this feat possible is a special component of Windows NT called the *Hardware Abstraction Layer* (HAL). HAL represents only a small (about 15–20 percent) portion of the entire Windows NT operating system and is the only part of NT's structure that is processor-specific. This design allows Windows NT to support a variety of today's most powerful processors, and also makes it easier to create NT support for faster processors developed in the future.

Out of the box, NT ships with a variety of HALs designed for different processor architectures, including

- The Intel x86 processor family, which includes the 80486, Pentium, Pentium Pro, Pentium II, and other x86-compatible processors

- The DEC Alpha family of processors, including the 21064, 21066, 21164 and 21264
- The MIPS R4X00, R5000, R8000, and R10000 processors
- The PowerPC processor, including the 601, 603, 604, and 620 versions

In addition, custom versions of NT with other HAL types are available from certain system manufacturers; these are used on computers with specialized hardware, such as systems with more than four processors (which require a vendor-developed HAL).

Comparing processor performance

One of the things many NT users are curious about is how various Intel x86- and RISC-based systems stack up against one another in terms of performance. Unfortunately, comparing the relative performance of different processor types in real-world terms is an inherently difficult task. This is because system performance is a very application-oriented concept and will vary greatly depending on a number of factors such as:

- The features and optimizations of the motherboard used to support the CPU
- The specific peripherals connected to the system, especially the disk and video subsystems
- The type of application being run to evaluate performance; that is, whether the application is 16- or 32-bit; whether it is natively compiled for the processor type it's being executed on (in the case of x86 applications running on RISC systems)
- In the case of native applications, whether the same level of code optimization was achieved by the developer on the Intel and RISC versions

These are but a few of the things to consider when doing system-to-system comparisons between various computers and/or hardware platforms. These issues aside, however, there are industry-standard tests available to benchmark each of the system's various components. In this section, we provide a sampling of the raw processor performance of the various CPU types, including their performance doing integer-based and floating-point operations (the two basic kinds of tasks a processor performs). Because there is an almost infinite number of possible combinations of CPUs, peripherals, and software one could compare, CPU performance is the best place to start when selecting, designing, or upgrading your system.

You should use the tables in each of the subsequent sections to gather a general idea of the raw processing capabilities of each type of CPU supported under

Windows NT. After identifying the CPU you want to base your system on, you should then use the information in the remainder of the chapter to choose the correct assortment of peripherals to construct your high-performance NT system. If you do this for each individual subsystem, you are virtually assured of ending up with a fast system that will be optimized for use with Windows NT.

CPU benchmarking notes

The comparative tables used in this chapter reference the SPEC95 suite of industry-standard benchmarks created by SPEC, a nonprofit organization that conducts independent research and performance testing. SPECint95 measures integer-based CPU performance, while SPECfp95 measures floating-point performance. These tests are designed strictly to test raw CPU performance, not to provide a composite system performance rating. Therefore, although different system configurations may yield slightly different SPEC95 figures, these variances should be minor from system to system.

Another item to remember regarding SPEC CPU performance figures is this: Because each set of system benchmarks submitted to SPEC by various companies reflects a specific implementation of the CPU in a specific environment (i.e., one particular computer), performance tests for the same processor in a different system can yield slightly different results. In addition, SPEC-based tests aren't normally performed under Windows NT, so these figures don't necessarily give an exact picture of the relative difference between these computers when running Windows NT. As previously mentioned, their primary purpose is to reflect raw processor performance.

Going the Intel way

The Intel processor family is a true dynasty in the personal computer industry. Since the introduction of the original 8086 processor in the early 1980s, Intel's processors have been the sole platform supported by modern PC operating systems such as MS-DOS, Windows 3.x, and Windows 95. It wasn't until the introduction of Windows NT 3.1 that the PC operating system market was opened to CPU architectures other than Intel's.

As a result of Intel's market dominance, the majority of today's Windows NT-based systems continue to be based on Intel x86 processors. The reason for this continued dominance is somewhat of an industry merry-go-round. Despite the significant performance advantages offered by RISC processors, software vendors are reluctant to develop applications for these platforms for fear of the added development costs and limited marketplace. Users, seeing the lack of software support (i.e., number of NT programs compiled specifically for that platform), choose Intel as a "safe bet." Unfortunately, this circle makes everyone a loser because it restricts the marketplace, allows Intel to keep its prices high, and limits the number of choices available to NT users.

This situation has already caused two casualties in the NT RISC camp, namely the PowerPC and MIPS processor. Motorola, the manufacturer of the PowerPC chip (as part of a joint-technology venture with IBM), and MIPS computing (a subsidiary of Silicon Graphics, Inc.) have both withdrawn their support for NT, blaming slow sales and inadequate developer support. This leaves only Intel and the DEC Alpha chips in the NT CPU market.

Currently, the offerings from Intel are these five processors: the 80486, the Pentium, the Pentium Pro, and the newest members, the Pentium MMX and Pentium II (a.k.a "Klamath"). The latter two chips, with their MMX capabilities, offer significant enhancement for floating-point and multimedia performance. More information on MMX technology appears later in this chapter in the "MMX: Multimedia Powerhouse" section.

THE 486: DON'T GO THERE!

My statement on the topic of the 80486 processor is a fairly simple one: yes, NT still supports it, and no, you shouldn't even consider running NT on a 486 if you want a fast NT system. Although less-CPU intensive operating systems such as DOS, Windows 3.x, and Windows 95 can run with decent performance on a fast 486 CPU, running NT is an entirely different matter. NT is a processor and disk-intensive environment that demands the kind of performance that only fast Pentium, Pentium Pro, and RISC-based CPUs can deliver.

In all fairness, there are a few uses to which you could put those old 486 systems if you really feel the need to use them. Specifically, you could put them to use in situations where you wish to deploy an NT system for a single, low-CPU utilizing task. One example of such a use is an NT system acting as a low-cost router or gateway, such as a multihomed computer (one with multiple network adapters) that routes network traffic between two or more network segments. Another example is an NT Server used strictly as a print server. A third example is an NT system running Internet proxy server software. These types of functions aren't inherently CPU-intensive and may allow you to save money for use on your higher-end NT systems. However, if you do this, don't forget to put lots of RAM on such a system; you don't want excessive paging (due to insufficient memory) slowing the system down even further.

THE PENTIUM

If you're considering an Intel processor for your NT system, the Pentium (aka the P5) processor is the baseline choice. It offers significant performance advantages over the 486 processor, and runs 32-bit operating systems such as NT, as well as 16-bit operating systems.

The Pentium processor was a landmark for Intel-based processors. It was the first CISC-based microprocessor to offer *superscalar* performance; that is, it was the first processor capable of executing more than one instruction per clock cycle (the Pentium is capable of executing two instructions per cycle). As a result, the Pentium offered PC users a level of performance never previously achieved by a CISC-based PC microprocessor. Most Pentium CPUs today have speeds from 75MHz to 200MHz. There are also some older 60 and 66MHz versions of the original Pentium chip floating around, but these aren't recommended for use with Windows NT for a number of reasons. Besides being significantly slower, older Pentium CPUs are notorious for overheating because of heat dissipation problems. This occurs because the original Pentium used an older 5.0-volt, 0.8-micron manufacturing process rather than the 3.3-volt, 0.6- and 0.35-micron technology used in faster versions. As if this weren't enough, many early versions of the Pentium (including some faster versions as well) have a number of bugs, including the now-famous floating-point division bug (where certain floating-point division operations can yield incorrect results on certain Pentium processors).

If you happen to own an older Pentium Processor and are concerned that the chip may contain the floating-point error, you can check this using a Windows NT utility called PENTNT.EXE. To check, simply type **PENTNT** at a command prompt; the utility will then report whether the system contains the bug. If it does, you should seek a replacement chip from Intel. In the meantime, you can also use this utility to tell NT to automatically turn off the Pentium's floating-point hardware under NT and use software-emulated floating-point operations instead. To do so, type **PENTNT /C** at a command prompt. This is the recommended switch to use in this situation, because it will conditionally enable software emulation at boot-up based on whether or not the bug is found.

In addition to superscalar performance, the Pentium also contains a number of other performance-related features. First, the Pentium extends the previous 32-bit data bus of its predecessors to 64 bits. It also separates the traditionally singular on-chip L1 cache into two separate 8K caches: one for instructions and one for data. A feature called Dynamic Branch Prediction enhances chip performance by predicting the most likely set of instructions to be executed next. To accomplish this, the chip implements two prefetch buffers, one to prefetch code in a linear fashion, and one that prefetches code according to a special buffer called the Branch Target Buffer (BTB). Using these mechanisms, instructions are almost always prefetched into the buffer before they're needed for execution. In addition, the floating-point performance of the Pentium is up to 10 times faster than that of the 80486 due to a completely redesigned and integrated FPU (Floating-Point Unit).

Finally, because the Pentium doesn't contain a built-in L2 cache (like the 486, motherboards using the chip must use an external L2 cache) you should purchase as much external cache as possible to optimize the chip's performance. Most motherboards only support up to 512K in external cache, but a few support 1MB or more. The amount of L2 cache is directly related to the amount of system RAM, because L2 cache memory services system RAM. Be sure that any system you have with more than 16MB of RAM has at least 512K of L2 cache; otherwise, the performance of your system will be unnecessarily diminished. In fact, you should fill your system with the maximum amount of L2 cache memory the motherboard supports because standard cache RAM is relatively cheap these days.

MMX: MULTIMEDIA POWERHOUSE

In early 1997, Intel took the wraps off a new technology designed to enhance their existing processor line. MMX (which probably stands for MultiMedia eXtensions, although Intel won't say for sure) technology is a set of 57 new instructions for the Pentium and uses a key new technology called SIMD (Single Instruction Multiple Data). SIMD allows each CPU instruction to operate on several pieces of data in parallel, which provides greater efficiency. The 57 new instructions operate on 64 bits of data at a time, which means they can operate on 8 bytes or four (2-byte) words or two 32-bit words – all in parallel. This translates into a tremendous performance boost during the compute-intensive performance loops common with multimedia data types such as video, audio, graphics, and animation. In addition, the Pentium MMX processor doubles the existing L1 cache of the regular Pentium CPU from 16K to 32K (divided as 16K instruction, 16K data), which further improves the chip's performance.

Although the MMX-enabled Pentium offers a new set of instructions, they are a superset of those found in the original Pentium rather than a redesign. Since the Pentium MMX is backwards compatible with the original Pentium, software designed for the regular Pentium CPU will run unmodified on the new chip. These programs simply see the MMX version as a normal Pentium, but applications written to take specific advantage of the new MMX extensions will detect the MMX's presence and take advantage of the new instruction set. Currently, the Pentium MMX is available in speeds of 166MHz and 200MHz.

If you're considering replacing your regular Pentium CPU with a Pentium MMX, be warned: although the two chips are software and pin compatible, they use different core voltages, and your motherboard must allow the voltage to be changed to accommodate this. Whereas the original Pentium processor had a unified voltage (3.3-volt core and 3.3-volt input/output), the Pentium MMX uses a split voltage (2.8-volt core; 3.3-volt input/output). To support the MMX version of the Pentium, your motherboard must have jumpers or other settings to configure the board for 2.8 volts. If you install the MMX in a socket configured for 3.3-volt operation, the processor could be damaged.

PENTIUM PRO

Despite its somewhat simplistic name, Intel designed the Pentium Pro processor (aka the P6) to be much more than a faster Pentium. In a leap of faith regarding the success of 32-bit operating systems such as NT, Intel specifically optimized the Pentium Pro for 32-bit code. The result is a chip that produces top-notch performance under Windows NT (and other 32-bit OSs such as UNIX and OS/2), but only mediocre performance on 16-bit operating systems such as Windows 95 and Windows 3.1/MS-DOS. In fact, the Pentium Pro is so 32-bit OS specific that it can actually run *slower* than a comparable Pentium running at the same speed when used with 16-bit operating systems.

Like the Pentium, the Pentium Pro uses a 64-bit data bus and a split 16K L1 cache design (one 8K instruction cache, one 8K data cache). In developing the Pentium Pro, Intel went beyond traditional CISC chip design, borrowing technologies and concepts from mainframe systems and even RISC-based systems. Ironically, the Pentium Pro is actually a combination of CISC and RISC technology together on one chip. As the old adage goes, "if you can't beat 'em, join 'em." Intel realized the limitations (namely, the number of transistors required) of CISC technology and decided that the only way to compete with the performance of high-end RISC processors such as the Sun UltraSPARC and DEC Alpha would be to incorporate RISC technology in the chip design. The result was a chip that not only met the performance of many RISC chips, but also bested many of them in raw performance (for integer operations). This sent shockwaves through the microprocessor industry and made many people reevaluate their notions about CISC-based chips.

To maximize the performance of your Pentium Pro/Pentium II system, choose a motherboard that supports the use of high-performance memory features such as bank interleaving and 128-bit memory access. Both of these features can greatly improve system memory performance.

As with the Pentium, the Pentium Pro introduces several new features that help it achieve its stellar performance. Among the most significant of these features is one called *Dynamic Branch Execution.* Like the Dynamic Branch Prediction feature found in the Pentium, Dynamic Branch Execution allows the Pentium Pro to optimally order the execution of instructions by predicting the flow of program code and making intelligent decisions about reordering it. However, the Pentium Pro improves upon the Pentium's implementation of this feature by using a more sophisticated, multipart engine system to handle execution. These three components, the Fetch/Decode Unit, the Dispatch/Execute Unit, and the Retire Unit, have access to a common "pool" of currently executing instructions; this allows the instructions to be examined for optimal processing order. This process is depicted in Figure 2-1.

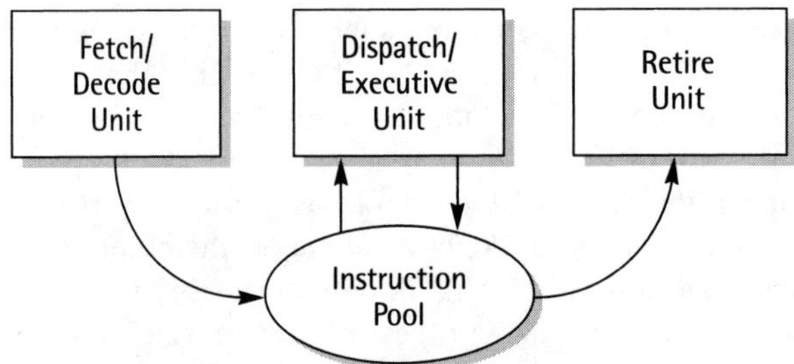

Figure 2-1: The Pentium Pro engine contains three separate components that communicate via a shared instruction "pool."

Dynamic Branch Execution is actually a combination of three processing techniques the Pentium Pro processor uses to speed up execution:

- *Multiple Branch Prediction*: similar to the Dynamic Branch Prediction of the Pentium processor, this allows the processor to look multiple steps ahead in the software and predicts which branches (groups of instructions) are likely to be processed next.
- *Dataflow Analysis*: this feature allows the Pentium Pro processor to analyze which instructions are dependent on each other's results, or data, to create an optimized schedule of instructions.

- *Speculative Execution*: instructions are carried out speculatively based on the optimized schedule arranged by the Dataflow Analysis feature, which helps to utilize the Pentium Pro's superscalar processing potential.

The Pentium Pro is superscalar like the original Pentium but is actually able to execute up to three instructions per clock cycle as opposed to the Pentium's limit of two. This earns the Pentium Pro the designation of a superscalar level 3 processor (the Pentium is level 2) and makes it among the fastest microprocessors currently available.

Finally, the Pentium Pro is also unique in that is does away with the notion of an external L2 cache. In the Pentium Pro, this cache is housed directly on the chip itself. This is also the reason for Pentium Pro's elongated, slightly rectangular shape – the chip actually contains two elements, the L2 cache and the CPU itself. This internal housing of L2 cache significantly improves the cache's performance and simplifies Pentium Pro motherboard design for board manufacturers. However, this also means you can't upgrade the L2 cache on a Pentium Pro CPU once you purchase it. Therefore, be sure to get as much on-board cache as you can afford. Currently, your choice is limited to 256K or 512K of built-in L2 cache, but future versions may include up to 1MB. Currently, the Pentium Pro processor is available in speeds of 150, 180, and 200MHz. In addition, the release of a new 300MHz version is said to be forthcoming.

PENTIUM II (A.K.A "KLAMATH")

No discussion of the Pentium family of processors is complete without mentioning the now-shipping heir to the Intel throne, the Pentium II. Formerly known by its code name "Klamath," this chip delivers amazing performance by integrating the best of the Pentium Pro and MMX technologies together in a single chip.

The Pentium II processor currently comes in 233MHz, 266MHz, and 300MHz versions, with faster versions already in the works for the near future. Although extending the Pentium II beyond these speeds will eventually be possible, it will probably present some serious design challenges to Intel due to the number of transistors required by the chip, as well as current limitations of Intel's submicron manufacturing process. However, even at speeds of 300MHz, the Pentium II gives even the fastest of today's RISC processors a run for their money. Like the Pentium Pro, the Pentium II is optimized for 32-bit operations and is a natural choice for Windows NT computers.

COMPARING INTEL PROCESSOR PERFORMANCE

To assist you in comparing the various Intel processors, a comprehensive listing of all currently available processors and speeds is provided in Table 2-1. Remember when reading this table that the figures represent only basic performance benchmarks. They are intended to provide a general comparison of the relative speeds of various Intel processors, and do not take into account real-world applications running on Windows NT or other operating systems. These benchmarks simply provide a processor-to-processor speed comparison and don't take into account performance variances caused by other factors such as the motherboard and chipset used, type of RAM, and so forth. It also doesn't take into account any software-related considerations such as the operating system or applications being used. Each of these factors can have significant impacts on actual system performance. In addition to Intel's own iCOMP 2.0 processor benchmark, the comparisons show relative processor speeds using the SPECint95/SPECfp95, Norton SI-32, and CPUMark-32 benchmark utilities.

TABLE 2-1 COMPARING INTEL PROCESSOR PERFORMANCE

Processor Type	Intel iCOMP2.0	SPEC int95	SPEC fp95	Norton SI-32	CPU Mark32
Pentium 100MHz	90	Not available	Not available	Not available	Not available
Pentium 120MHz	100	Not available	Not available	Not available	Not available
Pentium 133MHz	111	4.00	3.44	36.5	301
Pentium 150MHz	114	4.10	3.42	35.9	311
Pentium 166MHz	127	4.56	3.84	39.9	343
Pentium 200MHz	142	5.10	4.18	44.6	387
Pentium MMX 166MHz	160	5.59	4.30	50.7	390
Pentium MMX 200MHz	182	6.41	4.66	57.5	437
Pentium Pro 180MHz*	197	7.28	5.59	81.0	497
Pentium Pro 200MHz	220	8.58	6.48	97.6	611
Pentium II 233MHz	267	9.47	7.04	112.2	608
Pentium II 266MHz	303	10.80	7.68	127.8	692
Pentium II 300MHz	332	11.70	8.15	141.3	746

*Processor was tested with 256K L2 cache; unless otherwise noted, all others were tested with 512K L2 cache.

For additional information on Intel processor features and performance comparisons, visit Intel's Web sites at `http://www.intel.com/` and `http://mmx.com`.

SHIFTING INTO OVERDRIVE

Other than the standard, "true blue" Intel processor types, there are also a few other processors in this category you should be aware of. The first is the Intel OverDrive series of processors, which are upgraded CPUs designed to convert a 486 system to a Pentium Processor, or a Pentium system to a faster Pentium or Pentium MMX processor. There are a variety of OverDrive processors available in various speeds, and it's important to research which versions will work with your system before purchasing one (this information is available from Intel or your local Intel Processor Dealer).

To use an OverDrive in your existing 486 or Pentium system, the system must have been designed to be compatible with such processors. On a 486 system, this means that there is an additional empty row of holes around the outside of the 486 processor, which usually indicate that the socket is a Pentium OverDrive-compatible socket. The socket may even be labeled as such. On Pentium systems being upgraded to faster Pentium CPUs, it is important that the system support the system bus speed required by the OverDrive processor you intend to use (e.g., 50MHz, 60MHz, 66MHz, 75MHz, etc.). In addition, the Pentium CPU socket on your system's motherboard must also meet the requirements for the OverDrive processor. These sockets are labeled with names such as Socket 3, Socket 5, Socket 7, and so forth. Again, Intel or your local Intel CPU reseller can tell you what Socket level your motherboard will require to use the OverDrive you wish to install.

Don't expect a Pentium OverDrive-upgraded 486 system to perform the same as a true-blue Pentium system running the same speed CPU. The reason for this is that although the processor is an actual Pentium, other system peripherals such as the system bus and memory retain their original speeds and inherent limitations. The only benefit these kinds of upgrades offer is faster computational speeds (i.e., the internal processing speed of the CPU), which is only one of a variety of factors that contributes to a system's overall performance. To maximize the performance of a Pentium CPU, you'll want to use a motherboard and peripherals specifically designed around and matched to the capabilities of the Pentium.

INTEL-COMPATIBLE CPUS

It's also important to mention that Intel isn't your only choice for Intel-compatible processors. There are a variety of Intel 486 and Pentium-compatible CPUs on the market, many of which offer 100 percent software-compatibility with true Intel CPUs. These processors are available from several different manufacturers including AMD (manufacturer of the K6 x86-compatible microprocessor) and Cyrix, and come with a variety of different features and speed ratings. There are several potential advantages to purchasing Intel-compatible processors, because they often provide superior power to comparable Intel CPUs at a lower price. When using Windows NT on systems with these types of processors, NT normally installs and operates without a problem, because it believes the processor is actually an Intel CPU. Although Intel-compatible CPUs are often cost-efficient as compared to their true Intel counterparts, it is also worth noting that by playing "catch up" with Intel they are often six or more months behind in producing comparable offerings to Intel's.

Weighing the RISCs

One of the beauties of Windows NT is that is doesn't tie you down to a single type of processor. In addition to Intel and Intel-compatible CPUs, NT also supports a variety of RISC-based processors including the MIPS, DEC Alpha AXP, and PowerPC processors. In many cases, these processors offer superior performance to Intel-based CPUs in the same price range. However, there's a catch: this performance is dependent on the use of *native* applications compiled specifically for the RISC CPU you're using. This means that software vendors must do a special compile of their software for each RISC CPU platform they wish to support and provide these binaries to you in addition to the Intel version on their distribution media. Although Windows NT provides a 486 emulator to allow Intel binaries to run on these systems, this normally causes a major performance penalty for the software versus running it on a native Intel system.

Although many Windows NT applications and utilities support RISC versions of NT, many still do not. Therefore, never assume that just because a software package you're purchasing supports Windows NT that it will include binaries for RISC-based CPU platforms. Vendors tend to provide RISC support in a pecking order that reflects the overall market penetration of each product. This generally means that the order of RISC support is DEC Alpha AXP first, MIPS CPU second, and the PowerPC last. Some software supports every RISC platform, but this kind of support is becoming less and less frequent since the announcements of impending doom for the MIPS and PowerPC processors mentioned earlier (these processors won't be supported after Windows NT version 4.0).

CISC VERSUS RISC: PROCESSOR PHILOSOPHY

In a world full of duality, even PC microprocessors fall into one of two design philosophies: *CISC* and *RISC*. CISC (Complex Instruction Set Computing) microprocessor design is by far the more traditional and popular of the two. CISC processors are characterized by features such as small register sets, memory to memory operations, large instruction sets (with variable length instructions), and use of special hard-coded logic called *microcode*. Intel and Motorola have been the largest proponents of CISC-based CPU design, with Intel using CISC as the basis for all of its x86 processors and Motorola having used a CISC design in its 680X0 processor line (used in older models of the Apple Macintosh). Most other CISC-based chip designers are mainly Intel clone manufacturers (such as AMD and Cyrix) who produce x86-compatible processors. Computing tasks performed on a CISC-based architecture tend to result in large, complex sets of instructions. Although CISC instructions tend to be large, fewer CISC instructions are required to complete a given task.

Generally speaking, CISC design philosophy uses additional hardware wherever possible to reduce the number of processor instructions and increase performance. This additional hardware increases the overall complexity of the chip and the number of transistors required. The major disadvantage to this practice is that it's harder to increase the clock speed of a complex chip, and this creates limits on the maximum speed of CISC processors.

By comparison, the concept behind RISC (Reduced Instruction Set Computing) is that most tasks performed by the computer require simple instructions. RISC design calls for each instruction to be a single, fixed length and to execute in a single cycle, which is done with pipelines without using the microcode found in CISC chips. This has the effect of reducing a chip's complexity and increasing its overall speed. Although Intel dominates the worldwide market for processors on personal computers, there are more manufacturers producing RISC chips than there are producing CISC-based ones. Among the RISC-producing companies are Sun Microsystems (SPARC, UltraSPARC, and UltraSPARC2 processors), Motorola (the PowerPC chip), Digital Equipment Corporation (DEC Alpha AXP), MIPS (the MIPS family of processors), and Hewlett-Packard (PA-RISC processors).

RISC instructions are very small and efficient, and their design allows RISC processors to generally run at much higher speeds than CISC chips. This happens because RISC processors use fewer transistors than comparable CISC-based processors, making it easier to boost the chips to higher frequencies without causing heat dissipation problems. With CISC design, chip real estate for additional transistors and overheating problems are a constant challenge for chip designers. RISC's use of simpler instructions at faster speeds allows RISC to achieve equivalent and often faster performance than CISC processors.

The use of simpler instructions sometimes means that a given task may require more instructions to complete than the same operation run on a CISC-based CPU. However, conventional RISC wisdom maintains that very few (around 20 percent or so) of all instructions are of this type, so RISC designs should theoretically provide better overall performance than CISC designs. Finally, RISC designs call for each instruction to be a single, fixed length, and to execute in a single cycle, which is done with pipelines and without microcode (to reduce chip complexity and increase speed). RISC CPU operations are performed only on registers, with the only access of memory being loading and storing operations. In addition, some RISC designs use a large windowed register set or stack cache to speed subroutine calls.

A BLURRING LINE

The argument about which is better, RISC or CISC, is also becoming increasingly complex with the advent of hybrid chips such as the Intel Pentium Pro, which uses RISC-like technology for certain functions. Technology borrowing between the two platforms can be found in other places as well. For example, the use of pipelining (a method used in most RISC designs) can be found in the Motorola 68040 and Intel 80486 CISC processors. This allows the processors to execute instructions in a single cycle, even though they use microcode. In addition, the concept of windowed registers has been added to some CISC designs to speed them up in a similar fashion.

The performance battle between the RISC and CISC industries is a computer industry version of leapfrog: one camp comes out with the "fastest processor available" only to be bested by a chip with the opposite design a few months later. Until recently, the Pentium Pro 200MHz was the fastest PC microprocessor available running under Windows NT, having beaten out earlier DEC Alpha chips for the honor. However, a 600MHz version of the latest Alpha chip, the 21264, has turned the tables once again and re-throned the DEC Alpha as performance king under NT. This may change yet again with future release of the Intel "Merced" (P7) processor (but so it goes in the chip manufacturing business).

THE MIPS CHIPS

MIPS processors are probably best known for their use in Silicon Graphics computers, UNIX-based workstations commonly used in applications such as CAD, graphics, and engineering. MIPS support was the first non-Intel port of Windows NT, and currently includes support for all of the popular MIPS versions including the R4000, R5000, R8000, and R10000 processor families.

MIPS processors are 64-bit processors that use either a 64-bit, 128-bit, or 256-bit data path and separate data and instruction caches in their L1 cache design. In addition, the operational dynamics of MIPS processors (and most RISC-based processors, for that matter) require the use of larger L2 and L3 caches for optimal performance. For example, whereas Pentium Pro processors use from 256K to 512K of L2 cache, MIPS processors use anywhere from 4MB to a whopping 16MB of L2 cache. The highest-end MIPS processors, the R8000 and R10000, make use of a special "crossbar" bus architecture that is faster than the shared bus architecture used by many other microprocessors. In addition, the R10000 provides superscalar performance, executing up to four instructions per clock cycle. Finally, in a manner similar to the Intel Pentium Pro, the MIPS R10000 processor is able to reorganize the execution order of CPU instructions to optimize performance.

Table 2-2 shows the features of various MIPS processors, as well as their relative performance using the popular SPEC95 (or SPEC92 where listed) suite of CPU benchmarks.

TABLE 2-2 FEATURES AND PERFORMANCE OF VARIOUS MIPS PROCESSORS

MIPS Processor	Speed	Internal L1 Cache Size (Instruction/ Data)	L2 Cache Size	SPECint95 (*92)	SPECfp95 (*92)
R4400	200MHz	16K/16K	<=4MB*	141*	143*
R4400	250MHz	16K/16K	<=4MB	180.2*	177.5*
R4600	133MHz	16K/16K	N/A	113.5*	73.7*
R4700	175MHz	16K/16K	<=2MB	Not Available	Not Available
R5000	180MHz	32K/32K	<=4MB	4.82	5.42
R8000	75MHz	16K/16K	<=2MB	111.35	310.57
R8000	90MHz	16K/16K	<=16MB	Not Available	Not Available
R10000	200MHz	32K/32K	<=16MB	10.7	19.0

*The R4400MC and R4400SC models have an L2 cache interface, but the R4400PC version has none.

Although Windows NT support for MIPS processors looked strong when NT first hit the market as version 3.1, slow sales and the ensuing withdrawal of key MIPS-based system vendors such as NEC Technologies signaled the beginning of the end for MIPS support under NT. These days, MIPS-based systems are effectively "lame-duck" computers, because the termination of Microsoft's support for MIPS under Windows NT is imminent: Microsoft has verified that only the Intel and DEC Alpha microprocessor families will be supported under Windows NT 5.0.

THE POWERPC

In 1991, IBM, Motorola, and Apple launched a joint project to develop the next generation of PC microprocessor. The development team started with the POWER (Performance Optimized With Enhanced RISC) architecture, a second-generation

RISC architecture originally used in IBM's powerful RS/6000 workstations. One of the results of the team's efforts was the PowerPC processor.

One of the main attractions of the PowerPC is that it can run multiple operating systems, from the Apple Macintosh to UNIX and Windows NT. The processor was also originally intended as the basis for a new operating system being jointly developed by IBM and Apple (code-named "Taligent") which never appeared. Since its introduction, PowerPC-based systems have quickly become the de facto standard for Apple Macintosh systems. In addition, Microsoft announced early on that it intended to support the chip under Windows NT. With the introduction of Windows NT 3.51, the PowerPC chip officially joined the ranks of the x86, Alpha, and MIPS processors as an officially supported platform for Windows NT computers.

Despite its young age, there have already been several generations of the PowerPC, including the 601, 603, 604, and 620. The 60x versions of the PowerPC feature a 64-bit data bus, but are also capable of using a 32-bit data bus to provide backwards compatibility in certain environments. Like other high-end processors, the PowerPC is capable of superscalar performance, with some versions executing up to four instructions per clock cycle. The 601 and 603 versions are capable of three instructions per cycle, and the 604 and 620 versions are capable of up to four instructions per cycle. The 604e version of the PowerPC chip also sports separate 32K instruction and data caches; this is double the size of its direct predecessor, the 604. Finally, the 620 version of the PowerPC doubles the 64-bit data bus and 32-bit address bus of the other PowerPC family members to 128- and 64-bits, respectively, and also supports up to 128MB of L2 cache memory.

Table 2-3 lists the features of the various members of the PowerPC family and their relative SPEC95 performance benchmarks.

Unfortunately, the PowerPC's support under Windows NT has been short-lived. Shortly after the introduction of Windows NT 4.0, Motorola announced that it would discontinue support for the PowerPC under Windows NT, effectively killing any future the chip may have had with NT. Motorola cited poor sales of NT-compatible PowerPC systems and limited developer support for creating native PowerPC versions of NT applications as the primary reasons for this decision. One of the reasons for this lack of acceptance is the availability of comparable or higher-performance RISC and CISC processors at equal or lower prices. Basically, the PowerPC just never found its niche with NT.

The result is that many users' dream of multiboot systems running a combination of Windows NT, Macintosh OS, and UNIX has all but faded into oblivion. As with the MIPS processor family, it is currently unclear whether PowerPC support will continue with the introduction of Windows NT 5.0 in 1998. However, as with MIPS, it is difficult to recommend purchasing a PowerPC-based system for use with NT despite the chip's performance features. The most important aspect of any hardware is always its compatibility, and the future for PowerPC compatibility with NT currently looks bleak.

TABLE 2-3 FEATURES AND PERFORMANCE OF VARIOUS POWERPC PROCESSORS

MIPS Processor	Speed	Internal L1 Cache Size (Instruction/ Data)	L2 Controller	SPECint95 (*92)	SPECfp95 (*92)
601	66MHz	32K combined	External	62*	72*
603	66MHz	8K/8K	External	62*	54*
603	80MHz	8K/8K	External	75*	65*
603e	200MHz	16K/16K	External	5.6	4.1
603e	220MHz	16K/16K	External	6.1	4.5
603e	225MHz	16K/16K	External	6.3	4.6
603e	233MHz	16K/16K	External	6.0	4.1
603e	240MHz	16K/16K	External	6.2	4.2
604	100MHz	16K/16K	External	160*	165*
604	120MHz	16K/16K	External	180*	180*
604	133MHz	16K/16K	External	200*	200*
604e	166MHz	32K/32K	External	6.5	6.1
604e	180MHz	32K/32K	External	6.9	6.2
604e	200MHz	32K/32K	External	7.8	6.5
620	133MHz	32K/32K	>= 128MB	225*	300*

*These systems were benchmarked with SPEC92 rather than SPEC95; all test systems used a 1MB L2 cache configuration.

THE DEC ALPHA

Although it is a temporary title, Digital Equipment Corporation's Alpha AXP processor has the unique honor of being the fastest PC microprocessor you can buy for Windows NT. The Alpha is a 64-bit RISC-based processor developed by Digital for high-end workstations and servers running the Windows NT, UNIX, and VMS operating systems. In addition, the Alpha processor also enjoys excellent software support under Windows NT, because the Alpha has enjoyed significant sales and established a firm foothold in the high-end workstation market. The Alpha also benefits from a close relationship between Microsoft and DEC, the latter having been a staunch supporter of NT since its initial release.

Because there were no concerns about backward-compatibility with software or previous chip versions, DEC's engineers were able to take a "drawing board" approach in designing the Alpha. This unencumbered state (a rare situation in an industry of upgrades) allowed them to use the latest, cutting-edge technology in the new processor. This is reflected in the Alpha's screaming performance, which is virtually unrivaled by other PC processors. In fact, the fastest shipping version of the DEC Alpha (600MHz as of this writing) is capable of 2.4 billion instructions per second (BIPS)! This chip is, for now, the fastest PC microprocessor in the world.

There is also a new version of the Alpha processor, dubbed the 21264, which is in the final stages of development and should be shipping by the time you read this. This chip sports some amazing features: it is capable of executing up to six instructions per clock cycle, uses separate 64-bit instruction/data caches, and has a dedicated 128-bit L2 cache controller and separate 64-bit system bus capable of operating at speeds of up to 333MHz. The initial 500MHz version is reputed to have a SPECint95 rating in excess of 30 and a SPECfp95 rating in excess of 50.

In addition to the inherent RISC design and 0.35-micron manufacturing process that allow it to run at extremely fast speeds, the Alpha also uses other performance-enhancing features. These features include a 128-bit or 256-bit data bus, separate L1 caches for instructions and data (up to 64K in size with the latest 21264 Alpha processor), and superscalar performance that allows up to four simultaneous instructions to be executed simultaneously (up to six with the 21264 version). Level 2 cache support varies depending on the Alpha processor involved: the 21164 version of the chip includes a 96K, on-chip, set-associative write-back L2 cache, whereas other versions use an external L2 cache of up to 4MB or 16MB in size. Many Alpha chipsets also provide support for an additional L3 cache on the system motherboard.

Another advantage of the DEC Alpha platform is that unlike Intel-based systems, which only support 32-bit implementations of the PCI 2.1 expansion bus, many Alpha systems support a 64-bit PCI bus. This 64-bit PCI implementation effectively doubles the maximum theoretical throughput of bus from 132MBps to 264MBps (although real-world limits are closer to 200MBps due to bus latency and other factors).

Table 2-4 shows the features and performance figures for a sampling of Alpha-based systems running at various speeds.

TABLE 2-4 FEATURES AND PERFORMANCE OF VARIOUS ALPHA PROCESSORS

Alpha Processor	Speed	Internal L1 Cache Size (Instruction/ Data)	L2 Cache Size	SPECint95	SPECfp95
21064	166MHz	8K/8K	External; up to 16MB	2.95	3.64
21064A	233MHz	16K/16K	External; up to 16MB	4.27	5.09
21064A	300MHz	16K/16K	External; up to 16MB	5.23	5.81
21664	266MHz	8K/8K	On-chip; 96K	7.93	11.1
21664	333MHz	8K/8K	On-chip; 96K	9.82	12.5
21664	400MHz	8K/8K	On-chip; 96K	12.3	14.1
21664	500MHz	8K/8K	On-chip; 96K	15.4	21.1
21164	600MHz	8K/8K	On-chip; 96K	18.0	27.0
21164PC	400MHz	16K/8K	External; up to 4MB	10.7	13.0
21164PC	466MHz	16K/8K	External; up to 4MB	12.5	15.0
21164PC	533MHz	16K/8K	External; up to 4MB	14.3	17.0
21264*	500MHz	64K/64K	External; up to 16MB	30.0	50.0

*This is a forthcoming chip; SPECint/fp95 ratings are estimates only.

As evidenced by the failures of the MIPS and PowerPC chips, raw speed alone won't get you a following in the Windows NT market. To truly gain acceptance, a chip must offer both high performance for natively compiled applications and good performance when running 32-bit Windows applications compiled for Intel x86 platform as well (i.e., Windows 95 and NT applications written to the Win32 API). This is a practical consideration in most environments, because the majority of today's software is still Intel-compatible (although more and more natively Alpha versions of software appear all the time).

Foreseeing the need for high x86 performance under Alpha, Digital developed a special Intel x86 software emulator called *FX!32*. Put simply, FX!32 creates significant performance increases for 32-bit x86-based software running on DEC Alpha systems. Traditionally, the only way for RISC-based NT systems to run native Intel code was to use NT's built-in x86 code emulation subsystem. In versions of Windows NT prior to 4.0, this subsystem had fairly abysmal performance and poor compatibility offerings, largely due to its limited 80286-based emulation scheme. Despite the significant performance increase created by NT 4.0's upgrade of this subsystem to 486-based emulation, the performance of x86-based applications still tends to fall woefully short of execution on true Intel CPUs. With FX!32, Digital has created an NT subsystem that allows powerful RISC processors to run many x86-based applications at the same speeds they would run on fast Pentium or even Pentium Pro processors.

FX!32 installs a new client/server subsystem that provides three key components to support fast emulation: a run-time environment providing transparent execution, a binary translator that converts Intel code to high-speed Alpha code (this is the high-performance engine of FX!32), and a server component that coordinates the operation of the other two. The software works its magic by automatically optimizing and converting x86-based 32-bit applications "on the fly" as they are run. Once an application image has been optimized with Alpha-based code, FX!32 recognizes this and won't need to do the optimization again; this significantly enhances the speed of the translation process. Currently, more than 1,800 x86-based software packages have been certified as compatible under FX!32.

Another nice feature of FX!32 is that it is a "hands-off" product, requiring little or no maintenance by the user. Best of all, FX!32 is a free software package available from Digital Semiconductor, a division of Digital. The current version, 1.1, provides additional features and optimizations that enhance an already amazing product. This software is a definite "must have" for any user of an NT Alpha-based system, and gives the Alpha a large advantage over the other NT RISC platforms.

You can download the latest version of Digital's FX!32 (currently 1.1) for Alpha Systems running NT 4.0 from Digital's World Wide Web site: `http://www.service.digital.com/fx32/fx32_kit.htm`

SMP: THE MORE, THE MERRIER

In addition to its support of RISC systems, NT also offers the Windows community another powerful benefit: the capability of running the operating system on computers with multiple processors. Windows NT supports a form of multiprocessing known as *symmetric multiprocessing* (SMP), which allows multiple simultaneous code fragments called *threads* to be distributed evenly among all available processors. Symmetric multiprocessing allows the threads of any running process, including Windows NT itself, to execute on any available (i.e., idle) processor. In addition, multiple threads inside a single process can run on different processors simultaneously. This feature significantly enhances the performance of NT and NT applications, especially those that are written to use the multithreading features of the Win32 API.

Some other operating systems, such as Novell NetWare 4.1, use a different form of multiprocessing called *asymmetric multiprocessing*, which runs different tasks on specific CPUs. Asymmetric multiprocessing is generally less efficient, less scalable, and creates greater dependence on the particulars of the hardware being used.

So, how can you take advantage of this powerful NT feature? The answer is simple: purchase a multiprocessor system that is listed on the Windows NT Hardware Compatibility List. Being on the HCL means that a system has a specially written HAL that is provided on either the Windows NT CD-ROM or by the system's manufacturer. However, even if the system you're looking into isn't listed on the NT HCL, it may still work with Windows NT.

Because different vendors tend to do things in different ways when designing multiprocessor motherboards, several standards have emerged for the design and implementation of multiprocessor systems. The most popular of these is Intel's MP (MultiProcessor) specification, which defines a system BIOS enhancement for Intel-based systems that allows such systems to work with any MP-compatible operating system. In the case of Windows NT, MP support is implemented via an Intel MP HAL that ships with Windows NT. There are also other Intel-based systems (e.g., the AST Manhattan) that use custom, non-MP HALs provided on the NT CD-ROM. Still other systems, such as certain servers from Compaq and Hewlett-Packard, use non-MP HALs that are provided with the system by the manufacturer.

When shopping for an MP-compliant Pentium or Pentium Pro motherboard, be sure the board supports at least MP version 1.4 (the current version as of this writing). This version fixes several minor problems with previous versions of the specification and works well with NT's Intel MP HAL.

Does this mean that only Intel-based systems can use multiple processors? Heck, no! Although the MP specification is an Intel-specific standard, there are also a number of RISC-based systems, including DEC Alpha and MIPS-based systems, supporting multiple CPUs. In some cases, this support can go as high as 8, 16, or 32 processors!

Although NT can support a theoretical limit of 32 simultaneous processors, systems with more than 4 CPUs normally require a custom HAL provided by the system manufacturer.

If you're considering an upgrade from a uniprocessor to a multiprocessor system, it's important to remember that doubling the number of CPU's isn't necessarily going to translate into a doubling of performance. Multiple CPUs in a system must all compete (in most implementations) for the same system resources such as memory, external cache, and the system bus; this situation presents another natural limiting factor for many multi-CPU systems.

The optimal use of multiple processors requires software support in addition to hardware-level support. This essentially means that the application must be multithreaded and be optimized for use under multi-CPU systems. However, even if an application doesn't make heavy use of multithreading, it may still gain significantly from the presence of additional CPUs. The reason for this is that NT can still execute process threads generated by the operating system and other applications across the other CPUs, which still creates better performance than the same system with only one CPU.

Certain high-end systems (such as those from Sequent, Data General, Taligent, SGI, Digital, and HP) use a different system architecture called a *crossbar architecture* that provides system resources in such a way that contention between multiple CPUs for system resources is significantly reduced or eliminated altogether.

TWO SLOW CPUS OR ONE FAST CPU?

A typical question that arises regarding multiprocessor systems is whether it is faster to use two (or more) slower processors than to use a single, faster one. The answer depends largely on how the system will be used. If you normally run only one or a few applications at a time, you may not notice any real difference between the dual-CPU and the single-CPU system and may even find that the system with the single, faster CPU runs more quickly. The reason is that multiple CPU's increase the total available CPU *capacity*, not the CPU *speed*. The real benefits of a multiprocessor system come into play when the processor is put under heavy loads, running many applications and/or background services simultaneously. In this kind of situation, the single faster processor may process instructions more quickly than the multiple slower CPU system, but the faster CPU will become bogged down more easily under heavy loads (i.e., processor utilization will start to approach 100 percent). In addition, threads from multiple processes must wait in a single processor execution queue, whereas a multi-CPU system could spawn these threads off to multiple processors.

Another way of explaining this is by analogy: imagine that you had to take many people to a destination in one of your cars, either a fast sports car or a minivan. Having multiple, slower processors versus a single faster processor is essentially like having a slower car that can carry more people at a time (i.e., like the minivan) rather than a fast sports car that can make multiple trips back and forth more quickly (i.e., the fast CPU system). Both methods will get the people where they're going, but as soon as you need to carry more people than fit in the fast car, you're making multiple trips; at this point, the larger car starts to become a more efficient method of transportation.

If you're purchasing or building a multiprocessor Pentium Pro system, there are two criteria to use when selecting your processors. The first is to avoid early versions of the Pentium Pro that exhibited a special bug that afflicts multiprocessor systems; be sure that you are getting at least the A1 stepping version of the Pentium Pro (this problem is especially prevalent in systems with more than 2 CPUs). Second, to maximize performance, be sure to only purchase Pentium Pro CPUs with at least 512K of L2 cache on-chip. Versions of the Pentium Pro with 256K are notorious for poor performance in multiprocessor systems and will artificially inhibit your system's overall speed.

UPGRADING FROM A UNIPROCESSOR TO MULTIPROCESSOR SYSTEM

Contrary to what you might think, simply popping a second CPU onto a multiprocessor motherboard isn't going to make NT instantly recognize and use it. Making NT recognize an additional processor requires the use of a special HAL. If you're installing Windows NT for the first time on an NT-compatible multiprocessor system, enabling multiprocessor support is as easy as choosing the correct HAL during Windows NT Setup when Setup asks you to identify your computer type.

If, however, you've already installed NT and have added a second processor or replaced your single-processor motherboard with a multiprocessor one, there are two paths you can take to enable multiprocessor support. The first is to reinstall Windows NT, choosing the correct HAL type when Setup provides the option. This will preserve your existing NT installation but will effectively change the HAL to a multiprocessor one. However, there is also a shorter path available to this same result: a special utility available in the Microsoft Windows NT Resource Kit (both versions 3.5x and 4.0 of the kit) called UPTOMP.EXE (UniProcessorTOMulti-

Processor Upgrade Utility). This utility allows you to dynamically change your system's HAL and related support files without going through the hassle of a complete reinstallation.

You should never change your system's HAL, regardless of the procedure, without having first performed a complete backup of your Windows NT system and the NT registry database. You should also create or update your Windows NT Emergency Repair Disk before making this change.

The following steps describe how to use the UPTOMP.EXE utility to modify your Windows NT installation to enable multiprocessor support in Windows NT.

1. Install the Windows NT Resource Kit for whatever version of Windows NT you are using.
2. After closing all running applications, locate and execute the UPTOMP.EXE application (located in the directory in which you installed the Resource Kit files; the default is C:\RESKIT) by double-clicking its icon. At this point, UPTOMP will check to ensure that the system is currently a uniprocessor system; if it isn't, you'll receive an error message and the utility will not allow you to continue.
3. Once the system is verified as a uniprocessor system, the "Processor Upgrade Utility" main dialog window appears (NT 4.0 version shown in Figure 2-2 below). In this dialog, first specify a drive and directory location containing HAL files. This could be the platform directory on your Windows NT CD-ROM (e.g., `D:\I386`, etc.) or an alternate location such as a network drive location or floppy disk drive.

Be aware that the Uni-to-Multiprocessor conversion utility is currently a one-way affair and cannot be used to reverse the process (back to single processor configuration).

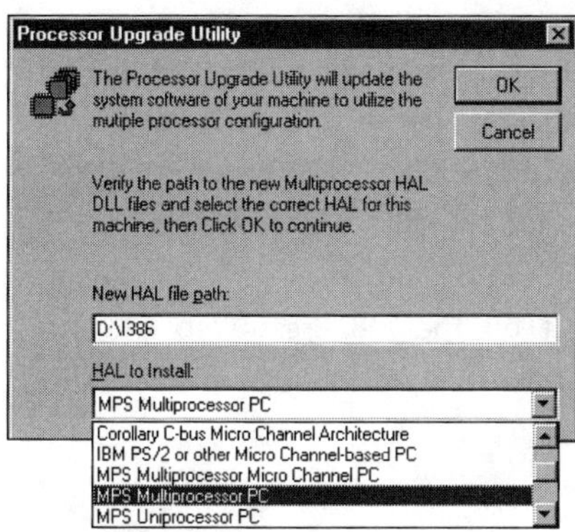

Figure 2-2: The `UPTOMP.EXE` **Processor Upgrade Utility initial dialog.**

4. Once you specify a valid location containing HAL files, use the "HAL to Install:" drop-down list box field to specify the HAL appropriate to your system. After you've selected the correct HAL, choose the OK button to continue.

5. At this point, you'll be informed that the upgrade process is not reversible and asked to confirm that you want to proceed. If you choose to continue, the utility will then copy the files from the previously specified source directory to a temporary directory on your hard disk. Before copying the system files from the temp dir to the *%SYSTEMROOT%\SYSTEM32* directory, the files being replaced are first moved to a subdirectory of the *SYSTEM32* (this allows the files to be restored in the event that the upgrade does not complete successfully). After the original system files have been safely moved, the files in the temporary directory are moved to the *SYSTEM32* directory and the temporary directory is then deleted.

6. Once the copy completes successfully, a dialog box stating that the upgrade was successful and that the system needs to be restarted to have the changes to take effect appears. It will also remind you that you should run RDISK after the system restarts to update the saved configuration. It is recommended that you do so, but that you create a new, separate Repair Disk rather than using the one you updated prior to the upgrade process. That way, a pre-upgrade copy of the original system configuration is preserved on this disk (useful in the event of an emergency). You are also presented with the choice of restarting the computer immediately or closing the application without restarting the computer. It is highly recommended that you reboot the system so that NT can be restarted with the new changes in effect.

The Windows NT Resource Kit, available for versions 3.5, 3.51, and 4.0, contains the UPTOMP.EXE utility along with a number of other must-have utilities and goodies to help you get the most from your Windows NT system. The kit is produced by Microsoft Press and is available in many bookstores or from Microsoft Press direct at (800)MS-PRESS. You can also find additional information about the Resource Kit on the MS Press Web site at: `http://www.microsoft.com/mspress`.

Motherboard

As the name implies, the motherboard is by far the most important aspect of your system; it is, after all, the "mother of all boards" in your computer. Therefore, you'll want to make sure that the system motherboard (or base system unit if you're purchasing a system from a hardware vendor) supports all of the latest, cutting-edge features. The criteria to use will also depend on your system's intended function; that is, workstation or server. There are also some features that are good to have on any NT system, regardless of its function.

Some of the features you should look for on any motherboard, regardless of its function, are the following:

- Boards using CPU daughtercards or passive backplane connectors. These designs separate the processor functionality from the main system board and often allow for easier upgrades to faster processor and memory technologies as they become available in the future.
- For systems that use external (off-chip) caches, also look for CPU daughtercards offering separate caches per CPU.
- A bridged PCI bus design with at least five PCI slots and three ISA slots (for compatibility with legacy cards). Also demand at least PCI 2.1 support (if not PCI 3.0); on DEC Alpha systems, look for 64-bit PCI connectors.
- Motherboards with a Plug and Play BIOS. Although Windows NT doesn't currently support Plug and Play, Windows NT 5.0 is expected to provide this support. Therefore, you'll want to have a system that supports it.
- Support for system bus speeds over 66MHz.
- For servers, a dedicated on-board I/O processor chip for system I/O operations (one implementation of this is the I20 initiative set forth by Intel and other manufacturers, which uses the Intel i960RD/RP RISC processor).

- A total of 8 to 12 SIMM sockets, or 6 to 8 DIMM sockets for DIMM-based boards.
- Try to stick with systems that use DIMMs (Dual In-line Memory Modules) rather than SIMMs (Single In-line Memory Modules) for system RAM; DIMMs offer a higher level of integration that increases your memory expansion ceiling.
- Memory bus architectures that use memory interleaving technology and/or 128-bit memory addressing (or 256-bit for Alpha systems), which optimizes the speed of system RAM access.
- Look for the motherboard to support the use of faster RAM types such as EDO and BEDO DRAM and SDRAM in addition to standard Fast Page Mode (FPM) DRAM.
- Support of Synchronous or Burst Synchronous Static RAM for the L2 and/or L3 cache subsystems (or, at minimum, the use of Pipelined Burst Mode Cache SRAM if synchronous SRAM isn't supported). Try to stay clear of systems using older, slower Asynchronous Static RAM (ASRAM) chips.
- At least 512K of L2 cache memory on Intel x86-based systems with 32MB or more of RAM; 2MB or more for RISC-based systems (or L3 if L2 cache is on-chip).
- The presence of a PS/2 Mouse Port (to avoid the use of serial mice on a COM port you may want to instead reserve for other functions, such as a UPS interface or modem).
- Bootable CD-ROM support (for x86-based systems; most RISC systems have this capability). This feature allows the system to be started from a CD-ROM that contains a special bootable format (this format is also sometimes referred to as the "El Torito" format). For IDE CD-ROMs, this support is in the BIOS as most x86-based motherboards include an IDE interface on the motherboard; for SCSI CD-ROMs, this support must be included in the SCSI host adapter's BIOS.
- IrDA (Infrared Digital Adapter) port to support infrared, wireless communication to devices such as printers. Many system boards support this option as an alternate configuration for the second built-in communications (COM) port.
- For systems with built-in parallel ports, be sure the port supports both the ECP (Extended Communications Port) and/or EPP (Enhanced Parallel Port) specifications. These are newer parallel port technologies that support higher data transfer rates and bidirectional communications features not present in the traditional, standard parallel port implementation.

- For systems with dual-channel IDE controllers, look for IDE controller chipsets that have busmastering, DMA Mode 3, and P/IO Mode 5 support. Also, look for IDE controllers that support dual IDE channel command queues/FIFO (first in, first out) buffers rather than a single one that's shared by both channels (more importantly, however, it is strongly recommended that you not use any IDE peripherals on your Windows NT system; SCSI devices are always the best choice).
- For Intel Pentium Pro-based motherboards, look for systems that use the newer 440LX/Bxchipsets. These provide superior performance and features over the older 440FX ("Natoma") and 450 GX/KX ("Orion") chipsets.
- Motherboards using a baby AT, ATX, or LPX form factor. These are the most modern system board designs and in the case of ATX and LPX, support useful power-off and integrated connector features.
- Desktop Management Interface (DMI) support in the system's BIOS. This is a management interface standard that allows for remote system monitoring and management.
- Only consider systems containing long-lasting low-voltage Lithium CMOS/clock batteries, which often have lifetimes of 5 years or more. This will likely prevent any need to replace the battery during the computer's lifetime.
- Only choose system boards that provide support, wherever possible, for the next generation of processors of that type. For example, only choose motherboards with a Voltage Regulator Module (VRM) that allows the CPU voltage to be adjusted for newer, lower-voltage CPU types (such as the new Pentium MMX chips using a 2.5-volt core voltage). On Pentium and Pentium Pro systems, try to stick with motherboards containing the latest Intel Socket type (Socket 8 as of this writing). NOTE: Pentium II systems use a newer type of CPU connector called a Slot 1 that is unique and has no backwards compatibility with previous CPUs; however, some motherboards do contain both a Slot 1 and a Socket-type connector.
- Finally, look for motherboards that support the latest and greatest modern I/O technologies, including AGP, Universal Serial Bus (USB), UltraSCSI or Ultra2SCSI, and FireWireFibreChannel. Although they are somewhat more difficult to find, these kinds of features are starting to become more and more available as these technologies experience higher demands.

In addition to the general motherboard features listed above, there are also some specific features you should consider for your NT server computers.

- Because memory reliability on servers is extremely important, be sure the server's motherboard supports the use of ECC (Error Correcting Circuitry) memory; this memory provides error correction technology that is superior to standard FPM memory using parity. Also look for the capability of having from 1GB to 4GB of main system memory; for a server, you may want to look for a motherboard with an even higher RAM capacity.

- If at all possible, use a motherboard that supports built-in SCSI-2 or UltraSCSI using an NT-compatible chipset. This will free a PCI slot and allow you to purchase a second SCSI card/channel for your fastest SCSI devices such as your disk subsystem; the on-board SCSI can be used for slower SCSI devices such as CD-ROMs, tape drives, and removable drives, which can slow down your faster devices if put on the same channel. Another way to accomplish this is to use a dual-channel SCSI controller such as those from Adaptec, QLogic, and other manufacturers; these provide two separate SCSI channels on a single card.
- On single- or dual-CPU motherboards, look for at least a 128-bit wide memory bus; for quad-CPU motherboards, double this requirement to a 256-bit wide bus.
- Support (e.g., additional motherboard jumpers) for an overheating alarm and an auxiliary case fan. You'll also want to use a case that takes advantage of these features.
- Since video is nonessential on servers, you may wish to consider a motherboard with built-in VGA. This saves an ISA slot (the only type of VGA card you should consider for servers) and frees it for use with another adapter type. On workstations, however, you'll want to forego this and choose a stand-alone PCI-based video adapter in order to get the best performance and features for your video subsystem. Even if you do choose a motherboard with a built-in video adapter for a server, be sure that it uses its own separate RAM and does not share main system RAM. Also be sure that the video can be disabled so that it may be bypassed in the event of video chip failure, or if the system requires a different video adapter or is relegated to another function in the future.

There are also specific motherboard features you should consider for use with your Windows NT computers acting as network workstations or stand-alone systems. These features are listed below.

- Advanced Configuration and Power Interface (ACPI) support.
- For NT systems acting as graphics or CAD workstations, Accelerated Graphics Port (AGP) support. This is a new Intel-led graphics standard that improves upon the bandwidth provided by the PCI bus for intensive graphics-oriented applications.
- Support for at least 1GB of main system memory (RAM).

About now you're probably wondering who makes the fastest motherboards (or systems). Unfortunately, this is a moving target. With new technology and chipsets arriving on an almost weekly basis, system board manufacturers and system vendors seem to be in a perpetual game of performance leapfrog. However, in our lab testing, we've had the opportunity to experiment with several boards that have demonstrated some amazing performance and merit a mention.

For DEC Alpha-based systems, we recommend checking out products from these vendors who produce their own custom system boards designed around the Alpha microprocessor:

Deskstation Technology	`http://www.deskstation.com/`	Product(s): Ruffian RPX system and RPX164-2 motherboard
The Panda Project	`http://www.pandaproject.com/`	Product(s): Archistrat 4s (workstation) or 5s (server) systems

For Intel x86-based systems, the fastest systems and motherboards we've tested to date are from these vendors:

Advanced Megatrends	`http://www.advancedmegatrends.com/`	Product(s): Apollo P6 Workstation system and the FX83-A Pentium Pro/II motherboard
SuperMicro	`http://www.supermicro.com/`	Product: Super P6DNH Dual Pentium Pro Motherboard with I20 Technology and Super P6DKF Dual Pentium II Motherboard

Expansion bus types

Another important feature of any system is the support provided for internal expansion cards. Motherboards normally support one or more bus types for the connection of peripheral boards such as storage controllers, network cards, video adapters, and the like. Over the years, a number of different bus standards evolved, each with different speeds, features, advantages, and disadvantages. However, an interesting development has occurred in an industry famous for the creation of competitive standards: hardware vendors have rallied around a single bus type – PCI (Peripheral Component Interconnect). This support reaches unprecedented levels by extending even to the Macintosh hardware community, who have also chosen PCI as the bus for modern Mac systems. The major advantage to this unified support is lower development costs for hardware vendors, which in turn translates to lower costs for users. Since vendors can focus on a single connector type, they can spend their resources and energy on the development of function logic rather than multiple implementations of their products on different bus types.

Although the PCI bus is by far the best bus choice for any modern NT system, there are several legacy bus types that must also be discussed, because many computers currently in operation use these connector types. In addition, the granddaddy of all PC buses, the ISA bus, continues to be deployed on virtually all modern PCs (including those using other buses such as PCI), because many cards do not requires the features or bandwidth provided by PCI. In the following sections, we give a brief description of each of the various PC bus types.

ISA

The ISA (Industry Standard Architecture) bus is the grandfather of all PC buses, having been around since the original IBM PC in the early 1980s. The ISA bus is a fairly slow bus by today's standards, running at 8.25MHz and achieving throughputs of 1.5Mbps to 5.0Mbps. The ISA bus specification supports either 8-bit or 16-bit peripherals (the latter using an additional slot just ahead of the primary slot). ISA's only advantage is that it is an industry standard that is well defined, and few compatibility problems arise with ISA devices. However, since ISA provides extremely limited bandwidth, its use should be restricted to peripherals that can't use more speed than ISA can deliver. Examples of these types of devices include items such as internal modems and fax devices, I/O boards containing parallel or joystick ports, bus mouse cards, sound cards, and the like. Under no circumstance should you use the ISA bus for high-throughput devices such as storage controllers, network adapters, or video cards; this can easily make those devices a bottleneck on your system and restrict its performance.

Although the ISA bus runs at 8.25MHz on most system boards, some boards (or BIOSs) make it possible to increase the ISA clock rate to 11MHz or higher. This is possible because the ISA clock rate is usually derived by dividing the PCI bus clock rate (usually 33MHz) by 4; however, some systems allow for the divisor to be changed to 3 (for 11MHz) or lower values. Although a faster clock rate can improve the performance of the ISA bus and peripherals, not all peripherals will work at frequencies higher than 8.25MHz.

MCA

IBM raised a lot of eyebrows when it introduced its successor to the ISA architecture, dubbed the MicroChannel Architecture (MCA) bus. MCA used a different connector slot and was completely incompatible with ISA peripherals, effectively rendering all previous ISA-based cards unusable in the new IBM PS/2 computers using MCA.

MCA uses either 16- or 32-bit connectors and is able to transfer data at speeds of up to 40Mbps. The MCA specification also enables MCA cards to act as *bus mastering* devices, meaning that they are capable of handling transfers to and from system memory without intervention from the system CPU. The MCA bus also offered other nice features, such as jumperless, software-based configuration of MCA devices. To accomplish this, an MCA configuration manager utility is used to view and manage the resources used by MCA devices. MCA cards ship with configuration disks that tell the configuration manager what resources they use and what alternate choices are available for each resource type. MCA is also capable of automatically configuring the system based on this information to prevent the resource conflicts that often plague ISA-based systems.

Although the MCA bus offers significant performance and configuration features as compared to the ISA bus, MCA support has been scarce in the industry. Because IBM owned the MCA patent and charged system vendors a hefty licensing fee to use MCA technology in their computers, most weren't interested in supporting the standard. Instead, many of these vendors banded together and set forth to develop an alternative replacement for ISA.

EISA

The research efforts of a vendor consortium dubbed the "Gang of Nine" and led by Compaq Computer Corporation led to the development of a new standard called EISA (Extended Industry Standard Architecture). EISA was developed as an alternative to IBM's proprietary MicroChannel architecture; one that would not only increase performance but also retain compatibility with previous ISA cards. The additional bandwidth was necessary to relieve the bottlenecks that typically occurred in several kinds of PC components, including video, disk, and network adapters.

The EISA specification defines a 32-bit slot running at 8.25MHz that is capable of delivering a maximum theoretical throughput of 32MBps. ISA cards can be placed in EISA slots, and EISA and ISA components can be freely intermixed in the same system. Although EISA solved the compatibility problem created by IBM's MCA bus, EISA motherboards and components were typically pricey and outside the reach of most users. However, EISA eventually found a niche in the PC server market, because it is able to provide the additional network and disk throughput these types of systems require. The use of EISA on workstation systems has been fairly limited, and the introduction of more modern buses such as VL-Bus and PCI all but eradicated the use of EISA in anything except server computers. Today, systems using EISA slots are quite rare.

As with ISA, the EISA bus clock rate is derived by dividing the PCI bus by a standard divisor, and can sometimes be changed to operate at a higher frequency (such as 11MHz). See the previous Tip in the ISA section for more information.

VL-BUS

Designed specifically for the additional video and disk requirements created by modern operating systems such as Windows, the VESA Local Bus (VL-Bus) standard was initially tied to the 486 CPU. It defines a 32-bit connector that gives VL-Bus peripherals direct access to the system CPU. VL-Bus devices are capable of a maximum throughput of 140MBps at 40MHz, far more than the speeds delivered by any previous standard. However, this direct-CPU access method (and more importantly, the lack of bus arbitration) limits the number of VL-Bus devices that can be present in a system. Most motherboards using the VL-Bus contain a maximum of two or three VL-Bus slots (in addition to regular ISA slots). The use of more than one or two of these slots, especially on motherboards running at system bus speeds of 33MHz or more, often overtaxes the CPU and causes severe bus contention problems.

Although some 486DX systems run at a 50MHz system bus speed and offer VL-Bus slots, speeds of over 50MHz aren't supported by the original VL-Bus specification and are likely to cause problems for many VL-Bus peripherals.

VL-Bus slots, like EISA slots, are backward-compatible with ISA devices because they use connectors that are in addition to the basic ISA connector. Unfortunately, because of its inherent tie to the 486 architecture, it was difficult for the VESA committee (the Video Electronics Standards Association, the standard's defining body) to quickly implement a version of the VL-Bus for Pentium systems when they arrived on the scene. Although a newer 64-bit version of VL-Bus, called VL-

Bus 2.0, was eventually released, this standard has been all but ignored by most peripheral vendors. The features and benefits of the Intel-backed PCI bus made the introduction of VL-Bus 2.0 a clear case of too little, too late.

Use caution when inserting a VL-Bus card. Because of its length and design, the insertion of a VL-Bus card tends to put more stress on the system board than does a card using another bus type. It is best to insert the card slowly and evenly, while simultaneously restricting the flex of the motherboard by applying counterpressure. Otherwise, you can easily overflex the system board and damage it.

PCI

The Peripheral Component Interface (PCI) bus first appeared in the original Pentium computers. PCI provides maximum data throughput rates comparable to VL-Bus (up to 132MBps), but without the problems that exist in the VL-Bus specification. Since PCI is a mezzanine bus (i.e., one level above) rather than a direct-to-CPU local bus architecture, the presence of multiple PCI adapters in a system doesn't overload the processor as it does in VL-Bus systems. In addition, the PCI bus uses shorter slots that don't cause insertion stress like VL-Bus adapters.

Despite the wonderful new features of PCI, early implementations of PCI-based devices were far from perfect. Incompatibilities between PCI motherboards and adapters were common, because many vendors implemented the specification incorrectly. Newer versions of the PCI bus have virtually eliminated these kinds of problems, and the PCI bus is currently the most popular bus type for personal computers (including modern Apple Macintosh systems, high-end RISC workstations, and many others).

The current version of the PCI specification, 2.1, defines either a 32-bit/33MHz implementation that yields a maximum throughput of 132MBps, or a 64-bit 33MHz version capable of up to 264MBps. In addition, the introduction of a new version of the PCI bus, version 3.0, is underway. This new version sports a 64-bit interface and signaling rates of up to 66MHz, yielding a maximum burst transfer rate of 264MBps at 64-bit/33MHz operation, and 528MBps at 64-bit/66MHz operation. This kind of bandwidth is necessary for extremely high-speed devices such as ATM adapters, high-end graphics/video adapters, and FibreChannel adapters. PCI 3.0 slots will also offer backward compatibility with PCI 2.x adapters and use lower-power 3.3-volt implementation rather than the 5.0-volt implementation used by previous PCI versions. This will be beneficial for laptops and energy-efficient desktop systems using low-voltage power supplies, and the lower heat dissipation will likely translate to longer service lives for PCI 3.0-based systems.

The following is a summary of PCI 3.0's new features and benefits:

- Faster data transfer rates (up to 528MBps)
- Frequencies up to 66MHz
- Backward compatibility with legacy PCI (2.x) adapters
- More efficient data transfers
- Long/short block support
- Larger buffers
- Lower latency
- Greater compatibility with non-Intel motherboards

Form factors and case design

When designing or selecting your system, you should also take some time to consider what type of form factor you want. Motherboards and cases come in a variety of different shapes and sizes, and it's important you choose one that's right for your needs. When considering the overall system design, be aware that there are several types of system board layouts available. The classic style is the "AT" or "Baby AT" style form factors, which places all system I/O ports (other than the keyboard) on remote leads that must be connected to slot brackets or cut-outs on the case. These types of motherboards also use a standard "AT" power supply. Most older style systems and many modern server motherboards use the AT style design.

An example of an AT-style motherboard is shown in Figure 2-3.

Figure 2-3: A baby AT form factor motherboard.

There are also several motherboard form factor types that use a more highly integrated approach. These motherboard designs, including the LPX and the newer ATX form factors, integrate the system's various I/O ports such as parallel, serial, and PS/2 mouse ports directly onto the board itself (or, in some cases, on a mezzanine level connector attached to the board but as a second tier above it). The most popular of these designs is the ATX design (currently in version 2.01), which is commonly used in workstation, business, and home machines.

In addition to the integrated ports, the ATX uses a special design that maximizes the board's efficiency. In addition to special layout dimensions and a dual-tier aperture at the rear of the case to accommodate the built-in connectors, the ATX design also moves the processor away from the expansion slots. This allows the expansion slots to more easily accommodate full-length cards. In addition, the ATX design uses a special power supply that directly cools the processor and I/O cards, eliminating in many cases the need for a second cooling fan. Also, because its design reduces the number of cables and components inside the system, the ATX design increases system reliability while simultaneously reducing manufacturing costs.

Figure 2-4 shows an example of an ATX-style motherboard.

Figure 2-4: An ATX form factor motherboard.

If the system is a server (or even a workstation with many internal peripherals), be sure to get a large tower case with plenty of internal drive bays and the capability of accommodating the larger "AT style" motherboard form factor used by many server motherboards. Also be sure your system's case has a sufficient power supply and adequate cooling for the devices you'll be installing. You may also want to consider the purchase of a case that supports dual-redundant power supplies, thus providing an additional level of fault-tolerance.

Memory

An often overlooked but extremely important component of any Windows NT computer is the memory, or RAM, that it uses. A single system may use many different types of RAM, including the system's primary Dynamic RAM (DRAM) memory, several different types of cache memory (used to speed up the access of the primary memory), and adapter-specific memory such as the RAM used on video cards, caching disk controllers, and other adapters.

There is a common misperception that "RAM is RAM," and that the performance differences between different types of RAM are so small as to be unnoticeable. Although this may be true in certain cases, generally it is not. RAM is without a doubt the most frequently accessed resource in your computer. Both the CPU and various system components make continual read and write operations to and from system RAM; any latencies or bottlenecks become greatly magnified. Therefore, the type of RAM you choose for your system is very important to the system's overall performance, and memory chips should be evaluated for their speed as well as their reliability.

Choosing your memory

Memory is easily the most precious resource on a Windows NT computer. NT has always been a memory-hungry operating system, and insufficient memory is one of the quickest ways to bring NT's performance to its knees.

As with just about any technology, there are choices to make when shopping for system memory. However, these choices are limited to the memory types supported by your particular motherboard. Thus, the first thing you should do when choosing memory is to consult your system or motherboard documentation to determine what types of RAM can be used. Then, after reading the following sections, you'll be able to choose the best type of RAM for your system.

MEMORY PACKAGES

Memory comes in many different shapes and sizes. From the original DIP (Dual Inline Package) format to the most modern DIMM (Dual Inline Memory Module), RAM modules have come a long way in their evolution. These days there are really only two types of memory packages you're likely to see: SIMM (Single Inline Memory Module) and DIMM. SIMMs are memory boards containing DRAM chips, and most often come in either a 30- or 32-pin, 8-bit format (9 bits if SIMM uses parity memory) or a 72-pin, 32-bit format (36 bits if SIMM uses parity memory). The 72-pin variety provides a higher level of integration and is usually the only type found on modern Pentium or RISC-based systems that use SIMMs.

DIMMs are identical to SIMMs except they are larger and provide an even higher level of integration. DIMMs use a 64-bit (72 bits if DIMM uses parity memory), 168-pin format and have separate contacts on either side of the board enabling them to provide twice the data of SIMMs. In addition, DIMMs offer some other technical advantages over SIMMs. The common address and control signals on DIMMs are buffered, which reduces the load on these signals when multiple DIMM modules are present. The result is that systems with large amounts of DIMM-based RAM are able to access memory more quickly than with SIMMs. The use of DIMMs is becoming more and more popular with the advent of 64-bit processors and processors capable of using data buses of up to 128 bits (including some Pentium Pro and many MIPS-based systems) or even 256 bits (including many DEC Alpha systems). DIMMs are a far better choice for these types of systems, and it is recommended that you go out of your way to find a motherboard that uses DIMMS; later on, you'll be glad you did.

DYNAMIC RAM TYPES

The primary memory used on virtually all personal computers is some form of Dynamic RAM (DRAM). DRAM memory is almost always the primary memory used in a computer and relies on the system to provide a continual cycle of power refreshes to enable DRAM to retain its memory image. Although this makes DRAM cheaper to manufacture, it also severely inhibits its performance potential.

Of the available DRAM types, Fast Page Mode (FPM) has been around the longest and thus makes up the majority of the RAM installed on existing systems. FPM DRAM is commonly found in lower-end systems and some servers, since faster DRAM types such as EDO (Extended Data Output) do not support the use of parity that servers need.

Although FPM has been around for a long time, its use is becoming rare because the prices for faster DRAM types are virtually on par with FPM. FPM memory comes in one of two formats: parity and nonparity. The difference is that parity memory uses an extra bit per byte (8 bits) as a parity bit that does a basic integrity check of the other bits to ensure accuracy. Although most Pentium and Pentium Pro systems are capable of supporting either type, the use of parity memory isn't as important for workstations as it is for servers. Servers should use either FPM parity or ECC (Error Correcting Circuitry) memory because they have greater reliability needs.

A successor to FPM DRAM on workstation and home systems, EDO memory has come into vogue. EDO offers minor performance gains over FPM DRAM (approximately 1–4 percent better performance), but costs approximately the same to manufacture as FPM memory. As a result, always select EDO over FPM DRAM whenever possible. Unfortunately, EDO memory doesn't support the use of parity, making EDO a poor choice for server systems.

BEDO (Burst Extended Data Output) memory is a newer type of memory that offers even better performance than EDO memory. Actually, BEDO is an adaptation of the very high speed Synchronous DRAM (SDRAM) used in many RISC-based systems, but one that is tuned to the lower bus speeds (i.e., up to 66MHz on most systems) of Intel Pentium and Pentium Pro systems. Therefore, the use of BEDO memory is most often found on these types of systems. The major functional advantage of BEDO over EDO is that BEDO offers a higher burst rate and lower latencies than EDO. BEDO is also very similar to SDRAM-lite, a low-end version of

SDRAM also intended for lower bus speed Intel-based systems. In fact, on many systems, BEDO and SDRAM-lite modules can be used interchangeably. Although BEDO costs about the same to manufacture as FPM and EDO (since it uses the same CMOS core), it is more difficult to find than these other two. BEDO memory is highly recommended if your system supports it and if you can find it.

ECC memory is an extension of FPM DRAM memory that, like EDO and BEDO memory, uses the same CMOS core. There are two primary types of ECC memory, those providing error correction on SIMM (EOS), and those that rely on the system's chipset to handle the error correction. ECC memory can correct a 1-bit error anywhere in memory and in some instances can correct two simultaneous errors. When implemented with good system firmware and supporting software, ECC memory can even mask out bad bits permanently, much like hard disk diagnostic software marks bad disk blocks. Due to its reliability features, ECC is an excellent choice for Windows NT server computers. Although it doesn't offer any speed advantages over FPM memory, its does provide the kind of mission-critical reliability that's far more important on a server. Although it's somewhat rarer, there is also a newer type of ECC memory that uses dual-porting (simultaneous reads and writes) and provides higher performance than regular, single-ported ECC.

SDRAM (Synchronous DRAM) is the speed demon of modern DRAM types. Unlike the previously mentioned RAM types that are asynchronous, SDRAM fully synchronizes all operations to the system clock, providing an enormous boost for memory access. SDRAM is most popular in RISC systems that use faster bus speeds (75MHz to 200MHz) that demand faster memory performance. Until Intel-based systems begin to reach system bus speeds over the current 66MHz barrier, it's unlikely that SDRAM will become common on Intel-based motherboards. However, there is a special variety of SDRAM, called SDRAM-lite, that is adapted for use on slower motherboards and is price and feature competitive with BEDO memory. If you're using a RISC-based system for Windows NT, you should actively seek motherboards that make use of SDRAM memory.

Cache memory

The term "cache memory" is heard often when discussing computer technology. Generally speaking, cache memory is a special, high-speed pool of memory designed to increase access to a higher-level memory by retaining recently accessed information in the higher-level memory. In regards to its use with processors and motherboards, cache memory is implemented at different levels, each with a different associated term. *L1* cache, which exists on virtually all modern processors, is a very small, on-chip cache used to cache data and instructions processed by the system CPU. Most of today's faster processors further separate the L1 cache into two distinct subcaches, one for instructions and one for data.

The second level of cache memory is *L2* cache memory, which can be either on-chip or external (located on the system motherboard). L2 cache memory is designed to improve the speed of access to system RAM by using memory faster than standard DRAM to cache recently accessed data in RAM. L2 cache typically involves the use of Static RAM (SRAM), a high-speed memory type that doesn't require the continual memory refreshes that slow down traditional DRAM. Due to its design and features, SRAM is significantly more expensive than DRAM. The minimum amount of L2 cache you should use on Pentium or Pentium Pro systems is 256K, but 512K or more is recommended for optimal performance on systems with 32MB or more of RAM.

Another level of cache, *L3*, is present on some systems using on-chip L2 caches. L3 cache is used to augment the L2 cache and further enhance the performance of system memory access. L3 cache is essentially a secondary L2 cache and uses the same types of Static RAM modules used in L2 cache arrangements. Although most L2 and L3 caches use Static RAM, not all Static RAM is created equal. The next section describes each of the most popular SRAM types and their respective features.

The use of cache memory doesn't stop with memory access. The concept of caching is useful whenever one, higher-speed technology can be used to speed access to another, lower-speed one. A good example is the use of main memory as disk cache memory; this provides exponentially faster disk speeds in most cases and serves to optimize system performance.

STATIC RAM TYPES

Unlike DRAM, which requires power refreshes from the system board to retain its data, Static RAM memory retains its data until the data is changed (thus the term "static"). Because it doesn't require the performance-killing refresh cycles of DRAM, Static RAM memory is far faster, and therefore well suited to use in L2 and L3 cache memory. As with DRAM, there are a variety of different SRAM types used in different systems.

Asynchronous SRAM (ASRAM) is akin to FPM DRAM in that it is by far the most traditional and extant category of Static RAM. Most ASRAMs chips come in 15ns (nanosecond) formats and support 3-wait state reads and 4-wait state writes. ASRAM modules can be found on a wide range of systems, from the lowliest of PCs to the fastest RISC-based systems with bus speeds greater than 100MHz. The use of ASRAM is slowly giving way to faster SRAM technologies, especially as these technologies become cheaper to manufacture. Today, most systems have gone away from using standard ASRAM, using instead one of the SRAM types discussed below.

Later-model Pentium motherboards were among the first to use a new type of Static RAM chip called Pipelined Burst Mode SRAM (PBSRAM). PBSRAM uses overlapping address and data phases that eliminate the tight address-to-data access times found in standard ASRAM. Apart from this, PBSRAM uses virtually the same technology as ASRAM and is otherwise identical.

SSRAM (SYNCHRONOUS SRAM)

Like SDRAM, Synchronous Static RAM (SSRAM) synchronizes all operations to the system's clock signal. These types of chips offer an approximate 15 percent performance gain over traditional ASRAM memory and are approximately 5–10 percent faster than PBSRAM. Unlike PBSRAM, which uses a pipelined architecture, SSRAM uses a flow-through design that allows for faster operation.

Burst Synchronous SRAM (BSSRAM) is another type of SRAM that is essentially an extension of SSRAM. BSSRAM enhances SSRAM's design by adding a burst counter with configurable addressing modes (a feature found in SDRAM memory), giving it a performance boost of approximately 5–8 percent over SSRAM. Like SSRAM, BSSRAM uses a flow-through rather than a pipelined design.

A newer, higher-performance type of SRAM called FSRAM (Flow-through SRAM, named after the cache access method it uses) promises the best performance yet and is just beginning to appear in system designs. This cache RAM is the type expected to be used on upcoming Pentium II systems running at speeds of 300MHz and higher, and systems using the newest member of the DEC Alpha processor family, the 21264.

Finally, when choosing a system or motherboard, look for SRAM sockets that use SIMM-style modules rather than DIP (Dual Inline Package) formats. These are far easier to install and reduce the likelihood of damaging the memory during the installation procedure. Although almost new motherboards use this type of SRAM, some older motherboards (e.g., Pentium motherboards using Neptune and early Triton chipsets) use the older style of chip.

Storage Devices

One of the most important decisions you'll make when configuring your Windows NT system is the choice of which components make up your mass storage subsystem. Since this subsystem includes vitally important components of your system, including your hard disk and CD-ROM, choosing the fastest devices you can afford is important for building a high-performance Windows NT computer.

Storage controllers

Even if you've spent only a short while with Windows NT, you're likely to have heard that SCSI (Small Computer Systems Interface) is the best choice for Windows NT computers. However, newer, enhanced versions of the IDE (Integrated Drive Electronics) specification such as EIDE/ATA-2, ATA-3, and Ultra ATA tout new and enhanced features that claim to give SCSI a run for its money. In addition, these newer, faster IDE-based drives can be had for significantly less money than comparable SCSI drives, making them far more attractive to NT users buying on a budget. Meanwhile, at the high end, an enormous host of new SCSI specifications has also arrived on the scene, themselves promising better performance and features than previous incarnations of SCSI. In this section, we examine the various flavors of both technologies, compare their features, and help you to separate facts from marketing hype.

SCSI'S ORIGINS

The SCSI interface, which first debuted on Sun Microsystems and Apple Macintosh computers, was designed to be a universal, multipurpose I/O bus for personal computers. Previous PC-based I/O solutions created a separate controller for almost every kind of device, meaning that a system might have one controller for the hard disk, one for a tape drive, one for a scanner, and so on. In addition, these other technologies typically defined specifications involving one or more "dumb" peripherals attached to a controller that handled all of the I/O operations. SCSI, on the other hand, introduced a specification that called for intelligent controllers and peripherals and could attach all of these devices to a single controller card. This is accomplished by daisy chaining up to seven devices on the SCSI bus, each of which has its own unique ID.

The first implementation of SCSI, dubbed SCSI-1, was an unofficial, "de facto" adoption of SCSI by various vendors in the mid-1980s. Among its various benefits, SCSI offered the capability to process multiple, overlapped commands simultaneously. This permitted SCSI devices to overlap read and write operations with other SCSI devices in the system, which meant that multiple devices could process data in a concurrent, parallel fashion rather than serially. It also offered an 8-bit wide data path and a 5MHz bus clock rate, yielding asynchronous transfer rates of up to 1.5MBps and synchronous transfer rates of up to 5MBps. (*Asynchronous transmission* requires a handshake, or signal, between the sending and receiving computers, for each byte transferred; *synchronous transmission* transfers a series of bytes before handshaking occurs, increasing the data transfer rate.) However, since SCSI-1 was never officially defined by any standards organization, it was plagued with incompatibility problems due to differing vendor implementations of the specification.

THE EVOLUTION OF SCSI

As a result of the early incompatibility problems of SCSI-1, the ANSI-approved SCSI-2 standard was introduced several years later to provide a unified SCSI implementation that would ensure interoperability between SCSI hardware from different vendors. In addition to increased compatibility, this new flavor of SCSI also offered a faster 10MHz-bus clock that yielded a maximum data transfer rate of 10MBps. Devices complying with the faster transfer rate were dubbed "Fast SCSI-2" devices. Also included in the new spec were provisions for a new 16-bit wide version of SCSI-2 (dubbed "Fast/Wide SCSI-2") that doubled bus throughput to 20MBps and increased the maximum number of devices on the SCSI bus from 7 to 15. Still other enhancements include features such as parity checking and an improved connector specification.

The continued popularity and success of the SCSI-2 standard later begat the SCSI-3 standard, which includes several popular implementations including the parallel UltraSCSI (8-bit data path at a 20MBps transfer rate) and UltraWide SCSI (16-bit data path at a 40MBps transfer rate) standards developed by Adaptec, Inc., and supported by a large number of SCSI vendors. Luckily, the Ultra and UltraWide SCSI implementations use the same connector types as with SCSI-2 (Fast and Fast/Wide) and are fully backward compatible with SCSI-2 controllers. This makes it possible to mix and match SCSI-1, SCSI-2, and UltraSCSI/SCSI-3 devices on the same controller, because all use the same physical connector types. Of course, it will require using the UltraSCSI/SCSI-3 controller to realize the maximum potential performance of an UltraSCSI device, but the capability to seamlessly intermix devices supporting different standards is certainly a nice bonus.

Although Ultra and UltraWide SCSI have become the most popular parallel implementation of SCSI-3, bear in mind that they are just that — an implementation (developed and trademarked by one vendor, Adaptec). The SCSI-3 standard itself is actually a very broad and multifaceted specification that incorporates many possible implementations, including those based on serial and parallel data transfers.

FC-AL: THE NEXT GENERATION

In addition to the more traditional parallel implementations of SCSI interface, the new SCSI-3 standard also supports serial versions, including the new FibreChannel Arbitrated Loop (FC-AL) specification. FC-AL is a subset of a larger technology known simply as FibreChannel and uses a loop rather than bus architecture. Although many associate FC-AL exclusively with optical fiber cabling, it is also capable of running over standard copper coaxial cable.

One nice thing about FC-AL's architecture is that FC-AL devices don't require jumper or switch settings; all FibreChannel devices have unique, worldwide addresses that can't be duplicated (similar to Ethernet network devices). Currently, FC-AL supports up to 126 devices and speeds of 200MBps or higher. FC-AL drives and controller products are already shipping from manufacturers such as Symbios Logic, Digital Equipment Corporation, IBM, Qlogic, Seagate, Hewlett-Packard, and Quantum.

The cabling and data throughput limitations of parallel SCSI are slowly moving the industry toward serial technologies. In the not-too-distant future, it is likely that most computers will use serial rather than parallel controller technology for their storage subsystem, because it offers faster throughput and longer maximum cable distances.

A summary of the various implementations of the various flavors of SCSI and their related technical specifications (including transfer rates, bit widths, number of devices, and maximum cable lengths with various numbers of devices) can be found in Table 2-5.

TABLE 2-5 TECHNICAL SPECIFICATIONS OF VARIOUS SCSI IMPLEMENTATIONS

SCSI Version	SCSI Bus Width (bits)	Maximum Devices	Data Transfer Rate (MB/s)	Maximum Single-Ended Cable Length (Meters)
SCSI-1 (unofficial standard)	8	8	5	6
Fast SCSI	8	8	10	3[1]
Fast/Wide SCSI	16	16	20	3[1]
UltraSCSI (aka UltraSCSI Fast 20)	8	8	20	3 with 1-4 devices, 1.5 with >4[1]
Wide UltraSCSI	16	16	40	3 with 1-4 devices, 1.5 with >4[1]
UltraSCSI Fast 40 (aka Ultra2 SCSI)[2]	8	8	40	12 (Using LVD)[3]
Wide UltraSCSI Wide Fast 80 (aka Ultra2 SCSI)[2]	16	16	80	12 (Using LVD)[3]
FibreChannel Arbitrated Loop (FC-AL)	N/A[4]	126	200-400	24 using coaxial cable, 10 kilometers using single-mode fiber-optic cabling

[1] Differential versions allow for overall cable lengths of up to 25 meters (82 feet).

[2] Proposed or emerging standard.

[3] No single-ended specification exists for Ultra2 SCSI at this time; implementation requires a new transceiver technology called Low-Voltage Differential (LVD).

[4] FC-AL uses a loop rather than a bus architecture.

FIREWIRE: A NEW KID IN TOWN

Another important new technology using the SCSI-3 command set is FireWire (in case you hadn't yet noticed, it's important that all new technologies have cool names to have a chance of succeeding!). Also known by its other name, IEEE P1394, FireWire is an initiative originally developed by Apple Computer to be a successor to traditional parallel SCSI implementations for the attachment of many different types of high-speed peripherals.

FireWire uses an *isochronous* (time-synchronized) delivery method that offers the low latency and high continuous bandwidth demanded by audio, video, and imaging applications, as well as other streaming data types. FireWire uses a high-speed serial bus rather than a parallel bus, and its fastest version (called S400) has a data transfer rate of 400Mbits/second (approximately 50MBps; this figure doesn't take into account bus command overhead). It also offers slower 100Mbits/second and 200Mbits/second versions called S100 and S200, respectively. FireWire uses three-pair (six-wire) shielded twisted-pair cabling with a braided outer shield much like coaxial cabling used in 10Base2 networks.

FireWire also uses 16-bit addressing that allows for up to 65,536 devices on a single FireWire system; this is accomplished by allowing up to 64 devices per bus, and up to 1,024 bus bridges per FireWire system. FireWire systems can be configured using several different topologies, including a "star" pattern or "tree" pattern. Tree patterns are particularly flexible, allowing you to daisy chain devices off of multiple "branches" of the tree (an example of this arrangement is shown in Figure 2-5).

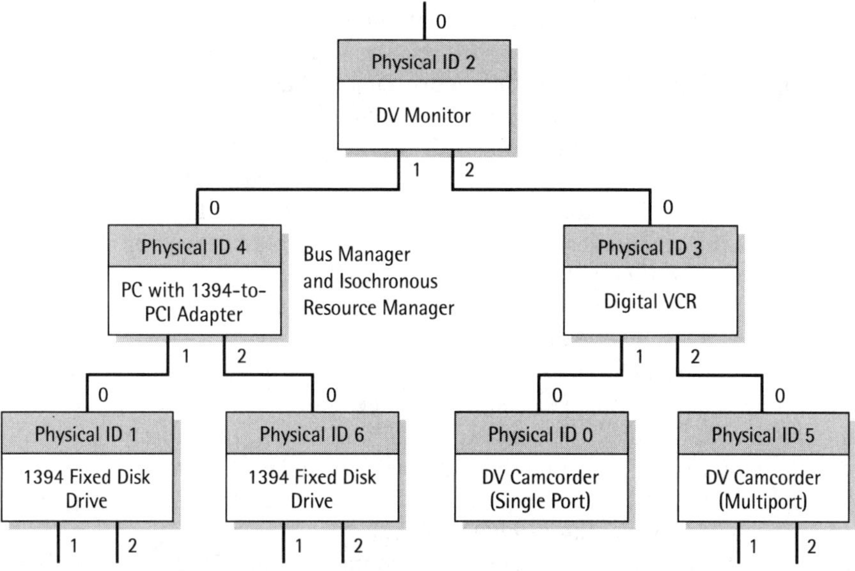

Figure 2-5: A FireWire "tree" topology.

The total length of the FireWire bus may be up to 72 meters in length (using shielded coaxial cable), and there can be up to 4.5 meters between each device on the bus.

Since it provides a bus capable of working with both low-speed peripherals as well as high-speed peripherals, FireWire has competition at both ends of the spectrum. At the low-end is Intel's Universal Serial Bus (USB), which has garnered a decent level of industry support but only supports a maximum 12Mbit/second transfer rate as compared to FireWire's 400Mbit/second. At the high end is the FibreChannel serial SCSI-3 implementation, which supports transfer rates of up to 1.6Gbit/second (approximately 200MBps). Although this is well beyond FireWire's fastest speed of 400Mbit/second, a new version of FireWire, S1600, is expected soon that will also deliver a 1.6Gbit/second data transfer rate. This kind of speed will almost certainly be a requirement if FireWire is to be considered a serious contender as the future of high-speed storage interfaces. It is also possible that FireWire, with its multimedia-oriented focus, will end up as a complement to other PC buses rather than being a replacement for them. Due to the relative newness of all these technologies, the winners of the PC peripheral bus wars are still yet to be determined.

UNIVERSAL SERIAL BUS: A CONTENDER AT THE LOW-END

Although not strictly a storage-oriented bus, the Universal Serial Bus (USB) architecture is another technology that's starting to gain a foothold in the PC market. Rather than being designed for a specific purpose, USB offers a higher-speed universal bus for connecting a wide variety of device types, including mice, modems, joysticks, speakers, digitizing tablets, scanners, and digital cameras.

USB offers significant advantages to traditional PC port types, allowing for the connection of up to 63 devices using a "tiered star" topology that is similar to the star topology used in 10BaseT Ethernet networking (a diagram of USB's topology is shown in Figure 2-6). This topology uses a system of hubs and nodes to allow for flexible configurations of USB devices. USB also has a few other things in common with Ethernet. USB uses a frame size that is nearly identical to Ethernet's and also uses half-duplex (one direction at a time) communication like Ethernet. However, USB uses signaling techniques that offer more than double the sustained throughput of 10Mbit/second Ethernet, which may eventually lead to the use of USB as a low-end networking solution in some environments (although no such specifications formally exist at this time).

USB offers both asynchronous and isochronous protocols, allowing it to support a wide variety of peripherals and applications including those requiring the delivery of real-time data (such as streaming audio and video). In addition, USB supports Plug and Play (PnP) functionality, which makes the configuration of USB-compliant devices far easier when using PnP operating systems such as Windows 95 and the upcoming Windows NT 5.0.

Most new Intel-based system include USB connectors, and USB may eventually be used in place of other low-bandwidth PC ports such as serial, parallel, game, and PS/2 mouse ports. However, since USB also offers significantly higher speeds than these other port types (up to 12Mbits/sec, approximately 1.5MBps), it is also a potential alternative to SCSI buses for the connection of certain peripherals traditionally used with SCSI.

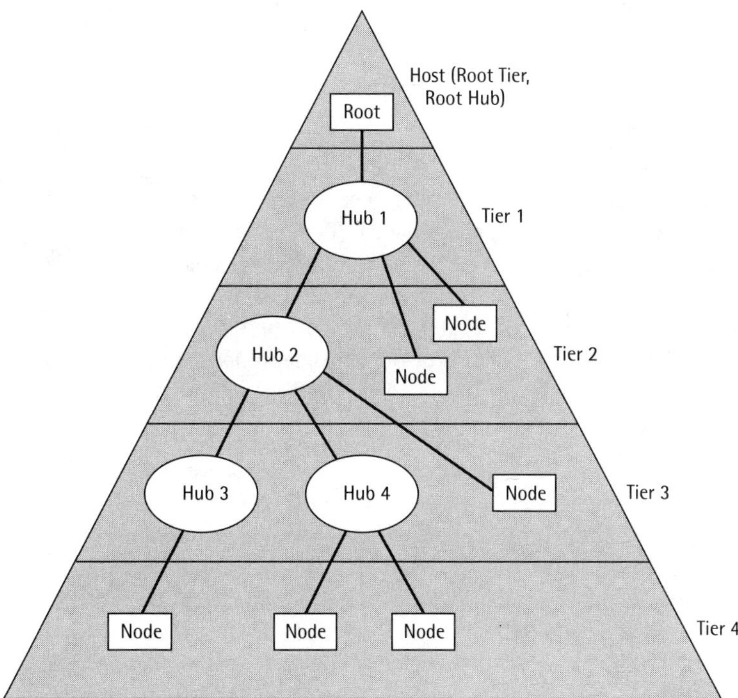

Figure 2-6: USB's tiered star topology.

SCSI + NT = POWER

Together, SCSI and Windows NT make a powerful combination. Without a doubt, the single most important feature of SCSI as it relates to performance under Windows NT is its capability of performing overlapped, multitasked I/O. One of NT's most important and touted benefits is its superior multitasking capabilities. These multitasking abilities are further enhanced by NT's asynchronous I/O model, in which multiple I/O operations can be conducted by the operating system concurrently with multiple devices. Unlike DOS and Windows 3.x, which serialize all I/O operations into a "one after the other" type of execution, NT can talk to multiple devices simultaneously. This in turn optimizes the overall efficiency of the system. After considering these facts, it starts to make sense why a storage technology that is itself capable of multitasking and asynchronous operations would provide the best performance on a multitasking system such as Windows NT.

In addition to its multitasking I/O capabilities, SCSI also provides a relatively low CPU utilization as compared to other disk controller standards such as IDE. This is because the various SCSI specifications incorporate specific features designed to maximize device performance while simultaneously minimizing the burden on the host system's processor. The most important of these features is by far the Bus Mastering DMA capability found on virtually all SCSI host adapters.

Data Transfer Methods Defined

One of the most important factors in a disk subsystem's overall speed is its method of data transfer. IDE and SCSI controllers can use any one of three methods to move data to and from system memory. The first, programmed I/O, relies entirely upon the host PC's CPU to conduct data back and forth between the controller and memory. Although cheap and easily implemented because it requires no special hardware, PIO-based disk I/O heavily taxes the host CPU and makes it unsuitable for multitasking environments such as Windows NT, UNIX, and NetWare. All implementations of the ATA/IDE specification can utilize PIO, whereas very few SCSI controllers (even older models) have ever employed this method.

The second and third methods of data transfer, which are more sophisticated than PIO, are both variants of a technology known as Direct Memory Access or DMA. DMA uses special hardware, either on the host system's motherboard or a controller card, to facilitate the transfer of data to and from system memory without requiring the involvement of the CPU. The less expensive and lower performance of the two DMA methods is known as third-party DMA. In third-party DMA, the specialized hardware used to accomplish these data transfers is the DMA controller chip found on all PC motherboards. The DMA controller is referred to as the third party since it transfers data between the first party, the drive controller, and the second party, the system's RAM. The various flavors of ATA/IDE specification support a variety of third-party DMA transfer methods, which are numbered from DMA mode 0 to DMA mode 3 in the new ATA-3 specification. Most SCSI adapters employ the DMA transfer method but use the first-party Bus Mastering DMA method rather than third-party DMA.

The second DMA transfer type and fastest data transfer method is known as first party or Bus Mastering DMA. In Bus Mastering DMA, the DMA controller chip is built onto the drive controller itself and enables the controller to directly transfer data to and from system RAM without requiring intervention by the host system's CPU or third-party DMA controller. This technology allows data to be transferred much faster than either PIO or third-party DMA, because only about half as many bus cycles are required. Both PIO and third-party DMA require the CPU or DMA controller to alternate between reading a word of data from one device and writing to the other. Each word of data transferred using this method requires two bus cycles: one for reading it from the source and one for writing it to the target. Bus Mastering DMA, on the other hand, only requires bus cycles when data is reading or writing to system RAM, thus cutting the number of required bus cycles in half. In addition, the Bus Mastering device is also capable of accessing system RAM using higher speed methods such as page mode access. All of this translates to significantly higher throughput and lower CPU utilization in Bus Mastering DMA devices. Virtually all SCSI controllers employ Bus Mastering for data transfer, but only later model ATA/IDE controllers (such as those found on Triton chipset-based Pentium motherboards and all Pentium Pro motherboards) are capable of using Bus Mastering DMA for data transfers.

One final note: the use of DMA and Bus Master DMA isn't limited to drive controllers — other types of adapters such as network interface cards may also employ these methods to transfer their data to and from RAM. It is important when configuring a system to not have too many Bus Mastering DMA peripherals because this could cause contention problems on the system resulting in lockups, instability, or data loss. Your hardware vendor should be able to tell you the maximum number of Bus Mastering devices your system can handle.

Unlike most IDE disk subsystems, which use a programmed I/O (PIO) method of data transfer that requires the system CPU to handle all I/O on behalf of the drive interface, SCSI uses Bus Mastering DMA to transfer data to system memory. Bus Mastering DMA uses DMA controller logic built onto the SCSI host adapter (rather than the system DMA controller) to take control of the bus and transfer data directly to system memory, thereby bypassing the system CPU entirely. For more information on the different data transfer methods used by disk controllers, see the sidebar, "Data Transfer Methods Defined."

SCSI also includes other features that help to improve other aspects of SCSI performance. For example, to improve the efficiency of SCSI bus utilization, SCSI provides features such as tagged queuing, scatter/gather, and disconnect/reconnect. In short, SCSI's efficient suite of protocols allows the maximum amount of work to be done with a minimal amount of strain on system resources.

The following is a summary of some of SCSI's more notable features and advantages:

- Extensive Device Support. SCSI supports an extremely wide array of devices, including everything from hard disks and CD-ROMs to items such as printers, floppy drives, scanners, optical drives, solid state drives, and hardware RAID systems. IDE on the other hand, is currently limited to support (via the ATAPI interface) for hard disks, tape drives, and CD-ROM drives. In addition, SCSI supports devices both internally and externally at the same high speeds, whereas ATA/IDE support is limited to internal devices only. Finally, SCSI can support either 7 (narrow/8-bit SCSI) or 15 (wide/16-bit SCSI) devices per SCSI channel, whereas IDE/ATA can only support four devices total split across two separate channels (each of which uses its own separate IRQ).

- Hot Sector Remapping. Hot sector remapping is a standard feature on virtually all modern SCSI drives and improves system fault tolerance by automatically and transparently moving data off of damaged sectors of the drive onto good sectors. In addition, this entire process is transparent to both the operating system and the end user. Although some higher-end ATA-X drives implement this feature, the majority of IDE drives do not.
- Disconnect/Reconnect. The SCSI disconnect/reconnect commands allow for better utilization of the common bus with multiple devices and improve efficiency by allowing SCSI devices to disconnect from the SCSI bus while they aren't using it (for example, to read a requested block of data), and then reconnecting as necessary to use the bus for data transfers (once the data has been located and is ready for transfer). In this way, a device doesn't hold up the bus while performing physical seeks in response to requests for data, which unnecessarily drags down performance. This feature makes sharing of the bus on SCSI systems far more efficient than devices on IDE-based systems, which tend to dominate the bus for long periods of time even when they aren't doing any actual transferring of data.
- Tagged Command Queuing. Tagged command queuing improves SCSI bus efficiency by allowing the SCSI host adapter to reorder and service queued commands in the most efficient order, rather than mechanically executing them in the order in which they were received. For example, if a command is looking for data in a certain area of a drive, and a command queued several steps later is looking for data in a neighboring area, the SCSI host adapter can reorder the commands to make the two occur sequentially, which is far more efficient than sequential execution. ATA/IDE always processes commands in the order received.
- Scatter/Gather. Another important contributing factor in SCSI's performance is the use of scatter/gather. Scatter/gather is a method for providing multiple host addresses for data transfer in one command packet. This feature improves SCSI I/O performance on operating systems like Windows NT that use virtual memory addressing, where one large amount of contiguous data from a device must often be broken up for transfer to multiple physical addresses in memory.
- Data Prefetching. Yet another feature that lends itself to superior performance of SCSI is its capability to perform a prefetch of data into the cache, which can improve sequential and random read performance. IDE drives don't offer data prefetching.

- Nonthermal Recalibration (A/V) Drives. Some higher-end disk drives, such as A/V certified drives, reduce or eliminate the slowing effects of constant thermal recalibration, or TCal, of the drive, which occurs to compensate for changes in head position due to heat. Although this technology is not inherently tied to SCSI, SCSI drives are currently the only drives found with this feature. Although it is theoretically possible to develop an non-TCal ATA drive, this is unlikely because ATA is a lower-end specification and suffers from other performance bottlenecks more serious than TCal; also, the additional expense of such drives would all but negate IDE's primary advantage over SCSI – lower cost.
- Higher Data Transfer Rates. In addition to the higher data transfer rates and wider data paths supported by the various SCSI specifications (such as Fast SCSI-2, UltraSCSI, and UltraWide SCSI), the highest drive spindle rates (up to 10,000rpms in some cases) are found on SCSI hard disks. Again, as with nonthermal recalibrating drives, this feature isn't inherently tied to SCSI; however, this availability makes SCSI a more appealing technology compared to the ATA/IDE specification whose drive spindle rates typically top out at around 5,400rpm.
- Support for (and availability of) Larger Drives. The SCSI specification supports extremely large drive volumes (usually up to 9GB or so), with some newer SCSI BIOSs providing support for volumes of up to 24GB or more in size. Nine-gigabyte SCSI drives are readily available on the market, with 18GB and 24GB models expected in the very near future. By comparison, even though the latest implementations of ATA support drives of up to 8GB in size, the largest ATA drives currently available are in the 6GB range.
- Low CPU Utilization. Last, but certainly not least, SCSI offers the lowest overall CPU utilization of any mass storage interface through a variety of features such as independent device data transfers, disconnect/reconnect, tagged queuing, and dynamic caching algorithms. This efficiency frees the CPU to perform other tasks. ATA/IDE drives, in contrast, make significant use of the system CPU for data transfer and make for poor performance in heavy multitasking environments.

SOME SCSI PITFALLS

The old saying goes, every rose has its thorn. Although SCSI-2 and SCSI-3 are high-performance, robust standards, implementing them can be a nightmare if done incorrectly. The three most common pitfalls for users implementing SCSI are improper electrical termination of the SCSI bus, incorrect cable lengths, and SCSI ID conflicts (two or more devices with the same SCSI ID number). If you've ever heard someone relate a story of a "nightmare SCSI experience" that had them tearing their hair out, it's likely that the problem was related to one of these two issues (however, it could also have been the rarer problem of a SCSI device manufacturer not adhering to a SCSI specification). Of the three, SCSI termination problems are by far the most difficult to diagnose and resolve.

A basic principle of SCSI says that a SCSI bus requires correct electrical termination at both ends to function properly. Proper termination ensures that the signal traveling down the SCSI bus doesn't reflect back, a situation that causes a variety of problems including "ghosted" SCSI devices, data errors, and other anomalies. Unfortunately, termination is implemented differently from SCSI device to SCSI device (most newer devices use jumpers or dip switches, while some older devices use removable terminating resistor packs or combinations of the two), and this can cause some headaches when configuring multiple devices on a SCSI bus. In addition, there are two types of SCSI termination: active and passive. It is important that all devices on the SCSI be configured to use the same type of termination. Of the two types, active termination is by far the better and more common choice.

Active SCSI termination requires three elements: at least one termination power source, and two terminating SCSI devices – one at each end of the SCSI bus. With active termination, one or more devices on the SCSI bus provide termination power to the bus, and devices at each end are configured with termination enabled. In most cases, the SCSI host adapter itself sits at one end of the SCSI bus and provides one side of the termination. The last SCSI device on the cable (whether internal or external) must also be terminated. In situations where both internal and external SCSI devices are attached to the host adapter, the SCSI host adapter must be configured with termination off (the most recent SCSI host adapters do this automatically, but you should always double-check the setting just to be sure).

Sounds simple, right? It can be, but sometimes you'll discover that not all devices are created equal in regards to termination. Some devices (generally the more expensive, higher quality ones) make good bus terminators and some do not. When they don't, it's generally because they use lesser quality components or different terminators with inconsistent Ohm ratings (SCSI-1 devices use 220–330 Ohm terminators, SCSI-2 devices use 90–110 Ohm terminators, and SCSI-3 devices use 90–95 Ohm terminators). As a result, it is possible that you could still experience problems even when the bus appears to be correctly terminated. Termination problems might manifest themselves in a number of ways, including duplicate or "ghosted" devices, missing devices, a hang at boot when the SCSI card initializes, or problems accessing SCSI devices attached to the bus. If a particular configuration doesn't work, try reterminating the bus with a different device (or devices) at the end(s). Also, it's probably a good idea to have more than one SCSI device providing termination power to the bus when many devices are present; furthermore, it is best to place these termination power sources as close as possible to the actual terminating devices themselves. A good rule of thumb is about one termination power source for every two to three devices on the bus. You don't have to worry about this causing an overvoltage problem because all SCSI devices have components to protect against this.

One way to circumvent SCSI termination hassles altogether is to use a separate external active terminator for your SCSI bus. Using one of these means you won't need to rely on the devices themselves to provide termination to the SCSI bus and can be assured that the proper termination is being supplied. One vendor of such products, Granite Digital (Union City, CA), makes both active terminators as well as special diagnostics cables that have LEDs telling you exactly what's going on with the SCSI bus. These products really take the guesswork out of SCSI troubleshooting and are highly recommended.

Granite Digital's SCSIVue Line of Products

The importance of good SCSI termination cannot be overstated. Granite Digital is a company that produces SCSI diagnostic cables and terminators that take the guesswork out of SCSI termination and ID conflict problems. They provide on-cable (or on-terminator) LED's that tell you exactly what's happening on the SCSI bus. In addition, their active terminators provide more reliable termination than those found on most SCSI devices.

Vendor: Granite Digital, Inc.

Product: SCSIVue Gold diagnostic cables and active terminators

Web site: `http://www.scsipro.com/`

IDE'S ORIGINS

Aside from SCSI, there's one other storage control standard: IDE (Integrated Drive Electronics). The original 1985 IDE (whose formal name is AT-Attachment or ATA) specification defined a 40-pin interface that ran on the ISA bus and offered a maximum throughput of 8.3MBps (although real-life average throughputs usually hovered around 2–3MBps). It also defined several modes of operation, including three programmed I/O modes (PIO modes 0, 1, and 2), and one DMA mode of operation (DMA mode 0). The specification, which was spearheaded by Compaq Computer and Western Digital, offered several major benefits to PC hardware vendors. However, the benefits of the IDE/ATA interface were inspired more by a desire for cost savings and simplicity rather than performance. By integrating drive controller electronics on the drive itself rather than on an expensive controller card, IDE allowed manufacturers to produce cheaper drives that offered users a decent level of performance. This still holds true: the IDE controller chipsets placed on virtually all modern motherboards are far less expensive for manufacturers to include than SCSI controller chipsets. As a result, the use of embedded SCSI controllers is generally relegated to high-end server motherboards. In addition, the electronics used on IDE drives themselves are also cheaper than those used on most SCSI drives, which is the reason why IDE drives tend to cost between 25 and 40 percent less than SCSI drives of similar capacities.

In addition to the cost saving features, IDE also offered features to simplify the process of configuring hard drives. IDE drives could be set up in a master/slave relationship without concern for electrical termination (unlike SCSI, which requires proper implementation of electrical termination), and drive configuration was simpler than with SCSI or the older ST-506–based drive interface standard. However, in a fashion similar to the early compatibility woes of the SCSI-1 specification, the original ATA/IDE specification was plagued by differing vendor implementations and drive incompatibilities: drives from one manufacturer would often fail to work with those from another. As with SCSI, however, the ease of ATA device interoperability has improved as the IDE/ATA specification has evolved and matured over the years.

EIDE AND BEYOND

With the advent of Windows 3.x in the early 1990s, the demand for faster PC performance grew to new levels and IDE began to show its age. In 1993, Western Digital Corporation, along with other key industry players, led the effort to strengthen the existing IDE interface. Their new specification, called Enhanced IDE (EIDE), breathed new life into the IDE specification by allowing for faster, higher capacity drives. It also supported the use of IDE on a local bus (e.g., VL-Bus) in addition to the slower ISA bus. EIDE offers new features to remove the four primary limitations of the original IDE specification: support for drives larger than the previous 528MB capacity limit; significantly faster data transfer rates (support for data transfer rates up to 13.3MBps for DMA mode 1 operation); an additional channel that allows for more IDE devices (upped to four from the two defined in the original specification); and a new interface specification, ATAPI, that allows connection of nondisk drive peripherals such as CD-ROMs and tape drives. Ironically, the ATAPI specification is essentially a simplified SCSI command set, and owes much to SCSI's design for device communication.

Since EIDE's introduction in 1993, there have been a number of additional extensions and improvements to the ATA/IDE specification, some of which are defined by standards organizations such as ANSI and the Small Form Factor (SFF) committee, and some of which are proprietary versions developed by drive vendors. The "official" second version of IDE, dubbed ATA-2, encompasses several of these proprietary implementations, including EIDE and two specifications promoted by Seagate and Quantum, Fast ATA and Fast ATA-2. The ATA-2 specification also defined two new PIO modes in addition to PIO modes 0, 1, and 2 introduced in the original ATA specification: PIO mode 3 at 11.1MBps, and PIO mode 4 at 16.6MBps. Also introduced were two new DMA-based modes, DMA mode 1 at 13.3MBps, and DMA mode 2 at 16.6MBps. In addition to ATA-2, there is also a newly ratified ATA-3 specification that has recently arrived on the market which defines still faster data transfer modes, including PIO mode 5 at 22.2MBps and DMA mode 3 at 33.3MBps. Quantum Corporation's implementation of ATA-3, dubbed "Ultra ATA," appears to be the early favorite and is being supported by a large number of hardware vendors. Together, these new specifications have conspired to extend IDE's lifespan and keep it a viable desktop technology for use with most modern operating systems.

THE LIMITATIONS OF IDE

Unfortunately, even with all of these new specifications, IDE still suffers from some inherent design limitations that make it less than appealing for use with Windows NT. Most importantly, IDE is highly CPU-intensive as compared to SCSI, burning precious CPU cycles to perform its work. With IDE PIO modes, the host system's CPU carries out all of the I/O operations for IDE devices. This causes a significant drain on CPU resources (an especially big no-no on any NT machine running compute-bound applications or as an applications server), and can result in lower overall system. In addition to the obvious undesirability of IDE's hogging of CPU resources, there is also another negative effect of this usage: it limits the effective speed of IDE. Why? To answer that question, let's take a look at how IDE does its work.

DOING THE IDE MATH

The most important thing to remember about published data transfer rates is that they are theoretical maximums and not the real-world, effective rates. The ATA-2/Fast ATA specification boasts a 16.6MBps rate for the transfer of data from a drive's buffer to system memory. However, this rate is virtually impossible to achieve under most IDE implementations due to the limitations of existing drives and the command overhead required by the ATA interface. To understand how the problem occurs, we must begin with some premises. First, even the fastest ATA/IDE hard disks aren't capable of much more than a 10MBps sequential transfer rate (drive to drive buffer). Furthermore, the buffer transfers on most IDE systems are 4KB in size. If we do the math, we discover that it takes around 400μs (μs = microseconds) or so for a drive to read 4KB of data into its buffer at 10MBps. Because we know ATA-2/Fast ATA's 16.6MBps transfer rate can easily keep pace with this, there should be no problem, right? Wrong!

Although the ATA interface is doing its job in this situation, there is a hidden factor limiting the 10MBps (the drive's maximum transfer rate in our example) performance ceiling: command turnaround time. Command turnaround time is essentially the overhead associated with the operations of the ATA/ATA-2 command set and is also affected to a small degree by the host system's CPU speed. Most PCs today have command overheads in the neighborhood of 275μs, and this figure remains fairly consistent between different computers. Unfortunately, this delay makes it impossible for the controller to keep pace with faster ATA/ATA-2 hard disks (most of which would require that the command turnaround overhead be closer to 150μs in order to keep pace with the drive). As a result, the ATA-2 controller can't grab data as fast as it arrives in the drive's buffer, resulting in a phenomenon known as "slipped revolutions." Because the drive's buffer is full and can't accept additional data, the drive platters must spin idly until the ATA interface can catch up and free room in the buffer. This in turn causes delays that limit the performance of ATA-2 drive subsystems.

Although the problem of "slipped revolutions" is prevalent in ATA and ATA-2-based systems, the new Ultra ATA and ATA-3 specifications all but remove this problem by doubling the burst transfer rate of the ATA interface to 33.3MBps. This allows the interface to keep pace with even the fastest ATA-based drives, and optimizes the performance of the IDE subsystem. One thing the new ATA-3/Ultra ATA specifications do not solve, however, is the CPU utilization problem of IDE. Despite enhanced ATA features such as DMA mode 2, Bus Mastering DMA, larger block sizes, and 32-bit addressing that were introduced to reduce CPU utilization of the ATA interface, the host CPU is still used to perform a significant amount of I/O as compared to SCSI. Table 2-6 summarizes the data transfer modes defined by various implementations of the ATA interface and their relative transfer rates.

TABLE 2-6 IDE P/IO AND DMA MODE TYPES

Mode Type	Affiliated Standard	Max. Synchronous Transfer Rate (MBps)
PIO Mode 0	ATA	<3.3
PIO Mode 1	ATA	5.2
PIO Mode 2	ATA	8.3
PIO Mode 3	ATA-2	11.1
PIO Mode 4	ATA-2	16.6
PIO Mode 5*	ATA-3/Ultra ATA	22.2
DMA Mode 0	ATA	4.2
DMA Mode 1	ATA-2	13.3
DMA Mode 2	ATA-2	16.6
DMA Mode 3*	ATA-3/Ultra ATA	33.3

*New standard recently ratified by the Small Form Factor (SFF) Committee.

IDE AND NT: OIL AND WATER

As was mentioned earlier, NT's asynchronous I/O model works most efficiently with a SCSI subsystem, due to SCSI's capability of handling multiple I/O requests simultaneously. Because all ATA/IDE systems are capable of handling only one I/O operation at a time, their performance is severely limited under Windows NT and other multitasking operating systems. Because the drive controller can only talk to one drive on a channel at a time, any other drive requiring I/O servicing at the same time must wait its turn in line until the first drive has finished. This aspect of IDE/ATA drives is also the reason you should never consider using them on NT systems acting as servers. Although even NT workstation computers will benefit from the use of SCSI over IDE (because the system itself is capable of multitasking file I/O requests), the situation becomes exponentially worse on machines with heavy file I/O demands.

On the other hand, these types of problems aren't nearly as prevalent under operating systems such as DOS and Windows 3.x that employ serialized I/O models. Even Windows 95 is prevented from taking full advantage of SCSI, because it lacks a fully asynchronous I/O model (like NT has) and maintains a significant degree of serialization in its low-level drivers. As a result, it isn't uncommon to see head-to-head comparisons of fast ATA-2 and SCSI-2 or UltraSCSI drives yield similar performance results under these operating systems. In these situations, choosing an ATA/IDE drive probably won't cause any significant performance loss. This is also true of single-tasking environments where a user typically only runs one application at a time, because SCSI's performance benefits don't really take off until two or more SCSI device-related tasks are run simultaneously. At that point, the multitasking features of SCSI are leveraged, creating a significant performance advantage over ATA-based systems.

Another note of interest on native ATA/IDE support under NT: Currently, NT's higher supported ATA PIO mode is PIO mode 2, which defines an 8.3MBps burst data transfer rate. This means that even if you're using a Fast ATA-2 subsystem capable of 16.6MBps with a PIO Mode 4-capable drive, under NT you're only realizing a maximum potential throughput of 8.3MBps. In addition, be sure to use only ATAPI v.1.2-compliant CD-ROMs and tape drives with Windows NT; this is the version that NT's ATAPI driver supports, and the use of ATAPI 1.1 or earlier devices could easily cause major headaches.

Also remember that the ATA/IDE specification relies upon the system's BIOS, and ATA/IDE features such as ATAPI support and >528MB disk capacities require a three-way support by the system BIOS, the peripherals, and the operating system. Although software BIOS enhancements exist to extend BIOS features and allow, for example, for hard disk partitions greater than 528MB on older systems, many of these utilities aren't compatible with NT. Fortunately, almost all modern PCs include Logical Block Addressing (LBA) support for IDE drives, which uses a logical addressing scheme similar to SCSI's to break the 528MB barrier. SCSI, on the other hand, has always used a logical block addressing/translation scheme to allow access to the full capacity of a drive. Also, because SCSI provides its own BIOS, this support is largely OS-independent – all the OS needs to do is provide a driver for the SCSI host adapter being used.

A final thought for the would-be IDE drive purchaser: Remember that IDE has other built-in limitations beyond those already mentioned. ATA/IDE specifications define a significantly shorter maximum cable length than is available in SCSI implementations. Whereas most SCSI implementations (differential SCSI excepted) provide for cable lengths of approximately 3 meters (approximately 10 feet), the maximum length for cables on ATA/IDE subsystems is a mere 45cm (just under 18 inches). To make matters worse, use of drives supporting the fastest PIO or DMA Modes cut even this distance in half, to just under 9 inches! With such cabling limitations, it's easy to understand why there are no defined specifications for connecting external ATA/IDE devices; there wouldn't be enough cable to connect them to the host system. One very important note: Don't forget to make provisions for the internal electronics inside the devices themselves when calculating cable distance; these invisible lengths count as part of the total bus length. In some cases, this distance can be as high as 6 inches or more (generally, however, it is safe to budget for around 2 to 4 inches per device).

Another "gotcha" with modern IDE is the difference between the primary and secondary IDE controllers on most motherboards. As you're probably aware, all modern implementations of the ATA interface include two separate IDE channels (normally built onto the motherboard), which are each capable of handling two devices. What you may not know, however, is that there are significant differences between these two channels. The primary channel (which normally uses IRQ14) is located on the system's faster PCI bus, which is capable of up to 33MHz operation. The secondary channel (which typically uses IRQ15), however, is located on the slower ISA bus and therefore limits the maximum data transfer rate of this channel to ISA's 8MHz transfer rate. This is good to remember if you are configuring an IDE drive subsystem, because you want to refrain from putting fast PIO Mode 4 drives on the slower channel whenever possible.

There can also be significant performance penalties when mixing different kinds of IDE devices on the same IDE channel. Unlike SCSI, which is capable of talking to peripherals communicating at differing speeds without incurring significant performance penalties, IDE will slow down when fast and slow ATA/IDE devices are combined on the same channel. For example, by combining a fast ATA-2 PIO Mode 4 hard disk on the same channel with a slower PIO Mode 2 IDE CD-ROM drive, you've effectively crippled the performance of the hard disk by forcing it to continually wait for I/O operations whenever the CD-ROM is active. Under these circumstances, the "fleet" effect takes place: the fleet can only go as fast as the slowest ship. A better solution is to place your slower IDE peripherals such as CD-ROMs and tape drives on the slower second channel, keeping them off the channel containing your faster hard disk(s). If you use more than two IDE hard disks on your system, however, you won't have a choice. With SCSI, these issues are virtually nonexistent.

Finally, as if all of this weren't enough, there are also a significant number of ATA/IDE controllers that use only a single command queue that is shared between the primary and secondary IDE channels. This can result in major performance delays when devices on both channels try to talk to the system simultaneously. This problem is further aggravated when the two channels are fully populated with IDE devices.

The maximum allowable length for a single IDE cable with two devices attached is 18 inches. In addition, achieving many of the higher PIO and DMA modes requires that this distance be cut in half to 9 inches (due to the higher data transfer rates involved).

Due to its extensive array of performance-related features and leveraging of NT's asynchronous I/O model, SCSI is clearly your best choice for disk subsystems on Windows NT computers. This is especially true of computers that are disk-bound by nature, such as fileservers and systems used for application development. However, any Windows NT system will benefit from SCSI's features and capabilities.

Hard disks

Unfortunately, just having a fast storage controller isn't going to make your disk storage subsystem a fast one. To create a truly optimal disk subsystem, you'll also need to put an equal amount of care into your choice of hard disks.

The most obvious place to start when choosing hard drives for your NT system is to choose drives that match the maximum capabilities of the system's disk controller. This means that if you've got an UltraWide SCSI controller, you should put only UltraWide SCSI drives on that controller; if you've got a Fast/Wide SCSI II controller, use Fast/Wide SCSI-2 drives; and so forth. Otherwise, you won't be taking advantage of the controller's capabilities and will be allowing this extra bandwidth to go to waste. In addition, try to keep all of your hard disks alone on the same drive channel wherever possible, and don't mix fast hard disks with other, slower devices. This will only serve to limit the drive's maximum throughput potential and create a less-than-optimal disk subsystem.

There are several criteria to keep in mind when purchasing hard disks, each of which affects a drive's overall performance. Each is described below, in the order of the significance of its impact on overall performance.

If you must share slow devices with fast ones on a SCSI bus, you should always place the slower devices at higher SCSI IDs. This will help to avoid "starvation" of the faster devices configured at the lower IDs.

MECHANICAL LATENCIES

The most important factor affecting any hard disk's performance is the drive's mechanical attributes. Unlike memory and processors, hard disks have actual moving parts that make them perform exponentially slower than these other components. The most important of these mechanical factors are *seek time*, *head switch time*, *cylinder switch time*, and *rotational latency*.

Seek time measures the amount of time it takes the drive's actuator arm to move a read/write head between tracks on the drive. Obviously, the impact of this factor on performance will depend on the number of tracks that exist on the disk. Many 3.5-inch disks these days contain upwards of 3,000 tracks, and it takes a lot longer for the drive to cross 2,999 tracks than it will to cross 1. This is the reason why you should only consider the *average* seek time of a drive (the average time it takes to locate a track on a random read request) and not the *track-to-track* seek time (which only measures the time it takes to move from one track to the next). All drive seek times are measured in milliseconds (ms). Seek times between adjacent drive tracks can be as small as 2ms or less, whereas *full-stroke* seeks (those going from the the drive's innermost to the outermost track) are normally in the neighborhood of 20ms or less. The average seek time for most of today's hard disks is usually in the 6–15ms range and is the only seek time figure to which you really need to pay attention.

Unfortunately, although a drive's average seek time measures only one dimension of the drive's overall performance, it has become the most common statistic cited by manufacturers when advertising their drives' features. This can lead to incorrect assumptions by unwary customers. It is easily possible, for example, for a drive with an advertised 12ms seek time to be faster than one with a 10ms access time. The reason is that there are many other factors that have a significant impact on a drive's overall performance. Therefore, when comparing drives, it is important to also look at these other factors.

One such factor affecting a drive's true performance is a type of mechanical latency referred to as *head switch time.* A drive's actuator arm moves all of the read/write heads over all platters simultaneously because they are not independent entities. However, only one of the read/write heads can be reading or writing data at a given time. The average time a drive takes to switch between two different read/write heads is referred to as head switch time. Like seek time, head switch time is measured in milliseconds.

A third and equally important factor in drive performance is the drive's *cylinder switch time* (aka track switch time). Cylinder switch time measures the time it takes for the drive's actuator arm to position the read/write head from one data cylinder to another. A drive cylinder is defined as all of the tracks located at the same relative position down through the different platters of the drive. Each of these factors is an important component of the time it takes for a drive to locate data on one of the disk's platters and should thus be examined when comparing different drives.

The final mechanical attribute you should examine about a drive is its *rotational latency.* Rotational latency is simply a measure of the average time (in milliseconds) a drive's read/write head must wait before the sector containing the desired data moves beneath the head. This figure will vary since the location of the disk's heads over its platters will be different at any given time. In a worst case scenario, the drive's read/write head will arrive at the desired track just after the desired sector has gone spinning by. In this case, the platters will have to make a full rotation before the sector can be accessed. However, the average amount of time this process takes, not surprisingly, is a one-half rotation of the drive's platters. This time is directly affected by yet another performance factor of the drive, the disk's *rotational speed* (measured in revolutions per minute or rpm).

Since a drive's rotational speed directly correlates to the drive's rotational latency, it would be nice to know what kinds of differences you can expect on drives with different rotational speeds. Table 2-7 shows some of the more common drive rotational speeds and their associated rotational latencies.

TABLE 2-7 COMMON DRIVE ROTATIONAL SPEEDS AND THEIR ASSOCIATED LATENCIES

Rotational Speed (rpm)	Rotational Latency (ms)
3,600	8.3
4,500	6.7
5,400	5.7
6,300	4.8
7,200	4.2
10,000	2.99

If you're looking for the fastest drives around, you should look into Seagate's new Cheetah family of disk drives. This line of UltraSCSI drives offer a 10,000rpm rotational speed, and are currently offered in 4.55GB and 9.1GB capacities. One tip, however, to remember: The extremely high rotational speed of these drives mean the drives will run hotter than those with lower rotational speeds and require direct cooling as a result. Therefore, you should be sure that the case you're using offers adequate cooling and should also ensure proper airflow over the drive using drive bezels or enclosures that incorporate fans directly inside them. Also, be sure to refer to the manufacturer's diagrams regarding the amount and direction of the airflow provided. Additional information on Seagate's Cheetah family of drives is available at: `http://www.seagate.com/disc/cheetah/cheetah.shtml`

Read and Write Caching Improves Performance

As it is with processors and RAM, the concept of caching is extremely important to a disk drive's performance. Virtually all modern disk drive contains an on-board cache buffer that is used both in disk-to-controller (read) and controller-to-disk (write) data transfers. Read caching is when a drive accesses data requested by the system from the appropriate sectors of the disk, and subsequently stores the data into the drive's

continued

Read and Write Caching Improves Performance *(Continued)*

internal cache memory. In this situation, the drive reads beyond the data requested and continues reading data into the buffer until it is full. This process of reading ahead is commonly referred to as "prefetching." This technique translates into much faster data access when additional requested data is located in the buffer, because data transfers from a drive's cache buffer are done at the maximum transfer rate of the drive. This transfer rate is exponentially faster (microseconds versus milliseconds) than situations where the drive must perform a physical seek of data using the drive's mechanics. Prefetching works well, because data is often (over 50 percent of the time) read from disks sequentially.

Write caching, used for I/O operations going to the drive, also offers performance benefits. Write caching allows system-to-buffer and buffer-to-disk transfers to occur simultaneously, which enhances performance by removing the rotational latencies that occur during sequential access. It also overlaps rotational latency and seek time with system processing during random write operations to the drive. These features translate to a performance increase of anywhere from 50 to 250 percent in sequential write operations and 30 percent or more during random write operations.

Although most drives offer read and write caching as standard options, it never hurts to double-check that these features exist on whatever drive you're considering for use with your NT system. In addition, the efficiency and performance of the read and write caching algorithms used by different drive manufacturers will vary, so it's also worth investigating whatever performance comparisons you can find about the techniques used by different manufacturers.

DATA TRANSFER RATE

Once a drive has positioned a read/write head over the appropriate sector of the disk, the drive is then ready to read or write the data from or to the disk platter. The speed of this transfer of data is yet another important factor in a drive's performance. In a disk-intensive environment such as Windows NT, especially when used in conjunction with disk-bound applications such as SQL databases, this factor will have an important impact on the speed of the system. The faster the data transfer rate, the better.

A drive's data transfer rate depends on two factors: the disk transfer rate (the rate at which data is transferred to and from the disk to the drive controller), and the controller transfer rate (the rate at which the drive controller passes data to the CPU). Data transfer rates are typically measured in terms of megabytes per second (MBps). To speed the host transfer rate and minimize mechanical delays (from seeking and rotational latency), many manufacturers make use of cache buffers that are placed directly on the disk drive (see the sidebar, "Read and Write Caching Improves Performance," for more information on this). In addition, many high-end disk controllers contain on-board cache RAM (typically from 1MB to 16MB or more) that also provides an enormous boost to the access of drive data.

DATA THROUGHPUT RATE

A disk drive's data throughput rate is a composite figure that measures both the drive's data access time as well as its data transfer rate. The data throughput rate, measured in kilobytes per second (KBps), indicates the total amount of data that the system CPU can access within a certain amount of time.

Data throughput rates can be subdivided into three distinct categories: *a minimum rate* (the worst case but guaranteed minimum rate); an *average rate* (a rate that can be achieved more than 50 percent of the time); and a *burst rate* (which is a theoretical maximum for the drive and is rarely achievable). Unfortunately, many drive manufacturers choose to quote burst rates when citing drive features, so be aware of this when comparing drive performance.

Although the average rate figure gives perhaps the truest picture of a drive's performance potential than do other individual figures (such as seek time), it and the other figures are also affected by the speed of the host system and are therefore not based solely on the drive itself. This fact should always be considered when reading data throughput rates for different drives. After all, if one drive is tested on a 200MHz Pentium Pro and another is tested on a Pentium 75MHz system, a significant part of any speed difference will be directly related to the differences between the two host systems used in the test. This aside, data throughput rates are still a good indicator of a drive's real-life performance; just be sure that the figures you're looking at are an apples-to-apples comparison.

THERMAL RECALIBRATION AND A/V DRIVES

Besides the mechanical latency factor inherent in disk drives, there is also another culprit that steals drive performance: thermal recalibration, also referred to as "TCal." Thermal recalibration is a routine housekeeping task performed by all standard hard disk drives, whereby the drive recalibrates the position of the drive's read/write heads to compensate for variances caused by heat. This process can result in interruptions during the data transfer process that can last anywhere from a few dozen milliseconds to up to 850ms in a worst-case scenario.

It's important to be aware of the real meanings of the terms used by the drive manufacturers when you're evaluating disk drive performance. Two commonly cited statistics are a drive's *average seek time* and its *average access time*. Average seek time is the average time it takes for the read/write head to move to a specific location on a disk platter. To compute the average seek time, a manufacturer divides the time it takes to complete a large number of random seeks by the number of seeks performed.

Average access time, on the other hand, is the average time interval between the time a request for data is made by the system and the time the data is available from the drive. Access time includes the actual seek time, rotational latency, and command processing overhead time. This includes SCSI command overhead time, which can add up to 2ms or more to the access time. Therefore, a drive advertised with a 4ms average seek time and an 8ms average access time may actually have a typical "real world" access time of 14ms after adding these factors together.

Although the TCal process doesn't cause major problems on regular disk I/O operations on most business-oriented applications, it can be fatal with high-end digital video and audio applications. This is because these types of applications require the disk drive to sustain a predetermined minimum data transfer rate, and disaster can result when the rate is not sustained. For example, full-motion video data requiring a continual delivery of data at 30 frames per second should not be used in conjunction with drives using TCal. Another example is CD-R drive mastering applications, which also require a high-sustained data throughput to correctly record on the CD-R media. Any hiccups during the data transfer process caused by thermal recalibration could easily ruin the CD-R media.

To address these problems and provide adequate sustained data throughput rates for these types of applications, several drive manufacturers produce special disk drives known as "A/V" drives. These drives eliminate the thermal recalibration process by using special features and components such as embedded servos. Embedded servos are timing and positioning signals on the disk's surface that also store data and allow the drive actuator to fine-tune the position of the read/write heads.

A/V drives also tend to offer other throughput-sustaining features such as on-the-fly error correction that minimize data transfer interruptions and guarantee the consistent delivery of data. The result is often sustained throughput rates of 4.0MBps or more without the fluctuations that plague regular drive types. If you are planning on using any A/V-oriented applications under Windows NT, you should give serious consideration to the purchase of an A/V drive. These drives are available from a variety of manufacturers, including Seagate, Micropolis, and Quantum.

THE ULTIMATE: SOLID STATE DISK DRIVES

Although they are still extremely pricey, the "Holy Grail" of fast drive storage is, without a doubt, the *solid state* drive (SSD). These drives are essentially lumps of DRAM memory chips integrated together in a drive-like package. They offer unbelievable speed because they literally eliminate mechanical latency factors and measure media access rates in nanoseconds (10^{-9}) rather than milliseconds (10^{-3}). SSDs provide consistent, submillisecond access to data stored on them, in many cases up to 100 times faster than comparable magnetic disk drives (the typical access times of SSDs range from 150ns to 230ns).

SSDs are typically used in conjunction with some form of battery backup, which are often long-life lithium batteries to prevent data loss. They also have MTBF (Mean Time Between Failure) ratings of twice that of standard magnetic disk drives (5–10 years versus 2–5 years).

Manufacturers such as IBM and Digital Equipment Corporation have been making solid state drives for years for midrange and mainframe applications, but their relatively high costs have kept them out of the PC market. However, as the price of RAM continues to drop, these drives are becoming more and more attractive all the time. If you are using Windows NT in an extremely storage-intensive environment and require the fastest storage access times available, then solid state drives are your answer.

REMOVABLE HARD DRIVES

Another choice when considering hard disk storage for your system is removable drives. Although they come in a variety of different capacities and capabilities, all of these drives essentially offer the same primary benefit: the ability to remove the drive or drive cartridge (for cartridge-based drives). This can have benefits in situations requiring either portability or security of data because the drive's contents can be removed from the system and transported to another location or drive.

Although a variety of removable cartridge drives exist on the market, drives from Syquest, including the SyJet 1.5GB, EZFlyer 230MB, and EZDrive 135MB products, offer some of the best price/performance ratios around. They are fast, relatively inexpensive, and offer excellent support for Windows NT. You can find additional information about Syquest's SyJet and EZFlyer products on its Web site at: `http://www.syquest.com`

Some of the most popular drives in the cartridge-based category include the Zip and Jaz drives from Iomega Corporation, and the EZDrive from Syquest Corporation. These drives use magnetic recording techniques on a drive cartridge that typically stores anywhere from 100MB to 1GB or more of data. Although not as fast as regular hard disk drives, most offer excellent data transfer rates and serve as excellent secondary storage, data archiving, or backup devices. Although many of these drives are offered in both parallel and SCSI versions, it is highly recommended that you stay clear of parallel versions and stick with the SCSI-based models because they offer far superior performance.

There are also a number of manufacturers making special drive/drive bay combinations that allow standard hard disks to be inserted and removed in a "hot swappable" fashion to achieve a similar result to cartridge drives. Although a primary application for such devices is use with RAID arrays that are made for hot swappability, workstation computers may also benefit from the use of these systems. The major disadvantage to this type of design is that the drives used are often less protected than drive cartridges, and thus have a greater exposure to damage while being removed. However, because they are standard hard disks (e.g., a 10,000rpm Wide UltraSCSI drive) that typically have much faster access times and data transfer rates than cartridge-based drives, this arrangement has the advantage of providing much better performance.

Optical drives

Luckily, magnetic media isn't your only storage choice for Windows NT. You can also choose from a variety of different optical-based drives. Optical drives are advantageous in that they offer removable formats, high storage capacities, and laser-based storage mechanisms that make optical drives far less prone to damage than magnetic media drives (i.e., hard drives). Optical drives have a higher reliability because their recording mechanisms don't ride close to the disk surface as with magnetic media drives, and therefore can't experience the data-damaging "head crashes" that occur with magnetic drives. In addition, many of the drive media formats used by optical drives are rated for long lives, with MTBF ratings of 30 years or more in some cases.

Some optical drives are capable of recording; others, like CD-ROM drives, are read-only by nature. Those that are write-capable are further divided into drives that allow data to be written and rewritten multiple times, and those that allow data to be written only once. In addition, write-capable optical drives generally use one of two different recording methods: Phase Change or Magneto-Optical. In the sections below, we take a look at several of the most popular optical drive technologies currently available.

CD-ROM DRIVES

CD-ROM drives have become somewhat of a commodity these days, and are found on virtually all modern PCs. They provide 650MB of read-only data storage or roughly 74 minutes of audio data (also called the CD "Red Book" Audio format) on a single-sided optical disc. In addition, many CD-ROM drives are capable of supporting a host of other data formats, including CD-ROM Mode 1, CD-DA, CD-I, Video CD (MPEG), CD-ROM XA Mode-2, Form 1, Form 2, Photo CD/Photo CD Plus, CD-G, and Karaoke. No Windows NT computer, except perhaps the most basic of network workstations, should be without a CD-ROM drive.

CD-ROM drives have come a long way since their 150KBps single-speed mechanism beginnings. Today, 12X, 16X, 20X, and 24X CD-ROM drives are commonplace, with data transfer rates of up to 3600 KBps and maximum (synchronous) burst transfer rates as high as 12MBps or more in some cases. When shopping for a CD-ROM drive for your system, remember the "numbers game" that manufacturers tend to play with their drive ratings. Specifically, remember that not all drives rated at the same spin rate (e.g., 12X) will deliver the same real-world performance, and the drive's interface type (i.e., SCSI or IDE) will also make an enormous difference.

Never assume that a CD-ROM with a faster speed rating will necessarily be a better choice than one with a slower one (e.g., 16X versus 12X). It isn't uncommon to find that the supposedly slower drive in this situation actually delivers better performance than the "faster" one in real-world performance testing. Another important factor to be aware of is that most CD-ROM discs aren't recorded at rates higher than 4X. For CD-ROM applications such as multimedia titles that are recorded using slower speeds, having a drive capable of faster data transfer rates won't make the CD-ROM access go any faster (although a faster drive will still speed up the copying of files from the CD-ROM using standard file copying procedures).

For the best CD-ROM performance, stick to the use of SCSI CD-ROM drives over IDE-based ones. This is due not only to the enhanced performance that the SCSI bus provides, but the reduced CPU utilization of SCSI versus IDE CD-ROM drives. It is not uncommon for some superfast IDE CD-ROM drives (i.e., those rated at 12X or higher speeds) to cause CPU utilization on some systems to jump to a whopping 55 percent or more! Although faster SCSI CD-ROM will also increase CPU utilization as compared to slower SCSI drives, this utilization will generally not exceed the 10–25 percent range; in any case, it will be far less than a comparable IDE-based drive.

For the reasons described earlier, it is an especially bad idea to share an IDE-based CD-ROM drive on a network server. When network users access the drive (especially if it is a fast drive), your server's CPU utilization will likely skyrocket, and this could easily drive your server's performance into the ground. If your network users tend to access this drive frequently, the problem will be exaggerated. If your network server has an IDE CD-ROM and you've noticed occasional, seemingly random performance lags, you may want to investigate this as a possible cause and either replace the drive or stop sharing it altogether.

Table 2-8 shows some sample CD-ROM spin rates and their corresponding theoretical (but not always actual) data transfer rates.

TABLE 2-8 CD-ROM DRIVE SPIN RATES AND DATA TRANSFER RATES

CD Spin Rate	Corresponding Data Transfer Rate (theoretical maximum in KB/sec)
1X	150
2X	300
4X	600
8X	1200
12X	1800
15X	2250
16X	2400
20X	3000
24X	3600

As with hard disks, there is far more to a CD-ROM than its maximum rated data transfer rate. This rate is a sequential "burst" rate for contiguous data that has already been located on the disc, but doesn't take into account other factors such as how long it takes to locate this data. To gain this information, you should also look into a drive's seek time, which is given in similar terms to hard disks. Full-stroke seek times describe a full inner-to-outer track head movement, while random seeks tell the average amount of time it takes for a drive to locate an arbitrary piece of information on the disc. Another important consideration with CD-ROM drives is the on-drive cache (data buffer) used by the drive; for optimum performance, look for drives with at least 512KB or, even better, 1MB of cache. Drives using smaller buffers will cost less, but will also sacrifice performance.

Personal testing has found drives from Plextor Corporation (formerly Texel) to be consistently faster than comparable drives rated at the same speed from other manufacturers. These drives, which are offered almost exclusively with SCSI interfaces, usually contain at least 512KB of buffer memory and currently come in versions up to 20X.

Information about Plextor's line of CD-ROM drives can be found on its Web site at:

`http://www.plextor.com`

CD-R DRIVES

Although CD-ROM drives broke new ground when they were introduced and created new possibilities for the distribution of applications and multimedia information, they have always had one major problem: you can't write to them. This fact led to the development of a new type of CD-ROM drive called CD-R (for CD-Recordable). CD-R drives are able to read and are backward-compatible with standard CD-ROM discs, but can additionally write data or audio information to special CD-R media. Most CD-R drives are offered in internal or external versions and almost always use a SCSI interface.

CD-R drives, in conjunction with CD mastering software, write data in "sessions" that are one-time recordings and that can contain a variety of different CD data formats. Although it isn't possible to rewrite CD-R media, it is possible to write multiple sessions to the same CD-R disc (however, the reading of such discs requires multisession-capable CD-ROM drives). It is critical to the successful creation of a CD-R disc that data be delivered to the CD-R drive in a smooth, continuous fashion without interruption during the mastering process. This means that the system should be fairly quick and that you use a fast source device (e.g., a hard disk or CD-ROM if copying information from CD-ROM to CD-R drive). Otherwise, buffer underruns can occur in the CD-R disc when it doesn't receive data quickly enough, ruining the CD-R disc being recorded to (these ruined discs are jokingly referred to as "coasters" by CD-R veterans, because that's about all they're good for).

To prevent the accumulation of "coasters" (ruined CD-R discs) when using a CD-R drive to record CDs, it is recommended that you only use it in conjunction with an extremely fast, fully defragmented hard disk. In addition, the drive should preferably use a SCSI or UltraSCSI interface to achieve an optimal maximum data transfer rate, and both the CD-R drive and the hard disk should ideally be located on the same SCSI controller and channel. In addition, you may also wish to consider the use of an A/V-rated hard disk that eliminates thermal recalibration, another potential cause of buffer underruns during CD-R recording sessions.

CD-R drives are available from a variety of different manufacturers and have different speed ratings: one for reading and one for writing. For example, the fastest CD-R drives currently offer a 6X speed for reading and a 4X speed for writing. Older drives offer 4X read/2X write or 2X read/1X write speeds. There are some CD-R drives on the market that don't offer NT support, so be sure to check with the manufacturer regarding NT drivers before buying a CD-R drive. Special drivers are required because CD-R drives use a different sector size than CD-ROM drives, so NT's default CD-ROM driver (CDROM.SYS) won't work.

CD-R drives are available from a number of manufacturers, including Hewlett-Packard, Pinnacle Micro, Plextor, Sony, Panasonic, and Philips.

PD/CD DRIVES

Although CD-R drives are good for one-time writing sessions (like WORM [write once, read many], described later) or making backup copies of CD-ROM discs, they aren't rewritable like hard drives: once you record over a portion of the disc, it can't be erased or rerecorded. However, the idea of having a single optical drive that is capable of reading CD-ROMs as well as writing data is still an attractive one. A newer type of optical drive, called Phase Change Dual (PD) drives, offers another approach to recordable CDs.

PD drives (also called PD/CD drives due to their backward compatibility with regular CD-ROMs) use a split head mechanism capable of writing to special rewritable 650MB PD cartridges as well as reading standard CD-ROMs. Although PD drives can't be used to create CD-ROMs like CD-R drives, their rewritability features make them especially attractive for those who want to use the drives for backing up, archiving, and transporting data. A PD/CD drive and PD cartridge are shown in Figure 2-7.

Figure 2-7: A PD/CD drive and PD cartridge.

Although Matsushita Electronics (Panasonic's parent company) developed PD technology and owns the patents for it, it has licensed the technology to a number of other manufacturers who have already started delivering PD/CD drives to the market. If you're looking for a single optical drive type that offers both CD-ROM compatibility and data rewritability at a reasonable price, PD/CD drives are well worth considering.

CD-REWRITABLE

The newest member of the CD family is the CD-ReWritable, or CD-RW, format. New drives capable of writing this format have just recently begun to appear on the market. CD-RW drives are capable of using special media that, unlike their CD-R cousins, are capable of being written and rewritten. CD-RW media is similar to CD-ROM and CD-R media in capacity (650MB data, or 74min of audio), but can be rewritten up to 1,000 times. Although most current CD-ROM and CD-R drives cannot read CD-RW media, new DVD-ROM (see below) drives and drives supporting Multi-Read (MR) can. In addition, CD-RW drives are capable of recording CD-R as well as CD-RW media.

Although CD-R is still normally the best choice for creating CDs for distribution and archiving (due to the lower cost of the media), CD-RW has the advantage of being usable as a data backup medium due to its rewritable nature. As Multi-Read capability becomes more and more pervasive in standard CD-ROM drives, CD-RW may also begin to replace CD-R as the writable CD format of choice.

DVD DRIVES

While CD-ROM discs are great for the delivery of many data types such as applications, audio, and graphics, they don't offer the capacities and data transfer rates required by certain data types such as digital video. To answer this, a new digital storage technology called DVD (Digital Versatile Disk, formerly Digital Video Disk, and pioneered by Panasonic Corporation) has been developed. DVD technology allows the storage of up to 4.7GB of information on a single high-density DVD-ROM disc and has a data transfer rate of 11 Mbits/second (1.4 MBps). DVD-ROM is poised to be the successor to CD-ROM drives on the desktop, because they offer backward compatibility with CD-ROM discs as well as enormous capacity.

DVD's scope isn't limited to use with computers, however. They are also targeted squarely at the consumer electronics market, providing well-defined audio and video formats that make them a formidable competitor to video laser disc players. In addition, DVDs may also end up replacing CD-ROM drives in home video game systems. Like CD-ROM, DVD-ROM is a media capable of supporting many different data types. The current flavors of DVD include a number of different data formats, some of which have been finalized and some of which are still under final development. There are currently two DVD-based formats that have been finalized:

- *DVD-ROM:* a high-capacity data storage medium, similar to CD-ROM
- *DVD-Video:* a specific application of DVD designed to deliver motion picture content

The DVD formats still under development but expected soon include:

- *DVD-Audio:* a specific application of DVD designed for audio-only uses, similar to CD-Audio (this specification is still under development)
- D*VD-R (Recordable):* a variation of DVD that permits one-time recording of data; a write once, read many (WORM) implementation
- *DVD-RAM:* a variation of DVD that is erasable and can be rewritten many times

DVD-ROM drives are expected to come initially in 8X and 10X speeds, with 12X speeds and greater speeds to follow shortly thereafter. However, remember that comparing DVD-ROM and CD-ROM spin rates isn't an apples-to-apples comparison, because DVD-ROMs use a greater data density and video-oriented data transfer technology that translates to superior performance to standard CD-ROM drives. As a result, an 8X DVD-ROM drive can easily best even a 12X CD-ROM drive when it comes to the delivery of streaming video and other data types.

Although DVD-based drives will initially be read-only like current CD-ROM drives, a new version called DVD-RAM is expected in the near future that will offer data recording at initial capacities of 2.6GB. In addition, enhanced DVD-ROM formats, including a 9.6GB double-sided format (requires flipping the disc over), an 8.5GB dual-layer version, and a 17GB double-side dual-layer format are expected by late 1997. If possible, try to find DVD-ROMs that will support the dual-layer media types. DVD-ROM drives are just beginning to hit the market as of this writing and are likely to start becoming standard equipment on desktop computers as their prices drop.

DVD-RAM is a forthcoming standard that promises to deliver us into optical heaven: a high-capacity, high data transfer rate coupled with rewritability. As of this writing, the standards committee working on the DVD-RAM standard had still not made a final decision as to whether Magneto-Optical (MO) or Phase-Change (PC) technology would be used as the recording method for DVD-RAM devices.

MAGNETO-OPTICAL DRIVES

In addition to the Phase Change technology used by many optical drives, there is also another optical drive recording method called magneto-optical (M-O). Magneto-optical drives use a technology that, like its name implies, uses a hybrid of optical and magnetic principles to read and write data. Magneto-optical disks are plastic or glass disks enclosed inside cartridges and coated with a compound that has special properties. The disk is read by shining a low-intensity laser onto the disk's surface and examining the magnetic polarization of the reflected light: one polarity reflects a "0" bit value, and the other reflects a "1." To write data, a higher intensity laser is used to heat the material to a specific temperature (called the media's *Curie point*) where it becomes susceptible to a magnetic field. When the media cools again, the recorded bits are "frozen" in place. When data needs to be rewritten, the process is started over again, and the media is heated and recooled.

Early implementations of magneto-optical technology used drives that performed writes in up to three separate passes (erase, write, and verify), which caused write performance to suffer as compared to hard disk drives. However, many of today's M-O drives use a new mechanism and media type that allow for a one-pass, direct overwrite write method called LIM-DOW (Light Intensity Modulation–Direct OverWrite) that greatly enhances write performance.

It may be possible to increase the performance on some M-O drives by eliminating the write-verify phase of the data write cycle. Many drives enable this feature using a jumper or DIP switch; others may require a firmware update to accomplish this. This setting is enabled on the majority of M-O drives even though the instance of write errors is relatively low on these drives. If you're willing to entertain a low risk by disabling this jumper, you will significantly enhance the drive's write performance.

M-O drives are currently offered in a variety of formats, from 130MB to 4.6GB. They are also available in both 3.5-inch and 5.25-inch media sizes, with the 3.5-inch versions offering greater convenience and faster spindle rates (up to 6,000 rpm or more in some cases), and the 5.25-inch versions offering higher data capacities. The fastest 5.25-inch M-O drives have spindle rates in the neighborhood of 4,000 rpm, but 5,400 rpm drives are expected to arrive shortly. Also, as the media densities are increased on the 3.5-inch versions, you can also expect to see new 3.5-inch M-O drives in the near future with capacities challenging those of the 5.25-inch models.

Pinnacle Micro is one of the leaders in the M-O drive market and makes M-O drives with capacities of up 4.6 GB, with synchronous transfer rates as high as 4 MBps. For more information on Pinnacle's M-O drives, point your Web browser to: `http://www.pinnaclemicro.com`

Using M-O for Ultrareliable Server Boot Drives

Although it may seem like a strange use for the technology, Magneto-Optical drives may have a use in your network file server. Due to their superior reliability, long MTBFs, and invulnerability to head crashes, M-O drives make an excellent choice as a boot drive for Windows NT Server computers requiring the utmost reliability and minimum downtime. Although not as fast as many SCSI and UltraSCSI hard disks, M-O drives are far less likely to fail than regular hard disks, making them a perfect choice for "zero-tolerance" environments that can't afford to have the server's drive fail. By using M-O or other optical drives as the boot partition, you are reducing the possibility of a failure ever occurring rather than taking precautions in the event that it does as with RAID. (Note: For this arrangement to work, the SCSI host adapter BIOS to which the optical drive is connected must support the use of removable drives as a boot device.)

WORM DRIVES

Although their use has diminished a great deal with the advent of newer optical technologies, WORM drives are another type of optical drive worthy of mention. Their write-once nature makes them similar to CD-R drives, but WORM drives predate CD-R technology by a number of years. Unlike CD-R drives, WORM drives don't offer an industry standard format, with different WORM drives using different formats to record data. However, many WORM drives offer much larger capacities (typically in the 2–9GB range) than CD-R and other optical media types, and are ideal for use in applications such as imaging and data archiving. However, a more important and practical point is that there is no support for WORM drives under Windows NT. However, it is possible that such support will be created in the future.

If your applications require a write-once procedure for security or other reasons, and you are able to find a drive with Windows NT support, you may want to consider the purchase of a WORM drive for your NT system. Manufacturers of these types of drives include Panasonic and Sony. Expect WORM prices to be slightly higher due to their specialized nature and the fact that they're primarily used in nonmainstream applications.

Tape drives

To accommodate you in backing up your system, Microsoft includes built-in tape drive support as well as a basic backup application (NTBACKUP.EXE) with Windows NT. Although a few lower-capacity tape drives are supported by NT (e.g., older QIC80-based 250MB drives), the majority of the drives supported are of the SCSI-based variety. Tape drives are installed in Windows NT via the Control Panel's Tape Device applet, shown in Figure 2-8.

As with just about every other kind of computer peripheral type, tape drive technology has gone through a significant amount of growth and enhancement during the past five years. The Quarter-Inch Cartridge (QIC)-based 120MB and 250MB drives of yesteryear have given way to higher capacity, higher reliability technologies such as DAT, DLT, and Travan. Microsoft has also steadily increased the number of tape drives supported under Windows NT, and other manufacturers have added to this support by writing NT drivers for their tape drives.

Although there are a variety of older, proprietary tape drive standards in existence that are still supported under NT, our discussion is limited to those tape drives that are still being actively supported and sold in today's market.

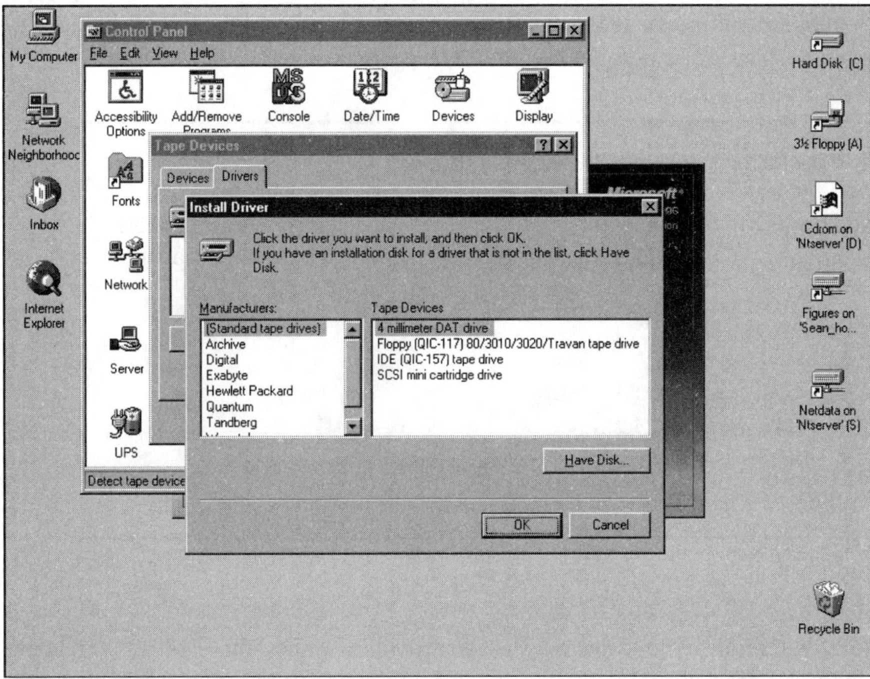

Figure 2-8: The Windows NT Control Panel Tape Devices applet used to install tape drive support.

MINICARTRIDGE DRIVES

Although the falling prices of more sophisticated DAT drives have put the squeeze on the minicartridge tape drive market, these drives still enjoy a loyal following and strong sales. Minicartridge drives come in several different flavors, the most popular of which are the newer QIC-Wide (QW, aka QIC-30XX formats) and Travan formats. Both offer superior reliability to previous minicartridge formats, but are still slower and less reliable than other tape formats such as DAT and DLT. Minicartridge drives typically work off of the system's floppy disk controller, although some newer models come in SCSI interface versions as well. The primary reason for their popularity is that minicartridge drives offer the lowest cost-per-megabyte of any tape drive on the market, making them popular for use in home and small business environments.

Capacities for minicartridge drives range from 250MB to 4GB or more. Although not very commonly seen on Windows NT computers, minicartridge drives have enjoyed considerable success on systems using other operating systems such as Windows 3.x and Windows 95. Of the various minicartridge formats, Travan drives are the most popular because they offer decent reliability, capacities of up to 4GB, and the broadest support from tape drive manufacturers and backup software developers. Travan drives come in several different varieties, each with a different "TR" number and associated capacity. The various Travan formats and their corresponding capacities are shown in Table 2-9.

TABLE 2-9 TRAVAN TAPE CAPACITIES AND DATA TRANSFER RATES

Travan Version	Capacity (Uncompressed/Compressed)	Data Transfer Rates* (Minimum/Maximum, in KBps)
TR-1	400MB/800MB	62.5/125
TR-2	800MB/1.6GB	62.5/125
TR-3	1.6GB/3.2GB	125/250
TR-4	4.0GB/8.0GB	567

*Depends on type of controller used.

Although minicartridge drives offer attractive low prices, they are far from being the highest performance tape drives you can purchase for a Windows NT computer. The superior reliability and speeds of higher end tape drives such as DAT, coupled with the rapidly decreasing price difference between low-end DAT and high-end minicartridge drives make it difficult to recommend minicartridge drives to any except the most budget-conscious of buyers. Minicartridge drives are available from a number of manufacturers, including Hewlett-Packard/Colorado, Seagate, and Exabyte.

DAT DRIVES

Digital Audio Tape (DAT) drives are without a doubt the most popular type of tape drive for Windows NT systems. DAT drives combine high capacities and fast data transfer rates with superior reliability and a relatively low cost per megabyte, making them a popular backup choice for servers and workstations alike.

DAT drives use a helical-scan recording method and store data on 4mm tapes certified under one of three levels of DDS (Digital Data Storage) compliance (DDS-1, DDS-2, and the newest, DDS-3 format). The maximum storage capacities of the tapes depend on the length of the tape and whether the drive supports compression: some do and some do not. DDS-1 tapes allow for the storage of up to 4GB with compression, DDS-2 tapes allow for up to 8GB with compression, and the latest DDS-3 tapes are capable of storing up to 24GB of data with compression.

Lengths of DAT tapes range from 60 to 125 meters. One nice thing about DAT drives is that regardless of their primary media type, they all offer backward compatibility with previous DDS levels, and are capable of automatically recognizing whatever DDS media type is placed in the drive.

Never use audio-grade DAT tapes in DAT drives; only use the proper DDS-certified tapes. Although the tape used for computer-grade DDS tapes and audio-grade DAT tape is basically the same, computer-grade tape is taken from the center of the roll (before slitting) and must meet strict ANSI standards to achieve its DDS certification. Computer-grade DDS DAT tapes also have a much lower BER (Bit Error Rate) than most audio DAT tapes and are significantly more reliable (unlike audio DAT tape, DDS tape is certified as "error free").

Finally, DAT drives are offered in special, high-capacity autoloader versions in addition to the regular single-tape versions. DAT autoloaders treat multiple DDS DAT tapes as a single "virtual" tape, so an autochanger's total capacity depends on the number of tapes supported. Many DAT autochangers based on DDS-2 tapes offer capacities up to 48GB or more; those based on the newly released DDS-3 format offer capacities starting at 144GB.

In addition to providing higher storage capacities, most DDS-3 tapes also use a better tape composition that provides higher quality and reliability of media; this had been a concern for some with earlier DDS standards.

DAT drives are available from a number of tape drive manufacturers including Hewlett-Packard and Seagate.

8MM DRIVES

Cousin to the 4mm DAT drive, 8mm tape drives are essentially like bigger DAT tapes that use the same helical scan recording method as their smaller relatives. The 8mm technology used with personal computers is also similar to the 8mm media used in consumer video technology, but has been modified to meet the more rigorous standard of computer data requirements. Eight millimeter tape drives typically offer capacities of anywhere from 7GB to 40GB, and data transfer rates from 0.5MBps to 6MBps.

Although they have been somewhat overshadowed by the popularity and lower prices of 4mm DAT, and the superior capabilities of DLT drives at the high end, 8mm drives still offer a solid backup choice for use with Windows NT. Although there are far fewer manufacturers producing 8mm drives than other tape drive types, several are still actively producing and selling the drives. However, before purchasing one of these drives, be sure to compare its features and benefits against comparable DDS-3 and DLT drives; DDS-3 drives typically offer comparable capacities at lower prices, while DLT drives offer higher performance at prices comparable to 8mm drives.

The primary vendor of 8mm technology is Exabyte, who makes the majority of 8mm drives currently on the market. Most, if not all, of Exabyte's 8mm drives are supported under Windows NT.

DLT DRIVES

Digital Linear Tape (DLT) drives are among the fastest and highest capacity tape drives in existence. First used in mid-range and mainframe systems, DLT drives have become popular as a high-end backup choice for PC networks as well. DLT offers a combination of high reliability and high performance, with DLT drives capable of a data transfer rate of 3MBps. DLT drives have been though several generations, from DLT2000 drives to the latest DLT7000 drives. DLT media are 0.5-inch cartridge-based tapes in a 5.25-inch form factor and as such are significantly bulkier than 4mm DAT or 8mm data cartridges. Table 2-10 shows several DLT drive types and their corresponding capacities and data transfer rates.

Most DLT drives currently in service have capacities between 10GB and 15GB and data transfer rates of up to 1.5MBps, although the latest DLT 7000 drives feature a data transfer rate of 5.0MBps and a native capacity of 35GB. Like DAT drives, DLT drives also come in autoloader versions that use multiple tapes that are treated as a single, logical tape. DLT autoloader drives are currently offered in capacities of up to 490GB. A significant advantage DLT holds over helical scan tape drives such as 4mm DAT and 8mm is the expected media and head life. Many DLT tapes are rated for over 1 million passes whereas most helical scan tapes are rated for only around 2,000 passes. In addition, most 4mm DAT and 8mm drives have 15K to 25K head life (MTBF), whereas DLT drives typically have a head life that is approximately 25 percent longer.

TABLE 2-10 DLT DRIVE CAPACITIES AND DATA TRANSFER RATES

DLT Drive Model	Capacity (GB)	Data Transfer Rate Uncompressed/Compressed* (MBps)
DLT-2000XT	15	1.25/2.5
DLT-4000	20	3.0/6.0
DLT-7000	35	5.0/10.0

*Most DLT drives offer some form of hardware compression.

There are three primary composition types used for DLT tapes, which vary in regards to capacity and reliability. These composition types are:

- MP (Metal Particle, standard type). This is the original type of tape used with earlier DLT drives and is still used today. It offers average capacities and reliability.
- AME (Advanced Metal Evaporate). This is the composition type used by DDS-3 tapes, as well as high-capacity 8mm and DLT drives. It is also currently the most common material for DLT tapes.
- AIT (Advanced Intelligent Tape). This composition has logic and is implemented with or without a 16K memory chip (MIC) for storing a directory index. AIT offers higher capacity, higher aerial density, and tougher tape composition than other composition types.

Quantum Corporation is the principle proponent and manufacturer of DLT tape drives, although they also license the technology to a variety of other companies including Digital Equipment Corporation, Overland Data, and GigaTrend.

A FINAL WORD ON TAPE DRIVES

Although the sequential access nature of tape drives makes them far less dynamic or glamorous than random access devices such as optical or removable hard drives, they are also far less expensive than these devices in terms of dollar-per-megabyte. Until rewritable optical drives reach a comparable price point for similar capacities, tape drives will continue to be the media type of choice for the archiving and backup of data.

Floppy drives

Of all the drive storage technologies in existence, floppy drives have probably progressed the least. The limitations of the standard PC floppy controller have limited the growth of these devices, with the largest available floppy drives being a puny 2.88MB in capacity (although most systems still use 3.5 inch 1.44MB floppy drives). However, floppy drives remain a necessity because they are a least common denominator on all systems for the distribution of information and storage of data. Although floppy drives per se haven't moved much in the past five years, there are some new floppy-like technologies that do offer the compactness and removability features of floppy diskettes, but in much higher capacities.

LS-120 and floptical drives

Several years ago, Iomega Corporation headed an ill-fated initiative to develop a special high-capacity floppy drive replacement dubbed a "floptical drive." This drive was to store 21MB of data and would read standard floppy diskette types as well. The new standard was touted as being the end to standard floppy diskette drives, a much-rued artifact still present in PC systems. Although some companies manufactured these drives, the idea never really caught on with system vendors or users and was fairly short-lived.

Recently, however, several manufacturers, including Compaq, 3M, and Matsushita, developed a new removable drive technology called LS-120 that has aspirations similar to the original floptical drive. LS-120 drives, which are capable of storing 120MB per disk, use an IDE interface and have the added advantage of being backward-compatible with regular 3.5-inch floppy diskettes. In addition, the latest incarnations of the LS-120 drives are also capable of writing standard floppy diskette formats at up to three times the speed of a regular floppy drive. Specifically, LS-120 drives deliver approximately 65ms average access times and 1MBps burst data transfer rates, with 500KBps sustained throughput rates. All of these statistics are far faster than any current floppy diskette drive.

Although they're beginning to receive some favorable press and several supportive manufacturers (and are faring better than their floptical predecessors), LS-120 drives still haven't received widespread use in the PC environment. This is largely due to the presence of other competitive products such as the Iomega Zip drive, which has stolen much of the limelight from these drives. Users are reluctant to buy LS-120 drives because they offer lower capacities and slower performance than low-end optical and magnetic-based removable drives. In addition, system vendors are reluctant to use them as standard equipment on their systems because they cost significantly more than regular floppy drives and haven't been in high demand by users as of yet. However, many modern BIOSs may be seen with LS-120 support, which is a promising sign for the future of this technology.

The fate of the LS-120 drive is still up in the air, but if its price drops to a low enough level, it may yet become standard PC equipment. Be sure if considering the purchase of one of these drives that you compare its price, performance, and features against other low-end removable drive types.

Video Subsystem

The graphics-intensive nature of a GUI (Graphic User Interface) environment such as Windows NT makes your choice of video graphics card an important factor in the overall performance of your NT system. Video graphics cards and accelerators offer a dizzying array of technologies and features, and different cards are targeted at different applications and uses. As a result, the price range for a Windows NT video card can range from $150 for a standard business applications-oriented card, to a whopping $1500 or more for the fastest OpenGL accelerator cards used in high-end NT graphics workstations. In this section, we help you understand the current state-of-the-art in video graphics technology so that you can make the appropriate choice for your system's needs.

Choosing a fast video adapter

Choosing a fast video adapter starts with a basic identification of what type of applications you'll be running under NT. In addition, you'll want to examine several physical attributes of any card you evaluate, including the coprocessor type or chipset used by the card, the video memory (RAM) used on the card, the bus/connector type, and the maturity of the Windows NT drivers provided by the card.

2D AND 3D TECHNOLOGY

There are two primary categories of video card technology: 2D and 3D graphics. Two-dimensional graphics are the type used by mainstream home and business applications. Three-dimensional graphics are the type used by heavy graphics-oriented applications such as animation, CAD, and even many of today's more sophisticated games. Three-dimensional graphics add the dimension of depth, represented by a Z-axis, to the height and width (i.e., X- and Y-axes) dimensions of traditional 2D technology. Although 3D graphics have traditionally been used in niche products, they have recently entered the mainstream and more 3D titles are appearing every day. Many cards combine 2D and 3D capabilities on a single card, while others are dedicated to either 2D or 3D functionality. It is also possible to use separate 2D and 3D cards together in the same system using the signal pass-thru technology supported by virtually all dedicated 3D cards; essentially, the card ignores all 2D instructions and doesn't kick in until an application specifically makes use of it.

As a result of this increased popularity of 3D, you may wish to consider a video graphics adapter that provides good 3D as well as 2D performance, especially if you foresee any 3D graphics or game applications in your future. Graphics and computer animation professionals using NT will want to stick with cards offering the highest possible performance for both 3D and 2D, and may even want to consider a card that supports NT's native OpenGL graphics language.

On the flip side of the coin, machines acting as NT server computers typically have little or no graphic needs at all. Typically, these types of systems sit in a back office or locked server closet and receive a minimal amount of direct use. It is a good idea to only use basic, ISA-based video cards on servers, to avoid soaking up the available bandwidth on fastest buses with unnecessarily fast video cards.

COPROCESSORS, CHIPSETS, AND DRIVERS

The most important aspect of any video card is the graphics coprocessor and/or chipset used by the card. Generally, the faster the chipset or coprocessor, the faster the card. Like most computer technology, video graphics processors and chipsets are a fast-moving market, with new technology coming out on an almost weekly basis. However, most cards at this time are using one of several different chipsets, including those from manufacturers such as Tseng Labs (the ET-6000 chipset), S3 Labs (the S3 ViRge 2D/3D chipset), Nvidia (NV1 3D chipset), 3Dfx (VooDoo and VooDoo Rush chipsets), and Rendition's Verite 1000 chipset. Several manufacturers also produce their own high-performance chipsets and coprocessors, some of which use 64-bit or even 128-bit dedicated coprocessors. These manufacturers include

ATI (the Rage 2D/3D), Matrox (the MGA 64-bit series of processors), and Number Nine (the Imagine 128 Series 2 chip).

Much of a graphic adapter's performance under NT (or any operating system for that matter) is also dependent on the optimization level of the drivers being used. Slow drivers can easily make a dog out of an otherwise fast adapter. Therefore, when researching adapters, try to stick with ones that have robust, mature drivers that the vendor has had some time to optimize. Otherwise, if you buy the latest and greatest video hardware using beta drivers, you'll likely experience less-than-optimal performance and perhaps even system crashes.

VIDEO RAM TYPES

Another important factor in video graphics performance is the type of video RAM used on the card. In addition to standard Dynamic RAM (DRAM) like that used for main system memory, there are a number of special RAM chip types developed specifically for use with graphics cards.

The first type, video-oriented RAM, is a special dual-ported version of standard DRAM called Video RAM (VRAM). VRAM chips use two I/O ports instead of the standard one used by DRAM chips, meaning that they can be sending and receiving data simultaneously. Since standard DRAM uses only a single port and can therefore only perform one type of operation at a time, this severely hampers their performance in graphics-intensive operations and makes cards using them undesirable.

DirectX5: High-Speed Graphics Performance Comes to NT

Windows 95 was the first Microsoft operating system to receive a net set of graphics and audio technology called DirectX. DirectX5, the latest version of DirectX, is made up of a number of other APIs including DirectDraw, DirectSound, Direct3D, DirectPlay, DirectInput, and DirectSetup. Each of these APIs allows high-end graphics applications and games to boost their performance exponentially over previously provided methods. The release of DirectX on NT is an especially important milestone for NT users because the hardware isolation and client/server graphics subsystem used by previous versions of NT have traditionally caused NT to offer abysmal graphics and game performance. Now, with DirectX, NT is able to enjoy much of the same support as is found with Windows 95.

Still other types of VRAM use even more than two ports, making them even faster than the dual-ported variety. One variant of VRAM doing this is known as 3DRAM, which can also be found on some higher-end 3D graphics cards (since it offers 3D-performance enhancements such as improved frame and Z-buffering). 3DRAM's performance goes well beyond that of the VRAM/WRAM (Window RAM) found on many display adapters, and its integrated ALU allows for drawing functions to be accelerated; this feature is particularly useful for high-end 3D video cards.

It is recommended that VRAM be the minimal type of RAM used by the graphics card you choose for your NT system; try to avoid those using regular DRAM. In addition, try to avoid cards using other single-ported memory types, such as MDRAM (Multibank Dynamic RAM), SGRAM (Synchronous Graphic RAM), or RDRAM (RAMBUS Dynamic RAM) memory.

Another popular video memory type is WRAM. Like VRAM, WRAM is dual-ported. However, due to its design, WRAM can be driven at higher frequencies than VRAM and typically delivers up to 30 percent better performance over VRAM at the same clock speeds. Despite its increased performance, WRAM is also cheaper to manufacture than VRAM and has thus replaced the use of VRAM on cards from several different manufacturers.

The amount of RAM you choose for your video card is similarly important, because it will determine the maximum resolution and number of simultaneous colors the card can display. When choosing a card, use the information in Table 2-11 to determine how much RAM you'll need on your video card. In addition, try to choose cards that allow you to install additional RAM (i.e., are upgradable), in case your needs change.

TABLE 2-11 MEMORY REQUIRED AT VARIOUS RESOLUTIONS AND COLOR DEPTHS

Resolution (pixels)	Color Depth (# of Colors)	Memory Required to Display (MB)
640x480	256	1MB
640x480	65,536	1MB
640x480	16.7 million	2MB
800x600	256	1MB
800x600	65,536	1MB
800x600	16.7 million	2MB
1024x768	256	1MB
1024x768	65,536	2MB
1024x768	16.7 million	3MB
1280x1024	256	2MB
1280x1024	65,536	4MB
1280x1024	16.7 million	4MB
1600x1200	256	2MB
1600x1200	65,536	4MB

When choosing a graphics adapter, don't forget to ask about the speed of the card's RAMDAC (Random Access Memory Digital to Analog Converter). Faster RAMDACs normally translate to crisper on-screen colors and support for higher maximum refresh rates (especially important for large monitors running at high resolutions). As a general rule of thumb, try to avoid cards using RAMDACs slower than 200MHz and try to stick with those using speeds of 220MHz or higher.

OpenGL: 3D for NT

One of the primary reasons that Windows NT can be an effective competitor to sophisticated (and expensive) graphics workstations such as those from Silicon Graphics (SGI) is NT's inclusion of the industry standard Open Graphics Library (OpenGL) API. OpenGL is a well-defined graphics API that is used in many high-end graphics, animation, and rendering packages. One example of OpenGL applications is the OpenGL-based screen savers that ship with all versions of Windows NT. These give a glimpse at the power of OpenGL-based rendering.

Although Windows NT will support the use of OpenGL on any video adapter, the effective use of these types of applications really requires the use of an OpenGL-based graphics card. These types of cards use dedicated coprocessors that provide native support of the OpenGL language and blazing performance for OpenGL applications. Without such cards OpenGL requires the host system's CPU to carry out all rendering tasks, which puts a severe performance drain on even the fastest of CPUs.

OpenGL cards are available from a number of system vendors, including Dynamic Pictures, ELSA, and Symmetric Corporation. They are also available in multiprocessor versions, with some using up to four processors on a single card.

3D/OpenGL Graphics Accelerators

For graphics professionals and others seeking the ultimate in graphics and 3D rendering performance, there are a number of high-end video adapters with Windows NT and OpenGL support that provide amazing performance. These cards have applications in CAD, 3D graphics development, multimedia authoring, and just about anything else that requires a high-octane 3D-rendering engine.

Two of the fastest cards we've seen and tested are the GLoria-L (Glint 500TX-based card) from ELSA, Inc. and the Oxygen 102/202/402 402 (one, two, and four processors, respectively) family of adapters from Dynamic Pictures, Inc.

Information on the ELSA GLoria-L can be obtained at:
http://www.elsa.com/

Information on the Dynamic Pictures Oxygen products can be obtained at:
http://www.dypic.com/

AGP and UMA: Video rides a new bus

Although the 64-bit, 66MHz PCI 3.0 bus would seem to be enough bandwidth for just about any application, the bandwidth-intensive nature of video has already precipitated the development of several new, graphics-specific technologies for PCs. One such technology, called Accelerated Graphics Port (AGP), is an Intel Corporation–led initiative to provide greater bandwidth for high-end video applications that can be provided by the PCI bus. AGP is a native 32-bit bus that runs at 66MHz, but uses a special "double-edged" signaling technique (using both the leading and trailing edges of the connector contacts) that significanty increases the available bandwidth. In addition to increasing bandwidth, AGP also reduces the latencies (i.e., inherent signal propagation delays) found in the PCI bus. AGP is characterized by the use of pipelined memory, a maximum theoretical data transfer rate of 532MBps at 133MHz (with an effective maximum of around 490MBps), and the demultiplexing of address and data signals.

Although AGP is the early favorite as the new high-bandwidth video bus, it also has some competition from the VESA (Video Electronics Standards Association)-led Unified Memory Architecture (UMA) standard. UMA defines an option for connecting the graphics controller, frame buffer, main memory, and main memory controller together across a special high-speed memory bus. This design allows graphics adapters to freely access video frame buffer or main system memory without intervention from the system's main chipset.

Although the 100MBps maximum sustained bandwidth potential of current PCI implementations are more than enough for most applications, it's likely that AGP and/or UMA technology will find their way into high-end graphics systems in the near future.

Network Adapters

If your Windows NT computer will participate on a local area network, be sure to obtain the highest-performance network adapter you can find. This is especially important for network servers, because the heavy network access on these machines often makes their network adapter cards a primary performance bottleneck.

Networking technologies

Before discussing the various network interface cards (NICs for short) available for Windows NT, it's probably best to begin with a discussion of the various networking technologies available. This is by far the most important aspect of any network, and the type of network card you choose is dependent on the networking technology used on your LAN.

ETHERNET

The granddaddy of all PC networking technologies is 10MBps Ethernet. Originally developed in 1973 at Xerox Corporation's Palo Alto Research Center (PARC), Ethernet enjoys the widest deployment of all network types in existence. It is estimated that well over 80 percent of the world's networks are implemented with Ethernet technology.

Although Ethernet is by far the most popular network type around, this doesn't necessarily mean that it is the best or only choice for your network. Ethernet uses a relatively crude media access scheme called *Carrier Sense Multiple Access with Collision Detection* (CSMA/CD for short) that has some significant drawbacks. Like many network technologies, CSMA/CD networks allow only one station to transmit data on the network at a time. However, it is also possible for two nodes to attempt to communicate data on the wire simultaneously; this event is known as a "collision." When collisions occur, both nodes wait for a randomly generated "back-off" period before attempting to communicate data again. Although this doesn't cause problems in low-traffic networks, collisions can become a major problem in highly congested Ethernet networks with many nodes. When a large number of nodes and large data types (i.e., multimedia data types such as audio and video information) are combined and wire utilization exceeds 60 percent, Ethernet can become a true nightmare, with high collision rates resulting in slow performance and other problems.

Ethernet is capable of running over a variety of different cable types, including various types of coaxial cabling (10Base2 and 10Base5 Ethernet) as well as unshielded twisted-pair (UTP) cabling (10BaseT Ethernet; requires the use of Category 3 or better cabling) and fiber-optic cabling (10BaseF). In addition, Ethernet can be run across either a bus (end-to-end as with 10Base2 and 10Base 5 Ethernet) or star (node-to-hub as with 10BaseT Ethernet) cabling topology.

FAST ETHERNET

Poised as a successor to the use of Ethernet on LANs, Fast Ethernet (also known as 100BaseTX or 100BaseT4, depending on the cabling type used) offers a 100MBps aggregate bandwidth that, like regular Ethernet, is shared by all nodes on the network. Fast Ethernet also uses the same CSMA/CD media access method as Ethernet, which means it is subject to the same collisions that occur in Ethernet networks. However, due to its higher bandwidth, Fast Ethernet is far less prone to experience collision-related problems in all but the most high-traffic network environments.

Unfortunately, although it offers significantly higher bandwidth, Fast Ethernet has several significant drawbacks in addition to the use of the CSMA/CD media access. First, it mandates a smaller overall network diameter than Ethernet (205 meters versus 2,500 meters), and it also prevents the use of regular 10MBps Ethernet devices on shared Fast Ethernet hubs. However, there are also some switching hubs on the market (albeit expensive ones) that do allow for the mixed use of Fast and regular Ethernet devices.

Full Duplex Doubles the Power

Another variation of Ethernet is provided by products capable of *full-duplex* operation. Normally, Ethernet uses a half-duplex mode of operation that allows communication in only one direction at a time. However, many of today's Ethernet adapters and switches are also capable of full-duplex communication, which allows communications in both directions simultaneously. Full-duplex essentially doubles the bandwidth of the Ethernet flavor in use; that is, 20MBps for regular Ethernet and 200MBps for Fast Ethernet. However, the capability to use full-duplex Ethernet is dependent on the capability of all network devices, including all switches and adapters, to support full-duplex operation. Full-duplex switches are also significantly more expensive than shared-media devices.

Fast Ethernet is capable of running over two different unshielded twisted-pair cable types in two different configurations: 100BaseT4 Fast Ethernet, which uses a minimum of Category 3 UTP cabling with four wire pairs; and 100BaseTX Fast Ethernet, which uses Category 5 UTP cabling with two wire pairs. One nice thing about Fast Ethernet is that it provides an easy upgrade path for existing 10BaseT networks that doesn't require recabling the network. Category 3-based networks can migrate to 100BaseT4 technology, while Category 5-based networks can migrate to the 100BaseTX version of Fast Ethernet.

SWITCHED ETHERNET

Switched Ethernet offers a different method of increasing the available bandwidth of Ethernet networks. Rather than using a shared media access control method like regular and Fast Ethernet, Switched Ethernet introduces the concept of Virtual LANs (VLANS). In Switched Ethernet, nodes do not share network bandwidth; each node is able to use the full rated specification of the Ethernet standard (i.e., 10MBps for Switched Ethernet and 100MBps for Fast Ethernet switches).

Switches are essentially multiport bridges that connect individual communicating nodes over a full, private 10MBps or 100MBps pipe. As a result, Ethernet switches deliver enormous performance benefits on congested networks, because they increase the available amount of network bandwidth exponentially. For example, although each port is capable of 10MBps maximum, a 12-port 10MBps Ethernet switch delivers a total aggregate bandwidth of 120MBps. Even when compared on a megabit-per-second basis, Switched Ethernet delivers better performance than Fast Ethernet due to the superior efficiency of switching technology as compared to shared technologies.

Switches can also be freely intermixed with shared Ethernet solutions, providing additional bandwidth for high-traffic network segments experiencing congestion. This flexibility, combined with the ability for switched Ethernet to use existing network cards and cabling, make it one of the best upgrade choices for Ethernet networks.

100VG-ANYLAN

Led by Hewlett-Packard Corporation, the 100VG-AnyLAN standard is an alternative to Fast Ethernet as the successor to Ethernet networks. This technology offers a 100MBps speed and shared media access similar to Fast Ethernet, but doesn't use the CSMA/CD protocol used by Ethernet. Instead, 100VG-AnyLAN uses a centrally controlled access method called *Demand Priority*. Demand Priority uses a deterministic request method that maximizes network efficiency by eliminating the network collisions that occur with CSMA/CD-based networks. In addition, Demand Priority uses two levels of priority for each user request to guarantee the timely delivery of time-critical data types such as those used in multimedia applications.

Like 10BaseT and Fast Ethernet, 100VG-AnyLAN networks use one or more central hubs or repeaters (referred to as a level 1, or root hub), connected to the various network nodes. An example of a 100VG-AnyLAN network layout is shown in Figure 2-9.

Although 100VG-AnyLAN is superior to Fast Ethernet in many respects, it hasn't received the same level of support or deployment as Fast Ethernet. This has been due in part to the fact that 100VG-AnyLAN products are typically more expensive than their Fast Ethernet counterparts. However, for networks using streaming data types (such as real-time video and audio for video conferencing or interactive video) and other applications requiring the consistent delivery of data, 100VG-AnyLAN is an excellent choice.

100VG-AnyLAN offers its 100MBps data rate using four-pair Category 3 (voice grade), Category 4, or Category 5 unshielded twisted-pair cable. Future implementations are in development that will also support two-pair UTP cabling, two-pair shielded twisted-pair (STP), and fiber-optic cabling.

The maximum node-to-node diameter on a VG-AnyLAN network is 205 meters using conventional Category 5 UTP cabling, the same as Fast Ethernet.

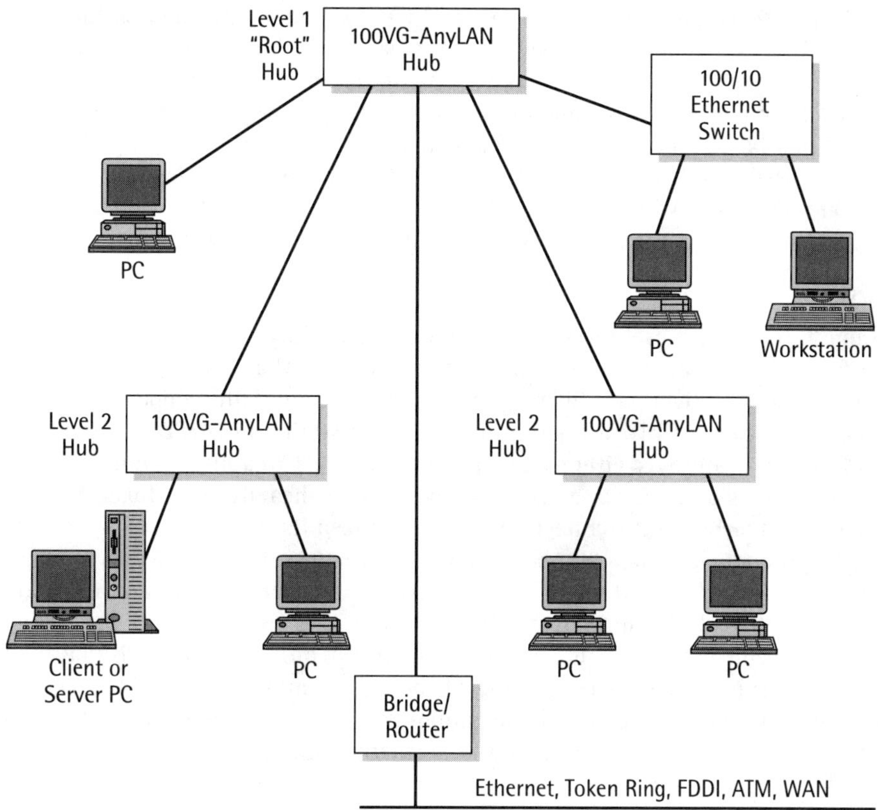

Figure 2-9: A 100VG-AnyLAN network.

TOKEN RING

Token Ring, which is primarily championed by IBM Corporation, is a networking technology that has seen deployment levels second only to Ethernet. It's estimated that Token Ring networks make up approximately 15 percent of all networks worldwide. Although Token Ring architecture uses a conceptual "ring" topology, it can physically be implemented using a star or bus technology as with Ethernet. However, Token Ring uses a token-passing methodology rather than Ethernet's collision-detection method to transmit data on the wire. In Token Ring, only the node possessing a special "token" is able to communicate data on the network, and only one network node may be in possession of the token at any given time. Nodes that wish to transmit data to other nodes place the data and destination address information with the token and pass this information on to the next node. Each receiving node checks to see if the token contains data for them, places any data it has to transmit, and then passes the token on to the next node in the ring.

Token Ring networks are available in 4MBps and 16MBps versions and are capable of using several different cable types including standard UTP cabling. Although it uses a more efficient and elegant communication method than Ethernet, Token Ring hasn't kept up with the 100MBps+ networking technologies that have developed over the past five years, and of late Token Ring has begun to show its age. To address this fact, several vendors offer switched Token Ring hubs that provide up to a full 16MBps of bandwidth to every Token Ring node. In addition, HP and IBM have announced new Token Ring standards that leverage HP's 100MBps VG-AnyLAN technology, although no such products have yet emerged.

FDDI

Although its name closely ties it to fiber-optical cabling, Fiber Distributed Data Interface (FDDI) is actually a higher-level technology that supports high-speed, robust networking over both fiber-optic and copper cabling (the copper implementation being called CDDI to distinguish it). Specifically, FDDI/CDDI provides a 100MBps data rate over either fiber or Category 5 UTP cabling using two-wire pairs. FDDI uses a media access scheme that borrows heavily from Token Ring; it uses a shared media ring architecture similar to Token Ring's.

FDDI products have actually been around since 1988, but their relatively high prices have kept them out of mainstream use. In addition, very few vendors are producing FDDI/CDDI equipment relative to the number of vendors producing Ethernet-specific products. Still another disadvantage of FDDI products is that their use often requires a complete rewiring of the organization, which translates to a higher net cost. For this reason, organizations moving from Ethernet are often better advised to stick with Switched and Fast Ethernet products, because they offer a more direct migration path.

GIGABIT ETHERNET

Another high-speed networking choice involves various flavors of Gigabit Ethernet, which is capable of running at speeds of 1GBps or more over a variety of different physical media types including copper and fiber. Since Gigabit Ethernet networking technologies are still fairly young and have only received limited deployment thus far, the jury is still out as to whether they will be significant players in the market. However, if the prices are right, Gigabit Ethernet could become a major contender to Fast and Switched Ethernet as the heir to the network desktop in the next few years. It is recommended that you keep an eye on the development of Gigabit Ethernet technologies and products as you research the choices for your organization's network.

ATM

Although other high-speed networking technologies such as 100VG-AnyLAN and Switched/Fast Ethernet offer high-speed networking, many believe that the future of voice and data networking lies in the hands of a technology called *Asynchronous Transfer Mode* (ATM). ATM uses a cell-switching technology rather than the shared-media access method used in other technologies such as Ethernet. In ATM, nodes are capable of using direct, point-to-point, full-duplex communication channels that do not require the sharing of bandwidth with other concurrent connections. As a result, ATM delivers the full rated speeds to each network connection made between nodes, which can be 25MBps, 155MBps, or even 1GBps and beyond in the fastest ATM implementations.

Although ATM adapters and switches are typically more expensive than those supporting other high-speed network types, their prices have begun to drop, and this has brought them within reach the reach of many organizations (especially at the slower 25MBps and 155MBps speeds). If your budget can afford it and you can find ATM adapters with Windows NT support, ATM is an excellent choice to carry your organization's network well into the twenty-first century.

Adapter types

Once you've determined the networking technology that your Windows NT system will use, you're ready to choose your network interface card. When choosing a network adapter, there are several very important considerations to remember, each of which can have a tremendous impact on your system's network performance.

The first criteria to consider when choosing a network card is the type of bus it uses. Whenever possible, use only network cards that use the PCI bus, and preferably those that support at least PCI revision 2.1. Although even ISA-based cards can fill a 10MBps network pipe with data, the use of PCI slots is always preferable because they use a faster, more efficient data transfer mechanism that works better under heavy system loads. For 100MBps or faster adapters, your only real choices are PCI and EISA-based adapters, although EISA adapters are rapidly becoming rare with the advent of PCI.

A second and equally important consideration for your system's network card is the data transfer method used by the card. Choose cards using bus-mastering DMA or shared memory methods over those that used programmed I/O. As with storage controllers, network controllers using programmed I/O will put significant burdens on the system CPU and slow the system down. The best choice of all is bus master-capable adapters (which aren't available for the ISA bus) because these are capable of directly transferring data between the card and system RAM without intervention from the host CPU. This translates to higher performance and far less stress on the system CPU.

It bears repeating that high CPU utilization is a big no-no for network adapters on Windows NT computers. Because Windows NT is already a compute-intensive environment, it doesn't make sense to use hardware devices that cause unnecessary drag on the CPU. Typically, this problem occurs with network adapters that use processor-intensive data transfer methods such as programmed I/O, but even some non-PIO cards can cause this. This situation is especially likely to cause performance problems on Windows NT applications servers, since many such servers run CPU-intensive tasks that exaggerate the net effect of this slowdown. When comparing the performance of different network cards, be sure to look at the average CPU utilization in addition to other factors; this in conjunction with the data throughput rate determines the overall efficiency of the card.

Other Recommended Hardware for NT

Although we've covered most of the important equipment you need to build your high-performance NT system, there are a few other hardware devices you should also consider for use with Windows NT:

- Uninterruptible Power Supply. As one of its fault-tolerance features, Windows NT provides the ability to directly communicate with Uninterruptible Power Supply (UPS) devices. These units make sure that clean power is provided to your NT system, protecting against spikes, sags, brownouts, and other power-related anomalies. In addition, they provide from 5 to 15 minutes of battery life, allowing you to gracefully shut down your system in the event of a total power outage. NT's ability to communicate directly with many UPS devices also allows you to have NT perform certain tasks automatically when power outages occur, such as logging off users, shutting down the system, sending pager alerts to system administrators, and so forth.
- Large Monitors (17–21 inches or more). There's nothing like having a large, crisp monitor for viewing your Windows NT desktop. This is especially important for those involved in graphics or CAD work because these environments are capable of using the higher resolutions that virtually demand larger screen sizes.
- Wavetable-lookup Sound Cards. Although Windows NT doesn't support nearly as many sound cards as Windows 95, there are a number of excellent sound cards that do have NT drivers available for them, including the SoundBlaster AWE-32 and 64 cards from Creative Labs, and the various cards from Turtle Beach including the Monte Carlo, Tropez, Tropez32, and TropezPlus cards. Also look for cards that contain on-board DSP (Digital Signal Processing) chips.
- Ergonomic Keyboards. With repetitive motion injuries becoming more and more common for those of us that consistently use computers, the purchase of an ergonomic keyboard (such as those from Microsoft, Curtis, and others) is definitely worth your consideration.
- Digital Joysticks. With its newly found DirectInput (part of DirectX) support, Windows NT is now capable of using joysticks and other controller devices attached to PC game ports. You may also want to check out some of the newer digital joysticks that don't require the constant recalibrations common with analog joysticks.

Summary

In this chapter, you were introduced to the fastest technologies available for Windows NT computers. Although the rapid pace of change in the computer industry means that any information on "state of the art" in computers automatically has a short shelf-life, this information was gathered from the latest technology white papers and technical reviews as of this writing. You can use this information when creating your "ultimate" Windows NT workstation or server, or when making choices about the hardware upgrades you choose for an existing one.

Once you've built the hardware for your NT system, you're ready to take the plunge into the software side of NT optimization.

Chapter 3

Optimizing Your Hardware Configuration

A GOOD PLACE TO START when tuning system performance is verifying that you've selected the optimal settings for the various hardware devices in your system. In Chapter 2, we helped you select the right types of equipment based on performance and features. In the following sections, we help you optimize that hardware for use under Windows NT.

Obviously, it will be impossible for us to cover every brand and model of hardware peripheral on the market (there is, after all, a virtually limitless number of different hardware products out there). However, we cover general hardware tuning concepts and some sample optimization settings for some of the more popular adapters on the market.

Optimizing the System and PCI Buses

Other than internal computations of the processor, the bulk of the work done by any computer is the constant transfer of data across several different "data highways" that exist on the system's motherboard. These data highways are referred to as *buses* because they are used to "bus" data back and forth between various system components (e.g., memory and the CPU, peripherals and memory, etc.). On any modern PC system the two most important of these buses are the PCI expansion bus (used to connect PCI-based peripherals such as SCSI controllers, video cards, network cards, etc.) and the system bus (which serves as a connector between system memory, the CPU, and the PCI bus). In the following sections, we discuss some tips and strategies for enhancing performance and reducing problems related to these buses.

Placement of PCI Cards

Believe it or not, the placement of your PCI adapter cards can actually affect their performance. This is especially true in situations where the PCI bus is heavily saturated; that is, when there are many PCI devices simultaneously competing for PCI bus bandwidth. This happens because most PCI buses assign a different priority level to each PCI slot, from highest to lowest. Although normally there is sufficient PCI bus bandwidth to go around, on a heavily saturated system with many active PCI devices, it's possible that high-priority devices placed in low-priority slots could cause less than optimal performance.

To reduce the possibility of such situations, put your highest priority cards (i.e., SCSI controller or network adapter) in the highest priority PCI slot on your system. On many Intel-based ISA/PCI systems, this is PCI slot 0 and is normally the connector nearest the keyboard connector. However, this is not guaranteed, so be sure to check your system documentation to verify its location. On DEC Alpha-based systems, PCI slot 0 is the location of the VGA card; all other cards can go pretty much anywhere you like without greatly affecting performance. Because slot priorities and the placement of particular adapter types aren't defined in the PCI specification, the implementation of PCI slot definitions and priorities varies widely from vendor to vendor.

On EISA/PCI systems, the situation is often the opposite of that with ISA/PCI systems (i.e., slot 0 starting near the keyboard connector side of the motherboard). With many of these motherboards, the EISA slots actually are the starting point (slot 0) and are farthest from the keyboard connector. The PCI slots come next and are sequentially numbered after the EISA slots. For example, in an eight-slot system, four slots are EISA, starting with EISA slot 0 and ending with EISA slot 3, while PCI starts with slot 4 and ends with PCI slot 7. However, as before, there are always exceptions: In this case, some non-Intel (i.e., RISC-based) EISA/PCI systems machines don't follow this rule and in fact assign slots numbers in the opposite direction. The position of PCI cards installed in the first bus slot will have first chance to allocate IRQ and memory I/O ports. Also, most adapters ship with an affinity for particular IRQ and port addresses. If the system BIOS does not allow explicit configuration of the PCI by slot number, you may have to move the controllers around until the resources are allocated correctly. However, most modern BIOSs allow you to explicitly configure the IRQ assigned to each PCI slot, so you should be able to make the interrupt assignments manually.

Again, remember that PCI slot priorities and IRQ assignments will vary from system to system, so be sure to check your system's documentation before making any assumptions. In addition, it's important to note that the placement of PCI cards is as important for avoiding resource conflicts (e.g., IRQ conflicts, as discussed in the next section) as it is for performance, and performance issues with PCI card placements will probably only be an issue if the PCI bus is heavily saturated.

System Bus Speed

One often overlooked factor of a system's performance is the clock speed at which the system's motherboard runs, known as the *system clock speed.* Although most people generally understand the concept of a CPU's internal speed (measured in megahertz – e.g., a Pentium Pro 200MHz CPU), many don't know that the system clock speed is at least as important to overall performance. PC motherboards use the system clock speed as a basis for the calculation of several important associated frequencies, including the CPU speed and the speed of the various peripheral buses (such as the PCI and ISA buses). The system bus also determines the speed at which the system transfers data to and from the various components of the system, the most important component being RAM.

Intel x86 systems

To determine the CPU clock speed on Intel x86-based systems, a system uses a clock *multiplier* to multiply the base system bus speed times a variable factor (such as 1.5, 2, 2.5, etc.). Likewise, a clock *divisor* is used to determine the speeds of slower buses such as the PCI and ISA bus speeds. On many Intel-based systems, the PCI bus is $^1/_2$ of the system bus speed and the ISA bus is usually $^1/_8$ the system bus speed. For example, a Pentium 133MHz system running with a 66MHz system bus would have a clock multiplier of 2.0, and would normally run the PCI bus at $^1/_2$ this speed at 33MHz, and the ISA bus at $^1/_4$ the PCI bus speed at 8.25MHz. (Note: Depending on the peripherals in use, you may also be able to successfully run the ISA bus at a higher speed such as 11.5MHz using a $^1/_6$ PCI bus clock divisor.) However, most systems are by default conservative in their autoconfigure settings, and will tend to choose the slower value. The only way to find out if the higher speed is possible is by trial-and-error.

Table 3-1 shows some sample CPU speeds on the x86 platform, and the available system bus speed(s) and CPU clock multiplier value(s) for each.

With some CPUs it is also possible to choose from one of several different system bus speeds. For example, a 150MHz Pentium CPU could run on a system with a 75MHz bus speed with a 2.0 CPU clock multiplier, a 60MHz system bus speed with a 2.5 CPU clock multiplier, or a 50MHz system bus speed with a 3.0 CPU clock multiplier. Other CPU speeds have only one or two choices for system bus speeds. When given the choice, always select the highest possible system bus speed available for the CPU you're using. On most Intel-based system boards, the on-board chipsets aren't rated by the manufacturer to exceed 66MHz, even if the motherboard supports higher speeds (such as the 75MHz or 83MHz support found on many modern Pentium and Pentium Pro motherboards). However, this doesn't mean that you're guaranteed to have problems running your system at these higher speeds; your success in these circumstances will depend entirely on the particular peripherals used in your system. Many users are successfully running systems with 75MHz system bus speeds without problems; however, there are a few adapters that don't like this and won't work properly in this configuration.

TABLE 3-1 STANDARD X86 SYSTEM CPU, SYSTEM BUS, AND PCI BUS SPEEDS

CPU Speed	Available System Bus Speed	CPU Clock Multiplier	Typical PCI Bus Speed
300MHz	66MHz	4.5	33MHz
266MHz	66MHz	4.0	33MHz
233MHz	66MHz	3.5	33MHz
200MHz	66MHz	3.0	33MHz
180MHz	60MHz	3.0	30MHz
166MHz	66MHz	2.5	33MHz
150MHz	75MHz*	2.0	37.5MHz
150MHz	60MHz	2.5	30MHz
150MHz	50MHz	3.0	25MHz
133MHz	66MHz	2.0	33MHz
120MHz	60MHz	2.0	30MHz
100MHz	66MHz	1.5	33MHz
90MHz	60MHz	1.5	30MHz
75MHz	50MHz	1.5	25MHz

*See the information elsewhere in this section and the sidebar "Overclocking: A Foray Into the Gray" for information concerning the use of a 75MHz bus speed on x86-based system.

It's also important when attempting to use these speeds that you use the fastest possible EDO SIMM or DIMM memory chips, preferably at least 60ns or faster. Fast Page Mode DRAMs or chips slower than 60ns are more likely to be problematic in such environments. If you truly want to leverage these faster system bus speeds, you should also consider motherboards that support faster RAM types such as BEDO (Burst Extended Data Output) and SDRAM (Synchronous DRAM).

For more information on the different type of DRAM chips available, see the "Memory" section of Chapter 2, "Killer Hardware for Windows NT."

Overclocking: A Foray into the Gray

As you can see, the system bus speed has an enormous effect on every aspect of your system, including the CPU, memory, and even the speed of your adapter cards. Therefore, it is beneficial to always achieve the highest bus speed possible that still allows the system to operate in a stable fashion. To this end, it is important to mention another way of eking still more performance out of your system: a technique known as *overclocking.* In a nutshell, overclocking is the practice of running a system board and/or CPU past its listed manufacturer rating to achieve higher performance.

Although the practice tends to be shunned by Intel and many Intel-based system board manufacturers (many of whom have financial agreements with Intel), it is often possible to run a system's CPU and motherboard past its maximum manufacturer-rated specification and achieve significantly higher performance. (In fact, due to high demand from users, many board manufacturers are now publicly supporting 75MHz bus speeds.) For example, you may be able to run successfully a Pentium 100MHz at 120MHz, or a Pentium 133MHz CPU at 166MHz or higher. In addition, running a system board at 75MHz or 83MHz will produce significantly faster performance for all system peripherals, assuming that all of the system's components work at the new speed. PCI cards utilizing the $^1/_2$ clock divisor on a 75MHz bus will run at 37.5MHz as opposed to the 30MHz or 33MHz speed of 60MHz and 66MHz system bus speeds, respectively, which increases the overall throughput of the PCI bus and reduces bus latency. It is also possible on some systems to run an 83MHz-system bus speed, which yields a 41.5MHz PCI bus speed. Again, the success of doing so depends entirely on the ability of the system RAM and PCI cards involved to work at the higher clock rate. Generally speaking, and not surprisingly, newer cards have a better chance of working than older cards. Alpha systems routinely run their system boards at 100MHz or greater, so changing the divisor for the PCI slots will yield the same results, though at 100MHz, the divisor for Alpha systems is usually the system bus clock divided by 3, or exactly 33MHz. Higher speeds and/or different clock divisors yield different PCI bus speeds.

Although overclocking is admittedly a "cutting edge" idea and can potentially introduce problems, it also opens the door to significantly higher system performance. In addition, and perhaps its most compelling benefit, it does so without incurring a dollar of additional expense. Although it takes some tweaking to implement and isn't for the technically faint of heart, overclocking may help you realize your system's true potential. Not all system boards support overclocking, and the ability to do so depends on several factors including the chipset used on your motherboard. Finally, don't expect support from your system vendor or motherboard manufacturer if you try to implement this technique: it's almost certain that they will discourage you from overclocking. In other words, you'll be on your own. However, don't despair, because there are several Internet sites that offer support to users interested in overclocking.

(continued)

Overclocking: A Foray into the Gray *(Continued)*

The place to start if you're interested in system bus speed issues and overclocking is Dr. Thomas Pabst's Web site ("Tom's Hardware Page"). This site, a haven for the PC hardware aficionados, is dedicated to the idea of maximizing PC hardware performance. There are a variety of interesting white papers, benchmark listings, and testimonials from other users who successfully implemented overclocking on their systems. One nice aspect to these testimonials is that each includes a detailed description of each user's system configuration; this allows you to compare notes with other users with similar configurations, and can also help you avoid configurations that are known to be problematic. The Web site can be found at:

`http://sysdoc.pair.com/`

The following information is intended for technically proficient users and is not recommended for production machines. DO NOT, under any circumstance, attempt to implement the methods described below without first backing up all of the data on your system. Also, these are not recommended procedures but rather a discussion of real-world practices that have been tested by other users. If you choose to attempt these procedures on your own machine, you do so at your own risk.

If you purchase or own a board supporting a bus speed higher than 66MHz and decide to enable overclocking, it is highly recommended that you use only the highest quality, fastest memory (RAM) chips you can obtain. For systems using standard DRAM chips, this means good quality memory of the 60ns or 50ns variety from a reputable manufacturer. In addition, be aware that many current SDRAM memory modules are fixed at a 66MHz maximum speed, so you'll likely encounter problems on SDRAM-based boards using these chips if you try to use a system bus speed higher than 66MHz.

DEC Alpha systems

The most immediately noticeable difference between DEC Alpha and Intel systems is the higher clock speeds of many Alpha CPUs. In fact, the fastest DEC Alpha processor, a 600MHz version, runs at over twice times the clock speed of the fastest Intel Processors on the market! Even faster versions of the Alpha chip are expected in the near future, including a 700MHz version that should be shipping by the time you read this.

In addition to running the CPU at faster speeds, DEC Alpha systems also run the system bus at speeds far higher than those found on Intel x86 systems. Whereas Intel-based systems boards tend to top out at 66, 75, or 83MHz, Alpha-based motherboards run at system bus speeds of up to 150MHz. The system bus speed on Alpha speed is determined by a divisor of the CPU speed, which is typically either $^1/_3$ or $^1/_4$ in most cases (however, most Alpha systems also leave this setting fully programmable from $^1/_{16}$ to $^1/_3$ of the CPU speed). This translates to extremely fast performance for all Alpha system components, including system RAM. The PCI bus, in turn, uses a divisor of the system bus speed, which is also usually either $^1/_3$ or $^1/_4$ of the system bus clock.

Upcoming DEC Alpha systems (and some current ones) use a special segmented bus architecture that separates the various buses on the system to allow for different data transfer rates between them. For example, systems based on the DEC Alpha 21264 processor communicate with the secondary (L2) cache at a speed of 333MHz, while the system bus runs at a speed of 133MHz. This design optimizes the performance of each system component and provides maximum performance versus "shared bus" architectures (such as those used with most Intel-based systems and older Alpha systems).

Table 3-2 lists a variety of Alpha CPUs and the typical system and PCI bus speeds on boards that use them.

TABLE 3-2 STANDARD DEC ALPHA 21164A SYSTEM CPU, SYSTEM BUS, AND PCI BUS SPEEDS

CPU Type/Speed	Maximum System Bus Speed*	PCI Bus Speed at 1/4	PCI Bus Speed at 1/3
21164a/433MHz	144MHz	27MHz	36MHz
21164a/466MHz	155MHz	29MHz	38MHz
21164a/500MHz	166MHz	31MHz	41MHz
21164a/533MHz	177MHz	33MHz	44MHz
21164a/600MHz	200MHz	37MHz	N/A

*The typical system bus clock speed on Alpha 21064 processors is usually 1/4 the CPU clock speed, while 21164-based system boards typically run at speeds of up to 1/3 the CPU clock speed.

Busmastering Issues

In Chapter 2, we discussed the benefits of devices that use busmastering DMA to bypass the system CPU and transfer data directly to system memory. Given the enormous performance benefits of this technology, you'd think that all modern video, network, and disk adapters would use busmastering by default. However, there are many PCI adapters/controllers that don't support busmastering, including Ethernet, SCSI, ATA/IDE, Token Ring, and VG-AnyLAN controllers and adapters. In addition, some older motherboards do not have busmastering support to all the PCI slots, often referring to one as a "slave" slot that shares its bracket with either an ISA, EISA, or VL-Bus slot. Be very careful about this, and be sure to check the system's documentation before buying it. Try to always stick with systems that support busmastering on all of their high-speed slots, whether they are PCI, VL-Bus, or EISA. Busmastering is the key to high performance with many adapter types, including disk, network, and video adapters. It allows the device to bypass the CPU entirely for direct-to-memory transfers that increase transfer speed and greatly reduce CPU utilization.

Another item to be aware of is that early chipsets for the Intel Pentium and Pentium Pro CPUs did not support more than two simultaneous busmastering devices on the system. Current chipsets for either can support as many as five concurrent busmasters. Alpha systems tend to start at 6 and go as high as 16. If you install and utilize more busmastering cards than your system has provisions for, chances are high that you will begin to experience a variety of different problems including system halts, poor performance, and/or boot failures.

Avoiding Interrupt Conflicts

IRQ is an acronym for "Interrupt ReQuest," and refers to the hardwired lines of communication that a system provides to allow system and peripheral devices to "interrupt" the processor to process a request from the device. IRQs are a precious resource on any system, because on most systems there are only 16.

In general, on Intel systems you want to avoid interrupts that map to interrupts either already in use by the system or any of several system devices. For example, the use of the system cascade interrupt pair IRQ2 and 9 (which are essentially the same interrupt) can cause problems on some systems but will work fine on others. If you do attempt to use IRQ2/9 with an adapter, it is recommended that you try it with a PCI rather than an ISA card; you'll have a better chance of success.

Also, on systems with a built-in PS/2 mouse port, conflicts can arise if a device attempts to use IRQ12, because this IRQ is used by that port. Even if you are using a serial mouse, be sure that the on-board PS/2 mouse port is disabled in the BIOS (and/or via jumper on the motherboard) before attempting to use IRQ12. On Alpha systems, the interrupts are different since there are no cascaded interrupt controllers as with Intel machines, although Alpha systems do offer a similar range of interrupts (i.e., 0–15).

In an effort to avoid duplicating the "IRQ challenged" nature of Intel-based PC systems, some DEC Alpha systems (those with the 21064a or later Alpha processor) offer a feature called Accelerator Mode that is capable of freeing up to four ISA interrupts by providing an additional four usable Interrupt Registers. This feature is only found on certain DEC PCI interrupt controllers and its use requires support in both the system firmware/BIOS as well as the operating system (OS), as it is a software-driven feature.

Table 3-3 maps the IRQ usage of modern Intel x86 and Alpha-based systems, the preassigned or typical uses for these IRQs, and comments regarding the potential usage of each on different platforms.

TABLE 3-3 COMMON IRQ ASSIGNMENTS

IRQ	Potential or Fixed Assignment	Comments
0	System Clock	This IRQ is used by the system clock and is unavailable for use.
1	Keyboard Controller (8042 chip)	On Intel-based systems, this IRQ is used by the system's programmable keyboard controller chip and is unavailable for use. On DEC Alpha systems, this IRQ is the one to which PCI IRQs are typically mapped and is unavailable for specific assignment by other system devices.
2	Cascade Interrupt to IRQ9	On Intel-based systems, this IRQ is used for a special interrupt/DMA "cascading" technique used by the PC architecture and is therefore not always capable of being used. On DEC Alpha systems, this IRQ is the one to which PCI IRQs are typically mapped and is usually unavailable for specific assignment by other system devices.
3	Serial Ports COM2 and COM4	This IRQ is typically used by COM ports 2 and 4 (if this many exist on this system), and systems with two or more COM ports probably won't have this IRQ available for use.
4	Serial Ports COM1 and COM3	This IRQ is typically used by COM ports 1 and 3 (if this many exist on this system), and systems with one or more COM ports probably won't have this IRQ available for use.

continued

IRQ	Potential or Fixed Assignment	Comments
5	Parallel Port LPT2, Sound Blaster Sound Cards, Alternate IRQ for COM3 or COM4	This IRQ is typically used for a second parallel (LPT) port, if one exists on the system. It is also the default for many Sound Blaster and compatible sound cards, although the IRQ settings for these cards are variable. Many internal modems also offer this IRQ as an alternative to IRQ's 3 and 4 for COM3 or COM4 settings.
6	Floppy Disk Controller	This IRQ is used for the system's floppy disk drive controller and is unavailable for use.
7	LPT1	This IRQ is normally used for the first parallel (LPT) port on the system. Therefore, unless the port has been disabled, this IRQ is generally unavailable for use by other devices.
8	Real-time Clock Chip	This IRQ is used for the system's real-time clock chip and is unavailable for use.
9	Cascade Interrupt to IRQ2	This IRQ is used for a special interrupt/DMA "cascading" technique used by the PC architecture and is therefore not always capable of being used.
10	Available	This IRQ has no standard system assignment and is generally available for use by other devices.
11	Available	This IRQ has no standard system assignment and is generally available for use by other devices.

continued

TABLE 3-3 COMMON IRQ ASSIGNMENTS *(Continued)*

IRQ	Potential or Fixed Assignment	Comments
12	PS/2 Mouse Port	The PS/2 Mouse Port uses this IRQ, if the mouse port is installed in the system. If you are using a serial mouse and wish to free this IRQ for use with another device, be sure to first disable the port completely in both the system BIOS and any jumpers on the system motherboard (if used).
13	Math Coprocessor	This IRQ is used by the math coprocessor found on all 486DX, Pentium, and Pentium Pro systems and is therefore generally unavailable for use.
14	IDE Disk Controller (Primary Channel)	The first IDE channel on a system uses this IRQ, if the channel is enabled in the system BIOS. Systems with IDE devices on this channel will not be able to use this IRQ for other devices.
15	IDE Disk Controller (Secondary Channel)	The secondary IDE channel on a system uses this IRQ, if the channel is enabled in the system BIOS. Systems with IDE devices on this channel will not be able to use this IRQ for other devices.

If you're using a SCSI controller on your NT system and have no IDE devices (a highly recommended situation!), then it is recommended that you disable both IDE channels in the system BIOS setup to free IRQ's 14 and 15 for use with other devices.

Interrupt Sharing

Another important issue in regards to system interrupts (IRQs) is the concept of IRQ sharing. The PCI bus specification was designed to allow for the sharing of hardware interrupts. However, the way in which this support is implemented in PCI cards varies from vendor to vendor, and it is an unfortunate reality that many Windows NT low-level device drivers don't contain support for this feature. As a result, PCI interrupt sharing doesn't usually work too well under Windows NT. It is an especially bad idea to try sharing interrupts between devices of a different type, for example, between Ethernet and SCSI, or SCSI and the video controller. A PCI SCSI controller and another PCI SCSI controller (or two or more SCSI channels on a single controller card) can sometimes share an IRQ without problems, but sharing a PCI SCSI card's IRQ with another type of controller will either make both devices run more slowly or cause one or both to stop working. Many boot-device controllers (SCSI and IDE) will not be able to boot the system if the interrupts are shared.

Interrupt Priorities

As with the prioritization given to Slot 0 on the PCI bus, there is a definite "pecking order" when it comes to the servicing of hardware interrupts by the system's chipset. Specifically, the higher-order interrupts 9–15 receive the highest priority on a PC system (in that order). Therefore, you should ensure that all of your high-demand adapters such as disk, video, and network controllers use interrupts in this range. The lower interrupt range of 3–7 should be reserved for slower devices such as serial (COM) ports, parallel (LPT) ports, sound cards, and modems.

One exception to this is IRQ2, which is electrically tied to IRQ9 for interrupt cascading and is therefore given the same priority as IRQ9. However, most systems won't allow you to use IRQ2/9 due to this predesignated purpose, and use of these interrupts should only be tried as a last resort, that is, when all other available IRQs have been exhausted.

Extended PCI Systems: Bridged/Dual-Peer PCI

As Mae West said, "Too much of a good thing is even better." Although the PCI bus is an excellent bus with strong features, a saturated PCI bus (one with many high-speed devices on it) can cause a bottleneck to occur on the PCI bus. This is common on high-end server systems using high-speed network cards and hardware RAID adapters, especially when more than one of these adapter types is installed. To alleviate this bottleneck, some systems use a "bridged" or "dual-peer" PCI design, where two separate PCI buses exist and are connected either to each other (bridged) or to the system bus (dual-peer). In bridged configurations, the primary benefit is an increase in the number of available PCI slots: you still have the same bandwidth, but typically get twice the number of slots.

With dual-peer PCI, the two buses run concurrently, each providing the full 132MBps of bus bandwidth (assumes 32-bit 33MHz, the typical configuration for most PCI buses). This can have the combined benefit of increasing the number of available PCI slots to eight (as with bridged PCI) and also increasing the maximum theoretical aggregate throughput for PCI devices to 264MBps (2x132MBps). However, a more real-world performance figure for these designs is closer to around 200MBps. On DEC Alpha systems using a 64-bit dual-peer PCI arrangement, the theoretical maximum jumps to a whopping 528MBps! This arrangement also reduces PCI bus latency because the total load is shared between two separate PCI buses.

Early systems implementing PCI bridges between the PCI bus and the system bus (as well as to legacy EISA, MCA, and ISA) were much slower than the maximum speed defined in the PCI specification, with many boards being limited to a mere 50MBps. However, newer bridge chipsets allow up to a 100MBps real-world data rate, twice the rate of the older implementations and closer to the maximum theoretical defined in the PCI specification.

If your system has dual-peer PCI buses, it is a good idea to place the video adapter on a different PCI bus than the disk and network controllers because these are typically the three most highly taxed adapters on an NT system. Also, this creates a better balance across the PCI buses because the nature of the data transfers used by these devices is also different: disk and network controllers tend to use long data bursts, while the video adapter tends to perform short bursts. Also, some video adapter chipsets are not fully compatible with the peer PCI bus arrangement and may cause problems if shared with these other devices on the same bus.

Another arrangement that is becoming more common is the presence of a second PCI bus that is bridged off of the first. Although it creates the ability to have additional PCI slots, it isn't as good as the previously discussed dual-peer arrangement because it doesn't really provide a separate bus. This ends up being slower because all of the devices are sharing the bandwidth of the existing PCI bus (i.e., 132MBps for a 33MHz 32-bit PCI bus) and so must contend for the limited bandwidth. This arrangement also increases PCI bus latency because more devices are competing for the same PCI bus.

Figure 3-1 depicts a bridged PCI bus arrangement.

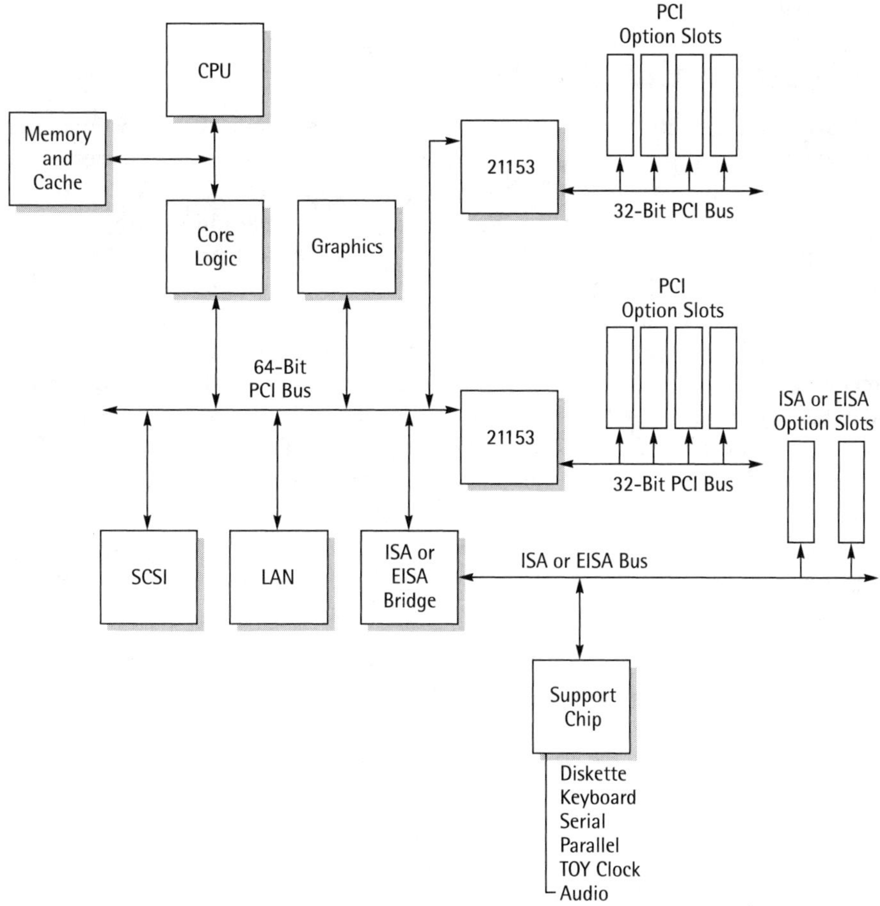

Figure 3-1: Block diagram of a system with two bridged PCI buses.

Configuring Legacy Expansion Slots

In addition to the PCI expansion slots common on most of today's personal computers, there are also a number of legacy connectors on many Intel x86 and RISC-based systems used with NT. These include ISA, EISA, MCA, and VESA VL-Bus, which we first discussed in Chapter 2. Each of these buses has its own set of issues, quirks, and features. Although it is highly recommended that you place all high-demand devices (i.e., disk, network, and video adapters) on the PCI bus, you may be forced to deal with these older bus types as well. Therefore, in this section we discuss a few of the issues surrounding these boards and provide some tips and tricks for configuring them.

Configuring the EISA bus

The EISA bus, originally backed by the "Gang of Nine" led by Compaq Computer Corporation, is by far the most common of the legacy high performance connectors. It is far more abundant than IBM's proprietary MCA (MicroChannel Architecture), mainly due to its capability of providing backward-compatibility with the large installed base of ISA 8-bit and 16-bit controllers. Before the arrival of the VL-Bus and PCI bus, EISA gained popularity as the fastest available nonproprietary bus for high performance workstations and servers. The EISA bus is much higher in latency than PCI and has a far higher CPU utilization under heavy use (CPU utilizations of 15–20 percent by the EISA bus aren't uncommon). EISA is also less efficient than IBM's MicroChannel Architecture (MCA) bus, which has a lower CPU utilization and better overall efficiency. However, MCA components also typically cost more to manufacture, produce more heat, and use more individual components and buffer memory.

EISA offers a high-performance feature known as DMA burst cycles. This feature lets the EISA bus be more efficient by allowing high-performance bus-mastering from an EISA controller, effectively doubling its rated performance. These burst cycles must be enabled for each device, as they are usually turned off by default. Not all systems have supported DMA burst cycles in the same way, so incompatibility problems were evident in many early EISA systems. However, EISA has been around long enough now that most such bugs are gone. In addition, most NT EISA drivers are well optimized, and virtually all modern EISA boards work flawlessly with DMA burst cycles enabled. A final note: A 1992 enhancement of this feature also exists, which allows for long block EISA burst cycles called EMB (Enhanced Master Burst) that can achieve data throughput rates as high as 66MBps (twice the standard EISA burst cycles at 33MBps). However, the majority of EISA systems do not support this particular revision.

EISA is still found on many of today's modern servers owing to its long-standing presence in the PC server market. The arrangement of most modern PCI/EISA systems has the EISA bus bridged to the PCI bus, while the PCI bus is, in turn, bridged directly to the system bus. The EISA bus also typically determines its clock rate by dividing off of the PCI bus clock rate, which is most typically either 30MHz or 33MHz. The EISA bus typically uses a divisor of $^1/_4$ (33 MHz divided by 4 = 8.25MHz) to arrive at its nominal clock rate. However, modern EISA computers can often safely push the EISA bus to $^1/_3$ or even $^1/_2$ the PCI bus for 11.5MHz and 16.5MHz clock rates, respectively (though far more can run at the more conservative 11.5MHz rate). At 11.5MHz, EISA can produce a theoretical burst rate of 46MBps with burst cycles, though most chipsets do not support EISA rates much over 40MBps. It's also worth noting that few server motherboards make it easy to change the EISA clock divisor, though with a little investigation of the system BIOS and/or system manuals you may be able to locate the proper BIOS or jumper settings to change this divisor.

Although it may be possible to overclock your EISA bus using this method, it doesn't generally result in noticeable performance increases. However, if overclocking can make the EISA bus more efficient and responsive, it may be worth trying regardless. If the card is older or cannot support higher clock rates, it is unlikely that testing it at the higher rate will damage it. In most cases, the worst that will happen is that the system or an EISA device will cease functioning properly; this can be solved by simply setting the bus back to its previous speed.

Like PCI, the EISA specification supports hardware interrupt sharing. However, not all EISA systems support this feature, despite its presence in the drafted specification. The default operation of EISA uses Edge-Triggered Interrupts (the method used by the ISA bus); a different method, called Level-Triggered Interrupts, is used for adapters sharing the same IRQ. The same problems that were previously discussed in regards to interrupt sharing on the PCI bus also unfortunately apply to EISA: most NT low-level drivers don't support this feature even when it is present in the EISA hardware being used.

One frustrating aspect of EISA is the continued need to use configuration disks to configure and support EISA adapters. This can be especially headache producing on systems that combine PCI and EISA together. Although a standard PCI bus can be set to automatically configure its devices, the presence of the EISA bus usually means that the EISA configuration utility must be run to register the positions of and resources used by the PCI cards (even if no EISA controllers are installed!). Also, the resources for each PCI card are registered on a slot-by-slot basis; if you move a card, the EISA configuration utility will have to be rerun to register the resource usage. Each time a board is changed, or memory or processors are added or subtracted from the system board, the EISA configuration utility must be rerun to reflect the changes.

Whenever changes are made to the installed cards in an EISA-based system, it is required that you run a configuration update via the EISA Configuration Utility (ECU). On Intel-based systems, this utility is normally started from a FAT-formatted DOS boot disk; RISC-based systems with EISA have a special ECU that is run from the console screen. Upon initialization of the EISA configuration utility, the system autodetects any changes or additions to the system and requests the appropriate configuration disks for any new or modified EISA cards. A reboot is then required to initialize the new changes.

EISA stores all of its information about the system board and option cards in Nonvolatile RAM (NVRAM), which has the potential to become corrupted during, for example, the boot process, configuration, firmware updates, or installing devices that support features the system does not. If this happens, it may be necessary to flash the entire NVRAM and start from scratch by pulling out the NVRAM/real-time clock chip (usually a large, black, plastic-encased rectangle with "Dallas" silk-screened on it, which is held on by a small retaining belt). Holding the NVRAM chip against a bare piece of metal for 5–10 seconds will flush the memory. Some EISA BIOS setup programs also have an option to flush the NVRAM from setup, which is the preferable method because it eliminates the need to open the case and risk destroying the NVRAM/real-time clock by bending its pins during extraction or reinsertion.

A final word of advice: when working with EISA-based systems, always be sure to use the most recent version of the EISA configuration utility from the system's manufacturer.

The ISA bus: An old dog and some new tricks

Industry Standard Architecture (ISA) slots continue to be the most common option board on Intel-based system motherboards, but are not as common on RISC machines. ISA is the original IBM PC bus, which typically runs at 8.25MHz. This speed is derived either from a $^1/_4$ divisor of the 33MHz system bus (on some 486 systems with a 33MHz system bus speed) or the 33MHz bus of the PCI bus to which it is currently bridged (on Pentium/Pentium Pro and some 486 systems using PCI). As stated in Chapter 2, it is best to use ISA for devices that use a 5MBps or lower data transfer rate, including I/O devices such as COM ports, parallel ports, sound cards, internal modems, and the like. If possible, you should always choose the PCI-based version of a peripheral over an ISA version whenever possible. The reason is that ISA peripherals typically hold the bus up to 10 times longer than PCI-based ones, which in turn translates to increased bus latency and slower system performance.

Configuring traditional, legacy ISA cards is a far more manual process than that of configuring PCI and EISA adapters, and usually involves manually setting jumpers or DIP switches on the cards. Although traditional ISA doesn't support autoconfiguration as with PCI and EISA, a newer flavor of ISA called Plug and Play (PnP) ISA is capable of automatically assigning system resources such as IRQ and DMA to ISA cards at system boot. However, Plug and Play requires a three-way combination of support, including the operating system, the system BIOS, and the cards themselves. Unfortunately, becauseWindows NT is not yet Plug and Play compliant (this is anticipated for NT 5.0), this means that NT can't participate in the Plug and Play process as well as true PnP-compliant operating systems like Windows 95.

When using PnP ISA cards with Windows NT, the PnP BIOS on your system handles the automatic assignment of system resources to all PnP ISA cards at boot, and NT uses whatever the BIOS has assigned. Unfortunately, with many cards this also means that you won't be able to modify the resources a card uses inside Windows NT, and this can cause some real configuration headaches when setting these adapters up on an NT system. Because they're Plug and Play compliant, most of these cards don't have any jumpers on them to allow you to override the PnP settings and manually assign system resources to the card. To accommodate configuring these types of cards in this situation, some cards come with a setup utility that allows you to configure the card through software without the need for jumpers or DIP switches.

In terms of maximum bus speed, many modern ISA cards can be safely pushed to speeds of 11.3MHz or faster by adjusting the ISA clock divisor. Depending on the types of cards involved, this may make the cards faster or more efficient. For example, an ISA VGA card or network or disk controller can benefit from this overclocking (although it is simultaneously true that none of these devices should be ISA-based if you want a truly optimized NT system). In many cases, the documentation (or even the product box itself) accompanying ISA boards list the maximum speed at which the board can run. ISA cards used in EISA or EISA/PCI systems will use the bus speed the EISA slot is set to, which is typically the standard EISA bus speed of 8.25MHz. ISA cards in these systems will generally not require EISA setup configurations to function, although because these cards share the slots and resources used by EISA cards, you may still want to register these cards and the resources they're using with the EISA configuration utility. This will explicitly inform the EISA bus about which resources are already in use so that conflicts can be prevented.

VL-Bus configuration issues

The VESA Local Bus (VL-Bus; VESA stands for the Video Electronics Standards Association, who developed the standard) is fully compatible with ISA and acts as an extension of this bus. VESA was the first PC bus that communicated at the full speed of the system bus available for the PC. It is functionally similar to the PDS

(Processor Direct Slot) of the Macintosh or the VME bus used in some RISC machines. As an independent bus tied directly to the processor local bus, it operates without regard for either the Plug and Play resource setup (if present) or features such as shared interrupts or multiple simultaneous busmasters. The VL-Bus is functionally a single busmastering bus with a 32-bit bus and support for up to 40MHz system bus speeds. It receives no arbitration (management of access and timing) by the system chipset. At its maximum speed, the VL-Bus is capable of delivering a maximum theoretical data rate of 160MBps. Some VL-Bus slots are also found on the 486DX50-based systems running at 50MHz, which exceeds the VL-Bus specification and is done to provide the maximum performance. However, many VL-Bus boards can't support the 50MHz frequency and will fail to operate properly when used at this speed.

Apart from the base local bus speed setting that drives it, there is really nothing you can do to optimize or modify the performance of VL-Bus adapters. Also, since it isn't a managed second level (or *mezzanine*) bus architecture like PCI, VL-Bus is more problem prone than other bus types. It is often difficult to get multiple VL-Bus cards to work concurrently on the same system due to the contention for the processor local bus. Often it is possible to only get a single VL-Bus adapter to work in a system, even those with two or three VL-Bus slots. The overclocking of ISA (discussed earlier) does nothing to increase the speed of the VL-Bus, because all the important signaling takes place in the extended part of the slot where most of the VL-Bus connectors reside. As with ISA, IRQ sharing is not supported on the VL-Bus. Windows NT does not treat the VL-Bus any differently than ISA, and support for it is therefore contained within the standard NT ISA/EISA HAL (Hardware Abstraction Layer).

MCA bus configuration issues

The MCA (MicroChannel Architecture) bus offers features, configuration, and performance similar to EISA, with the advantage of having a maximum theoretical throughput that is actually greater than many implementations of PCI. Like EISA, MCA cards come with a configuration disk that contains all the important information about the controller card. MCA also supports a technology called Programmable Option Select (POS) that allows for multiple simultaneous busmasters, advanced interrupt handling, and better bus arbitration than ISA, EISA, or VL-Bus. These features also allow MCA systems to easily support as many as 10 MCA slots.

MCA is also unique in that it uses a clock that is completely decoupled from the system bus clock. Regardless of the speed of the host CPU or system board, most MCA buses typically run at 10MHz (although later versions were double and even quadruple this number). Unlike EISA, which is capable of transferring data every other clock cycle, MCA can be configured to transfer data during each clock cycle; a feature also found in the PCI bus. It is also capable of supporting IRQ sharing between devices as do PCI and EISA. However the situation regarding low-level NT driver support for this feature is no better with MCA than it is with PCI or EISA. The block-size MCA uses for data transfers is double that of EISA (2K), and it is more efficient at arbitrating busmastering devices than EISA. In 1992, MCA was extended to 20MHz, giving it a 66MBps-bus performance, the same as the EMB EISA modes but with greater efficiency.

Like EISA, the MCA bus is usually found on high-performance systems from IBM or Motorola that feature POWER series processors, such as POWER 2, Power PC, and even some Intel-based PC servers. It is also found on the majority of the PS/2 line of systems. MCA uses a setup disk and utility much like EISA; configuration is only partially automated but the controllers are typically free of jumpers or DIP switches. Once registered, if the controller is moved from slot to slot, the utility must be rerun.

Many MicroChannel bus adapters made during the past few years may be pushed to as high as 40MHz, which yields a theoretical maximum data rate of 160MBps (higher than the 32-bit, 33MHz PCI). However, because this higher rate can cause problems with legacy 32-bit and 16-bit MCA cards, the lower 10MHz and 20MHz rates are the ones most commonly found on MCA systems. You can attempt to run MCA at the higher clock rates (i.e., 20MHz and 40MHz) to see if it can be supported on your system, provided there are BIOS level configuration options or board jumpers for doing so. As with other bus optimizations, experimentation is required to determine what works best on your system. MCA is fully supported under NT, and can be found on some PowerPC and Intel-based IBM and Motorola servers. As with EISA, always be sure to use the latest MCA setup utility from the system manufacturer.

Setting System CMOS Options

System BIOS parameters for both Intel and Alpha systems come in all manner of complexity or simplicity. This is because of the open nature of the PC hardware industry and the fact that there is a virtually limitless number of different BIOS manufacturers and BIOS revisions. Some BIOSs (such as those written by Intel and used on Intel-brand motherboards) tend to shield the user/administrator from difficult decisions by either not offering a configuration parameter or using auto modes by default. Such BIOSs can be vexing to the would-be optimizer because they restrict the ability to make advanced changes to the system's configuration.

Recently, differences between the BIOSs used on RISC and x86-based systems have also diminished. Most modern Alpha and PowerPC systems have adopted a graphical BIOS utility like those found on many x86-based motherboards. Some systems require an additional program be run to change some settings, particularly those which have legacy connectors such as MCA and EISA. Also, manufacturers making BIOSs for both platforms are widely using Flash BIOSs, which allow for the dynamic updating of the system firmware as new versions are released (it is highly recommended that you only purchases systems that offer this option).

Performance-Related Settings to Look For

Depending on your system's BIOS/firmware and chipset revision numbers (aka versions), options may exist for boosting the performance of your system. Several things can and should be enabled on a Windows NT system to increase available resources or improve device performance. It is an unfortunate reality that most system setup parameters are poorly documented, and furthermore that users and system integrators are often strongly discouraged from experimenting with different values. In addition to the fact that such settings are often enigmatic and difficult to comprehend, different system vendors with similar option screens may use totally different settings even when using an identical chipset and firmware. As a result, users must often find support on system BIOS settings from third-party sources or publicly available newsgroups and Web sites.

Miro Wikgren of Finland developed an interesting BIOS optimization utility called "TweakBIOS." This utility works with a wide array of systems, including those based on the Intel 430FX (Triton), Intel 430HX (Triton II), Intel 430VX (Triton III), Intel 430TX, Intel 440FX (Natoma), Intel 450KX/GX (Orion), Intel 430MX, AMD-640 (aka VIA VP-2), OPTi Viper & Vendetta, ALi Aladdin 2, and UMC 881 chipsets, and allows tuning parameters (i.e., memory timings, etc.) to be adjusted even on systems with BIOSs offering a limited number of BIOS tuning options. It is available in both shareware and commercial versions. A copy of the shareware version as well as general information about the utility can be downloaded from: `http://www.miro.pair.com/tweakbios`

Though it is less common than it used to be, many of the default settings on system BIOSs are just plain wrong as shipped from the manufacturers. In addition, those systems that have been set up according to factory specifications are often set up with highly conservative settings, which do not fully exploit the full performance possible with the system. The more important of these performance-related settings include those that affect the speed of communication between the CPU, cache memory, and main memory. For example, many BIOSs contain settings that pertain to important aspects of the system such as the buffering of the CPU to memory on reads and writes, the buffering between the expansion bus and the CPU through the system bus, and others. Generally speaking, the more buffering that is supported, the better. Buffering increases the cost of the board components, and this is the reason that many boards don't contain extremely large buffers. Other important performance-related settings found on many systems include those related to the system cache policy, cache cycle time, and cache speed; these affect the operation of the secondary (L2) and tertiary (L3) CPU caches, which are critical to system performance.

On PC systems where a single system board may employ various types of CPUs, cache, and DRAM types, the ability to change these features is extremely important to creating an optimally configured system. On ARC (Advanced RISC Computing) RISC machines, the memory and cache cycle times, speed, and policy are usually not configurable, but are usually set for the highest performance. This can generally be attributed to their traditional use in high-performance computing roles (such as graphics workstations or applications servers) that demand pre-optimized configurations, as well as the fact that many of these system manufacturers produce the motherboard, chipset, and the system firmware (providing better insight and ability to optimize performance). Other settings include BIOS shadowing and caching, support of delayed transactions and bus concurrency (PCI) through interleaving and buffering, systemwide parity enabling, and special features for embedded peripheral buses. Although most of these settings are usually configurable from the on-board system BIOS/Setup utility, some motherboards require that certain settings be altered from a disk-based configuration utility (such as EISA and MCA systems).

ARC RISC Configuration Primer

Because ARC-compliant RISC machines like the Alpha do not support DOS, they don't have to worry about the system BIOS taking up DOS memory. As a result, they tend to have large onboard environments stored in Nonvolatile RAM (NVRAM) and configured using the ARC/SRM console or the AlphaBIOS on DEC Alpha machines. The ARC console has a very UNIX-like feel to it, owing to the fact that the marriage between UNIX and Alpha has been somewhat longer than that between Alpha and NT. The AlphaBIOS uses a windowed configuration screen like many modern PC BIOSs, and is therefore easy to navigate. With the ARC console, devices are specified using UNIX-style device statements, which are the same conventions seen in the Windows NT BOOT.INI configuration file used in Intel x86-based NT installations. It is from this ARC Console or AlphaBIOS that the supplementary menus are chosen and the NT operating system installed directly from the CD without requiring the use of boot disks.

AlphaBIOSs of version 5.0 or greater also contain embedded support for the creation and formatting of partitions, and therefore serve the same functions as the partition management utility invoked by Windows NT Setup during an x86-based NT installation. Maintenance programs are also run directly from the AlphaBIOS or ARC console. For example, some older firmware did not support onboard partitioning and formatting functions, and required that a special program called ARCINST.EXE be executed from the >> (ARC) prompt. Long device names (e.g., scsi(1)disk(0)partition(1)) are used to specify devices during the boot process and during installation. Another example is the command for initializing a Windows NT installation on an ARC RISC system from the console:

```
cd:\alpha\setupldr
```

Listed below are examples of ARC statements one might see during the Windows NT boot process on an ARC-compliant machine:

- scsi(1)disk(0)fdisk(0)
- scsi(2)disk(1)hdisk(0)
- scsi(1)disk(2)cdrom(0)

This indicates the initialization of three devices; a floppy disk, a hard drive, and a CD-ROM drive.

Without direct changes to the CPU architecture, the single most important component to a systems CPU and expansion bus performance is its chipset/firmware. Two identical CPUs placed in different systems utilizing different chipsets and firmware will yield different performance figures, and in some cases the differences are drastic. An example of this kind of difference is the introduction of the Triton chipset for the Pentium CPU or the Alcor II chipset on the DEC Alpha platform. Each of these new chipsets delivered far better performance than their predecessors, in some cases as much as 20 percent higher. Many processors will have two, three, or more supporting chipsets developed for them during their life cycle, and each such chipset may experience a large number of firmware revisions during this same life cycle. This is yet another testimony for only purchasing systems that support user-upgradable FlashROMs (EEPROMs). Updating the system firmware on a regular basis can help you gain additional performance from your system. Most manufacturers offer these updates in the form of a software patch that can be downloaded from a BBS, FTP, or World Wide Web server.

Be aware that performing any BIOS/firmware flash upgrade is a potentially hazardous activity that, if not completed successfully (due to software bugs, power loss, or whatever) can render the system unbootable. Although many systems have a motherboard jumper setting or other special procedure to follow in these situations that can help recover the system, some do not. Although unlikely, it is possible that a failed flash BIOS update could render a system unusable to the point that it would have to be returned to the manufacturer for repair or reflashing. Therefore, minimize the number of flash BIOS updates you perform and try to save these procedures for important firmware updates that address specific problems in your environment.

Optimizing Memory Timings

Another issue to consider is the optimal timings to use for different RAM types running at different system bus speeds. Most RAM access happens as a "burst" type of access rather than a single memory location; that is, many locations are read at once because this is a more efficient way of retrieving data. In addition, most memory accesses occur with the L2 cache (Static RAM) rather than directly with main memory (Dynamic RAM). Every system has the capability to define exactly how many CPU clock cycles are required to read the initial memory location's Double Word (or DWord) value and consecutive adjacent DWord values in memory. The format for these memory timings is typically in the format x-y-y-y, where x is the number of cycles for the first memory address, and the y values are the number of clock cycles required for subsequent reads.

Although most systems will choose safe "default" settings for DRAM and SRAM burst mode read/write timing, you may want to double-check these settings with those shown in Table 3-4.

TABLE 3-4 OPTIMAL STATIC RAM CACHE TIMINGS AT VARIOUS SYSTEM BUS SPEEDS

System Bus Speed (MHz)	Asynchronous SRAM Cache	Synchronous SRAM Cache	Pipelined Burst Mode Synchronous
33	2-1-1-1	2-1-1-1	3-1-1-1
50	3-2-2-2	2-1-1-1	3-1-1-1
60	3-2-2-2	2-1-1-1	3-1-1-1
66	3-2-2-2	2-1-1-1	3-1-1-1
75	3-2-2-2	3-2-2-2	3-1-1-1
83	3-2-2-2	3-2-2-2	3-1-1-1
100	3-2-2-2	3-2-2-2	3-1-1-1
125	3-2-2-2	3-2-2-2	3-1-1-1

When used in reference to DRAM timings versus SRAM, the format is typically xXXX; e.g., x222, x333, x444, and so forth. On some Intel system BIOSs, the timings for different chip types may also be combined. For example the timing for Fast Page Mode versus Extended Data Output (EDO) DRAM may be listed together in different choices such as x222/x333, x333/x444, and so on, where the lower value is for EDO and the higher is for FPM memory. However, the choices and appropriate values will vary depending on the type of memory and chipset used on the motherboard. Although lower numbers are always preferable (because it will take less CPU cycles to access the data), it's important that the DRAM/SRAM you're using is capable of supporting the value chosen. Although the default values on most systems provide decent RAM performance, you may want to experiment with lower values to see if the RAM being used is capable of performing at the higher speeds. For standard FPM and EDO memory, this should generally only be done if you are using high-quality 50ns or 60ns chips; otherwise, setting lower values will likely cause operational problems on the system.

You should only experiment with memory timing change on nonproduction machines, because setting inappropriate values could potentially cause data corruption or loss on some systems. Also, be sure to perform a complete system backup, including the registry, prior to making system BIOS modifications of any kind.

For more information on doing system and registry backups and performing system maintenance, see Chapter 12, "Maintaining Your NT System."

If you want to benchmark your system's memory performance at different SRAM and/or DRAM timings, you can use U-Software's Bench32 benchmarking utility, included on the *Optimizing Windows NT* CD-ROM and described in Chapter 4. Bench32 allows you to select a full suite of system performance tests or only include certain tests (such as memory).

Optimal CPU, Memory, and Cache Settings (x86 Systems)

Intel x86-based system BIOSs are infamous for containing a wide array of settings related to CPU, memory, and cache. However, because many of these settings have little or no documentation in motherboard manuals and on-line help, you may be confused as to what each setting affects and what values are appropriate. To help, we've compiled a list of several common settings found in a majority of PC BIOSs that relate to these areas, and explain the function and optimal values for each.

- *Cache cycles/speed*: If available, these options allow you to set the cache cycle to an optimal setting. For example, asynchronous SRAM cache on Intel systems is ideal at 3-2-2-2, with the numbers indicating the wait states involved in each access. The first requires three cycles for activation of the CAS and RAS, while all other requests to the same pages are every other clock. Synchronous pipeline burst mode (PBM) cache memory is typically optimal at a 3-1-1-1 setting and is the most common cache type found on x86-based systems. Synchronous flow-through burst cache is optimal at a 2-1-1-1 setting. If these settings are available and match the cache installed, use them. The lower the wait states (what these numbers reflect), the faster the performance. An optimized cache can do more for improving processor scores than almost any other single feature.

Most DRAM and Static (cache) RAM require the use of intentional CPU delays called *wait states* to ensure that the CPU doesn't attempt to read data faster than the RAM in question can offer it. Wait states may be employed for both read and write memory operations. Because they introduce delays that impair RAM performance, you'll always want to ensure that you have the lowest wait state settings defined in your BIOS that your system and memory can safely support. This information may be available in your system documentation, or could also be derived by trial and error with different wait state settings (however, if using trial and error, be sure to have a complete system and registry backup because data could be corrupted if invalid settings are used).

- *DRAM cycles/speed*: If present, set the main memory down to its ideal cycle. FPM (Fast Page Mode) DRAM has an ideal cycle of 6-3-3-3 on many systems; in others it may be set to a more conservative setting of 7-4-4-4. On some systems, it may be as low as 5-3-3-3, though the requirement is for faster DRAM (below 60ns access time). EDO DRAM is optimal on many systems at 6-2-2-2, but may also be pushed to 5-2-2-2 at lower access times. BEDO DRAM is optimal at the same cycles as full SDRAM at 5-1-1-1 but can sometimes be pushed to 4-1-1-1, only one wait state longer on activation than pipeline burst mode SRAM. With SDRAM, the burst and latency counters are usually not accessible, and are handled by the manufacturer of the system board through its selection of chipset and firmware. Because optimal DRAM/SRAM timings are highly dependent on both the exact RAM chips in use (type and speed) as well as the system motherboard and chipset, there are no "hard and fast" general settings that will work best on all systems.
- *ECC enable*: This allows true parity memory to use the chipset for 1-bit error correction and 2-bit error detection. The setting is normally either parity or ECC. Although the use of parity memory or ECC has overhead that makes it somewhat slower than nonparity memory, it is important on systems that require maximum reliability such as network servers. Also, some chipsets don't support ECC calculations by the chipset and instead require the use of ECC memory modules to enable this functionality. When using parity memory on systems with ECC support in the chipset, choose ECC over parity; it is more reliable and uses a more sophisticated parity checking method.
- *Parity enable*: If the system is unable to automatically detect parity or nonparity DRAM, enable this option to explicitly inform the system that parity memory or special "parity generator" DRAM memory is in use.
- *Wait states*: Wait states incur intentional waiting periods during the access of memory and the system bus in order to allow the slower devices on these buses to keep up. The ISA and EISA buses also have special wait states called "recovery times" or "latency periods" during which the bus cannot be accessed. If these settings are higher (i.e., longer duration) than they need to be, the result will be an unnecessary performance hit. Although most boards configure this and other settings via an "auto" option in the BIOS, you may want to try experimenting with lower settings in an attempt to increase system performance. The best way to do this is to keep testing lower and lower (i.e., faster and faster) wait state settings until the system behaves erratically.

It is not recommended that you play with memory wait states or other system board settings on a production server or other machine with important data. Although the settings can always be reversed, there have been several instances where overly aggressive BIOS settings caused disk controllers to corrupt data on attached drives. Your best bet is to experiment with these settings on a nonproduction system that you have some benchmarking utilities installed on (e.g., Edmund Underwood's Bench32 that is found on the CD accompanying this book) to allow you to test the results of each setting change made.

- *CPU type:* Some CPUs offer special features (linear burst modes, special L1 or L2 cache interfaces) that should be configured to match the CPU. These types of options tend to apply more to x86 clone chips such as those manufactured by AMD and Cyrix.
- *Internal L1 cache policy:* If this option is accessible, set it to write-back, which is generally the fastest option available (some chipsets perform this as a read-around write, a more advanced and faster method).
- *L2 cache policy:* Use this setting to change the cache to write-back cache, a faster method than write-through (as with L1 cache policy, above, newer chipsets will perform this operation as a read-around write, an even faster caching method).
- *Pipeline support:* There is at least one, if not two, pipeline options; one is for pipelined CPU to DRAM support, the other is internal CPU pipeline enable. If available, both should be turned on.
- *Microcode:* This option allows for the update of CPU microcode via firmware updates/revisions and applies mainly to newer x86-type chips. This feature allows you to update your system's firmware to patch or enhance the CPU's internal microcode to fix bugs or improve performance. This feature is used with Intel Pentium II processors and is expected to continue being used in future processors from Intel and others.

- *Shadow option ROMs:* For Windows NT, it is best to disable all optional ROM shadow and caching (including system and video), because all functions of moving BIOS code to RAM is handled by NT's kernel. Shadowing wastes memory that could otherwise be used by the NT operating system, and leaving such options on can occasionally cause NT problems in detecting the amount of installed memory. The only exception to this rule is when NT is used in combination with another operating system that does benefit from ROM shadowing, such as DOS, Windows 3.x, or Windows 95. In these cases, it is beneficial to have at least the system BIOS ROM shadowed, because the system will be noticeably slower with system shadowing/BIOS caching disabled while using the non-NT operating system.
- *Cache system BIOS:* To cache the BIOS must be shadowed, but BIOS shadowing with NT is not valuable and wastes resources. Caching of BIOS allows the shadowed ROM to be cached by the system's fast L2–L3 cache to improve its performance even more. As with the discussion of ROM shadowing above, this option should only be enabled on NT systems that are dual-boot with another operating system that can benefit from the use of this feature.
- *Cache video BIOS:* Like system BIOS caching, it is not valuable with NT and must be used with shadowing of video BIOS. The same notes applicable to system BIOS caching apply here as well.
- *Drive voltage in milliamps:* This is a setting for determining the voltage sent to the memory array. If there is an AUTO setting, it is best that you use it. When set improperly this setting can actually damage memory; it is also a completely performance-neutral setting.
- *ISA/EISA bus clock divisor:* This is a setting to change the divisor of the EISA/ISA bus from its nominal of $^1/_4$ to a higher or lower clock divisor. Lower divisors reflect higher frequencies. Changing this setting will not always increase the performance of these connectors and may not be supported by the controllers installed. On some motherboards this setting may be a hardware jumper.
- *Recovery clocks:* For legacy peripheral expansion buses (e.g., ISA or EISA), this figure represents the number of clock cycles that must be used before the system can access the controller device again. The lower they are, the faster the device can be accessed again. As with other settings, you may wish to experiment with this figure to see if lower figures create faster system performance.

Optimal CPU, Memory, and Cache Settings (RISC Systems)

As mentioned in an earlier section, the CPU and cache settings for most RISC systems tend to be preoptimized and require little if any tweaking on the part of the user. For example, the proper memory timings for the system RAM are usually autodetected and are generally set in an optimal fashion. Users used to the wide variety of adjustments that exist in most Intel-based system BIOSs will discover that many of these setting modifications are either unnecessary or nonexistent in RISC-based system BIOSs (again, because many RISC-based systems are manufactured top-to-bottom by the same manufacturer rather than being a mishmash of mixed components from different manufacturers).

Optimal PCI Bus Settings

Many of the following PCI bus-related settings are found only on the most recent chipsets from VIA and Intel, especially on those used in more expensive systems targeted at the high-end workstation and server markets.

- *Write combine:* If available, the write combine setting should be enabled because it makes the PCI bus transactions more efficient by lumping multiple writes into a single more efficient write.
- *Delayed transaction*: This is one of the functions of PCI concurrency implemented through buffering of the PCI bus to main memory. All PCI configuration, I/O, and memory access can be performed much like a lazy write, without having to be performed immediately. Setting this feature on can result in better PCI bus performance in some environments.
- *Post Write:* Another feature associated with a buffering, usually between CPU and PCI. The "deeper" the buffer, the better the performance tends to be. It is closely related to buffering from main memory to PCI through read data buffering. Also note this is buffering, not caching memory, and the total amount of memory involved is usually less than 50 bytes.
- *PCI bus concurrency:* This feature allows traffic to be better managed on the PCI bus by providing interleaved access and does not require the presence of dual peer PCI buses to be enabled. It allows multiple commands and I/O to move on the bus simultaneously, mainly through buffering and the use of delayed transactions. Turning PCI bus concurrency on normally means better overall PCI bus performance.

- *PCI bus parity enable:* Allows the PCI bus to be fully parity checked for higher fault tolerance. Although this feature introduces some overhead that may slightly reduce PCI bus performance, it creates greater data reliability and is therefore recommended (like parity/ECC memory) on mission-critical machines such as network servers.
- *Passive release:* A function closely associated with PCI concurrency that allows interleaved access to main memory and reduces CPU utilization. This maximizes efficiency of the PCI bus and is a feature that should normally be enabled.
- *Latency Timer:* This value controls the latency in regards to access of the PCI bus. The figure represents the number of microseconds the PCI bus must remain idle after being accessed (during which time no system device may access the PCI bus). The typical setting is usually 32 or 64 microseconds for 4-slot PCI systems, and up to 96 microseconds for 6- or 8-slot PCI systems. The proper PCI bus latency timer setting is highly dependent on the number of concurrent devices operating on the PCI bus; that is, more devices and heavier bus saturation often require a higher latency timer setting to achieve optimal PCI bus operation.

Optimal Embedded IDE/ATA and USB Chipset Settings

The most common chipsets used for the embedded IDE/ATA and USB (Universal Serial Bus) controllers found on most modern motherboards are usually from either Intel or CMD. The most recent versions of both provide support for a number of higher-performance features, including busmastering, block data transfer modes, and support for 32-bit transfers. Although we strongly recommended that you choose SCSI over IDE for your NT system's drive subsystem, it is inevitable that some NT systems will continue to use IDE. The settings below detail some suggested settings that will help optimize the BIOS settings related to the IDE controller. Also included are some settings related to the Universal Serial Bus controller found on many of these motherboards.

- *PIO mode settings:* Many BIOSs will allow you to set the specific Programmed I/O (PIO) mode used by a particular IDE/ATA device such as a hard drive or CD-ROM drive. If you are unsure of the maximum speed supported by a drive, there is also usually an "auto" setting that interrogates the devices in an attempt to determine the correct settings. If you are sure a device supports a particular PIO mode, it is always best to manually select this mode rather than setting the auto option and taking the risk that the system will misidentify the maximum setting and communicate with the device at a less-than-optimal speed.

- *DMA mode settings:* IDE/ATA drives support DMA modes of operation in addition to Programmed I/O modes. As with PIO mode settings, these settings allow you to specify the particular mode supported by each IDE/ATA device in your system. If you're unsure, you can also select the "auto" value and let the system make the choice for you. As with PIO mode settings, you should always manually set the DMA modes for individual devices if you know them for sure; that way you're guaranteed to have the system communicate with the drive at the highest possible speed.
- *Busmastering support:* Allows the IDE/ATA controller to perform busmastering from the controller chipset directly to the host's main memory without intervention from the CPU. Busmastering occurs at the maximum rate for the PCI bus and ISA bus, respectively, because the dual channel controller is often embedded on the PCI bus for primary and ISA bus for secondary (however, some systems place both IDE channels on the PCI bus). Always have busmastering enabled whenever it is an available option; it makes an enormous difference to both the overall speed of data transfers and to the lowering of CPU utilization.
- *PIO Master/Slave independent drive timing:* Allows the devices on either channel to function with the full PIO modes enabled between slave and master devices, rather than being forced to use the PIO mode of the slowest device. Generally speaking, this option should be enabled, and you should only disable it if having it enabled results in problems.
- *32-bit transfer support:* This setting allows for full 32-bit transfers from drive's on-board controller through the system bus to memory. 32-bit transfers are more efficient than the default 16-bit transfers used when this option is disabled. To work, the IDE/ATA drive's onboard controller must support this feature.
- *Block mode:* Rather than triggering an interrupt for every 2K of data like the original IDE specification, block mode support allows a variable number of blocks (a group of sectors) to be transferred per interrupt; this greatly increases the overall efficiency of IDE/ATA data transfers. The larger the number of blocks, the lower the interrupt generation and the more efficient the transfer. You should experiment with different block mode settings (higher than 2K) to see which yields the best performance on your system.
- *IDE to CPU post:* This enables a buffer between the CPU and IDE controller to improve performance. This feature should generally be enabled.
- *ATA-33:* ATA-3/Ultra-ATA 33MBps DMA mode operation. DMA modes have nothing to do with busmastering. If you're using an ATA-3/Ultra-ATA-compliant hard drive, you should enable this feature.

- *USB passive release:* Like other passive release schemes, this setting allows interleaved access to memory while other busmasters are operating. The recommended setting is enabled.
- *USB clock frequency:* Set to either 24MHz or 48MHz. USB clock frequency sets the maximum rate at which the USB port can send/receive data. Change this setting to the higher rate if you're using USB devices that can take advantage of it.

Configuring the SCSI Subsystem

Another extremely important hardware subsystem that you should ensure is optimized is your system's SCSI controller. On most systems, this takes the form of a peripheral card adapter (preferably PCI if possible for maximum throughput), but on others it may be a SCSI controller embedded on the motherboard. Chipsets customarily used for on-board SCSI controllers include the NCR/Symbios Logic 53C8XXX SCSI chipset and Adaptec AIC-78XX. In many cases, the SCSI BIOS code for these controllers will actually be placed in the system BIOS itself.

Because these controllers are typically connected to the PCI bus, there is little performance difference between an on-board SCSI controller and a stand-alone PCI-based version using the same chipset. However, the stand-alone versions often provide additional connector options that the embedded versions don't have (such as an external connector or both narrow and wide connector types). The major advantage of the on-board versions is that they save a PCI slot for other uses. An excellent use for such embedded SCSI controllers is for your slower SCSI devices, such as CD-ROMs, tape drives, scanners, and other such devices. If you then place your faster SCSI hard drives on a separate stand-alone SCSI card (and therefore a separate SCSI channel), this will optimize the speed of these drives because the slower speeds of the other SCSI devices and additional SCSI channel contentions won't negatively affect them.

See the "Storage Controllers" section of Chapter 2 for additional information on the SCSI bus and information on optimizing SCSI channel usage.

SCSI devices utilize a simple ID system for determining priority, with higher priority allocated to higher ID numbers. Device ID 0 is the default ID on most systems of the boot drive, although Windows NT will allow either ID 0 or 1 to be used for the boot device. On some systems, it may even be possible to use higher

ID numbers as the SCSI boot device. This design is mainly used to provide backward compatibility and to remain consistent with existing hardware and software standards. Device ID 7 is almost always reserved for the SCSI controller (because it should always receive the highest priority), and this setting should normally not be changed.

If you have a mixture of SCSI and IDE hard drives in your system, you may wish to have your SCSI drives recognized by the system before your IDE drives (or vice versa). Although on most systems the default is for IDE devices to be enumerated first, many newer system BIOSs have an option that allows you to specifically designate the order in which the drives are recognized.

Although it seems somewhat counterintuitive, optimizing the performance of your SCSI bus is usually accomplished by placing high-speed, high-demand devices such as hard drives on lower SCSI IDs, and slower-speed devices such as CD-ROM and tape drives on higher SCSI IDs (5 and 6, for example) that receive higher prioritization on the SCSI bus. Although the result seems at first to be the exact opposite of what you might expect, the reason this works better is that low-speed devices placed on lower IDs often cause a "starvation" effect on the higher ID devices' ability to obtain SCSI bus access (especially when many devices are active on the SCSI bus at once). By placing the lower speed devices on higher IDs and the higher-speed devices on lower IDs, bus starvation can generally be avoided. Note also that this assumes that the fast and slow SCSI devices are being shared on a single SCSI channel; if they are separated onto separate SCSI channels this problem wouldn't exist.

The "starvation" phenomenon is one of the reasons that operating systems such as UNIX tend to make static assignments for certain SCSI device types; for example, ID 0 and 1 for hard drives, ID 2 for CD-ROMs, ID's 5 and 6 for tape drives, and so on. By standardizing these assignments, the chance of bus starvation is greatly reduced over the free-for-all SCSI ID implementations supported by other operating systems. Windows NT has no such SCSI ID restrictions, and only the SCSI chipset/firmware and SCSI miniport driver used limit recognition of the SCSI system devices.

Narrow SCSI (8-bit) implementations support 8 device IDs, 0 through 7, while Wide SCSI (16-bit) implementations support 16 IDs, 0 through 15. A special version of SCSI called Deep SCSI also exists on some high-end servers and supports 60 device IDs, due to its use of 4 bits rather than 3 bits for SCSI ID addressing.

General SCSI Controller Configuration Settings

Most SCSI chipsets and controllers have a BIOS configuration setup similar to that used by the main system BIOS. As with the system BIOS, these configuration screens are typically accessed during the system boot process by using a special key combination. Once pressed, you are then brought to the SCSI BIOS configuration menu for your controller. Most controllers announce the keystroke required to access this menu on-screen during the BIOS initialization process during system boot. For example, Adaptec controllers use the keystroke Ctrl-A to access their configuration menus, while most BusLogic controllers use Ctrl-B; the keystrokes for other cards vary depending on the manufacturer and product model. However, some SCSI BIOSs also have an option to hide this keystroke, so you may not see the key combination announced if you or the system vendor have turned on this option. Most motherboard-embedded SCSI controllers offer similar, if not identical, settings to their peripheral card-based cousins.

In addition to their graphical BIOS configuration utilities, some SCSI host adapters also contain software that writes directly to the card's NVRAM and allows you to perform low-level tuning of various operational parameters of the card. These utilities are provided by several manufacturers of high-performance SCSI and RAID controllers (one such vendor is Qlogic Corporation, who includes this utility with virtually all of their SCSI host adapter products).

Because there is a wide assortment of different SCSI card manufacturers and models on the market that are supported under Windows NT, we limit our discussion of chipset configuration settings to those that are common to a wide range of cards. There are two categories of SCSI-related settings, adapter-oriented (channel-oriented for multiple channel adapters) and device-oriented settings.

Common adapter/channel-oriented settings

Some adapter/channel-oriented settings are as follows:

- *UltraSCSI speed support:* UltraSCSI support is typically a global setting for the controller (or channel on multichannel cards) that informs the card to use the Fast-20 (UltraSCSI) protocol in support of UltraSCSI-compliant devices. This translates to a 20 MBps maximum synchronous transfer rate for narrow UltraSCSI, and 40 MBps for Wide UltraSCSI. If you are using UltraSCSI peripherals on your system, you should always enable this option to obtain optimal data transfer rates. In some circumstance, it is also possible that enabling UltraSCSI support will cause problems for other, non-UltraSCSI devices sharing the same SCSI bus. In these circumstances, you can either move such devices to another SCSI card or channel (if one exists) or disable UltraSCSI support. Although the latter isn't the fastest solution, it works because UltraSCSI devices are backward-compatible with slower SCSI protocols. Many UltraSCSI adapters have this setting disabled by default, so be sure to examine it if you're using UltraSCSI devices.
- *Host adapter termination:* This setting affects whether or not the SCSI adapter acts as a terminator at one end of the SCSI bus. The options on most cards typically include Enable, Disable, or Auto. Whenever possible, use Auto termination because this allows the controller to automatically reterminate the SCSI bus if external SCSI devices are connected or removed from the external SCSI connector.
- *Multiple LUN support:* This setting enables or disables support for Logical Unit Numbers, which are like a subclass of SCSI IDs and provide up to eight Logical Units per SCSI ID. For example, some CD autochangers use Logical Units numbers to assign independent IDs to each drive tray. However, the CD changer itself still uses only a single SCSI ID. Unless you know you have a device that requires LUNs, you can safely disable LUN support on your adapter.
- *SCAM support:* This enables support for the SCAM (SCSI Configured AutoMatically) protocol, which is a newer protocol (akin to Plug and Play found on newer system BIOSs) that allows SCSI adapters to automatically assign a SCSI device a device ID (SCAM 1) and in some cases termination (SCAM 2). Although it has no effect on performance, the use of SCAM is recommended because it relieves some of the headaches of SCSI ID configuration. The only exception to this is a situation where you wish to manually assign certain devices to higher priority SCSI IDs.

- *Tagged command queuing support:* This setting enables tagged command queuing, a special feature found on many SCSI host adapters. Tagged command queuing improves SCSI bus efficiency by allowing the SCSI host adapter to reorder and service queued commands in the most efficient order, rather than mechanically executing them in the order in which they were received. For maximum performance, this setting should always be enabled; it should only be disabled if problems are experienced.
- *SCSI parity checking:* This setting controls whether parity checking is used on the SCSI bus. Parity checking verifies the integrity of data passed between devices on the SCSI bus. Although it does impact SCSI performance somewhat, it should be left enabled in most environments (this is normally the default setting for most SCSI controllers).

Disabling SCSI parity could potentially cause problems with Windows NT (as well as other operating systems such as UNIX) and is not generally recommended.

- *BIOS enable/disable:* This setting turns the on-board SCSI BIOS on or off. Although SCSI channels or adapters used for boot devices should normally have this feature turned on, it isn't required for adapters/channels that only have devices that are supported by device drivers (e.g., CD-ROMs, tape drives, etc.) rather than the SCSI BIOS itself.
- *Load order:* In multiple adapter/channel systems, this setting controls the order in which multiple adapters or channels load their BIOS, and governs adapter/channel priority. It also changes which adapter/channel installs its BIOS first. This primary adapter/channel is normally the one containing the system boot drive, although this isn't a requirement with all adapters.

Common device-oriented settings

Here are some common device-oriented settings:

- *Initiate synchronous negotiation:* This setting controls whether the SCSI bus attempts to use synchronous negotiation with the device in question. SCSI supports the use of synchronous or asynchronous data transfers, with synchronous being the faster of the two. Generally speaking, it is best to leave this setting to yes, especially if you are unsure which data transfer method a device supports.

Although the controller will automatically detect and handle enabled initiate synchronous negotiation for asynchronous devices, this setting may cause problems with some older SCSI-1 devices that don't support synchronous negotiation. Although rare, this can sometimes cause the system to operate erratically; if this happens, simply change this setting to no for these devices.

- *Maximum synchronous transfer rate:* This setting defines the maximum synchronous data transfer rate that the SCSI adapter/channel can support.

As with synchronous negotiation, older SCSI-1 devices can sometimes cause the system to hang or act erratically if the maximum transfer rate for the device is set too high. If this happens, simply step the maximum transfer rate down until the problem goes away.

- *Enable disconnection:* Also referred to as Disconnect/Reconnect, this setting informs the SCSI adapter whether SCSI disconnection should be enabled for this device. Disconnection is a feature that allows a device to temporarily disconnect from the SCSI bus while not using it, so that other devices may have access to the bus. This optimizes the overall speed of the SCSI bus when multiple devices are present. However, this option should be disabled when there is only one device present on a SCSI adapter or channel; otherwise, the bus disconnections will introduce unnecessary delays for the device and actually end up reducing performance.
- *Initiate Wide negotiation:* On most cards, this setting is a per-device setting that informs the controller to attempt to negotiate a wide SCSI (16-bit) connection with the specified device. This option should always be enabled for your Wide SCSI devices in order to take advantage of their higher performance capabilities.
- *Active Negation:* Some cards offer an active negation feature, a process by which the SCSI bus is "cleaned" by an active signal to filter noise. This can improve SCSI bus performance if the cabling used is lower grade cabling (however, it is recommended that you always use the highest quality cables you can get for a SCSI subsystem because this will maximize performance and minimize the risk of data loss, corruption, and other problems).

- *Start Unit command enable:* This is a per-device setting that enables or disables the use of SCSI start unit commands. This is a logical SCSI instruction that informs SCSI devices to power up in a staggered fashion, a technique that can reduce the load on the system's power supply during power-on. When enabled, start unit commands are sent by the bus to SCSI device IDs in lowest to highest order (because most systems have the boot drive on the lower SCSI IDs such as 0/1). Normally, you can safely leave these settings disabled without problems; if you do wish to enable the use of start unit commands, many devices require a jumper setting on the device itself to support this feature.

Using multiple SCSI channels

As with everything else in computers, more is always better. In the case of SCSI, you can increase the performance of your SCSI subsystem by segmenting your SCSI traffic onto multiple channels or multiple physical adapters. Some SCSI controllers support two or three channels, which are each their own independent stand-alone SCSI bus. Although it is also possible to place multiple physical SCSI adapters in a computer to achieve the same result, using multiple channel cards has the added advantage of saving a PCI slot for other purposes. It can also eliminate the headache that sometimes arises when trying to get different cards of different models or makes to work together in a system.

When segmenting your SCSI traffic onto multiple channels or adapters, you should dedicate one channel to slow devices (such as CD-ROM drives, scanners, tape drives, SCSI floppy drives, etc.) and one or more channels to higher-speed devices such as hard drives and faster optical or removable drive types. The reason this scheme increases the speed of the SCSI system is twofold: first, having slower devices contend for the fixed amount of bandwidth on the SCSI channel (e.g., 10MBps, 20MBps, 40MBps, etc.). Second, many slower SCSI devices tend to incur a different traffic type (small, bursty, and short data transfers) than faster devices (even, fast, and long data transfers). Having disparate traffic types on the same channel will often bog the faster devices down and limit their performance. Although the flexibility of SCSI makes it tempting to fill a single SCSI adapter or channel with as many devices as will fit, this normally results in a less-than-optimal SCSI subsystem.

Obtaining the latest drivers

One of the easiest things you can do to improve the performance of a SCSI card is to visit the vendor's Web or FTP server to obtain the latest Windows NT drivers. Often, the default drivers shipped with Windows NT for a particular card are buggy, slow, or both. Although there is no guarantee a later driver will improve performance, this is the case more often than not. As time goes on, vendors improve the performance and efficiency of their NT drivers, and this can translate into reduced problems and/or improved speed.

Table 3-5 lists several of the most popular SCSI card manufacturers and their Web/FTP sites containing updated driver files.

TABLE 3-5 INTERNET SERVERS CONTAINING DRIVER UPDATES FOR POPULAR SCSI CARD MANUFACTURERS

Manufacturer	Web Site	FTP Site
Adaptec, Inc.	`http://www.adaptec.com`	`ftp://ftp.adaptec.com`
BusLogic/Mylex	`http://www.mylex.com`	`ftp://ftp.mylex.com`
QLogic, Inc.	`http://www.qlc.com`	`ftp://ftp.qlc.com`
Symbios Logic, Inc.	`http://www.symbios.com`	`ftp://ftp.symbios.com`
Distributed Processing Technology (DPT)	`http://www.dpt.com`	`ftp://ftp.dpt.com`
AdvanSys, Inc.	`http://www.advansys.com`	`ftp://ftp.advansys.com`
Diamond Multimedia, Inc.	`http://www.diamondmm.com`	`ftp://ftp.diamondmm.com`
AMI (American Megatrends Inc.)	`http://www.ami.com`	N/A*

*N/A = Not Available

Again, you should never assume that just because a driver is newer that it provides better performance. To determine the performance effects of the change, be sure to benchmark the performance of the SCSI/disk subsystem with both drivers. Although it's uncommon, we've actually seen new drivers provide worse performance in some cases. This usually happens when a vendor increases feature support in the driver or adds support for additional product models; the increase in overhead can translate into reduced performance.

When installing an updated driver for a particular card, it's usually a good idea to completely remove the existing driver prior to installing the new one (however, don't reboot in between the two steps or you may be unable to boot the system). This helps to ensure that any new subkeys or value settings related to the new driver are properly added into the registry. You should never, under any circumstances, simply replace a driver file manually even if the files have the same name.

Updated SCSI drivers may be installed in the SCSI Control Panel's Drivers tab, by first removing the existing driver and then installing the updated version (the SCSI Control Panel is shown in Figure 3-2).

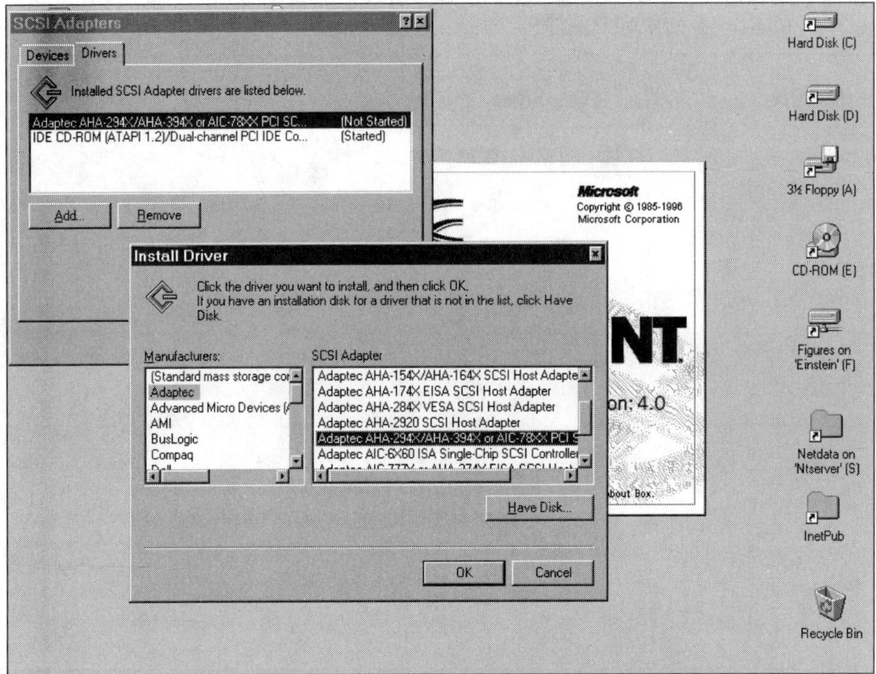

Figure 3-2: Installing an Updated SCSI Adapter Driver in the SCSI Control Panel.

Be certain when removing your existing SCSI driver that the new one you'll be installing is the correct one for your particular card; failure to do so could render your system unstartable, a situation that may require use of the Emergency Repair Process or Last Known Good Configuration option to fix (see Chapter 13 for explanations of these).

Notes on Specific SCSI Adapters

In the following sections, we discuss some driver-related performance tunings that apply to specific SCSI host adapter brands and models. You may wish to consider trying some of the modifications discussed on nonproduction machines to see if additional performance is obtained. Although all of these recommendations are straight from the individual card manufacturers, you should also consider checking the adapter's documentation and/or on-line resources (i.e., FTP or Web site information) to see if additional driver parameters have been released or discussed in a technical document from the vendor. As always, never try any modifications on a production machine without having first made a full backup of both the system hard drives and the NT registry.

Adaptec AIC-78XX SCSI adapters

On AIC-78XX chipset-based Adaptec controllers (such as the popular AHA-2940/3940 family of adapters), the disabling of SCSI disconnection on adapters/channels with one drive (in order to optimize performance) can result in system hangs. This is most likely to happen if the hard drive device supports tagged queuing. As a result, Adaptec recommends that with these adapters you always enable disconnection for hard drive devices. By default, disconnection is enabled so no action is required. If, for some reason, it is absolutely required that disconnection be disabled for hard drives in your system, you can turn off tagged queue requests by making these changes to the Windows NT registry:

1. In Windows NT 3.5x, select Run from Program or File Manager's File menu; in Windows NT 4.0, choose Run from the Start Menu accessible via the Start Button.
2. Enter **REGEDT32** to run the Registry Editor (in Windows NT 4.0, you can also use **REGEDIT**).
3. Open the following registry key by navigating down through the registry tree:

   `\HKEY_LOCAL_MACHINE\SYSTEM\CurrentControlSet\Services\aic78xx.`
4. Create a key named *Parameters* by selecting Edit → Add Key from the menus, and enter **Parameters** as the key name. Leave the Class box blank.
5. Open Parameters and create a key named *Device* by selecting Edit → Add Key from the menus. Enter **Device** as the key name. Leave the Class box blank.

6. Open the newly created Device key, and select Edit → Add Value option from the Edit pull-down menu. In the Value Name edit-box, enter **DisableTaggedQueuing**. Select a data type of *REG_SZ* from the drop-down list box.
7. Close the Registry Editor application and shut down and restart Windows NT; the change will take effect during the next system boot.
8. Set Enable Disconnection to No for your particular device(s) in the Adaptec SCSISelect utility during system boot (see your Adaptec host adapter manual for information on how to use the SCSISelect utility).

These Adaptec cards also have a number of command-line options that can be configured via Windows NT Registry entries for the SCSI miniport driver. Although making changes to these settings is somewhat risky, it could provide better performance in some environments. Therefore, Table 3-6 is provided for those interested in fine-tuning certain aspects of the AIC-78XX chipset-based adapters.

TABLE 3-6 SCSI MINIPORT DRIVER COMMAND-LINE ENTRIES FOR ADAPTEC AIC-78XX ADAPTERS

Switch Name	Description	Value Range	Default Value
/INSTRUMENTATION	Enable recording of I/O statistics and errors	None; not required	Disabled
/INSTR_ERRLOG_Z = *nnn*	If recording of I/O errors is enabled, sets maximum number of error log entries	0–128	32
/MAXIMUMSGLIST = *nnn*	Specify maximum number of scatter-gather elements	1–255	7
/MAXTAGS = *nnn*	Specifies tagged command queue depth	1–255	128

*Note: All data types in table are of type REG_SZ.

To enter these driver-specific parameters, it is necessary to edit the system Registry. To do so, follow these steps:

1. Select Run from the File pull-down menu (Windows NT 3.5x) or Run from the Start button (Windows NT 4.0).
2. Type **regedt32** and press Enter.
3. Open the registry list to the following location: *\HKEY_LOCAL_MACHINE\System\CurrentControlSet\Services\aic78xx\Parameters\Device\DriverParameters*

   If the *\Parameters\Device\DriverParameters* key already exists, skip to step 10 to begin entering parameters. If the keys do not yet exist, you will need to create them by continuing with step 4.
4. Click the aic78xx key.
5. Under the Edit pull-down menu, select Add Key.
6. Type **Parameters** as the name for the new key, and then press Enter.
7. Click the Parameters key.
8. Under the Edit pull-down menu, select Add Key.
9. Type **Device** as the new Key Name, and press Enter.
10. To specify a certain host adapter, append Device with the number of the host adapter. For example, type **Device0** for the first host adapter, **Device1** for the second, and so on. If you omit the host adapter number, the configuration information applies to all 7800-family host adapters.
11. Click the Device key.
12. Under the Edit pull-down menu, select Add Value.
13. Type **DriverParameters** as the name for the new key, and then press Enter. Make sure the Data Type is *REG_SZ* (or String value if using REGEDIT.EXE). This is shown in Figure 3-3.
14. A String Editor text box appears; enter parameters in the text box. When entering multiple parameters, each parameter must be separated by a space.

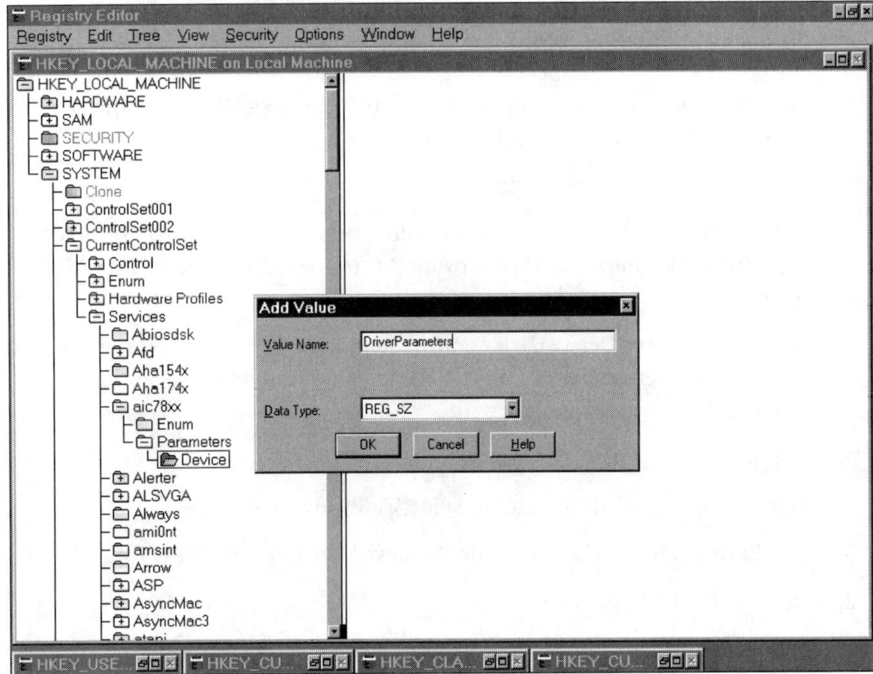

Figure 3-3: Adding the Parameters/Device/DriverParameters Value to the Adaptec AIC78XX.SYS Driver's Registry Configuration Using Registry Editor.

These and many of the other changes described in this chapter are very technically advanced and could potentially cause problems with your Windows NT installation. Therefore, as with any change to the system Registry, always be sure that you have first made a good backup of your system's configuration data by following the steps in Appendix B.

Buslogic/Mylex FlashPoint adapters

On BusLogic/Mylex FlashPoint adapters (including the FlashPoint LT, LW, DL, and DW models), the tunable (user-configurable) parameter, *MaxQueueTags,* is supported.

This parameter controls the maximum queue tag depth on tagged queuing devices attached to a given adapter. The driver defaults to a tag queue depth of 8, but the range of valid values is 1 to 60. Setting this value higher may produce better overall performance in some environments.

To modify this parameter under Windows NT, you must edit the Windows NT Registry following the instructions below. Also, note that Windows NT 3.51 does not support global parameters for this driver, so be sure to skip steps 7 through 11 if you're using NT 3.51.

(Note: Additional tunable parameters for these cards may be developed or released in the future; contact Buslogic/Mylex for additional information.)

1. Select Run from the File pull-down menu (Windows NT 3.5x), or Run from the Start button (Windows NT 4.0).
2. Type **REGEDT32** and press Enter.
3. Open the registry list to the following location: *HKEY_LOCAL_MACHINE\SYSTEM\CurrentControlSet\Services\FlashPnt*
4. Next, from the menus choose Edit → Add Key.
5. Now, enter **Parameters** for Key Name and choose OK. Leave the Class field blank.
6. Highlight the newly created Parameters subkey by left-clicking on it.
7. Next, choose Edit → Add Key again.
8. Enter **Device*X*** for the Key Name where *X* is 0 for the first SCSI host adapter (adapter 0), 1 for the second SCSI host adapter, and so on (e.g., Device0, Device1, Device2, and so on). Leave the Class field blank.
9. Highlight the newly created Device*X* subkey by left-clicking on it.
10. Next, from the menus choose Edit → Add Value.
11. Now, enter **DriverParameter** for Value Name and **REG_SZ** (the default) for Data Type. Leave the Class field blank. Choose OK when finished.
12. Type in the tunable parameter at the String prompt (multiple parameters must be separated by a semicolon). For example: To specify a maximum tag queue depth, where xx is a value between 1 and 60 inclusive, you would type MaxQueueTags=xx. (Note: under Windows NT 4.0, the parameter(s) will be applied to all BusLogic host adapters detected by the `FLASHPNT.SYS` SCSI miniport driver.)

Registry values are almost always case sensitive; therefore, be very sure to properly type in the key and value names for all entries that you add or modify.

QLogic SCSI adapters

This information applies to QLogic cards based on the ISP-1020 and ISP-104X chipsets.

The QLogic Fast!SCSI IQ/Ultra PCI miniport driver reads the onboard EEPROM and supports all of the customized configuration parameters for the adapter and the attached SCSI devices. You should use the QLogic Fast!Util program for changing these parameters. Windows NT Version 4.0 includes enhanced scatter/gather list support for doing very large SCSI I/O transfers. NT 4.0 will support up to 256 scatter/gather segments of 4,096 bytes each, allowing transfers up to 1,048,576 bytes. By default, transfers are limited to 65,536 bytes. Enabling larger transfers may increase SCSI I/O performance in some environments. As with most driver optimizations, this procedure involves a modification of the Windows NT Registry. Specifically, a new subkey must be added to the key related to the QLogic SCSI miniport driver, as follows:

1. Select Run from the File pull-down menu (Windows NT 3.5x), or Run from the Start button (Windows NT 4.0).
2. Type **regedt32** and press Enter.
3. Open the Registry list to the following location: *HKEY_LOCAL_MACHINE \SYSTEM\CurrentControlSet\Services\ Ql10wnt*
4. After opening the Ql10wnt key by left-clicking on it, choose Edit → Add Key from the menus.
5. Now, enter Parameters for the Key Name and choose OK. Leave the Class field blank.
6. Highlight the newly created Parameters subkey by left-clicking on it.
7. Next, choose Edit → Add Key again to create a subkey under the Parameters key.
8. This time, enter **Device** as the Key Name. If multiple QLogic adapters are installed on the system, you can specify separate subkeys for each adapter by using a subkey name of Device*X*, where *X* = the SCSI host adapter number (0, 1, 2, etc.).
9. Next, select the Device key and use Edit → Add Value to add a new value named **MaximumSGList**. Set the data type to **REG_DWORD** and enter a value from 16 to 255 (10 hex to FF hex). A value of 255 (FF hex) enables the maximum 1MB transfer size. Setting a value higher than 255 results in the default 64K transfer size. This registry subkey and value are shown in Figure 3-4.
10. Finally, exit Registry Editor and shut down and reboot the system so the changes can take effect.

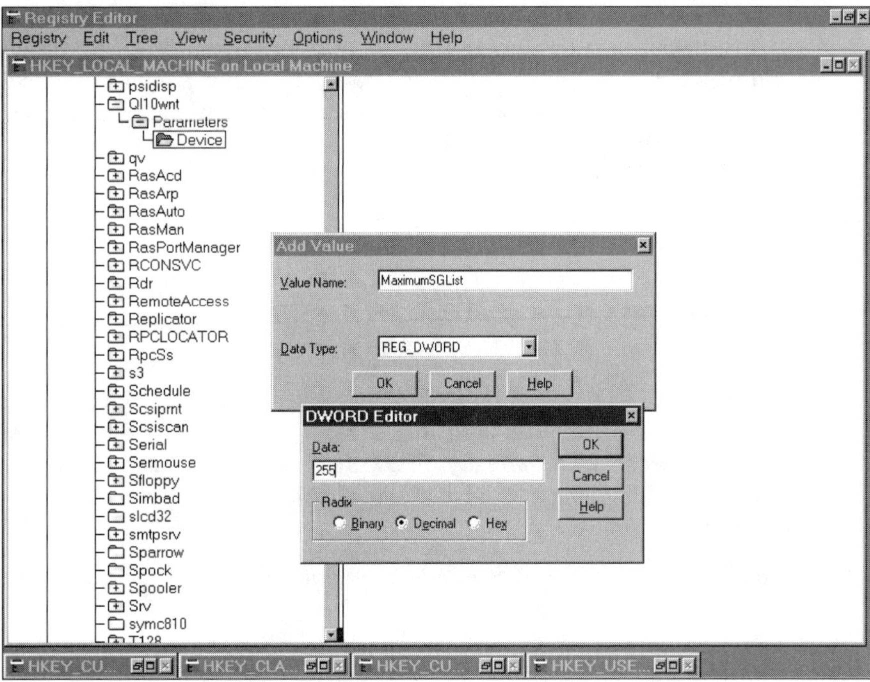

Figure 3-4: Editing the Qlogic `Q110WNT.SYS` Driver's Registry Configuration Subkey.

Symbios Logic adapters

For UltraSCSI-capable Symbios Logic adapters, one of the most important steps you can take to optimize adapter performance is to download a new Windows NT 4.0 driver that is now available for these cards on Symbios' Web site (`http://www.symbios.com/`). This driver contains additional optimizations and support for new features not included in previous versions of the driver.

Once you've obtained this driver, you can install it in Windows NT 4.0 using the following procedure:

1. Run the Windows NT Control Panel utility, located in the Start Menu/Settings folder.
2. Double-click on the SCSI Adapters icon.
3. Click the Drivers tab.

4. If NCRSDMS.SYS, NCRC810.SYS, NCRC8XX.SYS, or SYMC8XX.SYS drivers are listed here, select the driver(s) and choose Remove before adding the new driver. Select OK when prompted, "Are you sure you want to remove this driver?" Another message may also appear that says, "The SCSI Adapter has been marked as a boot device...." If so, choose OK.
5. Choose Add. A list of installed adapters is displayed.
6. Choose the Have Disk button.
7. When prompted, insert your Symbios Driver diskette. Type the proper path to the files (e.g., A:\) and select OK.
8. On the Select Manufacturer Driver menu, the Miniport driver, Symbios Logic PCI (53c8XX), is highlighted. If it is not highlighted, select it and choose OK. At this point, the following message may appear: "The driver(s) for this SCSI Adapter are already on the system. Do you want to use the currently installed driver(s) or install new one(s)?" Choose New to have the new driver be installed.
9. If prompted for a path to the OEM SCSI Adapter files, type the same path setting as before (the location of your newly downloaded driver; e.g., A:\) and select Continue.
10. A series of setup messages are displayed, giving you several options, including enabling the UltraSCSI (Fast 20), the PCI Cache Line, and the Prefetch support options. To enable a particular option, choose OK in that setup message window when it appears. To leave a particular option disabled, choose Cancel instead.
11. A message is then displayed saying that you must restart your computer before the new settings take effect and asking if you wish to restart now. Choose OK to restart and reboot NT. If you choose Cancel, remember that you must restart before the new driver will be loaded.

The Symbios Logic Miniport driver defaults to UltraSCSI (Fast 20) support, PCI Cache Line support, Tagged Queuing support, and Scripts Prefetch support turned OFF. Once the `SYMC8XX.SYS` driver is installed, support for these features can only be enabled or disabled using the Windows NT Registry Editor. Enabling these options only applies to Symbios Logic SYM53C8XX chips or boards that support them.

Use the following procedure to enable or disable the various miniport driver support options:

1. Select Run from the File pull-down menu (Windows NT 3.5x), or Run from the Start button (Windows NT 4.0).
2. Type **regedt32** and press Enter.
3. Open the registry list to the following location: *HKEY_LOCAL_MACHINE \SYSTEM\CurrentControlSet\Services\Symc8XX*
4. After opening the Symc8XX folder (by left-clicking on it), open the Device folder.
5. In the right-hand window, double-click on the DriverParameter entry. (Note: If this value does not exist, it can be added as a String (`REGEDIT.EXE`) or REG_SZ (`REGEDT32.EXE`) value with no class type.)
6. In the String Editor dialog box, do not change anything except the number just to the right of the equal sign(s). The entry(s) should appear as follows (multiple entries, if present, should be separated by a space):

   FAST20_Support=1 for UltraSCSI (Fast 20) enabled
   FAST20_Support=0 for UltraSCSI (Fast 20) disabled
   Cache_Line_Support=1 for PCI Cache Line support enabled
   Cache_Line_Support=0 for PCI Cache Line support disabled
   Prefetch_Support=1 for Scripts Prefetch Option enabled
   Prefetch_Support=0 for Scripts Prefetch Option disabled

   UseTags=1 for Tagged Queuing enabled

   UseTags=0 for Tagged Queuing disabled

Figure 3-5 shows this registry subkey and the DriverParameters value.

You should enable driver options only when you are positive that the installed adapter can support them. Consult the documentation accompanying your card to determine whether a particular feature is supported.

7. Click OK when done.
8. Exit Registry Editor and reboot your system in order to have the changes take effect.

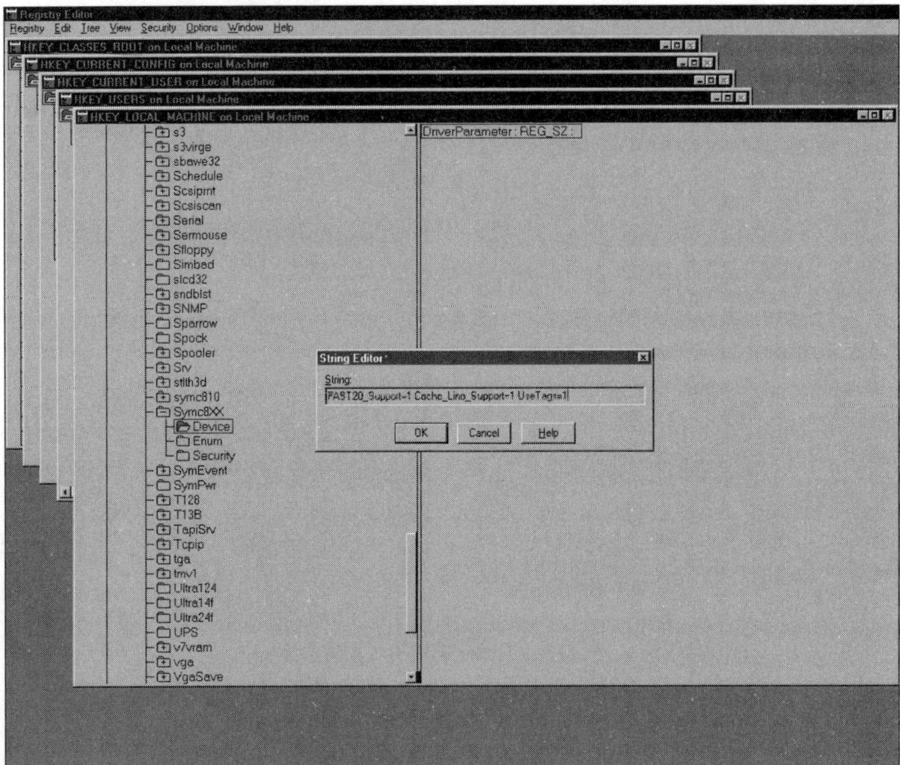

Figure 3-5: Editing the DriverParameters Value of the Symbios Logic SYMC8XX.SYS Driver's Registry Configuration.

Network I/O Subsystem

If your Windows NT computer participates on a Local Area Network (LAN), you'll want to spend some time ensuring that the network I/O subsystem is optimized for maximum performance. In this section, we discuss some of the issues involved with maximizing network performance, including common adapter options and some specific optimizations for particular network interface cards on the market.

Network and network adapter types

Without a doubt, the most important factor in network performance is the base media speed of the network type in use. Although most PC networks today are either 10MBps Ethernet or 16MBps Token Ring, there are a growing number of networks using faster network protocols that have far higher data transfer rates. These include technologies such as 100MBps Fast Ethernet (aka 100BaseTX or 100BaseT4

Ethernet), Switched Ethernet (which involves special switches that provide a full 10MBps to each port rather than sharing the 10MBps bandwidth between all ports), 100VG-AnyLAN, FDDI, and ATM (which comes in several different versions including 25MBps and 155MBps).

For more information on the different types of network technologies and media access schemes used on Local Area Networks see the "Network Adapters" section of Chapter 2, "Killer Hardware for Windows NT."

Although the base media speed supported by your network's hardware is the most important limiting factor in terms of network performance, the actual performance you experience on your system will also be affected to a great degree by the particular network adapter you're using. For Windows NT computers acting as servers, the capabilities of the network card in use impact both the performance of that machine and those accessing its resources over the network.

Like most categories of PC hardware, you've got lots of choices when it comes to choosing a network adapter for your system. However, when evaluating network adapters there are a few key features to keep a lookout for. Each of these features can potentially have a huge impact on your system's overall performance.

Busmastering

If you remember nothing else about the network adapter features we recommend here, at least remember to choose one that supports busmastering DMA operation. As discussed in Chapter 2, busmastering is a method employed by certain types of adapters to transfer data directly to system memory with minimal intervention by the CPU. As with busmastering disk controllers, busmastering network adapters are far faster and far less CPU-intensive than their nonbusmastering counterparts. Many of today's modern network adapters support busmastering, and you should always choose them over network adapters using Programmed I/O data transfers.

Low CPU utilization

The CPU utilization incurred by a network adapter is of great concern in the Windows NT environment, because NT and many NT applications tend to be CPU-hungry by nature. Although choosing a network interface card that supports busmastering is a good start, simply having such a card doesn't guarantee that the card will have low CPU utilization. Before buying a card, try to find out exactly what kind of CPU utilization should be expected by the card under different loads. This information should be available from the manufacturer, but may also be obtained through independent third-party product reviews (such as those conducted by magazines and independent testing laboratories).

Some of the fastest and lowest-CPU utilization network adapters are those produced by Adaptec/Cogent. These cards (including the ANA-69XX line of adapters) support both busmastering DMA and full-duplex operation and come in both 10MBps and 100MBps Ethernet varieties. More importantly, however, they incur among the lowest overall CPU utilization of any card on the market and are thus natural choices for NT file and application servers. As icing on the cake, there are also versions of these cards with features such as multiple channels (multiple Ethernet ports) and automatic failover capabilities (where one channel may take over if another fails). More information is available on these adapters at Adaptec's Web site at: `http://www.adaptec.com/`

Full-duplex support

Another network adapter feature that can have a significant impact on performance *is full-duplex* operation. Many network technologies, such as 10MBps Ethernet, by default use a "one-direction-at-a-time" communication method between network nodes called *half-duplex* operation. By contrast, full-duplex operation permits communication in both directions simultaneously. This feature effectively doubles the maximum throughput of the network. With 100MBps technologies such as Fast Ethernet and 100VG-AnyLAN, this means an increase of the maximum data transmission rate to 200MBps, an enormous performance boost to say the least!

So, what's the catch? Well, for your network to support full-duplex operation, all of the network cards and other network equipment must support full-duplex operation. Although most modern network adapters contain support for full-duplex operation, many older adapters and wiring hubs do not.

Generally speaking, with Ethernet, Fast Ethernet, and 100VG-AnyLAN, the implementation of full-duplex requires the use of a switch, which tends to be a bit pricey as compared to half-duplex shared media hubs. However, this means that if you do have a switch and enable full-duplex operation, you'll not only be getting the full rated media speed (i.e., 10MBps or 100MBps, etc.) per port, but will also be operating at twice that speed (i.e., 20MBps or 200MBps per port).

As a result, be sure to do a survey of all your existing network equipment to verify this support before trying to enable full-duplex operation on any of your network equipment. Most adapters offer full-duplex operation as a software-configurable option that can be enabled or disabled; some are even capable of automatically detecting which type of operation is in use and can set the card accordingly. Finally, some network technologies, such as ATM, use full-duplex communication by default and require no additional configuration or setting changes.

Incorrectly forcing a specific duplex mode may result in worse network performance and could even cause the network to stop functioning properly until the offending adapter is removed from the network or the machine is restarted. Find out the details of your network architecture before forcing a card into a particular duplex mode; if you're unsure about this information it's best to leave the duplex setting at its default (on most cards) of autonegotiate.

Bus types and interrupts

Another important choice for network adapters is the peripheral bus type used by the card. In most cases, you'll want to select a PCI-based network card for optimal performance. For faster network technologies such as ATM, and for 100MBps technologies such as 100BaseT, 100VG-AnyLAN, and FDDI, PCI is your only choice. This is because the additional bandwidth available on the PCI bus makes it capable of "filling the pipe"; that is, keeping up with the data transmission rate of these higher speed networks. This is also why you rarely see 100MBps network cards in ISA versions (although some do exist); they simply can't keep maintain the data rates required by these faster networks.

Although slower types of networks such as 10MBps Ethernet and 4MBps Token Ring can be adequately serviced by ISA, EISA, and MCA bus types, it is still best in these circumstances to choose PCI because of its greater efficiency and lower CPU utilization. Finally, whenever possible, try to set your network adapters to use IRQs 10–15, the higher-numbered PC hardware interrupts. As mentioned earlier, these interrupts receive a higher processor priority than do lower interrupts, and the use of these interrupts will help to ensure you achieve maximum network throughput.

Notes on Specific Network Adapters

This section details some adapter-specific information and configuration settings related to network driver performance. Due to the number of different adapter types, adapter versions, driver versions, and operating system versions that can be involved, the information provided may or may not be correct for your card. Always try to obtain the latest information and driver files for your card from the manufacturer's Web site, FTP server, or BBS before attempting to make advanced Registry changes. This will ensure that you have the latest information related to your card and have the best chance of making the correct driver modifications.

Intel EtherExpress Pro/100, Pro/100B, and Smart/100 adapters

For Intel EtherExpress Pro/100, 100/B, and Smart/100 network adapters, the following standard performance-related settings can be changed using the Intel PROset utility (which is normally installed in Control Panel automatically):

- *Coalesce Buffers:* This setting specifies the number of memory buffers available to the driver in case the driver runs out of available Map Registers. This buffer area is also used when a packet consists of many fragments. If no coalesce buffers or map registers are available, the driver will be forced to queue the packet for later transmission. The preferred method of transmitting data is to use map registers because it's the most efficient method. If you are using Windows NT 3.50 and having network performance problems, try increasing the coalesce buffers. The valid range of values for Coalesce Buffers is 1–16.
- *Receive Buffers:* This setting specifies the number of buffers used by the driver when copying data to the protocol memory. The recommended value is usually 16. In high network load situations, increasing receive buffers can increase performance. The tradeoff is that this also increases the amount of system memory used by the driver. If too few receive buffers are used, network performance will suffer. If too many receive buffers are used, the driver will unnecessarily consume memory resources. The valid range of values for Receive Buffers is 1–128.
- *Transmit Control Blocks:* This setting specifies how many transmit control blocks the driver allocates for adapter use. The recommended value is usually 16. This directly corresponds to how many outstanding packets the driver can have in its "send" queue. If too few transmit control blocks are used, performance will suffer. If too many transmit control blocks are used, the driver will unnecessarily consume memory resources. The valid range of values for Transmit Control Blocks is 1–80.

- *Map Registers:* Map registers are system resources used in physical-to-virtual address conversion with bus mastering cards. The Map Registers parameter specifies how many registers should be allocated to the driver. The recommended values for various operating system versions are:

  Windows NT 3.50: Map Registers = 8
  Windows NT 3.51: Map Registers = 64
  Windows NT 4.0: Map Registers = 64

As a rule, more map registers mean better performance. However, each map register consumes additional system resources. If too many are allocated, the driver will fail to load or your computer may behave erratically. In addition, increasing Map Registers in Windows NT 3.50 may cause problems. The valid range of values for Map Registers is 0–64.

The Intel EtherExpress Pro Smart/100 adapters are also capable of implementing a polled mode support in the drive that can dramatically reduce the adapter's CPU usage. To ensure that this mode of operation is turned on, use the REGEDIT.EXE Windows NT 4.0 Registry Editor (or a third-party Registry search utility) to perform a search through the data and values under the following subkey:

```
HKEY_LOCAL_MACHINE\SYSTEM\CurrentControlSet\Services\
e100snt
```

The search string you're looking for is *MODE=*. When you locate this data in the Registry subkey for the Smart/100 adapter driver, set the data (*REG_SZ* string value) to read MODE=1 to enable polled mode support.

Cogent/Adaptec ANA-69XX adapters

Unfortunately, the driver for these adapters offers virtually no configuration options when configured through the Network Control Panel utility. However, it is possible to modify certain aspects of the driver's configuration by editing the section of the Windows NT Registry related to the driver. To do so, run one of the Windows NT Registry Editor utilities (i.e., `REGEDT32.EXE` or `REGEDIT.EXE`) and locate the following key:

```
HKEY_LOCAL_MACHINE\SYSTEM\CurrentControlSet\Services\E
 MPCIXX\Parameters\
```

XX may be any of several number combinations, depending on the model of the card. There are two configuration parameters located in this key that you may wish to examine in regards to adapter performance:

- *FP_OFF:* This setting optimizes driver performance on some machines. Do not modify this value if you are using a motherboard based on the Intel 430FX PCI chipset (which includes Intel chips with the following part numbers: 82437FX, 82438FX, 82371FB, 82438FX, and possibly others as well). Set this parameter to "1" to activate optimization. The default value is 0 (disabled), and the possible range of values are 0 or 1.
- *BurstLength:* This setting determines the Packet Burst Length, the maximum number of DWORDs that are transferred in one DMA transaction. The default value is 32 DWORDS and the range of possible values is as follows: 1 DWORD, 2 DWORDS, 4 DWORDS, 8 DWORDS, 16 DWORDS, or 32 DWORDS. Normally the default value is optimal, but you may wish to experiment with different values to see if better results are yielded.

3Com Etherlink/Fast EtherLink XL adapters

Although 3Com Etherlink/FastEtherlink XL adapters are generally configured for best performance by default, there is an adapter optimization that is specific to Hewlett-Packard NetServers. When using these cards on HP NetServer 466LF and 466LC systems, optimal performance can be achieved by configuring the NetServer's BIOS/CMOS setup utility as follows:

In the Advanced Chipset Setup, set:

- DRAM Buffer Write to 0
- Snoop Ahead to 1

Although this optimization was originally tested on the HP NetServer 466 LF and 466 LC models, it may also apply to other models of HP NetServers offering these BIOS setup options.

3Com FDDILink FDDI adapters

Although not performance-related, there is an important feature available in 3Com's PCI FDDI adapters known as Resilient Home Architecture (RHA) that allows you to create high reliability on a server by installing two FDDI interface cards and enabling *dual-homing* on these adapters. When this feature is enabled, the second adapter can automatically take over for the first, should it experience a failure.

If you have 3Com Etherlink/FastEtherlink XL adapters and a 3Com switch supporting 3Com's special PACE (Priority Access Control Enabled) feature, you should use the 3Com PACE Config Control Panel to enable this option. This technology works by prioritizing the delivery of data based on the recognition of special data types used by certain high-bandwidth applications such as real-time video, multimedia, and so forth. PACE enhances the performance of these applications by optimizing network bandwidth utilization, reducing latency, controlling jitter, and supporting multiple traffic priority levels. PACE-enabled switches work by monitoring traffic and guaranteeing network access to devices on the network. Using this technology, PACE-enabled switches are capable of utilizing up to 98 percent of their capacity, which represents an improvement of roughly 25 percent standard switched links.

To enable dual-homing on 3Com FDDILink adapters, first be sure to load the most current FDDILink Windows NT driver. Next, you need to enable dual-homing by editing the dual-homing Registry variable parameter. Follow these steps to enable this feature:

1. Select Run from the File pull-down menu (Windows NT 3.5x), or Run from the Start button (Windows NT 4.0).
2. Type **regedt32** and press Enter.
3. Open the registry list to the following location: *HKEY_LOCAL_MACHINE \SYSTEM\CurrentControlSet\Services\flnkXX\Parameters* (where *XX* is the relative adapter number; e.g., flnk01, flnk02, etc.).
4. Next, double-click on the DualHoming value in the right window to edit its value (if the value doesn't exist, you can add it as a REG_DWORD value).
5. Set the DualHoming value to 1 for each installed adapter under its respective subkey name (i.e., flnk01\Parameters, flnk02\Parameters, etc.).
6. Finally, exit Registry Editor and reboot the computer to have the changes take effect.

After enabling the DualHoming Registry value, it's important that you take one additional step to properly configure the system for dual-homing. You must disable the network bindings for all but one of the FDDILink adapters in a dual-homing group. Use these steps to do this:

1. From the Control Panel applet, access the Network Settings dialog box.
2. Click the Bindings button.
3. In the Network Bindings dialog box, click on the FDDILink adapters to be disabled. (Note: You must leave one FDDILink adapter enabled. Be sure to disable all other FDDILink adapters.)
4. Click the Disable button to disable all binding for the selected adapter.
5. Exit the Network Control Panel and reboot the computer to have the changes take effect.

Dual-homing support requires the FDDILink Windows NT adapter driver version 1.0a or later.

HP VG-AnyLAN PCI adapter (J2585A/B)

One optimization for HP VG-AnyLAN PCI adapters that you may wish to implement is the enabling of high-priority operation. High priority is part of the demand-priority technology used by VG-AnyLAN to assign higher network access priorities to specific high-bandwidth data types such as for real-time voice, video, or other data types. When enabled, the adapter services high-priority requests before normal priority ones.

To control high-priority operation, a "Priority" parameter must be added to the Registry for each adapter. Follow the instructions below to add the priority parameter to the Registry and force high-priority operation:

1. Select Run from the File pull-down menu (Windows NT 3.5x) or Run from the Start button (Windows NT 4.0).
2. Type **regedt32** and press Enter.
3. Open the registry list to the following location: *HKEY_LOCAL_MACHINE\SYSTEM\CurrentControlSet\Services\HpfendX* (where *X* is the instance number of the driver for the adapter that you wish to enable for high-priority operation).
4. After opening the Hpfend*X* folder (by double-clicking on it), open the Parameters subkey.
5. Choose "Add Value" from the Edit menu.

6. In the "Add Value" dialog box, enter the word **Priority** in the Value Name field. Also, be sure that the first letter (P) is capitalized with subsequent letters in lowercase.
7. Select *REG_DWORD* for the Data Type and click the OK button.
8. Now double-click the newly created Priority value and enter a data value of 1 in the DWORD Editor dialog box and click OK (this setting enables high-priority operation).
9. Exit Registry Editor and reboot the system to have the changes take effect.

After the Priority registry value has been updated with a value of 1, the driver will always configure the adapter for high-priority operation. To disable high-priority operation, simply set the Priority keyword/value to a data of zero (0). Alternatively, the Priority keyword may be deleted from the Registry to disable the high-priority option. In step 9 above, single-click on the *Priority:REG_DWORD:0x1* line in the right pane and then choose Edit → Delete from the menus.

Compaq Netelligent 10/100TX adapter

Compaq Netelligent 10/100TX adapters have an optimization that is especially intended for Windows NT Servers acting as Internet/intranet Web servers (e.g., running Internet Information Server).

To optimize the Compaq Netelligent adapter for Web server operation locate the following Registry subkey using one of the Windows NT Registry Editors:

```
HKEY_LOCAL_MACHINE\SYSTEM\CurrentControlSet\Services\cpqnf3X\
  Parameters
```

(where *X* is the relative adapter number; e.g., cpqnf31, cpqnt32, etc.).
Once located, add the following REG_DWORD value to the Parameters subkey:

Value: **MaxReceives**
Type: REG_DWORD
Data: **0x1F4 hex / 500 decimal** (the default value is 0x064 hex/100 decimal)

This optimization improves the performance of the adapter under heavy loads by increasing the maximum number of receive lists the driver allocates for receive frames.

Fore systems ATM adapters

The following information relates to the ForeRunner PCA-200EPC model adapters.

The following adapter settings are related to performance and can be configured from adapter's installation/configuration utility:

- *Transmit Buffer Count:* This parameter determines the number of transmit buffers that are allocated by the driver when it is loaded, and thus significantly impacts the resources the driver consumes in the system. More transmit buffers allow more send operations to be in progress at one time, and thus potentially increases system performance, but also consumes more system resources. Setting this parameter too high can prevent the driver from loading, due to insufficient system resources. The default for this parameter is 36, which should be adequate for most installations. The range of possible values is 8–64.
- *Transmit Queue Size:* This parameter determines the number of transmit queue descriptors associated with the transmit buffers. The default for this parameter is 32. The range of possible values is 8–64.
- *Receive Buffer Count:* This parameter determines the number of receive buffers that are allocated by the driver when it is loaded, and thus significantly impacts the resources the driver consumes in the system. More receive buffers potentially increases system performance, but also consumes more system resources. Setting this parameter too high can prevent the driver from loading, due to insufficient system resources. The default for this parameter is 48, which should be adequate for most installations. The range of possible values is 8–64.
- *Receive Queue Size:* This parameter determines the number of receive queue descriptors associated with the receive buffers. The default for this parameter is 32. The range of possible values is 8–64.

Adaptec ATM adapters

On Adaptec ATM adapters, there are two values in the LANE (LAN Emulation) Configuration section of the adapter configuration screen that you may wish to examine:

- *MTU Size:* This value determines the Maximum Transmission Unit for the adapter and should be either set to "1516" or "9234" depending on the environment. Note: When choosing 9234, make sure the LES/BUS supports this value (see your ATM adapter manual for more information on this).
- *Peak Cell Rate:* This value selects the Peak Cell Rate (PCR) in Megabits/second. The values are 10, 155, 25, or LineRate. Setting LineRate as the value always uses the full line rate for the installed adapter.

Summary

In this chapter, we discussed some specific methods for optimizing your system hardware configurations to achieve maximum performance. We discussed motherboard configuration options, bus speed issues, and system BIOS settings. In addition, we also listed some product-specific tips and tricks for getting maximum performance from particular brands and models of SCSI and network adapters. Implementing these procedures will help ensure that you are getting the most from your hardware purchases, and that your Windows NT driver configurations are configured to their optimal settings.

In the next chapter, we dive into the software-side of Windows NT optimizing and teach you some of the basic skills you need to tune your Windows NT installation.

Chapter 4

NT Optimization 101

NOW THAT YOU'VE ASSEMBLED and optimized the ultimate assortment of hardware for your Windows NT computer, you're ready to delve into the process of tuning the actual Windows NT environment itself. In this chapter, we discuss some of the basic concepts of NT optimization, including an introduction to the various tools employed to optimize NT, and several fundamental procedures you should start with to increase system performance.

Due to the risky nature of the system modifications (such as changes to the system Registry database) discussed in this and other chapters, it's especially important that you first read Chapter 12, "Maintaining Your NT System," before making any changes. This chapter will help you to properly back up critical information, an insurance policy you'll definitely want to have before diving into any of the procedures discussed here and in other chapters.

Meet Your Toolkit

Throughout this book, we employ a number of different utilities to accomplish the job of monitoring, analyzing, and modifying your Windows NT system. This set of applications becomes your optimizing "toolkit," a set of utilities that assists in the optimizing process. Like any good mechanic, you should first become familiar with all of the tools in your kit before using them. In this section, we describe your NT optimizing "tools" and what each is used for.

Performance monitor: bottleneck sleuth

One of the most important tools for analyzing your system's performance is the Windows NT Performance Monitor. This application is a versatile and powerful monitoring utility that allows you to monitor and measure virtually every aspect of your Windows NT environment. Performance Monitor is a true boon to NT users and administrators, and has shipped with every version of Windows NT. To this day, it remains one of the most powerful diagnostic tools available for Windows NT.

Performance Monitor allows you to view the behavior of a wide variety of system objects such as processors, memory, cache, threads, and processes. Each of these system objects has an associated set of *counters* (analyzable elements) that provide information about various aspects of each component of the Windows NT environment, including devices, services, and applications.

Performance Monitor provides charting, alerting, and reporting features, and can be used for instantaneous views or to capture data over a period of time into a log file. When performing long-term monitoring, you can later open the log files and display them as if they reflected current activity.

Here's just a few of the feats that Performance Monitor can help you accomplish:

- Simultaneously view data from the local computer as well as other computers on a network.
- Export recorded data from charts, logs, alert logs, and reports to spreadsheet or database programs for analysis or processing.
- Add system alerts (in the Alert View) that can automatically notify you when certain thresholds that you've defined have been exceeded. This notification can take one or more forms, including: Reverting to the Alert view window, logging the event in Event Viewer's Application log, or issuing a pop-up administrative alert using the Windows NT Messenger service.
- Launch an application when a monitored counter value goes over or under a set value you've defined.
- Create log files containing data about objects on different computers.
- Append multiple log files into a single file to create a long-term performance archive.
- Create reports from existing log files.
- Save the defined performance monitoring settings you've created for either an individual view (chart, alert, log, or report) or for the entire Performance Monitor environment (called the workspace). This allows you to easily open these same environments in future Performance Monitor sessions.

If you truly wish to become proficient in diagnosing and resolving performance issues in the Windows NT, we recommend you begin by mastering the use of Performance Monitor. The best way to learn about Performance Monitor is to start using it, so let's fire it up and start analyzing data!

Because it was designed to be used by computer or network administrators, the Performance Monitor utility is located in the Administrative Tools (Common) Group. However, it's also possible for nonadministrators to run the utility as well and monitor most system object counters. There will, however, be a few counters or objects that require administrative access. If you don't have access to the Administrative Tools group on your Windows NT computer, you can easily create an icon for Performance Monitor. To do so, simply create a shortcut to the `PERFMON.EXE` file located in the *%SYSTEMROOT %\SYSTEM32* directory (e.g., `C:\WINNT\SYSTEM32`) by right-clicking the Desktop or a folder window, and then choosing New → Shortcut.

Launching the Performance Monitor application displays a window similar to Figure 4-1.

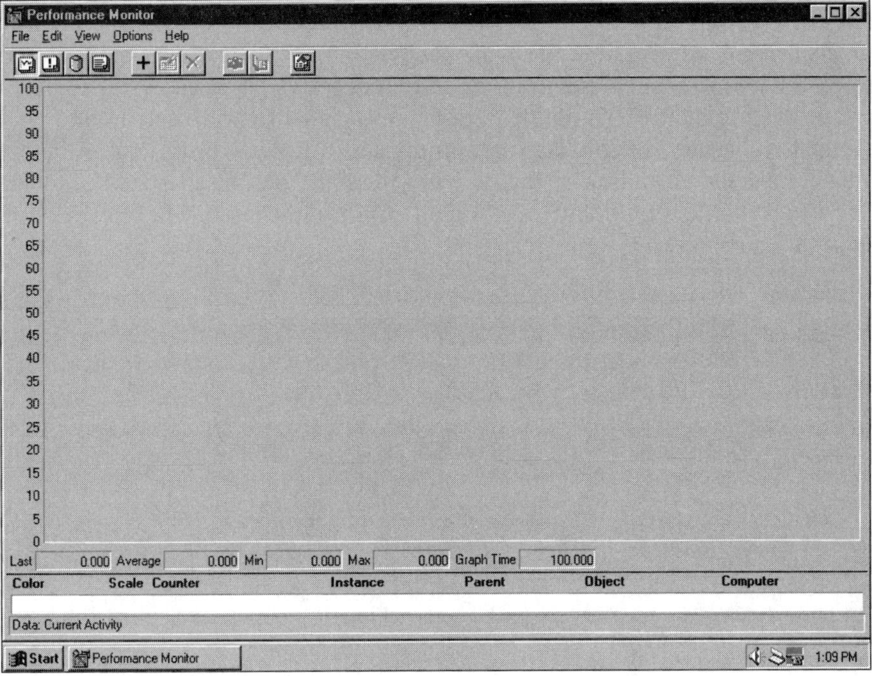

Figure 4-1: Performance Monitor's main window.

Now that Performance Monitor is started, you can see that it is not the most user-friendly of all Windows NT performance tools and that it is a little confusing for someone viewing it for the first time. For those with some NT experience it's easy to launch it and quickly start using some of the features. However, behind its seemingly simplistic interface lies a truly powerful tool, and the counters that it monitors are the heartbeat of the Windows NT operating system. Think of Performance Monitor as a doctor's stethoscope. It's a tool that lets you gather information on how well Windows NT is ticking.

The "organs" that Performance Monitor permits you to diagnose are *objects*, which include things such as memory, processor, cache, disks, and, in some cases, even individual applications. Objects, in turn, include a set of one or more *counters*, which are the actual items you track during a Performance Monitor session. Counters represent different aspects of an object. The memory objects for example, contain counters that represent the amount of free memory, the amount of memory currently in use, the number of memory pages per second that are being read to or written from the system's paging file, and other memory-related statistics. To monitor a particular counter or set of counters, you simply instruct Performance Monitor to add them to the current session. The system's ability to monitor performance using objects and counters is an important part of Windows NT's design, and is a boon for doing performance evaluations and system troubleshooting.

After opening Performance Monitor you see a blank window such as that shown in Figure 4-1. By default, Performance Monitor starts in the Chart View with no counters being monitored (thus the blank window). On the toolbar there are four buttons on the left, which represent the four different Views provided by Performance Monitor. We talk about views a little later, but let's gather some data to display.

To add a counter to Performance Monitor click on the + (Add) button on the toolbar, or use the menu by clicking on Edit, Add to Chart. The shortcut key to add an item to a chart is Ctrl-I. Once you add an object to the chart, you see a window similar to Figure 4-2.

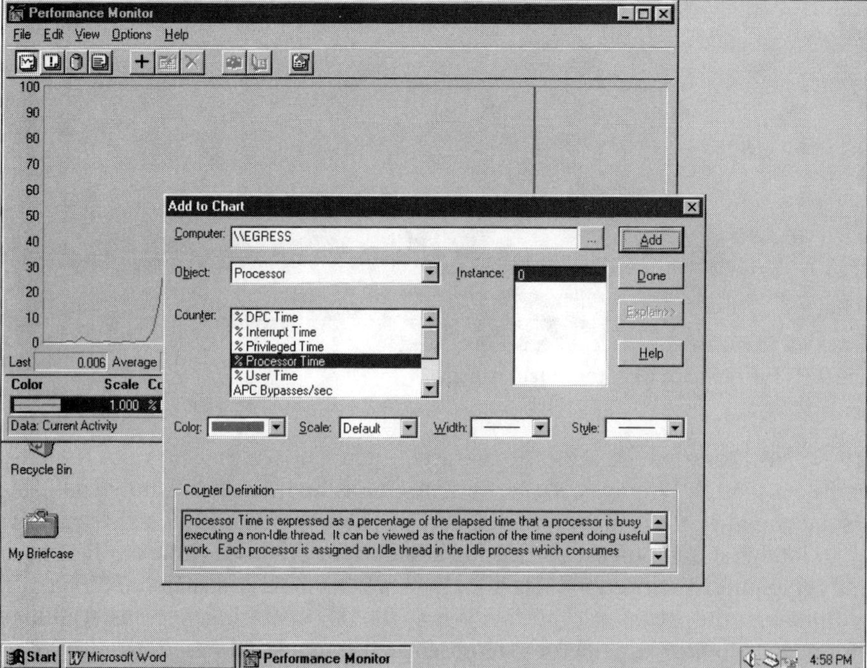

Figure 4-2: Adding counters to Performance Monitor.

By default, Performance Monitor selects the Processor object and the % Processor Time counter, which is a good place to start hunting bottlenecks in system performance. Click the Add button to add the % Processor Time counter to the chart.

As Figure 4-2 shows, Performance Monitor differentiates between multiple instances of an object. Instances are multiple occurrences of a particular object. If the computer in Figure 4-2 were a multiprocessing computer, there would have been more than one instance of the processor object. By only having one instance (Instance 0) of the Processor Object, we know that the computer in Figure 4-2 is a single-processor machine.

After adding the % Processor Time counter, look at Figure 4-3, which shows us the Performance Monitor chart monitoring the CPU (Central Processing Unit). We add more counters later, but for now let's take a close look at the screen while it's monitoring only one object.

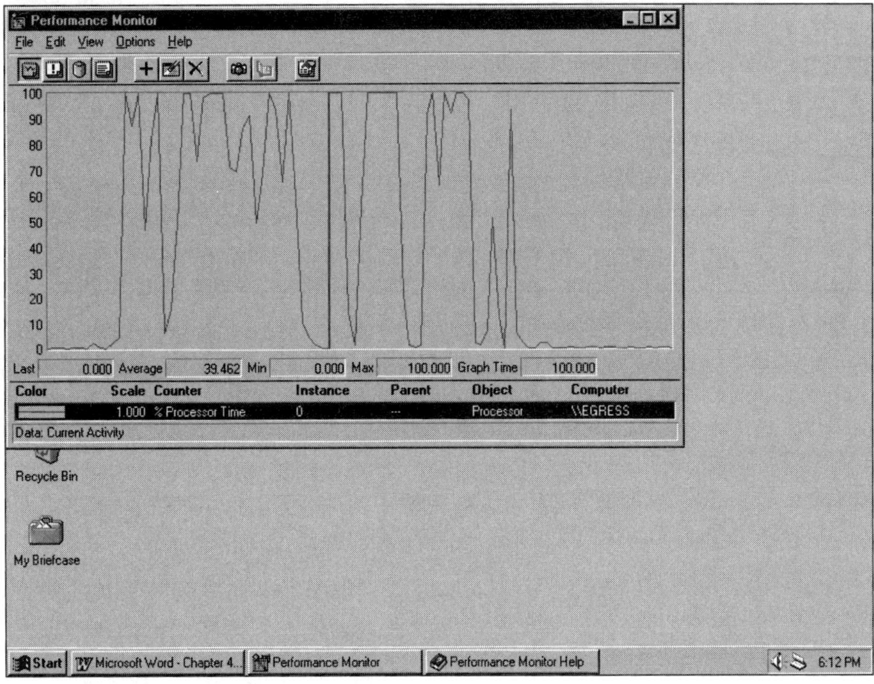

Figure 4-3: Monitoring CPU utilization.

After adding the % Processor Time counter notice that it was added to the legend at the bottom of the Performance Monitor screen, as shown in Figure 4-3, and the chart now displays the information gathered about the current state of processor. In addition to the line moving up and down as the processor load changes, notice the numerical information included in the Last, Average, Min, and Max boxes below the graph. These boxes display trends by showing the differences in the % Processor Time over a specified period of time (these items always apply to the counter currently selected in the bottom window).

Now let's add more object counters to our chart and save the configuration so we can recall the chart settings later. Click on the +, or Edit→Add to Chart to display the Add Counters dialog box. Click on the Objects drop-down list box to display other counters available on the local machine.

Add some of the counters listed in Table 4-1, which lists some of the common counters used when locating a suspected bottleneck. The table is organized by suspected bottleneck and the most common counters used for analysis.

For more information on the counters used in Table 4-1, and an analysis on how to use the counters to detect bottlenecks, see Microsoft Knowledge Base Article Q146005, located on Microsoft's support Web site: (`http://www.microsoft.com/kb/`) or Microsoft TechNet.

TABLE 4-1 IMPORTANT PERFORMANCE COUNTERS

Object	Counter	Description
Processor Bottleneck		
Processor	% Processor Time	Processor Time is expressed as a percentage of the elapsed time that a processor is busy executing a non-Idle thread. It can be viewed as the fraction of the time spent doing useful work. Each processor is assigned an Idle thread in the Idle process which consumes those unproductive processor cycles not used by any other threads.
Process	% Processor Time	This is the amount of processor time consumed by a particular instance of the Process object; that is, an individual process running on the system.

continued

Object	Counter	Description
System	% Processor Time	This counter is available only on systems using more than one processor. The _Total instance of this object always runs at 100 percent, because it includes the Idle thread (the amount of time the CPU spends not servicing any processes). Therefore, only individual processes should be monitored if you want to gain useful information.
System	Processor Queue Length	Processor Queue Length is the instantaneous length of the processor queue in units of threads. This counter is always 0 unless you are also monitoring a thread counter. All processors use a single queue in which threads wait for processor cycles. This length does not include the threads that are currently executing. A sustained processor queue length greater than two generally indicates processor congestion. This is an instantaneous count, not an average over the time interval.
Processor	Interrupts/sec	Interrupts/sec is the number of device interrupts the processor is experiencing. A device interrupts the processor when it has completed a task or when it otherwise requires attention. Normal thread execution is suspended during interrupts. An interrupt may cause the processor to switch to another, higher priority thread. Clock interrupts are frequent and periodic and create a background of interrupt activity.
Process (_Total)	% Processor Time	Processor Time is the percentage of elapsed time that all of the threads of this process used the processor to execute instructions. An instruction is the basic unit of execution in a computer, a thread is the object that executes instructions, and a process is the object created when a program is run. Code executed to handle certain hardware interrupts or trap conditions may be counted for this process.

continued

TABLE 4-1 IMPORTANT PERFORMANCE COUNTERS *(Continued)*

Object	Counter	Description
Memory Bottleneck		
Memory	Pages/sec	Pages/sec is the number of pages read from the disk or written to the disk to resolve memory references to pages that were not in memory at the time of the reference. This is the sum of Pages Input/sec and Pages Output/sec. This counter includes paging traffic on behalf of the system Cache to access file data for applications. This value also includes the pages to/from noncached mapped memory files. This is the primary counter to observe if you are concerned about excessive memory pressure and the excessive paging that may result.
Logical Disk	Avg. Disk sec/ Transfer	Avg. Disk sec/Transfer is the time in seconds of the average disk transfer.
Server	Pool Nonpaged Failures	The number of times allocations from nonpaged pool have failed. Indicates that the computer's physical memory is too small.
Server	Pool Paged Failures	The number of times allocations from paged pool failed. Indicates that the computer's physical memory or paging file is too small.
Server	Pool Nonpaged Peak	The maximum number of bytes of nonpaged pool the server has had in use at any one point. Indicates how much physical memory the computer should have.
Physical Disk Bottleneck		
Physical Disk	% Disk Time	Disk Time is the percentage of elapsed time that the selected disk drive is busy servicing read or write requests.
Physical Disk	Average Disk sec/ Transfer	Average Disk sec/Transfer is the time in seconds of the average disk transfer.
Physical Disk	Disk Queue Length	Average Disk Queue Length is the average number of both read and write requests that were queued for the selected disk during the sample interval.

continued

Object	Counter	Description
Physical Disk	Disk Bytes/sec	Disk Bytes/sec is the rate bytes are transferred to or from the disk during write or read operations.
Network Component Bottlenecks		
Redirector	Current Commands	Current Commands counts the number of requests to the Redirector that are currently queued for service. If this number is much larger than the number of network adapter cards installed in the computer, then the network(s) and/or the server(s) being accessed are seriously bottlenecked.
Redirector	Network Errors/sec	Network Errors/sec counts serious unexpected errors that generally indicate the Redirector and one or more Servers are having serious difficulty communicating. For example an SMB (Server Manager Block) protocol error will generate a Network Error. These result in an entry in the system Event Log, so look there for details.
Redirector	Reads Denied/sec	Reads Denied/sec is the rate that the server is unable to accommodate requests for Raw Reads. When a read is much larger than the server's negotiated buffer size, the Redirector requests a Raw Read, which, if granted, permits the transfer of the data without lots of protocol overhead on each packet. To accomplish this, the server must lockout other requests, so the request is denied if the server is really busy.
Redirector	Writes Denied/sec	Writes Denied/sec is the rate that the server is unable to accommodate requests for Raw Writes. When a write is much larger than the server's negotiated buffer size, the Redirector requests a Raw Write, which, if granted, permits the transfer of the data without lots of protocol overhead on each packet. To accomplish this, the server must lockout other requests, so the request is denied if the server is really busy.

continued

Table 4-1 IMPORTANT PERFORMANCE COUNTERS *(Continued)*

Object	Counter	Description
Server	Work Item Shortage	The number of times STATUS_DATA_NOT_ACCEPTED was returned at receive indication time. This occurs when no work item is available or can be allocated to service the incoming request. Indicates whether the initworkitems or maxworkitems parameters need tuning.
Server	Bytes Total/sec	The number of bytes the server has sent to and received from the network. This value provides an overall indication of how busy the server is.

By default, Windows NT does not enable the disk performance counters. If you plan on monitoring physical disk performance you need to enable disk counters using the DISKPERF.EXE utility located in the SYSTEM32 directory. To enable disk counters, open a Command Prompt and type to enable counters:

```
Diskperf -y
```

or to enable counters on a disk subsystem including a fault-tolerant/RAID volume using NT's FTDISK.SYS driver type:

```
Diskperf -ye
```

or to disable counters type:

```
Diskperf -n
```

After enabling or disabling disk counters using one of these commands, you need to reboot to have the changes take effect. The disk performance counters create a minor overhead (about 2 percent for slower machines) on system performance. On faster machines (e.g., Pentium or better processors), the overhead is negligible.

Certain standard objects such as Disk and Processor counters are available on all Windows NT systems; however, application-specific counters such as Microsoft Exchange are available only on the system in which the application is installed. One other special note is that to gather TCP/IP statistics the SNMP service must be installed and running. The SNMP service is not installed by default and can be added using the Network Services dialog box.

For a comprehensive listing of objects and counters that may be monitored using Performance Monitor, see Appendix C, "Index of Performance Monitor Objects and Counters."

There are a number of different objects available within Performance Monitor. If you're not sure what a particular counter represents, you can get a description of it by clicking the *Explain>>* button, which displays the Counter Definition box. The definition box includes a detailed description about each counter and, in many cases, will instruct you as to what a high or low value for the counter might mean in terms of system performance.

When displaying a chart with multiple counters, pressing Ctrl-H highlights the selected counter by turning the line bold while allowing you to see the line more clearly.

CHARTING PROCESSOR COUNTERS

Figure 4-4 shows that we added Table 4-1's suggested counters for troubleshooting a suspected processor bottleneck. To put the processor into a loaded state to get some usable information on the chart, we did something that is considered a big no-no when dealing with an NT server. We discuss it a little later in this chapter, but to put the processor under a little stress, we enabled the OpenGL Text screen saver that ships with Windows NT 4.0.

Now that we have a chart full of data to work off of, let's discuss some of the display and chart options available in Performance Monitor. We begin by saving the current chart settings so that we can recall this configuration at a later time.

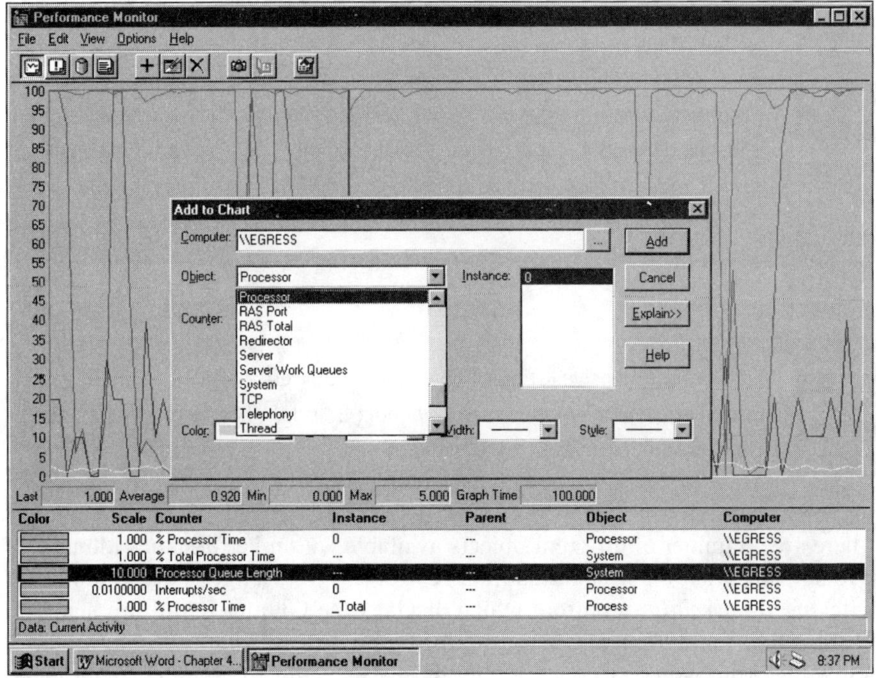

Figure 4-4: Monitoring additional processor-related counters in chart view.

There are two options when saving data in Performance Monitor: The first way to save the particular settings related to a specific chart is to click on File, Save Chart Settings As and give the chart settings a filename. For our purposes, let's save the active chart as C:\PROCESS.PMC. The second way of saving the configuration is to save the Performance Monitor Workspace (.PMW file). However, in this latter case, what's saved is not the actual chart data itself but rather the list of counters being monitored. This makes it easy to restore a particular environment (called a Performance Monitor *workspace*).

Performance monitor settings are saved with specific file extensions so that clicking on the saved file launches Performance Monitor and loads the saved counters automatically. It is also possible to do this by dragging a .PMC or .PMW file using the Windows NT Explorer into an empty Performance Monitor window. By clicking on File, and Save Workspace, all of the configuration settings for the Chart, Log, Report, and Alert views are saved in a single file. We discuss the Log, Report, and Alert views later in this section.

Now that we have our Chart settings saved as C:\PROCESS.PMC, let's change some of the Chart and Display options available. Clicking on the Options menu allows you to modify the Chart settings. Chart options allow you to change the refresh interval for the chart, add horizontal and vertical lines, and customize the overall look of the chart. The display settings can also be altered to hide much of the Performance Monitor application framework such as the menus and title bar, toolbar, borders, and status bar. Figure 4-5 shows the same counters as Figure 4-4 with the entire window framework removed.

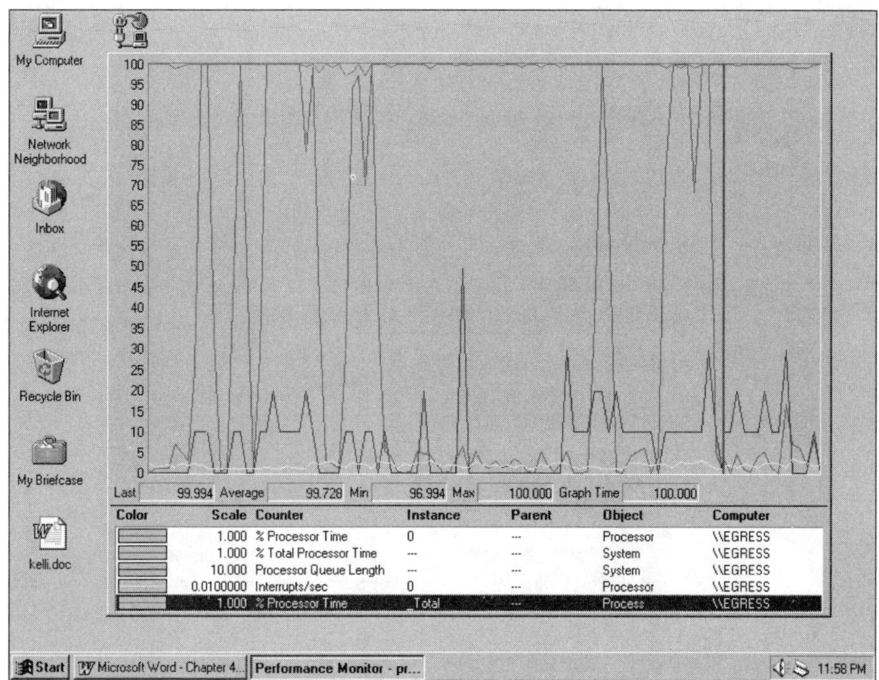

Figure 4-5: Performance Monitor's window with visual components removed.

Hiding all of the window components creates a more concise view of the data by reducing screen clutter.

You can hide or unhide the menu and title bar by double-clicking on the chart.

REMOTE MONITORING

Thus far we have measured counters on a local machine. You may have noticed the Computer Name field in some of the previous figures. Let's say we want to compare the CPU usage on a machine to that of another. One of the greatest benefits of Performance Monitor is the native ability to perform monitoring of remote counters located on different machines.

To take a look at remote monitoring, let's use the default *% Processor Time* counter for the *Processor* object. Click on the + button on the toolbar, or use Edit → Add to Chart. You should then see a window similar to Figure 4-6. Change the name in the computer field to the first computer you would like to monitor. This time there are two instances of the Processor object, meaning this is a machine with two processors.

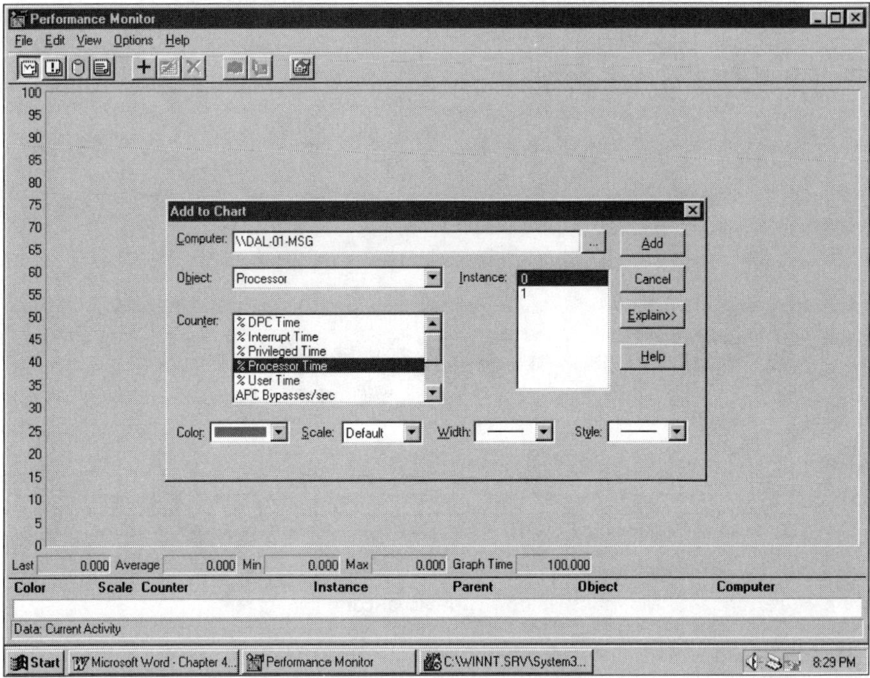

Figure 4-6: Monitoring two NT servers.

After adding the two instances of the processor on machine one, add a third counter as shown previously. This time type the second computer name of the machine you would like to monitor as shown in Figure 4-7.

Click on the Add button to add the third counter. Now we have a chart monitoring two processors on one machine and a single processor on a second machine. From the chart we can see that the dual processor machine shows a standard pattern in which the processors peak around 75 percent. This chart shows two healthy systems as far as the processor is concerned. Neither system ever peaks at 100 percent; in fact, the system with the single processor is actually underutilized (within the period of the chart data). This type of a view can be used to identify problems in which an application or network error may cause the processor to hang at a constant 100 percent utilization.

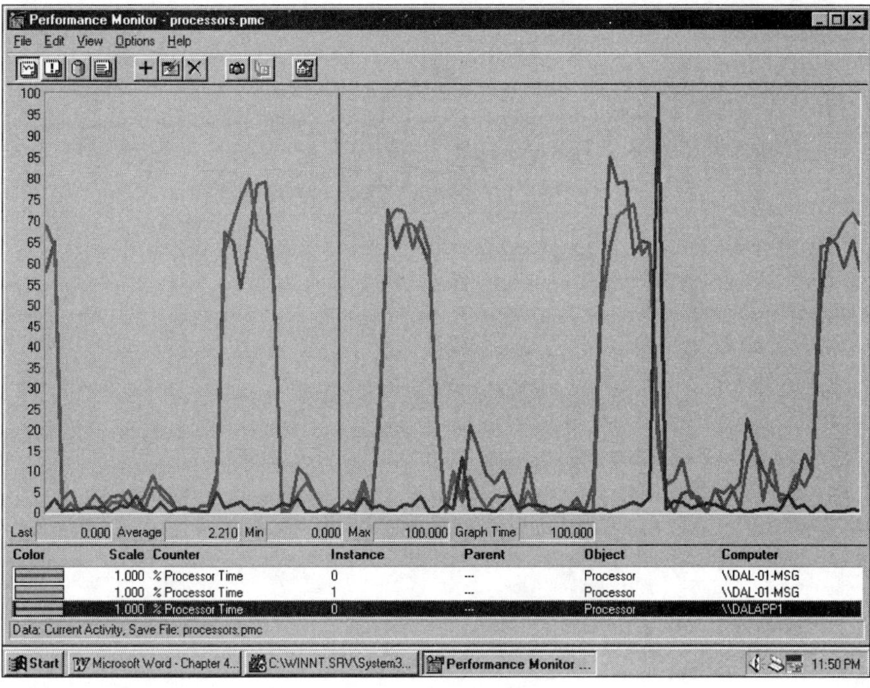

Figure 4-7: Adding a second machine to monitor.

Strange as it may seem, it actually creates more system overhead to run the Performance Monitor application locally than it does to run it remotely. Updating the screen requires more system resources than forwarding the information over the network. This effect is one reason that system administrators often prefer to run Performance Monitor remotely.

EXPORTING DATA

Performance Monitor also gives you the ability to export the current data. Data from the Chart view can be exported to either spreadsheet or database files. To export a chart, click on File → Export Chart Data. You should then see a screen similar to Figure 4-8. There are two types of files that the exported data can be saved to. The `.TSV` files are tab-delimited text files, and the `.CSV` are comma-delimited text files. For our example, choose to save the chart data as a `.CSV` file and call it `PROCESSORS.CSV`.

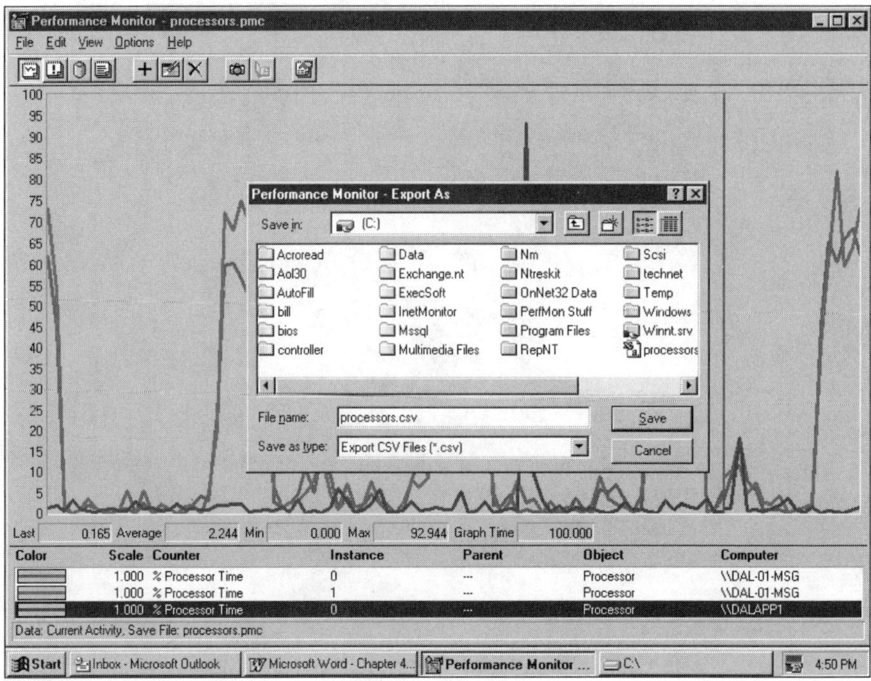

Figure 4-8: Exporting Performance Monitor chart data.

Once the data is exported to a file, you can use other applications to analyze the information. We can use an application such as Microsoft Excel to import the PROCESSORS.CSV file and see what type of information was exported. Figure 4-9 shows our sample data imported into Microsoft Excel. Once the data has been imported into an application such as Excel, it can be used to perform additional analysis on the objects that were exported.

APPLICATION MONITORING

We've taken a look at how to use Performance Monitor to diagnose operating system counters, but what about applications running on NT? The developers of Windows NT designed Performance Monitor to not only account for operating system counters, but also to account for server application counters such as Microsoft Exchange, IBM DB2, and Microsoft SQL server. The Windows NT Resource Kit 3.5 Volume 4 contained some of the most comprehensive for implementing counters into your server application. Unfortunately, this chapter did not make it into the Windows NT 4.0 Resource Kits so if you find an NT 3.5 Resource Kit, hang on to it!

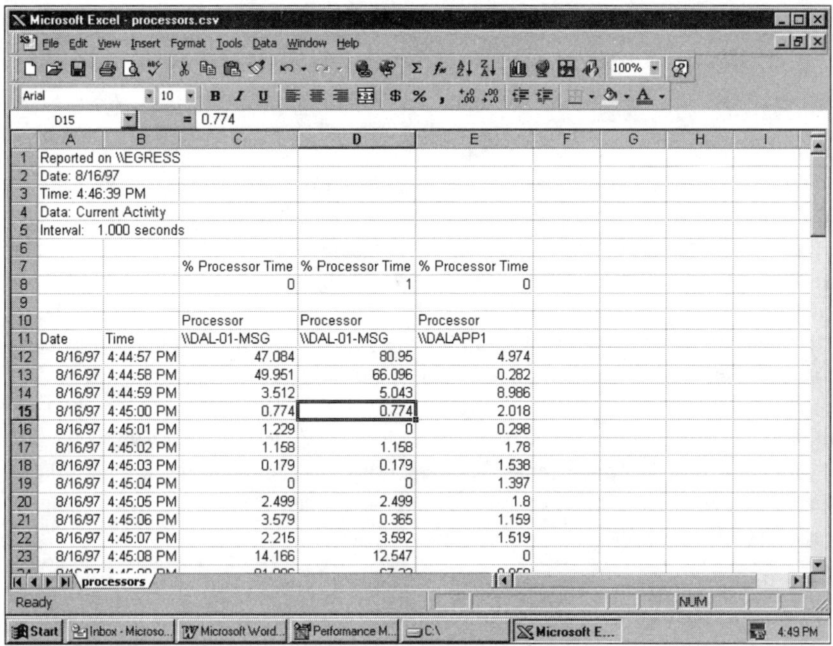

	A	B	C	D	E
1	Reported on \\EGRESS				
2	Date: 8/16/97				
3	Time: 4:46:39 PM				
4	Data: Current Activity				
5	Interval: 1.000 seconds				
6					
7			% Processor Time	% Processor Time	% Processor Time
8			0	1	0
9					
10			Processor	Processor	Processor
11	Date	Time	\\DAL-01-MSG	\\DAL-01-MSG	\\DALAPP1
12	8/16/97	4:44:57 PM	47.084	80.95	4.974
13	8/16/97	4:44:58 PM	49.951	66.096	0.282
14	8/16/97	4:44:59 PM	3.512	5.043	8.986
15	8/16/97	4:45:00 PM	0.774	0.774	2.018
16	8/16/97	4:45:01 PM	1.229	0	0.298
17	8/16/97	4:45:02 PM	1.158	1.158	1.78
18	8/16/97	4:45:03 PM	0.179	0.179	1.538
19	8/16/97	4:45:04 PM	0	0	1.397
20	8/16/97	4:45:05 PM	2.499	2.499	1.8
21	8/16/97	4:45:06 PM	3.579	0.365	1.159
22	8/16/97	4:45:07 PM	2.215	3.592	1.519
23	8/16/97	4:45:08 PM	14.166	12.547	0

Figure 4-9: Chart data imported into Microsoft Excel.

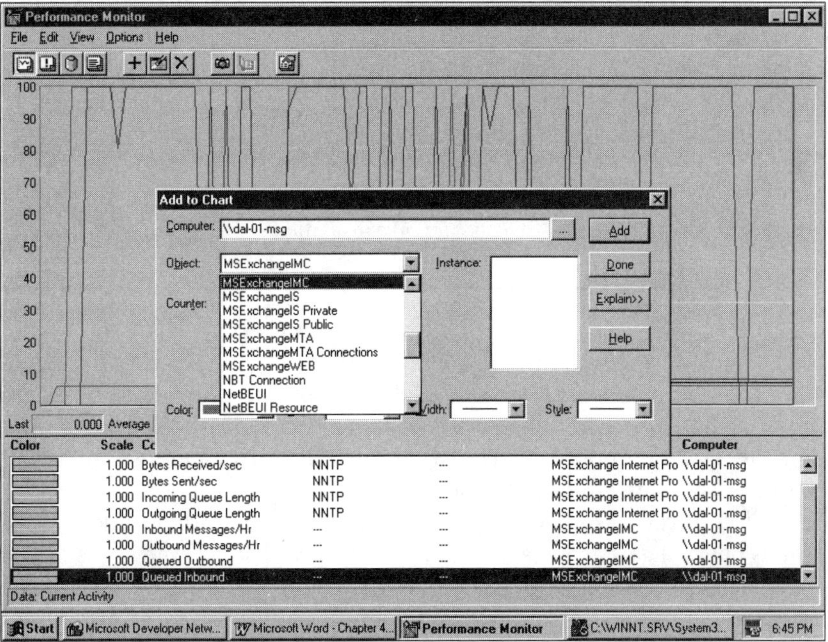

Figure 4-10: Using Performance Monitor to remotely monitor Microsoft Exchange.

Performance Monitor: A Journey Begins with a Single Step

Performance Monitor is a very powerful tool for diagnosing bottlenecks in a Windows NT system. The vast array of objects and counters tells the real-time story about the performance of the system. Most of the counters are presented in such a way that a Windows NT user can use the descriptions provided in the counter explanation box to detect a problem area such as memory or hard disk performance. Well, what about all those other counters like *Memory/Pool Paged Allocs*? Many of the counters available in Performance Monitor are difficult to understand for even experienced Windows NT Administrators. Quite a few of the counters are objects that only an operating system developer would understand. This type and depth of information (although a little overwhelming at first) allows you to drill down to even the most minute details of the operating system. As you can tell from the size of Table 4-1, explaining what all of these counters do and how to use them for analysis would take up quite a few shelves.

Those of us that have been around complex computers and operating systems for a while may remember the concept of the "big orange wall" that described the wall of technical books on DEC VAX Clusters (which had orange covers, thus the name). Fortunately we can get to this information more easily these days. Books such as the Windows NT Resource Kit, and CDs like Microsoft Developers Network and TechNet are available. There is also a vast amount of free information available on the Internet and elsewhere. The Microsoft Knowledge Base (`http://www.microsoft.com/kb`) on the Internet contains an abundance of information and can put a user well on the way to understanding and using these counters to pinpoint a problem. However, the best way to get familiar with advanced performance monitor is to simply jump in and start monitoring counters on your system. Remember to click the *Explain>>* button whenever you're unsure of what a particular counter monitors (or check out Appendix C, "Performance Monitor Counter Objects," for an explanation).

Let's take a look at some application counters in a real-world scenario. In Figure 4-10 we are going to add some Microsoft Exchange-specific counters to check the status of our Exchange server. Our server is computer `\\DAL-01-MSG`, and we want to monitor the SMTP (Simple Mail Transfer Protocol) traffic and also the NNTP (Network News Transport Protocol) traffic.

As Figure 4-10 illustrates, Performance Monitor can measure application statistics as well as operating system statistics. The drop-down list box shows just a few of the available counters to use with Microsoft Exchange. Figure 4-11 shows the NNTP traffic statistics and also a few counters to monitor the status of Internet Mail via the ExchangeIMC object (IMC stands for Internet Mail Connector).

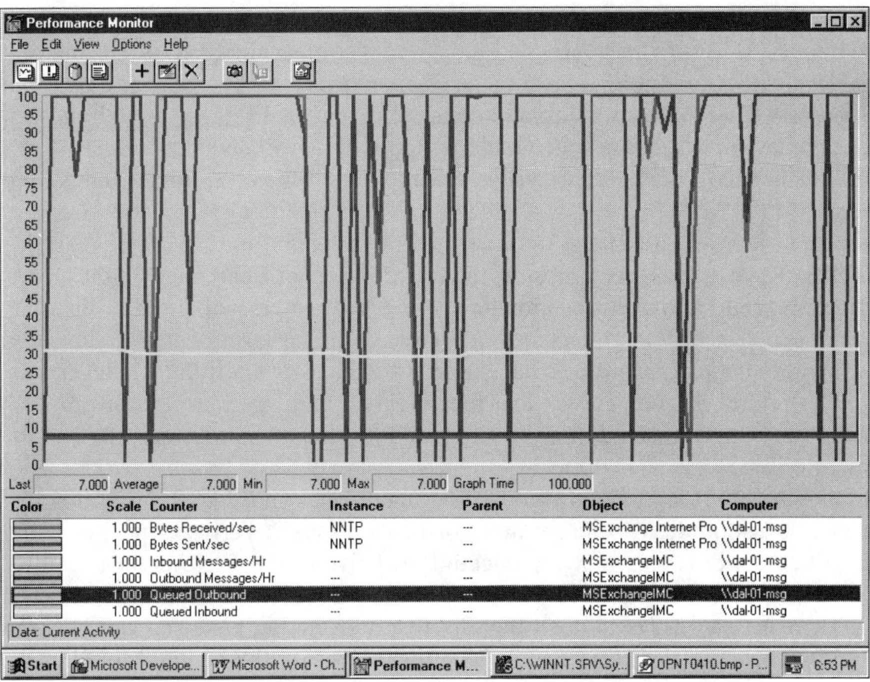

Figure 4-11: Performance Monitor graph monitoring Microsoft Exchange traffic.

The Queued Outbound Internet mail in Figure 4-11 shows that there are seven messages in the outbound queue waiting to be delivered (this value is shown graphically as well as numerically below the chart) . An administrator using this information could notice a potential problem area if the outbound message queue grows larger, indicating that the messages are not being delivered. This type of information should raise a flag that a problem may exist and intervention may be required.

There are all sorts of application counters that can be used. Which counters are available for your specific application depends on how the application was written and whether the developers included Performance Monitor code. Performance Monitor counters are required for an application to receive the Microsoft BackOffice Certified Logo.

Now that we know what type of information can be observed using Performance Monitor, let's take a look at some of the different methods that we can use to monitor and view performance data.

THE PERFORMANCE MONITOR VIEWS

Performance Monitor can be divided into four sections called Views. On the tool bar shown earlier in Figure 4-1, these views are represented by these buttons (from left to right): Charts, Alerts, Logs, and Reports. We covered Charts through most of our examples, but there are several additional options we haven't discussed. Let's take a deeper look at the chart view, and then we'll move to Alerts, Logs, and Reports.

CHART We've already seen most of the functionality of Chart View in our previous examples. Chart views provide a live, real-time view of data for the counters you select. When the chart lines move to the far right of the window, the charting automatically continues back again at the left (overwriting whatever was there). Therefore, charting is excellent for providing an instantaneous view of data, but not so great as a data collection tool (because the data is quickly overwritten).

In looking at a Chart View window, you may or may not like the way the data appears. For example, you might prefer using a different vertical scale, or using different colors to represent various counters. Fortunately, Performance Monitor provides a number of options for changing the appearance and behavior of charted data. There are two ways to open the Chart Options dialog box. You can click on the Options icon on the Performance Monitor toolbar on the far right, or click on Options → Chart from the menu bar. You then see a screen similar to Figure 4-12.

As Figure 4-12 shows, there are several options for customizing the chart options. Changing the value in the periodic update box customizes the chart Update Time; or the chart can be set to only perform a manual update. Other miscellaneous items allow you to add and remove certain objects from the Chart such as grid lines, Labels, the Value Bar, and the Legend.

The previous examples should have given you a fairly good overview of Chart View. There are three other very important views provided by Performance Monitor, which we examine next.

REPORT Report is essentially the same as Chart View except that it is a text representation of the data updated at configurable intervals (the default interval is five seconds). A sample report is shown in Figure 4-13.

ALERT Now that we know how to monitor objects and counters, we can apply these counters to build a customized monitoring system for your Windows NT environment. The monitoring system is the watchdog of Performance Monitor. An alert happens whenever a monitored counter exceeds or falls below a specified threshold. Let's add some counters to record an alert if any of our hard drive's free disk space falls below a certain point. From the View menu, click on Alert. You should see a blank Alert screen similar to a blank sheet of paper. To add the disk counters, click Edit → Add to Alert. You should see a screen similar to Figure 4-14.

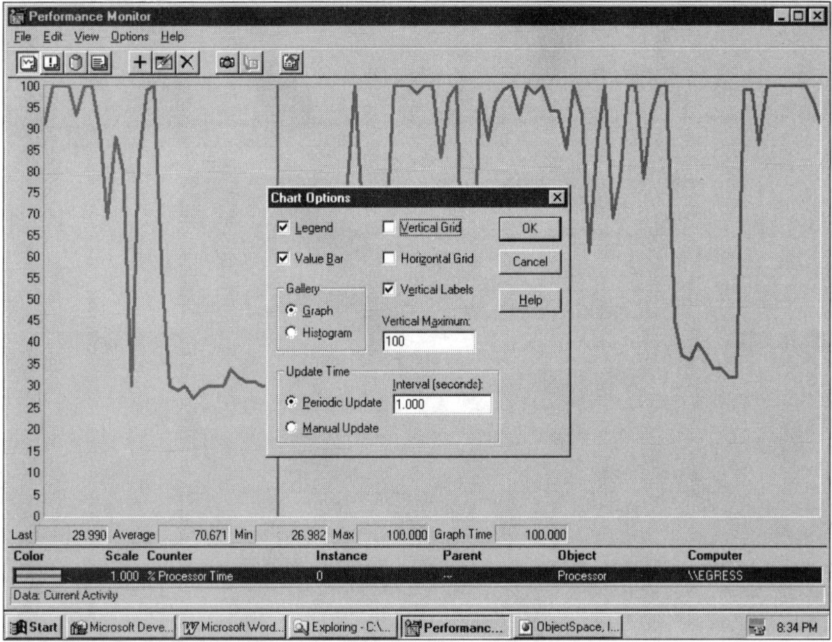

Figure 4-12: Graph options.

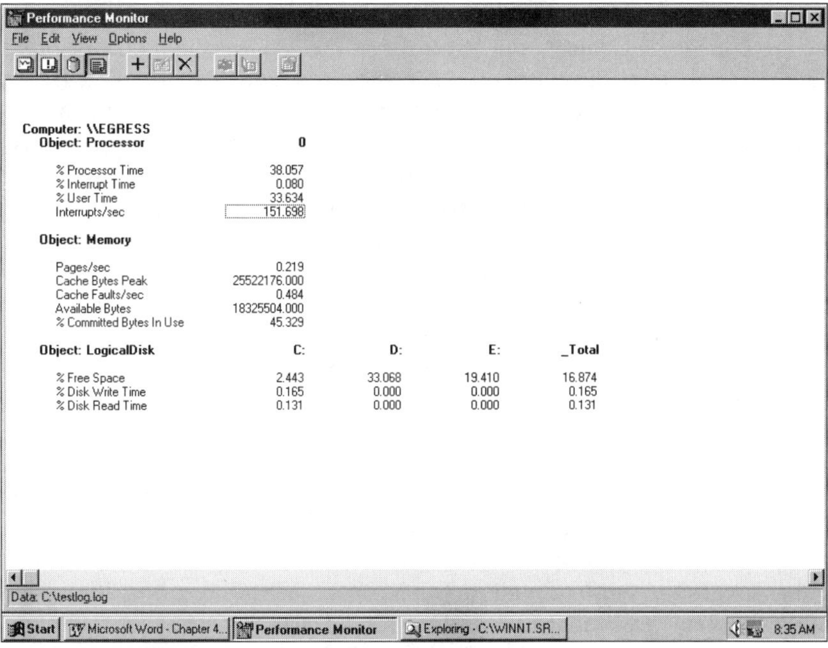

Figure 4-13: Performance Monitor Report View.

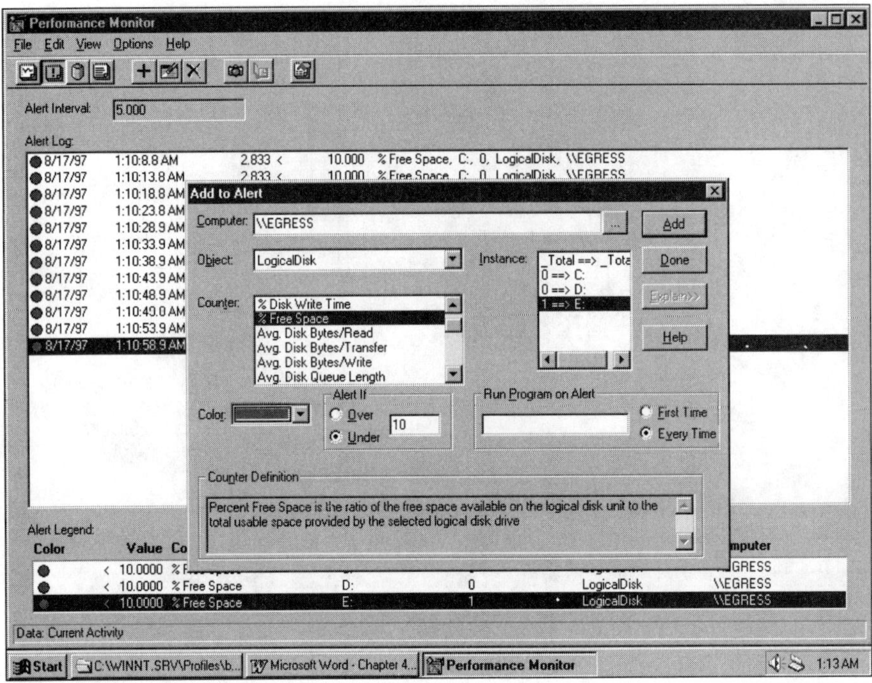

Figure 4-14: Adding alerts in Performance Monitor.

Locate the *Logical Disk* object, and select the % Free Space counter. Notice that there are four instances of this particular object. Three are logical drives C:, D:, E:, and _Total (cumulative drive space). In the Alert If frame, select the alarm threshold for the object you are adding. Let's set the alarm level to alert us if a particular drive has less than 10 percent free disk space. A major feature of Performance Monitor is its ability to run a program once, or continually, after receiving an alert. The ability to launch an application after receiving an alert can lead to all sorts of creative scripts and applications. For example, you could use a command line SMTP e-mail application (such as the *sendmail* utility popular on the UNIX platform but also available for Windows NT) after an alarm to send an Internet mail message to an administrator. Another example is sending an alert to the administrator via a command-line paging utility or an e-mail–based pager gateway. Alerts also include specific configuration options. Click on Options → Alert to view the Alert Options dialog box shown in Figure 4-15.

As Figure 4-15 shows, you can configure global Alert options. These options include the Update Interval, Network Alert, and the ability to log an event in the Application Event Log. Alert options also give you the ability to bring the Alert View to the foreground during an alert. The Network Alert dialog box allows the workstation running Performance Monitor to send a network message to another computer as long as the messenger service is running on the target computer.

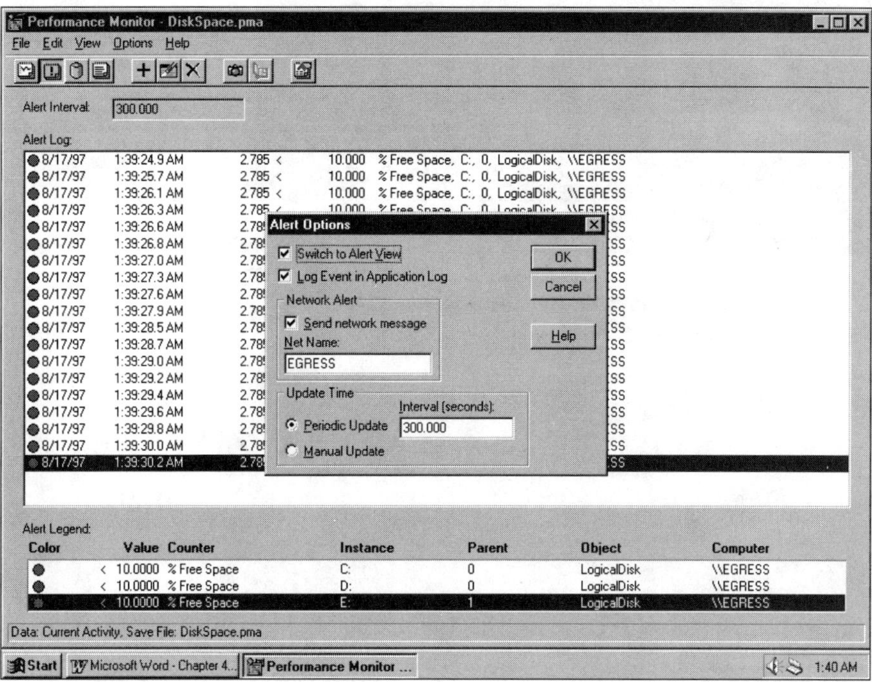

Figure 4-15: Alert Options dialog box.

LOG FILES To this point we have been working only with real-time data. But what if we want to record data over time for trend analysis? Log files allow you to record data at specified intervals for analysis in Performance Monitor or exported to more sophisticated applications. When adding objects to a log file, as shown in Figure 4-16, you don't actually select counters. In the case of log files, all counters associated with an object are automatically logged. As with other views you can log information from remote machines in the same log file. For our example, add the *Processor*, *Logical Disk*, and *Memory* objects.

After adding the objects, click Options → Log. You will see a screen similar to Figure 4-17. Once again, the Log Options screen looks different than the Chart and Alarm options we saw earlier. In the Log Options dialog box, we first need to give the log a filename. For our example let's use TESTLOG.LOG. In the update interval, put in 60 seconds so that our sample data is 1 minute apart. Click Save and the log file is ready to go – almost. Once you add the objects and give the log a filename and update interval, you have to manually start the log. Open the Log Options dialog box again and click on the Start Log button.

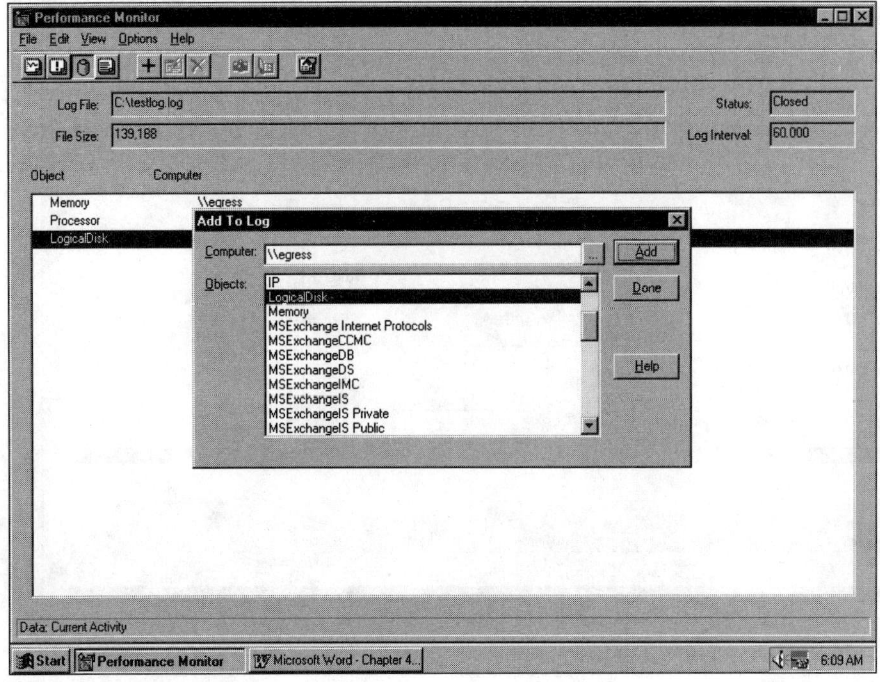

Figure 4-16: Adding objects to the Log.

You can tell that the log has started when the Status box says Collecting and the status bar shows a database icon in the lower right corner of Performance Monitor. While the log is running you can insert comments into the log by clicking on the Bookmark icon on the toolbar or clicking Options → Bookmark. The log can be stopped at any time by clicking Options → Log, and then clicking on the Stop button. After the log has stopped, restarting it appends data to the existing log file.

WORKING WITH LOG FILES Log files are one of the most important elements of Performance Monitor. We saw in the previous section that we can create log files that collect all counters and instances of an object at specified intervals. While in any view, click on Options → Data From, and select an existing log file. When working with existing log files instead of live data, you have the option of selecting a time window. You can set the window range by clicking on Edit → Time Window and selecting the start and stop points as shown in Figure 4-18. Reducing the time window can also drastically reduce the size of a log file if you are working with only a small section.

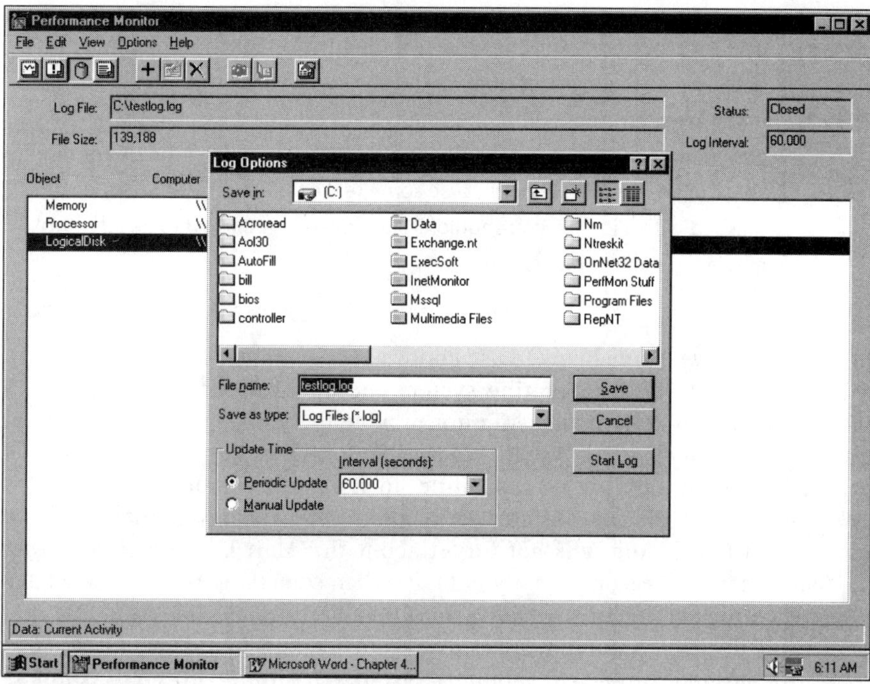

Figure 4-17: Creating and starting the Log file.

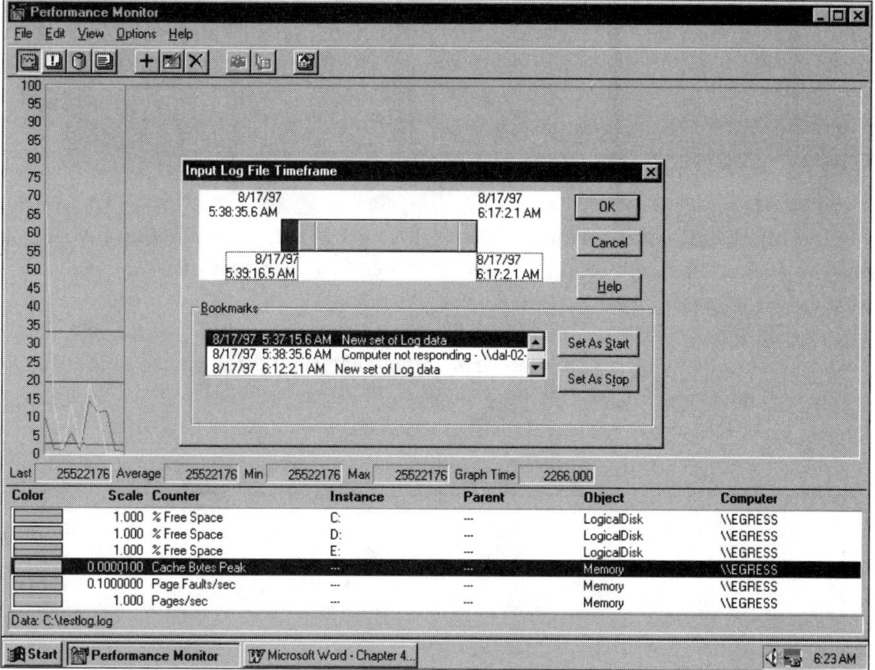

Figure 4-18: Reducing the Log window in Performance Monitor.

Be careful about disk usage when creating Performance Monitor log files because the files can get quite large; this is especially true when logging data over several days or weeks. When doing extended logging, you should periodically check the log file size to ensure that you don't run out of disk space (a situation that could cause some real headaches). Also, after you've finished with a log file you should either delete or archive it to an alternate media type to free disk space.

In this section, we learned how to use Performance Monitor like a stethoscope to peer into the Windows NT operating system and applications. The objects and counters available to Performance Monitor provide the vital signs in real-time on the health of the Windows NT system. We used Performance Monitor to take a look at real-time data and the logging capabilities to store information for later analysis. We exported Performance Monitor data to text files, which were then imported into Microsoft Excel. And let's not forget about the Alert Log, which acts as a Performance Monitor beacon letting you know when something is wrong. We have just scratched the surface of the many options to Performance Monitor. The real power from Performance Monitor comes from knowing how to use the tool to monitor and troubleshoot problems. Familiarize yourself with the different counters used by Windows NT. After installing an application, see if any counters were added that might assist in monitoring the application's performance. The time spent learning how to use Performance Monitor is time well spent and will give you an insight into the computer that will make you more effective as a troubleshooter.

PerfMan

After getting a taste of Performance Monitor's ability to create information such as charts and logs, those of us that are programmers envision an application that creates an entire Windows NT management system capable of being run from one console. Included on the Optimizing Windows NT CD-ROM is a copy of a utility with just this kind of functionality. PerfMan is an application that capitalizes on the ability to remotely monitor Performance Monitor counters. This data is then stored and used to detect bottlenecks and trends in your NT Servers and Workstations.

Extensible Counters Give PerfMon More Power

One of Performance Monitor's best features is its ability to have additional objects (and their associated counters) added to the system later on. These "add-ons" are known as *extensible performance counters*, and can be added for both hardware and software objects present on the system. For example, to enable a particular device driver, system service, or user application to display performance data in the Windows NT Performance Monitor (along with the standard system counters already present), software developers can use an API present in Windows NT to have their application, service, or drive provide performance-related data to the Performance Registry. This takes the form of a custom `.DLL` file that is installed to monitor the driver or application in question. After Performance Registry understands the object, it can be viewed in the Performance Monitor. It will also appear in the list of objects that can be monitored.

The Windows NT Resource Kit provides a handy utility for monitoring the list of extensible counters installed since the original installation of Windows NT (with its base PerfMon objects and counters). This utility is called the Extensible Performance Counter List Utility (`EXCTRLST.EXE`), and is located in the `\PERFTOOL\CNTRTOOL` subfolder of the Resource Kit's main installation folder. This utility displays a dialog that shows each of the additional extensible counters installed on the system and the `.DLL` files that support them. The Extensible Performance Counter List Utility's main dialog is shown in Figure 4-19.

One example of an application that installs new Performance Monitor objects and counters is the Windows NT Resource Kit itself. The Resource Kit automatically installs a number of new counters for measuring the performance of different system components in addition to those already included with Windows NT by default (for a list of these counters, see the `COUNTERS.HLP` file located in the same `\PERFTOOL\CNTRTOOL` subfolder as the `EXCTRLST.EXE` utility). There are also a few additional extensible counters (such as a number of advanced Pentium processor-related counters) that aren't installed by default, but may be manually added by following the instructions provided in the Resource Kit's documentation.

Another handy counter-related tool included in the Resource Kit is the Counter List Utility (`CTRLIST.EXE`), which is a text-based (nongraphical) tool that dumps a list of ALL installed Performance Monitor objects and counters to the screen. This can also be saved to a text file by using the ">" redirection symbol after the command to redirect the output to a text file (e.g., by typing **CTRLIST > COUNTERS.TXT**).

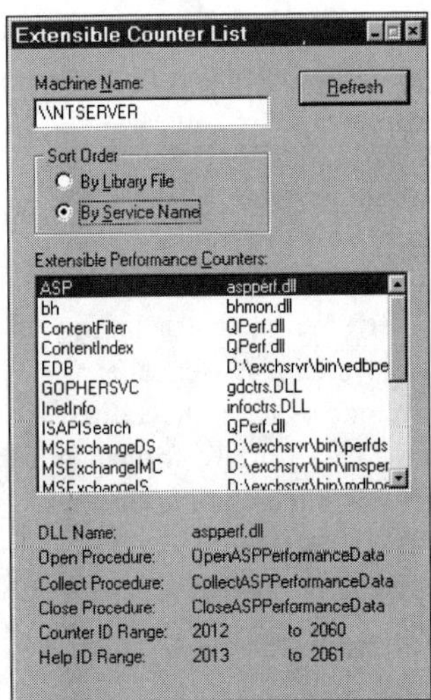

Figure 4-19: The Extensible Counter List utility included in the Windows NT Resource Kit.

Throughout this book we use Performance Monitor with a variety of different counters to detect system bottlenecks and monitor performance for the various Windows NT subsystems. Therefore, to get the most out of these chapters familiarize yourself with at least the basics of creating and viewing data using Performance Monitor.

The Windows NT Registry editors

The most critical component of any Windows NT installation is the Registry. The Registry is the Windows NT configuration database and is used by both the system and applications to store important configuration data. Any changes in your Windows NT environment, from screen saver settings to changes in installed hardware, are recorded in the Registry. The Registry consists of several different files, each of which stores information about a different aspect of Windows NT's environment.

Because all of Windows NT's vital data is stored in the Registry, it is critical that the Registry remain intact at all times. Invalid settings in the Registry, whether made by a user, system service, or application, can render the system unstartable. This situation can, in turn, require a restore operation or even a complete reinstall of Windows NT to fix.

WORKING WITH NT'S REGISTRY EDITORS

Despite the dangers of modifying the NT Registry database, it's also a necessary evil for many of the procedures relating to optimization. Therefore, the best thing to do is to embrace this process and garner some knowledge of the Registry's design and its management tools.

The primary Registry management utilities in Windows NT are the two Registry editors, REGEDT32.EXE and REGEDIT.EXE. Both allow you to view the various Registry database files and modify their contents.

The REGEDIT.EXE utility only applies to Windows NT 4.0; the REGEDIT.EXE in Windows NT 3.5x is the OLE Registration Database Editor. In Windows NT 3.5x, you must use the REGEDT32.EXE Registry editor.

As mentioned earlier, the use of a Registry-editing utility can cause severe system problems that can require the use of an Emergency Repair Disk or a reinstallation of Windows NT to fix. Also, it is important to understand that Microsoft does not support enduser use of the NT Registry editors and will probably not assist you with any problem caused by their use. Registry editing is done at your own risk.

Windows NT does not automatically create shortcut icons for the Registry Editor utilities. However, they are installed on every Windows NT System and can be accessed by choosing the Start menu's Run option and typing either **REGEDIT** (for the Windows 95-like version) or **REGEDT32** (for the original, standard version) and pressing Enter. You can use either version because both are capable of modifying the Registry.

On some systems the REGEDIT.EXE version of the Registry Editor doesn't get installed properly during the upgrade to Windows NT 4.0. In these situations, you instead get the OLE Registration Database Editor from an older version of Windows (e.g., Windows NT 3.5x, Windows for Workgroups, or Windows 3.x) that doesn't apply to Windows NT. If this is the case on your system, you need to manually copy the correct REGEDIT.EXE program from another machine or the *platform* folder on the Windows NT installation CD-ROM (where *platform* is the appropriate hardware platform directory for your system, such as \I386, \ALPHA, etc.) into the *%SYSTEMROOT%* folder (e.g., C:\WINNT).

For new NT users, it is recommended that you use the newer REGEDIT.EXE version of Registry Editor, because it sports an Explorer-style interface and has superior search capabilities to the older, original version (REGEDT32.EXE). The REGEDIT.EXE version is also the best choice for Windows 95 users, because of the similarities between it and Windows 95's Registry Editor. On the other hand, NT 3.x users may prefer to use the traditional REGEDT32.EXE version, because it is probably more familiar.

One advantage of the REGEDIT.EXE Registry editor is its capability to perform extended searches of the Registry, including values and data (REGEDT32.EXE allows you to search only on keys and subkeys). In addition, the entire Registry database is shown as one large tree, whereas REGEDT32 shows different segments of the Registry in their own separate windows. However, one advantage that REGEDT32.EXE has over REGEDIT.EXE is its default view of data such as string and numerical value. In general, REGEDT32's editors for data types are easier to read and interpret than the editors in REGEDIT. For example, certain types of string data are shown in REGEDIT in a somewhat bizarre-looking format with the readable text crammed into a few columns on the right, and the hex equivalents shown at left. REGEDT32, on the other hand, displays this type of data in a far easier to read format with the string displayed as one would expect. Finally, REGEDIT is incapable of creating certain types of Registry values that REGEDT32 is capable of creating (the REG_EXPAND_SZ and REG_MULTI_SZ string value types). As a result, the best approach is a mixed use of both; for example, using REGEDIT to search for values and REGEDT32 to create and edit those values that aren't handled well (or at all) by REGEDIT.

The REGEDT32.EXE version of the Registry Editor utility is shown in Figure 4-20 and the REGEDIT.EXE version is shown in Figure 4-21.

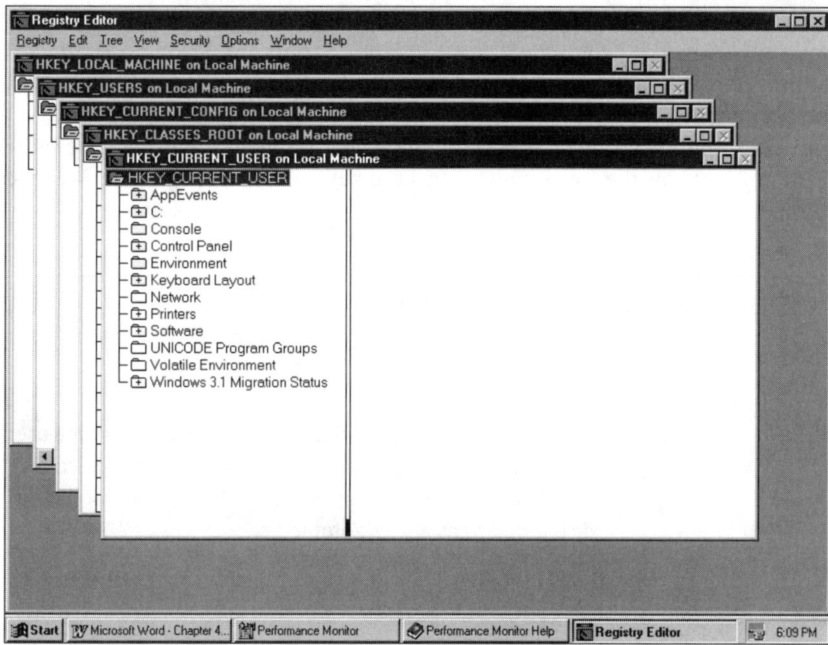

Figure 4-20: The REGEDT32.EXE version of the Windows NT Registry Editor utility.

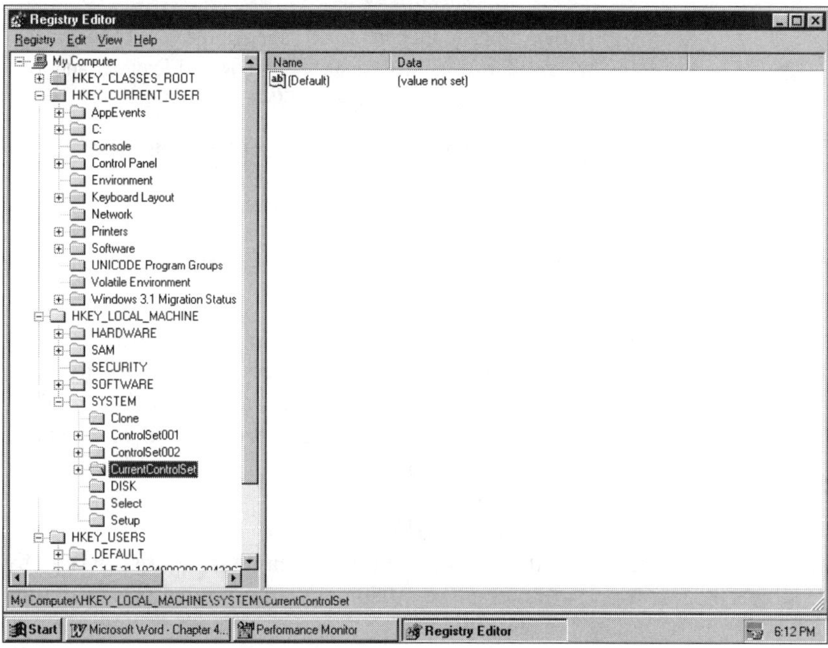

Figure 4-21: The REGEDIT.EXE version of the Windows NT Registry Editor utility.

THE REGISTRY EDITOR DISPLAY

When you run one of the Registry editors (REGEDIT.EXE or REGEDT32.EXE), several important sections of the Windows NT Registry are displayed within individual subwindows (REGEDT32.EXE) or branches of the My Computer "tree" (REGEDIT.EXE) inside the utility's main window. These subwindows or branches represent the individual Registry keys on the local computer. Five keys, described in Table 4-2, are displayed by default.

TABLE 4-2 THE WINDOWS NT REGISTRY EDITOR KEYS

Key Name	Description of Contents
HKEY_CURRENT_USER	This is the root of the configuration information for the user who is currently logged on. The user's folders, screen colors, and Control Panel settings are stored here. This information is referred to as a user's profile.
HKEY_USERS	This is the root key of all user profiles on the computer. HKEY_CURRENT_USER is a subkey of the HKEY_USERS key.
HKEY_LOCAL MACHINE	This key contains general configuration information for the local computer and is not specific to any one user.
HKEY_CLASSES_ROOT	This is a subkey of HKEY_LOCAL_MACHINE\SOFTWARE. The information stored here is used to open the correct application when a file is opened using the Windows NT Explorer and for COM/DCOM operations (aka OLE/Network OLE).
HKEY_CURRENT_CONFIG	This key contains information about the hardware profile used by the local computer at system startup. This key/window is a new feature in Windows NT 4.0.

Each of these individual keys is like a "branch" of the Registry Editor tree. The branches contained within each key window are also referred to as keys (or subkeys), and folder icons represent all keys. Each key can contain one or more values and subkeys. Each value is, in turn, assigned three characteristics: the value name, the value class, and the value's actual data contents.

NAVIGATING AND EDITING THE REGISTRY

Within either of the Registry Editor utilities, you can navigate Registry keys by simply double-clicking them; an opened key displays its nested subkeys and values. Whenever a key containing subkeys is unopened, its folder icon displays a plus (+) symbol. When the key is opened, its folder icon displays a minus (-) symbol, and the subkeys it contains are listed. Also, any values contained within that key are displayed in a window to the right (see Figure 4-22).

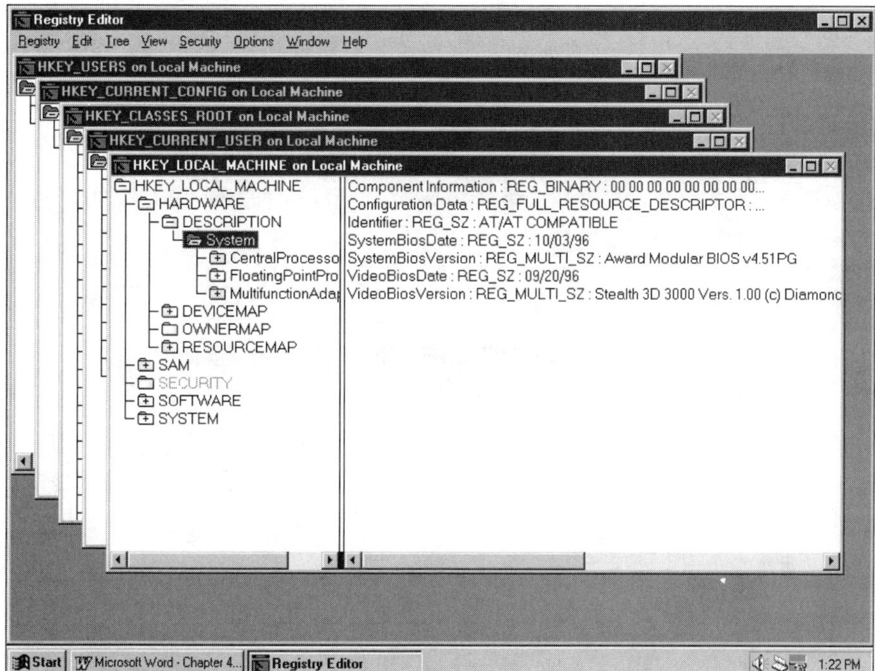

Figure 4-22: A Registry key with nested subkeys below and values displayed at right.

The class of a particular value displayed in the Registry Editor window is denoted by its prefix (e.g., REG_DWORD, REG_SZ, etc.), which is displayed next to the value name in capital letters. These five classes of values are found in the Registry:

- REG_BINARY values contain binary data (0 or 1).
- REG_SZ values contain string data (text).
- REG_DWORD values contain numeric data.
- REG_MULTI_SZ values contain multiple strings of text.
- REG_EXPAND_SZ values contain expandable strings of text.

In addition to a class type, each value has some type of data assigned to it. The data assigned to a value can be either a string or numeric data. To change the data assigned to a value, double-click the value name in the window to the right. This displays an editor window for the value type and shows the current data, which can then be changed (see Figure 4-23).

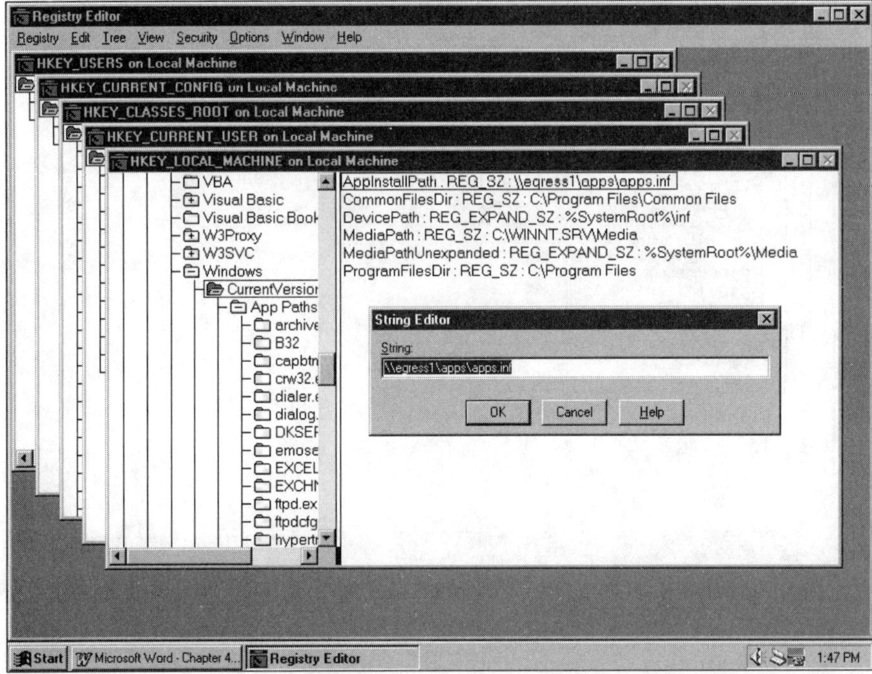

Figure 4-23: Editing a Registry value.

Using the Edit menu in Registry Editor, you can add subkeys and values to Registry keys. However, as with any Registry change, you should only do so under specific instructions from Microsoft, a third-party hardware or software vendor, or a qualified technician. And, as always, be sure to have a recent full backup of your Windows NT system and the Registry database before making any changes.

ACCESSING REMOTE REGISTRIES

Remember that powerful capability of Performance Monitor to monitor remote systems on the network? Well, a similar power is found in Registry Editor: one of its primary features is the ability to access the Registry of a remote computer on a network. To do so you must be a member of that computer's (or the domain's, if applicable) system administrators group. This feature can be especially handy for network administrators who need to diagnose and solve problems on remote workstations and servers across a LAN or WAN.

To access the Registry of a remote computer, choose Select Computer (if using REGEDT32.EXE) or Connect Network Registry from the Registry Editor's Registry menu. Then either select the computer from the list displayed or type its name in the Computer box.

When accessing the Registry of a remote computer, only the HKEY_USERS and HKEY_LOCAL_MACHINE keys will appear. Furthermore, it is recommended that you use the REGEDT32 version of Registry Editor rather than the REGEDIT version, because you are likely to have greater difficulty using REGEDIT to access remote registries than you will using REGEDT32. Specifically, REGEDIT will often issue an error message (that the Registry could not be accessed) when attempting to access a remote Registry; however, in these same situations, REGEDT32 will pull up the remote Registry without a hitch.

EDITING THE REGISTRY FOR FUN AND PROFIT

In typical day-to-day use, you don't want or need to directly edit the Registry using Registry Editor. In fact, doing so puts your system's integrity at risk because the Registry Editor utility has no syntax-checking features to ensure that an entry was entered correctly. However, many of the best system optimizations and configuration changes can only be made by editing the Registry directly – i.e., there's no standard Control Panel or system configuration dialog to make the change. As a result, a certain amount of Registry editing is necessary for any kind of system optimization. In reality, the Windows NT Registry editors are really the "keys to the NT kingdom." Without them, you are locked out of optimal system performance.

Throughout the book, we discuss a variety of tips, tricks, and techniques that require Registry modifications. Your best bet for getting the most out of this information (with the least amount of risk to your system) is to familiarize yourself with the Registry and the Registry Editor utility, and to have a basic understanding of Registry-related concepts and terms such as hives, keys, values, and data. Finally, be sure to have a good backup of your system's data and Registry before making any modifications to your system Registry.

For preventative maintenance tips and information on making system and Registry backups, see Chapter 12, "Maintaining Your NT System."

NT diagnostics: Information at your fingertips

Having a hard time determining why that new sound card or CD-ROM won't work? Wondering what IRQ (Interrupt Request) a particular piece of hardware is using? Although Plug and Play has made the installation of computer peripherals easier, it's still not perfect. Windows NT Diagnostics is a tool that lets you get "under the hood" of NT and see what's going on. It provides a snapshot of your system's configuration and resource usage, and can be very helpful when diagnosing problems or even when you're just trying to learn more about a particular system.

Among the information provided by Windows NT Diagnostics is the following:

- Windows NT version and user registration information
- CPU and BIOS type and version information
- Display-related information including both the physical adapter and the installed video driver
- Information about all drives installed on the system
- Network-related information, including current user and network configuration data
- Status of all system services
- System resource usage including IRQs, I/O Port, memory address, and DMA channels used
- Status of various memory pools, including paged and nonpaged pool kernel memory, physical memory, system cache, and the paging file
- Number of active handles, threads, and processes
- Installed device drivers (Devices)
- System environment variables and their values

One of the coolest things that Windows NT Diagnostics can tell you is the processor speed of the computer you're working on. This is shown in the System tab in the Processors section at the bottom of the dialog. This is especially handy if you're working with an unlabeled computer that doesn't display its speed in megahertz. Also shown in this window are the processor's family type and stepping version.

You will find Windows NT Diagnostics in the Administrative Tools section of the Programs menu. You can also create a shortcut to the program itself, `WINMSD.EXE`, which resides in the *%SYSTEMROOT%\SYSTEM32* subdirectory. Windows NT Diagnostics consists of nine different sections represented by the tab bars shown in Figure 4-24.

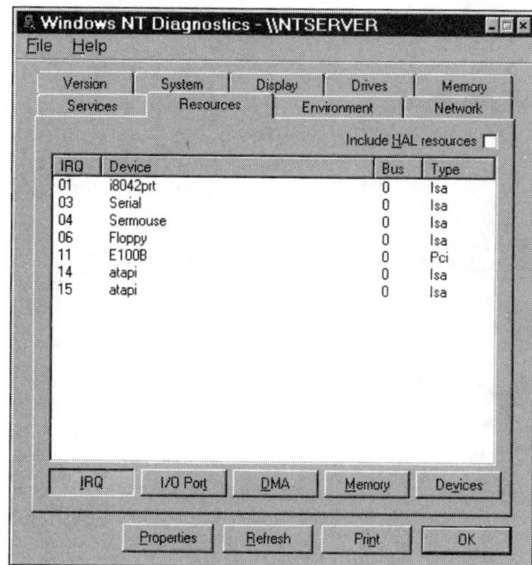

Figure 4-24: The Windows NT Diagnostics utility, which provides a snapshot of your system's configuration and resource usage.

Remember how Performance Monitor and the Registry Editor utilities worked across the network? Starting to see a trend? Yes, you guessed it – Windows NT Diagnostics also support the accessing of a remote machine. To do so, you simply choose File → Select Computer from the menus, which brings up a standard network browsing dialog box. From here you can either double-click the machine you wish to view or enter a machine's computer name manually in standard Uniform Naming Convention (UNC) format; e.g., *MACHINE_NAME*. This will bring up a Windows NT Diagnostics session for the selected remote system. This feature is especially handy for accumulating system inventory information on various machines on your network, without having to visit each and every single machine in person.

Managing applications with Task Manager

One of the most welcomed additions to Windows NT 4.0 is the enhanced Task Manager. The Task Manager in Windows NT 4.0 goes far beyond its counterpart in Windows NT 3.5x, providing process, memory, and performance-related information in addition to the capability of managing tasks (i.e., applications).

For the purposes of this book and the process of analyzing and maximizing Windows NT system performance, the Performance tab (shown in Figure 4-25) is by far the most important of Task Manager's features. It provides a "snapshot" of system performance-related data, including current and recent CPU utilization (including a chart-style graph that tracks utilization for each CPU in the system), memory statistics including those related to physical memory, paged and nonpaged pool Kernel memory, the NT file/system cache, and total committed memory.

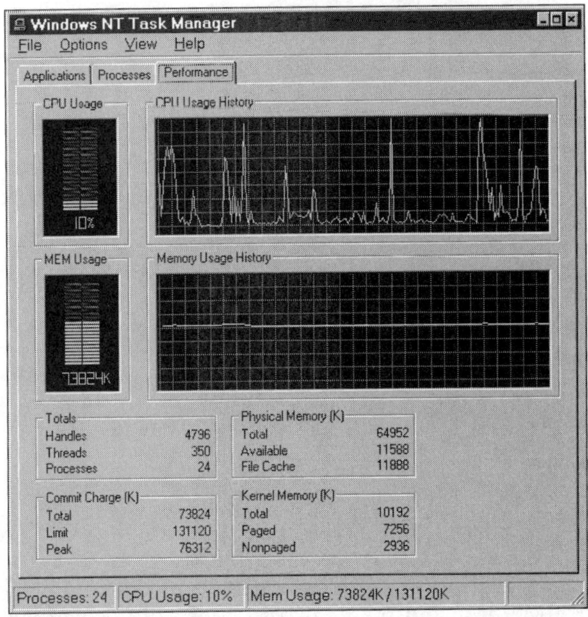

Figure 4-25: The Windows NT 4.0 Task Manager's Performance tab displays important system performance and resource usage information.

These statistics provide a quick and useful method for examining important system performance statistics without requiring the effort of firing up and configuring a Performance Monitor session. To obtain a quick view of the current status of CPU and memory statistics consider using Task Manager's Performance tab. However, for extended or in-depth performance analysis, use Performance Monitor because it provides a far more comprehensive set of counters and analysis features.

Another important aspect of Task Manager is its capability to shut down a hung application or system process. Although the Windows NT 3.5x version of Task Manager includes the capability to shut down user applications, the Windows NT

4.0 Task Manager goes beyond this and additionally provides control of individual system processes in addition to applications. It also provides CPU and memory usage statistics for each process running on the system, which can be helpful in identifying applications and system services that are hogging these precious resources. Task Manager's Processes dialog is shown in Figure 4-26.

Never use the End Task or End Process feature of Task Manager unless it's absolutely necessary for resumption of proper system operation. In addition, never shut down a process whose function you are unfamiliar with. Often processes have strange names that don't immediately identify the application or service to which they're connected. If the wrong process is abnormally terminated, it could result in a crashed application or even a loss of data.

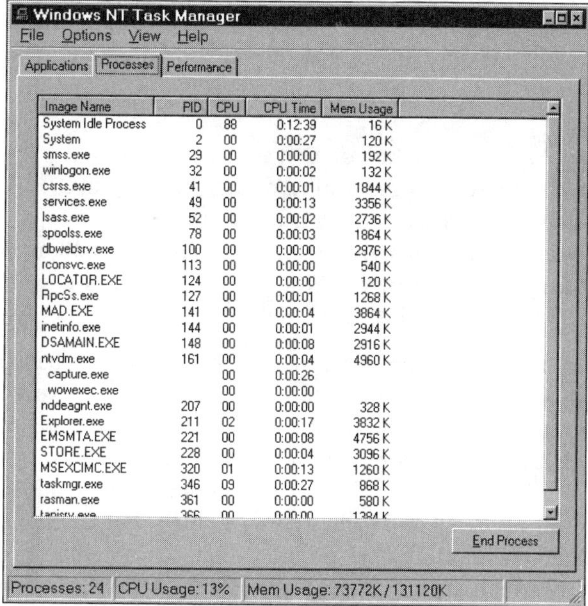

Image Name	PID	CPU	CPU Time	Mem Usage
System Idle Process	0	88	0:12:39	16 K
System	2	00	0:00:27	120 K
smss.exe	29	00	0:00:00	192 K
winlogon.exe	32	00	0:00:02	132 K
csrss.exe	41	00	0:00:01	1844 K
services.exe	49	00	0:00:13	3356 K
lsass.exe	52	00	0:00:02	2736 K
spoolss.exe	78	00	0:00:03	1864 K
dbwebsrv.exe	100	00	0:00:00	2976 K
rconsvc.exe	113	00	0:00:00	540 K
LOCATOR.EXE	124	00	0:00:00	120 K
RpcSs.exe	127	00	0:00:01	1268 K
MAD.EXE	141	00	0:00:04	3864 K
inetinfo.exe	144	00	0:00:01	2944 K
DSAMAIN.EXE	148	00	0:00:08	2916 K
ntvdm.exe	161	00	0:00:04	4960 K
capture.exe		00	0:00:26	
wowexec.exe		00	0:00:00	
nddeagnt.exe	207	00	0:00:00	328 K
Explorer.exe	211	02	0:00:17	3832 K
EMSMTA.EXE	221	00	0:00:08	4756 K
STORE.EXE	228	00	0:00:04	3096 K
MSEXCIMC.EXE	320	01	0:00:13	1260 K
taskmgr.exe	346	09	0:00:27	868 K
rasman.exe	361	00	0:00:00	580 K

Figure 4-26: The Windows NT 4.0 Task Manager's Applications and Processes tabs allow you to view and shut down running user applications and system processes.

Benchmarking Basics

Central to art of performance optimization is performance *benchmarking*. This simply means a standardized test that is applied to different system components to measure their performance. The results of the test become a "benchmark" of performance in the current environment, one that we can then use as a baseline for future comparisons. By benchmarking performance before and after you make changes to the system's configuration (hardware or software), you'll be able to properly evaluate the effectiveness and potential benefits of each change.

In *Optimizing Windows NT*, we use a number of different benchmarking utilities, including Bench32 (a shareware/commercial Win32 benchmarking utility), Response Probe (a part of the Windows NT 4.0 Resource Kit), and the Windows NT Performance Monitor utility.

When benchmarking the performance of any system component, it's very important that you follow certain procedural guidelines to ensure that you obtain accurate results. If you don't, you may end up with skewed or misleading results that will prevent you from making the best choices for your system's configuration.

By following the guidelines outlined next, you'll have an excellent chance of producing accurate and reproducible results that give a true picture of system performance:

- *Unload All Unnecessary Processes*: To ensure that no background applications or services interfere with the testing process, you should terminate everything that isn't absolutely necessary for the test to complete. This includes all applications visible on the Taskbar, as well as those that may be running invisibly (many of these have icons in the system tray area or can be stopped using Task Manager).
- *Reproduce*: When benchmarking system performance, it's important that you always run each iteration of a particular test at least twice to rule out any possible anomalies or "flukes." If the results are the same, you have a reasonable assurance that the results are accurate; if they are disparate, you should continue running the test until you can determine where and why the anomalous result occurred and can obtain a stable set of results. It's also important when benchmarking performance that you not change anything, including software, hardware, and system configuration settings, between tests. In other words, don't do things like swap the SCSI controller, load a new driver, or install the latest service pack, or you won't be able to accurately compare the results (unless, of course, these types of changes are what you're trying to benchmark).

- *Reboot Between Tests*: To ensure that your system is under a similar memory load during each test, it is advisable to restart the system prior to each test, wait until all background services have finished loading (this is often discernible by watching for the hard disk activity light to stop, indicating services are no longer loading into memory), and then immediately run the test. This helps duplicate the system's memory environment between tests and, more importantly, will clear the system cache from previously cached data (a factor that can skew some disk and network-based tests).
- *Run the Same Test on Different Machines*: When benchmarking the effects of a system configuration change (hardware or software), it's also a good idea to run the test suite on more than one machine to compare results. For example, if you were benchmarking the effects of a particular Registry modification on disk performance before and after the modification, you should run the same before and after tests on a machine with a different physical configuration. This will provide a better idea of how the change you've implemented works in different environments. In some cases, the differences may surprise you; e.g., a change that appeared radical on one machine might make only a minor or negligible difference on another.

Meet Bench32

One of the best benchmarking utilities available for Windows NT is U Software's Bench32. Bench32 is a utility designed to thoroughly test the performance of Win32-based systems (including both Windows NT and Windows 95). Bench32 is a fully configurable performance-testing tool that is capable of using a comprehensive set of tests to examine the performance of key system components. The tests Bench32 is capable of conducting are:

- Processor Test: tests the integer and floating point performance of your system's CPU/FPU (Floating Point Unit)
- Memory Test: tests your system's memory performance and bandwidth
- Disk Test: tests the I/O (Input/Output) performance of your system's disk subsystem
- Video Test: tests the 2D and 3D performance of the video subsystem

Using Bench32, you can first establish a baseline for your system's performance and later compare this baseline to other tests conducted after changes are made to the system. A sample Bench32 screen is shown in Figure 4-27.

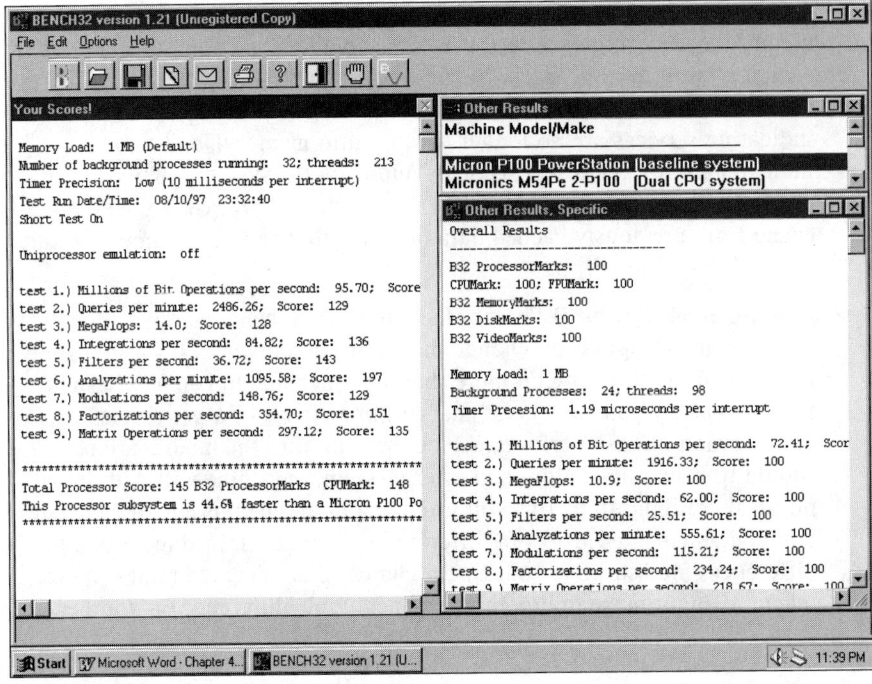

Figure 4-27: The Bench32 benchmarking utility.

Bench32 provides a number of different testing options, including short and long (more exhaustive) testing, different block and file sizes for disk tests, and larger memory load sizes for different machine types (e.g., workstations versus file or application servers). It also allows you to provide extensive descriptions of your system's configuration and save the results of each test for later comparison. Included with the software are a number of baseline tests that were conducted on different hardware platforms, which you can use as a basis of comparison for your own system.

The hardware and software requirements for running Bench32 are:

- CPU Requirements: Intel x86: 486DX/33 or faster; PowerPC: PowerPC 603 or better
- A monitor and video card capable of resolutions of 800x600 at 256 colors or higher
- Windows NT or Windows 95
- 24MB of RAM for Windows NT (16MB of RAM for Windows 95).

We refer to Bench32 throughout *Optimizing Windows NT*, especially in regards to the testing of disk subsystem performance (in Chapter 7).

Bench32 by U Software

We've included the shareware version of the Bench32 utility on the Optimizing Windows NT CD-ROM. To install Bench32, place the Optimizing Windows NT CD-ROM in your CD-ROM drive and point your Web browser to the location of the CD (if you have CD-ROM Autorun enabled, it will load automatically). Although the CD includes a functional shareware version of the Bench32 utility, we recommend that you obtain the registered version, which provides additional features and capabilities beyond the shareware version. Additional information on Bench32 and all of the utilities included on the Optimizing Windows NT CD-ROM is provided in Appendix A, "What's on the CD?"

Other benchmark utilities to consider

Although Bench32 provides a wide array of tests, there are other utilities you may wish to employ to round out this program's offerings (such as network-oriented tests, which Bench32 doesn't include). Although some of these utilities provide similar tests to those found in Bench32, others include unique tests designed to provide "real-world" performance testing. For example, the BAPCO SYSmark benchmarking utility opts to test system performance by running the system through a variety of popular applications in lieu of raw throughput exercises. Even where a particular utility provides a test similar to that found in Bench32, you may wish to run both tests on your system. This will provide yet another level of reassurance that you are receiving accurate and reproducible results.

These utilities and their respective features are listed below for your reference:

- **BAPCO SYSmark for Windows NT 4.0:** SYSmark is a system benchmarking utility with a different twist: it tests performance by applying workloads composed of several popular business productivity applications including word processing, spreadsheet, project management, computer-aided design (CAD), and presentation graphics programs. SYSmark/NT can generate performance metrics as a composite of all the different applications or for an individual application. In addition, SYSmark/NT automates the setup of the system's environment for consistent execution of the workloads, is capable of running the NT Performance Monitor in parallel to provide data for additional analysis and system tuning, and can be used across a network by multiple users. Another advantage of SYSMark/NT is its support of both the Intel and Alpha platforms.

- **Winstone 97 (Ziff-Davis):** Like BAPCO's SYSmark/NT, Winstone is a system-level, application-based benchmark that measures your PC's overall performance using real-world 32-bit Windows applications to generate a system workload. It runs a number of 32-bit business applications through prescripted activities and measures the time it takes the system to complete the tasks. Like SYSmark, this provides an idea of how the system performs in a real-world environment. Winstone is designed to run only on Intel-based Windows NT and Windows 95 computers.
- **WinBench 97 (Ziff-Davis):** WinBench is a subsystem-level benchmark from Ziff-Davis that, like Bench32, measures the performance of a PC's graphics, disk, processor, video, and CD-ROM subsystems. Also similar to Bench32, WinBench 97's tests are all 32-bit (with the exception of a 16-bit processor test) and are designed to run only on Windows 95 and Windows NT systems.
- **WebBench 97 (Ziff-Davis):** WebBench measures Web server software performance by running different Web server packages on the same server hardware or by running a given Web server package on different hardware platforms. WebBench's test suites produce two overall scores for the server: requests per second and throughput as measured in bytes per second. WebBench offers both static test suites, which strictly involve HTML pages, and dynamic test suites, which use dynamic executables and static requests. You can use this product to evaluate a number of different Web servers on a single NT Server to determine which is best for your application, or evaluate the relative performance of the same Web server software on an Intel versus an Alpha processor, and so forth. Although the Web server can be running on virtually any hardware platform and operating system (due to the use of standard CGI [Common Gateway Interface] scripts for the tests), the PC clients must be running either Windows 95 or Windows NT and the controller must be running Windows NT (Intel-based only).
- **NetBench 5.01 (Ziff-Davis):** NetBench is a portable benchmark program designed to test the performance of file servers. NetBench is able to use a mix of DOS, Windows 3.x, Windows for Workgroups, Windows 95, Windows NT, and Macintosh clients as the test clients. In the tests, the clients issue a steady stream of network file I/O requests. Each client keeps track of the total data throughput rate to and from the server during this process. NetBench then adds all of the client throughputs together to produce the overall throughput for a server. NetBench works only on Intel-based systems.

- **ServerBench 4.0 (Ziff-Davis):** ServerBench was designed to measure the performance of application servers in a client-server environment. The ServerBench test environment includes a server you're testing, a number of PC clients, and a single PC designated as the controller (which is responsible for executing and monitoring the testing process). ServerBench uses proprietary server, client, and controller programs that require Winsock 1.1-compliant TCP/IPs (Transmission Control Protocol/Internet Protocols) for the controller and clients to communicate with the server. The utility requires that the clients and the controller PC be running either Windows 95 or Windows NT, and works only on Intel-based systems.
- **Windows NT Resource Kit Performance Tools:** A final set of benchmarking utilities to consider are those in Microsoft's Windows NT Resource Kit. Although not nearly as sophisticated or user-friendly as those already mentioned, there are several useful performance tools in the Resource Kit. One, which we discuss in Chapter 7, is Response Probe. Response Probe is a script-based utility that measures the response of the computer and operating system to a predefined fixed workload. There are also a number of extra Performance Monitor counters and other performance measurement tools contained in the Resource Kit.

Additional information on and updates to the Ziff-Davis Benchmark Operation Project software (ZDBOp) including Winstone, WinBench, WebBench, NetBench, and ServerBench, are found at:

`http://www.zdbop.com/`

Additional information on the BAPCO SYSmark/NT utility is available at:

`http://www.bapco.com/`

Information on the Windows NT Resource Kit is available at Microsoft's Web site at:

`http://mspress.microsoft.com/`

As someone once said: "If you can't measure it, you can't manage it." By adding these tools to your arsenal of performance utilities, you'll be able to accurately measure the performance of every aspect of your Windows NT computer and network server. This will enable you to quantify and understand the performance differences that exist between different hardware components, platforms, and system configurations.

General Tuning Strategies

In upcoming chapters, we introduce you to optimization techniques for each of the critical Windows NT subsystems. For now, however, it's best if we begin by introducing some more basic optimization concepts – changes that you can implement quickly and easily on your Windows NT computers.

Even experienced NT users and administrators often neglect to make a few small changes to their systems that can make enormous differences in overall performance. Before we dive into advanced topics that involve Registry modifications and the like, we begin by covering these more basic optimizations to make sure you've got a good starting place for maximizing system performance. Although several of the optimizations mentioned in the following sections are covered elsewhere in the book, they are in the "basic" category and thus are provided here as well.

Memory, memory, memory

Although you've probably already heard it a million times before, it always bears repeating: the most important thing you can do to improve the performance of any Windows NT system is to give it lots of physical memory. There are two reasons why this is important: one is that increased memory means reduced paging file activity, which in turn translates to faster performance. The second is that Windows NT performs dynamic system tuning whereby additional memory is devoted to the system cache (which affects disk and network performance) automatically as the amount of available memory on the system is increased. Although there are methods to manually increase the system cache size, it is still beneficial to have a large pool of physical memory to spread between cache file usage, Windows NT Kernel components, and user applications.

So how much is enough? The answer, as you might have guessed, depends entirely on the role of your machine and the applications run on it. For an average Windows NT Workstation computer that runs only one or two simultaneous applications, 64MB is a good baseline figure (don't go less than 48MB in any case). If there are heavy application demands on the system, such as large engineering, graphics, or CAD applications, or the multitasking of a large number of programs, consider putting more than 64MB of memory. To monitor memory usage, you can use Performance Monitor to monitor the Memory Object's Committed Bytes figure over time or simply use the Chart View or Task Manager's Performance tab to obtain an instantaneous view of this figure. This figure represents the amount of memory committed (in use) by the system and user applications, and essentially amounts to the current memory "footprint" of your entire Windows NT environment, including applications. Another useful counter for gauging memory usage is % Committed Bytes In Use, which reflects the ratio of the Committed Bytes to the Commit Limit (the maximum amount of memory that may be committed for use before the paging file must be extended). This counter also provides you with a good idea of the current memory usage on the system, and can also expose situations where the paging file is being consistently increased due to insufficient memory.

Figure 4-28 shows the Performance Monitor utility charting the Memory object's Committed Bytes and % Committed Bytes In Use counters, along with several other important memory-related counters.

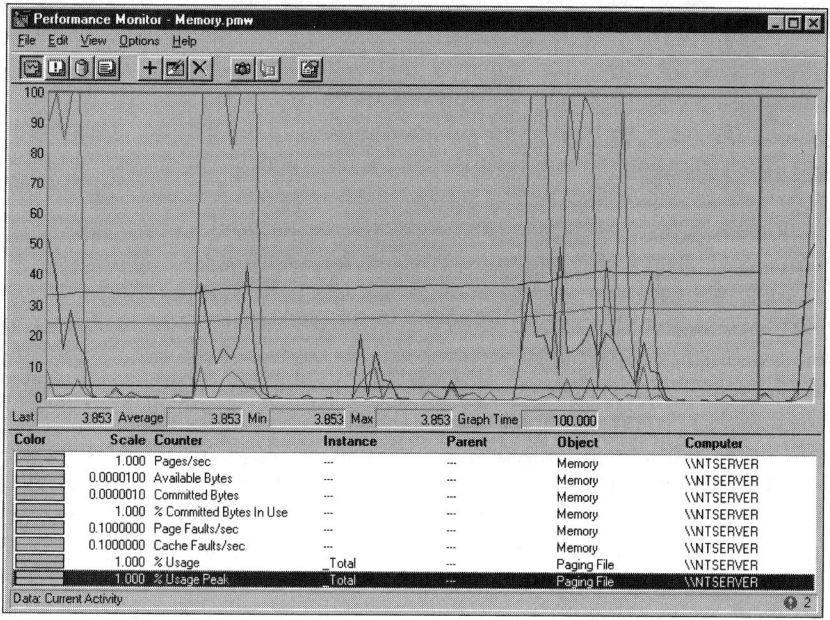

Figure 4-28: Using Performance Monitor to display important memory-related counters.

MEMORYBOTTLENECK.PMW

Included on the Optimizing Windows NT CD-ROM is MEMORYBOTTLENECK.PMW, a Performance Monitor workspace file that contains several important memory-related counters (including the Committed Bytes and % Committed Bytes In Use counters). To use this file, simply locate and double-click it using the Windows NT Explorer (it is located in the \PMWORKSPACE folder) or point your Web browser to the location of the Optimizing Windows NT CD-ROM (e.g., D:\). Then select the page for Performance Monitor Workspaces and follow the instructions given to load and use the file.

As a general rule of thumb for obtaining maximum performance, we recommend having an amount of physical RAM equal to approximately 1.5 to 2.0 times the average Committed Bytes figure on your system. You should also generate this average by monitoring the Committed Bytes figure over a period of time (e.g., using Performance Monitor's Log View) to obtain an accurate figure for average memory usage. Having ample memory keeps paging file usage at a minimum (even during times of peak usage), and also provides headroom for any later increases in application or data file sizes or the number of simultaneous programs run. It also provides extra room to accommodate later versions of NT, which will almost certainly have larger memory requirements. In addition, it maximizes the System Cache size and hit ratio (which, in turn, help to optimize disk and network performance) and allow you to implement additional optimizations that improve performance at the expense of additional memory usage. Remember, also, that having a bit of extra memory hanging around isn't such a bad idea, because we use some of it later to increase the performance of certain subsystems. If you don't have it to spare, you won't be as successful in trying to implement these techniques.

For Windows NT Server computers acting as a file and print server, the criteria used for determining the optimal amount of memory is somewhat different. With NT Servers supporting network users, you also need to be concerned with having sufficient memory to support the number of users in addition to the local applications and services running on the server. Simply monitoring the server's memory usage during idle or off-peak times can prove misleading, so be sure when monitoring the memory usage on servers to have the monitoring session include peak usage times (e.g., 8 a.m. on a weekday morning).

For a basic Windows NT file and print server, you can use Table 4-3 as a worksheet to estimate the amount of memory you need for each of your servers.

TABLE 4-3 ESTIMATING SERVER MEMORY REQUIREMENTS

Factor Impacting Memory Requirements	Value
Base system memory requirement (recommend 32MB for Intel-based; 48MB for RISC-based)	32–48MB
(Average size of data files open per user) * (Maximum number of users simultaneously connected to server)	_______MB
(Average size of executables run off of the server) * (Number of applications being run off of the server)	_______MB
Total server memory required (add above)	_______MB

Windows NT Servers running other BackOffice applications such as IIS (Internet Information Server), Exchange, and SQL (Structured Query Language) Server have their own additional sets of memory requirements beyond those discussed in Table 4-3. For these products, use the memory capacity planning guidelines set forth by Microsoft for each individual product (included with the product's documentation).

When deciding on the optimal memory configuration for your system, use NT's tools to help you; monitor your memory load index and Paging File with utilities such as the Windows NT Diagnostics Utility, Task Manager, and Performance Monitor. They help give you the real picture of your memory needs and answer the question of "how much is enough."

For additional information on optimizing system memory, see Chapter 5, "Optimizing Memory and Processing."

Removing/disabling nonessential protocols, services, and applications

One of the easiest things you can do to make an immediate difference in your system's performance is some good old-fashioned housecleaning. This essentially means going through your Windows NT configuration and disabling or removing unnecessary system and network services, network protocols, and user applications. The reason this improves performance is that each unnecessary software component installed and running on the system takes additional memory and CPU cycles that affect the performance of the whole system. By removing superfluous components, you increase the amount of memory available to the system cache and user applications and reduce the number of processes the CPU must service.

NETWORK PROTOCOLS

Start this process with the Network Control Panel's Protocols tab (shown in Figure 4-29). Remove any protocols that you don't absolutely need to function in your network environment. In a default installation, Windows NT installs several protocols, all of which may not be necessary in your environment. In addition, consider paring down the number of protocols used, and rethink your network design to see if it might be possible to accomplish more with fewer installed protocols.

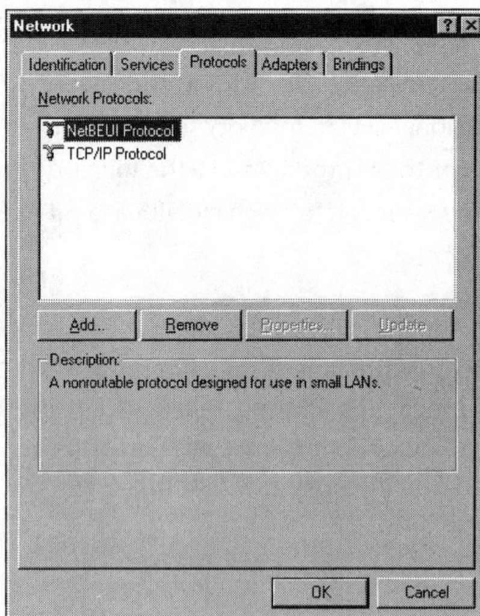

Figure 4-29: The Network Control Panel's Protocols tab allows you to add or remove protocols.

The following situations illustrate times when you may be able to reduce the number of network protocols installed:

- You're using TCP/IP for your primary file and print protocol and using the DLC (Data Link Control) protocol to control network printers (e.g., using HP JetDirect cards or similar devices). In this situation, it may be possible for you to use TCP/IP to also talk to the network printers, omitting the need for the additional protocol.
- You have machines on your network that connect to the Internet using TCP/IP for this purpose, but a different protocol (i.e., IPX/SPX or NetBEUI) for local network connectivity. In this situation, it is possible to implement TCP/IP as your sole network protocol to achieve all required connectivity.
- You have a number of individual Windows NT Workstations (or other Microsoft Windows clients) using one protocol for communication with local NT Servers, and another for access to a NetWare server or SNA-based server (such as an AS/400). In this situation, you could remove from each workstation the protocol used for access to the other server(s) (e.g., IPX/SPX for NetWare, and DLC or TCP/IP for SNA host connectivity), and instead use gateway software on the Windows NT Server to provide these services through the server itself. For example, you could use the Gateway Services for NetWare that ships with Windows NT Server for NetWare access, or Microsoft SNA Server (a separate BackOffice family product) for access to the SNA-based host.

If you choose to use TCP/IP internally on a network connected to the Internet, it is highly recommended that you implement some type of secure firewall on your network when using TCP/IP in this type of configuration, as it leaves your machine vulnerable to outside intrusion by hackers.

As an alternative to using protocol isolation (using one protocol for the local LAN and another, TCP/IP, for Internet access) to protect your network, consider the use of a proxy server application, which hides internal TCP/IP addresses from Internet users. With a proxy server, all traffic from the network is directed through the proxy, which translates all internal (usually private, nonroutable) IP addresses into a single, routable IP address (that of the proxy server).

One of the best available proxy servers is from Microsoft itself: Microsoft Proxy Server. This is a powerful yet easy-to-manage proxy server application that is closely integrated with Internet Information Server and leverages the Windows NT security model. It provides proxies for WWW (World-Wide Web) and FTP (File Transfer Protocol) services, as well as a number of other services through the included WinSock proxy component.

For more information about Microsoft Proxy Server, see Microsoft's Web site at:

`http://www.microsoft.com/proxy/`

NETWORK SERVICES

Another place where you can trim your system's memory and process "footprint" is the Network Control Panel's Service tab. This tab is where network-related services running on the system are installed, removed, and configured.

Once here, look for any installed network services that may not be necessary in your environment. Luckily, Windows NT is somewhat spartan about its default list of services when Windows NT is installed, so there isn't necessarily a lot of extra fat to trim here. However, we've found that many administrators and users new to NT tend to select lots of network services during NT's installation; perhaps because of confusion as to whether individual services were beneficial or necessary or in the hopes of checking them out later. If you've installed any network services that you aren't using or are unlikely to use in the near future, you should take this opportunity to remove them.

Of course, when considering the removal of a particular network service, be very careful that the service is not required for any other service or application running on your system or elsewhere on the network. For example, even though you may not be running SNMP (Simple Network Management Protocol) monitoring on a Windows NT computer, there may be another machine or device on the network that is. In this case, you wouldn't want to remove the SNMP service, because it is necessary to allow that station to be monitored.

A list of common network services that may be installed on your system (and may therefore be potential candidates for removal) and their respective descriptions and functionality are listed in Table 4-4.

Table 4-4 SOME COMMON NETWORK SERVICES

Service Name	Description	The Service Can Safely be Removed If...
DHCP (Dynamic Host Configuration Protocol) Relay Agent	Allows a Windows NT system to act as a DHCP/BOOTP Relay Agent	If the machine isn't a router that needs to forward DHCP/BOOTP packets
Microsoft DHCP Server	Allows a Windows NT Server to use Dynamic Host Configuration Protocol to automatically configure remote IP (Internet Protocol) clients	If you are statically assigning IP addresses to machines on your network, or don't require this machine to act as a DHCP server
Microsoft DNS (Domain Name System) Server	Allows a Windows NT Server to act as a Domain Name System server (provide Internet DNS name to IP address resolution)	If you aren't running an internal DNS server in your organization (i.e., are using external DNS servers housed at your ISP's (Internet Service Provider) or parent organization's site or don't require this machine to be a DNS server
Microsoft Internet Information Server (NT Server) or Microsoft Peer Web Services (NT Workstation)	Allows a Windows NT computer to act as a Web, FTP, and/or Gopher server on an intranet or the Internet.	If the machine doesn't act as an intranet/Internet server, and it is not supporting Web-based client access or administration tools (such as those available for NT Server, Exchange Server, and other products)
Microsoft TCP/IP Printing	Allows a Windows NT computer to act as an LPR (Line Printer Remote) -compatible client to, or LPD (Line Printer Daemon) - compatible server for a TCP/IP-based network printer	If you don't need to share or connect to TCP/IP-based network printers on your network

continued

TABLE 4-4 SOME COMMON NETWORK SERVICES *(Continued)*

Service Name	Description	The Service Can Safely be Removed If...
Network Monitor Agent	Provides the capability for the machine to be remotely polled by an NT Server running the Network Monitor utility	If you aren't using the Windows NT Server or SMS Network Monitor application on your network
Remote Access Service (RAS)	Provides the capability for the machine to run the Remote Access Service/Dial-Up Networking to make or receive dial-up network connections	If the machine is not a RAS server and doesn't need to connect to remote networks (including the Internet via dial-up device such as a modem or ISDN (Integrated Services Digital Network) Terminal Adapter)
RIP (Routing Information Protocol) for Internet Protocol or RIP for NwLink IPX/SPX (Internet Packet Exchange/Sequenced Packet Exchange) compatible transport	Allows a Windows NT Server to participate in RIP running on a IP or IPX network	If your network is using static routing, or another type of dynamic routing protocol other than RIP
SAP Agent (Service Advertising Protocol)	The SAP Agent is used to advertise services using NetWare's SAP Protocol	If you don't require that Windows NT machines on an IPX/SPX network advertise their services to NetWare clients
Services for Macintosh	Allows a Windows NT Server to act as a file and print server for Macintosh clients, and reshare Mac-based printers to Windows clients	If you have no Macintosh computers on your network, or if Mac clients do not need to connect to this server for file, print, or other services over AppleTalk

continued

Service Name	Description	The Service Can Safely be Removed If...
SNMP Service	Allows a Windows NT computer to be monitored by a remote SNMP manager such as HP OpenView, Sun Net Manager, or CA UniCenter TNG	If your network doesn't use SNMP monitoring, or this machine isn't included in the list of monitored devices
Windows Internet Name Service (WINS)	Allows a Windows NT Server to dynamically resolve NetBIOS names to IP addresses	If you aren't using WINS on your network (i.e., you're using DNS), or don't require this machine to act as a WINS server

If you're running the SAP Agent on a Windows NT machine to advertise the machine's services to computers on a NetWare network, be sure that the internal network number assigned to the machine's adapter isn't zero (the default setting). If it is zero, the machine may not be visible to other stations.

OTHER SERVICES

Apart from network-related services located in the Network Control Panel, there are other services running on your machine that may be unnecessary. To view these services, double-click the Services icon in Control Panel. Once there, examine the list of services running on your Windows NT system (i.e., those with a startup type of Automatic) to determine if any of the installed services are unnecessary or unused. Any services that you locate that are deemed extraneous should be removed to free additional memory for the operating system and user applications.

Table 4-5 describes a number of the services you're likely to see in this dialog, along with their descriptions and information regarding the effects of disabling each. Note that this information only applies to services that start automatically; those that have a startup type of Manual will only start once they are called on by the system or a user application. If a service that you don't require is already set to a startup type of Manual, it is recommended that you leave it this way rather than disabling it.

Never stop or disable a service unless you're sure of its function and the ramifications of doing so. Also, be aware that many services have dependencies on other services, and that disabling one service may cause another to stop functioning properly.

TABLE 4-5 SERVICES IN THE SERVICES CONTROL PANEL

Service Name	Description	The Service Can Safely be Disabled or Set to Manual Startup If...
Alerter	Allows a machine to send administrative alert messages to other machines or users on a Windows network	You don't need or want to have this machine issue administrative alerts. This service requires the Messenger service to operate. (Note: It is recommended that you leave this service running on a Windows NT Server.)
Clipbook Server	Allows a machine to share clipboard data with other machines on the network	You don't need this machine to share clipboard data with other computers.

continued

Service Name	Description	The Service Can Safely be Disabled or Set to Manual Startup If...
Computer Browser	Allows a machine to participate in browsing on a Microsoft Windows network	You don't want this machine (e.g., a workstation) to participate in browsing or to be capable of acting as a master, backup, or potential browser for its local subnet
Event Log	Causes a machine to record system, security, and application-related events in an event log (viewable with the Windows NT Event Viewer utility)	You don't want this machine to record any events. (Note: It is recommended that you leave this service running on a Windows NT Server.)
Messenger	Allows a machine to send and receive pop-up messages from local and remote applications on a Windows network	You don't need the machine to send or receive pop-up messages (including administrative alerts, which use this service). (Note: It is recommended that you leave this service running on a Windows NT Server.)
Net Logon	Provides authenticator - discovery and the pass-through authentication required for participation in a Windows NT domain	The machine is a stand-alone (nonnetworked) system or doesn't participate in a Windows NT domain.
Remote Access Autodial Manager	Manages automatic Dial-Up Connections to remote networks	You don't want Windows NT to automatically prompt you to use Dial-Up Networking phonebook entries to connect to remote networks.

continued

TABLE 4-5 **SERVICES IN THE SERVICES CONTROL PANEL** *(Continued)*

Service Name	Description	The Service Can Safely be Disabled or Set to Manual Startup If...
Schedule	Allows a machine to automatically execute tasks at predesignated times (this is configured using the AT command or the WinAT Resource Kit utility)	You don't run scheduled commands on this machine using the AT command/service.
Server	Allows a machine to share its file and printers with computers on a Microsoft network (i.e., allows the machine to act as an SMB (Server Message Block) server)	You don't want this machine to be accessible by others over the network and don't need to share any resources on it. (Note: Disabling this also prevents remote Registry access to this machine.)
Spooler	Allows a machine to print and also share and connect to printers on a network	The machine never needs to print to a local or network printer or share its printers on the network.
TCP/IP NetBIOS Helper	Provides NetBIOS-over-TCP/IP (NBT) functionality for Windows networking over the TCP/IP protocol	This is a stand alone machine or one that doesn't participate on a network using TCP/IP for file and print services. (Note: Stopping or disabling this service also stops the Computer Browser and Net Logon services.)

Fortunately, if you try to stop a service that has other dependent services, Windows NT will warn you before actually stopping the service. An example of this is shown in Figure 4-30.

Removing the OS/2 and POSIX Subsystems

Part of Windows NT's design is the ability to run nonnative Windows NT applications. In addition to its ability to run Win32, Win16, and MS-DOS–based applications, Windows NT also has OS/2 1.X (text-mode) and POSIX 1.0-compliant subsystems that allow these types of applications to run on a Windows NT computer. However, because most users will never need this functionality, these subsystems can be removed. Although these subsystems don't load into memory unless invoked by an application that uses them (and therefore aren't always stealing memory and CPU time), by removing them you will save disk space.

There are three methods you can use to remove these subsystems. The first, which is preferable, is to use the Windows NT Resource Kit's C2 Security Configuration Utility (`C2CONFIG.EXE`).

However, if you don't have the Resource Kit, you can also use one of the following two methods to accomplish the same thing:

Rename the files `OS2SS.EXE` and `PSXSS.EXE` in the `%SYSTEMROOT%\SYSTEM32` subdirectory to something different (e.g., `OS2SS.OLD` and `PSXSS.OLD`).

Use one of the Windows NT Registry editors to locate the following Registry subkey:

```
HKEY_LOCAL_MACHINE\SYSTEM\CurrentControlSet\Control\Session Manager\Subsystems
```

Once located, delete the "Posix" and "Os2" values. Any of these methods will effectively disable these subsystems.

For additional information on optimizing your Windows NT network configuration, see Chapter 9, "Optimizing Your NT Network."

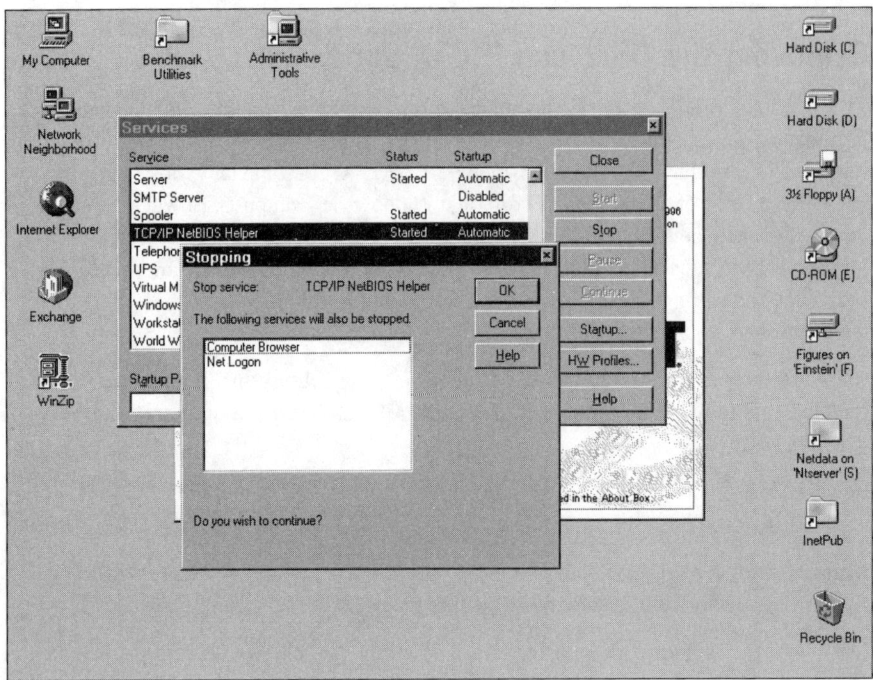

Figure 4-30: Warning when trying to stop or disable a service that has dependent services.

Limit the number of 16-bit applications run in separate memory spaces

Another method of minimizing memory usage is to minimize the number of 16-bit applications you run in a separate memory space. This feature (shown in Figure 4-31) provides greater stability and protection for a 16-bit application, but does so at the cost of additional memory. This is because each application run in this manner must receive an entire Virtual DOS Machine (VDM) devoted just to it, as well as a copy of all environment information; 16-bit applications running in a single shared VDM are able to share environment information and thus use memory more efficiently. Try to limit this method of running applications to those applications that are notoriously ill behaved or greedy for system resources.

For additional information on Virtual DOS Machines, see Chapter 6, "Optimizing Applications."

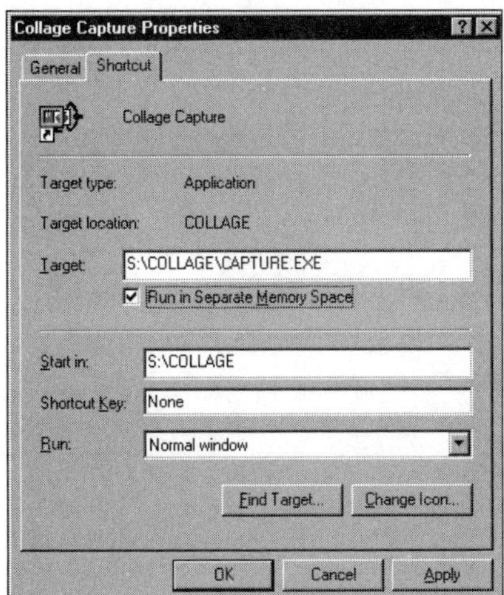

Figure 4-31: A shortcut's Properties dialog allows you to configure 16-bit applications to run in separate Virtual DOS Machines.

For more information on improving the performance of 16- and 32-bit applications, see Chapter 6, "Optimizing Applications."

Optimizing the paging file

The Windows NT paging file, created and managed in the System Control Panel's Performance tab, provides virtual (disk-based) memory that the system can use in additional to real RAM. The paging file is an important part of Windows NT's performance, because it is used even on systems with large amounts of RAM. Because of this, the performance of access to the paging file has an impact on the overall performance of your system. The paging file may be configured via the System Control Panel's Performance tab (this dialog is shown in Figure 4-32).

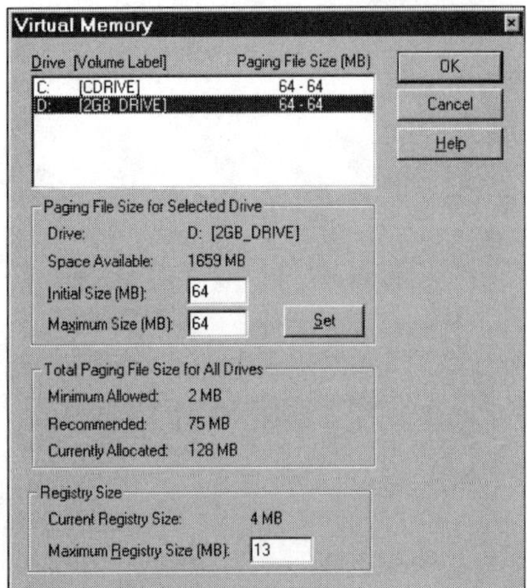

Figure 4-32: Configuring the Windows NT paging file.

You should take the follow steps to ensure that the paging file is being optimized on your system:

1. Make sure that your system's paging file is adequately sized. This means that you should always set the total size of the paging file (including all volumes across which it is spread) to at least the amount recommended by Windows NT in the paging file configuration dialog (in System Control Panel's Performance Tab).
2. Place the paging file on a volume that isn't heavily taxed with other uses and preferably on a partition other than that containing the operating system (i.e., not on the boot partition). The hard drive(s) housing the paging file should also be fast (i.e., have low disk access times and high data transfer rates). Wherever possible, spread the paging file across multiple physical disks, which can significantly enhance the speed of access to the file.
3. Last, but not least, set the paging file size on each member volume containing it to the same minimum and maximum size; that is, don't let Windows NT manage the upper size of the paging volume. By setting a single page file size that is adequate for your environment and that NT cannot resize, you prevent fragmentation of the paging file, which reduces performance. You also eliminate the disk and CPU overhead involved with constantly resizing a dynamic paging file that is set too small.

If you do set the minimum and maximum sizes for the paging file to the same size, make sure you don't set it too small; in other words, make sure that its size plus the amount of physical RAM on the system is adequate for the largest working set your system will incur. If you set it too small, your system could run out of virtual memory, which will result in unpredictable behavior and may even cause applications or system crashes.

The recommendation for spreading the paging file across multiple drives is for physical drives only, not multiple logical partitions on the same physical drive. Using multiple physical drives leverages the ability of each drive to transfer data concurrently (which is further enhanced by the strict use of SCSI-based hard drives rather than IDE-based hard drives, which do not operate concurrently). Spreading a Paging File between multiple logical volumes on the same physical disk will not improve performance and may even result in slower paging file performance.

The importance of a fast paging file cannot be underestimated; some heavily used systems dedicate a drive to the paging file (or even a paging file spread across a stripe set/RAID 0 volume). Finally, remember that no matter how fast a paging file is, it can never act as a substitute for physical RAM, which is always exponentially faster. If your system is experiencing heavy paging file usage on a regular basis, your first move should be to add additional RAM.

For more information and additional optimizations relating to the Windows NT paging file, see the "Disk Fragmentation and Optimization" section of Chapter 7, "Optimizing Disks."

Using disk striping for maximum speed

On a Windows NT Workstation computer, significant speed increases can be gained by using NT's disk striping (RAID 0) feature. This technology stripes data evenly across all multiple hard disks, which leverages the ability of NT's I/O system to issue concurrent reads to multiple drives. Note, however, that to reap the benefit of disk striping, your controller and disks must support asynchronous I/O, which essentially means the use of SCSI. IDE or EIDE (Enhanced IDE) drives are not recommended in striped configurations, because they are not capable of the device concurrence that makes this feature attractive. Finally, to fully maximize the speed of a stripe set, consider using a second SCSI controller – this will create a second SCSI channel, which can then share the disk I/O load with the first controller. Also, NT is capable of talking to both controllers simultaneously.

Figure 4-33 shows a sample Disk Administrator session configuring a stripe set (RAID 0) volume.

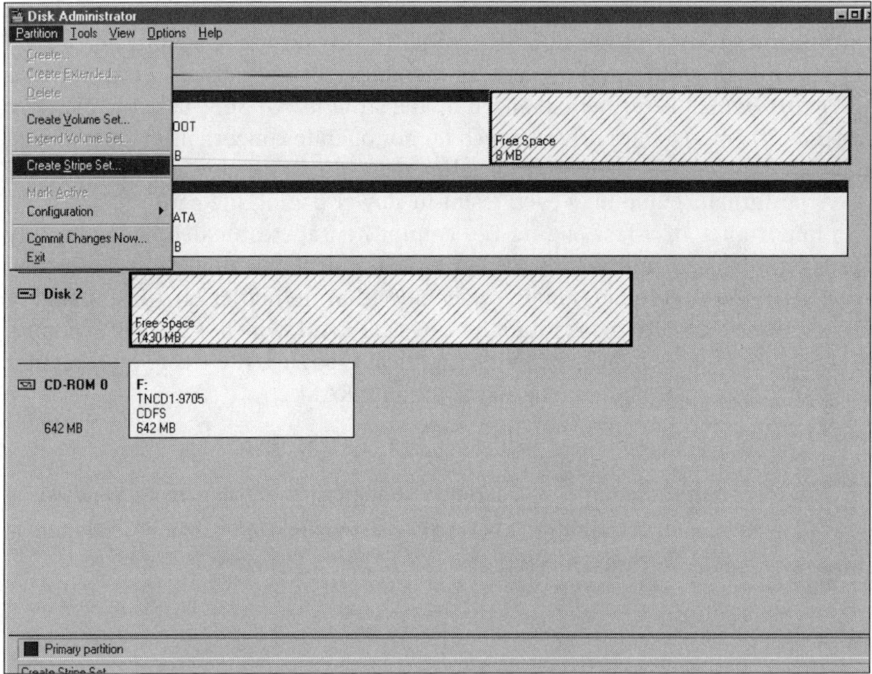

Figure 4-33: Configuring a stripe set/RAID 0 volume using Disk Administrator.

For more information on disk striping and other disk optimization topics, see the "Optimizing Multiple-Drive Configurations" section of Chapter 7, "Optimizing Disks."

The original disk defragmentation utility for Windows NT, Diskeeper by Executive Software is an excellent disk defragmentation tool that works with both FAT and NTFS volumes. Diskeeper also includes a handy disk fragmentation analysis tool, which informs you about the current level of file fragmentation on each of your disk volumes. Diskeeper Lite, the shareware version of Diskeeper, is included on the *Optimizing Windows NT* CD-ROM. To install the software, follow the directions outlined in Appendix A, "What's on the CD?," or point your Web browser to the index.html file on the *Optimizing Windows NT* CD-ROM and follow the links to install the software.

Speed Disk is another disk defragmentation utility for Windows NT and is included as part of Symantec's Norton Utilities for Windows NT. Speed Disk analyzes fragmentation and performs disk defragmentation. It also has a number of defragmentation, event logging, and thread priority tuning options. A live trial version of Speed Disk is included on the *Optimizing Windows NT* CD-ROM. To install the software, follow the directions outlined in Appendix A, "What's on the CD?," or point your Web browser to the index.html file on the *Optimizing Windows NT* CD-ROM and follow the links to install the software.

Defragmenting your hard disk

As with other operating systems, it is important that you keep your system's hard disks running at top speed by defragmenting them on a regular basis. Unfortunately, because NT does not include a defragmentation utility, you must purchase one. There are several NT disk defragmentation utilities on the market, including Executive Software's Diskeeper, Raxco's PerfectDisk NT, and Symantec's Speed Disk (part of the Norton Utilities for Windows NT). All of these products take advantage of the new disk defragmentation API included in Windows NT 4.0 and make no changes to the core kernel components (a trick that is required with 3.5x version of Windows NT; Executive Software's Diskeeper is the only product available for 3.5x versions of NT).

For more information on disk defragmentation and other disk optimization topics, see the "Disk Fragmentation and Optimization" section of Chapter 7, "Optimizing Disks."

Optimizing network access

Although the topic of optimizing network performance is a complex one (and one we address in its own section later in this book), there are a few basic things to consider doing to any networked Windows NT system from day one.

The place to start is to use the Protocols tab to be sure that no unnecessary protocols were installed. If there are any unnecessary protocols installed, remove them to increase the amount of available memory and improve network performance. In addition, be sure to select the fastest network protocol for your network configuration. If you are on a small network (200 machines or less) and do not require protocol routing between multiple network segments, NetBEUI is probably the fastest protocol for your configuration. However, for larger or routed networks involving a number of different physical networks tied together, you should consider using TCP/IP as your primary network protocol.

Because it doesn't offer any performance benefits over NetBEUI for non-routed networks or TCP/IP for routed networks, the IPX/SPX protocol is recommended only if your network's primary servers run Novell NetWare (which uses this as its native protocol for file and print services) rather than Windows NT. IPX/SPX uses broadcasts to advertise machine presence in a fashion similar to NetBEUI and can be particularly chatty when used on a Wide-Area Network (WAN) over routers (because of SAP packets that announce server resources).

In addition, for Windows NT computers with more than one type of client redirector installed (i.e., Microsoft Windows Network support and Client for NetWare), make sure that the Network Access Order in the Services tab of the Control Panel Services applet is set so that the most frequently used network is listed first. To access this configuration in Windows NT 3.5x, choose the Network button in the Network Control Panel; in NT 4.0, the dialog is accessible by choosing the Network Access Order button in the Network Control Panel's Services tab. The Windows NT 3.5x version of the Network Access Order dialog is shown in Figure 4-34, and the NT 4.0 version is shown in Figure 4-35.

The use of TCP/IP as the primary file and print service protocol on your network necessitates some form of NetBIOS-to-IP Address name resolution be in place so that network clients can resolve machine names. Unlike NetBEUI and IPX/SPX, TCP/IP doesn't rely solely on the use of broadcasts to announce and resolve machine names on the network (one of its performance advantages because of the decreased traffic). Instead, you need to use a method for resolving these names another way: this could be the use of an NT Server running as a WINS server, a DNS server, or the use of static Name-to-Address mappings in local or centralized `LMHOSTS` files.

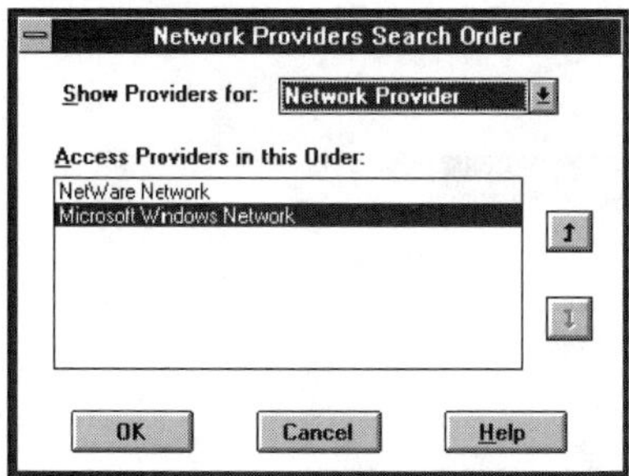

Figure 4-34: Adjusting the Network Access Order (client redirector priority) in the Network Control Panel in Windows NT 3.5x.

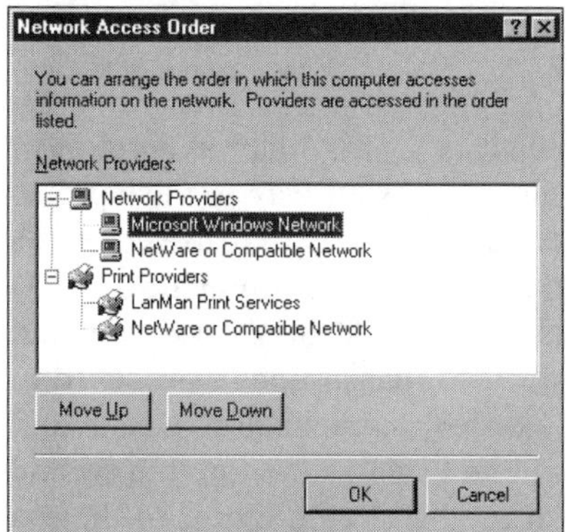

Figure 4-35: Adjusting the Network Access Order (client redirector priority) in the Network Control Panel in Windows NT 4.0.

The Network Access Order dialog in Windows NT 4.0 differentiates between file and print services and allows each to be prioritized separately; in Windows NT 3.5x, both services are lumped together and listed as a single service that may be moved up or down in the priority order.

An additional network-related optimization should be made via the Network Control Panel. Much as the Network Access Order determines which client redirector receives priority for the Workstation service, the Network Bindings order determines the priority order of protocols bound to each network adapter and service in the system. The configuration dialog for the Network Bindings order is accessible via the Bindings tab in NT 4.0 and via the Bindings button in NT 3.5x.

The Windows NT 3.5x version of the Network Bindings dialog is shown in Figure 4-36, and the NT 4.0 version is shown in Figure 4-37.

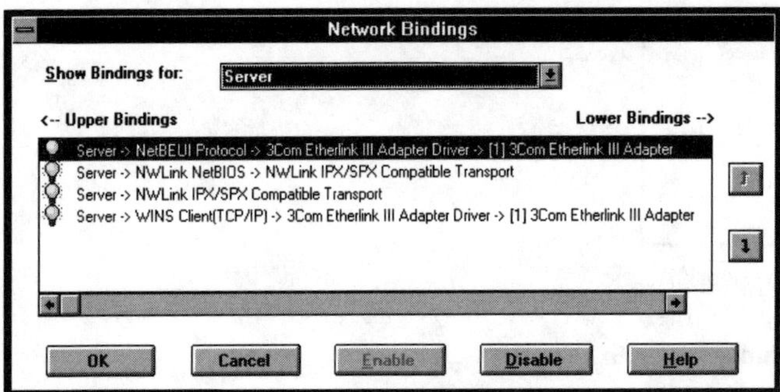

Figure 4-36: Adjusting the Network Bindings order in the Network Control Panel in Windows NT 3.5x.

Bindings may be viewed from different perspectives – by Adapter, Service, or Protocol. The Service-based view typically provides the easiest way to view protocol bindings and how they relate to the adapters and services that use them. To configure the bindings order for optimal operation in your environment, concentrate your attention on the order of the protocols listed under the Workstation and Server services. Specifically, set the bindings display so that protocols are listed in top-to-bottom order in the order of their priority on your system. This means that the most important protocol on the system should be listed at the top, the second most important should be next, and so on down the list. Being closer to the top means that Windows NT attempts to communicate using that adapter and service (in this case, the Workstation and Server services) via that protocol first before any others in the list. By placing the most frequently used protocol at the top of the list, you ensure that the time it takes NT to communicate using this protocol for a particular network operation is minimized.

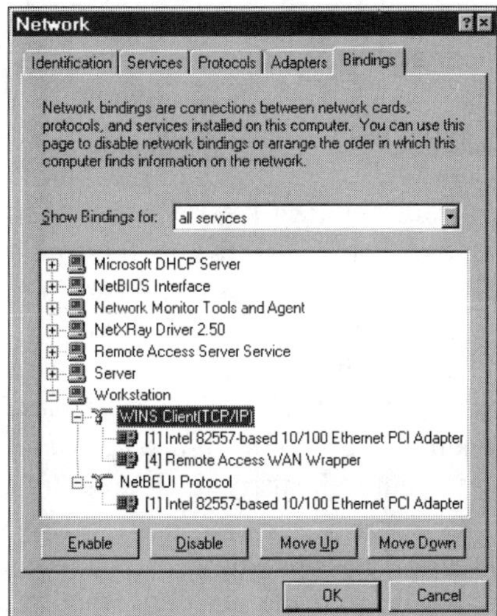

Figure 4-37: Adjusting the Network Bindings order in the Network Control Panel in Windows NT 4.0.

Recent information from Microsoft (which directly contradicts articles on the subject during the Windows NT 3.5x era) states that the Network Bindings order doesn't impact server service as it does the Workstation service, as the server service listens for client requests on all installed services in an equivalent fashion. However, we recommend that you optimize the Network Bindings order for each service, just in case Microsoft's wrong!

For more information on network optimization strategies, see Chapter 9, "Optimizing Your NT Network."

Keeping the Registry lean and mean

Ever notice how there's just nothing as fast as a fresh install of Windows NT? We are constantly amazed by the performance difference experienced when we perform a clean installation of Windows NT on a system that previously had an old, upgraded-a-million-times configuration. It just *blazes*. The increase in responsiveness that accompanies a fresh installation can make your computer feel like a brand-new machine. However, reinstalling NT from scratch is a fairly extreme proposition, because you will lose all your system and application configurations. Besides doing a clean installation, there are other things that can be done to gain some of these same benefits from your existing Windows NT installation.

One reason systems slow over time is that their Registry configuration database gets bigger. After all, each 32-bit Windows application, network service, and system driver you install adds additional Registry entries (which define how the application, service, or driver is configured), as well as files to the system. Over time, these additional Registry entries add up, and it's easy to have a Registry full of old, outdated entries for applications and drivers that no longer exist on the system. Because NT must load the Registry into memory as part of its operation, this means additional memory usage on the machine. In addition, the access to active, useful Registry keys is slowed because NT must search the entire Registry (including junk entries) to find a desired key or value.

Therefore, a small Registry is a happy (and fast) Registry, and your task is to keep the Registry as small as possible. The first thing to do is to avoid installing applications you're testing or evaluating on your primary production machines. Instead, create a separate installation of Windows NT designated for testing purposes, or install the application on a nonproduction machine. By doing so, you avoid clogging the system with files and Registry entries that you may not later need.

If you've already installed applications that you no longer have need of, you may be able to remove their files and Registry entries automatically using the Control Panel's Add/Remove Programs feature (shown in Figure 4-38).

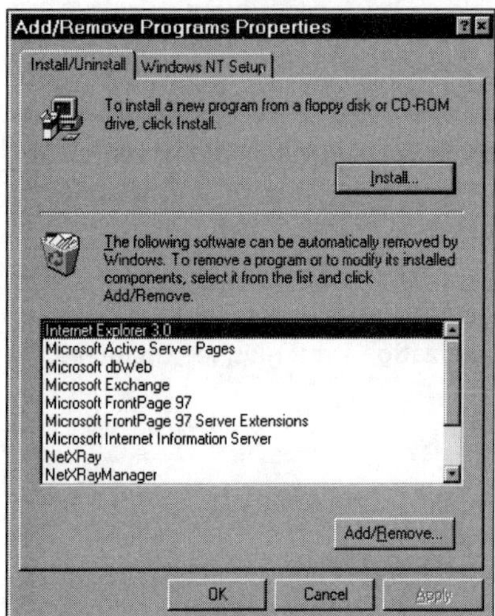

Figure 4-38: Use Control Panel's Add/Remove Programs feature to remove unwanted applications.

However, some programs either don't offer an uninstall option or don't cleanly remove themselves from the system even when their uninstal routine is invoked. For these unfriendly programs, there is little you can do but to obtain information directly from the software vendor as to which files and Registry entries are created by the applications, and whether or not they can be safely removed from the system without affecting NT or other applications. In the case of Registry entries, you can use one of the Windows NT Registry Editor utilities to manually remove the program's Registry subkeys if they remain after the program has been uninstalled. These keys are typically located as subkeys under the Registry subkey:

```
HKEY_LOCAL_MACHINE\SOFTWARE
```

Typically, the name of the subkey under this key is the name of the company that developed the software, but this is not always the case. Be careful when manually editing the Registry, because one software developer may have written more than one of the applications residing on your system (Microsoft is a good example of this) and these may all be configured under the subkey for the manufacturer in this location. In other words, check the branches underneath the subkey prior to deleting the entire key — if more than one application exists, you should delete only the subkey related to the application(s) you uninstalled.

Never delete or modify Registry keys for an application or service unless you have specific instructions from the manufacturer on doing so. Otherwise, you risk making invalid settings to the Registry that could render your system unstartable.

In addition, one or more of the user profiles (which are contained within the Registry) stored on the system may contain user-specific settings for the application under the following subkey:

```
HKEY_CURRENT_USER\SOFTWARE
```

The HKEY_CURRENT_USER key changes to point to the currently logged in user. Otherwise, you can access a user's profile in the Registry if you know their user SID — Security Identifier — which is used to denote the user's profile under the HKEY_USERS branch of the Registry in the format S-X-X-XX-XXXXXXXX-XXXXXXXXX-XXXXXXXXXX-XXXX, where the X's are 35 numbers representing the user's SID.

Wouldn't it be nice to have a utility that could automatically scan the Registry for old or invalid entries and remove them for you? Well, we have yet to find one that does exactly this. However, Microsoft produces an automated Registry cleanup utility called RegClean that you might want to check out. RegClean analyzes the Registry, looking for keys that contain erroneous values. After recording those entries into an undo file (UNDO.REG), it removes the entries from the Registry. Although it won't weed out keys from old, missing applications, it can help to maintain a healthy Registry free of garbage entries. As of this writing, Microsoft was writing an update to RegClean that should incorporate some additional features; hopefully, this will include a more aggressive "stale entry" key deletion feature. You may want to check Microsoft's Web site for an update to this utility (use the site's search function and search on "RegClean"). The Web site is located at:

```
http://www.microsoft.com/
```

There may also be other Registry locations created by the application; the only way to know for sure is to obtain information from the software developer who created the software and find out exactly what can be safely removed.

As always, remember that manually editing the Registry is a risky proposition and should be done with great care. You should also be certain to have a good backup of the system's data and the Registry (including a recently updated copy of the Emergency Repair Disk) prior to making any modifications.

Tuning foreground versus background application tasking

Another basic performance-related setting you should evaluate on any Windows NT computer running local user applications (i.e., Windows NT computers used as client workstations) is the foreground/background tasking option. This configuration, located in the System Control Panel's Performance tab, controls the process and thread priorities Windows NT automatically assigns to foreground versus background applications.

While both the 3.5x and 4.0 versions of Windows NT allow you to configure this setting, each shows the configuration dialog in a slightly different format. In Windows NT 3.5x, the choices for priorities of foreground versus background applications are made relative to one another, and there are three choices: "Best Foreground Application Response Time," "Foreground Application More Responsive than Background," and "Foreground and Background Applications Equally Responsive." However, in Windows NT 4.0, the wording (although not the functionality) was changed so that the setting indicates the amount of "boost" given to the foreground application (there are three settings configured via a sliding bar: None [left], Medium [center], and Maximum [right]). Table 4-6 shows the different settings in Windows NT 3.5x versus 4.0, what they mean, and how they relate to one another.

TABLE 4-6 FOREGROUND VERSUS BACKGROUND RESPONSE CONFIGURATION SETTINGS

Setting	Windows NT 3.5x Configuration for Setting	Windows NT 4.0 Configuration for Setting
Foreground and Background Applications Have Equal Performance	"Foreground and Background Applications Equally Responsive"	None (slide bar at left)
Foreground Application Has Slightly Higher Performance Than Background	"Foreground Application More Responsive than Background"	Medium (slide bar in center)
Maximum Performance for Foreground Application	"Best Foreground Application Response Time"	Maximum (slide bar at right)

The foreground/backup tasking configuration dialog for Windows NT 3.5x is shown in Figure 4-39, and for Windows NT 4.0 is shown in Figure 4-40.

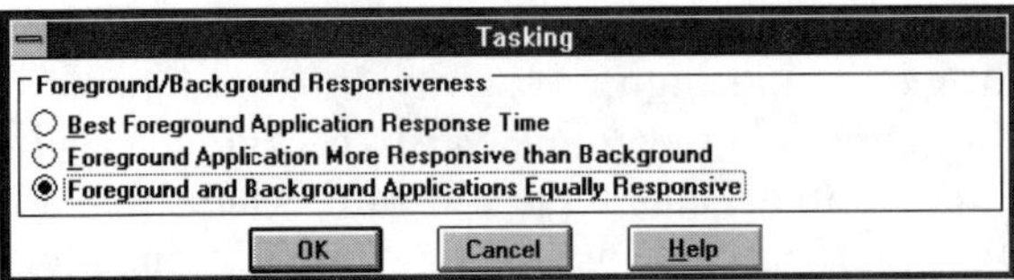

Figure 4-39: Changing foreground application boost (foreground versus background tasking priorities) in the System Control Panel's Tasking dialog (Windows NT 3.5x).

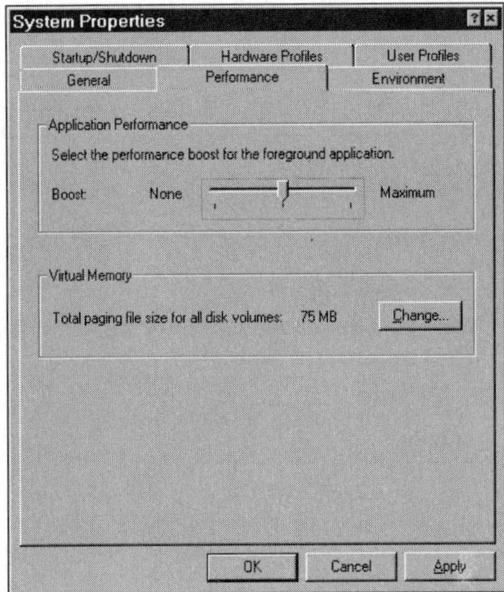

Figure 4-40: Changing foreground application boost (foreground versus background tasking priorities) in the System Control Panel's Performance tab (Windows NT 4.0).

Server Tuning Tips

In addition to the general tips provided above, there are also a few basic optimization tips directly related to machines acting as network servers. You should spend some time evaluating each of these settings to ensure that your server's basic performance settings are properly configured.

There are also other ways to boost the priorities of individual applications (processes) and even individual threads of execution within applications. To boost the process and thread priorities of applications that are already running, you can use the Process Viewer (PVIEWER.EXE) or Process Explode (PVIEW.EXE) utilities included with the Windows NT Resource Kit. You can also use the START command to start an application with a specific priority. The arguments for the command are /LOW, /NORMAL, /HIGH, and /REALTIME, followed by the command line for the program you're launching (e.g., START /HIGH C:\MYAPP\MYAPP.EXE). Note: Use of the /REALTIME switch is not recommended as it could cause your system to stop responding.

Configuring the server service

Apart from the basic network optimizations already discussed, there is also an NT Server-specific configuration option that directly relates to a server's network performance. You can configure the Windows NT Server service's allocation of memory to local applications versus network connections. The most important memory allocation controlled by this setting is that given to the system cache, which affects both disk and network performance. By configuring this allocation, you gain some control over how a server prioritizes its memory allocations and thread priorities for network services versus local applications and the size it allocates for the system cache.

Using the Network Control Panel's Service tab, highlight the Server service and click Properties. The dialog that appears is shown in Figure 4-41.

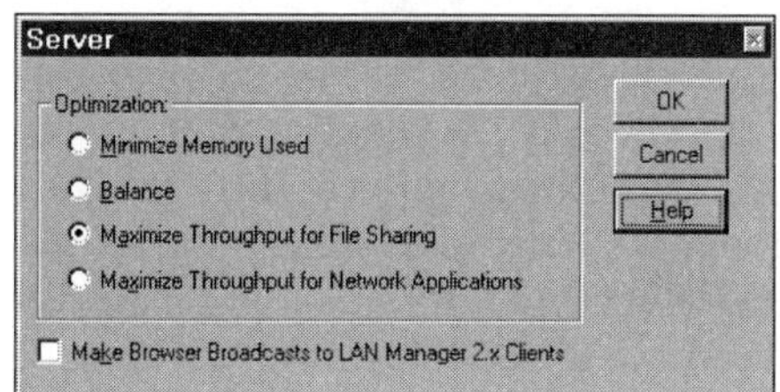

Figure 4-41: Configuring the Server service on a Windows NT Server.

The options shown in this dialog are described in Table 4-7.

Table 4-7 SERVER SERVICE CONFIGURATION SETTINGS

Setting	Description
Minimize Memory Used	This setting minimizes the amount of memory used for both the system cache and the working sets of applications (and is also the default setting for Windows NT Workstation computers). It is recommended that you never use this setting on a Windows NT Server because it inhibits network and disk performance.
Balance	This setting gives the system cache and working sets of applications equal memory allocation priority. Microsoft recommends this setting for servers servicing up to 64 simultaneous network connections, but we recommend that you only consider using this setting with nonfile servers such as application or communications servers.
Maximize Throughput for File Sharing	This setting gives the system cache a higher memory allocation priority than the working sets of applications and is the recommended setting for Windows NT Servers acting primarily as file and print servers.
Maximize Throughput for Network Applications	This setting gives the working sets of applications higher memory allocations priority than the system cache and is the best setting for application servers (with the exception of Microsoft SQL Server, which has its own internal memory management and is not optimal with this setting).

For Windows NT Servers, the default setting is Maximize for File Sharing. This is normally the best setting for a file server; however, if the server is also running many local applications (including client-server network applications) you may find that the Balance or Maximize Throughput for Network Applications setting provides the best overall performance for the server. The Balance option may also be the best setting to use if the server doesn't have a large amount of memory. If the server does no file and print serving and mainly runs client-server applications, the Maximize Throughput for Network Applications setting may be optimal. However, the only way to know for sure is to change the settings and benchmark, benchmark, benchmark.

Because Microsoft SQL Server performs its own memory management, the Maximize Throughput for Network Applications setting is not the best choice for servers running this application. Instead, consider the Balance or Maximize Throughput for File Sharing settings. The latter may be best because it provides the largest system cache value, which usually translates to the best disk and network performance.

In addition to its effect on the system cache size and memory access priority, this configuration setting also has a significant effect on the amount of memory allocated to key server resources such as InitWorkItems, MaxWorkItems, RawWorkItems, MaxPagedMemory, MaxNonPagedMem, ThreadCountAdd, BlockingThreads, MinFreeConnections, and MaxFreeConnections (all of which are located under the `HKEY_LOCAL_MACHINE\SYSTEM\CurrentControlSet\Services\LanManServer\Parameters` Registry subkey).

For more information on tuning the Server service configuration, and configuring this setting (via the Registry) for a Windows NT Workstation, see the "System Cache Tuning" section of Chapter 7, "Optimizing Disks." For more information on the values in the LanManServer parameters Registry subkey, see Chapter 9, "Optimizing Your NT Network."

Log off that server!

Another simple but important tip is to keep your servers logged out whenever possible. In addition to the possible security holes involved with leaving an administrative session locally logged in on an unattended Windows NT Server (unless the system has been locked via Task Manager or a protected screen saver), a locally logged in user on a server also burns a significant amount of CPU time. The reason for this is that NT must devote a certain percentage of CPU time to service a logged in user's session, which will naturally impact the CPU's availability (and therefore performance) for other applications and services running on the system.

In addition to the increased CPU usage, a logged in user session also impacts memory usage on the server, which may or may not have an impact on performance, depending on the amount of free memory on the system. In any event, you are always ensuring better performance by leaving your servers logged out as often as possible. There's also little reason to physically log in to a server because virtually all of Windows NT's administrative tools (including Server and User Manager, Performance Monitor, Registry Editor, and Event Viewer) are easily run from a remote administrative workstation.

One notable exception to the list of remote-capable administrative utilities is Disk Administrator, which must be run on a machine that is being configured.

OpenGL: A server no-no

There's no two ways about it: OpenGL screen savers are cool. They spin through space, they flip, they texture your favorite bitmaps in three-dimensional letters, and they run you though a 3D maze at headache-producing speeds. However, the CPU-intensive nature of these gems also means they have no place on your Windows NT server computers. On numerous occasions we've gone to a client's site to diagnose an unresponsive NT server, only to find 3D Pipes or some other OpenGL screen saver running on the server's screen. It isn't uncommon to see CPU utilization on systems running these kinds of screen savers at 75 percent to100 percent. To make matters worse, many of these same systems are logged in (usually under the Administrator account), which further exaggerates the slowdown of the system, never mind the security impacts of leaving a server logged in under the Administrator account!

The moral of this story is a simple one: never use OpenGL or other CPU-intensive screen savers on any computer acting as a server. Instead, use the Blank Screen screen saver – it may not be as exciting, but at least it won't bring your network's performance to its knees. Limit the use of these screen savers to NT systems in non-server (i.e., workstation) roles. However, even on these systems be aware of the potential interference that can occur with any background processes that may be running when the screen saver kicks in.

For more information on network optimization strategies, see Chapter 10, "Tuning NT Server Performance."

Before making any modifications to your system's configuration, we recommend that you first read Chapter 12, "Maintaining Your NT System," which provides important information on how to backup and protect your system's critical data and configuration information.

Summary

In this chapter, you started some basic Windows NT optimization concepts and techniques and were introduced to the software tools that we use throughout the book to monitor and improve performance. In the following chapters, we investigate the individual subsystems that comprise the Windows NT operating system and see what else can be done to improve performance.

Part II

Tuning the NT Subsystems

Chapter 5

Optimizing Memory and Processing

TWO OF THE COMPONENTS that greatly affect the performance of any computer operating system are the amount of physical memory (RAM) present and the speed of the system's processor(s). In fact, with Windows NT, memory is so vitally important that a deficiency easily impedes the performance of virtually every component of NT, including the application, hard drive(s), and network subsystems. Processor bottlenecks can be equally devastating because every process in the system is dependent upon the processor to carry out its threads of execution in a timely manner. When the processor becomes overloaded, the performance of the operating system and user applications are dragged to their knees as they wait for processor time.

Arming yourself with some of the techniques that allow you to identify situations where memory is a bottleneck ensures this situation doesn't occur. However, this isn't always easy; because memory shortages can show up as a symptom with many subsystems, it is often difficult to detect the true source of a performance bottleneck. In many cases, the symptoms may point to some other system component (such as the hard drive or system cache) rather than memory. Using the techniques in this chapter will enable you to properly identify whether memory is the problem and empower you to solve the problem quickly and efficiently, reducing the amount of time spent chasing performance "ghosts."

The Windows NT Memory Model

As part of its 32-bit design, Windows NT has processing, memory, and application management features that make it an extremely powerful and robust operating system.

Also as part of its design, NT contains two separate and distinct components that together comprise the core services of the NT operating system: the Windows NT *Kernel* and *Executive*. The Windows NT Kernel (also referred to as the *Microkernel*, the type of operating system architecture used by NT) is the set of core, essential services that perform a number of low-level operating system functions such as the scheduling of thread execution. The Kernel works in conjunction with the *Hardware Abstraction Layer* (HAL), which gains its name from the fact that it provides a middle layer (i.e., it *abstracts*) between Windows NT's core operating system services and the actual hardware in use on the system (e.g., Intel versus Alpha-based, uniprocessor versus multiprocessor, etc.).

There are three key components responsible for the processing and memory management features provided by Windows NT of the Windows NT operating system:

- Virtual Memory Manager (part of the Windows NT Executive): At the heart of Windows NT's memory management scheme is the *Virtual Memory Manager.* The Virtual Memory Manager maps virtual addresses in the process's address space to physical pages in the computer's memory. It hides the physical organization of memory from the process's threads to ensure that threads can access their own memory but not the memory of other processes.
- Process Manager (part of the Windows NT Executive): The *Process Manager* is the operating system component that creates and deletes processes (applications or modular parts of programs) and manages process and thread objects. It also provides a standard set of services for creating and using threads and processes in a particular subsystem environment.
- Thread Dispatcher (part of the Windows NT Kernel): Among the duties of the NT Kernel is the scheduling of execution for the threads of running processes on the system. Threads can also be executed in a uniform way across all available processors, which is part of NT's *Symmetric Multiprocessing* (SMP) architecture.

The Windows NT Architecture (for Windows NT version 4.0) is shown in Figure 5-1.

We touch upon each of these components and the roles they play in Windows NT system operation and performance throughout the rest of this chapter.

Virtual memory: Just like the real thing

As a 32-bit operating system, Windows NT is able to provide access to memory in a way that 16-bit operating systems simply cannot. NT uses a flat (linear) 4GB virtual memory model and address space that is available to all applications on the system. This 4GB-per-process availability is divided as follows: 2GB are visible to each process while it executes in *Kernel Mode* (where NT's low-level services execute, which runs in processor Ring 0), with the other 2GB being visible to the process while it executes in *User Mode* (the mode where user applications execute, which runs in the processor Ring 3).

However, unless you've got a really big budget for memory purchases, it's unlikely that you'll ever have a system with anywhere close to 4GB of memory. So, how does Windows NT provide this kind of memory to applications? The answer is *virtual memory.* One of the advantages of NT's 32-bit flat memory model is that it provides a logical view of system memory that is independent of the actual physical RAM installed on the machine.

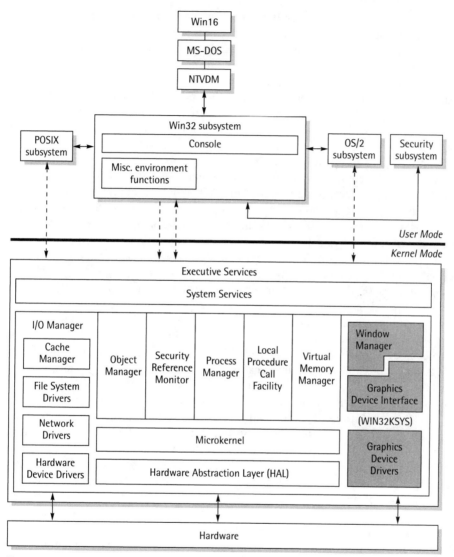

Figure 5-1: The Windows NT operating system architecture.

NT's 32-bit flat memory model is one of the reasons it is a portable operating system, because this memory architecture is compatible with the memory addressing of many processors, including Intel, DEC Alpha, MIPS, and PowerPC.

This logical view of memory is referred to as virtual memory because it isn't always composed of real, physical memory chips. However, Windows NT is capable of producing more memory for system functions and applications that are physically present in the machine through the Windows NT *paging file*, a topic we delve further into later. The nice thing about virtual memory is that applications treat it exactly as if it were real memory; it's up to the operating system to actually go out and do the legwork of identifying exactly where a particular referenced piece of memory is located. This creates enormous flexibility for both the operating system and user applications, and provides the ability for a Windows NT computer to extend beyond its physical memory (RAM) constraints.

With virtual memory, programs use virtual addresses rather than physical memory addresses to reference data in memory. Whenever an application attempts to access memory using a virtual address, the operating system invisibly goes out and performs a translation of the virtual memory address supplied to a real physical location, either in physical RAM or in virtual memory located on a system disk drive. The application is none the wiser and never knows what went on behind the scenes to resolve the memory reference.

In Windows NT, the system component responsible for managing the relationship between virtual memory and the physical organization of memory (on physical devices such as RAM and hard drives) is called the *Virtual Memory Manager.* The VMM is a component of the Windows NT Executive layer of services, which run in privileged or *Kernel* Mode. The VMM is Windows NT's memory management arm and makes it possible for applications to abstract physical memory addresses and use logical ones. To accomplish this, the VMM maintains data structures (such as lookup tables) that allow it to translate virtual memory addresses to physical ones.

The VMM maintains separate address translation tables for each process running on the system. These tables contain entries that determine how virtual addresses are translated to physical addresses, which essentially means the pages in RAM that the process may access (i.e., are within the process's address space). Although there are a few special cases where two or more processes will reference the same page of physical memory, generally speaking, each process on the system runs within a *private address space.* That is to say, the memory address space for each process is private to that process, meaning that each process's physical memory is generally protected from that of other processes. This memory protection feature is one reason for Windows NT's superior stability.

Paging Dr. Memory

Memory in Windows NT is divided into two separate types: *nonpaged* and *paged pool* memory. Nonpaged memory has the requirement that it must reside in actual physical memory (i.e., RAM) and cannot be written to or read from peripheral devices on the system (including hard drives, network adapters, and CD-ROM drives). Paged memory, on the other hand, is memory that the system can use to hold memory pages from peripheral devices such as hard disks, network adapters, and the like.

As you may have noticed, both of these terms incorporate the word *page*. A page is the basic unit of memory on a Windows NT system and varies depending on the hardware platform in use. For example, Intel-based systems all use a page size of 4096 bytes (4K), while RISC processors such as the Alpha and MIPS processors use a page size of 8192 bytes (8K). This is important to remember whenever a discussion of memory pages arises in relation to Windows NT, because ten pages of data on one system is not necessarily the same amount of information on another system.

Variable page sizes are used to optimize memory performance for a specific processor architecture. This variance in page sizes is also the reason why most (but not all) Performance Monitor counters refer to bytes rather than pages — bytes are absolute while pages are a relative reference.

PAGE FRAMES

Paged pool memory is further organized into structural divisions called *page frames*. When a memory page (either program code or data) is requested from a peripheral device, the Windows NT Virtual Memory Manager finds an available page frame in memory for the requested page. Once located, the memory manager then retrieves the page and processing continues. If there are no free page frames, the memory manager has to find one that it can reuse. When doing so, the memory manager will always try to use a page frame that is "stale"; that is, one that hasn't been used for a while. When the memory manager finds a page frame to reuse, it discards the page it contains (so long as the page hasn't been modified since it was put into RAM). If the page has been changed, it is first written back to the peripheral device before the new page is written into the frame to replace it.

PAGE FAULTS

While processing memory, if a request is made for a memory page that isn't currently within the set of pages visible to the process in RAM (known as the *working set* of the process), an event known as a *page fault* occurs. Page faults are resolved by the memory manager by locating the request page either elsewhere in RAM (known as a *soft page fault*) or from a peripheral device (e.g., virtual memory in the paging file located on a hard drive; this is known as a *hard page fault*).

Despite their harsh-sounding name, page faults are a fairly common event on any Windows NT computer. A page fault might occur because the requested page is currently in the working set of some other process, or it might have been removed from this process's working set by the memory manager in an attempt to free up memory for other processes on the system. Memory pages removed from a process's working set for the latter reason are referenced in a list of page frames called the *standby list*, which can be used to quickly locate and restore the page to the process's working set.

Although page faults are inevitable in Windows NT, excessive page faults (especially hard page faults, which must retrieve data from the hard drive) will slow performance. For soft page faults, the Virtual Memory Manager typically gives a temporary boost to the working set of the offending process in an effort to reduce the number of page faults. Excessive hard page faults, however, aren't quite so easy to fix. This situation typically occurs when the system is low on memory and the Windows NT memory manager is working furiously and continuously to balance the distribution of an insufficient amount of physical RAM between a number of different processes that are demanding it (a situation that involves a great deal of paging file activity, as memory pages are swapped back and forth from real physical RAM to disk). As a result, given the same total working set on the system, the only real solution to excessive hard page faults is adding more RAM.

Figure 5-2 depicts Windows NT's page fault handling mechanism.

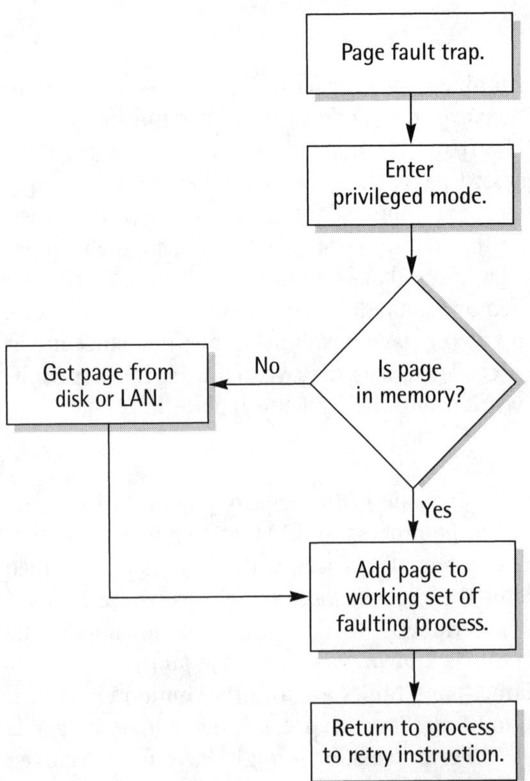

Figure 5-2: Windows NT's page fault handling mechanism.

The Segmented Memory Model: Rest in Peace

Windows NT's flat memory model is a far cry from the relatively primitive segmented memory model used in MS-DOS and Windows 3.x. With a segmented memory model, memory is broken into a number of 64K chunks called "segments." These segments create artificial boundaries that developers are forced to code around, an often difficult and tedious task. This limitation of the segmented memory model is the cause of many of the inherent limitations and problems with MS-DOS and Windows 3.x's designs, including the 64K resource heap limit that is imposed on the User, GDI, and Kernel heaps in Windows 3.x. Windows NT's 32-bit flat memory model eliminates this limitation and provides a 4GB linear memory model that is much easier to develop for.

DEMAND PAGING: I WANT MEMORY AND I WANT IT NOW!

Although virtual memory management is a cool concept, it is also important to note that a system's CPU can only access data directly when it resides in real physical memory. Because this is the only time that the data needs to be in physical memory, Windows NT's Virtual Memory Manager can take advantage of this fact to handle low memory situations efficiently. Specifically, the VMM moves less important information from physical memory to a system hard drive (in the Windows NT paging file) when the processor does not need the information. This process of moving information in memory back and forth between physical memory and hard drives is referred to as paging. By continually taking inventory of memory and performing memory "housekeeping," VMM optimizes the distribution of physical memory for all processes running on the system. In addition, the ability to use a disk-based paging file to house virtual memory increases the amount of total virtual memory that can be present on the system (because real physical RAM is still somewhat expensive as compared to disk-based storage).

Whenever a running process attempts to access information (program code or data) that is not in physical memory (e.g., because it was swapped to disk) it becomes VMM's responsibility to resolve the reference by reading or writing the data to or from a system hard drive. To accomplish this, VMM finds (or creates, if necessary) an available block of physical memory and copies the referenced data to that block so it can be accessed by the CPU. This concept of providing "memory on demand" is known as *demand paging*. The rules that Windows NT uses to calculate which memory pages are eligible for paging to disk are known as *demand paging algorithms*.

Although paging is a neat way of getting more memory than is physically installed on the computer, it can also become a significant performance bottleneck because hard drive access (measured in milliseconds, or thousandths of a second) is exponentially slower than physical RAM access (measured in nanoseconds, or billionths of a second). Therefore, it's important that to closely monitor disk-paging activity on your system and make sure that excessive paging activity isn't killing its performance. For more information on detecting memory and paging file bottlenecks, see the appropriate sections on both topics later in this chapter.

Memory Sharing: Play Nice Now

Occasionally two or more processes will require access to the same page of physical memory. As an example, two different applications might store a shared data structure in a section of memory so that both have access to it. The NT Virtual Memory Manager has special features to accommodate this type of memory sharing. In addition to adjusting the address translation tables for each process so that the required logical locations point to the same physical memory locations, it also uses special *synchronization objects* to manage and control the synchronization of this memory access between the two processes. The primary advantage to allowing processes to share memory is that sharing uses memory more efficiently: there is only one shared copy of the data being referenced rather than two separate ones.

Detecting Memory Bottlenecks

Now that we understand how Windows NT manages memory, we're ready to tackle the process of analyzing memory usage to ensure that memory isn't a system performance bottleneck.

The single largest enemy of the NT performance seeker is paging. Although a certain degree of paging file activity is expected on any Windows NT system, an excessive amount causes an immediate and noticeable slowdown in system performance because of the resultant disk activity (often referred to as *disk thrashing*). Excessive disk paging activity occurs when there is a shortage of physical RAM, a situation that forces the Virtual Memory Manager to utilize the paging file to produce additional memory. The importance of adequate physical memory for Windows NT can never be overstated: without it, you severely limit your computer's potential performance. In addition to the performance slowdown incurred by increased paging file usage, this situation also increases processor utilization as the Virtual Memory Manager is forced to handle this paging activity.

Finally, in addition to the increased paging file activity it incurs, an insufficient amount of physical memory also reduces the system cache size, which can adversely affect disk and network performance (because the system cache is used to cache both types of data). Together, these factors can quickly conspire to make your "hot rod" operating system feel like a 1928 U.S. Postal Service mail truck. It is our charge, therefore, to learn how to effectively use the available tools to analyze and identify memory bottlenecks when we suspect them.

In Chapter 4, we discussed a few quick and easy methods for examining your system's memory usage to determine if a memory shortage exists. Specifically, we discussed monitoring the system's *Committed Bytes*, either via Performance Monitor or in the Task Manager's Performance tab, to view the system's total virtual memory usage over time (including physical RAM and paging file usage). In addition, we discussed examining the Memory Object's *% Committed Bytes In Use* counter, which can reveal situations where the Committed Bytes figure is approaching or exceeding the *Commit Limit* – the memory limit at which NT must extend the paging file. The latter is a particularly bad situation, because constant resizing of the paging file is indicative of insufficient physical memory as well as the paging file and also fragments (and therefore degrades the performance of) the paging file as it is resized.

Examining available memory

Another useful Performance Monitor counter is the Memory object's *Available Bytes*. This figure tells us the total amount of free memory on the system. To ensure optimal performance, you want to be sure that this figure always indicates a healthy buffer zone even during peak system usage. As a general rule of thumb, you should never, under any circumstance, allow this figure to drop below 4MB on any system (including peak usage times). Dropping below 4MB is indicative of a low memory situation where excessive paging activity exists. In the ideal environment where paging file activity is minimal, this figure is 10MB or more.

Another method for examining the amount of available physical memory on the system is an easier and more direct one: simply start the Windows NT Task Manager and examine the *Available* figure in the Physical Memory (K) section of the Performance tab. The Available figure, along with the *Total* figure, lets us know the status of physical RAM on our system. The Available figure tells us the amount of free physical memory not currently allocated, and Total tells us the total physical memory available on the system. The Available figure should not be anywhere close to zero (preferably this should be 10MB or more, but absolutely no less than 4MB). If the Available figure is very low and remains this way on a regular basis, a memory bottleneck exists and additional memory should be added to the system.

Still another method for examining this statistic is the Windows NT Performance Monitor. For example, we can use Chart View to track the Memory object's Available Bytes counter for an instantaneous and historical representation over a short interval (for a longer view, use PerfMon's Log View instead and chart the logged data).

Figure 5-3 shows a Performance Monitor Chart session that reflects a desirable situation where the Committed Bytes figure isn't close to the Commit Limit (which also means that the % Committed Bytes In Use figure isn't close to 100%) and the Available Bytes figure is high (in this case, roughly 19MB). Making sure that you have plenty of memory "breathing room" is one of the most important things you can do to ensure optimal performance under Windows NT.

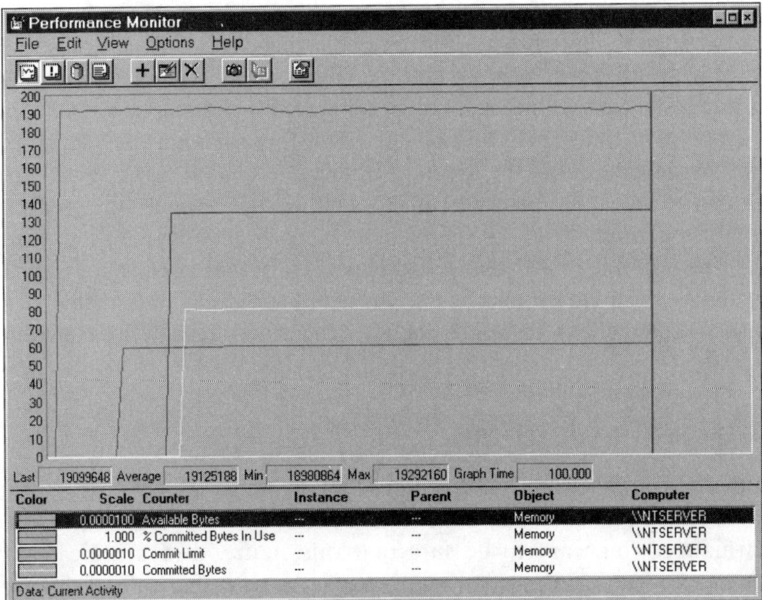

Figure 5-3: Observing Committed Bytes-related counters via Performance Monitor's Chart View.

Examining paging file activity

Although low memory situations certainly make the likelihood of excessive paging file activity much greater, it would be a lot better if we directly examined the paging file itself for usage and trends. Although paging activity is normally accompanied by tangible, physical signs that make it obvious to a person physically present at the computer in question (i.e., the continual grinding noises coming from the hard drive), this may not be the case if the machine is located remotely or disk activity isn't visible for some other reason. Also, not all excessive disk activity is paging-related, so it's a good idea to confirm that the cause of the disk activity is in fact the paging file and not some other source.

To quantify exactly how much paging file activity is occurring on the system, we can use any one of several methods, all of which will help determine if disk-paging activity is becoming excessive.

USING PAGES/SEC

The first method we can use is Performance Monitor to log values over time for the Memory object's *Pages/sec* counter. This counter tells us the number of pages the system has read from or written to the disk to resolve memory references to pages that were not in memory at the time the reference was made. After logging the value for a period of time (this should be long enough that a realistic profile of the system's workload is generated, preferably at least a day) you can view the data using Performance Monitor's Chart or Report View. In this case, either is usable because the figure we need to look at is the average of this counter over the logging period. Figure 5-4 shows a sample view of this data via Performance Monitor's Report View.

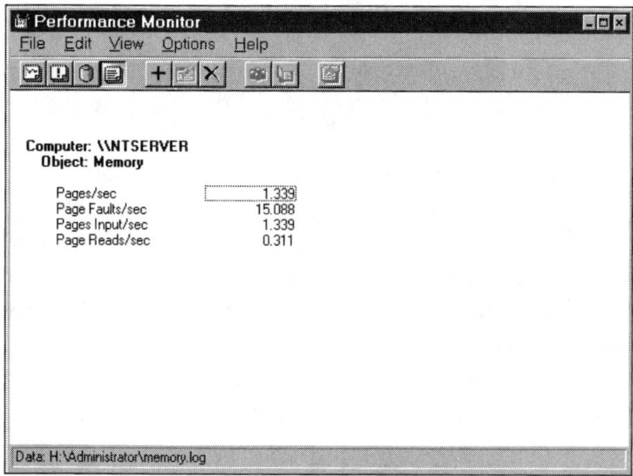

Figure 5-4: Viewing the Memory object's Pages/sec counter average value using logged data.

A general rule of thumb is that the average of this counter over time shouldn't be greater than five; if it is, then you probably have a memory bottleneck and need to add RAM. If the average is consistently equal to or greater than ten, your system's performance is severely affected and it's likely that there is a great deal of disk thrashing.

Don't automatically assume that a high Pages/sec number indicates the existence of a memory bottleneck. An application doing a number of disk read or write operations for data that is not currently in the system cache (such as a database application) can also produce high Pages/sec numbers. To determine if this is the case, also examine the Memory object's Available Bytes figure — if it isn't decreasing as Pages/sec is increasing, then the high Pages/sec figure may be the result of application-generated disk I/O and not a memory bottleneck.

USING AVE. DISK SEC/TRANSFER

Another method for detecting excessive paging is to combine and correlate the Memory Pages/sec counter with a physical disk counter, *Avg. Disk sec/Transfer*. This counter indicates the time, in seconds, of the average disk transfer (this is an average, not an instantaneous value). After using Performance Monitor to log data from the Memory and PhysicalDisk objects over a period of time (which should be long enough to accurately represent average system usage), determine the average value for the Memory Pages/sec counter and the figure for the PhysicalDisk object's Avg. Disk sec/Transfer counter. When selecting the instance for the Avg. Disk sec/Transfer counter, choose the instance representing the drive containing the paging file; if the paging file is spread across multiple physical drives, then use the _Total instance instead.

Next, multiply these two values together and examine the result. The figure generated is an approximation of the amount of disk time spent on paging file activity during the sampling period. As a general rule, this figure should not exceed 10 percent (0.1); if it does, this is probably indicative of excessive paging and a memory bottleneck. Figures of 20 percent or more indicate heavy disk thrashing and a major system performance problem.

Figure 5-5 shows a sample Performance Monitor Report View displaying the results of logged data for the Pages/sec and Avg. Disk sec/Transfer counters.

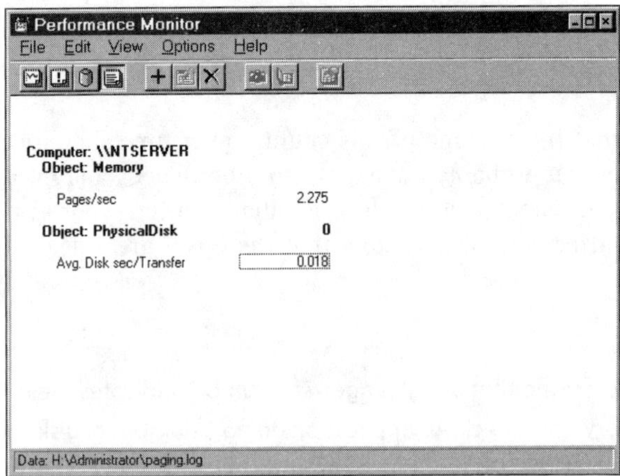

Figure 5-5: Viewing the Pages/sec and Avg. Disk sec/Transfer counters using Performance Monitor's Report View.

Multiplying the Pages/sec (2.275) by the Avg. Disk sec/Transfer (.018) gives a result of .04095. This indicates that approximately 4 percent of the disk's time was spent on paging activities during the sampling interval, which is within acceptable limits.

A final method you can employ to determine if excessive paging exists is to utilize three counters from the Performance Monitor's Memory object: Page Faults/sec, Pages Input/sec, and Page Reads/sec. These counters and their respective descriptions are given below:

- *Page Faults/sec*: This indicates the number of page faults that occur in the system's CPU. Page faults occur when a system process refers to a virtual memory page that is not currently within the working set in physical memory. If the requested page is on the standby list or a page currently shared with another process, a *soft page fault* is generated and the memory reference is resolved without physical disk access. However, if the referenced page is currently in the paging file, a *hard page* fault is generated and the data must be fetched from the disk.
- *Pages Input/sec*: The number of pages read from the disk to resolve memory references to pages that were not in memory at the time the reference was made. This counter also includes paging activity incurred by the system cache accessing file data for applications.
- *Page Reads/sec*: The number of times the disk was read to retrieve memory pages to resolve page fault (note that multiple pages can be read during a disk read operation).

Now that you've been introduced to these counters and their meanings, let's learn how to use them to determine if a memory bottleneck exists.

Figure 5-6 shows a sample Performance Monitor Chart View session charting a very busy (and overwhelmed) server.

This chart shows that we have a memory problem. One reason we know this is that more than half of our Page Faults/sec figure, which averages approximately 130 or so in the sample shown (note that the scale for this counter is 0.1 whereas the others are 1.0), are represented by Pages Input/sec; that is, hard page faults requiring disk access to resolve the memory reference. This means our disk is experiencing heavy paging activity. All other page faults can be considered to have been soft page faults, meaning that the referenced memory pages were found elsewhere in physical memory.

In this case, because the proportion of hard page faults to total page faults is extremely high, we know our system is spending far too much time on paging – a whopping 61.5 percent of the time to be exact! Although this is a somewhat extreme example, it serves to illustrate the pronounced effect of a memory shortage on disk paging activity and therefore system performance. Ideally, you don't want the percentage of hard page faults to total page faults to ever reach higher than five percent to ten percent; if the ratio goes higher, your system is spending too much time on paging activity and is in sore need of additional memory.

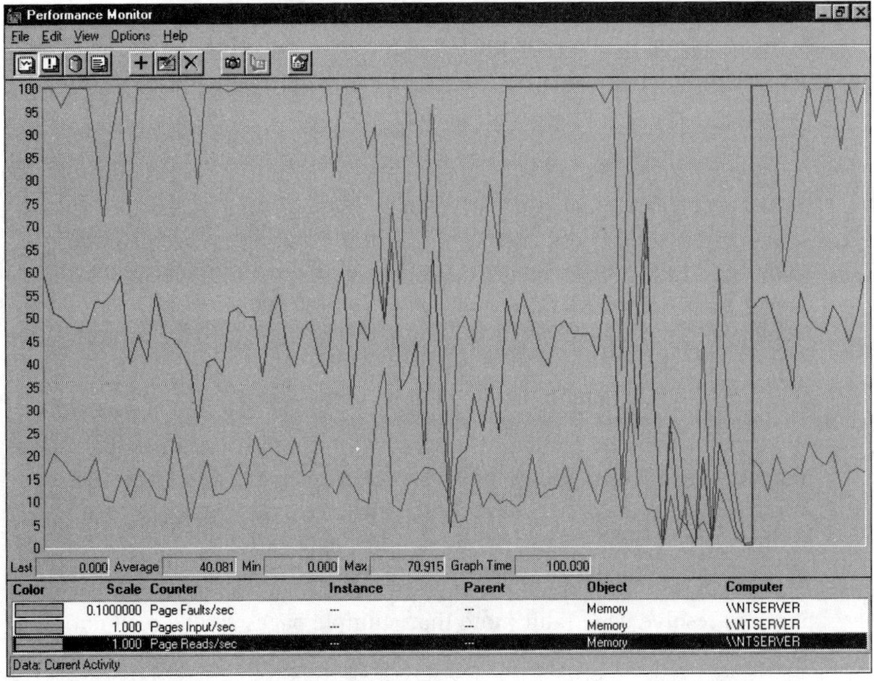

Figure 5-6: Charting key Memory object counters in Performance Monitor's Chart View.

Another interesting figure we can glean from our example is the number of pages being read by our disk per read operation. We determine this by dividing the Pages Input/sec figure by the Page Reads/sec figure. In this case, the Pages Input/sec figure averaged approximately 80 during the sampling session, whereas the Page Reads/sec figure averaged about half this, at 40. Dividing 80 by 40, we see that our disk was averaging about 2 pages per disk read during this session.

Included for you on the *Optimizing Windows NT* CD-ROM is a Performance Monitor workspace file, `PagingActivity.pmw`, that contains Page Faults/sec, Pages Input/sec, and Page Reads/sec counters. To use this file, simply locate and double-click it using the Windows NT Explorer (it is located in the `\PMWORKSPACE` folder), or point your Web browser to the location of the *Optimizing Windows NT* CD-ROM after inserting it in your CD-ROM drive (e.g., `D:\`). Then select the page for Performance Monitor Workspaces and follow the instructions.

Using Server Counters to Determine Memory Bottlenecks

In addition to telltale signs offered by disk and memory-related counters, some network-related counters can help to reveal memory bottlenecks as well. For example, the Performance Monitor's Server object contains two counters that can give an excellent indication of a memory problem: *Pool Nonpaged Failures* and *Pool Paged Failures.* Normally, both of these counters should be at zero, indicating that there have been no paged or nonpaged pool memory allocation failures (that is, sufficient memory of both types is available to the server service). If these figures indicate positive values, then a memory shortage on the machine is likely.

Detecting Paging File Bottlenecks

Although nothing will bring your system to its knees faster than a memory shortage (and the associated paging activity that inevitably accompanies it), there is another situation that can make this already bad situation even worse: a paging file bottleneck. A paging file bottleneck occurs when the system's paging file is inadequately sized for the paging activity the system experiences, creating an additional slowdown as the paging file is continually resized and expanded to accommodate the additional memory requirements.

Regardless of the level of paging activity your Windows NT computer experiences, you'll want to be very sure that your paging file is properly sized to prevent paging file bottlenecks. The default size that Windows NT uses for the system paging file is equal to the amount of physical memory present when Windows NT is installed, plus 11MB. Therefore, if you have 32MB of RAM present when you install Windows NT, the default paging file size will be 43MB. Although Windows NT can dynamically expand the maximum size of the paging file in an on-demand fashion, this is less than optimal if the paging file is continually being expanded past its default size. Instead, you should proactively set your paging file to a size that will accommodate the maximum size the paging file typically grows to. However, to do this you need some information in order to determine what the average paging file usage is and whether the current size represents a performance bottleneck on your system.

Fortunately, monitoring the paging file and discovering paging file bottlenecks is a fairly simple process. There are several methods that you can use.

Monitoring with Performance Monitor

One of the best ways to monitor the paging file to detect bottlenecks and observe its general behavior over time is via Performance Monitor. Performance Monitor includes an object specifically designed for this purpose: the Paging File object. This object contains two counters to ascertain paging file statistics:

- % *Usage*: This figure tells us the percentage of the paging file instance in question that is currently in use (or, for the _Total instance, the percentage of all paging files in use). It is an instantaneous value.
- % *Usage Peak*: This figure tells us the peak usage of the paging file during the given sampling period.

Included on the *Optimizing Windows NT* CD-ROM is a Performance Monitor workspace file, `PagefileUsage.pmw`, that contains *% Usage* and *% Usage Peak* counters. To use this file, simply locate and double-click it using the Windows NT Explorer (it is located in the `\PMWORKSPACE` folder), or point your Web browser to the location of the *Optimizing Windows NT* CD-ROM after inserting it in your CD-ROM drive (e.g., `D:\`). Then select the page for Performance Monitor Workspaces and follow the instructions.

A sample Performance Monitor session using Chart View to display paging file usage statistics is shown in Figure 5-7.

Although we can directly monitor "live" paging file statistics using Performance Monitor's Chart View, it is better to first log the Paging File object over time and then use the Chart or Report Views to examine this data afterwards (to do this, you need only log the Paging File object). Essentially, what you are looking for is a situation where either of these two counters approaches 100 percent at any given time (the % Usage Peak always represents the highest usage, whereas the % Usage counter represents the usage as compared to the paging file's maximum size at that time). Should this happen, Windows NT will expand the paging file (if the maximum size hasn't already been reached) to accommodate the additional memory requirement. This unnecessarily wastes disk and CPU time as the Virtual Memory Manager is forced to take additional time to expand the paging file from its current size. In addition, the file is likely to become fragmented if there is no space adjacent to the end of the current paging file on that volume, a situation that further degrades paging file performance.

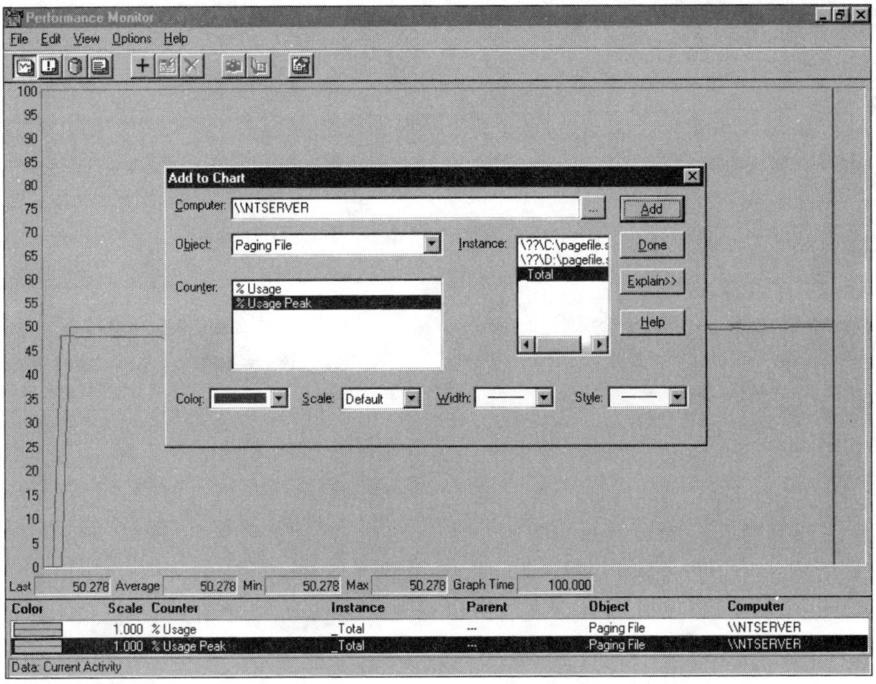

Figure 5-7: Monitoring paging file usage statistics with Performance Monitor.

If you find that the paging file's usage approaches 100 percent at any given time (anything over 85 percent), increase the file's size to better accommodate the memory usage on that system. This is done using the Change button located in the Virtual Memory section of the System Control Panel's Performance tab, shown in Figure 5-8.

Monitoring with Windows NT diagnostics

Another tool you can use to monitor the paging file is the Windows NT Diagnostics utility (WINMSD.EXE). In addition to its other useful statistics, NT Diagnostics contains a Memory section with statistics on the paging file. Similar to the Performance Monitor counters we observed earlier, this tab displays the usage and maximum usage of the paging file. However, in this case, these figures are shown as total kilobyte figures rather than as percentages. Also shown is the maximum paging file size, as well as a breakdown of the current, maximum, and peak sizes of each component volume housing the paging file.

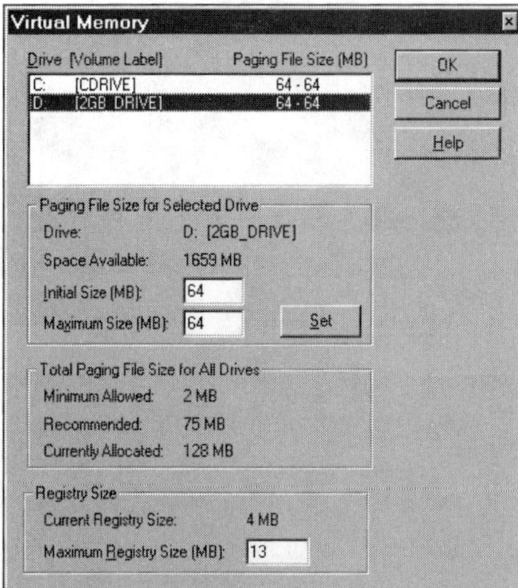

Figure 5-8: Using the change option of the System Control Panel's Performance tab to increase the size of the paging file.

The Memory tab of the Windows NT Diagnostics utility is shown in Figure 5-9.

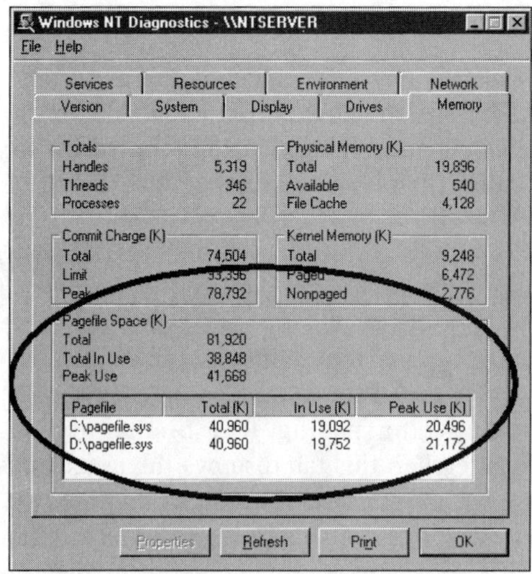

Figure 5-9: Observing the paging file's total size and usage via the Windows NT Diagnostics utility's Memory tab.

In addition to ensuring that the paging file is adequately sized, you should also optimize the paging file by spreading the paging file across multiple physical disks and setting the minimum and maximum size of the paging file on each physical drive to the same value to prevent it from becoming fragmented.

For more information on optimizing the paging file, see the "Optimizing the Pagefile" section of Chapter 7, "Optimizing Disks."

Detecting Processor Bottlenecks

Another important area of performance on any computer, regardless of its operating system or function, is related to the processor. The processor's performance and utilization levels are critical to system performance because, with relatively few exceptions, the system's processor (or processors) eventually handles everything that is done on your computer. Other than performance problems caused by memory shortages, one of the primary sources of bottlenecks on a Windows NT computer is the processor. The bottom line is that when the CPU is overloaded, everything grinds to a screeching halt.

Observing Processor Utilization with Task Manager and Performance Monitor

There are a number of resources available to determine if a processor bottleneck exists on a given system. The first and easiest method for observing a processor bottleneck is a new feature of the Windows NT 4.0 Task Manager that provides a graphical display of processor utilization. This display, found in Task Manager's Performance tab, is shown in Figure 5-10.

This screen shows both current CPU utilization as a bar graph (at left), and a recent history as a chart (at right). If multiple CPUs are present in the system, Task Manager displays separate graphs (distinguished by different colors) for each CPU.

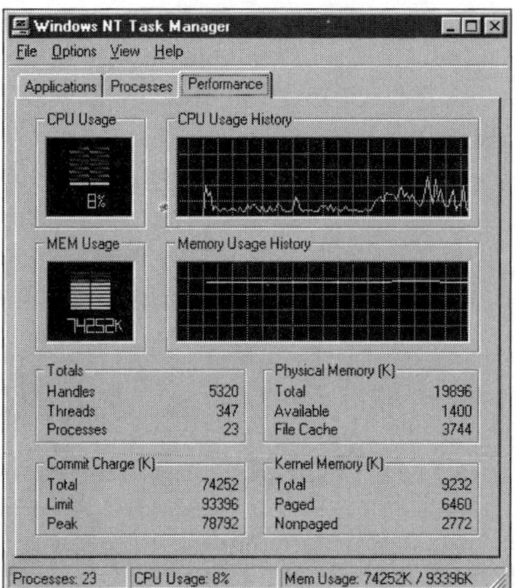

Figure 5-10: Observing processor utilization statistics via the Task Manager's Performance tab.

Although this is certainly a handy and neat little display, it isn't always adequate for extended processor monitoring and analysis. To get a better picture of what's going on with the processor, start Performance Monitor and monitor (or log) the key objects and counters that provide telltale information about CPU usage on the system.

Table 5-1 lists the objects and counters to monitor when you wish to analyze processor utilization and determine if a processor bottleneck exists.

By far, the most popular counters that are monitored in relation to processor utilization are the Processor object's % Processor Time and System object's % Total Processor Time counters. These provide, for single- and multi-CPU systems, respectively, a "quick and dirty" view of processor utilization. However, an equally important counter (included in Table 5-1) is the Processor Queue Length counter. This counter provides the number of instructions currently awaiting execution by the system processor(s). As a general rule of thumb, this figure should never rise above two; if it does, this is likely indicative of a processor bottleneck and may require the installation of a faster (or additional) CPU to alleviate the problem.

Included on the *Optimizing Windows NT* CD-ROM is `Processor Bottleneck.pmw`, a Performance Monitor workspace file that contains a variety of important processor-related performance counters. To use this file, simply locate and double-click it using the Windows NT Explorer (it is located in the `\PMWORKSPACE` folder), or point your Web browser to the location of the *Optimizing Windows NT* CD-ROM after inserting it in your CD-ROM drive (e.g., `D:\`). Then select the page for Performance Monitor Workspaces and follow the instructions given to load and use the file.

TABLE 5-1 PERFORMANCE MONITOR COUNTERS TO MONITOR PROCESSOR UTILIZATION AND BOTTLENECKS

Object Containing Counter	Counter Name	Description
Processor	% Processor Time	The percentage of a given time period that a processor is busy executing a non-Idle thread (each processor is assigned an Idle thread in the Idle process which consumes those unproductive processor cycles not used by any other threads). An instance of this counter is available for each processor present in the system.
Processor	Interrupts/sec	The number of device interrupts the processor is currently experiencing. A device interrupts the processor when it has completed a task or requires its attention. Normal thread execution is suspended when an interrupt occurs, and an interrupt may cause the processor to switch to another, higher priority thread. Note: System clock interrupts are a constant on every system and create a continual base level of interrupt activity regardless of other system activities.

continued

TABLE 5-1 PERFORMANCE MONITOR COUNTERS TO MONITOR PROCESSOR UTILIZATION AND BOTTLENECKS *(Continued)*

Object Containing Counter	Counter Name	Description
System	% Total Processor Time	The average percentage of time that all the processors on the system are busy executing non-Idle threads. This counter provides an instantaneous profile of the processor time for all installed processors, which is especially useful for multiprocessor systems.
System	Processor Queue Length	The instantaneous length of the processor queue; that is, the number of instructions awaiting execution by the processor in units of threads. This counter will always be zero unless you are also monitoring a thread counter. All processors use a single queue in which threads wait for execution. This length does not include the threads that are currently executing. An ongoing processor queue length of two or more is generally indicative of a processor bottleneck.
System	Context Switches /sec	The rate of switches from one thread to another. Thread context switches can occur either within an individual process or between separate processes. A thread switch may be caused either by one thread asking another for information or by a thread being preempted by another, higher priority thread becoming ready to run.
Process	% Processor Time (for a particular process instance)	Like the Processor object's counter of the same name, this counter provides an instantaneous value representing the amount of processor time consumed by an individual process on the system.

continued

Object Containing Counter	Counter Name	Description
Process	% Privileged Time (for a particular process instance)	The percentage of time that a particular process's threads spend executing code in NT's Privileged Mode (aka Kernel Mode or Ring 0). This statistic helps identify how much time a particular process spends executing in Privileged versus User Mode.
Process	% User Time (for a particular process instance)	The percentage of time that a particular process's threads spend executing code in NT's User Mode (aka Kernel Mode or Ring 0). This statistic helps identify how much time a particular process spends executing in User versus Privileged Mode.
Process	Priority Base (for a particular process instance)	For a given process (each process represents a separate instance of the counter), this counter gives the base priority assigned by the system to the particular process. Individual threads within a process can raise and lower their own base priority relative to the process's base priority, as can the operating system.
Thread	% Processor Time (for the Idle Instance)	Indicates the amount of time the processor spends on the Idle thread; that is, time spent not doing useful work due to system inactivity.
Thread	Priority Current	For a given thread within a process (each thread represents a separate instance of the counter), this counter gives the current priority assigned by the system to this process. A thread starts execution by default with the base priority of its parent process (that process which spawned it). Individual threads within a process can raise and lower their own base priority relative to the process's base priority, as can the operating system.

Figure 5-11 shows a sample Performance Monitor session charting these important processor-related counters.

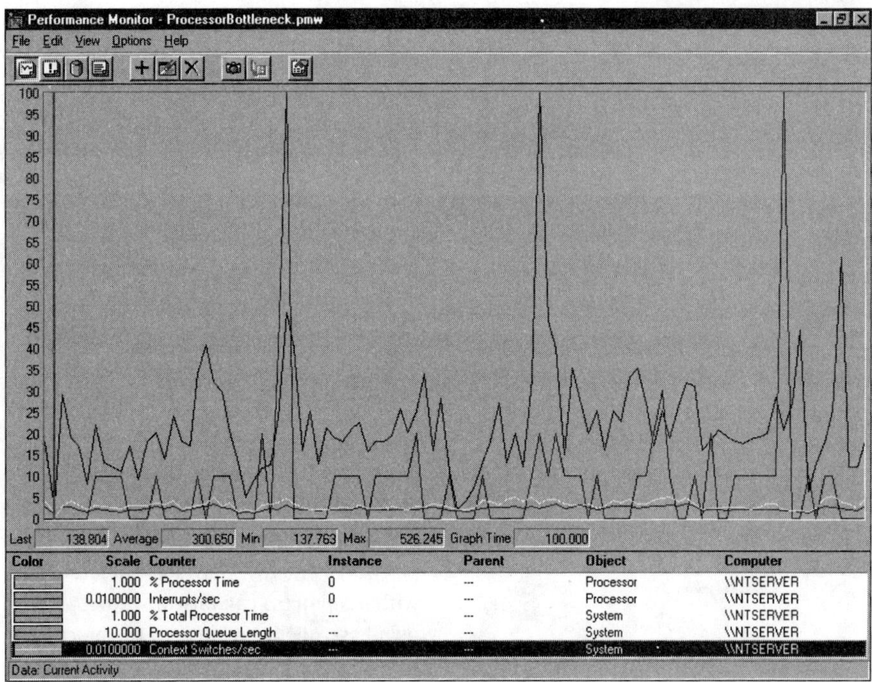

Figure 5-11: Observing processor-related counters in Performance Monitor to identify CPU bottlenecks.

Before you assume that a processor bottleneck exists (e.g., due to a consistently high CPU utilization or Processor Queue Length figure), first verify that no memory bottleneck exists on the system. If a memory bottleneck exists, the increased paging activity may be taxing the processor and masking what is essentially a memory-related bottleneck rather than a processor-related one (this is also true for suspected disk bottlenecks).

TotlProc, Part of the Windows NT Resource Kit

Occasionally, it is possible that Performance Monitor will show incorrect data for a given period of time. This happens when processor utilization is sampled rather than measured, which puts a minimal burden on processor resources. The problem can also occur when the sampling period, from which processor statistics are estimated, is so short that an insufficient amount of data was available to generate an accurate estimate. One way around this problem is to use the Windows NT Resource Kit's *TotlProc* utility. This program installs an extensible Performance Monitor counter designed to measure processor time more accurately than the other methods previously described. TotlProc is in the Performance Tools subfolder of the Resource Kit's main program folder and in the `\PERFTOOL\TOTLPROC` subdirectory of the Resource Kit's main installation folder. For more details on this utility, see the `RKTOOLS.HLP` file, which is part of the Resource Kit.

In addition to identifying the processor utilization level and queue length, the counters mentioned in Table 5.1 can also help to identify which process(es) is responsible for the majority of CPU usage, and the relative priority of each process and process thread. By monitoring what priority a process or thread is receiving from the system, you might be able to pinpoint a particular process that is receiving too low or too high a priority for its importance in your environment. These priorities may also be adjusted using any of several tools included with Windows NT and the NT Resource Kit.

For more information on identifying and adjusting process and thread priorities, see Chapter 6, "Optimizing Applications."

TotlProc is not compatible with other processor time counters found in other system tools and utilities. As a result, when TotlProc is running, the Performance Monitor and Task Manager utilities will always display processor time as 100%.

SMP: Processing in Parallel

One of Windows NT's more sophisticated and highly touted features is its capability to execute instructions across multiple processors in a uniform fashion, a feature referred to as *symmetric multiprocessing* (SMP). Although SMP is a key feature of Windows NT, many users misunderstand and often overestimate what effect the presence of multiple processors has on system performance. In fact, many users incorrectly assume that doubling the number of processors will automatically translate to a doubling of performance. Even if processor performance were the only component to overall system performance (which certainly isn't the case), this would be impossible because of several important mitigating factors that affect the real-world performance of multiprocessor machines. Let's look a little more closely at NT's brand of multiprocessing, and some of these real-world constraints that affect the performance potential of this technology.

While it is true that Windows NT may use multiple processors in a simultaneous fashion (thus the symmetric portion of the name), there are a few problems that inhibit the overall performance of SMP systems. One limiting factor is that most SMP systems share key system resources among all processors. For example, although multiple CPUs may exist, usually only one memory and disk subsystem is available for these CPUs. Because all CPUs are required to share these system resources, this sharing creates contention that in turn limits maximum performance. Of these shared resources, shared memory is by far the most limiting factor to multiprocessor system performance.

Windows NT Workstation computers are licensed for up to 2 processors, and Windows NT Server computers are licensed for up to 32 processors. Although the default shipping version of Windows NT Server currently only supports up to 4 processors out of the box, custom HALs are provided with systems containing more than 4 processors that allow NT to go beyond this figure; for example, there are a number of eight-way SMP servers available, and some with up to 16 or 32 processors.

The actual applications that are run on the system are another limiting factor to SMP performances. For Windows NT to fully exploit its multiprocessing capabilities, applications must be written in an efficient, multithreaded fashion that leverages the ability to concurrently process separate threads of execution. Unfortunately, many applications are not written this way, and processor resources on SMP systems are often underutilized as a result.

Although multiprocessor systems are certainly one of the primary beneficiaries of multithreaded applications, uniprocessor systems may also benefit from the use of multiple threads within applications. On these systems, the use of multiple threads allows the user to continue using a program while another thread is executing a different procedure.

These caveats and considerations aside, Windows NT's multiprocessing features are still impressive. The presence of multiple processors enables NT to execute multiple threads simultaneously, meaning that not only can different threads of different processes run concurrently on multiple processors, but even different threads from within the same process. This feat is made available by Windows NT's microkernel architecture and is handled at the lowest level by a Kernel component known as the *Thread Dispatcher*. The Thread Dispatcher schedules the execution of active threads across all available processors, to fully leverage the capabilities of the system hardware.

However, when purchasing or upgrading to a multiprocessor system, don't expect exponential leaps in performance. Instead, expect marked performance improvement only in situations where the majority of the applications running on the system use efficient multithreading. In addition, bigger improvements can be expected when systems are compute-bound by nature (applications are heavily processor-intensive rather than disk-intensive) and/or where processor performance has been a performance bottleneck. If you are not in one of these situations, you may be disappointed at the improvements you realize by upgrading to additional processors. This is why the process of ascertaining where performance bottlenecks lie is so important: among other things, it helps to prevent wasted hardware purchases!

When selecting multiprocessor systems that use external L2 or L3 caches, look for systems that provide separate caches per CPU rather than one L2/L3 cache that all processors must share. This provides higher system performance and is especially desirable for CPU-intensive systems such as high-end workstations or applications servers (e.g., a CAD or graphics machine, or an NT Server running Microsoft SQL Server).

Monitoring multiprocessor computer performance

Monitoring the performance of a multiprocessor system is similar, but not identical to that of a uniprocessor system. When examining the performance of a multiprocessor computer in Windows NT, there are certain counters that provide more accurate assessments of processor utilization and performance than others. As an example, take a particular process running on a multiprocessor system. If we use the Process object's % Processor Time counter that we used in our previous example on a multiprocessor system to monitor the process's CPU utilization, we may not receive accurate results. This is because although an individual process may use more than the equivalent of 100 percent of one processor (including all of its associated threads running on various processors), the total processor time reported can never go beyond 100 percent. Instead, if we add together the Thread object's % Processor Time counter for each thread instance within the process, we will have a more accurate reporting of the actual processor time consumed by the process.

Most of the other counters we used in our previous examples work equally well on a multiprocessor system. Remember that the Processor object's % Processor Time counter is a per-CPU counter and is only valid for the particular instance (CPU) it has been selected to monitor. To monitor the processor time for all processors as a single figure, use the System object's % Total Processor Time object instead.

The following is a summary of the counters you should use to monitor processor utilization and performance on multiprocessor systems:

- System: % Total Processor Time
- System: Processor Queue Length (this one queue is for all installed processors)
- Processor: % Processor Time (a separate instance is available for each installed CPU)
- Process: % Processor Time (each process is available as a separate instance; note that this is limited to 100 percent even if processor utilization is greater due to multiple threads on different processors)
- Thread: % Processor Time (each thread within a process is available as a separate instance)

Enabling multiprocessor support

Multiprocessor support in Windows NT requires only that a HAL be available for the system. When Windows NT is installed on a multiprocessor system that is supported by Microsoft (or by a third-party HAL available from the system vendor), Windows NT will autodetect the type of system in use and install the appropriate HAL (or you can manually inform NT of the appropriate HAL to use during the setup process).

However, if your Windows NT computer started life as a uniprocessor (single CPU) system, and later had an additional processor (or processors) added, you need to run a special utility to enable Windows NT to see the additional processors. Essentially, what is required is that Windows NT be informed of the appropriate new HAL to use for the new system configuration.

To make this process easier for endusers and administrators, Microsoft provides a uni-to-multiprocessor conversion utility as part of the Windows NT Resource Kit. This utility allows you to make a one-way change from a single- to multiprocessor system configuration. Although the nature of the utility sounds somewhat involved, running it is actually quite straightforward. The utility, UPTOMP.EXE, is located in the Resource Kit's main installation folder. After executing the program, you see a dialog similar to that shown in Figure 5-12.

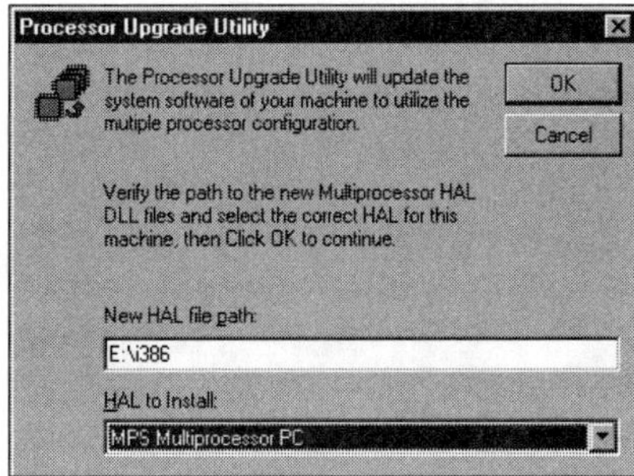

Figure 5-12: The uni-to-multiprocessor conversion utility.

It is recommended that you always make a full backup of the system as well as the Windows NT Registry prior to running the UPTOMP.EXE utility. In addition, be warned that this is a one-way trip — the utility does not allow you to later convert back to a uniprocessor configuration.

Summary

In this chapter, we examined Windows NT's memory and processing subsystems and the features and techniques NT uses to maximize the performance of each. In addition, we explored a variety of methods for monitoring memory and processor utilization levels, including physical memory (RAM), the Windows NT paging file, and the system processor(s). You can use these techniques to identify and resolve bottlenecks in each subsystem. In the next chapter, we discuss Windows NT's environment subsystems, how NT handles different types of applications, and what you can do to optimize the performance of the applications you run under NT.

Chapter 6

Optimizing Applications

IN CHAPTER 5, we discussed how Windows NT manages memory and processing, and some things that you can do to optimize these aspects of NT's performance. However, optimizing system performance isn't just about hardware. After all, using a computer is really about using *applications*. Without applications, our computers would be nothing more than an expensive (in some cases, really expensive!) hunk of metal and plastic. One of Windows NT's key design features is its capability to run many different types of applications, all within their own protected, 32-bit memory spaces. This design provides a great deal of flexibility and power, and also makes for an operating system that has a high level of stability. To get the most out of NT's application subsystems, you should first understand a little about their architecture and how they fit into NT's overall design. After that, we'll show you how to make some customizations and adjustments to these subsystems in order to get the most from them.

With this in mind, let's take at look at how Windows NT runs different types of applications, and what you can do to enhance the performance and efficiency of the applications you run on your system.

The Windows NT Environment Subsystems

As previously noted, one of Windows NT's key features is its capability to run many different types of applications. Specifically, Windows NT is capable of running all these types of applications:

- 32-bit Windows applications (via the Win32 subsystem)
- 16-bit MS-DOS applications (via a Virtual DOS Machine or VDM)
- 16-bit Windows applications (via the Windows-on-Windows32 or WOW subsystem, which runs within a Virtual DOS Machine)
- 16-bit OS/2 1.x character-mode applications (via the OS/2 subsystem)
- 32-bit POSIX.1 applications (via the POSIX subsystem)

Windows NT gains its multilinguistic capabilities from special operating system components called *environment subsystems.* Environment subsystems are essentially a set of separate system processes, each of which can fully emulate a particular operating system environment. By identifying an application's type and running it within the appropriate environment subsystem, Windows NT can make the application believe that it is actually running on its native operating system – the application has no idea it is actually running under Windows NT.

Although it might sound like lumping support for a bunch of different operating systems together makes NT into a bloated, overweight operating system, this really isn't the case (although NT's healthy memory requirements would surely cause some to disagree with me!). To prevent wasted memory and CPU resources, NT uses a method of application support that implements an on-demand loading of required environment subsystems. Apart from the Win32 subsystem (which is essential to NT's operation and always available), each of the optional subsystems is loaded only when you run an application that requires it. This "just in time" loading of subsystem support keeps the system's memory footprint leaner than if all support was automatically enabled when the system boots.

In addition, these environment subsystems are also efficient due to the fact that Windows NT uses them only for the highest-level functions available in each operating system. For lower-level device driver calls and the like, functions within each operating system are mapped to their corresponding functions in the Win32 subsystem (NT's primary subsystem). This means that there is less duplication of code, because all low-level program functions, regardless of the type of application that initiated it, are handled by the Win32 subsystem. This design also has the additional benefit of making new subsystems relatively easy to develop and existing ones easier to maintain.

Figure 6-1 provides a graphical representation of the Windows NT environment subsystem architecture.

Like just about everything else in Windows NT's operating system design, applications and their respective environment subsystem use a *client-server* methodology for their communication. The subsystem acts as the server and provides the high-level application programming interfaces (APIs) that the clients, or applications in this case, require. This communication is facilitated via message passing between the application clients, running in User Mode, and the server subsystems, running alongside the Windows NT Executive in Kernel Mode. This design provides superiority system stability because the applications are physically isolated from the environment subsystems in memory and therefore cannot corrupt their memory spaces. In addition, even if a particular subsystem were to crash, this would not affect other subsystems for a similar reason: each subsystem runs in its own protected memory space that is separate from other subsystems.

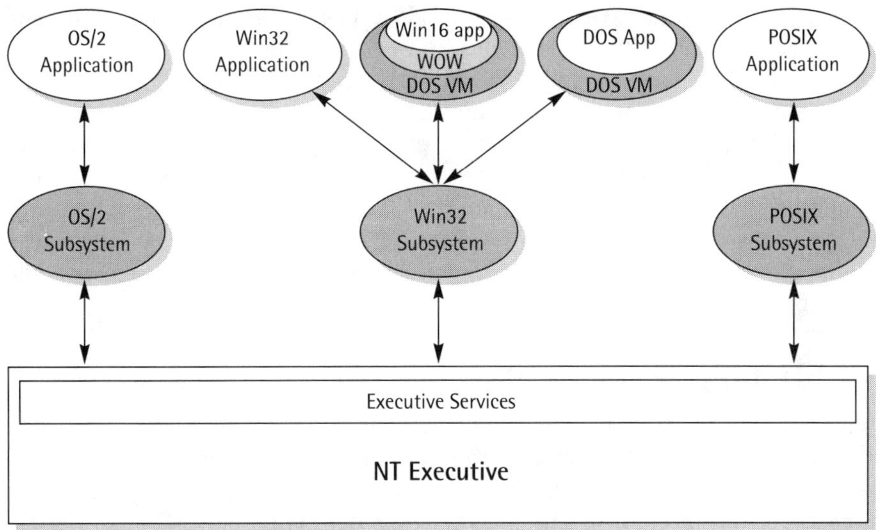

Figure 6-1: The Windows NT environment subsystem architecture.

In the following sections, we discuss each of the Windows NT environment subsystems in-depth and give you some tips on how to tune each for your needs.

Optimizing the NT Environment Subsystems

NT incorporates five application environment subsystems on the Intel x86 platform and four subsystems on RISC systems (OS/2 is not supported). These subsystems allow you to run applications across Windows versions and operating system platforms. The subsystems supported by NT are:

- DOS
- Win16 Over Win32 (WOW)
- OS/2 (not supported on RISC platforms)
- POSIX
- Win32

Figure 6-1 shows the close interrelationship between Win32 and the WOW and DOS VDM (Virtual DOS Machine) application environments. As the figure depicts, the POSIX and OS/2 subsystems (optional subsystems) communicate directly with NT's Executive services where the applications perform their I/O functions. The WOW and DOS application environments, on the other hand, use calls which NT translates in Win32 API calls; this allows for the relatively seamless operation of DOS and Win16 applications running under Windows NT.

Of the subsystems mentioned, DOS and Win16 use a VDM (Virtual DOS Machine). WOW (Win16 Over Win32) can be configured to use either a shared memory or separate memory space per VDM.

The Virtual DOS Machine (VDM)

To support 16-bit DOS-mode applications running under Windows NT, NT provides a special entity known as the Virtual DOS Machine (VDM). A Virtual DOS Machine is not really a subsystem at all, but rather a user mode program that makes it more like an "application environment." Optimizing the emulated DOS environment includes setting the environment size for the specific application for the amount of memory that the application actually requires. Every DOS application runs in a 1MB virtual machine. In addition to this conventional memory allocation, memory conforming to the various extended and expanded memory standards (e.g., XMS, EMS, and DPMI memory) can also be provided for applications that require them.

DOS programs can also still make use of .PIF files (Program Information Files) similar to those found in Windows 3.x, which are provided to maintain consistency and backwards compatibility. However, it's also true that the functionality of PIF files has been largely automated in Windows NT, so that PIF files are usually not necessary. If you ever do need to custom-configure the startup environment for a DOS application, you should do so using the shortcut properties for the DOS application rather than using a PIF file. Under NT 4.0, PIF files are only created when you make a shortcut for the DOS application. Windows 3.x PIF file options ignored under NT include:

- All video related parameters, except windowed or full-screen options
- All advanced memory options
- All advanced multitasking options
- All execution settings including Background and Exclusive

A DOS VDM can also run on a RISC-based machine (Alpha, and the now unsupported MIPS and PPC machines) that fully emulates an Intel 80486 processor.

DOS VDM applications can only run within a window on the desktop of a RISC-based machine; they cannot run full-screen. Only Intel x86-based machines can run DOS applications in full-screen mode.

You may either increase or decrease the amount of memory a DOS application requires (and therefore uses) by tweaking the various memory types allocated to the application, including conventional, XMS, EMS, DPMI, and environment memory space. Each of these memory types is adjustable by editing the properties of the shortcut used to launch the application, or can be configured using `CONFIG.NT` or a custom CONFIG file specifically defined for that application (which can be called anything you like; e.g., CONFIG.JOE, CONFIG.BIG, CONFIG.DOS, or whatever). `CONFIG.NT` and its companion, `AUTOEXEC.NT` (both of which are stored in the *%SYSTEMROOT%\SYSTEM32* folder) are not parsed during system boot, but are equivalent to the `CONFIG.SYS` and `AUTOEXEC.BAT` files used to set the default environment when DOS applications are started. To adjust the default environment size through the desktop on an NT 4.0 Server or Workstation, do the following:

1. Right-click on the application's shortcut.
2. Select Properties and then select the Memory tab (this screen is shown in Figure 6-2).
3. For each type of memory, enter a new value or select one from the drop-down lists. The default settings for most entries are "AUTO." This directs NT to reference the SHELL= line in CONFIG.NT if it is present. You can set the conventional, expanded, extended, DPMI, and initial environment size here, with values for extended, expanded, and DPMI going up to 16MB. It is very rare that you need to change the AUTO parameter for something else because all but the most stubborn DOS applications should be satisfied with the memory they receive automatically.

By default, all DOS applications running under Windows NT run in separate memory space (i.e., are launched in a separate VDM) and are therefore protected from each other in the event that one errant application should try to write to memory that it does not own.

USING CONFIG.NT TO SET THE ENVIRONMENT SIZE

The `CONFIG.NT` file may also be used to adjust the default environment size. This will affect all DOS applications that start from then on (that do not have an alternate `CONFIG.NT` file specified in their shortcut's properties — this is described below). You can change the DOS environment through the `CONFIG.NT` file by doing the following:

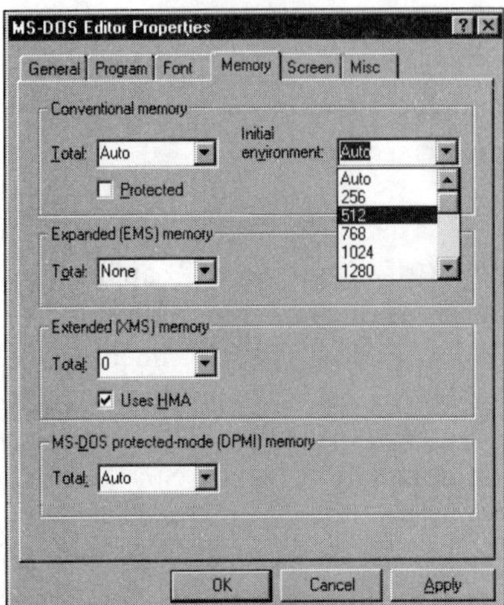

Figure 6-2: Configuring the memory allocations for an MS-DOS application.

- You can add or edit the `SHELL=` line in the `CONFIG.NT` file. For example, you could create an environment size double the default size of 256 bytes by using this line:

```
shell=%systemroot%\system32\command.com /e:512
```

- The maximum size for the environment is 32K. This is more than large enough for handling commands and long path statements.
- Also, you can specify a specific CONFIG.*XX* file (which can have a different extension than NT) for a specific application by right clicking on the shortcut and selecting the properties for it, choose the program tab, and select the Windows NT button (this dialog is shown in Figure 6-3).

MONITORING DOS APPLICATIONS

One problem with DOS applications running under Windows NT is that it can be very tricky to figure out which DOS application is using what resources on the system. This is because all DOS applications launched under Windows NT appear as a process called "NTVDM" rather than the actual name of the application being run (e.g., via the Windows NT Task Manager). As a result, it may be much easier to simply rename the NTVDM for each application (which does not require a reboot to perform) so that each application can be uniquely identified. Because DOS applications run in separate VDMs, the issue is not performance of the application threads, but of the ease with which you can monitor those threads from their parent processes.

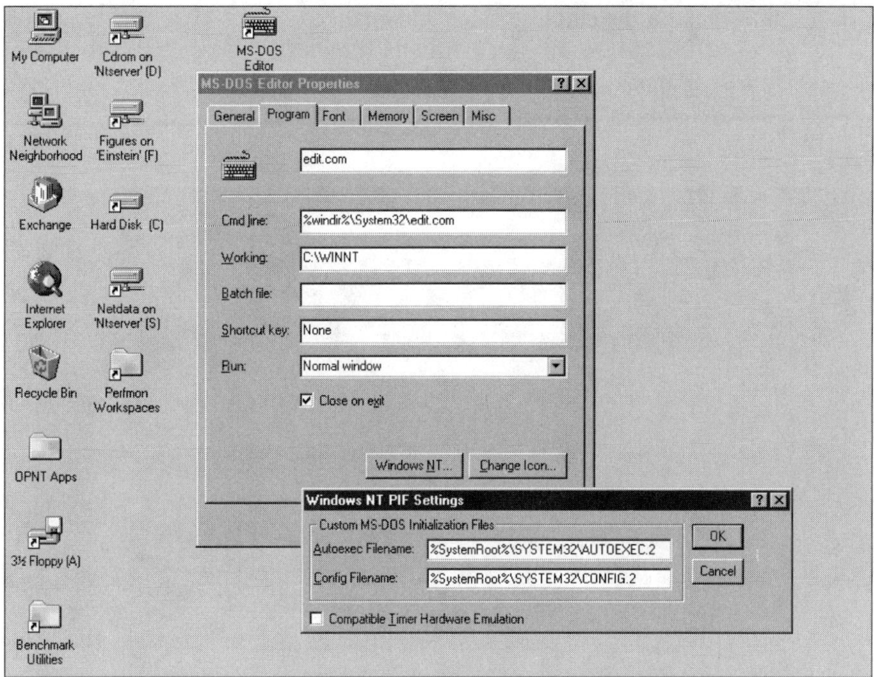

Figure 6-3: Setting a custom CONFIG.NT and AUTOEXEC.NT File for a DOS application.

STEPS TO CREATE A NEW PROCESS NAME FOR AN NTVDM

To create a new process name for an NTVD, follow these steps:

1. Start by copying the `NTVDM.EXE` in the *%SYSTEMROOT%* folder (e.g., `C:\WINNT\SYSTEM32`) to a different name while retaining the .EXE extension.
2. Start one of the Windows NT Registry Editors (`REGEDIT.EXE` or `REGEDT32.EXE`) to change the cmdline value for that NTVDM to point to the new name.
3. To make the registry changes, go to:

   `HKEY_LOCAL_MACHINE\System\CurrentControlSet\Control\WOW`

   Value Name: `cmdline`

   Default Value: `%SystemRoot%\system32\ntvdm.exe`

   Type: `REG_DWORD`

   Value Range: Whatever new filename to which you've copied `NTVDM.EXE`

4. Double-click on the cmdline value and change NTVDM.EXE to the name you copied NTVDM.EXE to in Step 1 (this is shown in Figure 6-4). When you start a DOS application, it will start in the VDM of the name you have chosen. This makes monitoring the processes easier.

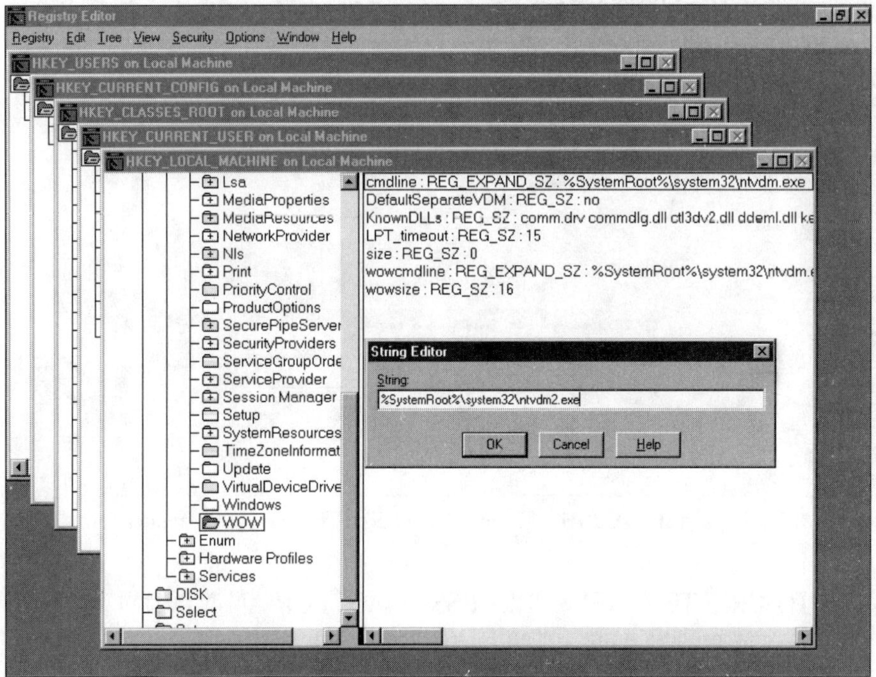

Figure 6-4: Using Registry Editor to edit the cmdline value to reference a custom NTVDM executable.

You don't have to restart the computer for the cmdline Registry change to take effect. The new name will apply to the new DOS application and will not affect DOS applications that were previously loaded. This functionality allows you to monitor each DOS application instance under a different process name, which simplifies auditing of the applications resource usage.

CUSTOMIZING NTVDM.EXE'S BEHAVIOR

As we've already seen, it's possible to change the name of the NTVDM.EXE for different DOS applications so that they may be easily monitored while running. In addition to referencing the name of the appropriate VDM executable (i.e., NTVDM.EXE or another custom filename you've copied it to), this value can also be modified with certain command line switches that modify its behavior.

The default value of the cmdline value is *%SystemRoot%\system32*\ntvdm.exe, and you can add any of these switches at the end of this string:

-a = Specifies a command to pass to the VDM

f = Specifies the directory of NTVDM.EXE

m = Hides the VDM console window

w = Specifies the WOW VDM

In addition to the custom command line switches, there is also another value that may be of use to you. This value is another listed under the WOW subkey containing the cmdline value and is described below:

Value Name:	size
Default Value:	0
Type:	REG_SZ
Value Range:	Amount of memory, in megabytes, from 0 to available memory.

This value sets the maximum possible size of the VDM created for DOS-based applications. This includes all conventional, extended, expanded, and DPMI memory required by the application. Although typically, you wouldn't need to modify this value, it may be useful if you wish to manually limit the maximum size for all DOS applications (or a particular one) to conserve memory on the system for other processes.

Tuning the WOW subsystem

WOW stands for "Win16 On Win32" and is closely related to the Virtual DOS Machine we discussed earlier (and even configured and referenced from the same Registry key). The WOW subsystem is an application environment that runs as a User Mode program (its filename is WOWEXEC.EXE), which also invokes, by default, a single Virtual DOS Machine (VDM) for all Win16 applications to run in. On RISC-based systems, WOW can be tweaked to alter the amount of memory that WOW is allowed to allocate for its VDM. On Intel- and RISC-based systems, it is also possible to edit the command line parameters issued to its executive. Win16 applications (by default) run in the same VDM using separate threads, which differs from the behavior of DOS applications, which run in separate VDMs.

The WOW application environment is designed to make the differences between 16-bit and 32-bit applications transparent. WOW, in combination with NT's native x86, emulation allows RISC systems (Alpha and the no longer supported MIPS and PPC) to run Win16 applications without having to purchase specialized hardware or use advanced emulation like Digital Equipment Corporation's FX!32 translator/emulation software.

THE ANATOMY OF A WIN16 VDM

Win16 VDMs include two system threads: the `WOWEXEC.EXE` thread, which starts Win16 applications, a heartbeat thread to emulate timer interrupts to the application, and one thread for each Win16 application running in the process. Figure 6-5 shows the components of the Win16 VDM.

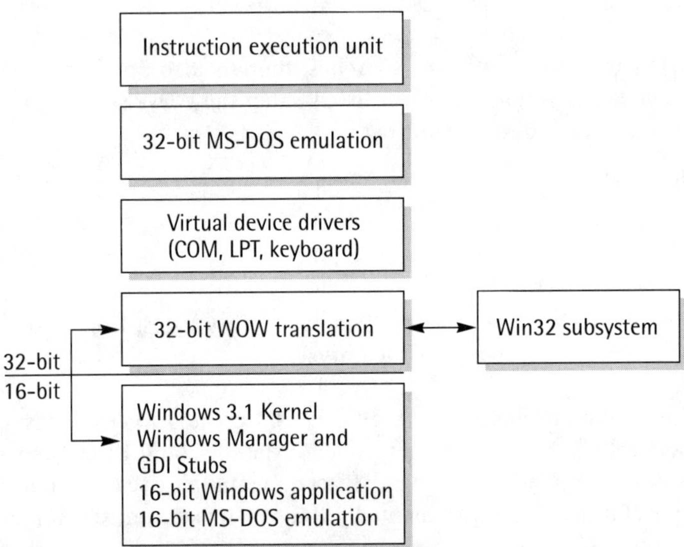

Figure 6-5: The Win32/WOW subsystem interaction used for 16-bit Windows applications.

IMPROVING WIN16 APPLICATION STARTUP SPEED

The WOW application environment is not started until the first time a Win16 application is invoked. One of the shortcomings of the design of the WOW application environment is that even after all Win16 applications are closed, WOW remains in memory until the system is either shut down or the user logs off.

Because the WOW application environment does not start until the first Win16 application is run, it takes longer for the first Win16 application to start than any subsequent Win16 applications. You can reduce the amount of time it takes the first Win16 application to start by preloading the WOW executive. To do this, you can add a shortcut to the file `WOWEXEC.EXE` to the Startup group, which will preload the WOW application environment whenever a user logs on. Placing the file in the per-machine (or common) Startup folder will cause this to happen for all users on the machine, whereas placing it in a per-user (or personal) Startup folder for a single user will cause this to happen for only that user. Placing the shortcut in a Startup group should only be done in situations where Win16 applications (which trigger the initialization of the WOW environment) are frequently run.

In addition, you can also free the memory and CPU resources used by WOW by manually terminating the `WOWEXEC.EXE` process after you're done running all Win16 applications during a session. To do this, run the Windows NT Task Manager by pressing Ctrl-Alt-Del or right-clicking an empty space on the Taskbar and choosing Task Manager. Next, choose the Processes tab and locate the instance of the `NTVDM.EXE` process containing `WOWEXEC.EXE` underneath it (no other applications should appear under this instance of `NTVDM.EXE`; if other applications appear, you need to close them first). This dialog is shown in Figure 6-6. Finally, select this instance of the `ntvdm.exe` process and click the End Process button. Windows NT will issue a warning about terminating processes this way, to which you must answer "Yes" to have the WOWEXEC process terminated. Doing this can actually free a significant amount of memory, because on most systems a basic VDM plus `WOWEXEC.EXE` session uses in the neighborhood of 3MB of system memory. If you won't be running any other Win16 applications in the near future, this memory can be far better used for the system or other applications.

If you've started and are still running one or more Win16 applications in their own separate memory spaces (discussed in the following section), then multiple instances of `NTVDM.EXE` and its child `WOWEXEC.EXE` process will appear in the Processes dialog. However, after exiting all Win16 applications, only one instance will remain.

Never terminate the `NTVDM.EXE` process (and its child `WOWEXEC.EXE` process) unless you are positive that no active applications are running within it (applications running within the WOW subsystem appear as indented entries along with `WOWEXEC.EXE` underneath `NTVDM.EXE` in the Processes tab).

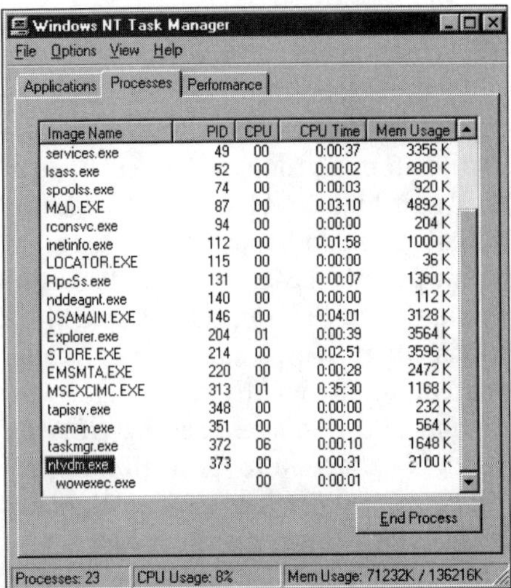

Figure 6-6: Terminating the WOWEXEC.EXE process after all Win16 applications have been closed to free system resources.

WOW's application environment is very similar in functionality to the 386 Enhanced mode of Windows 3.1. These similarities between WOW and 386 Enhanced mode include:

- Support for Virtual Memory
- Support for Object Linking and Embedding (OLE)
- Support for Dynamic Data Exchange (DDE)

These similarities create a seamless and compatible environment for 16-bit Windows applications to run in under Windows NT.

RUNNING WIN16 APPLICATIONS IN SEPARATE MEMORY SPACES

Like the MS-DOS VDM, the Win16 VDM is a multithreaded process wherein each of the Win16 applications is a different thread of execution. A Win16 VDM is multitasked just as with any other system process, allowing the shared WOW VDM to be run at the same time as threads of other system processes (Win32 processes). However, because of the design of the Win16 VDM, only one thread (representing one Win16 application) may run at a time from a single VDM/WOW process. While the thread for one Win16 application is being serviced, all others within the same shared WOW environment are blocked. Whenever this thread is preempted (for example, by a higher priority thread), the Thread Dispatcher (aka Thread Scheduler) will resume with the thread that was last preempted.

For better performance, memory isolation, and application protection, it is better to run all 16-bit Windows applications in separate VDMs, allowing simultaneous Win16 application threads to run concurrently. This is of particular benefit on multi-processor machines, which are capable of executing multiple threads simultaneously. The major advantage of doing so (as with many performance enhancement modifications) is memory usage. Because a separate VDM (and WOW environment) is launched for each Win16 application, more memory is used than would be the case if all Win16 applications were running in a single shared VDM/WOW process. Therefore, you should only enable this behavior if you have plenty of available RAM.

You can specify that a 16-bit application (including both Win16 as well as MS-DOS applications) run in its own memory space from the NT desktop by choosing the application icon, selecting properties, and selecting the checkbox for running the application in its own separate memory space, using the Start menu's Run command (which also offers this checkbox option), or via a special command line option from an NT command prompt session. In Figure 6-7, you can see that the checkbox for Run in Separate Memory Space has been chosen from the Start Menu's Run command so that the Win16 application being executed will be isolated from any other occurrence of Win16 applications.

You should always configure crash-prone applications or those requiring maximum stability to run in their own separate memory spaces. By not having to share memory address space (which can be violated by errant applications in the same shared environment) and system resource pools (memory heaps) with other Win16 applications, the application will be far less likely to experience problems.

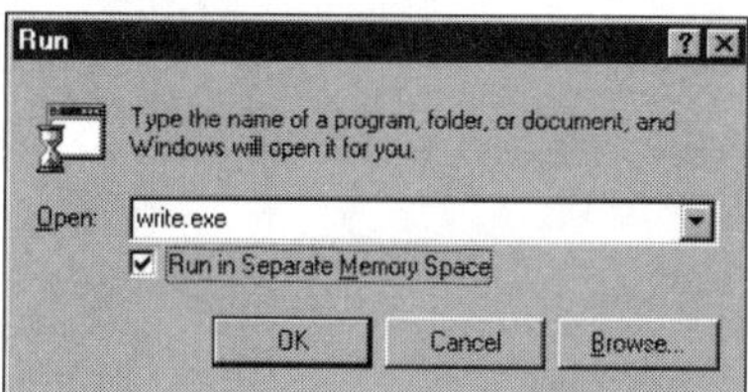

Figure 6-7: Configuring a Win16 application to run in its own separate memory space (and separate instances of NTVDM.EXE and WOWEXEC.EXE).

To issue the same command at the command line in an NT command prompt session, type:

start /separate *<Application Filename>*

Alternatively, you can enable the opposite behavior, using the command line to run a Win16 application in a shared memory space (where all Win16 applications use a shared pool of memory and instance of `NTVDM.EXE` and `WOWEXEC.EXE`) by typing:

start /shared *<Application Filename >*

Depending on your needs, you may want to create two separate shortcuts for each of your 16-bit applications: one that is configured to run in a separate memory space and another that is configured to run in a shared memory space.

One possible problem that running individual Win16 applications in their own separate memory spaces can introduce is that it can cause interoperability problems for applications that use shared memory to communicate. Although most applications that share data use methods such as Dynamic Data Exchange (DDE) and Object Linking and Embedding (OLE, also knows as Component Object Model or COM), which are supported by this feature, some older applications may use shared memory. If you encounter any such applications, you should configure them to run in a shared memory space rather than separate ones to solve the problem.

To create two shortcuts to a Win16 application, one of which invokes the Win16 application in shared memory, while another shortcut brings up the Win16 application in separate memory, do the following:

1. Create two shortcuts to the Win16 application and give each a name that indicates its shared/nonshared memory status (e.g., "Accounting (Shared)" and "Accounting (Separate)").
2. On the shortcut for the instance to be run in a separate memory space, right-click the shortcut, then choose Properties.
3. Choose the Shortcut tab, and select the Run in Separate Memory Space option.

CONFIGURING WOW TO USE SEPARATE MEMORY SPACES BY DEFAULT

Configuring Win16 applications on a case-by-case manner using shortcuts or command line entries is useful if only some of your applications should be run in separate memory spaces. However, if you're really sold on the idea of always running Win16 applications in their own separate memory spaces, have plenty of memory to enable this behavior, and don't have any applications using shared memory to communicate with one another (and thus won't work when configured this way), you'll be interested to know that it is possible to configure this as the default behavior for all Windows 16 applications. To enable this configuration, you need to use Registry Editor to locate and modify the following value in the Registry:

```
HKEY_LOCAL_MACHINE\SYSTEM\CurrentControlSet\Control\WOW
```

Value Name:	`DefaultSeparateVDM`
Default Value:	No
Type:	`REG_SZ`
Value Range:	Yes or No

As the name indicates, this value specifies whether or not each Win16 application runs with its own separate instance of `NTVDM.EXE` and `WOWEXEC.EXE` and in its own separate memory space. As we discussed earlier, this setting can improve performance and reduce problems with potentially troublesome 16-bit applications, but may also prevent applications using shared memory from interoperating correctly. Change the value from No to Yes to ensure that all future Win16 applications start with separate memory space enabled by default. This section of the Registry and value are shown in Figure 6-8.

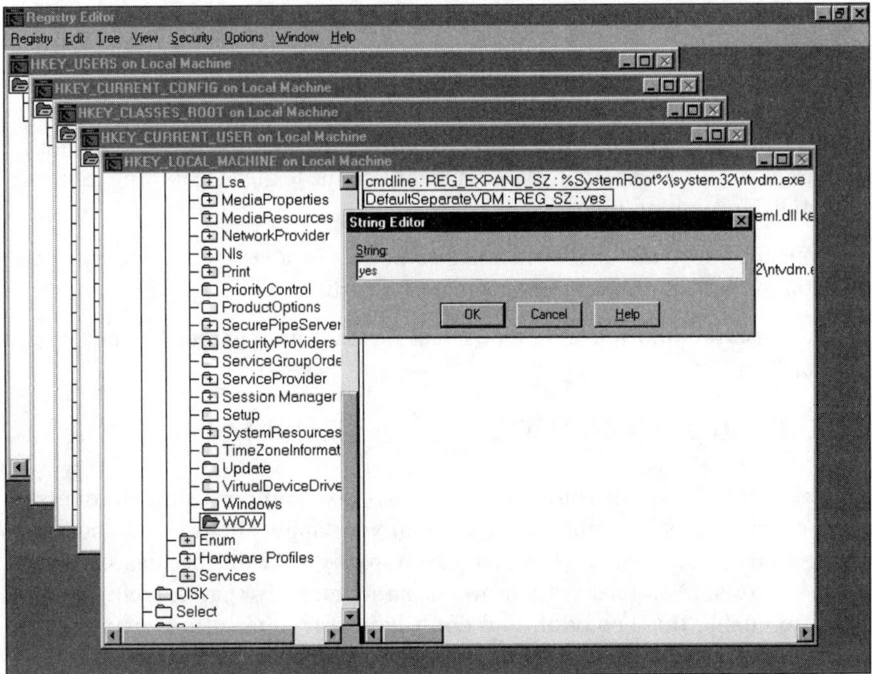

Figure 6-8: Configuring NT to run all Win16 applications in a separate VDM by default.

OTHER WOW-RELATED REGISTRY ENTRIES

In addition to the DefaultSeparateVDM value, the WOW application environment's configuration in the Registry has several other values that may be of interest to you. Some of these values are located in the previously discussed WOW subkey underneath the `SYSTEM` hive, while others are located in different subkey underneath the `SOFTWARE` hive. First lets look at some of the additional values contained in the aforementioned subkey:

```
HKEY_LOCAL_MACHINE\SYSTEM\CurrentControlSet\Control\WOW
```

To change settings such as the cmdline options and the size of the environment (for RISC machines), locate the following value under this subkey:

Value Name: `wowsize`

Default Value: For RISC systems depends on the amount of installed memory (for Intel x86-based systems, the value is ignored but will default to 16)

Type: `REG_SZ`

Value Range: 0–16MB

This setting is only used on RISC-based systems (Alpha and the now unsupported MIPS and PPC). Intel systems do not use this setting, and all memory is provided on these systems on an as-needed basis. This value sets the size of the WOW environment; the default is based on the system configuration. Also, due to overhead from the VDM itself, each megabyte that is specified actually uses 1.25MB, so a wowsize value of 4MB would actually be using 5MB even though applications only have access to 4MB.

Table 6-1 shows the recommended WOW VDM sizes for various systems according to the amount of installed memory. You can use this table as a guide when selecting the size of the wowsize value for your RISC-based NT machine:

TABLE 6-1 RECOMMENDED WOW VDM SIZES FOR RISC MACHINES BASED ON MEMORY SIZE

System Memory Configuration	WOW VDM Size
Less than 16MB system memory (small)	3MB
20–32MB system memory (medium)	6MB
32–63MB system memory (large),	8MB
64MB or more of system memory (very large)	16MB

Setting the wowsize value lower than 3MB will cause most applications to fail when you attempt to run them; therefore, always set this value to at least 3, but preferably higher.

It is highly unlikely that an NT RISC system user will need to be concerned about these values because it is very rare to find RISC-based computers with less than 32MB of memory. A large WOW value is only going to cause problems when memory resources are short and there is little or no memory available for other applications or NT itself. Also, remember that the WOW VDM will only be running when the Win16 application that invoked it has started.

Another value under this Registry subkey is similar to the cmdline value we saw in the section dealing with DOS VDMs. This value is listed below:

Value Name:	`wowcmdline`
Default Value:	`%SystemRoot%\system32\ntvdm.exe -a %SystemRoot%\system32\krnl386`
Type:	`REG_SZ`
Value Range:	Path to `NTVDM.EXE` plus any command line switches

This value is the same as cmdline described for DOS VDM but used only by WOW VDMs (those invoked by Win16 applications rather than DOS applications). The value specifies the command line parameters that are issued when a 16-bit Windows application is invoked. The supported switches are also the same as the cmdline value, which are repeated below for your convenience:

`-a` = Specifies a command to pass to the VDM

`-f` = Specifies the directory to find Ntvdm.exe

`-m` = Hides the VDM console window

`-w` = Specifies the WOW VDM

The second Registry location containing WOW-related entries can be found at:

```
HKEY_LOCAL_MACHINE\SOFTWARE\Microsoft\Windows NT\CurrentVersion\WOW
```

This Registry subkey references the Windows 3.x `SYSTEM.INI` file. The values contained in these keys are the same items that would be found under the corresponding `SYSTEM.INI` headings and are maintained for backward compatibility with Win16 applications.

OS/2 and POSIX: The optional subsystems

Windows NT's optional subsystems include POSIX and OS/2. We refer to POSIX and OS/2 as "optional" subsystems for two reasons: (1) they are not very popular or widely used; and (2) they are only loaded when they are needed by NT – they are not required for Windows NT to start. Although the latter is also technically true for DOS and Win16 applications that initiate an NT VDM, these types of applications are still used frequently enough that they aren't really an optional item in most environments. In addition, even if it were possible to do so, disabling VDM support in NT would almost surely cause major problems with your Windows NT installation at some point (and we therefore don't recommend trying it).

Unless you have some very esoteric needs in your environment, the POSIX and OS/2 subsystems are pretty much worthless and do nothing but take up valuable disk space on your system. In addition, OS/2 bound-mode applications (16-bit applications which were written to run under an MS-DOS environment as well as native OS/2) will often run equally well (if not better) in a NT VDM than they will within OS/2 subsystem, and without the additional memory usage incurred by initiating the OS/2 subsystem.

On RISC-based NT machines, the only type of OS/2 applications that can run are bound-mode applications, because these can be run in a DOS VDM through the included 80486 emulation in RISC versions of NT.

POSIX

NT includes a subsystem that is compliant with the IEEE standard of the Portable Operating System Interface (POSIX) version 1. The POSIX kernel interfaces (IEEE 1003.1) are designed to provide a very basic set of APIs (Application Programming Interfaces) in order to provide a development platform for applications that are portable across POSIX-compatible operating systems such as UNIX. Support for POSIX in NT is POSIX.1 only, which is not a full environment and which requires the Win32 API for such things as input/output (I/O). POSIX.2 is a far more robust subsystem, although it must be purchased separately from a third-party vendor. To date, Microsoft has made no public commitments for incorporating POSIX.2 functionality into NT, leaving this market completely to third-party developers.

Several years ago, Microsoft announced an intention to have an open system within the Windows Open Services Architecture (WOSA) incorporating XPG4 (aka X/Open). However, this has not come to pass, and there are no known plans for this in the immediate future.

REPLACING NT'S POSIX SUBSYSTEM WITH THIRD-PARTY TOOLS

POSIX.1, the version found in NT, is generally useless for most modern computing needs. If you are a user or developer and want to get any serious development work done, it is suggested that you remove NT's default POSIX subsystem and either replace it with POSIX.2 from a third party company or use a UNIX work-alike such as the GNU Win32 tools, which use the Win32 API rather than the POSIX subsystem. These types of products offer significantly enhanced functionality over that offered in NT's default POSIX subsystem. For example, the POSIX.2 Toolkit from Software Systems Inc. includes such features as true UNIX shells and the capability to run X Windows on Windows NT.

OpenNT from Software Systems Inc. and GNU Win32 from Cygnus

These packages add functionality to the somewhat "broken" and limited POSIX.1 built into NT with these features:

- POSIX.1, POSIX.2, and ANSI C interfaces
- Available for Intel and Alpha
- BSD sockets
- SVID shared memory and semaphores
- X11R5 clients, libraries, and headers
- OPENNTIF (OSF/Motif 1.2.4 window manager and development libraries)
- Color curses
- Full shell job control
- Tape device support
- UNIX development tools: make, rcs, yacc, lex, cc, c89, nm, ar, strip, and more

The GNU Win32 tools are ports of the popular GNU development tools to Windows NT/95 for the x86 and PowerPC processors. Applications built with these tools have access to the Microsoft Win32 API as well as the Cygwin32 API which provides additional UNIX-like functionality including UNIX sockets, process control with a working fork, and select.

With either of these tools installed, it is possible to have enhanced UNIX functionality, including the capability of:

- Writing Win32 console or GUI applications that make use of the standard Microsoft Win32 API and/or the Cygwin32 API
- Easily configuring and building many GNU tools from source (including rebuilding the GNU Win32 development tools themselves under x86 NT)
- Porting many other significant UNIX programs to Windows NT/95 without making significant changes to the source code
- Having a fairly full UNIX-like environment to work in, with access to many of the common UNIX utilities (from both the bash shell and `command.com`)

For more information and to keep up to date with OpenNT software, check out this URL on the Internet:

```
http://www.softway.com/OpenNT/home.htm
```

For more information on the state of the GNU Win32 project, go to:

```
http://www.cygnus.com/misc/gnu-win32/
```

OS/2

The other subsystem in NT, which is of even less value than POSIX, is the OS/2 subsystem. If you're thinking that OS/2 support means the ability to support OS/2 2.Xx or OS/2 Warp or Merlin applications, think again. This subsystem is intended to support text-only 16-bit OS/2 applications that are designed for the OS/2 1.2 and 1.3 operating systems. Put another way, it's pretty much a lame duck. It can also support 16-bit OS/2 bound-mode applications that can run in either MS-DOS or OS/2 environments. As mentioned earlier, these applications may run better in a DOS VDM than in an OS/2 virtual machine, and so the subsystem may be safely disabled without fear of affecting these types of applications. OS/2 will not be supported in future versions of NT, and its native file system, HPFS, ceased being supported as of Windows NT version 4.0.

You can force bound applications to use the DOS NTVDM by using the `FORCEDOS` command. For help on using this command, type **FORCEDOS /?** at the command line.

Disabling the optional subsystems

OK, now for the fun part – disabling these subsystems (after all, using Windows NT is about Windows applications, not prehistoric OS/2 1.Xx and POSIX.1 applications!). Disabling OS/2 and POSIX subsystems is as easy as renaming the subsystem files `OS2SS.EXE` and `PSXSS.EXE` to some other names (such as `PSXSS.BYE` and `OS2SS.BYE` or whatever you like). If an application requiring these subsystems is attempting to load with these files renamed, the load will abort and the application will not be able to start. Again, optional subsystems do not load until invoked by an application that requires them. For POSIX-based applications, a better alternative is a more full-featured and up-to-date POSIX subsystem replacement.

Another method for disabling these subsystems, and the recommended method, is to use the C2 Configuration Utility (`C2CONFIG.EXE`) found in the Windows NT Resource Kit. As part of its security audit and configuration features, this utility allows you to completely remove these subsystems. This can be done by simply double-clicking the OS/2 and POSIX entries where they appear in the C2 Configuration Manager display window (this utility is shown in Figure 6-9). This is the simplest, most thorough, and least risky method for removing these subsystems.

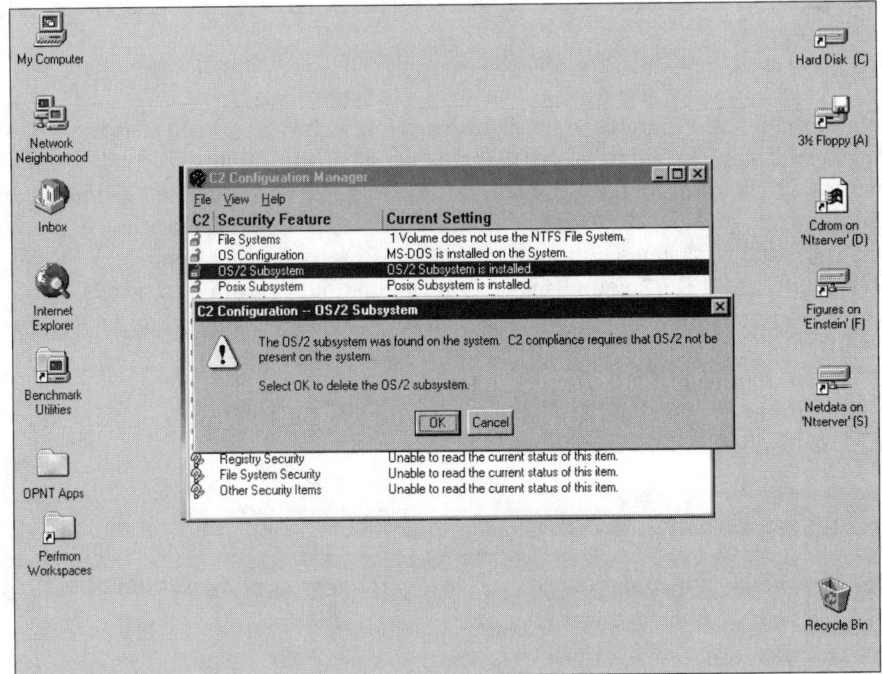

Figure 6-9: Using the Windows NT Resource Kit's C2 Configuration Utility to remove the optional POSIX and OS/2 subsystems.

Tuning the Win32 subsystem

The Win32 subsystem is NT's own native subsystem that supports the all-important Win32 API. The Win32 subsystem sees memory in a flat, 32-bit address all the way up to 4GB. Due to NT's design, 2GB of the total of 4GB is reserved for the system while the remaining 2GB can be used for program data. Most of the optimization techniques which are performed with Win32 applications running on the Win32 subsystem are priority and quantum (time slice) related, because these affect the likelihood and the frequency that a process's threads will run.

With versions of Windows NT prior to 4.0, priority boosting was the primary method for increasing performance for a particular application; this was accomplished by increasing the priority base of the parent process. Windows NT 4.0, however, changed this methodology by introducing the concept of longer thread quanta (time slices) rather than priority boosts to reduce the number of context switches and cache cycles that can reduce performance.

Unlike 16-bit x86-based Windows applications, which run fairly quick on both Intel and RISC platforms, 32-bit x86-compiled Win32 applications run on RISC machines such as the Alpha with a significant performance hit using NT 4.0's native 80486 software emulation. This is important to consider if you're thinking of migrating to a RISC-based Windows NT platform. The best way to avoid this performance hit is to ensure that there are native versions of the software you wish to run that are specifically compiled for your hardware platform (in today's NT RISC market, this essentially means DEC Alpha support, because the MIPS and PowerPC chips are all but dead on the NT platform and will not be supported in Windows NT 5.0 and later versions). Natively compiled applications require no translation, and should take excellent advantage of the power of your system's RISC processor. The other way around this on the DEC Alpha platform is to obtain a copy of a special Intel-to-Alpha binary translation produced by Digital Equipment Corporation called FX!32 (see the sidebar on FX!32 for more information on this product).

FX!32: x86 Compatibility for the Alpha

Digital created FX!32 to provide a fast, efficient, and transparent means of executing Intel x86-based Win32 applications on the Alpha NT platform. One of the best things about FX!32 is its price: since its inception, it has been a free download from Digital. The performance provided by FX!32 with x86 applications in comparison with actual native Alpha-compiled applications is quite impressive; often, FX!32 can deliver between 60 and 80 percent of the speed of the native Alpha applications. X86-based programs that make significant use of the floating point unit (FPU) will see the greatest performance increases, because FX!32 delivers floating point performance that far exceeds that of the 80486-in-software emulated version built into RISC versions of Windows NT 4.0. These types of applications will also derive greater benefits than similar FX!32-translated x86-based applications that make heavier use of integer instructions.

Unlike other methods for dealing with executing code compiled for a different platform, FX!32 uses both emulation and translation to achieve the highest degree of performance. Its first component, like most other software emulators, is generally slow

(*continued*)

FX!32: x86 Compatibility for the Alpha *(Continued)*

but transparent to the user running the application. However, the translation component of FX!32 can produce fast native code from x86 code but requires that the application be run several times for the libraries to be built. When the application is run, FX!32 performs a dynamic code translation of the Intel x86 code into native Alpha code, which is then used in subsequent executions of the application.

When you install FX!32, running x86 Win32 applications becomes transparent. From then on, any x86-compiled Win32 application you try to start will automatically start FX!32, allowing you to run the application and let the program work its magic. FX!32 contains an emulator that uses the entire x86 User Mode instruction set, as well as the complete x86 Win32 environment.

The first time an application is run, FX!32 runs the x86 application very slowly because the entire program must be run through the emulator. With each successive use of the application, more of the original code will be "swapped" for Alpha native code through the background translator. Ideally, very little x86 native code should remain after the process is run several times, though the emulator will always remain active due to the remaining x86 code that could not be translated (the use of x86 machine code by the software vendor is often the cause of this).

The translator portion of FX!32 uses a unique background optimization technique that carefully groups basic blocks into considerably larger (and more efficient) units called translation units. This allows for full utilization of global optimization methods of x86 into Alpha native code. By providing the user with a slow but transparent emulator at the front end while the translation occurs in the background provides the best compromise to running native Alpha programs.

Though it doesn't solve all of the problems of software support for Alpha/NT computers, FX!32 provides a great deal of compatibility with most mainstream software titles. Many applications won't run properly or operate at all using FX!32, particularly if the application is older or incorporates a significant amount of x86 specific machine code. Performance using x86 programs on Alpha/NT is anywhere from acceptable to surprising, although it never equals the performance of true native-compiled Alpha code. As a tool to provide access to the wide variety of x86-compiled Win32 programs, FX!32 is an invaluable tool for extending the software palette available to Alpha-based Windows NT machines.

For more information on specific options for configuring the FX!32 subsystem, go to Digital's Web site at:

```
http://www.digital.com/semiconductor/amt/fx32/index.html/fx32_k
it.html
```

SETTING WIN32 APPLICATION PRIORITIES

As described earlier, thread priorities and time slices (or quanta) govern the performance that a particular Win32 program can achieve. Manually increasing priorities is a somewhat tricky business and requires that you be a member of either the Administrators or Power Users group on the system (or domain). Priority levels can be changed temporarily from the command prompt, the Start menu's Run command, or the Windows NT Task Manager. They can also be set from within a batch file or a shortcut. In the following sections, we look into how NT assigns thread priorities to processes and threads, and some methods you can apply to make adjustments to these priorities.

THREAD EXECUTION: DYNAMIC BY DESIGN

In Windows NT, the smallest execution unit that is dispatched (scheduled to run) is the thread. Thread dispatching selects the next ready and waiting thread to execute on the next available processor. The time units used by the scheduler are called a time slice or quantum. In defining a process priority level, remember that only a certain number of high priority threads can run before contention and system thread "starvation" (lack of attention) causes the system to become unresponsive and performance to plummet. Context switching from one thread to the other is caused by the preemption of one thread and the execution of another. Too many context switches can sap performance, because changing from one thread to another while retaining the former thread's state takes time.

NT's thread scheduler component may boost the thread priority for foreground applications according to the priority set when it was started, such as starting an application with a `START /HIGH` command (more on this command in a bit). NT has 32 thread priority levels, with values ranging from 0 to 31 (however, priority level 0 is reserved for system use and cannot be defined manually by a user).

When an interactive thread voluntarily gives up executing on the processor before its defined time slice has ended, the dispatcher will increase the thread in priority from its base priority. When the thread that was running is very CPU-bound and uses up its entire time slice, the process priority is decreased (although never below the base level) to allow other threads to run. This is an efficient method for dealing with the potential for thread starvation (where a lower priority thread fails to receive any processor attention) and ensuring that all applications receive sufficient CPU time.

NT can also add additional priority adjustments based on certain system events, such as the brief, but significant, boosting of the thread priority, which occurs after it returns from a call such as a keyboard input. When the "real-time" thread priorities of 16 through 31 are used for a thread, the scheduling is much more deterministic and consistent, and the dynamic boosting and cutting of thread priority does not occur at all. The highest priority thread in the queue always wins for contention with the processor. Hardware events cause the state of threads to be checked frequently, and the process of selecting and servicing a particular thread takes only 10 to 32 milliseconds.

Because of the flexibility provided for a Power User or Administrator to configure priority bases, it is possible to configure a system for very high performance when running a particularly demanding application (such as a 3D graphics-rendering application). However, the process and inherited thread priority levels will not really have much of a significant effect unless the processor becomes highly utilized. Priority levels force some threads to wait longer in the queue than others, which can cause slower overall system performance. What you want to avoid is having the performance of the entire system compromised for the sake of a single high priority process. To avoid this, you should not be too liberal with priority changes for applications, or NT may become unresponsive or even hang. This is particularly true of attempting to run an application with a real-time priority (i.e., levels 16–31) that wasn't designed for that priority level. The rest of the system, including NT itself, may become so starved for processor time that system performance will greatly deteriorate rather than improve.

You should also remember that only Win32 applications can be scheduled for real-time and high priority. Win16, DOS, OS/2, and POSIX applications are only capable of running with normal priority (a maximum base priority of 7). If the process is set with a low priority, any processes and threads spawned from it will inherit the low priority. Conversely, a process set with a high priority will spawn processes and threads with only a normal priority.

Table 6-2 shows the base priority levels tied to the four priority-class types for processes running under Windows NT.

TABLE 6-2 PROCESS PRIORITY BASE LEVELS AND THEIR ASSOCIATED PRIORITY VALUES

Priority Base Levels	Default Priority Value Associated with Level
Low	4
Normal	7
High	13
Real-time	24

Many factors influence the base priority of a process, including the group membership (such as Domain User or Administrator) of the user account under whose security context the process is launched, the tasking options defined in the System Control Panel's Performance tab, and whether or not the process is running in the foreground or the background.

The foreground process is the application whose window is currently active on the Windows NT desktop. All other running processes are defined as background processes.

Figure 6-10 shows the priority levels available to User and Kernel Mode programs in Windows NT. Note that each class has several priority levels within them.

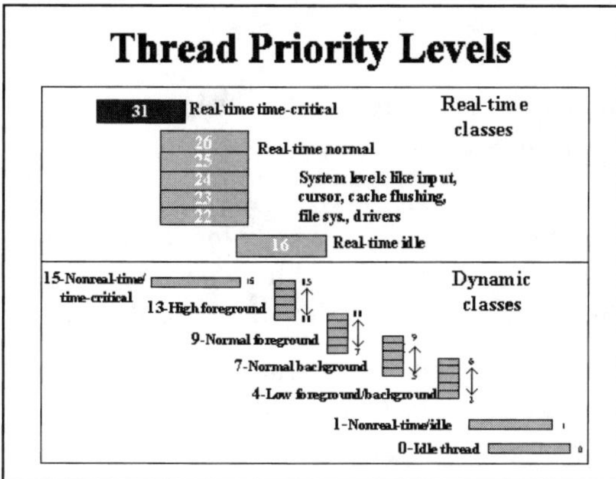

Figure 6-10: The dynamic and real-time priority levels available to User and Kernel Mode processes in Windows NT.

"Real-Time" NT

NT has some "near" real-time system capabilities, though applications must be specifically developed to take advantage of real-time priority or NT will not be able to supply itself with enough processor time to service the application. True real-time applications, such as mission control at NASA or a shop running mechanical devices such as bottling machines, generally use embedded systems that have a very high degree of precision. NT is close enough to a true real-time OS (operating system) to be able to provide real-time services in less exacting roles. The highest priority that can be assigned to any User Mode process is a priority of 15. Levels in this range and below can be dynamically increased and decreased as necessary by the scheduler. Priority levels above this point are in the real-time class and cannot be dynamically altered.

Priorities are arranged in classes and have ranges within each class. All priorities from 1 to 15 fall into the *dynamic* class of priorities while those above 15 are not dynamically configurable and are considered *real-time*. In Figure 6-10, we can also see that each class has a range of priority values, including relative priorities within the class, including idle, normal, high priority, and time-critical.

NT dynamically alters thread priority to ensure that thread starvation (a state in which a thread is unable to run due to overt contention for the processor) does not occur. This boost or cut is orchestrated by the Dispatcher and can be up to two levels, either up or down. Additionally, every thread that is present has a Dispatcher state that changes through the duration of the thread's lifetime. The most important of these states are:

- *Running*: This state means that a thread is executing on the processor. Despite the term "multitasking," only one thread per processor can be executing at the same time.
- Ready: The ready state indicates that the thread is ready for execution the next time the kernel dispatches a thread. The thread from the pool of ready threads that will execute is determined by the priority of the thread.
- Waiting: A waiting thread is waiting for another event (such as keyboard input) to occur before the thread can become ready again.

MONITORING THE WIN32 SUBSYSTEM

Fortunately, all Win32 applications have their own name, and it is therefore not difficult to monitor the processes or the individual threads within processes. In addition, the main physical component of the Win32 subsystem is a process named `CSRSS.EXE` (stands for Client SeRver Runtime SubSystem). You can monitor individual applications running on the system or the `CSRSS.EXE` process to monitor the Win32 subsystem itself.

You can use Performance Monitor to view (but not alter) the following objects and counters which relate the priority levels of various processes and threads currently running on the system:

- Process: Priority Base
- Thread: Priority Base
- Thread: Priority Current

Note that these are generic counters and are available for each process and thread currently being executed; the various processes and threads are accessible as separate instances of the Process and Thread objects, respectively.

SETTING APPLICATION PRIORITIES

To set the priority for a particular application to boost its performance on a busy or moderately busy system, you can use a number of different methods, including (but not limited to) the Windows NT Task Manager, a program's shortcut, the START command issued manually at the NT command prompt, and the Run command.

To make things simpler, you may want to start by having Task Manager display the base priority of all processes as a separate column in the Processes windows (it is not shown by default). To do so, follow these steps:

1. Run Task Manager (e.g., using Ctrl-Shift-Esc, right-clicking the Taskbar, and choosing Task Manager, or pressing Ctrl-Alt-Del and choosing Task Manager).
2. Select the Processes tab.
3. From the View menu selection, choose Select Columns.
4. In the Select Columns dialog that appears (shown in Figure 6-11), place a checkmark in Base Priority box (you may also be interested in viewing other process-related data that are selectable for display in this dialog).

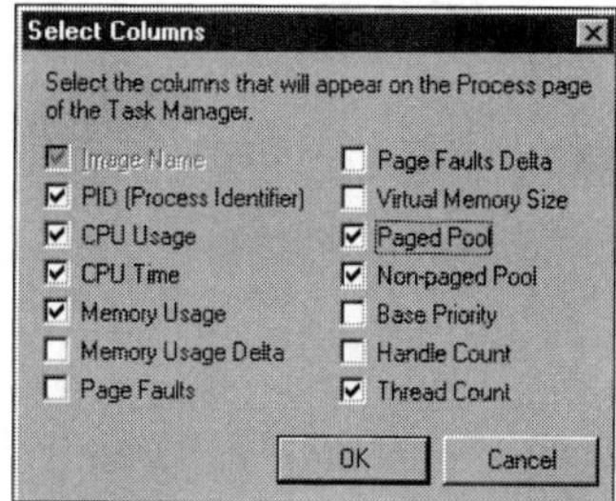

Figure 6-11: The Select Columns dialog of the Processes tab in Task Manager.

In addition, you can also use the Processes tab in Task Manager to change the base priority of an existing process. To do so, follow these steps

1. Launch Task Manager and choose the Processes tab.
2. Select a process name with the right mouse button.
3. Select Set Priority → Base and select a new base priority level for the process (this is shown in Figure 6-12).

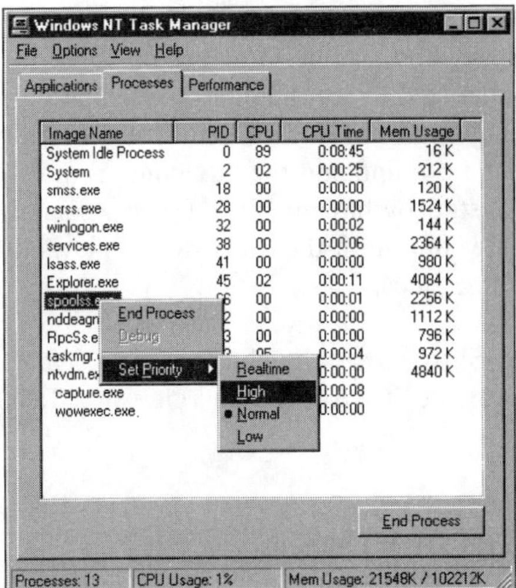

Figure 6-12: Changing the base priority for a process in Task Manager.

Changes made to a process's priority level occur immediately; you do not need to restart the process or computer for the change to take effect.

Figure 6-12 also shows that the base priority differs depending on the priority class in which the process was started. If the counters indicated the other priority levels within the dynamic class, the chart would look different, indicating which threads were boosted and which were cut to lower priorities.

Whenever a user works in an application (i.e., switches to its window), the application becomes the "focus" and moves the application's process to the foreground where NT boosts the base priority of the process to improve the application's responsiveness. When a different application becomes the focus, the original application returns to a background priority level.

It is possible to change the degree of boost given to foreground applications while simultaneously changing the relationship between foreground and background priority. By reducing the foreground boost, it is possible to improve background execution of commands. To make this adjustment, you can use the System Control Panel's Performance tab (shown in Figure 6-13). By simply sliding the Application Performance bar from right to left, you change the performance relationship of foreground versus background processes. The default setting of maximum boost for foreground applications (far right setting) is usually best for Windows NT Workstation computers, because the foreground application is generally the one whose performance you will be most concerned with (and therefore to which you want to give the maximum amount of CPU time). However, if you tend to run a number of background applications that are continually doing useful work (i.e., are not just sitting idle) such as the downloading of data, compiling of programs, calculations of data, and the like, you may find that the middle or far left setting gives the best mix of performance. You should experiment with different values to determine which works best for you.

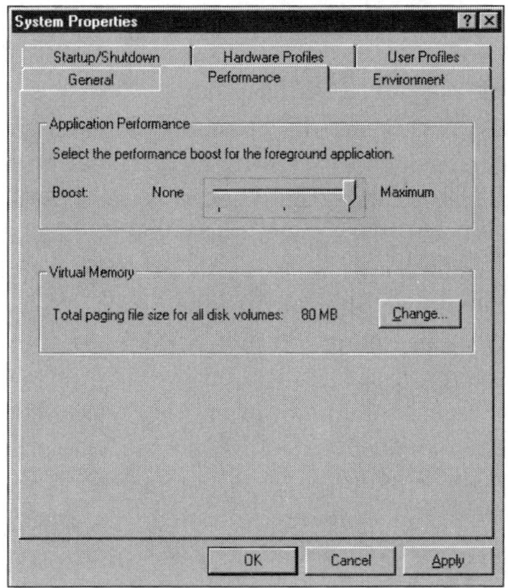

Figure 6-13: Changing the boost given to the foreground application.

When Windows NT 4.0 was first released many users thought that NT's thread scheduler was broken because it always showed a priority base of 8 from within Task Manager and Performance Monitor, even after following the steps to boost foreground responsiveness found in Microsoft's documentation for both the new product and the older 3.51 products. The reason for this behavior is that the function of the Application Performance slider was changed in NT 4.0. Instead of adding or "boosting" the foreground base priority up a level to 9 (as was the case with NT 3.51 and earlier), NT now adds to the length of the quantum (time slice) to give each thread running in the foreground more time to execute before being preempted for another process. You can easily observe this phenomenon using Performance Monitor. Open Performance Monitor, select Add to Chart, choose the Win32 process from the list under the process counters and select priority base. Under NT 4.0, the priority for the process remains at 8 regardless of the position of the Foreground Boost slider in the Performance tab (however, under NT 3.5x the base priority will increase to 9). The reason for this change was that Microsoft discovered that increasing the time slice/quantum was a more efficient method for boosting foreground application performance than increasing the base priority level.

STARTING APPLICATIONS WITH THE START COMMAND

All applications can be started with the Windows NT START command from either the command prompt, or with this command added in front of the application's executable file name in a batch file or application shortcut. When you use START to open an application from the command prompt, the application will start within its own window. This behavior allows the command prompt to be used for issuing a new command. When you start an application without using the START command, the application opens and the original command prompt window used to launch the application is no longer available until the application is exited (however, other NT command prompt sessions can be started and run in other windows).

To use the START command to also start an application with a specific base priority, you can use the special switches `/LOW`, `/NORMAL`, `/HIGH`, and `/REALTIME`. These switches (with the exception of `/NORMAL` and `/LOW`) are restricted to use with Win32 applications and can be changed only if you have sufficient user privileges. Though START can be used with any available subsystem or application environment, most of the options apply only to Win32 applications running under the Win32 subsystem. Like changes made from within the Task Manager, priority changes made from the command prompt are immediate, but only affect that execution of the application.

Other than the full pathname of the application being started (which should appear at the end of the START command line), the following command line parameters are available for the START command:

- "title": This displays the text of your choosing in the window title bar.
- `/Dpath`: Directory where program is located.
- `/I`: This sets the new environment be passed to the `CMD.EXE` as the original environment and not the current environment. This is useful for allowing different environment parameters to be used.
- `/MIN`: Opens the program with the window minimized.
- `/MAX`: Opens the program with the window maximized.
- `/LOW`: Opens the program with the IDLE priority class.

- /NORMAL: Opens the program with NORMAL priority class.
- /HIGH: Opens the program with HIGH priority class. Only Administrators and Power Users can set this priority level.
- /REALTIME: Opens the program with REALTIME priority class. Only Administrators and Power Users can apply this priority level; furthermore, use of this setting is not recommended as it is likely to make the entire system unresponsive.
- /B: Start application without creating a new window. This makes Start act more like the default application open.

To get additional information about the START command, type **START /?** at the command prompt or use the Windows NT help file to find more information about the command's usage, features, and limitations.

As mentioned earlier, you can use the START command directly from an NT command prompt or enter the command using the Start menu's Run command. However, the base priority level changes you make using these methods will only be temporary for that one session; future instances run normally will return to the default priority for that application. For a more permanent solution, you should change the application's shortcut or create a batch file so that the application is started using the START command followed by the desired base priority level switch (e.g., /LOW, /NORMAL, /HIGH, or /REALTIME).

If you try to enter the START command from the Start menu's Run command or in the command line for an application's shortcut, you'll quickly notice that it doesn't work the same way as it does when used manually from the command line or a batch file. The trick to making this work is to preface the entire command line (beginning with "START...") with CMD.EXE /C. For example, you might enter the following to run NotePad with a priority of HIGH from the Start menu's Run command:

```
CMD.EXE /C START /HIGH NOTEPAD.EXE
```

This instructs CMD.EXE (the NT Command Prompt executable) to launch, run the command prompt listed after it, and then terminate. Issuing the command in this manner will allow the application to run properly at the desired priority.

WIN32 REGISTRY ENTRIES

As with virtually every component of Windows NT, the Win32 subsystem has its own section of the Registry containing configuration information. The configuration data related to the Win32 subsystem is located in the Registry under:

```
HKEY_LOCAL_MACHINE\SYSTEM\CurrentControlSet\Control\Session
Manager\SubSystems
```

in the Required and Windows entries. This portion of the Registry is discussed in more detail in the Setup module's Boot Sequence section.

The Windows NT and Windows NT System32 directories are defined under:

```
HKEY_LOCAL_MACHINE\SYSTEM\CurrentControlSet\Control\Windows
```

Another section containing a number of parameters related to the Win32 subsystem is located at:

```
HKEY_LOCAL_MACHINE\SOFTWARE\Microsoft\Windows NT\CurrentVersion
```

Although a number of values within this subkey relate to Win32, not all of them do. For instance, the WOW subkey (as mentioned in the WOW section earlier) contains settings for the WOW subsystem.

It is recommended that you never make changes to Registry values related to the Win32 subsystem (or any other Registry values, for that matter) unless you are sure of their meaning and effect. Otherwise, you might make changes that render your system unstartable.

Faster Backups with NT Backup under Windows NT 3.5x

If you use Windows NT Backup under NT versions earlier than 4.0 (i.e., 3.1 or 3.5x), you should know about a problem that severely impacts the performance of this application. The problem is mainly related to the situation where you are backing up data using UNC (Universal Naming Convention) names (such as \\BIGSERVER\BIGSHARE) rather than a mapped drive letter. Due to a typographical error in a Registry key, the performance of NT Backup in this situation is significantly impaired.

The reason the problem occurs is that whenever NT Backup encounters a file that could be a POSIX file, it requests that Windows NT open the file in a POSIX-compatible manner (the path and filename match the filename case exactly). Because the workstation service has the wrong case for the device path Registry settings (as you can see below, where the first character is lowercase instead of uppercase), Windows NT refuses to open the file when Windows NT Backup requests a POSIX-compliant format. As a result, Windows NT returns an error message. At that point, NT Backup then tries to open the file without specifying POSIX semantics, which works correctly. However, these continual failed file open attempts and subsequent errors impede performance because NT Backup tries to open each file twice rather than once.

To correct the problem, follow these steps:

1. Run Registry Editor (`REGEDT32.EXE`).
2. Locate the following registry key: `HKEY_LOCAL_MACHINE\SYSTEM\CurrentControlSet\Services\LanmanWorkstation\networkprovider`.
3. Edit the `Devicename` value, which will have a type of `REG_SZ` and a default value of `\device\LanmanRedirector`.
4. Change the string data for this value from `\device\LanmanRedirector` to `\Device\LanmanRedirector`. (Note: Change only the case of the first letter d in device) — do not change anything else!)

This situation exists only in NT versions 3.x and does not affect Windows NT 4.0 computers.

Optimizing the Desktop Environment

If your primary use of Windows NT is from a client workstation perspective, then your biggest concerns in regards to system performance are probably with respect to the speed and responsiveness of the NT desktop environment itself. Fortunately, there are a number of things you can do to enhance the Windows NT desktop environment, including configuration changes that can enhance both performance and stability.

Let's begin by looking at some of the more important components of the Windows NT desktop environment.

Environment variables

Like MS-DOS, OS/2, UNIX, and other operating systems, Windows NT incorporates the ability to define special global system-, application-, and user-oriented settings known as *environment variables.* Environment variables are provided in Windows NT to improve NT's compatibility and cross-platform support. Although it's unlikely that the setting of environment variables will have any effect on the actual performance of your Windows NT system, they are an important aspect of your system's environment and overall configuration, and are therefore worth a bit of discussion.

Three levels of environment variables exist within Windows NT, including system environment variables, user environment variables, and the environment variables that are set in the `AUTOEXEC.BAT` file. Also provided are predefined environment variables that are set when the system boots and when a particular user logs on (for example, the system's base installation directory or *SYSTEMROOT* variable, the user's log in name or *USERNAME* variable, etc.).

You can manually set environment variables in Windows NT using the SET command, followed by the environment variable name and value. The format of the command is:

```
SET [variable=[value]]
```

However, variables set in this manner will only stay in effect until the user typing them logs off. To permanently set or change an environment variable, you should instead use the System Control Panel's Environment tab.

You can also type SET by itself to display a list of all currently defined environment variables and their values, or SET followed by a variable name to display the value for that particular variable. To reference the actual value assigned to a variable, place "%" symbols around the variable name as in the following example: *%SYSTEMROOT%*. This is the method for referencing an environment variable's value within a batch process (e.g., a system log in script) or within an NT command prompt session.

SYSTEM ENVIRONMENT VARIABLES

System environment variables are the same regardless of the user that logs on. User environment variables set environment parameters for that particular user, and the AUTOEXEC.BAT environment variables set the environment for particular subsystems such as DOS or Win16 (which are often required by applications running in these subsystems).

System environment variables can be viewed from Control Panel by choosing the System icon and then choosing the Environment tab. This dialog is shown in Figure 6-14. System environment variables, which are displayed in the top window of the dialog, are called such because they are global or systemwide — they are always set no matter who logs on. In addition, only a system administrator can modify these values — regular users cannot.

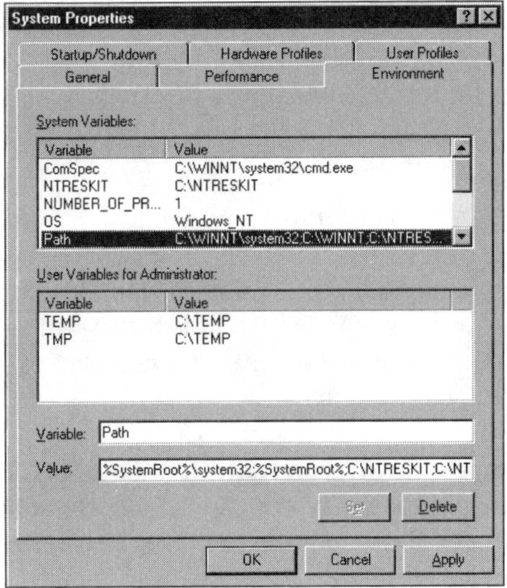

Figure 6-14: Setting system environment variables in the System Control Panel.

Even if you are logged on with an administrative-level account with sufficient privileges to do so, you should normally never make modifications to system environment variables. These values are generated by NT during setup and are usually correct; changing them to invalid settings could cause systemwide problems.

In addition to the system environment variables displayed in the System Control Panel, there are also a few additional predefined environment variables that are set when the user logs in that do not appear in this dialog box:

- USERNAME: the name of the currently logged-in user
- USERDOMAIN: the name of the domain containing the user account
- NTVERSION: the version of NT: Note that this is no longer available as of Windows NT 4.0
- WINDIR: the Windows NT installation folder, e.g., `C:\WINNT`, etc.
- OS: the operating system; typically, this is set to `Windows_NT`
- PROCESSOR_ARCHITECTURE: hardware platform; one of the following: x86, PPC, MIPS, or ALPHA
- PROCESSOR_LEVEL: type of processor(s) installed: values for x86 systems: 486, 586,686, 786; values for MIPS: 4400, 4600, 5000, 8000, 10000; values for PPC: 601, 603, 604, 620, X704; values for Alpha: 21066, 21064, 21164, 21164PC, 21264
- HOMEPATH, HOMEDRIVE, HOMESHARE: These three environment variables are set based on the value of the home directory. The user's home directory is specified in User Manager (in the Profile section). If the home directory uses universal naming conventions (UNC), then they will have the following values: HOMESHARE=\\<*server name*>\<*share name*>, HOMEPATH=\<*path*>, and HOMEDRIVE=<*drive letter*>:

All the home references shown above are always present on Windows NT machines and as such can always be used to direct a system to use a particular share or drive from within a logon script stored on an authenticating server. In addition, these values may be queried using batch files or other programs to determine the configuration of the current system.

USER ENVIRONMENT VARIABLES

Like system environment variables, user environment variables can be viewed from within Control Panel or directly from the Registry. Variables set in the user environment variable can be easily changed to suit the needs of a specific user without affecting the environments of other users. These variables override any equivalent system environment variables which are applied globally (default settings). The user path is always added to the system path. By default, only two variable parameters are defined, one for the location of the TEMP directory, and the other for TMP (which is specified on the next line to be the equivalent of TEMP). This looks like:

```
TEMP    d:\TEMP
TMP     d:\TEMP
```

(where *d:* is some drive letter on the system)

As with system environment variables, user environment variables can be referenced in login scripts and can also be queried by user batch files or applications that need to determine values related to the currently logged-in user.

AUTOEXEC.BAT ENVIRONMENT VARIABLES

Although the `AUTOEXEC.BAT` file is a vestige of MS-DOS and is largely ignored by Windows NT, there is one function NT uses it for: parsing environment variables set by DOS and Win16 applications that use them. Because older applications don't realize they're running under NT and may, as part of their operation, place SET statements for environment variables in the `AUTOEXEC.BAT` that are required for proper operation, it's important that NT process this file to read any values. All of the environment variables set in the `AUTOEXEC.BAT` are parsed at boot time and configured to be globally available in the NT environment (for all users). In addition, any directory paths listed in the `AUTOEXEC.BAT`'s `PATH` statement are added to the system path at the same time.

CONFIGURING PARSING OF THE AUTOEXEC.BAT FILE

Although the `AUTOEXEC.BAT` parsing feature is nice for backward compatibility with legacy applications, it may not be desirable in some environments. This functionality can be turned off if you do not wish to have the system parse the `AUTOEXEC.BAT` file at boot.

To change the parsing of the `AUTOEXEC.BAT` characteristic of NT, perform the following:

1. Start one of the Windows NT Registry Editors (`REGEDIT.EXE` or `REGEDT32.EXE`).
2. Locate the following Registry subkey: `\HKEY_LOCAL_MACHINE\SOFTWARE\Microsoft\Windows NT\CurrentVersion\Winlogon`.
3. The value within this key that you're looking for is ParseAutoexec. The default of 1 means `AUTOEXEC.BAT` is parsed. Change the value to 0 to instruct NT not to parse the `AUTOEXEC.BAT` file at boot.

Changing the behavior of parsing for `AUTOEXEC.BAT` has no effect on the parsing of `AUTOEXEC.NT` or `CONFIG.NT` by the DOS or 16-bit Windows environments (VDMs).

In addition to preventing potentially unwanted values from appearing in Windows NT's global environment, disabling this feature also creates a small increase in startup speed, because the AUTOEXEC.BAT file does not need to be checked for environment variables.

ENVIRONMENT VARIABLE PRIORITIES

Environment variables under Windows NT also have a priority order in which they are processed and understood. This order affects which environment variable is considered the actual value if a duplicate variable name exists between one or more types of variables (e.g., system, user, and AUTOEXEC.BAT varieties).

This order is:

1. System Environment Variables
2. AUTOEXEC.BAT Environment Variables (SET statements)
3. User Environment Variables

INCREASING ENVIRONMENT SPACE FOR LARGE ENVIRONMENTS

Like all data structures on a computer system, environment variables need a chunk of memory real estate in which they can be stored. When you start an NT Command Prompt session (an instance of the CMD.EXE program), Windows NT automatically allocates a certain amount of memory for the storage of environment variables. This storage pool is known as the *environment space* available to that session. Occasionally, you may run into situations where there is insufficient environment space available, and either you or an application are unable to create or expand environment variables (this is usually accompanied by an "Out of Environment Space" error message). To rectify this situation, you can increase the amount of memory the environment has for environment variables by performing these steps:

1. In Control Panel, click the System icon.
2. Click the Environment tab.
3. In the System Environment Variable list, select the ComSpec variable (this dialog is shown in Figure 6-15).
4. To increase the amount of environment space, change the data in the Value box using this syntax:

   ```
   ComSpec = <drive:\windir>\system32\cmd.exe
   /e:<envsize_in_bytes>
   ```

   where *<drive:\windir>* is the drive and directory where the Windows NT installation is located.

   (Note that the maximum size for the environment is 32768 bytes.)

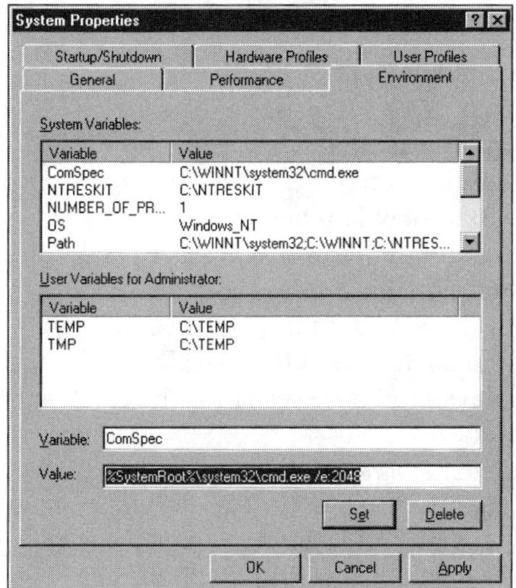

Figure 6-15: Increasing the default environment space available in a Windows NT command prompt session.

Be aware that changes made to environment variables via the System Control Panel's Environment tab take effect immediately and are visible to all new applications and command prompt sessions launched after the change is made. However, any applications already running won't see the change until the next time they are started. In addition, permanent changes to environment variables should always be made via the System Control Panel rather than within an NT Command Prompt session, because changes made in individual command prompt sessions only take effect for that session and are not permanently recorded.

Optimizing the Windows NT Explorer

Using a Windows NT computer as a workstation is really about using Windows NT's shell, the Windows NT Explorer. Explorer is NT's default desktop shell and is used to handle all aspects of desktop management, including:

- Presentation of the User Interface (the NT GUI)
- Launching and Control of Applications

- File and Folder Management
- Configuration of File Associations and File Type Definitions

Part and parcel of the Windows NT Explorer (which is an actual application whose filename is `EXPLORER.EXE`) is the Taskbar, the gray bar which appears by default at the bottom of the Windows NT 4.0 display (although you can also move it to any edge of the screen you like by dragging it). The Taskbar is a part of the Windows NT Explorer interface and is responsible for displaying and switching to running applications, as well as displaying the Start button (which contains program shortcuts and other selections) and the System Tray (that small area on the opposite side of the Start button that displays miniature icons for the clock and other various applications and utilities).

In the following section, we examine some issues surrounding the optimization of Windows NT Explorer interface, and some tips and tweaks that you can employ to improve performance and troubleshoot a variety of problems that can occur.

SOLVING OUT OF MEMORY ERRORS

If you ever receive "Out of Memory" errors or errors related to `USER32.DLL`, and are sure that you have plenty of free memory on the system, you may wish to consider making a modification to the Registry which may help to alleviate the problem.

If you are receiving these errors, locate the following Registry value, which configures the Win32 subsystem's startup properties:

```
HKEY_LOCAL_MACHINE\SYSTEM\CurrentControlSet\Control\Session
Manager\SubSystems
```

Value Name:	`Windows`
Default Value:	`%SystemRoot%\system32\csrss.exe` ObjectDirectory=\Windows SharedSection=1024,3072 Windows=On SubSystemType=Windows ServerDll=basesrv,1 ServerDll=winsrv:UserServerDllInitialization,3 ServerDll=winsrv:ConServerDllInitialization,2 ProfileControl=Off MaxRequestThreads=16
Type:	`REG_EXPAND_SZ`

Scan the value's data for the part that says "SharedSection=*X*,*Y*." Here, *X* is the size of the desktop heap created by interactive programs (in Kilobytes or K) and *Y* is the size of the systemwide heap. There is also a third possible value here that isn't enumerated by default. To enumerate (and increase) this value, add ",*Z*"after the other two numbers listed. *Z* represents the size of the hidden desktop heap created by noninteractive processes. The recommended value to start with is 512 (Kilobytes); this will probably solve the problem you're experiencing. If not, try increasing the value in increments of 128 until the problem goes away.

When you're finished, the string should appear as follows: "...SharedSection=1024,3072,512...." If you've got a large amount of installed memory on your system you may also want to experiment with increasing the sizes of *X* and *Y*. In some situations, this may increase the responsiveness or stability of the desktop environment. Again, it is recommended that you start with only small increases, and that you don't get too carried away. As an example, my own configuration reads: "...SharedSection=1536,4096,512...."

Be aware that increasing the values in the SharedSection portion of the Windows value increases the amount of memory used by Windows NT, and more specifically, the Windows NT Explorer application (EXPLORER.EXE). For example, the command line used on my own system (SharedSection=1536,4096,512) causes Explorer to use almost 5MB of RAM (this memory usage can be viewed using the Processes tab of Task Manager). Therefore, you should only increase these values if your system has plenty of memory; in the case of the hidden desktop heap (*Z*) value addition, you should only add this value if you are experiencing errors or wish to takes proactive steps to help prevent the possibility that this might occur in the future.

SOLVING PROBLEMS RELATED TO THE IRPSTACKSIZE VALUE

Another Registry modification, which is also related to artificial low-memory errors, may help in situations where you receive errors (or Event Viewer notifications) indicating that your system has insufficient resources. Specifically, if you receive any of the following error messages, you may wish to consider making this modification:

- "Not enough server storage is available to process this command" message appears in the Windows NT System Event Log (typically, this occurs after a service or driver is added to the system).
- The error "The server's configuration parameter irpstacksize is too small for the server to use a local device. Please increase the value of this parameter" occurs when printing using the HP Print Monitor over the DLC protocol (e.g., to an HP JetDirect card in a network printer).
- The status of a printer managed using the HP Print Monitor over DLC is listed as "not available" in Print Manager even though the printer itself works fine.

IRPstackSize is a Server service-specific parameter that specifies the number of stack locations in I/O request packets (IRPs) used by the Server service on an NT Server or Workstation. It may be necessary to increase this number for certain transports, MAC drivers, or local file system drivers. You may experience problems related to this value right after adding a device or service to the system, because that driver or service may push this heap past its default size limit.

To increase this value, first locate the following in the Registry:

```
HKEY_LOCAL_MACHINE\SYSTEM\CurrentControlSet\Service\LanmanServer\
Parameters
```

Change or add the following value within this subkey:

Value Name:	`IRPstackSize` (note that capitalization should be exactly as listed)
Default Value:	Varies; but most likely will be 6
Type:	`REG_DWORD`
Range of Values:	0 to 12 (decimal)

If you are experiencing any of the above errors, try setting this value to at least 7, or, if it is already at 7, try increasing it by increments of 1 until the problem disappears. Do not set the value any higher than 12, which is the maximum allowed value.

If you will be installing the Norton NT Tools or Norton Utilities for Windows NT on your system, you must be sure not to set the IRPstackSize value higher than 10 (decimal); otherwise, the utilities are likely to fail to install properly.

ALLOWING NT TO AUTOMATICALLY DETERMINE REGISTRY AND PAGEDPOOL MEMORY SIZES

Another possible cause of the "Not enough server storage to process this command" Event Viewer message (in the System Event Log), as well as various kinds of Remote Procedure Call (RPC) errors and errors related to paged pool memory, are often related to a special Windows NT configuration value known as the RegistrySizeLimit (RSL). The value set for the RSL limits the total amount of space that may be consumed in paged pool and disk space by Windows NT Registry data (the Registry hives). You can think of the RSL as a sort of global quota for the NT Registry.

The Registry Size Limit value doesn't indicate the actual size of the Registry, just the maximum size to which it can grow. Therefore, the Registry's size doesn't grow just because the RSL value does.

By default, Windows NT sets the Registry Size Limit to 25 percent of the current paged pool memory allocation. Because these figures are inherently tied and may be set too low, it is usually beneficial to configure them so that NT dynamically allocates them (e.g., they aren't set to specific values, and NT automatically configures them as necessary).

Paged pool memory is configured in this Registry location:

```
HKEY_LOCAL_MACHINE\SYSTEM\CurrentControlSet\Control\Session
Manager\Memory Management
```

Value Name: `PagedPoolSize`
Default Value: 0 (NT automatically configures) or may be set to an actual hard-coded number
Type: `REG_DWORD`
Value Range: 0, or 0x00000001 - 0x0C000000 bytes (192MB)

The RSL value, if one exists, is found in this Registry location:

```
HKEY_LOCAL_MACHINE\SYSTEM\CurrentControlSet\Control
```

Value Name: `RegistrySizeLimit`

Default Value:Doesn't exist; however, it may be set to an actual hard-coded number if you've adjusted it via the Virtual Memory dialog in the Performance tab of the System Control Panel or directly via the Registry.

Type: `REG_DWORD`
Value Range: 0 or 4 – 0xFFFFFFFF megabytes (Actual range: 4MB – 80 percent of paged pool memory)

The RegistrySizeLimit value is not listed by default; however, it may appear if you've ever configured the Maximum Registry Size value in the Performance tab of the System Control Panel (this dialog is shown in Figure 6-16).

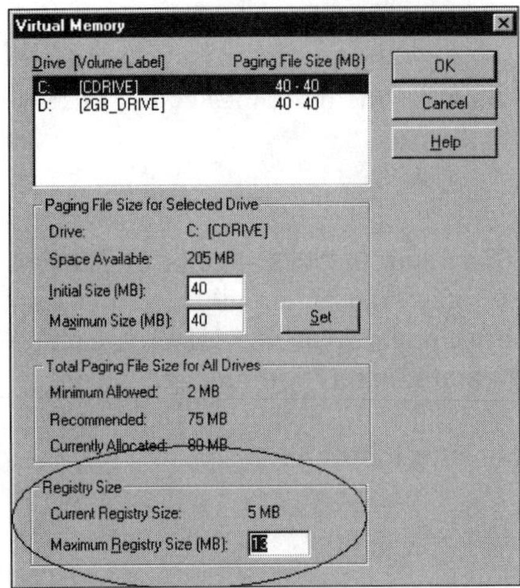

Figure 6-16: Configuring the Registry Size Limit via the Performance tab of the System Control Panel.

The best way to ensure that the paged pool value is always optimal is to simply set its data to 0 (which is also the default, but may have changed at some point). For the RegistrySizeLimit value, the best way to ensure that Windows NT is in control of automatically sizing the value is to verify that the RegistrySizeLimit value doesn't exist. If it does, you can simply delete it.

Note that you will need to reboot to have any changes made to these values take effect.

For different versions of Windows NT, the maximum paged pool memory/Registry Size Limits are as follows (the RSL can be up to 80 percent of the paged pool memory size): NT 3.1: 32MB/8MB; NT 3.5x:128MB/102MB; NT 4.0: 192MB/154MB. Among other things, the maximum size of the Registry affects the maximum number of users that can be supported on Windows NT domain. In NT 3.1, this limit was around 5,000 users, in NT 3.5x it was around 20,000 users, and in NT 4.0, it is around 30,000 users (however, other system limitations and real-world factors often limit the maximum number of users to an even lower figure).

RUNNING EXPLORER AND TASKBAR IN SEPARATE PROCESSES

One of the coolest modifications we've come across for the NT desktop environment relates to execution of the various components of the NT desktop environment, including the Windows NT Explorer, the Desktop, and the Taskbar. By default, Windows NT uses a single process to run the Taskbar, Desktop, and multiple instances of the NT Explorer, where each of these elements runs as an individual thread within this same shared process. As a result of this design, it is possible for problems with any one of these threads to crash the entire shared process. This can make for a less-than-stable desktop environment and can also affect the performance and responsiveness of these desktop elements.

To minimize the possibility that this situation can occur, you can make a Registry modification that will force NT to create separate processes for the Desktop and Taskbar, and also one for each instance of Explorer that is run.

To enable this functionality, first locate this Registry subkey:

```
HKEY_CURRENT_USER\SOFTWARE\Microsoft\Windows\CurrentVersion\
Explorer
```

To this subkey, add the value `DesktopProcess`. The value type is `REG_DWORD`, and the value should be set to 1 to enable separate processes (0 or a missing value disables this feature).

As with many other system optimizations, this one has the negative side effect of costing memory. As a result, make sure you've got plenty of extra memory before enabling this feature. The memory usage may be especially significant if you've enabled the previously discussed SharedSection memory increase.

OPTIMIZING FONT USAGE AND CACHING

If you're a person that just loves to have tons of fonts installed on your system, be aware of the potential performance impact of doing this. The bottom line is that more fonts use more memory and slow overall system performance. This is because NT must process every installed font at startup, load them into memory, and then sift through them every time a font dialog is popped up within an application. The moral to the story is don't load any more fonts than you absolutely need for your applications.

Also, you can opt to use a font manager utility such as Adobe Type Manager Deluxe (the only font manager available for NT as of this writing, and only for Intel x86 systems). This type of application is capable of optimizing font and font memory management by placing fonts together into font groups and loading them only when called for by the user.

Recapturing a Lost NT Desktop

Although not strictly a performance-related feature, there is one modification that you might find very useful if you've ever had the experience of losing your NT desktop shell after Explorer crashes. If this happens to you and the shell doesn't automatically restart, there is an answer to your problem. Through a specific Registry modification, you can instruct Windows NT to always automatically restart the Windows NT Explorer should it crash.

To enable this feature, locate this Registry subkey:

```
HKEY_LOCAL_MACHINE\SOFTWARE\Microsoft\Windows
NT\CurrentVersion\Winlogon
```

Once located, modify (or add if it doesn't exist) this value: AutoRestartShell. The value should be set to type `REG_DWORD`, and the data should be set to 1 to enable automatic restarting of the shell (0 disables the feature).

A good idea when using ATM Deluxe for NT is to have a group of system fonts loaded that remain active but are paired down to the absolute bare minimum number that you need. You can then also maintain a separate group for fonts you rarely use but may need on occasion.

Each font takes approximately 35K of memory, something to keep in mind when you have 1,000 fonts loaded on your system (which would use around 34MB!).

Larger, "Multiple Master" PostScript fonts use more memory than simple PostScript fonts which have more limited character sets and features. Postscript fonts in general use more memory than TrueType fonts, but are also more accurate and are the standard in desktop publishing. The included font functionality in NT is lacking in many features and is a primary candidate for replacement if you are involved in desktop publishing in one form or another. Currently, ATM Deluxe is only available in Intel-only builds.

If you are a publisher using a large number of typefaces, or using an international version of Windows NT with a large character set, it may be beneficial to increase various parameters related to NT's font cache. This can be accomplished by directly editing the font cache-related values in Registry. To do this, locate the following Registry subkey, which contains entries that define parameters for font caching:

```
HKEY_LOCAL_MACHINE\SOFTWARE\Microsoft\Windows
 NT\CurrentVersion\FontCache
```

The value entries in the `FontCache` subkey can greatly influence the amount of memory used by the system. However, these values should not be modified, except in the rare case where you must tune the performance for an international version of Windows NT or for specialized cases such as a print shop, where you may be manipulating large character sets.

The values you may wish to modify are:

Value Name: `MaxSize`
Default Value: 0x80 (hex) or 128 (decimal)
Type: `REG_DWORD`
Range: Number of kilobytes

This value specifies the maximum amount of address space reserved per font cache.

Value Name: `MinIncrSize`
Default Value: 0x4
Type: `REG_DWORD`
Range: Number of kilobytes

This value specifies the minimum amount of memory committed each time a font cache is grown.

Value Name: `MinInitSize`
Default Value: 0x4
Type: `REG_DWORD`
Range: Number of kilobytes

This value specifies the minimum amount of memory initially committed per font cache at the time of creation.

Adobe Type Manager Deluxe 4.0 for NT (Intel only)

The Deluxe version of Adobe Type Manager (ATM) software offers powerful new features that let you custom organize all of your Type 1 and TrueType fonts. Using interactive control panels, you can install typefaces with point-and-click simplicity. Easily create custom sets of fonts that apply to different projects, users, or any other classification you choose. In seconds, you can activate only the typefaces you need, and then deactivate them when you're finished. Like any good manager, ATM Deluxe can take care of many tasks for you, including font activation, font smoothing, and font substitution; preview typefaces on-screen or print a sample page; and create multiple master typeface instances quickly and easily. As millions have come to expect from award-winning ATM software, ATM Deluxe provides crisp, clear type at any point size on Adobe PostScript printers and non-PostScript printers alike.

Identifying problem applications and applications bottlenecks

When it comes right down to it, each application running on your Windows NT system uses two major resources: memory and CPU time. Although other resources such as disk space and video subsystem resources also receive heavy use by certain application types, memory and CPU are typically the most important in regards to overall performance.

Exceptions to this include extremely disk-intensive applications such as heavily loaded transactional database systems, or video-intensive applications used in specialized applications such as CAD, linear or nonlinear video editing, and 3D animation. These types of applications may cause those subsystems to be the major bottleneck rather than CPU or memory.

As you might expect, some applications are well-behaved in regards to CPU and memory usage, while others gobble up far more than their fair share of system resources. This latter type of application is your classic resource hog, one of the greatest enemies of a high performance Windows NT system. Resource hogs are also something that you should be able to quickly identify and deal with should one appear in your Windows NT environment.

In addition to the standard memory and CPU time an application uses, there are also times when an application will crash or "hang" in such a way that its processor utilization shoots sky high, sometimes approaching 100 percent. Depending on the system involved, this may have an effect ranging from a noticeable sluggishness to a complete seizure of activity on the system. Luckily, Windows NT and its companion Resource Kit provide a number of tools that you can use to identify and manage these situations.

IDENTIFYING RESOURCE HOGS USING TASK MANAGER

One of the quickest and easiest ways to monitor the resource usage of processes in Windows NT is the multifaceted Windows NT Task Manager. Specifically, you can use Task Manager's Processes tab to examine the memory and CPU time consumed by each process, all of which appear in a list within this tab. By default, Task Manager displays the following information about each process running on the system:

- *Image Name*: This displays the executable file name of each running process (or, in the case of the System and System Idle Processes, a descriptive name).

- *PID*: The Process ID (PID) Number is the internal process identification number assigned to that process by Windows NT.
- *CPU*: This is the current CPU utilization incurred by that process, shown as a percentage. This is an instantaneous value that is continually updated, so there is no need to refresh the display to see the current CPU usage of various processes. This indicates how much of the CPU's resources are currently being consumed by each process and can help you to quickly isolate applications that have been hoarding the system's CPU(s). When the system is mainly idle, the System Idle Process should be just less than 100 percent; this entry represents the Idle Thread, or time spent doing no useful work (because there isn't any to do).
- *CPU Time*: This figure is a cumulative value representing the total amount of CPU time (in hours, minutes, and seconds/HH:MM:SS format) that has been consumed by this process since it was started. This indicates how much total CPU time has been used to execute threads related to this process and can help you to quickly isolate applications that have been hoarding the system's CPU(s).
- *Mem Usage*: This displays the total memory usage by each process, in kilobytes (K). This is an instantaneous value for the total memory footprint of the process, including both its paged and nonpaged pool memory usage.

The Task Manager dialog is shown in Figure 6-17.

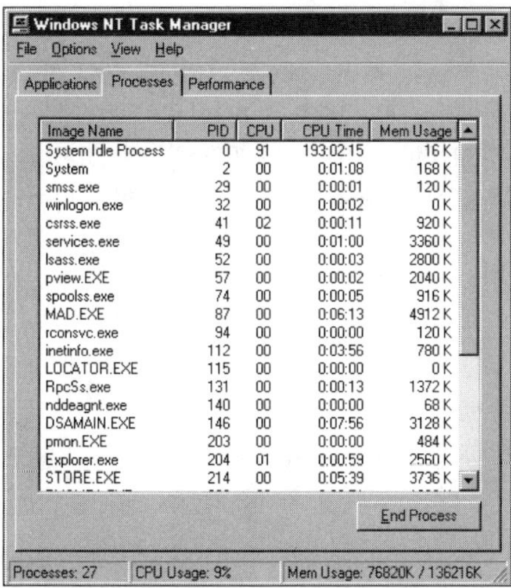

Figure 6-17: Using Task Manager to view process-related resource usage statistics.

Be sure when using Task Manager that the Show 16-bit Tasks option is turned on (checked) in the Options menu if you want to view 16-bit as well as 32-bit applications. Otherwise, 16-bit applications will be hidden from the Processes tab display window.

Additionally, you may wish to add the following columns to the display (via the View→Select Columns from the menu bar), which provide additional useful information about each process:

- *Memory Usage Delta*: The change in memory use since the last update, in kilobytes (Note: This column is capable of displaying negative values for this column when appropriate.)
- *Virtual Memory Size*: The amount of virtual memory used by each process
- *Paged Pool*: The paged pool (user memory) usage of each process
- *Nonpaged Pool*: The nonpaged pool (system memory) usage of each process
- *Base Priority*: The proccss's base priority level (Low/Normal/High)
- *Thread Count*: The number of threads associated with each process

The size of the paged and nonpaged pool memory values shown on the Processes tab are not 100 percent precise. This is because the values are taken from internal system counters which count duplicated object handles as well as space for the object. In addition, they are rounded to the page size of the processor (4K for Intel and 8K for Alpha), resulting in rounding up if a process is using only part of a page. By contrast, the global paged and nonpaged pool sizes for the entire system, shown on the Performance tab, are 100% correct. As a result, the sum of values for each process might not match the count for the whole system. Task Manager, Performance Monitor, Process Explode (`PVIEW.EXE`), Process Monitor (`PMON.EXE`) and Process Viewer (`PVIEWER.EXE`) all use the same internal system counters to monitor paged and nonpaged memory usage.

IDENTIFYING RESOURCE HOGS USING PROCESS VIEWER AND PROCESS EXPLODE

Several others useful methods for viewing application resource usage are available to those who own the Windows NT Resource Kit. Included in the Resource Kit are several utilities that allow you to view process-centric information including CPU and memory usage, and other important statistics such as page pool versus non-paged pool memory usage, process and thread base and current priority levels, the amount of time the thread spends in User Mode versus Kernel (or Privileged) Mode.

Process Monitor (`PMON.EXE`) is actually included with the Windows NT Resource Kit as well as the latest shipping versions and Service Packs of Windows NT. It is a fairly basic but informative text-mode application that displays basic process data, including CPU utilization, CPU time spent, memory usage, a memory delta (difference figure) since the last refresh, page faults, paged and nonpaged memory pool usage, handle and thread counts, and several other items. It is very useful for obtaining quick pictures of process performance; however, it isn't capable of managing processes.

Process Monitor is shown in Figure 6-18.

```
C:\NTRESKIT\pmon.exe
 Memory:   64952K Avail:  12816K  PageFlts:     71 InRam Kernel: 2880K P: 7332K
 Commit:  76388K/  55900K Limit: 136216K Peak:  78268K  Pool N: 3276K P: 7424K

                  Mem  Mem    Page   Flts Commit  Usage   Pri  Hnd Thd   Image
CPU  CpuTime    Usage Diff   Faults Diff Charge NonP Page      Cnt Cnt   Name

                15644    0    27110    5                                File Cache
95 193:02:45       16    0        1    0      0    0    0  0     0   1 Idle Process
 0   0:01:08      168    0     1702    0     36    0    0  8  1418  44 System
 0   0:00:01       32    0     1983    0    164    1    0 11    30   6 smss.exe
 0   0:00:12      916    0     1066    0   1260    4   53 13   422   7 csrss.exe
 0   0:00:02        0    0     1002    0    592   10   19 13    46   2 winlogon.exe
 0   0:01:00     3360    0     4105    0   1388  232   18  9   282  19 services.exe
 0   0:00:03     2800    0     2423    0   1068   28   12  9   121  13 lsass.exe
 0   0:00:05      916    0     1410    0   1976  691   14  8   105   8 spoolss.exe
 0   0:00:00      120    0      317    0    380   14   13  4    36   4 rconsvc.exe
 0   0:00:00        0    0      393    0    492   14   10  8    41   5 LOCATOR.EXE
 0   0:00:13     1372    0     2959    0    840 1012   14  8   101   7 RpcSs.exe
 0   0:00:00       28    0      314    0    312    1    9  8    16   1 nddeagnt.exe
 0   0:06:13     4912    0     9215    0   2524  695   25  8   147  17 MAD.EXE
 0   0:03:56      684    0     1250    0   1744 2892   60  8   323  31 inetinfo.exe
 0   0:07:56     3128  -16    99562    0   5136 5088   21  8   348  25 DSAMAIN.EXE
 0   0:05:39     3540    0     3731    0  14736 7356   26  8   412  51 STORE.EXE
 0   0:00:51     1544    0     5155    0  12620 1947   25  8   448  45 EMSMTA.EXE
 0   1:11:08     1104    0     3607    0   1720 1144   25  8   194  30 MSEXCIMC.EXE
```

Figure 6-18: Viewing process-related statistics with Process Monitor (`PMON.EXE`).

You aren't limited to viewing only the processes that appear in the first screen that Process Monitor shows you — use the up and down arrow keys to scroll through the list of processes.

A second utility that is very handy when you wish to monitor and/or control system processes is Process Viewer (`PVIEWER.EXE`), available only with the Windows NT Resource Kit. It displays similar data to that shown in Process Monitor, but does so via a graphical display. In its primary screen, only basic process data, such as CPU time, thread priority, and working set memory, are shown. However, extensive memory usage statistics for any process can be viewed by clicking the Memory Usage Detail button available on the left side of the dialog. This button displays a memory detail dialog for the selected process, including figures related to user address space, mapped and private memory commit values, and virtual memory figures. The Process Viewer dialog, including the Memory Detail dialog, is shown in Figure 6-19.

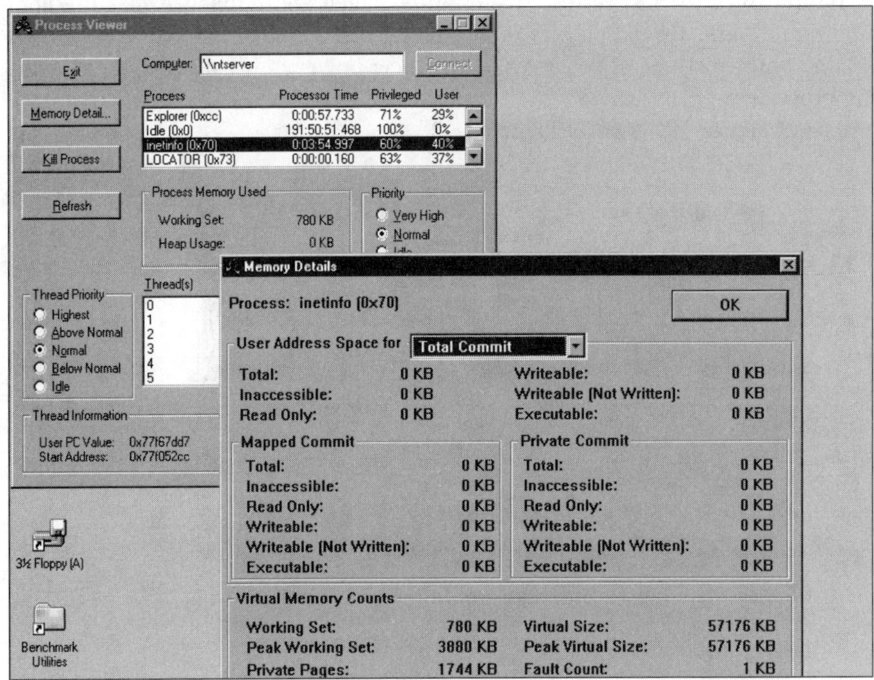

Figure 6-19: Viewing process-related statistics with Process Viewer (PVIEWER.EXE).

Process Viewer also provides a number of controls, including a Kill Process button and the capability to enter a computer name anywhere on the network for remote monitoring of other systems (a very handy feature for network administrators!).

A third utility for viewing process-related data, which is also available only with the NT Resource Kit, is an abbreviated version of Process Viewer called Process Explode (which has the seemingly unrelated executable file name of PVIEW.EXE; this also makes it easy to confuse this program with Process Viewer's PVIEWER.EXE). Process Explode offers similar information to both Process Monitor and Process Viewer; however, its methodology is different. Although it uses a graphical display like Process Viewer, it dumps all of the information related to each process in a single dialog (rather than using a separate dialog as with Process Viewer). The result is an informational utility, but one that only a programmer could love (or perhaps someone with really good detail vision). Like Process Viewer, Process Explode also contains a process termination button, labeled tersely as Kill App.

The Process Explode dialog is shown in Figure 6-20.

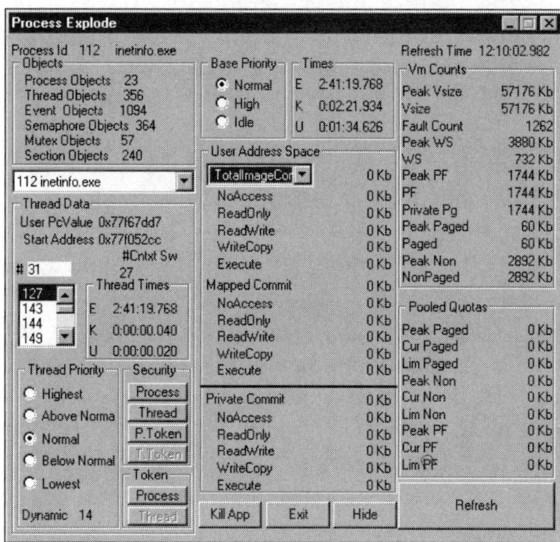

Figure 6-20: Viewing process-related statistics with Process Explode (PVIEW.EXE).

What to do if you identify a resource hog

Unfortunately, as an enduser, there isn't a whole lot you can do about an application that is hogging system resources. Your choices are limited to these: (1) notify the developer of the situation and hope it is addressed in a future release or patch; (2) stop using the program altogether and switch to a competitive product that is kinder on system resources; (3) live with it as-is; or (4) increase your system resources to accommodate the hogginess (however, this is akin to the tail wagging the dog, unless the application happens to be one that is "mission critical" and indispensable in your environment). Employing the methods described in this section will at least empower you to identify these programs so that you can make informed decisions about how the applications run on your system and what requirements they generate.

If, on the other hand, you're a developer of an application, this information gives you valuable insight into the resource usage of your application and can help you identify problem areas. By combining Performance Monitoring with regular application debugging tools, you can create applications that are not only robust and rock-solid, but efficient as well.

A final concept to consider when monitoring and evaluating application performance in Windows NT is generating a "performance baseline" for your system. This baseline is essentially a snapshot of your system's resource load for various subsystems and components and defines the environment in which your applications are running. This is important, because changes in your environment will have at least as much effect on your application performance as changes to the applications or environment subsystems that run them. By creating a baseline early on, you'll be able to more intelligently judge the performance of your system over time (because you'll have something to compare it to).

To get an initial performance baseline for a Windows NT system, you should use Performance Monitor to monitor some key objects and counters. These objects and counters are shown in Table 6-3. If you generate the same Performance Monitor view later on after making changes to your software or hardware configuration, you'll be able to instantly judge the effects of these changes on your overall system. As you see trends in the system performance curve pointing to bottlenecks in one subsystem or several, you can then employ more specific "vertical tools" (those designed to evaluate a specific aspect of system performance) to further analyze the problem area to determine exactly what is going on.

TABLE 6-3 PERFORMANCE MONITOR OBJECTS AND COUNTERS TO CREATE A PERFORMANCE BASELINE

Object Name	Counter Name	Description
Cache	Data Map Hits %	How often requested data is found in cache.

continued

Object Name	Counter Name	Description
Logical Disk	Avg. Disk Queue Length	Measure activity of each logical partition of the disk. Avg. disk queue length of 1.0 indicates that the disk is too busy to service the request at the time it was made and requests were queued.
Memory	Pages/sec	The number of pages between main memory and the disk drives in each second. If this counter is consistently high, memory is in short supply.
Objects	Processes	An instantaneous count of the number of processes running.
Physical Disk	Avg. Disk Queue Length	A measure of the activity of the disk subsystem. It is the sum of Avg. Disk Queue Length for all logical partitions of the disk.
Process	% Processor Time	A measure of each process's use of the processor.
Processor	% Processor Time	A good indicator of the demand for and efficiency of a processor.
System	% Total Processor Time	Include this counter to monitor multiprocessor systems. It combines average processor usage of all processes into a single counter.
Thread (for a particular thread instance or all instances)	% Processor Time	Threads are the components of a process that execute its code on the processor. This counter indicates how much processor time individual threads are receiving.

(continued)

TABLE 6-3 PERFORMANCE MONITOR OBJECTS AND COUNTERS TO CREATE A PERFORMANCE BASELINE *(Continued)*

Object Name	Counter Name	Description
Thread (for a particular thread instance or all instances)	% Context Switches	Measure rate of switches from one thread to another. Thread switches can occur either inside of a single process or across processes. A thread switch may be caused either by one thread asking another for information, or by a thread being preempted by another awaiting execution.

You may wish to first log the objects containing these counters over a day or several days, and then use Chart or Report View to analyze the data collected. A sample Performance Monitor session displaying these values is shown in Figure 6-21.

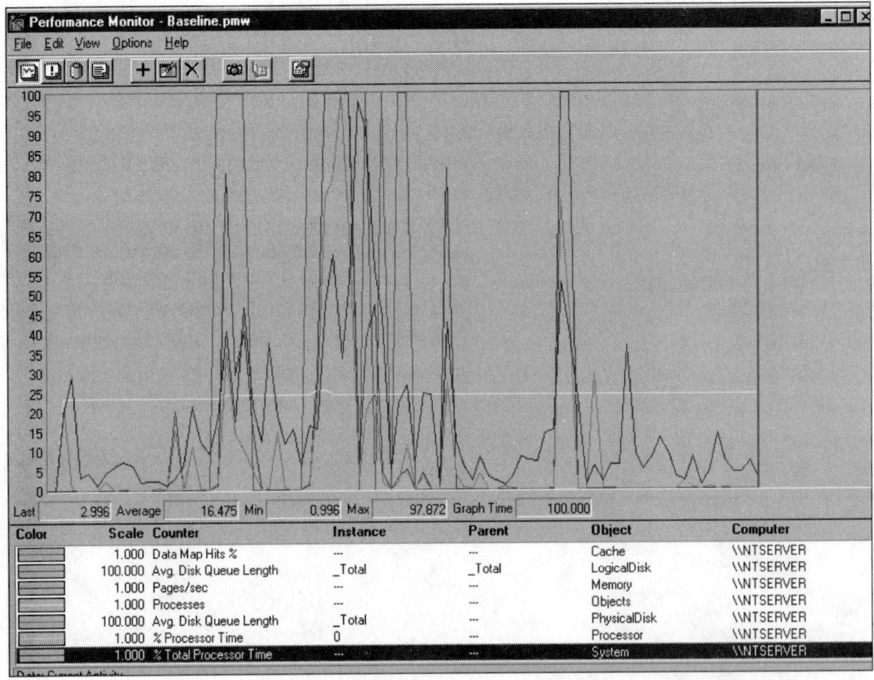

Figure 6-21: Charting a system's performance baseline in Performance Monitor.

An extensive list of Performance Monitor objects and counters is provided in Appendix C,"Index of Performance Monitor Objects and Counters."

Included on the *Optimizing Windows NT* CD-ROM is `BASELINE.PMW`, a Performance Monitor workspace file that contains a basic set of counters (those shown in Figure 6-21) to help you create a baseline of system performance. (Note:The only counters not included in this file are individual thread-related counters, because these will be different from system to system.) To use this file, simply locate and double-click it using the Windows NT Explorer (it is located in the `\PMWORKSPACE` folder, or point your web browser to the location of the *Optimizing Windows NT* CD-ROM after inserting it in your CD-ROM drive (e.g., `D:\`). Then select the page for Performance Monitor Workspaces and follow the instructions given to load and use the file.

It is often a good idea to monitor individual processes (and even threads within processes in some cases) to discover which are demanding the greatest resources. This helps profile system and process performance, and pinpoint which processes may be causing problems. After profiling the overall system, you can focus on finding "bad apps" or budgeting more system resources after discovering which areas are presenting the largest performance bottlenecks.

Setting process/processor affinity

In addition to its process monitoring abilities we examined in the previous section, Task Manager has another interesting trick: the capability to tell Windows NT which processes run on which processors. Recalling our discussion of NT's symmetric multiprocessing (SMP) features from Chapter 5, we know that NT is capable of executing threads across multiple processors in a parallel fashion. When scheduling threads, NT uses a process called *soft affinity* to distribute the thread load across the available processor resources. Soft affinity basically means that in most circumstances, NT will associate a particular process with a particular processor and continue to schedule threads from that process to run on that same processor for the duration of its execution. This methodology is beneficial to performance for one very simple but important reason: the local cache of the processor which first executed the process will have cached code and data related to that process within it. Therefore, it is much more efficient for the process to continue operating on that processor rather than losing the benefit of the cached information to run on a different CPU.

Although normally Windows NT handles the distribution of threads and processor affinity automatically and in a highly optimal fashion, you may use Task Manager's Processes tab to manually configure a particular process to be able to run only on a specific processor or processors. This option, of course, is only available on SMP Windows NT computers and is configured via the same right-click action on a process we used earlier to change its base priority. However, on an SMP machine, an additional menu option appears when right-clicking a process: Set Affinity. This dialog is shown in Figure 6-22.

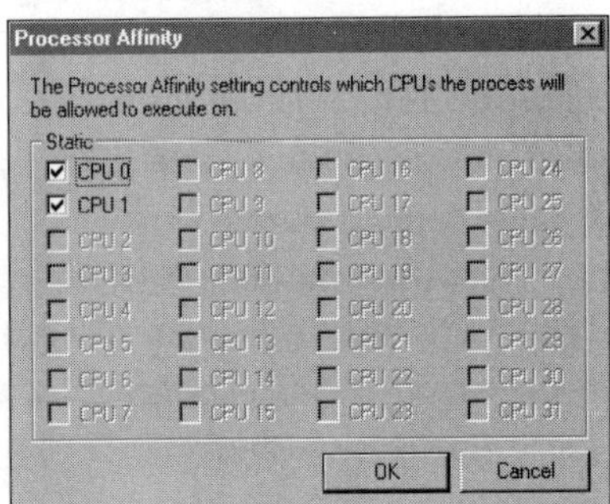

Figure 6-22: Manually configuring a process's Processor Affinity in Task Manager's Processes tab.

By checking certain CPUs in the list shown, you ensure that that process only runs on the selected CPU(s). Again, Windows NT typically handles thread execution and distribution in an efficient manner that won't benefit from this type of configuration. However, if you are running an applications server or other machine that uses a CPU-intensive application, you may want to experiment with dividing CPU time between that application's process and others running on the system (e.g., set a certain application to run only on one or more processors, and set all other processes to use any processors *except* those processors selected for the other application). In some circumstances, you may find that doing so provides additional performance benefits for the application.

Setting processor affinity is a dynamic, nonpermanent change that affects only that instance of a running process. Future executions of the same process will revert to the default behavior in Windows NT; that is, being able to run all processes across any available processor.

Summary

In this chapter, we examined Windows NT's application architecture and the individual NT environment subsystems and discussed some strategies for optimizing the performance of applications that run within them. In addition, you gained some tools that allow for the identification of applications that cause a negative impact on performance or system resources. In the next chapter, we discuss a topic that is paramount to the successful optimization of any system: the disk subsystem.

Chapter 7

Optimizing Disks

IT IS AN UNFORTUNATE FACT that, despite the existence of PC microprocessors measured in BIPS (Billions of Instructions Per Second) and memory chips capable of synchronous operation at speeds of 10 nanoseconds (ns) or less, most systems have one major limitation that has been difficult to overcome: the disk subsystem. No matter how fast your processor(s), memory, and video subsystems may be, it's an unfortunate reality that most of the delays you experience while using Windows NT are directly related to the mechanics of your system's disk drive(s). After all, even the fastest hard drives are only capable of transfer rates in the 5–7 MBps range, which pales in comparison to the transfer rates of most CPUs, memory chips, and I/O buses (often measured in hundreds of megabytes per second or more). This disparity makes disk drives the most immediate and identifiable bottleneck on most systems.

In addition, since cheap, high-capacity secondary storage devices are not available, it is also unlikely that this situation will change radically in the immediate future. Therefore, the best that you can do to mitigate this problem is to ensure that your NT disk subsystem is highly efficient, and reduce the amount of disk usage on your system as much as possible. In this chapter, we discuss various aspects of the Windows NT disk and file subsystems and explore ways in which you can increase your overall disk performance.

Specifically, we focus on:

- The Windows NT disk subsystem architecture
- NT file system architecture and comparisons
- NT disk and file system optimization techniques

Understanding NT's Disk Subsystem

Because disks play such an important role in any operating system, Windows NT has a sophisticated and highly capable disk subsystem that includes a number of important components. The most important of these components are:

- The Virtual Memory Manager (VMM)

- Miniport drivers (e.g., the low-level driver for a particular SCSI adapter or chipset)
- The Windows NT File Systems (including their respective file system drivers – NTFS.SYS for NTFS and FASTFAT.SYS for FAT volumes)
- The Windows NT File Cache Manager
- The Fault-Tolerant Subsystem Driver (FTDISK.SYS)
- The Windows NT Paging File

Each plays a special role in delivering NT's disk subsystem features. In the following sections, we examine various aspects of each component and see what we can do to tune its performance.

The asynchronous I/O model: NT's performance engine

As we discussed in Chapters 1 and 2, Windows NT has an asynchronous I/O model that is capable of communicating with multiple devices simultaneously. This nonlinear approach to system I/O gives Windows NT a significant performance increase over systems using serialized I/O models (such as DOS, Windows 3.1, and Windows 95), where each system I/O transaction occurs in a one-after-the-other fashion. In the case of the disk subsystem, this feature allows Windows NT to perform disk I/O operations to multiple disks and disk controllers simultaneously.

However, to fully reap the benefit of this capability, you must have a disk subsystem capable of supporting this feature. This means that the most important step you'll take is selecting the correct type of disk subsystem for your Windows NT system. Currently, this essentially means using SCSI-based disk controllers and drives (including all of the various flavors and derivatives of SCSI such as Fast/Wide SCSI, UltraSCSI, Ultra2SCSI, FibreChannel, etc.). The fact that most IDE disk subsystems are only capable of communication with one device at a time and have much higher CPU utilization than comparable SCSI subsystems, generally makes them a bad choice for Windows NT computers.

For more information on SCSI and IDE disk subsystems and a comparison of them, see the "Storage Device" section of Chapter 2, "Killer Hardware for Windows NT."

The Windows NT file cache

Another key feature of Windows NT's disk and memory subsystems is Windows NT's file cache (a.k.a disk cache) manager. A disk cache stores recently accessed disk data in a memory pool known as a "cache." This optimizes disk performance by retrieving data from the cache instead of physically retrieving it from a hard drive. Due to the relatively slow performance of even the fastest hard drives, the existence of disk caching is key to decent disk performance under any operating system. The NT cache manager is an especially dynamic and intelligent entity. It continually maintains a balance between available system RAM and memory used for disk caching, relinquishing memory back to the system from the cache as needed. By dynamically resizing the cache on the fly, NT's cache manager is capable of optimizing disk performance under whatever memory load the system is experiencing.

In fact, NT's cache manager is rather aggressive by default, and uses a large amount of memory for the disk cache until forced to relinquish it to other system processes. Because of the nature of disks and disk caching, the configuration of NT's file cache is extremely important to system performance. Reading through the Windows NT documentation gives you very little information on how to configure the size of NT's file cache and even less on advanced cache parameters that the NT file cache manager controls. However, in this chapter we give you some tips on how you can better control the NT file cache to help optimize its performance in your environment.

More RAM Equals Less Disk

As you have probably already figured out, Windows NT is extremely fond of memory. In fact, you could say that it's downright memory hungry. This isn't necessarily a bad thing, because it also knows how to use additional memory when available, and how to scale back on system features and component sizes when memory is at a premium. However, for optimal performance, you will want to put as much RAM in your Windows NT system as possible. Generally speaking, the more you give it, the better it will perform (to a certain point). This performance increase is directly related to the disk subsystem for two reasons:

1. More physical RAM means results in reduced paging file activity (contents of memory being paged to and from the disk instead of being left in physical RAM) and therefore a reduced disk bottleneck.

2. More physical RAM means automatically increased quotas for various autotuned operating and file system components, the most important of which being the file system cache size. These increased quotas translate to enhanced disk and file system performance. In particular, a larger file cache increases cache hit ratios (where requested objects are retrieved from system memory rather than requiring physical disk access), significantly enhancing the speed of disk I/O operations.

As mentioned in the chapter's introduction, the physical limitations of disk drive mechanics automatically make disks a primary system bottleneck. It therefore stands to reason that one of our primary objectives in optimizing NT's performance is to reduce physical disk access as much as possible. For the reasons described earlier, the best place to start is by ensuring that your system has as much physical RAM as possible. By doing so, you'll automatically increase the performance of the disk subsystem and the entire system as a whole. Windows NT detects the additional memory and automatically performs certain system parameter tunings that reduce disk access. Although it's a good place to start, simply throwing additional RAM into your system isn't the only thing you can do to maximize disk performance. Now that you've beefed up your RAM, you're ready to delve deeper into the dynamics of NT's disk and file system components to identify bottlenecks and do some performance tweaking.

Detecting Disk Subsystem Bottlenecks

Unlike some system performance problems, disk-related bottlenecks aren't usually that difficult to identify: a disk-bound system will usually give itself away by the continual grinding noises of the hard drive and/or flashing disk access LEDs. If you are seeing a great deal of disk activity (or continual disk activity) on your system, or feel that disk-related operations are happening more slowly than they should, you should start by examining the disk subsystem as a possible performance bottleneck.

The first step in solving any problem is verifying the problem's exact cause. If you suspect that your system is suffering due to a disk-related performance bottleneck, you need some quick and reliable methods to verify that the problems are in fact disk-related. Furthermore, you want to determine whether the problem is the physical disk subsystem itself, or a configuration problem related to either another system component (such as processor or memory) or to the configuration of your Windows NT installation itself. Specifically, you should follow the steps outlined in the "Detecting Memory Bottlenecks" section of Chapter 5, "Optimizing Memory and Processing." This will help you to ascertain whether the excessive disk activity you are seeing is due to a lack of physical RAM (and the paging activity that normally results from this) or the actual disk subsystem itself.

Detecting excessive disk activity

The first thing to do when diagnosing a disk subsystem problem is to define a standard for what comprises "excessive" disk activity on an NT system. Because every Windows NT computer has a certain amount of disk access under any circumstance, we need to generate some rules of thumb that we can use to determine whether what we're seeing is excessive or out of the ordinary.

Before we can do any disk-related performance monitoring in Windows NT, we must first issue a special command to instruct NT to turn disk-related counters on; they are off by default on all versions of Windows NT. To enable disk-related performance counters, open an NT Command Prompt window and issue the following command:

```
DISKPERF -Y
```

If your system uses stripe sets, mirror sets, or stripe sets with parity that you will be performance monitoring, you should instead use the DISKPERF command with the *-YE* switch, which enables counters for volumes using the FTDISK.SYS fault tolerant disk driver:

```
DISKPERF -YE
```

After entering either of these commands, you'll receive a message that disk performance counters will be active the next time the system is booted. At this point you should shut down and restart your system. If you want to disable disk counters later on, you can simply issue the command again with the *-N* option to turn the counters off. If you switch between measuring standard and striped/mirrored/striped with parity volumes, you can also alternatively issue the *-Y* and *-YE* switches before testing each. (Note: A reboot is required each time a different DISKPERF command is issued, since the configuration is read when the system boots.)

The reason disk counters are turned off by default goes back to an issue that has become somewhat dated by today's standards: that disk counters can cause a 1.5 percent performance hit on slower 386 systems. Because 386 systems are no longer supported and the average Windows NT system these days is a Pentium-based system, this has become a moot issue.

Once disk counters are enabled, you're ready to fire up the trusty Windows NT Performance Monitor and examine some disk performance-related counters.

For more information on the use of the Windows NT Performance Monitor utility, see the "Meet Your Toolkit" section of Chapter 4, "NT Optimization 101."

With Performance Monitor open, we'll want to open the Chart View and add the counters shown in Table 7-1 to the display (these can be added using the ""+"" icon on the toolbar or Edit → Add to Chart from the menus):

TABLE 7-1 DISK PERFORMANCE-RELATED PERFORMANCE MONITOR COUNTERS

Object	Counter	Instance	Description
PhysicalDisk	% Disk Time	The relative physical drive number of individual drive (starts with 0)	The percentage of time that the specified disk(s) is busy handling disk I/O requests, including time spent waiting in the disk queue.
PhysicalDisk	Current Disk Queue Length	The relative physical drive number of individual drive (starts with 0)	The number of outstanding (unserviced) requests on the disk at the present time; this includes requests in service at the time of the snapshot.
PhysicalDisk	Avg. Disk seconds/Transfer	The relative physical drive number of individual drive (starts with 0)	The time, in seconds, it takes to complete an average disk transfer.
Memory	Pages/second	N/A	The number of pages read from the disk or written to the disk to resolve memory references to pages that weren't in memory at the time of the reference.

The cache bottleneck chart monitors are automatically set up for you if you use the `CacheBottleneck.pmw` Performance Monitor Workspace file, which is included on the book's CD. To use this file, simply locate and double-click it using the Windows NT Explorer (it is located in the `\PMWORKSPACE` folder, or point your Web browser to the location of the *Optimizing Windows NT* CD-ROM after inserting it in your CD-ROM drive (e.g., `D:\`). Then select the page for "Performance Monitor Workspaces" and follow the instructions given to load and use the file.

For descriptions of the various counters viewable with the Performance Monitor utility, see Appendix C, "Performance Monitor Counters."

A sample Performance Monitor session including these counters is shown in Figure 7-1.

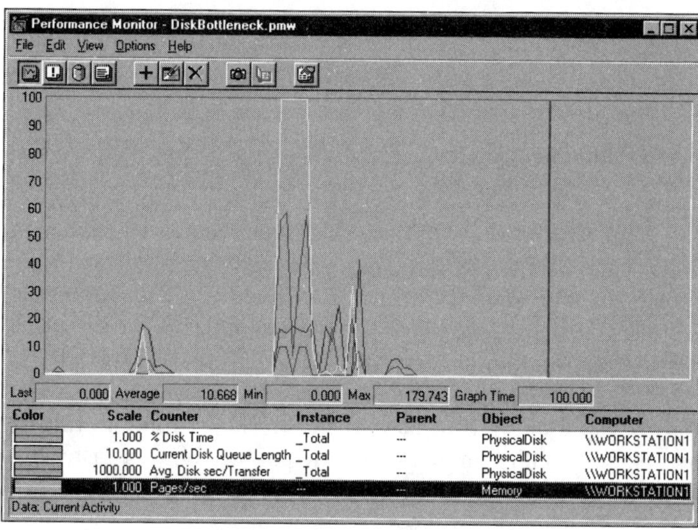

Figure 7-1: Using Performance Monitor to identify disk bottlenecks.

Once the Chart View (or, for a longer-term picture of performance, the Log View) is used to monitor and log these counters under a regular system load (i.e., typical day-to-day activities), we can use some formulas and rules to determine if and where bottlenecks exist.

As a rule, figures for the PhysicalDisk: % Disk Time counter reaching values of 66 percent or higher indicate that the physical disk drive itself is the performance bottleneck. Because this figure represents the total time the drive spends servicing disk I/O requests, it means that the drive is busy most of the time ($^2/_3$ of the time or more, to be exact); this is likely the result of a slow disk drive or controller card. In these situations, you should strongly consider immediate replacement of the disk drive(s) and/or drive controller with faster versions.

For more information on recommended disk and controller hardware for Windows NT systems, see Chapter 2, "Killer Hardware for Windows NT."

The next item we can examine is the PhysicalDisk: Current Disk Queue Length counter. This counter indicates the current disk I/O queue; that is, the number of disk I/O requests that are waiting to be serviced by the disk drive hardware. As is true with any system I/O device, this number should generally never increase past a value of 2; if it does, this may also indicate that the physical disk subsystem itself is the bottleneck. Again, the solution is to replace the disk drive and/or controller with faster versions that are capable of servicing disk I/O requests more quickly (which we would expect to result in a lower average Current Disk Queue Length value).

Another use for this information is determining exactly how much time, as a percentage, the disk spends servicing paging file activity. To compute this, we can use the following formula:

% Disk Time Used for Paging = 100 * (Pages/second * PhysicalDisk/Average Disk seconds/Transfer)

As a general rule of thumb, you shouldn't see this figure rise to more than 10 percent of the total disk time being spent on paging file activity. Higher numbers wouldn't necessarily indicate a problem with the disk subsystem per se, but instead indicate that system RAM is deficient and needs to be increased. However, if a slow disk subsystem exists in this situation (as determined by our previous guidelines), the problem will be further exaggerated due to the slow servicing of relatively high amount of paging file activity that's occurring on the disk. The solution for this situation is to increase system memory and/or move the paging file to a faster disk on the system; the paging file could also be spread across multiple physical disks if they are available.

Included on the CD-ROM accompanying this book are a number of Performance Monitor workspaces with predefined counter selections. To duplicate the Performance Monitor environment discussed here, open the CD using your Web browser and choose the `DiskBottleneck.pmw` workspace from the Performance Monitor Workspaces section.

Testing disk throughput

Part of optimizing the performance of any piece of equipment is to determine what its maximum speed is. If you've ever bought a "high performance" vehicle, you probably took it for a high-speed test drive to see how fast it *really* went; not just what the salesperson told you. In a similar fashion, it's a good idea to take your disk subsystem for a "test spin" to see where it tops out. Not only will this give you an idea of the actual data transfer rates your disks are capable of delivering, but it will also provide you with a baseline of comparison if optimizations are made later.

There are several methods for testing your disk subsystem performance in Windows NT, including using the utilities provided with the Windows NT Resource Kit, as well as the CD accompanying this book.

TESTING DISK THROUGHPUT WITH RESPONSE PROBE

A very useful performance-related tool included with the Windows NT Resource Kit (from Microsoft Press) is the Response Probe utility. This utility allows you to put various types of loads on your NT system and is intended to be used with the Windows NT Performance Monitor that analyzes the results of the Response Probe process.

Diskmax is one of the predefined tests included with Response Probe. Diskmax tests a disk's maximum speed by having the drive read large, 64K records in a sequential fashion from a large, 20MB file. The reason this test exercises the drive's maximum speed is because it represents a "best case" scenario (large records in a sequential fashion from a large file means the drive can read data in a virtually continuous stream). The use of sequential records and a single, large file minimizes the amount of overhead from drive mechanics that would exist if multiple, smaller files or random records were used.

Response Probe and the Diskmax test will only be available on your system if you selected the "Performance Tools" option during the Windows NT Resource Kit installation process. If you did not install these tools, you can reinstall the Resource Kit over the existing copy and select this option.

The Response Probe utility is located in the PERFTOOL subfolder of the Resource Kit installation folder (e.g., C:\NTRESKIT\PERFTOOL), and the Diskmax files are located in the EXAMPLES folder underneath this folder. To run this test you need these files:

```
Probe.exe
Probeprc.exe
Diskmax.scr
Diskmax.scp
DISKMAX.SCT
```

In addition, you need the actual test file itself, which isn't installed by default but can be found on the Resource Kit CD-ROM in the \COMMON\PERFTOOL\PROBE \EXAMPLES\WORKFILE folder. The filename is WORKFILE.DAT and is a 20MB file filled with zeroes. This file contains the records that Response Probe will read during the Diskmax test.

Although the default WORKFILE.DAT test file is 20MB in size, you can also create a test file of any size for use with Response Probe. To do so, run the Createfile Utility (CREATFIL.EXE) located in the PERFTOOL\PROBE subfolder of the Resource Kit installation folder. Once you're at an NT command prompt in this folder, type the following:

```
CREATFIL filename [filesize]
```

filesize is optional and should be given in Kilobytes (K); if you don't specify a value for it the default size will be 1024K.

Follow these steps to run Diskmax and test your disk's maximum throughput:

1. If you haven't already done so, enable disk counters by typing **DISKPERF -Y** (or -YE if you are testing a mirror, stripe, or stripe set with parity volume) at an NT command prompt and then restart the system.
2. Close all open applications.
3. Launch the Performance Monitor utility located in the Administrative Tools (Common) program folder and choose View → Log.
4. Add the System object and Logical Disk object to the list of monitored objects for this Performance Monitor session; this is done using the Edit → Add to Log... menu option or the "+" menu bar icon. Then choose Done.

5. Next, choose Options → Log. Enter a filename for the log file. If possible, you should instruct Performance Monitor to write the log to a different physical drive so that there is no interference with the drive being tested. In the Update Time selection box, select a Periodic Update of one-second intervals. When ready to start logging, click Start Log. This dialog is shown in Figure 7-2.

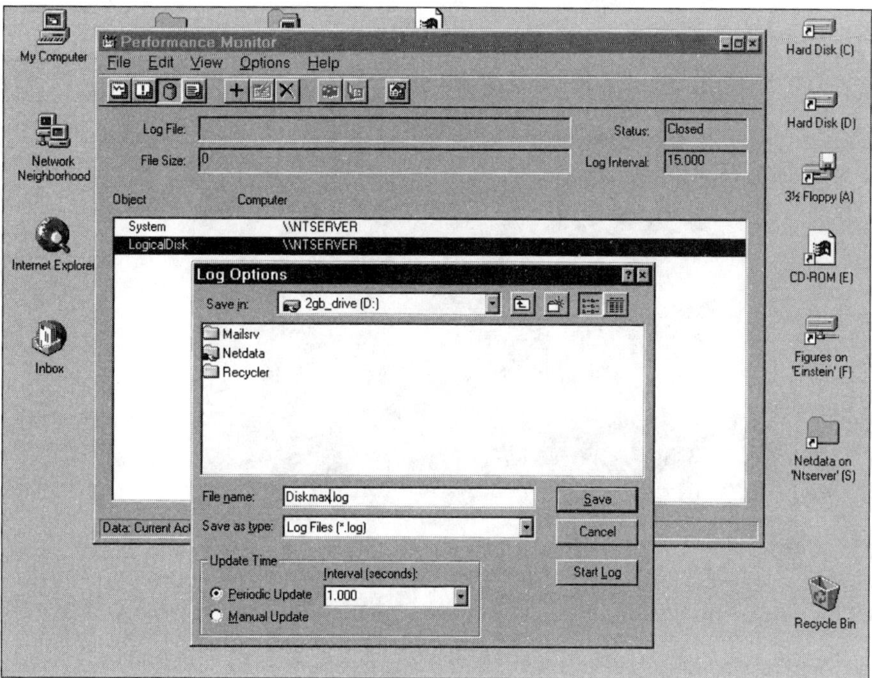

Figure 7-2: Starting a Performance Monitor log for the Diskmax test.

6. Now run the Diskmax Response Probe test by opening an NT command prompt window, changing the default directory to the `\PERFTOOL\PROBE\EXAMPLES` subfolder of the Resource Kit installation folder. With this as the default folder, type the following command: ..\PROBE DISKMAX.SCR *time_in_seconds*

7. In this command, *time_in_seconds* is the duration of the test; it is recommended that you set this value to a minimum of 120 (or set it higher) for proper results. Also note that this command assumes that the default directory is one below the PROBE folder, the default location; if not, substitute the full path name of the folder containing the PROBE.EXE utility in the above command line. This command launches the Diskmax Response Probe test for the specified duration. Figure 7-3 shows a sample session running Response Probe with the Diskmax test.

```
C:\WINNT\System32\cmd.exe
03/01/96  12:00a                   740 4096.SCR
03/01/96  12:00a                 2,156 4096.SCT
03/01/96  12:00a                   622 4MSU.SCP
03/01/96  12:00a                   833 4MSU.SCR
03/01/96  12:00a                 1,817 4MSU.SCT
03/01/96  12:00a                   743 512.SCP
03/01/96  12:00a                   754 512.SCR
03/01/96  12:00a                 2,379 512.SCT
03/01/96  12:00a                   621 8KSU.SCP
03/01/96  12:00a                   831 8KSU.SCR
03/01/96  12:00a                 1,814 8KSU.SCT
03/01/96  12:00a                   596 DISKMAX.SCP
03/01/96  12:00a                   650 DISKMAX.SCR
03/01/96  12:00a                 1,818 DISKMAX.SCT
03/01/96  12:00a                 3,670 DISKMAX.TXT
03/01/96  12:00a                   608 DOPROBE.BAT
03/01/96  12:00a                   735 MINREAD.SCP
03/01/96  12:00a                   773 MINREAD.SCR
03/01/96  12:00a                 2,254 MINREAD.SCT
03/01/96  12:00a                 4,333 MINREAD.TXT
03/01/96  12:00a                   978 SIZEREAD.BAT
03/01/96  12:00a                 4,206 SIZEREAD.TXT
07/22/96  01:15p            20,480,000 WORKFILE.DAT
              41 File(s)      20,531,762 bytes
                             254,836,736 bytes free

C:\NTRESKIT\PerfTool\Probe\Examples>..\probe diskmax.scr 120

Multi-Processor Response Probe.
Copyright 1990-1996, Microsoft Corporation.
Version 2.3  (96.07.31)

Fri Jun 27 03:02:30 1997

Script File:               diskmax.scr
Trial Time:                120 seconds
Stable interval : [50%..100%] of Trial Time == [60..120]  (60 seconds)
Relative Processor Speed:        10.91

C:\NTRESKIT\PerfTool\Probe\Examples>
```

Figure 7-3: Running Response Probe with the Diskmax test from an NT command prompt window.

8. When the command prompt returns, the test is complete. At this point, immediately stop Performance Monitor logging by choosing Log → Stop Log from the menus.

Now that we've got a log of the Diskmax test, we can analyze the data to generate some information. To do so, change the Performance Monitor view to Chart View (View → Chart).

Next, we'll need to instruct Performance Monitor to generate the Chart View from our previously recorded log file rather than current activity. To do so, choose Options → Data From from the menus, and use the dialog to locate the logfile we recorded during the Diskmax test.

Once we've done this, we're ready to include the counters we want to look at from our Performance Monitor session. Using Edit → Add to Chart or the "+" menu bar icon, add each of the following counters (shown in Table 7-2).

For more information on using the Windows NT Performance Monitor, see the "Meet Your Toolkit" section of Chapter 4, "NT Optimization 101."

TABLE 7-2 PERFORMANCE MONITOR COUNTERS FOR THE DISKMAX THROUGHPUT TEST

Object	Counter
System	% Total Processor Time
System	Total Interrupts/sec
System	% Total Interrupt Time
LogicalDisk	Average Disk Read Queue Length
LogicalDisk	Average Disk Bytes/Read
LogicalDisk	Average Disk sec/Read
LogicalDisk	Disk Read Bytes/sec
LogicalDisk	Disk Reads/sec

A predefined Performance Monitor workspace environment file, `Diskmax.pmw`, has been provided on the *Optimizing Windows NT* CD-ROM to expedite this process.

This will generate a Performance Monitor Chart display similar to the one shown in Figure 7-4.

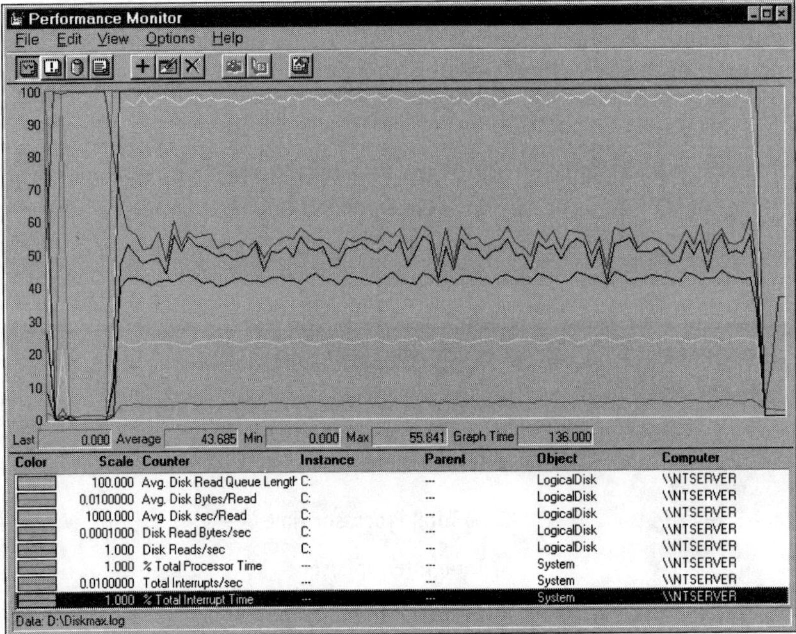

Figure 7-4: The results of the Diskmax test in Performance Monitor's Chart View.

As an alternative, we can display a text-based summary of the data collected using Performance Monitor's Report View. To do this select Options → Data From as in the previous example, but instead select View → Report to set Performance Monitor into Report View. The display will be similar to that shown in Figure 7-5.

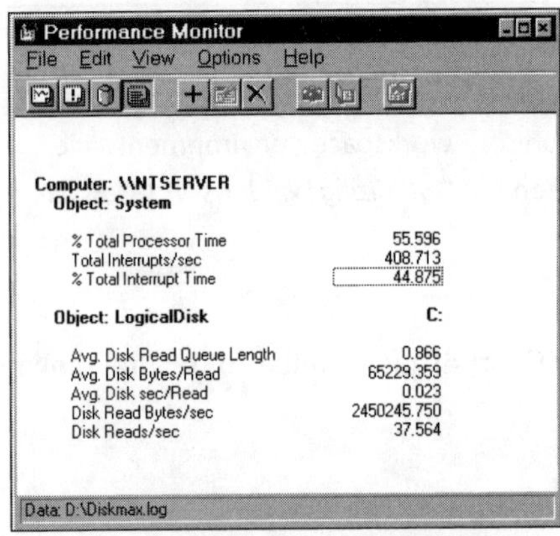

Figure 7-5: The results of the Diskmax test in Performance Monitor's Report View.

As you can see, we got a lot of interesting looking data during our test. So what do the data mean and what do we do with them? Well, first, we convert the Disk Read Bytes/sec figure (which is an average over the test period) from bytes to megabytes. This shows that the disk achieved 2.37MB/second, a respectable speed. In addition, we see that the disk read an average of 37.6 records per second (each record being 64K in size), and that each read took an average of .02 seconds. Not too shabby at all! However, further investigation reveals an ugly but important truth: although the average processor utilization was relatively moderate (55.6 percent), a whopping 44.8 percent of this time was generated by the interrupts being generated by the disk subsystem. Ouch! This sounds like an IDE drive subsystem at work. In fact, this particular machine was using a 630MB EIDE drive running with NT's default IDE device driver in IDE PI/O Mode 2.

So, just for the heck of it, let's see what happens if we conduct the same test on an identically configured system with a Fast/Wide SCSI-2 drive subsystem instead of an IDE-based one. Of course, for the sake of proper comparison, we want to use the same set of parameters for our Response Probe Diskmax test, with the same exact size for `WORKFILE.DAT`.

After completing this test, the results shown in Figure 7-6 were generated.

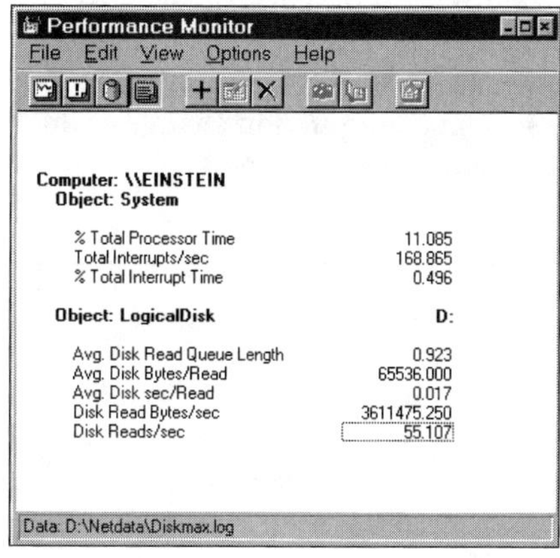

Figure 7-6: Running a comparative Diskmax test on a SCSI drive.

Wow, big difference! In this test, we see that our disk performance has skyrocketed while our CPU utilization has simultaneously plunged (a good thing). Specifically, we achieved a maximum throughput during the test of 3.4MB/second, around 33 percent faster than the previous test. Our average processor utilization has also gone from the previous 55.6 percent to a mild 11.1 percent. In addition, we see that our test only generated an average of 168.9 interrupts/second, down from 408.7 in the previous test. These interrupts also only accounted for 0.5 percent of the total processor time, a far cry from the 55.6 percent CPU utilization we saw using the IDE drive subsystem. This is a clear demonstration of the CPU-friendly and high-throughput nature of SCSI, and the potential problems inherent in the use of IDE. This should be remembered when considering the type of drive subsystem to deploy on systems that will incur heavy disk utilization, or on those systems whose CPU power is at a premium and cannot afford to be stolen to service the disk subsystem.

TESTING DISK THROUGHPUT WITH BENCH32

Although the Diskmax test is good for determining our disk subsystem's maximum throughput, it uses a single "best case" scenario, and is somewhat two-dimensional by nature. Although we can vary the file size used in the test, we aren't able to test multiple aspects of the drive's performance, such as write performance, raw, uncached drive performance versus performance with NT's file cache enabled, and performance using nonsequential I/O tests (unlike Diskmax's purely sequential test).

We could use Performance Monitor to glean some of this information, but it is somewhat awkward for this purpose due to the number of variables we want to introduce. Instead, it is far easier to use a commercial benchmarking utility that accommodates these kinds of tests. Included on the CD with this book is Bench32 from U Software, a benchmark utility that is designed specifically to run performance benchmarks on Windows NT and Windows 95 systems. In fact, we use Bench32 throughout this book to execute a variety of performance benchmarks on the various Windows NT subsystems. This enables us to quickly and easily generate performance figures before and after we make system configuration changes, which helps us determine the effects and value of each optimization we perform.

Bench32 by U Software

Included on the *Optimizing Windows NT* CD-ROM is an excellent benchmarking utility called Bench32 from U Software. Written by Edmund Underwood, this utility allows you to perform a wide variety of performance benchmarks on the most important components of your system, including CPU, memory, disk, and video. To install Bench32, place the *Optimizing Windows NT* CD-ROM in your CD-ROM drive and point your Web browser to the location of the CD. Although the CD includes a functioning shareware version of the Bench32 utility, it is highly recommended that you obtain the registered version, which provides additional features and capabilities beyond the shareware version. Additional information on Bench32 and all of the utilities included on the *Optimizing Windows NT* CD-ROM is provided in Appendix A, "What's on the CD?"

For more information on Bench32 and general benchmarking tips, see the "Benchmarking Basics" section of Chapter 4, "NT Optimization 101."

Once you've installed Bench32 from the *Optimizing Windows NT* CD-ROM, you're ready to run some disk benchmarks. Let's start by configuring Bench32 for the disk tests we'll be running. To configure the disk test options in Bench32, choose Options → Preferences from the Bench32 menus, select the Benchmark Settings tab, and click Disk Test Options. You'll see the screen shown in Figure 7-7.

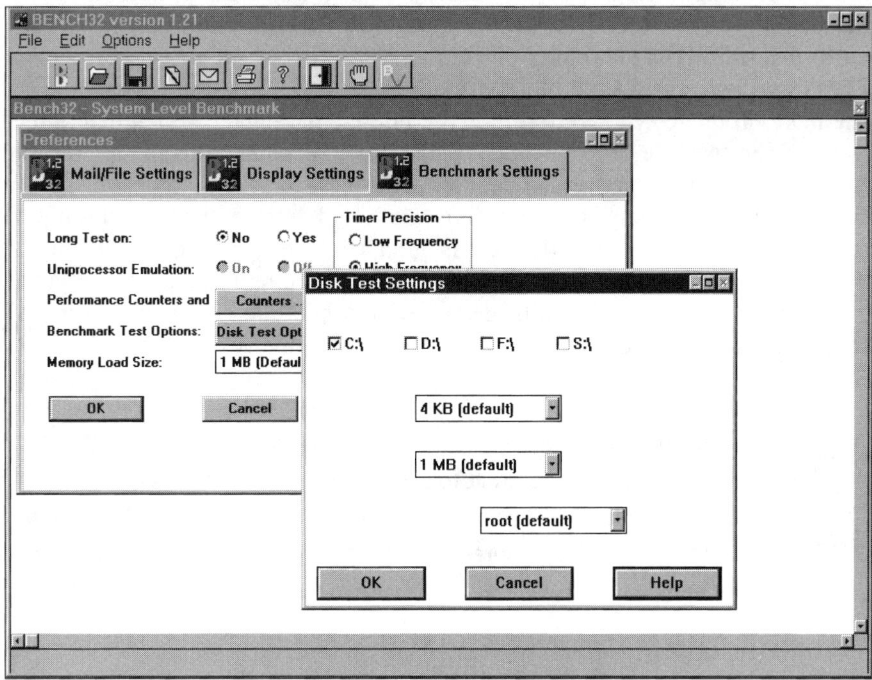

Figure 7-7: Bench32's Disk Test Settings configuration screen.

The Default Drive(s) Selection checkboxes allow you to select which disk(s) to include in the disk test. Place a checkmark next to each disk drive to test when Bench32 runs a disk test (the options you select are saved for future runs and will remain until changed).

Although the available drive selections will include network drives, it is recommended that you only test local drives using Bench32. If you wish to test the performance of a network drive, run Bench32 locally on the server containing the drive(s).

The Default Test Selection section is where you configure the actual test parameters themselves. The *Blocksize* parameter is used to set the block size used during the test, and ranges from 512 bytes to 16KB. Generally speaking, larger block size values will generate higher performance values, but this is not a guarantee. However, if you are trying to duplicate the Diskmax maximum performance test, you should start by selecting the largest block size (16KB) and working your way down to determine the maximum performance values for the drive. For general disk tests start with the default block size of 4KB.

The next parameter you configure is the *Filesize* parameter, which determines the size of the test file used during the disk test. Although the size of the file doesn't normally affect performance, it's usually best to select larger file sizes to ensure that the test is complete and comprehensively exercises the drive during the benchmark. As you may recall, the Diskmax test we generated earlier using Response Probe used a file size of 20MB; therefore, if you're trying to duplicate this test, you should start with a 20MB file size. For general disk tests, however, you can probably use a smaller file size such as the default of 1MB.

One situation where the file size may affect test results is a disk with significant fragmentation. As a result, to generate accurate results it is always best to run a complete disk optimization using a disk defragmentation utility prior to each test. This ensures that disk fragmentation doesn't affect your test results.

The final parameter on this screen, *Default Directory*, informs Bench32 which directory should be used as the location to generate the test data. The available options are root, temp, or *%homepath%*. Root is the root directory of the drive; temp is the location of the Windows NT temp directory (as defined by the TEMP variable defined in the System Control Panel Environment tab); and *%homepath%* is the location of the currently logged user's home directory on this drive. It is generally recommended that you select root because this guarantees that the test will occur on the proper drive and also guarantees maximum performance for large volumes or those using the FAT file system.

As we discussed in Chapter 4, test consistency is the key to generating accurate test figures. This means that when running disk tests, take steps to ensure that an identical environment is provided for each test's iteration. To maximize the usefulness of your disk tests, you should also follow these guidelines:

- Run a disk defragmentation utility (a thorough defragmentation run) before each test to ensure that the same approximate level of disk fragmentation exists during each test. Have as few background services and applications running as possible during the test; only run those services that are necessary for proper system operation
- To ensure the same approximate amount of available physical memory, start the test immediately after restarting the system (preferably after running the disk defragmentation) and logging in. In addition, bypass any startup group programs that may exist by holding down the Shift key during the login process (after entering login credentials).
- To keep test environments "apples to apples," always use the same test parameters for tests intended to compare a particular system configuration change or optimization.
- Make sure that the benchmark utility remains as the foreground application during the entire test (i.e., don't switch away from the application or perform other system operations during the test), and set the priority boost for foreground applications to the maximum (this can be done in the System Control Panel's Performance tab by setting the sliding bar to the far right).
- Run every test at least twice to ensure that no anomalous results were obtained during a particular test. In addition, if possible, run a test on two identically configured systems to reduce the possibility of a machine-related test anomaly (such as faulty hardware).

Once you have the test environment configured, you're ready to start generating data. To begin a new test, select File → New Test from the menus. By default, when Bench32 completes a test it generates a screen displaying a graphical representation of the test results. This graphical depiction also compares the test results to a baseline system, which includes a 100MHz Pentium system running with a 2GB EIDE hard drive (using IDE Mode 2 Programmed I/O with NT's default IDE device driver).

Figure 7-8 shows the results of a test using Bench32's disk test configured for the default settings of a 4K block size and a 2MB file size.

If you only want to test the disk subsystem and not run the other Bench32 tests (video, CPU, etc.) be sure to instruct Bench32 of this prior to running the test. By default, all tests are run during a benchmark. To configure Bench32 to run only the disk test, select Options → Run Disk Test from the menus.

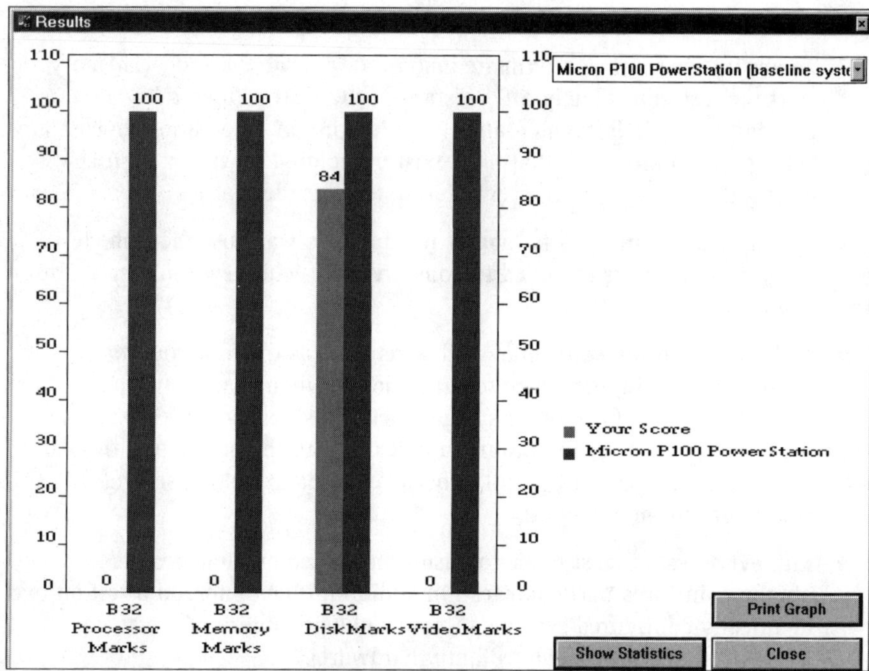

Figure 7-8: Bench32's graphical display of disk test results.

Once you're done viewing the graphical display, you can view the benchmark report generated by Bench32 for the current test. Click the Close button and you'll see a screen similar to that shown in Figure 7-9.

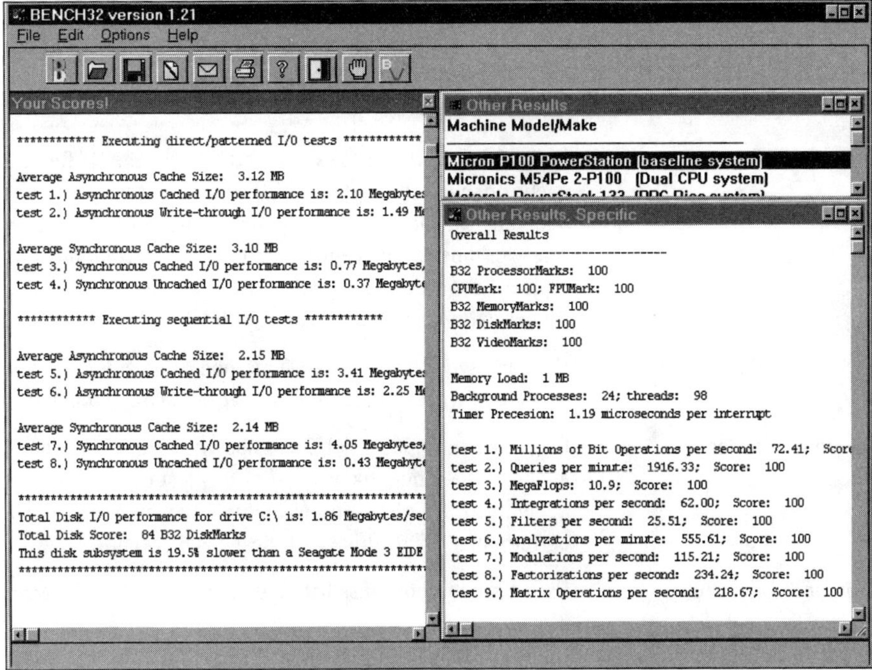

Figure 7-9: Bench32's test results screen with comparisons to baseline systems.

This screen shows the various test results for your disk subsystem during each of Bench32's tests at left (the "Your Scores!" window) and the results for similar tests on any of a variety of baseline systems at right. This is an especially handy feature because it allows you to compare your system's performance to that of a similarly configured system. Another nice feature of Bench32's disk test is that it runs a variety of different tests on the disk drive(s) being tested, including both cached and uncached performance, as well as tests using both asynchronous and synchronous I/O data transfer methods. The various tests run by Bench32's disk benchmark and their descriptions are listed in Table 7-3.

TABLE 7-3 THE BENCH32 DISK TESTS

Test Type	Description
Asynchronous Cached	Uses an asynchronous disk I/O method with the NT file cache enabled; the patterned I/O version of the test is generally the most accurate representation of the drive's real-world performance for most environments (and is typically the second highest score, bested only by the sequential synchronous cached I/O test)
Asynchronous Write-Through	Uses an asynchronous disk I/O method using NT's file cache in a write-through (i.e., no write-caching) manner
Synchronous Cached	Uses a synchronous disk I/O method with the NT file cache enabled; the sequential version of this test generally generates the highest figures and the maximum possible performance of the drive in a "best case" scenario
Synchronous Uncached	Uses a synchronous disk I/O method with the NT file cache disabled

Sequential I/O tests are similar to those generated by the Diskmax Response Probe test we used earlier; that is, sequential access to records in a file (as a result, this version of the asynchronous cached I/O test is the one most likely to approximate the Diskmax test). The direct/patterned I/O tests, on the other hand, provide a more random file access method that gives a better representation of real-life disk performance than the sequential I/O tests.

Generally, the sequential, synchronous cached I/O tests can be referred to as an indicator of your drive's maximum theoretical performance, and the direct/patterned I/O version of the asynchronous cached I/O test can be referred to as the best indication of the average “real world” performance of your drive. Also worth noting are the synchronous uncached I/O tests, which give a decent indication of the raw throughput capabilities of the drive, without the benefit of NT's file cache (however, note that virtually all drives, and some disk controllers, contain on-board cache memory that cannot be disabled by this test).

The results screen for your scores file can be saved for later reference using the File → Save option in the Bench32 menus. The file is saved as a plain ASCII text file with a .BMF (BenchMark File) extension.

Drive subsystems, such as EIDE, that use Programmed I/O (PIO) modes of operation are dependent on the CPU to carry out disk I/O operations. As a result, the CPU speed of the system is likely to have a significant impact on the disk subsystem's performance.

Now that we have a tool to test our disk subsystem, we can compare performance of our "baseline" configuration; that is, our current system configuration. As you modify your system configuration (such as by adding new driver, installing additional system RAM, or implementing any of the other optimizations discussed in this book), you can generate additional test results to determine the effects of the optimization on your system's performance. When generating additional tests to compare performance, it is also a good idea to run tests at multiple block and/or file sizes to get a wide range of data to use as a basis for comparison. In some cases, performance could theoretically go up for one test and down for another (smaller versus larger block sizes, etc.).

Throughout the rest of this chapter, we refer to the Bench32 test results screen to evaluate and demonstrate the results of various disk-related performance optimizations.

Optimizing the NT System Cache

Without a doubt, the most important aspect to disk drive performance (and system performance in general) under Windows NT is the NT system cache, also known as the file cache. As we discussed at the beginning of the chapter, Windows NT uses an adaptive caching mechanism that attempts to always deliver the best possible disk performance regardless of the amount of the system's available physical memory. As a result, Windows NT increases the system cache size as more physical RAM becomes present on the system; this is why it is so important to put as much RAM as possible in a Windows NT system for maximum disk performance.

The Windows NT system cache is a dynamic memory pool used to stored recently accessed data for all cacheable peripheral devices; this includes data transferred between hard drives and CD-ROM drives, as well as network cards over a Local Area Network. The NT Virtual Memory Manager (VMM) copies data to and from the cache as though it were an array in memory, and because these references don't invoke the file system driver (and therefore the disk drive containing the data) system performance is significantly increased.

By far, the most important advantage of the NT system cache is its effect on hard drive performance, because these devices are relatively slow by nature and greatly benefit from the presence of a cache (sometimes increasing performance by 500 percent or more!). However, given that you have provided Windows NT with sufficient RAM for the system cache, is there anything else that can be done to increase the performance of the disk subsystem? You bet there is! In this section, we examine some of the methods you can employ to ensure you're getting the most out of NT's file cache, and to determine if a system cache bottleneck exists on your system.

Viewing the system cache size

NT automatically scales the amount of memory devoted to the system cache as it becomes available to the operating system. However, it would be nice to know exactly how much memory NT is devoting to the cache at any given time so that we can track and correlate this information as we optimize our disk subsystem.

One way to view the currently allocated system cache size is to use Windows NT Task Manager's Performance tab. In addition to displaying CPU and memory usage graphs, Task Manager provides a summary of various memory size values for the system. The current size of the NT file cache is found in the Physical Memory section of the Performance tab windows, and is listed as File Cache. This figure gives the number of kilobytes (KB) currently allocated to the file cache (to convert this figure to megabytes divide the number by 1024). This screen is shown in Figure 7-10.

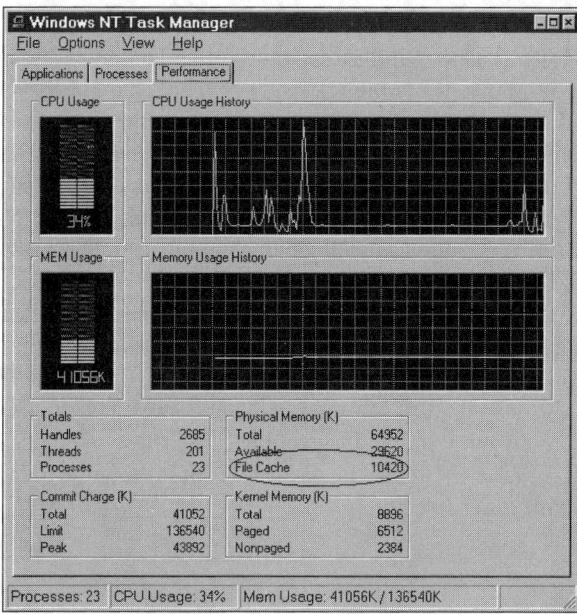

Figure 7-10: Viewing the current system cache size via Task Manager's Performance tab.

A second method for observing the cache size is to use the Windows NT Diagnostics utility (WINMSD.EXE) located in the Administrative Tools (Common) program group in the Start Menu's Programs submenu. The value is listed as File Cache in Windows NT Diagnostics' Memory tab (shown in Figure 7-11).

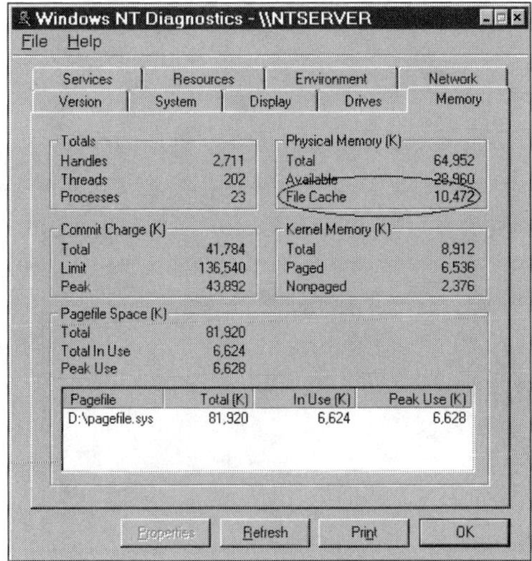

Figure 7-11: Viewing the current system cache size via the Windows NT Diagnostics' Memory tab.

Still another method for observing this value is to use Performance Monitor in a Chart or Log view for instantaneous or long-term monitoring of the cache's size. Two counters, which are part of the Memory object, may be of interest here: one is the Cache Bytes, which gives an instantaneous value of the current system cache size (in Bytes), and the other is Cache Bytes Peak, which always represents the peak value for the system cache. These counters are shown in Figure 7-12.

You may find it helpful when tuning the system cache to log the Cache Bytes value during each step; this allows you to correlate the ongoing changes in system cache size to both the optimization steps you take as well as the performance levels achieved at each step.

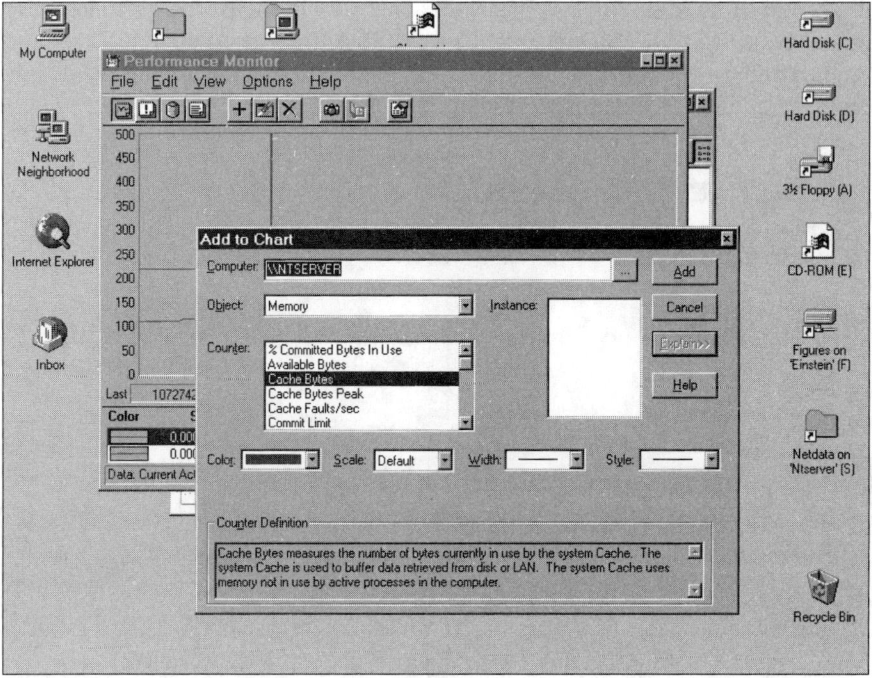

Figure 7-12: Adding the Cache Bytes and Cache Bytes Peak counters to a Performance Monitor session (Chart View).

One major difference between the Windows NT Diagnostics and Task Manager file cache size displays is that Task Manager provides a live, "real-time" view of the current cache size, while NT Diagnostics shows a current figure as of when the program was run. Thus, when using Windows NT Diagnostics to observe the system/file cache size, you should periodically click the Refresh button to observe any changes in the cache size since the program was started.

System cache tuning

Other than improving disk subsystem hardware, the most important modification we can make on an NT system to improve disk performance is to ensure that NT's file cache has been optimized for our operating environment. However, let's start by examining how NT manages the file cache and what criteria are used to determined the size of this cache.

Although we know that NT will automatically increase the system cache size as more memory becomes available, how does it figure out how much to use? To determine how much memory should be allocated to the cache, Windows NT uses certain criteria that are part of the system's configuration and instruct NT how to prioritize memory allocations between the system cache and the working sets of system processes (services and applications). This dynamic allocation process is a continual juggling act between memory used for the system cache and memory used for processes.

On Windows NT Server computers, we can adjust this prioritization by editing the properties of the Server service in the Network Control Panel's Services tab. This configuration dialog is shown in Figure 7-13.

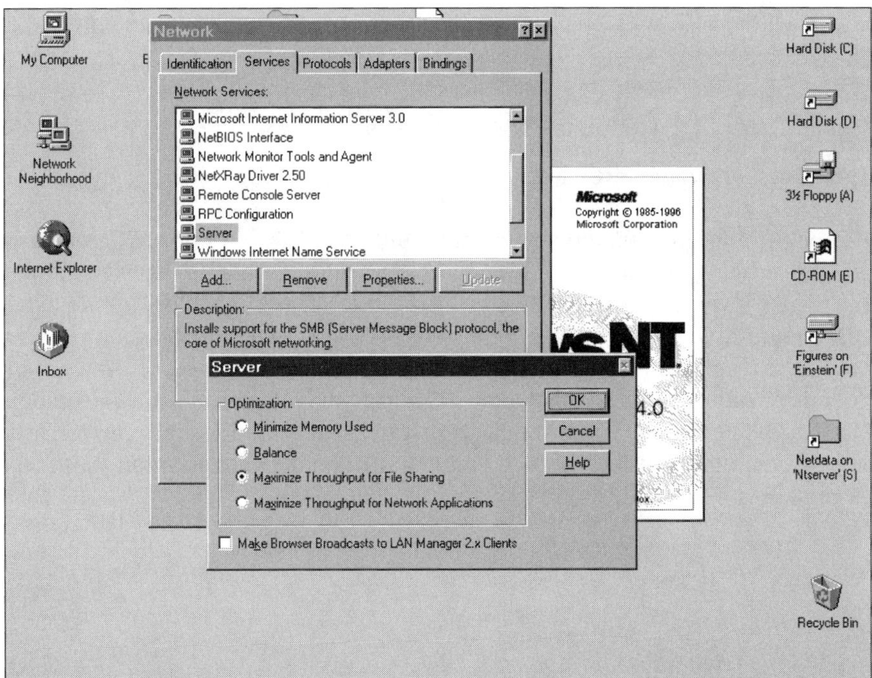

Figure 7-13: Configuring system cache priorities via Server Properties in the Network Control Panel's Services tab.

Depending on the setting, NT will either minimize the memory used for the system cache ("Minimize Memory Used" setting), balance the distribution of memory between the cache and the running processes ("Balance" setting), favor the use of memory for the system cache ("Maximize Throughput for File Sharing" setting), or favor the use of memory for applications over the system cache ("Maximize Throughput for Network Applications" setting).

While this procedure works fine for Windows NT Server, what about NT Workstations? If you attempt to configure the Server service on an NT Workstation, you're informed that the service isn't configurable. However, this is not true! In fact, NT Workstation can be configured with the same entries as NT Server; however, in the case of Workstation, this requires manually editing the Registry. The two settings that control this prioritization can be found in the following locations in the Registry:

```
HKEY_LOCAL_MACHINE\SYSTEM\CurrentControlSet\Control\Session
 Manager\Memory Management
```

Value: LargeSystemCache
Default Data: 0 for Workstations; 1 for Servers
and

```
HKEY_LOCAL_MACHINE\SYSTEM\CurrentControlSet\Services\LanmanServer
 \Parameters
```

Value: Size
Default Data: 1 for Workstations; 3 for Servers

These keys and values are shown in Figures 7-14 and 7-15.

Although in Microsoft's documentation, only the LargeSystemCache value is referenced as being affected when the Server Service is configured, an examination of the Registry while actually doing so (using the NTInternals' RegMon Registry monitoring utility included on the Optimizing Windows NT CD-ROM) shows that in fact both of these values are modified in conjunction with each of the various server prioritization options. This seems to indicate that Microsoft's documentation on the LargeSystemCache value and Server service configuration are incorrect; as a result, we recommend using Table 7-4 in lieu of the documentation on these settings contained in the NT Resource Kit and on-line help files.

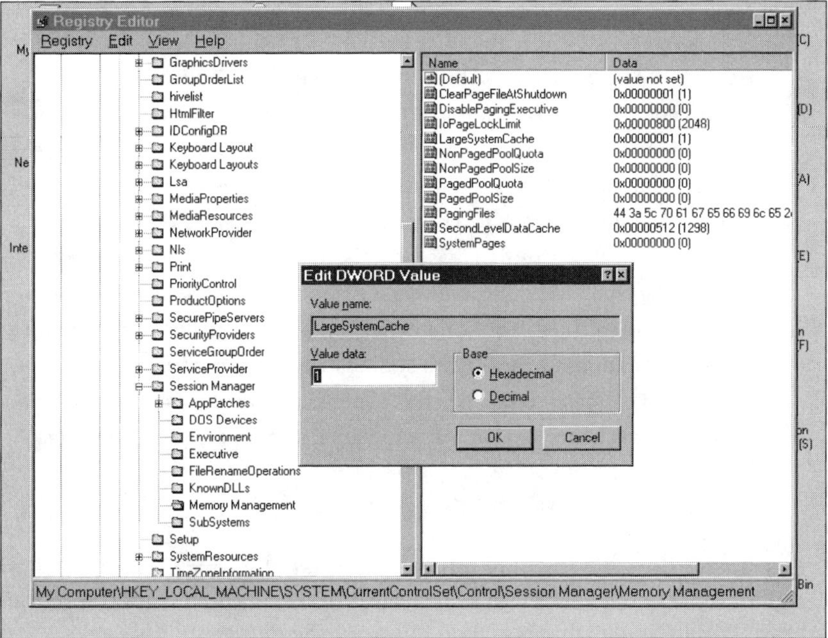

Figure 7-14: Changing the Session Manager's LargeSystemCache Registry value.

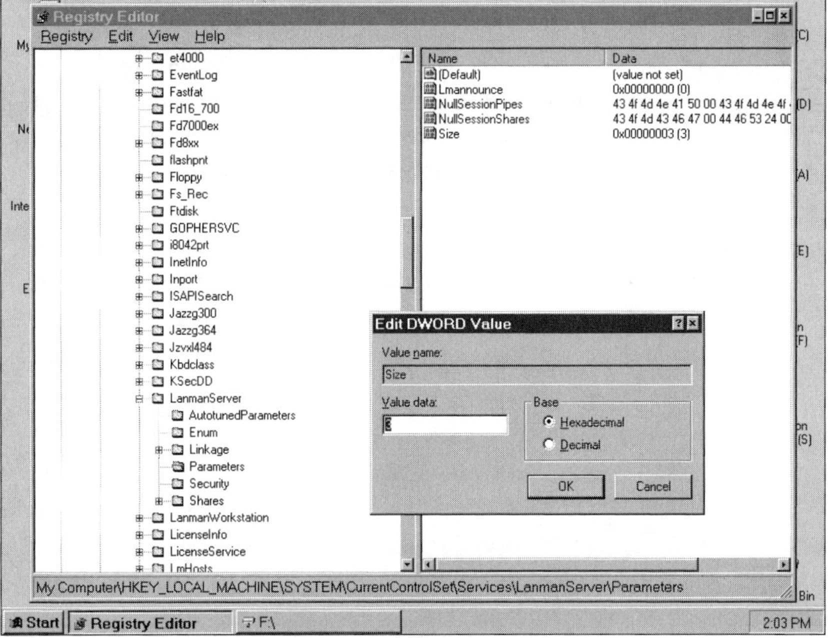

Figure 7-15: Changing the LanmanServer's size Registry value.

While conducting disk optimization experiments in the lab, we began to suspect that the LargeSystemCache/Server Service configuration documentation provided by Microsoft was in error after having made various changes to the Server service on an NT Server that did not change the LargeSystemCache value as advertised. For example, where we expected the LargeSystem to change to a value of 3 for the "Maximize Throughput for Network Applications" setting (based on the information in the regentry.hlp Registry Entry help file in the NT Resource Kit), we instead saw the value set to 0. The changes made to the LargeSystemCache value were starting to look almost random as we made settings to a variety of machines and checked the corresponding Registry changes. It was only after discovering the additional changes being made to the Size parameter did things start making sense.

Table 7-4 summarizes the possible settings for these Registry values and their associated meanings. Using this Table as a guide, you can experiment with setting an NT Workstation to values that correlate to one of the entries in this Table.

Increasing the values for the LargeSystemCache and Size Registry values on Windows NT systems with insufficient amounts of free physical memory is likely to result in increased paging file activity. This happens because the System Cache size increases and system memory usage is prioritized in favor of the cache over the working sets of running processes; therefore, if additional memory is needed for applications and services it will likely come from the paging file. The resulting increase in paging file activity will probably reduce overall system performance rather than increase it in these situations. As a result, this modification should be performed only on systems with plenty of available RAM. If you see a drastic increase in paging file activity after making one of these changes, you should restore the settings to their original values.

TABLE 7-4 SERVER SERVICE CONFIGURATIONS AND RELATED REGISTRY VALUES

Server Service Configuration	Corresponding LargeSystem Cache Registry Value	Corresponding Size Registry Value	Effect/Meaning Setting
Minimize Memory Used	0	1	This setting minimizes the amount of memory used for the system cache, in order to maximize the amount of memory available for running processes; this is the default setting for Windows NT Workstations.
Balance	0	2	This setting instructs NT to give the system cache and the working sets of system processes equal priority; that is, balance memory allocation between the two.
Maximize Throughput for File Sharing	1	3	This setting instructs NT to give the system cache a higher priority than the working sets of applications; this is normally the best setting for NT file servers. This is the default setting for Windows NT Servers.
Maximize Throughput for Network Applications`	0	3	This setting instructs NT to give the working sets of applications higher priority than the cache; this is normally the best setting for NT applications servers.

On Windows NT Workstations, the default value is LargeSystemCache: 0/Size: 1, which instructs NT to minimize the amount of memory used for the system cache and process working sets. However, if you have plenty of RAM on your system (48MB or more on Intel-based systems, 64MB or more on RISC-based systems) and want to significantly increase disk performance, try setting the Size value to 1. This tells NT to balance memory usage between the system cache and process working sets and, more importantly, to use a larger file system cache than the default setting.

In the lab we assembled for researching this book, some of the most impressive disk-related performance increases our test systems achieved resulted from modifying the LargeSystemCache and Size Registry values. The increase observed ranged from 5 percent to 40 percent. The results also varied depending on other factors such as the version of Windows NT in use, whether the system was using NT Workstation or Server, the amount of installed RAM, the type of file system in use, and type of disk subsystem installed. For NT Workstations with at least 32MB of installed RAM, it is recommended that you try setting the Size value from 1 to 2 and test the results after restarting the system. In most cases, you should experience a significant increase in disk performance.

You should experiment with different values and benchmark the performance both before and after each modification. In most cases, you'll probably find that a LargeSystemCache value of 0 and a Size value of 2 provides the best overall balance of disk and application performance for a typical NT Workstation. Windows NT Servers should be tuned according to their particular role on the network: dedicated file servers or those with significant disk I/O will probably be best with a setting of LargeSystemCache 1/Size 3 (which corresponds to the Server Service's configuration setting of Maximize Throughput for File Sharing). NT application servers are often best configured with a setting of LargeSystemCache 0/Size 3 (which corresponds to the Maximize Throughput for Network Applications setting).

The Maximize Throughput for Network Applications setting doesn't help the performance of Microsoft SQL Server because this product performs its own memory management. This is also the case for some other network database applications. With these products, the best performance is often realized by selecting other choices such as the File Sharing or Balance settings.

Cacheman: Ultimate file cache control

Although adjusting the LargeSystemCache value will give you additional control over the NT system cache, you may be interested in taking this level of control even further. Cacheman is a utility that allows you to do just this. Dr. Mark Russinovich and Bryce Cogswell wrote Cacheman. It allows you to manipulate virtually every aspect of Windows NT's cache and the cache manager.

Cacheman performs its magic by making unexported (i.e., hidden) cache-related variables and functions available for manipulation by the user. Normally, these parameters are not accessible to users and can only be internally managed by the system. However, this utility effectively circumvents this restriction and provides a graphical interface for manipulating various file cache values and parameters. The Cacheman utility's main window is shown in Figure 7-16.

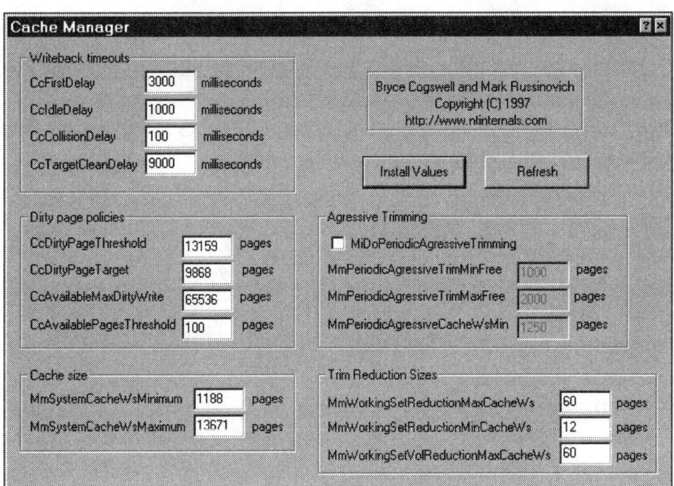

Figure 7-16: Cacheman's main window.

Table 7-5 contains a list of the cache control variables that Cacheman allows you to manipulate. Note that these descriptions are not guaranteed to be 100 percent accurate and represent a "best guess" by the utility's designers; this is because all such functions and variables are undocumented by Microsoft.

TABLE 7-5 FILE CACHE VARIABLES EXPOSED BY CACHEMAN

Cache Variable	Description
CcFirstDelay	Delay before writing back a page after first access to the page (in milliseconds)
CcIdleDelay	Idle period to wait before writing back dirty pages in the cache (in milliseconds)
CcCollisionDelay	Amount of time to delay if cache writeback is not possible (in milliseconds)
CcTargetCleanDelay	Standard delay before writing back dirty cache pages (in milliseconds)
CcDirtyPageThreshold	Maximum number of dirty pages to allow in cache
CcDirtyPageTarget	Desired number of dirty pages in cache
CcAvailableMaxDirtyWrite	Maximum number of dirty pages to write back at a time
CcAvailablePagesThreshold	Require at least this many pages available in the cache
MmSystemCacheWsMinimum	Minimum size of the working set of the cache
MmSystemCacheWsMaximum	Maximum size of the working set of the cache
MmDoPeriodicAgressiveTrimming	When turned on (checked in the Cacheman window and applied), instructs NT to aggressively reduce working sets of all tasks
MmPeriodicAgressiveTrimMinFree	Trims the working set of cache if available number of cache pages is greater than the specified amount
MmPeriodicAgressiveTrimMaxFree	Trim working set of cache if available pages less than this amount
MmPeriodicAgressiveCacheWsMin	Trim the cache to this amount periodically
MmWorkingSetReductionMaxCacheWs	Trim cache by this amount if larger than the specified maximum size
MmWorkingSetVolReduction MaxCacheWs	Trim cache by this amount if larger than max size during volume reduction

Note: When referring to pages as references in the Table, remember that the page size for Intel x86-based machines is 4K; Alpha machines use an 8K page size.

Once values in the Cacheman dialog have been set, they are applied using the Install Values button. Also, because the cache is a dynamic entity by nature, these values change on the fly and may change while the window is open. To refresh the current values for the cache, click the Refresh button. Because there is no way to undo changes made to the cache during a Windows NT session, you may want to make note of the values as they existed when the utility was first run; this will enable you to quickly reset the values back to their original state. Finally, remember that any changes made in the Cacheman window apply only during this Windows NT session; once the system is rebooted, the values will be dynamically reinitialized by Windows NT.

Additional information on the Cacheman utility and the other utilities produced by Dr. Russinovich and Bryce Cogswell are available at the NTInternals Web site at:

`http://www.ntinternals.com/`

You may also wish to visit NTInternals' sister site containing their retail, commercial utilities at:

`http://www.winternals.com/`

There are a few important caveats to remember when using Cacheman. First is that it is an experimental utility that was primarily designed to demonstrate the capability of exposing and manipulating unexported system cache functions and variables. In its current state, Cacheman does not perform any validity checking on the cache values you set to see if they are outside permissible boundaries because these are unknown, so it is possible that entering inappropriate settings will result in the system becoming unstable or crashing. Therefore, it's probably a good idea to be conservative when making changes to Cacheman variables; this means incrementing/decrementing values by small amounts rather than making radical changes all at once. It's also important to note that changes to most of these variables will not have an immediate or noticeable effect on cache behavior, size, or system performance unless the system memory is very high.

Finally, because Cacheman uses an unorthodox method to obtain pointers to internal NT variables, Microsoft neither condones nor supports the method or this utility. As a result, don't expect support from Microsoft Product Support Services if you're running Cacheman on your system: you're on your own if you use it.

Cacheman

Several of the NTInternals utilities, including the Cacheman disk cache manager, are included on the *Optimizing Windows NT* CD-ROM. To get more information about this utility or to install it, point your Web browser to the location of the *Optimizing Windows NT* CD-ROM after inserting it in your CD-ROM drive. Then select the page for NTInternals Utilities and follow the instructions given to install the utility on your system.

Cacheman is a powerful low-level utility, and as such should be used only on an experimental basis on nonproduction machines to gain a better understanding of NT file cache behavior. If you choose to implement any of the run time modifications possible via Cacheman, you do so at your own risk.

Turbocharging the disk subsystem with SuperCache and SuperDisk

Although we've given you a few methods to enhance the performance of the Windows NT system cache, generally speaking, you can't really make any earth-shaking changes to the Windows NT system cache because it is primarily controlled and managed by the operating system and not the user. Or can you?

Two applications that can help you make radical changes to Windows NT's disk subsystem performance are SuperCache-NT and SuperDisk-NT from EEC Systems, Inc. EEC Systems has developed caching and RAM Disk products for OpenVMS in the past and recently created similar products for Windows NT.

SUPERCACHE: CACHING DYNAMO

SuperCache-NT is a software device driver that essentially augments the standard Windows NT system cache. The utility's vendor claims that the utility is capable of enhancing NT disk performance between 500 percent and 2000 percent. Although we can't testify to having achieved quite these levels of performance increases during our own limited testing of SuperCache in the Optimizing Windows NT lab, we did see some substantial gains (typically between 20 percent and 300 percent on most systems, which is still a significant increase).

SuperCache-NT has two modes of operation that it is capable of using:

- Write-Through Mode: This is the safer mode and provides enhanced data protection. In Write-Through Mode, data is written through to the Windows NT lazy write mechanism synchronously when it is written to cache.
- Write-Back Mode (aka Lazy Write Mode): This mode of operation is faster than the Write-Through Mode, but should only be used in conjunction with an uninterruptable power supply (this will help protect against data loss in the event of a power failure that prevents data from being written back properly to the disk). In this mode, data is written into a proprietary cache and later written to the Windows NT lazy write mechanism.

SuperCache-NT can use from 25 percent to 75 percent of physical memory as a cache for a single disk partition, up to a maximum (as of this writing) of 512MB of memory. It supports the final release versions of Windows NT 3.51 and Windows NT 4.0, and 24MB of RAM is recommended as a minimum. SuperCache supports both the FAT and NTFS file systems. In addition, a SuperCache-enabled volume can be mounted and shared over a Local Area Network just as with a standard drive volume.

As with the standard Windows NT system cache, SuperCache-NT dynamically allocates memory between the cache and the system depending on the current memory environment on the system. In addition, SuperCache-NT has an adaptive read-ahead caching mechanism that increases cache read performance during sequential file accesses. You select which partition is to be cached by SuperCache using the SuperCache Configuration utility `SCCONFIG.EXE`.

Although SuperCache also provides a number of fine-tuning options for advanced users, one of the major benefits (and best features) of the product is that it was designed to be usable out of the box in its default configuration.

SUPERDISK: A RAM DRIVE FOR NT

SuperCache's sister product is SuperDisk-NT, a utility that creates a RAM drive for Windows NT systems. Users of other operating systems such as MS-DOS or OS/2 may have had some experience with the concept of a RAM disk: a virtual disk drive contained in system RAM. This disk appears to the system and applications as a standard disk drive but operates at the speed of RAM rather than at the speed of a conventional disk drive.

SuperDisk-NT lets you create a RAM disk on any Windows NT that has 24MB or more of physical RAM. In addition, the RAM disk created can be anywhere from 25 percent to 75 percent of the total available physical memory on the machine, up to a maximum of 512MB. Like SuperCache, SuperDisk supports both the FAT and NTFS file systems. Also like SuperCache, SuperDisk drives can be accessed and mounted over a Local Area Network by remote users.

One of the most amazing capabilities of SuperDisk, and important to point out, is its ability to allow the running of all of Windows NT in RAM (the only stipulation being that you have at least 32MB of memory). Having the operating system reside completely in RAM means that it won't be paged to disk, and all operating system services will always be found in system RAM. This should translate to significant performance increases in most environments.

SuperDisk has three modes of operation under which it can run:

- *Write-Through Data Protection*: This mode offers the safest operation and slowest performance
- *Lazy Write Protection*: This mode offers a moderate safety level but faster performance
- *RAM Disk Only* (without backing disk update): This mode offers the lowest safety factor but delivers fastest performance

Another interesting feature of SuperDisk is that it can be mirrored to a physical disk drive. This means you can store data on the RAM disk and have it mirrored to a physical disk or a disk partition. In this configuration, the use of SuperDisk is far safer and more fault-tolerant than running the RAM disk alone, because data is protected even in the event of a power failure. Also, in the event that a power failure or crash does occur, the SuperDisk software has a feature to automatically restore the contents of the RAM disk (during the system boot process) to its previous state prior to the outage or crash.

Although it is true that the use of products such as SuperCache and SuperDisk introduce the possibility of more problems than a standard Windows NT installation without them, they also offer the potential for enormous performance increases. As a result, anyone seeking absolute maximum performance under Windows NT should definitely evaluate and consider the use of these products. However, as with any new product that makes major system changes, it is always recommended that you first test these products on a nonproduction machine that serves as an evaluation testbed. Once you've determined that the products don't introduce any problems in your environment, you can deploy them on your production systems and enjoy their benefits.

Evaluation versions of both SuperCache-NT and SuperDisk-NT utilities are included on the *Optimizing Windows NT* CD-ROM. However, as with all of the software included on the CD, use of these utilities is done at your own risk. Observe all standard precautions when using utilities that modify your system configuration or modify the behavior of Windows NT, including having a full backup of the system, as well as the Registry. For more information on doing preventative maintenance to your system, refer to Chapter 12, "Maintaining Your NT System."

Although SuperCache and SuperDisk can deliver an excellent performance boost to system performance in some environments, there are some extremely important caveats that you need to pay attention to before installing them; these come straight from the utility's vendor. First, DO NOT use this utility to cache either your system partition or any partition containing the paging file. In addition, do not use SuperCache together with the SuperDisk product, or any disk defragmentation tools, including Executive Software's Diskeeper or Symantec's Speedisk (part of the Norton Utilities for Windows NT), and do not run SuperCache on a removable disk. Finally, do not install SuperCache-NT on a system running the Beta 1 version of Windows NT 4.0, as this may cause the system to crash. EEC Systems, Inc. recommends that you run SuperCache only on the final release versions of Windows NT 3.51 or 4.0. Failure to observe these cautions could result in any of a variety of problems, including data corruption, data loss, or rendering your Windows NT installation unstartable. It is also imperative that you read the installation README file for either application before installation; these files contain important compatibility and installation notes. You should also check the vendor's Web site for any updated compatibility- or bug-related information before installing the products in your environment.

Detecting cache bottlenecks

In addition to being able to optimize and tune the Windows NT system cache, another important skill to master is the ability to identify whether a system cache bottleneck exists on your system. Typically, this situation occurs as a result of limited system RAM, and tends to be more pervasive on server rather than workstation computers (because workstations don't usually experience the severe network and disk workloads that are common with servers).

Essentially, a cache bottleneck is really just a mirror reflection of a memory bottleneck. This makes sense, because the cache resides in physical memory, and NT will automatically reduce the size of the cache, as less physical memory is available on the system. However, you may at some point be interested in looking specifically at cache-related statistics rather than the more general memory object; the information provided here will help you do this.

To monitor the cache in Windows NT, use the Performance Monitor application to log the following objects over a decent period of time (at least a day or two):

- Memory
- Cache
- Logical Disk

After you've logged this data, use Performance Monitor's Chart View mode to chart the data listed in Table 7-6.

A predefined Performance Monitor workspace environment file, `CacheBottleneck.pmw`, is provided on the *Optimizing Windows NT* CD-ROM to expedite this process.

TABLE 7-6 CACHE BOTTLENECK-RELATED PERFORMANCE MONITOR COUNTERS

Object	Counter
Memory	Cache Bytes
Memory	Cache Faults/sec
Memory	Page Faults/sec
Memory	Pages Input/sec
Cache	Copy Reads/sec
Cache	Data Flushes/sec
Cache	Copy Read Hits%
Cache	Lazy Write Pages/sec
Cache	Lazy Write Flushes/sec
Cache	Read Aheads/sec
LogicalDisk	Disk Reads/sec

For descriptions of the various counters viewable with the Performance Monitor utility, see Appendix C, "Performance Monitor Counters."

Other than those described for memory bottlenecks, there aren't really any hard and fast rules regarding expected values for cache-related counters. However, there are some general trends you can watch for that might indicate that the system cache is becoming a bottleneck. For example, a significant decrease in the Cache Bytes value (the total size of the cache) coupled with a simultaneous increase in the Cache Faults/sec (which indicates the number of times per second that the VMM was unable to resolve memory references using the cache) counters may indicate that the system cache is both decreasing (probably due to a memory shortage) and becoming less efficient. You can also analyze the overall efficiency and performance of the cache using the steps outlined in the "Analyzing Cache Performance" section later in this chapter and correlate this to the cache size (as indicated by the Cache: Cache Bytes counter) to determine if the cache is a system bottleneck.

Figure 7-17 shows a sample Performance Monitor session observing these counters.

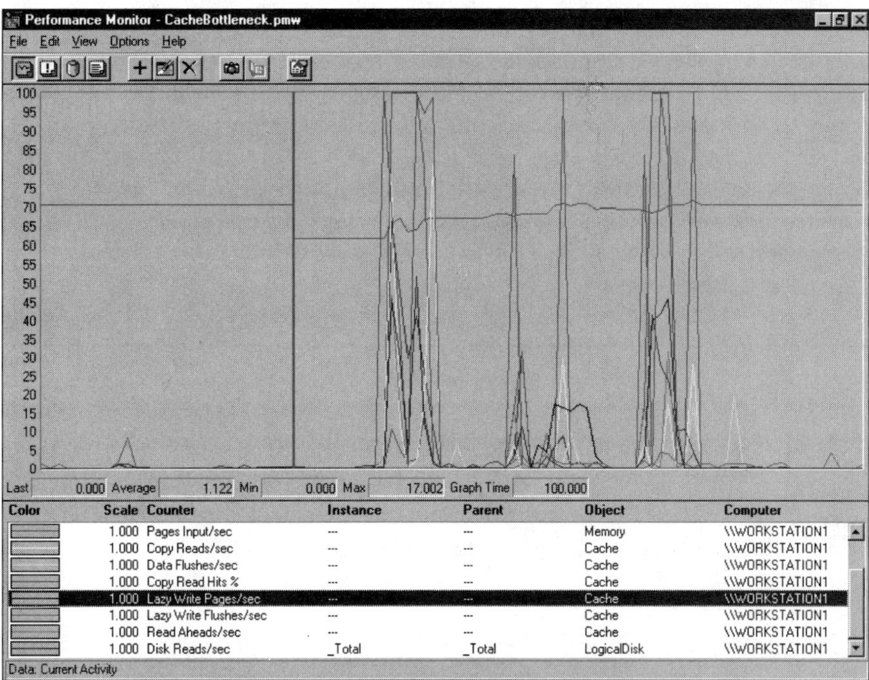

Figure 7-17: Using Performance Monitor to identify cache bottlenecks.

Cache Bottlenecks and Applications

The biggest victim of a system cache shortage, other than the disk subsystem, will be applications that were written to use the system cache effectively. This will become the case especially in situations where the cache becomes particularly anemic (e.g., a cache size of 5MB on a workstation or server running a number of applications or with insufficient physical memory).

However, normal rates of reads, hits, and cache flushes also tend to range widely depending on the particular application(s) involved. Thus, to monitor a particular application you must establish cache-related benchmarks for your primary applications; this allows you to establish a set of baselines for individual applications that can be used as a point of reference and for later comparison.

To monitor the effect of a cache bottleneck on an application, log the Cache and Memory objects over a period of time while the application is active (preferably with few or no other applications running simultaneously), and then chart these counters:

- Cache: Copy Reads/sec
- Cache: Copy Read Hits%

In this situation, a cache bottleneck will appear in regards to a particular application as a steady decrease in Copy Read Hits while the Copy Reads/sec counter stays relatively flat. Monitoring them in regards to a particular application will let you compare the effectiveness of individual applications in their use of the NT system cache. If you remonitor an application when system memory, and therefore the system cache size, are reduced, you will see a drop in the Copy Read Hits% figure if the cache is a bottleneck. Again, there aren't any hard-and-fast recommended levels for these values; however, in general, a hit rate of over 80 percent is considered to be excellent, and a 10 percent decrease in the Copy Read Hits% figure is cause for concern; it probably also indicates a cache and overall memory shortage.

For more information on detecting memory bottlenecks, see the "Detecting Memory Bottlenecks" section of Chapter 5, "Optimizing Memory and Processing." For descriptions of Performance Monitor counters in Windows NT, see Appendix C, "Performance Monitor Counter Objects."

Analyzing cache performance

In addition to viewing, and to a certain degree, manipulating the NT system cache, it is also possible to analyze its performance. Cache performance, regardless of the type of cache, is measured in terms of hit and miss ratios (percentage figures); the higher the hit ratio, the more effective the cache. This provides yet another tool to track the effectiveness of our system configuration and to monitor and optimize the performance of the disk subsystem.

To analyze NT system cache performance, first run a Performance Monitor logging session of these objects:

- Memory
- Cache

Next, in order to analyze cache performance statistics, use Performance Monitor to chart these counters:

TABLE 7-7 CACHE PERFORMANCE-RELATED PERFORMANCE MONITOR COUNTERS

Object	Counter
Cache	Copy Reads/sec
Cache	Copy Read Hits %
Cache	Data Maps/sec
Cache	Data Map Hits %
Cache	Fast Reads/sec
Cache	Read Aheads/sec

A predefined Performance Monitor workspace environment file, `CachePerformance.pmw`, has been provided on the *Optimizing Windows NT* CD-ROM to expedite this process.

Figure 7-18 shows a sample Performance Monitor session observing these counters in Chart View.

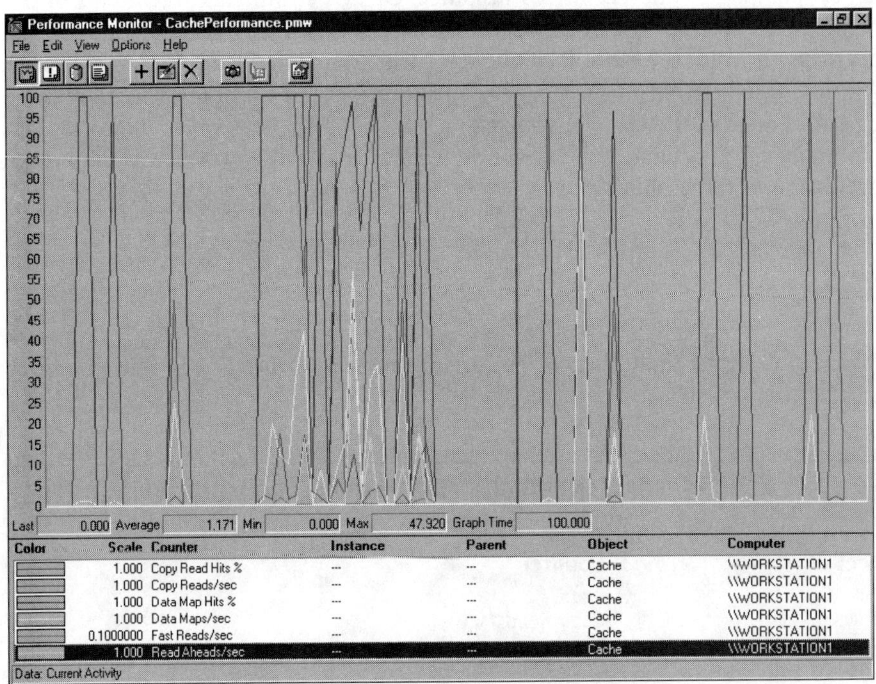

Figure 7-18: Observing cache performance via Performance Monitor.

When trying to interpret these counters, you should pay particular attention to the following counters and keep the following information in mind:

- For regular file read operations, the Copy Read Hits% counter is the one to watch; it gives us the best idea of the cache hit ratio for this type of file access. Specifically, it tells us how often, when looking to read data from the disk, the Virtual Memory Manager is finding a requested page in the cache (located in RAM) rather than physically accessing the disk.
- For file write operations, the cache's level of activity is revealed by the Data Flush Pages/sec and Data Flushes/sec, the frequency with which the cache manager is flushing pages from the cache back to disk. The system or a user application via a special function call can trigger these data flushes.

- The Data Map counters are indicative of operations on the directory or many small files; therefore, a high cache hit rate (as determined by the Data Map Hits% counter) should not be taken as an overall indication of the cache's effectiveness.

In addition to these counters, there are also several others that provide good information. For example, the Fast Reads/sec tells us the frequency of memory page reads that bypass the file system and retrieve the data directly from the system cache (as opposed to a Copy Read, which is typically the type of cache read that occurs when a process first accesses a file that is located in the cache).

Another informative counter is Read Aheads/sec, which gives the frequency of cache reads where the cache detects sequential access to a file (this is the type of access used by the Diskmax test we used earlier to test disk's maximum throughput). A read-ahead permits the data to be transferred in larger block sizes than is being requested by the process calling for the data; this in turn makes access to the data faster than it normally would have been if the read-ahead hadn't occurred.

When monitoring and attempting to understand the information provided by these cache-related Performance Monitor counters, it's important to remember that applications running under Windows NT are capable of using any of four different methods for reading data (which explains the different counters that are available):

- In *copy reads*, data mapped in the cache is copied into memory so it can be read (an application's first read from a file is usually a copy read).
- Subsequent reads from the cache are normally a special type called *fast reads*, which is where the process calls the cache directly rather than calling upon the file system to retrieve the requested data.
- *Pin reads* are instances where data is mapped into the cache just so that they can be modified and then written back to disk. They are said to be *pinned* in the cache; that is, held at the same memory address and made nonpageable. This is done to reduce the number of page faults that occur.
- Cache *read-aheads* occur when the NT Virtual Memory Manager determines an application or other process is reading a file sequentially and, in anticipation of the read pattern, starts mapping larger blocks of data into the cache than are being requested by the application. Although there is no guarantee that they'll always be more efficient, read-aheads usually deliver faster performance when they occur.

Another way to monitor file cache performance is to run the Performance Meter applications (`PERFMTR.EXE`) included in the Windows NT Resource Kit. Once the application is running, simply press **r** to display real-time cache performance statistics (which are updated every few seconds).

Optimizing the File System

The question many NT users and system administrators who seek optimal disk performance for their servers and workstations ask is: Which is better for performance, NTFS or FAT? The answer, as it usually tends to be in these cases, is "it depends." Although the primary determinant is size of the volume in question, there are also other important factors in making this decision. For example, we also need to look at factors such as the role of the system (stand-alone PC, network server, workstation, etc.), the security needs of the environment in which the system lives, the recoverability needs for the volume, and so on.

In Windows NT 3.5x, the choice of disk file systems includes the NT File System (NTFS), File Allocation Table (FAT), and the OS/2 High-Performance File System (HPFS). Although the decision as to which file system to use when setting up an NT system is extremely important, this choice has been made easier as of Windows NT version 4.0, because there are only two real choices left: NTFS and FAT. As of Windows NT 4.0, HPFS support has been permanently dropped. Before we can decide which file system is appropriate for a particular volume on our system, it's best to start with an overview of the features and capabilities of each. Only then can we make an intelligent, informed decision about which is best for a given situation.

Technically, there is one other file system supported in NT: the CD-ROM File System (CDFS), used to access data on ISO-9660 PC-compatible CD-ROMs.

A quick disk primer

Before we jump into a comparison of file systems, we need to get some terminology and disk-related concepts straight.

All usable disks must contain one or more *partitions,* which are basic structural divisions of the disk. There are two types of partitions: primary and extended. A *primary partition* is the only type that can contain an operating system such as

Windows NT. You can assign each primary partition a drive letter such as C or D and have up to four primary partitions on one physical drive. An *extended partition* is a special type of partition that you can subdivide into one or more *logical drives*. Each logical drive within an extended partition is normally assigned its own drive letter. You can have multiple extended partitions per physical drive, and each extended partition can contain multiple logical drives. In addition, there is no practical limit to the number of logical drives that an extended partition can contain. Each primary partition and logical drive is formatted independently and can use different file systems.

Volume is a term used to refer to a primary partition or logical drive that has been formatted with a file system (e.g., FAT or NTFS). A volume is a logical entity that appears to the system as a single drive letter; volumes can consist of one or multiple partitions (spanning multiple drives in some instances). The term volume isn't restricted to hard drives, either: removable media such as floppy disks, CD-ROMs, or optical cartridges containing a valid file system format are also referred to as volumes.

Windows NT gives special names to particular disk partitions. For example, the *System Partition* contains hardware-specific files needed to boot the system. These files include the NT Boot Manager and `BOOT.INI`, `NTDETECT.COM`, and `NTLDR` (`OSLOADER` on RISC-based systems). Although the System Partition can (and often does) contain the NT installation directory, it doesn't necessarily have to.

On Intel x86-based computers, you can format the System Partition with either the FAT or NTFS file system. However, with RISC-based systems, you must format the System Partition with FAT.

Because FAT partitions don't have NTFS's security capabilities, Windows NT includes a feature that lets administrators secure the FAT System Partition on a RISC-based NT system. From the NT Disk Administrator's partition menu, choose Secure System Partition. The system will ask you to confirm the request. Click OK, and reboot the system to activate security on the system partition. When you specify this feature, only members of the Administrators group can access the FAT System Partition.

Another special partition in NT is the *Boot Partition*. Although it sounds a little confusing at first, the boot partition isn't necessarily the drive the system boots from. Instead, Boot Partition indicates that this is the volume containing the Windows NT installation directory. In this case, *boot* refers to the files required to start NT, not the computer itself. The Boot Partition can be the same partition as the System Partition, but this isn't a requirement. On both RISC and Intel NT systems, the Boot Partition can be on either a FAT or NTFS partition.

Now that we've got our disk terminology down, we're ready to compare the relative features and capabilities of our two file systems to determine which is best for our system's disk volume(s). However, because performance isn't the only thing that matters (after all, we can't only be speed freaks and ignore security), we also evaluate additional features of each operating system and weigh these factors in making our decision.

The FAT file system

The FAT (File Allocation Table) file system is the aged veteran of PC file systems and is used by more operating systems than any other single file system. MS-DOS, OS/2, Windows 3.x, Windows 95, Windows NT, and even Macintosh systems are all capable of reading and writing to FAT volumes. This makes it the most compatible file system; but does this mean it's the best choice for your disk volumes? To answer that question, we need to dig into the constructs of FAT and evaluate its features.

Anyone who has used MS-DOS in the past will recognize some of the FAT file system's distinguishing characteristics. FAT uses a special table (the file allocation table, FAT's namesake) to keep track of files and directories on the volume (this table is stored near the beginning of the FAT volume). As a fault-tolerance measure, FAT volumes automatically store a second copy of the file allocation table on the disk at all times; this second copy can then be used in the event that the primary copy becomes corrupted or otherwise damaged. On FAT volumes, the file allocation table and the volume's root directory must be in specific locations on the disk so the system can access files needed to boot from a FAT volume.

The file allocation table requires constant updates, which in turn requires that the hard drive heads continually return to the beginning of the volume. As a result, FAT can cause a severe performance hit on large volumes – the larger the volume, the greater the performance penalty. This is the first strike against FAT volumes – the physical head movement requirements for updating the volume's table.

Another thing to remember about FAT volumes is that they store their files on a first-come, first-served basis; that is, the system writes files to disk in the first available area. There is very little dynamic intelligence used to determine the best location for a file in regards to its read performance on the back end. Over time, this method results in heavy file fragmentation (files are in multiple, noncontiguous disk blocks), another performance-killer. To remedy this problem, you have to run a disk defragmentation program that makes all the fragmented files contiguous again. For more information on disk defragmentation, see the "Disk Defragmentation and Optimization" section later in this chapter.

Another disadvantage to FAT is that its directory structure has no formal organization. So FAT has no way to automatically sort folders and filenames in a directory. As a result, locating a file on a FAT volume, especially a very large one, often takes longer than locating the same file on an NTFS volume with automatic directory sorting.

FAT ADVANTAGES

Why then would anyone want to use FAT? Well, to start with, FAT is the most popular and widely used PC file system, mainly because for a long time it was the only file system choice for PC-compatible computers. Even though alternative file systems such as OS/2's HPFS and NTFS arrived on the scene later, MS-DOS was by far the most popular operating system, having the majority of the PC market. As a result, using FAT on a Windows NT disk volume provides one very big advantage: the ability to have other operating systems on the computer access data on the volume (the MS-DOS, OS/2, Linux, Windows 3.x, Windows 95, and Windows NT operating systems are all able to use FAT volumes). If you choose to use NTFS on a volume, the only operating system able to access it is Windows NT.

In addition, FAT can be the best choice for smaller volumes because its relatively simple nature and low operational overhead make it fast on these volumes. This is also why FAT is the only choice for floppy formats in NT. The overhead of NTFS, a more complex file system, makes its use on a floppy disk almost ridiculous (it would be very slow and there would be much less free space on the disk due to NTFS' structural and security overhead).

A final advantage of FAT is its ability to store programs that you can access when the system boots under DOS. These programs include setup utilities for configuring hardware devices and peripheral cards.

Although Windows NT can access FAT volumes up to 4GB, MS-DOS can only recognize FAT volumes of up to 2GB. Therefore, keep the volume size to 2GB or less when you create FAT volumes for use by both DOS and Windows NT.

FAT DISADVANTAGES: CLUSTER SIZES AND WASTED DISK SPACE

When you consider FAT's advantages, you also need to remember that FAT is not as secure as NTFS. This inferior security can be unacceptable for some organizations. You can easily access FAT volumes with a DOS boot floppy, and FAT provides only basic directory-level access security that is limited compared to the security features of NTFS. For these reasons, it is not recommended that you use FAT on network shared volumes. You should, instead, consider NTFS, which has file-level security and superior protection against physical access, for such volumes.

If you maintain a large disk volume (i.e., one that is greater than 1GB in size), another issue to consider is the minimum cluster size used for NTFS versus FAT file systems at various volume sizes. Specifically, you should remember FAT's potential to affect performance and usable disk space.

Every FAT and NTFS volume uses clusters, the basic unit of allocation, to store disk files. FAT can have large minimum cluster sizes that reduce the usable storage space on the volume. Regardless of how small a file or part of a file is it must take up at least one cluster of disk space. When a file doesn't take up an entire cluster, the portion of the cluster that contains no data is wasted space. The larger the cluster, the larger the waste. The amount of disk space wasted by minimum cluster sizes on FAT volumes becomes exaggerated the larger the volume is, because larger volumes have larger minimum cluster sizes. Therefore, large volumes that store many small files will lose a lot of storable space because of the minimum cluster size problem.

Table 7-8 shows the default minimum cluster sizes for various FAT volume size ranges. With large FAT volumes (256MB to 2048MB), the wasted drive space is substantial and is reason enough to choose NTFS on these volumes.

TABLE 7-8 DEFAULT CLUSTER SIZES ON FAT VOLUMES

For Volumes in This Range...	The Default Cluster Size Is...
0MB to 15MB	4K*
16MB to 127MB	2K
128MB to 255MB	4K
256MB to 511MB	8K
512MB to 1023MB	16K
1024MB to 2047MB	32K
2048MB to 4095MB	64K
4096MB to 8191MB	128K**
8192MB to 16384MB	256K**

*FAT volumes under 16MB use a 12-bit rather than a 16-bit FAT; thus the reason for the nonsequential cluster size.

**These volume sizes are possible only under Windows NT version 4.0 and later.

CONVERTING FAT VOLUMES: A ONE-WAY TRIP

If you use FAT with another operating system and later add Windows NT to your system, you can keep your volumes formatted as FAT until you're ready to completely switch to NTFS. However, after you convert a volume from FAT to NTFS, you can use that volume only with NT – you can't convert that volume back to FAT without backing up, reformatting, and restoring the volume.

To convert a FAT volume to NTFS, type **CONVERT** at the command prompt. The format of the CONVERT command is:

```
CONVERT <drive:> /fs:ntfs [/v]
```

Here *<drive:>* is the drive designation of the drive you want to convert. The */v* option tells CONVERT to run in verbose mode, which gives detailed command output.

The NTFS file system

One of the cornerstones of the Windows NT operating system is its high-performance file system, NTFS (NT File System). NTFS has a number of unique features and capabilities that make it a good choice for many environments. In this section, we take a close look at these features and compare them to the feature of the FAT file system.

NTFS SECURITY

NTFS's integration with NT security makes NTFS the best choice for disk volumes requiring high levels of security. NTFS provides file-level security, which lets you set permissions on folders and files. These permissions make the most of the existing local or domain NT accounts database, and you can even have different sets of permissions on different files in the same folder. Several types of file and folder permissions are available, including *No Access*, which prevents all access to a file or folder for a specified user or group, and *Full Control*, which grants full control over a file or folder, including the ability to set permissions on and take ownership of it. File and folder permissions use the accounts database of the local NT computer or NT domain. You can apply permissions to individual users, user groups, or everyone.

NTFS volumes also have somewhat better protection against unauthorized physical access than FAT volumes. For example, users can't access NTFS volumes by booting the system from a regular MS-DOS disk. This is because the NTFS file system driver that allows access to an NTFS volume loads with NT. However, it's important to note that a second installation of NT can easily access an NTFS partition, and several utilities have been developed that allow read access of NTFS volumes from different operating systems (including the NTFSDOS utility included on the Optimizing Windows NT CD-ROM and another utility developed for the Linux operating system). As a result, this particular "security" feature of NT is easily circumvented, making NTFS volumes far from impervious to intrusion.

Because NTFS can't prevent *physical* access to files on NTFS volumes, the only way to prevent such access is to either physically lock the computer containing the data or use file encryption, which NTFS doesn't support (however, there are third-party products available that allow data encryption on NTFS volumes).

Another NTFS security-related feature prevents users from undeleting files or folders removed from NTFS volumes (or, in NT 4.0 terminology, emptied from the Recycle Bin). Even if the files still exist on the drive, NT doesn't give undelete programs physical disk access to do their magic on an NTFS volume. (You can, however, use a third-party undelete program such as Norton Utilities for Windows NT which does allow for undeletion on NTFS volumes.) Although NTFS's security features can be inconvenient for users with little or no security needs, these features are central to NTFS and NT security and required for its C2-level security certification.

NTFS RELIABILITY

In addition to its extensive memory and application protection features, NT offers a reliable file system. This is a key feature of NTFS, because the corruption or loss of data as a result of damage to the disk's logical structure is a common disaster.

When storing data to disk, NTFS records file I/O events to a special transaction log. If the system crashes or encounters other interruptions, NT can reference this log to restore the consistency of the volume and prevent corruption in the event of abnormal program termination or system shutdown. NTFS doesn't commit an action to disk until it can verify the successful completion of the action. This precaution helps prevent corruption of an NTFS volume and makes NTFS especially solid for data storage on stand-alone systems and network file servers.

NTFS also supports a fault-tolerance feature called *hot fixing.* With hot fixing, the OS (operating system) automatically blocks out bad disk sectors and relocates data from these sectors. This process occurs transparently in the background, requiring no intervention by the user. An application attempting to read or write data to an area that is hot fixed on the fly will never know that there was a problem.

NTFS PERFORMANCE

Ahhh...performance; this is what we're really most interested in, isn't it? In addition to its security and reliability features, NTFS was designed for speed. NTFS provides impressive disk I/O performance on large volumes such as those typically found in file servers or advanced workstations, and is therefore usually the best file system choice for these systems. However, it's important to remember that this performance gain typically won't kick in until the volume size is 1GB or larger in most cases. The reason is that on smaller volumes, the overhead from NTFS' security and reliability features tends to negate the performance benefits. On every system, there will be a "break-even point" between NTFS and FAT under a particular load. However, there aren't any hard and fast rules for where this point will occur, because it depends on factors such as the disk hardware and the nature of the applications running on the system.

Although results from system to system will vary, we have generally found during our testing that FAT provides the best performance for volumes under 1GB in size. However, as we discussed earlier, performance isn't the only criterion to consider when selecting a file system; security and reliability are at least as important, and NTFS offers better features in both categories. In addition, FAT tends to become fragmented more quickly than NTFS due to its design, which means its performance is likely to diminish more quickly. Be sure to weigh all of these factors before making your selection.

NTFS uses a binary tree structure for all disk directories, which reduces the number of times the system has to access the disk to locate files. This system is best for large directories, and NT easily outperforms FAT in these situations. In addition, NTFS automatically sorts files in a folder on the fly.

Another performance-related feature of NTFS is its resistance to file fragmentation. Note that we're saying "resistance" and not "immunity." Although it tends to become less fragmented than a comparable FAT volume under the same usage, NTFS does still fragment over time. The reason NTFS is less prone to fragmentation is that it makes intelligent choices about where to store file data on the disk. In contrast to FAT's first-come, first-served method, NTFS's method of writing files minimizes, but does not eliminate, the problem of file fragmentation on NTFS volumes. NT also gains an edge over FAT by using relatively small disk allocation units (cluster sizes) for NTFS volumes. Smaller clusters prevent wasted disk space on volumes, especially those with numerous small files.

Table 7-9 lists the default cluster sizes for various NTFS volume sizes.

TABLE 7-9 DEFAULT CLUSTER SIZES ON NTFS VOLUMES

For Volumes in This Range...	The Default Cluster Size Is...
0MB to 512MB	512 bytes
513MB to 1024MB	1KB
1025MB to 2048MB	2KB
2049MB or greater	4KB

As Table 7-9 illustrates, the largest NTFS cluster size is 4KB, even on volumes larger than 2GB. Because NTFS uses small clusters better and has a more efficient design, its performance doesn't degrade with large volumes as does performance with FAT.

The maximum theoretical size for an NTFS partition is 2 exabytes (2^{64} bytes); however, the current limitations of disk drive technology place the practical limit somewhere around 2 terabytes (2^{41}).

Still another performance-related feature of NTFS is its ability to store very small files in the NTFS volume directory itself. This is a feature exclusive to NTFS and makes access to these files much faster because they are stored close to the directory where their location is referenced.

When you format an NT volume, NT automatically chooses a cluster size to fit the volume size. With NTFS, you can manually select the cluster size for the volume when you use the FORMAT command from the NT command prompt (this solution is not possible from Disk Administrator). To set the cluster size, use the */A* switch with the FORMAT command as follows:

```
FORMAT <drive:> /fs:ntfs /a:<clustersize>
```

Here, *<drive:>* is the drive to be formatted, and *<clustersize>* is the cluster size to be assigned to the volume, which should be one of the following: 512, 1024, 2048, 4096, 8192, 16K, 32K, or 64K.

Although NT won't automatically assign a cluster size larger than 4K to a volume, it is possible for you to do so manually using the FORMAT command. However, before overriding the default cluster size for a volume you should always experiment with and benchmark a sample configuration on a nonproduction machine to determine the possible performance values of increasing the cluster size. Also, note that the use of larger cluster sizes will necessarily incur an increased amount of wasted disk space for all files of sizes that are nonmultiples of the cluster size.

Despite the flexibility this feature provides, you generally don't need to worry about manually specifying NTFS cluster sizes. NT automatically configures cluster sizes for you, and its settings usually deliver excellent, if not optimal, performance. However, as with any system default, there is always the possibility that overriding the default and choosing a custom setting will enhance performance. Therefore, if you wish to explore the possibility that alternate cluster sizes might improve performance on your NTFS volumes, you should experiment with different cluster sizes on a nonproduction machine. Be sure to exhaustively benchmark each iteration of cluster size you test. Furthermore, be sure that the nature of the data files on the volume are representative of those that will actually be stored on the volume once it is in actual use in your environment.

The reason for this is that performance under different cluster sizes is directly related to the average file size on the volume; for example, you may find that larger cluster sizes deliver better performance than smaller ones or vice versa. However, you should always experiment thoroughly before committing to a custom cluster size choice. The nice thing here is that if you choose to just go ahead with NT's default size and not bother, you'll still get good performance. The major benefit of smaller cluster sizes is that there is less disk space wasted; it's unlikely that you'll see large performance differences between different cluster sizes.

NTFS COMPRESSION

Another important feature of NTFS, which was new with Windows NT version 3.51, is the ability to selectively compress individual files and folders on a disk. Although most people think of compression strictly in terms of disk space savings, you might be interested to know that compression can also have major performance benefits. However, these benefits come at a price: CPU utilization.

In our lab experimentation with NTFS compression during the writing of this book, we tested a number of machines with and without NTFS compression. On smaller volume sizes (generally sub-2GB non-RAID volumes), we were amazed to discover that volumes using NTFS compression delivered overall performance increases of up to 50 percent. It seemed too good to be true until we simultaneously monitored CPU utilization during a subsequent run of the same benchmarks using a compressed NTFS volume. We saw average CPU utilization on these tests jump from a mild 10–18 percent range on the uncompressed NTFS volume tests to a whopping 30–80 percent range on the compressed NTFS volume tests. Therein lies the rub. Additionally, we saw major performance decreases when using NTFS compression on large volume sizes (between 4GB and 17GB) and software-based fault-tolerant RAID volumes (which already incur a CPU hit due to the RAID redundancy operations).

To summarize, you can significantly increase disk performance using NTFS compression in some cases on smaller volume sizes, but you'll likely do so with a significant hit in CPU utilization. However, this effect might be tolerable on systems with extremely fast processors or multiple installed processors. As always, it is recommended that you test this feature on a nonproduction machine to experiment with it prior to deploying it "live" in your environment.

If you do choose to employ compression on your NTFS volume, you'll be glad to know that compression can be done on a selective basis. In fact, NTFS compression goes down to the file level, meaning that you can compress individual files and directories on a case-by-case basis; you don't have to compress the entire volume as is the case with compression methods used by other operating systems. However, if desired, you can also compress an entire NTFS volume simply by compressing the volume's root folder. With NT 3.5x, you compress files and folders with File Manager. In NT 4.0, you select a file or folder's Properties dialog by right-clicking on the file or folder and choosing Properties.

To compress an entire drive, open the My Computer desktop folder, right-click on the NTFS volume to be compressed, and choose Properties. In the dialog that appears, check the Compress <*drive:*> box and choose OK. You will be asked if you wish to also compress all the subfolders of the drive as well; if this is the case, choose Yes. Otherwise, only the root folder of the volume will be compressed.

Figure 7-19 is an example of the dialog to compress an NTFS volume.

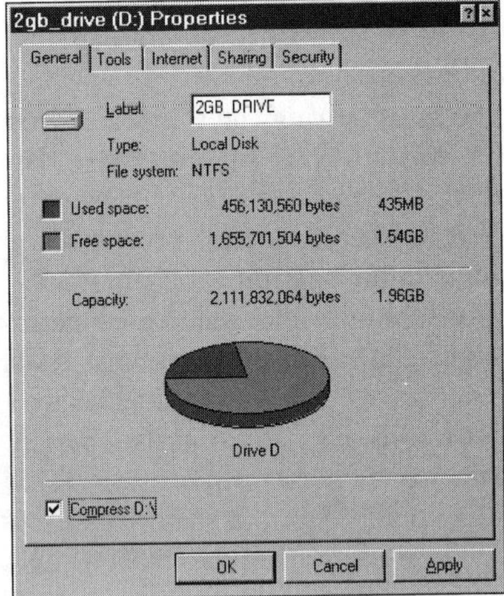

Figure 7-19: Compressing an entire NTFS volume.

Figure 7-20 is an example of the dialog to compress an individual folder on an NTFS volume.

You can also compress a file or folder with the command-line utility `COMPACT.EXE`. The command format to do this is:

```
COMPACT [/c | /u] [/s[:dir]] [/a] [/i] [/f] [/q] [filename [...]]
```

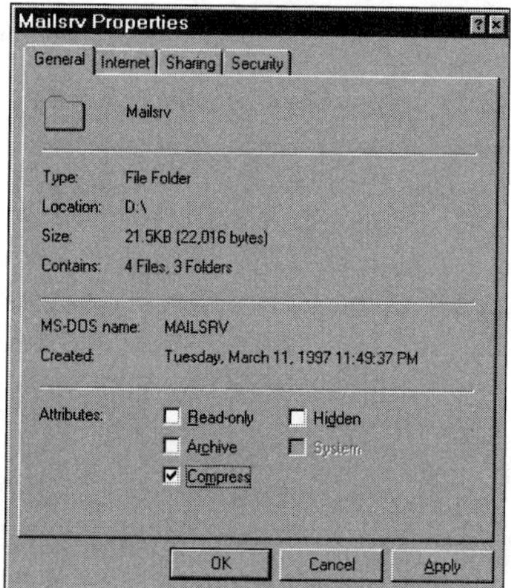

Figure 7-20: Compressing an individual folder on an NTFS volume.

where:

- */c* Compresses the specified files. Directories are marked so that files added afterward are compressed.
- */u* Uncompresses the specified files. Directories are marked so that files added afterward are not compressed.
- */s* Performs the specified operation on files in the given directory and all subdirectories. Default "dir" is the current directory.
- */a* Displays files with the hidden or system attributes. These files are omitted by default.
- */i* Continues performing the specified operation even after errors have occurred. By default, COMPACT stops when an error is encountered.
- */f* Forces the compress operation on all specified files, even those that are already compressed. Already compressed files are skipped by default.
- */q* Reports only the most essential information.
- *filename* Specifies a pattern, file, or directory.

When used without any command-line parameters, COMPACT displays the compression status of the current directory and any files it contains. You can also use multiple filenames and wildcards (however, you must put spaces between multiple parameters).

NTFS TUNING

In addition to what has been described elsewhere in this chapter, there are a few other things you can do to optimize the performance of NTFS volumes. Specifically, there are several Registry modifications you can make to disable certain features of NTFS that may not be necessary in your environment.

The first such modification is a system change that disables NTFS's automatic creation of MS-DOS style 8.3 format "short names" for files stored on NTFS volumes. As you probably know, Windows NT supports the use of long filenames on both NTFS and FAT volumes. In both cases, NT automatically creates a short name version of each file stored on a volume in 8.3 naming format. This maintains compatibility with 16-bit operating systems and applications that access the volume (such as MS-DOS, Windows 3.x, Windows for Workgroups, and applications that run under these operating systems). However, this procedure also incurs additional write overhead to add the second Master File Table entry for each file and directory. With NTFS volumes, it is possible to disable this automatic name generation via a Registry modification (there is no such equivalent for FAT volumes).

You may want to consider making this modification if your network is in pure 32-bit networking environment with 100 percent 32-bit operating systems and applications. To enable this change, open one of the Windows NT Registry Editor utilities and locate the following key and value:

```
HKEY_LOCAL_MACHINE\SYSTEM\CurrentControlSet\Control\FileSystem
```

Value: NtfsDisable8dot3NameCreation
Default Data: 0 (false)

To disable 8.3 short-name generation, set the data for this value to 1.

There are several important points to remember if you're considering making this change. First, be very sure that your network does not now contain, and will not in the future contain, any systems that use DOS, Windows 3.x, or Windows for Workgroups 3.x. These systems cannot use files on an NTFS volume without 8.3-style names. Also, be aware that using 16-bit applications (e.g., MS-DOS or Win16 applications) on an NTFS volume without 8.3 names may cause application incompatibilities or crashes. Finally, be aware that changing this Registry value affects only future files stored on the volume. Existing files retain their previously created 8.3 version names until you remove the files from the volume. If you want to start with a clean slate, you'll have to set the Registry value to 1, move all the files to another volume or tape, and then move the files back to the original volume.

Disabling NTFS 8.3 short-name creation on a Windows NT 3.51 Server running Microsoft Exchange Server may prevent Exchange Custom Forms from working properly. If you are using these products in this configuration, it's recommended that you leave 8.3 name creation enabled.

In addition to the 8.3 name generation feature, there is one other Registry modification that we can make to create some improvement in NTFS's performance. A value named *NtfsDisableLastAccessUpdate* controls whether NTFS updates the LastAccess time/date stamp on directories as NTFS traverses the directory structure. Disabling these last access updates can reduce NTFS's overhead without significantly impairing functionality. The default value is 0 (NTFS updates directory time/date stamps); change the value to 1 to disable updates. If you don't see the *NtfsDisableLastAccessUpdate* value listed, you can manually add it as a REG_DWORD value and then set the value's data as 1. However, if you add it, be very certain to spell the value name correctly including capitalization.

Disk Fragmentation and Optimization

One of the most important practices in maintaining a well-optimized disk subsystem under any operating system is minimizing the level of file fragmentation that exists on the system's various drive volumes. This can be accomplished by regularly running a disk defragmentation utility that defragments — that is, makes contiguous — every file on the volume. In addition, these utilities are also capable of defragmenting the free disk space on the volume, which is also beneficial to improving volume performance.

Fragmentation adversely affects performance because additional head and platter movements are required to access a file which is stored in multiple, noncontiguous locations on a disk. On the other hand, when a file is contiguous, it can be read sequentially in one long burst without requiring additional drive re-positioning.

To maintain optimal disk performance on your Windows NT system, you should regularly run a disk defragmentation tool. The frequency of this process should be proportionate to the level of disk usage on the machine; that is, heavily-accessed network servers should probably have this process run once per week at minimum, whereas workstations with relatively light disk usage may be fine with a monthly or semimonthly disk defragmentation. You can use the disk fragmentation analysis tool included with your defragmentation software to determine the level of fragmentation that currently exists on each volume.

Figure 7-21 shows a Windows NT disk defragmentation utility at work.

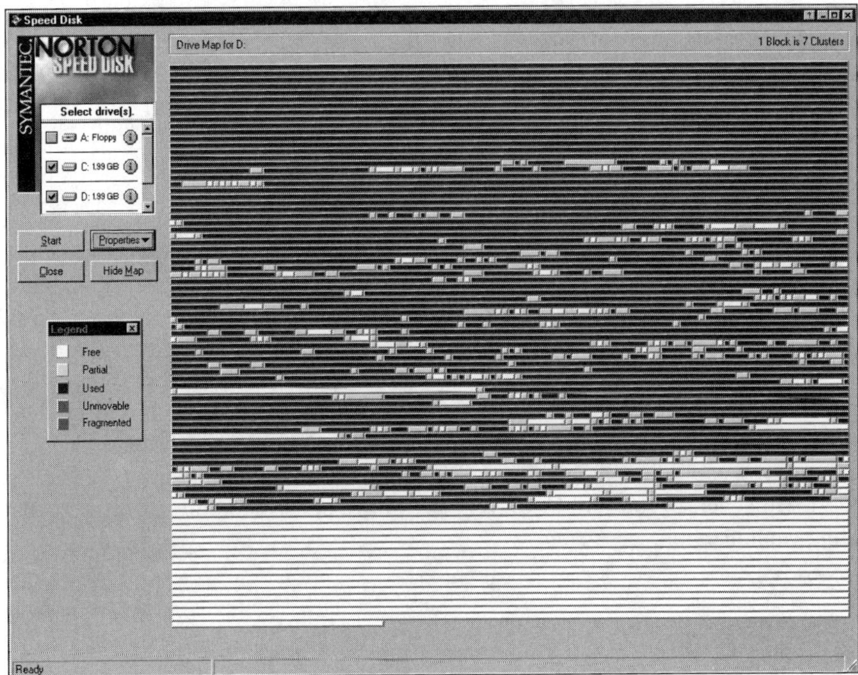

Figure 7-21: Running a Windows NT disk defragmentation utility to optimize volume access speed.

At the time of this writing, there are three commercial disk defragmentation utilities available for Windows NT: Executive Software's Diskeeper for Windows NT, Norton Speedisk, part of the Norton Utilities for Windows NT available from Symantec Corporation, and Perfect Disk NT by Raxco Software. Information on Diskeeper can be found on Executive Software's World Wide Web site at:

`http://www.execsoft.com/`

Information on Diskeeper can be found on Executive Software's World Wide Web site at:

`http://www.execsoft.com/`

Information on Perfect Disk NT can be found at Raxco's Web site at:

`http://www.raxco.com/`

Diskeeper by Executive Software, the original disk defragmentation utility for Windows NT, is an excellent disk defragmentation tool that works with both FAT and NTFS volumes. Diskeeper also includes a handy disk fragmentation analysis tool, which informs you about the current level of file fragmentation on each of your disk volumes. Diskeeper Lite, the shareware version of Diskeeper, is included on the *Optimizing Windows NT* CD-ROM. To install the software, follow the directions outlined in Appendix A, "What's On the CD?," or point your Web browser to the location of the *Optimizing Windows NT* CD-ROM in your system and follow the links to install the software.

When running disk-related benchmarks on your system, don't forget to run a full file and free space defragmentation before each benchmark test iteration. Otherwise, varying levels of fragmentation may affect your tests and produce skewed or misleading results.

Optimizing the paging file

One of the most important components in Windows NT system performance is the paging file. The paging file, as you know from Chapter 5, serves as virtual memory and is used to swap pages to and from memory to balance the use of physical RAM between various processes on the system. The paging file provides supplemental memory to physical RAM and is used as part of Windows NT's total memory address space. However, because it is disk-based memory and not actual physical RAM, the paging file is exponentially slower than real RAM and can become a performance bottleneck when it is heavily used by the system.

As a result, one of the most important things we can do in optimizing a Windows NT system is to ensure that we are achieving maximum performance from the paging file. Although job #1 in optimizing a Windows NT computer is to ensure that paging file activity is at a minimum (which basically means that there is plenty of memory available on the system), any Windows NT system, regardless of the amount of installed physical memory, is going to experience some degree of paging file activity (due to the construction of NT's Virtual Memory Manager). However, we certainly don't want to exacerbate a memory bottleneck with a slow paging file! Even on systems with plenty of memory, we want to be sure that the paging file isn't slowing us down unnecessarily.

For information on detecting memory bottlenecks and the Windows NT paging file, see Chapter 5, "Optimizing Memory and Processing."

Because the paging file is stored on one or more system volumes, the volumes themselves become a factor in paging file performance (and therefore, in overall system performance when paging file activity occurs). This means that to properly optimize the paging file, we must consider the following about any volume that stores the paging file:

- File system: Is the NTFS or FAT file system used on the volume(s)?
- Volume location: Is the volume on a physical disk with many partitions (and therefore a potentially high degree of activity), or is the sole volume on the physical disk?
- How many physical disks are available containing free space that we can utilize for the paging file?

GENERAL PAGING FILE CONFIGURATION TIPS

The first thing we can do to optimize paging file performance is to spread the file across multiple *physical* drives. Using more than one physical drive for the paging file provides multiple disk spindles that can be accessed by the operating system simultaneously; this translates to better paging file performance. However, to truly leverage the performance possibilities of using multiple drives, these drives should ideally be SCSI, because SCSI drives are better equipped to utilize NT's asynchronous I/O capabilities than are (E)IDE drives. It is still advantageous in most instances to use a combination of SCSI and IDE drives if present in the system, and even the use of multiple IDE drives may yield better performance than a single drive. To determine which is best for your environment you need to do some experimentation and run benchmarks to evaluate the performance of each configuration.

When using multiple drives for the paging file, be sure that you use multiple physical drives and not multiple logical drives on the same partition, because using multiple logical drives on the same partition won't yield any performance benefits.

The Windows NT paging file is configured via the System Control Panel's Performance tab. This dialog allows you to define a paging file on one or more drives and to set the minimum and maximum sizes on each volume.

Figure 7-22 shows this configuration dialog.

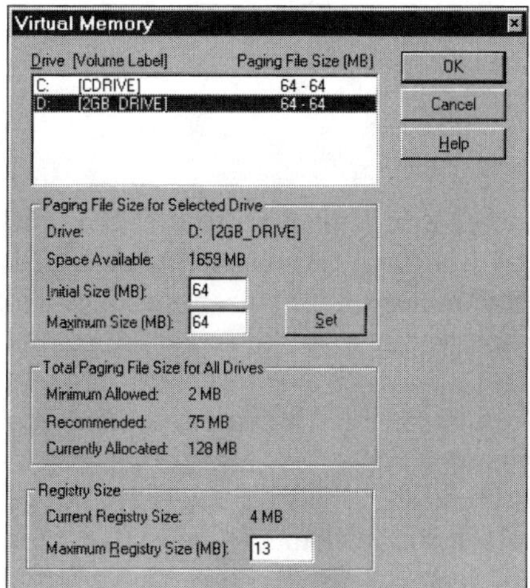

Figure 7-22: Optimizing the paging file using multiple physical drives and equivalent minimum/maximum sizes.

In this dialog, we set the minimum and maximum size for the paging file on each partition to the same size. Preventing NT from dynamically adjusting its size by setting the same minimum and maximum size for the paging file is another method for improving paging file performance. This prevents the paging file from becoming fragmented (a natural result of being extended and reduced), a condition that slows the paging file's performance. When configuring the paging file in this manner, you should ensure that the total size of the paging file is at least the minimum recommended size as displayed in the paging file configuration dialog box. Although the downside of doing this is that it will use more disk space (because it doesn't allow NT to dynamically increase the file on an as-needed basis), it will prevent page file fragmentation and thus optimize its performance.

Although Windows NT will generally recommend a paging file size of physical RAM + 11MB, if disk space permits you should consider making the paging file 150 percent of physical RAM size. This will provide a higher ceiling in the event of extremely heavy paging usage, and act as a hedge against situations where physical memory is increased but a corresponding increase in the paging file size (which should coincide with such a change) is inadvertently omitted.

Creating a paging file that is guaranteed to be unfragmented requires that you either (1) have (or create) a new partition with a fresh format or (2) run a disk defragmentation program on a nonpaging file volume to defragment both files and free space on the volume. Once you've done this, you're ready to create the paging file in the contiguous free space you've created.

To create a new, unfragmented paging file on a newly formatted volume or a fully defragmented volume, follow these steps:

1. Open the Performance Tab of the System Control Panel (Note: in NT 3.5x, you should instead choose the Virtual Memory button).
2. Select a new partition on which to locate the paging file.
3. Using the dialog, set the minimum and maximum paging file sizes to the same value (preferably greater than or equal to the recommended size listed) and click Set to commit the changes.
4. Next, select the existing paging file and set the minimum and maximum paging file sizes to zero; then choose Set to commit the changes.
5. Shut down and restart the system as instructed; when you reboot, the paging file should be contiguous.

Another important aspect to paging file performance is the activity of the drive(s) used for the paging file. When selecting a drive (or drives) for the paging file, make sure that the drive is one that isn't heavily bogged down with other system tasks. This helps balance the load on the disk subsystem and ensures the paging file receives faster servicing by the disk subsystem. If possible, place the paging file on its own dedicated partition with little or nothing else on the partition (or at least no data that is actively referenced by the system or applications on a continual basis). This eliminates the possibility of contention with other system processes accessing the disk, ensuring the fastest possible access to the paging file.

The only other thing you can do to further optimize paging file (other than increasing the speed of the disk hardware involved) is to place it on a RAID 0/striped set volume (a single logical volume consisting of two or more equally sized partitions across multiple physical disks). Although at first it may seem somewhat decadent and unnecessary to do, systems with heavy paging file usage may benefit greatly from this type of configuration.

If you do decide to place the paging file on a dedicated partition and are concerned about wasting disk space, consider placing static files that receive minimal access on the same volume. For example, you might place data such as hardware support files or even the contents of the Windows NT CD-ROM (or a portion of it) on this partition. The key criterion for the files you place here is that they be infrequently accessed files that are usually accessed in a read-only fashion. This will make better use of disk space on the volume and will not create contention with paging file access.

The last general tip regarding the paging file relates to the type of file system volume(s) you store the paging file on. Microsoft recommends placing the paging file on an NTFS partition. However, except in cases where this is necessary for security reasons, we recommend that you place the paging file on FAT volumes for maximum performance. Because FAT is generally faster than NTFS on smaller volume sizes, placing the paging file on a smaller, dedicated FAT volume will yield faster performance than placing it on a comparable NTFS volume. Again, this recommendation assumes that the volume(s) used are under 2GB in size where FAT maintains a performance advantage over NTFS.

You should never place your paging file on a stripe set with parity (RAID 5) volume, because doing so will degrade its performance. If you want to place the paging file on a fault-tolerant volume, choose a mirror set (RAID 1) volume instead.

DEFRAGMENTING THE PAGING FILE

Although we've discussed ways to prevent paging file fragmentation (namely, setting the minimum and maximum size to the same value when creating the file on a new or fully defragmented partition), you may be in a situation where the paging file is already fragmented. For example, you may have already created your paging file, in which case setting the minimum and maximum sizes equally may not create an unfragmented paging file (i.e., the file is already fragmented or there is insufficient contiguous disk space to create a new, contiguous paging file). Another possibility is that you have disk space limitations that prevent you from setting the minimum and maximum paging file sizes to the same value; as a result, your paging file becomes fragmented over time as it expands and reduces in size.

In any case, it is possible defragment the paging file using a special procedure. However, as you might have already guessed, defragmenting the paging file using this procedure requires access to a commercial disk defragmentation utility (Executive Software's Diskeeper Lite is included on the CD and can be used for this purpose). We can't just run the defragmenter and have the paging file be automatically defragmented along with the volume because the file is constantly in use by the system and therefore cannot be fragmented. The following procedure allows you to defragment the paging file using a roundabout method.

This method requires at least two partitions and adequate free space to install a second, temporary copy of Windows NT.

To defragment an existing paging file, follow these steps:

1. Install a second, temporary installation of Windows NT in a separate directory. If possible, this should be a partition other than the one(s) containing the existing fragmented paging file.
2. Boot the temporary installation of Windows NT.
3. While booted under this temporary copy of NT, set the paging file location for that installation of Windows NT to a volume other than the one containing the paging file for your original Windows NT installation.
4. Install a commercial disk defragmentation utility on the system.
5. Rename the original fragmented paging file, called `PAGEFILE.SYS` and located in the volume's root folder, to another name of your choosing (e.g., `PAGEFILE.ORI`.)
6. Defragment the partition where the original fragmented paging file (now renamed) exists. This will defragment not only that volume but the paging file as well.
7. Rename the now defragmented original paging file back to `PAGEFILE.SYS`.
8. Reboot your system back into your original Windows NT installation (assuming the system boots properly, it is now also safe to remove your temporary second copy of NT).

Directory optimization

In addition to optimizing files, volume free space, and the paging file, there is one other disk entity that you may wish to optimize: the directory. The directory is basically a database of all of the files and folders on a volume, including information such as the starting and ending cluster for each folder and file.

Like these other entities, a volume's directory becomes fragmented over time as many folders and files are created, modified, and deleted. Because the directory is constantly being updated, it is beneficial to have it be as unfragmented as possible. In addition, it is also beneficial to move the directory to the *outside* of the disk's platters, because it is always preferable to have frequently accessed data on the outside of the disk's platters.

The reason for this preference is simple: the outside of a disk has a higher rotational rate, and therefore a faster data transfer rate than the inner parts of the disk. If you don't believe us, try this experiment: go to your local playground and stand on one of those spinning carousels, first sitting on the inside, and then the outside. You'll quickly see which makes you feel more seasick.

As a result of this phenomenon, it would be ideal if we could move the directory to the outside of the disk where the performance is faster. However, there is no easy way to do this, because under NT even defragmentation utilities aren't allowed to move the directory; doing so risks data corruption and isn't supported by the operating system. However, if you are really interested in optimizing a volume's directory, there is a method to accomplish this. Although it's somewhat tedious to implement, it does work.

To defragment a volume's directory and move it to the outside of the disk, follow these steps (this method can't be used for the Windows NT system partition):

Be certain that you have a known good full backup of your system and Registry before following the procedure to optimize the directory, because the procedure involves the deletion of files and could, if done improperly, result in data loss.

1. Copy all of your files (and only the files) to another partition or to a tape drive.
2. Next, delete the files only from the original, source partition. Note: Do not move the files in one step – first copy them and then delete them as a second step.
3. Now copy all of your directories (and only the directories) to another partition or to a tape drive. Again, be sure to copy the directories, don't move them.

4. Next, delete your directories from the original source partition.
5. If you intend to create a paging file on this partition, you should do so now so that it is unfragmented; in addition, it is recommended that you set the paging file to the same minimum and maximum size to prevent future fragmentation of the file.
6. Next copy all of the directories back to the original partition.
7. Now copy all of the files back to the original partition.
8. After following this procedure, all of the volume's directories should be contiguous, and should be at or near the beginning of the volume (and thus the outside of the disk).

If you employ this procedure to optimize an NTFS volume and wish to preserve NTFS security information, you should use two NTFS volumes and use the SCOPY utility included with the Windows NT Resource Kit rather than the COPY or XCOPY command (or the Windows NT Explorer). This is because SCOPY preserves security information during a copy operation; by default, NTFS uses the security of the recipient directory for permission during a copy operation. If you also copy the files back, you should once again use SCOPY to preserve the existing security information on the files.

There are also some steps you can take to proactively prevent directory fragmentation in Windows NT. Whenever you install any large application software on the system, take these three steps in the order listed: (1) defragment the volume fully, including free space; (2) reboot the system; (3) install the application. This helps minimize the amount of directory fragmentation that occurs on the volume, because testing has shown that there is a greater tendency for new directories to be written toward the beginning of the disk after the system has been rebooted. It is suspected that this occurs because the "next directory allocation" pointer (which tells NT where to write the next directory on disk) is reset to the beginning of the volume after a reboot.

Optimizing Multiple-drive Configurations

One of the most powerful methods of improving the performance of any disk drive subsystem, regardless of the operating system, is to employ multiple drives working in tandem. The reason for this is simple: there will always be limits to the performance that a single drive, no matter how fast, can achieve. This limit is derived from the fact that one drive can still only perform one operation at a time, having only one set of read/write heads. However, when used with an operating system such as Windows NT, which supports an asynchronous I/O model supporting device concurrency (talking to multiple devices simultaneously), a multidrive configuration can deliver some amazing performance gains.

Defining RAID levels

The most common reason for using multiple drive sets is their use in Redundant Array of Independent Disks (RAID) configurations. A RAID array is a collection of disks that provide a single logical volume to the operating system and user, faster performance than a single drive by itself, and in most implementations, some form of *fault-tolerance*. In the case of RAID disk arrays, fault-tolerance means that one member disk in a set can fail and the operating system or RAID hardware can recover and rebuild the information from the data contained on the other member drives in the set.

RAID is defined in a series of levels (starting with level 0), most of which provide some form of data fault-tolerance in addition to their speed advantages. Because both the data redundancy and performance implications of RAID are so significant, their use warrants consideration by anyone looking to achieve maximum disk subsystem performance.

Windows NT goes far beyond most other workstation and server operating systems by internally supporting three separate levels of RAID in software:

- RAID 0 (Disk Striping): RAID 0 is the only common implementation of RAID that offers no fault-tolerance. It does, however, offer the fastest performance of any RAID level; it works by striping data evenly across two or more drives in the RAID 0 set. This concurrent drive usage translates to excellent read and write performance and is the best choice for maximum performance where data fault-tolerance on the drive array itself is neither a concern nor a requirement.

- RAID 1 (Disk Mirroring or Duplexing): In a RAID 1/Mirror volume, two drives of equivalent capacity are used; one is a "mirror" or "shadow" of the second. RAID 1 provides the best fault tolerance of all RAID configurations because no rebuilding is required in the event of a failure; the failed drive can simply be decommissioned and the mirror drive used in its stead. When two controllers are used in RAID 1 (one for each drive), this is referred to as disk *duplexing*.
- RAID 5 (Disk Striping with Parity): RAID 5 uses a method of data storage similar to RAID 0 (Disk Striping) but adds a new twist: it uses an amount of space equal to one of the member drives in the set to store *parity* information. Parity data is error-checking information that can be used in the event of a failure of any single member of the set to rebuild the set with no loss of data. Due to this feature, RAID 5 sets require a minimum of three physical drives. RAID 5 volumes generally offer the fastest read performance but the slowest write performance of all the RAID levels supported by Windows NT.

Figure 7-23 displays a graphical representation of the data storage methods used by each RAID level.

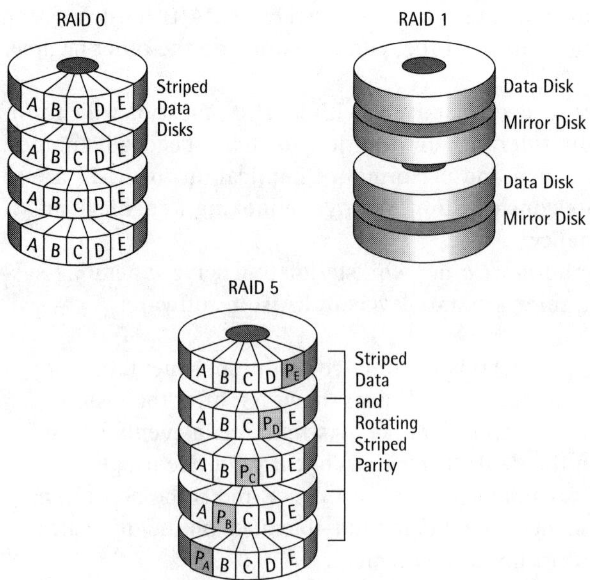

Figure 7-23: The three RAID levels supported internally by Windows NT.

An excellent source of information on RAID terminology, concepts, and technology is the "RAID Book," produced by the RAID Advisory Board. Information about this book and other RAID-related information can be found at:

`http://www.raid-advisory.com/`

Hardware versus software RAID

Although it's wonderful that Windows NT includes internal support for RAID, this doesn't mean that it is your best choice for establishing RAID volumes on your systems. This is because Windows NT's support for RAID is a software-based one that relies on the host computer's CPU to carry out all of the redundancy-related work (e.g., parity calculations for RAID 5). This in turn means that the performance of the RAID array is dependent on the speed of the host CPU and causes a significant increase in processor utilization on the host system (this is especially true of a RAID 5 array, which is more CPU intensive by nature than RAID 0 or 1). The major benefit to using NT's built-in RAID is cost. Because nothing more than a standard disk controller and a bunch of disks are required to get it up and running under NT, the world of RAID becomes available to those even on the tightest of budgets. However, from a performance standpoint, it is recommended that you limit the use of software RAID under Windows NT to RAID 0 Stripe Set configurations on workstations and similar noncritical machines. The processor utilization impact will be minimized, and the performance increase in most cases will be significant.

A much better choice for fault-tolerant RAID configurations and maximum performance on workstations is hardware-based RAID solutions. Typical hardware RAID solutions include one or more dedicated on-board processors, which perform the RAID logic operations in lieu of the host system's CPU. In addition, most processors found on hardware RAID controllers are specifically designed for I/O such as disk drive/RAID operations, which translates to much higher performance than could ever be possible using Windows NT's built-in RAID support. Hardware RAID controllers also tend to offer additional flavors of RAID with capabilities beyond the RAID levels 0, 1, and 5 offered by NT. The most significant of these is any type of RAID 0+1 offering (Mirrored Stripe Sets), which offers the best performing fault-tolerant RAID configuration for most environments.

Finally, hardware RAID controllers offer additional recovery and other features that aren't included in Windows NT's FTDISK.SYS driver and Disk Administrator management software. Hardware RAID controllers usually provide management utilities that make the job of configuring and administrating the RAID arrays attached to the controller a simple one. The bottom line: If you want maximum RAID performance for your Windows NT system, go with a dedicated RAID controller.

There are typically two types of hardware RAID products: SCSI-to-Host and SCSI-to-SCSI. With SCSI-to-Host, a dedicated internal SCSI-based RAID controller card (containing the RAID logic) is used to communicate with a number of standard SCSI hard drives. With SCSI-to-SCSI RAID systems, the RAID controller intelligence is typically built into the external enclosure housing the drive subsystem, which attaches to a standard SCSI adapter on the host computer rather than a special RAID controller card.

In our lab tests for this book, we had the pleasure of working with two dedicated hardware RAID controllers that demonstrated both impressive performance as well as strong fault-tolerance features. The Mylex DACPDU960, an UltraWide SCSI-based controller sporting an Intel i960 RISC I/O processor, is an excellent choice for hardware RAID and has full Windows NT support. More information on this product can be obtained from the vendors Web site at:

`http://www.mylex.com/`

The other controller we were impressed with was the SmartCache IV and SmartRAID IV products from Distributed Processing Technology (DPT), which offers a number of upgradeable, modular RAID controllers that provide excellent performance and compatibility with Windows NT. More information on DPT's RAID products can be obtained at their Web site at:

`http://www.dpt.com/`

Both of these products merit consideration for anyone seeking a Windows NT hardware RAID solution.

When configuring RAID arrays using hardware or software methods, try to always purchase controllers with multiple channels, and limit the number of drives per channel to three or four at maximum (as a general rule of thumb). Otherwise, the command overhead of the drives may saturate the channel and cause a performance bottleneck.

Comparing RAID performance

Now that we understand a little about how the different levels of RAID supported by Windows NT store their data, let's compare their relative performances to see how we can best deploy them in our environment.

When deciding which RAID level(s) to deploy on the Windows NT computers in your organization, you should first do a thorough comparison of the advantages and disadvantages of each level, including features related to fault-tolerance and performance. In addition, because some RAID levels are good for one type of drive I/O (i.e., read or write) and not for another, it's important to be sure that the RAID level selected is appropriate for the kinds of data to be stored on the volume.

A comparison of the most widely implemented RAID levels is provided in Table 7-10.

As you can see from Table 7-10, you'll want to evaluate the nature of the data to be stored on a volume before you choose a RAID level for the volume. For example, RAID 5 or 6 wouldn't be a good choice for write-intensive volumes due to the performance penalty of the parity generation on these drives; in these cases, you would probably want to use RAID 1 or a proprietary RAID 0+1 implementation that provides better write performance. RAID 0+1 is always the best choice for maximum performance and fault-tolerance and should be used in any situation where maximum performance in a fault-tolerant configuration is required (and the cost per megabyte disadvantage of these configurations is not a major issue).

Because Windows NT supports currently only RAID levels 0, 1, and 5, there's also a natural performance boost involved with any implementation of RAID levels 6 or 0+1. The use of these levels implies the use of a hardware-based, dedicated RAID controller that supports these RAID levels, which will provide far better performance than the use of NT's internal RAID support.

Table 7-10 FEATURE AND PERFORMANCE COMPARISON OF VARIOUS RAID LEVELS

RAID Level	Advantages	Disadvantages
RAID 0 (Disk Striping)	Fastest RAID level; provides superior read and write performance; lack of fault-tolerance provides 100 percent disk utilization (but no redundancy)	No fault-tolerance features; failure of any one drive set member will cause the entire set to fail; as a result, should only be used in conjunction with a backup system
RAID 1 (Disk Mirroring/Duplexing)	Provides the highest fault-tolerance in the event of a single drive failure in the set; offers write performance equivalent to a single drive and superior read performance; performance and fault tolerance can be increased further with the use of a second controller for the second drive	Achieves only a 50 percent net disk space utilization, making the cost per megabyte the highest of all the RAID levels
RAID 5 (Disk Striping with Parity)	Offers a good balance of disk utilization (usable space = C*N-C where C is the drive capacity of the member drives and N is the number of member drives), performance, and fault-tolerance; offers superior read performance because all disks can read, especially for sequential data access	Has relatively poor write performance as compared to the other RAID levels

continued

RAID Level	Advantages	Disadvantages
RAID 6*	As with RAID 5, except that additional fault-tolerance is gained by use of second set of parity information; as a result, can suffer two failures without data loss; best for read-only or read-oriented volumes	As with RAID 5; however, write performance is even slower than RAID 5 due to additional parity calculations
RAID 0+1 (Striped Mirrors) and RAID 10 (Mirrored Stripes)*	Offers the best of RAID 0 and RAID 1; the high performance of striping coupled with the strong fault-tolerance of RAID 1; the fastest fault-tolerant RAID configuration; offers good read and write performance	As with RAID 1, a 50 percent net disk space utilization is achieved, making the cost per megabyte high

*These are proprietary RAID levels and are only supported on hardware RAID equipment from specific manufacturers.

When using a hardware RAID-based array with Windows NT, you won't use Disk Administrator to configure any fault-tolerance — only to partition and format the volume. Disk Administrator will see each array defined as if it were a single physical drive. The drive pack is configured and defined using the software included with the hardware RAID controller, which then presents each array as a single logical unit to Windows NT.

Volume Sets: A RAID-less Multidrive Set

Another potential use of multiple drives under Windows NT, which isn't any form of RAID, is a type of disk volume known as *volume set*. Volume sets are essentially concatenations of free space on two or more partitions, which may be contained on one or more physical drives. These multiple, scattered areas of free space are joined together to create one logical, "virtual" drive that appears to the user and applications as a single drive letter (just like RAID volumes do).

However, volume sets are very different from RAID 0 and 5 configurations (stripe sets and stripe sets with parity, respectively) because volume sets use space sequentially and not striped across multiple physical volumes concurrently (which is the feature that delivers the real performance benefits of having multiple drives). Windows NT will write data on a volume set sequentially; that is, it writes data to the first drive in the set until that drive is full, and then continues to the next drive. Although in some circumstances this could deliver some simultaneous drive use, such usage would be relatively sporadic and thus limits the performance advantages of this configuration.

Creating RAID configuration with Disk Administrator

If you decide to use Windows NT's built-in RAID capabilities, then you'll need to use Disk Administrator to configure the volumes. Disk Administrator is located in the Start Menu → Programs → Administrative Tools (Common) program folder and can be used to define RAID 0 (Disk Stripe), RAID 1 (Mirrored/Duplexed), or RAID 5 (Stripe Set with Parity) volumes.

CREATING A RAID 0 STRIPE SET OR RAID 5 STRIPE SET WITH PARITY

To use Disk Administrator to create a RAID 0 Stripe Set or RAID 5 Stripe Set with Parity, you must first have either two physical drives (RAID 0) or three physical drives (RAID 5) with free space on them. The total size of the volume is the smallest amount of free space on all of the drives. For RAID 0, the total usable space is the sum of all the drives. For RAID 5, the sum is the total of all the drives minus one drive's capacity (used to store parity information). From 2 to 32 partitions can participate in a stripe set, and when creating the set Disk Administrator automatically makes all the partitions approximately the same size.

To create a stripe set using the Windows NT Disk Administrator follow these steps:

1. Run Disk Administrator, located in the Start Menu → Programs → Administrative Tools (Common) program folder.
2. Next, select from 2 to 32 areas of free space, making sure all are on separate drives. To select multiple areas of free space, select the first area of free space on the first disk and then hold down the CTRL key while left-clicking on a second area of free space on another (physical) drive. Repeat the CTRL-click maneuver for each area of free space area you wish to combine in the stripe set. All areas selected will have a highlighted border around them.
3. To create a stripe set, choose Partition → Create Stripe Set; to create a stripe set with parity, choose Fault Tolerance → Create Stripe with Parity.
4. In the Create Stripe Set/Stripe Set with Parity dialog (shown in Figure 7-24), type the size of the stripe set that you want to create and choose OK. The selected size must be a number between the minimum and maximum sizes displayed.

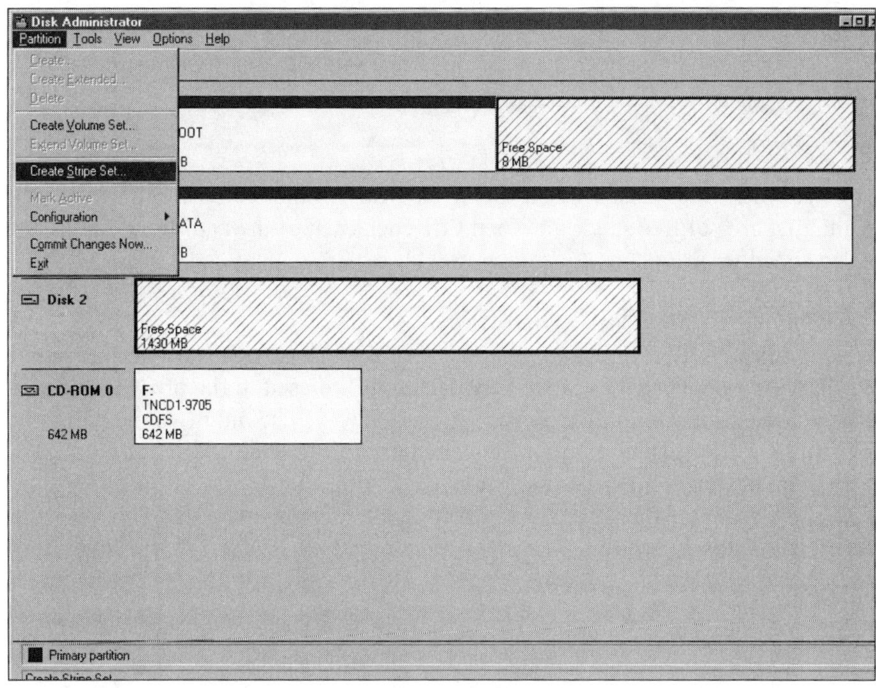

Figure 7-24: Creating a stripe set using Disk Administrator.

At this point, the stripe set is created, and the display window changes to indicate that the selected areas are now part of a stripe set.

Once the Stripe Set/Stripe Set with Parity has been created, you can choose Partition → Commit Changes Now to commit the changes to disk and then use Tools → Format to format and prepare the volume for use.

When you create a stripe set, Disk Administrator divides the total amount of space selected by the number of physical disks, creating equally sized unformatted partitions on each of the selected disks. If the resulting number cannot be divided equally, Disk Administrator will round to the closest higher or lower value. Depending on your drive configuration, this can leave small amounts of free space on one or more drives. The additional free space can be left unused, used to create additional partitions, or combined to create a volume set.

Operating systems such as MS-DOS, Windows 3.x, and Windows 95 aren't capable of recognizing stripe sets created using Windows NT's built-in RAID support. Therefore, if you create a stripe set on a multi-boot Windows NT system, any defined stripe sets or stripe sets with parity will be unusable while the system is booted under these other operating systems.

To select each free space area on the member drives that comprise the stripe set, click the first area of free space and then Ctrl-click each of the additional free space areas on the other drives.

CREATING A RAID 1 MIRROR SET

Creating a mirror set is similar to creating a stripe set or stripe set with parity but somewhat less complicated because only partitions are used in the process of creating the volume. However, unlike stripe sets, you always use only two components: an existing partition which may or may not currently contain data but must contain an existing format (this is the primary partition that you wish to have "mirrored") and an area of free space as the secondary component.

To use Disk Administrator to create a mirror set (see Figure 7-25) follow these steps:

1. Run Disk Administrator, located in the Start Menu → Programs → Administrative Tools (Common) program folder.
2. Next, select two areas on two separate physical drives; one is an existing, formatted partition, which is the primary partition you wish to mirror; the second is an area of free space you wish to use as the "mirror" of the primary. (Note: The mirror's area must be at least as big as the primary partition.) To select multiple areas of free space, select the first area of free space on the first disk and then hold down the CTRL key while left-clicking on a second area of free space on another (physical) drive. Repeat the CTRL-click maneuver for each free space area you wish to combine in the stripe set. All areas selected will have a highlighted border around them.
3. From the menus, choose Fault Tolerance → Establish Mirror. When you are done, Windows NT informs you that you've made changes requiring that the system be shut down immediately. Once you click OK, the system will shut down and restart so that the new disk configuration change may take effect.

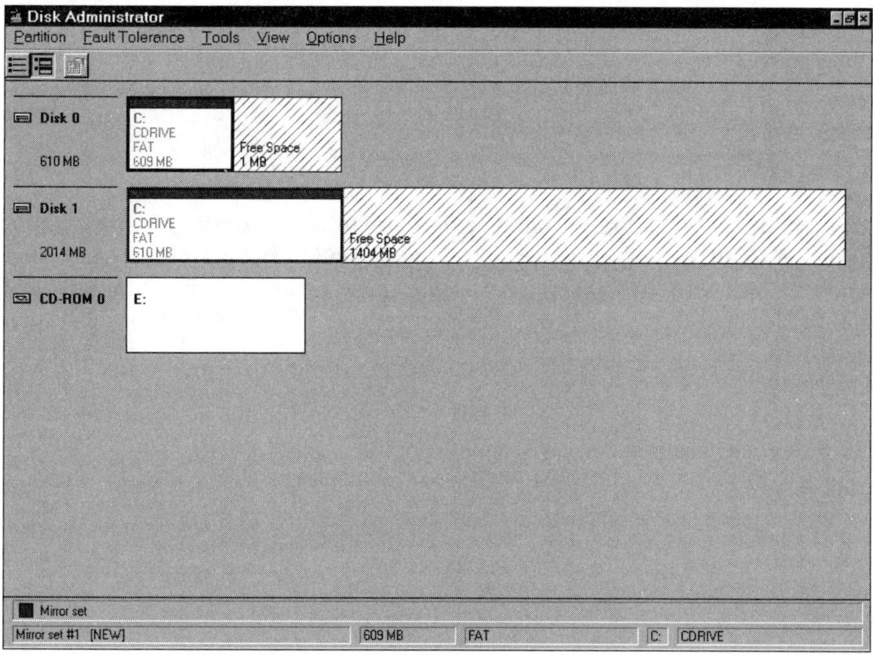

Figure 7-25: A mirror set created with Disk Administrator.

Once the system restarts, NT automatically begins the background process of mirroring the data from one drive to the other. While the primary drive is still synchronizing with the shadow/mirror drive, both drives are shown in red in the Disk Administrator display window. Once this process is complete, a notification entry is placed in the System Event Log (viewable with Event Viewer) and the drive color turns to purple (indicating a synchronized mirror set).

When we say "free space" we mean just that. Don't fall into the trap of trying to use a partition with a format on it as part of a RAID volume — NT won't let you. If you have already partitioned and formatted a volume that is to become a member of a fault-tolerant disk set, you'll need to first delete the partition (after first backing up any data on the volume) before it can be included in the new set.

Immediately after creating or modifying your disk configuration using Disk Administrator, update your Emergency Repair Disk (ERD), because Disk Administrator modifies important system configuration information, which is recorded on the ERD, in the process.

Summary

In this chapter, we explored a number of ways to optimize the performance of Windows NT's disk subsystem, easily the most important performance-related component of a Windows NT system. Using these methods in conjunction with the proper hardware selections will ensure that your Windows NT disk subsystem provides excellent performance at all times and will minimize the bottleneck of disk access.

In the next chapter, we explore methods for optimizing the performance of yet another subsystem: printing.

Chapter 8

Optimizing Printing

ALTHOUGH YOU MIGHT NOT initially think of it as a potential candidate for performance optimization, the Windows NT printing subsystem is another aspect of the NT environment you can teach a few new tricks. Windows NT has a sophisticated client/server printing model that is capable of utilizing server resources to maximize performance while minimizing the administrative and system resource burdens on the client.

Windows NT also includes flexible and powerful features for sharing network and local printer resources. This functionality includes the capability of browsing for available printers, making direct connections to shared Windows NT printers (i.e., local printer drivers are not required), printing support for all supported NT hardware platforms (Alpha, Intel, MIPS, PPC), UNIX systems, Macintosh clients, and clients printing through NetWare networks. Also provided are tools that allow for remote administration and configuration of printers attached to Windows NT computers.

In this chapter, we take a look at these aspects of printing under Windows NT:

- Overview of the Windows NT printing system and printer driver model
- Printer-related settings and modifications for enhancing performance and functionality
- Optimizing printer browsing on the network
- Using printer pools to increase printing performance

Printer Hardware

As with the performance of other systems, printing performance under Windows NT is determined first and foremost by the actual hardware used. This means that to create an optimal printing environment, you should start by purchasing the fastest printer(s) you can that support the features required in your environment.

The most important performance-related aspects that you should look for in any printer are:

- Page per Minute (PPM) Rating: This indicates the maximum number of pages a printer can generate under ideal circumstances, and is usually subdivided into two separate categories: Graphical Pages per Minute (GPPM), which is the maximum speed for printing a page of graphics, and Text Pages Per Minute (TPPM), the speed at which the printer can print a page of straight text. These statistics are the most common method for judging a printer's expected performance.

For dot matrix printers, be sure to find out if a referenced performance figure is for draft (quick, one-pass character formations) or letter-quality printing modes (multipass, high-quality character formations), because print times between the two will vary greatly.

- Resolution: When considering a printer's PPM rating (whether text-based or graphics-based pages), be sure to remember what resolution (typically measured in dots per inch or dpi) the given PPM rating was tested at, and (for color printers) whether the rating is for black-and-white print jobs or those involving multiple colors. The dpi factor is especially important, because basing a decision to buy a 600dpi printer that you'll be using at its maximum resolution based on its 300dpi PPM rating doesn't really give you a true picture of what the printer's real-world performance will be in your environment.
- Availability of High-speed Interface(s): No matter how fast a printer is, you'll want to be sure that the interface through which the printer receives data doesn't limit its potential performance. This means you'll want to look for a printer that supports a network interface (e.g., Ethernet, Fast Ethernet, Token Ring, etc.) or another type of high-speed port such as Universal Serial Bus (USB) or parallel interfaces. If you choose a parallel interface printer (by far the most common and popular type) also look for compatibility with high-speed, intelligent parallel interface standards such as ECP, EPP, or Bidirectional (aka PS/2 Mode) parallel interfaces. Whenever possible, try to avoid using slower printer interface types such as serial or Infrared (IRDA), which have lower maximum throughput rates.

Although there are some proprietary printer controller cards on the market that promise higher print rendering speeds, it is recommended that you steer clear of these. Their functionality is dependent on the specialized hardware that they use, which can easily become outdated with a new version of Windows NT (or with a Service Pack update, for that matter). Instead, stick with printers and printer interfaces that use popular, industry-accepted standards.

Although having a very fast printer connection such as a network-based (e.g., Ethernet, Fast Ethernet, or Token Ring) or EPP/ECP interface is nice, it won't make a printer print any faster than its physical capabilities. Regardless of how fast it receives data, a printer is limited by its page per minute rating. With high-speed interfaces such as these, the bottleneck will likely be the printer's physical printing mechanisms and not the interface itself. However, the other major advantage to remember about such interfaces is that they allow the printer to be centrally available on the network rather than locally connected to a single machine. This can be especially useful in mixed environments where multiple operating systems require access to the same printer, or situations where the printer needs to be situated in a location that isn't in physical proximity to a system acting as a print server.

Extended Capability Port (ECP) and Enhanced Parallel Port (EPP) are bidirectional parallel port specifications that have features and transfer rates beyond those defined by the unidirectional "Centronics" parallel port standard. Both of these specifications are implementations of the newer parallel port specifications defined by the IEEE 1284 specification. A good source of additional information on these standards and their capabilities is available at: `http://www.fapo.com/1284int.htm`

Table 8-1 lists the transfer rate ranges for various printer interface types.

TABLE 8-1 TRANSFER RATES OF VARIOUS PRINTER INTERFACE TYPES

Interface Type	Minimum/Maximum Data Transfer Rates
Serial Interface (RS-232/422)	38 to 14,400 characters/second
Standard Parallel ("Centronics")	10,000 to 125,000 characters/second
Enhanced Parallel Port (EPP)	500,000 to 1,000,000 characters/second
Extended Control Port (ECP)	500,000 to 1,000,000 characters/second
Network (10Mbps Ethernet)	Up to 1,250,000 characters/second
Network (100Mbps Fast Ethernet)	Up to 12,500,000 characters/second
Network (4Mbps Token Ring)	Up to 500,000 characters/second
Network (16Mbps Token Ring)	Up to 2,000,000 characters/second

If you know you are not going to need the parallel port on a particular NT system and would like to free the interrupt used for this port (typically IRQ7), you can disable the parallel port driver used by Windows NT for the port. To do so, go to the Devices Control Panel and set the startup type for the "Parallel" device to Disabled. Should you ever need to use the parallel port in the future, simply set the startup type back to Automatic. When disabling the parallel port on your system, you should also disable the port on the I/O card or motherboard (this is done using the BIOS setup utility or via a jumper on the board).

Again, it's important to remember that past a certain data transfer rate it will be the printer itself that becomes the bottleneck and not the interface over which the data is sent. At least for now, there are no printers capable of keeping pace with the data rates of your average network interface.

Even if you've got a fast printer and a high-throughput printer interface, there are still a few techniques that will further improve printing performance. Before we delve into this topic, however, let's start with a brief overview that will give us a better understanding of printing under Windows NT.

In the following sections, we examine how printers are created and managed by the user, and the underlying model used by Windows NT to implement the printing of data.

Automatic Printer Driver Sharing

One of the nicest print-related features in Windows NT is its ability to automatically download print drivers from Windows NT computers acting as print servers (i.e., those sharing printers on a network). Instead of having to install a local printer driver on each Windows NT computer that needs to use a particular printer on the network, the driver need only be installed once — on the machine sharing the printer. Windows NT client workstations that wish to attach to and use the printer will automatically download the appropriate driver when they connect. In addition, it is also possible to store drivers for hardware platforms, versions, and even operating systems that are different from the Windows NT computer sharing the printer. Currently, print drivers for Windows NT 3.5x or Windows NT 4.0 can be stored on any of the four supported hardware platforms (Intel x86, Alpha, MIPS, and PowerPC) and for Windows 95 computers. These drivers are then automatically downloaded to those types of clients when they connect to the shared printer.

Windows NT Printing Concepts and Terminology

Since it was first released, Windows NT has offered an impressive array of printing features. Printing in Windows NT was designed to be flexible, powerful, fast, efficient, and easy to use.

Before continuing, we should define some of the terminology and concepts involved in Windows NT printing. This is important because some of the terms used in Windows NT printing have meanings that are different than their names imply.

The following is a list of printing terms and concepts used in Windows NT and explanations for each:

- *Printing Device*: A Windows NT printing device is a physical output device (i.e., a printer such as a laser printer, inkjet printer, or plotter); this is what you would normally be referring to when you use the term "printer."
- *Print Driver*: A print driver is the software that communicates with the Windows NT Graphics Device Interface (GDI32) to render print jobs created by applications. Each printer defined in Windows NT uses a print driver to prepare jobs in the proper format for the connected printing device.
- *Printer Port*: The port the printing device is connected to. This can either be a *physical port* on the local computer (such as LPT1, COM2, etc.), or a *logical port*, which refers to the Uniform Naming Convention (UNC) name of a network connection to a remote printing device (e.g., \\SERVER\PRINTER).

- *Printer*: In Windows NT, the term *printer* refers to the software setup of a printer entity in the Printers folder. It is the software interface between the application and the printing device, and it is possible to have multiple printers defined for the same physical printing device, each with different option settings. For example, you might have two printers defined for a printing device capable of both PostScript and PCL printing: one setup for PostScript jobs, and the other for PCL jobs. Printers may be created for both local printers (using a local print driver) and shared network printers on other machines (which may or may not use a local print driver). When you install a local printer on your computer, you will have an opportunity to specify the print driver, physical or logical port name, and printing options for the printer.

In other operating systems, including NetWare and OS/2, shared printers are equivalent to logical printer ports, also referred to as *print queues*. A print queue is simply a network batch process connected to a printing device that can accept incoming jobs from network clients and pass them on to the device. This process is known as *print spooling*. In most network operating systems, client workstations interact with the print queue rather than directly with an actual printer.

However, Windows NT printer sharing goes far beyond the capabilities of traditional print queues. Unlike other network operating systems, Windows NT uses the (software-created) printer as the primary interface between applications and a printing device rather than a print queue. This allows users and administrators to manage intelligent printer entities rather than dumb printer queues, giving them greater power and flexibility.

Although Windows NT printers can print to print queues (logical printer ports) created by these other operating systems, it is capable of more interesting feats when printing is done in conjunction with other Windows NT computers.

Managing Printers Via the Printers Folder

Another important and essential element of Windows NT printing is the process of creating, configuring, and managing printers. This is accomplished using a special utility called the Printers folder. This folder (which is really a utility) can be accessed from any of several places:

- The Windows NT Control Panel
- The Start Menu Settings Submenu
- Inside the Network Neighborhood, by double-clicking the icon for a Windows NT computer that is sharing a printer on the Local Area Network
- The My Computer desktop icon

The Printers folder is shown in Figure 8-1.

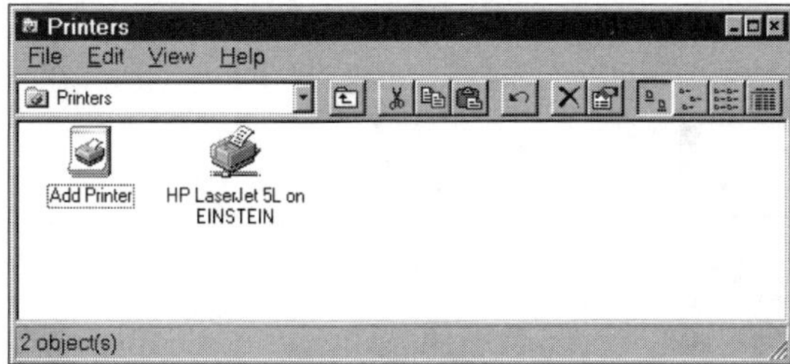

Figure 8-1: The Windows NT Printers folder.

After you double-click the Printers folder, you see a list of icons representing the various printers installed on the system (or shared printers if using the Network Neighborhood method). Even if there are no printers currently defined, you'll always see at least one icon: the Add Printer icon. Double-clicking this icon launches the Add Printer Wizard (shown in Figure 8-2), which takes you step-by-step through the process of configuring a new printer. After you've added a new printer, an icon representing that printer appears in the Printers folder.

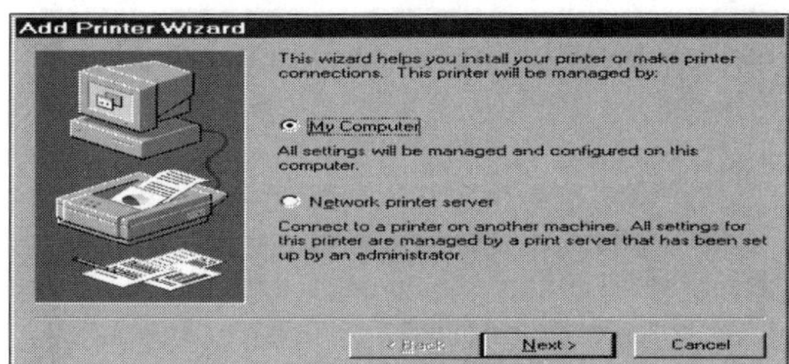

Figure 8-2: Running the Add Printer Wizard.

When you add a printer using the Add Printer Wizard, you're initially given two choices: adding a locally connected printer (i.e., a printer physically connected to a port on the local computer) or a printer shared by a remote print server on the network. When installing a locally connected printer, you'll be asked about what port(s), drivers, and settings you want to use with it.

After you have installed a printer using the Add Printer Wizard, you can then use the Printers folder to configure and manage it. Most of the options are accessible by either double-clicking or right-clicking the icon for the printer you want to control. Right-clicking a printer's icon displays a context-sensitive menu related to that printer; the most important choice on this menu is Properties, which allows you to examine and modify the printer's configuration. Most of the items we discuss in this chapter are related to options contained within the Properties dialog for a printer. This dialog is shown in Figure 8-3.

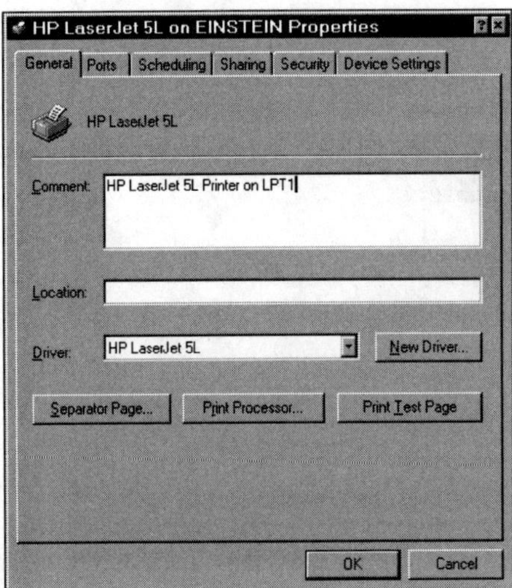

Figure 8-3: A printer's Properties dialog.

Table 8-2 provides brief descriptions of each of the tabbed sections within the printer Properties dialog.

TABLE 8-2 TABS IN THE PRINTER PROPERTIES DIALOG

Tab Name	Description
General	The general tab provides options to enter a comment about the printer and its location, select the driver that should be used for the printer, or add a new print driver not already installed on the system. There are also several options at the bottom of the dialog: Separator Page allows you to configure a separator page to be printed at the beginning of each print job; Print Processor allows you to set which print processor and datatype are used for print jobs; and Print Test Page.
Ports	This tab lists the currently available printer ports on the system, and allows you to add and/or configure these ports. Configuring a COM port brings up the Settings portion of the Control Panel Ports applet, and configuring LPT ports allows you to change the Transmission Retry timeout period for the port (the amount of time to wait before notifying you that a printer connected to the port is not responding). The Enable bidirectional support checkbox allows bidirectional communication between Windows NT and this printer.*

continued

Tab Name	Description
Scheduling	The Scheduling tab allows you to configure print scheduling related options, such as when the printer is available to users and what priority level is assigned to printed documents by default. In addition, it provides printer spooling options such as whether print jobs are spooled or printed directly to the printer, whether spooled jobs print first, whether mismatched print jobs (e.g., those set for a different orientation than the printer is currently configured for) are printed or held in the print queue, and whether documents should be deleted or retained after being printed.
Sharing	The Sharing tab allows you to share the printer on a Local Area Network. There is also an option that allows you to specify additional print drivers for other operating systems that should be installed for client computers that will connect to and share this printer. Doing so allows the client attaching to this printer to automatically download the required driver for the printer.
Security	This tab lets you set an access control list (ACL), auditing options, and ownership for a printer. To do so, you must be a member of the Administrators or Power Users group, or another group with the right to assign permissions to the printer. It is important that everyone needing to use the printer be given at least the Print permission, while the Full permission is reserved for system administrators.
Device Settings	The Device Settings tab is unique in that it changes depending on the particular printer involved. It contains printer-specific configuration options (e.g., printer resolution, installed memory, fonts, tray/form assignments, etc.) — a configuration "tree" that divides the printer options into various sections such as Soft Fonts, Installed Memory, and so forth. The top section of the dialog is used to select the option to be modified while the bottom window displays the list of possible choices for the current option.

*For bidirectional communication to work properly, you must have a printer, printer cable, and parallel port capable of bidirectional communication.

The actual options available in the Properties dialog for a particular printer vary depending on the particular printer and its features and capabilities.

The Device Settings tab typically contains an option for setting the printer's output resolution. Remember that resolution and print speed are always inversely proportional: higher resolution means slower print speeds (because high-resolution jobs require processing more data, and the formation of the actual image takes longer). Therefore, if you're looking for maximum performance and are willing to sacrifice some quality, one of the best ways to increase printer performance is to reduce the printer's output resolution.

Most of the options in this context-sensitive menu are also available inside of the menus in the printer's window, which appears when you double-click the printer's icon in the Printers folder window.

Stopping Unwanted Printing Behavior

Although printing under Windows NT is highly sophisticated and powerful, it also exhibits a few behaviors that can be annoying and unwanted. One such behavior is the print job logging that occurs by default in NT. If you are tired of logging hundreds of print job events on your file/print servers, you can ensure that they never show up in your log again (however, you will still be alerted when there is trouble via the messenger service and alerter). This is of particular importance to administrators who set up their NT boxes with C2-level security considerations and have the system set to halt when a log file fills to a set size (because it will serve to help keep the log file size smaller). To disable print event logging in Windows NT 3.5x, use one of the Windows NT Registry Editors and locate the following subkey:

```
HKEY_LOCAL_MACHINE\SYSTEM\CurrentControlSet\Control\Print\Providers
```

Once here, you want to add the following value (it doesn't appear by default):

Value Name: **EventLog**
Default Value: **3 for Workstations; 7 for Servers**
Data Type: **REG_DWORD**
Range of Values: **0 through 7**

The data for this value acts as a "bitmask" and is a sum of the values for three different logging options: errors, warnings, and informational events. These three event types represent the first, second, and third bits (one's, two's, and four's places), respectively, so that the data value of the Registry key represents which bits/print event logging types are currently turned on. For example, if only error logging was enabled, the value is 1 (bit 1 on); if error and warning event logging are on (the default), the value is 3 (bits 1 and 2 on; 1 + 2 = 3); or, if all three options were on, the data value is 7 (bits 1, 2, and 3 on; 1+2+4=7).

To add this value, start Registry Editor and open to the Edit menu and choose Add → Value (in REGEDT32; for REGEDIT, use New → DWORD Value). Enter the Value Name as **EventLog** and set the data type as **REG_DWORD**. Finally, double-click the new EventLog value you've created and enter a value of **0** (disable). To reenable print event logging, simply change the value to 1.

In Windows NT 4.0, it is also possible to accomplish this using a non-Registry method. To do so, open the Printers folder. Next, from the File menu, select Server Properties. Choose the Advanced tab, select the desired logging options you want (there are three event types that can be logged: errors, warnings, and informational), then choose OK. Because it is safer to use this dialog box rather than editing the Registry directly, it is recommended that you always set these options here in Windows NT 4.0.

Another annoying habit of Windows NT printing is its predilection to constantly pop up message dialogs informing you that a print job has printed when printing to remote printers. In many cases, this information is redundant and unnecessary, and is annoying.

To disable print notification for a particular printer under Windows NT 4.0, simply open the Printers folder, and choose File → Server Properties from the menus. Then choose the Advanced tab and uncheck the box labeled "Notify when remote documents are printed."

For Windows NT 3.5x, it is also possible to disable this behavior by directly editing the Registry entry related to this setting. To do this, locate the following Registry subkey using one of the Windows NT Registry Editors (or create it if it doesn't already exist).

```
HKEY_LOCAL_MACHINE\SYSTEM\CurrentControlSet\Control\Print\Providers
```

The value to modify (or add) is as follows:

Value Name: **NetPopup**
Data Type: **REG_DWORD**
Range of Values: **0** or **1**
Default Value: **1 (enabled)**

To disable remote print notification, simply edit the value using the DWORD editor and change the 1 to a 0. After restarting the machine, you will no longer receive print notification messages when printing to remote printers.

The NT Printing Process

To better understand how we can maximize Windows NT printing performance for our applications, we must first understand how NT handles the printing process. Specifically, we need to understand how Windows NT computers interact with each other during the printing process. We should also note that the actual steps that take place during the print process vary depending on whether the client is running Windows NT or another operating system. However, because we're most concerned with NT-to-NT print jobs, let's examine the step-by-step process that occurs when one NT system prints to another:

1. After a user selects the print function inside an application, the printing application calls the graphics device interface (GDI) component of Windows NT. GDI in turn makes a call to the printer driver associated with the target print device. Using information from both the application and the print device information from the printer driver, GDI renders the print job in the native printer language of the target print device.

One of the major changes to Windows NT version 4.0 was the move of the GDI32 component from User Mode to Kernel Mode. This move means that GDI now runs as a part of the Windows NT Executive at processor Ring 0 and translates to faster video and print rendering times. By contrast, Windows NT 3.x versions ran GDI as part of Win32 in User Mode, which makes GDI somewhat safer but at the price of performance.

2. The application then calls the client side of the spooler (`WINSPOOL.DRV`), which delivers the print job to the Windows NT computer acting as the print server. It does so by making a remote procedure call (RPC) to the server side of the spooler (`SPOOLSS.EXE`), which makes a direct application programming interface (API) call to the print router (`SPOOLSS.DRV`). The print router then contacts the remote print providers, and the Windows remote print provider (`WIN32SPL.DLL`) makes an RPC to `SPOOLSS.EXE` on the Windows NT computer acting as the print server, which receives the print job over the network.

3. On the print server, print jobs from Windows NT clients running Windows applications are received in enhanced metafile format (EMF) by default. Some print server services for non-Windows NT clients assign other datatypes and still others leave the datatype blank. Print jobs with no datatype set will use the default datatype specified in the Print Processor dialog box on the print server (see the "Printer Tuning Tips" section later in this chapter for more information on datatypes and defining the default datatype).
4. The router or print server service passes the print job to the *local print provider* on the server (which is itself a component of the spooler service), which then spools the print job to disk.
5. The local print provider polls the installed *print processors* on the system. When a particular print processor recognizes the job's datatype, that print processor receives the print job and handles it according to its datatype to ensure that the job prints correctly.
6. The *separator page processor* receives control of the print job and adds a separator page (if one has been specified) to the front of the job.
7. The job is despooled to the *print monitor* monitoring the port for the specified printer. (Note: If the print device is bidirectional, the job first goes to a *language monitor*, which handles bidirectional communication with the printer and then passes the job to the port monitor.)
8. The print device receives the print job, translates each page into a bitmap, and prints it out onto the specified media type.

The Windows NT printing process is illustrated in Figure 8-4.

Printer Tuning Tips

Now that we understand a little of how Windows NT printing works, we're ready to examine some of the individual steps in this process that we can modify to improve performance.

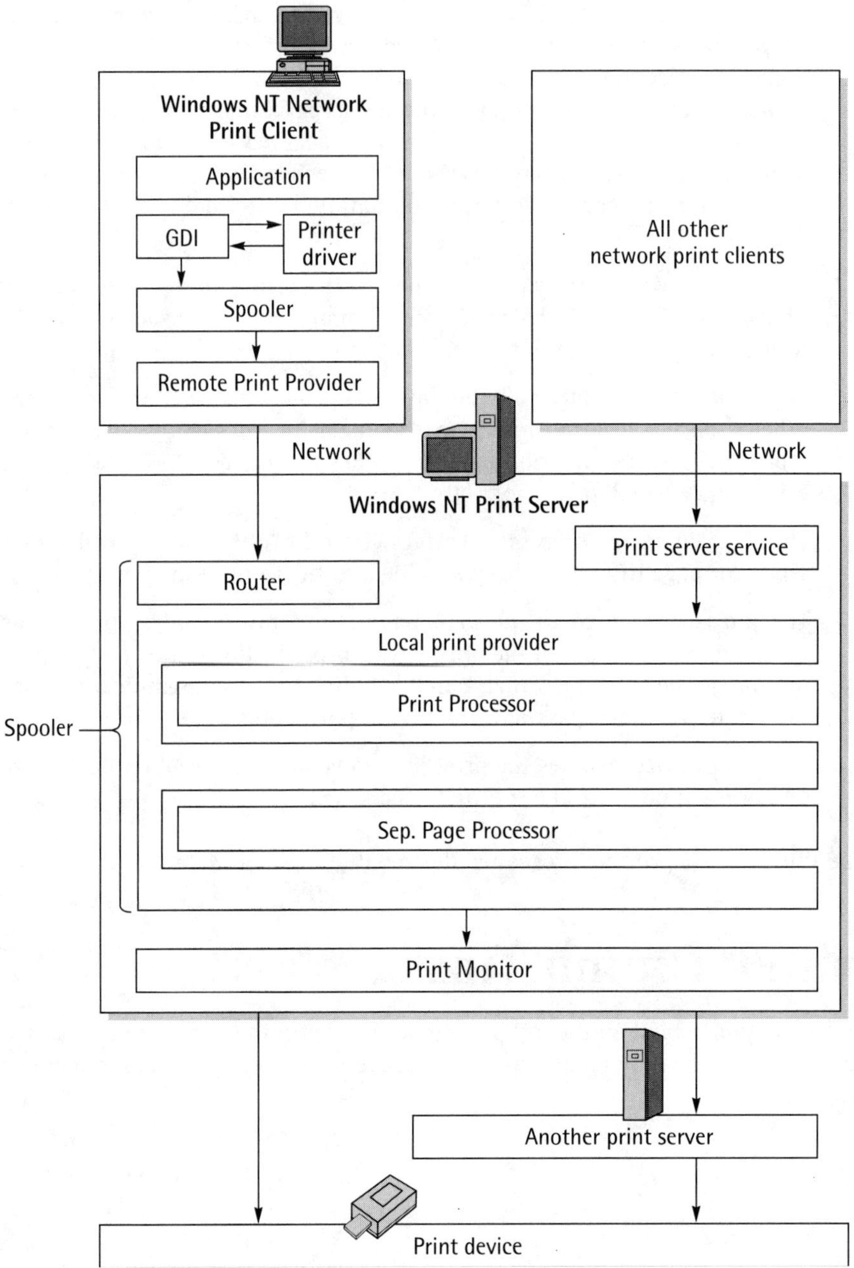

Figure 8-4: The Windows NT print process.

When considering the concept of printer performance, the first question to ask is, "What defines fast?" For example, does fast mean a speedy return to the application, a maximized data throughput stream to the printer, or a print server that's operating at maximum efficiency? The answer determines exactly which adjustments (if any) you'll want to make on your system. Therefore, in the following sections, we describe the ramifications of each modification and what types of optimization they help us achieve.

Printer options settings

When using the Printer folder to modify a printer's configuration, you should take note of one area that provides several performance-related settings.

In the Scheduling tab of a printer's Properties dialog (shown in Figure 8-5), there are several options that can have an effect on printing performance. These options are:

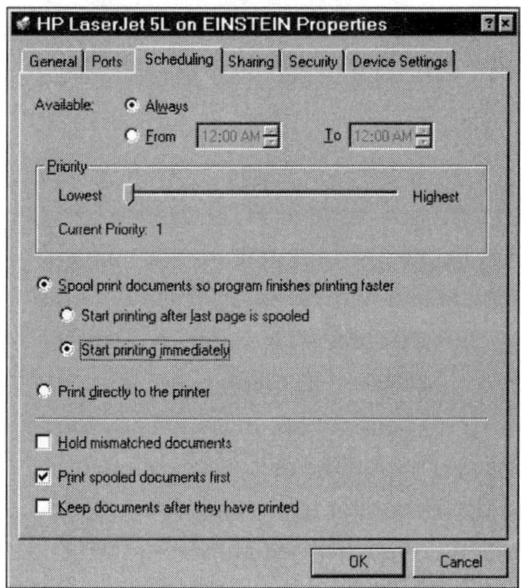

Figure 8-5: The Scheduling tab of a printer's Properties dialog.

- *Priority*: The priority sliding bar sets the *default priority* for documents printed to the printer; that is, what base priority level each document starts out with. The default setting is 1 (lowest priority), although you can increase this number and then decrease the print priorities of individual jobs that should receive lower priorities. A common approach is to create one "common use" printer (i.e., a printer used by the majority of users) with the default setting of 1 and then create a separate "high priority" printer that sends output to the same printing device but has a higher priority setting. Print jobs from this printer will receive precedence over those with lower priorities printed using other printers. This is especially useful for high-priority print jobs when sharing a printer or when key personnel require faster access to a printer. Because priorities are relative to other jobs currently printing, they are only relevant when multiple jobs are present simultaneously and vying for access to the printer (see the "Increasing Print Job Priorities" section later in this chapter for more information on increasing the print priority of individual print jobs).

- *Spool print documents* so program finishes printing faster: This option instructs Windows NT to spool printed documents to disk where they are despooled to the printer. This option should always be selected because it provides the quickest return of application control to the user and doesn't have any negative performance impacts. This option, when selected, also has two suboptions: Start printing after last page is spooled, which will wait until a job has been completely spooled to disk prior to sending it to the printer; and Start printing immediately, which begins despooling a print job immediately after it begins queuing. The latter option is generally preferred because it provides both a quick return of application control and the fastest printing of documents.

One situation in which you might not want to use the "Start printing immediately" spooling option is when you are in a networked environment and many users are printing from programs that take a long time to generate each page of an output document (e.g., a CAD or 3D graphics application). This kind of a situation can result in inefficient printer utilization and long waiting periods, especially with large print jobs. The reason this happens is that the printer is completely tied up waiting for the application to spool each page, because it will have begun printing immediately after the first page was spooled. At this point, the printer will then be waiting for the application to generate each additional job rather than just spooling data to the printer that's ready for printing. In these environments, it is usually best to choose the "Start printing after last page is spooled" option, which ensures that the entire print job is available to the printer and is printed without waiting for the application. However, the side effect is that the printing application remains unavailable until the last job has been spooled to the printer.

- *Print directly to the printer*: The alternative to the "Spool print documents" option, this option instructs Windows NT to send documents directly to the printer rather than queuing them to a disk file. It is generally recommended that you not select this option in most environments, because it causes significant delay in the return of application control after print jobs are sent. However, if you want to ensure the fastest possible time-to-output and are willing to sacrifice the ability to continue using the system while the print job is in progress, you may want to consider enabling this option.
- *Print spooled documents first*: This option instructs the Windows NT print spooler to favor documents that have completed spooling over those that are still in the process of spooling, even when the completed documents have a lower print priority than the spooling documents. If no documents are completely spooled, the spooler favors larger spooling documents over smaller ones. This option provides the best overall printer efficiency and it is generally recommended that you leave it selected. When this option is disabled, the print spooler prioritizes the printing of documents based on their priorities.

In summary, in the majority of environments (but not all), setting the "Spool print documents so program finishes printing faster," "Start printing immediately," and "Print spooled documents first" options will ensure that documents print as quickly as possible to your printer and maximize the printer's overall efficiency. The question of which options are best will be determined by a number of factors: whether you require the ability to continue using the system during print jobs, whether the printer is shared on a local area network (LAN), and the length and typical page generation time of the kinds of print jobs normally sent to the printer.

Understanding print job datatypes

Another area for potential optimization is the datatype used by the print processor associated with a given printer. In the Windows NT printing process, an application sends data to a printer in a particular data format. The print processors on the print server (or local computer if printing locally) are then responsible for identifying the datatype in use and deciding which processor should handle the processing of the data stream.

The following datatypes are handled by the WinPrint print processor, the default processor used by printers in Windows NT:

- *Raw*: This datatype indicates that the job is in a ready-to-print format in the printing device's native language, and that the spooler should not alter the job at all. RAW is the default value for jobs with no specified datatype. RAW spool files are device-dependent. It is assumed with this datatype that all rendering was performed by the GDI and device driver interface. There are cases where this is the fastest datatype because it does not require encoding and decoding both from the server and client (e.g., PostScript, which uses this datatype by default).
- *Raw [FF Appended]*: This datatype informs the spooler to assume that the job originated from an application that did not append a form-feed character to the end of the print job. It is usually only necessary where the lack of a trailing form-feed character string prevents the last page of the job from printing when sent to a print device. The print server's spooler appends this form-feed to the trailing end of the print job without making any additional changes. None of the Windows NT print processors will apply this datatype by default, though it can be defined as a default datatype in the print processor options box.
- *Raw [FF Auto]*: This datatype is similar to RAW [FF Appended] except that RAW [FF Auto] instructs the spooler to look for a form-feed character at the trailing end of the job. This datatype will add no form feed character if one is already present, but it will append one if none is found. As with RAW [FF Appended], none of the Windows NT print processors will apply this datatype by default, though it is definable as a default datatype under the printer processor options box.
- *Text*: This datatype indicates a print job that consists of ANSI text. With jobs using this datatype, WinPrint uses GDI and the printer driver to create a new job that prints the text correctly. This option can be useful when an application produces text as a print job but the target print device requires a printer-language type of job such as PostScript. In this case, WinPrint automatically creates a new job that handles formatting the appropriate printer language.

If a job composed of printer-language commands (e.g., the actual language of a PostScript job output) is identified with this datatype, the result is a print job that prints the text of the printer commands on the page rather than using the instruction to create the page image. Most UNIX LPR (Line Printer Remote) clients send print jobs with an "f" control command by default, which causes Windows NT's LPD service to automatically assign the job the TEXT datatype.

◆ *PSCRIPT* (PostScript support for Macintosh clients using non-PostScript printer): This setting is used for Macintosh clients printing (through the Windows NT Service for Macintosh print spooler) to non-PostScript printers shared by a Windows NT computer. It does not affect Windows clients. One limitation of this datatype is due to the TrueImage RIP (Raster Image Processor) which can only produce 300dpi output. However, this limitation can be overcome with third-party replacement RIPs that can support higher resolutions and color options.

Graphics and prepress shops often require higher-end print processors than those available natively in Windows NT. Two products that provide replacement Raster Image Processors for advanced printing features and capabilities (e.g., increased color, resolution, and image rendering speed) such as those required for prepress, are Color Central for Windows NT (version 3.5x or 4.0, but for Intel-based systems only) by Luminous, and the Taipan RIP Software by Agfa (available for both Intel and Alpha platforms).

Information on Luminous' Color Central for Windows NT is available at:

`http://www.luminous.com/`

and information on Agfa's Taipan RIP Software is available at:

`http://www.agfa.com/`

◆ *Journal*: This datatype, which exists only with 3.x versions of Windows NT, indicates that the job was created by a locally run Windows application, and GDI has done a partial render of the job. WinPrint then uses GDI in conjunction with the printer driver to finish the rendering process. The resulting job, which is output-ready, is then returned to the local print provider for further processing.

◆ *EMF*: A new feature of Windows NT 4.0, the EMF datatype is similar to Windows NT 3.x Journal files in that they indicate that the job was created by a Windows application and that GDI has partially rendered the job. As with jobs using the Journal datatype, WinPrint uses GDI and the printer driver to complete the rendering process. However, unlike the Journal datatype, which only works for locally printed jobs, EMF has client/server capabilities that allow EMF-formatted jobs to be transmitted across a Local Area Network and rendered at a remote print server. As a result, the use of the EMF datatype offers performance benefits for many printers (such as PCL-based laser printers). One exception is PostScript printers, which are more efficient using the RAW datatype (due to the nature of their print job data).

Using EMF Files to leverage server resources

Other than the move of GDI from User Mode to Kernel Mode, the EMF datatype is one of the most important new printing-related features of Windows NT 4.0. Whenever a Windows NT 4.0 client computer prints to a Windows NT 4.0 print server, and the client's driver has the EMF option enabled (checking/setting this option is described later), the client sends EMF files to the print server, and WinPrint on the print server completes the rendering. By using the remote print server's resources in this fashion, the resource load for document printing is distributed across the LAN, which frees the client workstation more quickly after jobs are printed. It also takes better advantage of the capabilities of the remote print server whose CPU resources may be heavily underutilized even when handling a large number of print jobs (especially when the majority of these jobs were previously using the RAW datatype rather than EMF format).

By default, print jobs from Windows NT 4.0 clients are in EMF format when printed remotely to a PCL or HPGL/2 language printer on a Windows NT 4.0 print server. PostScript printers use the RAW datatype by default. In addition, the EMF format will only be generated if the client is printing using the remote print server's print driver rather than a locally created printer (i.e., the "Network Printer Server" option was selected during the Add Printer Wizard process rather than the "My Computer" option).

Table 8-3 shows the various types of print clients and which datatypes Windows NT uses by default with each.

TABLE 8-3 DEFAULT DATATYPES USED FOR VARIOUS CLIENTS

Client Type	Default Datatype Used
Windows NT 4.0 (using remote server's print driver)	EMF
Windows NT 4.0 (using locally created printer pointed to remote server's UNC sharepoint)	RAW
Windows NT 3.x (using remote server's print driver)	RAW
Windows NT 3.x (using locally created printer pointed to remote server's UNC sharepoint)	RAW
Windows 95	RAW
Windows for Workgroups	RAW
Windows 3.x	RAW
Non-Microsoft Client Operating Systems	RAW

Although Windows 95 computers are capable of using EMF datatypes, these files are always rendered locally and sent to the network printer as RAW.

Although NT uses the information listed in Table 8-3 to determine which datatype to use for a particular job, it is also possible to override this setting and choose a particular datatype for a printer you create. For example, you might decide to have client workstations always use the RAW datatype to relieve a heavily taxed print server by having the clients do all job rendering locally. To change the default datatype generated by the client workstation for a particular printer, open the Printer's Properties window in the Printers Folder and click to the General tab. Next, click the Print Processor button which opens the Print Processor dialog shown in Figure 8-6.

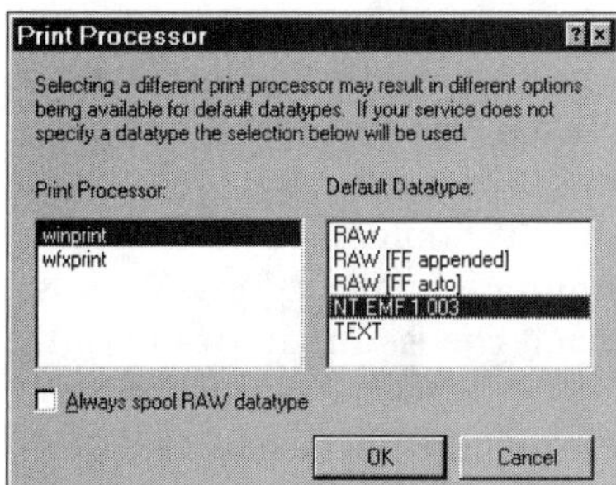

Figure 8-6: Defining the default datatype via the Print Processor dialog.

In this dialog, you can select the desired datatype for jobs generated using this printer that don't specify a datatype. In addition, you can instruct the client to always generate RAW datatype print jobs using this printer by clicking the "Always spool RAW datatype" option.

In addition to their other advantages, EMF files are also more portable than RAW datatype files. An EMF file is printer language-independent and can be printed on any print device, but a RAW file can only be printed to one particular type of printing device (the type whose language the RAW data is rendered in). Still another advantage of EMF files is size: in most cases, EMF files for a particular print job are smaller than the same print job rendered in the RAW datatype. On a LAN that services many remote print jobs (or very large ones), this smaller file size also helps to reduce overall network congestion.

A final advantage to EMF files is that they ensure that fonts specified on the client computer are the same ones used by the print server because the rendering process is split between the client and the server computers.

Although the EMF datatype is best for many graphics-capable printers, PostScript printers default to using a datatype of RAW. This is because PostScript printers receive data in a different format than most other types of printers. Instead of receiving a binary image of a page rendered by Windows NT's print processor in the printer's native language, PostScript printers receive what amounts to a "program" that defines the page using text commands (using the PostScript language). The printer then interprets these textual programming commands into a definition of each page in the print job. As a result, the optimal datatype for PostScript printers differs from that of other printer types.

Increasing print job priorities

In addition to allowing for the configuration of printers, the Printers folder also allows you to view the current print queue and manage documents in the queue. One of the management options available to the owner of a printer, or anyone with the Windows NT "Manage Documents" privilege on the printer (such as a member of the Print Operators group), is to change the priority of a queued job. To do so, simply right-click the job's listing in the queue and choose Properties from the pop-up menu that appears (alternatively, you can also select the document whose priority you want to change and choose Properties from the Document menu).

In the Properties dialog for the print job, you can change the job's priority in the queue (so that it will print faster) by moving the Priority sliding bar to the right. The range of priorities goes from 1 to 99, where 1 is the default priority assigned to all jobs in Windows NT. By increasing a job's priority in a backlogged print queue, you can make a job "cut in line" in the queue to print more quickly.

Figure 8-7 is an example of using the document Properties dialog to change the priority of a queued document.

Although you can change document print priorities on a case-by-case basis using this method, it is also possible to change the default priority assigned to printed documents from a particular printer. A good example for doing this would be setting the boss's printer for a shared network printing device so that the boss's jobs always received higher priority and thus are printed ahead of other jobs (a smart political move for any IS Manager!).

To set the default priority for all jobs printed from a particular printer, open the printer's Properties window in the Printers folder and click the Scheduling tab. In this tab, the same sliding bar is shown as appears in a document's Properties dialog, except that the priority set here affects all new documents printed using this Printer. This dialog is shown in Figure 8-8.

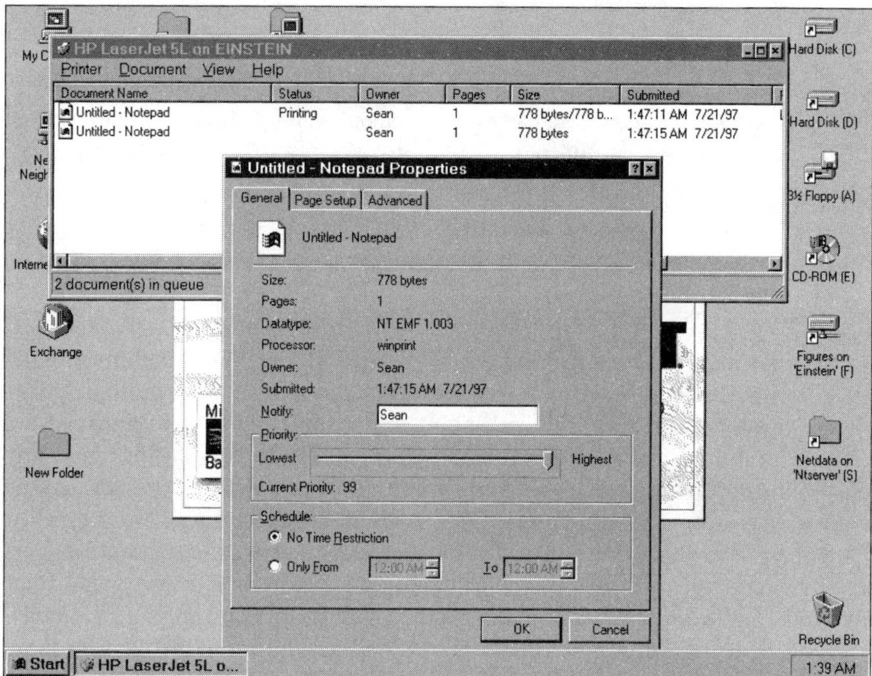

Figure 8-7: Changing a queued document's print priority via the document's Properties dialog.

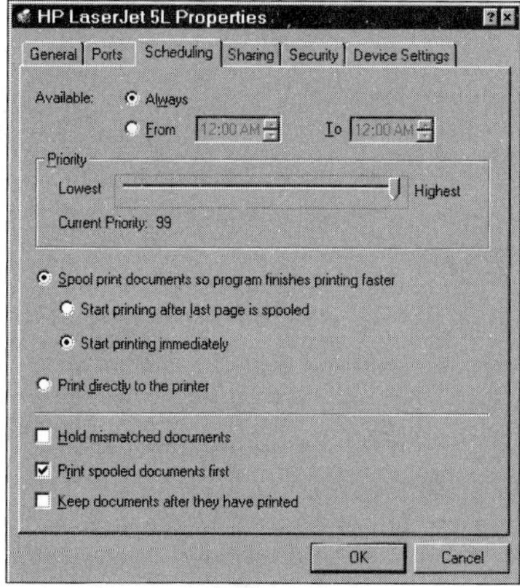

Figure 8-8: Changing the default priority for all print jobs created by a printer.

To use this option effectively, you need to create a local printer for the user receiving the higher priority print jobs and point this printer to the shared network location (UNC name) of the remote printer. Otherwise, if you install the printer using the "Network printer server" option of the Add Printer Wizard, any changes you make to the default job priority level will be the same for all machines sharing the printer in this manner (i.e., it will make this change on the printer server's copy of the Printer).

Another method for implementing this solution (and one that doesn't require the use of a locally created printer on the client workstation) is to create multiple printers in the printers folder, all of which point to the same physical printer and are offered under different share names. By assigning different default document priorities and group permissions to each printer, you can control who can use the low-priority version of the printer (e.g., the Users group or some other local or global group) and who has access to the higher-priority version (e.g., the Managers group). Because high-priority jobs will always print before low priority ones (that aren't already printing), this accomplishes the same feat as our previous example. In addition, this solution is better in that it allows the solution to be scaled as more high-priority printer users are added to the network.

SuperPrint, from Zenographics, Inc., is a product that replaces most of the included NT printing software with a faster 32-bit printing engine. Output times with this software tend to run two-thirds of the time or less than printing the same job with NT's default print engine. Along with enhanced performance, SuperPrint also offers much more flexibility in output quality with independent controls for sharpness, contrast, lightness, saturation, grayscale, and dot gain.

SuperPrint is available in a high-end form that allows NT to interact with more sophisticated continuous tone, thermal wax and dye sublimation printers. Other features include Internet files support, preview of all print jobs, and full support of PostScript Level 2. This last feature allows you to turn your non-PostScript printers into fully PostScript-capable devices.

SuperPrint also includes tools such as SuperQueue, which gives you more control of print job processing and provides far more information on job status than you can view with NT's default printer utilities. SuperQueue also allows you to preview and print bitmap and PostScript files with simple drag-and-drop procedures without any additional application support required.

Probably the most interesting thing about SuperPrint is the inclusion of Zenographics' SuperDrivers, which are drivers that have been optimized for most of the popular non-PostScript printers. In addition to these features, GIF, JPEG, TIFF, Targa, BMP, and PCX files are supported directly by the SuperDrivers so you can generate compact image files very quickly from any Windows application. All preview features are on-screen and show how your image file fits on the page, whether fonts are correct, and how your colors look.

The most significant feature for NT users is the improved efficiency of network printing using a proprietary SuperMetafile format that is even more compact than the EMF format used by Windows NT 4.0. High-end devices supported by SuperPrint include film recorders, large format printers, thermal printers, and continuous tone devices. Each copy of SuperPrint also includes support for laser, dot matrix, inkjet, and thermal printers.

Information on SuperPrint can be obtained at Zenographics' Web site located at:

`http://www.zeno.com/`

Included on the *Optimizing Windows NT* CD-ROM is a trial/evaluation version of the SuperPrint printing utility for Windows NT. This utility provides faster printing and enhanced printing support for most printers in the Windows NT environment. To install the utility, place the *Optimizing Windows NT* CD-ROM in your CD-ROM drive and point your Web browser to the location of the CD. Although the CD includes a functional shareware version of the SuperPrint utility, it is recommended that you obtain the registered version, which provides additional features and capabilities beyond the shareware version. Additional information on the utilities included on the *Optimizing Windows NT* CD-ROM is provided in Appendix A, "What's on the CD?"

Understanding printer pools

One of Windows NT's more interesting printing features is the capability to create a special type of printer called a *printer pool.* A printer pool is essentially a single "virtual" printer that is associated with multiple physical printing devices, each of which is connected to a different logical (network or local) port. This arrangement is used to create a "round robin" arrangement for a heavily loaded print destination (e.g., the central printer in an office that produces a large amount of printed output). Once defined, Windows NT can automatically spool waiting documents to the next available printer rather than queuing all jobs for a single printer.

It's important to note that when creating printer pools, each of the printers used in the pool should be an identical print device. At the very least, all of the member printing devices should be capable of emulating the same type of print device (i.e., they can all use the same printer driver). When print jobs are sent to this printer, NT routes the job to the first available print device, using the printers more efficiently.

Windows NT printer pools have these general characteristics and features:

- All print devices in the printer pool share the same printer name (i.e., the icon shown in the Printers folder) and act as a single device. For example, pausing the printer will pause the entire printer pool, and changing any properties will affect all print devices in the printer pool.
- The destination ports for the member printing devices can be of mixed types (i.e., serial, parallel, network, etc.).
- When a job arrives for the printer pool, the spooler checks to see which print device is available. The spooler checks for available devices based on the order in which they were added to the printer pool in Print Manager. Therefore, if the printer pool consists of mixed print destinations, for optimal performance make sure that the fastest port is selected first when setting up the printer pool.
- Windows NT doesn't pose any effective limits on the number of print devices that can be in a printer pool.

CREATING PRINTER POOLS

The process of creating a printer pool in Windows NT is actually quite easy. First you want to ensure that your printer configuration meets the pool criterion; that is, two or more printers capable of using the same emulation mode and print driver. Next, you want to make sure the printers are hooked up and available and connected to separate local or network-based ports (in the case of network printer ports, you want to be sure to add and define these ports ahead of time). Once this is done, you can create the printer pool using these steps:

1. Open the Printers Folder.
2. Choose "Add Printer" if the printer isn't already defined, or double-click an existing printer using one of the ports that will be associated with the printer pool.
3. On the screen used to identify the port(s) to which the printer is connected (Step 2 of the "Add Printer Wizard" process or the Ports tab if editing an existing printer's properties) be sure to check the "Enable printer pooling" option at the bottom of the screen. This is important because the next step won't work unless this is done first.
4. Select all of the ports to which members of the printer pool are connected. When doing so, be sure to select the ports in a fastest-to-slowest order, because this is the order NT will use when determining which port to send a job to. The port selection dialog is shown in Figure 8-9.
5. If desired, share the printer on the network using the Sharing tab (or the step of the Add Printer Wizard process that asks if you wish to share the printer) of the Printer Properties dialog and provide a share name so that remote users can access the printer pool.
6. Click OK to close the Printer Properties dialog (or finish the Add Printer Wizard steps if creating a new printer); you're now ready to start using the printer pool.

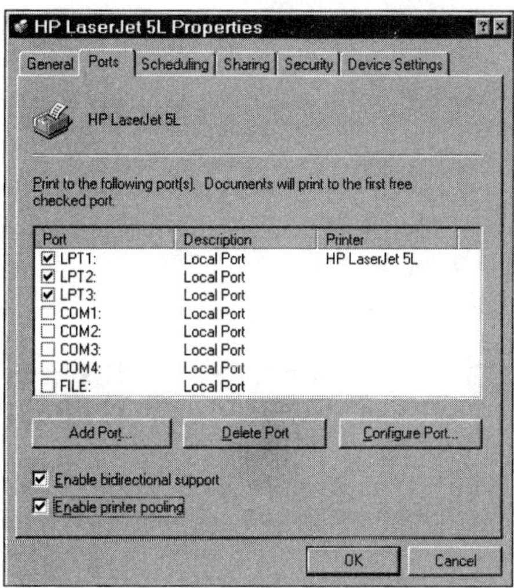

Figure 8-9: Creating a printer pool.

A FEW PRINTER POOL CAVEATS

Although printer pools can help improve printing efficiency in high-output environments, there are a few caveats to remember when considering their use. The first is that, as mentioned earlier, printer pools act as a single logical unit. One disadvantage of this is that there is no way to be notified as to which printer in the pool printed a particular job. Therefore, when using printer pools, try to keep the printers together in relatively close proximity. This will help prevent users from becoming frustrated after having to play the "where's the print job" game. You should also be sure to have similar forms and trays available on all printing devices in the pool; this ensures that the proper forms are available regardless of which printer is used to print the job.

Another negative effect of the printer "unification" created by pooling occurs when one of the configured printers goes off-line. In this situation, any jobs sent to this port by the pool may become stuck and time out; a situation that requires the job be deleted. Because printer pools can't redirect jobs from failed ports to healthy ports, the only real solution is to either repair the malfunction or delete the job and remove the port connected to that printing device from the pool temporarily, until the malfunction is repaired.

Fonts and font caching

Another aspect of printer optimization relates to fonts. Although Windows NT usually handles font printing and caching in an acceptable fashion, you may want to modify font caching behavior in certain situations involving fonts used with large character sets. This is a consideration with some international versions of Windows NT (using large character sets), for example, or with print/prepress shops that deal with a number of fonts and extended character sets.

There is a special Registry subkey that specifically defines parameters related to fonts and font caching. This subkey is located in the following location in the Registry:

```
HKEY_LOCAL_MACHINE\SOFTWARE\Microsoft\Windows
 NT\CurrentVersion\FontCache
```

The values in this key can greatly affect the amount of memory the NT system requires for font caching (the memory "footprint") and can have negative effects on performance when values are set too high. Therefore, only users requiring very large numbers of fonts, prepress and print shops, and users of international versions of NT with large extended character sets should consider experimenting with these values.

The three values defined in this subkey, their value ranges, and descriptions are:

- MaxSize (REG_DWORD): This value specifies, in kilobytes, the largest size the font cache can grow to. The default data is 0x80 hex (128 decimal).
- MinIncrSize (REG_DWORD): This values specifies, in kilobytes the largest interval that the font cache is grown. When changing this value, remember that most fonts are 40KB in size. The default data is 4 (KB).
- MinInitSize (REG_DWORD): Specifies the minimum size, in kilobytes, reserved for the font cache. The default data is 4 (KB).

Optimizing the Spooler Service

As you probably know by now, the Spooler service is responsible for much of the work that goes on during the Windows NT printing process. Due to its importance, it is sometimes beneficial to make adjustments to the Spooler service to enhance its performance and ensure that it is running in an optimal environment.

In essence, the Windows NT Spooler service is a print job scheduler and is part of the local Print Provider service of a particular machine. The Spooler service has these printing process-related responsibilities:

- Keeping track of what jobs are going to which printers
- Keeping track of which ports are connected to which printers
- Routing print jobs to the correct ports
- Prioritizing print jobs

In Windows NT, a separate process thread is used for each port to which a printer is attached. The spooler is called by any of these threads whenever a thread completes a job, or when an external thread initiates a print job.

Increasing spooler thread priorities

Because the Spooler service is just another application running on a Windows NT computer, its worker threads receive a default thread priority, which is comparable to that of other noncritical system services. However, it may be beneficial for print server performance to increase the default thread priority assigned to the Spooler service and its various components. This might be helpful, for example, on a heavily taxed or dedicated Windows NT print server that handles a very large number of jobs on a daily basis.

Printing-Related Registry Keys and Values

As with all of the Windows NT subsystems, the important low-level settings that control functionality and performance of the printing subsystem are located in the Registry. Although many may be changed using the graphical dialogs contained in the Printers folder, others must be edited directly in the Registry using one of the Windows NT Registry Editor utilities (`REGEDIT.EXE` or `REGEDT32.EXE`, discussed in Chapter 4).

The most important printing-related Registry entries are located under the following Registry subkeys:

```
HKEY_LOCAL_MACHINE\SYSTEM\CurrentControlSet\Control\Print
```

This key contains values related to print browsing and other print-related features and options. Under this key, there is also an Environments subkey that contains subkeys for each of the currently supported Windows NT hardware platforms. Each of these subkeys in turn contains the name of the directory in which the drivers for that platform are stored. Each Drivers key contains subkeys for any and all locally installed printer drivers for that platform. Under the key for each printer driver there is information about which files make up the components of that particular printer driver, as well as the driver's version information.

The per-user settings (i.e., those for the currently logged-on user) for the current default printer are stored under this key:

```
HKEY_CURRENT_USER\Printers
```

The hardware-specific information about drivers and print processors is stored under the following key (where *<platform>* represents the subkey for a specific Windows NT hardware platform, such as "Windows NT x86" for Intel or "Windows NT Alpha_AXP" for Alpha):

```
HKEY_LOCAL_MACHINE\SYSTEM\CurrentControlSet\Control\Print
  \Environments\<platform>
```

Finally, values that control print spooling and other aspects of printer support are found in this Registry location:

```
HKEY_LOCAL_MACHINE\SYSTEM\CurrentControlSet\Control\Print
```

In this section, we discuss a number of the values found in these Registry subkeys, and how they can be manipulated to improve printing efficiency and performance.

In these situations, you may discover that making adjustments to some or all of the three print-related Registry values helps print server speed and efficiency. These Registry values are found in this Registry location:

```
HKEY_LOCAL_MACHINE\SYSTEM\CurrentControlSet\Control\Print
```

Figure 8-10 is a view of this key and its default values (using Registry Editor).

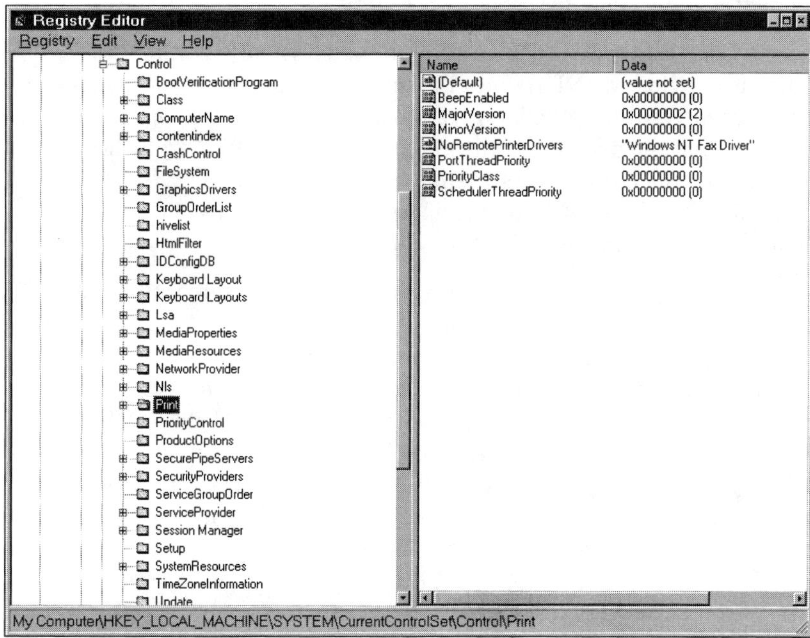

Figure 8-10: The `HKEY_LOCAL_MACHINE\SYSTEM\CurrentControlSet\Control\Print Registry` subkey containing parameters related to print browsing and other features.

Inside this key, you will find a number of printing-related values; however, the values that we're primarily concerned with are the PortThreadPriority, PriorityClass, SpoolerPriority, SchedulerThreadPriority, FastPrintSlowDownThreshold, FastPrint-ThrottleTimeout, FastPrintWaitTimeout, and NetPrinterDecayPeriod values. Each of these values can have a bearing on some aspect of print (or print browser) performance. These values, their default data, and their possible data ranges are:

- PortThreadPriority (REG_DWORD): As mentioned earlier, each defined printer port in Windows NT has its own associated thread which is responsible for sending data to the port. This value's data defines the priority used for these port threads. The default value is 0, which indicates that the default priority should be used (7 for NT Workstations, 9 for NT Servers). The valid range of values are: THREAD_PRIORITY_ ABOVE_NORMAL, THREAD_PRIORITY_ NORMAL, and THREAD_ PRIORITY_BELOW_NORMAL. See Table 8-4 for descriptions and numerical equivalents for each of these thread priorities.
- PriorityClass (REG_DWORD): This value, which is only used in 3.x versions of Windows NT, defines the priority class; that is, the associated thread priority, of the Windows NT spooler. The default value is 0, which indicates that the default priority should be used (THREAD_PRIORITY _NORMAL, which translates to 7 for NT Workstations and 9 for NT Servers). In Windows NT 4.0, this value has been replaced by the SpoolerPriority value (described below).
- SpoolerPriority (REG_DWORD): This value, which is used in Windows NT 4.0 and replaces the previous PriorityClass value used in NT 3.5x, sets the priority class for the print spooler. By default, this value doesn't appear in the Registry, and will have to be added manually if the data is to be changed. By default, the print spooler is set to NORMAL_PRIORITY _CLASS. The valid range of values are IDLE_PRIORITY_CLASS, NORMAL_PRIORITY_CLASS, and HIGH_PRIORITY_CLASS (any other values are ignored). See Table 8-4 for descriptions and numerical equivalents for each of the priority classes.
- SchedulerThreadPriority (REG_DWORD): This value sets the priority of the scheduler thread, which is responsible for assigning print jobs to ports. The default data for this value is 0, indicating that a normal thread priority should be used. The valid range of values is 0 (Normal), 1 (Above Normal), and 0xFFFFFFFF (Below Normal; note that this is a hexadecimal number and not a string value).
- FastPrintThrottleTimeout (REG_DWORD): When the "Start printing immediately" option (the "Jobs print while spooling" option in Windows 3.x-speak) in the Scheduling tab of a printer's Properties dialog is enabled, some printers pause if they don't receive data for a time out period (time varies depending on type of printer; for example, this period is around 15 seconds for a PostScript printer). To counteract this, the spooler throttles back on data sent to the printer when the data contained in the FastPrintSlowDownThreshold value is reached. At that point, FastPrintThrottleTimeout causes 1 byte per defined period to be sent to the printer until the threshold defined by FastPrintSlowDownTheshold is exceeded. This value is entered in milliseconds (thousandths of a second), and the default data is 2,000 (2 seconds).

- FastPrintWaitTimeout (REG_DWORD): When the "Start printing immediately" option in the Scheduling tab of a printer's Properties dialog is enabled, the port thread must synchronize with the application spooling the print job. The FastPrintWaitTimeout value determines how long the port thread will wait before giving up, pausing the current print job, and moving to the next print job. This value is entered in milliseconds (thousandths of a second), and the default data is 24,000 (24 seconds).
- FastPrintSlowDownThreshold (REG_DWORD): This value is used with the FastPrintThrottleTimeout value to determine at what point the spooler should begin throttling back on data sent to the printer (to maintain a continuous flow of data to the printer and not trigger a printer time out). The default value is the FastPrintWaitTimeout value divided by FastPrintThrottleTimeout value, but can also be manually set (the value is entered in milliseconds).
- NetPrinterDecayPeriod (REG_DWORD): This value specifies how long a network printer should be cached for local machine's client browser. The cache is used to present a list of network shared printers when you browse for available printers (e.g., using the Network Neighborhood or during the Add Printer Wizard when searching for a network printer to add). The range is in milliseconds, and the default data is 3,600,000 (1 hour).

When modifying these values, you can use the thread priorities and priority classes described in Table 8-4 as a guideline. As with any type of Registry modification, any changes you decide to experiment with should be made in small increments and benchmarked along the way using a standard test to determine their effectiveness.

It is unlikely that modifications to these Registry values will produce significant benefits except on the very busiest print servers serving a large number of printing devices. Also, when increasing the priorities of print-related threads on NT servers that aren't dedicated to print serving (i.e., those being used as file and/or application servers or for local applications) deprioritizes the access of other process threads.

Table 8-4 THREAD PRIORITIES AND PRIORITY CLASSES USED BY PRINTING-RELATED THREADS

Thread Priority (range is 1–31)	Priority Class*	Descriptive Name of Thread Priority
14	High	THREAD_PRIORITY_ABOVE_NORMAL
13	High	THREAD_PRIORITY_NORMAL
12	High	THREAD_PRIORITY_BELOW_NORMAL
10	Foreground normal	THREAD_PRIORITY_ABOVE_NORMAL
9	Foreground normal	THREAD_PRIORITY_NORMAL
8	Foreground normal	THREAD_PRIORITY_BELOW_NORMAL
8	Background normal	THREAD_PRIORITY_ABOVE_NORMAL
7	Background normal	THREAD_PRIORITY_NORMAL
6	Background normal	THREAD_PRIORITY_BELOW_NORMAL
5	Idle	THREAD_PRIORITY_ABOVE_NORMAL
4	Idle	THREAD_PRIORITY_NORMAL
3	Idle	THREAD_PRIORITY_BELOW_NORMAL

*Note: This relates to the foreground/background tasking.

Optimizing the print spooler file

Another system configuration change that may produce increased performance in some situations is related to the location of the default spool file used for printer spooling. Windows NT spools print jobs to disk prior to printing them (as long as the print spooling option is turned on for the printer in question). By default, jobs will be spooled to the following disk folder:

%SYSTEMROOT%\SYSTEM32\SPOOL\PRINTERS
(e.g., `C:\WINNT\SYSTEM32\SPOOL\PRINTERS`)

Deprioritizing the Print Server

Although the information provided in this section is focused on how to increase the thread priorities of print-related services, occasionally there are situations where you may wish to decrease these priorities.

Specifically, you may want to set the thread priority on some servers to give file server-related threads higher priority than those related to print serving. This may be required to properly balance the load distribution on the server, or even to resolve problems that occur because the file server threads do not receive adequate CPU attention (this is called thread "starvation").

By default, the file server service runs at foreground process priority, which is a value of 8. Other threads in the system service, such as the print service, run at foreground process priority +1, which is 9. This includes such services as the XACTSRV service and the threads it spawns. The XACTSRV is used to fulfill printing requests, and so a file server also serving double duty as a print server may suffer the throes of thread starvation due to the lower priority the server service threads default to in comparison with the XACTSRV threads. If the logs indicate this trend, a move from the default to one priority point higher may remedy the problem.

You can find the value in:

```
HKEY_LOCAL_MACHINE\SYSTEM\CurrentControlSet\Services\Lanman
  Server\Parameters
```

The value to modify (or add) is:

Value Name: **ThreadPriority**

Data Type: **REG_DWORD**

Range of Values: **0, 1, 2, or 15**

Default Value: **1** (equivalent to foreground execution priority)

Set ThreadPriority to 2. This will automatically steal priority from the print server so that the fileserver can perform more optimally when utilization of the server is high. Like the other optimizations we've discussed, this priority shuffling will do nothing if the server is running at relatively low utilization with few clients interacting with the server; it will only prove helpful when the server is heavily taxed (and thread responsiveness needs to be increased to meet the demand).

However, on servers that experience a heavy disk load on the Boot Partition (the drive where the %SYSTEMROOT% folder is located) due to application and paging file activity, disk spooling activities may be slowed down due to contention. This in turn may adversely affect overall printing performance as the disk spooling thread is forced to wait for other system activities before receiving disk time to write spool data.

To alleviate this problem, consider moving the default spool file location on a print server to an alternate drive. In Windows NT 4.0, this is easy to accomplish – simply follow these steps:

1. Open the Printers folder.
2. Select File → Print Server Properties from the menus; you may also view Print Server Properties by right-clicking an empty space in the Printers folder window and selecting Print Server Properties from the pop-up menu that appears.
3. Select the Advanced tab.
4. To move the spool location, simply change the value listed in the Spool Folder option to an alternate folder. Note: Before doing so, make sure that this folder exists and that all users who will print to this machine have at least Change permissions on the folder (if it is located on an NTFS partition).

The Print Server Properties dialog is shown in Figure 8-11.

This dialog contains three tabbed sections, Forms, Ports, and Advanced. The one we're most interested in is the Advanced tab, which contains an option to set the spool file directory for this server.

Changing the Spool Folder location can also be accomplished in Windows NT 3.x, but doing so requires that you use Registry Editor to edit the Registry directly. The value for the default Spool Folder for all printers is found in the following location (this is also the same Registry location in Windows NT 4.0):

```
HKEY_LOCAL_MACHINE\SYSTEM\CurrentControlSet\Control\Printers
```

The value to modify (or add) is:

Value Name: **DefaultSpoolDirectory**
Data Type: **REG_SZ**
Range of Values: Any valid directory pathname
Default Value: *%SYSTEMROOT%\SYSTEM32\SPOOL\PRINTERS*

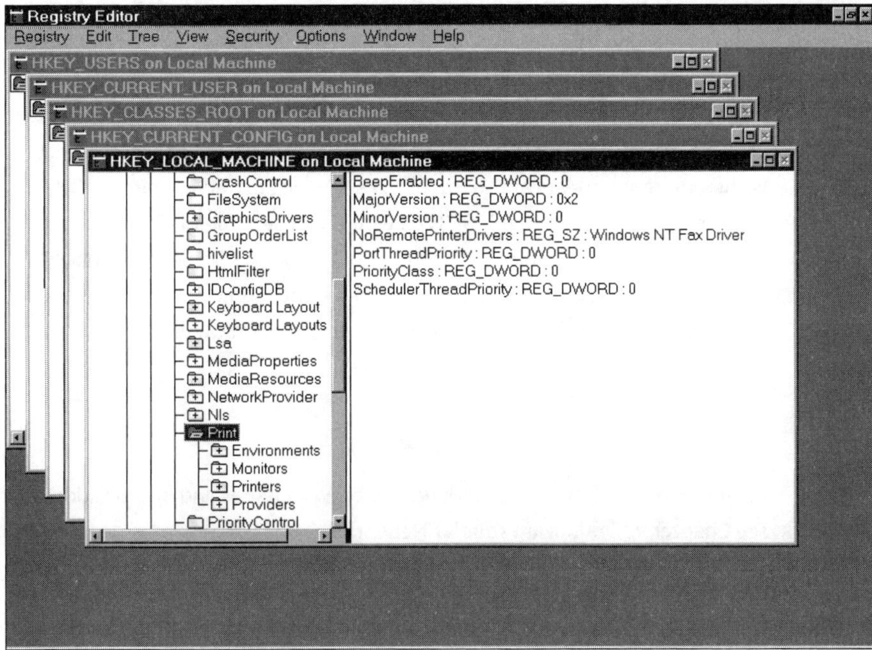

Figure 8-11: Changing the Spooler Folder location via the Print Server Properties dialog.

The DefaultSpoolDirectory value can be modified by editing the associated string data and replacing it with the name of an alternate directory for printer spool files. Again, be sure that any users who will be printing to that machine have at least Change permissions (if located on an NTFS volume) and that the folder already exists.

Optimizing Network Printing

The final area of printer-related optimizations we discuss is related to improving the performance and efficiency of printing over a Local Area Network.

Tuning print browsing

Whenever a printer is shared on a Windows NT computer, the Windows NT Spooler service issues a broadcast message to all other print servers on the network about the existence of the new printer share. The other print servers are then informed of the new printer share and add it to their printer browse lists. In addition, all print servers automatically rebroadcast their entire list of available print servers and shares every 10 minutes to all other print servers on the network. This can cause excessive traffic on large networks with many active print servers.

As an interesting side note: Windows NT uses a different system for electing master printer browsers (those maintaining print server and share lists) than it does with file share-browsing. On a Windows NT network, NT automatically uses the server with the lowest alphabetical value to its NetBIOS name (that is, the one that appears at the top of the server list in Server Manager). For example, a server named APPSERVER would be used ahead of one named BIGSERVER. The reason for the default use of a Windows NT Server is that NT assumes that as a server the machine will have both sufficient resources and network availability to fit the role of the master printer browser.

For more information on networking and browser issues and optimizations, see Chapter 9, "Optimizing Your NT Network."

To reduce this traffic, you can implement any of several Registry modifications that relate to print browsing. All of these entries are located in the same Registry subkey we examined earlier in regards to print browsing:

```
HKEY_LOCAL_MACHINE\SYSTEM\CurrentControlSet\Control\Print
```

There are several values within this Registry subkey that relate to print browsing:

- DisableServerThread (REG_DWORD): This value, which has a default value of 1 (enabled), can be set to 0 which effectively disables the print browser thread (which notifies other print servers of the shared printers on that computer).
- ServerThreadTimeout (REG_DWORD): This value specifies the amount of time that the server thread waits before sending announcements about available printers on the machine. The data is in milliseconds and the default value is 36,000 (10 minutes). Setting this number higher reduces network traffic by reducing the frequency of print browser announcements.

- NetPrinterDecayPeriod (REG_DWORD): This value specifies the amount of time that the machine should cache print server/share lists obtained from print servers on the network. If you adjust the ServerThreadTimeout value above, you want to set a longer decay period value to correspond to the longer announcement intervals. The data is in milliseconds and the default value is 3,600,000 (1 hour).
- RefreshTimesPerDecayPeriod (REG_DWORD): This value specifies the number of times per decay period that the machine should refresh the browse lists of browse masters and backup browsers. The default data is two (times per hour, the default decay period) and the possible range of values is 1–5.

By disabling the print browser thread by changing the DisableServerThread value, you prevent other print servers and clients on the network from seeing the printers on that computer. This means that any connections to shared printers on the machine will have to made manually (via UNC names such as `\\PSERVER\BIGPRINTER`) rather than via the Network Neighborhood.

By disabling this thread or at least reducing its announcement frequency, you can significantly reduce network traffic on a large network containing a number of print servers ("print servers" includes any Microsoft Windows-based machine sharing a printer on the network, not just Windows NT Server computers).

Improving print server performance

A final Registry modification that may improve the network performance of a print server is to increase the Server service's network request buffer. This can aid in network printing performance because all network print jobs from remote clients are handled via the Server service.

The Server's request buffer size is defined in the SizReqBuf value, which can be found at the following Registry location:

```
HKEY_LOCAL_MACHINE\SYSTEM\CurrentControlSet\Services\LanManServer\
  Parameters
```

Value Name: SizReqBuf
Data Type: REG_DWORD
Range of Values: 512-65536 (bytes)
Default Value: 4356

If the value doesn't appear, you can add it using Registry Editor's Add Value option (it is type REG_DWORD). You may want to experiment by increasing this value in 64-byte increments (e.g., 4410, 4474, etc.) to see if additional printer performance is realized (be sure to perform a system reboot after each change so that it takes effect).

For more information on optimizing network server performance, see Chapter 9, "Optimizing Your NT Network," and Chapter 10, "Tuning NT Server Performance."

Summary

In this chapter, we looked into some methods for improving printing performance under Windows NT, including printer settings and printer pools.

Stay tuned, because in Part III, we delve into another all-important area of Windows NT performance: Networking.

Part III

Optimizing Your NT Network

Chapter 9

Optimizing Network Performance

TUNING WINDOWS NT'S NETWORK PERFORMANCE (and network performance in general, for that matter) is one of the most complex subjects that a network administrator has to contend with. The selection of the best NT hardware, disk, and memory configurations will have a significant impact on the ability of the NT networking components to perform optimally. With this tight interrelationship in mind, we enter into this chapter on networking with the goal of reducing overhead and increasing network throughput and responsiveness. Our objective is to dispel the myth that new hardware, and new hardware alone, can help improve NT performance. However, the obligatory references to cool hardware are provided (after all, who can resist fast new hardware toys?). Some of the NT tuning you will perform will have more of an effect on response time than throughput, especially where items such as bindings and service priorities are concerned. The main goal in tweaking NT networking components is to reduce the overhead generated by network services, and balance and control network traffic.

Understanding NT Networking Architecture

To the Windows NT operating system there is no difference between opening a file locally and opening it on a remote system; this is the result of an underlying network architecture that is designed to mask the differences. For a user, a logon script which maps drives and printer shares at startup can abstract the location of the files to the user in such a way that the user is not really aware of the actual location of the files and the objects they're working with. Often the only noticeable difference between locally stored and remote files is the speed at which the file is retrieved or the desired application started. The complexity of interactions that exist at the lower level of the network driver software is abstracted by higher level layers of programming interfaces. Network driver components are implemented as file system drivers in order to take advantage of NT's caching and simplify network component driver design. The components that are implemented as file system drivers are:

- Redirector (RDR)
- Server (SVR)
- Named Pipe File System (NPFS)
- Mail Slots File System (MSFS)

Figure 9-1 shows the various components involved in Windows NT networking, and their relation to the seven-layer Open Systems Interconnect (OSI) networking model.

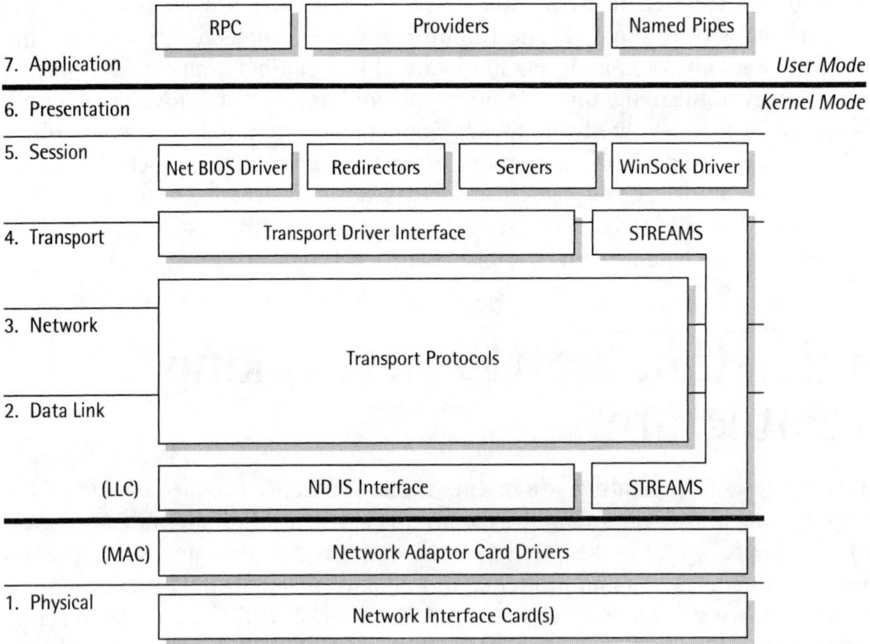

Figure 9-1: Windows NT networking components in relation to the OSI networking model.

NT provides network functionality for sharing resources through two main components: The Server and Workstation services. These services control NT's networking subsystem and provide access to file shares and other resources. Figure 9-2 shows the Redirector and Server components in relation to NT's User and Kernel modes. As you can see, both components are divided into two separate pieces, one that runs as a User Mode program and another that runs in Kernel Mode, which acts as a trusted part of the operating system. Kernel Mode programs run in privileged mode, a level that permits higher performance and direct access to NT Executive services. User Mode programs, on the other hand, must use a message-passing methodology to communicate with NT Kernel Mode services. This means that a buggy User Mode process cannot affect the operating system or other running applications. User Mode is also a slower mode of operation, and the mode in which most user applications in Windows NT are run. This division of the Server and Workstation components has the benefit of allowing the Kernel Mode portion of the driver to be very small, efficient, and portable.

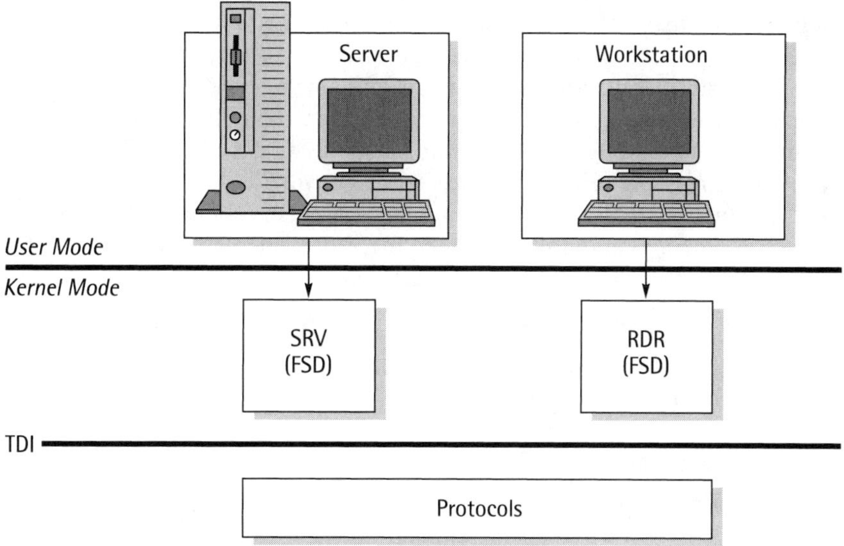

Figure 9-2: The Windows NT Server and Redirector services.

Workstation service

The Workstation service's name is actually a bit misleading. The service's actual job is that of network redirector, meaning that it establishes logical connections to other computers on the network. As we mentioned already, the Redirector is composed of two parts, a User Mode and a Kernel Mode component. This was done to make the porting of code simpler and to make the Kernel Mode portion that runs as a file system driver as small as possible. The Redirector communicates with the protocol stacks to which it is bound via the Transport Driver Interface (TDI) and the Network Driver Interface Specification (NDIS) layers. It is dependent on the Multiple Uniform Naming Convention Provider (MUP) for servicing any UNC (Uniform Naming Convention) commands, and on the MPR (Multiprovider Router) for servicing network commands. The Redirector resides above the TDI layer, which itself resides above the NDIS layer. The TDI layer is really a conceptual division rather than an actual driver. NDIS controls the network interface controller miniport drivers, which form the lowest level of the vertical software communication stack through which data and commands must traverse. All packets the NDIS layer transmits are raw, and it is the responsibility of the transport protocol stacks to format packets into the format required for the media type in use on the network (Ethernet, FDDI, TokenRing, etc.).

The Redirector (RDR.SYS, the Kernel Mode portion of the Workstation/Redirector service) is implemented as a file system driver that allows transparent access to resources without regard to whether the file or program is local or remote. This design also allows the networking drivers to run in the faster Kernel Mode of operation, allowing the Redirector to call directly on other device drivers and Kernel Mode NT components such as the Cache Manager. NT's ability to cache all I/O through the Cache Manager (whether disk or network) greatly improves network performance. Because of its design, the Redirector can also be loaded and unloaded from memory dynamically, just like any other driver. In addition, the Redirector can coexist easily with other network redirectors (e.g., Client Service for NetWare) to allow multiple network providers to access the network.

Finally, the Redirector service has a number of Registry values, which may be altered to allow for maximum performance in your particular environment. The primary Registry values that relate to the Workstation/Redirector service are stored in these Registry subkeys:

```
HKEY_LOCAL_MACHINE\SYSTEM\CurrentControlSet\Services\
  LanmanWorkstation\Parameters
```

and

```
HKEY_LOCAL_MACHINE\SYSTEM\CurrentControlSet\Services\Rdr
```

For more information on configuring the Workstation/Redirector service, see Chapter 10,"Tuning NT Server Performance."

Server service

The Windows NT Server service is the component that provides file and print serving on a Windows NT computer and is responsible for servicing requests made by other computers for resources residing on the local computer. The Server service communicates using SMB (Server Message Block), which is the core of NT's networking services. This is a higher level protocol for packaging commands than that of the transport protocols and is, in fact, completely protocol-independent. All native Windows NT file and print operations using the Server and Redirector services (and their equivalents in other operating systems such as Windows for Workgroups and Windows 95) on a Windows network are conducted using SMB sessions between computers.

Like the Workstation service, the Server service is divided into both User and Kernel Mode components. The Server Kernel Mode component is provided by the Windows NT file named `SRV.SYS`. The Server component coordinates both print and file service requests as well as providing part of the base platform for application services. The Server service has several advanced properties that can be configured from the Network Control Panel or directly via the Registry.

For descriptions of the various counters viewable with the Performance Monitor utility, see Appendix C, "Performance Monitor Counters."

For more information on the Registry values which the Server optimization level actually alters, see the "System Cache Tuning" section of Chapter 7, "Optimizing Disks."

The primary location of Server service-related entries in the Windows NT Registry is:

```
HKEY_LOCAL_MACHINE\SYSTEM\CurrentControlSet\Services\LanmanServer\
  Parameters
```

TDI

The Transport Driver Interface is the single programming interface specification (a "standard") through which Redirector, Winsock, and NetBIOS directly communicate. The upper boundary of the network layers that the TDI creates is a conceptual division rather than an actual software boundary. The TDI also prevents the Redirectors and Server services from becoming dependent on transport protocols.

MULTIPLE UNC PROVIDER

In addition to the components Server and Workstation provide to the network subsystem, there are also several Kernel and User Mode programs that provide key network services. One such program, MUP, is designed to locate UNC names by selecting an appropriate redirector that can then set up the connection to the system on which the UNC-named resource resides. Figure 9-3 shows the Kernel Mode MUP in relation to NT's architectural design.

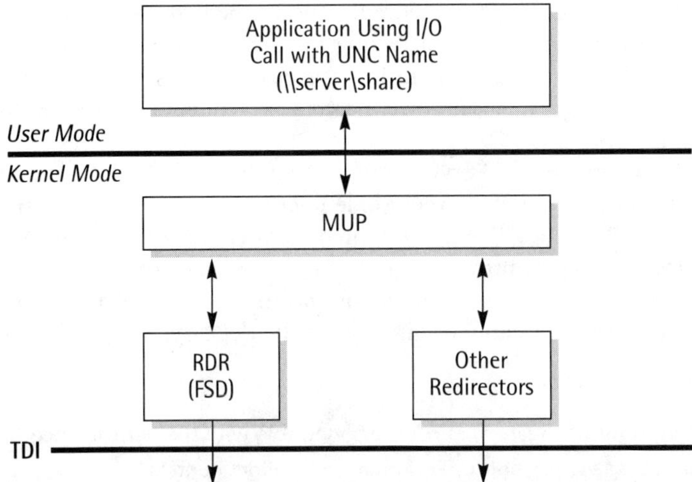

Figure 9-3: The MUP in relation to NT's architectural design.

UNC names make identifying resources on a network easier. All UNC path names contain double backslashes followed by the name of the machine and any shared object, printer, directory, or subdirectory name. UNC names appear in these formats:

For file shares:

`\\SERVER_NAME\SHARE_NAME\SUBDIRECTORY\FILENAME` (where *SHARE _NAME* is the name of the directory share being served by the server).

In the case of a simple printer or printer pool, a UNC name would appear simply as:

`\\SERVER_NAME\SHARE_NAME` (where *SHARE_NAME* is the name given to the shared printer being served by the server).

MULTIPROVIDER ROUTER

MPR is another high-level network component designed to support those network requests that do not contain UNC names. The types of commands that communicate with MPR are called WNet (Windows Network) commands and are based on the Win32 network API (Application Programming Interface). Figure 9-4 shows the position of MPR in relation to MUP and the installed network redirectors.

Unlike MUP, MPR is a User Mode component. MPR receives incoming commands (WNet commands) and determines an appropriate redirector which can dispatch the request. Different vendors provide different redirectors, so there are several provider DLL files between the MPR and the redirectors. MPR has no Registry-tunable parameters.

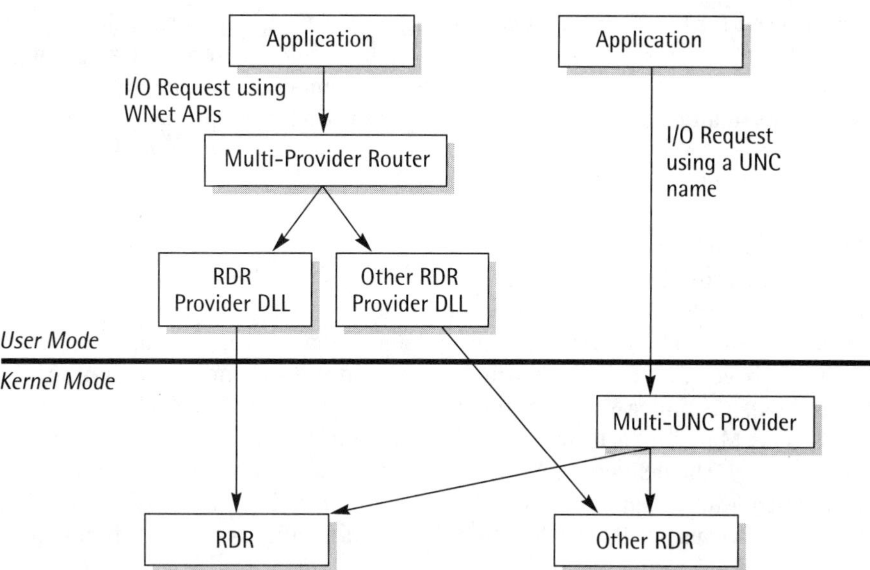

Figure 9-4: The MPR User Mode program with redirectors.

IPC and IPC mechanisms

IPC stands for Interprocess Communication (IPC) and is the mechanism for providing distributed processing for applications that support it. Applications designed to take advantage of IPC are divided into two parts: the client and the server. Most of the processing for the application is performed on the server rather than on the local client system on the premise that the server can provide significantly more power for running large and complex applications. This allows the client to be "thin," that is, having much smaller requirements for memory and processing power. This is the client-server model that became a global buzzword a few years ago.

IPC also provides network applications with the ability to communicate over the network. IPC includes such components as Named Pipes, Remote Procedure Calls, and Mailslots.

RPC

Remote Procedure Call (RPC) is used to establish communications between client and server. It is the most flexible of the IPC mechanisms and can use TCP/IP sockets, Named Pipes, and NetBIOS. If both the client and server portions of an application reside on the same computer, Local Procedure Call (LPC) is used for transferring information between processes and even subsystems.

RPC is used for the distributed computing mechanism, which provides support for the client-server shared-processing model. A custom-designed application could run a simple interface on the client and the remainder of the program could be shared by many users and run on the server. One example of RPC usage is Master Browsers on a Windows network, which update the backup browsers using RPC over Named Pipes.

MAILSLOTS AND NAMED PIPES

Named Pipes provide a high-level interface for communicating between two processes on remote machines. Mailslots provide an interface for one to many communications via broadcasts. Both Mailslots and Named Pipes are implemented as file system drivers, and share security and configuration options with other file systems. Mailslots under NT are restricted architecturally to second-class Mailslots. Second-class Mailslots are *connectionless*, meaning that they are for broadcast messaging only. The delivery of Mailslots is not guaranteed by the protocol, but the rate at which Mailslots are transferred tends to be very high while remaining low in overhead. Because of its broadcasting, it is used for things like identifying other computers and delivering wide-scale messages.

NetBIOS and Windows Sockets

NetBIOS provides the mapping between NetBIOS applications and TDI transport protocols. It is also extremely important to the proper operation of NT networking. Disabling the NetBIOS support (as is occasionally suggested in some NT security documents) has the effect of disabling many of NT's network services including file and printer sharing functionality. Network transport protocols such as NetBEUI (NetBIOS Extended User Interface) include the NetBIOS-compatibility API in the driver, eliminating the need for running the protocol (as is required with the IPX/SPX and TCP/IP protocols) under the NetBIOS API. The NetBIOS and Windows Sockets interfaces are supplied by separate DLLs which communicate with drivers in Kernel Mode. This design allows NetBIOS and Windows Sockets to bypass the redirector completely and communicate directly with the transport protocols utilizing the TDI.

Version 5.0 of Windows NT will allow you to completely drop the NetBIOS layer (and the associated overhead it represents) from NT's network subsystem. However, it will also be possible to retain NetBIOS for backward compatibility with existing applications.

In Figure 9-5, we can see how Windows Sockets and NetBIOS interact with their respective Kernel Mode drivers within the NT kernel and direct communication to the transport protocols directly without any redirector services.

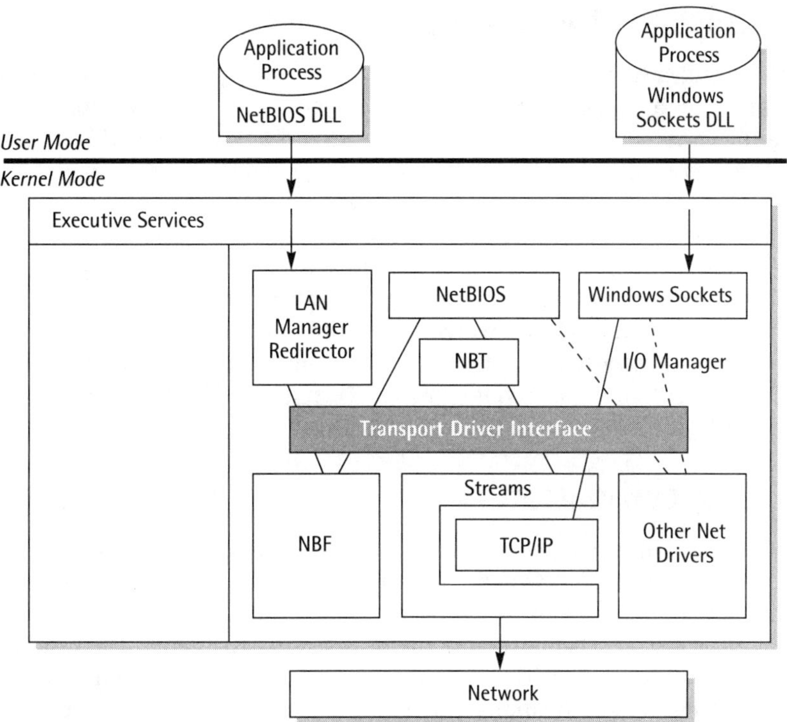

Figure 9-5: The NetBIOS and WinSock API layers in relation to NT Kernel Mode services.

Network component dependencies

For the networking components to load properly, a number of network services must start in a particular order. The failure of one network driver or service upon which others are dependent usually prevents access to the network. For example, the LanmanWorkstation (NT Redirector) service depends on such things as the successful loading of transport protocols and the MUP and NDIS components. Although this order of loading is important for the initial startup of network services, sometimes there are also cross-dependencies between various services. As an example, the MUP component is dependent on the Redirector for its operation, which it relies on to perform redirection routines necessary to MUP's operation.

To troubleshoot the failure of networking services in Windows NT, use the NT Event Viewer application in the Administrative Tools group. The System Log section of Event Viewer shows an audit trail of each component which failed to load at boot, allowing you to trace the failures back to the individual component that started the domino effect of failures.

NT transport protocol support

Windows NT includes support for a number of network transport protocols, which can be combined on a single machine and used concurrently in any combination. However, doing so is also one of the quickest ways to kill your network's performance. Using many transport protocols concurrently generates more network traffic, incurs delays from binding priorities, and uses more memory and processor resources. In addition to its performance benefits, having fewer protocols also means less troubleshooting when trying to isolate network problems. Data sent on the network will be sent by default over all available network transport protocols bound to the NIC on that segment, which is a wasteful duplication. The network transport protocols supported under Windows NT include NetBT (NetBios over TCP/IP), NBF (NetBEUI Frames), NWLink (IPX/SPX), and DLC. We discuss the benefits and drawbacks of each of these protocols later in the chapter.

The NDIS specification

The layer of software drivers below the transport protocols includes NDIS (Network Device Interface Specification) which allows for support of concurrent transport protocols and binding of transport protocols to an unlimited number of NICs. NDIS sends and receives raw packets only; it is the responsibility of the transport layers to format the packets to the specific media access protocol (such as Ethernet, FDDI, and TokenRing). Several specifications of NDIS have evolved with NT, with the latest version being 4.0. To take advantage of the latest NDIS specification, you must use miniport NIC drivers specifically designed for the latest revision. Most NIC miniport drivers remain compliant only with NDIS specification version 3.0. Listed below are some of the features for the more recent versions of NDIS that exist:

- NDIS 3.0: A 32-bit protected-mode driver interface specification that supports an unlimited number of NICs, which must be on different networks (either physically separate networks or different logical networks with different transport stacks). No software routing is provided between network adapters. NDIS 3.0 also has basic support for SMP systems and allows for flexible protocol bindings on a per NIC basis. On SMP machines, IRQ generation is not evenly distributed between or among CPUs.
- NDIS 4.0: Builds on version 3.0 with better SMP optimizations by realizing NIC IRQ distribution, as well as new features like packet prioritization and Quality of Service support (QOS). Unfortunately, very few NDIS 4.0-compatible NIC drivers have been released, except from large vendors with a significant investment in Windows NT (e.g., Intel, Digital, Adaptec). To use the special prioritization capabilities, you must have switches and routers that support the prioritization and quality of service protocols as well as the latest NIC drivers supporting NDIS 4.0.

- NDIS 5.0: A proposed and upcoming standard slated for NT 5.0 and Windows 98, this new specification will include support for Microsoft's Zero Administration Windows initiative, and includes a more mature priority and QOS mechanism. It will also fully support the Plug and Play network card operation, as well as the fully dynamic removal of NIC drivers and transports without requiring a system reboot.

Support for non-Windows systems

In addition to the Server and Redirector services, and the SMB core protocol they use for native Windows networking support, Windows NT also supports several other networking environments. Separate redirectors and/or servers capable of native communication with these other systems are provided with Windows NT, and installing the appropriate services activates the drivers to enable communication with the foreign system. Several of these optional networking services are described below.

CLIENT SERVICES FOR NETWARE (CSNW)

Microsoft created Client Services for NetWare in order to allow Windows NT workstations to access resources on Novell Netware servers using NCP (NetWare Core Protocol, NetWare's native file and print service protocol akin to SMB under NT). A client dependency for this software is the NWLink IPX/SPX transport protocol.

GATEWAY SERVICES FOR NETWARE (GSNW)

GSNW is an NT service that provides NT Servers with the ability to access files, printers, and directories on NetWare servers and reshare these resources to SMB-based clients on a Microsoft Windows network. As such, the service provides a gateway for the Windows clients to the NetWare network's resources. Clients on the Windows network may access redirected NetWare shares through the NT Server as though the shares were actually local to the NT Server. Like CSNW, GSNW requires the NWLink IPX/SPX protocol to be loaded.

SERVICES FOR MACINTOSH (SFM)

Services for Macintosh is a collection of NT services that together provide print and file service for Macintosh OS computers on a Windows NT Server computer. The service utilizes the AppleTalk Filing Protocol (AFP) to allow connection to native Macintosh computers and printers. From a Macintosh client, the NT Server appears to be a standard AppleShare server in the same AppleTalk zone. Printers are accessed and print jobs processed through a special RIP (Raster Image Processor) that converts PostScript print requests to a different format (e.g., PCL) if the NT attached printer is not a native PostScript printer. From the chooser, NT Macintosh shares appear just like ordinary AppleShare resources. SFM filename support is up to 31 characters, just like other Macintosh systems. NTFS security supports

Macintosh security natively, so there is none of the overhead associated with mapping one system to the other. The resources that this server component provides are tunable via the Registry.

For more information on tuning Windows NT file and print services, see Chapter 10,"Tuning NT Server Performance."

Identifying Network Bottlenecks

Windows NT has some excellent integrated tools that can help you determine if and where problems are developing on your NT network. These tools include Performance Monitor (a "horizontal" tool) and the Network Monitor utility (a "vertical" tool). Performance Monitor is an excellent tool for general information on many subsystem components, whereas Network Monitor provides in-depth information related to the network subsystem (specifically, network traffic analysis) down to the packet level. In addition, full-blown network "sniffer" tools like those produced by Cisco, HP, Intel, and Microsoft (vis-à-vis the full and extended version of Network Monitor found in Microsoft's SMS Server) can collect even more information on network traffic patterns, problems, and performance.

The major limitation of the Network Monitor application provided with Windows NT Server is that it is only capable of monitoring network traffic to or from that server, whereas a full-blown network monitoring or "sniffer" tool is capable of examining all network traffic on the local segment.

The first step to optimizing any component is to baseline its existing performance and its impact on the performance of the rest of the system. A network bottleneck can occur anywhere in the networking subsystem and may be indicated by unusual activity in the following components:

- Redirector
- Server
- Network Interface
- Network Segment

Telltale signs of network bottlenecks

Signs of network problems include complaints about the speed at which files are opened from and saved to the server, as well as the speed of interaction with application servers such as SQL servers. Telltale signs of potential hardware or network software problems include high network utilization, high interrupt generation, and excessively long queues for such resources as processor, disk, and network interface. Other signs include large numbers of context switches per second and high processor utilization. Context switches reflect the number of times in a given time unit that the processor(s) has to stop servicing one thread and start processing another. The transition from one to the other takes a long time and requires that the processor save the volatile contents of its internal registers before performing any action on the new thread. High processor usage gives an overall measure of the remaining capacity of the processors for executing other threads, a capacity that may be drastically reduced by an improperly configured network subsystem.

The high utilization of a network object as measured by Performance Monitor is not necessarily indicative, in and of itself, of a network bottleneck; long queue lengths (the queue for network commands which forms when they cannot be performed immediately) are the real indicator of a bottleneck. Queue lengths of 2 (which applies to several other NT subsystems, including processor and disk) are indicative of either a slow NIC or a congested network. Sustained high queue lengths of 3 or more should warn you that your network is not keeping up with demand and may require additional hardware and network software component changes.

To get useful Performance Monitor objects such as Network Interface, you must install the SNMP Management and Network Monitor Tools and Agent services, both of which may be added via the Network Control Panel's Services tab. Installing the Network Monitor Agent also provides Network Segment, a new Performance Monitor object that can be used to monitor various aspects of network segment performance (without these services installed, you are limited to the base NT Performance Monitor objects). After installing the services, you will need to reboot for the new drivers and performance objects to be available.

See the "Meet Your Toolkit" section in Chapter 4 for instructions on how to build a baseline set for Performance Monitor.

A predefined set of Performance Monitor workspace environment files for detecting network bottlenecks called `NetworkBottleneck.pmw` is provided on the *Optimizing Windows NT* CD-ROM.

Figure 9-6 shows a sample Performance Monitor session using important network-related counters.

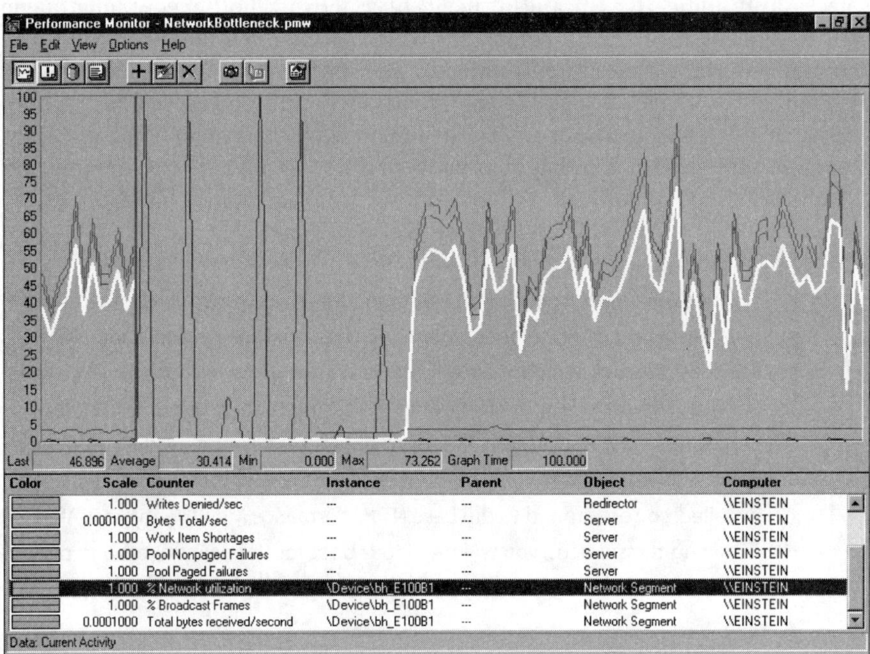

Figure 9-6: Using Performance Monitor to examine network performance statistics.

Monitoring and benchmarking methodology

Although there are many methods for improving network performance, you must first know and understand the elements you'll be dealing with. Two methodologies exist for accomplishing the goal of maximum performance. The first is stress testing using a workload generator to produce the highest possible scores with your environment's native overhead. However, this method can sometimes produce inaccurate (or "colorized") results because these tests tend to use an *approximation* of data access. In some cases, these approximations may not accurately simulate the work that is really being done on your network by real users and applications. Tools like ServerBench tend to produce less-than-real-world results because of their use of a relatively static synthetic work generator. Products such as BlueCurve Corporation's Dynameasure, on the other hand, measure performance based on rules that can be changed to govern the way in which "engines" simulate real users and workloads. This provides a better workload simulation, and therefore a better test of your servers' maximum performance and capacity. The Windows NT Resource Kit also contains a tool called Response Probe that has a programmable workload generator with some basic functionality for testing I/O characteristics of your network. Although not nearly as sophisticated as commercial products such as Dynameasure, this utility can provide some basic performance statistics that may be helpful in assessing server performance.

One of the best means to measure and optimize a network remains the tried and true science of systems analysis with data logging over a period of weeks or months to isolate trends. This reflects the real usage of the network and is almost impossible to beat in the information it reflects. Discovering the maximum amount of work that a server can perform is invaluable in combination with actual usage logs to help in determining when and if new hardware must be added.

Measuring individual component performance

Now it's time for some real-time charting of the activity on your network. Start the Performance Monitor from the Administrative Tools program folder. With the Performance Monitor open, pull down the Chart View (default) and add the counters listed in the next section to the display for the selected system. It will default to the current computer on which you are running Performance Monitor. Choose a server or use your own workstation. The objects listed in the next section can be added using the + icon on the toolbar or Edit→Add to Chart from the menus.

REDIRECTOR SERVICE COUNTERS

This group of Redirector counters determines if it is a network component that is bottlenecking the network.

- *Bytes Total/sec*: This object gives the total number of data bytes being processed by the Redirector. This includes all packet data and protocol overhead, and gives an accurate measure of the amount of work Redirector is performing. This number should not reach the maximum rated speed of the network medium (the maximum speed achievable by a particular network technology, such as MB10MB Ethernet, or MB100MB FDDI) or a sustained value greater than 50 percent of its capacity over a sustained amount of time. Such a high utilization on the network medium indicates that the network is being pushed too hard. Consider NT-based or hardware-based segmentation either by using a router (small scale, rather complex) or employing switches (fast and relatively simple).
- *Current Commands*: This counts the number of requests to the Redirector that are currently queued for service. Ideally, this value should not be more than one command per installed NIC. If a value higher than one is present, the redirector may be the bottleneck. This can happen if there is an asymmetry between the speed of server and the redirector which is causing inefficient communication between the local and remote systems. This can also indicate that the network capacity is being pushed to its limits and that it may be necessary to break the network into subnetworks to reduce traffic.
- *Network Errors/sec*: Counts the number of serious errors that generally indicate the Redirector and one or more servers are having serious communication difficulties. For example, an SMB (Server Manager Block) protocol error will generate a Network Error. These result in an entry in the system Event Log, so look there for details. If errors appear in the chart, check the Event Log for more detailed error messages. This can be a sign of problems with the NIC or NIC driver, the hub or switch, or the cabling.
- *Reads Denied/sec*: This specifies the number of read attempts to the server, which rejected requests for RAW Reads. When the Redirector read request is larger than the server's negotiated buffer size, the Redirector will request a RAW read instead. When the server permits RAW reads, the performance of the connection can be significant because it occurs without all of the protocol overhead on every packet. RAW reads are accomplished by locking out all other requests and giving the transfer its full attention. The server will deny RAW read transfers if it is too busy to lock out other requests.
- *Writes Denied/sec*: Like Reads Denied/sec, this is a request for a RAW write to the server, which if granted can permit a high degree of performance. If the server is busy, it will reject the request. Both Reads and Writes Denied/sec are measures of how efficient the server you are monitoring is performing and how busy it is.

SERVER SERVICE COUNTERS

This group of server counters determines if it is the server network component that is bottlenecking the network. This is the service primarily responsible for conveying client data from the server to the client computers.

- *Bytes Total/sec*: Specifies the total number of bytes the server has sent and received over the network. The values this object monitors gives a good idea of how busy a server is. If this number is consistently at or above 50 percent of the network capacity, you may need to break the server off onto a faster switch or hub, or you could subnetwork using NT's routing capability and a second NIC.
- *Work Item Shortages*: This is the number of times that a "STATUS_DATA_NOT_ACCEPTED" message was returned. When no work items are available to service the network request, this message is returned to the system making the request. This value specifies whether modifications need to be made to InitWorkItems or MaxWorkItems parameters. A busy server that is getting close to its limits for memory will suffer more shortages, so this can be used to indicate a very busy server and a lack of physical memory resources. You may want to take off some services from the server to better service the remaining requests.
- *Blocking Requests Rejected*: This server counter measures the number of times that a blocking SMB request has been rejected as a result of insufficient free work items. This can help to determine if the MaxWorkItem or MinFreeWorkItems parameters may need to be modified. A busy server will reject blocking requests for RAW transfers more often, giving an indication of how busy the server is.
- *Context Blocks Queued/sec*: This server counter measures the rate at which work context blocks were placed in the server's FSP queue because they could not be executed immediately. High values reflect a server component bottleneck.
- *Pool Nonpaged Failures*: This counter measures the number of errors experienced by the server service due to exhausting memory resources that were originally allocated. Increasing numbers of this counter indicate a physical memory shortage.
- *Pool Paged Failures*: This counter measures the number of allocation errors experienced by the server service due to an insufficient pagefile. Failures indicate that the pagefile is too small and needs to be increased. This counter in combination with the Pool Nonpaged Failures and Context Blocks Queued/sec can indicate a bottleneck in the server component as a result of an improper server optimization level (minimize, balance, maximize).

NETWORK INTERFACE

This group of counters is only available if you install SNMP support with TCP/IP. Network Interface determines if it is the network itself that is congested and bottlenecked. The Network Interface object will have one instance for each NIC installed.

- *Output Queue Length*: This is the number of packets in the output queue. This value should not sustain more than 2 or the network is bottlenecked and the underlying hardware may need to be reconfigured or replaced. Contrary to documentation that states that this counter always remains at zero, it does, indeed, give useful information.
- *Bytes Total/sec*: This counter reflects the number of bytes that are sent and received through the interface, including all framing characters. This counter measures all net traffic that moves through the NIC and includes overhead from media access protocol and transport protocol. If this counter is observed to sustain (converted) 390 to 586K and grow above these rates while your output queue lengths continue to increase, the NIC and media access protocol is bottlenecking the system and segmentation/subnetworking may be required.
- *Current Bandwidth*: This counter is an estimation of the current bandwidth on the interface in bps (bits per second). For interfaces that do not vary in bandwidth (like Ethernet and FDDI), this is a nominal bandwidth value.

NETWORK SEGMENT

This group of counters is only available when you install the Network Monitor Agent. Unlike the other counters, this group actually uses the agent and converts the information for Performance Monitor.

- *% Network Utilization*: This is the percentage of the network bandwidth that is in use. By comparing this counter's value to that of the Network Interface object, Current Bandwidth counter, you can determine how much of the network capacity is actually being used.
- *% Broadcast Frames*: This counter counts the percentage of frames that are broadcast traffic (and potentially wasted bandwidth) as opposed to multicast and unicast traffic. If this or % Multicast Frames reaches anywhere near 100 percent (combined) in a second, you should look for the source of the traffic immediately. Large numbers of broadcasts can be caused by a misconfigured bridge, a chattering NIC, or a large NT network using transport protocols that are resolving NetBIOS names to physical addresses. Segmenting the network using subnetworks or switches can reduce this traffic. Other changes include using transport protocols, which do not generate as many broadcasts (TCP/IP).

◆ *Total Bytes Received/sec*: This counter indicates the total number of bytes received from a particular network segment. This is a good indicator of the amount of work that the server is doing. If the total is getting close to the maximum for the speed of the medium (MB10MB Ethernet, MB100MB Ethernet, TokenRing 16) pay close attention to the Output Queue length counter of the Network Interface object. If the number is too high, you may add NICs and subnetwork the network, or you may choose to add switches. Sustained numbers of more than half the rated maximum speed of the network medium is an indication of overutilization and need for breaking the network up and/or adding faster network components.

Once you have monitored your network for a few days and gotten a feel for what each counter is indicating and how the Performance Monitor objects interrelate, you should be able to start identifying problem areas and isolating whether the bottleneck is occurring at the network segment, the network interface, or within the network components themselves.

See Chapter 10,"Tuning NT Server Performance" for additional Performance Monitor objects related to server performance.

Identifying network interface card bottlenecks

The Network Interface counter (installed when you choose to install SNMP support under TCP/IP options) is the best tool for determining whether your bottleneck is on the network interface controller, on the network itself, or caused by improperly configured or overtaxed network software components. From the Network Monitor, you can also view the percentage of network utilization as well as the frames/second and bytes/second. Consistently high numbers from either tool monitoring the appropriate objects (those for Network Segment and Network Interface) indicate that the performance problem is being caused by a source outside of NT's network subsystem software.

Other measures for determining if the NIC itself is causing trouble include measuring System Total Interrupts/sec and Network Interface packets/sec. Sustained figures of 150 interrupts per second are troublesome. A high packet rate with a processor interrupt rate in the sub-100 range is ideal. Six hundred interrupts per second or higher is a good indication of a hardware level problem with the NIC or NIC driver. Context switches (thread service switching) will also reflect a high number, which will be close to the rate of interrupts per second from miniport driver servicing by the processor(s). As mentioned, queue lengths are the most important measure for determining bottlenecking. If a component is getting close to 100 percent usage while the output queue remains empty, the component is providing work at the rate it is requested without having to delay service by placing the request in the queue. If the network interface queue is four or higher, then your network interface is becoming the bottleneck. Causes for this include a slow NIC or a very busy network in which the NIC must wait to transmit/retransmit.

A good NIC will incorporate features to reduce contention on the network as well as provide good performance with the minimum interrupt generation. Busmastering PCI NICs provide the best performance with the lowest processor utilization. The efficiency of an NIC is the measure of raw throughput divided by the processor utilization as a percentage. A higher efficiency rating is indicated by the lowest processor usage accompanied with throughput rates at close to the rated speed of the medium in a switched environment using cached data transfers. The driver should fully support the latest NT networking component revisions and the other network hardware installed on the network.

Because NT now supports the enhanced NDIS 4.0 spec, get in touch with your vendor to find out if they have updated NDIS 4.0 miniport drivers for the NIC you already use. All the major vendors now support this specification, though older NICs may not have an updated driver that supports NDIS 4.0. Most good NICs have a driver setup utility that allows you to set up the parameters for the NIC explicitly. As already described, it's good to leave nothing to chance, and if you are reading this book you are probably not one for allowing much in the way of automatic configuration.

For large networks, you may want to keep your duplexing and line speed set for autonegotiate. This should prevent serious problems from occurring if you move machines around on the network and add or remove switches.

Though it isn't possible to tell you all of the possible driver parameters for all of the available network cards, cards based on the Digital Semiconductor network accelerator chips tend to have very high performance and are found on some of the highest rated cards (like the Adaptec Quartet Fast Ethernet adapters). Intel and 3COM also make very good cards, with driver parameters that are generally more tweakable than those based on the Digital chipset. Parameters such as send and receive buffers should be increased in small increments. Map registers (when available) allocate memory for the driver and give the best performance. If you see this parameter, try to increase it as much as you can without logging errors (memory used is often less than 32K).

Monitoring Network Performance with Network Monitor

Windows NT's included monitoring tools are great for quick and easy identification of network bottlenecks. You don't have to buy an expensive third-party tool for providing information on network performance, even if your investigation leads you down to the packet level. For this kind of low-level network monitoring, you can use the Network Monitor utility included with Windows NT Server. To use Network Monitor, you have to install the agent and the Network Monitor tool from within `Control Panel\Networks`. See Figure 9-7 for a view of the Network Control Panel, Services tab.

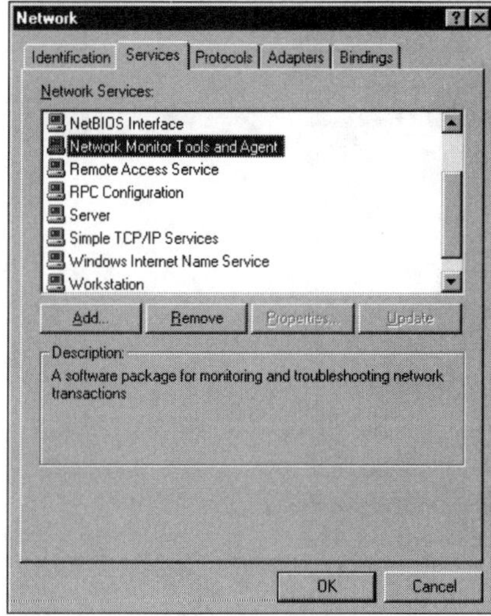

Figure 9-7: Services tab with Network Monitor Tools and Agent listed.

Network Monitor interface

Network Monitor automatically opens to the Capture Window. The screen is divided into four frames: the graph pane, the session pane, the station statistics pane, and the total statistics pane.

The graph pane, which is visible in the upper left-hand corner, shows all current network activity in bar graph form. The top is labeled "% Network Utilization," which is the same counter that can be accessed from within Performance Monitor. Just below this is the Frames Per Second graph followed by Bytes Per Second and then Broadcasts Per Second. The upper right is the home of the Total Statistics pane. This is a statistical display of all frames, bytes, and adapter statistics. See Figure 9-8 for a view of the Network Monitor.

The Session Statistics pane is situated to the middle and left. This is summary information of network activity, which also indicates the source of broadcast and multicast traffic. The Station Statistics Pane occupies the bottom of the frame. It displays a summary of total frames and bytes that are sent by a particular system and any broadcast and multicast traffic initiated by the system.

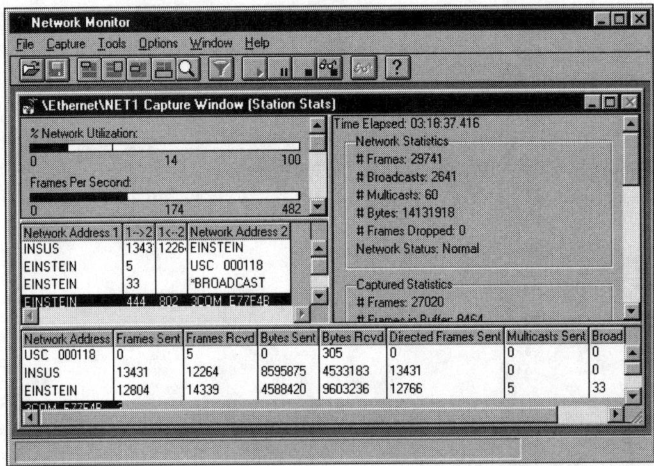

Figure 9-8: Network Monitor's default window.

SETTING UP TO CAPTURE

Without changing any default settings, you can start monitoring. The small 1MB default buffer will fill quickly on a busy network, so you may wish to increase this to something more useful, like 4 to 5MB. You can change this simply by going to the Capture menu and selecting Buffer Settings. Change the value to a setting between 3MB and your total available memory (remember to be conservative here, because allocating too much memory may cause other system problems while the utility is running). Increasing the buffer size helps prevent the loss of frames during the capture session. Once this is done, choose Capture→Start to begin capturing network traffic.

ANALYSIS

If you notice values of 50 percent network utilization on an ongoing basis, then you should consider segmenting the network either by adding NICs to the server and enabling routing (good for small environments on tight budgets) or by purchasing a switch. The switch is the faster option and is more scalable. You can also use the Network monitor on a per-server basis to see which systems are using the network most heavily to determine where to break the network into further segments.

Packet level information can help you determine if the network is being bombarded with broadcasts which may be reduced by installing a WINS server (for TCP/IP) and removal of broadcast-based protocols like NetBEUI. You could also determine whether IPX is the better option if Internet connectivity is not an issue.

Comparison of the NT and SMS network monitors

Though it is essentially "free," Network Monitor is still a very versatile tool. NT's included Network Monitor is a less feature-rich version of the Cisco co-developed version found in SMS 2.0. The Network Monitor included with NT 4.0 is limited to seeing the network only in relation to the system on which Network Monitor runs where the full SMS version is able to see any system which has a Network Monitor Agent installed.

For Network Monitor to perform its capture functions, it configures the NIC(s) for "promiscuous mode", allowing the NIC to see all the packets that pass through the segment to which it is attached. Normally, NICs ignore any packet that does not have its MAC address in the header.

Packet Sniffers Provide Network Insight

Packet sniffers allow you to gain valuable insight on your network, such as finding network intruders, exposing internal and external security holes, and even figuring out where all your network bandwidth is going. These are often expensive devices using such exotic things as software-based neural networks, artificial intelligence and "fuzzy logic" supplemented with a set of rules for identifying what a particular kind of traffic indicates. Depending on the particular product involved, these systems can often fix a problem before you even know it exists, or at least notify you of a potential problem before it becomes a full-fledged disaster. Although the cost of these little network helpers is often a bit high, it may be a worthwhile investment if the size, complexity, and uptime needs of your network environment warrant having one. These products are available from companies such as Hewlett-Packard, Computer Associates, and Novell, among others.

Logging data over the long haul

To get a sense of what is happening on your network at different times during the day, week, and month, you should consider logging your network activity to a local log file using Performance Monitor. Logs you create here can be played back for review and bookmarked in the significant sections. You can review these files and bookmark the activity of interest and create a screenshot of the file to help others visualize the network activity. Because watching endless graphs of network data is about as interesting as watching paint dry, set your update frequency to a much higher value than the default of 15 seconds for the log view. A good starting point is every 5 to 10 minutes, which will add data to the log at a much slower and less granular rate. Many events may slip by the log if the value is set too high and you have a large number of very small jobs that occur sporadically throughout the day. If you find your logs are showing little activity but you are experiencing short periods of slow service, you will need to reduce the interval until the activity that is causing the slowdown shows up on the log. You can change this by going to the Options menu, choosing Log, and changing the interval in the dialog box.

For more information on using Performance Monitor's Log view, see the "Performance Monitor: Bottleneck Sleuth" section in Chapter 4, "NT Optimizing 101."

Specify the name of the file and location where you want to put the log file (use your local drive, don't save a log across the network when what you are monitoring is network performance). When finished, hit "Start Log." The log will then begin to capture an array of statistics that you can later examine to view the trends that are occurring on your NT systems.

To playback the log, you must first stop the logging process. To stop collecting data, select the Options menu and go to Log→Stop Log. To read it, go back to Options and choose Data From and select the file location and name (make sure you include a `.log` extension or you won't see the file). Next, select View→Chart to chart statistics based on the log file (rather than live data). You should then select the counters (available within the objects that you logged) that you want to observe.

You can use Performance Monitor's Bookmark feature to mark the areas of interest for determining at what point in a day or week that a component is in the greatest demand.

Logging activity using Performance Monitor or the datalog service requires that you have sufficient disk space for containing the log file. Each counter instance ranges in size from 4 to 8 bytes depending on the counter and object. When measuring, be aware that each time the activity is measured using these counters, the total size of the log will increase according to the size of each counter added together. For the counters in the .PMW file included on the CD, the total size added to a log file at each interval is less than 100 bytes per measurement. Longer intervals between samples mean less disk space will be used. Using more counters with more instances (as with multiple disks, network adapters, processors, etc.) will increase the amount of disk space used. It is a good idea to choose an empty partition or removable disk for storing and generating log files to avoid the possibility that data files may compete for space with the log file.

Using the datalog service

Should you set up Performance Monitor logging on a remote station, you can save the log file to the local hard drive and avoid costly network usage. Performance Monitor has a companion tool for remote station logging called the Data Logging Service (DATALOG.EXE).

Datalog is an NT service that can perform the same functions as the Performance Monitor Alert and Logging capabilities. This is useful for monitoring many remote NT systems.

This first step to using the Data Logging Service is to create settings for Performance Monitor to use. Add all the objects you want to have in the Alert or Logfile and then specify a name for the log file (must end with .LOG) and set the time interval. However, don't start logging yet! You first need to save the settings file you just created as a .PMW that must be stored in the *%SYSTEMROOT%*\SYSTEM32 directory of the system where Datalog will be running. Save the workplace by choosing File→Save Workplace.

The next step is to move the DATALOG.EXE into the target system's *%SYSTEMROOT%*\SYSTEM32 directory. You must then install the Data Logging Service using a command prompt from within the *%SYSTEMROOT%*\SYSTEM32 directory. To do this, you will have to be at the machine's console. Type **monitor setup.**

The command will register the service with the Service Manager so that it now has all the standard startup options and option for a special user name. To use the workplace (.PMW) file that you created, open the command prompt again and type **monitor filename.**

To start logging the specified events to the log and alerts type **monitor start.**

To stop logging and view the contents of the log file that was created, type **monitor stop.**

Once the monitor has stopped and all logging has ceased, you can view the log file from Performance Monitor as described earlier. To view remote logs on your local system, you can use Server Manager to stop the remote monitor service on the target machine and open the log from Performance Monitor's Chart view (or Alerts, or Reports).

Alleviating Network Bottlenecks

Has desktop ATM's time finally come on your network? Or, perhaps you've been considering deploying Gigabit Ethernet on your network backbone – perhaps even all the way to the desktop? Big pipes don't always yield the kinds of results you might think, especially if you add the right hardware to the wrong place. Often a simple and relatively inexpensive 10MB Ethernet (or more recently, Token Ring) switch can alleviate the bandwidth problems to most desktops, until of course advanced bandwidth hogging applications are added to the mix. Bottlenecks that occur on a network can come from anywhere from the user's perspective, because users are generally at the logical end of the line.

A bottleneck at the backbone between several LAN segments or at a switch between servers can wreak as much havoc as a slow NIC on the client system. Replacing all your client NICs with 100MB and above network technologies may not provide any improvement in network responsiveness without the all-important changes at the server, client, and topological level. It is often better to have one fast PCI NIC in the server than four typical NICs in versions of NT prior to NT 4.0. The addition of the RandomAdapter Registry parameter, along with the new NDIS 4.0 specification, allows for much better utilization of the NICs in the server. You should use multiple NICs in your server if you discover that you are sustaining very high (close to 50 percent) utilization on an Ethernet, and segment the network into subnetworks through NT routing with multiple NICs installed. This works for smaller installations up to about 100 typical users total. More than that and you are better off with a dedicated device.

Using workgroup switches is the fastest option for segmenting your LAN when sustained values for the network interface and queue lengths remain high. Try to stay with one NIC vendor that has proven performance and features. Mixing NICs often has the result of differing NIC performances on the network. Plus, every new device means you have to maintain and update a new set of miniport drivers, which means more work for you.

In addition, you should improve the efficiency of your reduced number of transport protocols using Registry values that increase window sizes, maximize the MTU, and set up packet buffering.

Servers that show signs of bottlenecking at the network interface (and not just somewhere else such as the disk drives) benefit from special NICs that have large physical cache sizes as well as a good local processor (like the Intel I960 RISC processor). These NICs cost more but will improve overall server efficiency to the client by increasing throughput and reducing server CPU utilization.

On the software side, you should make sure that your Server and Workstation services are performing optimally using the Performance Monitor workspace file (`.PMW`) provided on the CD-ROM with this book. Once you have, you can issue two simple commands from the command prompt to enumerate all Redirector and Server service entries for easy modification.

By default, very few of the value parameters for the Windows NT Server and Redirector services are displayed in the Registry. To enumerate the parameters available for these services, open an NT command prompt window and issue these commands:

```
net config workstation /charwait: 3600
net config server /srvcomment: "text"
```

The commands are nondestructive, and do not overwrite any of the existing (hidden) parameters. These simple commands will enumerate most (but not all) the tunable parameters for each service. However, be aware that once you use these commands, the autotuning (NT's mechanism for altering resource allocation, primarily based on the size of installed memory) for these services will be disabled, putting the burden of optimizing them for a given purpose entirely in your hands. For example, if you later install memory on the machine, NT would normally perform an automatic increase of the Redirector and Server Registry parameter values to maximize performance under that memory environment. However, with the above enumerations in effect, you will have to either increase these values manually or remove the settings added when you enumerated the key for each service. Once these settings are removed, NT again utilizes its autotuning for these services. As a result, it's a good idea to write down the exact list of values (and respective data) for the LanmanServer (Server) and Lanman Workstation (Redirector) services prior to issuing the NET CONFIG commands listed above.

The location of the keys enumerated for each service is as follows:

Workstation service:

```
HKEY_LOCAL_MACHINE\SYSTEM\CurrentControlSet\Services\
LanmanWorkstation\Parameters
```

Server service:

```
HKEY_LOCAL_MACHINE\SYSTEM\CurrentControlSet\Services\
LanmanServer\Parameters
```

For more information on improving server performance through changes to the Server service, see Chapter 10,"Tuning NT Server Performance."

If the information gathered by the `NetworkBottleneck.PMW` file (which can be used to isolate a broad range of network bottlenecks and is included on the *Optimizing Windows NT* CD-ROM) indicates that the Workstation (Redirector) service is causing a bottleneck, you can change a few values for the Workstation service once you have enumerated its parameters. There are two main parameters that can be adjusted based on information you find in Performance Monitor: MaxCmds and KeepConn (the LockQuota value can also occasionally make a small performance contribution).

One parameter you might want to experiment with when you are benchmarking for maximum network performance is the UtilizeNtCaching parameter, which is set to "on" by default. This value instructs NT whether it should use the system file cache. Try turning this off and see what happens to your network I/O. Although you'd never want to turn the value off permanently, doing so temporarily can help you appreciate the performance gained by the NT system cache. In addition, it is also useful to turn this value off when conducting server-benchmarking tests, because local caching at the workstations can interfere with the test results.

Value Name:	`MaxCmds`
Default:	15
Type:	`REG_DWORD`
Value Range:	0 to 255

The Registry parameter for MaxCmds can be increased to improve performance by increasing the maximum number of work buffers Redirector can allocate. Higher values should increase your network throughput. The more operations an application performs, the more important it is to increase this value.

Value Name: KeepConn
Default: 600
Type: REG_DWORD
Value Range: 1 to 65,535 seconds

KeepConn controls the length of time that a connection to another system can remain dormant. This parameter does for the Redirector what the Disc parameter does for Server in the \LanmanServer\Parameters subkey by reducing disconnect/reconnect delays between client and server.

Increase the default value to decrease the number of reconnections made to a server.

Value Name: LockQuota
Default: 4,096 (bytes)
Type: REG_DWORD
Value Range: Bytes of data

This is a read optimization parameter which sets the maximum amount of data read for each file provided that the UseLockReadUnlock (which is enabled by default) is set to "on." You can try to increase the value if the network application you use performs many simultaneous lock-and-read type operations. Lock-and-read operations are defined as any file operation that is performed with a lock operation immediately followed by reading the contents of data that was locked. Be conservative at first with this; if you see no meaningful result it is because the type of file read operations your network application performs does not benefit from changes to this parameter.

Value Name: UtilizeNtCaching
Default: 1 (True)
Type: REG_DWORD
Value Range: 0 or 1 (False or True)

This parameter indicates whether the Redirector uses the cache manager to cache the contents of files. Disable this value entry only to guarantee that all data is flushed to the server immediately after it is written by the application.

Comparing and optimizing NT's transport protocols

Keep your transport protocols to a minimum. Too many protocols will make life difficult by requiring frequent troubleshooting and maintenance. Additionally, every transport protocol has its own browse lists and Master Browser so there is additional work for servers to perform to keep each of the frequently duplicated browse lists current.

TCP/IP has become the single most important protocol available to the industry, having both comparable speed to IPX/SPX with reduced broadcasting (mostly caused by name resolutions) and routability. NetBEUI is the lowest in overhead and still the fastest protocol for NT on small networks.

The protocol you choose has much to do with what you are intending to do. You can isolate a network using multiprotocol routing from say TCP/IP to IPX/SPX and keep your network secure or build a network with a single simple nonroutable protocol like NetBEUI. NetBEUI is on its way out with NT 5.0; TCP/IP is fast becoming the standard protocol by which all others are judged. IPX/SPX is slightly more compact than TCP/IP but no longer has any performance advantages and lacks the distinction of being the most open and ubiquitous protocol.

TCP/IP features

TCP/IP stands for Transmission Control Protocol/Internet Protocol. It contains a suite of software and diagnostic tools that are common to most UNIX systems as well as other TCP/IP supporting operating systems. TCP/IP was designed during the cold war as a protocol meant to survive bombs dropping on part of its network paths, and so has a lot of provision for bad or lost connections. The TCP portion always tests the link, and so starts with slower performance until it is sure that the "coast is clear" and that data is arriving safely at the other end. The User Datagram Protocol (UDP), on the other hand, is a low overhead, high-level, "best attempt" protocol that does not guarantee delivery at all.

TCP/IP protocol includes such advantages as:

- Open connectivity across hardware platforms and operating systems
- Access to the Internet, intranet, Extranet, and networking equipment such as network printers and routers
- Support for routing
- Support for SNMP (Simple Network Management Protocol)

From a configuration standpoint, TCP/IP can get complex, because it requires you to learn the arcane IPv4 32-bit addressing scheme. The new IPv6 which NT 5.0 is slated to support (if the specification is finished by the time it ships) will provide for 128-bit IP addressing, allowing something like 1 quadrillion devices to connect to the Internet through about 1 trillion networks. However, until IPv6 comes out, the current implementation of TCP/IP (IPv4) remains the standard method of connecting to the Internet. Figure 9-9 shows Windows NT's TCP/IP address configuration dialog, available by choosing the Properties for the TCP/IP protocol in the Network Control Panel's Protocols tab.

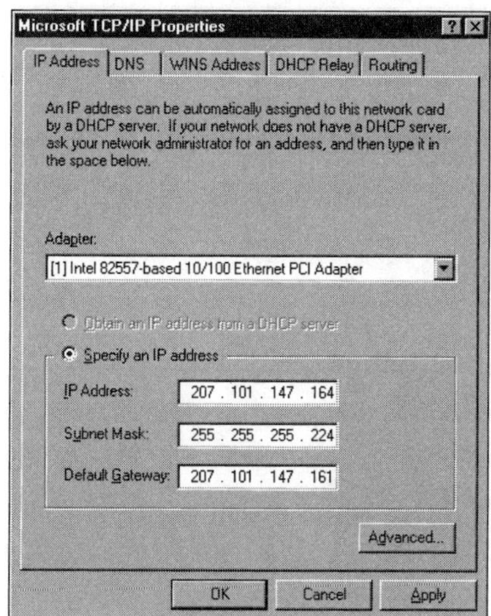

Figure 9-9: Configuring the TCP/IP protocol via the Network Control Panel.

When using TCP/IP on your network, you must provide both an explicit IP address and subnetwork, or point the workstation to a DHCP server where both can be automatically provided and "leased" by a DHCP server. You also need to fill in the default gateway address if you are configuring TCP/IP on multisegment network (however, this, too, can be provided automatically by a DHCP server if automatic addressing is configured).The default gateway specifies for routers that maintain routing tables which direction the datagram should take to reach its destination. Without the default gateway filled in, routing from that machine will limit destinations to inside the local network. The scope ID is designed to let NetBIOS know how to separate traffic. The scope ID is a character string that is added to the end of the NetBIOS name. For machines on the same network to communicate, they must have the same scope ID. NT uses a null string by default. Certain UNIX flavors will use different strings.

Table 9-1 provides a description of the three classes of IP addresses and their associated default subnetwork masks.

TABLE 9-1 IP ADDRESS CLASSES AND THEIR DEFAULT SUBNETWORK MASKS

Address	Class	Default Subnetwork Mask
Class	A	255.0.0.0
Class	B	255.255.0.0
Class	C	255.255.255.0

TCP/IP performance tweaks

TCP/IP has a lot of features which ensure delivery of packets and reassembly of packets that had to be fragmented by a noncompatible MTU size by a router. An example of transport protocol optimizations for TCP/IP would include changing the MTU size, the window size, and setting error control to assume that the network is solid and error-free (after you have established this is true). Increasing the size of the TCP/IP forwarding buffers helps routing performance. Other ways of improving TCP/IP performance in a Windows environment deals with the mapping of NetBIOS names to IP addresses and that of host names to an IP address as with DNS. You can also configure the system to use an LMHOSTS file that is centrally located on a server and automatically downloaded as a backup to the name servers. This improves performance (because the files are stored locally) as well as ensuring that a failure in a name server won't keep your client systems from attaching to network shares.

The following is a summary of the primary modifications that can have the most pronounced impact on TCP/IP performance in most network environments:

- Maximize window size (Defines the number of packets which can be sent without an ACK [acknowledgment]. Generally the higher the value, the better the performance.)
- Maximize MTU (Specifies the Maximum Transmission Unit. Use the largest size your underlying network can support. Ethernet uses a default of 1,500 bytes.)
- Don't allow fragmentation (This may include making sure all your routers are set with the same permitted MTU sizes.)

- Set TCP/IP to attempt to retransmit with the "don't fragment" bit set if it comes across a "black hole" router that does not respond with its MTU size.
- Buffer packets appropriately to the medium involved (slower links demand smaller buffers).
- Ensure SYN attacks cannot tie up resources.

There are also modifications to TCP/IP that occurred as of Windows NT Service Pack 2 which prevent SYN attacks from tying up resources on your server when transmitted from a malicious source with a spoofed IP address. SYN attacks are attacks that begin like any other TCP communication, with the computer sending a TCP connection request (SYN) to initiate communication with a target machine. The IP source address is "spoofed" (using an IP address that is already assigned or using an address that is not in use on the Internet). The difference between a SYN attack and a normal connection request is the sheer number of requests made. The sending computer will attempt to send as many SYN requests as it can to tie up as many resources at the target computer as possible. Information on reducing the affect of these attacks is given in the following sections.

TCP/IP nodes in Windows NT are configured through the NetBT (NetBIOS over TCP/IP) section of the Registry rather than the TCP/IP Registry subkey. This subkey may be found in the following Registry location:

```
HKEY_LOCAL_MACHINE\System\CurrentControlSet\Services\NetBt\Parameters
```

To enable LMHOSTS usage (especially useful for decreasing WAN traffic) you must first set this option in the TCP/IP Properties dialog of the Network Control Panel's Protocols tab. This checkbox setting in turn changes the following Registry value:

Value Name:	`EnableLMHOSTS`
Default:	0 (False)
Type:	`REG_DWORD`
Value Range:	0 or 1 (False or True)

In Figure 9-10, you can see that the WINS Address tab of the TCP/IP properties allows you to enable LMHOSTS and DNS-based name resolution, as well as giving you a button to search for the appropriate LMHOSTS file on a network share.

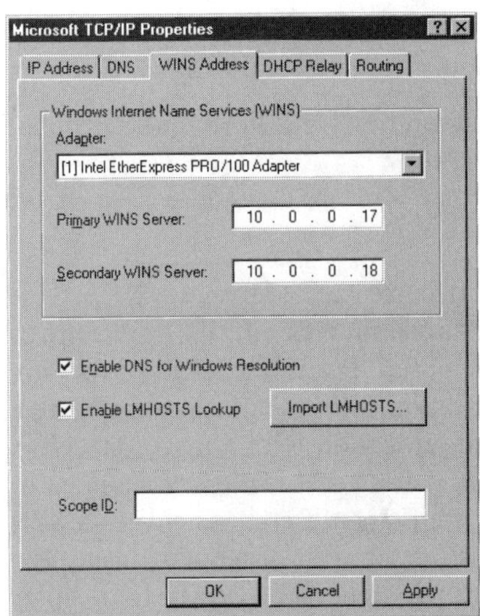

Figure 9-10: Enabling the LMHOSTS lookup option in the TCP/IP Properties dialog.

TCP/IP can be configured to use four different methods for resolving IP addresses to NetBIOS computer names. Some of these methods involve broadcast-based resolution and some involve point-to-point name registration/resolution with a WINS server. Still others use a mix of methods in a priority order. The thing to remember is that you want to avoid broadcasts at all costs, because this unnecessarily wastes network bandwidth. Even if you use WINS for point-to-point (non-broadcast-based) name resolution, you may want to consider using a centralized LMHOSTS file as a local backup should WINS fail. This is because systems will always check LMHOSTS first prior to using broadcasting to resolve names. If you keep an up-to-date, centralized copy of an LMHOSTS file containing the IP addresses and names of all of your network servers, this will reduce network traffic in the event of a WINS service failure.

You can also specify the WINS node type that you would like to use explicitly provided you also install and enable the services which are required to provide a particular node type. The node types are given below, along with the Registry value that controls the WINS node setting:

Value Name:	`NodeType`
Default:	1 or 8 depending upon the WINS server configuration
Type:	`REG_DWORD`
Value Range:	1 (B-node), 2 (P-node), 4 (M-node), or 8 (H-node)

This parameter sets the method NetBT uses to register and resolve NetBIOS names in the presence of an LMHOSTS file or if DNS resolution is enabled, NetBT will also use these methods. If there is no NodeType, DhcpNodeType, or WINS server entries, then NetBT will use the default node type of 1 (B-node). The default is 8 (H-node) if at least 1 WINS server is configured.

- *B-node:* Broadcasts are used for name registration and name resolution, but the workstation first checks the LMHOSTS cache which, if found, returns. If the first method fails, the workstation will attempt broadcasting to resolve the NetBIOS name which, if found, returns. If all other methods fail, then the workstation will check the local LMHOSTS file in the `\%SYSTEMROOT%\SYSTEM32\DRIVERS\` directory.
- *P-node:* Broadcasts are not used for name registration or name resolution. The workstation will instead register with a NetBIOS Name Server at start-up. It is the name server that is responsible for mapping NetBIOS computer names to IP addresses ensuring there are no duplicate names on the network. All workstations must have the address to the NetBIOS name server or name resolution will not work.
- *M-node:* M stands for "mixed" node type, which uses a combination of B-node and P-node to resolve NetBIOS names. M-node uses B-node first, followed by P-node, which should theoretically improve network performance and reduce traffic.
- *H-node:* Like M-node, H-node uses both B-node and P-node for resolution. The difference is it only uses B-node broadcasting as the very last resort. The workstation will always try to resolve using P-node first before resorting to B-node, and only then if P-node fails. H-node allows a system to be configured to utilize the LMHOSTS file even after a P-node resolution query fails and before a B-node resolution is attempted. The H-node type does not require successful P-node NetBIOS name registration for the workstation to initialize though the workstation will use B-node broadcasts only until a P-node resolution succeeds.

For a view of the contents of a centralized LMHOSTS file and appropriate syntax, see Figure 9-11. To allow the use of the centralized LMHOSTS file as a fast backup to the nameservers, you must specify the location of the file through the NullSessionShares parameter found in the key:

```
HKEY_LOCAL_MACHINE\SYSTEM\CurrentControlSet\Services\LanManServer\
  Parameters
```

```
lmhosts - Notepad
File Edit Search Help
#GATEWAY  #routes to ISP, NEOSOFT through ISDN 2xB 64k
206.109.7.98      KIPLING

#USERS

10.0.0.1          TI600
10.0.0.2          P5-100-4
10.0.0.3          P5-100-1
10.0.0.4          P5-100-2
10.0.0.5          P5-100-3
10.0.0.6          P6-200-1
10.0.0.7          P5-100-2
10.0.0.8          P5-100-5
10.0.0.9          P6-200-2
10.0.0.10         P5-100-6
10.0.0.11         P5-100-7
10.0.0.12         P5-100-8
10.0.0.13         INSUS

10.0.0.16              EINSTEIN       #PRE    #DOM:LN1   #COMMSERV and BDC
10.0.0.17              HAWKING        #PRE    #DOM:LN1   #PDC
```

Figure 9-11: Centralized LMHOSTS file format.

Append to the end of the existing NullShares the directory path to the LMHOSTS file. This allows the changes you make to the centralized file to be used by all workstations once they have been configured to import the LMHOSTS file from within TCP/IP setup.

Speeding up NetBT

TCP/IP is implemented in Windows NT as TCP/IP over the NetBIOS API (aka NetBT or NetBIOS over TCP/IP). As a result, the Registry parameters for TCP/IP are not all in one place. To get the most out of this protocol, you can increase the amount of memory resources allocated and change its error-checking behavior. Though the names of the following Registry modifications differ, as does their affect on NetBT performance, the resource involved here is always memory. Be sparing when increasing values; part of optimizing is providing the amount of memory for a component that is actually useful, not excessive. Monitor the effect your changes have on network performance using the provided Performance Monitor counters and keep an eye on memory usage.

MAXIMIZING DATAGRAM BUFFERING

If you find in the Registry that the output queue from the Network Interface object in Performance Monitor is sustaining at close to 2, you may wish to increase this value in order to improve the performance for the queued commands.

Value Name: `MaxDgramBuffering`
Default: 0x20000 (128K)
Type: `REG_DWORD`
Value Range: 0 to 0xFFFFFFFF bytes

This parameter specifies the maximum amount of memory that NetBT can dynamically allocate for all queued datagrams waiting to be sent. If this limit is reached, transmissions will fail due to lack of memory resources. Because this is not a fixed buffer and is dynamically used up to its maximum size, large values will not hurt available memory if these resources are not required by NetBT to transmit.

INCREASING CONNECTION BLOCK INCREMENT

You can increase the number of Connection Blocks created for users at one time in order to improve the speed with which a large number of users can connect to the server.

Value Name:	`BacklogIncrement`
Default:	3
Type:	`REG_DWORD`
Value Range:	1 to 20

This determines the increment of connection blocks that is added each time that the server must create new connection blocks. This is only valid on NT 4.0 Service Pack 2 systems and later. NetBt has been revised as of Service Pack 2 to automatically allocate additional connection blocks to reduce connection setup time. Whenever a connection occurs, if the available number of connection blocks is two or less, NT will create the number of new connection blocks specified by BacklogIncrement.

The NetBT used in NT 3.51 and 4.0 (pre-Service Pack 2) also maintains a backlog of available connection blocks. This number of blocks available is equal to two plus the incremental number that depends on the number of NetBT-dependent services, such as server, Redirector, and NetBIOS applications. Most of the time, the increment for new connection blocks is 7 to 11. Setting this value too high wastes resources, but will increase the speed at which connections are made available when they are requested.

SETTING MAXIMUM CONNECTION BLOCKS

If you are experiencing memory shortages for certain applications or services, you may need to reduce this value to conserve memory.

Value Name:	`MaxConnBackLog`
Default:	0x3E8 (1000 decimal)
Type:	`REG_DWORD`
Value Range:	0x1 to 0x9C40 (1 to 40,000 decimal)

This parameter defines the total number of connection blocks that NetBT may allocate. Every block connection block requires about 78 bytes of memory. These connection blocks are reused when the SYN-ACK timer expires and TCP fails to make a connection.

RANDOMIZING NIC USAGE ON MULTIHOMED SYSTEMS

Value Name: `RandomAdapter`
Type: `REG_DWORD`
Default: 0 (False)
Value Range: 0 or 1 (False or True)

This parameter allows NetBT to randomly select the IP address to apply to a name query response from any of its bound interfaces. The response will typically contain the address of the interface on which the name query was received. This is a feature to balance the load between two or more server interface cards that are connected to the same network.

The RandomAdapter parameter was designed to optimize the performance of the NetBT protocol on a multihomed computer (one with more than one network interface). This parameter is ignored unless you also specify SingleResponse value as 1 (true).

SINGLERESPONSE, A COMPANION TO RANDOMADAPTER

Value Name: `SingleResponse`
Default: 0 (False)
Type: `REG_DWORD`
Value Range: 0 or 1 (False or True)

This parameter specifies for a nonzero value that NetBT only supply a single IP address from one of its available interfaces in response to name queries. Its default value sends the IP address of all the interfaces bound to NetBT. The RandomAdapter parameter requires that you set this parameter to 1. The computer must be multihomed for this parameter to have any effect.

Other TCP/IP performance tweaks

The Registry location for TCP/IP parameters is:

```
HKEY_LOCAL_MACHINE\System\CurrentControlSet\Services\Tcpip\Parameters
```

DHCP may have configured many of the TCP/IP settings for you if it was available. A system reboot is required after every change to the TCP/IP parameters.

MAXIMIZING THE TCP WINDOW SIZE

As described in the opening text for optimizing the TCP/IP protocol, this modification is high on the list for improving the performance of the NT TCP/IP stack. Because this reduces protocol overhead by eliminating part of the safety net and shaving some of the time involved in the turnaround of an ACK, you must be sure that you only perform this on solid networks. Don't adjust this setting upward unless you have tested the network rigorously and are sure that it is error-free.

Value Name:	`TcpWindowSize`
Default:	The smaller of 0xFFFF or larger than four times the maximum TCP data size or 8,192 rounded up to an even multiple of the TCP data size (default size is 8,760 for Ethernet)
Type:	`REG_DWORD`
Valid Range:	0 to 0xFFFF (in bytes)

This parameter will determine the maximum size of the TCP receive window size. This specifies the number of bytes that a sending computer can transmit without receiving an ACK. This is a time saving feature that improves performance over known good links. If you have either very high bandwidth (100MB or higher) or very high latency (analog modem lines controlled by RAS), you should consider increasing this value as specified. To attain the highest performance, set the receive window to an even multiple of the TCP Maximum Segment Size (MSS).

PROTECTING YOURSELF FROM SYN (DENIAL-OF-SERVICE) ATTACKS

Though not a direct performance modification per se, there are certain security measures that can be beneficial in that they protect against certain types of performance-crippling Denial-of-Service (DoS) attacks. One such attack is called a SYN flooding attack, whereby a system is overrun with fake TCP-based connection attempts from a "spoofed," or fake, IP address. SYN attacks can quickly turn your system into a slug unless you install the latest Windows NT Service Pack and ensure the proper setting of the following Registry value:

Value Name:	`TcpMaxConnectResponseRetransmissions`
Default:	3
Type:	`REG_DWORD`
Value Range:	0, 1, 2, 3

This value and its data set the number of times the system should respond to a TCP connection request (SYN-ACK) before it is retransmitted. This value entry is implemented in TCPIP.SYS for Windows NT 4.0 Service Pack 2 and later. The parameter is designed to prevent SYN flooding of an NT system which will bog down the network connection. As mentioned earlier, SYN flooding is a condition in which many TCP connection requests are made which contain spoofed IP addresses. The problem results because the system will try to send acknowledgments to an IP which does not exist. This causes numerous retries to the fake address, with each retry requiring twice as much time as the last.

Every time a computer running TCP/IP receives a connection request, it will allocate memory resources to manage the new connection. The target computer will then respond to the request with a SYN-ACK (request acknowledgment). Because the computer which is sending these malicious SYN requests is using a spoofed IP address, the target of the attack is not able to respond and will continue to retry the SYN-ACK until it finally times out the connection (keep in mind a very large number of these is occurring at once).

The default value for retransmission of the SYN-ACK packet for NT 3.51 and NT 4.0 is five times. The initial timeout value for the first retransmission is three seconds; this doubles every time the retransmission fails (which, with a spoofed IP address, will never succeed). This means that for every SYN connection request received there will be a retry every 3, 6, 12, 24, and 48 seconds. After the last retransmission, a full 96 seconds must pass before the target of the SYN attack finally gives up on the transmission with the computer that issued a spoofed IP address. In this time period, the resources that were set up during the initial SYN connection request have been tied up. After this time period expires, the resources are deallocated. The total amount of time that has passed from the initial request until the final timeout is 189 seconds. While this is happening for each of the many SYN connection requests that were issued by the attacking computer, the target computer's performance slows to a crawl and legitimate connection requests cannot be serviced efficiently, if at all. Table 9-2 shows the length of time that resources are tied up by a malevolent SYN attack for the default retry count and duration.

TABLE 9-2 TCPMAXCONNECTRESPONSERETRANSMISSIONS VALUES AND POTENTIAL EFFECTS OF A SYN-ACK ATTACKS ON EACH

Value	SYN-ACK Retransmission Times	Elapsed Time	Result
0	No SYN-ACKs are retransmitted.	0	*All will timeout in 3 seconds. This value might cause legitimate connection attempts from distant clients to fail.*
1	3 seconds	9 seconds	*Cleans up 6 seconds after last retransmission.*
2	3 and 6 seconds	21 seconds	*Cleans up 12 seconds after last retransmission.*
3	3, 6, and 12 seconds	45 seconds	*Cleans up 24 seconds after last retransmission.*

To determine if a particular system is the subject of a SYN attack, you can use this command to view the number of half-open (`SYN_RECEIVED`) connection requests.

```
netstat -n -p tcp
```

You may see something like the following if the system is being attacked:

```
Active Connections
Proto  Local Address Foreign Address      State
TCP 127.0.0.1:1026   127.0.0.1:1028       ESTABLISHED
TCP 127.0.0.1:1028   127.0.0.1:1026       ESTABLISHED
TCP 206.109.7.65:21  207.68.156.16:1256 SYN_RECEIVED
TCP 206.109.7.65:21 207.68.156.16:1257 SYN_RECEIVED
TCP 206.109.7.65:21 207.68.156.16:1258 SYN_RECEIVED
TCP 206.109.7.65:21 207.68.156.16:1259 SYN_RECEIVED
TCP 206.109.7.65:21 207.68.156.16:1260 SYN_RECEIVED
TCP 206.109.7.65:21 207.68.156.16:1261 SYN_RECEIVED
TCP 206.109.7.65:21 207.68.156.16:1262 SYN_RECEIVED
TCP 206.109.7.65:21 207.68.156.16:1263 SYN_RECEIVED
TCP 206.109.7.65:21 207.68.156.16:1264 SYN_RECEIVED
TCP 206.109.7.65:21 207.68.156.16:1265 SYN_RECEIVED
TCP 206.109.7.65:21 207.68.156.16:1266 SYN_RECEIVED
TCP 206.109.7.65:4803 207.68.156.81:139 TIME_WAIT
```

INCREASING FORWARD BUFFER MEMORY FOR IP ROUTERS

If you are implementing NT with software IP routing and multiple NICs to break up your network, this modification can give your router a boost.

Value Name:	`ForwardBufferMemory`
Type:	`REG_DWORD`
Range:	Number of Bytes
Default:	74,240 (enough for fifty 1,480-byte packets, rounded to a multiple of 256)

This parameter determines the amount of memory that IP can allocate to store packet data in the router's packet queue. When this amount is reached, the router will randomly discard packets from the queue. Packet queue data buffers are 256 bytes in length, so all increments must be made in multiples of 256. When larger packets are sent, multiple buffers are chained together. IP headers are stored separately. If there is no buffer memory specified or routing is not enabled, the parameter is ignored.

SETTING THE MAXIMUM FORWARD BUFFER MEMORY

This parameter complements the previous parameter, and like ForwardBuffer Memory, larger values may improve IP routing through NT.

Value Name:	`MaxForwardBufferMemory`
Default:	0xFFFFFFFF
Type:	`REG_DWORD`
Range:	Number of Bytes (Network MTU – 0xFFFFFFFF)

MaxForwardBufferMemory specifies the maximum number of memory bytes that IP can use to allocate as a packet data store in the router packet queue. The value specified must be at or above the ForwardBufferMemory.

SETTING THE MAXIMUM NUMBER OF FORWARDING PACKETS

Because packet data and headers are stored separately by the NT IP or IPX router, you may need to increase the size of the memory store for packet headers to improve routing through NT software routing.

Value Name:	`MaxNumForwardPackets`
Type:	`REG_DWORD`
Default:	0xFFFFFFFF
Value Range:	Packet headers (1 to 0xFFFFFFFF)

This specifies the maximum number of IP packet headers (which are stored separately from the packets themselves) that may be allocated for use by the router packet queue. The value specified must be greater than or equal to the NumForwardPackets value.

USING DNS TO SPEED INTERNET NAME TO IP RESOLUTION

NT includes support for DNS servers by providing a dynamic DNS server that works with WINS as well as supporting standard DNS from external networks or non-NT machines. Having a DNS server can improve the startup time of Exchange clients and other network-connected client systems. To use DNS, you need to enable DNS resolution from within the TCP/IP configuration. You have to specify the IP addresses of the DNS primary and secondary servers for this option to take effect. DNS requires that you set the information for enabling the resolution method and the actual IP addresses of the DNS servers in two separate locations. To enable DNS, you must return to the NetBT key where you made other modifications.

```
HKEY_LOCAL_MACHINE\SYSTEM\CurrentControlSet\Services\NetBT\Parameters
```

Value Name:	`EnableDNS`
Default:	0 (False)
Type:	`REG_DWORD`
Value Range:	0 or 1 (False or True)

Once you have set the EnableDNS bit to on, go to the TCP/IP key and set the IP addresses for the DNS servers; these are under:

```
HKEY_LOCAL_MACHINE\SYSTEM\CurrentControlSet\Services\Tcpip\Parameters
```

The order in which the values are added, from left to right, governs the search order. IP addresses for the DNS servers are separated by spaces.

Value Name:	`NameServer`
Default:	None
Type:	`REG_SZ`
Value Range:	Any primary and secondary DNS server you want queried

Adapter-specific TCP/IP entries

The following are adapter-specific TCP/IP-related Registry options, all of which are located in the following Registry subkey:

```
HKEY_LOCAL_MACHINE\System\CurrentControlSet\Services\adapter
 name#\Parameters\Tcpip
```

SETTING THE MAXIMUM PACKET QUEUE SIZE

This is another parameter for boosting performance for an NT system setup for IP routing.

Value Name:	`MaxForwardPending`
Default:	20
Type:	`REG_DWORD`
Value Range:	Packets (1 to 0xFFFFFFFF)

This parameter sets the maximum number of packets the IP forwarding engine can send to a specific network interface at one time. Any additional IP packets are queued until they can be forwarded. On slow links, such as multiplexed RAS serial lines, larger values may improve performance. The speed and the number of connections determine the amount of increase, though the default setting will work most of the time.

TWEAKING THE SIZE OF THE MTU TO THE MAXIMUM SUPPORTED VALUE

This is another tweak high on the list for boosting TCP/IP performance, though it is used more often to reduce the MTU size for slow WAN devices such as modems and ISDN terminal adapters.

Value Name:	MTU
Type:	`REG_DWORD`
Default:	0xFFFFFFFF
Value Range:	From 68 to the MTU of the underlying network in bytes

This parameter sets the MTU (Maximum Transmission Unit) which is the maximum packet size that the transport will transmit across the network. The size of the MTU includes the size of the header.

Because this is an adapter-specific setting, each network interface can have its own explicitly set MTU. It is usually not necessary to change this setting because the MTU is negotiated with the lower level drivers that communicate with the NIC. This autonegotiation is overridden when this parameter is specified. If you set this parameter too high, the MTU will be set to that of the network's default size. If the value is less than 68 bytes, then the MTU will automatically be set at 68 bytes. Remember that an IP datagram can span multiple packets.

What you are trying to achieve is the ideal of a one-to-one relationship whereby each datagram is contained within a single packet. This is the most efficient method for transferring data across the network. The network technology in use will be the governing factor in just what size can be used. For example, Ethernet uses up to a 1,500-byte packet, FDDI uses over an 8,000-byte packet. If the datagram is larger than the MTU packet size, then the datagram is automatically broken into fragments with a size the multiple of eight. Reassembly of fragmented datagrams takes time, as the fragments travel separately and must be reordered; lost fragments require the entire datagram to be resent.

NT uses PMTUD (Path Maximum Transmission Unit Discovery) which automatically queries the NIC miniport driver for the maximum MTU size. Because most interoperable components use standardized MTU sizes, it may not be necessary to change this setting unless you are dealing with a situation in which you want to ensure the largest possible size or reduce the size for slow WAN link applications.

NetBEUI features

Unlike TCP/IP, NetBEUI can't use a name server for address resolution, instead relying on the use of broadcasts to resolve NetBIOS names to MAC (Media Access Control) physical addresses. Though it is small, fast, and low in overhead, it lacks the routability, configuration options, and global acceptance of TCP/IP, and to a lesser extent IPX/SPX. As a result, its use is best limited to small, non-routed LANs (under 200 PCs) requiring the fastest access possible. However, even in these environments, TCP/IP may still be the best choice, especially if Internet connectivity is required and you wish to streamline the number of protocols used on the network.

Most of the optimization of NetBEUI is accomplished automatically via NT's preallocation of resources for the transport. The transport is also capable of dynamically and automatically increasing these values, but it takes a little more time than if you were to establish them yourself manually via the Registry. The speed you gain by this is somewhat negligible, though if many connections to the system occur concurrently the preallocated resources for NBF may make those alterations worthwhile.

NetBEUI is designed and optimized for small LANs. It is the fastest protocol you can use with NT but has no routing support and is broadcast heavy. It is also said by Microsoft to be completely self-tuning with good error control and a very small memory footprint.

Most of the important values in NBF are set to a value of zero, a good indicator in NT regspeak of an autotuned parameter. Self-tuning claims not withstanding, here are some ways to tweak NetBEUI to the utmost.

The Registry location for NetBEUI parameters is:

```
HKEY_LOCAL_MACHINE\System\CurrentControlSet\Services\Nbf
```

INCREASING INITIAL CONNECTION COUNT

The preallocation of resources for connections will improve the rate at which new connections can be made, but will not affect the performance of the actual transfers using NBF.

Value Name:	`InitConnections`
Default:	1
Type:	`REG_DWORD`
Value Range:	1 or higher; 0 = no limit

This parameter defines the initial number of connections (NetBIOS sessions) to allocate. Set this value if you know that many connections are needed. This value automatically increases as new connections are required.

INCREASING INITIAL LINK COUNT

Value Name:	`InitLinks`
Default:	2
Type:	`REG_DWORD`
Value Range:	1 or higher; 0 = no limit

This parameter sets the initial number of LLC links to preallocate. As a matter of course, you have one connection per LLC link to another NIC, because the Redirector service aggregates all links to a workstation into a single connection. This number may be higher if several systems are communicating or NetBIOS programs are running. Preallocate links if you know several will be required, otherwise they will be automatically increased as needed.

INCREASING INITIAL PACKET COUNT

Value Name:	`InitPackets`
Default:	30
Type:	`REG_DWORD`
Value Range:	1 or higher; 0 = no limit

This parameter sets the number of initial number of transport packets that are preallocated when the system starts and is the minimum number of packets maintained during operation. NBF uses these packets to send data about connections to a workstation. This parameter automatically increases as needed, but if you know that many transport packets will be required you can increase the value. This is the value to change if you receive "send packets exhausted" messages or if you experience unusually high value results monitoring the NetBEUI object Times Exhausted counter.

INCREASING INITIAL RECEIVE BUFFERS

Value Name: `InitReceiveBuffers`
Default: 5
Type: `REG_DWORD`
Value Range: 1 or higher; 0 = no limit

Specifies the number of initial receive buffers to allocate. Receive buffers are used by NBF when it calls NDIS TransferData for received datagrams. Usually, this value is allocated as needed, but you can use this value entry to preallocate memory if you know a large number of datagram frames will be received.

INCREASING INITIAL RECEIVE PACKETS

Value Name: `InitReceivePackets`
Default: 10
Type: `REG_DWORD`
Value Range: 1 or higher; 0 = no limit

This parameter sets the initial number of transport packets that are allocated when the system starts and also the minimum number of transport packets maintained (and not freed) during the system's operation. This parameter is used by NBF to request data from the NDIS driver. The value is automatically adjusted as needed, but preallocation of the resources can improve performance if the amount of user data is very small or very large. Adjustment of this parameter is indicated by many "receive packets exhausted" messages or the presentation of unusually high values for the Performance Monitor NetBEUI object Times Exhausted counter.

INCREASING INITIAL REQUESTS

Value Name: `InitRequests`
Default: 5
Type: `REG_DWORD`
Value Range: 1 or higher; 0 = no limit

This parameter sets the initial requests to improve performance if a large number of requests occur simultaneously. InitRequests are used by in-progress connect requests, remote NIC status requests, name queries, and other network request types. Set this parameter to a higher value if you are expecting a large number of these types of requests. The requests are increased as needed automatically by the system, though preallocation of requests can boost performance if the number of requests in a short time period is very large.

NWLink features

NWLink is an IPX/SPX protocol stack designed for interoperability with Novell Netware. This protocol can be used with or without a Novell server on the network. NWLink is used in conjunction with a Netware-specific redirector like Client Services for NetWare (CSNW) or the Novell equivalent thereof. To gain NT's network functionality, you must run IPX/SPX over NetBIOS because so much of the NT network architecture is dependent on this API.

NWLINKIPX PARAMETERS

The Registry location for NWLink is in three parts. IPX parameters are in:

```
HKEY_LOCAL_MACHINE\System\CurrentControlSet\Services\NwLnkIpx\
  Parameters
```

SETTING SYSTEM TO DEDICATED IPX ROUTER

Value Name:	`DedicatedRouter`
Default:	0 (False)
Type:	`REG_DWORD`
Value Range:	0 or 1 (False or True)

This sets the system to perform dedicated IPX routing and assumes that there are no additional services running on it. The performance for this setup is surprisingly high, though spending almost $1,000 on a software router using Windows NT for this one single function is probably a bit wasteful.

DISABLING THE NETBIOS LAYER FOR DIAL-IN USERS

If you want to lose some overhead, dumping NetBIOS when the packets are destined for a non-Windows computer can spare you some bandwidth.

Value Name:	`DisableDialinNetbios`
Default:	1
Type:	`REG_DWORD`
Value Range:	0 to 3

This parameter specifies if the forwarding of IPX type-20 (NetBIOS session layer) packets between remote RAS clients, the LAN, and the RAS server is enabled or disabled. This parameter only exerts control over dial-in on RAS servers. Table 9-3 provides details on support of the different packet types.

TABLE 9-3 BROADCAST IPX PACKETS OVER LOCAL AREA AND REMOTE NETWORK LINKS

0	IPX type-20 packets will broadcast from the RAS server to remote clients, from the remote clients to the RAS server, and then through the IPX router for broadcast on the LAN (if the router is configured to forward IPX NetBIOS packets).
1	IPX type-20 packets will broadcast only from remote clients to the internal net and to the RAS IPX router. This setting disables broadcasts from the internal net to the remote clients. This is the default.
2	IPX type-20 packets will broadcast from the internal net to the remote clients.
3	All IPX type-20 broadcasts are disabled.

DISABLING USE OF SAP ADVERTISEMENT FOR DIAL-OUT USERS

For even more reduction in overhead, you can eliminate broadcast-ridden SAP advertisement over your slow WAN connections with this parameter.

Value Name: `DisableDialoutSap`
Default: 0 (False)
Type: `REG_DWORD`
Value Range: 0 or 1 (False or True)

The parameter specifies for a nonzero value that all SAP announcements and responses on slow dial-out connections be disabled. This greatly reduces the potential costs and reduced performance from router-to-router SAP communications. It also allows GSNW or CSNW configured on the system to discover servers over the WAN.

INCREASING INITIAL DATAGRAM COUNT

Value Name: `InitDatagrams`
Default: 10
Type: `REG_DWORD`
Value Range: 1 to 65,535

This parameter specifies the number of datagrams that are initially allocated by IPX. See also MaxDatagrams. Higher values tend to boost performance by preallocating resources for the stack.

INCREASING MAXIMUM DATAGRAM COUNT

Value Name:	`MaxDatagrams`
Default:	50
Type:	`REG_DWORD`
Value Range:	1 to 65,535

This defines the maximum datagram count that IPX is able to allocate. Also see InitDatagrams. This sets the upper range for the number of IPX datagrams that can be transmitted at once.

SETTING IPX TO COMMUNICATE WITH ONLY THE LAN OR WAN

Value Name:	`SingleNetworkActive`
Default:	0 (False)
Type:	`REG_DWORD`
Range:	0 or 1 (False or True)

This parameter specifies for a nonzero value that only the LAN or the WAN connection is allowed to be active on the system at one time. This setting gives the GSNW or CSNW the capability to correctly connect to NetWare servers on the WAN when a connection is made.

Adapter-specific IPX settings

Just like the TCP/IP adapter specific settings, these parameters reflect the specific settings on a per NIC basis. This gives you flexibility if you have different speed networks being connected through an IPX router with two separate interfaces.

```
HKEY_LOCAL_MACHINE\System\CurrentControlSet\Services\NWLinkIPX\
 NetConfig\Driverx
```

SETTING MAXIMUM FRAME SIZE

Value Name:	`MaxPktSize`
Default:	0
Type:	`REG_DWORD`
Value Range:	0 to 65,535

MaxPktSize sets the maximum frame size the NIC is permitted to transmit. When set to zero (default) this information is negotiated with the NIC driver. This allows you to reduce the size of the frame beyond what the NIC driver would allow. This is useful when the frame size is converted from one to the other, as in an Ethernet connecting to an FDDI ring.

NWLink SPX parameters

The other half of the IPX/SPX protocols is the SPX component, which provides dutiful delivery.

The parameters for the SPX portion of NWLink is stored under:

```
HKEY_LOCAL_MACHINE\System\CurrentControlSet\Services\NWLinkSPX\
  Parameters
```

SETTING SPX WINDOW SIZE

Like TCP window size, this allows you to increase the number of good data packets sent before the computer must receive an ACK. Larger values tend to improve performance at the cost of your safety net. Don't slide this value up if you are unsure of the quality of the network interconnects.

Value Name:	`WindowSize`
Default:	4
Type:	`REG_DWORD`
Value Range:	1 to 10 SPX packets

This parameter defines window size to use with SPX packets. The WindowSize parameter assigns the value to use in the SPX allocation field. This parameter can improve performance by reducing the number of ACKs required in proportion to the number of packets sent. However, this should only be increased if the connection is known to be highly reliable.

SETTING INITIAL SPX PACKET COUNT

Value Name:	`InitPackets`
Default:	5
Type:	`REG_DWORD`
Value Range:	1 to 65,535

Specifies the initial number of packets that SPX allocates.

INCREASING MAXIMUM PACKET COUNT

Value Name:	`MaxPackets`
Default:	30
Type:	`REG_DWORD`
Value Range:	1 to 65,535

Specifies the maximum number of packets that SPX will allocate.

INCREASING MAXIMUM PACKET SIZE

Value Name: `MaxPacketSize`
Default: 4096
Type: `REG_DWORD`
Value Range: 1 to 65,535

Specifies the maximum packet size that SPX-2 protocol will use when negotiating for a packet size with the remote network node. SPX-2 will size the packet correctly provided it is smaller than MaxPacketSize.

NWNBLink features and tweaks

Microsoft extended Novell NetBIOS to enhance its performance and gave it the capability of automatically detecting whether the system it is communicating with can use these extensions or not. In the event that the system cannot use the NWNBLink extensions, NWNBLink falls back to the standard NetBIOS used in most NetWare environments. You can gain significant performance over the conventional NetWare NetBIOS if these extensions can be used.

The Registry path for these value entries is:

```
HKEY_LOCAL_MACHINE\System\CurrentControlSet\Services\NWNBLink\
  Parameters
```

SETTING ACKNOWLEDGMENT DELAY PERIOD

Value Name: `AckDelayTime`
Default: 250 (no entry = default)
Type: `REG_DWORD`
Value Range: 50 to 65,535 milliseconds

This parameter sets the value for delayed acknowledgment. Generally, the longer the delay, the less effect ACKs have on network performance.

SETTING ACKNOWLEDGMENT WINDOW SIZE

One more window size entry that allows you to adjust the ratio of data to ACK traffic. Increasing this value can improve performance by allowing more data frames to pass before the ACK is received.

Value Name: `AckWindow`
Default: 2 (no entry = default)
Type: `REG_DWORD`
Value Range: 0 to 65,535 frames

This configures the window size, which specifies the number of frames that can be sent before acknowledgment must be sent. AckWindow entry can be used to improve the performance between a sender that resides on a fast LAN with a receiver connected by a slower link. Forcing acknowledgments allows the sender to keep sending frames continually. In the event that both stations are located on a fast LAN, AckWindow can be set to 0 to disable acknowledgments. NWNBLink can be configured to automatically determine if AckWindow should be used based on the values in the AckWindowThreshold.

SETTING ACKNOWLEDGMENT WINDOW THRESHOLD

Value Name: `AckWindowThreshold`
Default: 500 (no entry = default)
Type: `REG_DWORD`
Value Range: 0 to 65,535 milliseconds

This parameter sets the threshold for turnaround time that specifies when the AckWindow value will be ignored. The round-trip is an estimation based on the amount of time from sending to receiving a frame sent by a workstation. Depending on the length of time this round-trip takes, NWNBLink will determine if and when an acknowledgment is sent. When the AckWindowThreshold parameter is set to 0, NWNBLink will rely solely on the AckWindow parameter value.

ENABLING THE USE OF MS EXTENSIONS

Value Name: `Extensions`
Default: 1 (True; no entry = default)
Type: `REG_DWORD`
Value Range: 0 or 1 (False or True)

This parameter sets NWNBLink to use the extensions described under NWNBLink which improve performance.

SETTING MAXIMUM SIZE OF THE RECEIVE WINDOW

Value Name: `RcvWindowMax`
Default: 4 (no entry = default)
Type: `REG_DWORD`
Value Range: 1 to 49,152 frames

This parameter sets the maximum number of frames the receiver can receive at once. This number is given to the sender to establish the maximum number. Higher values tend to improve performance. Other entries related to RcvWindowMax include AckWindowThreshold, EnablePiggyBackAck, RcvWindowMax, AckDelay Time, and AckWindow.

DLC features

DLC is not a primary protocol and only provides functionality to those applications that have direct access to the data link layer. Direct access with the data link layer prevents the Redirector from establishing communications between machines. The only reason DLC is supported is to allow for access to older HP network printers and other simple device communications falling under the legacy department. If you can use an alternative protocol, which is used by the rest of the network, use it instead and eliminate DLC.

Simple Network Tweaks

Not everything in NT's network configuration is as complex as component level Registry tweaking or peculiar sounding parameters in the NIC driver setup. Simple changes at the graphical level through the Control Panel can make significant improvements in network performance. Changes as easy as modifications to your transport protocol bindings and name to address mapping schemes can be made in minutes (though you must reboot for the changes to take effect).

Configuring network bindings

Bindings control the priority and status (on or off) of transport protocols which communicate through your installed NICs. First decide which transport protocols you really need and disable all other transports. This will reclaim memory resources and slightly reduce processor usage. This is easier and more flexible than removing the protocols completely in the event you should have to reload them. Protocol stacks are prioritized from top to bottom. The higher the protocol, the better the opportunity to attempt to transmit on the network and the faster the response time from that stack. If you are using a network with both NetBEUI and TCP/IP installed, but most of the applications and services you use are based on TCP/IP, set TCP/IP to the top of the bindings list by selecting the protocol under Workstation in the Control Panel/Network/Bindings tab. See Figure 9-12 for a view of the Network configuration applet for configuring bindings.

From within the network binding tab, choose the "Show Bindings for" drop-down box to select all services. Then select a protocol bound to any of the services listed (server and workstation, for example) and move them up or down using the appropriate buttons at the bottom of the dialog box. Move your higher priority protocols to the top of the list and hit OK. You will need to reboot for the changes to take effect (in Windows NT 5.0 and later versions of NT, the reboot step won't be necessary, since network binding will be able to be done "on the fly").

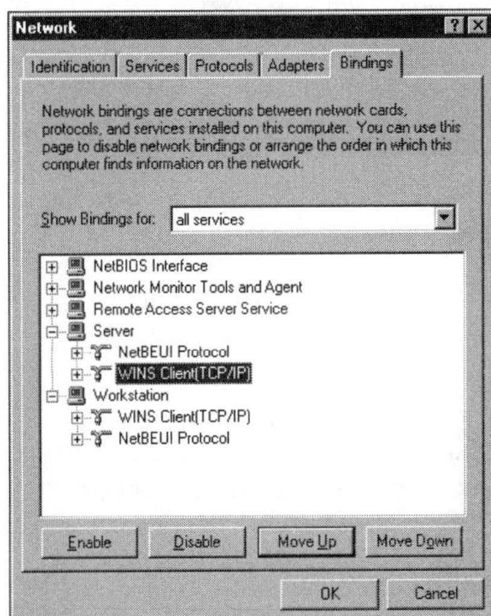

Figure 9-12: The Bindings tab of the Network Control Panel.

Bindings can be enabled and disabled depending on the networking components installed on your system and your intended applications. In this day and age, TCP/IP is fast becoming the standard by which all others are judged, and so if you have several TCP/IP applications, you may wish to move this transport to the top of the bindings list.

The Server service, unlike the other components in the bindings dialog box, is not affected by changes in binding priority. The Server service listens to all installed protocols simultaneously in an equivalent fashion.

Overhead in NT Networking Defined

There are two competing and mutually exclusive objectives existing in every network installation: to provide as many services as possible to make users more productive while somehow managing to remove any excess junk that will slow down the system. Anything that can consume server resources or network bandwidth that doesn't prove its worth is fair game for removal. Once again, we invoke the writ of balance that states that everything has its place so long as it is moderated.

Things that can bog down an NT server or the network itself include such NT housekeeping as:

- PDC/BDC Security Accounts Manager and Local Security Authority (SAM/LSA) domain synchronization
- Extensive and complex trust relationships
- Domain Master Browser and Master Browser synchronization and broadcast announcements
- Printserver browse list announcements
- WINS push/pull partner replication updates (WINS can add system overhead from running on the server, but also helps reduce broadcast resolutions on the wire)
- DHCP lease expiration/allocation (very little overhead)
- SNMP monitoring traffic (especially across a WAN)
- Directory replication at peak hours (if it is enabled at all)
- NT Backup schedulers running at peak times
- Disk defragmenters running at peak network usage times
- Extensive and verbose event logging of system events and services

Reducing the effects of domain synchronization

Domain synchronization is when the Primary Domain Controller (PDC) and Backup Domain Controller (BDC) communicate with each other and exchange all or part of the user database (Security Access Manager and Local Security Authority, or SAM/LSA). Changes that are appended to the database are called partial synchronizations. When a sufficient amount of time has passed, the entire database is sent to each BDC, which can consume a lot of network bandwidth and domain controller resources. The PDC pulses BDCs that it knows are not up-to-date after a set amount of time in order to inform them it is time to synchronize. The BDC then requests any updates and new user information to append to the user database. Avoid frequent full synchronizations that can bring all or parts of your network to a crawl. We are fortunate that there are plenty of tunable parameters in the Registry for controlling synchronization through the Netlogon service, which is responsible for all SAM/LSA synchronization activity.

If the values for the replication governor (the mechanism which sets PDC/BDC updates) are set too high, then the domain will be out of synch and its member servers will have information which is not reflected in the other SAM/LSA databases on the domain. Setting the value too low will cause the bandwidth of the network to be absorbed by SAM/LSA update activity. A full synchronization sends the entire user database from the PDC to all BDCs. The bandwidth consumed by user database updates can completely swamp slow WAN connections (like X.25, ISDN, switched 56K, or even fractional T1 in large domains).

The BDC has a parameter called ReplicationGovernor that defines both the size of the data transferred on each call to the PDC and the frequency of those calls. Adjusting the ReplicationGovernor percentage can make the process more efficient and have less of an impact on the network or servers. The ReplicationGovernor parameter reduces the size of the buffer used on each call from the BDC to the PDC so that a single call for synchronization does not consume too much bandwidth (which as stated could be the entire WAN link). The parameter also causes the Netlogon service to go into an idle state between calls. This reduces network bandwidth consumed and will free both the local network and the link to a remote site for other applications in between calls for synchronization to the PDC.

The ReplicationGovernor value can be configured in the Registry to control the BDC under the following key:

```
HKEY_LOCAL_MACHINE\SYSTEM\CurrentControlSet\Services\Netlogon\
  Parameters
```

CONFIGURING THE BDC FOR REPLICATION FREQUENCY

Value Name:	`ReplicationGovernor`
Default:	100
Type:	`REG_DWORD`
Range:	0 to 100

This value can be set anywhere from 0 to 100. The default is 100 and represents a percentage that defines both the size of the data transferred on each call to the PDC and the frequency of those calls. For example, setting the ReplicationGovernor value to a value of 50 percent will use a 64K buffer rather than the full 128K buffer. In addition, the BDC will only have a synchronization call outstanding on the network a maximum of 50 percent of the time.

Caution must be taken in setting this value because if the ReplicationGovernor is set too low, synchronization may never complete. A value of 0 will cause Netlogon to never synchronize, and the user account database can become completely out of sync.

The ReplicationGovernor value must be set *individually* on each BDC because values from one BDC do not alter the ReplicationGovernor values of another BDC.

It is possible to alter the ReplicationGovernor value via a script, which could change the value for optimal values at different times during the day or week. The script would contain the change and be run through the `REGINI.EXE` file included in the NT Resource Kit as well as the WinAT command (scheduler). The script would need to include the following:

```
net stop netlogon
regini scriptfile
net start netlogon
```

The *scriptfile* must contain the full path for the Registry parameter for ReplicationGovernor and the new value you want to use.

For more information on the usage and syntax of the `REGINI.EXE` program as well as creating a scheduled script, refer to the Windows NT Resource Kit's Resource Kit Tools Help (`RKTOOLS.HLP`).

Table 9-4 contains values that may be added to alter the partial synchronization rate for the SAM/LSA database. It also has descriptions of the default, and minimum and maximum frequencies for domain synchronization.

The following information describes the effect of each of the values listed in Table 9-4.

- *Pulse*: This parameter sets the pulse frequency in seconds. Any changes made to the SAM since the last pulse are collected into a single pulse. When the pulse time finally expires, all BDCs that do not already have updated SAMs are pulsed and the changes appended to the database.

TABLE 9-4 ALTERING NETLOGON SERVICE PARAMETERS TO TUNE PARTIAL SYNCHRONIZATION REQUESTS

Value Name	Default Value	Minimum Value	Maximum Value
Pulse	300 (5 minutes)	60 (1 minute)	3,600 (1 hour)
PulseConcurrency	20	1	500
PulseMaximum	7200 (2 hours)	60 (1 minute)	86,400 (1 day)
PulseTimeout1	5 (5 seconds)	1 (1 second)	120 (2 minutes)
PulseTimeout2	300 (5 minutes)	60 (1 minute)	3,600 (1 hour)
Randomize	1 (1 second)	0 (0 seconds)	120 (2 minutes)

- *PulseConcurrency*: This parameter establishes the number of simultaneous pulses sent to the BDCs on the network. The Netlogon service actually pulses BDCs one at a time, so the value reflects the number of pulses that are pending. To reduce the load on the PDC to service BDC SAM updates, set this value lower. The compromise is that on a large domain with many changes to the user database, lower values will extend the amount of time required for the domain to be synchronized.
- *PulseMaximum*: This is the rate at which any and all BDCs will be pulsed, whether or not their user database is up-to-date. Setting this to a higher value can reduce the load on the PDC to do full updates to the BDCs but will also increase the time it takes to fully synchronize a large domain. Higher values work best with small domains.
- *PulseTimeout1*: This value defines the duration in seconds that a PDC will wait for an unresponsive BDC to respond. A BDC must respond to the pulse within this time period. If the BDC times out, it is passed over. Unresponsive BDCs are not subtracted from the PulseConcurrency value, allowing the PDC to service other BDCs while it waits. If the value is set too high, a large domain with several unresponsive BDCs may cause the partial synchronization of the domain to take a long time. If the value is set too low, then a functioning BDC may be incorrectly deemed unresponsive. When the BDC finally does respond, it will have a forcible partial synchronization initiated by the PDC, unnecessarily increasing the load on the PDC.

- *PulseTimeout2*: This value determines how long a PDC will wait for a BDC to complete each step in the replication process. The BDC must complete each step within the time defined by PulseTimeout2, or the PDC will deem it unresponsive and continue on to other BDCs in the domain. If the number is set too high, a slow-to-respond BDC (or a BDC that has had its ReplicationGovernor rate reduced) will subtract from the PulseConcurrency value and take an otherwise useful slot away from another more responsive BDC. If the value is set too low, the PDC may become overly burdened due to the large number of BDCs performing partial synchronizations.

The PulseTimeout2 parameter only affects scenarios in which the BDC cannot retrieve all of the changes to the database in a single call. This type of problem will only occur if a large number of changes have been made to the user database.

- *Randomize*: The Randomize parameter specifies the number of seconds the BDC should wait before making a call to the PDC. When the BDC receives its pulse, the BDC will wait between a value of zero and the Randomize value before calling the PDC. The Randomize parameter is an outside figure used as a maximum range and should always be smaller than the PulseTimeout1. When the Randomize parameter's value is not specified, the Netlogon service determines optimal values depending on the domain controller's workload. In other words, this is an autotuned feature by default. Changing any of the values turns off autotuning. To figure out how long it will take to synchronize all BDCs in domain, remember it will take longer than (Randomize/2) * NumberOfBDCsInDomain / PulseConcurrency.

Additional Netlogon tweaks

In addition to controlling network synchronization and bandwidth consumed by those synchronizations, Netlogon includes a host of other parameters that can be used to maximize domain server performance while minimizing the effect on the network.

Value Name:	`ChangeLogSize`
Default:	65,536 (64K)
Type:	`REG_DWORD`
Value Range:	65,536 to 4,194,304 bytes

This parameter specifies the size of the change log which maintains a list of all the changes made to the SAM/LSA up until the last overwrite. The change log occupies both memory and disk space, its log of changes residing in %SYSTEMROOT%\NETLOGON.CHG. Changing the size of this parameter will increase the amount of disk space and nonpaged pool (virtual memory) it uses. The significance of the change log is that if a BDC does a partial synchronization and requests an entry that has already been overwritten, it is forced to perform a full synchronization with the PDC.

Typical size for a change entry is about 32 bytes. This means that the default change log size of 64K can maintain about 2,000 changes before the oldest entry is overwritten.

You should consider setting the ChangeLogSize parameters to avoid full database synchronization as much as possible. You should also consider increasing its value if you expect that one or more of your BDCs will not request a partial synchronization within the 2,000 changes that the default log size maintains.

ChangeLogSize only needs to be set on the PDC; the BDCs do not need this value changed unless you are planning to promote one of the BDCs to domain controller. You must reboot for the changes to take effect.

Value Name: Update
Default: No
Type: REG_SZ
Value Range: Yes or No

When the Update Parameter is set to "Yes," the Netlogon service fully synchronizes the SAM/LSA database with the PDC each time it is started. This can help when machines are brought down out of production often, but will also increase boot times, particularly on large domains.

Browser traffic

One of the biggest bandwidth-wasters on a Microsoft Windows network is browser traffic, a result of broadcast announcements and sharing of NetBIOS names for available network servers and resources. Browser traffic results in both network overhead and host system overhead because of the system impact of maintaining the list (you get a hit for the updates, then a hit for all requests to search for resources off the list by network users). NT workstations and Windows machines can suffer severe performance penalties if they are elected as the Browse Master.

Browse lists are divided into file and device shares, which are maintained on one list, and one browse list, which maintains a list of available printers and print resources. The Domain Master Browser (DMB) contains the master lists and is responsible for updating all local Master Browsers (MBRs) which are themselves responsible for updating Backup Browsers. Printservers maintain the separate lists of printers. Each transport protocol on an NT or Windows machine has its own browse lists, so each transport protocol adds additional overhead to maintain them. The best way to keep your Windows and NT Workstation machines from being elected the Browse Master or Backup Browser is to disable the Computer Browser service (easily accomplished via the control panel/services applet). Disabling this service does not prevent your NT server or workstation from browsing for network resources; it will however prevent any network browsing from occurring if you get overzealous and there is no Master Browser on the network. You may also wish (more for security reasons than performance) to hide NT machines from the Domain Master Browser via a simple Registry change. NT 5.0 will see the much-deserved death of the NetBIOS-based browser service and its associated overhead.

Master Browser elections are held every time a system boots. There is a cascading order in which systems receive priority to become Master Browsers, moving down from NT Servers (all depending on version number), to NT Workstations, Windows 95 machines, and even Windows 3.11 machines. NT Servers which are not the PDC (which always wins DMB elections) are elected depending on both the time which they have been available on the network and their NetBIOS name (Alphabetical, A to Z). The time duration between when a Domain Master Browser and a Master Browser update is 12 minutes by default. Network announcements to keep this list current start immediately after boot followed by announcements at intervals of 2, 4, 8, and finally every 12 minutes. Every subnetwork contains its own Master Browser. Browser traffic accounts for some pretty massive percentages of network bandwidth (as much as 30 percent in some cases) so reduce it as much as possible. Good old log on scripts which map directory shares to drive letters and network printers to LPT ports solve most of these problems painlessly.

Parameter values for configuring the Browser service are found in:

```
HKEY_LOCAL_MACHINE\SYSTEM\CurrentControlSet\Services\Browser\
  Parameters
```

GROOMING THE SYSTEM FOR DOMAIN MASTER BROWSER DUTY

Value Name:	`IsDomainMaster`
Default:	0
Type:	`REG_SZ`
Value Range:	1 or 0

When the IsDomainMaster value is set to 1, the server receives a priority boost that will improve its likelihood of winning a Master Browser election. However, it does not automatically make the server the Domain Master Browser (DMB). The value can be set with any Boolean value: Yes/No, True/False, or 1/0.

SETTING THE SYSTEM BROWSER ELIGIBILITY

Value Name:	`MaintainServerList`
Default:	Auto
Type:	`REG_SZ`
Value Range:	Yes, No, Auto

This value, when set to its default of Auto allows the server to run in a Master Browser election if asked to do so by the DMB. When set to No it refuses to run at all. When set to Yes, it will always run for election.

SETTING THE MBR TO DMB SYNCHRONIZATION PERIOD

Value Name:	`MasterPeriodicity:`
Default:	720
Type:	`REG_DWORD`
Value Range:	300 to 4,294,967 seconds

This value specifies the interval in seconds that an MBR synchronizes with a DMB. Default for this value is 720 seconds (12 minutes). Minimum value for this parameter is 300 seconds (5 minutes) with a maximum value of 4,294,967 seconds (49 days and 8 hours). The parameter can be altered dynamically, allowing you to change Browser traffic characteristics without a reboot. You can write a script file and schedule the new value to run using the AT command or WinAT tool with the help of `REGINI.EXE` (from the Resource Kit). This would allow multiple announce/synchronize rates over the course of a day or week to reduce bandwidth wasted on these services.

The MasterPeriodicity parameter must be set individually on each MBR. If you set these parameters on the DMB be aware that it will also affect the interval it communicates with WINS for the domain list of NetBIOS names. This can also increase WAN traffic that could increase leased line costs and slow WAN performance. Smaller values reflect more traffic generation.

SETTING THE BACKUP TO MBR SYNCHRONIZATION PERIOD

Value Name:	`BackupPeriodicity`
Default:	720
Type:	`REG_DWORD`
Value Range:	300 to 4,294,967

This value sets the time interval in seconds that a backup Browser (which is a separate machine that backs up the MBR in case it is shutdown) synchronizes with the MBR. Default value for this parameter is 720 seconds (12 minutes). The minimum value is 300 seconds (5 minutes) with a maximum value of 4,294,967 seconds (49 days and 8 hours). Unlike the MasterPeriodicity, this value is not dynamically read and you must reboot for the change to take effect. It also does not affect WAN performance, because traffic is restricted to only one subnetwork.

BackupPeriodicity is used to determine when an entry in the browse list will expire and be removed. Expiration and removal is performed after three consecutive BackupPeriodicity iterations.

To avoid losing entries due to a low value, ensure that BackupPeriodicity is set to at least a third of the maximum value of MasterPeriodicity. You must implement this on every computer that could become the PDC.

DISABLING PRINTSERVER BROWSER ANNOUNCEMENTS

The Printservers on your network will broadcast announcements of available printers every 12 minutes. Disabling the printer Browser can reduce these pesky broadcasts that soak up a small amount of network bandwidth. The chatter between print servers is not really helpful; printer resources rarely change. To disable the Printserver announcements go to:

```
HKEY_LOCAL_MACHINE\SYSTEM\CurrentControlSet\Control\Print
```

Value Name:	`DisableServerThread`
Default:	0 (False)
Type:	`REG_DWORD`
Value Range:	0 or 1 (False or True)

Set this to 1 (True) to disable the browse thread. This thread is used to call other Printservers to notify them that this printer exists. Even though the Printservers will no longer have browse lists, the printers remain available and any mapped connection to a printer will remain completely intact. The DisableServerThread parameter is for all out elimination of the traffic that is caused by Printserver announcements. See the following parameters for reducing the traffic without eliminating the service.

CONFIGURING PRINTSERVER BROWSER SYNCHRONIZATION

Value Name:	`ServerThreadTimeout`
Default:	36,000 (10 minutes)
Type:	`REG_DWORD`
Data:	3,600,000 (1 hour)
Value Range:	Milliseconds

This specifies the time in which the ServerThread idles before calling all other print servers to notify them of the existence of printers on that particular print server. Longer values mean less traffic.

SETTING THE PRINTSERVER BROWSER CACHE

Value Name:	`NetPrinterDecayPeriod`
Default:	3,600,000 (milliseconds; equals 1 hour)
Type:	`REG_DWORD`
Data:	28,800,000 (8 hours)
Value Range:	Milliseconds

This value specifies for how long a printer should remain in the cache before its listing expires. Longer values mean less traffic to update, but also mean that any printer or print server added to the list recently may not be reflected.

SETTING THE FREQUENCY OF PRINTSERVER BROWSE SYNCHRONIZATION WITH MBR AND BACKUP BROWSERS

Value Name:	`RefreshTimesPerDecayPeriod`
Default:	2
Type:	`REG_DWORD`
Value Range:	1 to 5 hours

This parameter specifies the number of times the Printserver should inform the Browse Masters and Backup servers during a decay period. The default value is twice per hour. Don't set this to a zero value if you specify both a RefreshTimesPerDecayPeriod and ServerThreadTimeout. The system will simply wait for the maximum ServerThreadTimeout or the RefreshTimesPerDecayPeriod. Larger values mean less traffic, but increase the chances of invalid entries in the printer browse list.

BROWSER TRAFFIC OVER SLOW LINKS

You can ensure that the browse overhead is low over your ISDN WAN links while maintaining availability of the complete domain browse list:

```
HKEY_LOCAL_MACHINE\\SYSTEM\CurrentControlSet\Services\
 LanmanWorkstation\Parameters
```

Value Name:	KeepConn
Default:	600
Type:	REG_DWORD
Value Range:	1 to 65,535 seconds

Set the parameter KeepConn to a small value of seven seconds or less. A good value for most environments seems to be around five seconds. This value will prevent network traffic between browse refreshes to disconnect the connection established during the browse list exchange.

WINS performance tweaks

WINS (Windows Internet Naming Service) is used to map all Windows networking NetBIOS names (like `\\Parisian`) to IP addresses. This proprietary nameserver can get a bit of a performance boost by reducing its overhead and increasing its thread priority. You may wish to have a few dedicated WINS servers in a large domain rather than several dozen servers pulling double or triple duty with other services to provide. WINS is important because it reduces wasted bandwidth lost to broadcast resolutions by client systems when a WINS server is not running or there is no updated LMHOSTS file. Broadcast resolution should be avoided if at all possible. WINS performs slightly better when it doesn't have to log everything it does. When a backup path is specified for the database, the database is protected and the logging is really not necessary. Figure 9-13 shows the WINS Manager window with logging options being disabled.

Figure 9-13 shows the WINS Manager advanced options. We have enabled "backup on termination" to protect the database while disabling logging to speed up name mapping. When the WINS server has been running for a while, the database file may need compaction to improve its performance. This is particularly true if and when the file approaches a size of 30MB or more. Versions of NT prior to NT 4.0 used an earlier version of the Jet database engine, which required more frequent compaction. To do this, stop the WINS service and run the `JETPACK.EXE` program from the *%SYSTEMROOT%*`\SYSTEM32` folder. When finished restart the service in its freshly compacted state. Using WINS Manager forgoes the persistent danger of using the Registry Editor to perform the same actions, but you may want to be able to alter them directly.

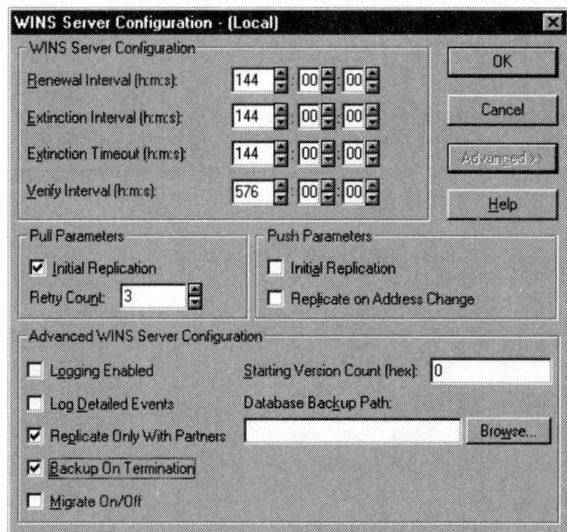

Figure 9-13: WINS Manager advanced options.

Remember that it is still possible to bypass WINS altogether and instead maintain a centralized LMHOSTS file (refer to the NT Server manuals or the Windows NT Resource Kit documentation for information on how to do this). The major disadvantage to this is that LMHOSTS requires manual editing and maintenance, and isn't very user-friendly (or administrator-friendly, for that matter). However, the net per-system overhead for the centralized LMHOSTS method is extremely small in comparison with other methods. When performed correctly (as per instructions given earlier under the "TCP/IP Features" section), it won't matter if the WINS servers all die off; the LMHOSTS file will be in the NetBios name cache and will be reloaded when the system reboots. WINS allows for a level of flexibility you may need if you have a large TCP/IP network that changes often. Database integrity checks will also slow things down, so if you can avoid them, do so. Values for WINS are found in:

```
HKEY_LOCAL_MACHINE\SYSTEM\CurrentControlSet\Services\Wins\Parameters
```

SPECIFYING THE WINS DATABASE BACKUP DIRECTORY

Even though it is recommended that you disable logging to improve the number of resolutions WINS can perform per minute, you do not have to lose your ability to recover from a failure. Set the backup directory and ensure that the database backs up every time the system is shut down.

Value Name:	`BackupDirPath`
Default:	*%SYSTEMROOT%*`\system32\wins\backup`
Type:	`REG_SZ`
Value Range:	Path name of the WINS backup directory

This value specifies the path to the WINS backup directory.

SETTING DATABASE NAME

Value Name: `DbFileNm`
Default: *%SYSTEMROOT%*`\system32\wins\wins.mdb`
Type: `REG_EXPAND_SZ`
Value Range: Path name of the WINS database file

This parameter specifies the full path for the WINS database file and name.

INSTRUCTING WINS TO BACKUP

Value Name: `DoBackupOnTerm`
Default: 0 (False)
Type: `REG_DWORD`
Value Range: 0 or 1 (False or True)

This parameter sets the WINS database to backup automatically to the path specified in BackupDirPath upon WINS service termination. This provides more useful protection and lower overhead than logging or verbose logging (described below).

DISABLING WINS LOGGING

Value Name: `LoggingOn`
Default: 1 (True)
Type: `REG_DWORD`
Value Range: 0 or 1 (False or True)

This parameter specifies whether WINS event logging of any database changes are saved to the `JET.LOG`. The more logging, the slower the WINS server performs.

DISABLING VERBOSE WINS LOGGING

Value Name: `LogDetailedEvents`
Default: 0 (False)
Type: `REG_DWORD`
Value Range: 0 or 1 (False or True)

This value specifies whether WINS event logging is verbose (and overhead-ridden). It is highly recommended that you always leave this value off (disabled) unless you need to enable it for temporary diagnostic purposes.

INCREASING WORKER THREADS

Value Name: `NoOfWrkThds`
Default: Number of processors on the system
Type: `REG_DWORD`
Value Range: 1 to 0x28

This value specifies the number of worker threads that will handle name lookup packets from client systems. This value is dynamic and can be changed without restarting the system though you must restart the WINS service. Higher values may improve performance but may also cause a CPU bottleneck if the number of context switches gets too high. Be conservative and don't cause any undue context switches trying to push WINS performance to the limits.

INCREASING WINS PRIORITY CLASS

Value Name:	`PriorityClassHigh`
Default:	0 (False)
Type:	`REG_DWORD`
Value Range:	0 or 1 (False or True)

This parameter specifies the priority class of the WINS service. A setting of 1 will set the service for high priority. This setting is dynamic and can be set without system reboot though you must restart the WINS service. The point of changing priority is when a multipurpose server is already bogged down performing other duties and the WINS service is more important to provide. This setting will do nothing on a server that is not busy servicing other requests (like an applications server or a busy PDC).

TURNING OFF WINS REPLICATION PARTNER ANNOUNCEMENTS

When you start the WINS service it automatically sends IGMP packets to multicast address 224.0.1.24. This is a multicast packet sent by the WINS service looking for possible replication partners. WINS periodically sends information about itself by means of these packets.

If you do not want these multicast packets to be sent, set UseSelfFndPnrs in the Registry under `WINS\PARAMETERS` to `DWORD` 0 and also set McastIntvl to some very large value (DWORD FFFFFFFF, for example; by default the interval is 2,400, that is, 40 minutes).

TIME INTERVAL FOR WINS TO SEND MULTICAST ANNOUNCEMENTS

Value Name:	`McastIntvl`
Default:	2,400 (seconds)
Type:	`REG_DWORD`
Value Range:	2,400 seconds (40 minutes)

This parameter specifies the time interval (in seconds) at which the WINS server sends a multicast announcement to announce its presence to other WINS servers. The more announcements the system makes, the more bandwidth is consumed (especially in large shared network environments).

WINS MULTICAST TIME TO LIVE

Value Name:	`McastTtl`
Default:	6
Type:	`REG_DWORD`
Value Range:	1 to 32

This parameter specifies the number of router hops a WINS multicast announcement can make. Lower values can reduce multicast traffic across a WAN but may also prevent successful communication between WINS servers.

Optimizing WAN-Based Domains

Though it would be very nice to connect all your remote networks over a fast ATM or Frame Relay network, the reality of associated costs to rent, build, and maintain these networks makes them less accessible to the smaller installation. Fortunately, NT has several built-in features that allow networks to dial into each other to maintain such things as the user database in synch. Because WAN traffic is generally the domain of the standard routable protocol TCP/IP, this will mainly deal with issues associated with integrating NT's network services over the TCP/IP transport for use on a WAN.

Optimizing Remote Access Services

Most of the guidelines which apply to optimizing TCP/IP over WAN links apply here (After all, RAS is often the mechanism of delivery). Over slow links like ISDN, Switched-56 and analog modems tend to benefit from using smaller numbers of packets per TCP window. This often results in reduced delays from timeouts and so forth.

If you are using RAS as an Internet gateway and have IP routing enabled, you should use the settings described earlier in the "Optimizing TCP/IP" section for improving router performance.

You may also optimize your serial ports configurations by avoiding hardware handshaking (which NT is emulating) that slows things. Use XON-XOFF handshaking for all serial ports and set the maximum BPS (Bits Per Second) that the port can support. Enable all FIFOs to improve the flow of information through the modem or serial board.

Whenever possible, opt for multiport serial cards with dedicated ASICs, MPUs, and buffer memory; they can save you a lot of time and energy during setup and troubleshooting. A single software driver can control up to 12 serial ports with minimal CPU usage when these special cards are used. This is preferable to the slower performance of standard 16550-based UART chips.

```
HKEY_LOCAL_MACHINE\SYSTEM\CurrentControlSet\Services\Tcpip\Parameters
```

The values for EnablePMTUDiscovery are described in the Optimizing TCP/IP section.

The recommended value is 0, which disables this feature on DUN clients (you will be setting the MTU explicitly to a lower value). TcpWindowSize is also discussed in the Optimizing TCP/IP section, and should be reduced to a value of 2,144 or less (decimal).

```
HKEY_LOCAL_MACHINE\System\CurrentControlSet\Services\RemoteAccess\
  Parameters\NetbiosGateway
```

Value Name:	MaxDgBufferedPerGroupName
Default:	10
Type:	REG_DWORD
Value Range:	1 to 255

This value establishes the number of datagrams that can be buffered within a group name, a concept used by multicast traffic. By increasing the value, you may achieve better performance but you will use more paged pool memory.

Value Name:	MaxDynMem
Default:	655,350
Type:	REG_DWORD
Value Range:	131,072 to 4,294,967,295

This parameter specifies the maximum amount of paged pool (virtual memory) that can be used to buffer NetBIOS session data. This is an important parameter because of the function it serves – fast data from the LAN must be stored temporarily in the buffer while it waits to be transmitted on the slow WAN link. RAS Server only locks 64K for each client, allowing you to increase this setting with minimal impact.

The following parameter may improve incoming packet performance for PPTP sessions:

```
HKEY_LOCAL_MACHINE\System\CurrentControlSet\Services\RasPptpe\
  Parameters\Configuration
```

Value Name:	RxPacketWindow
Default:	3
Type:	REG_DWORD
Value Range:	Number of packets

This parameter sets the maximum number of packets that can be received before an ACK must be sent.

The value is automatically negotiated upon establishment of a new PPTP session. The value is used on both ends of the PPTP connection. Try increasing the value on WAN connections (particularly digital services like xDSL, ISDN, and T1). This value is global and used for all PPTP connections for the local machine.

An excellent Web site with information on improving the performance of Win95 and NT 4.0 DUN was designed and is maintained by Patrick Pang, and is located at:

`http://www.geocities.com/Tokyo/Towers/3315/tips_mtu.html`

Designing Your Network

Though most network administrators inherit their networks from their predecessors, the network should be viewed as a living, breathing organism. Networks are continuous works in progress, changing and growing as the needs of the business change. Nothing remains static for long, especially where technology and the driving force of competition are involved.

Always build your network to grow; any changes you make to your existing network should be made to ensure that future changes will not be unnecessarily difficult or costly. Build in extra capacity for network services and users on your network. Leaving room for "the toes to wiggle" will save you pain in the long run by avoiding the pitfalls of underestimating the changing requirements of your network. Another thing to remember is the KISS principle (Keep It Simple, Stupid!). Complex networks can become job security, but they are also cumbersome to deal with and make you more susceptible to office politics (which can *reduce* job security).

Never steer your network design into a deadend with single vendor solutions or technology that may not be supported or in existence in a few years. Even if you have to pick your "standards" watch what other organizations similar to yours are doing within their budgets. Don't limit your long-term functionality in order to keep initial costs down or to bandage a very specific and current dilemma. Flexibility, modularity, manageability, security, and performance should govern the way in which you layout your network (priority for these is entirely up to you). These are all conceptual elements, and therefore no single software or hardware widget or doodad can provide you with all of them.

A *flexible* network is one in which the network is dynamic, allowing configuration and layout changes with minimum pain. This concept is intimately tied with *modularity,* which is the ability to add and remove components individually, and provides a migration path to newer-better-faster equipment. *Manageable* networks allow for easy monitoring and measuring, allowing you to easily keep tabs on and logically view your network. This capability is of particular importance with the current move to switching technology and the use of VLANs (which are themselves single vendor solutions). Using VLANs makes monitoring and measuring very difficult without the support of the vendors who actually built the hardware. *Security* insures that your network resources are only accessed by those individuals and systems whom you wish to access them. This is accomplished with numerous layers of security ranging from user privileges to protocol firewalls.

Designing a network for performance alone is impractical, because other requirements often add features at the expense of some overhead but are too important to do without (error control and security, for example). The difficult goal of network performance optimization is *balance.* A well-planned attack on the problem of network performance (such as deploying ATM instead of Fast Ethernet for large campuses), now and in the future, should reduce the costs of maintaining the network. "Patchwork" networks consisting of multiple disparate components are a thing of life but should be treated as a transition with a clear course for the future. Coordinating a mixed bag of TokenRing, FDDI, switched Ethernet, and ATM backbones is not uncommon in large organizations. Implementing a "slick" simplified network is always 90 percent politics and 10 percent implementation, so bring the bean counters and the number crunchers into it with pretty graphs of network utilization and pesky problems (which directly affect them) and they will likely back your case.

There are two basic methods of increasing network performance: switching and routing. When you use the routing method, you subnetwork the network using the IPX/SPX or TCP/IP protocols (which are routable) and install multiple NICs in the servers. Routing is slower and more complex to build and maintain, as well as being less scalable as the size of the network increases. Alternatively, you can deploy switching hubs to connect workstations and servers either directly to the switch or through a shared media hub that radiates off the switch. You can easily balance performance by providing servers with switched ports at maximum speed and zero contention while workstations and less performance-sensitive servers can use slower speed network connections (like a connection to a 10MB shared or switched hub radiating from the 10/100/1000 switch). You can purchase larger numbers of smaller switches to avoid creating a single point of failure for your network. You should place redundant servers (such as BDCs) on separate hubs or switches.

Concepts for Fast Network Building

Always assume that your network is imperfect until you check it to the ground wires. Cable testers are an essential (but costly) tool to have on hand when you are building or adding to your network. Some polls suggest that as much as 1 bad cable drop exists for every 100; finding that 1 bad drop can be a miserable undertaking. Patch panels, patch cables, and the wall plate are all suspect. Optical cabling can pay for itself when it comes time to figure out how to deal with an interference or distance problem. Optical cabling never suffers the kinds of interference problems (Radio Frequency and Electromagnetic) that plague UTP and even improperly shielded BNC and STP cabling, especially when sources of interference are not identified in advance. Problems with optical fiber installation include the cost of the optical NICs (including 100baseFX) and the much greater cost of optical hubs. The cable installation of optical fiber also requires that specialists be called on, because only a few cable installers have either the equipment or the experience to drop or "blow" fiber (using special tools, you can use bursts of air to push the cable through a conduit).

Some of the things that will make your network slower than you think it should be are protocol overhead, delays in media access (contention), and error rates/retries from bad installation or frayed contacts.

Network design checklist

To take advantage of your existing network investments, you should always have a plan for where you are going with the network in the next few years. What changes can you expect in the next two to four years? Sometimes answering these questions is difficult, but defining a game plan allows a degree of flexibility you just can't get by reacting to a sudden problem.

A checklist of things to be aware of and practices to use for developing high performance systems is given below.

- Use tools like Bluecurve Dynameasure (a demo version of which is included on the CD accompanying this book) for pushing the limits and Performance Monitor and Network Monitor for monitoring the trends.
- Find out exactly what your current shared Ethernet segments are capable of and determine which systems are experiencing the greatest delays or lack of bandwidth. For example, the maximum value for a 100MB Ethernet is 12.5 megabytes/sec, a figure which includes about 15 percent protocol overhead at its peak, giving you about 10 megabytes/sec, at least on a switched port.
- When using switches, ask yourself how many segments do you really need? You can answer the question by monitoring client and server systems individually for bandwidth used and output queuing.

- Install CAT 5 wiring or multimode fiber of the highest quality you can buy. Connect all copper conductors on punchout panels so that rewiring will not have to occur later when more pairs of the copper wire are used. This ensures that future networks will be able to use the existing cable plant, even as speeds exceed gigabyte speeds. Companies that installed CAT 4 wiring instead of CAT 5 are feeling the pinch now with 100MB Ethernet and with so few products supporting the older cable.
- Reduce the number of subnetworks to the minimum to avoid the costly act of reconfiguring subnetworks as the network grows.
- Using stackable hubs and switches allows you a modular approach to network growth. This also cuts down on the dreaded "rats nest" of patch cables.
- Switches can connect networks together at much higher speeds than routers are capable of providing while serving much of the same purpose in network infastructure.
- Always use busmastering NICs which have proven specifications for efficiency (high throughput is meaningless if it costs you 90 percent of your processor). Efficiency is a measure of CPU usage to throughput.
- Try to use NICs from the same vendor and keep your NIC drivers up to date (about once every four to six months search for driver updates). Using NICs from the same vendor also reduces the number of support libraries of drivers and configuration tools you must maintain to support your networks NICs.
- Set all NIC and hub/switch options for the driver explicitly, such as frame type (802.3, SNAP, etc.), line speed, full-duplex or half-duplex, and processor efficiency. Leave nothing to chance.
- Use server-targeted NICs in your servers rather than just standard NICs. Many server-targeted NICs have additional features, such as local processors to reduce interrupt generation and processor usage. In addition, these NICs often integrate large caches that can slightly improve packet transfer rates to the clients.
- Use multichannel NICs whenever possible for best performance. Multichannel network adapters can improve performance by offering the ability to send data to two or four channels and network segments simultaneously from a single server expansion slot. This can reduce the number of interrupt lines used (each individual network I/O chip is masked behind a bridge chip), and save several PCI slots for other devices.
- Attach your multiple NICs or multichannel NIC to a single segment for fault tolerance to improve availability using adapters which offer this functionality (such as Adaptec's Duralink).

FACTORS OF NETWORK PERFORMANCE

Network performance is as much about response time as throughput. High throughput can be accompanied with poor response time and vice versa, so always remember to keep these issues in balance. Prioritize your protocols, explicitly set NIC frame types and network media speed (100MB for example). Don't leave anything to chance. The move to lower latency and faster response time has been underscored with the move to network switching technologies. Faster networks often use smaller segments/collision domains to restrict the amount of contention and turnaround that can occur. Having higher bandwidth does not mean that your network will respond more quickly.

BANDWIDTH-HUNGRY APPLICATIONS

Applications driving the need for higher bandwidth include fully network-aware multimedia applications such as groupware applications incorporating streaming audio and video, smooth, full color, broadcast quality video (e.g., for desktop videoconferencing), multichannel digital sound, telephony applications, and data warehousing.

Many user interfaces will soon be dominated by 3D graphics, as will the increasingly high degree of integration from many data sources, all of which will push the need for bigger and faster pipes. Other bandwidth munching changes to today's networks are the increasing trends for simpler administration using "thin" clients where client applications, desktop preferences, and portions of the operating system itself will run across the network and less and less will reside on the client workstation.

Comparing network media protocols

NT has quite a few media access protocols that it natively supports, including all versions of Ethernet, TokenRing, LocalTalk (Macintosh support), and FDDI. ATM is only supported through LANE (LAN Emulation) and VG-AnyLAN support falls under Ethernet, even though the two technologies differ in how the shared media is accessed.

ETHERNET ISSUES

By far the most common network technology in the world, Ethernet is not exactly the most technically refined method of dealing with the problems of attaching computers together, but it is generally well understood and here to stay. Ethernet is one of the granddaddies of the media access protocols, having ties with earlier topologies like StarNet, which included the same collision-based mechanism called CSMA/CD (Carrier Sense Multiple Access/Collision Detection). Ethernet (IEEE 802.3) is described as a "fair" protocol because it allows any node on the network access to the media without a fixed time slot or the need for an access token. The downside of CSMA/CD is that it is easy to saturate on the most common, somewhat erratic, bursty networks. On lightly used networks, Ethernet can be very responsive, though its responsiveness plummets rapidly as more nodes are added to the network and traffic increases. It is very rare that you can push Ethernet beyond 60 percent of its capacity without causing serious performance problems for other users on the network due to the greatly escalated number of packet collisions.

CAN YOU REPEAT THAT?

In a very real sense, Ethernet is like a very crowded room full of people where anyone can talk without any special permission. When too many people talk at once, the conversations between people get jumbled and its becomes progressively harder to communicate, especially with people on the other side of the room. The frustrated individuals involved are forced to make several attempts to get their point across by waiting for the loudest people to stop talking before they attempt once again to communicate.

Like the crowded room, packets from one network node can be transmitted at the moment another transmission has already started. The Ethernet NIC detects that both sets of packets have destroyed each other and waits a random amount of time before reattempting a transmission. As the number of network stations trying to transmit increases, the number of collisions also increases, reducing the total efficiency that an Ethernet can achieve.

FAST ETHERNET ISSUES

Fast Ethernet (IEEE 802.3u) is an extension of the original flavor with 10 times the theoretical bandwidth of the 10MB specification. Fast Ethernet borrowed the electrical signaling of another 100MB copper-based technology called CDDI (Copper Distributed Data Interface, based on FDDI). This new Ethernet constitutes the bulk of the 100MB network technologies, far outstripping the number of nodes in place using FDDI and CDDI. The primary driver for this success has been cost and familiarity. 100MB Ethernet suffers from the same CSMA/CD protocol that made earlier Ethernet specifications less efficient. Pushing the Ethernet to 60 percent of its bandwidth on a shared 100MB LAN results in significantly reduced response time and throughput. In most installations, Fast Ethernet is around 2.5 times faster in practice than 10MB Ethernet, in part because of the speed of components such as the disk drives, which transfer data on both ends.

There are currently three versions of the 100MB "Fast" Ethernet specification: TX, T4, and FX. TX uses two pairs of CAT 5 wiring, where T4 uses four pairs (all eight wires) over CAT 3 or CAT 4 wiring. A less common option is 100baseFX, a multimode fiber based Ethernet with distance limitations for the segment of 412 meters (turnaround time made it necessary to reduce the normally long distances associated with fiber). FX Ethernet equipment costs about one-third the price of FDDI equipment minus the fault tolerance and efficiency characteristics of that specification.

Maximum distance from hub to port is 100 meters (328 feet). This distance is slightly less for T4 (CAT 3 or 4) due to the lower grade of wiring. Remember that things like patch cables and breakout boxes subtract from that total (figure on 90 meters for the network, leaving 10 meters for the rest). Fast Ethernet is limited to 100 meters end-to-end. Most companies have not implemented 100MB technology to the desktop yet, but will as the number one subject talked about at board meetings starts to see significant adoption: Desktop videoconferencing.

The biggest innovation in dealing with the problems of Ethernet bandwidth utilization has been the incorporation of switching technology. Each network node can be connected to a switch port providing it with its own isolated collision domain. A single user with a single port can monopolize almost the entire bandwidth of the Ethernet (excluding some protocol overhead). The downside of this collision domain isolation is that monitoring the network becomes much more complex, because most software, and even some hardware-based products, requires the capability to see all the activity happening on the entire physical network in order to report meaningful findings. The other downside is the cost per port for a decent fast switching (sub-20 microseconds) workgroup switch, which is generally much higher than a passive hub, often in the neighborhood of $600 per port.

It is still more efficient and cost-effective to use 10MB Ethernet switches to segment off your nonmultimedia, word processor-oriented users from your large file junkies/power users with 100MB pipes to either a shared hub or Ethernet switch. The server really should have a 100MB connection to the hub or switch to avoid bottlenecking the servers network interface. It is also important to note that to use the full-duplex operation that many NICs support, you must use an Ethernet switch; ordinary hubs won't support it, and the option will remain disabled. Full-duplex allows you up to 200MB total bandwidth with 100MB upstream and 100MB downstream. For best performance, consider using switches for at least some of your stations and servers to improve performance.

Adaptec/Cogent Fast Ethernet Adapters and DuraLink Technology

Adaptec/Cogent PCI Quartet Fast Ethernet adapter boasts four RJ-45 connectors for supporting four separate network segments independently on NT. Autosensing capability allows each port to support 10MB, 20MB, 100MB, and 200MB full-duplex speeds. When the adapter is connected to full-duplex Fast Ethernet switches, it can produce a maximum theoretical rate of 800MB. One of its more important features is its Duralink Failover and load balancing software which offers a near FDDI-like port resiliency for enhanced availability. The adapter uses a Digital Equipment Corporation bridge chip to mask off the interrupts and provide high efficiency with reduced CPU usage.

Gigabit Ethernet on the horizon

All the specifications have not been formalized for Gigabit Ethernet, but it is known that the signaling over the multimode or single-mode fiber is based on that of another gigabit + network technology called FibreChannel. Gigabit Ethernet will use the same CSMA/CD that virtually every LAN integrator has grown to know (and in some cases, despise) which is used by traditional Ethernet LANs. Most of the "first to market" products are actually 10/100 switches with a 1,000MB uplink port rather than an actual 10/100/1,000-capable device. In its early form, the Gigabit Ethernet Alliance has drawn up several specifications that are awaiting acceptance by the IEEE. Its initial signaling will be restricted to multimode fiber installation, but may eventually include twisted-pair copper wiring. The investments made in software, training, and mindshare ensure that Ethernet, warts and all, will still be with us in the twenty-first century.

One of the problems with adopting other network technologies is the current widespread use and dependency on the broadcasting and multicasting of frames using various transport protocols. This level of functionality and transparent support of multicast delivery has been slow in coming with other technologies such as ATM and FibreChannel. Though it won't happen overnight, it is expected that Gigabit Ethernet will take some of the market share for backbones away from ATM. It is not likely that Gigabit Ethernet will end up on the desktop any time soon. Gigabit Ethernet should also support 1GB rates in full-duplex mode, allowing a 2GB simultaneous upstream and downstream (though your mechanical disk drive will never keep up). It will add support for RSVP (a protocol for reserving bandwidth for time sensitive transmissions) and some amount of QOS (Quality of Service), but there will be no real guarantee of jitter-free real-time video or audio.

VG-ANYLAN BLUES

VG-AnyLAN was a development of Hewlett Packard (HP) and was later turned over and modified by the IEEE 802.12 committee. Among its large (but few) backers are IBM with its promise of a migration path from their proprietary and not-so-new-and-sheik TokenRing. The 100VG-AnyLAN standard involves a different wiring scheme and the use of different network management tools than Fast Ethernet. Despite its support of a highly efficient demand priority scheme, which is in many ways superior to conventional Token passing and Fast Ethernet, VG-AnyLAN has not gained much support.

Because VG does not use a contention protocol to allow access to the shared network, VG-AnyLAN cuts down on traffic and improves available bandwidth for users, reducing the need to segment or switch. The 100MB rate of its current incarnation is better utilized than on 100MB Ethernet LANs and has much more available bandwidth than 16MB TokenRing. VG-AnyLAN has a more flexible scheme for cascading hubs in a tree form with up to seven such repeaters supported. Because VG-AnyLAN represents a small but devoted segment of the market, it will be interesting to see what new developments come out of it. HP is the only vendor that offers a full product line of VG-AnyLAN components, most of which are for connecting Ethernet and Token Ring switches and hubs together.

TOKENRING ISSUES

TokenRing was a development of IBM that was handed over to the IEEE where it became a formal standard under the 802.5 committee. A long-time alternative to the less expensive and nonproprietary Ethernet, TokenRing uses an organized method for dealing with traffic control using an access token. If you want to transfer or load a file from across the network, you must wait until the token comes around to you to allow you access. TokenRing has the advantage over Ethernet in heavily utilized networks owing to its design. Pushing TokenRing to up to 85 percent of its capacity is fairly common with minimal disturbance in network performance. TokenRing can still be had in 4MB as well as 16MB options though the latter has become far more common.

An advanced 100MHz TokenRing was proposed but never implemented. All TokenRing NICs must connect to a MAU (Multistation Access Unit) which serves as the concentrator for the attached stations. Though it is described as a ring, it takes the form of a star, with all looping to form the ring performed by the MAU. Recently, TokenRing saw the advent of TokenRing switching to improve its performance and segment the network into smaller, more high-speed segments. TokenRing allows up to seven bridges to be used to extend the network, though a large network using TokenRing can result in turnaround delays from the circulation of the single token. TokenRing has been used on STP (Shielded Twisted-Pair), UTP (Unshielded Twisted-Pair), and multimode fiber.

ATM – A SLEEPY RUNAWAY TRAIN

Asynchronous Transfer Mode has been the sleeper network technology of 1997, with such cute new acronyms as “After The Millennium” (reminiscent of snide acronyms for NT – look what happened there!). Formalizing specifications as well as rolling out new products has proved a much slower process than anticipated. Additionally, convincing MIS people that they need the new technology has proved even more daunting. ATM is available in 155MB and 622MB for applications such as backbones, and even as an option up to the desktop. Gigabyte speeds are expected by late 1998. Projects such as the ATM 25 desktop product were disbanded in 1996 because of the lack of interest by the network community. In the backbone department,155MB ATM has been gaining some acceptance.

ATM is a cell-switching network topology that uses either permanent virtual circuits (PVCs, which are a pain to set up) or switched virtual circuits (SVCs). SVCs can establish and tear down connections between hosts as needed. Using a software technology called LANE (LAN Emulation, currently a 1.0 product) allows ATM networks to act as backbones to repeaters, bridges, routers, and workgroup switches. This capability allows for ATM-based VLANs to communicate with Ethernet workstations and network devices without having to go through any additional hardware (but with TONS of overhead). In addition to generating plenty of CPU usage on the host system, important features such as QOS are not available in emulation mode. LANE 2.0 should be a significant improvement allowing multiple LANE backup servers whose job it is to provide MAC (Media Access Control) address to ATM address conversion, as well as establishing the connection between the systems which are attempting to communicate.

Among its other features, ATM support of QOS is at a level at which all other topologies are judged. You can assign different data types different levels of QOS to ensure timely and uninterrupted delivery. One thing ATM will benefit by is the fact that, because of this feature, it has received remarkable levels of adoption by large telecommunication companies even though its implementation at the corporate LAN level has been slow.

FIBRECHANNEL – FASTER AND FATTER

Though it is going to remain pretty restricted to the niche markets for a while, FibreChannel is an example of true integration of channel and network. Though recently its derivatives such as FCAL (FibreChannel Arbitrated Loop) are seeing use for connecting large disk arrays and certain clustering options, FibreChannel is meant to be a singular device attachment connecting everything from client and server systems to high-speed disk drives. FibreChannel may play an important role in server clusters before moving on to other network uses. Most of the speed of FibreChannel comes from transferring packet data between memory buffers at both the source and the destination hosts. Switching between the source and destination over the network gives it higher efficiency. It is especially good for large data streams but FibreChannel has a lot of overhead using small, time sensitive data. The buffering of data from station to station reduces the complexity at the client and moves it to the network.

FibreChannel can extend out to 11km over single mode fiber and is part of the ANSI X3T9.3 committee which includes such specifications as HIPPI (High Performance Parallel Interface) FireWire and SCSI III.

Adaptec ATM Adapters

Adaptec PCI based ANA-5930A and 5940A are full-duplex 155MB ATM adapters. They support LAN Emulation (LANE 1.0) and Classical IP over ATM for transparent integration with existing LANs. Up to 1,024 virtual circuits are supported with either SVCs or PVCs. The adapters are manageable through SNMP and ATM Forum ILMI MIB. These adapters are excellent for workgroup server or workstation applications.

Its current signaling rates include 1.06Gbit and 1.6Gbit (100 and 200 MBps respectively) with rates over 2Gbit planned. All of these rates double with its native support of full-duplex operation. Support for dual-attached nodes with self-healing capability like that of FDDI are all defined and in production. Switches, adapters, and hubs are already available and configuration is much simpler than most ATM devices. Problems with FibreChannel include the lack of QOS in its existing revisions and a high degree of overhead from mapping command sets. It also has a large number of version subsets, which can make interoperability complex from one vendor and subset to another.

FDDI/CDDI ISSUES

Fiber Distributed Data Interface (IEEE 802.6) has been around for several years and is primarily used in large campuses and LAN backbones where fault tolerance and efficiency are paramount. FDDI is a token passing scheme that incorporates some added features that enhance its efficiency when it covers large (2km or more) distances. This technique is called "piggybacking" in which a single token circulates but allows multiple messages to be appended onto each other as they are given access to the network. FDDI stations can be used with a special dual-attachment (B node) adapter that allows the station to be on both of the counter rotating rings to allow fault tolerance and self-healing as well as higher performance. Computers connected as an A node connect to only one of the rings and are less costly to implement (FDDI PCI controllers are still over $1,000). The distances FDDI was designed to cover are vast, 2km between repeaters and 200km total. CDDI came about as a lower cost option that could use the existing UTP copper wiring while taking advantage of most of the other aspects of FDDI.

FDDI was designed around the concept of a MAN (Metropolitan Area Network) with distance considerations for such a network defining the long maximum length. FDDI is still in use in many campuses as a backbone connecting and aggregating traffic from several LANs. FDDI 2 includes the capability to partition 64K of bandwidth for analog voice and video streams. With full-duplex support, FDDI can achieve near 200MB performance. FDDI/CDDI remains more efficient in the 100MB network types than Fast Ethernet but costs for implementing and maintaining FDDI networks is still very expensive. Switched Fast Ethernet, VG-AnyLAN, ATM, and even Frame Relay have taken over many of its backbone duties.

Network devices

There are several network devices that serve to interconnect different networks or break apart a network into more manageable and faster segments. Some devices serve only to provide a passive means for attaching clients to a common low-speed connection, while others possess logic and protocol specific programming to allow high-speed transfer of data from one device or network to another.

HUBS

Hubs are devices which are used to concentrate the network connections and for regeneration and amplification of signals to extend the total size of a network (cascading of hubs). Hubs may be daisy-chained or connected to other devices, but have limits to the number of concurrent hubs allowed on any one segment according to the specifications defined by the media access protocol (100baseTX, FDDI, etc.). This is primarily due to added delays in turnaround time. There is a limit of 4 repeaters on a 10MB Ethernet, and up to 2 repeaters on a 100MB Ethernet.

SWITCHING TECHNOLOGIES

Switches allow you to connect workstations and servers to each other through a high-speed virtual circuit that partitions off broadcast and multicast traffic to improve efficiency by reducing collisions and wasted bandwidth. Contention for the network is reduced on the segments created by attaching devices to the switch ports. Switches may be used to break a large shared network into several segments containing a smaller number of computers which increases the amount of bandwidth available for each computer. As an expensive option, each workstation and server may receive its own dedicated port for maximum bandwidth.

The hottest news in the switching department is the development of high-speed, cost-effective Layer 3 switching. Layer 3 on the OSI model corresponds to the session layer, which establishes a dialog between applications. ASIC (Application Specific Integrated Circuit)-based switching forgoes the messy and expensive multipurpose processors (such as the I960) for a dedicated ASIC, which can perform its job of switching faster than any microprocessor-based switch. Manufacturers can also cut out some local memory that is normally associated with using microprocessor-based switching and further reduce costs. This ASIC technology is destined for high-performance IP-based Ethernet switching. Though this technology is not yet officially standardized by any of the major standards bodies, it will have significant impact on the way switches are built in the coming years. Layer 3 switching will significantly reduce prices while providing high-speed IP routing for everything from the small LAN to the telecommunication company's WAN backbone.

ROUTERS

Routers are network layer devices (they use layer 3 of the OSI model) which connect networks together that employ the same network-level protocols (like TCP/IP or IPX/SPX). Routers use standardized protocols like RIP (Router Information Protocol) to move packets to their intended destinations. Routers provide better security and control over paths than bridges do, but are harder to set up and maintain than bridges. They are also significantly slower than switches at performing the same duties, and particularly at the same price points as switches. Though routers have traditionally been used for breaking up networks, they are less ideal than switches because of the scalability and performance switches offer and the recent introduction of layer 3 switching.

BRIDGES

Bridges allow the easy interconnection of two or more LANs using the same media access protocol (CSMA/CD, TokenRing, etc.). Bridges are protocol-ignorant (they live on layer 2 of the OSI model). Broadcast traffic flows freely through the bridge, and thus larger installations with many bridged networks may experience traffic from the circulation of unchecked broadcast overhead.

Summary

In this chapter, we explored NT's network architecture, hardware issues, and ways to optimize NT's network subsystem. We discussed means for removing networking overhead and explored transport protocol parameters. We also developed some tools for measuring NT's network performance and means to coax secrets from the network's inner workings. The network hardware suggestions made in this chapter, in concert with the measuring tools discussed, provide you with the means to achieve maximum network performance. In the chapter that follows, we will apply the tools learned here directly to modify yet another important NT function: NT server role optimization.

Chapter 10

Tuning NT Server Performance

NT SERVER WAS DESIGNED from the outset to be a multipurpose network operating system, providing file, print, and application services capabilities in a distributed computing environment. The problem with this is that from a practical standpoint, a "Jack of all trades, master of none" factor can come into play. At the current time, many of the most powerful application servers remain UNIX flavored while NetWare is still (by a small margin) the most popular Intel-based file and print server around. However, provided with the proper hardware and software configurations and specific performance optimizations, NT can meet or exceed the performance of even these more "dedicated" operating systems at the very roles they were designed to excel in.

To get the most out of Windows NT Server, you should first determine what role you would like it to play and what its most important service or services should be on your network. If you must provide many services on a single server, which service is the most important? The fastest way to run NT systems is to dedicate them to a single role with a group of related functions and literally strip everything else out that is nonessential to that role. Once again, we have to arrive at a balance: You don't want to have to manage a very large number of "dedicated" NT Server configurations when what you would really like is great performance in the minimum number of boxes. With careful monitoring, you can establish which systems should be dedicated to a particular role while other servers continue to provide a manually prioritized mix of different services. Having only a few systems that provide all your network functionality creates the kind of "single points of failure" that NT was specifically designed to avoid. With the new commitment to availability and scalability shown by Microsoft and its partners, it is expected that low cost but resilient clustering options will be available very soon. The clustering API has already been made part of the NT operating system, and Microsoft has come out with its own "phase 1" of the clustering program (Microsoft Cluster Server, formerly known by its code name "Wolfpack").

Server Tuning Concepts and Objectives

It can be very beneficial to purchase a large number of inexpensive Intel PCs and alternately load NT Server onto some and NT Workstation on others, giving every workgroup their own NT Server. Other environments may require the greater capacity made available by powerful SMP (multiprocessor) DEC Alpha-based NT Servers with their ability to move massive amounts of data through their CPUs and memory arrays. A system like this could support hundreds, even thousands of users for a particular application. The needs of the users on the network govern the choices you make.

One of the major benefits of NT is the capability to run powerful servers alongside more low-key systems.

You can dedicate a system or two for special applications or delegate performance-sapping domain responsibilities to less expensive machines which don't require the more "exotic" hardware the application servers often do. Typically, using larger numbers of less powerful systems allows you to more easily refine the role of the server, and in the event of a system failure, allows simpler reinstallation. More powerful machines are often set up to perform multiple duties, making the process of enhancing performance at any one task a complex job of monitoring and prioritizing system services.

In this chapter, we discuss both the optimization of key NT network services, which were briefly covered in the previous chapter, as well as NT Server roles which will tune NT to better suit a particular requirement.

Unfortunately, there is no secret Registry key that will unlock your server's performance. Each environment possesses unique requirements that require unique solutions to achieve maximum performance. This is often an all-out barrage of long-term logging of activity, as well as a focused scrutiny of individual subsystem performance. The results you gain from this assault on NT's well-protected internal workings will let you plan a decisive surgical strike on bottlenecks and bloat within the system.

Improving NT's performance to suit a particular need often requires some changes to both hardware and the Registry. Turning off services you don't need is also an important step in reclaiming lost resources. Just as an Indy race car team will tune the car's components to improve scores by hundredths of a second at a time, optimizing an NT server involves monitoring server activity, assessing network trends, and tuning individual subsystems to achieve small but important performance improvements. Individually, these changes may account for only a small percentage of the total improvement you can achieve. Each change you make individually may only improve the performance for a particular resource by a few percent, but when aggregated together, these small, and often subtle, improvements can make a big difference. In some cases, your system may end up as much as several times faster doing a particular chore than an unoptimized "stock" system with default settings. The downside of any optimization is that if the server changes roles, but its optimizations for the old role remain intact, the previously "fast" system may actually be crippled.

Fiddling with a server that is active in a production environment (that is, providing services that users require) can be a quick shortcut to an unexpected job change. Be sensitive to the fact that most users (and managers, for that matter) just want to get their job done and don't care about what kind of server they save their files to every day or how long you spent tweaking it. At the very most, you may hear a casual comment from a user about how great the network is performing, but that beats the awful alternatives. Always test the Registry modifications and hardware changes suggested in this chapter in a test environment before deploying them in a production environment.

Tuning NT Server Within Its Role

NT, though designed as a general purpose Network Operating System, can provide more optimal performance if you understand the desired tasks it will be performing and assign it to a role. Any modifications to the system you make will be to make it more efficient at the role you assign.

The three basic roles NT Server falls into are of these types:

- File and print server
- Application server
- Domain Controller

It is difficult to know how an NT Server that you are installing or upgrading is going to be deployed. A server's role often changes over its lifetime to reflect the changing needs of the network. There is more involved with deploying a new or upgraded server on the network than just Registry tweaks and hardware. You must understand that a particular system may end up being used for a completely different role than it was originally assigned. Make management aware of everything you are doing and explain why to avoid miscommunication. If you are tweaking the system, let them know about it and assure them that it will not affect anyone on the network; in a case where it does affect users, give them an estimate for how long. When planning and deploying, always refer to the NT Server by the role it plays in the network. Make management aware of the consequences of changing the role of a server that has been optimized for a particular purpose. Explain to them that this could result in degraded performance, wasted investment, and lost man-hours.

Defining the NT Server's roles on the network

A Windows NT Server can always provide multiple server roles but will tend to perform multiple roles (particularly those that require totally different sets of modifications) at the cost of performance. This is that "Jack of all trades, master of none" concept we discussed earlier. You can make NT into a single function thoroughbred, or keep it as a more multipurpose mule. Even when an NT Server must provide a broad assortment of services, there is statistically more demand on one type of service than on another. Using Performance Monitor, you can log data to provide you with useful information on what services are being used the most. Once you've determined what your existing multifunction NT Server is doing the most of, you can prioritize its services to provide more processor time, memory, and disk to help perform them better.

A server role defines how an NT Server will be used, how it will be tweaked, and thus the efficiency that the server will be able to provide in servicing that role. Once you have decided what role a particular machine should play, you can get more into the specifics of how each NT Server role's needs differ. The fork in the road begins here.

APPLICATION SERVER DEFINED

Application servers provide services that use the local processing power of the server to do such things as generate results to query or execute code from a particular Web page whose results are then returned to the user. On NT Servers, "applications" generally refers to programs designed to run as services, which run above the NT operating system's kernel layer and operate regardless of whether or not an administrator or user is logged in. Application services include products such as many of the members of the Microsoft BackOffice product suite (including Systems Management Server, Exchange Server, Proxy Server, and Site Server) or SQL (Structured Query Language) servers such as Microsoft SQL Server and competitive products from Oracle, Informix, and others.

NT Servers assigned the role of application server require better optimization of such low-level hardware as processors, caching, and memory. Multiple processors (through NT support of SMP, Symmetric Multiprocessing) provide an application server with the ability to execute multiple threads simultaneously, a capability that can only be achieved when multiple processors are present (otherwise, only one thread can run at a time). A close second in priority to processor and memory requirements is the performance of the disk subsystem with its dual role to provide both virtual memory and the rapid retrieval of data for processing. Application servers benefit from disk subsystem arrangements that improve response time, a property more important to application service than file throughput. Disk arrays and dedicated disks provide improved application server performance by separating the load on relatively poky disk drives into multiple parallel units, feeding the memory and processors with data and code more quickly than with a single drive. As an alternative to (or in combination with) the use of disk arrays, RAM disk software can be used to provide both vastly improved application response time as well as throughput. The only disadvantages of this kind of utility are the cost of the extra DRAM and the potential loss of some fault tolerance if you are not protected by effective power backup and power filtration. Paramount to application server performance is the amount of memory available for the applications, NT operating system, and file system cache. The more memory you have, the more NT will use, and the more memory NT system components will have to work with.

For information on optimizing the disk subsystem including the file system cache, see Chapter 7, "Optimizing Disks."

The best way to optimize Windows NT Server as an application server is to make it as transparent to the chosen server-side application as possible. All system resources then become dedicated to providing the best possible performance for the application.

Application servers include just about any kind of NT service that provides users with interaction where most of the work is being performed on the server. Because of the difference in priority for internal network components, application servers tend to provide reduced performance when used in a fileserver role. The most common server-side applications that application servers provide are:

- Internet server providing WWW (World-Wide Web) server/Search engine/Gopher Server/FTP Server/Mailserver, etc.
- Database/transaction server
- Telephony applications
- High-speed routing (steelhead) and proxy service
- RAS Server
- Multimedia streaming of audio and video

For more information on optimizing Internet Information Server, see Chapter 11, "Optimizing Your NT Internet Server."

Niche markets where the application server role is used include use as a rendering engine for 3D graphics applications; an application server running a client-server transaction processing system for a large organization; a development system for running large background binary compilations; and the server-side transaction processor for a secure credit card ordering system.

FILESERVER ROLE DEFINED

A fileserver's main job is dealing with network input/output (I/O) requests for user files and printing requests. These files are passed back to the user workstation from server storage without modification. In some cases, the spooler service may account for a greater percentage of the percent of disk time used than file requests if the size and frequency of print jobs are very large.

Larger file sizes associated with "graphically rich" environments also tend to produce large and complex print jobs, so the need for a more potent disk subsystem becomes top priority. Rendering of most print jobs destined for PCL printers will be performed on the client workstation. Most PostScript jobs will be partially rendered at the workstation and passed on to the printer whose own local processor will finish rendering the job.

For more information on improving printing performance, see Chapter 8, "Optimizing NT Printing."

Processor performance is not nearly as significant on fileservers as on application servers, because the main use of the server's processor is from servicing the operating system and interrupts generated by the network adapters and disk controllers. A small amount of processor time is also spent completing the rendering of print jobs. Fileservers greatly benefit from disk arrays consisting of striped disks (including RAID levels 0, 5, 01, and 10) as well as individual disks dedicated to particular functions to improve their disk I/O capacity. Throughput is more of an issue than response time in this role (the amount of data it can transfer as opposed to how quickly it responds). Fileservers can be dedicated or nondedicated, and also have the option of participating in domain security if configured to do so during the installation of NT. Because fileservers emphasize the disk subsystem and the performance of the network adapters, the processing power of an SMP machine will not benefit performance much, wasting resources that could otherwise be put to good use elsewhere. This brings us to another important aspect of performance optimization – providing what is needed for the job now and into the future, but not wasting money on resources that will never be used. Better that you instead spend the money saved on other subsystems that can actually benefit performance. Deploying a system assigned for file service with 4x 533MHz processors while pushing a maximum sustained processor usage of less than ten percent represents an awful waste of hardware. In regards to file services, keep your focus on the disk controllers and network adapters.

Fileservers provide print service in addition to file access. At its simplest, a fileserver is a file repository for large numbers of relatively small data and text files, and serves as a print server, perhaps controlling large numbers of printers or printer pools. In some cases, it may be necessary to further break down the division of file and print server into dedicated print server, especially if a relatively low powered system is required to provide the highest possible performance for a particular print server related function. This would include such advanced uses of NT as using third-party server software to make NT into a RIP (Raster Image Processor) for a color proofer or imagesetter (a device which prints to film and is used by commercial print shops to make the printing plates used in the printing process). In the case of the last two items, multiple fast processors could relieve the burden of the processor-intensive rendering routines found in complex full-color jobs.

DEFINING DOMAIN CONTROLLER

Domain controllers are the unsung heroes of a Windows NT network, providing such necessary functions as user and group information as well as providing security. Domain controllers have the unglamorous role of providing user log on validation and controlling access to network resources such as files, printers, and the like. The goal of the domain controller is to make access to files and other resources as transparent to the user as possible. If the domain controller slows to a crawl, access to otherwise stable and fast resources can grind to a halt. A smoothly functioning domain controller with adequate capacity is key to achieving high performance NT networking.

As network sizes grow, it often becomes desirable to dedicate the domain controllers to servicing log on and authentication requests alone with no additional roles to perform. A relatively small system can service many thousands of log on requests per hour, with the most important aspect of its operation being the rate at which it can process those authentication and security policy requests. NT's domain structure, though in many ways dense and cumbersome, does allow you to relieve the overhead and fault tolerance across many machines. The Primary Domain Controller (PDC) is backed by Backup Domain Controllers (BDC) that provide load balancing and fault tolerance domain controller activity. A dead PDC can be replaced by a BDC through promotion of the machine, reducing potential downtime.

Frequently, domain controllers (Primary Domain Controllers and Backup Domain Controllers) are also used to provide file and print services in addition to security duties, particularly in small networks. If the network is small enough and the capacity of the server still great enough even after providing all its required services, there is nothing wrong with adding additional services to the server, though as the load grows, the compromise for performing one task over another becomes greater. It is generally safer on a large network (300 users or more) to provide dedicated functions or at the very least prioritizing domain control over the file and print services. Using a domain controller in a dual role with application services is only wise on the lightest of loads, because both the domain controller and application service will be competing for processor time, an often precious commodity for application services. Your use and loading will determine which course is better to take.

The domain controller role is one in which the server acts as the gateway to network resources, logging on users, and providing access control to available resources. In addition, these servers often provide additional functionality such as name service and browse lists, which include all available resources.

The following is a list of some of the more common services provided by Windows NT domain controllers:

- Primary Domain Controller/Backup Domain Controller Services (including user logon authentication and user accounts database synchronization)
- Name Resolution Services (DNS, WINS, etc.)
- Browser Services (Domain Master Browser, Master Browser, Backup Browser, etc.)
- Time services

Balancing multipurpose servers

Often times, budgets and management issues do not permit the use of a large number of NT systems with dedicated functions. In this scenario, the act of optimizing NT becomes a juggling act of prioritizing different services. Optimizing NT in this scenario becomes a game of compromise in which services are prioritized for the server to perform those services that are requested the most. Not surprisingly, multiuse NT servers constitute the bulk of NT Server installations and also tend to be the most difficult to tweak. You must figure out how to balance the performance between or among the required services in such a way that the effect of the compromise is felt by the users the least.

For example, a BDC may provide in addition to its domain security functions basic file and print services. In many small networks, this is a completely acceptable solution because neither the user nor the BDC is impacted by the additional overhead (file services are overhead if the main role is domain security functions). As long as no one is complaining about performance and the server has extra capacity remaining to service any increase in demand for its resources, the extra services the system is providing means that a greater return on the hardware and software investment has been achieved. As discussed earlier, the greatest drawback is that tweaking the server to provide the best performance for servicing a particular task impairs its capability to perform its other tasks well if the system is taxed by heavy usage of a service you neglected to account for. In addition, should the system fail or a reinstallation/restore ever be required, you will have to go through considerably more to reestablish the system to the state it was in before it went comatose. For an example of distributing multipurpose services across multiple servers in a domain, see "Delegating Server Duties" later in this chapter.

Non-Windows network support

Windows NT Server also has built-in support for the Macintosh operating system so that it may be used by Macintosh clients as though it were an Appleshare server (however, this is far from a high-performance network environment – Appleshare runs over the top of the MacOS about as well as LAN Manager did over OS/2, if not worse). Additional capabilities include NetWare connectivity tools to provide access for NT Workstation (CSNW) and NT Server (GSNW) and NetWare server emulation (FPNW). NT does not have any built-in support for UNIX clients, but support for these operating systems is available through third parties such as Hummingbird and Intergraph, as well as via freeware applications available on the Internet.

SERVICING MACINTOSH CLIENTS

Once Services for Macintosh (SFM) is installed, NT Server can fully support Macintosh clients natively with similar performance to Windows-based clients. MacOS clients can view resources from the Chooser as easily as Windows clients can view resources through Network Neighborhood.

The AppleTalk Filing Protocol (AFP) is implemented to allow users to share data files and applications stored on the NT Server. SFM is designed for use as a file-server service for servicing Macintosh clients, and can be tweaked to provide better performance at the expensive of fileserver responsiveness to non-Macintosh clients. While NTFS has native support for Macintosh file resources and naming conventions, it does not pay to use the same fileserver on a busy network for both Macintosh and Windows clients unless you can properly balance the load placed on the server by both sets of clients. To give maximum performance to the Macintosh clients, you need to tweak the Registry settings that set memory usage for the SFM services. Keeping your Macintosh services on a few dedicated machines will reduce the complexity of restoration in the event a system fails and provide the most efficient service for Macintosh clients. SFM appears as a separate network provider, allowing you to choose the more frequently used network provider based on system usage to improve responsiveness.

SERVER SERVICES FOR CONNECTING TO NETWARE SERVERS

Three services exist for connecting NT Workstation and NT Server to NetWare servers. Client Services for NetWare (CSNW) is an NT service for providing NT Workstation with access to NetWare fileservers shared directories and printers. It requires IPX/SPX as its dependency and installs as a separate network provider/redirector.

Gateway Services for NetWare (GSNW) is an NT Server service which provides servers and Windows clients with access to NetWare resources as though they were located on the NT Server. Like CSNW, this service requires IPX/SPX to install and operate. There is some overhead involved in the way that mapping is performed, and the tool was not designed for allowing fast access to the NetWare servers.

File and Print Service for NetWare (FPNW) is a service for emulating a NetWare 3.12 server or a NetWare 4.x server using bindery emulation. NT does not support the newer Novell Directory Service (NDS) despite the benefits of having such a directory service. FPNW provides seamless access to clients configured for communication with NetWare servers without any changes to client software. This is a migration tool and has a lot of overhead. Long-term use should be avoided. All the NetWare connecting services, FPNW, GSNW, and CSNW can get a performance boost by changing the network provider order to allow the provider component redirector for NetWare first chance at the communication on the network.

What about autotuning?

NT Server is said to have self-optimizing mechanisms, so you may ask just how well they perform. Autotuning is performed on most components very conservatively, mainly to avoid wasting memory resources. The autotuning design comes with a price; the consequences of overriding the parameters NT automatically adjusts often means disabling autotuning for that particular component. This is done in part because NT may actually autotune your changes right out of existence. The autotuning features are component specific; overriding the server service entries won't affect the redirector service if it remains untouched.

Generally, NT's autotuning features are better than those of other operating systems at providing improved performance based on usage, but can never replace hand tweaking of parameters to adjust performance for a specific NT implementation. Many of the autotuning functions of such things as transport protocols continue to function, even after you have made significant changes to default values. Most values which are dynamically changed by NT's autotuning mechanism have a value of "0." This does not indicate that the actual value is zero, but that NT is free to change the value to meet the constantly changing demand and resource availability.

The resources the autotuner and manual Registry tweaks consume include the paged and nonpaged pool. Higher performance settings are almost always at the expense of an amount of one or both of these memory pools. NT's autotuning features use the installed memory as a guide to help determine component parameters for increasing memory "breathing room" with higher performance as a result. When you make manual changes which disable autotuning of system level components, NT will not automatically slide up the memory bracket to increase the amount of memory allocated for components when you install additional memory.

You can use the net config server command to enumerate server parameters normally hidden from view by issuing a nondestructive command from the command prompt. Using the command `NET CONFIG SERVER /SRVCOMMENT` will dump the hidden values in the Registry into the parameters key, but will not enumerate *all* the available values. Those that you need to be aware of will, however, be visible. To enumerate (that is, write Registry parameters that are autotuned to the `LanManserver\parameters` key) type:

```
CONFIG SRV /SRVCOMMENT
```

As a warning, the act of enumerating the server service Registry entries will automatically turn off the autotuning feature of the server service, leaving you to make the important changes by hand from then on. NT disables autotuning for a particular key in order to avoid overwriting your hand set values. As a consequence of disabling autotuning, neither Control Panel settings nor the addition of new system memory will affect performance, and no changes will actually be made. To allow NT to make better use of the memory added to the system, you will have to delete all enumerated values except these:

- EnableSharedNetDrives
- Lmannounce
- NullSessionPipes
- NullSessionShares
- Size

In addition to those entries presented here, you may also have additional values installed by a service. Do not remove these additional static entries, either. Once you have removed all these values (by selecting and deleting) the autotuning feature will be enabled and any memory you added will be recognized.

Typing the `NET CONFIG SERVER` command by itself will not disable autotuning without passing it a switch, but will show you what is already configured.

System size as calculated by NT for the purposes of autotuning various parameters is based on a fairly simple formula. A system size of "small" is defined as an NT Workstation with the minimal 12MB of memory for the x86 platform or 16MB memory for RISC machines. A "small" system size for NT Server starts with the minimum of 16MB on the x86 platform, and 16 to 20MB of memory for RISC systems. A "medium" system size is an NT Workstation with 24MB of memory on the x86 platform or 32MB of memory for the RISC platform. A "medium" size server for the x86 platform is 32MB while RISC systems are 32 to 48MB of memory. A "large" NT Workstation on the x86 platform is any amount over 32MB, while RISC-based systems are considered "large" at 48MB memory and up. A large server size is 64MB or more for the x86 platform or 64MB or more for the RISC platform.

See the "Keeping System Modification Logs" section of Chapter 12, "Maintaining Your NT Server," for information on protecting your Registry by logging all changes.

Simple stuff to avoid

It is a common situation that the most sophisticated IS departments armed with powerful measuring and benchmarking techniques can also occasionally fail to see the obvious. Among the simple things to avoid doing on any NT server installation is using performance sapping features like the 3D screen savers (as discussed in Chapter 4, "NT Optimizing 101"). NT 4.0 Workstation and Server ship with OpenGL 3D screen savers that can simultaneously make your server much more attractive to look at the expense of server responsiveness and processing power. One pretty OpenGL screen saver can bring an otherwise efficient server to its knees. The cause of this performance penalty is simple: Because you are not using a hardware-accelerated OpenGL video card in your server (which is true about 99% of the time because such cards are specialized and somewhat expensive items), the routines for modeling and rendering the 3D image will use your host processor(s) to perform these routines. The result of all this behind the scenes number crunching is a processor usage that may be consistently hitting 90 or 100 percent, even on a fast system. The best method to avoid this is to simply delete 3D screen saver files (or simply not install them at all), leaving only nonsapping ones such as Blank Screen (a highly recommended one for any server). You can do this by deleting all screen saver files with names of the format SS*.SCR in the *%SYSTEMROOT%\SYSTEM32* folder. If you were monitoring the server when one of these screen savers kicked in, all you would be likely to see initially would be a massive jump in processor usage at the moment the screen saver kicked in.

NT Clustering for Maximum Performance and Availability

Clustering has gotten a lot of attention recently as NT moves closer and closer to replacing or running alongside the last vestiges of "big iron" mainframes and minicomputers in the dark, raised floor recesses of the corporate MIS departments. The concept of connecting multiple servers together to share the load or provide fault tolerance (or both) is not new; DEC's VMS had this functionality upwards of 16 years ago. Moving NT up to the enterprise has meant adding availability and fault resilience that systems supporting thousands of users and running 24 hours a day, 7 days a week require. In its simplest form, clustering consists of a pair or small group of independent servers that are managed as a single resource, each providing additional power to cluster, each backing the other. As the load on the resource being shared increases, the servers in the cluster all share the burden, allowing capacity beyond that of any individual server. If a server fails within the group, the remaining members "take up the slack" to continue servicing requests. Many of the existing low-cost clustering solutions for NT can provide either simple availability with no performance scaling, or satisfying scaling issues within a simple two- or three-way cluster. Microsoft and its business partners ported the concept of clustering to NT and created "WolfPack," a means by which to open the door to higher performance enterprise-level NT. Microsoft developed a simple three-phase plan to incorporate clustering in NT, starting with adding an API to allow applications and services to be "cluster aware." One very basic clustering solution is from Microsoft itself in the form of MCS (Microsoft Cluster Server).

Microsoft Cluster Server provides such features as:

- *Availability*: MCS can automatically determine that a failure occurred at either the software or hardware level and moves key services onto the remaining server (it only supports a two-server cluster at this time). The fail-over period is measured in seconds and allows the users connected to the cluster to continue working without downtime.
- *Manageability*: Also provided for in the MCS product is the capability for administrators to check on the status of resources connected to the cluster and assign workload onto each individual server within the cluster. An added benefit of assigned duties is that you can perform "rolling updates" where a new software revision is added without having to take the shared application off-line.

- *Scalability*: This is the big word MS jocks tote about in lieu of new cluster-aware applications designed to use the MCS API to perform dynamic load-balancing of an application across many servers. Without support at the application level (cluster-aware), scalability of a shared application across many servers cannot be achieved. In addition, MCS will support (in Phase 2) the adding of servers to the existing cluster groups transparently. The entire process will be self-configuring once the option for automatically adding new servers is enabled. Scaling performance across multiple machines within a cluster is managed and set using friendly GUI tools and fairly basic concepts, making it easy to build powerful clustering solutions.

Several of the early adopters of "WolfPack" who contributed to the specification also have designed and implemented vendor-specific enhancements to the specification that go well beyond the initial capabilities included in phase 1 of Microsoft's WolfPack clusters. This includes Tandem, HP, Digital, and IBM, among others.

One of the companies most seasoned in clustering solutions, having invented the concept in the 1980s, is Digital Equipment Corporation. In the early 1980s, VMS was already providing VMS clustering on VAX minicomputers. Today, Digital can leverage its experience with its Digital Clusters for NT.

In addition, don't add insult to injury and punish the server even further by boosting the screen resolution to workstation levels (1024x768 and up). This results in the need to draw even more pixel information on the screen. Doing so is also wasteful of processor resources, and therefore a bad idea. Therefore, don't waste money by using high-performance video cards in your server, and don't use its native drivers set to high resolution. Instead, opt to run at no more than 800x600 (or even better, 640x480) using NT's stable, built-in drivers. The reason the latter is important is that Windows NT 4.0 introduced an architecture change that brought the GDI (Graphical Device Interface) components into the kernel where they could be run faster than in versions prior to NT 4.0. This added speed came at a price, because it becomes possible that a bad video or printer driver can cause performance problems and even system crashes, something that wasn't possible under Windows NT 3.5x (which ran these services in User, rather than Kernel, Mode). Do yourself a favor and use the standard VGA or SVGA driver, and only use new third-party printer drivers after you have tested them rigorously on a nonserver or non-production system.

Cutting the fat

Windows NT comes with several default services that you may wish to disable if the purpose they serve doesn't coincide with your intended use for the system. Such components consume small amounts of processor time and a reasonable amount of memory when they are started, and eliminating them can regain some performance lost to bloat and reduce NT's memory footprint (you can never have too much memory!). Suitability to role governs which services you can ax and which must stay.

Some of the easiest changes you can make involve the number of services you load at boot. Figure 10-1 shows a list of NT services, some of which may be little more than extra fat in your system. The Services applet shows the startup parameters for each service, and the state of each service (started or not started). The services for NT Workstation and NT Server are functionally identical with only a few additions to the base server product. Most of the services listed only occupy roughly 200 to 300K of memory each and wake up to perform housekeeping such that they generally require little CPU attention. Then again, every little bit helps. See Table 10-1 for a full description of the base services.

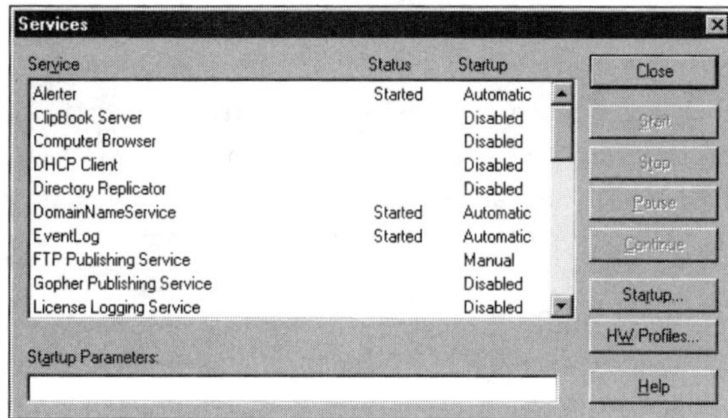

Figure 10-1: The Windows NT Control Panel with some of its more common, default services.

In addition, you may find such things as third-party services and services added by installing components such as DNS, DHCP, WINS, IIS, or the TimeServer included on the Resource Kit CD. If you are not using the FTP or Gopher services from within the IIS suite of services, disable them and free some memory, or set them to a startup type of manual.

TABLE 10-1 A LIST OF COMMON SERVICES AND WHAT EACH PROVIDES

Service	Description
Alerter	This service notifies administrators (by default) and users (which you have to add in Server Manager) what alerts are occurring on the machine where alerter is running. To receive notification of these alerts, you must have the messenger service set to load automatically at boot. This is useful and doesn't take up much space.
ClipBook Server	This allows a user to share the contents of the ClipBook (Clipboard), and is not too useful for a server in most environments. Although the service is set to manual by default, you may want to disable it altogether to prevent applications running on the server from being able to start it.
Computer Browser	This is the service that provides a list of servers and server resources to clients that request it. Maintaining it on NT Workstations and NT Servers constitutes a major performance sapper. This is a chatty and cumbersome server that definitely constitutes fat; however, it also happens to be required for any dialog-based browsing of network resources (e.g., the Network Neighborhood and many application dialogs). If you can get your users to manually type server names (e.g., \\BIGSERVER) rather than relying on browse lists provided by the Browser service, you'll improve server performance and reduce network traffic. However, many environments will likely encounter resistance to this idea and be forced to retain it; after all, it is a more "user friendly" method of finding network resources than memorizing Universal Naming Convention (UNC) names.
DHCP Client	This is the service that establishes and connects to Dynamic Host Configuration Protocol (DHCP) Servers that lease IP addresses. It is set to manual if you tell it at boot (after installing TCP/IP during an installation) that you do not want to see any more DHCP messages. If you do not use DHCP, then this service is not required.
Directory Replicator	Not enabled by default, this service allows you to transfer files and directories between defined NT systems. As hardly anyone uses it and it's not enabled by default, it's not a problem.

continued

Service	Description
Event Log	This service records all system, security, and application events in a log file where the events can be viewed later. Event log is an essential component that lets you know what is going on with the internals of NT components and hardware. Disable this only when absolutely necessary, or to see what it's like to live without it.
License Logging Service	This service establishes the number of client and server licenses and the method of counting them. Because this is a tool for helping you stay legal, it is not essential and qualifies as definite fat. It is enabled by default and gets in the way.
Messenger	This server provides a functional equivalent to the Windows pop-up program, providing pop-up messaging for NT systems.
Net Logon	On NT Workstation computers, this service supports domain pass-through authentication. This service is used when the NT Workstation participates on a domain. On NT Servers, this service provides account authentication and keeps the LSA/SAM up-to-date and synchronized with all other domain member servers.
Network DDE	This service provides both a transport driver and security for Dynamic Data Exchange (DDE) communications. This service is set to manual by default, so the system can start it if it is invoked by an application.
Network DDE DSDM	This service manages DDE communications. The service is used by Network DDE service. DSDM stands for DDE Share Database Manager. This service is set to manual by default, so the system can start the service if it is needed by an application.
NT LM Security Support Provider	This service provides security to Remote Procedure Call (RPC) services which use transports other than named pipes. This service is set to manual by default.
Plug and Play	This service allows such things as network adapters to be automatically configured at boot. This service is not yet fully functional. Though you can turn it off to save some memory, you will not be able to open Control Panel if you do.

continued

Table 10-1 A LIST OF COMMON SERVICES AND WHAT EACH PROVIDES *(Continued)*

Service	Description
Remote Procedure Call (RPC) Locator	This service allows distributed programs to use RPC name service. This service manages the RPC name database. It is set to manual by default.
Remote Procedure Call (RPC) Service	This service is the RPC subsystem of Windows NT that provides the endpoint mapper and miscellaneous RPC functions. This service is set to manual by default.
Schedule	Enables the capability to run AT and WinAT (WinAT is a resource kit GUI AT commander) to schedule a particular action to take place at a particular time. Schedule is an important service for permitting you to perform scheduled tasks on NT. The service is manual by default.
Server	Service provides RPC as well as file, print, and named pipes sharing. On NT Workstations, this can be disabled to free some memory, which can increase performance.
Spooler	This is the service that controls the print spooler. This constitutes fat on a system that does not have any printers attached and does not provide print spooling for any clients. This service is on by default and set to automatic (start at boot).
UPS	This is a basic Uninterruptible Power Supply (UPS) management utility. This service is disabled by default.
Workstation	This is the redirector service and provides network connections and communications. If you disable this on any NT machine, your network disappears completely.

You can also use the Server Manager to control (i.e., disable, stop, or configure the startup type of) services on a local or remote server. Figure 10-2 shows the Services option available within Server Manager, which allows you to administer the Service Control Panel on remote NT servers and workstations. To disable or modify the properties of a service, start by choosing the server you wish to configure from the list of servers, and then select Computer from the menu followed by Services.... You can then set the properties for the services and choose the ones you want to retain.

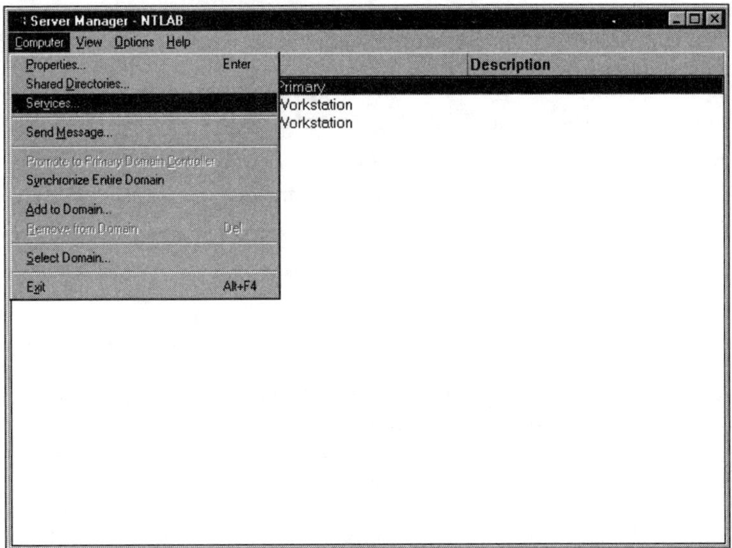

Figure 10-2: The Services option of Server Manager may be used to manage services on remote servers and workstations.

In Windows NT 4.0, many users and administrators have noticed that systems (especially servers) often have extremely long shutdown times. This is sometimes caused by a problem with a driver or service improperly closing. One of the most common services to cause this behavior is the spooler service. The service sits idly waiting for jobs and upon receiving a shutdown message may require several minutes to respond. Additionally, video drivers can cause shutdown delays that require driver update, though on most file servers the default VGA or Super VGA drivers are the best choice both for stability and simplicity.

To address the spooler issues, you can write a batch file with either a `.BAT` or `.CMD` extension with the following command contained within it (or you can simply type the command at an NT command prompt):

net stop spooler /y

This will down the spooler on the local system and allow you to shut down the system without having to wait the several minutes it normally takes for the shutdown process to complete. To further enhance the usefulness of the batch file, you can also create a shortcut to it and place it on your desktop for easy and convenient access. In many cases, running this batch file prior to shutting down the system will greatly reduce the amount of time it takes for the system to shut down.

For a full list of networking components and network architecture, see Chapter 9, "Optimizing Your NT Network."

Identifying Server Bottlenecks

By monitoring NT using such tools as the included Performance Monitor, you can discover unexpected things about your server's utilization and the traffic patterns that occur throughout the day, week, and month. Obvious signs of server bottlenecking include slow or reduced network I/O and reduced packet transfer rates. Server processors may be swamped with excess activity from handling too many or unnecessary services. A heavily burdened server may also experience disk bottlenecks due to memory shortages, which cause paging to the disk. The network interface may also be absorbing so much of the processor that additional requests cannot be satisfied because too little free processor time remains. The problems may also be less obvious; performance has not yet suffered but capacity for handling work has been reduced from what the server is actually capable of by either a single or group of components which aren't keeping up with demand.

See the "Meet Your Toolkit" section of Chapter 4, "NT Optimizing 101," for more information on using Performance Monitor to create charts, alerts, reports, and logs.

Included on the *Optimizing Windows NT* CD-ROM are two Performance Monitor workspace files, `ServerBottleneck.pmw` and `Server Advanced.pmw`, that contain a basic set of counters that will help you monitor NT Server performance. To use these files, simply locate and double-click them using the Windows NT Explorer (the files are located in the `\PMWORKSPACE` folder), or point your Web browser to the location of the *Optimizing Windows NT* CD-ROM after inserting it in your CD-ROM drive (e.g., `D:\`). Then select the page for Performance Monitor Workspaces and follow the instructions given to load and use the files.

There are a number of useful Performance Monitor objects that can help determine if the server is suffering a bottleneck. Build a new chart and monitor these counters at the default interval with the target system being your server (not the workstation you run Performance Monitor from). Items that are useful for this chart are shown in Table 10-2.

Deciphering Performance Monitor results

If you notice high rates of errors and rejected requests for blocking SMB (Server Message Block), you may want to try increasing the minworkitems and maxworkitems based on the workitem shortages value. When the counters Pool Paged, Pool Nonpaged Failures, Blocking Requests Rejected, and Work Item Shortages are showing values which continue to rise, the server software component is bottlenecking the rest of the server system, and the server service is not keeping up with demand. Context Block queue/sec can also indicate a server bottleneck if it averages 20 or more. Work items are the means by which a server is able to store SMB, the core component of NT network messaging. Larger numbers of work items (within the limit of the system resources) can help reduce the slowdown associated with large numbers of concurrent users using up the existing supply of work items. The two values for paged and nonpaged pool are indicative of insufficient memory resources. Nonpaged pool is system memory while paged pool is represented by the pagefile; if either is experiencing failures from reaching their limits, you should consider increasing both.

TABLE 10-2 SERVER PERFORMANCE-RELATED COUNTERS

Object	Counter	Instance	Description
Server	Blocking Requests Rejected	N/A	Counts the number of times the server has rejected blocking SMBs as a result of insufficient number of free work items. You may need to increase maxworkitem or minfreeworkitems.
Server	Context Block queue/sec	N/A	This is the rate that work context blocks had to be placed in the FSP queue to await server processing.
Server	Pool Nonpaged Failures	N/A	The number of times allocations from nonpaged pool have failed. Indicates that the computer's physical memory is too small.
Server	Pool Paged Failures	N/A	The number of times allocations from paged pool have failed. Indicates that the computer's physical memory of pagefile is too small.
Server	Work Item Shortages	N/A	This is the number of times that a STATUS_DATA_NOT_ACCEPTED error was returned to the client. This indicates that no more workitems were available. Increase initworkitems or maxworkitems

Work items increase depending on the installed system memory and the optimization bias of the server service (as with the Maximize Throughput...) and as long as autotuning for the server service is still enabled. The value will fluctuate in use between the minimum and maximum number specified by MaxWorkItems and InitWorkItems. Increasing the work items will not improve performance if the server is encumbered with too many services, so try to establish which services are in the highest demand and which are simply preventing the rest from functioning optimally. Objects and counters for obtaining this information are given in the advanced section later in this chapter. You may want to move these services (such as a database, Webserver, mailserver, etc.) onto another machine, which is not as busy.

Logging activity

To get information for long-range planning and analysis of shifting trends, you should consider regularly starting logs with fairly long intervals (say 5 minutes to 15 minutes) and recording these results to the local drive (or removable disks) to dump into a database such as Access for later review. You don't want so much information over a long period that you experience data overload, but you don't want too little information reflected in the logs either. Brief, sporadic bursts of activity that bottleneck the server and then disappear may not appear frequently (or at all) if they occur within a small enough interval while the update for the log is several times greater (a period in which the log is not being written to).

For more information on installation of the Datalog service, see Chapter 9, "Optimizing Your NT Network."

Advanced Performance Monitor objects

In Table 10-3, objects and counters for a more detailed picture of your server's performance and activity are given. The objects for such non-Windows network services as FPNW and SFM closely mirror those for the Windows networking components. FPNW and SFM objects have corresponding counters that allow you to use most of the same familiar counters from one network provider to the next. You can use the objects used in both the bottleneck detection .PMW file and the more advanced file after you change the server group for the non-Windows server components.

In addition to the general, advanced, and specific server role counters, see Chapter 9, "Optimizing NT Networking," for more information on monitoring the network subsystem of NT and incorporating its objects for more detailed analysis of network performance.

Table 10-3 ADVANCED SERVER COUNTERS

Object	Counter	Instance	Description
Server Work Queues	Context Blocks Queued/sec	one per processor	This is the rate at which work context blocks had to be queued to await processing.
Server Work Queues	Queue Length	one per processor	The current length of the server work queue for the selected processor. Sustained queue length of 4 or more is a good sign of a processor bottleneck. The count is instantaneous.
Server Work Queues	Bytes Send/sec	one per processor	This is a measure of server workload. It measures the amount of data being sent to clients from the selected processor.
Server Work Queues	Available Work Items	one per processor	This is the number of available work items used by clients to connect to the server for the selected processor. Keeping extra work items speeds processing. This count is instantaneous and not a running total. If the value sustains close to 0, you may need to increase the MinFreeWorkItems Registry value for the Server service.
Server Work Queues	Work Item Shortages	one per processor	This is the number of work items that were not available at the time a client tried to connect. A sustained value greater than 0 suggests that increasing MaxWorkItems may fix the problem.

continued

Object	Counter	Instance	Description
System	Total Interrupts /sec	N/A	This is the rate that the system services hardware interrupts from system devices (such as NICs and SCSI controllers).
System	Processor Queue Length	N/A	This measures the instantaneous length of the processor queue; it is expressed as a number of threads. You must also measure a thread object or the value will remain 0. There is only one processor queue, even on SMP systems. The count only includes ready threads, not those already running. A processor queue of more than 2 on average is a processor bottleneck.
System	% Total Interrupt Time	N/A	This is the sum of the percentage of interrupt time for all installed processors divided by the number of processors
Server	Bytes Total/sec	N/A	This provides an overall indication of server workload. The counter reflects the number of bytes sent and received from the server.

continued

Table 10-3 ADVANCED SERVER COUNTERS *(Continued)*

Object	Counter	Instance	Description
Server	Work Item Shortages	N/A	This is the number of times that the STATUS_ DATA_NOT_ACCEPTED error was returned to the client. This happens when there are no free work items remaining. This may require tweaking of the initworkitems and/or maxworkitems parameters.
Server	Pool Paged Failures	N/A	This counts the number of times that attempts to make new allocations in the paged pool have failed. It suggests that physical memory or pagefile are insufficient.
Server	Logon/sec	N/A	Logon/sec is the rate that all server log on requests are serviced.
Server	Logon Total	N/A	Logon Total counts and adds all interactive logons, network logons, service logons, successful logons, and failed logons and keeps a running count from the last reboot.
Server	Files Opened Total	N/A	Counts all successful attempts to open files that are performed by the server for the client requesting the file to be opened. This is a good tool for determining file I/O, overhead, and the effect of opportunistic locking (opplocking).

continued

Object	Counter	Instance	Description
Server	Errors System	N/A	This counts the number of times an unexpected internal error was detected. These problems are usually caused by a problem with a server component.
Server	Blocking Requests Rejected	N/A	This counts the number of times a blocking request was rejected due to a lack of free work items. This suggests that the maxworkitem and/or minfreeworkitems should be tuned.
Redirector	Bytes Total/sec	N/A	This counts the rate the redirector is processing data bytes. This includes all overhead.
Redirector	Current Commands	N/A	This counts the number of requests to Redirector that are currently queued for service. The number should mirror the number of NICs installed in the system. If this number is much larger than the number of network adapter cards installed in the computer, then it is likely that the server is seriously bottlenecked.
Redirector	Network Errors /sec	N/A	This counts serious errors, which generally indicate a communication problem between a remote server and local redirector components.

continued

TABLE 10-3 ADVANCED SERVER COUNTERS *(Continued)*

Object	Counter	Instance	Description
Redirector	Reads Denied/sec	N/A	The rate that the server cannot honor requests for Raw Reads. When read size is much larger than the server's negotiated buffer size, the redirector requests a Raw Read which, if the server permits, transfers to the client with the absolute minimum overhead that can be achieved. To do this, the server must lock out all other requests. If the server is too busy, the request will be rejected.
Redirector	Writes Denied /sec	N/A	This is the rate at which Raw Writes are rejected. When the write request is much larger than the server's negotiated buffer size, redirector requests a Raw Write. If permitted, the data can be sent with the smallest overhead in addition to the data. To do this, the server must lock out all other requests. It will reject this request if it is too busy.

Interpreting advanced counter scores

Note that for the Server Work Queues counters, the Blocking Queue instance was omitted from the table because it remains at 0. If queues for any queue-measuring items exceed four or sustain at two threads, you know that your processor is becoming a bottleneck. Reduced performance will occur if the redirector is attempting Raw Reads and Raw Writes but is being rejected frequently. High values for either will be indicative of a busy server, other counters can help pinpoint where the problem lies. The measure of work items is another indication of server workload, if the values for Available Work Items are going down while Work Item Shortages are going up, increase the InitWorkItems and MaxWorkItems in the Registry as described later in this chapter.

The total interrupts per second and total interrupt time are two indications of hardware efficiency. Total interrupts for the system should not exceed 200 for any length of time; busy systems often hover between 150 and 200 interrupts/sec. If this value goes as high as 600, a hardware problem must be resolved immediately. Total Interrupt time represents the percentage of the processor time that was used servicing interrupts. If this is much above 30 percent for any length of time, you have a hardware problem that you should feel compelled to fix. Similarly, those counters which count errors, such as network errors, can help you isolate where the problem is with sending network data from the server to the workstations. If error counters have any sustainable values at all, then a persistent network or component problem is present which needs to be resolved. Occasional errors are unfortunately a part of life. If one shows up in your logs, don't panic. Even older networks develop hiccups every now and then.

Application server counters

Application servers are defined by their use of processor-bound services which can make significant memory and processor demands. By monitoring the specific server-side applications that the application server runs, you can determine such things as whether or not you have overcommitted memory to a service, such as SQL Server, which is not using the memory (because it performs its own memory management), or indicating a problem with your installed memory size and the size of the working set for the application process. On SMP machines, processor usage may outstrip available processing power, requiring either additional processors or faster processors. Additional system component counters can give additional help to isolate where your problem is. Refer to Table 10-4 for a list of counters for the application server role.

Table 10-4 APPLICATION SERVER COUNTERS LIST

Object	Counter	Instance	Description
System	% Total Processor Time	N/A	This is the percentage of time that the processor was used by a thread to execute instructions.
System	Processor Queue Length	N/A	Instantaneous measurement of the length of the processor queue expressed as a number of threads. To make it work, you must monitor a thread counter or the value remains 0. Installed processors all use a single queue in which threads wait. This only includes ready threads, not running threads. If the value sustains above 2 the processor is bottlenecking.
System	% Total interrupt Time	N/A	This is the total percentage of all interrupt time for the installed processors divided by the number of processors in the system.
System	Context Switches	N/A	The rate of switching execution of one thread to another. Higher priority threads are often the cause of this preemption. Too many context switches slow performance.
Server Work Queues	Available Work Items	one per processor	All client requests to the server are expressed as a server work item. NT stores a group of work items for every processor to speed processing. The value is instantaneous. If the value is sustained close to a value of 0, MinFreeWorkItems may need to be increased. Blocking Queue instance is always 0.

continued

Object	Counter	Instance	Description
Server Work Queues	Borrowed Work Items	one per processor	All client requests to the server are expressed as a server work item. NT stores a group of work items for every processor to speed processing. When a processor finally runs out of free work items, it borrows work items from another processor (if available). If the value continues to increase for this running counter, you may need to increase MaxWorkItems and/or MinFreeWorkItems. The Blocking Queue instance is always 0.
Server Work Queues	Queue Length	one per processor	This is the current length of the server work queue for the selected CPU. Sustained queue lengths greater than 4 may indicate processor bottlenecking. The measurement is instantaneous, and not an average.
Processor	Processor Queue Length	one instance per installed processor	Represents the number of threads in the processor queue. Only one queue exists, even for SMP machines. This counts ready threads only, and not threads already running. Sustaining a queue length of longer than 2 is indicative of a processor-related bottleneck.
Processor	% Processor Time	one instance per installed processor	This is a percentage of time that a processor is busy executing a thread.

continued

TABLE 10-4 **APPLICATION SERVER COUNTERS LIST** *(Continued)*

Object	Counter	Instance	Description
Process	Working Set	one instance for each running process	This is the current number of bytes in the working set of the selected process. This indicates the number of memory pages used by the process. If the amount of free memory in the system is above a certain threshold, memory pages are retained in the working set of a process even if they are not in use.
Process	Working Set Peak	one instance for each running process	This is the maximum number of bytes in the working set of this process at any point in time. The working set is the set of memory pages touched recently by the threads in the process. If free memory in the computer is above a threshold, pages are left in the working set of a process even if they are not in use.
Process	% Processor Time	one instance per running process	% processor time for the application service you are running.
Process	Priority Base	one instance per running process	The current base priority of the selected process.
Thread	% Processor Time	one instance per thread (multiple threads exist for each process)	This is the percentage of time that a thread used the processor to execute instructions. There is one instance per processor, so a four-processor system could monitor all four processor usage percentages independently.

continued

Object	Counter	Instance	Description
Thread	Priority Base	one instance per thread (multiple threads exist for each process)	This is the current base priority for the thread. Thread priority can be boosted above the base if the thread is responsible for user input. It can also be reduced if the thread requires its entire time slice to execute.
Thread	Priority Current	one instance per thread (multiple threads exist for each process)	This is the current dynamic priority of the thread. Thread priority can be boosted above the base if the thread is responsible for user input. It can also be lowered if the thread uses the entire time slice provided to execute.

Interpreting application server counter values

There are three counters which register waiting threads as viewed from the system, processor, and server work queues objects. System Processor Queues should not sustain over two threads, nor should Processor Queues sustain over two threads and Server Work Queues should not sustain over four threads. If any of these conditions exist, the processors in the system are being bottlenecked. Available Work Items should not decrease, and Borrowed Work Items should not continue to increase, because this is an indication that the MinWorkItems and MaxWorkItems values are probably set too low. The System object counters dealing with the processor include all processors as a whole rather than individually. The System Context Switches are a good indication of whether or not Registry changes you may decide to make based on the information in Performance Monitor has had a negative effect on the number of Context Switches being generated. Context switches require that the processor save the volatile contents of its internal registers, pick up the new task, execute the code in the thread, restore the previous register settings for the last thread that was run, and execute the last thread run again. This takes several milliseconds of time to accomplish. If this number has increased significantly based on your recorded system baselines, consider reducing the values you tweaked to reduce needless context switching.

For more information on creating a performance baseline and the use of Performance Monitor, see Chapter 4,"NT Optimizing 101."

Monitor the Process objects for your server-side applications and monitor the peak size of the working set as opposed to the current size of the working set for that process. If the current size exceeds the peak size, then (with an application like SQL Server) you should reevaluate the amount of memory that you should lock down for use with the application, if it provides this option. This is also a good indicator of whether the installed memory in the system is enough to adequately service the NT operating system and the application services that are installed, as well as provide sufficient remaining memory for caching.

Use the Process Priority Base counter to check on the priority set by the configuration utility for the server-side application. Use the Process % Processor Time counter to evaluate if the processor configuration of your system is sufficient for servicing both the server-side application and the operating system along with any other system events. If Process % Processor Time is remaining at 90 percent, your services may have outgrown the machine, or you may be able to eliminate any additional processor cycle robbing service or move them to another machine. A sustained 75 percent Processor time from any of the object counters suggests an overall processor congestion. Use the individual object counters provided to isolate which process or component is using the most processor time and try to eliminate it.

An additional counter from the System object group is % Total Interrupt Time. This gives you an idea of how much time the processors are spending servicing hardware interrupts from disk controller, network adapters, and so forth. If this number climbs above a sustained 30 percent on a dedicated application server, then some hardware component is using too much of the processor time and is reducing the processing capacity of the system. Technologies like I20 should reduce this figure, as will hardware RAID controllers with large amounts of hardware cache and specialized processors to unload parity calculations from the host system processors. Make sure all devices are operating as efficient busmastering devices on the PCI bus, and eliminate any devices in the system that could be slowing the rest of the bus down (ISA or EISA bus bridged off PCI will slow the PCI bus as well). Any ISA or EISA controllers should be replaced by PCI alternatives. If you have to purchase new PCI controllers to replace inefficient, older PCI 2.0 specification controllers, find a more recent PCI 2.1 specification alternative with a high efficiency index for low CPU usage and high transfer rates from memory through busmastering DMA. Disk configuration was discussed earlier in this book, so we won't repeat that information here.

See Chapter 7, "Optimizing Disks," for more information on the configuration and maintenance of disks in Windows NT.

Application server optimization

Application servers have special requirements that can make them less straightforward to configure than more simplistic file and print servers. First of all, NT application servers may run on top of NT Server but provide their own memory management, making changes to NT's Registry harmful to the performance of the application that runs on top of it. MS SQL and Oracle are good examples of this kind of independence from some of NT's memory manager. Making as much memory and disk time as possible available for these applications will improve performance. Segment the disks according to their function, and group the access type (such as sequential or random) to the portions of the application that you separate off.

Both Exchange Server and SQL have log files and data sets. The data sets are read/written randomly while log files are written to sequentially. To get the performance you need from both, you should strongly consider separating these components onto separate disks or disk sets (i.e., RAID volumes).

Another useful suggestion on SQL Server is that you can lock down the memory it uses as a percentage of the total installed memory. This partitioned memory can't be touched by NT, which is one reason you should be careful to measure it twice to make sure you are not stealing memory NT could have used (measure twice, cut once). Monitor SQL server's memory usage within this locked-down memory partition by opening Performance Monitor, choosing the Process object, then the SQL executable. If the amount of memory actually committed is much less than the partition you locked down, then you should rethink the size you gave SQL and give it back to NT.

Applications that make full use of NT application server optimizations include IIS, Transaction Server, SMS, and Exchange Server.

For application servers running memory-hungry applications (other than those providing their own memory management previously discussed), one of the most significant optimizations you can make is to configure the Server service to give memory allocation preference to applications over the system cache. This guarantees applications the lion's share of memory on the server. This option may be configured in the Services tab of the Network Control Panel, by choosing the Properties for the Server service (this configuration dialog is shown in Figure 10-3).

For more information on optimizing Internet Information Server, see Chapter 11,"Optimizing Your Windows NT Internet Server."

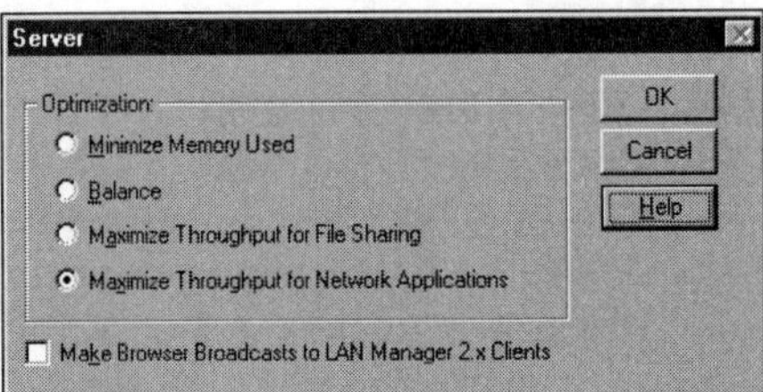

Figure 10-3: Configuring the Server service's Maximize Throughput for Network Applications option via the Network Control Panel.

Application servers using SMP can benefit from the affinity many applications have for the processor on which they were last run. This was deliberately engineered to avoid wasting the data and instructions already stored in processor cache and also to reduce the delays in context switching.

There are many places in the Registry where you can give Registry values such as "-1" in the Registry keys for some server-side applications in order to ensure that a particular application always runs on a particular "soft" dedicated processor. Conversely, you can use additional Registry modifications to ensure that all applications and the NT operating system threads go to whatever processor is available (potentially with a loss of performance from the loss of processor cache data).

Because memory and CPU performance are so critical to good application server performance, you need to know all you can about identifying bottlenecks in these subsystems. See Chapter 5, "Optimizing Memory and Processing," for more information on these topics.

With application servers such as Exchange, you should move the information store onto the fastest drive or array at your disposal. Use a dedicated disk or striped set for the logs that can be read very quickly.

Exchange Server includes a performance-monitoring tool called LoadSim (Load Simulator) which can help you balance system performance for the Exchange Server platform. This is a vertical tool specifically designed for probing and tuning the Exchange Server service. In addition, Exchange includes an optimization utility that can (and should) be run to determine the most efficient locations for the various components of Exchange, including transaction log files and the Directory and Information Store databases.

Fileserver counters

As we discussed earlier, fileservers are very sensitive to disk and network interface problems. Objects for monitoring the performance of the fileserver must always include objects from the logical disk, physical disk objects, as well as the network interface. Your processor objects or system objects (especially useful in SMP systems) do not need to be very focused, a generalized % utilization is sufficient, because it is not a high-demand resource in the fileserver in comparison with other components. What matters most in judging the values the objects are capturing is the average amount of time that a server must queue requests because the device is bottlenecking. Mild queue lengths of 2 or less on a sustained basis are quite reasonable, though remaining capacity for performing work, at least from the component you are monitoring, is probably reaching its limits.

For information on optimizing disk configurations, see Chapter 7, "Optimizing Disks."

Some good counters for determining if the fileserver is operating to its full potential and satisfying needs include those in Table 10-5.

Table 10-5 FILESERVER PERFORMANCE COUNTERS

Object	Counter	Instance	Description
Logical Disk	Avg. Disk Bytes Transfer	one per disk	This is the average number of bytes transferred to and from disk.
Logical Disk	Avg. Disk Queue Length	one per disk	This is the average number of read/write requests that were queued for a particular disk.
Logical Disk	Current Disk Queue Length	one per disk	This samples the length of the disk command queue. It is an instantaneous length.
Physical Disk	% Disk Time	one per disk	The percentage of time that the disk drive is busy servicing read/write requests.
Physical Disk	Avg. Disk Bytes Transfer	one per disk	This measures the number of bytes transferred to and from disk during write/read.
Physical Disk	Avg. Disk Queue Length	one per disk	This is an average queue length which includes both read and write requests that were queued for the disk.
Physical Disk	Current Disk Queue Length	one per disk	This is the number of requests unfulfilled on the disk at sample time. It is an instantaneous count and not an average.
Network Segment	%Network Utilization	one per attached segment	This is the percent of bandwidth in use on the measured segment.

continued

Object	Counter	Instance	Description
Network Interface	Output Queue Length	one per NIC	This is the length of the output packet queue for the NIC. If the value goes above 2 and stays there, there are either delays from the network medium itself, or the NIC.
Network Interface	Current Bandwidth	one per NIC	This is an estimate of NIC current bandwidth in bps (bits per second).
Server	Pool Non-Paged Bytes	N/A	This counts the number of bytes in nonpageable memory that the server is currently using. This counter can assist in assessing proper settings for max nonpagedmemoryusage parameter.
Server	Pool Paged Bytes	N/A	This is the number of bytes of pageable memory the server is currently using. This counter can help determine optimal maxpage dmemoryusage parameter.
Server	Session Sessions	N/A	This is an indication of server activity.
Server	Files Open	N/A	This counts the number of files currently opened on the server. This is an indicator of server activity.
Server	Directory Search	N/A	This counts the number of searches for files that occurred in the sample period. It is an indicator of server workload.

continued

TABLE 10-5 FILESERVER PERFORMANCE COUNTERS *(Continued)*

Object	Counter	Instance	Description
Server	Files Open Total	N/A	This counts the total number of files opened on the server. This indicates server workload.
System	Processor Time %Total	N/A	This measures the amount of time that a thread spent being executed by the processor.
System	%Total Interrupt Time	N/A	This is the sum of percent of interrupt time for all installed processors divided by the number of processors in the system.

Fileserver counter results

As with so many other things in NT, the objects which monitor queue lengths are the most important to watch; percentages of utilization are not a serious issue unless the queue lengths increase as well. A queue length of 2 for disk, processor, or network interface will tell you that the component is no longer able to keep up with demand. If you can achieve close to 100 percent utilization without queuing commands, you're getting the maximum out of the component (theoretically true but difficult to achieve in practice). Logical Disk counters differ from Physical Disk counters in that logical disk counters include partitions and disk sets created by Disk Administrator. Physical disks deal only with the physical drives on an individual basis, regardless of how they might be configured. The counters for the fileserver chart include the Server: Work Item Shortages counter, which tells you if you need to modify the values for initworkitems and maxworkitems. The two counters for monitoring paged and nonpaged pool can help you to tweak the size of these pools to enhance the performance of the Server service. Server: Paged Pool and Server: Non-Paged Pool reflect the pools that were described in previous chapters on optimizing memory and processing. The values for increasing the server service are all within the parameters subkey of the LanManserver key, which is discussed in a later section on Registry modifications.

Processor usage is reflected by the rather general System: Processor Time, which is all you really need for fileservers most of the time. If the processor should for some reason start getting anywhere near sustaining 50 percentage processor usage, start adding application and service processes to your chart or log and look for unusual amounts of activity. Be very aware of your disk controller and network adapter efficiency. Adding NICs, disk controllers, and RAID controllers is great for improving performance through segmenting the workload across several buses and components, but only if they are functioning normally. The System counter % Total Interrupt time can let you know if your processor is being unnecessarily used by a malfunctioning or poorly configured controller card. If your percent of network utilization climbs above a sustained 50 percent of the total network bandwidth, your network interface is being pushed too hard (unless you run to a switch). Find out what is causing the serious network traffic and eliminate it using Network Monitor and Performance Monitor.

For more information on improving the performance of the NT network subsystem for maximum throughput, see Chapter 9, "Optimizing Your NT Network."

There really are no hard and fast rules for determining NT fileserver memory requirements, so use this as a guideline rather than a rigid formula.

This formula will give you a rough estimate that you can use to determine an amount of memory appropriate for your installation. This does not take into account any application services you may wish to run and assumes a cache size that is very small.

System memory (minimum required for NT Server is 16MB for Intel, 20MB for Alpha) = A

User data:

Average size of data files open per user = B

Number of users = C

Multiply B by C = D

Applications:

Average size of executables being run off the server = E

Number of applications being run off the server = F

Multiply E by F = G

The total system memory recommended= A + D + G

File/print server optimization

Monitoring NT Server may reveal high disk utilization that may be caused by the spooler service. Shops that churn out several thousand print jobs from a single NT Server per day should consider moving the spool directory to a disk other than the disk where the pagefile resides; this is covered in Chapter 8. The pagefile itself ideally should not reside on the disk with the NT operating system or data files, and with the current cost for 2GB and 4GB SCSI disks, what reason remains not to move the pagefile? Figure 10-4 shows the `Control Panel\Network` server parameters. If you have not already gotten ahead of yourself and used the command to enumerate all parameters in the server registry key, this server parameter change will no longer work.

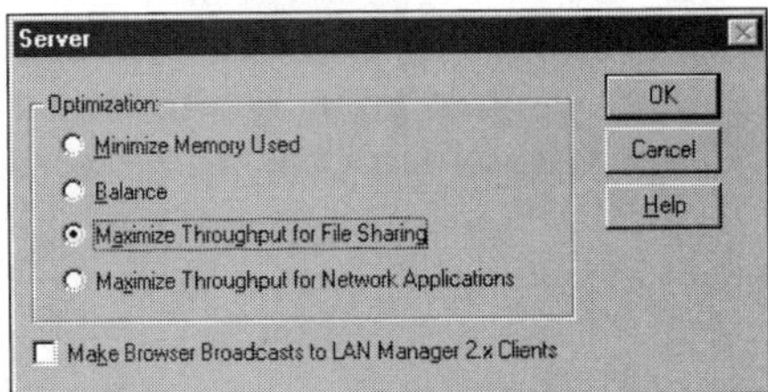

Figure 10-4: Configuring the Server service's "Maximize Throughput for File Sharing" option via the Network Control Panel.

Using a Multipart Disk Subsystem

To get the most out of your NT Server, consider the benefits of a multipart disk subsystem that allows fast concurrent access to data files, spooler, pagefile, and the operating system. Disk configurations which benefit NT fileservers in relatively busy to very busy networks include three- and four-part RAID disk subsystems where a different RAID level is used for each data type to attain the highest degree of fault tolerance and performance. RAID 1 (disk mirroring or duplexing) is an excellent choice for the boot drive containing the NT operating system. RAID 1 has slightly less write performance than a single disk, but an improved read performance. Its write performance is considerably faster than the standard RAID levels 1 to 5. It is a good idea to install NT twice so that the extra copy can fix any damage to your production installation. Generally, this should be on a different disk than the original one in the event of serious disk problems. The location of the second installation on the other disks doesn't matter much (except from the standpoint of losing 120 to 250MB of space) because it will only be used in an emergency. RAID level 0 is the best choice for the pagefile, because it has the highest read and write performance of the NT-supported RAID levels and can be set up and managed by NT software with minimal overhead.

A two-disk stripe dedicated to the pagefile provides the best performance for when memory resources run low. You can also store application archives and other support files, which are infrequently used, there to avoid wasting the extra disk space, if that is a concern. Set everything on the disk except the pagefile to read-only to avoid changes to the disk that could cause the disk to fragment and slow down your pagefile. Additionally, make the initial size and maximum size of the pagefile the same; this avoids the costly process (from a performance viewpoint) of resizing the pagefile. Set it to three or four times the memory size. With a dedicated disk set, you have the capacity to do it. RAID 0 is also a good choice for the spooler files because they require rapid low-overhead access. Some print jobs from programs like QuarkXpress and Adobe PageMaker can easily be over 500MB in size. If you have an art department or marketing department that produces large-format, high-resolution print jobs, you should consider a dedicated RAID volume for their work as well. Move the spooler files to the new disk as detailed in Chapter 8, "Optimizing Printing," and isolate it from the pagefile and any additional data files which see high demand. Because concurrent users spooling 300 to 500MB PostScript jobs can easily fill a 4 or 8GB stripe, you may need to invest in more disks to accommodate the workload. Both the pagefile and spooler file are read and written to sequentially. If you must add additional files or software components to disk volumes to justify the cost of implementing them, try to make sure that they are also sequential read/write types (such as SQL and Exchange Server log files). This will keep performance high.

Databases require fault tolerance as much or more than raw speed. Small concurrent random reads are the norm for this type of access. RAID 5 is the best choice for databases and most user file archives. The capacity used on the disks is efficient and cost effective, its only downside being comparatively slow write performance. Though NT can create a software-managed RAID 5 (striping with parity) fault-tolerant volume, the impact on processor and memory resources may not make it worthwhile (unless done temporarily). RAID 0/1 is a better choice for performance sensitive database and data files. It is the fastest of all RAID levels but has half the total capacity of the disks used as a mirror. RAID 0/1 has the benefits of RAID 1 fault tolerance (no parity, full copy) and RAID 0 performance (no overhead). Two RAID 0 stripes are mirrored together (as in RAID 1) and the performance of each individual stripe is multiplexed together to get close to double the performance of a single stripe set. Because it is expensive, you only want to use it when performance is paramount. A minimum of four disks are required to get the benefit of RAID 0/1.

As with good NT workstations, a fast RISC processor-equipped multitasking and busmastering SCSI controller should be used whenever possible. The quality of the controller is actually more important than buying the best disk drives. The reason for this is that the differences between slow and fast disk drives is small enough that using a larger number of "slower" disks will produce better results than the same amount of money spent on a smaller number of fast disks. Burst rates, which is one of the primary differences between slow and fast drive technology, is of little use in the random seek environment of the fileserver. There just isn't enough constant streaming access to justify a high burst rate when the random uncached read rate is the rate governing the speed of the disk transfer better than 75 percent of the time.

A fileserver which has many concurrent users logged on may have a highly active pagefile if system memory becomes limited. If your system starts starving for more physical memory, give it what it needs; the price of skimping on memory is reduced efficiency for NT across the board. To provide NT with a good safety net in the event system memory runs dangerously low, create a pagefile twice the size of the installed memory and make the initial and maximum sizes the same (this avoids fragmenting the pagefile if the size must be grown). If you have multiple disks installed (which is strongly recommended), place a pagefile the same size as the installed memory with initial and maximum values set the same on *each* disk in your system. You may want to avoid placing a pagefile on a disk performing supporting large and frequent print jobs, or a disk where frequently accessed and time-sensitive data files are stored to avoid contention. As mentioned, the more memory you have, the less pagefile you use and the better your performance is.

Large onboard disk caches (ranging from 512K to 2MB) are also not too useful, though they may complement disk performance by a small margin if disk access is regular and sequential. If any of the data access to the fileserver is composed of large sequentially read files, then these large onboard caches may help improve performance by a small amount. RAID controllers also use separate caching that is often configurable to a particular cache "policy." Default policy is usually the safer write-through mode in which data is written to the physical platter at the same time it is written to the cache. Write-back cache policy provides the highest performance, but removes the safety net of the data being written to disk at the same time the cache is written to. You must rely heavily on the UPS which protects the server in order to safely utilize this cache policy.

NT's native file system cache provides caching for all supported file systems (including the redirector, which is implemented as a file system driver). For more information on optimizing the NT cache, see Chapter 7, "Optimizing NT Caching." Chapter 7 also contains information on how to configure and monitor the performance of the disk subsystem.

One of the things that you may want to know is how does your out-of-the-box clone server (Data General, Intergraph, HP, etc.) compare with customized installations of NT and with a highly hand-tweaked installation of NT running on similar hardware. Some of the design decisions made by major companies are the product of endless hours of research. Others are just tried-and-true methods that worked under previous operating systems and work just as well now. If you benchmark your system using tools such as Bluecurve Dynameasure, you can test using the same rules on a factory-tweaked system to see how well your system performs.

Included on the *Optimizing Windows NT* CD-ROM is a demonstration/evaluation version of Bluecurve Dynameasure, an advanced tool for measuring the performance of fileservers (versions also exist for monitoring application server performance). It is a well-designed workload generator which uses several "engines" to simulate real users work with included "think time." The engines can run simultaneously on a small number of workstations provided you have enough memory on the client system. This use of multiple engines per client allows you to simulate a much larger number of clients without the need for individual machines. Because in normal situations, the client system does not take advantage of its own capacity, this is a reasonable, and generally colorless, method of determining fileserver performance with more modest testing facilities.

Domain controller counters

The things that must be monitored on a DC (Domain Controller) include the number of log ons it is processing, DMB (Domain Master Browser) requests, and synchronization. Monitor memory to ensure that you have sufficient memory for containing the entire SAM/LSA (Security Accounts Manager/Local Security Authority) in physical RAM as well as the core NT operating system components. Disk performance and even network throughput are not high on the list. Response time to logon and security requests, as well as frequency of full synchronization requests, is more of an issue. Table 10-6 lists the counters for monitoring such things as domain controller efficiency at logon servicing, browser request fulfillment, and general system-level efficiency.

TABLE 10-6 DOMAIN CONTROLLER SPECIFIC COUNTERS

Object	Counter	Instance	Description
Browser	Announcements Domain/sec	N/A	Measures the rate that the domain announces itself to the rest of the network.
Browser	Announcements Server/sec	N/A	Measures the rate that the servers in the domain are announcing themselves to the server being measured.
Browser	Announcements Total/sec	N/A	This is the sum total of both Announcements Server/sec and Announcements Domain/sec.
Browser	Election Packets /sec	N/A	This is the rate that browser election packets are broadcast and received by the system being measured.
Browser	Enumerations Domain/sec	N/A	This is the rate that domain browser requests have been processed by the measured system.
Browser	Enumerations Server/sec	N/A	This is the rate of server browser requests that were processed by the measured system.
Browser	Enumerations Total/sec	N/A	This is the total number of combined browser requests processed by the measured system. This includes Enumerations Server, Domain, and Other.
Browser	Missed Server Announcements /sec	N/A	This is the number of server announcements which were missed because of configuration problems or memory limits.
Browser	Missed Server List Requests/sec	N/A	This is the count of requests to retrieve a list of browser servers that were received but could not be processed due to configuration problems or memory limits.

continued

Object	Counter	Instance	Description
Browser	Server List Requests/sec	N/A	The count that measures the rate of requests to retrieve a list of browser servers that have been properly processed by the target machine.
Memory	Page Faults/sec	N/A	Counts the number of Page Faults in the processor. Page faults occur when a process points to a virtual memory page that is no longer in its working set. It will be a "soft" fault if the page can be found in the standby list, because it will still be resident in memory and can often be shared with another process. If it is not found here, the page will have to be retrieved from disk.
Memory	Pages/sec	N/A	This is a count of the number of pages read or written to disk to fix references to pages in memory that were no longer present at the time they were requested. This is the sum total of Pages Input/sec and Pages Output/sec. The counter also includes any paging from the system cache as well as the pages to and from noncached mapped memory. This is the best counter for measuring the cause of "disk thrashing."
Memory	Commit Limit	N/A	This is the size in bytes of the virtual memory that the system can commit without having to extend the pagefile.
Memory	Committed Bytes	N/A	This is the amount of virtual memory out of the total commit limit that the system is actually using. The less it uses, the better.

continued

Table 10-6 DOMAIN CONTROLLER SPECIFIC COUNTERS *(Continued)*

Object	Counter	Instance	Description
Server	Errors System	N/A	This is a measure of the number of times an internal error occurred. This indicates that there is a low-level problem with the server.
Server	Logon Total	N/A	This is the sum total of all interactive, network, service, and successful and failed logons. The measure starts from the last time the system was rebooted.
Server	Logon/sec	N/A	This is the measure of all server logons.
Server	Timed Out	N/A	This counts the number of sessions that were closed when their idle time limit expired. (defined by autodisconnect). This can help show if your new autodisconnect value saved resources by closing the idle connection.
Server	Logged Off	N/A	This counts the number of sessions that were logged out normally. Used in combination with Time-out, Errored-out, you can calculate statistically how much of one or the other is going on and tweak autodisconnect values from that information.
Server	Errored Out	N/A	This counts the number of sessions closed due to errors. This can tell you how often network problems are dropping connections.
System	%Total Processor Time	N/A	This counts the average percentage of time that all the processors on the system are running threads. This thread measures processor time as an accounting of performing real work.

continued

Object	Counter	Instance	Description
System	%Total Interrupt Time	N/A	This is the sum total of the percentage of interrupt time for all installed processors which is divided by the number of processors in the system.

Interpreting domain counter data

When interpreting the data for the role of Domain Controller, remember that neither the disk nor the processor is particularly burdened under realistic loads. The disk is the least affected of the system components, only providing virtual memory when physical memory is in short supply. The biggest issue with Domain Controller optimization is the amount of memory the system has for accommodating the entire user database (SAM/LSA) while providing room for the NT operating system as well as some cache (for network and disk). The cache has little overall impact on a pure Domain Controller system, but little things can add up and help when you need them most. Don't skimp on memory for the domain controller if you can avoid it, especially considering current memory prices are downright cheap. According to Microsoft's own documentation, it is possible to comfortably support a 10,000-user domain on a single domain controller with 48MB of RAM, a 96MB pagefile, and a Pentium 133MHz processor (which would be very likely maxed out much of the time). While it is possible to do this, as it is possible to run NT on an Intel 486SX25, it is not going to get you anything resembling ideal performance. A few inexpensive systems can be set up as dedicated BDCs and share the load of domain administration. If your logons per second, total logons, and memory and processor counters all appear to be showing signs of stress, add a new BDC to the network to give the PDC some breathing room.

You can use the Server Logged Off, Errored Out, and Timed Out counters for determining if error conditions on the server are causing users to be disconnected from the network. Use this in combination with the Server: Errors System counter to determine if the domain controller you are monitoring is experiencing internal errors (possibly memory related).

The Commit Limit and Committed Bytes counters from the Memory object let you view the amount of virtual memory the system is using in relation to what has been made available. For more information on setting up virtual memory for a domain controller, see "Domain Controller Optimizations" later in this chapter.

One of the more serious problems in setting up domain controllers is that the amount of memory provided for them to perform their duties is too limited to really allow them to operate efficiently without significant paging to disk. To determine if more hard drive than physical memory is being used to satisfy demand, use the aforementioned Memory objects Committed Bytes, Commit Limit, Page Faults, and Pages/sec. If Pages/sec sustains at five or more, the system does not have sufficient memory and "disk thrashing" is occurring. Page Faults can be soft or hard; occasionally the page is found elsewhere in memory and therefore does not result in a much slower search for the page on disk. See "Domain Controller Memory Requirements" Section later in this chapter for a handy guide on determining the amount of memory a Domain Controller requires.

Domain controller optimizations

Because the domain controller is technically an application server, modifying the priority of the process set using the server optimization "Maximize Throughput for Network Applications" can give a slight boost to domain controller performance when other services are concurrently running. This will, of course, do little or nothing if the server is dedicated and there are no competing services trying to steal processor time. Microsoft published a guideline for implementing domain controllers across a precalculated number of users and stated the amount of memory, disk, and CPU required for each bracket. Refer to Table 10-7 for more information on hardware requirements.

In Chapters 2 and 3, we made reference to cool new NT hardware that can serve as an excellent base for a new NT Server installation. We can't say enough good things about hardware RAID, particularly with the existing gap between the performance of CPUs, system/memory buses, and the lowly mechanical hard drive.

Virtually no aspect of NT Server performance (regardless of role) can go unaffected by a sluggish disk subsystem. In addition to providing a safer and more fault-tolerant configuration, you should consider at least a mirrored NT boot disk with the mirror managed by NT's own native Disk Administrator fault tolerance. Mount these drives in removable drive shuttles or external enclosures and standardize on SCSI controllers. The resulting mirrored disks could then be moved painlessly to a new system in the event that the system died some mysterious death when you needed it most. If you have enough installed memory, you may even decide to keep the pagefile on the disks with the operating system (usually a no-no). Another nice thing about a clean, dedicated PDC is that you can dump close to half the default services by disabling each one that didn't help your PDC or BDC provide domain security and free several megabytes of memory. After all of your housekeeping on the Domain Controller, you should save multiple copies of its Registry to large removable disks so that you can restore the user database if you have to directly from the removable disk using Regrest (from the NT 4.0 Resource Kit).

For more information on RAID levels and configurations, see the "Defining RAID Levels" section of Chapter 7, "Optimizing Disks."

When selecting a computer for use as a PDC or BDC, use the hardware guidelines in Table 10-7. The table assumes that the computers will function only as PDCs and that no other major Windows NT operations will occur, such as moderate file server, SQL server, SNA server, and remote access server. All numbers are in megabytes (MB) and it is assumed that the computer's pagefile size is at least 250MB.

TABLE 10-7 DOMAIN CONTROLLER HARDWARE REQUIREMENTS

# of User Accounts	SAM Size	Registry Size	Paged Pool	Min CPU Needed	Pagefile	RAM
<3,000	5	25 (default)	50 (default)	486DX/33	32	16
7,500 (default)	10	25	50	486DX/33	64	32
10,000	15	25	50	P5, Alpha	96	48
15,000	20	30	75	P5, Alpha	128	64
20,000	30	50	100	P6, Alpha	256	128
30,000	45	75	128	P6, Alpha	332	166
40,000	60	102	128	SMP system	394	196
50,000	75	102	128	SMP system	512	256

For more information on domain planning, refer to the "Large Domain Testing Overview" document, which is available from Microsoft Product Support Services.

If you have offices separated by slow links in a single domain, you better have at least one BDC per site to prevent WAN-based log ins to the PDC (an especially bad thing if the link to the PDC is slow or heavily congested). There are no hard and fast rules for the number of BDCs to users you have, even if they are all localized within a relatively small geographic location. Use the Performance Monitor Counters for measuring domain controller efficiency to see if it is time to dedicate the domain controllers or add new BDCs.

Fine-Tuning Via the Registry

No investigation into NT Server performance could be complete without a Registry-tuning session. We provide the scalpel; you provide the patient. While we are on the subject of a medical procedure, a malpractice insurance policy is in order:

Using the Registry Editor incorrectly can cause serious systemwide problems that could cause instability, blue screens, or prevent you from rebooting the system at all. Neither IDG nor the authors of this book can guarantee that the Registry parameters in this book are 100 percent safe. The chance of an operating room mortality is always present in the realm of experimental Registry surgery. Take precautions before you begin cutting to ensure adequate protection against corruption (REGBACK, NTBackup, image backup, etc.) and "operator error." Also, see to it that the system is taken gently and quietly off-line and out of production. Always allow several days under observation before returning the system to the production environment.

Registry modifications for server service

Once you have monitored the servers for a while and gotten a feel for where the bottlenecks are (or just want to see how much damage you can do now), open the Registry. These changes are applicable to NT Server in any role. To remedy any problems you might have discovered via Performance Monitor while monitoring for server activity, go to:

```
HKEY_LOCAL_MACHINE\SYSTEM\CurrentControlSet\Services\LanmanServer\
  Parameters
```

Table 10-8 lists some Registry Editor parameters.

TABLE 10-8 REGISTRY EDITOR PARAMETERS

Value Name	Default Value	Type	Value Range	Description
MaxWork Items	(depends on server optimization and installed memory)	REG_ DWORD	1 to 64 on Windows NT Work-station; 1 to 65,535 on Windows NT Server	This value sets the outer limit on the number of work items (receive buffers) the server is able to allocate. When this limit is reached, the transport must begin utilizing flow control, which greatly reduces performance.
MaxWork ItemIdle Time	300	REG_ DWORD	10 to 1,800 seconds	Sets the amount of time a work item can remain in the idle queue before it is recycled.
InitWork Items	(depends on configuration)	REG_ DWORD	1 to 512	This parameter defines the initial number of work items (receive buffers) used by the server. The preallocation of work items consumes memory, but allocating more buffers later will require more.
InitConn Table	8	REG_ DWORD	1 to 128	Sets the initial number of tree connections to be used in the connection table. The server automatically increases this number, but a higher initial value should improve its performance.

continued

Table 10-8 REGISTRY EDITOR PARAMETERS *(Continued)*

Value Name	Default Value	Type	Value Range	Description
MaxFree Connections	(depends on server optimization setting and memory)	REG_ DWORD	2 to 8 items	This parameter sets the maximum number of free connection blocks that must be maintained per endpoint. Higher values ensure that free connections will always be available.
MaxLink Delay	60	REG_ DWORD	0 to 100,000 seconds	This parameter sets the time threshold that is permitted for link delay. RAW I/O for this connection will be disabled if delay exceeds this value.
MaxMpxCt	50	REG_ DWORD	1 to 100 requests	This parameter establishes the outer range for the number of outstanding requests from clients to the server. Higher values will increase performance at the cost of more server work items.

continued

Value Name	Default Value	Type	Value Range	Description
Max Nonpaged Memory Usage	(depends on server optimization and installed memory)	REG_ DWORD	1MB to infinite	This sets the maximum size of the nonpaged memory pool that the server can use at any time. If you want to ensure that the server only uses a certain amount of memory, you can set this value. Infinite values grow dynamically as available memory grows.
MaxPaged Memory Usage	(depends on system and server configuration)	REG_ DWORD	1MB to infinite	Like MaxNonPaged Memory Usage, this value should be modified only if you want to restrict the amount of memory that the server service can use. The value can move up to an infinite amount if it is provided with enough resources.
MinFree Connections	(depends upon configuration)	REG_ DWORD	2 to 5 items	Sets the minimum number of free connection blocks retained. Increase this value to ensure free connections are always available. This ensures that there is little delay when new users connect.

continued

Table 10-8 REGISTRY EDITOR PARAMETERS *(Continued)*

Value Name	Default Value	Type	Value Range	Description
MinFree WorkItems	2	REG_ DWORD	0 to 10 items	Sets the minimum number of receive work items which the server needs in order to begin processing an SMB which could turn out to be a blocking request. Larger values ensure that work items are available for quickly servicing nonblocking requests. The downside is that it will also increase the probability that a blocking request will be rejected.
MinRcv Queue	0	REG_ DWORD	0 to 10 items	This sets the minimum number of receive work items which remain free before the server begins to allocate more receive work items. Larger values ensure that work items will always be available. Values set too high will simply waste resources.

continued

Value Name	Default Value	Type	Value Range	Description
Auto Disconnect	15	REG_ DWORD	Minutes: 0 to 0x FFFFFFF	This sets the amount of time that a client is allowed to remain idle before being disconnected. If there are any open files or searches, the client is not disconnected. Lower values reduce server resource usage but cause overhead as the number of disconnect/reconnects on the server increase. A value of 0xFFFFFF ensures the circuit never drops and no overhead from having to reconnect is incurred. The cost is memory resources.
MaxRaw WorkItems	(depends on server optimization level and installed memory)	REG_ DWORD	1 to 512 items	This parameter sets the maximum raw work items the server can allocate for use. When this limit is reached, the server will reject all raw I/O requests from the client.

continued

Table 10-8 REGISTRY EDITOR PARAMETERS *(Continued)*

Value Name	Default Value	Type	Value Range	Description
`OplockBreakWait`	35	REG_DWORD	10 to 180 seconds	Sets the amount of time that server waits for a client to respond to an oplock (Opportunistic Lock optimization) break request. A smaller value allows server to discover a crashed client connection more quickly, but can cause a loss of cached data.
`RawWorkItems`	(depends on the server optimization level and installed memory)	REG_DWORD	1 to 512 items	Specifies the number of special work items for raw I/O that the server uses. A larger value for this value entry can increase performance but uses more memory.
`SizReqBuf`	4356	REG_DWORD	512 to 65,536 bytes (64K)	Sets the size of server request buffers. Larger values improve performance at the cost of memory usage.
`XactMemSize`	1MB	REG_DWORD	64K to 16MB	Specifies the maximum amount of virtual memory used by the Xactsrv service (which handles such things as print requests). A larger value for this value entry helps ensure that memory is available for clients but uses virtual address space and pageable memory.

continued

Value Name	Default Value	Type	Value Range	Description
ThreadCountAdd	(depends on server optimization and memory)	REG_DWORD	0 to 10 threads	This defines the number of worker threads per processor that should be added to the default of one thread per processor. Adding threads can improve performance but will consume more memory. Values that are too high can hurt performance by causing excessive context switching (task switching).
ThreadPriority	1	REG_DWORD	0, 1, 2, 15	This adds priority to the base priority of the process. Higher server priority gives better server performance at the expense of local responsiveness. The values 0 to 2 are relative to normal or background process priority. A value of 1 is equivalent to the foreground process. A value of 15 runs the server threads at real-time priority, which can cause serious performance problems.

continued

TABLE 10-8 **REGISTRY EDITOR PARAMETERS** *(Continued)*

Value Name	Default Value	Type	Value Range	Description
				A ThreadPriority value of 2 gives the server a priority boost 1 higher than XACTSRV, which is the service that services print requests. Most of the time it is more logical to prioritize fileservice over printservice because these delays are more noticeable. This will do nothing if the server is not already very busy.
Scav Timeout	30	REG_ DWORD	1 to 300 seconds	This sets the time that the scavenger remains idle before waking up to service requests. Using smaller values will increase responsiveness by invoking the scavenger more often, but will cost an amount of processor utilization.

Workstation Registry tweaks

Because the workstation service provides all redirector services to the server (as described in Chapter 9, "Optimizing Your NT Network"), the performance of this service also affects the server's overall performance. Table 10-9 lists some Registry values that can help you boost performance for this service. These values are valid for the following Registry location:

```
HKEY_LOCAL_MACHINE
    \SYSTEM
        \CurrentControlSet
            \Services
                \LanmanWorkstation
                    \Parameters
```

Table 10-9 REGISTRY EDITOR VALUES

Value Name	Default Name	Type	Value Range	Description
LockQuota	4096 (bytes)	REG_DWORD	Bytes of data	This sets the maximum amount of data read for each file using this optimization parameter if UseLockReadUnlock parameter is also enabled. If the network applications you are using perform a large number of lock and read type operations you should increase this value. This is particularly true of many application servers such as databases or message stores. Setting the value too high could use most or all of the paged pool memory.

continued

TABLE 10-9 REGISTRY EDITOR VALUES *(Continued)*

Value Name	Default Name	Type	Value Range	Description
MaxCmds	15	REG_ DWORD	0 to 255	This parameter specifies the maximum number of work buffers the redirector maintains to achieve optimal performance. Increasing this value can increase network throughput. You can monitor the number of commands used by the redirector from the Performance Monitor. Because this value actually controls the number of execution threads that can be outstanding on the network, your performance may not always improve.
Max Collection Count	16	REG_ DWORD	0 to 65,535 bytes	This parameter sets the threshold for named-pipe writes. Writes smaller than this value will be buffered. Increasing this value can improve performance for a named-pipe application that does not perform its own memory management.

continued

Value Name	Default Name	Type	Value Range	Description
ReadAhead	0xffffffff	REG_ DWORD	Kilobytes/ sec	This sets the throughput necessary over the network, which will set the cache manager to enable read-ahead buffering. Lower values will trigger read-ahead buffering at lower speeds.
UtilizeNt1 Caching	(true)	REG_ DWORD	0 or 1	This instructs the redirector to use cache manager to cache file contents. This has significant performance improvements, so don't turn it off.

Server service tweaks for other platforms

Computers running operating systems other than Windows and NT can benefit from Registry values used to tweak NT Server in the fileserver role. Almost all of the additional fileserver services which provide cross-platform compatibility are fileserver service products and benefit from hardware configurations such as those already discussed for NT Server in the fileserver role.

TUNING SERVICES FOR MACINTOSH (SFM)

NT Server's native support for Macintosh (known as Services for Macintosh or SFM) is a significant and important feature. However, certain management features of SFM are somewhat clunky to deal with, and some still require the use of the old Windows NT 3.5x File Manager utility to perform. Not surprisingly, running a cross-platform server service such as SFM on the same machine with a server also providing shares for Windows systems will lead to a certain amount of contention for server resources. Once you determine who should receive the lion's share of the NT Server's resources (e.g., Do you have a 1,000-user network with 900 Windows users and 100 Mac users, or vice-versa?), you can set up the system to provide the best access for one or the other set of client computers. Conceptually, the same things that make NT Server excel as a fileserver for Windows clients will make it perform well for Macintosh clients. The only difference is that the Performance Monitor counters are found under the MacFile object. The Registry keys for the service are under MacFile as well. The primary ingredient in making SFM run swiftly on NT Server is a larger allocation size for the paged and nonpaged pool greater than the one that is supplied by default. NT Server Service For Macintosh is quite efficient in the speed and consistency with which it handles Macintosh clients in small workgroups without modification. Add a few hundred more Macs to the mix and the need to optimize the server to provide the best performance for them becomes paramount.

MACFILE REGISTRY PARAMETERS

The paged/nonpaged values for the Macintosh file server service (SFM) are similar to those of the server service. The MacFile PagedMemLimit, like that of the server service, sets maximum allocable paged pool memory that the SFM can use. Higher values reflect better performance. This and other values may be found in the following Registry location:

```
HKEY_LOCAL_MACHINE
\SYSTEM
\CurrentControlSet
\Services
\MacFile
\Parameters
```

Table 10-10 lists some MacFile Registry parameters.

TUNING NETWARE SERVICES

Interaction with Novell NetWare and InterNetWare servers is still a significant concern to many network administrators working in mixed NetWare/NT environments. Therefore, in the following sections, we'll discuss a few optimization tips related to NetWare services and interoperability under NT that you can use to enhance network performance in these environments.

TABLE 10-10 MACFILE REGISTRY PARAMETERS

Value Name	Default Value	Type	Value Range	Description
PagedMem	0x4e20 (20,000K)	REG_ DWORD	0x3e8 to 0x3e800 (1,000 to 256,000K)	This sets the outside value for determining the amount of virtual memory SFM can use. MacFile service performance increases proportionately with this value. Increasing either or both values for SFM service will improve performance but will reduce the performance of all other services on the system.
NonPaged MemLimit	0xfa0 (4,000K)	REG_ DWORD	0xff to 0x3e80 (256K to 16,000K)	

CHANGING NETWORK PROVIDER PRIORITY

In the event you have loaded support for Novell NetWare on a Windows NT computer, you should consider changing the network provider to the network most often used. Specifically, make sure that the Network Access Order in the Services tab of the Control Panel Services applet is set so that the most frequently used network is listed first. To access this configuration in Windows NT 3.5x, choose the Network button in the Network Control Panel; in NT 4.0, the dialog is accessible by choosing the Network Access Order button in the Network Control Panel's Services tab. The Network Access Order dialog is shown in Figure 10-5.

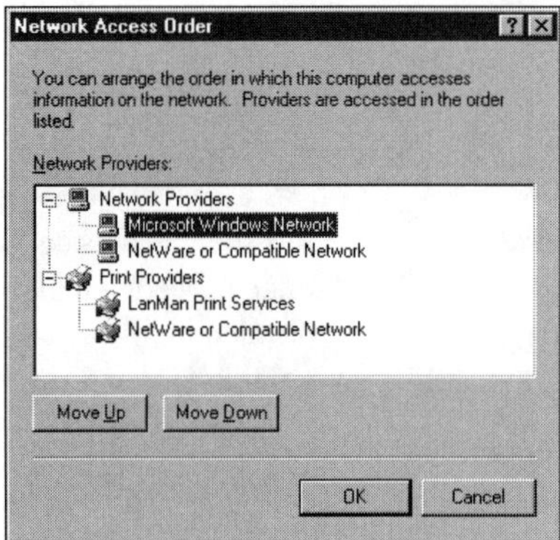

Figure 10-5: Adjusting the Network Access Order (client redirector priority) in the Network Control Panel.

The Network Access Order dialog in Windows NT 4.0 differentiates between file and print services and allows each to be prioritized separately; in Windows NT 3.5x, both services are lumped together and listed as a single service that may be moved up or down in the priority order.

In addition to Network Access Order priority, there is an additional network-related optimization that should also be made via the Network Control Panel. Much as the Network Access Order determines which client redirector receives priority for the Workstation service, the network bindings order determines the priority order of protocols bound to each network adapter and service in the system. The configuration dialog for the network bindings order is accessible via the Bindings tab in Windows NT 4.0, and via the Bindings button in Windows NT 3.5x.

The Network Bindings dialog is shown in Figure 10-6.

Bindings may be viewed from different perspectives: by Adapter, Service, or Protocol. The Service-based view typically provides the easiest way to view protocol bindings and how they relate to the adapters and services that use them. To configure the bindings order for optimal operation in your environment, you should concentrate your attention on the order of the protocols listed under the Workstation and Server services. Specifically, you should set the bindings display so that protocols are listed in a top-to-bottom order of priority on your system. This means that the most important protocol on the system should be listed at the top, the second most important should be underneath this, and so on down the list.

Being closer to the top means that Windows NT will attempt to communicate using that adapter and service (in this case, the Workstation and Server services) via that protocol before attempting to use any others in the list. By placing the most frequently used protocol at the top of the list, you ensure that the time it takes NT to communicate using this protocol for a particular network operation is minimized.

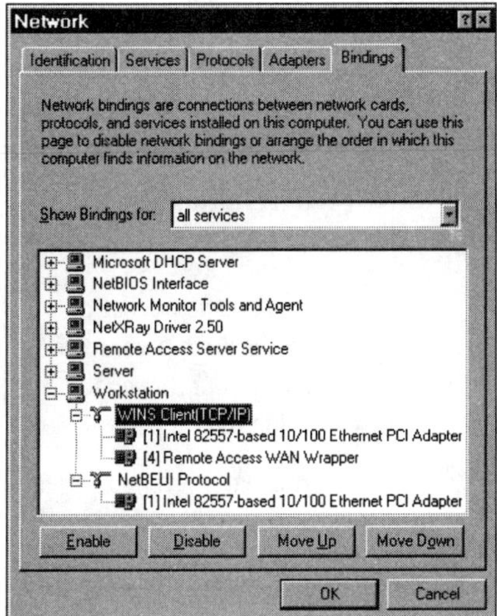

Figure 10-6: Adjusting the Network Bindings Order in the Network Control Panel.

Recent information from Microsoft (which directly contradicts previous articles on the subject in the Windows NT 3.5x era) state that the network bindings order doesn't impact the Server service as it does the Workstation service, as the Server service listens for client requests on all installed services in an equivalent fashion. However, we recommend that you optimize the network bindings order for each service, just in case they're wrong!

FPNW REGISTRY PARAMETERS

This set of parameters is for File and Print services for NetWare, a NetWare 3.1x server emulator/migration tool. Use the Network Provider Registry values given earlier to improve performance for non-Windows network clients. These values may be found in the following Registry location, and are described in Table 10-11.

```
HKEY_LOCAL_MACHINE\SYSTEM\CurrentControlSet\Services\FPNW\Parameters
```

TUNING CSNW AND GSNW

One of the key optimization points with any of the NetWare-related services is explicit selection of frame types used on your network, and of selecting the correct Network Provider. You may get slow performance and throughput for the various NetWare connectivity services (including Client Services for NetWare or CSNW, and Gateway Services for NetWare or GSNW) if you have multiple frame types enabled on your NetWare servers.

TABLE 10-11 FPNW REGISTRY PARAMETERS

Value Name	Default Value	Type	Value Range	Description
EnableBurst	0x00000001	REG_DWORD	0 or 1	This allows packet burst mode. With a value of 1, packet burst is enabled. A value of 0 is none.
Size	3	REG_DWORD	1 to 3	This parameter specifies amount of work the system is expected to perform. Size sets the maximum number of receive buffers which can be allocated, initial number of receive buffers to allocate, and the number of worker threads to allocate. Possible values are 1 (minimize memory usage), 2 (balance memory with performance), and 3 (maximize performance).

continued

Value Name	Default Value	Type	Value Range	Description
BlockingWorkerThreads	Depends on memory installed and optimization level	REG_DWORD	1 to 64	Sets the number of threads FPNW reserves to service requests that can block the thread for a significant amount of time. Larger values can increase performance but use more memory. Higher values can improve performance but require more memory. If this value is set too high, performance can be sapped by excessive task switching.
CoreCacheBuffers	Depends on server optimization level and installed memory	REG_DWORD	0 to 1,024 buffers	Extra buffers (separate from the Windows NT Server cache manager) used to cache small sequential reads and writes.
CoreCacheBufferSize	This is the page size of the architecture, 4K for Intel, 8K for Alpha	REG_DWORD	0; 4,096; and 8,192	Specifies the size of the buffers specified in CoreCacheBuffers. Default is based on the size of the system page, which is platform specific.
InitialReceiveBuffers	Defaults for size = 1,2, 3 or 2,20,40	REG_DWORD	Default up to MaxReceiveBuffer value	This sets the number of receive buffers initially allocated and the minimum number of receive buffers that the server will maintain. These resources are only freed when the system is either unloaded or rebooted.

continued

TABLE 10-11 **FPNW REGISTRY PARAMETERS** *(Continued)*

Value Name	Default Value	Type	Value Range	Description
				The minimum is the default value. The maximum value is the value of MaxReceive Buffers.
MaxCached OpenFiles	4	REG_DWORD	0 to -1 (unlimited)	This parameter sets the maximum number of files FPNW is capable of having open and in cache per client.
Max Receive Buffers	For size 1,2, 3 or 64, 128,256	REG_DWORD	10 to infinite	The maximum number of receive buffers the server will keep committed. When processing burst requests the server may go over this amount, but this is normal behavior. It frees the excess buffers later.
MaxWork ItemIdle Time	300 seconds	REG_DWORD	0 to -1 (unlimited)	This parameter sets the amount of time (in seconds) that a work item (receive buffer) can stay in the idle queue before it is recycled.

NetWare servers can provide router and translation duties, allowing you to convert one frame type to another. If the frame type for the NT machine is different from the NetWare clients and NetWare server, then all traffic will have to go through the NetWare server. The condition is exacerbated if the NetWare server is separated by a slow WAN link.

1. Verify that the correct frame type is set for NWLink, which will be the same type used by the NetWare server.
2. Check that NWLink is binding properly to the correct network adapter. Once the frame type is changed and the system rebooted, performance should improve.

Delegating Server Duties

Based on what we have learned about server roles and service delegation, we can create a model which illustrates what duties each server will perform depending on its role and its capacity. Some services make sense to have on the same machine for management reasons, while others should not share the machine because their optimization levels would conflict and negate the effect of optimization (such as an application server and a fileserver sharing the same box).

Some of the decisions about which services a PDC should have were provided for you, such as making it the default DMB (Domain Master Browser). Disabling the browser can change this default behavior. Other decisions on what will be used where, you will have to make. The objective is to build a well-balanced network by leveraging the strengths of the installed systems to make them the best they can be with what is available. An inexpensive server can provide dedicated service for a particular function, while additional low-cost servers can be added to back the dedicated server's functions. Distributing the workload this way is less expensive than buying a smaller number of much more powerful systems, but there is a breaking point between the cost of the hardware, the cost of maintaining the systems (often 85 percent of your network budget), and the potential for creating a single point of failure.

Table 10-12 shows an example of a Master Domain model supporting a theoretical 600-user network that consists of the following server configurations with their resources and services:

Table 10-12 MASTER DOMAIN MODEL SUPPORTING A 600-USER NETWORK

Server 1	Server 2	Server 3	Server 4	Server 5	Server 6
PDC and DMB	BDC and MBR	BDC and backup browser	Resource Server	Resource Server	Resource Server
Secondary WINS Server	Primary WINS Server	DHCP Server	Exchange Server	File and print Service	Macintosh File and Print services
Secondary DNS Server	Primary DNS Server	RAS	IIS		Cluster 1 (2 way)
Time Server (source)	DHCP Server	limited file and print service	RAS		Resource Server
	Time Server		Proxy		SQL Server
					SMS Server
					Transaction Server

In this environment, the applications and file service that users required resulted in several servers dedicated to a particular role which provides several essential services such as domain management and name service. The servers which are not configured as domain controllers are configured for dedicated file/print service and application services. Because they do not share the overhead of domain management, they are free to perform their duties more optimally, with all resources committed to those tasks.

Summary

In this chapter, we explored the issues surrounding the optimization of Windows NT Server within its role on the network. We discussed some important Performance Monitor objects to examine, as well as some Registry keys for modifying the values you measured. We also discussed the important role that disk, network, memory, and processing all have on server performance. Having built up to the base platform for serving up files, printers, and applications, we'll now delve into a more specific optimization topic: optimizing Windows NT-based Internet servers.

Chapter 11

Optimizing Your Windows NT Internet Server

ONE OF WINDOWS NT 4.0'S GREATEST ASSETS is its native ability to perform as an Internet/intranet server. As industries look for more inexpensive ways to collect and distribute information, the Internet Information Server (IIS) is a perfect fit. IIS consists of three Windows NT services that allow any Windows NT server or workstation to become an HTTP (Hypertext Transport Protocol), FTP (File Transfer Protocol), and Gopher server. These services are built upon a collection of TCP/IP (Transmission Control Protocol/Internet Protocol) protocols that are the language of the Internet. These services require that the TCP/IP protocol be installed and operating.

For a more in-depth look at TCP/IP see Chapter 9, "Optimizing Your NT Network."

Some of these protocols such as the HTTP server, which is the basis of the World Wide Web (WWW), have been around for only a few years. Others such as FTP have been around for decades, since the birth of the Internet in the 1960s when it was known as ARPANet. The Internet supports many different protocols, which are defined in Requests For Comments (RFC's); however, the WWW service has set the stage for a total change in the way people use computers and find information.

A Little IIS History

Microsoft first released Internet Information Server version 1.0 in April 1996 to gain a presence on the Internet and to promote its flagship industrial operating system, Windows NT 3.51. Other Internet Servers such as EMWAC's, O'Reilly's WebSite, and NetScape were already entering the market with servers based upon Windows NT. IIS version 1.0 was succeeded by version 2.0 when other vendors started releasing HTTP servers that would run on NT and give better functionality such as connections to Open Database Connectivity (ODBC). IIS 2.0, which ships standard with Windows NT 4.0, was also optimized for better speed and ran 40 percent faster than version 1.0. This gave IIS 2.0 better speed and also removed one major limitation in IIS 1.0: in version 1.0 you could only perform one database command per page change. This limitation created major problems due to the market shift from static to dynamic Web pages using the Common Gateway Interface (CGI), which we discuss later in the chapter. IIS 2.0 gave Web developers the ability to perform up to 25 database queries in one script. This allows for richer dynamic content without sending the user through a virtual maze to obtain the necessary data to create a Web page.

IIS 3.0, code named "Denali," began to arrive on the market in beta form in late 1996. Denali provided something that very few Web servers could offer, a Web programming environment. The primary feature of IIS 3.0 is the addition of Active Server Pages. Active Server Pages give IIS the ability to host Web applications by creating a development environment in which a user session can be tracked and decisions can be made using session variables. IIS 3.0 provides access to what are referred to as objects (nothing new to our developer audience). The objects available in IIS provide a direct programming interface to items such as databases, other ActiveX servers, Java Applications, and the built-in VBScript and JScript (JavaScript) scripting languages to give Web pages thinking power. These objects make programming Web pages much simpler and give the programmer enormous flexibility in presenting dynamic content. That's enough history, let's get into how to make sure you are getting the best possible performance out of your NT Web server.

General Web Server Tuning Strategies

The Web optimization strategies mentioned in this section can be applied to any HTTP server running on Windows NT 3.51, 4.0, or 5.0. We take a more in-depth look at specific optimization techniques for Microsoft Internet Information Server a little later in this section.

Hardware (memory/CPU)

It is important to remember that HTTP servers run as a service under the Windows NT operating system. As a service, IIS (or any other vendor's software) can only run as smoothly as the operating system. Any bottlenecks in the server will make a direct, and usually substantial, performance impact on any application the server is hosting.

For more information on Windows NT CPU and memory optimization see Chapter 5,"Optimizing Memory and Processing."

During the setup of any Windows NT Server, you have the option of making the machine a Primary Domain Controller (PDC), a Backup Domain controller (BDC), or a Standalone server. The optimal configuration for an Internet server is to install it as a Standalone server but have it participate in a domain so that the NT domain database can be accessed for user control. This configuration applies to any servers running specific applications such as Internet, SQL, Exchange, or Lotus Notes. Domain controllers (PDC's and BDC's) have the additional overhead of performing domain database maintenance, replication, and other networking outlays such as fulfilling domain log-on requests. These types of activity steal CPU, memory, and network resources, which loss we want to minimize, from our application.

Another subtle limitation is that domain controllers aren't capable of performing specific logging and auditing processes on a per machine basis. When setting up logging or auditing on a domain controller, the properties set in User Manager apply to all the domain controllers. This makes it impossible to perform a particular type of audit or log on a specific machine.

In Windows NT 4.0 Server the Domain Users Group was removed from having the privilege of Logon Locally. What this did was remove the capability for a standard domain user to log directly into a server console, yet they can access the server from over the network. In many organizations, Web developers may need to have local log on or administrative access to a server, or group of servers. By setting up your Internet servers as Standalone, you can grant the developers specific permissions by server. An example of this situation would be to grant a specific user, or group of users Administrative rights over a particular machine. If the machine were a PDC or BDC, you would have to grant them Administrative rights over all PDC's or BDC's in the domain, which may not be an acceptable security practice in your organization.

To determine the proper amount of memory to devote to your IIS Server, we must take a look at what applications will be running on the machine. If your server will only be used as an IIS server, with no other major applications on it, 32MB of RAM on a fast 486 or a low-end Pentium is a good start. As other applications such as a SQL (Structured Query Language) server or Exchange Server are added to a machine running an Internet service, more memory and CPU power will be required.

Network (LAN/WAN)

Network speed is crucial to any high performance NT server. With an Internet or intranet server, there are two sides to consider when determining how to optimize networking: your Wide Area Network (WAN) connection and your Local Area Network (LAN) connection.

WAN

The Internet is a good example of a Wide Area Network. Also good examples are the vast number of private networks running through both national and international phone companies.

WAN connections come in a vast array of speeds using different types of technology and vary widely depending on your country. We limit our discussion to common services used in the United States.

The most common WAN connection a user could make is the act of dialing an Internet Service Provider (ISP) using a standard modem. This may be fine for the average user, but we're here to optimize by locating any bottlenecks in the communications of the Web server, which will rarely operate using this type of WAN connection.

WAN connections come in two basic types, dialup and dedicated. These can also be referred to as asynchronous and synchronous, respectively.

DIALUP

Regular dialup connections start at V.34 28.8 KBps modem rates, although some users still use 14.4 KBps connections. Faster connection rates kilobytes per second are also available. This connection is reasonably slow, only good for about one person, and is available to just about anyone anywhere because the connection is made over standard telephone service lines, also known as POTS (Plain Old Telephone System).

The next step up from POTS, but not available in all areas, is the Integrated Services Digital Network (ISDN) which comes in two types, Basic Rate Interface (BRI) and Primary Rate Interface (PRI).

For additional information on ISDN, one of the most popular resources on the Internet is the Dan Kegel ISDN home page at `http://www.cerf.net/dank/isdn`.

ISDN BRI

A BRI is a fully digital connection that comes into your home or business just like a regular telephone line. It consists of two B Channels and one D channel. The D channel speed is 16 KBps and is usually reserved for switching; however, it can be used for X.25 connections. The other two channels are the paths used for either voice or data.

Because we are talking about Web servers, we'll discuss B channel data use in 64KBps digital mode.

Dialing from one ISDN device to another with one channel would produce a bandwidth of 64KBps; connection with two channels would double the bandwidth to 128KBps. By using dialing protocols such as Multilink PPP, a direct digital connection can exist at 128KBps. This much bandwidth is sufficient to support from 10 to 50 Web clients at once depending on the file sizes being requested by the client. Small file sizes allow for a quick transmission, while larger file sizes take longer to transfer causing connections for other users to slow down. ISDN BRI should only be considered for small or personal sites with a low number of users. ISDN can also be used as a backup connection in case of a faster primary connection failure.

ISDN PRI

A domestic Primary Rate Interface (PRI) line is similar to a BRI except there are 23 B channels and 1 D channel. Speeds this high produce 1.544MBps of dedicated bandwidth. This produces a signal that is designed to run over standard North American T1 lines. This much bandwidth is sufficient to support from 100 to 500 users.

DEDICATED

Dedicated connections can be leased from the local telephone company. These types of phone lines are permanent (or nailed) connections between your location and your Internet Service Provider. The physical connection from your location to the ISP Point of Presence (POP) is called the local loop. Determining the proper amount of bandwidth for the local loop depends on the number of connected users and your budget. Some common Internet connection types are listed in Table 11-1.

TABLE 11-1 COMMON U.S. INTERNET SERVICE DEDICATED CONNECTIONS

Connection Type	Bandwidth	Supported Users (approximate)
56KB	56 KBps	10–25
Frame Relay	Varies (56KBps to 1.544MBps)	10–500 depending on bandwidth
T1	1.544MBps	100–500
Fractional T1	Varies (128KBps up to T1 Speeds)	15–500 depending on bandwidth
T3	45MBps	5,000 or more

LAN

The LAN side becomes important to optimize when the Web server needs to communicate with other machines on the same LAN (such as database servers), and when it's being used as an intranet server.

Allowing HTTP servers to communicate with other types of information providers such as databases on just about any platform has shifted the way HTML (Hypertext Markup Language) pages are written and used. This type of communication is called Server Side Scripting and is covered later in this chapter.

Although many Web servers simply deal with static HTML pages, both the Internet and the intranet are shifting to providing dynamic pages with active content that include the capabilities of streaming audio and video. Products such as Microsoft NetShow rely on the speed of the LAN connection to distribute high quality (and bandwidth consuming) data streams.

IIS includes capabilities to limit network bandwidth as shown in Figure 11-1. because we want to optimize our network, the default full throttle network usage permitted would probably not cause any problems. However, to help balance the load on high traffic networks, IIS gives you the capability of lowering (or throttling) the allowed network bandwidth that all IIS services consume.

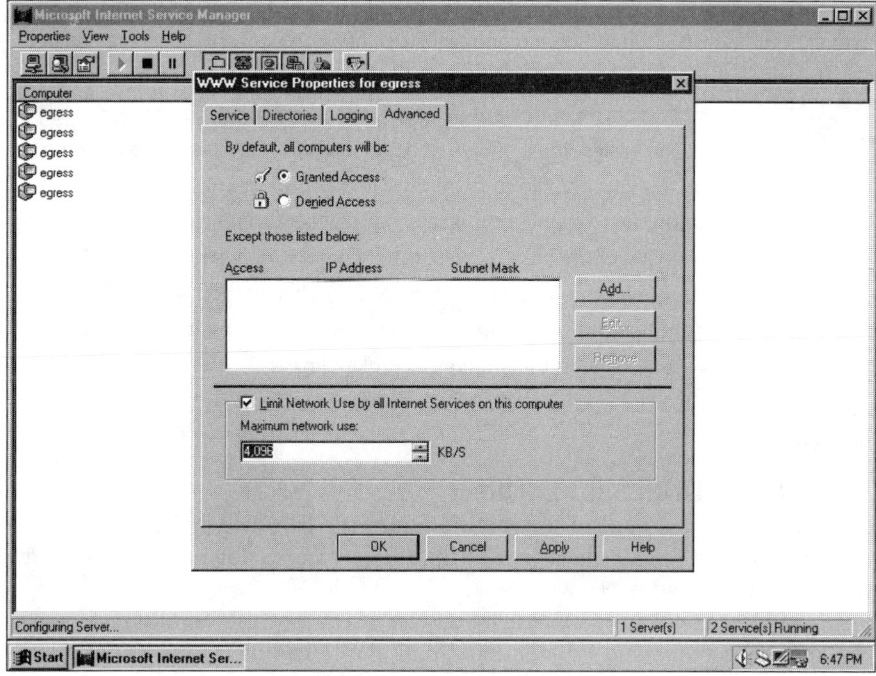

Figure 11-1: Limiting bandwidth with the IIS Manager.

For a more in-depth look at LAN connections and how to determine your needs, be sure to see Chapter 9 "Optimizing Your NT Network".

Load balancing (DNS Round Robin)

One of the best ways to optimize your Web site is to distribute the client load between multiple computers that have identical content. DNS Round Robin is described in RFC 1794.

When a client makes a request to attach to a specific Web site, a Domain Name System (DNS) server answers the request. The purpose of DNS servers is to provide the client the IP address of the host to which they would like to connect. Once the client machine has an IP address, all of the networking information needed to route the user to the host has been received. For very high traffic Web sites, a supercomputer is needed to handle the traffic. The answer to the problem is to have the DNS server respond with an IP address by circling through a pool of IP addresses. The Microsoft DNS server that ships with Windows NT 4.0 is one DNS server that supports this type of virtual router approach.

Using DNS Round Robin requires the use of a content replication system. By rotating network connections between different servers, the content on the different servers must be kept in sync. Many synchronization schemes can be used. The easiest is a simple batch file copy from one server to the next. The problem with the file copy method is that broken links can appear in a Web during the copy procedure causing the client to receive Error 404, File not found. One of the more sophisticated content replication systems is the Microsoft Content Replication System (MCRS). This method uses routines to stage content on one or more servers, then bulk copy it to production servers using a means that minimizes broken links.

MULTIPLE A (ADDRESS) RECORDS

One way of creating a pool of alternating addresses is to use multiple A or Host records. Using this form you enter multiple host records for each of your Web servers as shown in Figure 11-2.

Once the records have been entered, you can test to see if Round Robin is working by opening a Command Prompt and typing the following.

```
C:\>ping www.mycompany.com
Pinging www.mycompany.com [172.16.0.1] with 32 bytes of data:
Reply from 172.16.0.1: bytes=32 time<10ms TTL=128
Reply from 172.16.0.1: bytes=32 time<10ms TTL=128
Reply from 172.16.0.1: bytes=32 time<10ms TTL=128
Reply from 172.16.0.1: bytes=32 time<10ms TTL=128
C:\>ping www.mycompany.com
Pinging www.mycompany.com [172.16.0.5] with 32 bytes of data:
Reply from 172.16.0.5: bytes=32 time<10ms TTL=128
Reply from 172.16.0.5: bytes=32 time<10ms TTL=128
Reply from 172.16.0.5: bytes=32 time<10ms TTL=128
Reply from 172.16.0.5: bytes=32 time<10ms TTL=128
C:\>ping www.mycompany.com
Pinging www.mycompany.com [172.16.255.229] with 32 bytes of data:
Reply from 172.16.255.229: bytes=32 time<10ms TTL=128
Reply from 172.16.255.229: bytes=32 time<10ms TTL=128
Reply from 172.16.255.229: bytes=32 time<10ms TTL=128
Reply from 172.16.255.229: bytes=32 time<10ms TTL=128
C:\>
```

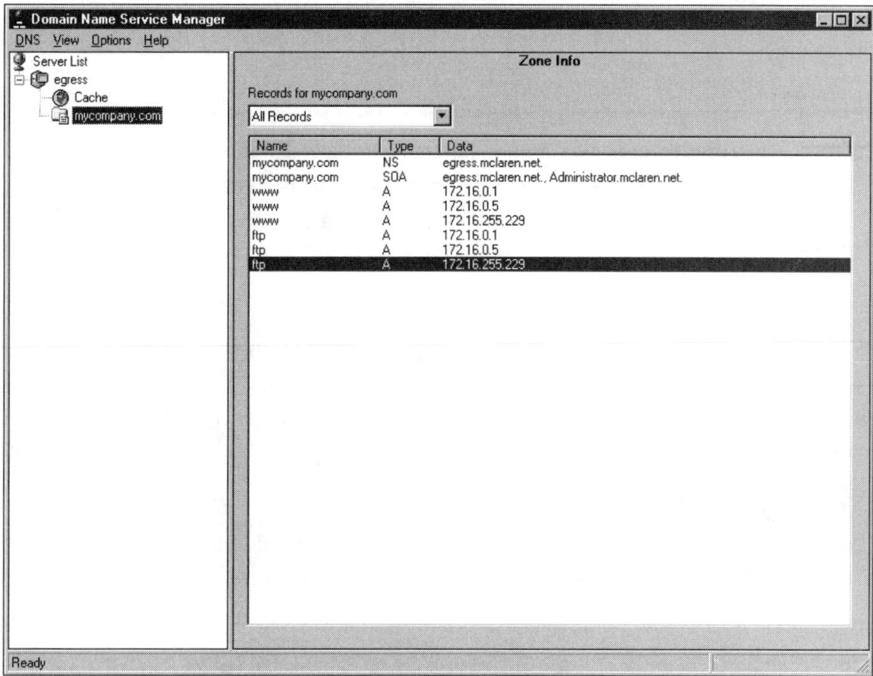

Figure 11-2: DNS Manager with multiple A records.

Once the records have been entered, you can test to see if Round Robin is working by opening a Command Prompt and typing the following.

```
C:\>ping www.mycompany.com
Pinging www.mycompany.com [172.16.0.1] with 32 bytes of data:
Reply from 172.16.0.1: bytes=32 time<10ms TTL=128
Reply from 172.16.0.1: bytes=32 time<10ms TTL=128
Reply from 172.16.0.1: bytes=32 time<10ms TTL=128
Reply from 172.16.0.1: bytes=32 time<10ms TTL=128
C:\>ping www.mycompany.com
Pinging www.mycompany.com [172.16.0.5] with 32 bytes of data:
Reply from 172.16.0.5: bytes=32 time<10ms TTL=128
Reply from 172.16.0.5: bytes=32 time<10ms TTL=128
Reply from 172.16.0.5: bytes=32 time<10ms TTL=128
Reply from 172.16.0.5: bytes=32 time<10ms TTL=128
C:\>ping www.mycompany.com
Pinging www.mycompany.com [172.16.255.229] with 32 bytes of data:
Reply from 172.16.255.229: bytes=32 time<10ms TTL=128
Reply from 172.16.255.229: bytes=32 time<10ms TTL=128
Reply from 172.16.255.229: bytes=32 time<10ms TTL=128
Reply from 172.16.255.229: bytes=32 time<10ms TTL=128
C:\>
```

Notice that each time the Web server is pinged, the DNS server returns a different IP address.

In a production environment, the rotation of the IP addresses may vary from the examples. The DNS server rotates the address on each client request. If you have more than one client making DNS queries, the results in the example may not be in the exact order shown.

This also allows for a crude fault-tolerant approach because your Web site doesn't rely on a single machine or IP address. If your Web site consisted of five servers, and the third server in the address pool goes down, every fifth connection attempt would fail; a retry, however, would have an 80 percent chance of succeeding.

CNAME APPROACH

A CNAME record is an alias for a host record (CNAME stands for Canonical NAME). You add a CNAME record and then an alternate address as shown in Figure 11-3.

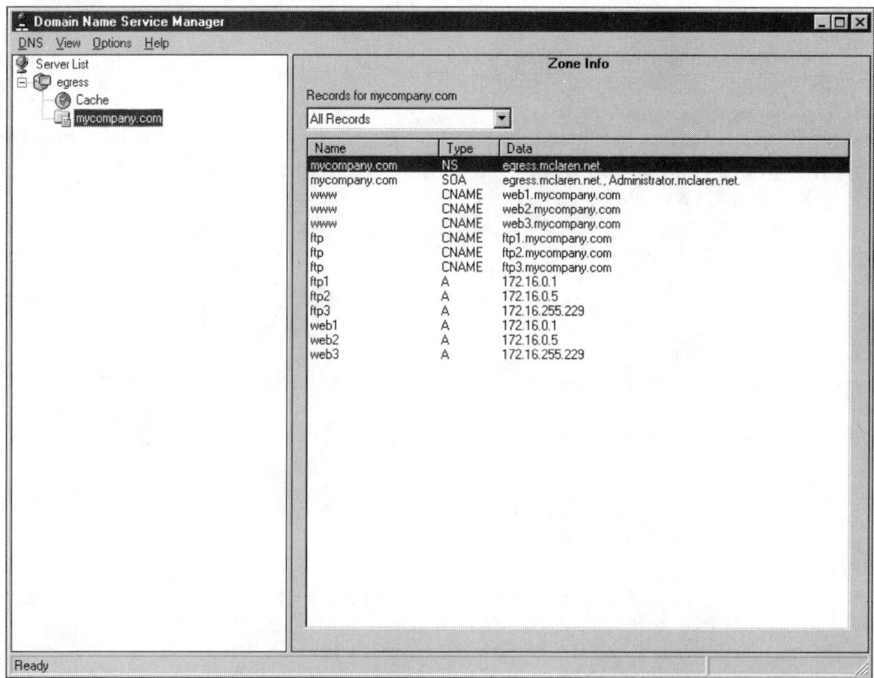

Figure 11-3: DNS Manager using CNAME rotation.

As in the previous implementation, multiple CNAME records are created that substitute host names instead of raw IP addresses.

```
C:\>ping www.mycompany.com
Pinging web1.mycompany.com [172.16.0.1] with 32 bytes of data:
Reply from 172.16.0.1: bytes=32 time<10ms TTL=128
Reply from 172.16.0.1: bytes=32 time<10ms TTL=128
Reply from 172.16.0.1: bytes=32 time<10ms TTL=128
Reply from 172.16.0.1: bytes=32 time<10ms TTL=128
C:\>ping www.mycompany.com
Pinging web2.mycompany.com [172.16.0.5] with 32 bytes of data:
Reply from 172.16.0.5: bytes=32 time<10ms TTL=128
Reply from 172.16.0.5: bytes=32 time<10ms TTL=128
Reply from 172.16.0.5: bytes=32 time<10ms TTL=128
Reply from 172.16.0.5: bytes=32 time<10ms TTL=128
C:\>ping www.mycompany.com
Pinging web3.mycompany.com [172.16.255.229] with 32 bytes of data:
Reply from 172.16.255.229: bytes=32 time<10ms TTL=128
Reply from 172.16.255.229: bytes=32 time<10ms TTL=128
Reply from 172.16.255.229: bytes=32 time<10ms TTL=128
Reply from 172.16.255.229: bytes=32 time<10ms TTL=128
C:\>
```

Repeating the sequence of pinging the WWW host produces the results shown above. Notice that using the CNAME approach, the actual host name of the Web server is substituted producing essentially the same effect. The problem with using the CNAME approach is that many users save bookmarks or favorites to places they find interesting. When the browsers save the bookmark, the fully qualified URL is saved which points the user back to the same host every visit. This defeats the purpose of using the virtual router approach by distributing the users across servers on an ongoing basis. If a particular host name were down for maintenance, this would also cause the client to receive an error even though the rest of your Web "site" is functioning.

USE OF SSL

The Secure Sockets Layer (SSL) was implemented to encrypt information as it travels across the Internet. Most users are not aware that as they send information across the Internet, it is not encrypted and is transmitted as clear text. Any self-respecting hacker can intercept the packets, reassemble them, and read the information. Domestic international Internet users have access to 128-bit SSL encryption. SSL encryption is paving the way for secure Internet purchasing because credit card numbers and personal information can be encrypted. You can tell when your browser is in secure mode by looking for a locked key icon in one corner of your browser, or if the titlebar turns a different color. Encrypting information helps protect the security of a message as it travels across the Internet. If intercepted by a hacker, the SSL packets would not contain easily readable information. Only force the browser into SSL mode when retrieving information that needs to be encrypted. Encrypting large graphics files and other objects can create a substantial overhead for both the server and the browser. SSL should be used with discretion to prevent unnecessary download times.

DISK FRAGMENTATION

By its very nature, Web servers usually consist of a large amount of small files. These files are usually text, with additional multimedia files mixed in to provide sound and graphics. Whether you are using FAT or NTFS volumes to store this information, quick disk access is always a necessity when optimizing performance under Windows NT. File fragmentation occurs whether you are using a single drive or a sophisticated drive array. Both NTFS file partitions and FAT partitions are affected by fragmentation; however, NTFS uses better mechanisms than does FAT to reduce the amount of fragmentation. Because Windows NT does not include any built-in mechanism for disk defragmentation, a third party utility should be used.

To help eliminate disk fragmentation, be sure to check out Diskkeeper Lite by Executive Software on the CD. For more information on the effects and performance gain of disk defragmentation see Chapter 7, "Optimizing Disks."

DISK CACHE

Disk cache has two different forms. Which form it takes depends whether or not you are using Microsoft's Internet Information Server. Windows NT performs its own native disk caching, and most Internet server software also allocates a specific amount of memory for caching Internet server information. Because two cache systems are used, optimal performance can only be obtained by ensuring that both cache systems are optimized. With the cache system as two separate entities, each has its own object monitoring system that can be analyzed using the Performance Monitor (Figure 11-4).

A lot of adjustments can be made to optimize the Windows NT file cache if you know the right tricks and know where to look. Options are available to change the cache priorities, cache size, and other properties. These settings affect not only Windows NT Server systems, but in some cases, Windows NT Workstations and Windows 95 systems also. For a thorough look at the Windows NT system cache, and some cache tuning utilities, see "Optimizing the NT System Cache" in Chapter 7, "Optimizing Disks."

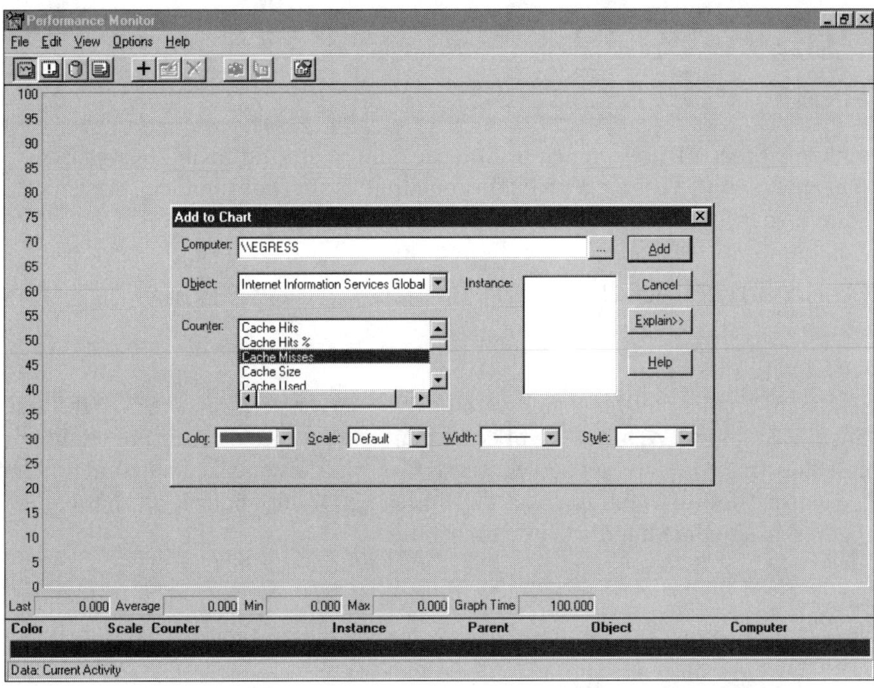

Figure 11-4: Using Performance Monitor to analyze the Windows NT file cache.

One of the most useful Performance Monitor counters for analyzing the efficiency of IIS interaction with the file system cache is the MDL Read Hits %. MDL stands for Memory Descriptor List, and these types of reads are often used to retrieve cached FTP and Web files. Start Performance Monitor and add a chart or log with the Cache: MDL Read Hits % counter. The MDL Read Hits % is operating optimally when the hit rate is at or around 100 percent. The MDL Miss % can be calculated by subtracting the Read Hits % from 100. Other counters can then be used to determine the exact type of read causing the cache miss.

More information on analyzing IIS specific file system data can be found in Windows NT 4.0 Server Resource Kit, Supplement Two.

When analyzing performance logs, be sure to run the test long enough to see how the cache memory varies over a controlled period of time at different intervals. The more data you have for analysis, the better.

Performance Monitor is used to analyze cache information specific to Internet Information Server cache in the next section.

Optimizing Internet Information Server

As with Windows NT itself, much of Microsoft Internet Information Server is self-tuning. However, there are client-load simulating applications you can measure to make sure your IIS server is operating at peak performance.

Measurement tools

WEBSTONE

The standard application for benchmarking Web server performance is WebStone by Silicon Graphics. WebStone works by configuring one or multiple clients to request files from the Internet server. These files can vary in size and content. The Web client portion of WebStone is a multithreaded 32-bit application that can be configured to simulate hundreds of connections.

WebStone can be downloaded from the Silicon Graphics Web site at: `http://www.sgi.com`.

While WebStone is good for performance ratings between different types of Web servers, a more effective tool for troubleshooting and measuring the performance specific to Microsoft IIS is the Web Capacity Analysis Tool (WCAT).

WCAT

The WCAT application is found on the Windows NT 4.0 Server Resource Kit Supplement 1 compact disc.

WCAT integrates very well with IIS and improves measurement statistics by allowing for startup and cool-down routines to ensure all cache objects have time to perform properly. Using WCAT requires the use of at least three different machines, the Web server, a controller, and the Web clients. The controller is what makes WCAT unique in that the clients wait for instructions from the controller about what type of files to request from the Web server. The different tests include simple transfer of HTML text files and graphics to more complex CGI ISAPI script testing. We discuss CGI and ISAPI in a later section of this chapter. Here is an example of a WCAT report:

```
WebCat Version = 3.1
ConfigFile = scripts\FILEMIX.cfg
ScriptFile = scripts\FILEMIX.scr
DistribFile = scripts\FILEMIX.dst
PerfCounterFile =
LogFile = scripts\FILEMIX.log
Author =
```

```
Creation Date =
Test Run Date = Sun Jun 08 15:18:01 1997
Comment = Configuration For File Size Mix
Server [IpAddr:Port] = 172.16.0.5 [172.16.0.5:80]
Clients = 1
Threads = 5
Buffer Size = 131072 bytes
Duration = 300 seconds (Warmup 30 seconds, Cooldown 30 seconds)
Results:
Data, Summary, Rate, 172.16.255.229,
Client Id, 0, 0.00, 1,
Duration, 300, 1.00, 300,
Pages Requested, 2528, 8.43, 2528,
Pages Read, 2528, 8.43, 2528,
Total Responses, 2528, 8.43, 2528,
Avg Response Time, 592, 1.97, 592,
Min Response Time, 10, 0.03, 10,
Max Response Time, 17064, 56.88, 17064,
StdDev Response Time, 1286, 4.29, 1286,
Total Connects, 2528, 8.43, 2528,
Avg Connect Time, 21, 0.07, 21,
Min Connect Time, 0, 0.00, 0,
Max Connect Time, 3005, 10.02, 3005,
StdDev Connect Time, 188, 0.63, 188,
Connect Errors, 0, 0.00, 0,
Read Errors, 0, 0.00, 0,
Data Read, 41065728, 136885.76, 41065728,
Header Bytes, 503309, 1677.70, 503309,
Total Bytes, 41569037, 138563.46, 41569037,
Avg Header per Page, 199, 0.66, 199,
Avg Bytes per Page, 16443, 54.81, 16443,
Files Requested, 2528, 8.43, 2528,
Files Read, 2528, 8.43, 2528,
```

WCAT is a must-have utility to stress a machine that needs to be 100 percent optimized. There are many different configuration files included with WCAT. There are modules designed to measure specific applications such as CGI, ISAPI, standard text, and image transfer. The reports are logged in a comma-delimited format for easy batch monitoring operations, which can be imported into a spreadsheet or database for analysis. Keeping extensive logs in this manner will help you easily identify when there is a problem with a particular machine or possible problems and bottlenecks on specific ISAPI or CGI routines.

INETLOAD

At the time of this writing, Microsoft released a beta version of "InetLoad" on their Web site at `http://www.microsoft.com`. InetLoad differs from both WebStone and WCAT by providing a simple graphical user interface with access to Internet protocols such as NNTP, SMTP (Simple Mail Transfer Protocol), IRC (Internet Relay Chat), LDAP, and many other protocols commonly used by Internet Service Providers. InetLoad works by simulating hundreds or thousands of connections to one or more servers. By using the graphical interface, profiles are constructed that establish how many connections are to be made and which protocols are to be used. By providing access to protocols not supported by WebStone or WCAT, InetLoad gives an administrator the ability to analyze one or more protocols that are possibly causing a bottleneck in the server when the server is under a load. InetLoad has a very extensive macro facility for automating test script routines and the flexibility to use different authentication procedures. Results from InetLoad can be logged and monitored using Performance Monitor, or by using the extensive InetLoad logging capabilities.

INETMON

InetMon is a newly released utility at the time of this writing. The application can be downloaded from the Microsoft Web site. InetMon provides a real-time snapshot of server resources critical to performance. The four areas of focus are processor, memory, network utilization, and disk utilization. By default InetMon presents you with a real-time graph of the critical resources as shown in Figure 11-5. Warning lights on the lower left of the screen trigger when a particular threshold has been exceeded. InetMon also includes scheduled logging of performance statistics over a specified period of time. For network monitoring to work, the Network Monitor Agent must be installed on the server.

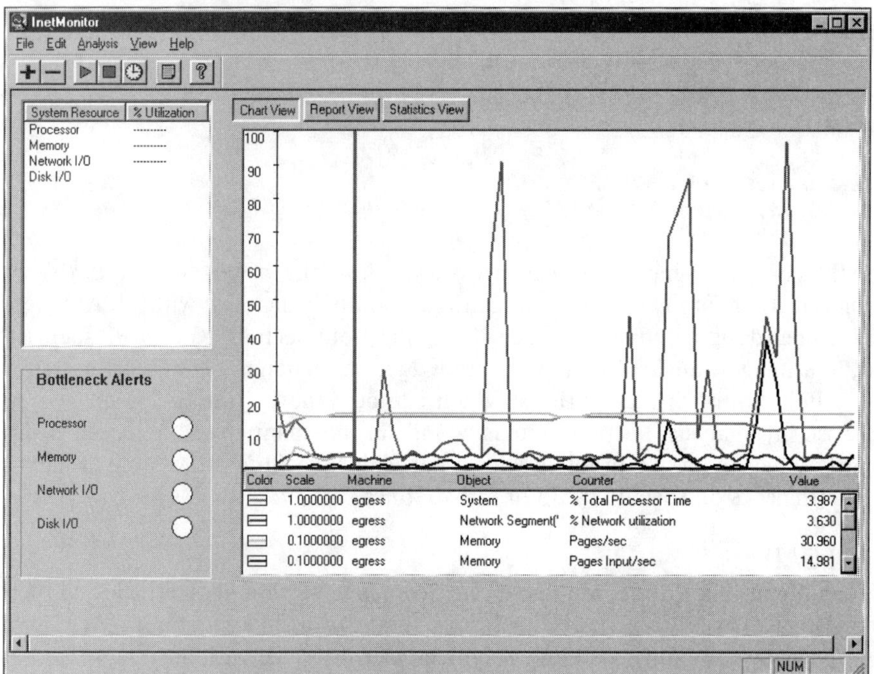

Figure 11-5: Using InetMon to monitor server resources.

The IIS Registry Subkeys

All of the IIS configuration parameters are stored in the Windows NT Registry. Most of these settings are made available through the IIS Administrator interface or are self-tuning. There are, however, one or two settings that can only be changed by directly editing the Registry. With a basic IIS installation, there are four Registry subkeys that are located in the `HKEY_LOCAL_MACHINE\System\CurrentControlSet\Services` tree. These subkeys are:

- `Inetinfo`: Shared Registry with FTP, WWW, and Gopher services
- `W3SVC (WWW)`: Contains the parameters specific to the WWW service
- `MSFTPSVC (FTP)`: Contains the parameters specific to the FTP Service
- `GOPHERSVC (Gopher)`: Contains the parameters specific to the Gopher Service

We discuss specific Registry settings in the "Monitoring IIS Memory Objects" later in this section.

For specific details on the IIS Registry Parameters, see Knowledge Base articles Q143180, Q147621, and Q147623 on the Microsoft Product Support Web site, or Microsoft Technet.

Memory requirements

When installing IIS, three services can be installed: the WWW, FTP, and Gopher. During installation choose only those services required. A server running only Web server services doesn't need the FTP or Gopher services. Installation of these three services requires about 400KBps of memory. It is important to remember that the IIS process (`inetinfo.exe`) has full access to the Windows NT virtual memory system, which allows the operating system to use hard disk space as virtual memory. When measuring IIS performance, it is important to ensure that the server has enough physical memory to keep IIS's working set of objects in physical memory instead of paging to disk.

For an application service, IIS requires a fairly small amount of memory. To reduce IIS memory requirements, you can disable any unused IIS services such as FTP or Gopher if the server is not performing these functions. This assumes the services were installed during setup. To disable specific IIS services use the Services application in Control Panel to set specific services to disabled or manual as shown in Figure 11-6. Further memory requirements for IIS that relate to cache and other objects, which we describe in the next section, can be tuned.

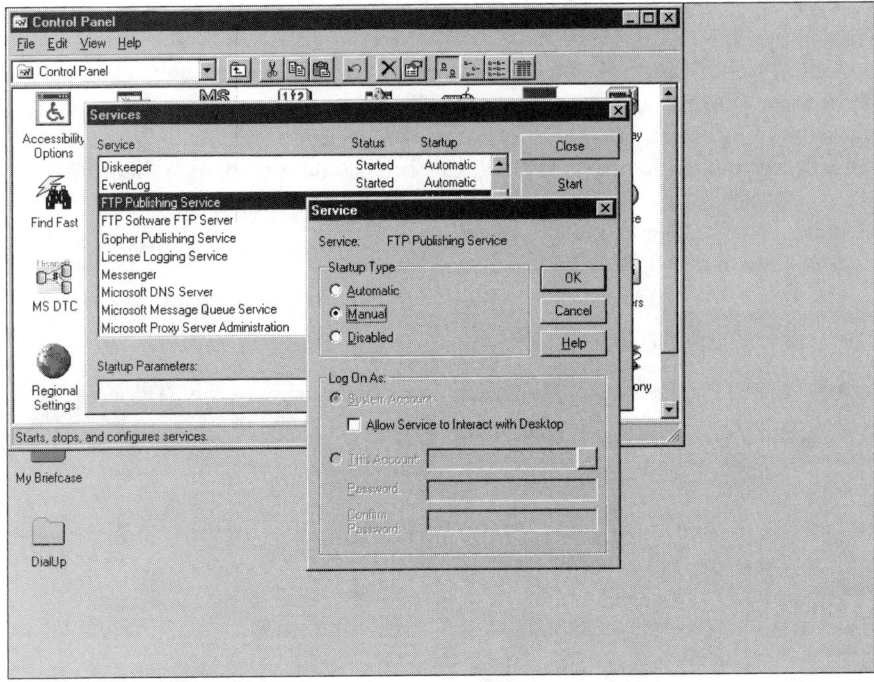

Figure 11-6: NT Service manager.

Monitoring IIS memory objects

SERVER MEMORY

As stated earlier, IIS can only perform as well as the overall operation of the Windows NT system. When optimizing IIS, it is important to locate any memory bottlenecks caused by the server, without relation to the IIS code itself. These types of measurements include monitoring the available memory, disk paging and page faults, the size of the file system cache, and the size of the paging files.

Optimizing server memory and locating processor or memory bottlenecks is described in more detail in Chapter 5, "Optimizing Memory and Processing."

Once any server bottlenecks have been addressed and corrected, it's time to look at the memory used by IIS. Most of the IIS memory objects are tuned by the operating system, which is why it is very important to make sure that any server bottlenecks have been removed. By removing server memory limitations, the memory available to the IIS working set will self-tune for better performance.

The physical memory available to IIS is called its *working set*. The IIS process (`inetinfo.exe`) is a pageable User Mode application that performs best when its code can be stored in physical memory instead of being paged to disk. The IIS process continually monitors and adjusts the working set of IIS memory, which can be measured using the Windows NT Performance Monitor.

The IIS working set must be large enough to hold many of the cache objects associated with IIS and other data running in the IIS process. The IIS current working set can be monitored using the Process: Working Set: Inetinfo counters in the NT Performance Monitor as shown in Figure 11-7. To effectively use this information, the working set counters should be compared to the Memory: Available Bytes and be logged over a period of several days to obtain the most accurate information.

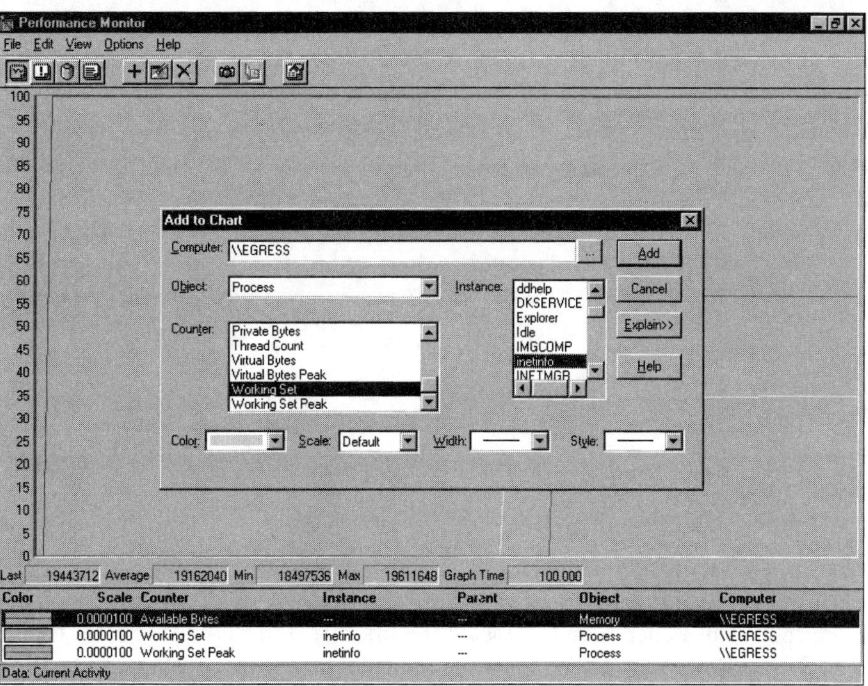

Figure 11-7: Performance Monitor display of available memory and the IIS working set.

IIS OBJECT CACHE MEMORY

One of the most important parts of the IIS working set is the Object Cache. The IIS Object Cache is a collection of commonly used objects IIS stores in RAM. Items such as directory listings, file handles, and large binary objects are kept in memory to improve overall performance. This cache is part of the working set of IIS and can therefore be paged to disk. To improve performance, ensure the system has enough memory to keep it in physical memory.

Most of the IIS Object Cache is revealed through the Internet Information Services Global object as shown in Figure 11-8. These Objects consist of counters used in two areas: cache usage, and bandwidth measurements.

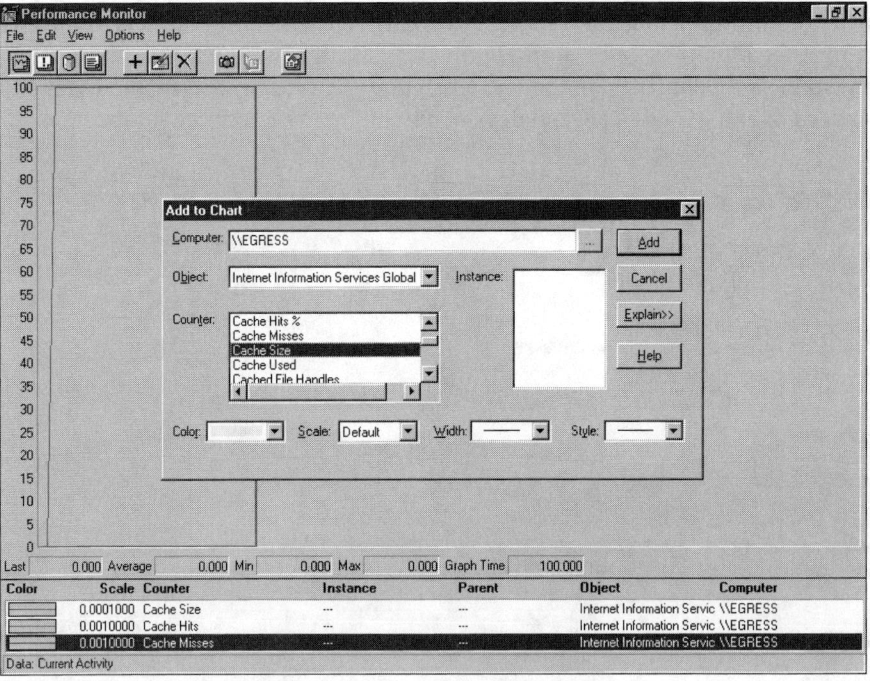

Figure 11-8: Internet Information Server Global Memory Objects.

Performance Monitor is a powerful tool for analyzing this Object Cache. After starting the Performance Monitor, locate the Internet Information Services Global Object. Set the Counter to Cache Misses to analyze the number of times a file open, directory listing, or binary object request was not found in the cache. Other counters allow you to analyze the amount of cache in use and the effectiveness of the cache.

The size of the Object Cache can only be changed by directly editing the Registry as described below:

Location in Registry:

```
HKEY_LOCAL_MACHINE\SYSTEM\CurrentControlSet\Services\InetInfo
 \Parameters
  Value: MemoryCacheSize
  Description of Function:   Determines the size of the IIS Object Cache
Possible Data Values:        0 - 0xFFFFFFFF Default - 10 percent of
                             physical memory
```

By default this setting is set to 10 percent of physical memory and caches all file handles, directory listings, and large binary objects. Sites that have a large amount of files will want to set this to a higher setting depending on available system memory.

IIS FILE CACHE

IIS uses the operating system file cache and the IIS object cache together. IIS requests files sequentially which allows Windows NT to use algorithms that speed disk operations by predicting ahead of time which file will be requested next. If the file cache has enough room in memory, it stores the file and passes the handle to the file to the IIS Object Cache, which then reads the file from the disk cache. Getting the file from the cache will make a substantial performance improvement over reading the file from disk.

IIS LOG BUFFERS

When configuring IIS logging, there are two options. You can either log to a file or to an ODBC system data source to have connection information written to a database. File logging is the faster of the two options. When using file logging, all network connection information is written to a file. As IIS receives connection requests, it stores this information in a memory buffer. By default, this buffer is 64KB and is configurable only in the Registry. The higher the setting, the less disk activity for logging will be used because it takes longer to fill the buffer. On the other hand, those sites interested in a higher level of real-time information can lower this buffer setting to cause the buffer to flush sooner, which will increase the disk activity and performance will drop. The Registry setting to tune the log file buffer size can be configured as follows:

Location in Registry:

```
HKEY_LOCAL_MACHINE\SYSTEM\CurrentControlSet\Services\InetInfo\
 Parameters
  Value: LogFileBatchSize
  Description of Function: This parameter sets the log file batch
size. As network connection information is passed to the IIS service,
data is stored in memory, then written to disk. Increasing this value
reduces disk writes, while decreasing it yields better real-time
data.
```

```
Possible Data Values: The default buffer size is 64*1024 (64KB),
possible data values are 0 – FFFFFFFF.
```

You should raise the number to increase the buffer size and enhance performance, or lower the buffer size to get better real-time data.

More information on this parameter can be found in Microsoft's Knowledge Base article Q143180 found at `http://www.microsoft.com` or Microsoft TechNet.

Real-time data can also be achieved by using the ODBC logging capability. Logging to an ODBC database such as SQL or Access presents additional overhead on system performance because connection data is written to the database in real-time. The database will always be current because no buffering is used, but this severely impacts the system's performance and throughput capabilities. If real-time data is not important in your situation, it is best to use file logging and raise the buffer level to decrease disk activity. When shutting down the server, the information in the file-logging buffer is flushed to disk so that information in the buffer is not lost. More information on this subject can be found in Microsoft's Knowledge Base article Q142557.

Optimizing Server Scripting

The creation of dynamic content by an Internet server has made a substantial impact on how companies do business. It is now possible to track your packages, order flowers, place an auction bid, or get a bus route on-line. The smoke and mirrors behind the screen lie in the fact that the page contents are generated on the fly. Page contents can contain information such as your bank balance or a stock transaction by giving the Web client an interface, or communications path, to the data to query or change.

There are currently three different approaches that HTML writers use to access external information. Let's take a look at these methods and their advantages and disadvantages.

CGI: The Common Gateway Interface

By far, the most popular method to use when communicating with a Web server is through the use of the Common Gateway Interface (CGI). The emergence of CGI established bidirectional communications between the Web browser and the server. CGI was introduced to add dynamic content to Web pages by acting as a gateway, or bridge, between the HTTP server and other resources such as SQL databases. This gateway is actually an executable file that accepts environment variables from the server, and also *stdin*, which is the communication path from the server to the executable. Once the application has executed, it processes and returns the requested information through *stdout*. CGI applications can be written in many different programming and scripting languages. Let's take a look at an example written in Perl.

```
print "HTTP/1.0 200 OK\n";
print "Content-Type: text/html\n\n";
print "<HTML>\n";
print "<HEAD>\n";
print "<TITLE>Hello World!</TITLE>\n";
print "</HEAD>\n";
print "<BODY>\n";
print "<H4>Hello World!</H4>\n";
print "<P>\n";
print "Your Hostname is $ENV{HTTP_HOST}.\n";
print "<P>";
print "Your IP Address is $ENV{REMOTE_ADDR}.\n";
print "<P>";
print "</BODY>\n";
print "</HTML>\n";
```

Because the CGI script actually invokes an executable file on the server operating system, CGI scripts can be written in many popular languages. Many CGI scripts are targeted at the Unix operating system, which has many script interpreters available. One of the most popular CGI scripting languages is Perl because it makes scripting very simple. Perl stands for Practical Extraction and Reporting Language. It is available for virtually all Unix operating systems as well as Windows NT and Windows 95.

In the above script example, there are variables being passed from the server to the client such as the IP address. Other server variables are listed in Table 11-2.

Using sophisticated page programming you can customize your Web pages around what was revealed about the client through the server variables. For example, different objects, such as HTML pages or images files, can be given to different clients based on their capabilities.

One of the most utilized IIS environment variables is LOGON_USER. However, this field will be blank if the client has attached as an anonymous user.

TABLE 11-2 INTERNET INFORMATION SERVER ENVIRONMENT VARIABLES

Server Variable	Value
AUTH_TYPE	
CONTENT_LENGTH	0
CONTENT_TYPE	
GATEWAY_INTERFACE	CGI/1.1
LOGON_USER	
PATH_INFO	/test/scripts/debug.asp
PATH_TRANSLATED	e:\InetPub\wwwroot\Test\Scripts\debug.asp
QUERY_STRING	
REMOTE_ADDR	172.16.0.1
REMOTE_HOST	172.16.0.1
REQUEST_METHOD	GET
SCRIPT_NAME	/test/scripts/debug.asp
SCRIPT_MAP	
SERVER_NAME	Egress
SERVER_PORT	80
SERVER_PORT_SECURE	0
SERVER_PROTOCOL	HTTP/1.0
SERVER_SOFTWARE	Microsoft-IIS/3.0 URL /test/scripts/debug.asp
HTTP_ACCEPT	image/gif, image/x-xbitmap, image/jpeg, image/pjpeg, application/vnd.ms-excel, application/msword, application/vnd.ms-powerpoint, */*
HTTP_ACCEPT_LANGUAGE	En
HTTP_CONNECTION	Keep-Alive
HTTP_HOST	Egress
HTTP_UA_PIXELS	1024x768
HTTP_UA_COLOR	color16

continued

Server Variable	Value
HTTP_UA_OS	Windows NT
HTTP_UA_CPU	x86
HTTP_USER_AGENT	Mozilla/2.0 (compatible; MSIE 3.02; Update a; Windows NT)
HTTP_COOKIE	ASPSESSIONID=NSQFOJPGDXFIRCVS

Perl for Win32 ships with the Windows NT 4.0 Resource Kit. If you don't have the resource kit, you can also download it from the Internet at `http://www.activeware.com`. ActiveWare also has two other versions of Perl. Perl for Internet Server API (ISAPI) communicates directly with Windows NT Internet service as an in-process DLL instead of CGI, making it very fast. We discuss ISAPI in the next section. PerlScript is another form of Perl useful for scripting Web pages.

Although CGI is highly portable across platforms, the drawback is that it's slow. Work is being done to incorporate new features into CGI to correct some of its performance problems.

Other solutions such as FastCGI are designed to offload or distribute CGI processing to other systems, leaving the Web server more process time to handle HTTP requests. More information on FastCGI can be found at `http://www.fastcgi.com`.

Many languages are used to create CGI scripts, including Sun Microsystems' Java, C, Microsoft Visual Basic, and most Unix shells. CGI remains very popular, however, because the operating system and Web server combination usually is a much more efficient means of requesting information from another applications.

When using Perl under Windows NT, you must setup an association between the *.pl* extension and the physical location of the *perl.exe* file. This entry must be made directly in the Registry.

Location in Registry:
`HKEY_LOCAL_MACHINE\SYSTEM\CurrentControlSet\Services\W3SVC\Parameters\ScriptMap`
After locating the ScriptMap Key in the Registry, click on the Edit menu, then Add Value.
The Data type for this entry is `REG_SZ`.
Enter the Value Name: **.pl.**
Next, enter the full path to *perl.exe* followed by a **%s.**

Example: `c:\perl\bin\perl.exe %s`

After restarting the WWW service, executing a Perl script with the *.pl* extension launches the *perl.exe* interpreter.

For more information about installing and testing Perl under WindowsNT, be sure to check out article Q150629 on the Microsoft Web site or Microsoft TechNet.

ISAPI: Internet Server API

The Internet Server API (ISAPI) is a collection of run time Dynamic Link Libraries (DLLs) that actually make up the Web server on Windows NT. These libraries have the ability to load and unload from memory as needed. ISAPI has several major advantages over CGI. One of ISAPI's best features is its superior speed over CGI. The speed improvement is substantial due to how the process (or the threads of execution) get created on the server. Let's take a closer look.

When executing a CGI script, an entirely new process is created, executed, and terminated for every request. There are as many processes as there are active requests. This type of interface drastically increases the processing time and requires large amounts of server RAM.

ISAPI, on the other hand, uses run time DLLs that are compiled function libraries that can be dynamically loaded and unloaded during run time. The major speed advantage that run time DLLs have is that they can be loaded into the same memory address space, running under the same process as the HTTP server. When a function out of an ActiveX control or DLL is called, the library is loaded into the same memory address space as the IIS server. By running in the same memory space, there is a lot less work to do in the NT memory subsystem, which increases performance.

Programming ISAPI components requires extra care in testing and debugging. An errant in-process component can cause the Internet service to become unstable or fail.

Capabilities exist to preload certain DLLs to speed response time and to unload others to conserve server resources. These in-process DLLs, now called ActiveX components, were previously called OLE Automation Servers. ActiveX components can be created using a variety of programming languages including Visual Basic 4.0 Professional and Enterprise Editions, Delphi, Visual C++, and Java.

For more information on creating ActiveX Server Components, refer to Module 3 of the tutorial documentation that ships with the Active Server Pages at `http://www.microsoft.com/iis`. ActiveX technology has also been turned over to the Open Group. More information can be found on the ActiveX Web site at `http://www.activex.org`.

Server side includes

Anyone who has ever built a Web page or entire Web project from scratch will immediately recognize the convenience of server side includes (SSI). Software developers have been using something similar for years called reusable code. If your project has the same footer or copyright notice on the bottom of every page, then changing one file is much easier than changing all of the pages manually. An example SSI statement looks like this example:

```
<HTML>
<HEAD><TITLE>Example SSI Page</TITLE></HEAD>
<BODY>
<!—#include virtual="/test/disclaimer.html"—>
</BODY>
</HTML>
```

In this example, the `#include` tag tells the server to include the contents of *disclaimer.html* as though it were part of the file in use. Some Web servers require that the include file have a different file extension such as .inc, or .stm. Be aware of your server's requirements for include files. Internet Information Server only supports the `#include` directive. All other SSI tags are ignored. Although rudimentary, this did provide a stepping stone for adding dynamic content to Web pages. While making coding easier for the developer the trade-off is that SSI decreases performance due to the extra processing that must take place on the server.

Since IIS does not support any SSI directives except `#include`, this can make a substantial impact on the time required to migrate a Web site to IIS that currently uses unsupported SSI directives.

IIS 3.0: Active Server Pages

Internet Information Server 3.0, also known by its code name "Denali," has put a very powerful twist on Web scripting by embedding two very robust scripting language interpreters into the Active Server Pages code. IIS executes what are referred to as Active Server Pages or .ASP files. These pages use a combination of HTML and two very powerful languages, VBScript and JScript. VBScript is a subset of the more powerful Visual Basic. Table 11-3 describes the Java, JavaScript, and JScript.

TABLE 11-3 JAVA JARGON

Language	Description
Java	Java is an object-oriented programming language with minor similarities to C++. Java was developed by Sun Microsystems and uses machine-independent multithread-enabled code, which gives it the ability to run across many platforms including Unix and Windows NT.
JavaScript	JavaScript was developed by NetScape Communications and is a scripting language that can be embedded into HTML pages and interpreted by NetScape Navigator. It is important to note that JavaScript is independent of Java and Sun Microsystems.
JScript	JScript is Microsoft's open implementation of Netscape's JavaScript. JScript has extended functionality to link JScript code to ActiveX controls and Java programs.

Both VBScript and JScript allow Web developers to create objects such as a buttons, check boxes, or text boxes on a form that is more interactive than the standard HTML form controls. Both provide quite a bit of functionality, yet, for security reasons, they have a rather limited access to operating system functions. We take a more in-depth look at VBScript and JScript in the following sections.

Before IIS 3.0, deciding on a scripting language was a little easier because these scripting languages could only be interpreted by the client. Both NetScape and Microsoft browsers support JavaScript, while VBScript is only supported by Microsoft Internet Explorer.

With the arrival of IIS 3.0 and the Active Server Pages component, both VBScript and JScript can be interpreted and executed either on the client browser, or, using IIS 3.0 Active Server Pages, have the script executed on the server. By executing the code on the server, transmission times are shorter, while providing dynamic pages with processing power that are platform-independent. This is accomplished by having the script execute on the server and returning to the client only the HTML code comprising the page. All of the valuable background code-performing operations are not revealed to the client. Because all of the code execution takes place on the NT server, a Web developer can standardize on one coding language and not have to worry about native browser support for the scripting code. An example of the power of this capability lies in the fact that a dynamic page can be executed on the server using VBscript routines that are not supported by NetScape or Mosaic browsers.

Executing scripts on the server side is demonstrated in the VBScript sample shown here:

```
<HTML>
<HEAD>
<TITLE>Hello World</TITLE></HEAD>
<BODY BGCOLOR=#FFFFFF>
<% for x = 4 to 6 %>
<FONT SIZE=<% = x %>Hello World</FONT>
<BR>
<% next %>
</BODY>
</HTML>
```

The following script will work whether the client is NetScape Navigator, Mosaic, or Internet Explorer running on a PC, Macintosh, or a Unix workstation. This is because the server interprets the script and only the HTML code is returned to the client.

```
<HTML>
<HEAD>
<TITLE>Hello World</TITLE></HEAD>
<BODY BGCOLOR=#FFFFFF>
<FONT SIZE=4>Hello World</FONT>
<BR>
<FONT SIZE=5>Hello World</FONT>
```

```
<BR>
<FONT SIZE=6>Hello World</FONT>
<BR>
</BODY>
</HTML>
```

Server-side scripts that run under Internet Information Server 3.0 require an extension of .ASP. That's the easy part. What is buried just a little deeper in the documentation is that the virtual directory that the script will be residing in must have Execute privileges enabled. A quick sign that it is not enabled is when you go to a page that should execute and instead you see the raw HTML text of the page. The cool tip: Microsoft FrontPage97 makes it easy to set a folder for Execute privileges. Just right click on the folder that contains the files requiring execute permissions, then click on Properties and turn on the Allow Scripts to be Run checkbox. FrontPage97 will remove the read rights from the folder and enable the execute rights. This is for security reasons that are discussed later.

It is a recommended security practice to keep files that execute and files that are read-only in different directories. By placing the script files and active server pages in a directory with only execute and no read privileges, a client can't download the actual text of an active server page. Information contained in the page script might contain user login information for the ODBC connection or formulas for configuring a product discount. This information might be confidential and should be protected in this environment.

VB versus Java scripting

With the release of Microsoft Internet Explorer 3.0 and NetScape Navigator 2.0, HTML pages took on an entirely new form. Both Navigator and Explorer include the capability to execute JavaScript code embedded into HTML pages. It is important to note that the embedded code executes on the client machine. Because the code executes on the client, complex scripts can drastically slow a client with limited memory or CPU speed. This is very noticeable when using extensive graphic animation. Internet Explorer 3.0 also included the first version of VBScript (Visual Basic Scripting Edition), as well as JScript. Let's take a closer look at both of these languages.

VBSCRIPT

VBScript is a subset of Microsoft Visual Basic with limited functionality for computer and network security reasons. VBScript is perfect for lightweight HTML scripting to create form items such as command buttons and text boxes with better event handling than is currently available through standard HTML objects. VBScript objects contained in an HTML page also have the capability of communicating directly with ActiveX controls on the client or the server. The following code example illustrates some simple VBScript.

```
<html>
<head>
<title>VBScript Sample Page</title>
</head>
<body bgcolor="#FFFFFF">
<script language="VBScript">
<!-
Sub window_onLoad()
txtBox.value = Now()
end sub
-></script>
<p><input type="text" size="20" name="txtBox"> </p>
</body>
</html>
```

Figure 11-9 shows how the page will look in the browser when executed by the client.

One of the limitations of using VBScript on the client side is that the controls are event-driven. As the example shows, program output must go to an object instead of being written straight to the page output. Server-side VBScript, which is part of IIS 3.0 Active Server Pages, has quite a bit more functionality than the client-side scripting and handles page layout and program flow control in a much better fashion.

JSCRIPT

As stated earlier, JScript is an open and full implementation of NetScape JavaScript. JavaScript and JScript are functionally compatible. JScript, however, also includes enhancements for Internet Explorer. As with VBScript, JScript can be run on the server side, making it browser-independent. The following is a sample JScript that will print the date and time on an HTML page. The script results are shown in Figure 11-10. Notice that JScript allows a developer to print output directly to the page, something that is not possible with VBScript.

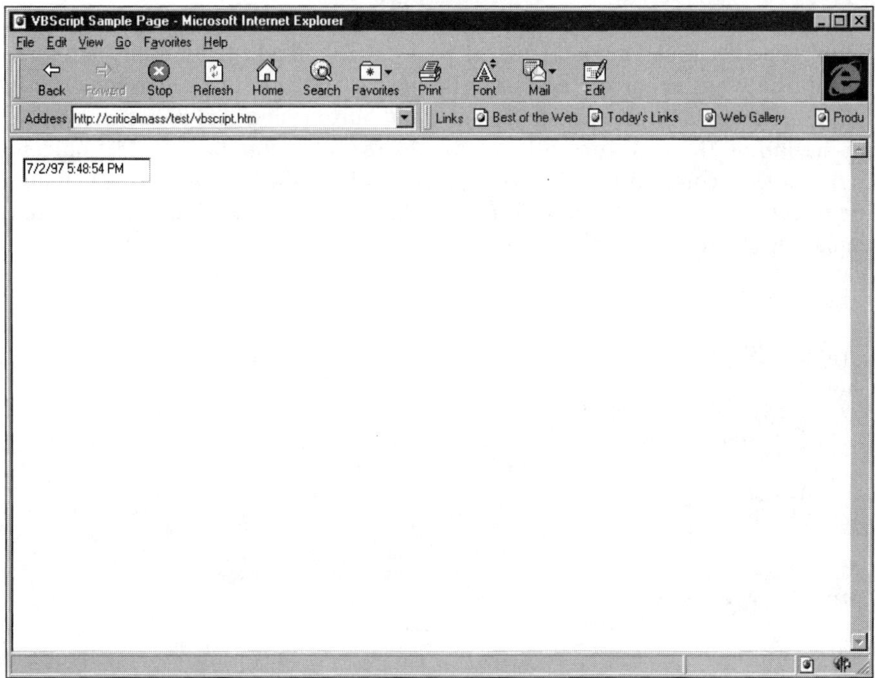

Figure 11-9: The sample VBScript running in a browser.

```
<html>
<head>
<title>Sample JScript Page</title>
</head>
<body bgcolor="#FFFFFF">
<p><script language="JavaScript"><!—
// create a date object
Today = new Date()
// output some HTML text for the time
document.write ("The current time is: ");
// gets the hour
document.write(Today.getHours(),":");
// gets the minutes
document.write(Today.getMinutes());
// put the date on a new line
document.write("<BR>");
// output some HTML text for the date
document.write("The date is: ");
document.write(Today.getMonth()+1,"-");
document.write(Today.getDate(),"-");
document.write(Today.getYear());
// —></script></p>
</body>
</html>
```

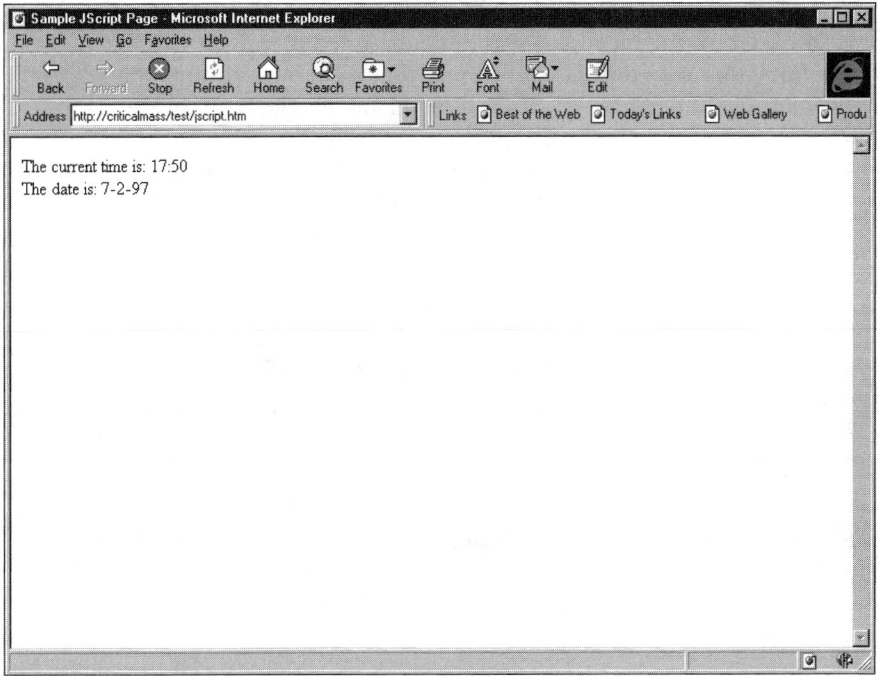

Figure 11-10: Page showing the results of the sample JScript.

Choosing a Back-End Database

Dynamic HTML pages usually use information stored in some form of database to create the document contents. These databases come in many different forms with different requirements, capabilities, and complexity. By using database results to generate dynamic Web pages, high traffic sites will usually require a high-end database that has been optimized for speed such as Microsoft SQL Server, Oracle, or Sybase. What should you look for when choosing a database to power your Web site? There are a couple of considerations.

First, the database should be ODBC (Open Database Connectivity) compliant. Let's take a closer look at ODBC.

ODBC database access

The first thing to consider when selecting a back-end database is how well it communicates with other data sources. ODBC is part of the Windows Open Systems Architecture (WOSA). ODBC does for databases what the operating system does for the PC: it provides a uniform, controlled access to a resource. An ODBC database driver uses a standard set of commands called Structure Query Language (SQL) to access information independent of the database being used. ODBC drivers can access information stored in just about any type of database format. Some of the more popular ODBC database types are listed in Table 11-4.

TABLE 11-4 SAMPLE ODBC-COMPLIANT DATABASES

Text Files	Microsoft FoxPro	Btrieve
Microsoft Access	Microsoft SQL Server	IBM DB/2
Lotus Notes	Sybase	Paradox
xBase (dBase) Files	Oracle	Informix Online

There are many, many different types of databases in the computer industry. Some of these databases, such as those listed in Table 11-4, are considered "open" and comply with the ODBC specification. Each database offers different features such as speed, security, size, portability, and scalability.

The IS Challenge

In the real world, companies merge and new technologies come along that challenge any developer. Mergers produce bigger companies that possibly use different information systems, across different platforms and networks. Information managers and software developers are faced with merging all of this data into meaningful information. ODBC isn't a solution for all of these problems in itself, but it does go a long way toward being able to query and report on information stored on different systems. Distributed computing solutions are now being built around object-oriented technology such as Microsoft's Distributed Common Object Model (DCOM) and the Object Management Group's Common Object Request Broker Architecture (CORBA) specifications. Using object-oriented code allows developers to invoke method objects whether the code is local or on a network machine that may be running a different operating system. Combining the power of ActiveX and the portability of Java with DCOM and CORBA will, in the future, make a substantial impact on eliminating cross-platform problems. More information on DCOM can be found on the Microsoft Web site, and information about CORBA can be located on the Object Management Group Web site at `http://www.omg.org`.

SETTING UP AN ODBC CONNECTION

ODBC data sources are configured using the ODBC control panel application as shown in Figure 11-11.

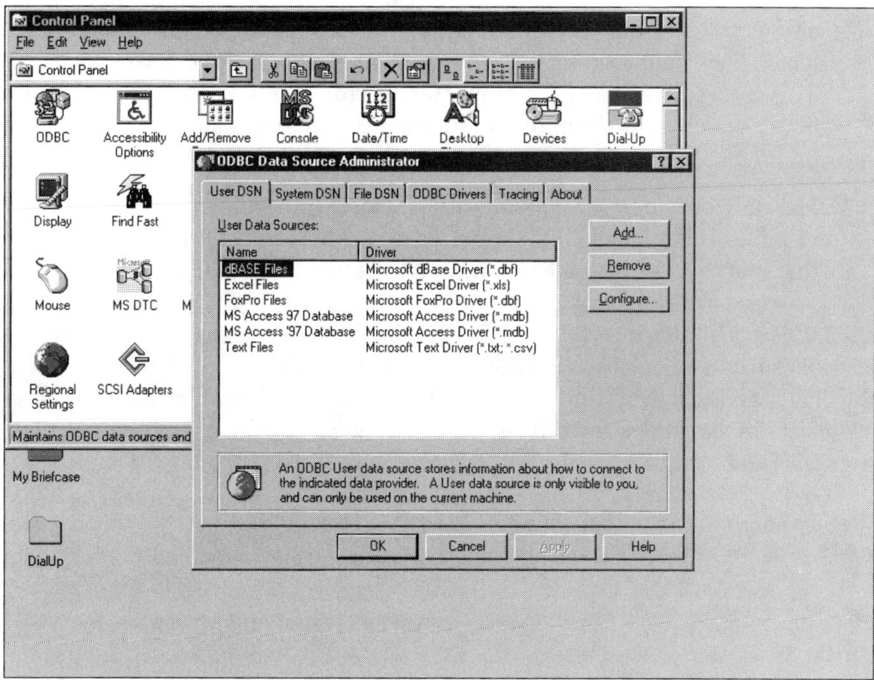

Figure 11-11: The ODBC Data Source Administrator.

As shown in the Data Source Administrator, there are three different ODBC connection types. The Data Source Name (DSN) type determines where the database connection information is held.

1. User DSN: A User DSN is a single data connection owned by a single user account on an NT system. Because the connection is owned by a user account, the data connection and its configuration are removed from memory when the user logs off. This assists with Windows NT security because another user logged onto the same machine won't see the data connection of another user. User DSN connection information is stored in the `HKEY_CURRENT_USER_` Registry key.

2. System DSN: When writing applications that require the system have access to a data connection even when no one is logged on, you use a System DSN. System DSNs are independent of who is logged onto the console. The connection information for a System DSN is stored in the `HKEY_Local_Machine\` Registry. The drawback about using System DSN connections is that the connections are dependent on the machine on which they have been set up. This usually presents a problem when moving a Web application from one server to another, or moving from development to production environments. For Web applications running on IIS 3.0, it is best to use the File DSN described below.

3. File DSN: A File DSN maintains all database connection information inside of a file. This type of DSN should be used when creating Web applications that make use of the global.asa, which is supported by IIS 3.0. .

IIS 3.0 uses a file in the Web root called global.asa. Web application development tools such as Microsoft Visual InterDev automatically configure the content of the global.asa such as setting up database connections. The following code from a global.asa file illustrates the differences in using a file DSN connection versus a System DSN connection.

```
<SCRIPT LANGUAGE=VBScript RUNAT=Server>
Sub Session_OnStart
 '==Visual InterDev Generated - DataConnection startspan==
 '—Project Data Connection
      Session("AccessFile_ConnectionString") = "DBQ=C:\Program
 Files\Microsoft
 Office\Office\Samples\Northwind.mdb;DefaultDir=C:\Program
 Files\Microsoft Office\Office\Samples;Driver={Microsoft Access
 Driver (*.mdb)};DriverId=25;FIL=MS
 Access;ImplicitCommitSync=Yes;MaxBufferSize=512;MaxScanRows=8;PageT
 imeout=5;SafeTransactions=0;Threads=3;UID=admin;UserCommitSync=Yes;
 "
      Session("AccessFile_ConnectionTimeout") = 15
      Session("AccessFile_CommandTimeout") = 30
      Session("AccessFile_RuntimeUserName") = "admin"
      Session("AccessFile_RuntimePassword") = ""
 '—Project Data Connection
      Session("SQLFile_ConnectionString") = "DRIVER={SQL
 Server};SERVER=egress;UID=sa;PWD=;APP=Microsoft (R) Developer
 Studio;WSID=EGRESS"
      Session("SQLFile_ConnectionTimeout") = 15
      Session("SQLFile_CommandTimeout") = 30
      Session("SQLFile_RuntimeUserName") = "guest"
      Session("SQLFile_RuntimePassword") = ""
 '—Project Data Connection
      Session("AccessDSN_ConnectionString") =
 "DSN=AdvWorks;DBQ=E:\inetpub\ASPSamp\AdvWorks\AdvWorks.mdb;DriverId
 =25;FIL=MS Access;MaxBufferSize=512;PageTimeout=5;"
```

```
        Session("AccessDSN_ConnectionTimeout") = 15
        Session("AccessDSN_CommandTimeout") = 30
        Session("AccessDSN_RuntimeUserName") = "RuntimeUser"
        Session("AccessDSN_RuntimePassword") = "Password"
  '==Visual InterDev Generated - DataConnection endspan==
End Sub
</SCRIPT>
```

There are three separate ODBC database connections listed in this code. The first is called AccessFile, which is a File DSN connected to an Access database. The second is a File DSN connected to a SQL server, and the third is a System DSN connection to an Access database.

Notice that there are extensive configuration parameters describing the Access and SQL File DSN connections. The IIS Active Data Object (ADO) interprets these parameters to establish a connection, which is independent of the ODBC data source administrator. Visual InterDev maintains the configuration settings in the global.asa during development cycle by using a File DSN on the developer workstation. If a change is made to the File DSN, the global.asa is automatically updated. Once the Web application is published, the global.asa no longer needs the File DSN.

The final database connection, called AccessDSN, uses a System DSN connection, which is shown by the different parameters in the global.asa file.

Web applications written using the IIS 1.0 and 2.0 database interface can only use a System DSN because the global.asa and the Active Data Object (ADO) were not introduced until IIS 3.0.

DISADVANTAGES

The functionality provided by ODBC doesn't come without a price. The additional overhead of the ODBC layer takes its toll on performance when compared to using native drivers. Native drivers such as the SQL DB-Lib are faster and can be accessed from a run time DLL.

SQL server database

As stated earlier, SQL is an industry standard data access method. An SQL server is a very fast database server usually connected to a network that can process thousands of transactions per minute.

ODBC 3.0 now ships with the ODBC Trace utility. This utility traces and logs all SQL calls made to the ODBC driver. Security concerns may arise because many HTTP servers and other applications use standard SQL log in procedures through ODBC. This log keeps all information, including the username and password, in a file capable of being read by any text editor. Microsoft has published procedures, which can be found at `http://www.microsoft.com/odbc`, describing how to disable tracing on both Windows 95 and Windows NT.

As an alternative to standard SQL log in, Microsoft SQL Server and other BackOffice-logo products use an integrated or mixed authentication process. The NT integrated authentication process uses information from your domain and username to establish a session and set your permissions for data access.

MICROSOFT SQL SERVER

SQL servers such as Microsoft SQL Server for Windows NT are high-performance database servers capable of serving thousands of clients. As more Web content is converted from static to dynamic, it is important not to overlook any bottlenecks that are being created on the data server and which might cause the Web server to wait before returning content to the client.

Optimizing a Microsoft SQL Server takes training and experience. Performance tuning is more of an art than a science. It is impossible to tune the server for optimum performance without identifying the actual cause of a specific performance problem. However, it is possible to make some general recommendations about system configuration. These changes can be made in the SQL Enterprise Manager as shown in Figure 11-12.

- TempDB in RAM: SQL Server has a temporary database used to store the results of intermediate database operations. This information is stored in TempDB on the hard disk by default. By allocating physical memory for TempDB, you can dramatically improve the performance of sorting, GROUP BY calculations, joins, and queries that require temporary workspace.

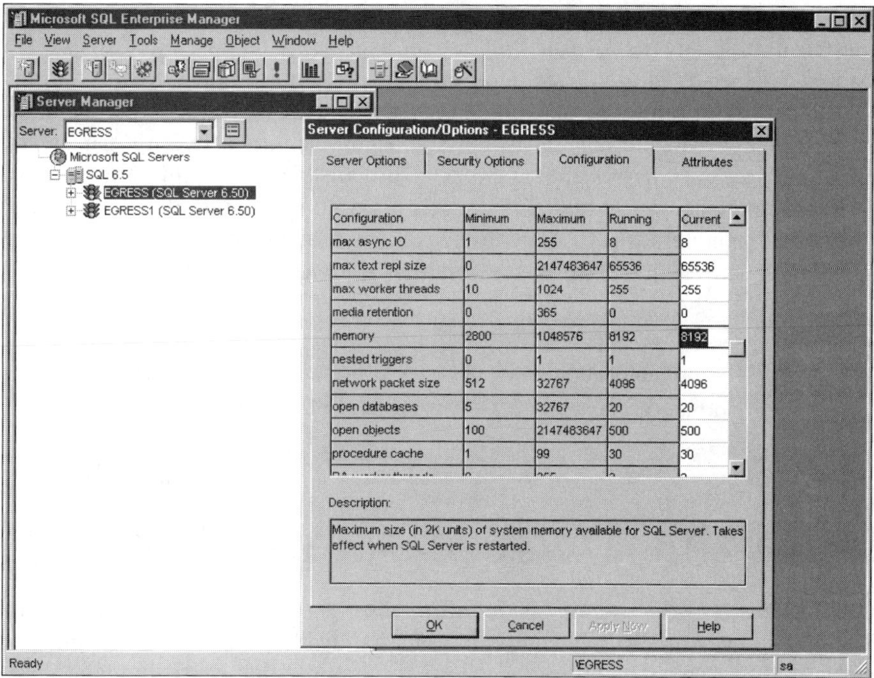

Figure 11-12: SQL Enterprise Manager.

- Memory Allocation: Determining the amount of physical memory to devote to SQL server can be a complex subject depending on how your server is used. As a rule of thumb, you should reserve 16MB of memory strictly for Windows NT Server and allocate the rest to SQL Server (assuming the machine is dedicated to SQL Server). A system with 64MB of RAM would have 48MB allocated to the SQL service, leaving 16MB for the Windows NT operating system. You can specify the memory used by SQL Server in the Server Configuration dialog box as shown in Figure 11-12. Memory is specified in 2K pages. The number of pages can be calculated by multiplying the amount of RAM by 512 (48MB × 512) = 24,576 pages.
- Locks: During installation, SQL Server defaults to 5,000 locks. In a medium-sized environment, this should be raised to at least 15,000 locks.
- Procedure Cache: By default SQL Server allocates 30 percent of its memory to Procedure Cache once the SQL memory requirements are met. Adjusting the size of this cache up or down can yield significant performance advantages. See the Microsoft SQL server documentation for more details about this topic.

Our purpose in analyzing and optimizing the SQL server is to ensure that the requested data is returned to the Web server as quickly as possible. Our last tip regarding SQL server is to not overlook the network connection if you aren't running SQL and IIS on the same machine. In most cases, the Web server and the database server will be on the same LAN. For stable connections between LAN servers, take a look at optimizing the network protocols for LAN communications. Microsoft's implementation of TCP/IP is very flexible in its configuration. Tuning the TCP/IP parameters for a LAN connection, such as by increasing the Sliding Window size, can yield significant network performance improvements.

For more information on network protocols, see "Optimizing TCP/IP Performance" in Chapter 9, "Optimizing Your NT Network."

Optimizing Microsoft Proxy Server

The rapid growth of the Internet as an information gathering and communications tool is limited by available bandwidth. Internet bandwidth problems affect both the clients and the servers. The Internet has peak usage times that cause dramatic slowdowns. Part of the solution to the bandwidth issue is to implement a proxy server as a performance enhancement and as a security tool. In this section, we discuss the Microsoft Proxy Server.

A proxy server acts as a relay agent for browser requests. When a user types a URL (Uniform Resource Locater), the proxy server intercepts and fulfills the request without the client actually establishing direct communications with the destination server. Proxy servers are primarily used to allow clients outbound connectivity while securing the internal network.

Performance benefits

Because clients make all requests to the proxy server, a sophisticated proxy will implement some form of caching to reduce the traffic to popular sites. The Microsoft Proxy server implements two forms of caching.

For performance reasons, it is recommended that cached information always be stored on an NTFS volume.

PASSIVE CACHING

Passive caching is based on Time To Live (TTL). When a client makes a request to the proxy server, the pages and other objects such as graphics are placed in the proxy cache for a specified amount of time. This time length can be adjusted by setting the cache expiration policy as shown in Figure 11-13.

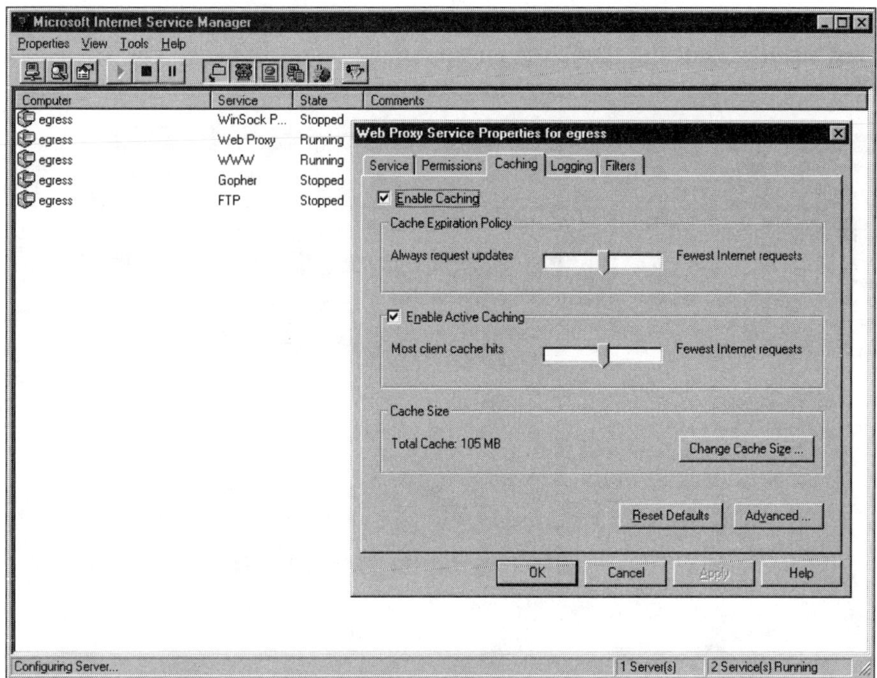

Figure 11-13: Setting the cache expiration policy using the Web Proxy Service Properties dialog.

ACTIVE CACHING

Active caching allows the proxy server to use sophisticated statistical analysis on cached objects. These objects are then requested from the server without the assistance of the client to perform more of a proactive cache based on the analysis. Active caching is also optimized to refresh the cache during off-peak periods by analyzing server load patterns.

Security benefits

FILTERS

As stated earlier, a proxy server denies access to internal network resources from outside sources. With the push to get onto the Internet, it has also become necessary to restrict access to outside sources. Microsoft Proxy Server allows packet filtering targeted at a single computer, multiple computers, or an entire domain. Filtering options administered with the IIS Administrator are shown in Figure 11-14.

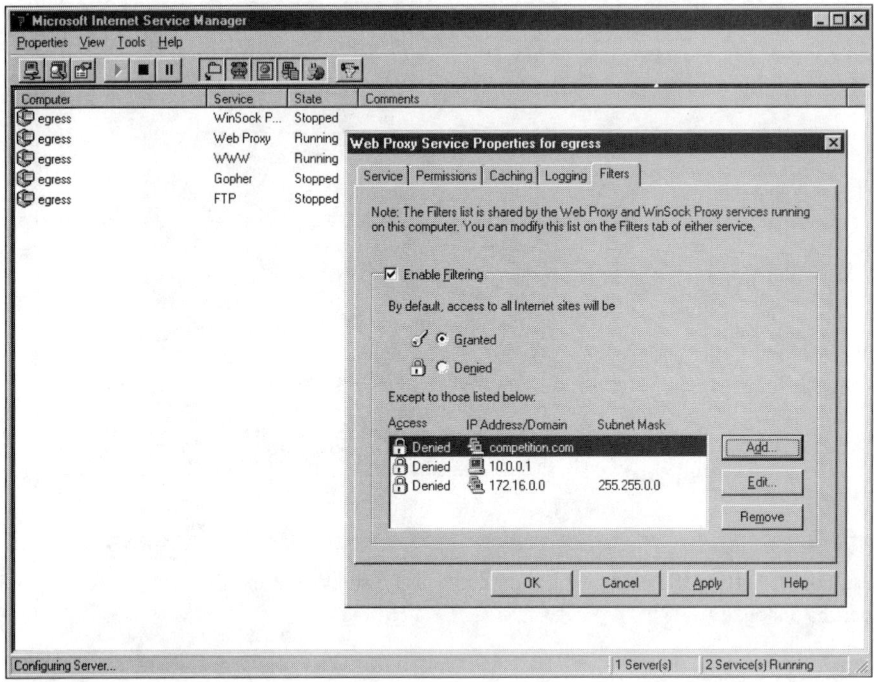

Figure 11-14: Proxy Service filter options.

PERMISSIONS

Because Windows NT powers Microsoft Proxy Server, using the integrated security mechanisms you can grant and restrict access to specific users or entire groups. Filtering options administered with the IIS Administrator are shown in Figure 11-15. Options can be set for specific types of access such as FTP Read, Gopher, WWW, and Secure access.

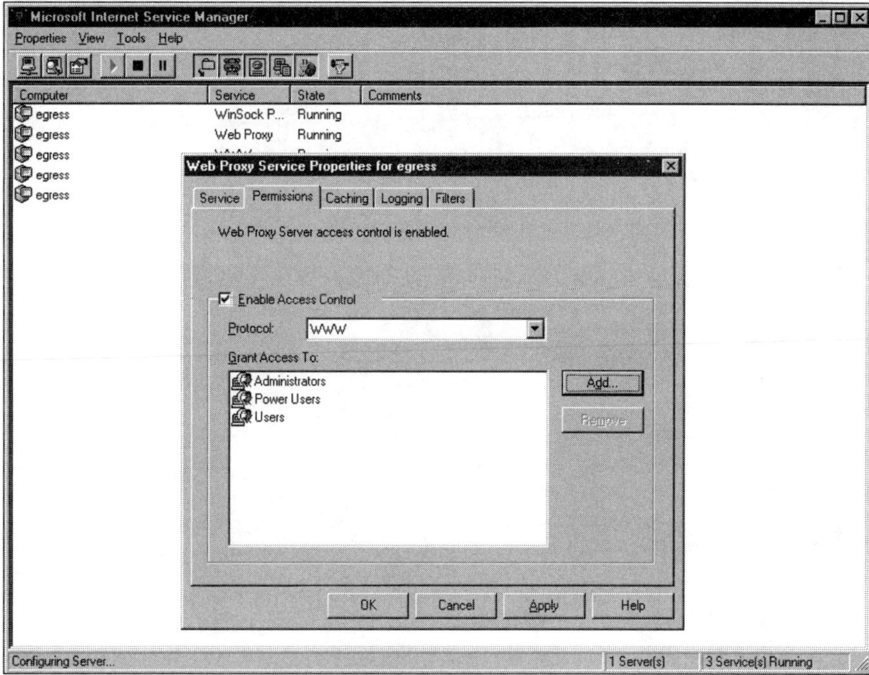

Figure 11-15: Web Proxy Service permissions.

LOGGING

As part of Internet Information Server and the ISAPI specification, Microsoft Proxy Server logs all connection information either to a file or to an ODBC connection. Performance enhancements can be made by increasing the size of the buffer size to reduce disk writes. For more information on changing the buffer size of IIS, review the section on IIS log buffers earlier in the chapter.

Summary

In this chapter, we examined issues surrounding the performance of Internet and intranet servers running on Windows NT servers, including those related to the protocols, scripting methods, database, and add-on products used with your server. You can use this information to evaluate and estimate the usefulness of each of these technologies, methods, and tools in your particular environment (or to reevaluate for servers that are already deployed). You can also use this information to make immediate changes that can greatly enhance your server's overall performance.

In the next chapter, we discuss maintaining and recovering Windows NT systems.

Chapter 12

Maintaining Your NT System

TO HELP PREVENT DISASTERS, you'll want to make sure that there is a good maintenance plan in place for your NT systems. This plan should include several proactive, preventive maintenance tasks that will make it easier for you to recover your system in the event of a disaster such as hard drive failure or Registry corruption. Although these procedures are always an important part of using any Windows NT computer, they are especially important if you implement any of the Registry changes mentioned in this book. The reason is that any Registry change, no matter what it affects, has the potential to cause problems with your Windows NT installation. Although every effort has been made to ensure the accuracy of the modifications discussed in this book, it is still possible that a Registry change will cause unpredictable results on some systems. Therefore, as the old sports saying goes, the best defense is a good offense. In this case, your "offense" can be the implementation of the procedures described below, in addition to any others you may already be using.

Installing System Updates

All software has bugs and Windows NT is no exception. However, the good news is that Microsoft actively responds to bugs discovered in NT and regularly releases operating system updates to fix them. Microsoft refers to these updates as *Service Packs* and *Hotfixes*. Service Packs are usually large collections of fixes and enhancements that are created over a period of time, whereas Hotfixes are narrowly focused fixes targeted at one specific bug or problem. Read on for more information about how to obtain and install these updates on your system(s).

Windows NT Service Packs

Although the major reason for Service Packs traditionally has been to fix problems in the operating system, Microsoft recently has been using them to add or enhance operating system features. In some cases, these feature additions or changes are minor; in others, they are significant. In addition to problem fixes, Service Packs can also contain feature upgrades or enhancements to the Windows NT operating system. Service Packs make it possible for Microsoft to repair bugs and add functionality without going through the development costs associated with a new version release. Windows NT Service Packs are available for download from Microsoft's FTP (File Transfer Protocol) server or on the Microsoft TechNet CD-ROM.

Microsoft numbers Service Packs sequentially, in the order of their release (e.g., Service Pack 1, Service Pack 2, and so on). In addition, each Service Pack level is cumulative and contains both the new fixes and enhancements of that Service Pack as well as those contained in all previous Service Pack releases. This means you only need to load the most recent Service Pack to obtain all of the fixes and enhancements that were developed since the base version was released.

Although all NT Service Packs to date have been cumulative, this is not always true of other Microsoft products. Therefore, never assume (even with future Windows NT Service Packs) that the fix is cumulative, and always read the instructions that accompany the Service Pack before installing it. One notable exception to the cumulative Service Pack idea is Microsoft Exchange Server Service Pack 3; it requires the presence of Exchange Service Pack 2 to install properly. As Service Packs grow in size, Microsoft may elect to use this strategy with other products as well.

Hotfixes

Sometimes, problems are discovered that are urgent enough that they can't wait for the next Service Pack release to be fixed. To address these situations, Microsoft developed a special type of patch for NT called a hotfix. Hotfixes are different than Service Packs in that normally they address only a single issue or problem and are usually much smaller in size. Also, the installation procedure for hotfixes differs from that of regular Service Packs (see the "Installing Hotfixes" section later in this chapter for more information on how they are installed).

Finally, hotfixes differ from Service Packs in that they do not always receive the same level of testing as a Service Pack does. This means that although they may fix one problem, they could potentially cause another problem somewhere else. This fact is evident from the disclaimer that accompanies all NT hotfixes:

STATUS: Microsoft has confirmed this to be a problem in Windows NT version 4.0. A supported fix is now available, but is not fully regression-tested and should be applied only to systems experiencing this specific problem. Unless you are severely impacted by this specific problem, Microsoft recommends that you wait for the next Service Pack that contains this fix. Contact Microsoft Technical Support for more information.

Often there's not much of a choice: If a hotfix is available for a particular problem, it's probably a fairly severe one that affects a large number of users (thus the urgency in releasing it before a Service Pack). If you're one of these users, you'll probably find it difficult to wait for the next Service Pack.

Obtaining Windows NT Service Packs and hotfixes

The best way to obtain Service Packs and hotfixes is by download from the Internet via Microsoft's FTP server using a Web browser (such as Microsoft Internet Explorer or Netscape Navigator) or an FTP client application. Microsoft always makes NT Service Packs available on this server, which is located at `ftp.microsoft.com`. The actual Service Pack files are inside subdirectories within the /`bussys/winnt/winnt-public/fixes` directory. Underneath this subdirectory are subdirectories for various countries for each international version of Windows NT(/USA for the US, /FRN for France, etc.). Inside the country-specific directory you must choose the version-specific directory representing the version of NT the Service Pack is for (/NT40, /NT351, /NT35, etc.). Inside this directory you must specify the directory containing the Service Pack level you're looking for (e.g., /SP1, /SP2, etc.). Finally, once inside this directory, you must select the directory representing the hardware platform of your Windows NT computer (/I386, /MIPS, /ALPHA, /PPC, etc.). The self-extracting archive file containing the Service Pack will be located in this directory (it should be the only .EXE file there), with a name specific to the version of NT, the Service Pack level, and the hardware platform chosen. Although not a hard and fast rule of any kind, Microsoft usually manages to release about one NT Service Pack per quarter.

Hotfixes are located in the same area on Microsoft's FTP Server as Service Packs, but are stored off of the base NT fixes directory in a subdirectory starting with "hotfixes-post*N*," where *N* is the number of the Service Pack the hotfixes are for (e.g., the Windows NT 4.0 post-Service Pack 2 hotfixes are located in the directory `/bussys/winnt/winnt-public/fixes/usa/nt40/hotfixes-postSP2`). Unlike Service Packs, hotfixes for all platforms (i.e., Intel, Alpha, MIPS, and PowerPC) are usually contained within the subdirectory, so be sure to download the correct version for your system. The platform type can be identified by the last letter of the hotfix file name; e.g., a RAS hotfix file for Windows NT 4.0 on the Intel platform might be named something like RAS40I.EXE.

Here's a cool tip for anyone wanting an easy way to keep up-to-date on new hotfixes and Service Packs: create an Internet URL shortcut on your desktop for the Service Pack (SP) directory of your NT version on your desktop (e.g., a shortcut to `ftp://ftp.microsoft.com/bussys/winnt/winnt-public/fixes/usa/nt40/`, the SP directory for users of the English version of NT 4.0). Once you've established your connection to the Internet, you can select this shortcut to automatically load the NT fixes/patches directory display in your Web browser. To further enhance the usefulness of this shortcut, place it on your desktop. If you're using Internet Explorer, this is as simple as loading this location as the current page, and then choosing File → Create Shortcut from the menus. This trick always keeps you a double-click away from seeing the latest contents of the Service Pack directory.

Installing Service Packs

Once you have downloaded the Service Pack .EXE file, you should place it in its own directory and execute the program. Execution decompresses the archive file's contents into the same directory as the archive file itself (you can also specify a directory to unpack to as a command line argument (e.g., `SP2_400I.EXE C:\SERVPACK`). All Windows NT Service Packs come in a self-extracting archive file format (.EXE) that automatically unpacks into the directory containing it when executed. This is the format provided on the Microsoft FTP server for downloading. However, you may also find the Service Pack in an already unpacked form on any of several different CD-ROMs of applications that require that Service Pack level to operate correctly.

There is one inconvenience with Service Packs for Windows NT 3.51 and Service Pack 1 for Windows NT 4.0: once installed there is no way to uninstall them. The only way to do so is to either reinstall Windows NT from scratch and reapply the previous Service Packs (if any), or to run the Repair option of Windows NT setup to restore the base version of Windows NT. However, beginning with Windows NT 4.0 Service Pack 2 it is possible to instruct the Service Pack Installer to create an uninstall directory that allows you to return to the previous Service Pack revision of Windows NT 4.0 (or base version if SP1 is installed).

The sections below detail the procedure for two different types of Service Pack installations; which one you use depends on the particular Service Pack you're installing. It is recommended that you always create an uninstall directory for every Service Pack you install. In addition, you should not delete this directory until you have verified that the new Service Pack is not causing problems in your environment.

Before installing a Service Pack or hotfix, make sure that there are no open applications and that no one is connected to your computer if you are on a local area network (LAN). To view the current network connections to your computer, use the Users button in the Server applet of Control Panel.

Additionally, you may use Server Manager to send a message alerting users of your intentions and then forcibly disconnect any stray users from the network using the "disconnect" or "disconnect all" radio buttons.

INSTALLING WINDOWS NT 3.51 SERVICE PACKS OR WINDOWS NT 4.0 SERVICE PACK 1

Once you have verified there are no open applications or connected users on the NT system you're updating, follow these steps to install the NT 3.51 Service Pack or the NT 4.0 Service Pack 1 update:

1. If you obtained the service pack in a self-extracting archive file format, copy the file (e.g., `SP1_400I.EXE`, etc.) to a temporary hard drive directory with plenty of free space and execute the file by typing its name followed by the **-D** command line option to unpack included subdirectories, if any (for example, **SP1_400I -D**). The disk space required depends on the particular Service Pack and whether or not the Uninstall feature is requested. This step is unnecessary if the Service Pack is already in an uncompressed format (e.g., on a CD-ROM containing an application requiring the Service Pack).
2. Next, in the directory containing the Service Pack files execute the file `UPDATE.EXE`. For example, you could use the Start Menu/Run... command and enter **<path>\update**, where *<path>* is the directory path of the Service Pack update files.
3. The Update program will inform you that it will upgrade your Windows NT installation to that Service Pack level (Figure 12-1). Choose OK or press Enter to begin the installation process.

4. When the installation has finished, you will be informed that the system must be rebooted – this is your only choice. When the system is restarted, it will be updated to the new Service Pack level. Although it is possible to return to the desktop (or Program Manager if using NT 3.51) if you need to, it is generally recommended that you restart your system immediately after installing a Service Pack update.

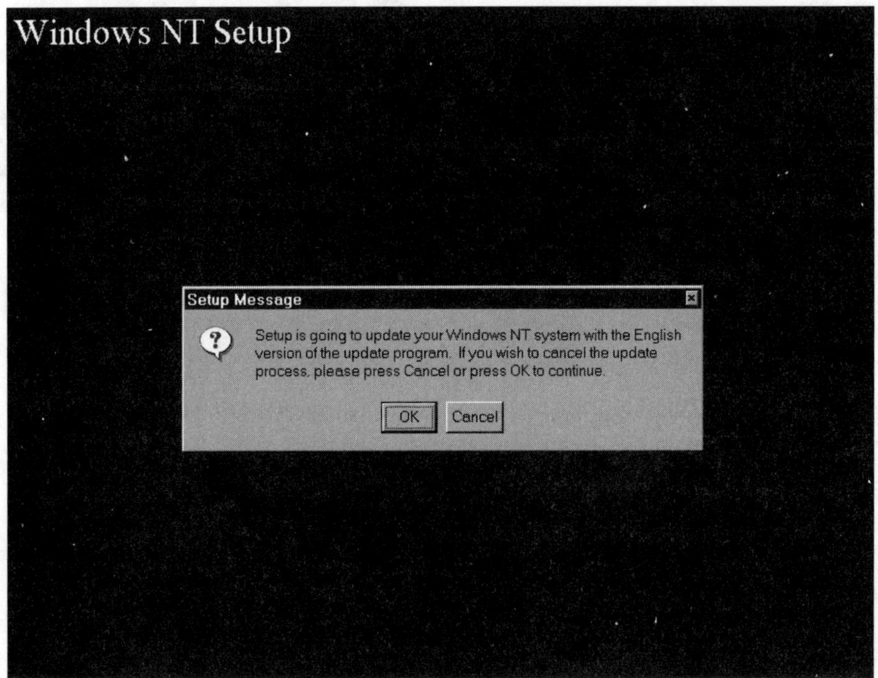

Figure 12-1: Setup message when installing a Windows NT 3.51 Service Pack or NT 4.0 Service Pack 1 update.

INSTALLING WINDOWS NT 4.0 SERVICE PACK 2 OR LATER

Once you have verified there are no open applications or connected users on the NT system you're updating, follow these steps to install the Service Pack update:

1. If you obtained the service pack in a self-extracting archive file format, copy the file (e.g., `SP2_400I.EXE`, etc.) to a temporary hard drive directory with plenty of free space and execute the file by typing its name followed by the -D command line option to unpack included subdirectories, if any (for example, **SP2_400I -D**). The disk space required depends on the particular Service Pack and whether or not the Uninstall feature is requested. This step is unnecessary if the Service Pack is already in an uncompressed format (e.g., on a CD-ROM containing an application requiring the Service Pack).

2. Next, in the directory containing the Service Pack files execute the file `UPDATE.EXE`. For example, you could use the Start Menu/Run... command and type **<path>\update**, where *<path>* is the directory path of the Service Pack update files (e.g., `C:\SERVPACK\UPDATE`). This launches the Service Pack Installation Wizard, which prompts you step-by-step through the update process (Figure 12-2). The Installation Wizard will inform you that it will upgrade your Windows NT installation to that Service Pack level (Figure 12-1). Choose OK or press Enter to begin the installation process.

3. Click the Next > button to step through the installation process. If you wish to have the option of later uninstalling the Service Pack , be sure to choose this option when it's presented (Figure 12-3).

4. When the installation is finished, you are informed that the system must now be rebooted — this is your only choice. When the system is restarted, it will be updated to the new Service Pack level. Although it is possible to Alt-Tab back to the desktop if you need to, it is generally recommended that you restart your system immediately after installing a Service Pack update.

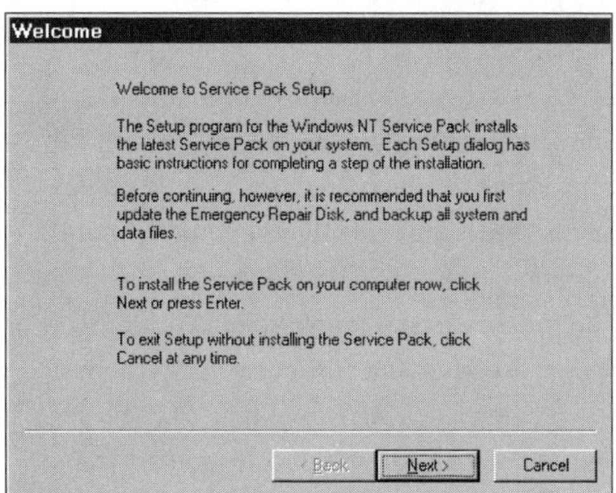

Figure 12-2: Installing a Windows NT 4.0 Service Pack 2 or later update.

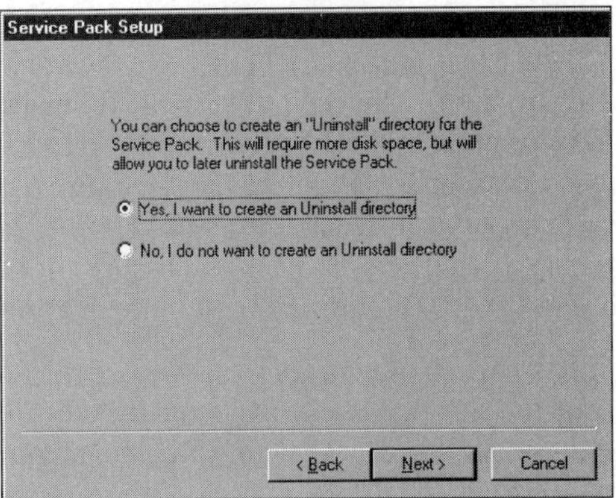

Figure 12-3: Telling the Service Pack installation Wizard to create an uninstall directory.

If you're using Microsoft Exchange Server, be aware that applying some NT Service Pack updates may overwrite the special Exchange-aware versions of User Manager (USRMGR.EXE or MUSRMGR.EXE) and Windows NT Backup (NTBACKUP.EXE) that ship with Exchange Server. A good way to avoid this problem is to back up these files before applying the Service Pack update; once the Service Pack is installed you can copy or restore these files back over the new Exchange-ignorant versions.

When installing the "international" versions of NT Service Packs, you will encounter one or several dialogs asking you to confirm the overwrite of your existing 128-bit encryption schemes for various components with 40-bit export-grade ones. The reason is that the encryption schemes in domestic versions of NT are illegal to distribute outside the United States. Therefore, if you obtain an international version of the Service Pack (i.e., the ones available for download on the Internet), it won't be able to upgrade the 128-bit components and can only offer 40-bit versions (which is considered safe for export by the government). If you wish to obtain a 128-bit version of the Service Pack, you must contact Microsoft directly and ask that a domestic version be sent to you.

Uninstalling NT 4.0 Service Packs

Windows NT 4.0 Service Packs 2 and later also contain an uninstall feature to remove the Service Pack from your system. This process restores your system to its previous state; for example, if you install Service Pack 2 after Service Pack 1, uninstalling Service Pack 2 will leave Service Pack 1 on your system. For this option to be available, you must have checked the "Yes, I want to create an Uninstall directory" button during the Service Pack installation process. This creates an uninstall directory that can be used to restore the system files that were present before the Service Pack was applied. The only disadvantage to this choice is that it requires at least 60MB of free space on the drive containing your Windows NT system installation, which can be problematic if disk space is at a premium.

If at any time you wish to uninstall the Service Pack, follow these steps:

1. Rerun the `UPDATE.EXE` utility that came with the Service Pack to relaunch the Service Pack Installation Wizard.
2. Choose Next > to proceed to the second step in the installation process.
3. In this dialog, check the "Uninstall a previously installed Service Pack" button (Figure 12-4) and choose the Finish button to proceed. (Be sure you're ready to proceed before clicking this button, because the uninstall process begins immediately after choosing this button without further warning.)
4. Reboot your system as per the instructions at the end of the uninstall process. Once your system has rebooted, UPDATE will have replaced the files updated by the Service Pack with the files from the previous installation and will also restore your Registry settings to what they were before the Service Pack was installed.

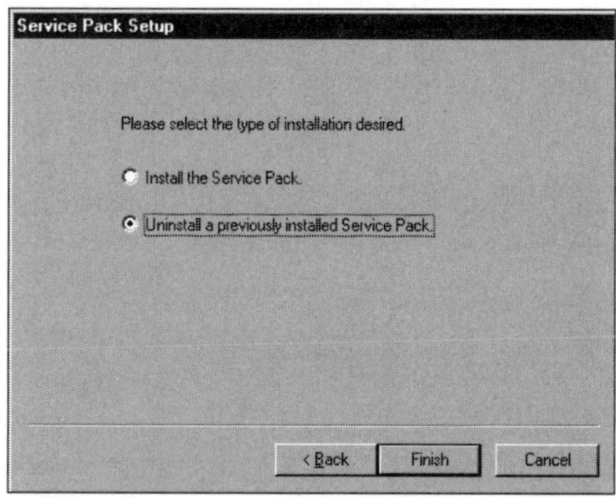

Figure 12-4: Selecting the Service Pack Uninstall option.

If you install any applications that require Service Pack 2 or later, or have bug fixes contained in Service Pack 2 or later, uninstalling the Service Pack will likely cause problems for those applications.

There's a fairly serious bug related to Windows NT 4.0 Service Pack 2 that affects systems that have NT reinstalled over a Service Pack 2 NT 4.0 system. The problem relates to the `TCPIP.SYS` driver, which should be manually replaced by the base version of the file located on the NT 4.0 CD-ROM before you start the reinstallation process (this file resides in the *%SYSTEMROOT%\SYSTEM32\DRIVERS* folder. Otherwise, failure to do so will result in your system issuing a STOP error (blue screen) at boot during the reinstallation process.

To check the Service Pack level of a Windows NT computer, you can use the Version tab of the Windows NT Diagnostics program, located in the Start Menu's Administrative Tools program folder. You can also choose Run... from the Start Menu and type winver to display version information about the Windows NT system.

Installing hotfixes

Windows NT hotfixes are installed differently than Service Packs. In addition, hotfixes tend to include only one or several updated files whereas Service Packs typically include a larger number of files (often 25 to 50 or more). Like Service Packs, hotfixes are contained within a single, self-extracting archive file that you download and execute (to unpack) in a temporary directory. Every hotfix includes the `HOTFIX.EXE` utility, which is used both to install hotfixes and to track which hotfixes have been already installed. Help for the use of the hotfix utility can also be obtained by typing **hotfix /?** in the directory containing the `HOTFIX.EXE` file.

Windows NT hotfixes can be installed by following these steps:

1. If you obtained the hotfix in a self-extracting archive file format, copy the file (e.g., RASI.EXE.) to a temporary hard drive directory that has plenty of free space and execute the file to start the unpacking process. The space required depends on the particular Service Pack and whether or not the Uninstall feature is to be requested. This step is unnecessary if the Service Pack is already in an uncompressed format (e.g., on a CD-ROM containing an application that requires the Service Pack).
2. Next, in the directory containing the hotfix files type this command: **hotfix /install**. You should then receive a message that the hotfix was installed (Figure 12-5).
3. After installation, type **hotfix** by itself (this accomplishes the same thing as the */list* or */l* option) to verify that the hotfix was installed correctly. You should see a display of all currently installed hotfixes along with information on when they were installed and by whom.
4. When the installation has finished, for the hotfix to take effect you must shut down and restart your system. Although it is possible to continue using the computer after the hotfix is installed, it is generally recommended that you restart your system immediately after installing any hotfix update.

A sample hotfix installation process is shown in Figure 12-5.

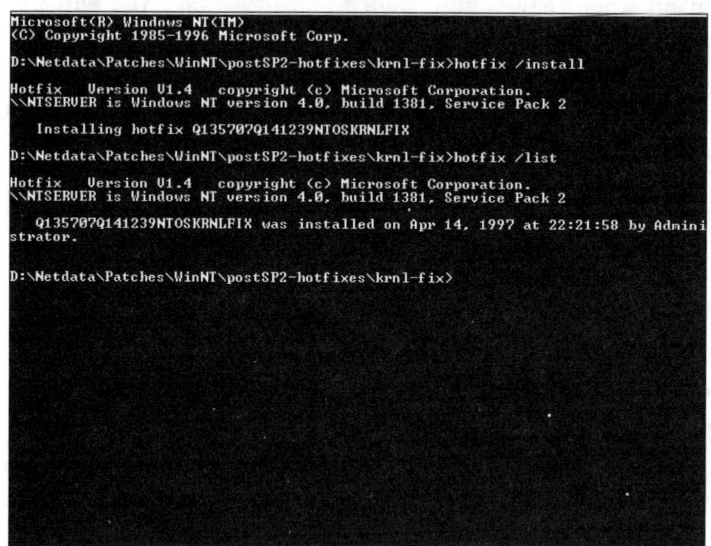

Figure 12-5: Installing a Windows NT hotfix.

Hotfixes for Windows NT 4.0 Service Pack 3 and later now offer an easier, graphic-based installation routine that requires only that you run the .EXE file containing the hotfix. The fix is then automatically installed and you are asked to simply press OK to restart the system to have the changes take effect. As with previous hotfix installations, you aren't asked to confirm after executing the hotfix installer; therefore, be sure you have a good backup of your system and Registry.

Uninstalling hotfixes

To uninstall a Windows NT hotfix, you need to have the `HOTFIX.EXE` file you used to install the hotfix originally. If you no longer have `HOTFIX.EXE` on your system, you can get it by redownloading the same hotfix self-extracting archive file you originally downloaded from Microsoft's FTP Server (you can actually use any `HOTFIX.EXE` file from any hotfix archive for your version of NT).

To remove a Windows NT hotfix, follow these steps:

1. In the directory containing the `HOTFIX.EXE` program file, type **hotfix** by itself (this accomplishes the same thing as the */list* or */l* option). This command displays a list of all currently installed hotfixes along with information on when they were installed and by whom. You will use information on this screen in the next step.
2. In the directory containing the `HOTFIX.EXE` program file, type the following command: **hotfix /remove "hotfix_name"** or **hotfix /r "hotfix_name"** where *hotfix name* is the exact name of the hotfix as displayed in step 1 (e.g., "Q142027 AND Q162927 DNS.EXE FIX"). The quotation marks are very important if the hotfix name contains any spaces; otherwise, they aren't necessary. If you typed the name correctly in the command line, you should then receive a message that the hotfix was removed. This procedure is shown in Figure 12-6.
3. Type **hotfix** by itself again (this accomplishes the same thing as the */list* or */l* option) to verify that the hotfix was successfully removed (it should no longer be displayed in the list of installed hotfixes).
4. When the installation has finished, you must shut down and restart your system for the hotfix removal to take effect. Although it is possible to continue using the computer after the hotfix is removed, it is generally recommended that you restart your system immediately after removing a hotfix.

```
Microsoft(R) Windows NT(TM)
(C) Copyright 1985-1996 Microsoft Corp.

D:\Netdata\Patches\WinNT\postSP2-hotfixes\dns-fix>hotfix

Hotfix   Version V1.5   copyright (c) Microsoft Corporation.
\\NTSERVER is Windows NT version 4.0, build 1381, Service Pack 2

   Q135707Q141239NTOSKRNLFIX was installed on Apr 14, 1997 at 22:21:58 by Admini
strator.
   Q142047 AND Q162927 DNS.EXE FIX was installed on Apr 14, 1997 at 22:25:49 by
Administrator.

D:\Netdata\Patches\WinNT\postSP2-hotfixes\dns-fix>hotfix /remove "Q142047 AND Q1
62927 DNS.EXE FIX"

Hotfix   Version V1.5   copyright (c) Microsoft Corporation.
\\NTSERVER is Windows NT version 4.0, build 1381, Service Pack 2

Hotfix: Fix Q142047 AND Q162927 DNS.EXE FIX was removed.

D:\Netdata\Patches\WinNT\postSP2-hotfixes\dns-fix>hotfix

Hotfix   Version V1.5   copyright (c) Microsoft Corporation.
\\NTSERVER is Windows NT version 4.0, build 1381, Service Pack 2

   Q135707Q141239NTOSKRNLFIX was installed on Apr 14, 1997 at 22:21:58 by Admini
strator.

D:\Netdata\Patches\WinNT\postSP2-hotfixes\dns-fix>
```

Figure 12-6: Uninstalling a Windows NT hotfix.

It is also possible to view the list of hotfixes on a remote computer on your network. To do so, type **hotfix\\computer_name** where *computer_name* is the name of the remote computer you wish to view.

Preventative Maintenance for NT

Job number one for any serious Windows NT user or system administrator is the design and implementation of a proper system backup plan. In addition, the implementation of any type of Registry modification, such as those mentioned in this book, represents a natural increase in the likelihood of system problems. Therefore, if you plan to implement these types of changes in your system(s), you are urged to follow the precautions set forth in this chapter.

Although most people consider themselves adequately protected by doing tape backups, this alone may not be enough to restore functionality. There are additional procedures that we introduce you to in this section that provide additional disaster protection at several different levels. These procedures back up information that is not included on a standard tape backup, even one that includes the Registry. Implementing these procedures increases your chances of being able to recover your system in the event of disaster.

Doing tape backups with NT Backup

The baseline disaster prevention method for any individual or organization is a full system backup, which is normally done to tape. To accommodate this procedure, Windows NT includes (and has included since its inception) a tape backup utility called NT Backup. However, there are also a number of excellent third-party backup solutions on the market, including Seagate Software's BackupExec, Cheyenne's ArcServe, BEI's UltraBAC, and Legato's Networker. All of these utilities provide a wide range of backup options beyond those found in the basic NT Backup utility. However, any backup is better than no backup at all, and NT Backup provides a solid and usable backup utility for NT users on a budget. To address the widest audience, we stick with NT Backup which all NT users have.

NT Backup is a GUI (Graphical User Interface)-based utility that supports a number of different tape drives, from floppy-based QIC drives to SCSI-based minicartridge, DAT, and DLT drives. The tape drives themselves are configured using the Tape Devices Control Panel shown in Figure 12-7.

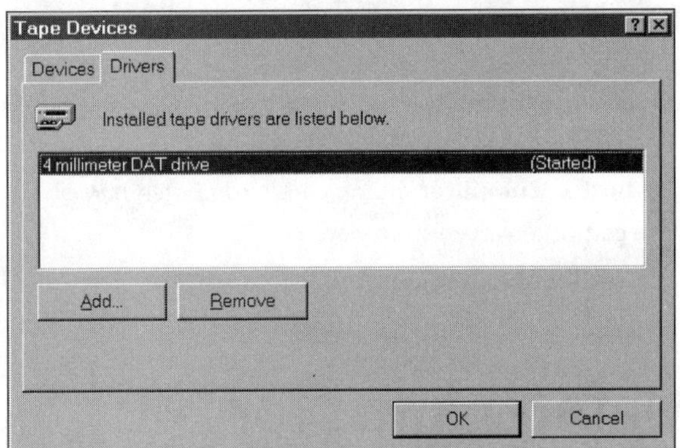

Figure 12-7: The Tape Devices Control Panel used to install tape drive support.

Once tape support has been installed, you can use the NT Backup utility to back up one or more system drives, including both local drives and remote drives over a Local Area Network. Use of the NT Backup utility requires that the user running the backup have Backup privileges on the system. Backup privileges include the ability to read files as well as special users rights such as Bypass Traverse Checking (which bypasses file and directory security to allow the user to back up all files and directories, including those on which they have no rights). The NT Back up utility (labeled "Backup") is located in the Administrative Tools Common Program Folder in the Start Menu Programs folder. The utility's main window is shown in Figure 12-8.

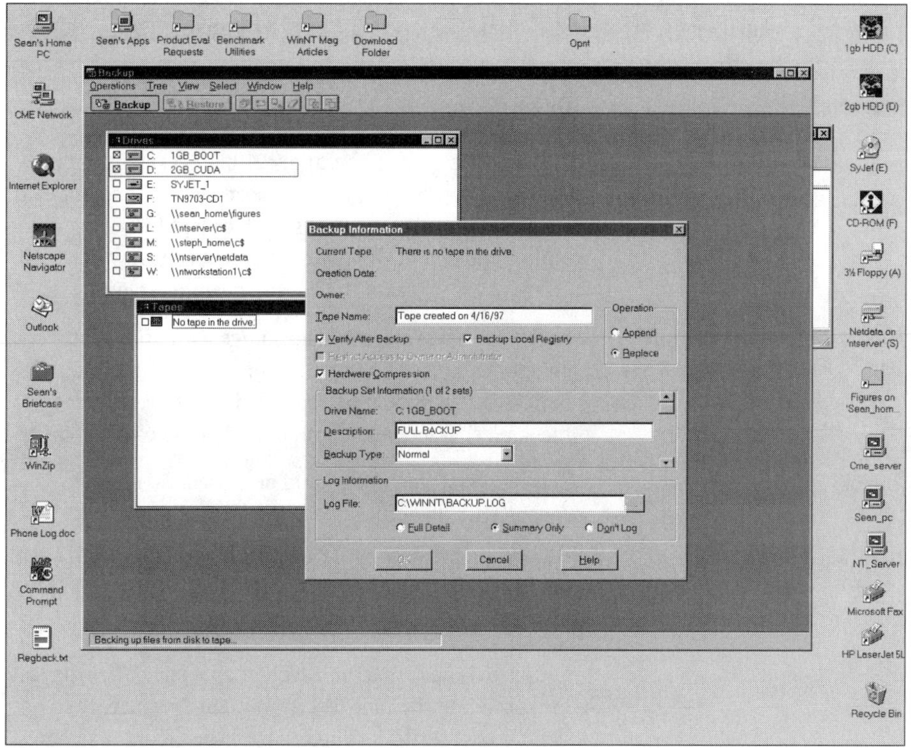

Figure 12-8: The NT Backup Utility main window.

When performing full system backups of your Windows NT system with NT Backup, always check the Backup Local Registry option in the Backup Information dialog shown when configuring a backup job (also shown in Figure 12-8). This instructs NT Backup to back up the Windows NT system Registry, something you definitely want to have stored on your backup volume.

Although NT Backup can be operated strictly via its GUI interface, it can also be launched via the command line or placed inside of batch files. The general format of this command is:

```
NTBACKUP operation path [/a][/v][/r][/d "text"][/b][/hc:{on | off}]
 [/t {option}][/l "filename"][/e][/tape:{n}]
```

As you can see, there are a number of startup switches that you can pass to NT Backup to control how it starts and what operation is performed when run in this manner. These command line switches are described in Table 12-1.

Table 12-1 WINDOWS NT BACKUP COMMAND LINE STARTUP SWITCHES

Startup Switch	Description
operation (backup or eject)	Specifies the type of operation; either backup or eject. (The eject parameter should be used by itself and not in conjunction with any other switch except the */tape* option; the rest of the switches described below are intended for use with the backup operation type.)
Path (drive and/or directory)	Specifies one or more backup source path drives and directories to backup (e.g., `C:\` or `D:\BACKME`). Multiple path locations should be separated by a space. Wildcard filename characters are not allowed in the path option.
/nopoll	Specifies that the tape should be erased. Do not use */nopoll* with any other command line parameters.
/missingtape	Specifies that a tape is missing from the backup set when the set spans several tapes. Each tape becomes a single unit as opposed to being part of the set.
/a	Causes backup sets to be added or appended after the last backup set on the tape. When */a* is not specified, the program overwrites previous data. When more than one drive is specified but */a* is not, the program overwrites the contents of the tape with the information from the first drive selected and then appends the backup sets for the remaining drives.
/v	Instructs NT Backup to verify the backup operation when completed.
/r	Restricts access of the backup set to the backup set owner or system administrator.
/d "*text*"	Adds a description to the backup set as defined in the "*text*" string.
/b	Instructs NT Backup to back up the machine's local Registry.
/hc:on or /hc:off	Specifies whether or not tape drive hardware compression is turned on or off.

continued

Startup Switch	Description
/t {*option*}	Specifies the type of backup operation to be performed: normal (regular backup including reset of archive bit), copy (normal backup with no reset of archive bits), incremental (all files since the last normal or incremental backup, resets archive bit), differential (all files since the last full backup, does not reset file archive bit), and daily (all files added/modified that day).
/l "*filename*"	Specifies the filename for the backup log.
/e	Specifies that the backup log include exceptions only.
/tape:{*n*}	Specifies which tape drive to back up the files to. *N* is a number from 0 to 9 that corresponds to the number the drive was assigned when the tape drive was installed.

One difference between NT Backup and full-blown, third-party backup utilities is the lack of an internal backup job scheduler. While most backup utilities can be set to run automatically at a certain time of the day, NT Backup doesn't have this option. However, scheduling NT Backups is possible with the Windows NT "AT" command. The AT command, which requires that the Windows NT Schedule service be running (by default, this service does not run; if you wish to enable it, go to Services, change its startup type to Automatic, and click the Start button to have it start immediately).

To schedule a backup job for automatic execution, use the AT command in conjunction with the normal command line you'd use to run the utility. For example, let's say you want to schedule a full backup of your system's C: drive so that it occurs every day at 11:00 p.m. Furthermore, you want to set a number of options about how the backup is done; path to backup, add to the existing volumes on the tape, turn hardware compression on, verification, and so forth. To schedule this command via the AT scheduling service on a computer named `\\MY_PC`, you could type a line similar to this:

```
AT \\MY_PC 23:00 /EVERY:1 "ntbackup backup c:\ /a /hc:on /b /d /t
 normal /e"
```

An easier way to manage the scheduling of backup jobs and other automated tasks is to use a graphical version of the AT command provided in the Windows NT Resource Kit called WINAT. This utility provides a graphical front end to manage the scheduling of commands and lets you add, delete, and modify scheduled commands.

For descriptions of the various counters viewable with the Performance Monitor utility, see Appendix C, "Performance Monitor Counters."

For additional information on the Windows NT AT command, type AT /? at the Windows NT Command Prompt.

To graphically schedule command lines to execute via the AT command, check out the WINAT scheduler which is part of the Windows NT Resource Kit (versions 3.5x and 4.0).

Although NT's built-in backup utility is certainly convenient, its feature set and capabilities are limited. Luckily, there are a number of excellent third-party backup applications available that address these shortcomings and offer more sophisticated backup features. One of the finest of these programs is a backup utility called UltraBAC from BEI Software. In addition to being one of the fastest backup utilities around, this program has extended capabilities that go far beyond many other backup applications. These features include the capability to create and restore an "image" backup of a system drive (rather than a file-based backup), the capability to boot and restore from a special "disaster recovery" floppy (that allows for data to be restored without requiring that NT be loaded), and options to backup to either tape or disk devices (including Network, Optical, and Removable Media Drives).

An evaluation copy of the UltraBAC backup utility is found on the CD-ROM that accompanies *Optimizing Windows NT.*

Maintaining the Emergency Repair Disk

When you first installed Windows NT, Setup gave you the chance to create a special recovery disk called the *Emergency Repair Disk*. This disk records vital information about your Windows NT configuration, including a majority of the Windows NT Registry and several other files. It's extremely important for you to create these disks (if you didn't already during installation) and to update it for each of your Windows NT computers on a regular basis. The reason this is so important is that the Emergency Repair Disk (ERD) can help you recover your Windows NT installation should it ever become damaged. The disk can be used in conjunction with the "Repair a Damaged Windows NT Installation" feature of the Windows NT Setup program. This feature of NT Setup can inspect various aspects of your Windows NT environment for problems and can use information on the Emergency Repair Disk to recover damaged components. Although it may be possible to recover an installation without the ERD, your chances are greatly improved by having one handy.

The information backed up by the Emergency Repair Disk changes as you make changes to your Windows NT configuration, so it is very important that you frequently update the Emergency Repair Disk to keep it in sync with your current Windows NT configuration. It is recommended that you update the Emergency Repair Disk whenever you make any significant changes to your Windows NT Environment, including these events:

- Changes to your disk configuration (i.e., changes made with NT's Disk Administrator Utility)
- Installation of a new Windows NT application that runs as a service
- Installation of new devices that install new Windows NT device drivers or services
- Changes to the NT user accounts database (if you are telling the ERD to back this information up with the */s* option)

The Emergency Repair Disk is created and maintained using a special Windows NT utility called the Repair Disk Utility (`RDISK.EXE`). Unfortunately, this utility has no shortcut icon on the desktop or in the Start Menu. To run the Repair Disk utility, you must either run it manually using the Start Menu's Run command, or create a shortcut to it and use the shortcut to start the utility. The Repair Disk Utility is shown in Figure 12-9.

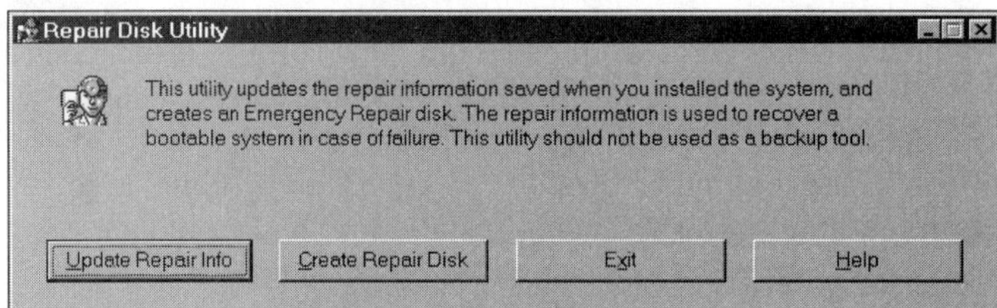

Figure 12-9: The Repair Disk Utility is used to create and maintain system repair information and the Emergency Repair Disk.

The Repair Disk Utility actually has two operation stages:

- To update the repair information that is stored on your hard drive. This information is stored in the *%SYSTEMROOT%\REPAIR folder* (e.g., `C:\WINNT\REPAIR`).
- To copy the repair information stored in the above folder to a floppy disk that can be used to help recover a Windows NT installation that has become damaged; this disk is the Windows NT Emergency Repair Disk.

Therefore, the first step performed by the Repair Disk Utility is always to update the repair information stored in this directory. The second step, which is optional, copies this updated information to the Emergency Repair Disk. The Repair Disk Utility has these two menu options that relate to these two functions:

- Update Repair Info: updates the Windows NT repair information stored in the *%SYSTEMROOT%\REPAIR* folder. This option makes a backup of the Registry in compressed format in the *%SYSTEMROOT%\REPAIR* folder on the Windows NT boot partition. This option should be done prior to creating the repair disk, and when complete it will ask if you wish to create the repair disk.

- Create Repair Disk: this option formats a floppy disk and then copies the latest repair information stored in the *%SYSTEMROOT%\REPAIR* folder to the disk (the Emergency Repair Disk).

To provide even better protection against disasters, you should really create two Emergency Repair Disks: one prior to the change and one afterwards. That way, if anything should go wrong during the change, you'll have an Emergency Repair Disk reflecting the NT environment beforehand.

To update your Emergency Repair Disk, or create it if you skipped this process during Windows NT Setup, follow these steps:

1. Open the Start Menu and choose Run.
2. Type **rdisk** to run the Repair Disk Utility. Alternately, you can type **rdisk** /s if you also wish to have security-related information updated (see below for more information on the */s* command line option).
3. Choose Update Repair Info to update the repair information saved on your hard drive. Windows NT will confirm that you want to replace the old repair information; choose Yes to update the information. A status window appears displaying the progress of the repair information update process.
4. When the update process is complete, you are asked if you wish to create/update the Emergency Repair Disk. If so, choose Create Repair Disk to create/update the disk.
5. Windows NT will prompt you to label and insert a disk in your floppy drive. The disk should be a high-density (i.e., 1.44MB) floppy disk. It doesn't matter whether the disk is formatted or unformatted, or if it contains previous Emergency Repair information; Windows NT will format it in either case and overwrite the existing contents. Insert a disk and choose OK or press Enter.
6. The disk is now formatted and the current repair information is copied to the disk. Be sure to put the Emergency Repair Disk in a safe place.

After running the RDISK command to update system repair information, the contents of the *%SYSTEMROOT%\REPAIR* folder (and the Emergency Repair Disk, if created) will look similar to that shown in Table 12-2.

Table 12-2 **FILES UPDATED IN THE %SYSTEMROOT%\REPAIR FOLDER BY REPAIR DISK**

File Name	Description
AUTOEXEC.NT	Similar to the AUTOEXEC.BAT file of MS-DOS, this file contains commands used to initialize 16-bit Virtual DOS Machines (VDMs). It is stored in uncompressed form.
CONFIG.NT	Similar to the CONFIG.SYS file of MS-DOS, this file contains commands used to initialize 16-bit Virtual DOS Machines (VDMs). It is stored in uncompressed form.
DEFAULT._	The contents of the HKEY_USERS\DEFAULT Registry key stored in compressed form.
NTUSER.DA_	The NTUSER.DAT user profile data, which is equivalent to the HKEY_CURRENT_USER key of the user logged in when the repair disk utility was run. The file is stored in compressed format.
SAM._	The Security Accounts Manager (SAM) user accounts database, located in the HKEY_LOCAL_MACHINE\SAM Registry key. The file is stored in compressed format. This information is only updated if the RDISK/S command is used.
SECURITY._	Contains the security-related information stored in the HKEY_LOCAL_MACHINE\SECURITY Registry key and is stored in compressed format. This information is only updated if the RDISK /S command is used.
SETUP.LOG	Contains a log of the files installed during Windows NT Setup, along with checksums for each file to allow the repair process to identify which files have changed. By default this file is hidden in the folder display window (unless the Windows NT Explorer has been configured to show hidden files or the DIR /AH command is issued at the NT command prompt).
SOFTWARE._	Contains software-related information for the local computer located in the HKEY_LOCAL_MACHINE\SOFTWARE key. The file is stored in compressed format.
SYSTEM._	Contains system-related information for the local computer located in the HKEY_LOCAL_MACHINE\SYSTEM key. The file is stored in compressed format.

Because they are stored in a special compressed format, the files on the Emergency Repair Disk and in the *%SYSTEMROOT%\REPAIR* folder should never be manually copied over the "live" Registry hive files in the *%SYSTEM-ROOT%\SYSTEM32\CONFIG* folder. Instead, use the Repair option of Windows NT Setup to restore these files.

The first time the Repair Disk utility is run it saves all of the Windows NT Registry hive files and the `AUTOEXEC.NT` and `CONFIG.NT` files in the *%SYSTEM-ROOT%\REPAIR* folder. By default, successive executions of the Update Repair Info option update all Registry information except the security and user account information contained in the SAM and SECURITY Registry hive files. Unfortunately, this means that should you ever need to restore your Windows NT system using the repair information stored by Repair Disk, you won't be able to retrieve this information. Instead, you will receive the original SAM and SECURITY files that were saved the first time the Repair Disk utility was run.

There is another reason why you might not want to update the security-related information in the Registry, or at least preserve a copy of the first Emergency Repair Disk you created that contains the original SAM Registry hive file. This original disk can come in handy if the Administrator password was changed from the original and then forgotten, or if the administrator of the NT machine or domain leaves without informing anyone of the system password. Because the original Emergency Repair Disk (or any disk not created with the */S* option) contains the original Administrator password, it could be used to reset the SAM database back to its original state — only the Administrator and Guest accounts and their original passwords (this would mean, however, the loss of other user accounts which would need to be reentered). Even if you choose to always use the */S* option to update the Emergency Repair information, it is recommended that you keep a copy of the original Emergency Repair Disk and the original Administrator password in a secure location.

However, there is a little known switch for the `RDISK.EXE` utility that addresses this issue. To save the contents of the SECURITY and SAM Registry hives in addition to other Registry information, use the */S* option in the command line or shortcut used to launch the Repair Disk utility. Using this switch causes Repair Disk to automatically and immediately update the repair information in the *%SYSTEMROOT%\REPAIR* folder, including the SAM and SECURITY Registry hives. After doing so, it will ask if you wish to create the Emergency Repair Disk. The only impracticality to the use of the RDISK /S command is where there is a large number of user accounts on the system. In this case, the SAM Registry hive file may be quite large and may not fit on a floppy disk. If this is the case, you have the option of either manually copying the contents of the *%SYSTEMROOT%\REPAIR* folder to another type of removable media (such as a floptical drive or removable hard drive).

Remember that the Windows NT Emergency Repair Disk is not a bootable disk and cannot be used to start the system should a boot or NT startup failure occur. It must be used in conjunction with the Windows NT Setup program's "Repair an Existing Windows NT Installation" to compare and recover information on the hard drive from that stored on the diskERD. For information on creating an NT Startup Disk, see the section in this chapter entitled "Creating a Windows NT Startup Disk."

Although creating and updating the Emergency Repair Disk are vitally important activities for every Windows NT system, doing so can also be a real hassle when you have a large number of Windows NT computers on your network. Thankfully, there is a utility available that allows you to perform a centralized execution of the Emergency Repair Disk creation process (i.e., execution of RDISK -S) from a single system on the network. This utility, called ERDisk, is produced by MWC, Inc. and available in a downloadable 30-day evaluation version from its Internet Web site at:

`http://www.ntsecurity.com/Products/ERDisk/index.html.`

The utility automatically generates a list of computers on the network and allows you to automate the execution of RDISK -S on each machine using a special "agent" utility. This utility is an administrative godsend, and is highly recommended to anyone maintaining a large number of NT systems.

Keeping system modification logs

One of the most valuable preventative maintenance measures you can take for your Windows NT systems requires nothing more than a pencil and a piece of paper. By keeping a log of modifications that are made to each Windows NT computer you administer, you can create an "audit trail" of events related to those computers. These logs can prove extremely helpful when trying to track down the source of a problem. In addition, by enhancing these logs to include information about the hardware and software installed on each computer, you also end up with a useful inventory of your systems. Although a pencil and paper would certainly work, it's obviously a better idea to enter this type of information in a database application or table. Better yet, you may wish to purchase a commercial software package specifically designed to accommodate the entry of this kind of information.

There are a number of network diagramming and system inventory packages on the market. Many of these include features to draw network schematics that include network topology and machine hardware specifics, and that allow you to log modifications made to each device on the network. Microsoft System Management Server (SMS) goes a step further by querying each system on the network and automatically constructing a hardware and software inventory database. This product also has a host of other remote-management features, including "push" software installations to client PCs and remote control. Information on SMS Server can be found at:

```
http://www.microsoft.com/backoffice/sms/
```

In the network diagramming software category, there are two products that provide excellent network diagramming and modification logging features. The first is ClickNet Professional from PinPoint Software. Information on ClickNet is available at:

```
http://www.pinpt.com/
```

The second product is NetViz from Quyen Systems, which also provides network diagramming and maintenance logging features. Information on NetViz is available at:

```
http://www.quyen.com/
```

The reason these logs can be so helpful is that the "audit trail" they provide can help you pinpoint exactly which event caused a particular problem to start on a Windows NT computer. Therefore, it is important that you log each and every software- and hardware-related event that occurs on a system, from the addition of new peripheral cards to modifications of the system Registry (such as those mentioned in this book). Although a failure that occurs immediately after a configuration change makes it fairly obvious what caused the problems, some problems don't always surface immediately. However, by maintaining a log of events to that system, you should be able to reverse recent changes by restoring a backup of the Registry made prior to the modification (from the Emergency Repair Disk or by using the REGBACK utility). For this reason, it is also recommended that you make a backup of the Registry prior to every modification you make to a system; this includes both hardware-related changes as well as changes to network services or direct modifications of the Registry. Otherwise, without a Registry backup that predates the change, you may not be able to repair the problem even if you identify the problem's exact starting point.

The following are some of the changes and configuration information that should be included in your system maintenance logs:

- The computer brand, model, and serial number
- Contact information of the vendor the system was purchased from
- The system's BIOS version (Intel x86 computers) or firmware revision level (RISC-based systems)
- CMOS configuration settings from the BIOS setup utility (Intel x86-based systems) or NVRAM configuration settings (RISC-based systems)
- A map of hardware resource usage on each machine, including IRQ, DMA, Upper Memory, and I/O Base Addresses used by each card in the system
- For MicroChannel or EISA-based systems that use configuration disks to store system configuration settings, have a backup of the current configuration
- The brand, model, and BIOS revision level of the system's SCSI controller, and what version of the driver is in use (the Windows NT default driver, an updated driver from the manufacturer, etc.)
- A map of SCSI bus configurations, including the location of active termination power sources, SCSI ID and LUN (Logical Unit Number) assignments, and as much information as is known about each attached SCSI device (such as asynchronous versus synchronous handshaking support, SCSI interface type used, SCSI protocols support such as SCSI-2 or SCSI-3, and the maximum data transfer rate of each device)

- The version of Windows NT installed on the system, including any installed Service Packs and/or hotfixes
- Information about the various third-party devices drivers and services installed on the system
- Historical list of service repair and troubleshooting activities on each machine, including the date, name of the technician or administrator attending to the problem, the problem's symptoms, the steps taken to resolve the problem, and the final resolution (if any)
- Information on the system's disk subsystem, including a map of all drive partitions on the various drives as well as information about each partition's size, volume type, file system, and installed operating systems

Performing Registry backups

With poetic license to recoin a famous phrase, it would read: "You can never be too rich, too thin, too good looking, or have too many backups." Given its critical importance to your Windows NT installation, the Windows NT Registry is an especially good candidate for multiple backups. Although the Emergency Repair Disk and full system backups using NT Backup can back up the Registry, it's never a bad idea to have an extra copy lying around somewhere – just in case. It's also nice to be able to copy the Registry in an uncompressed format that's not on a backup tape; this makes it more readily accessible in the event of an emergency.

There are a variety of tools available to do Registry backups. If your Windows NT installation is on a FAT partition, the easiest way is to simply boot the system using an MS-DOS boot disk and copy the contents of the *%SYSTEMROOT%\SYSTEM32\CONFIG* folder to an alternate source. Of course, if your Windows NT system partition is an NTFS volume or the drivers required to access the destination drive you're using as a backup destination aren't installed at DOS, you'll instead need a Windows NT utility capable of performing this task while Windows NT is loaded. This section describes several methods for accomplishing this.

BACKING UP THE REGISTRY USING REGBACK

The Windows NT Resource Kit contains a number of invaluable utilities for Windows NT system administrators. One such utility is REGBACK, which is part of the Windows NT Resource Kit utilities. REGBACK allows a user with backup privileges on the Windows NT system to perform a "hot" backup of the NT Registry while NT is running. REGBACK allows you to backup either the entire Registry or a particular hive file, and the backup can be stored on any destination drive with sufficient space to contain it. REGBACK is used to back up the Registry, while REGREST, it's mirror image utility, allows you to reverse the process and do a hot restore of the Registry. (Always immediately follow any restore of the Registry by a system reboot.)

Despite the fact that it is somewhat less secure, we generally recommend the use of FAT file system over NTFS for Windows NT system and boot partitions (i.e., the disk partitions used to boot the system and where the Windows NT installation directory is stored, respectively; on RISC systems, the system partition must be FAT). The reason is that it is far easier to repair boot problems such as corrupted disk/file structure or a damaged Registry on a FAT partition than it is on an NTFS partition. With NTFS, you're reliant on the ability to boot NT in order to run a repair utility to fix problems. However, if NT cannot boot from an NTFS partition and if NT's built-in tools (CHKDSK and Windows NT Setup's Repair option) cannot solve the problem, you're forced to do a complete reinstall of NT. Although rare, there have been cases where the problem remains even after a reinstallation and full restore. On FAT partitions, it is easier to diagnose and repair such problems and to restore the Windows NT Registry. However, in environments where the use of FAT is not an option (e.g., for security reasons), you can also install a second, minimal installation of NT on the system to ease the recovery process in the event of disaster. This second installation of NT allows access to an NTFS system/boot partition if the primary installation cannot be accessed, which in turn will allow you to diagnose and recover the primary installation.

Assuming you have Windows NT Resource Kit installed, you can run REGBACK (the file is located in the main Resource Kit directory) at a Windows NT command prompt. In addition, you can use this command with any of the following options in Table 12-3:

REGBACK (and its counterpart, REGREST) requires that you have administrative privileges on the Windows NT computer you are running them on. Also, it should be noted that REGBACK will not copy the files in *%SYSTEMROOT%\SYSTEM32\CONFIG* folders that are not currently open and in use by Windows NT. For inactive Registry hive files, you instead use a command such as XCOPY to back up any inactive hive files.

You can get additional information on the REGBACK and REGREST utilities in the `RKTOOLS.HLP` help file that is included with the Windows NT Resource Kit.

For more information on restoring the Registry using the REGREST utility (REGBACK's counterpart) see the "Restoring the Registry" section of Chapter 13, "Troubleshooting and Recovery Techniques."

TABLE 12-3 REGBACK USAGE EXAMPLES

Command	Description
`REGBACK` or `REGBACK /?`	Displays command help information.
`REGBACK` *<destination_folder>*	Backs up all of the open Registry hives to the specified destination folder (normally, this will be all Registry hives). After the command has run, it will also warn of hives that must be backed up manually or of errors. In most cases, the current user profile (the NTUSER.DAT file, located in the `HKEY_CURRENT_USER` key) cannot be backed up and REGBACK issues the command you'll need to type to back it up as a separate step. This secondary command must include the 14-character Security Identifier (SID) of the user whose profile is to be backed up.
`REGBACK` *<filename> <hivetype> <hivename>*	This command will backup the named root hive type/ name to the specified destination filename: <hivetype> name must be either machine or users; <hivename> is the name of an immediate subtree of the particular hive type specified (i.e., either of the HKEY_LOCAL_MACHINE or HKEY_LOCAL_USERS hive types). For example, these commands would backup the System subkey of the `HKEY_LOCAL_MACHINE` Registry hive type to the `C:\REGBACK` folder, and the user profile data for the user with SID S-1-1234-1234-1234 to the file `C:\REGBACK\CRAIG.DAT` folder.
`REGBACK C:\REGBACK machine System`	`REGBACK C:\REGBACK\CRAIG.DAT` users S-1-1234-1234-1234.

BACKING UP THE REGISTRY WITH NT BACKUP

In addition to Repair Disk and REGBACK, there are other ways of backing up the Windows NT Registry. One way is to ensure that the "Backup Local Registry" option is selected when doing a tape backup of your system using NT Backup or a third-party Windows NT backup application. All Windows NT backup utilities provide the option to back up the system Registry as part of the backup process. This dialog is shown in Figure 12-10.

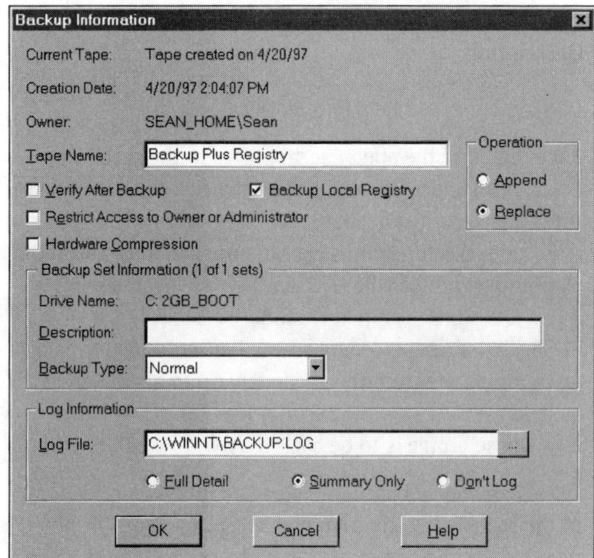

Figure 12-10: The Backup Local Registry option of Windows NT Backup.

See the "Doing Tape Backups with NT Backup" section earlier in this chapter for more information on the NT Backup application.

BACKING UP THE REGISTRY WITH THE REGISTRY EDITORS

In addition to the other methods described for doing Registry backups, it is also possible to save all or part of the Registry as a disk file using one of the Windows NT Registry Editor applications, `REGEDIT.EXE` and `REGEDT32.EXE`. Both utilities contain features for exporting Registry information to disk files. In the `REGEDIT.EXE` version of Registry Editor, use the Registry → Export Registry File option; in the `REGEDT32.EXE` version of Registry Editor use the Registry → Save

Key option. REGEDIT's export feature can be extremely handy because it allows you to later restore portions of the Registry or even entire Registry hives for troubleshooting, comparisons between registries of different machines, and so forth. Although both utilities have options to export information to disk, there are slight differences between the two: the `REGEDT32.EXE` version only allows you to save individual Registry hives or keys, whereas the `REGEDIT.EXE` version allows you to save both individual hives/keys or the entire Registry.

To use the `REGEDT32.EXE` Registry Editor to save Registry information to a disk file, follow these steps:

1. Run Registry Editor by using the Start Menu Run option, typing **REGEDT32**, and pressing Enter.
2. In the Registry editor display window, select the hive window containing the key you wish to back up and then the key itself.
3. With the key highlighted, select Registry → Save Key from the menus (as shown in Figure 12-11).
4. Select the folder and filename for the exported Registry key and choose OK. The file is then saved to the specified location.

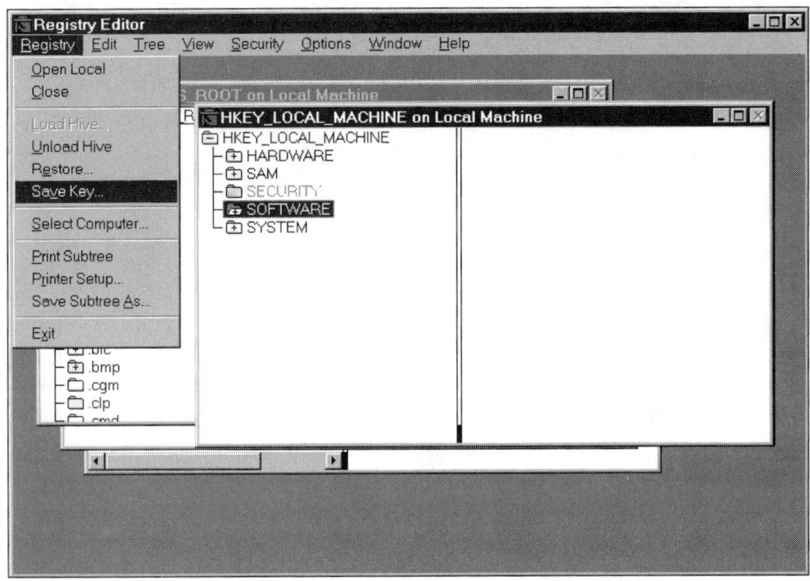

Figure 12-11: The REGEDT32 Registry Editor option to save Registry information to disk.

This option does not automatically assign a file extension to the export file unless specifically given one by you during the save operation.

The export file formats of the REGEDIT and REGEDT32 Registry editors are incompatible; therefore, you should not attempt to import files into one that was originally exported using the other.

To use the `REGEDIT.EXE` version of Registry Editor to save Registry information to a disk file, follow these steps:

1. Run Registry Editor by using the Start Menu Run option, typing **REGEDIT**, and pressing Enter.
2. In the Registry editor display window, select the Registry key you wish to export to a disk file.
3. With the key highlighted, select Registry → Export Registry File from the menus (as shown in Figure 12-12).
4. Next, select the folder and filename for the exported Registry key. If you wish to save only this key, leave the default entry in the "Selected branch" alone (it reflects the currently selected key). If, instead, you wish to save the entire Registry, click the "All" option.
5. Once you've made your selections, choose OK. The selected Registry information is then saved to the specified file.

Selecting to export the "My Computer" (root) branch of the REGEDIT display is the equivalent of selecting the "All" option when saving the file.

To back up a section of the Registry, you need to have sufficient access privileges to that key and any subkeys beneath it. Because the default on most keys is for the Everyone group to have read access, this normally isn't a problem. However, some keys, such as the user profile keys (`HKEY_USERS\`*<userSID>*), do not assign any access to the Everyone group and require either that user or the administrator be logged on in order to back them up.

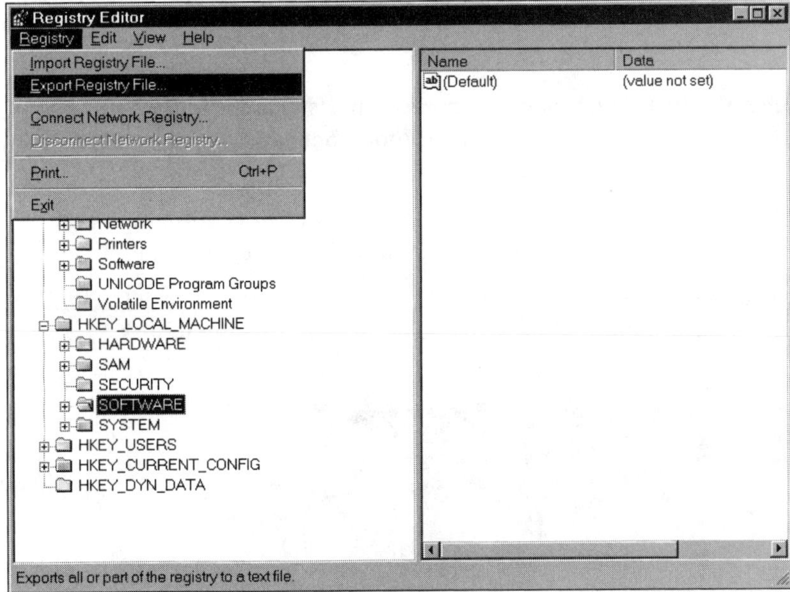

Figure 12-12: The REGEDIT Registry Editor option to save Registry information to disk.

Another important section of the Registry to make extra backups of is the `HKEY_LOCAL_MACHINE\SYSTEM\DISK` Registry key. This key contains configuration information related to disk drive letters, volume sets, stripe sets, fault-tolerant disk sets, as well as network and CD-ROM drive mappings. Whenever you make changes to your disk configuration, Windows NT updates this key. Therefore, you should make backup copies of this key before making changes such as creating, modifying, or deleting a disk partition, changing a drive letter, or creating or deleting a volume or stripe set to your system's disk configuration.

BACKING UP THE SYSTEM HIVE WITH DISK ADMINISTRATOR

Another method for backing up the all-important `SYSTEM` portion of the NT Registry (the `HKEY_LOCAL_MACHINE\SYSTEM` key) is by using the Windows NT Disk Administrator utility. This utility manages disk configuration information on your Windows NT system and contains an option to save the current system configuration to a disk file. Unfortunately, one limitation of this utility is that it only allows you to save this information to a floppy disk drive, whereas the Registry Editor methods described earlier allow you to save to any disk location, including hard disk drives.

To use Disk Administrator to save the SYSTEM key to a floppy disk, follow these steps:

1. Launch the Disk Administrator application; its icon is located in the Start Menu → Programs → Administrative Tools common program group.
2. From the menus, choose Partition → Configuration → Save (shown in Figure 12-13). Disk Administrator informs you of the information that will be saved and prompts you to insert a formatted floppy disk into drive A:.
3. Insert a blank formatted floppy disk into drive A: and choose OK to have Disk Administrator save the SYSTEM Registry information to disk.

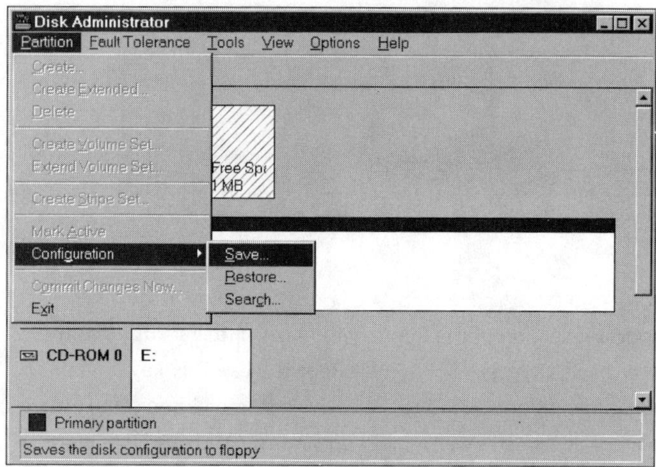

Figure 12-13: The Disk Administrator option to save the current system configuration to disk.

You must be logged in as an administrator to run the Disk Administrator utility.

One of the handiest utilities for making system configuration backups is a program called ConfigSafe NT from Artisoft, Inc. (the makers of LANtastic networking software). This program can automatically create and maintain updated backups of key system configuration files including the Registry, `AUTOEXEC.BAT`, `CONFIG.SYS`, and various `.INI` files. The program can be used to backup and restore these configuration files, as well as to instantly compare previous and current versions of each file to determine what changes were made (the changes are highlighted).

A time-expiring demonstration copy of the Artisoft ConfigSafe NT utility is on the CD-ROM that accompanies *Optimizing Windows NT*.

Creating a Windows NT startup disk

Although the Emergency Repair Disk can be a real lifesaver should your Windows NT installation be damaged, it won't help you boot your system because it isn't a startable disk. Therefore, it is a good idea to supplement your data recovery resources by creating a special Windows NT Startup Disk. In a situation where the NT boot process is failing, you may be able to use this disk to access resources on your system's hard drive(s), even if they are formatted under NTFS! This type of disk can be especially handy in any one of these circumstances:

- The Partition Boot Sector (PBS) of the boot drive has become corrupted
- The Master Boot Record (MBR) of the boot drive has become corrupted
- The MBR or PBS is infected by a virus
- `NTLDR` or `NTDETECT.COM` are missing or corrupt
- An incorrect copy of `NTBOOTDD.SYS` (for RISC systems or Intel systems with SCSI cards that use a SCSI device driver rather than the system BIOS to boot)
- Booting from the mirrored drive in a mirrored/duplexed RAID 1 volume (however, making this work may require modification of the `BOOT.INI` file on the floppy disk)

There are also a few categories of boot problems that the startup disk may not be useful in resolving, such as problems caused by incorrect or corrupt device drivers in the Windows NT *SYSTEM32* or *SYSTEM32\DRIVERS* directory, or any other type of problem that occurs after the NT Boot Loader screen has completed.

How you create the Windows NT Startup Disk depends on the hardware platform used by your Windows NT system. In the following sections, we describe the process for creating this disk on both Intel x86-based systems as well as RISC-based systems. The first step, in either case, is to format a floppy disk while booted under Windows NT using Windows NT's format command. This is vital because NT places the Windows NT Partition Boot Sector on the floppy, which is required for the disk to be capable of serving as an NT boot disk.

Several of the files that you need to copy to this newly formatted disk have their Hidden, System, and Read-Only attributes (H, S, R) set by default. As a result, you need to take a preliminary step to be able to view and copy these files to the Startup Disk. Follow these steps to make these files visible so that you can copy them.

1. Using My Computer or Windows NT Explorer, open the root folder of the drive containing the Windows NT startup files. (On RISC systems you should instead open the folder containing the `OSLOADER.EXE` and `HAL.DLL` files; e.g., `\OS\WINNT40`.)
2. In the Explorer folder window, select View → Options.
3. Select the View tab; select the Show all files radio button; click OK.
4. Select all the files that are to be copied by left-clicking the first one and Ctrl–left-clicking the additional files until all are highlighted (each Ctrl–left-click on a file adds or removes the file from the list of selected files).
5. For Windows NT 3.51, choose File → Properties from Program Manager's menu; for Windows NT 4.0, right-click one of the selected files and choose Properties from the pop-up menu that appears.
6. In the Attributes section of the General tab, clear the Read Only, System, and Hidden check boxes and click OK. This clears these attributes for all selected files.

FILES TO COPY FOR A STARTUP FLOPPY ON X86-BASED SYSTEMS

To create a Windows NT Startup Disk for Intel x86-based systems, you need to copy these files to the disk:

- NTLDR – The Windows NT boot loader utility.
- BOOT.INI – File describing the location of the various boot partitions on the system, which are specified using ARC (Advanced RISC Computing) pathnames.
- NTDETECT.COM – This file is used by NT for automatic hardware detection.
- BOOTSECT.DOS – This file contains the boot sector for an alternate operating system other than Windows NT (e.g., MS-DOS, Windows 95, etc.) on a multiboot system.
- NTBOOTDD.SYS – This file is a copy of the SCSI controller driver (.SYS file) used for the system's SCSI boot controller. This file is required only if your boot controller/drive uses the scsi() syntax in the ARC pathname inside the Windows NT BOOT.INI file that resides in the root folder of the NT System Partition. If the syntax is multi(), this file is not necessary.

These files can be found in the root folder of the system's boot drive.

FILES TO COPY FOR A STARTUP FLOPPY ON RISC-BASED SYSTEMS

To create a Windows NT Startup Disk for RISC-based systems, you need to copy these files to the disk:

- OSLOADER.EXE – This file is equivalent in functionality to the x86-based NTLDR, NTDETECT.COM, and BOOTSECT.DOS files combined.
- HAL.DLL – The Windows NT Hardware Abstraction Layer (HAL).
- *.PAL – All files with a .PAL extension (this applies to DEC Alpha AXP-based systems only).

Unlike Intel x86-based system which use the BOOT.INI file to define the location of primary partitions (those containing operating systems), RISC systems use a firmware configuration utility to maintain this list. The configuration is verified automatically at system startup, and the utility can be used to quickly recreate the entries in the event of a lost configuration. With Intel-based systems using BOOT.INI (especially on an NTFS partition), the loss of the BOOT.INI file can be far more difficult to resolve.

These files should be to the exact same relative folder path as they are on the system's boot drive; for example, if the startup files (`OSLOADER.EXE`, `HAL.DLL`, etc.) on a RISC system are stored in a hard disk directory `C:\OS\WINNT40`, then they should be copied to the floppy in the directory `A:\OS\WINNT40`. Failure to do so will prevent the Startup Disk from booting the system successfully.

Once the files have been successfully copied to the disk, you should test your new boot disk by rebooting your system with the disk in the A: drive. For Intel x86-based systems be sure the system's BIOS is configured to boot first off of A: and not C:. Many BIOS are configured to boot first from C:. For RISC-based systems, there is also an option to set the floppy as the first boot device but it won't use the A:/C: nomenclature because these aren't ARC-compliant names.

Using DiskSave and DiskProbe to backup critical disk information

Last, but not least, another preventative maintenance you should do on all your important Windows NT systems is make backups of two special disk structures that are critical to the systems' proper operation. These are the *Master Boot Record* and the *Partition Boot Sector* of the partition containing the Windows NT installation (referred to as the Windows NT *System Partition*). It is possible for these files to become corrupted in a variety of ways, including viruses, bugs in drivers or the operating system, power outages, faulty hardware or hardware configurations, or from a disk head crash. Unfortunately, because these types of events are often outside of NT's capability to control, the only way to be protected is to have an up-to-date backup of each.

It is highly recommended that you purchase a commercial Windows NT antivirus application to prevent against virus-related attacks. This is especially important because many viruses specifically target the Master Boot Record and Partition Boot Sectors, and damage to these vital areas can wreak havoc on your Windows NT system. All partitions, including those formatted with the NTFS file system, are vulnerable to boot-sector virus infection.

The Master Boot Record is a special record on the disk containing information about the partitions contained on the disk. The system BIOS on Intel x86-based computers uses this record to read the disk's Partition Table and find the Partition Boot Sector of the Windows NT system partition (bootable partition). This sector also contains the Partition Table. If the MBR becomes damaged in any way, it's likely that the computer will not be able to locate the System Partition to boot Windows NT. The Partition Boot Sector, on the other hand, is a special sector on every disk partition that instructs the computer to load either an operating system kernel or a boot loader (such as the Windows NT Boot Loader that appears when the system boots). As with the MBR, a corrupt or Partition Boot Sector can also prevent your system from booting properly.

Be very careful to ensure that the sectors you restore match the current configuration of your system's disk subsystem. If you were to accidentally restore invalid or outdated versions of these sectors, you could actually end up making your problems worse. To prevent this, always save the Master Boot Record and the Partition Boot Sector whenever you make changes that affect them. The Master Boot Record should be updated whenever changes are made to the disk partitions on your system (such as adding, deleting, or modifying partitions, or setting a different active boot partition). You should back up a partition's Boot Sector whenever you perform actions such as formatting a volume, installing Windows NT on a volume, or converting a volume from the FAT file system to the NTFS file system.

Furthermore, if you have multiple hard drives, or more than one partition per disk, then back up every Master Boot Record and Partition Boot Sector on every disk. However, the Master Boot Record for the boot drive and the Partition Boot Sector of your Windows NT System Partition are the most critical. Although the MBRs and PBSs on other drives/partitions aren't necessarily critical to the boot process, you may not be able to access files on those drives if the disk's Master Boot Record or Partition Boot Sector for the volume is corrupted or damaged.

You can back up these special areas of the disk sectors using either of two utilities included with the Windows NT Resource Kit: the Windows NT-based program DiskProbe or the MS-DOS-based program DiskSave. These utilities are included on the CD-ROM accompanying both the Server and Workstation versions of the Windows NT Resource Kit.

USING DISKSAVE TO BACK UP THE MBR AND PBS

DiskSave is an MS-DOS utility that allows you to back up the Master Boot Record and Partition Boot Sector as files. To use DiskSave you have to boot your system from an MS-DOS boot floppy. If you don't have a DOS boot floppy or your system isn't capable of running MS-DOS, you must instead use the Windows NT-based DiskProbe utility.

You must boot the system under MS-DOS to run DiskSave; it will not run from a Windows NT command prompt session.

The files you create using DiskSave should be saved to your Windows NT startup disk or your MS-DOS bootable floppy disk. If your computer experiences boot problems at some later date as a result of damage to the MBR or PBS, you can restore them using one of these disks to try and restore functionality to the system. Another feature of the DiskSave utility is that it allows you to turn off the Fault Tolerance (FT) bit in the System ID field of the Windows NT System Partition. This is helpful for mirrored (RAID 1) or duplexed disk volumes when the primary drive fails. In this situation, you can use the DiskSave utility to turn off the FT bit on the System Partition on the mirror disk if Windows NT fails to start after the primary drive fails.

The DiskSave program is a file named DISKSAVE.EXE and is located in the primary installation folder of the Windows NT Resource Kit on your hard drive or network drive. It is a good idea to copy this utility to a floppy disk because it won't be readily accessible if the drive holding it is the one to fail. To execute the program, first boot the system using an MS-DOS boot disk, and then type **disksave** at the MS-DOS command prompt (e.g., `C:\RESKIT>`). If the volume is not a FAT volume, you need to have a copy of the DiskSave program on a floppy so that it can be run.

DiskSave's main menu options are:

- F2: Back up the Master Boot Record. This function saves cylinder 0, head 0, sector 1 of the startup disk to the filename that you enter. You need to save a new copy of this record any time that you create or delete a partition, or change the file system used on a partition.
- F3: Restore the Master Boot Record. This function copies the file that you specify to cylinder 0, head 0, sector 1 of the startup disk. Restoring this sector also replaces the Partition Table. There are no checks to determine if the sector is a valid Master Boot Record.
- F4: Backup the Partition Boot Sector. This function saves the first sector of the system partition on disk 0 to the filename specified.
- F5: Restore the Partition Boot Sector. This function replaces the first sector of the system partition with the contents of the specified file. There are no checks to determine if the sector is a valid Partition Boot Sector.

- F6: Disable fault tolerance on the startup disk. This function is useful when Windows NT will not start from a mirror set of the system partition. The function looks for the system partition. It then checks to see if the System ID byte has the high bit set. Windows NT sets the high bit of the System ID field if the partition is a member of a fault-tolerant volume. Disabling this bit has the same effect as breaking the mirror set. DiskSave does not allow you to reenable the bit once it has been disabled.

When using DiskSave to back up the MBR (F2 menu option) or PBS (F4 menu option), you'll be prompted to enter the full name for the backup destination file, including the folder path. This name can be any name you like that conforms to the 8.3 MS-DOS file-naming convention.

The DiskSave utility will only save the Master Boot Record on disk 0 and the Partition Boot Sector for the System Partition (partition used to boot the system) on disk 0.

USING DISKPROBE TO BACK UP THE MBR AND PBS

Although the Windows NT-based DiskProbe utility allows you to perform all of the same functions as the DOS-based DiskSave utility, it also goes far beyond the capabilities of DiskSave. In fact, the DiskProbe utility (also included with both the Server and Workstation versions of the Windows NT Resource Kit) is a complete low-level disk editor and is therefore similar to commercially available programs such as Symantec's Norton DiskEdit. Like most other low-level disk editing utilities, DiskProbe allows you to save, restore, locate, view, and modify data on a disk. Essentially, DiskProbe gives administrators physical access to every byte of data on a drive without regard to security.

Because of the potentially harmful nature of the DiskProbe utility, it is especially important that you have a current full system backup, including the Registry, before using DiskProbe to make any changes to a disk.

Although DiskProbe provides enormous troubleshooting and diagnostics power to system administrators, in this section we limit our discussion of DiskProbe to its MBR/PBS backup features.

Follow these steps to back up the Master Boot Record using the DiskProbe utility:

1. Start the DiskProbe utility by selecting its shortcut, normally located in the Start Menu → Programs → Resource Kit 4.0 → Disk Tools menu. This will display DiskProbe's main window, which is shown in Figure 12-14.

2. From the menus, select Drives → Physical Drive. You will see the Open Physical Drive dialog box shown in Figure 12-15. Each physical drive on the system is listed as PhysicalDrive*n*, where *n* = 0 is the first hard drive, *n* = 1 is the second, and so on. Double-click the drive that contains the Master Boot Record you want to save (because it is the most important, the first MBR you should save is the one on the physical disk containing the System Partition). On Intel x86-based systems, this drive is almost always PhysicalDrive0; on RISC-based systems it could be a different drive.

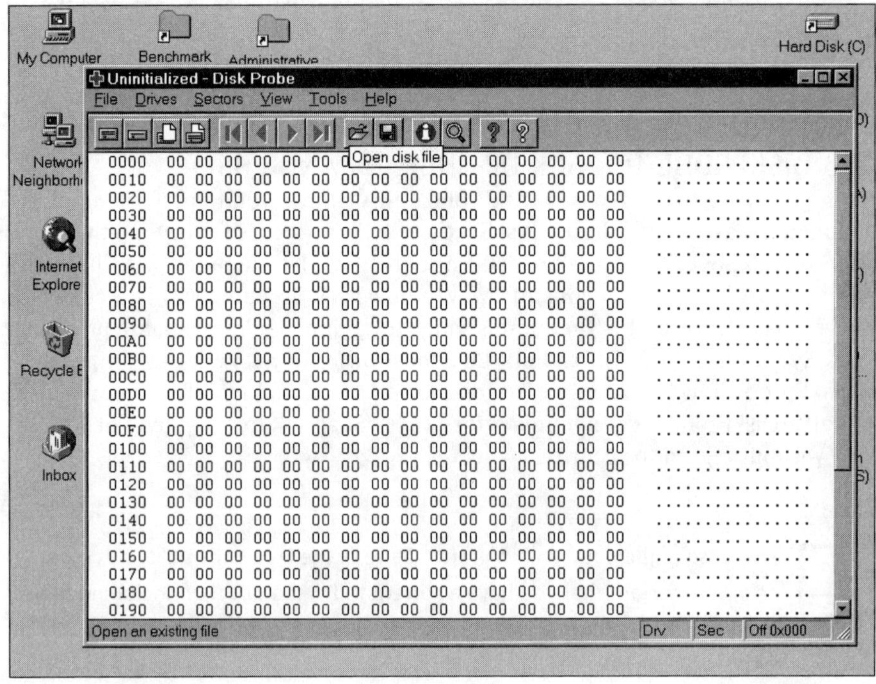

Figure 12-14: The DiskProbe Utility main window.

3. In the Handle 0 group box, choose the Set Active button and then click Close.
4. Next, select Sectors → Read from the menus. This opens the Sector Range dialog box, shown in the Figure 12-16. In this dialog window, set the Starting Sector box to 0 and Number of Sectors box to 1. Then click Read. This should display the Master Boot Record for that drive.
5. From the menus, select File → Save As.
6. Next enter a filename for the MBR backup. It is recommended that you save this file to the Emergency Repair Disk, Windows NT startup floppy disk, or an MS-DOS bootable floppy disk (or more than one place if desired). If you have more than one disk whose Master Boot Record you are backing up, it is also OK to save multiple MBRs to the same disk; however, be sure to use a different name for each disk's MBR (e.g., `MBRDISK0.DSK`, `MBRDISK1.DSK`, etc.).

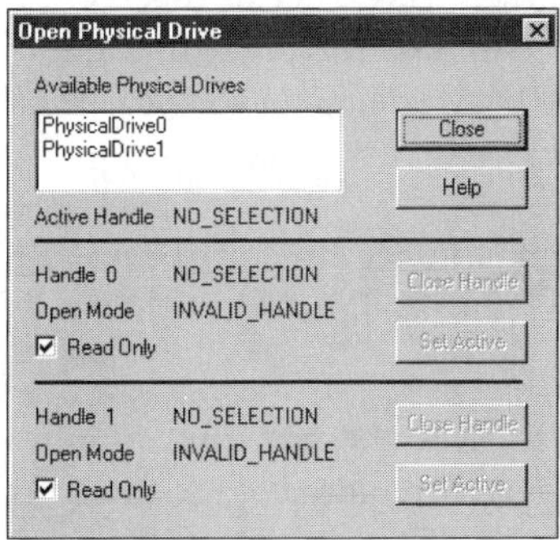

Figure 12-15: DiskProbe's Open Physical Drive selection dialog.

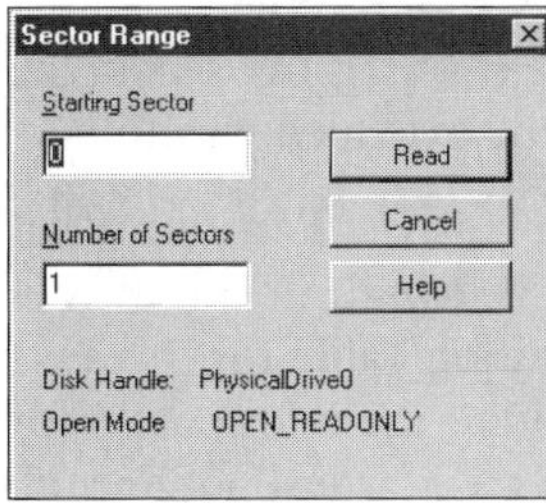

Figure 12-16: DiskProbe's Sector Range selection dialog.

It is also possible to back up Partition Boot Sectors of drive partitions using the DiskProbe utility. There are actually two different methods you can employ to accomplish this: one using the physical drive and one using the logical drive. In addition, a different method is used depending on whether the partition in question is a primary or extended partition.

A *primary partition* is the only type that can contain an operating system. You can assign each primary partition a drive letter such as C: or D: and may have up to four primary partitions on one physical drive. An *extended partition* is a special type of drive partition in addition to the primary that you can subdivide into one or more logical drives.

To use DiskProbe to back up any type of Partition Boot Sector using the Physical Drive method, you need to use the same steps each time to view a drive's Partition Table. This process is a continuation of the process described earlier in this section to view a drive's Master Boot Record. Follow steps 1 to 4 of the preceding numbered list that describes the process for backing up the Master Boot Record. Then perform the following steps to view a Partition Table:

1. Select View → Partition Table from the menus to see the Partition table displayed in a dialog box. You will see a screen similar to that shown in Figure 12-17.
2. In the Partition table index list box, double-click the partition number containing the Partition table you wish to view. If required, click the Next Partition button to see the information in the first sector of the next partition. When viewing a primary partition, clicking the Next Partition button reads the Partition Boot Sector of the next partition. When the next partition is an extended partition, clicking Next Partition reads the Partition Table sector for the first logical drive in the extended partition.
3. For a primary partition, clicking the Go button reads the Partition Boot Sector for the current partition. However, when the System ID field is of type EXTENDED, clicking the Go button reads the Partition Table for the next logical drive in the extended partition. When you view the information for an extended partition in the Partition Table area of the Master Boot Record, the Total Sectors field represents the total size of the extended partition.

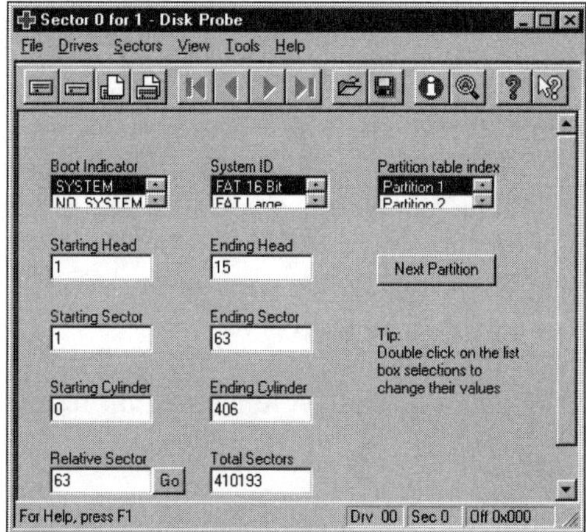

Figure 12-17: DiskProbe's Partition table dialog.

If you make any changes to a Partition table, you must write the sector back to disk by selecting Sectors → Write from the menu. This will only work if the session for the drive wasn't read-only (i.e., the session is read/write).

To back up a Partition Boot Sector for a partition by using the Physical Drive method follow these steps:

1. Read and view the Partition table using the steps outlined in the preceding procedural listing.
2. In the Partition table index list box, double-click the partition number for the Partition Boot Sector that you want to save. For example, to save the Partition Boot Sector for the system partition, double-click the partition number that has the Boot Indicator set to SYSTEM.
3. To read the Partition Boot Sector, click the Go button next to the Relative Sector field. On the View menu, click NTFS BootSector or FAT BootSector to see the information displayed appropriately. Make sure that the sector you just read looks like a Partition Boot Sector.
4. From the menus, select File → Save As.

5. Next, enter the destination filename for the Partition Boot Sector backup. It is recommended that when saving a Partition Boot Sector you use a name that includes the relative disk and sector number of the Partition Boot Sector being backed up in the format PBSssssssssDISKn.dsk, where sssssss is the relative sector of the Partition Boot Sector and n is the disk number. This makes it easier to later associate backup copies with the Partitions they are from. It is also recommended that you save this backup file to the Emergency Repair Disk, Windows NT startup floppy disk, or an MS-DOS bootable floppy disk (or more than one place if desired).

To back up the Partition Boot Sector by using Logical Volume method follow these steps:

1. Start the DiskProbe utility by selecting its shortcut, normally located in the Start Menu → Programs → Resource Kit 4.0 → Disk Tools menu.
2. Select Drives → Logical Volume from the menus. In the Logical Volumes list box, double-click the drive letter for the Partition whose Partition Boot Sector you wish to back up.
3. In the Handle 0 group box, click the Set Active button and then click Close.
4. Select Sectors → Read from the menus. This should display the Partition Boot Sector for that drive.
5. From the menus select File → Save As.
6. Next, enter the filename for the destination backup file. It is recommended that when saving a Partition Boot Sector, you use a name that includes the logical drive letter and disk number; for example, PBSdDSKn.DSK, where d is the drive letter of the logical drive, and n is the disk number. This will make it easier to associate backup copies with the partitions they are from later on. It is also recommended that you save this backup file to the Emergency Repair Disk, Windows NT startup floppy disk, or an MS-DOS bootable floppy disk (or more than one place if desired).

To back up the Partition Boot Sectors in extended partitions using the Physical Drive method follow these steps:

1. Read and view the Partition table using the steps outlined previously.
2. In the Partition table index list box, double-click the partition number for the extended partition that you want to save and then click Go. Doing this reads the first Partition Table entry in the extended partition.

3. This dialog allows you to "walk" the extended partition to find the logical drive whose Partition Boot Sector you want to back up. When you walk the extended partition, view the information for Partition 1 and click Go to read the Partition Boot Sector. You can also use the Search function on the Tools menu to find each Partition Boot Sector. Finally, it is also possible to print a map of the disk by using the DiskMap utility (also included with the Windows NT Resource Kit) which lists the address of the Partition Table entry for every logical drive on the system. Once you have this information, you can use DiskProbe to read the first sector of the logical drive whose Partition Boot Sector you want to back up and then click Go.
4. Once you have read a Partition Boot Sector, on the View menu click NTFS BootSector or FAT BootSector to see the information displayed appropriately. Make sure that the sector you just read looks like a Partition Boot Sector.
5. From the menus select File → Save As.
6. Next, enter the filename for the destination backup file. It is recommended that when saving a Partition Boot Sector you use a name that includes the logical drive letter and disk number; for example, PBSdDSKn.DSK, where d is the drive letter of the logical drive, and n is the disk number. This makes it easier to later associate backup copies with the Partitions they are from. It is also recommended that you save this backup file to the Emergency Repair Disk, Windows NT startup floppy disk, or an MS-DOS bootable floppy disk (or more than one place if desired).

Having copies of the MBR and PBS for all drives and partitions makes it far easier to recover your system in the event that these disk structures become damaged or corrupted. This information, in conjunction with a good backup of the system and the NT Registry, provides excellent protection against data loss.

For information on troubleshooting and recovering a damaged Windows NT installation, refer to Chapter 13, "Troubleshooting and Recovery Techniques."

Configuring STOP error behavior

STOP errors, or "blue screens of death" as they are more affectionately known by many NT users, are easily one of the most dreaded events in Windows NT. Although there is nothing you can do to regain control of Windows NT after a STOP error (save restarting the system), you can prepare the system ahead of time to provide additional information or take specified actions if a STOP error occurs. For example, you can have the system capture the contents of physical memory at the time of the STOP into a memory "dump" file, or automatically reboot after a STOP error occurs. It is also possible to install special software that may help to provide better information (on the STOP error screen itself) about the problem and its cause.

SYSTEM RECOVERY OPTIONS

To configure your system's behavior when a STOP error occurs, you can use the options found in the Recovery section of the Startup/Shutdown tab in the System Properties dialog (shown in Figure 12-18).

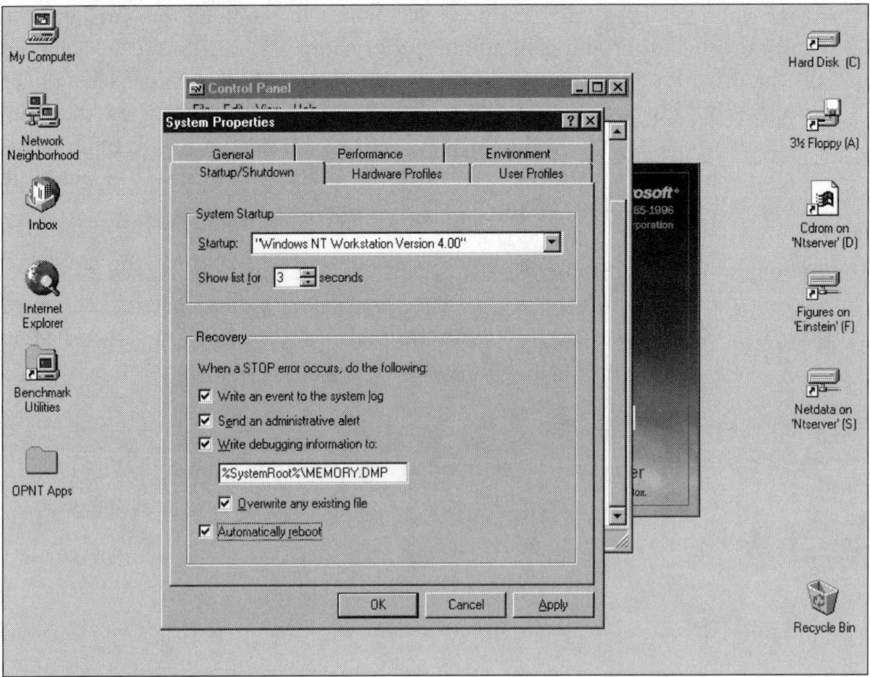

Figure 12-18: Configuring STOP error behavior via the Startup/Shutdown tab of the System Properties dialog.

To have Windows NT log an event for the STOP event (which may be later viewed using Event Viewer) check the "Write an event to the system log" box. To have Windows NT send an alert message to all users/computers set to receive alerts, check the "Send an administrative alert" option. The list of users/computers that should receive alerts can be set via the Alerts button on the Server Control Panel (or the Server Manager application on Windows NT Server computers). To have the system create a memory dump file (`MEMORY.DMP`) containing the contents of system memory at the time of the STOP error, check the "Write debugging information to:" box. If you want the file automatically overwritten if it already exists, check the "Overwrite any existing file" box. Enabling this option can be helpful to developers when diagnosing the cause of a STOP error; occasionally, application developers or Microsoft may request this file to aid them in determining the source of a problem. If you call Microsoft Product Support in reference to a STOP error and they request a copy of the `MEMORY.DMP` file, it should be submitted to this directory on Microsoft's FTP server (`ftp.microsoft.com`): `/transfer/incoming/bussys/winnt`.

For the "Write debugging information to" (aka CrashDump) option to work, the following criteria must be met: the paging file must be on the Windows NT system partition (the partition containing the hardware-specific files required to boot the system) and must be at least 1MB larger than the amount of physical RAM on the system. In addition, the system partition must have an amount of free space greater than or equal to the size of the paging file. The dump file (`MEMORY.DMP`) created by this option will be equivalent in size to the amount of installed RAM on the system; for example, a system with 128MB RAM will produce a 128MB `MEMORY.DMP` file. As a result, it is advisable to always select the "overwrite existing file" option when using this feature on systems with a large amount of installed RAM (i.e., 128MB or greater). Otherwise, multiple memory dump files will be created during successive system STOPs, which can quickly fill a hard drive.

Finally, to have your system automatically reboot after a STOP error occurs, check the "Automatically reboot" box. This causes the system to restart automatically after the STOP error occurs and the `MEMORY.DMP` file has been created (if this option is selected).

It is recommended that you always check the "Automatically reboot" option on a system acting as a network server. That way, if the system experiences the STOP error while the admin.istrator is away, it will automatically reboot and continue to provide services to network users.

For more information on restoring the system Registry, refer to the procedures described in the "Restoring the Registry" section of Chapter 13, "Troubleshooting and Recovery Techniques."

INSTALLING DEBUGGER SYMBOL FILES

In addition to configuring your system's response to STOP errors, you can take proactive measures to increase the amount of useful information that NT provides when these errors occur.

Many software developers use special debugging versions of Windows NT called *checked builds* that include versions of the Windows NT installation files that contain extra code to diagnose the cause of kernel STOP errors and make the process of debugging easier. One benefit of checked build versions of NT is that they often provide additional information about STOP errors. Because these debugging versions of NT tend to be slower than the normal versions (also called nonchecked or *free* versions) due to their extra baggage, they aren't generally recommended for use by endusers. However, it is possible to get the additional information benefits of the checked version on a normal Windows NT installation by installing *symbol files*. Symbol files are essentially the extra debugging information not found in the normal, retail version of Windows NT used by most people. All of the important Windows NT installation files (such as `.EXE`, `.DLL`, `.COM`, `.DRV`, `.SYS`, etc. files) have a corresponding symbol file (with a .DBG file extension) that contains debugging information. If a STOP error occurs in relation to that file, the symbol file is used by the system to provide specific information about the problem and its cause.

The Windows NT symbol files are located on the Windows NT CD-ROM in the `\SUPPORT\DEBUG\platform\SYMBOLS` folder (where *platform* is either I386, ALPHA, MIPS, or PPC). For the symbol files to work, the symbol tree underneath this folder must be copied to a `SYMBOLS` folder underneath your Windows NT installation folder (e.g., `C:\WINNT\SYMBOLS`).

The easiest way to install the debugging symbol files is to use EXPNDSYM. CMD, a special batch installation routine provided in the CD-ROM's \SUPPORT\ DEBUG folder. The format of this command is:

EXPNDSYM *<CD-ROM Drive Letter>* *<NT Installation Folder>*

(e.g., EXPNDSYM F: C:\WINNT).

This command automatically creates the appropriate folders in your Windows NT installation directory and then expands and copys the debugger symbol files to them.

The only real disadvantage to the use of symbol files is that they take up a significant amount of hard drive space. For example, in the Intel x86-based version of Windows NT 4.0, the debugger symbol files take up approximately 93MB of disk space. However, if disk space is not an issue it may be a good idea to install these files; if and when STOP errors occur, you may be able to garner more information about the problem than you would without them.

If you have installed debugger symbol files on your Windows NT system, be sure when obtaining Service Packs to obtain the version containing updated versions of the symbol files. This will be listed as a separate file on Microsoft's FTP server and will be larger in size. For example, the regular version of the Windows NT 4.0 Service Pack 3 file for Intel system is named `NT4SP3_I.EXE`, whereas the version containing the updated symbol files is `NT4SYM3I.EXE`. Once this file has been downloaded and installed, it may be necessary to manually install the updated symbol files. Information on doing so is located in the `README.TXT` file that accompanies the Service Pack.

Summary

In this chapter, we discussed a variety of steps you can take to maintain your Windows NT system. Following these procedures will not only keep your system up-to-date and healthy, but will also help to prevent disasters. By being proactive and preparing for problems before they occur, you increase your chances for a successful recovery. At minimum, you should have an up-to-date copy of the Emergency Repair Disk and apply the latest Service Pack of Windows NT (including any hotfixes appropriate to your environment). However, if you go beyond these basic steps and follow the other maintenance and backup procedures outlined in this chapter, you can make your Windows NT computer far more disaster-proof.

In the next chapter, we discuss system troubleshooting and recovery techniques for Windows NT, including many which use the resources you created in this chapter.

Chapter 13

Troubleshooting and Recovery Techniques

THIS CHAPTER ASSISTS in resolving some of the problems that can occur with your Windows NT installation. There are a number of different events that can cause problems on your system, including hard drive failure or corruption, a buggy application or application installer, a problematic Registry modification, or a virus attack. There are also a number of problems that are directly caused by bugs or incompatibilities related to the Windows NT operating system itself.

The information in this chapter may also prove useful should you encounter a situation where your NT system refuses to boot. Assuming that you've taken the precautionary steps outlined in Chapter 12 to prepare yourself for such situations, there is an excellent chance that you'll be able to recover your system to its original state. Even if you haven't made the preparations outlined in Chapter 12, you may still be lucky enough to perform a successful system recovery. However, the chances are much better when you have your "Break Glass in Case of Emergency" materials at the ready; these materials should include at least a full system backup and an updated Emergency Repair Disk. An even better set of disaster recovery tools includes several generations of the Emergency Repair Disk, a Windows NT startup disk, a backup of the Master Boot Record (MBR) and partition tables of every hard drive on the system, and extra copies of the Windows NT Registry hive files on a removable storage device.

Service or Driver Failing to Load

The most commonly seen problem in Windows NT is the failure of a service or driver at system startup. This circumstance results in the appearance of the dialog box shown in Figure 13-1.

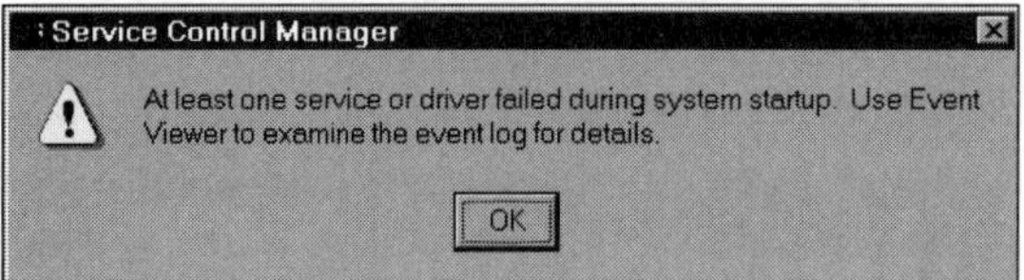

Figure 13-1: Notification that a Windows NT service or driver failed to load.

This situation often occurs after a hardware change of some kind such as the installation of a new video or SCSI card or changing your CD-ROM drive from an IDE version to a SCSI version. It can also occur after an application has been added to or removed from the system or if a device fails to initialize properly when its driver loads.

The first thing to do in such situations is identify exactly which driver(s) or service(s) are failing. This is accomplished with the Windows NT Event Viewer application. After running Event Viewer, examine the System and Application logs to see which services or drivers have red stop signs next to events related to them. For example, let's say you just replaced one SCSI card in your system with a different SCSI card and successfully installed the driver for the new card. However, on starting the system you receive the "At least one service or driver failed during system startup. Use Event Viewer to examine the event log for details" message (Figure 13-1). An examination of the Event Viewer System log would reveal something similar to the screen shown in Figure 13-2.

Event Viewer - System Log on \\NTSERVER (Filtered)

Log View Options Help

Date	Time	Source	Category	Event	User	Computer
5/12/97	7:41:38 PM	Service Control Mar	None	7026	N/A	NTSERVER
5/12/97	7:32:27 PM	Rdr	None	3012	N/A	NTSERVER
5/12/97	7:20:26 PM	Rdr	None	3012	N/A	NTSERVER

Figure 13-2: Event Viewer System Log screen identifying the failed event.

The System log displays events related to system services and drivers, whereas the Application log displays user application-related events. The third log is the Security log.

Here, we see that a service is failing to load at startup (as indicated by the red Stop icon and the event type of Service Control Manager next to it). Double-clicking the entry brings up the event detail window shown in Figure 13-3 that provides us with additional information about the problem.

Examining this Event Detail window, we recognize the driver name, aic78xx, as the driver for the SCSI card we just removed. Now that we've identified the source of the boot-up error message, we can diagnose the problem further and determine its cause. In this case, we forgot to tell NT that we're no longer using the old card so it's still trying to load its driver at boot. Because we know this card is no longer in the system, we know that we can safely remove its driver without causing boot problems. Normally, this procedure is accomplished using the SCSI Adapters Control Panel to remove the driver for this card. However, it is possible that even when you have properly removed a device's driver, Windows NT may continue to try loading its driver at startup. This happens because the device's startup type does not get changed to Disabled or Manual, and NT therefore attempts to initialize it during each system boot.

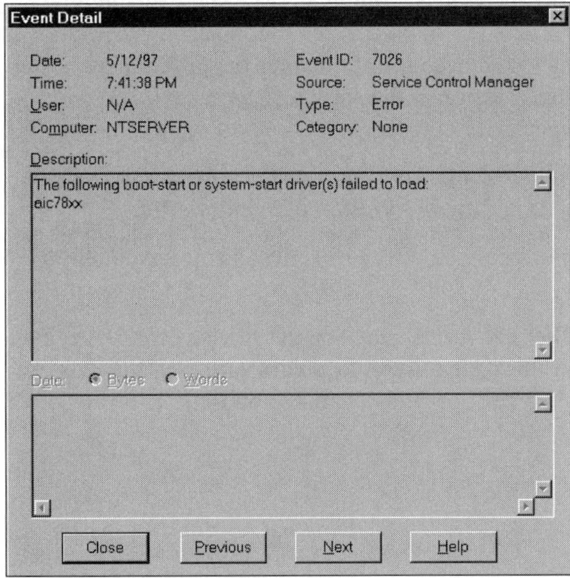

Figure 13-3: Event Detail window.

In these situations, the remedy is to manually disable the appropriate device driver or service in either the Services or Devices Control Panel (whichever is appropriate). Once there, locate the service or device in question and use the Startup... button to reconfigure the device/service's startup type to either Manual or Disabled. This configuration dialog is shown in Figure 13-4.

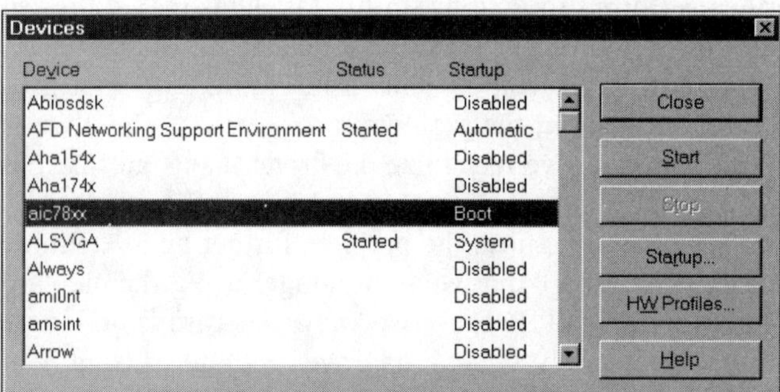

Figure 13-4: Reconfiguring a device's startup type.

Although the example related to a driver failure for a device that was no longer in the system, there are many other types of service and driver failures as well. The causes of these failures include all of these reasons:

- Service log on failure. This occurs for a number of reasons, including a service's logon account password changing, the logon account being deleted altogether, or the logon account not having the proper permissions required or not having been assigned the special "Logon As a Service" user right in User Manager.
- One or more of the files related to a service or device driver was moved, deleted, corrupted, or is for a different version of Windows NT.
- A service or device driver on which a service is dependent has failed to load.
- There is a resource conflict between the device the service or driver relates to and another device in the system (such as a hardware IRQ, I/O Base address, Upper Memory address, or DMA channel conflict).

If you receive the "At least one service or driver failed during system startup. Use Event Viewer to examine the event log for details" message for a device driver whose device you're certain is no longer installed, you can stop the error message from occurring by setting the device's Startup type to Disabled in the Devices Control Panel.

If you believe the problem could be related to a hardware resource conflict of some kind, try assigning different resources (e.g., IRQ, I/O Base Address, DMA channel, or Upper Memory Address range) to one or more cards on the system. After this, reboot the system and see if the error message repeats. Also try removing cards one by one and restarting the system after each removal to see if the service(s) or driver(s) in question begins to work properly.

There are many different types of service and device driver-related Event Viewer errors you might see when examining the Event logs, ranging from informational to extremely serious in nature. Because Windows NT automatically notifies you about any device driver or service (with an Automatic startup type) that failed to load, you always know at boot when something has gone awry. The next step is to examine the Event Viewer application to get additional information about exactly which services or drivers failed and why. More often than not, you'll get specific information that will allow you to diagnose and solve the problem.

Resolving Application Crashes with Dr. Watson

If you've used Windows NT for any length of time, it's likely that you've encountered one or more application crashes that resulted in the appearance of a special Windows NT utility called Dr. Watson. Dr. Watson is a Windows NT application error debugger that Microsoft ships with Windows NT. This utility's primary job is to detect application errors when they occur and to help you, Microsoft, and/or the application's developer to diagnose and determine the cause of the error. It does this by automatically, at the time of the crash, creating an error log file and, optionally, a binary application "dump" file. These files log diagnostic information that provides helpful clues about why the crash occurred. When an application is consistently crashing, a programmer or technical support representative at the software vendor's organization can often use this information to resolve the problem.

Windows NT automatically configures Dr. Watson as the system's default crash debugger during installation. When a user application crash occurs, a Dr. Watson dialog box automatically appears and informs you that a log file is being generated. By default, the log file is named DRWTSN32.LOG and stored in the *%SYSTEMROOT%* (Windows NT installation) folder; for example, `C:\WINNT`. Once generated, you can either examine log file or forward it to technical support personnel at Microsoft or the application's vendor for further examination.

Although Dr. Watson is automatically installed for you, it is possible to customize the program's operation by running it manually. The program file is DRWTSN32.EXE and is located in the *%SYSTEMROOT%\SYSTEM32* folder. To run it, go to an NT command prompt or the Start Menu Run option, type **DRWTSN32**, and press Enter. The Dr. Watson main dialog, shown in Figure 13-5, should appear.

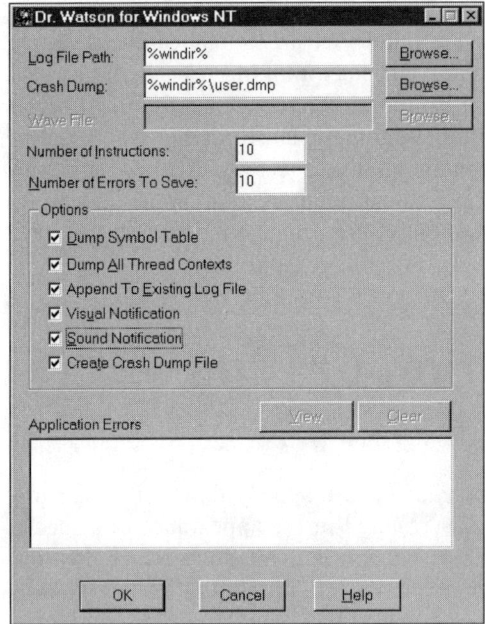

Figure 13-5: The Dr. Watson application debugger configuration dialog.

The options found on this screen are:

- *Dump Symbol Table*: This option determines whether Dr. Watson for Windows NT includes the symbol table for each involved module in the log file. Symbol table dumps contain the address and name for each symbol and require that the kernel debugger symbol files have first been installed (see the "Configuring STOP Error Behavior" section of Chapter 12 for information on installing these files). This option can provide a greater level of detail regarding the problem, but also increases the overall size of the resulting DRWTSN32.LOG file. This option is off by default.
- *Dump All Thread Contexts*: This option controls which application threads Dr. Watson will dump information on. If checked, Dr. Watson will dump information on each thread in the application causing the error; otherwise, it will only log information about the thread that caused the error. This option is on by default.
- *Append to Existing Log File*: Determines whether Dr. Watson appends log file information to the end of the existing DRWTSN32.LOG file (if any exists) or creates a new log file for each new application error. As with the symbol table option, be aware that this can significantly increase the size of the log file over time; if selected, be sure to periodically check the log file and delete it if necessary to save disk space. This option is on by default.
- *Visual Notification*: Determines whether Dr. Watson displays a pop-up window with an OK button after an application error occurs. Even if selected, the box automatically disappears if the OK button isn't selected within five minutes of the error being issued. This option is on by default.
- *Sound Notification*: This option determines whether Dr. Watson plays a sound (.WAV file) when an application error occurs. The sound played is either the file specified in the Wave File option, or a standard beep if no .WAV file is selected. This option is off by default.
- *Create Crash Dump File*: This option determines whether Dr. Watson creates a binary crash dump file. A support technician might request this file when diagnosing a problem, or it can be loaded into a debugging utility for examination. If you mark this checkbox you must also specify a filename for the crash dump file in the Crash Dump option box. This option is on by default.

To ensure that Dr. Watson generates a binary memory dump file in addition to the DRWTSN32.LOG file, make sure that at least the Create Crash Dump File option is selected and that a valid path and filename are listed in the Crash Dump field. By default, this file is named USER.DMP. This file should not be confused with the MEMORY.DMP file, which is a different memory dump file that is generated when a system STOP blue screen error occurs (see the next section for additional information on this topic).

Dr. Watson is normally configured to start automatically whenever an application crashes. However, if Dr. Watson doesn't appear on your system, it is possible that it was disabled for some reason. To reset Dr. Watson as the default debugger on your system, run the utility with the */I* switch as follows:

```
DRWTSN32 /I
```

After being run (e.g., from a command prompt session or the Start Menu Run dialog box), Dr. Watson is reinstated as the default system debugger.

STOP Errors (a.k.a. "Blue Screens of Death")

It seems that every operating system has its dreaded error message that users never want to see. In MS-DOS, it is the EMM386 Exception Errors 12 and 13; in Windows 3.1, it is the "General Protection Fault." Novell system administrators are loathe to see crash-indicative server "Abend" errors, and Linux users will tell of their experiences with "Kernel Panic" error messages. For Windows NT users, the dreaded message is the infamous STOP error, also affectionately known as a "Blue Screen of Death." These are operating system–generated bug checks that purposefully bring the system to a halt when severe error conditions are encountered. The resulting blue text screen includes some type of STOP error message and often other information as well such as one or more hexadecimal codes and a list of all system drivers active in memory at the time of the STOP error. An example of a STOP error/bug check is shown in Figure 13-6.

```
          BSR CTS
*** STOP:  0x0000000A (0x00000000, 0x0000001a, 0x00000000, 0x00000000)
IRQL_NOT_LESS_OR_EQUAL

p4-0300 irql:1f  SYSVER:0xf000030e

Dll Base DateStmp - Name                Dll Base DateStmp - Name
80100000 2e53fe55 - ntoskrnl.exe        80400000 2e53eba6 - hal.dll
80010000 2e41884b - Aha154x.sys         80013000 2e4bc29a - SCSIPORT.SYS
8001b000 2e4e7b6b - Scsidisk.sys        80220000 2e53f238 - Ntfs.sys
fe420000 2e406607 - Floppy.SYS          fe430000 2e406618 - Scsicdrm.SYS
fe440000 2e406659 - Fs_Rec.SYS          fe450000 2e40660f - Null.SYS
fe460000 2e4065f4 - Beep.SYS            fe470000 2e406634 - Sermouse.SYS
fe480000 2e42a4a4 - i8042prt.SYS        fe490000 2e40660d - Mouclass.SYS
fe4a0000 2e40660c - Kbdclass.SYS        fe4c0000 2e4065e2 - VIDEOPRT.SYS
fe4b0000 2e53d49d - ati.SYS             fe4d0000 2e4065e8 - vga.sys
fe4e0000 2e406655 - Msfs.SYS            fe4f0000 2e414f30 - Npfs.SYS
fe510000 2e53f222 - NDIS.SYS            fe500000 2e40719b - elnkii.sys
fe550000 2e406697 - TDI.SYS             fe530000 2e47c740 - nbf.sys
fe560000 2e5279d9 - nwlnkipx.sys        fe570000 2e53a89e - nwlnknb.sys
fe580000 2e494973 - tcpip.sys           fe5a0000 2e5256b8 - afd.sys
fe5b0000 2e5279d3 - netbt.sys           fe5d0000 2e4167f7 - netbios.sys
fe5e0000 2e4066b3 - mup.sys             fe5f0000 2e4f9f51 - rdr.sys
fe630000 2e53f24a - srv.sys             fe660000 2ef16062 - nwlnkspx.sys

Address    dword dump Build [1057]                             - Name
FF541E4c   fe5105df fe5105df 00000001 ff640128 fe4a8228  000002fe - NDIS.SYS
ff541e60   fe501368 fe501368 00000246 00004002 00000000  00000000 - elnkii.sys
ff541eb4   fe481509 fe481509 ff6688c8 ff668288 00000000  ff668138 - i8042prt.SYS
ff541ee0   fe481ea8 fe481ea8 fe482078 00000000 ff541f04  8013c58a - i8042prt.SYS
ff541ee4   fe482078 fe482078 00000000 ff541f04 8013c58a  ff6688c8 - i8042prt.sys
ff541ef0   8013c58a 8013c58a ff6688c8 ff668040 80405900  00000031 - ntoskrnl.exe
ff541efc   80405900 80405900 00000031 06060606 06060606  06060606 - hal.dll

Restart and set the recovery options in the system control panel
or the /CRASHDEBUG system start option if this message reappears,
contact your system administrator or technical support group.
CRASHDUMP: Initializing miniport driver
CRASHDUMP: Dumping physical memory to disk:  2000
CRASHDUMP: Physical memory dump complete
```

Figure 13-6: A STOP error/bug check (aka "Blue Screen of Death") screen.

STOP errors appear when a fatal error condition occurs on a Windows NT system. Because of NT's robust memory protection model, these messages are usually not related to a User Mode application but to a problem with a hardware device or a system-level service or driver. These types of services are known as "trusted" code because they are run in NT's protected Kernel Mode along with the Windows NT operating system and device drivers. Fortunately, because NT is adept at protecting the operating system from events that would crash most other operating systems, STOP errors are relatively rare.

Why STOP errors occur

As with service and device driver failures, there is a wide variety of STOP error types (each represented by a different, unique STOP error code) and causes. However, the majority of STOP errors occur for one of these reasons:

- A bug in the Windows NT operating system
- A malfunctioning hardware device (e.g., bad memory chips, a damaged video or SCSI adapter, etc.)
- A system with BIOS settings that exceed the capabilities of the installed hardware (e.g., memory timing settings have too few wait states, etc.)
- Corrupted or missing files related to system startup, or critical system services, or device drivers
- Buggy third-party services or device drivers (sometimes referred to as "trusted code") that crash or cause conflicts with other operating system services or device drivers.

These are just a few of the items that can cause the system to issue a STOP. They are commonly seen after a major change is made to hardware, system services, or device drivers, although this isn't the only circumstance under which they can occur. Another situation in which you might see such an error is immediately after the installation of a Windows NT Service Pack or version upgrade because both of these operations change a number of important system files.

For more information on Service Packs, see the "Windows NT Service Packs" section of Chapter 12, "Maintaining Your NT System."

Interpreting STOP error screens

One of the first things you'll notice about STOP error blue screens is that they aren't particularly pretty to look at. In fact, some would say they look downright scary.

However, most of these screens do offer a decent amount of information about the problem that caused the STOP error, although this information is somewhat masked by an apparent array of gibberish. Armed with a little information, you can interpret this gibberish to make the information intelligible; this helps you better understand why the error occurred and therefore resolve it.

Generally speaking, STOP blue screens offer the following information:

- A specific STOP error code and four hexadecimal parameters in parentheses at the very top of the screen
- A list of the kernel modules (typically `NTOSKRNL.EXE` plus a number of `.SYS` driver files) that were loaded and initialized at the time the STOP error occurred
- A list of the kernel modules that were on the system memory stack at the time of the STOP error

Together, these tidbits of information offer clues as to where the problem occurred and why. In all but a few cases, STOP errors occur because a piece of trusted system code (i.e., a driver or `NTOSKRNL.EXE` itself) attempts to access a memory address that is outside of its address space. However, there are also STOP errors that occur for completely different reasons such as a faulty piece of hardware (e.g., a bad RAM module).

The first and most important piece of information on a STOP error screen is the STOP error code itself. Each STOP code represents a unique problem, and the code is the piece of information that identifies the problem and its source. The next most important piece of information on a STOP screen is the parameter list to the right of the STOP error code. In most cases, this is a list of four hexadecimal parameters, each of which identifies a different aspect of the problem. These parameters are:

- First Parameter: This code identifies the memory address that was improperly referenced by the offending driver or module.
- Second Parameter: This code identifies the process internal request level (aka IRQL) that was required by the system to access the memory address listed in the first parameter.
- Third Parameter: This code identifies the type of memory access that was being made to the address listed in the first parameter as a write (0x00000001) or read (0x00000000) operation.
- Fourth Parameter: This code identifies the exact instruction address that attempted to access the memory address identified in the first parameter.

Occasionally, there will also be a third piece of information at the top of the screen (normally on the next line after the STOP code and its parameters): a textual description of the STOP error code listed. Although not all STOP errors provide such descriptions, many do. For example, you might see: "IRQL_NOT_LESS_OR_EQUAL," "KMODE_EXCEPTION_NOT_HANDLED," or "INACCESSIBLE_BOOT_DEVICE." These describe some of the general categories of STOP errors that can appear on a system. See the "Resolving STOP Errors" section later in the chapter for more information on some of the more common STOP error types and possible solutions for each.

Although there are a significant number of different STOP error codes that can appear in Windows NT, some are more common than others. Although you've learned how to interpret the STOP code and its parameters, it's unlikely this information will have much meaning to you unless you are a developer. Therefore, the first thing you should do when you receive a STOP error message is research the error code listed at the top of the screen using the Microsoft Knowledge Base. The Knowledge Base is an on-line database of common problems and answers related to Microsoft products. This may help shed light on the cause of the STOP error and help you resolve the problem. Microsoft TechNet CD subscribers can also search on the Knowledge Base included on every TechNet CD.

The on-line version of the Microsoft Knowledge Base is located at:

```
http://www.microsoft.com/kb/
```

To enhance the amount of information that Windows NT can provide when STOP errors occur, you should install the kernel debugger symbol files as described in the "Installing Debugger Symbol Files" section of Chapter 12.

Resolving STOP errors

Table 13-1 summarizes some common STOP error codes, their potential causes, and, where possible, solutions to remedy the problem. Many STOP error messages relate to bugs in third-party drivers or the Windows NT operating system itself. In the case of Windows NT operating system bugs, the solution is often to apply a Service Pack (for boot-time STOP errors, this may require first restoring the Registry using the procedures described later in this chapter). Because many STOP errors have similar resolution methods, these have been abbreviated in the table with keywords. These keywords are:

- LKG: Boot Windows NT and choose the "Spacebar to Restore the Last Known Good Configuration" option when the option appears during the boot process (this occurs after the NT Boot Loader menu and before the blue text-mode screen displaying the Windows NT version appears). From the menu displayed, select the option to restore a previous system configuration.

- LD: Obtain and install the latest version of the driver causing the STOP error. This may require booting to MS-DOS on FAT volumes or the IN method below for NTFS volumes if the STOP error occurs at boot-time.
- SP: Install the latest Windows NT Service Pack for your version of Windows NT. This is only possible if the STOP error isn't occurring at boot, because you must be booted into Windows NT as an administrator to install a Service Pack. The procedure for installing Service Packs is described in Chapter 12.
- HF: Install a hotfix developed by Microsoft specifically to solve the particular problem. The procedure for installing hotfixes is described in Chapter 12.
- SRV: Run the Windows NT Setup "Repair an existing Installation" option and select the "Verify Windows NT system files." This will compare the existing files to the original installation files and offer to replace each that differs.
- SRR: Run the Windows NT Setup "Repair an Existing Installation" option and select the option to "Inspect Registry files." This will verify the integrity of the system Registry database and offer to restore individual Registry hive files if necessary (from a backup copy on the hard drive or the Emergency Repair Disk, the preferred method).
- SRB: Run the Windows NT Setup Repair an Existing Installation option and select the option to Inspect Boot Sector. This will verify that the Windows NT Boot Sector is intact and repair it if necessary.
- SRS: Run the Windows NT Setup Repair an Existing Installation option and select the option to "Inspect startup environment." This will verify the integrity of the files required for Windows NT to boot such as NTLDR, NTDETECT.COM, and so forth, and offer to repair them if necessary.
- IU: Reinstall Windows NT over the top of the existing version (this is performed as an Upgrade installation even though it is the same version).
- IN: Install a new, parallel version of Windows NT into a separate directory from the original installation. This is sometimes required to gain access to NTFS volumes on systems that are receiving STOP errors at boot-time. This allows the access required to attempt a repair of the problem with the problematic Windows NT installation (e.g., manual replacement of an operating system file or driver).

TABLE 13-1 COMMON STOP ERRORS AND RESOLUTIONS

STOP Error Code	Description/ Explanation of Possible Causes	Possible Solution(s)
0xC0000221 Unknown hard error *<path>\<file name>*	Appears when a critical system file or other file needed to load Windows NT (identified by *<path>\<filename>*) is corrupted or an incorrect version (e.g., a RISC binary on an Intel system).	SRV, IU
0x00000051 REGISTRY_ERROR	Typically occurs when the Registry is badly damaged or the system is unable to read the Registry files due to a hardware or software problem.	If corruption is the problem, LKG (for SYSTEM hive only) or SRR; otherwise, if the problem is a faulty driver, SRV, IU, or IN; if hardware is the problem, the faulty component should be replaced.
0x00000077 and 0x0000007A KERNEL_STACK_INPAGE_ ERROR *Parameter2*	Caused when NT attempts to load a page into memory from the paging file on the hard drive but is unable to access the page due to a software or hardware failure. Can be a result of any of the following: The paging file contained a bad block, improper SCSI termination, bad drive cabling, a disk controller or driver error, or insufficient physical RAM. Additional information about the exact cause may be determined from the value listed in *Parameter2*.	If the problem is a bad block located within the page file, NT's CHKDSK command will attempt to locate and map out the block when it runs automatically after the system restarts. If *Parameter2* is 0xC000009A, the problem may be a lack of nonpaged pool memory resources; if it is 0xC000009C or 0x000016A, the problem could be a bad block on the drive; 0xC0000185 indicates improper SCSI termination. For other problems, the resolution depends on the exact cause (see Microsoft Knowledge Base article Q130801 for more information on this error).

continued

TABLE 13-1 COMMON STOP ERRORS AND RESOLUTIONS *(Continued)*

STOP Error Code	Description/ Explanation of Possible Causes	Possible Solution(s)
`0x00000079 MISMATCHED_HAL`	Caused by the Hardware Abstraction Layer component of NT not matching the installed hardware (the HAL file is `HAL.DLL`). Can occur if the wrong machine type is selected during NT Setup or when running the NT Resource Kit's Uni-to-Multiprocessor conversion utility (`UPTOMP.EXE`).	SRV and SRR, IU, or LD if a custom or updated HAL is required from the manufacturer.
`0X0000001E KMODE_EXCEPTION_NOT_HANDLED - TCPIP.SYS` or `0x0000000A IRQL_NOT_LESS_OR_EQUAL - TCPIP.SYS`	This is caused by the infamous "PING of death" caused by a PING command with specific parameters being issued to certain versions of Windows NT.	SP
`0x0000001E (`*parameter1, parameter2, parameter3, parameter4*`) KMODE_EXCEPTION_NOT_HANDLED`	Occurs due to a corrupted handle table in the `AFD.SYS` driver when Dr. Watson (`DRWTSN32.EXE`) is run after an application crashes. The parameters vary depending on the particular system.	SP
`0x00000019 (`*parameter1, parameter2, parameter3, parameter4*`) BAD_POOL_HEADER`	Many possible sources; one reason is an error that occurs in the NTFS driver in Windows NT 3.51.	For NT 3.51 NTFS driver error, SP; otherwise, search TechNet or the Microsoft Knowledge Base

continued

STOP Error Code	Description/ Explanation of Possible Causes	Possible Solution(s)
0x00000024 NTFS_FILE_SYSTEM	An error occurred in relation to the NTFS file system on a volume; the screen will also contain a 32-bit code, the first 16 bits of which identify the offending file, and the second 16 bits of which identify the source line in the file where the bug check occurred.	It is likely that a disk repair utility will need to be run on the drive to repair the file system; if CHKDSK is unable to resolve the problem when the system reboots, this may require a third-party disk repair utility or placement of the drive in another NT system (or the same system as a secondary drive) to run a thorough CHKDSK or other disk utility on the volume.
0x0000007B INACCESSIBLE_BOOT_DEVICE	Inaccessible boot device; often indicative of a disk or disk controller hardware or configuration problem, resulting in a driver initialization failure. Can also occur after any of several events, including removing an IDE CD-ROM drive, installing Windows NT 4.0 Service Pack 2 to a system with IDE hard disks, damage to the Partition Boot Sector of the boot drive, or a boot sector virus infection.	SRB, SRV, Antivirus Software (if boot sector virus).
0x0000007F UNEXPECTED_KERNEL_TRAP	Indicates that a trap occurred in the processor's privileged mode (aka Kernel Mode or Ring 0) and the NT kernel is unable to handle	Depends on cause; if hardware, replace faulty component; if file system driver, SRV; if file system, run disk diagnostics on

continued

TABLE 13-1 **COMMON STOP ERRORS AND RESOLUTIONS** *(Continued)*

STOP Error Code	Description/ Explanation of Possible Causes	Possible Solution(s)
	the trap. Can result from memory modules that are faulty, mismatched, or of the incorrect speed; can also be due to BIOS problems or a corrupted file system or file system driver. The first number after the STOP code is the actual processor trap; further information may be available on this trap in an Intel processor technical reference guide.	volume; if BIOS, get updated BIOS from system manufacturer; for NT bugs and conflicts, SP may fix problem.
`0x0000004E PFN_LIST_CORRUPT` or `0x0000000A IRQL_NOT_LESS_OR_EQUAL`	Bug in `AFD.SYS` driver that occurs under heavy computer usage under Windows NT 3.51.	SP
`0x0000000A` (*parameter1, parameter2, parameter3, parameter4)* `IRQL_NOT_LESS_OR_EQUAL`	Indicates that an attempt was made to access a memory address (in *parameter1*) at a process internal request level (IRQL) that was too high and therefore invalid. One common situation in which this error occurs is during removable drive access on some NT 4.0 systems running antivirus software after applying Windows NT 4.0 Service Pack 2.	HF, SP, SRV; if occurring after system configuration change, LKG or LD; if during setup, see Knowledge Base articles Q165863 and Q130802 for additional information on this error.

continued

STOP Error Code	Description/ Explanation of Possible Causes	Possible Solution(s)
0x00000093 INVALID_KERNEL_HANDLE	Boot-time error caused by some parallel port "dongle" security adapter drivers.	LKG or rename driver file (requires IN procedure if on NTFS partition).
0x0000000A IRQL_NOT_LESS_OR_ EQUAL NTOSKRNL.EXE	NT kernel-related STOP error caused by bug in original version of Windows NT 4.0.	SP, SRV
0x00000050 PAGE_FAULT_IN_NON PAGED_AREA AFD.SYS	Occurs under heavy use of WinSock applications due to bug in Windows NT 4.0.	HF, SP
0x0000001E (0xC0000005, 0xFF1BBD79, 0x00000000, 0x00000038) KMODE_EXCEPTION_NOT_ HANDLED Address FF1BBD79 has base at FF1AE000 – TCPIP.SYS	Occurs when reinstalling Windows NT 4.0 over top of a Windows NT 4.0 installation with Service Pack 2 applied due to a conflict with the SP2 TCPIP.SYS driver.	For systems with FAT boot partitions, manually expand the TCPIP.SYS driver from the Windows NT 4.0 CD-ROM to the *%SYSTEMROOT%*\SYSTEM32\DRIVERS folder; for NTFS Boot partitions, first do procedure IN.

For information on preparing your system for STOP errors, see the "Configuring STOP Error Behavior" section of Chapter 12.

What happens if you can't find any information about the STOP error that you're receiving? If this happens, don't despair: you may not be out of luck. Because most errors occur immediately or shortly after a software or hardware change is made to the system, the first thing to do is reverse whatever the most recent changes were that you made to your system. For example, you may have recently installed or removed a piece of software or hardware. If you've kept good maintenance logs about changes to your system (as recommended in Chapter 12), it should be fairly easy to identify the recent changes you've made. If the change was a hardware-related one, you should try returning the system to its previous configuration (including both the piece of hardware itself as well as any related drivers and/or services) to see if that alleviates the STOP error. If the change was software-only in nature, then you should try using the "Last Known Good Configuration" boot option or take another of the steps described in the "Repairing a Damaged NT Installation" or the "Restoring the Registry" sections later in this chapter.

If none of the above STOP error messages or descriptions help you to solve the problem, your next step (if you haven't done so already) is to research the problem via the Microsoft Knowledge Base (MSKB) or the TechNet CD-ROM. You may wish to reference MSKB article number Q103059 (Descriptions of Bug Codes for Windows NT). This article provides a numerically sorted list of all STOP error/bug check types that occur in Windows NT and their descriptions. If this research doesn't yield any useful information, you should call Microsoft Product Support Services (PSS) for further assistance with the problem.

Submitting memory dump information to Microsoft

If you ever have to contact a software developer or Microsoft Product Support Services regarding a troublesome STOP error, you may be asked to provide information that will aid the technician in diagnosing the problem. As we discussed in the "Configuring STOP Error Behavior" section of Chapter 12, the System Control Panel allows you to have NT automatically create a dump of physical memory to a file when a STOP error message occurs. The file created is, by default, placed in the Windows NT installation folder (*%SYSTEMROOT%* folder) as `MEMORY.DMP`. This is a binary file containing the raw physical contents of memory at the time of the STOP error.

The first thing to do is read the "Configuring STOP Error Behavior" section of Chapter 12 to ensure that this option is configured on your system. Although this creates the MEMORY.DMP file, it may be difficult or impractical to send this file to Microsoft. This is because the MEMORY.DMP file is always the same size as the amount of the physical RAM on the machine; for systems with large amounts of RAM, this results in extremely large files that may be difficult or costly to send electronically or on removable media.

As an alternative to sending MEMORY.DMP, you can use a special utility called DUMPEXAM to convert the binary MEMORY.DMP file into a smaller (and more readable) text file. DUMPEXAM interprets the information in MEMORY.DMP into a text file that summarizes the most important information contained within the memory dump. The resulting file is usually significantly smaller than the original binary file (five percent of the original size, or less in some cases).

To use DUMPEXAM, you first need to copy it from the Windows NT installation CD-ROM to your system (it isn't installed during Windows NT Setup). The files you'll need are located in the *\SUPPORT\DEBUG\platform* folder of the CD-ROM, where *platform* is the hardware platform of your system (I386, ALPHA, MIPS, or PPC). Once in this folder, you need to copy three files to a folder on your hard drive:

- DUMPEXAM.EXE
- IMAGEHLP.DLL
- KDEXT???.DLL (where ??? represents the hardware platform of the system being used; either X86, ALP, MIP, or PPC; e.g., the file for Intel systems would be KDEXTX86.DLL)

Once these files have been copied, you can run DUMPEXAM.EXE at an NT command prompt session to create a summary text file. The syntax of this command is:

```
DUMPEXAM [options] filename
```

where *filename* is the name of the binary crash dump file (normally MEMORY.DMP; this isn't necessary if the file is named this and located in the *%SYSTEMROOT%* folder), and *options* is any of these command options:

- *-?* Displays help for the DUMPEXAM command
- *-v* Runs the program in verbose mode
- *-p* Prints the header only

```
-f filename
```

specifies the name of the output text file for DUMPEXAM to create; if omitted, DUMPEXAM creates a file named `MEMORY.TXT` in the same directory as the binary memory dump file (`MEMORY.DMP`).

```
-y path[;path2;path3;etc]
```

path specifies a folder containing debugger symbol files for installed Service Packs and/or hotfixes; if multiple Service Packs and hotfixes are installed, the paths for the debugger symbol files of each should be listed as *path2*, *path3*, and so on, separating each by a semicolon.

For more information on Service Packs and hotfixes, see the "Installing System Updates" section of Chapter 12; for information on debugger symbol files, see the "Installing Debugger Symbol Files" section of Chapter 12.

Repairing a Damaged NT Installation

If you suspect that one or more components of your Windows NT installation is corrupted or damaged, you'll want to take steps to repair the installation. Although there are several ways for you to accomplish this, the best is usually to start with Windows NT Setup's Repair option. This process analyzes various aspects of the Windows NT installation, such as the boot sector, the Registry, and the Windows NT installation files, and offers to fix problems or replace files that are determined to be damaged or different than the original Windows NT installation files. Because some of these determinations are made by comparing the current Windows NT installation to the configuration stored on the Emergency Repair Disk, it is important that you regularly update your system configuration and the Emergency Repair Disk using the Repair Disk utility discussed in Chapter 12.

Repairing via the Windows NT setup repair option

To run the Windows NT Setup Repair process, follow these steps:

1. Boot the system with the Windows NT Setup Boot Disk in Drive A:. Alternately, if your system supports booting from a CD, you can insert the Windows NT CD-ROM into your CD-ROM drive.
2. Begin the Windows NT Setup process. When you get to Disk 2, you will see the "Welcome to Windows NT Setup" screen that gives several options including the option to press R to repair a damaged Windows NT installation. Press R to repair your existing installation.

3. Next, you will receive a screen (shown in Figure 13-7) asking which optional tasks you want the repair process to perform during its operation. To select an option, move the up/down arrow keys to highlight it, and press Enter to toggle the option on or off. When you select an option, an X appears in the box next to it. When you have selected all desired options, highlight the option to Continue and press Enter.

4. When the repair process is complete, Windows NT informs you that the system must be rebooted.

```
As part of the repair Process, Setup will perform each of the optional
tasks shown below with an "X" in it's check box.

To perform the selected tasks, press ENTER to indicate "Continue." If you
want to select or deselect any item in the list, press the UP or DOWN arrow
key to move the highlight to the item you want to change.

Then press ENTER.

    [X]   Inspect registry files.
    [X]   Inspect startup environment.
    [X]   Verify Windows NT system files.
    [X]   Inspect Boot Sector.
       Continue (perform selected tasks)

F1=Help       F3=Exit       ESC=Cancel

ENTER=Select/Deselect
```

Figure 13-7: The Windows NT Setup Repair process allows you to select which tasks you want performed as part of the repair process.

Even with an updated Emergency Repair Disk, the repair process is ignorant of any installed Service Pack files and will always recommend that updated files be replaced with the originals from the CD-ROM. As a result, after running the repair process immediately reapply your current Windows NT Service Pack.

The following is a description of each repair process option:

- *Inspect Registry files*: This option, when selected, will inspect each Registry file to determine if it is corrupt. If any files are determined to be corrupt, you will receive a screen that allows you to choose which files should be restored.

- *Inspect startup environment*: This option checks the integrity of the NT boot files such as NTLDR, NTDETECT.COM, and so forth. If these files are damaged, NT will fail to boot properly.
- *Verify Windows NT system files*: This option compares every file installed by the Windows NT Setup process to the files currently on the hard drive. If a file is missing, corrupt, or different than the original installed version, NT notifies you of this and offers to replace the file with an original copy from the Installation CD. When restoring files, you are prompted to confirm each replacement or you can choose to automatically replace all files that are different than the original installation files. Any Service Packs installed on the system should be immediately reapplied if any files are restored using this option.
- *Inspect Boot Sector*: This option verifies that the Windows NT boot sector is intact and still references NTLDR. If it does not, the boot sector is restored to its original state. This is handy if the boot sector becomes damaged or overwritten (for example, by a virus program or an accidental execution of the MS-DOS SYS command that replaced the NT boot sector with an MS-DOS boot sector).

Recovering with a Parallel Installation of NT

Windows NT systems with NTFS system or boot partitions present some unique challenges in terms of recovery. Although it is easy enough to boot to another operating system such as MS-DOS or Windows 95 to restore Registry or system files on a FAT-based NT boot or system partition, this isn't possible if the partition is NTFS because these other operating systems do not have the ability to access NTFS partitions. This creates a catch-22 situation: you can't recover the system until you boot NT, but you can't boot NT because the system is damaged. One common method for repairing a Windows NT installation in these circumstances is to install a separate, parallel copy of Windows NT on the system. Once this is done, you are then able to access the NTFS partition containing the original Windows NT installation and perform the necessary operations to recover the system (such as restoring system files or Registry hives).

When doing a parallel installation of Windows NT to perform a recovery, it is best to do a minimum installation of NT because you won't need anything more than the basic operating system to access the NTFS partition. Therefore, don't install components such as accessories, games, networking, and other extraneous options. This is also important if the system is low on disk space and you are having difficulty fitting an additional copy of NT on the system.

Manually Expanding Installation Files

Although the Windows NT Setup process is a comprehensive utility capable of repairing many different types of problems, it may not be necessary for you to run it if you only need to replace one or several files in your NT installation.

Restoring the Registry

As you already know, the Registry is "configuration central" for Windows NT. As a result, it should come as no surprise that the most common solution to the more severe problems that happen to Windows NT systems is a restore of a previous copy of the system Registry database. This is because most changes that precipitate problems (such as conflicts, STOP blue screens, boot failures, failed services or drivers, etc.) are recorded through a change in the system Registry. It isn't usually that the Registry itself is corrupt or damaged, but that the change (usually to the SYSTEM hive) that has caused the system to stop working properly is reflected inside the Registry. This fact underscores the importance of having previous copies of the Registry handy (including an updated copy of the Emergency Repair Disk) at all times.

Although it solves many problems, restoring the Registry is by no means a panacea for problems you encounter. For example, it won't help in situations where the problem is a damaged or missing file, there is physical damage to the hard disk drive, and so forth. It should only be done as a last resort when you are experiencing severe problems such as boot failures or STOP errors, and you believe the problem is being caused by a recent system configuration change.

Restoring the last known good configuration

To restore the Registry there are several methods you can use. The first and easiest method is to use the "Last Known Good" configuration option that occurs during the Windows NT boot process. First, a little background on how Windows NT uses system configurations to boot.

Each time you successfully boot Windows NT and log in, NT automatically makes a copy of the system's current configuration, called a *control set*, that was used to boot the system. All control sets are subkeys of the HKEY_LOCAL_MACHINE\SYSTEM\ Registry key (Figure 13-8) and have names such as ControlSet001, ControlSet002, etc. In addition, there is also a subkey called CurrentControlSet that is a pointer to the configuration the system used to boot the current session of NT.

By default, a system control set (startup configuration) used to boot the system is declared "good" when there are no Severe or Critical errors while starting system services and at least one successful log on.

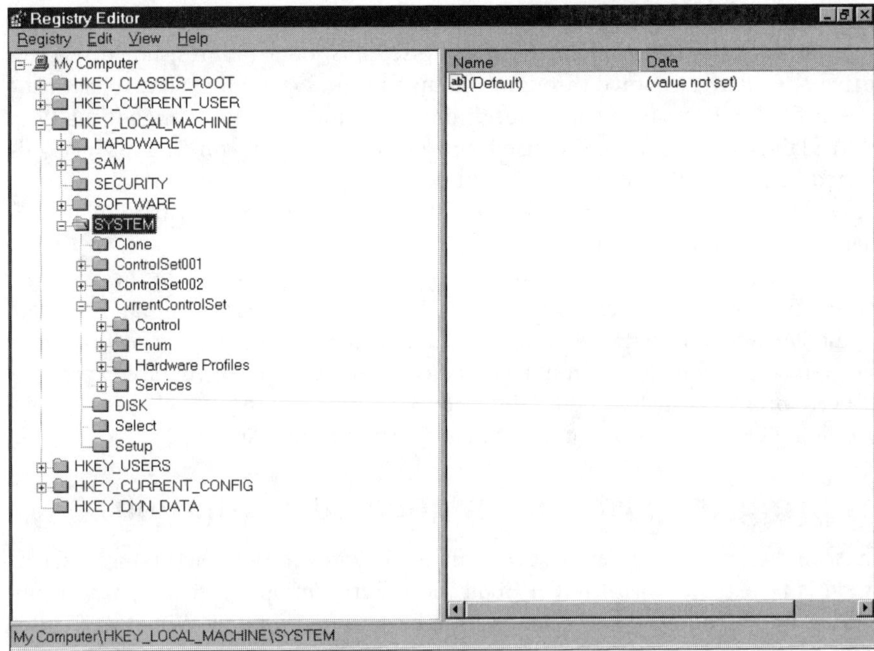

Figure 13-8: The control sets in the HKEY_LOCAL_MACHINE\SYSTEM **Registry key.**

When making any modifications to the Windows NT Registry, you should only modify the `CurrentControlSet` key and not the others listed. If you were to accidentally propagate an invalid or harmful change throughout all control sets, you might eliminate the ability to restore using the Last Known Good configuration option.

Each control set key contains a group of subkeys that reference different aspects of the control set. These subkeys are described in Table 13-2.

Table 13-2 REGISTRY CONTROL SET SUBKEYS

Subkey Name	Description
Control	Contains static configuration parameters for various aspects of the NT operating system
Enum	Contains dynamic information collected when various system device drivers and services are started
Hardware Profiles	Contains configuration information related to the video subsystem
Services	Contains startup and configuration parameters for Windows NT device drivers and services

If you ever need to restore to a previous "known good" working copy of the Registry, you can tell NT to revert to the last known good control set by following these steps:

1. Boot the system. After selecting the option to boot Windows NT from the NT Boot Loader menu, a message will briefly appear informing you to press the Space Bar to restore the last known good configuration. At this point press the Space Bar.
2. The Hardware Profile/Configuration Recovery screen appears. This screen is used to select hardware profiles at startup, but is also used to select the last known good Registry. Press L to select the Last Known Good system configuration. The only reflection of your selection will be that the menu option for L changes to instead say press D for the default configuration (the one that NT was originally going to use).

3. Press F3 to have the Last Known Good control set become the current control set and automatically restart the computer using the new configuration.

Restoring the Registry via the setup repair process

Restoring the previous working system configuration using the Last Known Good option is the preferred method because it is easy, quick, and solves many system configuration-related problems. However, if the system continues to experience problems after restoring the last known good configuration, the problem may not be the control set configuration or you may need to restore another version of the control set using a different method.

If you wish to try restoring an alternate system control set or wish to restore other Registry hives, there are several other methods you can use. One is to use the Repair option of Windows NT Setup as described earlier in this chapter. After choosing the "Inspect registry files" option on the Repair screen, you are asked to specify which Registry hive files to restore. This menu of choices is similar to that shown here:

```
[X] SYSTEM (System Configuration)
[X] SOFTWARE (Software Information)
[ ] DEFAULT (Default User Profile)
[ ] NTUSER.DAT (New User Profile)
[ ] SECURITY (Security Policy) and
SAM (User Accounts Database)
Continue (perform selected tasks)
F1=Help ENTER=Select/Deselect F3=Exit
```

From the options displayed, select the individual Registry hive files you wish to restore and then choose Continue and press Enter. Depending on whether or not you told Setup you had the Emergency Repair Disk, the selected Registry hive files are then copied from either the Emergency Repair Disk or the *%SYSTEM-ROOT%\REPAIR* folder. If using the Emergency Repair Disk, it is especially important that the Emergency Repair Disk is both the correct one for that machine and recent. If you restore the wrong Registry, or one that is very out-of-date, the cure may end up being worse than the disease.

Restoring the Registry from backups

Although it won't help you much if you are unable to boot Windows NT, you may also wish to restore your Registry from a tape or other backup. Many Windows NT-based backup utilities, including the `NTBACKUP.EXE` application that ships with NT, include the option of backing up the system Registry with backup volumes. If you wish to return to a previous Registry configuration as of the date of a backup set, you can use your application's restore option to do so. Unfortunately, few backup utilities allow for the selection of individual hive files and instead restore the entire set of hives at once. Therefore, when using this method with such backup utilities, be aware that all system configuration changes, including software-related configurations, user accounts database (SAM) changes, and user preference settings made after the backup volume will be lost.

To restore the Registry using the Windows NT Backup utility you simply check the appropriate box when running a restore job. This option is shown in Figure 13-9.

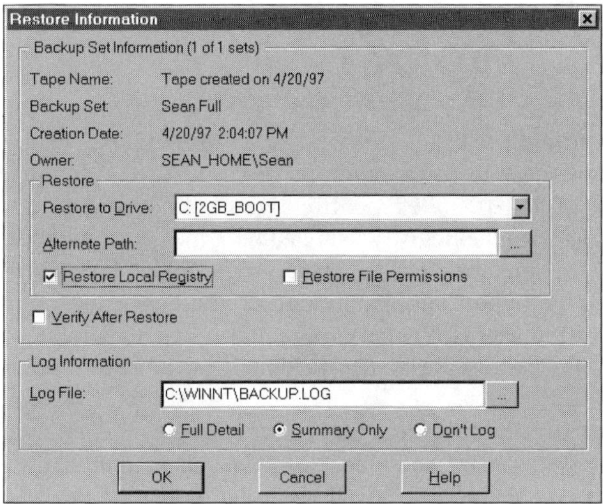

Figure 13-9: Restoring the Registry using NT Backup.

One quirk of NT Backup is that it forces you to select at least one file to restore when performing a restore of the Registry. If you select no files and only check the Restore Local Registry option, you are given an error message when you choose the Restore button to proceed. The way around this is to simply select one file that you're sure hasn't changed since the backup was done; to be safe, you should select an unimportant file such as a `README.TXT`, a `.BMP` (graphics file), or similar file.

Whenever you restore the Registry using a backup utility (or any other method), you should always immediately shut down and restart the system to enable the changes. Failure to do so could cause problems on your system (e.g., if applications in memory are maintaining invalid pointers to now nonexistent Registry entries).

Restoring individual keys using the Registry editors

Another method for restoring portions of the Registry is the use of one of the Windows NT Registry Editor utilities: REGEDIT.EXE and REGEDT32.EXE. As we discussed in Chapter 12, both of these utilities have options to restore individual Registry keys (or, in the case of REGEDT32.EXE, entire hive files). These files can then be manually imported back into the Registry using either a file copy operation (however, the files must have the same name as the actual Registry hive files themselves for this to work) or via the Import options present in both Registry editors. In REGEDIT.EXE, the import option is Registry → Import Registry File; in REGEDT32.EXE, this option is Registry → Restore. An example of the latter option is shown in Figure 13-10.

Because the use of a Registry editor requires that NT be running, this method won't be of much help if the system isn't bootable. However, this method can be handy for those comfortable with the use of the Windows NT Registry editors in solving noncritical or application-related problems. It also has the added advantage of allowing individual key replacements whereas other methods only allow you to restore individual hive files or the entire Registry at once.

For more information on the use of the Windows NT Registry Editors, see the "Meet Your Toolkit" section of Chapter 4, "NT Optimization 101." For more information on using the Registry Editors to perform Registry backups, see the "Performing Registry Backups" section of Chapter 12, "Maintaining Your NT System."

Although both Registry editor utilities can be used to restore individual Registry keys, only REGEDT32.EXE is capable of restoring entire hive files at once. Furthermore, it is even possible to open hive files as separate, temporary keys in the Registry editor display window for comparisons between configurations, copying and pasting data, and so forth. As discussed in Chapter 4, the major advantage to using the REGEDIT.EXE Registry editor is its advanced searching capabilities.

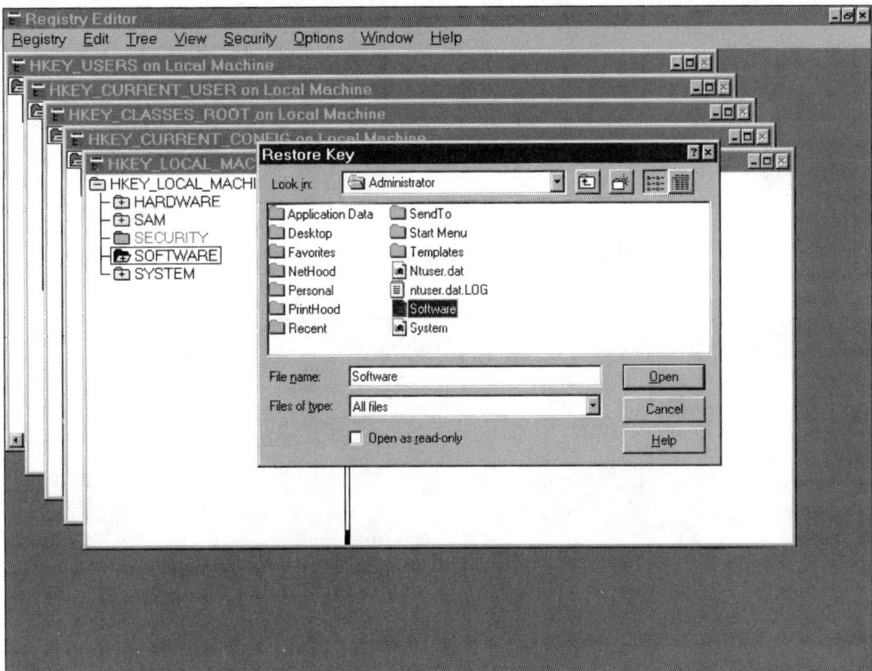

Figure 13-10: Using the REGEDT32 Registry Editor to restore a previously saved Registry key.

Manually restoring Registry hive files

Another, more direct method of restoring the Windows NT Registry is to manually replace the Registry hives files. Although this requires a slightly higher level of expertise than the other methods described, it also allows for greater flexibility and more direct control over the restore process. If you wish to restore only certain hive files or a set of uncompressed hive files you have saved in a special location (such as a hard drive folder, floppy disk, or other removable drive type), you can use this method in lieu of the other restore procedures.

The bulk of the Windows NT Registry is essentially just a collection of files (called Registry *hives*) stored in the *%SYSTEMROOT%\SYSTEM32\CONFIG* folder. Each hive is a combination of a single file with no extension and an associated `.LOG` file (e.g., `SYSTEM` and `SYSTEM.LOG`) located in the *%SYSTEMROOT%\SYSTEM32\CONFIG* folder or the %SYSTEMROOT%\PROFILES\username folders (where *username* is the user account name of a system user). The majority of the Registry hive files (Default, Sam, Security, Software, and System) are stored in the *%SYSTEMROOT%\SYSTEM32\CONFIG* folder. The exceptions are the user profile-related files, `NTUSER.DAT` and `NTUSER.DAT.LOG`, which are stored in the *%SYSTEMROOT%\PROFILES\username* folder of each system user.

If you inspect the *%SYSTEMROOT%\SYSTEM32\CONFIG* folder, you may also notice that there are .SAV files in addition to the hive files and the .LOG files. These files are backups of each hive file made after the text mode portion of Windows NT Setup was completed during the installation process.

The Registry files and their descriptions are listed in Table 13-3.

TABLE 13-3 THE WINDOWS NT REGISTRY HIVES

Registry Hive	Related File(s)	Description
HKEY_LOCAL_MACHINE\SYSTEM	SYSTEM and SYSTEM.LOG	The most important NT hive; contains setup, disk, and system configuration information
HKEY_LOCAL_MACHINE\SOFTWARE	SOFTWARE and SOFTWARE.LOG	Contains global (i.e., those not related to any single user) software-related settings for user applications; user-oriented software settings are stored in the HKEY_CURRENT_USER\SOFTWARE key of each user
HKEY_USERS\.DEFAULT	DEFAULT and DEFAULT.LOG	Contains the system's default user profile
HKEY_CURRENT_USER	NTUSER.DAT and NTUSER.DAT.LOG*	Contains the user profile of the currently logged in user
HKEY_LOCAL_MACHINE\SECURITY	SECURITY and SECURITY.LOG	Contains user and group policy information
HKEY_LOCAL_MACHINE\SAM	SAM and SAM.LOG	Contains local and domain (if applicable) user account and group information; information is stored in an encrypted format

*The NTUSER.DAT is the user profile and normally resides in the *%SYSTEMROOT%\PROFILES\username* folder; a copy exists for each user on the system.

There are several methods you can use to restore these files. Some may be done while booted under NT; others require access of the hard drive from another operating system such as MS-DOS or a separate installation of Windows NT. If you have a FAT boot partition (the one containing the Windows NT installation folder), you can simply boot from an MS-DOS boot disk and copy the backup set of Registry hive files to the *%SYSTEMROOT%\SYSTEM32\CONFIG* folder. If, on the other hard, you have an NTFS-based boot partition, you need to install a separate, parallel copy of Windows NT to gain access to the NTFS volume containing the Registry hive files to use this method. Because this can be somewhat cumbersome, it is usually preferable to use another method for restoring the Registry such as the Last Known Good boot option or the Windows NT Setup Repair option.

A DOS-based utility called NTFSDOS, created by Mark Russinovich and Bryce Cogswell of NTInternals, allows you to access to NTFS partitions while booted under MS-DOS. Although as of this writing it is still a read-only utility, a write-capable version of NTFSDOS (version 2.0) is expected in the near future. With this utility, it will be possible to replace Registry hive files from an MS-DOS boot disk. For current status on the development of this utility, see the NTInternals Web page at:
`http://www.ntinternals.com/`

If for any reason you choose to restore Registry hive files in this manner, it is recommended that you first make a backup copy of the existing files. That way, if the fix ends up being worse than the original problem, you can reverse what was done.

The Registry hive files are in use while the system is booted under NT and cannot (and should not) be replaced by straight file copy operations. Instead, boot to MS-DOS (FAT drives), another installation of NT (NTFS drives), or use the Resource Kit's REGREST utility to replace the Registry hive files.

If you have used the REGBACK utility from the Windows NT Resource Kit to manually back up your Registry hive files, another method you can use to restore the Registry is to use REGREST (the use of the REGBACK utility is described in Chapter 12). Like REGBACK, REGREST is a command line utility that normally issues at an NT command prompt session. REGBACK allows you to perform a live restore of the Windows NT Registry while booted under NT. The command has this format:

```
REGREST <sourcefolder> <savefolder>
```

where *<sourcefolder>* is the folder containing a Registry hive file set previously backed up (e.g., using REGBACK utility), and *<savefolder>* is the name of a backup folder to which REGREST will copy the existing Registry hive file set being replaced (a precautionary measure). For example, if you saved a copy of the Registry in a folder called `C:\REGBACK` and wish to replace the existing Registry with these files and save the existing ones into a folder called `C:\REGSAVE`, you would type:

```
REGREST C:\REGBACK C:\REGSAVE
```

Another way you might use the REGREST utility is to restore individual hive files or hive file backups that were given names other than their default names when they were backed up (e.g., a `SYSTEM` hive backup in a file called `GOODCONFIG`). The format of the REGREST command in these situations is:

```
REGREST <newfilename> <savefilename> <hivetype> <hivename>
```

where *<newfilename>* is the name of the file containing the Registry hive file to be restored, *<savefilename>* is the name of the file to be given to the automatic backup of the Registry hive being replaced, *<hivetype>* is the name of the primary hive containing the hive being replaced, either machine or users (representing `HKEY_CURRENT_MACHINE` and `HKEY_CURRENT_USERS`, respectively), and *<hivename>* is a hive contained within the hive specified in *<hivetype>*. For example, to replace the existing SOFTWARE Registry hive with a backup hive file named `NEWSOFT`, and to make a backup copy of the current `SOFTWARE` hive in the file `OLDSOFT`, you would type:

```
REGREST NEWSOFT OLDSOFT machine software
```

REGREST doesn't restore hives that aren't loaded in memory (e.g., user profiles for users who aren't currently logged in and therefore aren't represented by the current `HKEY_CURRENT_USER` hive. For regular Registry hive files, you can simply copy them manually to restore them; for user profiles, you must specify the filename containing the user profile and the user's Security Identifier (SID) on the REGREST command line. For example, to restore the user profile hive for user Craig with SID S-1-5-21-62146109-1959755064-1038892726-1000, you would type:

```
REGREST C:\REGBACK\CRAIG C:\REGBACK\CRAIG.BAK users S-1-5-21-
  62146109-1959755064-1038892726-1000
```

This would first back up the existing user profile for this user (the NTUSER.DAT file typically stored in the *%SYSTEMROOT%\PROFILES\username* folder) as `C:\REGBACK\CRAIG.BAK` and then replace it with the user profile hive stored in the file `C:\REGBACK\CRAIG`. An error is returned if an incorrect filename or SID is issued, or if the user profile hive specified contains invalid data.

To backup user profiles, it's easiest to simply back up each user's NTUSER.DAT file in their respective profile directory (e.g., C:\WINNT\PROFILES\CRAIG\NTUSER.DAT). However, if you wish to use REGREST as described above, you need to know the user's SID. You can find out a user's Security Identifier (SID) when logged in as that user and when the REGBACK command is issued to back up the Registry hive files. After the primary hive files are backed up, you're told that the user profile must be backed up manually and you are given the user's SID (as well as the exact format of the command line that should be issued to perform the backup — a nice bonus).

Resolving Boot Failures

One of the most disconcerting and debilitating problems that happens is a system that refuses to boot properly. There are myriad reasons why this occurs, ranging from damaged, buggy, or corrupted software (i.e., system configuration) to plain old hardware failures. The more common causes for boot failures are:

- A hardware failure, such as the hard drive, hard disk controller, system motherboard, memory, or other system component.
- Misconfigured/invalid system CMOS settings due to corruption, low battery, user configuration error, and so forth.
- A damaged or missing Master Boot Record (MBR), partition table, or partition boot sector on the hard drive containing the system partition.
- A damaged, invalid (i.e., wrong or incompatible version), or missing file critical to the Windows NT startup process. This includes the Windows NT boot-related files such as `NTLDR` (or `OSLOADER` on RISC-based systems), `NTDETECT.COM`, `NTBOOTDD.SYS` (on systems not using the SCSI adapter's BIOS), `NTOSKRNL.EXE`, and `HAL.DLL`. It also includes all system devices and services critical to the boot process, such as video and SCSI card drivers and the `BOOT.INI` file which is read by the NT Boot Loader and used to define the bootable partitions that exist on the system.
- Virus infection (e.g., of the boot sector).
- Corrupted or missing Windows NT Registry hive files, or a Registry with invalid or problematic settings.

Although this list covers the most common reasons for boot failure, there are also other, less obvious causes of such problems. For example, your system might fail to boot properly if the system or boot partition has no free disk space, or if the Windows NT Registry's size has exceeded the maximum Registry size defined in the Performance tab of the System Control Panel. Still another potential cause of boot problems is extreme levels of file fragmentation on systems with NTFS-based boot volumes. Each of these problems has its own associated set of symptoms accompanying it.

There are also two distinct and separate categories of boot problems that we can define: those that occur before the NT Boot Loader Menu appears, and those that occur after the Boot Loader menu appears (after you have selected to boot Windows NT from this menu). The reason for this categorization is that these two types of problems tend to have very different root causes. Problems occurring before the Boot Loader tend to be related to physical or logical damage to the drive's Master Boot Record (MBR), Partition Table, or Partition Boot Sector (PBS), whereas those occurring after the Boot Loader menu are usually related to the Windows NT operating system files themselves (including the startup boot files located on the system partition such as NTLDR and BOOT.INI).

Understanding the Windows NT boot process

Resolving boot problems on Windows NT system is a lot easier when you understand the individual steps that occur during NT's boot process. Understanding this process may help you pinpoint exactly where a problem is occurring, making it easier to remedy.

The NT boot process, like the boot process of any operating system, is essentially just a sequence of loading files required to initialize the system. Therefore, if any of these files are missing, damaged, or mismatched versions, the boot process is likely to fail.

In general terms, the NT boot process can be summarized by the following steps, which happen sequentially:

- The Power On Self Test (POST) process. On Intel x86 systems, this is the initialization of the video BIOS, system BIOS, and all other installed system ROMs; on RISC-based system, this is the initialization of the ARC firmware (or AlphaBIOS found on some DEC Alpha systems).
- Initial startup procedure. On Intel x86 systems, this involves locating and executing the Master Boot Record on the first installed hard drive (i.e., drive C: or 80 hex); on RISC-based system, this involves the selection of the Windows NT operating system from the ARC firmware menu.

- Execution of a boot loader menu (NTLDR.EXE on Intel x86 systems; on RISC-based systems, this is handled by the system's BIOS firmware) and selection of Windows NT as the operating system by the user (or by default if the boot loader has a countdown that times out).
- The system's hardware is detected (on Intel x86 systems, this is done by NTDETECT.COM; on RISC-based systems, this is handled by the ARC firmware in an earlier step, and at this point the OSLOADER.EXE program is executed).
- A system control set (Registry configuration) is selected to use as the default control set for the boot process.
- The Windows NT kernel (NTOSKRNL.EXE) and system device drivers are loaded into memory and then initialized.
- A user logs onto the system after receiving the Windows NT log in prompt.

The order of the events varies slightly depending on the type of system; that is, Intel- or RISC-based and whether it is an Alpha, PowerPC, or MIPS RISC system. In the following sections, we describe the individual boot processes on Intel and RISC systems in more detail.

BOOT PROCESS FOR INTEL-BASED SYSTEMS

On Intel x86-based systems, this whole boot process is able to start because the system hardware knows to automatically look for a special disk entity called the Master Boot Record (MBR) which is located on the first sector of the first installed hard disk. This ability to self-start is the origin of the term "bootstrap" (the analogy being that the system is essentially pulling itself up by its own bootstraps). The MBR, in turn, contains information about the various partitions on the boot drive, and also about which partition is currently designated as the Windows NT system partition (the partition from which the system boots). Specifically, the MBR performs these tasks:

- Reads all Partition Table entries for the drive
- Determines the location of the Partition Boot Sector (PBS) of the drive (the partition containing the Windows NT system volume, from which the system boots)
- Loads and executes the code in the Partition Boot Sector

After loading the Partition Boot Sector into memory, the NTLDR utility executes and in turn reads the BOOT.INI file containing the list of operating system choices on the computer. These choices are then displayed in the familiar Windows NT Boot Loader menu. When you choose to start Windows NT, the Windows NT kernel and system device drivers are loaded and initialized in memory.

BOOT PROCESS FOR RISC-BASED SYSTEMS

Things happen a little differently during the boot process on RISC systems than they do on Intel-based systems. It also varies somewhat depending on the particular type of RISC system being used. Like Intel x86-based systems, RISC systems have a POST process that initializes the various system ROMs, but this is where the similarity ends.

At this point, a special Nonvolatile RAM (NVRAM) utility executes and displays a menu of operating system choices (the Boot Selection menu) that were previously defined by the user. Each entry points to a particular disk and partition, each of which contains the startup files for an operating system. When executed, the menu choice then loads the executable program specified in the table's entry and which is located on that partition. In the case of Windows NT, this executable file is OSLOADER.EXE.

FILES LOADED DURING THE BOOT PROCESS

Table 13-4 describes the files loaded during the Windows NT boot process for both Intel x86-based and RISC-based systems.

TABLE 13-4 FILES LOADED DURING THE WINDOWS NT BOOT PROCESS ON INTEL AND RISC SYSTEMS

Filename (Intel x86 System)	Disk Location	Filename (RISC System)	Disk Location
`NTLDR`	Root folder of system partition (e.g., `C:\`)	`OSLOADER`	`\OS\NT40` folder of system partition
`BOOT.INI`	Root folder of system partition (e.g., `C:\`)	N/A	N/A
`BOOTSECT.DOS`	Root folder of system partition (e.g., `C:\`)	N/A	N/A

continued

Filename (Intel x86 System)	Disk Location	Filename (RISC System)	Disk Location
NTDETECT.COM	Root folder of system partition (e.g., C:\)	N/A	N/A
NTBOOTDD.SYS (SCSI disk controllers not using own BIOSs)	Root folder of system partition (e.g., C:\)	N/A	N/A
NTOSKRNL.EXE	*%SYSTEMROOT%* \SYSTEM32 folder of boot partition	NTOSKRNL.EXE	*%SYSTEMROOT%*\ SYSTEM32 folder of boot partition
HAL.DLL	*%SYSTEMROOT%* \SYSTEM32 folder of boot partition	HAL.DLL	\OS\NT40 folder of system partition
N/A	N/A	*.PAL files (Alpha-based systems only)	\OS\NT40 folder of system partition
SYSTEM Registry Hive File	*%SYSTEMROOT%* \SYSTEM32\ CONFIG folder of boot partition	SYSTEM Registry Hive File	*%SYSTEMROOT%*\ SYSTEM32\DRIVERS folder of boot partition
System Device Driver Files	*%SYSTEMROOT%* \SYSTEM32\ CONFIG folder of boot partition		ERS folder of boot partition

Because all of these files are essential to a proper system boot, it is likely that NT will fail to boot should any of them become damaged, deleted, or replaced with incorrect versions. If the problem occurs after the selection to boot Windows NT is made (from the NT Boot Loader menu on Intel systems or the Boot Selection menu on RISC systems) then the problem may be a faulty `NTOSKRNL.EXE` or system device driver. Therefore, it may be helpful to instruct NT to display each driver filename as they are being loaded using the `[VGA Mode]` boot selection from the boot loader menu (which uses the `/SOS BOOT.INI` option).

For more information on how to get Windows NT to display each system device driver file as it is loaded, see the "Troubleshooting with BOOT.INI Switches" section later in this chapter.

The hardware detection process

Occasionally, problems during the Windows NT boot process occur during the hardware detection process. On Intel x86-based systems, this process occurs after the Windows NT boot selection is made and is handled by NTDETECT.COM. This may be the case if the system is locking up after the system displays the message:

```
NTDETECT V1.0 Checking Hardware . . .
```

If this occurs, you'll want to get more information about exactly which hardware component is causing the detection process to hang the system. The best way to do this (rather than using guesswork and randomly removing or swapping individual hardware components and peripherals) is to use the special checked version of `NTDETECT.COM` called `NTDETECT.CHK` located on the Windows NT installation CD-ROM.

For more information on installing the `NTDETECT.CHK` file to force NT to display additional information during the hardware detection process, see the "Using NTDETECT.CHK to Troubleshoot Boot Failures" section later in this chapter.

Once you've located the hardware that is causing the problem, you can either remove it or replace it with another and attempt to boot the system again. Also, it is important to note that this problem can result from incompatibilities between specific hardware devices and system BIOS revisions. In this case, the solution may be to obtain the latest BIOS firmware update available from your system's manufacturer. These days, most BIOSs are stored on Erasable Programmable ROMs (EPROMS) and have the ability to be "flashed" to a later version simply by running a special BIOS Flash/Update utility available from the manufacturer. However, on some systems, updating the BIOS may actually require obtaining a new chip (or set of chips).

Using the NT hardware query tool

Another method for troubleshooting problems that occur during the hardware detection process is to use a special utility that ships on the Windows NT CD-ROM called the Windows NT Hardware Query Tool (aka NTHQ). NTHQ is an MS-DOS utility (which, not surprisingly, uses a Windows 3.1-style GUI interface) that detects system hardware and generates a report of its findings both graphically and in a log file. Using NTHQ may yield different results than the Windows NT NTDETECT.COM program (i.e., it may not lock up the system during the detection process even if NTDETECT does).

To run NTHQ, you first need to install the necessary files onto a 3.5 inch 1.44MB floppy disk. This disk will automatically be formatted and have MS-DOS system files installed on it to make it bootable.

To create the NTHQ utility boot disk, follow these steps:

1. Insert a 1.44MB floppy disk into your 3.5 inch floppy drive.
2. While booted under Windows NT, run the `MAKEDISK.BAT` file located in the `\SUPPORT\HQTOOL` folder on the Windows NT installation CD-ROM.
3. Follow the steps presented by the installer to create the disk. The disk will automatically be formatted and have the appropriate files copied to it.

Once the NTHQ floppy has been created, you need to boot your system using the disk in order to run the utility. During the boot process, a custom MS-DOS boot process takes over and creates a RAM drive to which the necessary files are copied and from which they are executed.

Next, the system prompts you to begin the detection process and then attempts to identify all system hardware. Specifically, NTHQ does the following:

- Identifies PCI devices and resources used by each
- Identifies ISA Plug and Play devices and resources used by each
- Identifies EISA and MCA devices

- Identifies Legacy ISA (non-Plug and Play) devices, system components, and resources used by each
- Creates a log file (NTHQ.TXT) where the results of the detection process are recorded

After NTHQ executes, it offers a graphical screen displaying a summary of the system hardware detected and buttons to zoom in on individual component categories. It also offers options to print a report of its findings to a local printer or to save the results to a file on a disk of your choosing (however, because this file is automatically created no matter what and stored on the NTHQ boot floppy, this step isn't mandatory). The saved filename with the utility's results is NTHQ.TXT. In addition, there is a README.TXT file on the NTHQ boot disk that gives hints as to how to interpret the log information recorded in NTHQ.TXT. This information may be very helpful to either you or a Microsoft Product Support Services representative in diagnosing a hardware detection problem.

NTHQ will not run under Windows NT or Windows 95; it will only run under MS-DOS. It should only be run by using the special boot disk created by the MAKEDISK.BAT file on the NT CD-ROM because this disk contains a special startup environment that creates the resources needed by the utility.

A Boot Failure Checklist

When faced with a boot failure, you need to take some diagnostic steps to determine the source of the problem. Listed below are "checklists" of steps to take if your system fails during the boot process.

Problems occurring before the NT Boot Loader menu

The first category of boot failure is problems that occur prior to the Windows NT Boot Loader menu appearing. Typically, such problems are related either to hardware or to damage to one of the boot drive's physical structures.

For problems that occur before the NT Boot Loader menu appears, take these steps to recover the system:

- Attempt to boot the system from a Windows NT boot floppy (the procedure for creating this disk is described in Chapter 12). If you are able to boot and access the system using this disk, it is likely that the problem is one of the following: a damaged Master Boot Record or Partition Boot Sector; or an invalid, damaged, or missing `NTLDR` or `BOOT.INI` file. In this case, you need to take steps to repair the affected files or disk structures. See the following sections for more information on how to repair a damaged MBR or PBS.
- If you are unable to access the system using an NT boot floppy, try running the Windows NT Setup Repair process in conjunction with the Emergency Repair Disk. When prompted, choose to inspect all aspects of the Windows NT installation, including the startup environment, NT boot sector, Registry files, and Windows NT installation files. Follow the prompts and replace any files Setup recommends be replaced.
- If the above steps fail, try reinstalling Windows NT in the same folder as the existing version to see if this fixes the problem. When prompted, tell NT Setup that you are doing an upgrade installation and NOT a new installation; if you choose to do a new installation into the same directory, you will overwrite the existing Windows NT Registry database and lose your previous system configuration.
- If all else fails, try to recover data (if possible) from your Windows NT installation. If NT is installed on a FAT partition, you can simply boot to MS-DOS and use a DOS-based utility to copy the information to another location (such as a removable drive or tape backup). If the volume is NTFS, you need to install a second, parallel copy of Windows NT and use this to access the data in the original installation.
- If this is an NTFS-based NT installation and there is insufficient room on the drive for a second installation, you can take the drive to another machine and install it as a secondary drive; this will allow you to access and recover information from the drive.

Although in most cases one of the procedures described in this section will allow you to recover a Windows NT installation that fails to boot properly, there is an alternate method that is helpful where these circumstances exist:

- The machine is the sole domain controller of a Windows NT domain
- The Windows NT installation is on a FAT volume
- All attempts to repair a boot failure (such as a STOP blue screen error) have failed and the problem persists

- The option of restoring a full system backup is either undesirable (e.g., due to age of backup) or unavailable

The reason this situation is so difficult is that there is no backup domain controller with a replica of the domain user database. This means that any reinstallation of NT on the machine will wipe out the domain's SID and user account database (otherwise, another machine could have been promoted to the Primary Domain Controller [PDC] and the machine could be brought up as a Backup Domain Controller when being reinstalled). Although this situation is easily remedied by reinstalling a new copy of Windows NT and reinstalling a recent backup, the procedure discussed here is handy when this option is not desirable (or available).

This procedure essentially involves a "patching" of the SAM and SECURITY Registry hive files from the original Windows NT installation into the *%SYSTEMROOT%\SYSTEM32*\CONFIG folder of a new Windows NT installation. To minimize the amount of reconfiguration that is necessary, this procedure works best if the new installation of NT is done into the same folder as the damaged version (this assumes that attempts to recover NT using the upgrade reinstallation procedure failed). To do this, first make sure you have uncompressed backup copies of the SAM and SECURITY Registry hive files from the NT installation that refuses to boot. Next, reinstall NT, this time choosing to perform a new installation into the existing Windows NT installation folder rather than an upgrade installation. Then install the machine as a PDC for the same domain as the original installation of NT. When finished with the new installation, reboot the system using a DOS boot disk to access the FAT volume containing the NT installation. Next, copy the SAM and SECURITY files from the original Windows NT installation to the *%SYSTEMROOT%\SYSTEM32\CONFIG* folder of the new installation. This will preserve the system-related configuration settings, but replace the security-related information including the original domain's SID and the user accounts database. Although it may seem a strange procedure, this normally works perfectly and gives a clean Windows NT installation with all of the original domain and security information from the previous NT installation. The only other activities left to do are the reinstallation of any services and applications on the server.

NOTE: This procedure is not necessary if you have a Backup Domain Controller (BDC) in the domain (highly recommended) or are willing to restore from a full system backup. It is only provided to help in situations where a PDC installation is unrecoverable and no other options exist. If you have at least one BDC and maintain your system using the recommended procedures in Chapter 12, you'll never face this situation.

Problems occurring after the NT boot loader menu

The other category of boot failure is those failures that occur after the NT Boot Loader menu appears and you have selected the option to boot Windows NT. Because this portion of the boot process involves a large number of Windows NT installation files (including the NT kernel, drivers, and services) there are a larger number of potential problems than exist for pre-Boot Loader startup problems.

For problems that occur before the NT Boot Loader menu appears, the first step to take is to gather as much information as possible on the problem. Your course of action depends largely on the specifics of the situation. How far does the boot process get before the problem occurs? Does the blue screen (the normal operating system loader screen, not a STOP blue screen) indicating the normal NT system loading process appear? Are you receiving a STOP error during the boot process? If the answer to this last question is "yes," proceed to the section of this chapter dealing with STOP errors for information on how to proceed. Otherwise, the next step is to try to further identify the source of the problem so you can decide how to proceed.

Although it isn't totally unheard of for a hardware problem to cause a post-Boot Loader boot failure, most such problems tend to be problems with either the Windows NT system files or the Registry. Therefore, we focus on some of the software-related methods you can use to diagnose the source of a post-Boot Loader failure.

One hardware-related problem that causes boot problems that occur after the NT Boot Loader is bad RAM chips. Typically, this problem results in random STOP errors that occur sometime during the process of loading the NT operating system (often during the blue screen portion of the load process, when `NTOSKRNL.EXE` and drivers are loaded). If this is a new system you're installing and the memory is as yet unproven, you should try swapping the installed RAM with a different set of modules. You may also want to try using the `/MAXMEM` option in `BOOT.INI` (as described in the next section) to determine if bad RAM is the problem. It is also possible for these types of problems to be caused by a bad motherboard or invalid CMOS configuration settings.

Using NTDETECT.CHK to troubleshoot boot failures

There are several tricks you can use to enhance the amount of information Windows NT provides about the boot process. This additional information can be very useful for troubleshooting boot-related problems. The first of these involves the use of a special version of NTDETECT.COM. NTDETECT.COM is responsible for identifying system hardware during the boot process and is the first program that runs after you select Windows NT from the NT Boot Loader menu.

Normally, NTDETECT.COM displays only a terse message indicating that it is "checking the system" when the system boots. However, it is possible to temporarily replace NTDETECT.COM with another version that is specially written to provide verbose information on the hardware detection process. This can be especially helpful if the boot problem is occurring during the NTDETECT process. This might happen because of a conflict between NTDETECT.COM and a hardware component, a corrupted NTDETECT.COM, or a faulty hardware component. This special checked version of NTDETECT is named NTDETECT.CHK and is located in the \SUPPORT\DEBUG*platform* folder of the CD-ROM, where *platform* is the hardware platform of your system (I386, ALPHA, MIPS, or PPC). Much like the debugger symbol files described in Chapter 12, this file is capable of generating more information when problems occur than is the regular version of NTDETECT.COM.

To use this file, you need to replace your existing NTDETECT.COM file in the root folder of your system volume (boot drive) with NTDETECT.CHK. However, because NTDETECT.CHK requires you to press a key to continue after it has completed the detection process, you won't want to use it long-term and will want to restore your original version once the problem is solved. Therefore, make a backup copy of your original NTDETECT.COM file before replacing it.

Follow these steps to replace NTDETECT.COM with the .CHK version on your system:

1. Remove the System, Read Only, and Hidden attributes of the existing NTDETECT.COM file (use the Windows NT Explorer or the command ATTRIB NTDETECT.COM -R -S -H from an NT command prompt session).
2. Copy or rename the existing NTDETECT.COM file in the root folder of your system volume (boot drive) to another filename such as NTDETECT.ORI or NTDETECT.BAK.
3. Copy the NTDETECT.CHK file from the appropriate platform folder in the Windows NT CD-ROM's \SUPPORT\DEBUG folder as NTDETECT.COM in the root folder of the system volume.
4. Boot the system with the new NTDETECT.COM file now in place and diagnose the problem.

5. When done using the checked version, copy the original version of NTDETECT.COM (now NTDETECT.ORI, .BAK, etc.) back to NTDETECT.COM in the root folder of the system volume.
6. Finally, reset the System, Read Only, and Hidden attributes of the NTDETECT.COM file using either the Windows NT Explorer or the command ATTRIB NTDETECT.COM +R +S +H from and NT command prompt session.

When the checked version of NTDETECT.COM runs after you select Windows NT from the Boot Loader menu, you'll see a slightly different output than you're used to. Your screen output may appear similar to this:

```
NTDETECT V1.0 Checking Hardware . . .
Detecting System Component . . .
Reading BIOS date . . .
Done reading BIOS date (1/10/97)
Detecting Bus/Adapter Component . . .
Collecting Disk Geometry . . .
Detecting ROM Blocks . . .
Detecting Keyboard Component . . .
Detecting ComPort Component . . .
Detecting Parallel Component . . .
Detecting Mouse Component . . .
Detecting Floppy Component . . .
8649d064-0000000-A
Detection done. Press a key to display hardware info . . .
```

Once this process is complete, press Enter to continue with the boot process. On the next screens, NTDETECT will display detailed information about each individual, listed component (called node information); press Enter after each of these screens to continue to the next.

This information can be extremely useful for either you or a Microsoft Product Support Services engineer helping you resolve a boot failure. It can identify a piece of hardware that is failing to initialize properly, whereas the normal version of NTDETECT.COM might just leave you with a black frozen screen and no additional information.

If your system volume is NTFS rather than FAT, you need to create a Windows NT boot disk containing the NTDETECT.CHK version of NTDETECT.COM because the boot failure will prevent you from accessing your NTFS volume. See the "Creating a Windows NT Startup Disk" section of Chapter 12 for more information on creating a system startup diskette.

Troubleshooting with BOOT.INI switches

Another method you can use to gain additional information about boot problems is to modify the BOOT.INI used by NTLDR to identify and load the Windows NT installation on your machine (and other installed operating systems in some cases). There are two switches in particular, /MAXMEM and /SOS, that can be helpful when diagnosing NT boot failures. These switches are used on the lines that instruct NTLDR to load the operating system. /MAXMEM=*X* switch instructs Windows NT to only use *X* megabytes of memory, as if the system only had that much memory installed. This can be helpful if the problem is bad memory and the bad memory is above the amount specified in /MAXMEM. If the system boot failure goes away once /MAXMEM is reduced to a certain number, then it's likely that the problem is RAM. As an example, the BOOT.INI line to instruct NT to load and use only 12MB of memory would appear similar to the following:

```
multi(0)disk(0)rdisk(0)partition(1)\WINNT="Windows NT Workstation
 4.0" /MAXMEM=12
```

/MAXMEM should never be reduced below 12MB on an Intel x86-based Windows NT Workstation system and 16MB on an NT Server system, because these are bare minimum figures required for NT to load properly. On RISC systems, the minimum number you should supply for /MAXMEM is approximately 16MB for NT Workstation and approximately 20MB for NT Server. You may be able to get away with using smaller figures in some cases (depending on your system's configuration and the particular services and drivers installed), but doing so may cause the system to issue error messages and exhibit other strange behavior.

Another helpful switch is the /SOS parameter. This instructs Windows NT to display each component of Windows NT, including the kernel and system driver files, as they're loaded. This is especially handy for identifying a particular system component (such as a driver) that is causing the boot process to fail. If you've ever run the special [VGA Mode] option of Windows NT from the NT Boot Loader menu, then you've already seen what this option does. However, this option also includes a special /VGA switch which forces NT to load in 16-color VGA mode. If you want the /SOS parameter to apply to your normal boot of Windows NT, you can simply add this switch to the end of the BOOT.INI startup line for the regular boot of Windows NT. For example, your new line might read:

```
multi(0)disk(0)rdisk(0)partition(1)\WINNT="Windows NT Workstation
 4.0" /SOS
```

Although it will display additional information even when there are no problems present, this can be helpful to have if a boot problem occurs later on. As an alternative, you can leave the `BOOT.INI` file unchanged and simply choose the `[VGA Mode]` option of Windows NT from the NT Boot Loader menu, which includes the `/SOS` option.

Repairing a Damaged Disk Structure

It may happen that after troubleshooting a system boot failure, you determine that the problem may be related to a damaged disk structure such as the Master Boot Record or Partition Boot Sector. If this is the case, you may be able to restore the affected structure if you previously made a backup of it using the procedures described in Chapter 12.

Although any significant damage to either the MBR or PBS will cause the boot process to fail, there may be telltale signs indicating which structure is damaged. For example, a missing or damaged MBR might cause one of these error messages to appear during the boot process:

```
Missing Operating System
Invalid Partition Table
```

However, the following message might be indicative of a problem with the Partition Boot Sector:

```
Couldn't find NTLDR
A kernel file is missing from the disk
```

If you receive one of these messages, it's very possible that a restore of the Partition Boot Sector will fix your problem. There are also a number of other messages that might appear, but these are by far the most common. If you are experiencing a boot failure prior to the appearance of the NT Boot Loader menu and suspect damage to the MBR or PBS, try using the procedures below to repair the affected structure(s).

Using DiskSave to restore the MBR or PBS

If you have an MS-DOS boot disk available, the easiest way to repair a damaged Master Boot Record or Partition Boot Sector is to use the Windows NT Resource Kit's DiskSave utility discussed in Chapter 12. This program provides an easy-to-use menu that provides options for both saving and restoring critical disk structures.

To restore the Master Boot Record or Partition Boot Sector using DiskSave, follow these steps:

1. Have an MS-DOS boot disk ready as well as a disk containing the `DISKSAVE.EXE` program file. Note that the latter step is only necessary if the NT system volume is NTFS, because an accessible FAT volume will contain the `DISKSAVE.EXE` program inside the folder containing the Windows NT Resource Kit files.
2. DiskSave presents you with a menu of choices. Two options, F3 and F5, are for restoring the MBR and PBS. Press F3 to replace the MBR or F5 to replace the PBS.
3. You are prompted for the filename of the saved MBR or PBS. Enter the full pathname (e.g., `A:\MBRDSK0.DSK`) and press Enter.

As mentioned in Chapter 12, DiskSave will only save and restore the MBR or PBS on physical disk 0 — other drives are not supported.

After restoring the MBR or PBS using DiskSave, you should immediately quit the application and restart your system. If a corrupted MBR or PBS was the problem, your system should now boot properly.

Using DiskProbe to restore the MBR or PBS

The best and easiest way to restore the MBR or PBS is using the MS-DOS-based DiskSave utility because it can be used even if the system fails to boot. However, you might also be able to use the DiskProbe utility (also part of the Windows NT Resource Kits) in some situations to accomplish the restoration of the MBR or PBS. For example, you could do this if you booted Windows NT from a different drive on the system, or even on another system to which you have transported the damaged drive. If you prefer this method, then you should be able to use the DiskProbe utility to repair the damaged MBR or PBS. DiskProbe also has another advantage over the DiskSave utility: it is able to restore the MBR or PBS of any disk or partition, not just the first ones. In addition, DiskProbe is also capable of restoring the Partition Boot Sector for special partition types, including logical drives in an extended partition, volume sets, stripe sets, mirror sets, and stripe sets with parity. However, because our discussion is focused on boot-related problems, we show you how to use this utility to restore the MBR and PBS on a Windows NT system partition.

If you have determined that your Master Boot Record has become damaged or virus-infected and wish to restore the Master Boot Record using DiskProbe, follow these steps:

1. From the Start Menu, run the DiskProbe icon located in the Programs → Resource Kit 4.0 → Disk Tools menu.
2. From DiskProbe's menu bar, choose File → Open. Enter the filename of the previously saved MBR and choose OK. At this point, verify that the file is 512 bytes in length (DiskProbe will display a message if the size of the file is not a multiple of 512 because this would normally indicate the file is invalid).
3. Next, choose Drives → Physical Drive from the menus. The Available Physical Drives are listed as PhysicalDrive*n* (where $n = 0$ for the first hard drive, and so on). Select the disk that contains the Master Boot Record you want to restore by double-clicking it in the window.
4. Clear the Read Only check box in the Handle 0 group box, and click the Set Active button. Then click Close.
5. From the menus, choose Sectors → Write. This opens the Write Sector dialog box. Set Starting Sector to Write Data to 0.
6. Finally, click the Write It button to write the data to disk.

To restore the Partition Boot Sector on a primary disk partition, follow these steps (we will use the logical drive method rather than the physical drive method because it is easier):

- From the Start Menu, run the DiskProbe icon located in the Programs → Resource Kit 4.0 → Disk Tools menu.
- Next, choose Drives → Logical Volume from the menu bar. In the Open Logical Volume dialog box, there will be a Logical Volumes list box; in the box, double-click the logical drive whose Partition Boot Sector you want to restore.
- In the Handle 0 group box, clear the Read Only check box, click Set Active, and then click Close.
- Choose File → Open, and then enter the filename of the file that contains the Partition Boot Sector. Once the file is open, verify that it looks like a Partition Boot Sector and is 512 bytes in length (DiskProbe displays an error if the file size is not a multiple of 512 because this would normally indicate an incorrect size for a Partition Boot Sector).

- Next, choose Sectors → Write from the menus. This displays the Write Sector dialog box. In the Starting sector to write data, enter 0 for the Starting sector to write data. Then click the Write it button to write the Partition Boot Sector information to the disk.
- Finally, restart your system after restoring the Partition Boot Sector so that the changes make take effect.

Repairing a Boot Failure on a Mirrored Drive Set

Another boot-related failure is that of one of the components in a fault-tolerant RAID 1 mirror set. How you recover from this situation depends on the exact nature of the failure. If the problem is the disk controller (or one of the disk controllers if this is a duplexed RAID 1 configuration with two controllers and two drives) then all you probably need to do is replace the failed controller. If, however, one of the disks has ceased to function properly, you need to take different steps to solve the problem.

Failure of the secondary drive

In a RAID 1 configuration, the primary drive is the drive the system operates from; all data written to this drive is automatically "mirrored" to a second drive called the *shadow drive*. Although no disk failure is a good one, failure of the mirrored shadow drive is always preferable to having the primary drive fail. In the event that this happens, Windows NT should continue to boot normally, but after NT is booted you'll probably see a message similar to the one shown in Figure 13-11.

Figure 13-11: Message indicating that a member of a fault-tolerant disk set failed.

After receiving this message immediately replace the failed drive. The replacement drive should (whenever possible) be an identical brand and model to the working drive, and be configured with identical settings to the failed drive it is replacing. If, however, replacing the drive is something you cannot do immediately, you should use the Windows NT Disk Administrator utility to break the mirror set and temporarily disable the fault-tolerant disk configuration. After doing this, you can safely remove the dead drive until a replacement is obtained. This prevents the previous error message from displaying and avoids potential problems that can occur by leaving the system with the fault-tolerant configuration enabled (especially if both drives aren't present).

Perform these steps to break a fault-tolerant mirror set using Disk Administrator:

1. Open Disk Administrator and select the mirror set you want to break by clicking on one of the member drives in the graphical display window.
2. From the menu bar, choose Fault Tolerance → Break Mirror.
3. In the Confirm message, select Yes.

This effectively breaks the mirror set and redefines NT's disk subsystem configuration. Once the replacement shadow drive is obtained, you can use Disk Administrator to reestablish the mirror volume in conjunction with the primary drive.

Failure of the primary drive

If the primary drive in a mirrored fault tolerant set fails, Windows NT may or may not make a graceful recovery. If the primary and shadow drives are SCSI drives and are sequentially numbered SCSI ID 0 and 1 respectively, the chances are good that NT will automatically skip the dead drive and boot from the shadow drive. However, if the drives aren't numbered sequentially (e.g., the primary is ID 0 and the shadow is ID 3, perhaps with other SCSI devices between the two), don't expect your system to automatically jump over and start using the other drive to boot from; it probably won't. This situation can also occur when the RAID 1 configuration is a duplexed configuration with two separate controllers serving the two different drives. In these situations, it is unlikely that NT's `FTDISK.SYS` (the fault-tolerant disk driver) will be able to gracefully recover the system. Instead, you need to manually reconfigure the system so that Windows NT attempts to boot from the shadow drive (and controller) rather than the primary.

It is recommended that you always configure a RAID 1 mirror set with the primary and shadow drives set to SCSI ID's 0 and 1, respectively. For duplexed configurations, it is recommended that you set both drives to the same SCSI ID (e.g., ID 0 for a mirrored system partition). These configurations make the recovery process much easier in the event of primary drive failure.

There are several methods, both hardware- and software-based, that you can use to recover from a failure of the primary drive in a mirror set. The hardware method for resolving this problem is to swap the good shadow drive with the primary drive, while simultaneously replacing the failed drive (and setting it up as the new shadow drive). For example, if using SCSI drives, simply set the SCSI ID of the shadow drive to that of the previous primary drive and install the new replacement for the failed primary drive with the configuration of the previous shadow drive. When NT boots again, the `FTDISK.SYS` fault-tolerant disk driver will detect that the new drive requires resynchronization with the primary and perform the operation. You can check the Windows NT Event Viewer's System log to view all entries related to this process (they will be listed under the FTDISK service).

When using the physical method to replace a failed primary SCSI drive and restore a mirror set, be very sure to double-check that you have configured the correct SCSI ID and SCSI bus termination settings on both drives. Often, these settings are swapped between the two drives (but this depends on the exact configuration of your disk subsystem). Likewise with IDE drives, be certain that you have configured the correct master/slave settings between the two drives.

There are also several other ways of instructing NT to boot from the shadow drive that don't require making physical changes to the hardware (however, you'll still want to replace the failed drive as quickly as possible). One is to use a modified version of your Windows NT Startup Disk as described in Chapter 12. For Intel x86-based systems, this specially modified version of the Windows NT Startup Disk must have the necessary changes in its `BOOT.INI` file to tell NT to use the shadow drive rather than the primary drive as the location of the Windows NT boot partition and installation directory. RISC systems usually won't need to use a startup floppy because their ARC firmware can be configured with a new or modified entry that points to the shadow drive rather than the primary drive of the mirror set. For more information, see the sidebar, "Creating a Shadow Drive Boot Entry on RISC Systems."

Creating a Shadow Drive Boot Entry on RISC Systems

If you are using a RISC system and experience a failure of the primary drive of a mirrored system volume, you'll need to create a boot entry that points to the shadow drive of the mirror set. This procedure requires that the system partition and the boot partition be the same partition (or that both the system and boot partitions be mirrored), and uses the ARC firmware setup on RISC systems that defines the system's boot options. Firmware screens vary from manufacturer to manufacturer; we use a DEC Alpha system as an example. This method is described below:

1. After booting the system, the System Boot Menu appears. From this menu, select the Manage Boot Selections option.
2. From the Manage Boot Selections menu, select Add a Boot Selection.

You are prompted for various information about the new boot entry as follows:

- Prompt: "Select a system partition for this boot selection"
- Select: New system partition
- Prompt: "Enter location of the system partition for this boot selection"
- Choose: SCSI Hard Disk
- Prompt: "Enter the osloader directory and name"
- Type: **\os\winnt40\osloader.exe** (example for Windows NT 4.0)
- Prompt: "Enter the location of the OS partition"
- Prompt: "Select media"
- Choose: SCSI Hard Disk
- Prompt: "Enter SCSI bus number"
- (Type in the appropriate bus number; e.g., **0**)
- Prompt: "Enter SCSI ID"
- Type in the appropriate SCSI ID of the shadow drive; e.g., **1**)
- Prompt: "Enter partition"
- (Type in the appropriate partition number; e.g., **0**)
- Prompt: "Enter the operating system root directory"
- (Type in the path; e.g., **\winnt40**)

- Prompt: "Enter the name for this boot selection"
- Type in a name; e.g., **Boot Shadow Drive)**
- Prompt: "Do you want to initialize the debugger at boot time:"
- (Choose Yes or No)

After entering all of the above information, the Setup menu appears again. Select Supplementary Menu, and then Save Changes to exit the Setup menu. The changes are stored in NVRAM. The new boot selection becomes the default for the system. The Manage Boot Selections menu also has an option to reorder system boot selections if you do not want the new selection to be the default. You may wish to reorder the system boot selections if you are creating this entry as a fallback option rather than in response to an actual boot failure (a highly recommended procedure).

The `BOOT.INI` file uses ARC (Advanced RISC Computing) pathnames to indicate the relative location of the Windows NT installation directory. Understanding these ARC pathnames is important if you are attempting to recover from a failed drive in a mirror volume.

The ARC pathnames in the Windows NT `BOOT.INI` file have the following format:

scsi(x)disk(x)rdisk(x)partition(x)
or
multi(x)disk(x)rdisk(x)partition(x)

where:

- *multi*: this indicates a disk adapter which is using its own BIOS (e.g., an IDE/EIDE adapter or a SCSI adapter whose BIOS is enabled); *x* is the adapter's ordinal number. For example, if there are two adapters in the system, the first to load and initialize is assigned 0 and the next is assigned 1.
- *scsi:* this indicates a SCSI disk adapter whose BIOS either doesn't exist or is disabled (this is the default on all RISC-based systems). The syntax and ordinals are the same as they are for *multi*, but the device driver for the SCSI adapter card must be copied to the root of the boot drive (or root of the floppy if booting from a Windows NT Startup Disk) as `NTBOOTDD.SYS` for the system to boot.
- *disk*: for *scsi* syntax (or *multi* where the controller is a SCSI adapter with an enabled BIOS) this is the SCSI ID of the disk; for *multi* with non-SCSI adapters it is always 0.

- *rdisk*: for *scsi* syntax this is always 0; for *multi* it is the ordinal of the disk – that is, the order in which the disk appears in Disk Administrator (disk 0, disk 1, etc.).
- *partition:* the partition where NT is installed. (Partition numbers begin with 1, not 0; all other entries in an ARC pathname use 0 as their starting number.)

For example, a SCSI-based system using its own adapter BIOS (i.e., not a RISC-based system using ARC firmware to boot or an Intel-based system with a SCSI adapter configured to use `NTBOOTDD.SYS`) with the primary drive at ID 0 and the shadow drive at ID 3 might have the following line in its `BOOT.INI` file for the normal startup of Windows NT:

```
multi(0)disk(0)rdisk(0)partition(1)\WINNT="Windows NT Server 4.0"
```

This would indicate that the Windows NT boot partition is located on the first partition of the first disk of the first adapter on the system.

In the event that the primary drive/partition in a mirror set fails, all we need to do to have the Windows NT Startup Disk boot from the shadow drive is modify this line so that it refers to the second (shadow) drive. In this case, this would mean changing `disk(0)` to `disk(3)`. However, if this were a duplexed mirror set (two controllers) we would instead need to change `multi(0)` to `multi(1)` to refer to the second controller. Assuming the drive's relative number on this controller was the same as the primary controller (i.e., also `disk(0)`) then no further changes would be necessary.

Use of DiskSave when a shadow drive won't boot

Occasionally, situations occur where the shadow drive of mirror set fails to boot properly even when the system has been correctly configured to boot from this drive. This happens because when NT starts it checks to see if the System ID byte of the boot drive has the high bit set. Windows NT sets the high bit of the System ID field if the partition is a member of a fault-tolerant volume (such as a mirrored volume). If this bit is set on a drive that is no longer a member of a mirror volume, the system may refuse to boot from the drive.

To get around this problem, you may be able to use a feature of the DiskSave utility discussed earlier in this chapter. In addition to its capability to back up and restore the Master Boot Record and Partition Boot Sector on the boot drive, DiskSave also has an option to disable the Fault Tolerance (FT) bit of a boot drive that was previously a member of a fault-tolerant disk set.

Creating a Fault-Tolerant Boot Floppy in a Pinch

If the primary drive of your mirror set is lost, but you don't have a Windows NT Boot Floppy or another NT system from which to create one, you may not be totally out of luck. Here are steps you can take to create a fault-tolerant Windows NT Boot Floppy "in a pinch":

1. Boot to MS-DOS, either at another system or with a floppy on the current system.
2. Copy the Windows NT Server Setup Boot Floppy (Disk 1) to a blank floppy disk using the DISKCOPY utility or another disk copy utility that copies the entire disk image.
3. Delete all files on the copied disk except `NTDETECT.COM` and `NTLDR`.
4. Expand `NTLDR` as `SETUPLDR.BIN` using the command:

   ```
   EXPAND NTLDR SETUPLDR.BIN
   ```
5. If the mirrored drive is a SCSI disk requiring a SCSI driver to work with Windows NT (i.e., it uses the *scsi(x)* keyword rather than the *multi(x)* keyword in `BOOT.INI`), copy and expand the appropriate SCSI driver from the Windows NT Server Setup Boot Disk and rename it NTBOOTDD.SYS.
6. Using a text editor such as `EDIT.COM`, create a `BOOT.INI` file with an ARC path that points to the Windows NT directory on the mirror partition. You should now be able to use this disk to boot the system from the shadow drive of the mirror set.

To use this option, first follow the directions in the "Using DiskSave to Restore the MBR or PBS" section earlier in this chapter to locate and run the DiskSave utility (which is part of the Windows NT Resource Kit and does not come with Windows NT). After starting DiskSave, choose the F6 – Disable FT on the Boot Drive option from the main menu. Disabling this bit effectively breaks the mirror set and should permit the system to boot from the shadow drive.

You cannot use DiskSave to reenable the FT bit once it has been disabled; however, you can use Disk Administrator to re-enable the FT bit once the failed drive is replaced. Also, if you use the F6 option to turn off the Fault Tolerance bit in order to start a system with a mirror set whose primary drive has failed, you still need to break the mirror using the Windows NT Disk Administrator utility the next time you start Windows NT (this turns off the FT bit in the mirrored drive's partition). This is important because it synchronizes the Registry and disk information, which is essential to proper system operation.

NTRecover: Remote Recovery for Dead NT Systems

One of the more serious problems that can occur on any PC is corruption or a failure of the hard drive subsystem. Because they are software-related in nature, it is likely that the previous methods of recovery described in this chapter won't be of much help in this type of situation. Fortunately, however, there are third-party utilities available to assist you in attempting to repair an NT system that is "dead."

A favorite is the NTRecover utility produced by Mark Russinovich and Bryce Cogswell at NT Internals. This utility is essentially a dead-system recovery utility that works only with x86-based NT systems (RISC versions may become available in the future). Using NTRecover, NT machines that fail to boot because of data corruption, improperly installed software or hardware, or faulty configuration, can be accessed and recovered using standard administrative tools as if the machine were up and running. Using an adjacent NT-based computer connected by a serial cable, NTRecover allows a system administrator to:

- Copy files between the nonbooting system and the working NT system
- Edit or delete files that may be preventing the system from booting
- Run virus detection and removal programs
- Repair damaged file system structures using the CHKDSK utility

NTRecover consists of host and client software, where the host software runs on a working NT system, and the client software executes on the dead system in need of repair. The "dead" system is booted off a floppy disk directly to the NTRecover program, so repair is possible even when basic startup code in NT, such as NTLDR, fails. The host and client machines are connected with a standard null-modem serial cable.

The NTRecover host software creates virtual disk drives on the host machine that represent the drives present on the client computer. When native NT file systems, such as NTFS and FAT, access the drives, NTRecover manages communications over the serial cable to the client software to transfer disk data back and forth between the two machines. As far as Windows NT on the host machine is concerned, the drives created by NTRecover are indistinguishable from the local drives present on the host, so they can be manipulated with Windows NT disk utilties including high-level tools such as the Windows NT Explorer, and low-level tools such as CHKDSK.

The *Optimizing Windows NT* CD-ROM includes a free trial version of NTRecover that behaves just as the retail version, except that it permits only read-access to the damaged system. However, this type of access is sufficient for salvaging data off dead NT systems in situations where no access is otherwise possible. The retail version has the additional capabilities of restoring files or repairing drives (e.g., running CHKDSK, etc.) on a dead system.

Summary

In this chapter, we discussed a number of strategies and techniques for troubleshooting and recovering Windows NT. As you've probably already figured out, an ounce of prevention is truly worth a pound of cure when it comes to Windows NT systems. The ounce of prevention is the creation and maintenance of a complete set of backups and emergency resources for your Windows NT computer; these can become lifesavers should you ever experience a major problem with your system.

Appendix A

What's on the CD-ROM

THE SOFTWARE INCLUDED on the *Optimizing Windows NT* CD-ROM is referenced throughout the book, and provides extended functionality and performance enhancement for your Windows NT system. To view the contents of the CD-ROM, simply insert it into your CD-ROM drive. If you have CD-ROM AutoPlay enabled, your default web browser utility will launch and automatically load the CD's main page.

If you have AutoPlay disabled, you can launch your browser manually and point it to the `INDEX.HTML` file in the root directory of the CD-ROM. If you wish to re-enable CD-ROM AutoPlay, change the data for the following registry value from 0 (disabled) to 1 (enabled): `HKEY_LOCAL_MACHINE\SYSTEM\CurrentControlSet\Services\Cdrom\Autorun`.

The CD-ROM contains third-party tools that can add configuration and performance options to NT, providing functionality beyond that offered with NT's built-in tools. These utilities, in addition to the recommendations and optimization techniques detailed in the book, will provide you with the necessary building blocks to get the most out of your existing hardware and software investments. These tools cover everything from low-level firmware and driver-related settings that can make system hardware run at the limits of its design, to high-level tools and techniques that keep your configuration database safe from harm. Included throughout the chapters are illustrations and screenshots demonstrating the use of these tools.

The author and IDG Books Worldwide make no warranties, expressed or implied, regarding the functionality or suitability of any of these products to a particular task. Furthermore, neither the author nor IDG Books Worldwide shall be liable for any harm to your system or data resulting from the use of these tools. All software provided on the *Optimizing Windows NT* CD-ROM and mentioned within the book is used by you at your own risk.

You must have System Administrator privileges to run most of the programs on this CD-ROM.

To learn more about a particular piece of software, choose its link in the Contents pane on the left side of the screen while viewing the CD, and read through the documentation and any specific installation notes for that application. To install the software for a particular platform, simply click on the "Install Software!" link for the appropriate machine type (i.e. Alpha or Intel).

For example, you might see a listing at the bottom of a page similar to the following:

Install Diskkeeper lite 2.0 for Alpha!
Install Diskkeeper lite 2.0 for Intel!

Clicking one of these links will start the installation routine or self-extracting installer. For programs that use self-extracting installers, you may first need to extract the installation files to a temporary directory on your hard disk (e.g. `C:\TEMP`, etc.) and then run the main installation program which is extracted to this directory (usually this will be `SETUP.EXE` or `INSTALL.EXE`, but could be different for a particular application). Others will automatically launch the program's setup routine for you.

After clicking the link, your browser may ask if you wish to open the file or save it to disk; in this case, choose Open to launch the installer or self-extracting archive utility. Some browsers (e.g. Microsoft Internet Explorer 3.02 or later) will also issue an additional warning about the fact that programs downloaded via browser can contain viruses; choose Yes to continue installing the software.

Most of the software utilities included on the CD are trial, evaluation, or demonstration versions. Some applications are fully functional programs with a self-timed expiration date, while others may have reduced functionality and no expiration date. The choice for how this software is bundled and the length of time the trial software operates is completely up to the software vendor that developed the program. If you should have questions regarding a particular software package, you should direct them to the software vendor and not IDG Books. Before attempting to install any of the programs included on this CD-ROM, be sure to first read the included `README.TXT` file, which provides other important installation information.

The software index is arranged into groups based on product type. This can help you isolate where you want to start if you are reading through a chapter and come across an "On the CD" reference.

For updates, revisions, and/or corrections related to the book or the CD-ROM contents, check the IDG Books Worldwide website at `http://www.idgbooks.com/`, and the author's (Sean Daily) website at `http://www.ntsol.com/books/ownt/`.

You should check the vendor's website link listed at the bottom of each product page for more detailed information, updated software and possible changes in licensing or distribution.

Bench32

Bench32 is a system benchmarking utility that supports the Windows NT platforms (versions 3.51 and 4.0) as well as Windows 95. Bench32 is used throughout Optimizing Windows NT to benchmark the effects of system performance tuning and configuration changes. Bench32 doesn't just run a few loops to verify that your components exist; it is a high level, statistical, analysis tool. Bench32 will perform statistics on all tests performed (if a long test is specified) so that you receive a score that is accurate as possible. Means, distributions, standard deviations, weighting schemes, rejection analysis, error propagation, and regressional algorithms are all subjected on the data that is taken from benchmarking. Bench32 can even tell you if the benchmark performed accurately or not within three levels of accuracy.

Features

Bench32 uses a very wide range of the Win32 API to fully test the capabilities of a Win32 based system. This includes:

- 2-D and 3-D animation
- 3-D rendering, photoeffects
- Other special effects
- Bezier and other advanced API drawing
- Synchronous and Asynchronous Disk I/O
- Cached and Uncached Disk I/O

- Direct and Sequential Disk I/O
- True System RAM Performance testing
- CPU and FPU testing
- Single Processor and Multiple Processor Testing (up to 32 processors)
- And much, much more

Bench32 also adds the usefulness of saving files while still retaining the ability to integrate those files back into the benchmark. This means that a person sending his scores for his SMP machine to another person who uses Bench32 on a single processor machine with different hardware will view the data as if he were on the SMP machine (from the single processor machine).

Bench32 adds many useful graphs whose data is saved with each file. These graphs can also be printed out. Bench32 doesn't just stop here as far as data analysis goes; it allows you to run real-time counters to detect how much CPU time is being used by each and every processor in the system, how many context switches are being made per second, how many interrupts each processor is experiencing per second, how many times an application has to page out to auxiliary memory, how much memory is available at any given instant, and how often an application pages out to disk (thrashing). These figures can often be used to analyze any deviations that might have been seen in benchmarking. Bench32 can allow you to properly analyze your system with very thorough and precise tools. It also makes it simple to view and share the data with others. Bench32 can help you pinpoint any problems that you are experiencing in your system, or give you insurance that your system is performing up to par.

System requirements

Bench32 requires that you have the following present on your system:

- A 486DX/33 microprocessor or higher
- A floating point unit
- Support for 800×600 or higher graphics resolution at 8-bit colors or higher.
- At least 1MB of Video Memory
- Windows 95 or Windows NT
- Minimum of 16MB RAM for Windows 95 (24 recommended) and 24MB for Windows NT
- Windows NT 4.0 (This product will not run under DOS, Windows 3.x, Windows 95, or Windows NT 3.51.)

During the installation of Bench32, you will be asked for an unlocking code. The code you should use is listed below:

SpxLw7-NsOqGB752-4SetuP-v120B32 (note that letters are case-sensitive)

Additional information about Bench32 can be obtained at the vendor's website, at the following URL:

`http://www.usoftware.com/bench32/bench32.html`

Dynameasure

Dynameasure is a high-end server benchmarking and performance evaluation system from Bluecurve, Inc. Included on the *Optimizing Windows NT* CD is an evaluation version called Dynameasure Demo. With Dynameasure Demo, you can explore Bluecurve's new generation of capacity planning and performance measurement software for Microsoft Windows NT and see how this utility can help you proactively manage these system management problems.

Dynameasure Demo includes everything you need to put a measurable, controlled stress on your Windows NT or Windows 95 computer using a real Microsoft Access database, and real database transactions. Dynameasure Demo is a working version of Dynameasure. It includes the same read-only SQL database tests included in Dynameasure for SQL and Dynameasure Enterprise. Dynameasure Demo is different in that it uses a Microsoft Access test database instead of Oracle or Microsoft SQL Server, and the test database must reside on the same computer where Dynameasure Demo is installed.

The purpose of this demo version of Dynameasure is to show you, with your help, how the Dynameasure product family works. And while Dynameasure Demo is not intended to solve capacity and performance problems, it is capable of exploring and teaching you much about the capacity of your system. Dynameasure Demo comes complete with online help and is approximately 5MB in size. You'll need a Windows 95 or Windows NT system, with 16MB of memory to run and operate the demo.

Please be sure to visit the Bluecurve Web site at http://www.bluecurve.com/ for complete information on Bluecurve's complete family of commercially available products including:

- *Dynameasure Enterprise*, the proactive capacity and performance measurement solution over multiple Windows NT services, which is the industry's first and only measurement tool available that supports concurrent testing of multiple Windows NT services
- *Dynameasure for File Services*, the proactive capacity and performance measurement solution for Windows NT file services
- *Dynameasure for SQL*, the proactive capacity and performance measurement solution for SQL with Windows NT, which offers tunable online transaction processing (OLTP) SQL tests with support for Oracle7 Server and Microsoft SQL Server

Additional information about Dynameasure can be obtained at the vendor's website, at the following URL:
http://www.bluecurve.com/

PerfMan

PerfMan, a product of The Information Systems Manager, Inc. (ISM), delivers full control of performance metrics from a complex network of servers and workstations, identifying exception conditions in the network and providing early warning of future performance problems. PerfMan supplements Microsoft's NT Performance Monitor with significant data management, trend analysis, and reporting capabilities, resulting in proactive performance management and capacity planning.

In environments where service levels are critical to success, PerfMan provides these essential elements:

- Data Management
- Centralized Administration
- Data Accessibility
- Early Warning
- Management Reporting

- Open Interface to Database
- Enterprise Scalability
- Automation
- Low Overhead, Non-Intrusive
- Flexible, Change-Friendly Last
- Integrated with Solutions for Other Platforms

Additional information about PerfMan can be obtained from the Sunbelt Software (a distributor of the product) website, at the following URL:

`http://www.ntsoftdist.com/perfman.htm`

or the vendor, The Information Systems Manager's website, at:

`http://www.infosysman.com/perfman/`

Performance Monitor Workspaces

Throughout the Optimizing Windows NT book, we reference specific Performance Monitor counters and objects that can be monitored to determine if particular bottlenecks exist on the system. Once a group of Performance Monitor counter objects have been added for charting or logging, the environment can be saved into a file called a Performance Monitor Workspace (`.PMW` extension) file.

To make it easier for you to create the Performance Monitor sessions discussed in the text, we have included `.PMW` files containing these counter objects. To determine what a particular workspace environment is intended to monitor or what kind of bottleneck it is meant to detect, these data files may be used with Performance Monitor in Windows NT on any platform.

The .PMW files are located on the Optimizing Windows NT CD-ROM in the `\PMWORKSPACE` folder. To open and use one of the `.PMW` files and have Performance Monitor utilize the included counter objects, you have two choices:

1. Open Performance Monitor and use the File→Open option to locate the specific `.PMW` file you wish to open on the CD-ROM.

2. Use the Windows NT Explorer to open the CD-ROM folder containing the .PMW files contained on the CD-ROM (in the \PMWORKSPACE folder) and then use drag and drop to drop the desired workspace file into an empty Performance Monitor window. This will cause Performance Monitor to load the contained counter objects (and, in the case of Chart View, immediately begin charting them).

Despite there being an automatic association between PerfMon and .PMW files, simply clicking on a .PMW file in an Explorer window may not always properly launch Performance Monitor and load the workspace environment. Due to a long filename support issue that exists on some systems, you may find that instead Performance Monitor will load with an empty session. If this happens, choose the View→Options menu item of any Explorer window and select the File Types tab. Next, locate the Registered file type labeled 'Performance Monitor File' and choose Edit to edit the associations for those file types. In the Actions list at the bottom of this dialog, highlight Open and choose Edit. At the end of the command line that is listed in the 'Application used to perform action' box, add the following string: "%1" (including the double quotes). For example, the finished command line might appear as follows: `C:\WINNT\system32\perfmon.exe "%1"`. After making this change, you should be able to double-click any .PMW file and successfully have Performance Monitor launch and load the workspace.

TcpSpeed

TcpSpeed is a utility that allows you to measure the bandwidth that flows over your Internet connection. It works by measuring how many bytes can be blasted over your connection in a given amount of time. This is especially useful for measuring the connection to your local access provider.

Please note that since it really taxes the bandwidth of your computer, the remote computer that you're connecting to, and all intervening computers on the Internet, test durations are limited to 12 seconds. Be kind to the 'net!

The use of TcpSpeed requires `VBRUN300.EXE`. Download this from Microsoft if you don't already have it and put it into your Windows System directory.

Additional information about TcpSpeed can be obtained at the vendor's website, at the following URL:

`http://www.maximized.com/`

Diskeeper Lite

Diskeeper Lite is a high-speed, manual disk defragmentation utility designed specifically for Windows NT 4.0 (build 1381 or higher). Diskeeper was the first commercial defragmentation utility available for Windows NT, and has a large and loyal following among NT users worldwide. Diskeeper makes it easy for you to restore and maintain Windows NT disk subsystem performance.

Diskeeper 2.0, the current version, is ten times faster than Diskeeper v1.0x, has five different priority settings, and installs without modifying any system files (it utilizes the disk defragmentation API built into Windows NT 4.0). For Diskeeper 1.0x users, a free upgrade pack is also available from the Executive Software website, but you must have your original Diskeeper 1.0x CD available.

Additional information about Diskeeper can be obtained at the vendor's website, at the following URL:

`http://www.execsoft.com/`

Speed Disk Live Trial Edition

Speed Disk is a disk defragmentation utility that is part of the Norton Utilities 2.0 for Windows NT, available from Symantec Corporation. Included on this CD is a free Live Trial Edition of Speed Disk. This software runs only on Intel systems.

Speed Disk frees up space and rearranges files into contiguous blocks so you can access them quickly. Monitor the process on-screen or run Speed Disk in the background as a Windows NT service. Adjust the amount of CPU time that Speed Disk uses to accomplish this process. Speed Disk rearranges your files and free space into contiguous blocks. The payoff is faster access to your critical information.

Additional information about Speed Disk can be obtained at the vendor's website, at the following URL:
`http://www.symantec.com/`

SuperCache-NT

SuperCache-NT is a software device driver that can significantly enhance disk drive performance. SuperCache-NT is designed to improve the disk I/O performance of a system by using free physical memory as a disk cache. Whenever the system reads an area of data or code more than once, the data is returned to the requester at fast memory bus speed. The cache saves most of the latencies caused by mechanical actions, controller overhead, I/O bus overhead, and low, level drivers associated with disk access. The effective response times for users or batch jobs on the system can be improved by a factor of over 25 times, depending on the power and number of CPUs in the system, and the amount of free memory available for the cache. SuperCache-NT is a multi-threaded device driver that enhances hard disk drive performance. No changes are made to the Windows NT operating system kernel.

PLATFORM SUPPORT

SuperCache-NT is supported on Windows NT V3.51 and V4.0 on both Intel and Alpha AXP platforms. Both NTFS and FAT partitions are supported by the software. Both the Server and Workstation versions of Windows NT are supported. In addition, all current releases of standard disk device driver software are supported, including shadowing, striping, and RAID. In order to make use of SuperCache-NT, at least 24MB of main memory is required. EEC Systems, Inc. recommends that customers add as much memory as possible to their systems. Windows NT currently supports a maximum of 2GB of memory. SuperCache-NT will use up to 75 percent of system memory as a device cache. Use of memory beyond the current 2GB limit is planned in a future release. Please contact your distributor or EEC Systems, Inc. for further details.

SuperCache-NT supports the following hardware platforms:

- Intel Pentium, Pentium Pro, Pentium II-based Systems
- Alpha AXP-based Systems
- All SMP configurations are supported by multi-threaded code in the device driver

FEATURES

SuperCache-NT dynamically caches disk partitions. The system manager selects which partition is to be cached using the setup tool ScConfig.exe. The partition can be either NTFS or FAT. With the current release, caching of the system partition is supported. During setup, the system manager selects either write through mode or lazy write mode. When the system is re-booted SuperCache-NT is automatically started on the selected partition and immediately allocates 25 percent of the physical memory on the machine to the cache. The cache will grow on demand, using up to 75 percent of the available system memory for data caching. SuperCache-NT has a built-in mechanism for automatically returning memory to the rest of Windows NT when the operating system requires it for other uses. This operation is automatic and transparent to the rest of the system.

In Write Through Data Protection Mode, SuperCache-NT writes data synchronously to the Windows NT lazy write mechanism. If a power failure or system failure were to occur in this mode of operation, data would be protected from loss in exactly the same way as it would be without SuperCache-NT being loaded. In Lazy Write (or Write Back) Data Protection Mode, SuperCache-NT uses a proprietary write caching mechanism to enhance performance even further. Lazy write mode will dramatically improve the performance of write intensive applications. EEC Systems, Inc. recommends the use of an uninterruptible power supply in this mode. If a power failure or system failure occurs while using lazy write mode, the data which has not been flushed to the backing partition will be lost. Use of an uninterruptible power supply will greatly reduce the likelihood of data loss, since SuperCache-NT automatically performs a write flush once a second in the background.

SuperCache-NT has a built-in adaptive read-ahead mechanism. This is useful if sequential file accesses occur. For advanced users, many tuning commands are also available to obtain the very best possible performance from SuperCache-NT. These include adjusting the size of disk transfers which are to be cached by each of the two internal caches in SuperCache-NT, and adjusting the amount of memory used by the lazy write mechanism. Several other parameters may be adjusted by advanced users. For most users, however, SuperCache-NT can be used just as it's delivered.

Once installed, SuperCache-NT is completely transparent to all user and system applications. The only difference users will notice is the increased speed of their applications. No further action by the system manager is required to obtain Super Performance automatically.

RESTRICTIONS

All current releases of standard disk device driver software are supported, excluding software shadowing and software striping. Hardware RAID configurations are supported. In order to make use of SuperCache-NT, at least 24MB of main memory is required. EEC Systems, Inc. recommends that customers add as much memory as possible to their systems.

GUIDELINES FOR USING SUPERCACHE-NT

SuperCache-NT will take 25 percent of the total physical memory at boot time, and from then on automatically allocate or de-allocate memory, based on the needs of the system. It takes 0.4 percent of the size of the partition you choose to cache to map the disk into memory. That is 4MB for every 1GB of storage. This does not include the memory that will be used to cache the data.

For caching to be successful, you have to have available CPU cycles and memory to store the cached data. If you have both of these, then the amount of improvement you will see depends upon how I/O intensive your application is, and how frequently the same data is reread.

An average rule of thumb for calculating memory needs is 48MB of total system memory for the first 1GB of storage you wish to cache, and 16 to 48MB for each additional gigabyte of storage in the partition you wish to cache. Usually more memory is always better. (Of course, there are some applications that have small hot files that are reread so frequently that they can see tremendous gains with less memory than this rule of thumb, but this is not the norm.) Currently there is a limit to the memory the cache can use: the upper limit is 192MB on Intel systems, and 240MB on Alpha systems. (This memory limit also applies to SuperDisk-NT.) The goal is to have an unlimited cache size available within the next 3 to 12 months.

As of this writing, EEC Systems is currently working on a 64-bit VLM (very large memory) version of SuperCache-NT product. Be sure to check the EEC web site at `http://www.eecsys.com/` for the very latest information and versions of their products. With the upcoming VLM versions, NT workstation and server customers will be able to allocate 2GB for RAM Disks and/or the cache. On the Enterprise version of the product, the size of the cache and RAM Disk will be virtually unlimited.

Additional information about SuperCache-NT can be obtained at the vendor's website, at the following URL:

`http://www.eecsys.com/`

SuperDisk-NT

SuperDisk-NT is designed to improve the disk I/O performance of a system by using free physical memory as a RAM Disk. Whenever the system reads an area of data or code, the data is returned to the requester at fast memory bus speed. SuperDisk-NT eliminates all of the latencies caused by mechanical actions, controller overhead, I/O bus overhead, and low-level drivers associated with disk access. The effective response times for users or batch jobs on the system can be improved by a factor of over 30 times, depending on the power and number of CPUs in the system, and the amount of free memory available for SuperDisk-NT. SuperDisk-NT is a multi-threaded device driver that enhances hard disk drive performance. No changes are made to the Windows NT operating system kernel.

PLATFORM SUPPORT

All current releases of standard disk device driver software are supported, excluding software shadowing and software striping. Hardware RAID configurations are supported. In order to make use of SuperDisk-NT at least 16MB of main memory is required. EEC Systems, Inc. recommends that customers add as much memory as possible to their systems. Windows NT currently supports a maximum of 2GB of main memory. SuperDisk-NT will use up to 75 percent of system memory as a RAM disk. Use of memory beyond the current 2GB limit is planned in a future release. Please contact your distributor or EEC Systems, Inc. for further details.

SuperCache-NT supports the following hardware platforms:

- Intel Pentium, Pentium Pro, Pentium II-based Systems
- Alpha AXP-based Systems
- All SMP configurations are supported by multi-threaded code in the device driver

FEATURES

SuperDisk-NT has three modes of operation. It may be configured as a plain RAM Disk, a RAM Disk with write through data protection to a partition, or a RAM Disk with lazy write data protection to a partition. The system manager selects which partition is to be used with the setup tool `SdConfig.exe`. The partition can be either NTFS or FAT. During setup, the system manager selects either a simple RAM Disk, a

RAM Disk with write through data protection, or a RAM Disk with backing to a partition using lazy write mode. When the system is re-booted SuperDisk-NT is automatically started on the selected partition and immediately allocates up to 75 percent of the physical memory on the machine to the RAM Disk.

In Write Through Data Protection Mode, SuperDisk-NT writes data synchronously to the Windows NT lazy write mechanism. If a power failure or system failure were to occur in this mode of operation, data would be protected from loss in exactly the same way as it would be without SuperDisk-NT being loaded. In Lazy Write (or Write Back) Data Protection Mode, SuperDisk-NT uses a proprietary write caching mechanism to enhance performance even further. Lazy write mode will dramatically improve the performance of write intensive applications. EEC Systems, Inc. recommends the use of an uninterruptible power supply in this mode. If a power failure or system failure occurs while using lazy write mode, the data which has not been flushed to the backing partition will be lost. Use of an uninterruptible power supply will greatly reduce the likelihood of data loss, since SuperDisk-NT automatically performs a write flush once a second in the background.

RESTRICTIONS

All current releases of standard disk device driver software are supported, excluding software shadowing and software striping. Hardware RAID configurations are supported. In order to make use of SuperDisk-NT, at least 16MB of main memory is required. EEC Systems, Inc. recommends that customers add as much memory as possible to their systems.

SuperDisk-NT may NOT be used with the system partition. However, it is possible to load many of the system DLLs into memory. SuperDisk-NT allows you to move the system DLLs to the SuperDisk-NT partition (hard disk backing mode only) using the RELODLLS utility included with the product. This will copy the DLLs and make the necessary registry changes to use the frequently accessed DLLs with SuperDisk-NT. If you really want to run the entire system root directories with improved performance, EEC recommends you use their product SuperCache-NT on your system partition. SuperCache-NT now supports caching of the system partition, and caching of the partition containing the page file.

Additional information about SuperDisk-NT can be obtained at the vendor's website, at the following URL:

`http://www.eecsys.com/`

SuperPrint

SuperPrint 5.0 is a print subsystem replacement for Windows NT (and other Windows products), and comes in both standard and high-end versions. SuperPrint standard is for popular desktop printers and transforms Windows into a true 32-bit printing subsystem for smoother multitasking and better background processing. In addition, SuperPrint improves the output quality of graphic and image files. SuperPrint allows you to output Internet-ready files from any Windows application and view/print Web images (GIF, JPEG, & PostScript) with drag-and-drop ease, do PostScript Level 2 printing to non-PostScript devices, and do screen previews of documents to be printed. SuperPrint's use of compact metafiles improves client PC performance and reduces traffic across networks. SuperPrint supports Windows 3.1x, 95, NT 3.51, and NT 4.0.

SuperPrint is a set of advanced printing tools for windows designed to provide faster, better, and smoother printing. SuperPrint replaces Windows' 16-bit print subsystem with 32-bit technology for smoother multitasking and better background processing. Included are SuperDrivers for Windows 3.1x, 95, NT 3.51 and NT 4.0, with controls for sharpness, contrast, lightness, saturation, dot gain, and hue matching. You can drag and drop bitmaps into SuperPrint's image filters to print without other applications. The automatic lightness and contrast enhancements provide the best possible output when you print.

Additional information about SuperPrint can be obtained at the vendor's website, at the following URL: `http://www.zeno.com/`

NTInternals utilities

The NTInternals utilities are a group of excellent Windows NT-related applications written by Dr. Mark Russinovich and Bryce Cogswell. These utilities provide advanced functionality, control, and monitoring capabilities in the Windows NT environment. Each utility is described below along with notes on system requirements, warnings, and other important information. The *Optimizing Windows NT* CD includes a number of NTInternals utilities, including Cacheman, NTFilemon, NTFrob, NTRecover, NTRegmon, NTSync, NTFSDOS, and more.

Additional information about the NTInternals utilities can be obtained at the vendor's website, at the following URL:

`http://www.ntinternals.com/`

TweakBIOS

TweakBIOS is an advanced BIOS configuration utility supporting systems using the Intel FX, HX, VX, TX, and Natoma chipsets (versions for other chipsets are expected soon). This software runs on Intel platforms only and will only run while the system is booted under MS-DOS boot. The program cannot be run from a Windows NT Command Prompt window due to direct hardware access used by the program. This shareware program lets you tune your chipset, probably more than any "real" BIOS. And using it is simple; you don't have to worry about "flashing" your BIOS, you can run it from the DOS prompt.

This program works with most computers using one of the following chipsets, regardless of the BIOS: Intel 430FX (Triton), Intel 430HX (Triton II), Intel 430VX (Triton III), Intel 430TX, Intel 440FX (Natoma), Intel 450KX/GX (Orion), Intel 430MX, AMD-640, VIA VP-2, OPTi Viper and Vendetta, ALi Aladdin 2, and UMC 881 chipsets.

Here's just a few of the motherboards using these chipsets:

- Most Asus Pentium, Pentium Pro, and Pentium II motherboards
- Most Abit Pentium, Pentium Pro, and Pentium II motherboards
- Most Intel Pentium, Pentium Pro, and Pentium II motherboards
- Micro Star, Supermicro, Tyan, Shuttle/Spacewalker, Gigabyte, Soyo, Biostar, FIC, CMC, and many other motherboards

You can change all the settings on the left side of the TweakBIOS display (without rebooting your computer), regardless of what motherboard or BIOS you have. On the right side of the display is information about your DRAM and Cache configuration, and also the actual DRAM and Cache timings, based on the current configuration.

Additional information about TweakBIOS can be obtained at the author's website, at the following URL:

`http://www.miro.pair.com/tweakbios/`

ConfigSafe

Artisoft ConfigSafe enables you to easily recover from PC crashes with one-step system restoration and advanced tracking features. ConfigSafe can automatically track changes to important system configuration files including the system Registry, `.INI` files, `AUTOEXEC.BAT`, `CONFIG.SYS`, and others. It also allows you to easily view changes that have been made and restore previous configurations from backups.

ConfigSafe is a life-saver for growing businesses as operating systems become more complex, technical support more expensive, and downloadable software more common. It costs less than one service call and saves you dozens of future support charges and many hours of expensive downtime. (Note: ConfigSafe is a trademark of imagine LAN, Inc.)

Additional information about ConfigSafe can be obtained at the vendor's website, at the following URL:
`http://www.artisoft.com/`

ULTRABAC

ULTRABAC from BEI Software is a high-performance backup software for expedited disaster recovery. ULTRABAC incorporates Image Backup Technology with Boot Floppy Restore for Windows NT version 4.0. Now both image and file-based backups can be scheduled together during the same session to tape. ULTRABAC is NT 4.0 compliant and supports all O/S versions. Other major enhancements include Optional Microsoft Exchange and SQL Agents, which allow either full or incremental backup of active databases, media rotation and password protection, and an upgraded ULTRAVUE network backup administration module.

Additional information about ULTRABAC can be obtained at the vendor's website, at the following URL:
`http://www.ultrabac.com/`

Appendix B

Other Sources of Information

IN THIS APPENDIX, I'll introduce you to a number of resources that are available for Windows NT users and administrators. These resources include training materials such as books, CD-ROMs, and videos, as well as on-line resources such as web sites and FTP servers that contain NT FAQs (Frequently Asked Questions lists) and utilities. There are also a number of USENET newsgroups, e-mail list discussion groups, and regional NT user groups you can join to share thoughts, questions, and information with other Windows NT users.

Microsoft TechNet CD-ROM

A "must have" for any Windows NT power user or system administrator is a subscription to the Microsoft Technet CD. Technet is easily one of the most valuable informational resources available to people using or administrating systems running Microsoft software. The CDs include a wealth of valuable information, tips, patches, utilities, products descriptions, whitepapers, technology primers, and current events. In addition, each CD contains the entire contents of the Microsoft Knowledge Base, a database of all of the technical questions and answers about every imaginable Microsoft product. More often than not, I have found the answers to my questions and problems on the TechNet CD.

TechNet is sold on a subscription basis, both from Microsoft directly and through booksellers and other retail outlets. To order it, visit your local computer reseller or bookseller, or contact Microsoft Product Sales directly. You can also get more information on TechNet from Microsoft's World Wide Web server at http://www.microsoft.com/technet/.

Windows NT Server and Workstation Resource Kits

The Windows NT Resource Kit, which is available in both Server and Workstation versions, is a collection of extremely useful information and utilities for Windows NT. The Workstation version is a 1,350 page tome chocked full of NT Workstation-related information that isn't included in the Windows NT Workstation product documentation. It also includes a CD-ROM that contains a number of very useful utilities and supplemental help files. The Server version includes three volumes ("Internet Guide," "Resource Guide," and "Networking Guide") that cover in-depth topics about the architecture and design of Windows NT, as well as advanced networking concepts. Like the Workstation version, it includes a CD-ROM full of useful utilities and information. The Server CD is a superset of the NT Workstation Resource Kit CD, containing several additional utilities such as a Remote Console application, a Telnet Daemon, and a POP3 Mail Server. You'll find many of the Resource Kit utilities to be invaluable tools, and probably end up wondering how you ever got along without them!

Since the Windows NT 4.0 Resource Kits first shipped, Microsoft has also shipped two important updates: Supplement One and Supplement Two. These contain important updates that address new Service Pack releases of Windows NT that shipped after the Resource Kit was released, and new topics of interest. They are usually available in the same bookstores that carry the base Resource Kit. It is recommended that you purchase both of these supplemental updates in addition to the base Resource Kit, so that you'll have the most up-to-date copies of the Resource Kit utilities and information.

Here's a quick list of just a few of the gems located on the Resource Kit CD-ROMs:

- Shutdown utility for shutting down and restarting NT systems remotely (both graphical and command-line versions)
- AutoLogon utility for configuring a system to automatically login without prompting for username and password
- Telnet daemon (service) for allowing client access to an NT system via Telnet
- Perl 5 Scripting Language
- Time server service for automatic time synchronization with public time servers
- C2 security auditing and configuration utility
- "AT" command (command scheduling) graphical front end/management utility
- Disk probe disk sector editor
- Fault tolerance configuration editor

- Windows NT Setup management utility for creating unattended answer files (UAFs)
- File and directory comparison utility
- Graphical TCP/IP configuration viewer

The NT Resource Kits are available from Microsoft Press or at your local bookstore, and information about it can be found on Microsoft's World Wide Web server at `http://www.microsoft.com/`.

Windows NT 3.51 Training Kit and 4.0 Upgrade Training Kit

Another useful learning tool is the Windows NT Training Kit, another Microsoft Press offering. It is a self-paced training kit which helps you learn basic and advanced concepts about Windows NT, and is particularly helpful for individuals studying to take Microsoft's Windows NT Certified Professional exams. It includes information on the installation, configuration, optimization, and troubleshooting of NT, as well as advanced topics related to Windows NT networking. It comes with two books, several disks containing practice files, support and troubleshooting utilities, and a video that demonstrates Windows NT networking concepts. Unfortunately, the base training kit has not yet been updated to version 4.0 of NT; instead, Microsoft ships an NT 4.0 version as an "upgrade" to the base training kit. The 4.0 Upgrade Training Kit contains no books and instead comes on a CD-ROM and uses a Computer Based Training (CBT) format.

Internet Resources

Many of the most valuable Windows NT-related resources are available for free on the Internet. There are a number of FTP servers with Windows NT-related files and World Wide Web servers with pages dedicated to Windows NT and NT users. In addition, there are also several e-mail list discussions that a variety of users participate in to exchange information about Windows NT and other Microsoft BackOffice products.

World Wide Web and FTP servers

When searching the Internet for Windows NT-related sites, try the locations listed in Table B-1. Many of these sites also contain links to other useful NT-related sites on the Internet.

Table B-1 WINDOWS NT-RELATED INTERNET RESOURCES

Description of Resource	Internet Location (URL)
Microsoft's WWW Home Page	`http://www.microsoft.com/`
Microsoft's FTP Server (NT-related Files)	`ftp://ftp.microsoft.com /bussys/winnt/`
Microsoft KnowledgeBase On-line	`http://www.microsoft.com/kb/`
Microsoft BackOffice Home Page	`http://backoffice.microsoft.com/`
NT Seek (NT Utilities Search Database)	`http://www.ntseek.com/`
Windows NT Magazine Web Site	`http://www.winntmag.com/`
The Windows NT Resource Center at Beverly Hills Software	`http://www.bhs.com/`
NT Internals (NT Utilities and Information)	`http://www.ntinternals.com/`
The iNformaTion Page	`http://www.rmm.com/nt/`
Digital's Windows NT Info Center	`http://www.windowsnt.digital.com/`
Coast to Coast Software Repository (NT-related Files)	`ftp://ftp.coast.net/coast/nt/`
European Microsoft Windows NT Academic Center (EMWAC)	`http://emwac.ed.ac.uk/`
JSI, Inc. (Registry Hacks & Tweaks)	`http://www.jsiinc.com/`
SomarSoft (NT Utilities)	`http://www.somarsoft.com/`
Sunbelt Software Distribution (NT Utilities)	`http://www.ntsoftdist.com /ntsoftdist/`
Network Specialist NT Home Page	`http://infotech.kumc.edu/`

E-mail List Discussion Groups

There are a number of excellent e-mail list discussion groups on the Internet that are dedicated to Windows NT and Microsoft BackOffice-related topics. These are great places to ask questions, help out fellow NT users, and generally learn more about NT issues and technology. When you join an e-mail discussion group, all messages posted by a user to the list's e-mail address are automatically copied to all of the list's members. That way, you can post questions and information and have these messages seen by other list members, who can also then respond to your post either privately or via a group post to the list.

Table B-2 WINDOWS NT-RELATED INTERNET E-MAIL LIST DISCUSSIONS GROUPS

List Name	List Posting Address (use to send mail to the list)	List Server Administration Address (for join/ leave requests)	Subscription/Join Command (Place in Body of Subscribe Message)
The International Windows NT Users Group	`Iwntug@bhs.com`	`list@bhs.com`	Join iwntug
Windows NT Discussion List	`Windows-nt@ mailbase.ac.uk`	`Mailbase@ mailbase.ac.uk`	Windows-nt *firstname lastname*
NT Lanman List	`Lanman-l@ list.nih.gov`	`Listserv@ list.nih.gov`	Subscribe lanman-l
Windows NT Give-and-Take Forum	`Winnt-l@peach. ease.lsoft.com`	`Listserv@peach. ease.lsoft.com`	Sub winnt-l *firstname lastname*
NT List	`Nt-list@netspot. city.unisa. edu.au`	`Listproc@ netspot. city.unisa. edu.au`	Subscribe nt-list *your email address*
Windows NT Consultants Forum	`Ntconsult@bhs.com`	`list@bhs.com`	Join ntconsult
NT Developer List	`Ntdev@atria.com`	`Majordomo@ atria.com`	Ntdev *your email address*

To join an e-mail discussion group, you must send a subscribe/join request to the list server which administrates the list. Note that this is usually a separate address from the actual address where list e-mail is sent (the list posting address); try to avoid sending join requests to the list posting address, since it won't do anything except annoy list members.

Several Windows NT list discussion groups, along with their posting address, list server request address, and list server request commands, are listed in Table B-2. To join a list, send an e-mail message to the e-mail address listed in the "List Server Administration Address" column, and put the information in the "Subscription/Join Command" column as the body of the message. Do not put any other information in the body of the message, such as signature lines, etc., or the request may not be processed properly by the list server. To send mail to the list, use the address listed in the "List Posting Address" column.

USENET Newsgroups

Another e-mail-related forum for Windows NT information and assistance is USENET (NNTP) newsgroups. Newsgroups are public discussion forums which you can view messages on and post messages to. To view newsgroups, you must use an Internet newsreader application (such as the Internet News utility included with Microsoft Internet Explorer 3.0) and have access to a news server. Most Internet Service Providers provide an NNTP news server as part of their basic service.

Here are a few of the groups available on most news servers that relate to Windows NT:

- `comp.os.ms-windows.nt.misc`
- `comp.os.ms-windows.nt.setup`
- `comp.os.ms-windows.nt.admin.misc`
- `comp.os.ms-windows.nt.admin.networking`
- `comp.os.ms-windows.nt.software.backoffice`
- `comp.os.ms-windows.nt.software.compatibility`
- `comp.os.ms-windows.nt.software.services`

Additional newsgroups are available via news servers run by Microsoft Corporation themselves. Like the previous newsgroups, these groups are publicly available, but require that you point your news reader to the following server: microsoft.public.windowsnt.

Using this server, the following newsgroups may be of interest to you:

- microsoft.public.windowsnt.apps
- microsoft.public.windowsnt.dfs
- microsoft.public.windowsnt.dns
- microsoft.public.windowsnt.domain
- microsoft.public.windowsnt.dsmnfpnw
- microsoft.public.windowsnt.fsft
- microsoft.public.windowsnt.mac
- microsoft.public.windowsnt.mail
- microsoft.public.windowsnt.misc
- microsoft.public.windowsnt.personalfax
- microsoft.public.windowsnt.print
- microsoft.public.windowsnt.protocol.ipx
- microsoft.public.windowsnt.protocol.misc
- microsoft.public.windowsnt.protocol.ras
- microsoft.public.windowsnt.protocol.tcpip
- microsoft.public.windowsnt.setup

Windows NT users groups

There are many Windows NT users groups across the globe. NT users groups are excellent places for avid Windows NT users to share information, ideas, and problems with other NT users, see previews of current and upcoming products, and occasionally receive group purchasing discounts.

Check the Windows NT users groups listed in Table B-3 to see if one is located near you; if not, consider starting one!

TABLE B-3 WINDOWS NT USERS GROUPS WORLDWIDE

State/Country	Users Group	World Wide Web Home Page Contact E-mail or Phone
	International Windows NT Users Group	http://iwntug.org/
	Worldwide Association of NT Users Groups	http://www.wantug.org/
Alabama	Birmingham Windows NT Users Group	http://www.ortho.uab.edu/bwntug/
Alaska	Anchorage Windows NT Users Group	http://rmm.com/awntug/
	Fairbanks Windows NT Users Group	http://tmg.imagi.net/nt/ rmarty@imagi.net
	Interior Alaska Windows NT Users Group	http://www.iawntug.org/iawntug/
Arizona	Phoenix PC Users Group Windows NT SIG	http://www.phoenixpcug.org/sigs/nt/
	Phoenix Windows NT Users Group	http://budman.cmdl.noaa.gov/RMWNTUG/User_Groups/PHXNTUG.HTM majordomo@tsiung.dist.maricopa.edu, send "subscribe pintouch"
Arkansas	Central Arkansas NT Users Group	Cantug@arkansas.net
Australia	Brisbane NT Users Group	http://www.ozemail.com.au/~dkowald/bntug.htm M.Miller-Crispe@eas.gu.edu.au or dkowald@ozemail.com.au
	Canberra NT Users Group	neil.pinkerton@cao.mts.dec.com

continued

State/Country	Users Group	World Wide Web Home Page Contact E-mail or Phone
	Melbourne NT Users Group	comelb@yarra.vicnet.net.au or woodcock@ariel.ucs.unimelb.edu.au
	Melbourne-Australian NT Users Group	Rcomg@chucich.cse.rmit.edu.au
	Newcastle NT Users Group	barclay@msmailnt.bhpese.oz.au
	Sydney NT Users Group	robg@pactok.peg.apc.org
	Tasmania NT Users Group	n_alam@postoffice.utas.edu.au
	Wollongong NT Users Group	phil.p.m.evans@msmail.bhp.com.au
Austria	Windows User Group Austria (WUG)	http://www.wug.or.at/wug/
Belgium	Belgium NT Users Group	Wim.VanHolder@econ.kuleuven.ac.be
California	Bay Area (northern California) Local Users Group	http://bayvax.decus.org/
	Bay Area Windows NT User Group	http://wyp.net/users/ntgroup/
	Belmont NT Users Group	http://www.actioninc.com/winntug.htm
	Berkeley	erutsch@sirius.com
	Hayward PC Club/NT SIG	Jchrist@ccnet.com
	Los Angeles NT Users Group	http://budman.cmdl.noaa.gov/RMWNTUG/User_Groups/LAMEET2.HTM markkap@cerfnet.com

continued

Table B-3 WINDOWS NT USERS GROUPS WORLDWIDE *(Continued)*

State/Country	Users Group	World Wide Web Home Page Contact E-mail or Phone
	Los Angeles Windows NT Microsoft Networking Users Group	http://www.lantug.org/
	Northern California Windows NT Users Group	http://www.actioninc.com/winntug.htm
	Oakland NT Users Group	kenh@TFS.COM
	Orange County Windows NT User Group	http://www.ocntug.org/
	San Diego County Windows NT Users Group	http://www.bhs.com/sdug/
	San Diego NT Users Group	clbrown@netcom.com
	Ventura NT Users Group	JKashihara@AOL.COM
	Windows NT Engineering Association of Silicon Valley (NTEA)	Michael@maserson.com
Canada	GEANT Quebec: Le Groupe des Experts en Administration NT du Quebec	http://www.geant.org/
	GUBOQ: Group des Utilisateurs BackOffice du Quebec	Eric@zenon.com
	Ontario NT Users Group	http://www.ontug.org
	Vancouver NT Users Group	http://www.vantug.com/
Colorado	Northern Colorado Windows NT Users Group	Brian@ataman.com
	Rocky Mountain SQL Server Users Group	Sonnyhdrk@aol.com
	Rocky Mountain Windows NT Users Group	http://budman.cmdl.noaa.gov/rmwntug/rmwntug.htm

continued

State/Country	Users Group	World Wide Web Home Page Contact E-mail or Phone
Florida	Florida Developer/System Engineer Users Group	http://www.homnick.com /ugnews.htm
	Greater Orlando NT Users Group	Pmod@magicnet.com
	Orlando NT Users Group	pmod@magicnet.net
	Tampa Bay NT Users Group	Sharkeyman@aol.com
	Windows NT SIG, Tampa Bay Paradox Users Group	http://www.infep.com /tbug.htm
France	French NT Users Group (Utilisateurs Français et Francophones de Windows NT)	http://fwntug.org/
Georgia	Atlanta NT Users Group	74777.2127@compuserve.com
	Greater Atlanta BackOffice Users Group	Lisa@intelli.net
Germany	Bonn NT Users Group	siegfried@nibelungen. rhein.de
	Paderborn NT Users Group	gruss@syskoplan.de
Hawaii	HINTUG: Hawaiian Islands NT Users Group	http://www.aloha.com/ ~brettc/hintug.html
Illinois	Champaign NT Users Group	kashi@uiuc.edu
	Chicago Area Internet Society NT SEG (CAIS NT SIG)	Dawn@uhost.com
	Chicago Area NT Business Users Group (CANTBUG)	Pkauppi@specgrp.com
	Chicago Computer Society Windows NT SIG	http://ww.mcs.com/ ~thomas/www/ntsig/
	Chicago NT Users Group	burger@sphinx.ece.wisc.edu
	Great Lakes SQL Server User Group	Don@rdisoft.com

continued

TABLE B-3 WINDOWS NT USERS GROUPS WORLDWIDE *(Continued)*

State/Country	Users Group	World Wide Web Home Page Contact E-mail or Phone
Indiana	Windows NT Users Group of Indianapolis	http://www.wintugi.org/
Japan	Japan Windows NT Users Group (JWNTUG)	http://www.t3.rim.or.jp/~rkaneko/
Kansas	Kansas City Windows NT Users Group	http://www.sound.net ~/darksol/masug/ nw7301@tyrell.net
	Topeka/Kansas City NT Users Group	lad@tinman.dot.state.ks.us or srodgers@kumc.wpo.ukans.edu
	Wichita NT Users Group (WNTUG)	http://www.nvt.net/wntug/
Kentucky	NT Bluegrass User Group	http://www.orb-bit.com/ntbug/
Maine	Aroostook NT User Group	http://www.aroostook.org/
Maryland	Columbia Baltimore User Group (CBUG) NT SIG	http://www.techarchitects.com/
Massachusetts	New England Windows NT Users Group	http://www.nentug.org/
Michigan	Detroit NT Users Group	jeff@oak.oakland.edu
	Southeastern Michigan Windows NT User Group	http://ourworld.compuserve.com:80/homepages /MI_WINNTUG/
Minnesota	Microsoft Windows NT Server User Group	http://www.skypoint.com/subscribers/dpmadson/wintug.html
	Minneapolis	quadling@mnhepo.hep.umn.edu
	Minneapolis-Windows NT Users Group	http://tomys.ecology.umn.edu/ntug/

continued

State/Country	Users Group	World Wide Web Home Page Contact E-mail or Phone
	Minnesota Windows NT Users Group	http://mnntl.hep.umn.edu/mwntug.htm
Missouri	St. Louis CAD/NT Users Group	http://www.direct-data.com
Montana	Big Sky Users Group	http://www.softworx.com/nt/
Nebraska	NT Omaha	Jpashan@neonramp.com
Nevada	Las Vegas PC User Group Windows NT Advance User SIG	Mark_Scarborough@lasvegas-nexus.com
New Jersey	New Jersey NT Users Group	djs@cnj.digex.net
	NJ BackOffice User Group	http://www.msboug.org/
New Mexico	Albuquerque Windows NT Users Group	http://mack.rt66.com/jheald/ntuser.htm jheald@RT66.com
New York	Capital District NT/ BackOffice User Group	http://www.albany.net/~capnt/
	Gotham Windows NT User Group	http://wwwntweb.org/gwntug.html
	Long Island PC User Group (LIPCUG)	http://www.i.net/-lipcug/
	New York City NT Developers SIG	Tony@dhbrown.com
	New York City NT Users Group	http://budman.cmdl.noaa.gov/RMWNTUG/User_Groups/NYNTSIG3.HTM lee_t@access.digex.net or iams@smosna.cs.nyu.edu
	New York PC Windows NT Developers Group	http://budman.cmdl.noaa.gov/rmwntug/User_Groups/nyntsig3.htm
	New York Windows NT Users Group	71052.2677@compuserve.com

continued

Table B-3 WINDOWS NT USERS GROUPS WORLDWIDE *(Continued)*

State/Country	Users Group	World Wide Web Home Page Contact E-mail or Phone
	NYC/Long Island NT Users Group	anthonyc@QUEENS.LIB.NY.US
North Carolina	Asheville NT Users Group	mcmurtry@mail.montreat.edu
	Triangle NT Users Group	http://www.nando.net /ads/ncs/
Ohio	Greater Cleveland PC User Group/Windows NT SIG	http://www.gcpcug.org/
Oregon	Portland Area Windows NT User Group (PANTUG)	http://www.involved.com /pantug/
	Portland Area Windows NT Users Group	http://www.inprot.com/nt/
Pennsylvania	Philadelphia Area Windows NT User Group (PANT)	http://www.pant.reohr.com/
	Philadelphia NT Users Group	http://www.netaxs.com/ ~aengel/PHLNTUG/welcome. html aengel@netaxs.com or arnie@pond.com
	Philadelphia Windows NT Users Group	http://www.netaxs.com/ ~aengel/PHLNTUG/welcome. html
Rhode Island	Rhode Island NT User Group	http://www.wsbinc.com/
Russia	Russian Windows NT User Group	http://www.quarta.msk.u/
Singapore	DECUS NT Special Interest Group	Murali@csn.st.com.sg
Slovenia, Republic of	Slovenian Windows NT Users Group	http://WWW.SWINTUG.SI/

continued

State/Country	Users Group	World Wide Web Home Page Contact E-mail or Phone
South Carolina	Greenville NT Users Group	pp000106@interramp.com
Switzerland	CERN Windows NT Users Group	http://www.cern.ch/NTUG/
	Switzerland NT Users Group	deffer@eunet.ch
Taiwan	Microsoft Windows NT Taiwan Users Group (TWNTUG)	http://ntcda.tl.ntu.edu.tw/
Tennessee	Chattanooga-River Valley NT User Group	James@press.southern.edu
	Memphis NT Users Group	bill-spencer@mail.psyc.memphis.edu
	Nashville NT Users Group	foxhunter@telalink.net
Texas	Austin NT Users Group	pasha@austin.ibm.com
	Central Texas LAN Association (CTLA) CTLA's Windows NT SIG	http://www.ctla.org/
	Dallas BackOffice User Group (DBUG)	http://www.debug.org/
	Dallas NT Users Group	http://budman.cmdl.noaa.gov/RMWNTUG/User_Groups/DLSUGAN.HTM deborahl@microsoft.com
	El Paso NT Users Group	chuckko@primenet.com
	Houston NT Users Group	vandusen@NeoSoft.com
	Microsoft Networking SIG	http://www.ntpcug.org/sigs/msnetwrk/index.htm
	North Texas PC Users Group	http://budman.cmdl.noaa.gov/rmwntug/User_Groups/dlsugan.htm
United Kingdom	Windows NT UK User Group (WINNTUUG)	NTUSER@TSAUK.DEMON.CO.UK

continued

Table B-3 **WINDOWS NT USERS GROUPS WORLDWIDE** *(Continued)*

State/Country	Users Group	World Wide Web Home Page Contact E-mail or Phone
Virginia	Northern Virginia NT Users Group	Prrtap@erols.com
	Richmond BackOffice Users Group (RichBUG)	Listorj@infi.net
	Virginia NT Users Group	sova@infi.net
Washington	BackOffice Professional Association (BOPA)	http://BOPA.ORG
	Spokane NT User Group (NeTUG)	http://netug.skywalk.com/
Washington, D.C.	Exchange Users Group	Spyros@paradigms.com
	Metro Area SQL Server Users Group	Brian@datafocus.com
	Mid-Atlantic VC++ User Group	Brossart@rdaconsultants.com
	Washington, D.C. SQL Server Users Group	brian@datafocus.com
	Enterprise Server Integration Local Users Group (ESILUG)	http://www.decus.org/decus/lugs/esilug/
	NT Pro	http://www.ntpro.org/
	Washington, D.C. NT Users Group	ckelly@cpcug.org
Wisconsin	Green Bay NT Users Group	bvoltmer@online.dct.com
	Wisconsin NT User Group (WINTUG)	http://www.wintug.org/
	Wisconsin NT Users Group	burger@sphinx.ece.wisc.edu

Commercial Training Products

In addition to the free resources available on the Internet, there are also a large number of commercial training products available for Windows NT training. They range from cheap to very expensive, and many include discussions of areas not covered in the Microsoft Press products. Table B-4 lists a number of these NT training products, their focus, and important information on the manufacturer/distributor of each.

TABLE B-4 COMMERCIAL WINDOWS NT TRAINING PRODUCTS

Vendor	Type of Product	World Wide Web Address	Phone Number
LearnKey Systems, Inc.	Video and CD-ROM Training Products	`http://www.learnkey.com/`	(800) 865-0165
KeyStone Learning Systems	Video Training Products	`http://www.klscorp.com/`	(800) 748-4838
CBT Systems, Inc.	CD-ROM CBT Training Software	`http://www.cbtsys.com/`	(800) 387-0932
Transcender Corp.	Exam Preparation Software	`http://www.transcender.com/`	(615) 726-8779
Wave Technology, Int'l.	Book and Video Training Products	`http://www.wavetech.com/`	(888) 204-6143
Mastering Computers	Videos, CBT Software, and Training Seminars	`http://www.masteringcomputers.com/`	(800) 800-9686

Another excellent source of Windows NT information is any of a number of commercial "snail mail" newsletters delivered by the good old USPS. One such newsletter is *Exploring Windows NT*, by the Cobb Group, which contains a number of handy NT tips, tricks, and information in each monthly issue.

You can obtain additional information about the *Exploring Windows NT* newsletter at The Cobb Group's website, at:

`http://www.cobb.com/ewn/`

Appendix C

Index of Performance Monitor Objects and Counters

THIS APPENDIX PROVIDES a listing of performance-related Performance Monitor objects and the counters related to those objects. You can monitor these counters using the Windows NT Performance Monitor application to determine where bottlenecks and other problems lie in your system. Windows NT 4.0 provides a superset of those objects and counters found in version 3.51; both are included in this table.

For information on using the Windows NT Performance Monitor utility, see the "Meet Your Toolkit" section of Chapter 4, "NT Optimization 101."

TABLE C-1 PERFORMANCE-RELATED OBJECTS AND COUNTERS IN THE WINDOWS NT PERFORMANCE MONITOR

Object/Counter Name	Description	Default Scale	Counter Type	Counter Size
AppleTalk Object	**AppleTalk Protocol-related counters**			
AARP Packets/sec	Number of AARP packets per second received by AppleTalk on this port.	0.1	PERF_COUNTER_COUNTER	4 bytes
ATP ALO Response/sec	Number of ATP At-least-once transaction responses per second on this port.	1	PERF_COUNTER_COUNTER	4 bytes
ATP Packets/sec	Number of ATP packets per second received by AppleTalk on this port.	0.1	PERF_COUNTER_COUNTER	4 bytes
ATP Received Release/sec	Number of ATP transaction release packets per second received on this port	0.1	PERF_COUNTER_COUNTER	4 bytes
ATP Response Timeouts	Number of ATP release timers that expired on this port.	1	PERF_COUNTER_RAWCOUNT	4 bytes
ATP Retries Local	Number of ATP requests of a local origin retransmitted on this port.	0.1	PERF_COUNTER_RAWCOUNT	4 bytes
ATP Retries Remote	Number of ATP requests of a remote origin retransmitted to this port.	0.1	PERF_COUNTER_RAWCOUNT	4 bytes

ATP XO Response/Sec	Number of ATP Exactly-once transaction responses per second on this port.	0.1	PERF_COUNTER_COUNTER	4 bytes
Average Time/AARP Packet	Average time in milliseconds to process an AARP packet on this port.	1	PERF_AVERAGE_BULK	8 bytes
Average Time /ATP Packet	Average time in milliseconds to process an ATP packet on this port.	1	PERF_AVERAGE_BULK	8 bytes
Average Time/DDP Packet	Average time in milliseconds to process a DDP packet on this port.	1	PERF_AVERAGE_BULK	8 bytes
Average Time/NBP packet	Average time in milliseconds to process an NBP packet on this port.	1	PERF_AVERAGE_BULK	8 bytes
Average Time/RTMP packet	Average time in milliseconds to process an RTMP packet on this port.	1	PERF_AVERAGE_BULK	8 bytes
Average Time/ZIP Packet	Average time in milliseconds to process a ZIP packet on this port.	1	PERF_AVERAGE-BULK	8 bytes
Bytes In/sec	Number of bytes received per second by AppleTalk on this port.	0.0001	PERF_COUNTER_BULK_COUNT	8 bytes
Bytes Out/sec	Number of bytes sent per second by AppleTalk on this port.	0.0001	PERF_COUNTER_BULK_COUNT	8 bytes
Current NonPagedPool	The current amount of nonpaged memory resources used by AppleTalk.	0.0001	PERF_COUNTER_RAWCOUNT	4 bytes
DDP Packet/sec	Number of DDP packets per second received by AppleTalk on this port.	0.1	PERF_COUNTER_COUNTER	4 bytes

Object/Counter Name	Description	Default Scale	Counter Type	Counter Size
AppleTalk Object				
NBP Packets/sec	Number of NBP packets per second received by AppleTalk on this port.	0.1	PERF_COUNTER_COUNTER	4 bytes
Packets dropped	Number of packets dropped due to resource limitations on this port.	1	PERF_COUNTER_RAWCOUNT	4 bytes
Packets In/sec	Number of packets received per second by AppleTalk on this port.	0.1	PERF_COUNTER_COUNTER	4 bytes
Packets Out/sec	Number of packets sent per second received by AppleTalk on this port.	0.1	PERF_COUNTER_COUNTER	4 bytes
Packets Routed In/sec	Number of packets routed in on this port.	1	PERF_COUNTER_COUNTER	4 bytes
Packets Routed Out/sec	Number of packets routed out on this port.	1	PERF_COUNTER_COUNTER	4 bytes
RTMP Packets/sec	Number of RTMP packets per second received by AppleTalk on this port.	0.1	PERF_COUNTER_COUNTER	4 bytes
ZIP Packets/sec	Number of ZIP packets per second received by AppleTalk on this port.	0.1	PERF_COUNTER_COUNTER	4 bytes
Browser Object	**Browser Statistics**			
Announcements Domain/sec	The rate at which a Domain has announced itself to the network.	1	PERF_COUNTER_BULK_COUNT	8 bytes

Announcements Server/sec	The rate at which the servers in this domain have announced themselves to the server.	1	PERF_COUNTER_BULK_COUNT	8 bytes
Announcements Total/sec	The sum of Announcements Server/sec and Announcements Domain/sec.	1	PERF_COUNTER_BULK_COUNT	8 bytes
Duplicate Master Announcements	The number of times that the master browser has detected another master browser on the same domain.	1	PERF_COUNTER_RAWCOUNT	4 bytes
Election Packet/sec	The rate of browser election packets that have been received by this workstation.	1	PERF_COUNTER_COUNTER	4 bytes
Enumerations Domain/sec	The rate of Domain browse requests that have been processed by this workstation.	1	PERF_COUNTER_COUNTER	4 bytes
Enumerations Other/sec	The rate of browse requests processed by this workstation that were not domain or server browse requests.	1	PERF_COUNTER_COUNTER	4 bytes
Enumerations Server/sec	The rate of Server browse requests that have been processed by this workstation.	1	PERF_COUNTER_COUNTER	4 bytes
Enumerations Total/sec	The rate of browse requests that have been processed by this workstation. This is the sum of Enumerations Server, Enumerations Domain, and Enumerations Other.	1	PERF_COUNTER_COUNTER	4 bytes

Object/Counter Name	Description	Default Scale	Counter Type	Counter Size
Browser Object				
Illegal Datagrams/sec	The rate of incorrectly formatted datagrams that have been received by this workstation.	1	PERF_COUNTER_BULK_COUNT	8 bytes
Mailslot Allocations Failed	Number of times the datagram receiver has failed to allocate a buffer to hold a user mailslot write.	1	PERF_COUNTER_RAWCOUNT	4 bytes
Mailslot Opens Failed/sec	The rate of mailslot messages received by this workstation that were to be delivered to mailslots that are not present on this workstation.	1	PERF_COUNTER_COUNTER	4 bytes
Mailslot Receives Failed	Number of mailslot messages that could not be received due to transport failures.	1	PERF_COUNTER_RAWCOUNT_	4 bytes
Mailslot Writes Failed	Total number of mailslot messages that have been successfully received, but that were unable to be written to the mailslot.	1	PERF_COUNTER_RAWCOUNT	4 bytes
Mailslots Write/sec	The rate of mailslot messages that have been successfully received.	1	PERF_COUNTER_COUNTER	4 bytes
Missed Mailslots Datagrams	Number of Mailslot Datagrams that have been discarded due to configuration or allocation limits.	1	PERF_CONTER_RAWCOUNT	4 bytes

Missed Server Announcements	Number of server announcements that have been missed due to configuration or allocation limits.	1	PERF_COUNTER_RAWCOUNT	4 bytes
Missed Server List Requests	Number of requests to retrieve a list of browser servers that were received by this workstation, but could not be processed.	1	PERF_COUNTER_RAWCOUNT	4 bytes
Server Announce Allocations Failed/sec	The rate of server (or domain) announcements that have failed due to lack of memory.	1	PERF_COUNTER_COUNTER	4 bytes
Server List Requests/sec	The rate of requests to retrieve a list of browser servers that have been processed by this workstation.	1	PERF_COUNTER_COUNTER	4 bytes
Cache Object	**The Cache object type manages system cache memory under Windows NT. Files on Windows NT are cached in 4k units called pages. Physical memory pages not used in the working sets of processes are available for use by the Cache. The Cache preserves file page memory as long as possible to permit access to the data through the file system without having to access the disk.**			

Object/Counter Name	Description	Default Scale	Counter Type	Counter Size
Cache Object				
Async Copy Reads/sec	The frequency of reads from Cache pages that involve a memory copy of the data from the Cache to the application's buffer. The application will regain control immediately even if the disk must be accessed to retrieve the page.	1	PERF_COUNTER_COUNTER	4 bytes
Async Data Maps/sec	The frequency that an application using a file system such as NTFS or HPFS to map a page of a file into the Cache to read the page, and does not wish to wait for the Cache to retrieve the page if it is not in main memory.	1	PERF_COUNTER_COUNTER	4 bytes
Async Fast Reads/sec	The frequency of reads from Cache pages that bypass the installed file system and retrieve the data directly from the Cache. Normally, file I/O requests will invoke the appropriate file system to retrieve data from a file, but this path permits direct retrieval of Cache data without file system involvement if the data is the Cache. Even if the data is not in the Cache,	0.1	PERF_COUNTER_COUNTER	4 bytes

	one invocation of the file system is avoided. If the data is not in the Cache, the request (application program call) will not wait until the data has been retrieved from disk, but will get control immediately.			
Asyn MDL Reads/sec	The frequency of reads from Cache pages using a Memory Descriptor List (MDL) to access the pages. The MDL contains the physical address of each page in the transfer, thus permitting Direct Memory Access (DMA) of the pages. If the accessed page(s) are not in main memory, the calling application program will not wait for the pages to fault in from disk.	1	PERF_COUNTER_COUNTER	4 bytes
Async Pin Reads/sec	The frequency of reading data into the Cache preparatory to writing the data back to disk. Pages read in this fashion are pinned in memory even if the disk must be accessed to retrieve the page. While pinned, a page's physical address will not be altered.	1	PERF_COUNTER_COUNTER	4 bytes

Object/Counter Name	Description	Default Scale	Counter Type	Counter Size
Cache Object				
Copy Read Hits %	The percentage of Cache Copy Read requests that hit the Cache, i.e., did not require a disk read in order to provide access to the page in the Cache. A Copy Read is a file read operation that is satisfied by a memory copy from a Cache page to the application's buffer. The LAN Redirector uses this method for retrieving Cache information, as does the LAN Server for small transfers. This is a method used by the disk file systems as well.	1	PERF_SAMPLE_FRACTION	4 bytes
Copy Reads/sec	The frequency of reads from Cache pages that involve a memory copy of the data from the Cache to the application's buffer. The LAN Redirector uses this method for retrieving Cache information, as does the LAN Server for small transfers. This is a method used by the disk file system as well.	1	PERF_COUNTER_COUNTER	4 bytes
Data Flush Pages/sec	The number of pages the Cache has flushed to disk as a result of a request to flush or to satisfy a write-through file write request. More than one page can be transferred on each flush operation.	1	PERF_COUNTER_COUNTER	4 bytes

Data Flushes/sec	The frequency the Cache has flushed its contents to disk as the result of a request to flush or to satisfy a write-through file write request. More than one page can be transferred on each flush operation.	1	PERF_COUNTER_COUNTER	4 bytes
Data Map Hits %	The percentage of Data Maps in the Cache that could be resolved without having to retrieve a page from the disk, i.e., the page was already in physical memory.	1	PERF_SAMPLE_FRACTION	4 bytes
Data Map Pins/sec	The frequency of Data Maps in the Cache that resulted in pinning a page in main memory, an action usually preparatory to writing to the file on disk. While pinned, a page's physical address in main memory and virtual address in the Cache will not be altered.	1	PERF_SAMPLE_FRACTION	4 bytes
Data Maps/sec	The frequency that a file system maps a page of a file into the Cache to read the page.	1	PERF_COUNTER_COUNTER	4 bytes
Fast Read Not Possibles/sec	The frequency of attempts by an application program interface (API) function call to bypass the file system to get at Cache data that could not be honored without invoking the file system after all.	1	PERF_COUNTER_COUNTER	4 bytes

Object/Counter Name	Description	Default Scale	Counter Type	Counter Size
Cache Object				
Fast Read Resource Misses/sec	The frequency of Cache misses necessitated by the lack of available resources to satisfy the request.	1	PERF_COUNTER_COUNTER	4 bytes
Fast Reads/sec	The frequency of reads from Cache pages that bypass the installed file system and retrieve the data directly from the Cache. Normally, file I/O requests invoke the appropriate file system that retrieves data from a file, but this path permits direct retrieval of Cache data without file system involvement if the data is in the Cache. Even if the data is not in the Cache, one invocation of the file system is avoided.	0.1	PERF_COUNTER_COUNTER	4 bytes
Lazy Write Flushes/sec	The frequency the Cache's Lazy Write thread has written to disk. Lazy Writing is the process of updating the disk after the page has been changed in memory, so the application making the change to the file does not have to wait for the disk write to complete	1	PERF_COUNTER-COUNTER	4 bytes

	before proceeding. More than one page can be transferred on each write operation.			
Lazy Write Page/sec	The frequency the Cache's Lazy Write thread has written to disk. Lazy Writing is the process of updating the disk after the page has been changed in memory, so the application making the change to the file does not have to wait for the disk write to complete before proceeding. More than one page can be transferred on a single disk write operation.	1	PERF_COUNTER_COUNTER	4 bytes
MDL Read Hits %	The percentage of Cache Memory Descriptor List (MDL) Read requests that hit the Cache, i.e., did not require disk accesses in order to provide memory access to the page(s) in the Cache.	1	PERF_SAMPLE_FRACTION	4 bytes
MDL Reads/sec	The frequency of reads from Cache pages that use a Memory Descriptor List (MDL) to access the data. The MDL contains the physical address of each page involved in the transfer, and thus can employ a hardware Direct Memory Access (DMA) device to effect the copy. The LAN Server uses this method for large transfers out of the server.	1	PERF_COUNTER_COUNTER	4 bytes

Object/Counter Name	Description	Default Scale	Counter Type	Counter Size
Cache Object				
Pin Read Hits %	The percentage of Cache Pin Read requests that hit the Cache, i.e., did not require a disk read in order to provide access to the page in the Cache. While pinned, a page's physical address in the Cache will not be altered. The LAN Redirector uses this method for retrieving Cache information, as does the LAN Server for small transfers. This is usually the method used by the disk file systems as well.	1	PERF_SAMPLE_FRACTION	4 bytes
Pin Read/sec	The frequency of reading data into the Cache preparatory to writing the data back to disk. Pages read in this fashion are pinned in memory at the completion of the read. While pinned, a page's physical address in the Cache will not be altered.	1	PERF_COUNTER_COUNTER	4bytes
Read Aheads/sec	Read Aheads/sec is the frequency of Cache reads where the Cache detects sequential access to a file. The read aheads permit the data to be transferred in larger blocks than those being requested by the application, reducing the overhead per access.	1	PERF_COUNTER_COUNTER	4 bytes

Sync Copy Reads/sec	The frequency of reads from Cache pages that involve a memory copy of the data from the Cache to the application's buffer. The file system will not regain control until the copy operation is complete, even if the disk must be accessed to retrieve the page.	1	PERF_COUNTER_COUNTER	4 bytes
Sync Data Maps/sec	The frequency that a file system such as NTFS or HPFS maps a page of a file into the Cache to read the page, and wishes to wait for the Cache to retrieve the page if it is not in main memory.	1	PERF_COUNTER_COUNTER	4 bytes
Sync Fast Reads/sec	The frequency of reads from Cache pages that bypass the installed file system and retrieve the data directly from the Cache. Normally, file I/O requests invoke the appropriate file system to retrieve data from a file, but this path permits direct retrieval of Cache data without file system involvement if the data is in the Cache. Even if the data is not in the Cache, one invocation of the file system is avoided. If the data is not in the Cache, the request (application program call) will wait until the data has been retrieved from disk.	0.1	PERF_COUNTER)COUNTER	4 bytes

Object/Counter Name	Description	Default Scale	Counter Type	Counter Size
Cache Object				
Sync MDL Reads/sec	The frequency of reads from Cache pages that use a Memory Descriptor List (MDL) to access the pages. The MDL contains the physical address of each page in the transfer, thus permitting Direct Memory Access (DMA) of the pages. If the accessed page(s) are not in main memory, the caller will wait for the page(s) to fault into memory from the paging file.	1	PERF_COUNTER_COUNTER	4 bytes
Sync Pin Reads/sec	The frequency of reading data into the Cache preparatory to writing the data back to disk. Pages read in this fashion are pinned in memory at the completion of the read. The file system will not regain control until the page is pinned in the Cache, in particular if the disk must be accessed to retrieve the page. While pinned, a page's physical address in the Cache will not be altered.	1	PERF-COUNTER_COUNTER	4 bytes

FTP Server	**The FTP Server object contains counters specific to the FTP Server service (part of the Internet Information Server on NT Server, or Peer Web Services on NT Workstation).**			
Bytes Received/sec	The rate at which data bytes are received by the FTP Server.	0.0001	PERF_COUNTER_BULK_COUNT	8 bytes
Bytes Sent/sec	The rate at which data bytes are sent by the FTP Server.	0.0001	PERF_COUNTER_BULK_COUNT	8 bytes
Bytes Total/sec	The sum of Bytes/Sent/sec and Bytes Received/sec. This is the total rate of bytes transferred by the FTP Server.	0.0001	PERF_COUNTER_BULK_COUNT	8 bytes
Connection Attempts	The number of connection attempts that have been made to the FTP Server.	1	PERF_COUNTER_RAWCOUNT	4 bytes
Current Anonymous Users	The number of anonymous users currently connected to the FTP Server.	1	PERF_COUNTER_RAWCOUNT	4 bytes
Current Connections	The current number of connections to the FTP Server.	1	PERF_COUNTER_RAWCOUNT	4 bytes
Current NonAnonymous Users	The current number of non-anonymous users (i.e., those with valid NT user accounts) currently connected to the FTP Server.	1	PERF_COUNTER_RAWCOUNT	4 bytes
Files Received	The total number of files received by the FTP Server.	1	PERF_COUNTER_RAWCOUNT	4 bytes

Object/Counter Name	Description	Default Scale	Counter Type	Counter Size
FTP Server				
Files Sent	The total number of files sent by the FTP Server.	1	PERF_COUNTER_RAWCOUNT	4 bytes
Files Total	The sum of Files Sent and Files Received. This is the total number of files transferred by the FTP Server.	1	PERF_COUNTER_RAWCOUNT	4 bytes
Logon Attempts	The number of logon attempts that have been made by the FTP Server.	1	PERF_COUNTER_RAWCOUNT	4 bytes
Maximum Anonymous Users	The maximum number of anonymous (guest) users simultaneously connected to the FTP Server.	1	PERF_COUNTER_RAWCOUNT	4 bytes
Maximum Connections	The maximum number of simultaneous connections to the FTP Server.	1	PERF_COUNTER_RAWCOUNT	4 bytes
Maximum NonAnonymous Users	The maximum number of non-anonymous (i.e., those with valid NT user accounts) users simultaneously connected the FTP Server.	1	PERF_COUNTER_RAWCOUNT	4 bytes
Total Anonymous Users	The total number of anonymous users that have ever been connected to the FTP Server.	1	PERF_COUNTER_RAWCOUNT	4 bytes

Total NonAnonymous Users	The total number of non-anonymous (i.e., those with valid NT user accounts) users that have ever been connected to the FTP Server.	1	PERF_COUNTER_RAWCOUNT	4 bytes
Gateway Service For NetWare	**Gateway Service for NetWare object type**			
Bytes Received/sec	The rate of bytes coming into the Redirector from the network. It includes all application data as well as network protocol information (such as packet headers).	0.0001	PERF_COUNTER_BULK_COUNT	8 bytes
Bytes Total/sec	The rate the Redirector is processing data bytes. This includes all application and file data in addition to protocol information such as packet headers.	0.0001	PERF_COUNTER_BULK_COUNT	8 bytes
Bytes Transmitted/sec	The rate the bytes are leaving the Redirector to the network. It includes all application data as well as network protocol information (such as packet headers,etc.).	0.0001	PERF_COUNTER_BULK_COUNT	8 bytes
Connect NetWare 2.x	Counts connections to NetWare 2.x servers.	1	PERF_COUNTER_RAWCOUNT	4 bytes
Connect NetWare 3.x	Counts connections to NetWare 3.x servers.	1	PERF_COUNTER_RAWCOUNT	4 bytes

Object/Counter Name	Description	Default Scale	Counter Type	Counter Size
Gateway Service For NetWare				
Connect NetWare 4.x	Counts connections to NetWare 4.x servers.	1	PERF_COUNTER_RAWCOUNT	4 bytes
File Data Operations/sec	The rate the Redirector is processing data operations. One operation includes (hopefully) many bytes. We say hopefully here because each operation has overhead. You can determine the efficiency of this path by dividing the Bytes/sec by this counter to determine the average number of bytes transferred/operation.	1	PERF_COUNTER_COUNTER	4 bytes
File Read Operations/sec	The rate the applications are asking the Redirector for data. Each call to a file system or similar Application Program Interface (API) call counts as one operation.	1	PERF_COUNTER_COUNTER	4 bytes
File Write Operations/sec	The rate the applications are sending data to the Redirector. Each call to a file system or Application Program Interface (API) call counts as one operation.	1	PERF_COUNTER_COUNTER	4 bytes

Packet Burst IO/sec	The sum of Packet Burst Read NCPs/sec and Packet Burst Write NCPs/sec.	1	PERF_COUNTER_COUNTER	4 bytes
Packet Burst Read NCP Count/sec	The rate of NetWare Core Protocol requests for Packet Burst Read. Packet Burst Read is a windowing protocol that improves performance.	1	PERF_COUNTER_COUNTER	4 bytes
Packet Burst Read Timeouts/sec	The rate the NetWare Workstation Compatible Service needs to retransmit a Burst Read Request because the NetWare server took too long to respond.	1	PERF_COUNTER_COUNTER	4 bytes
Packet Burst Write NCP Count/sec	The rate of NetWare Core Protocol requests for Packet Burst Write. Packet Burst is a windowing protocol that improves performance.	1	PERF_COUNTER_COUNTER	4 bytes
Packet Burst Write Timeouts/sec	The rate the NetWare Workstation Compatible Service needs to retransmit a Burst Write Request because the NetWare server took too long to respond.	1	PERF_COUNTER_COUNTER	4 bytes
Packets Received/sec	The rate at which the Redirector is receiving Server Message Block (SMB) packets. Network transmissions are divided into packets. The average number of bytes received in a packet can be obtained by dividing Bytes	0.1	PERF_COUNTER_BULK_COUNT	8 bytes

Object/Counter Name	Description	Default Scale	Counter Type	Counter Size
Gateway Service For NetWare				
	Received/sec by this counter. Some packets received may not contain incoming data; for example an acknowledgment to a write made by the Redirector would count as an incoming packet.			
Packets/sec	The rate the Redirector is processing data packets. One packet normally includes many bytes. You can determine the efficiency of this path by dividing the Bytes/sec by this counter to determine the average number of bytes transferred/packet. You can also divide this counter by Operations/sec to determine the average number of packets per operation, another measure of efficiency.	0.1	PERF_COUNTER_BULK_COUNT	8 bytes
Packets Transmitted/sec	The rate at which the Redirector is sending Server Message Block (SMB) packets. Network transmissions are divided into packets. The average number of bytes transmitted in a packet can be obtained by dividing Bytes Transmitted/sec by this counter.	0.1	PERF_COUNTER_BULK_COUNT	8 bytes

Read Operations Random/sec	The rate at which, on a file-by-file basis, reads are made that are not sequential. If a read is made using a particular file handle, and then is followed by another read that is not immediately the contiguous next byte, this counter is incremented by one.	0.1	PERF_COUNTER_COUNTER	4 bytes
Read Packet/sec	The rate at which read packets are being placed on the network. Each time a single packet is sent with a request to read data remotely, this counter is incremented by one.	0.1	PERF_COUNTER_COUNTER	4 bytes
Server Disconnects	The number of times a Server has disconnected your Redirector. See also *Server Reconnects*.	1	PERF_COUNTER_RAWCOUNT	4 bytes
Server Reconnects	The number of times your Redirector has had to reconnect to a server in order to complete a new active request. You can be disconnected by the Server if you remain inactive for too long. By default, even after all remotely opened files have closed, the Redirector will keep your connections intact for ten minutes (these are referred to as *dormant connections*). High numbers may reflect a need to increase the Server's Autodisconnect parameter configured via the **NET CONFIG SERVER /AUTODISCONNECT:nnn**	1	PERF_COUNTER_RAWCOUNT	4 bytes

Object/Counter Name	Description	Default Scale	Counter Type	Counter Size
Gateway Service For NetWare				
	command (type **NET HELP CONFIG SERVER** for more information on this command).			
Server Sessions	The number of active security objects the Redirector is managing. For example, a Logon to a server followed by a network access to the same server will establish one connection, but two sessions.	1	PERF_COUNTER_RAWCOUNT	4 bytes
Write Operations Random/sec	The rate at which, on a file-by-file basis, writes are made that are not sequential. If a write is made using a particular file handle, and then is followed by another write that is not immediately the next contiguous byte, this counter is incremented by one.	0.1	PERF_COUNTER_COUNTER	4 bytes
Write Packet/sec	The rate at which writes are being sent to the network. Each time a single packet is sent with a request to write remote data, this counter is incremented by one.	0.1	PERF_COUNTER_COUNTER	4 bytes

ICMP	**The ICMP Object Type includes counters that describe the rates that ICMP Messages are received and sent by a process using the ICMP protocol. It also includes counters to monitor error counts for the ICMP protocol.**			
Messages Outbound Errors	The number of ICMP messages that this process did not send due to problems discovered within ICMP such as lack of buffers. This value should not include errors discovered outside the ICMP layer such as the inability of IP to route the resultant datagram. In some implementations there may be no types of error that contribute to this counter's value.	1	PERF_COUNTER_RAQWCOUNT	4 bytes
Messages Received Errors	The number of ICMP messages that the process received but determined as having errors.	1	PERF_COUNT_RAWCOUNT	4 bytes
Messages Received/sec	The rate at which ICMP messages are being received by the process. The rate includes those messages received in error.	0.1	PERF_COUNTER_COUNTER	4 bytes
Messages Sent/sec	The rate at which ICMP messages are attempted to be sent by the process. The rate includes those messages sent in error.	0.1	PERF_COUNTER_COUNTER	4 bytes

Object/Counter Name	Description	Default Scale	Counter Type	Counter Size
ICMP				
Messages/sec	The total rate at which ICMP messages are received and sent by the process. The rate includes those messages received or sent in error.	0.1	PERF_COUNTER_COUNTER	4 bytes
Received Address Mask	Number of ICMP Address Mask Request messages received.	1	PERF_COUNTER_RAWCOUNT	4 bytes
Received Address Mask Reply	Number of ICMP Address Mask Reply messages received.	1	PERF_COUNTER_RAWCOUNT	4 bytes
Received Destination Unreachable	The number of ICMP Destination Unreachable messages received.	1	PERF_COUNTER_RAWCOUNT	4 bytes
Received Echo Reply/sec	The rate of ICMP Echo Reply Message received.	0.1	PERF_COUNTER_COUNTER	4 bytes
Received Echo/sec	The rate of ICMP Echo message received.	0.1	PERF_COUNTER_COUNTER	4 bytes
Received Parameter Problem	The number of ICMP Parameter Problem messages received.	1	PERF_COUNTER_RAWCOUNT	4 bytes
Received Redirect/sec	The rate of ICMP Redirect messages received.	0.1	PERF_COUNTER_COUNTER	4 bytes
Received Source Quench	The number of ICMP Source Quench messages received.	1	PERF_COUNTER_RAWCOUNT	4 bytes

Received Time Exceeded	The number of ICMP Time Exceeded messages received.	1	PERF_COUNTER_RAWCOUNT	4 bytes
Received Timestamp Reply/sec	The rate of ICMP Timestamp Reply messages received.	0.1	PERF_COUNTER_COUNTER	4 bytes
Received Timestamp/sec	The rate of ICMP Timestamp (request) messages received.	0.1	PERF_COUNTER_COUNTER	4 bytes
Sent Address Mask	The number of ICMP Address Mask Request messages sent.	1	PERF_COUNTER_RAWCOUNT	4 bytes
Sent Address Mask Reply	The number of ICMP Address Mask Reply messages sent.	1	PERF_COUNTER_RAWCOUNT	4 bytes
Sent Destination Unreachable	The number of ICMP Destination Unreachable messages sent.	1	PERF_COUNTER_RAWCOUNT	4 bytes
Sent Echo Reply/sec	The rate of ICMP Echo Reply messages sent.	0.1	PERF_COUNTER_COUNTER	4 bytes
Sent Echo/sec	The rate of ICMP Echo messages sent.	0.1	PERF_COUNTER_COUNTER	4 bytes
Sent Parameter Problem	The number of ICMP Parameter Problem messages sent.	1	PERF_COUNTER_RAWCOUNT	4 bytes
Sent Redirect/sec	The rate of ICMP Redirect messages sent.	0.1	PERF_COUNTER_COUNTER	4 bytes
Sent Source Quench	The number of ICMP Source Quench messages sent.	1	PERF_COUNTER_RAWCOUNT	4 bytes
Sent Time Exceeded	The number of ICMP Time Exceeded messages sent.	1	PERF_COUNTER_RAWCOUNT	4 bytes

Object/Counter Name	Description	Default Scale	Counter Type	Counter Size
ICMP				
Sent Timestamp/sec	The rate of ICMP Timestamp request messages sent.	0.1	PERF_COUNTER_COUNTER	4 bytes
Sent Timestamp Reply/sec	The rate of ICMP Timestamp Reply messages sent.	0.1	PERF_COUNTER_COUNTER	4 bytes
Image	**The Image object type displays information about the virtual address usage of the images being executed by a process on the computer.**			
Executable	Image Space is the virtual address space in use by the selected image with this protection. Executable memory is memory that can be executed by programs, but may not be read or written. This type of protection is not supported by all processor types.	1	PERF_COUNTER_RAWCOUNT	4 bytes
Exec Read Only	Image Space is the virtual address space in use by the selected image with this protection. Execute/Read Only memory is memory that can be executed as well as read.	1	PERF_COUNTER_RAWCOUNT	4 bytes

Exec Read/Write	Image Space is the virtual address space in use by the selected image with this protection. Execute/Read/Write memory is memory that can be executed by programs as well as read and written.	1	PERF_COUNTER_RAWCOUNT	4 bytes
Exec Write Copy	Image Space is the virtual address space in use by the selected image with this protection. Execute Write Copy is memory that can be executed by programs as well as read and written. This type of protection is used when memory needs to be shared between processes. If a sharing process desires write access, then a copy of this memory will be made for that process.	1	PERF_COUNTER_RAWCOUNT	4 bytes
No Access	Image Space is the virtual address space in use by the selected image with this protection. No Access protection prevents a process from writing or reading these pages and will generate an access violation if either is attempted.	1	PERF_COUNTER_RAWCOUNT	4 bytes

Object/Counter Name	Description	Default Scale	Counter Type	Counter Size
Image				
Read Only	Image Space is the virtual address space in use by the selected image with this protection. Read Only protection prevents the contents of these pages from being modified. Any attempts to write or modify these pages will generate an access violation.	1	PERF_COUNTER_RAWCOUNT	4 bytes
Read/Write	Image Space is the virtual address space in use by the selected image with this protection. Read/Write protection allows a process to read, modify, and write to these pages.	1	PERF_COUNTER_RAWCOUNT	4 bytes
Write Copy	Image Space is the virtual address space in use by the selected image with this protection. Write Copy protection is used when memory is shared for reading but not for writing. When processes are reading this memory, they can share the same memory, however, when a sharing process wants to have read/write access to this shared memory is made for writing to.	1	PERF_COUNTER_RAWCOUNT	4 bytes.

IP	**The IP Object Type includes those counters that describe the rates that IP datagrams are received and sent by a certain computer using the IP protocol. It also describes various error counts for the IP protocol.**			
Datagrams Forward/sec	The rate of input datagrams for that this process was not their final IP destination, as a result of which an attempt was made to find a route to forward tem to that final destination. In entities that do not act as IP Gateways, this rate will include only those packets that were Source-Route option processing was successful.	0.1	PERF_COUNTER_COUNTER	4 bytes
Datagrams Outbound Discarded	The number of output IP datagrams for which no problems were encountered to prevent their transmission to their destination, but which were discarded. This counter would include datagrams counter in Datagrams Forwarded if any such packets met this discard criterion.	1	PERF_COUNTER_RAWCOUNT	4 bytes
Datagrams Outbound No Route	The number of IP datagrams and their destination. This counter includes any packets counted in Datagrams Forwarded that meet this 'no route' criterion.	1	PERF_COUNTER_RAWCOUNT	4 bytes

Object/Counter Name	Description	Default Scale	Counter Type	Counter Size
IP				
Datagrams Received Header Errors	The number of input datagrams discarded due to errors in their IP headers, including bad checksums, version number mismatch, other format errors, time-to-live exceeded, errors discovered in processing their IP options, and so on.	1	PERF_COUNTER_RAWCOUNT	4 bytes
Datagrams Received Address Errors	The number of input datagrams discarded because the IP address in their IP header's destination field was not a valid address received at this entity. This count includes invalid addresses (for example, 0.0.0.0) and addresses of unsupported Classes (for example Class E). For entities that are not IP Gateways and therefore do not forward datagrams, this counter includes datagrams discarded because the destination address was not a local address.	1	PERF_COUNTER_RAWCOUNT	4 bytes

Datagrams Received Delivered/sec	The rate at which input IP datagrams are successfully delivered to IP user-protocols.	0.1	PERF_COUNTER_COUNTER	4 bytes
Datagrams Received Discarded	The number of input IP datagrams for which no problems were encountered to prevent their continued processing, but which were discarded. This counter does not include any datagrams discarded while awaiting re-assembly.	1	PERF_COUNTER_RAWCOUNT	4 bytes
Datagrams Received Unknown Protocol	The number of locally-addressed datagrams received successfully but discarded because of an unknown or unsupported protocol.	1	PERF_COUNTER_RAWCOUNT	4 bytes
Datagrams Received/sec	The rate at which IP datagrams are received from the interface, including those in error.	0.1	PERF_COUNTER_COUNTER	4 bytes
Datagrams/sec	The rate at which IP datagrams are received from or sent to the interfaces, including those in error. Any forwarded datagrams are not included in this rate.	0.1	PERF_COUNTER_COUNTER	4 bytes
Datagrams Sent/sec	The rate at which IP datagrams are supplied to IP for transmission by local IP user-protocols (including ICMP). This counter does not include any datagrams counted in Datagrams Forwarded.	0.1	PERF_COUNTER_COUNTER	4 bytes

Object/Counter Name	Description	Default Scale	Counter Type	Counter Size
IP				
Fragmentation Failures	The number of IP datagrams that have been discarded because they needed to be fragmented at this entity but could not be (usually this happens when a datagram's 'Don't Fragment' flag is set).	1	PERF_COUNTER_RAWCOUNT	4 bytes
Fragmented Datagrams/sec	The rate at which datagrams are successfully fragmented at this entity.	0.1	PERF_COUNTER_COUNTER	4 bytes
Fragments Created/sec	The rate at which IP datagram fragments have been generated as a result of fragmentation at this entity.	0.1	PERF_COUNTER_COUNTER	4 bytes
Fragments Received/sec	The rate at which IP fragments that need to be reassembled at this entity are received.	0.1	PERF_COUNTER_COUNTER	4 bytes
Fragment Re-assembled/sec	The rate at which IP fragments are successfully re-assembled.	0.1	PERF_COUNTER_COUNTER	4 bytes
Fragments Re-assembly Failures	The number of failures detected by the IP re-assembly algorithm. This is not necessarily a count of discarded IP fragments since some algorithms (such as that defined in RFC 815) can lose track of the number of fragments by combining them as they are received.	1	PERF_COUNTER_RAWCOUNT	4 bytes

LogicalDisk	**A Logical Disk object type is a partition on a hard or fixed disk drive and assigned a drive letter, such as C. (NOTE: In order to monitor disk counters, you must have previously typed DISKPERF -Y at an NT Command Prompt and rebooted your system; this is also discussed in Chapter 7, "Optimizing Disks").**			
% Disk Read Time	The percentage of elapsed time that the selected disk drive is busy servicing read requests.	1	PERF_COUNTER_TIMER	8 bytes
% Disk Time	The percentage of elapsed time that the selected disk drive is busy servicing read or write requests.	1	PERF_COUNTER_TIMER	8 bytes
% Disk Write Time	The percentage of elapsed time that the selected disk drive is busy servicing write requests.	1	PERF_COUNTER_TIMER	8 bytes
% Free Space	The ratio of the free space available of the logical disk unit to the total usable space provided by the selected logical disk drive.	1	PERF_RAW_FRACTION	4 bytes
Avg. Disk Bytes/Read	The average number of bytes transferred from the disk during read operations.	0.01	PERF_AVERAGE_BULK	4 bytes

Object/Counter Name	Description	Default Scale	Counter Type	Counter Size
LogicalDisk				
Avg. Disk Bytes/Transfer	The average number of bytes transferred to or from the disk during write or read operations.	0.01	PERF_AVERAGE_BULK	4 bytes
Avg. Disk Bytes/Write	The average number of bytes transferred to the disk during write operations.	0.01	PERF_AVERAGE_BULK	4 bytes
Avg. Disk Queue Length	The combined average number of read and write requests queued for the selected disk. This counter is helpful for monitoring the performance of multi-disk sets, including striped and mirrored RAID volumes.	10	PERF_COUNTER_RAWCOUNT	4 bytes
Avg. Disk Read Queue Length	The average number of read requests queued for the selected disk. This counter is helpful for monitoring the performance of multi-disk sets, including striped and mirrored RAID volumes.	10	PERF_COUNTER_RAWCOUNT	4 bytes
Avg. Disk Write Queue Length	The average number of write requests queued for the selected disk. This counter is helpful for monitoring the performance of multi-disk sets, including striped and mirrored RAID volumes.	10	PERF_COUNTER_RAWCOUNT	4 bytes

Avg. Disk sec/Read	The average time in seconds of a read of data from the disk.	1000	PERF_AVERAGE_TIMER	8 bytes
Avg. Disk sec/Transfer	The time in seconds of the average disk transfer.	1000	PERF_AVERAGE_TIMER	4 bytes
Avg. Disk sec/Write	The average time, in seconds, of a data write to the disk.	1000	PERF_AVERAGE_TIMER	4 bytes
Disk Bytes/sec	The rate bytes are transferred to or from the disk during write or read operations.	0.0001	PERF_COUNTER_BULK_COUNT	8 bytes
Disk Queue Length	The number of requests outstanding on the disk at the time the performance data is collected. It includes requests in service at the time of the snapshot. This is an instantaneous length, not an average. Multi-disk sets can have multiple requests active at one time, but other concurrent requests are awaiting service. This counter reflects a transitory high or low queue length, but if there is a sustained load on the disk drive, it is likely that this will be consistently high. The figure, minus the number of disk spindles, indicates the delays that disk read/write requests experience. Normally, this difference should average less than 2; otherwise, it could indicate a disk-related bottleneck.	10	PERF_COUNTER_RAWCOUNT	4 bytes

Object/Counter Name	Description	Default Scale	Counter Type	Counter Size
LogicalDisk				
Disk Read Bytes/sec	The rate bytes are transferred from the disk during read operations.	0.0001	PERF_COUNTER_BULK_COUNT	8 bytes
Disk Reads/sec	The rate of read operations on the disk.	1	PERF_COUNTER_COUNTER	4 bytes
Disk Transfers/sec	The rate of read and write operations on the disk.	1	PERF_COUNTER_COUNTER	4 bytes
Disk Writes/sec	The rate of write operations on the disk.	1	PERF_COUNTER_COUNTER	4 bytes
Disk Write Bytes/sec	The rate bytes are transferred to the disk during write operations.	0.0001	PERF_COUNTER_BULK_COUNT	8 bytes
Free Megabytes	Free Megabytes displays the unallocated space on the disk drive in megabytes. One megabyte = 1,048,576 bytes	1	PERF_COUNTER_RAWCOUNT	4 bytes
MacFile Server	**Services for Macintosh AFP File Server counters**			
Current Files Open	The number of internal files currently open in the MacFile Server. This count does not include files opened on behalf of Macintosh clients.	1	PERF_COUNTER_RAWCOUNT	4 bytes
Current NonPaged Memory	The current amount of nonpaged memory resources used by the MacFile Server.	0.0001	PERF_COUNTER_RAWCOUNT	4 bytes

Current Paged Memory	The current amount of paged memory resources used by the MacFile Server.	0.0001	PERF_COUNTER_RAWCOUNT	4 bytes
Current Queue Length	The number of outstanding work items waiting to be processed.	1	PERF_COUNTER_RAWCOUNT	4 bytes
Current Sessions	The number of sessions currently connected to the MacFile Server. Indicates current server activity.	1	PERF_COUNTER_RAWCOUNT	4 bytes
Current Threads	The current number of threads used by MacFile Server. Indicates how busy the server is.	1	PERF_COUNTER_RAWCOUNT	4 bytes
Data Read/sec	The number of bytes read from disk per second.	0.0001	PERF_COUNTER_BULK_COUNT	8 bytes
Data Received/sec	The number of bytes received from the network per second. Indicates how busy the server is.	0.0001	PERF_COUNTER_BULK_COUNT	8 bytes
Data Transmitted/sec	The number of bytes sent on the network per second. Indicates how busy the network is.	0.0001	PERF_COUNTER_BULK_COUNT	8 bytes
Data Written/sec	The number of bytes written to disk per second.	0.0001	PERF_COUNTER_BUL_COUNT	8 bytes
Failed Logons	The number of failed logon attempts to the MacFile Server. Can indicate whether password guessing programs are being used to crack the security on the server.	1	PERF_COUNTER_RAWCOUNT	4 bytes

Object/Counter Name	Description	Default Scale	Counter Type	Counter Size
MacFile Server				
Max NonPaged Memory	The maximum amount of nonpaged memory resources used by the MacFile Server.	0.0001	PERF_COUNTER_RAWCOUNT	4 bytes
Max Paged Memory	The maximum amount of page memory resources used by the MacFile Server.	0.0001	PERF_COUNTER_RAWCOUNT	4 bytes
Maximum Files Open	The maximum number of internal files open at one time in the MacFile Sever. This count does not include files opened on behalf of Macintosh clients.	1	PERF_COUNTER_RAWCOUNT	4 bytes
Maximum Queue Length	The maximum number of outstanding work items at one time.	1	PERF_COUNTER_RAWCOUNT	4 bytes
Maximum Sessions	The Maximum number of sessions connected at one time to the MacFile Server. Indicates usage level of server.	1	PERF_COUNTER_RAWCOUNT	4 bytes
Maximum Threads	The maximum number of threads used by the MacFile Server. Indicates peak level of server.	1	PERF_COUNTER_RAWCOUNT	4 bytes

Memory	**The Memory object type includes those counters that describe the behavior of both real and virtual memory on the computer. Real memory is allocated in units of pages. Virtual memory may exceed real memory in size, causing page traffic as virtual pages are moved between disk and real memory.**			
Available Bytes	Available Bytes displays the size of the virtual memory currently on the Zeroed, Free, and Standby lists. Zeroed and Free memory is ready for use, with Zeroed memory cleared to zeroes. Standby memory is memory removed from a process's Working Set but still available. Note that this is an instantaneous count, not an average over the time interval.	0.00001	PERF_COUNTER_RAWCOUNT	4 bytes
Cache Bytes	Cache Bytes measures the number of bytes currently in use by the system Cache. The system Cache is used to buffer data retrieved from disk or LAN. The system Cache uses memory not in use by active processes in the computer.	0.00001	PERF_COUNTER_RAWCOUNT	4 bytes

Object/Counter Name	Description	Default Scale	Counter Type	Counter Size
Memory				
Cache Bytes Peak	Cache Bytes Peak measures the maximum number of bytes used by the system Cache. The system Cache is used to buffer data retrieved from disk of LAN. The system Cache uses memory not in use by active processes by the computer.	0.00001	PERF_COUNTER_RAWCOUNT	4 bytes
Cache Faults/sec	Cache Faults occur whenever the Cache manager does not find a file's date in the immediate Cache and must ask the memory manager to locate the page elsewhere in memory or on the disk so that it can be loaded into the immediate Cache.	0.1	PERF_COUNTER_COUNTER	4 bytes
Commit Limit	The size, in bytes, of virtual memory that can be committed without having to extend the paging file(s). If the paging file(s) can be extended, this is a soft limit.	0.000001	PERF_COUNTER_RAWCOUNT	4 bytes
Committed Bytes	Committed Bytes displays the size of virtual memory (in bytes) that has been Committed (as opposed to simply reserved). Committed memory must	0.000001	PERF_COUNTER_RAWCOUNT	4 bytes

	have backing storage available, or must be assured never to need disk storage (because main memory is large enough to hold it). This is an instantaneous count, not an average over the time interval.			
Demand Zero Faults/sec	The number of page faults for pages that must be filled with zeroes before the fault is satisfied. If the Zeroed list is not empty, the fault can be resolved by removing a page from the Zeroed list.	0.1	PERF_COUNTER_COUNTER	4 bytes
Free System Page Table Entries	The number of Page Table Entries not currently in use by the system.	0.01	PERF_COUNTER_RAWCOUNT	4 bytes
Page Faults/sec	A count of the Page Faults in the processor. A page fault occurs when a process refers to a virtual memory page that is not in its Working Set in main memory. A Page Fault will not cause the page to be fetched from disk if that page is on the standby list, and thus already in main memory, or if it is in use by another process with whom the page is shared.	0.1	PERF_COUNTER_COUNTER	4 bytes
Page Reads/sec	The number of times the disk was read to retrieve pages of virtual memory necessary to resolve page faults. Multiple pages can be read during a disk read operation.	1	PERF_COUNTER_COUNTER	4 bytes

Object/Counter Name	Description	Default Scale	Counter Type	Counter Size
Memory				
Page Write/sec	The number of times pages have been written to the disk because they were changed since last retrieved. Each such write operation may transfer a number of pages.	1	PERF_COUNTER_COUNTER	4 bytes
Pages Input/sec	The number of pages read from the disk to resolve memory references to pages that were not in memory at the time of the reference. This counter includes paging traffic on behalf of the system Cache to access file data for applications. This is an important counter to use if you're trying to determine if memory is a bottleneck, since high numbers reflect excessive paging activity and normally indicate insufficient system RAM.	1	PERF_COUNTER_COUNTER	4 bytes
Pages Output/sec	The number of pages that are written to disk because the pages have been modified in main memory.	1	PERF_COUNTER_COUNTER	4 bytes
Pages/sec	The number of pages read from the disk or written to the disk to resolve memory references to pages that were not in memory at the time of the	1	PERF_COUNTER_COUNTER	4 bytes

	reference. This is the sum of Pages Input/sec and Pages Output/sec. This counter includes paging traffic on behalf of the system Cache to access file data for applications. This is the primary counter to observe if you are concerned about excessive memory pressure, and the excessive paging that may result.			
Pool Nonpaged Allocs	The number of calls to allocate space in the system Nonpaged Pool. Nonpaged Pool is a system memory area where space is acquired by operating system components as they accomplish their appointed tasks. Nonpaged Pool pages cannot be paged out to the paging file, but instead remain in main memory as long as they are allocated.	0.01	PERF_COUNTER_RAWCOUNT	4 bytes
Pool Nonpaged Bytes	The number of bytes in the Nonpaged Pool, a system memory area where space is acquired by operating system components as they accomplish their appointed tasks. Nonpaged Pool pages cannot by paged out to the paging file, but instead remain in main memory as long as they are allocated.	0.00001	PERF_COUNTER_RAWCOUNT	4 bytes

Object/Counter Name	Description	Default Scale	Counter Type	Counter Size
Memory				
Pool Paged Allocs	The number of calls to allocate space in the system Paged Pool. Paged Pool is a system memory area where space is acquired by operating system components as they accomplish their appointed tasks. Paged Pool pages can be paged out to paging file when not accessed by the system for sustained periods of time.	0.01	PERF_COUNTER_RAWCOUNT	4 bytes
Pool Paged Bytes	The number of bytes in the Paged Pool, a system memory area where space is acquired by operating system components as they accomplish their appointed tasks. Paged Pool pages can be paged out to the paging file when not accessed by the system for sustained periods of time.	0.00001	PERF_COUNTER_RAWCOUNT	4 bytes
Pool Paged Resident Bytes	The size of paged Pool resident in core memory. This is the actual cost of the paged Pool allocation, since this is actively in use and using real physical memory.	0.00001	PERF_COUNTER_RAWCOUNT	4 bytes

System Cache Resident Bytes	The number of bytes currently resident in the global disk cache.	0.00001	PERF_COUNTER_RAWCOUNT	4 bytes
System Code Resident Bytes	The number of bytes of System Code Total Bytes currently resident in core memory. This is the code working set of the pageable executive. In addition to this, there is another ~300k bytes of non-paged kernel code.	0.00001	PERF_COUNTER_RAWCOUNT	4 bytes
System Code Total Bytes	The number of bytes of pageable pages in ntoskrnl.exe, hal.dll, and the boot drivers and file systems loaded by NTLDR/OSLOADER.	0.00001	PERF_COUNTER_RAWCOUNT	4 bytes
System Driver Resident Bytes	The number of bytes of System Driver Total Bytes currently resident in core memory. This is the code working set of the pageable drivers. In addition to this, there is another ~700k bytes of non-paged driver code.	0.00001	PERF_COUNTER_RAWCOUNT	4 bytes
System Driver Total Bytes	The number of bytes pageable pages in all other loaded device drivers.	0.00001	PERF_COUNTER_RAWCOUNT	4 bytes
Transition Faults/sec	The number of page faults resolved by recovering pages that were written in transition, that is, being written to disk at the time of the page fault. The pages were recovered without additional disk activity.	0.1	PERF_COUNTER_COUNTER	4 bytes

Object/Counter Name	Description	Default Scale	Counter Type	Counter Size
Memory				
Write Copies/sec	The number of page faults that have been satisfied by making a copy of a page when an attempt to write to the page is made. This is an economical way of sharing data since the copy of the page is only made on an attempt to write to the page; otherwise, the page is shared.	1	PERF_COUNTER_COUNTER	4 bytes
NBT Connection	**The NBT Connection Object Type includes those counters that describe the rates that bytes are received and sent over a single NBT connection connecting the local computer with some remote computer. The connection is identified by the name of the remote computer.**			
Bytes Received/sec	The rate at which bytes are received by the local computer over an NBT connection to some remote computer. All the bytes received by the local computer over the particular NBT connection are counted.	0.1000	PERF_COUNTER_COUNTER	4 bytes

Bytes Sent/sec	The rate at which bytes are sent by the local computer over an NBT connection to some remote computer. All the bytes sent by the local computer over the particular NBT connection are counted.	0.0001	PERF_COUNTER_COUNTER	4 bytes
Bytes Total/sec	The rate at which bytes are sent or received by the local computer over an NBT connection to some remote computer. All the bytes sent or received by the local computer over the particular NBT connection are counted.	0.0001	PERF_COUNTER_COUNTER	4 bytes
NetBEUI	**The NetBEUI protocol handles data transmission for that network activity which follows the NetBIOS Extended User Interface standard.**			
Bytes Total/sec	The sum of Frame Bytes/sec and Datagram Bytes/sec. This is the total rate of bytes sent to or received from the network by the protocol, but only counts the bytes in frames (packets) which carry data.	0.0001	PERF_COUNTER_BULK_COUNT	4 bytes
Connection Session Timeouts	The number of connections that were dropped due to a session timeout. This number is an accumulator and shows a running total.	1	PERF_COUNTER_RAWCOUNT	4 bytes

Object/Counter Name	Description	Default Scale	Counter Type	Counter Size
NetBEUI				
Connections Canceled	The number of connections that were canceled. This number is an accumulator and shows a running total.	1	PERF_COUNTER_RAWCOUNT	4 bytes
Connections No Retries	The total count of connections that were successfully made on the first try. This number is an accumulator and shows a running total.	1	PERF_COUNTER_RAWCOUNT	4 bytes
Connections Open	The number of connections currently open for this protocol. This counter shows the current count only and does not accumulate over time.	1	PERF_COUNTER_RAWCOUNT	4 bytes
Connections With Retries	The total count of connections that were made after retrying the attempt. A retry occurs when the first connection attempt failed. This number is an accumulator and shows a running total.	1	PERF_COUNTER_RAWCOUNT	4 bytes
Datagram Bytes Received/sec	The rate at which datagrams are received by the computer. A datagram is a connectionless packet whose delivery to a remote computer is not guaranteed.	0.0001	PERF_COUNTER_BULK_COUNT	4 bytes

Datagrams Sent/sec	The rate at which datagrams are sent from the computer. A datagram is a connectionless packet whose delivery to a remote computer is not guaranteed.	0.1	PERF_COUNTER_COUNTER	4 bytes
Datagrams/sec	The rate at which datagrams are processed by the computer. This counter displays the sum of datagrams sent and datagrams received. A datagram is a connectionless packet whose delivery to a remote system is not guaranteed.	0.1	PERF_COUNTER_COUNTER	4 bytes
Disconnects Local	The number of session disconnections that were initiated by the local computer. This number is an accumulator and shows a running total.	1	PERF_COUNTER_COUNTER	4 bytes
Disconnects Remote	The number of session disconnections that were initiated by the remote computer. This number is an accumulator and shows a running total.	1	PERF_COUNTER_RAWCOUNT	4 bytes
Expirations Ack	The count of T2 timer (acknowledgment) expirations.	1	PERF_COUNTER_RAWCOUNT	4 bytes
Expirations Response	The count of T1 timer (response) expirations.	1	PERF_COUNTER_RAWCOUNT	4 bytes

Object/Counter Name	Description	Default Scale	Counter Type	Counter Size
NetBEUI				
Failures Adapter	The number of connections that were dropped due to an adapter failure. This number is an accumulator and shows a running total.	1	PERF_COUNTER_RAWCOUNT	4 bytes
Failures Link	The number of connections that were dropped due to a link failure. This number is an accumulator and shows a running total.	1	PERF_COUNTER_RAWCOUNT	4 bytes
Failures No Listen	The number of connections that were rejected because the remote computer was not listening for connection requests.	1	PERF_COUNTER_RAWCOUNT	4 bytes
Failures Not Found	The number of connection attempts that fails because the remote computer could not be found. This number is an accumulator and shows a running total.	1	PERF_COUNTER_RAWCOUNT	4 bytes
Failures Resources Local	The number of connections that failed because of resource problems or shortages on the local computer. This number is an accumulator and shows a running total.	1	PERF_COUNTER_RAWCOUNT	4 bytes

Failures Resources Remote	The number of connections that failed because of resource problems or shortages on the remote computer. This number is an accumulator and shows a running total.	1	PERF_COUNTER_RAWCOUNT	4 bytes
Frame Bytes Received/sec	The rate at which data bytes are received by the computer. This counter only counts the frames (packets) that carry data.	0.0001	PERF_COUNTER_BULK_COUNT	8 bytes
Frame Bytes Rejected/sec	The rate at which data bytes are rejected. This counter only counts the bytes in data frames (packets) that carry data.	0.0001	PERF_COUNTER_BULK_COUNT	8 bytes
Frame Bytes Re-Sent/sec	The rate at which data bytes are re-sent by the computer. This counter only counts the bytes in the frames (packets) that carry data.	0.0001	PERF_COUNTER_BULK_COUNT	8 bytes
Frame Bytes Sent/sec	The rate at which data bytes are sent by the computer. This counter only counts the bytes in frames (packets) that carry data.	0.0001	PERF_COUNTER_BULK_COUNT	8 bytes
Frame Bytes/sec	The rate at which data are processed by the computer. This counter is the sum of data frame bytes sent and received. This counts the byte in frames (packets) that carry data.	0.0001	PERF_COUNTER_BULK_COUNT	8 bytes

Object/Counter Name	Description	Default Scale	Counter Type	Counter Size
NetBEUI				
Frames Received/sec	The rate at which data frames are received by the computer. This counter only counts the frames (packets) that carry data.	0.1	PERF_COUNTER_COUNTER	4 bytes
Frames Rejected/sec	The rate at which data frames are rejected. This counter only counts the frames (packets) that carry data.	0.1	PERF_COUNTER_COUNTER	4 bytes
Frames Re-Sent/sec	The rate at which data frames (packets) are re-sent by the computer. This counter only counts the frames (packets) that carry data.	0.1	PERF_COUNTER_COUNTER	4 bytes
Frames Sent/sec	The rate at which data frames are sent by the computer. This counter only counts the frames (packets) that carry data.	0.1	PERF_COUNTER_COUNTER	4 bytes
Frames/sec	The rate at which data frames (packets) are processed by the computer. This counter is the sum of data frames sent and data frames received. This counter only counts those frames (packets) that carry data.	0.1	PERF_COUNTER_COUNTER	4 bytes

Packets Received/sec	The rate at which packets are received by the computer. This counter counts all packets processed, control as well as data packets.	0.1	PERF_COUNTER_COUNTER	4 bytes
Packets Sent/sec	The rate at which packets are sent by the computer. This counter counts all packets sent by the computer, control as well as data packets.	0.1	PERF_COUNTERR_COUNTER	4 bytes
Packets/sec	The rate at which packets are processed by the computer. This count is the sum of Packets Sent and Packets Received per second. This counter includes all packets processed, control as well as data packets.	0.1	PERF_COUNTER_COUNTER	4 bytes
Piggyback Ack Queued/sec	The rate at which piggybacked acknowledgments are queued. Piggyback acknowledgments are acknowledgments to received packets that are to be included in the next out-going packet to the remote computer.	0.1	PERF_COUNTER_COUNTER	4 bytes
Piggyback Ack Timeouts	The number of times that a piggyback acknowledgment could not be sent because there was no outgoing packet to the remote on which to piggyback. A piggyback acknowledgment is an acknowledgment to a received packet	0.1	PERF_COUNTER_RAWCOUNT	4 bytes

Object/Counter Name	Description	Default Scale	Counter Type	Counter Size
NetBEUI				
	that is sent along in an outgoing data packet to the remote computer. If no outgoing packet is sent within the timeout period, then an ack packet is sent and this counter is incremented.			
Window Send Average	The running average number of data bytes that were sent before waiting for an acknowledgment from the remote computer.	1	PERF_COUNTER_RAWCOUNT	4 bytes
Window Send Maximum	The maximum number of bytes of data that will be sent before waiting for an acknowledgment from the remote computer.	1	PERF_COUNTER_RAWCOUNT	4 bytes
NetBEUI Resource	**The NetBEUI Resource object tracks the use of resources (buffers) by the NetBEUI protocol.**			
Times Exhausted	The number of times all the resources (buffers) were in use. The number in parentheses following the resource name is used to identify the resource in Event Log messages.	1	PERF_COUNTER_RAWCOUNT	4 bytes

Used Average	The current number of resources (buffers) in use at this time. The number in parentheses following the resource name is used to identify the resource in Event Log messages.	1	PERF_COUNTER_RAWCOUNT	4 bytes
Used Maximum	The maximum number of NetBEUI resources (buffers) in use at any point in any time. This value is useful is sizing the maximum resources provided. The number in parentheses following the resource name is used to identify the resource in Event Log messages.	1	PERF_COUNTER_RAWCOUNT	4 bytes
Network Interface	**The Network Interface Object Type includes those counters that describe the rates that bytes and packets are received and sent over a Network TCP/IP connection. It also describes various error counts for the same connection.**			
Bytes Received/sec	The rate at which bytes are received on the interface, including framing characters.	0.0001	PERF_COUNTER_COUNTER	4 bytes
Bytes Sent/sec	The rate at which bytes are sent on the interface, including framing characters.	0.0001	PERF_COUNTER_COUNTER	4 bytes

Object/Counter Name	Description	Default Scale	Counter Type	Counter Size
Network Interface				
Bytes Total/sec	The rate at which bytes are sent and received on the interface, including framing characters.	0.0001	PERF_COUNTER_COUNTER	4 bytes
Current Bandwidth	An estimate of the interface's current bandwidth in bits per seconds (bps). For interfaces that do not vary in bandwidth or for those where no accurate estimation can be made, this value is the nominal bandwidth.	0.000001	PERF_COUNTER_RAWCOUNT	4 bytes
Output Queue Length	The length of the output packet queue (in packets). If this is longer then 2, delays are being experienced and the bottleneck should be found and eliminated if possible. Since the requests are queued by NDIS in this implementation, this will always be 0.	1	PERF_COUNTER_RAWCOUNT	4 bytes
Packets Outbound Discarded	The number of outbound packets that were chosen to be discarded even though no errors had been detected to prevent their being transmitted. One possible reason for discarding such a packet could be to free up buffer space.	1	PERF_COUNTER_RAWCOUNT	4 bytes

Packets Outbound Errors	The number of outbound packets that could not be transmitted because of errors.	1	PERF_COUNTER_RAWCOUNT	4 bytes
Packets Received Discarded	The number of inbound packets that were chosen to be discarded even though no errors had been detected to prevent their being deliverable to a higher-layer protocol. One possible reason for discarding such a packet could be to free up buffer space.	1	PERF_COUNTER_RAWCOUNT	4 bytes
Packets Received Errors	The number of inbound packets that contained errors preventing them from being deliverable to a higher-layer protocol.	1	PERF_COUNTER_RAWCOUNT	
Packets Received Non-Unicast/sec	The rate at which non-unicast (i.e., broadcast or multicast) packets are delivered to a higher-layer protocol.	0.1	PERF_COUNTER_COUNTER	4 bytes
Packets Received Unicast/sec	The rate at which unicast packets are delivered to a higher-layer protocol.	0.1	PERF_COUNTER_COUNTER	4 bytes
Packets Received Unknown	The number of packets received on a network interface that were discarded because of an unknown or unsupported protocol.	1	PERF_COUNTER_RAWCOUNT	4 bytes
Packets Received/sec	The rate at which packets are received on the network interface.	0.1	PERF_COUNTER_COUNTER	4 bytes

Object/Counter Name	Description	Default Scale	Counter Type	Counter Size
Network Interface				
Packets Sent/sec	The rate at which packets are sent on the network interface.	0.1	PERF_COUNTER_COUNTER	4 bytes
Packets Sent Non-Unicast/sec	The rate at which packets are requested to be transmitted to non-unicast (subnet broadcast or subnet multicast) addresses by higher-level protocols. The rate includes the packets that were discarded or not sent.	0.1	PERF_COUNTER_COUNTER	4 bytes
Packets Sent Unicast/sec	The rate at which packets are requested to be transmitted to unicast addresses by higher-level protocols. The rate includes the packets that were discarded or not sent.	0.1	PERF_COUNTER_COUNTER	4 bytes
Packets/sec	The rate at which packets are sent and received on the network interface.	0.1	PERF_COUNTER_COUNTER	4 bytes
Network Segment	**Provides Network Statistics for the local network segment via the Network Monitor Service**			
% Broadcast Frames	Percentage of network bandwidth which is made up of broadcast traffic on this network segment.	1	PERF_AVERAGE_BULK	8 bytes

% Multicast Frames	Percentage of network bandwidth which is made up of multicast traffic on this network segment.	1	PERF_AVERAGE_BULK	8 bytes
% Network Utilization	Percentage of network bandwidth in use on this network segment.	1	PERF_COUNTER_COUNTER	4 bytes
Broadcast Frames Received/sec	The number of Broadcast frames received per second on this network segment.	0.1	PERF_COUNTER_COUNTER	4 bytes
Multicast Frames Received/sec	The number of Multicast frames received per second on this network segment.	0.1	PERF_COUNTER_COUNTER	4 bytes
Total Bytes Received/sec	The number of bytes received per second on this network segment.	0.0001	PERF_COUNTER_COUNTER	4 bytes
Total Frames Received/sec	The total number of frames received per second on this network segment.	0.01	PERF_COUNTER_COUNTER	4 bytes
NWLink IPX Object	**The NWLink IPX transport handles datagram transmission to and from computers using the IPX protocol.**			
Bytes Total/sec	The sum of Frame Bytes/sec and Datagram Bytes/sec. This is the total rate of bytes sent to or received from the network by the protocol, but only counts the bytes in frame (packets) which carry data.	0.0001	PER_COUNTER_BULK_COUNT	8 bytes

Object/Counter Name	Description	Default Scale	Counter Type	Counter Size
NWLink IPX Object				
Connection Session Timeouts	The number of connections that were dropped due to a session timeout. This number is an accumulator and shows a running total.	1	PERF_COUNTER_RAWCOUNT	4 bytes
Connections Canceled	The number of connections that were canceled. This number is an accumulator and shows a running total.	1	PERF_COUNTER_RAWCOUNT	4 bytes
Connections No Retries	The total count of connections that were successfully made on the first try. This number is an accumulator and shows a running total.	1	PERF_COUNTER_RAWCOUNT	4 bytes
Connections Open	The number connections currently open for this protocol. This counter shows the current only and does not accumulate over time.	1	PERF_COUNTER_RAWCOUNT	4 bytes
Connections With Retries	The total count of connections that were made after retrying the attempt. A retry occurs when the first connection attempt failed. The number is an accumulator and shows a running total.	1	PERF_COUNTER_RAWCOUNT	4 bytes

Datagram Bytes Received/sec	The rate at which datagram bytes are received by the computer. A datagram is a connectionless packet whose delivery to a remote computer is not guaranteed.	0.0001	PERF_COUNTER_BULK_COUNT	8 bytes
Datagram Bytes Sent/sec	The rate at which datagram bytes are sent from the computer. A datagram is a connectionless packet whose delivery to a remote computer is not guaranteed.	0.0001	PERF_COUNTER_BULK_COUNT	8 bytes
Datagram Bytes/sec	The rate at which datagram bytes are processed by the computer. This counter is the sum of datagram bytes that are sent as well as received. A datagram is a connectionless packet whose delivery to a remote computer is not guaranteed.	0.0001	PERF_COUNTER_BULK_COUNT	8 bytes
Datagrams Received/sec	The rate at which datagrams are received by the computer. A datagram is a connectionless packet whose delivery to a remote computer is not guaranteed.	0.1	PERF_COUNTER_COUNTER	4 bytes
Datagrams Sent/sec	The rate at which datagrams are sent from the computer. A datagram is a connectionless packet whose delivery to a remote computer is not guaranteed.	0.1	PERF_COUNTER_COUNTER	4 bytes

Object/Counter Name	Description	Default Scale	Counter Type	Counter Size
NWLink IPX Object				
Datagrams/sec	The rate at which datagrams are processed by the computer. This counter displays the sum of datagrams sent and datagrams received. A datagram is a connectionless packet whose delivery to a remote computer is not guaranteed.	0.1	PERF_COUNTER_COUNTER	4 bytes
Disconnects Local	The number of session disconnections that were initiated by the local computer. This number is an accumulator and shows a running total.	1	PERF_COUNTER_RAWCOUNT	4 bytes
Disconnects Remote	The number of session disconnections that were initiated by the remote computer. This number is an accumulator and shows a running total.	1	PERF_COUNTER_RAWCOUNT	4 bytes
Expirations Ack	The count of T2 timer (acknowledgment) expirations.	1	PERF_COUNTER_RAWCOUNT	4 bytes
Expirations Response	The count of T1 timer (response) expirations.	1	PERF_COUNTER_RAWCOUNT	4 bytes

Failures Adapter	The number of connections that were dropped due to an adapter failure. This number is an accumulator and shows a running total.	1	PERF_COUNTER_RAWCOUNT	4 bytes
Failures No Listen	The number of connections that were rejected because the remote computer was not listening for connection requests.	1	PERF_COUNTER_RAWCOUNT	4 bytes
Failures Not Found	The number of connection attempts that failed because the remote computer could not be found. This number is an accumulator and shows a running total.	1	PERF_COUNTER_RAWCOUNT	4 bytes
Failures Resource Local	The number of connections that failed because of resource problems or shortages on the local computer. This number is an accumulator and shows a running total.	1	PERF_COUNTER_RAWCOUNT	4 bytes
Failures Resource Remote	The number of connections that failed because of resource problems or shortages on the remote computer. This number is an accumulator and shows a running total.	1	PERF_COUNTER_RAWCOUNT	4 bytes
Frame Bytes Received/sec	The rate at which data bytes are received by the computer. This counter only counts the frames (packets) that carry data.	0.0001	PERF_COUNTER_BULK_COUNT	8 bytes

Object/Counter Name	Description	Default Scale	Counter Type	Counter Size
NWLink IPX Object				
Frame Bytes Rejected/sec	The rate at which data bytes are rejected. This counter only counts the bytes in data frames (packets) that carry data.	0.0001	PERF_COUNTER_BULK_COUNT	8 bytes
Frame Bytes Re-Sent/sec	The rate at which data bytes are re-sent by the computer. This counter only counts the bytes in frames (packets) that carry data.	0.0001	PERF_COUNTER_BULK_COUNT	8 bytes
Frame Bytes Sent/sec	The rate at which data bytes are sent by the computer. This counter only counts the bytes in frames (packets) that carry data.	0.0001	PERF_COUNTER_BULK_COUNT	8 bytes
Frame Bytes/sec	The rate at which data bytes are processed by the computer. This counter is the sum of data frame bytes sent and received. This counter only counts the bytes in frames (packets) that carry data.	0.0001	PERF_COUNTER_BULK_COUNT	8 bytes
Frames Received/sec	The rate at which data frames are received by the computer. This counter only counts the frames (packets) that carry data.	0.1	PERF_COUNTER_COUNTER	4 bytes

Frames Rejected/sec	The rate at which data frames are rejected. This counter only counts the frames (packets) that carry data.	0.1	PERF_COUNTER_COUNTER	4 bytes
Frames Re-Sent/sec	The rate at which data frames are re-sent by the computer. This counter only counts the frames (packets) that carry data.	0.1	PERF_COUNTER_COUNTER	4 bytes
Frames Sent/sec	The rate at which data frames are sent by the computer. This counter only counts the frames (packets) that carry data.	0.1	PERF_COUNTER_COUNTER	4 bytes
Frames/sec	The rate at which data frames are processed by the computer. This counter is the sum of data frames sent and data frames received. This counter only counts those frames (packets) that carry data.	0.1	PERF_COUNTER_COUNTER	4 bytes
Packets Received/sec	The rate at which packets are received by the computer. This counter counts all packets processed, control as well as data packets.	0.1	PERF_COUNTER_COUNTER	4 bytes
Packets Sent/sec	The rate at which packets are sent by the computer. This counter counts all packets sent by the computer, control as well as data packets.	0.1	PERF_COUNTER_COUNTER	4 bytes

Object/Counter Name	Description	Default Scale	Counter Type	Counter Size
NWLink IPX Object				
Packets/sec	The rate at which packets are processed by the computer. This count is the sum of Packets Sent/sec and Packets Received/sec. This counter includes all packets processed, control as well as data packets.	0.1	PERF_COUNTER_COUNTER	4 bytes
Piggyback Ack Queued/sec	The rate at which piggybacked acknowledgments are queued. Piggyback acknowledgments are acknowledgments to received packets that are to be included in the next outgoing packet to the remote computer.	0.1	PERF_COUNTER_COUNTER	4 bytes
Piggyback Ack Timeouts	The number of times that a piggyback acknowledgment could not be sent because there was no outgoing packet to the remote on which to piggyback. A piggyback acknowledgment is an acknowledgment to a received packet that is sent along in an outgoing data packet to the remote computer. If no outgoing packet is sent within the timeout period, then an ack packet is sent and this counter is incremented.	0.1	PERF_COUNTER_RAWCOUNT	4 bytes

Window Send Average	The running average number of data bytes that were sent before waiting for an acknowledgment from the remote computer.	1	PERF_COUNTER_RAWCOUNT	4 bytes
Window Send Maximum	The maximum number of bytes of data that will be sent before waiting for an acknowledgment from the remote computer.	1	PERF_COUNTER_RAWCOUNT	4 bytes
NWLink NetBIOS	**The NWLink NetBIOS protocol handles the interface to applications communicating over the IPX transport.**			
Bytes Total/sec	The sum of Frame Bytes/sec and Datagram Bytes/sec. This is the total rate of bytes sent to or received from the network by the protocol, but only counts the bytes in frames (packet) which carry data.	0.0001	PERF_COUNTER_BULK_COUNT	8 bytes
Connection Session Timeouts	The number of connections that were dropped due to a session timeout. This number is an accumulator and shows a running total.	1	PERF_COUNTER_RAWCOUNT	4 bytes
Connections Canceled	The number of connections that were canceled. This number is an accumulator and shows a running total.	1	PERF_COUNTER_RAWCOUNT	4 bytes

Object/Counter Name	Description	Default Scale	Counter Type	Counter Size
NWLink NetBIOS				
Connections No Retries	The total count of connections that were successfully made on the first try. This number is an accumulator and shows a running total.	1	PERF_COUNTER_RAWCOUNT	4 bytes
Connections Open	The number of connections currently open for this protocol. This counter shows the current count only and does not accumulate over time.	1	PERF_COUNTER_RAWCOUNT	4 bytes
Connections With Retries	The total count of connections that were made after retrying the attempt. A retry occurs when the first connection attempt failed. This number is an accumulator and shows a running total.	1	PERF_COUNTER_RAWCOUNT	4 bytes
Datagram Bytes Received/sec	The rate at which datagram bytes are received by the computer. A datagram is a connectionless packet whose delivery to a remote computer is not guaranteed.	0.0001	PERF_COUNTER_BULK_COUNT	8 bytes
Datagram Bytes Sent/sec	The rate at which datagram bytes are sent from the computer. A datagram is a connectionless packet whose delivery to a remote computer is not guaranteed.	0.0001	PERF_COUNTER_BULK_COUNT	8 bytes

Datagram Bytes/sec	The rate at which datagram bytes are processed by the computer. This counter is the sum of datagram bytes that are sent as well as received. A datagram is a connectionless packet whose delivery to a remote is not guaranteed.	0.0001	PERF_COUNTER_BULK_COUNT	8 bytes
Datagrams Received/sec	The rate at which datagrams are received by the computer. A datagram is a connectionless packet whose delivery to a remote computer is not guaranteed.	0.1	PERF_COUNTER_COUNTER	4 bytes
Datagrams Sent/sec	The rate at which datagrams are sent from the computer. A datagram is a connectionless packet whose delivery to a remote computer is not guaranteed.	0.1	PERF_COUNTER_COUNTER	4 bytes
Datagrams/sec	The rate at which datagrams are processed by the computer. This counter displays the sum of datagrams sent and datagrams received. A datagram is a connectionless packet whose delivery to a remote computer is not guaranteed.	0.1	PERF_COUNTER_COUNTER	4 bytes
Disconnects Local	The number of session disconnections that were initiated by the local computer. This number is an accumulator and shows a running total.	1	PERF_COUNTER_RAWCOUNT	4 bytes

Object/Counter Name	Description	Default Scale	Counter Type	Counter Size
NWLink NetBIOS				
Disconnects Remote	The number of session disconnections that were initiated by the remote computer. This number is an accumulator and shows a running total.	1	PERF_COUNTER_RAWCOUNT	4 bytes
Expirations Ack	The count of T2 timer (acknowledgment) expirations.	1	PERF_COUNTER_RAWCOUNT	4 bytes
Expirations Response	The count of T1 timer (response) expirations.	1	PERF_COUNTER_RAWCOUNT	4 bytes
Failures Adapter	The number of connections that were dropped due to an adapter failure. This number is an accumulator and shows a running total.	1	PERF_COUNTER_RAWCOUNT	4 bytes
Failures Link	The number of connections that were dropped due to a link failure. This number is an accumulator and shows a running total.	1	PERF_COUNTER_RAWCOUNT	4 bytes
Failures Not Listening	The number of connections that were rejected because the remote computer was not listening for connection requests.	1	PERF_COUNTER_RAWCOUNT	4 bytes

Failures Not Found	The number of connection attempts that failed because the remote computer could not be found. This number is an accumulator and shows a running total.	1	PERF_COUNTER_RAWCOUNT	4 bytes
Failures Resource Local	The number of connections that failed because of resource problems or shortages on the local computer. This number is an accumulator and shows a running total.	1	PERF_COUNTER_RAWCOUNT	4 bytes
Failures Resource Remote	The number of connections that failed because of resource problems or shortages on the remote computer. This number is an accumulator and shows a running total.	1	PERF_COUNTER_RAWCOUNT	4 bytes
Frames Bytes Received/sec	The rate at which data bytes are received by the computer. This counter only counts the frames (packets) that carry data.	0.0001	PERF_COUNTER_BULK_COUNT	8 bytes
Frame Bytes Rejected/sec	The rate at which data bytes are rejected. This counter only counts the frames (packets) that carry data.	0.0001	PERF_COUNTER_BULK_COUNT	8 bytes
Frame Bytes Re-Sent/sec	The rate at which data bytes are re-sent by the computer. This counter only counts the frames (packets) that carry data.	0.0001	PERF_COUNTER_BULK_COUNT	8 bytes

Object/Counter Name	Description	Default Scale	Counter Type	Counter Size
NWLink NetBIOS				
Frame Bytes/sec	The rate at which data bytes are processed by the computer. This counter is the sum of data frame bytes sent and received. This counter only counts the frames (packets) that carry data.	0.0001	PERF_COUNTER_BULK_COUNT	8 bytes
Frame Bytes Sent/sec	The rate at which data bytes are sent by the computer. This counter only counts the frames (packets) that carry data.	0.0001	PERF_COUNTER_BULK_COUNT	8 bytes
Frames Received/sec	The rate at which data frames are received by the computer. This counter only counts the frames (packets) that carry data.	0.1	PERF_COUNTER_COUNTER	4 bytes
Frames Rejected/sec	The rate at which data frames are rejected. This counter only counts the frames (packets) that carry data.	0.1	PERF_COUNTER_COUNTER	4 bytes
Frames Re-Sent/sec	The rate at which data frames are re-sent by the computer. This counter only counts the frames (packets) that carry data.	0.1	PERF_COUNTER_COUNTER	4 bytes

Frames/sec	The rate at which data frames are processed by the computer. This counter is the sum of the data frames sent and data frames received. This counter only counts the frames (packets) that carry data.	0.1	PERF_COUNTER_COUNTER	4 bytes
Frames Sent/sec	The rate at which data frames are sent by the computer. This counter only counts the frames (packets) that carry data.	0.1	PERF_COUNTER_COUNTER	4 bytes
Packets Received/sec	The rate at which packets are received by the computer. This counter counts all packets processed, control as well as data packets.	0.1	PERF_COUNTER_COUNTER	4 bytes
Packets/sec	The rate at which packets are processed by the computer. This count is the sum of Packets Sent/sec and Packets Received/sec. This counter counts all packets processed, control as well as data packets.	0.1	PERF_COUNTER_COUNTER	4 bytes
Packets Sent/sec	The rate at which packets are sent by the computer. This counter counts all packets processed, control as well as data packets.	0.1	PERF_COUNTER_COUNTER	4 bytes

Object/Counter Name	Description	Default Scale	Counter Type	Counter Size
NWLink NetBIOS				
Piggyback Ack Queued/sec	The rate at which piggyback acknowledgments are queued. Piggyback acknowledgments are acknowledgments to received packets that are to be included in the next outgoing packet to the remote computer.	0.1	PERF_COUNTER_COUNTER	4 bytes
Piggyback Ack Timeouts	The number of times that a piggyback acknowledgment could not be sent because there was no outgoing packet to the remote on which to piggyback. Piggyback acknowledgments are acknowledgments to received packets that are to be included in the next outgoing packet to the remote computer. If no outgoing packet is sent within the timeout period, then an ack packet is sent and this counter is incremented.	0.1	PERF_COUNTER_RAWCOUNT	4 bytes
Window Send Average	The running average of number of data bytes that were sent before waiting for an acknowledgment from the remote computer.	1	PERF_COUNTER_RAWCOUNT	4 bytes

Window Send Maximum	The maximum number of bytes of data that will be sent before waiting for an acknowledgment from the remote computer.	1	PERF_COUNTER_RAWCOUNT	4 bytes
Objects	**The Objects object type is a metaobject that contains information about the objects in existence on the computer. This information can be used to detect the unnecessary consumption of computer resources. Each object requires memory to store basic information about the object.**			
Events	The number of events in the computer at the time of data collection. This is an instantaneous count, not an average over the time interval. An event is used when two or more threads wish to synchronize execution.	0.1	PERF_COUNTER_RAWCOUNT	4 bytes
Mutexes	The number of mutexes in the computer at the time of data collection. This is an instantaneous count, not an average over the time interval. Mutexes are used by threads to ensure only one thread is executing some section of code.	1	PERF_COUNTER_RAWCOUNT	4 bytes

Object/Counter Name	Description	Default Scale	Counter Type	Counter Size
Objects				
Processes	The number of processes in the computer at the time of data collection. This is an instantaneous count, not an average over the time interval. Each process represents the running of a program.	1	PERF_COUNTER_RAWCOUNT	4 bytes
Sections	The number of sections in the computer at the time of data collection. This is an instantaneous count, not an average over the time interval. A section is a portion of virtual memory created by a process for storing data. A process may share sections with other processes.	0.1	PERF_COUNTER_RAWCOUNT	4 bytes
Semaphores	The number of semaphores in the computer at the time of data collection. This is an instantaneous count, not an average over the time interval. Threads use semaphores to obtain exclusive access to data structures that they share with other threads.	0.1	PERF_COUNTER_RAWCOUNT	4 bytes

Threads	The number of threads in the computer at the time of data collection. This is an instantaneous count, not an average over the time interval. A thread is the basic executable entity in a processor.	0.1	PERF_COUNTER_RAWCOUNT	4 bytes
Paging File	**Displays information about the system's Paging File(s).**			
% Usage	The amount of Page File instance in use in percent. See also Process: Page File Bytes.	1	PERF_RAW_FRACTION	4 bytes
% Usage Peak	The peak usage of the Page File instance in percent. See also Process: Page File Bytes Peak	1	PERF_RAW_FRACTION	4 bytes
Physical Disk	**A Physical Disk object refers to a physical hard disk drive, which contains one or more logical partitions (NOTE: In order to monitor disk counters, you must have previously typed DISKPERF -Y at an NT Command Prompt and rebooted your system; this is discussed in Chapter 7, "Optimizing Disks").**			
% Disk Read Time	The percentage of elapsed time that the selected disk drive is busy servicing read requests.	1	PERF_COUNTER_TIMER	8 bytes

Object/Counter Name	Description	Default Scale	Counter Type	Counter Size
Physical Disk				
% Disk Time	The percentage of elapsed time that the selected disk drive is busy servicing read or write requests.	1	PERF_COUNTER_TIMER	8 bytes
% Disk Write Time	The percentage of elapsed time that the selected disk drive is busy servicing write requests.	1	PERF_COUNTER_TIMER	8 bytes
Avg. Disk Bytes/Read	The average number of bytes transferred from the disk during read operations.	0.01	PERF_AVERAGE_BULK	8 bytes
Avg. Disk Bytes/Transfer	The average number of bytes transferred to or from the disk during write or read operations.	0.01	PERF_AVERAGE_BULK	4 bytes
Avg. Disk Bytes/Write	The average number of bytes transferred to the disk during write operations.	0.01	PERF_AVAERAGE_BULK	4 bytes
Avg. Disk Queue Length	The combined average number of read and write requests queued for the selected disk. This counter is helpful for monitoring the performance of multi-disk sets, including striped and mirrored RAID volumes.	10	PERF_COUNTER_RAWCOUNT	4 bytes

Avg. Disk Read Queue Length	The average number of read requests queued for the selected disk. This counter is helpful for monitoring the performance of multi-disk sets, including striped and mirrored RAID volumes.	10	PERF_COUNTER_RAWCOUNT	4 bytes
Avg. Disk Write Queue Length	The average number of write requests queued for the selected disk. This counter is helpful for monitoring the performance of multi-disk sets, including striped and mirrored RAID volumes.	10	PERF_COUNTER_RAWCOUNT	4 bytes
Avg. Disk sec/Read	The average time in seconds of a read of data from the disk.	1000	PERF_AVERAGE_TIMER	4 bytes
Avg. Disk sec/Transfer	The time in seconds of the average disk transfer.	1000	PERF_AVERAGE_TIMER	4 bytes
Avg. Disk sec/Write	The average time is seconds of a write of data to the disk.	1000	PERF_AVERAGE_TIMER	4 bytes
Disk Bytes/sec	The rate bytes are transferred to or from the disk during write or read operations.	0.0001	PERF_COUNTER_BULK_COUNT	8 bytes

Object/Counter Name	Description	Default Scale	Counter Type	Counter Size
Physical Disk				
Disk Queue Length	The number of requests outstanding on the disk at the time the performance data is collected. It includes requests in service at the time of the snapshot. This is an instantaneous length, not an average over the time interval. Multi-spindle disk devices can have multiple requests active at one time, but other concurrent requests are awaiting service. This counter may reflect a transitory high or low request length, but if there is a sustained load on the disk drive, it is likely that this will be consistently high. Requests are experiencing delays proportional to the length of this queue minus the number of spindles on the disks. This difference should average less than 2 for good performance.	10	PERF_COUNTER_RAWCOUNT	4 bytes
Disk Read Bytes/sec	The rate bytes are transferred from the disk during read operations.	0.0001	PERF_COUNTER_BULK_COUNT	8 bytes
Disk Reads/sec	The rate of read operations on the disk.	1	PERF_COUNTER_COUNTER	4 bytes
Disk Transfers/sec	The rate of read and write operations on the disk.	1	PERF_COUNTER_COUNTER	4 bytes

Disk Writes/sec	The rate of write operations on the disk.	1	PERF_COUNTER_COUNTER	4 bytes
Disk Write Bytes/sec	The rate bytes are transferred to the disk during write operations.	0.0001	PERF_COUNTER_BULK_COUNT	8 bytes
Process	**The Process object type is created when a program is run. All the threads in a process share the same address space and have access to the same data.**			
% Privileged Time	The percentage of elapsed time that this process's threads have spent executing code in Privileged Mode. When a Windows NT system service is called, the service will often run in Privileged Mode to gain access to system-private data. Such data is protected from access by threads executing in User Mode. Calls to the system may be explicit, or they may be implicit such as when a page fault or an interrupt occurs. Unlike some early operating systems, Windows NT uses process boundaries for subsystem protection in addition to the traditional protection of User and Privileged modes. These subsystem processes provide additional protection. Therefore, some work done by Windows NT on behalf of your application may appear in other subsystem processes in addition to the Privileged Time in your process.	1	PERF_100NSEC_TIMER	8 bytes

Object/Counter Name	Description	Default Scale	Counter Type	Counter Size
Process				
% Processor Time	The percentage of elapsed time that all of the threads of this process used the processor to execute instructions. An instruction is the basic unit of execution in a computer, a thread is the object that executes instructions, and a process is the object created when a process is run. Code executed to handle certain hardware interrupts or trap conditions may be counted for this process.	1	PERF_100NSEC_TIMER	8 bytes
% User Time	The percentage of elapsed time that this process's threads have spent executing code in User Mode. Applications execute in User Mode, as do subsystems like the window manager and the graphics engine. Code executing in User Mode cannot damage the integrity of the Windows NT Executive, Kernel, and device drivers. Unlike some early operating systems, Windows NT uses process boundaries for subsystem protection in addition to the traditional protection of User and Privileged modes. These subsystem	1	PERF_100NSEC_TIMER	8 bytes

	processes provide additional protection. Therefore, some work done by Windows NT on behalf of your application may appear in other subsystems in addition to the Privileged Time in your process.			
Elapsed Time	Total time in seconds this process has been running.	0.0001	PERF_ELAPSED_TIME	8 bytes
ID Process	The unique identifier of this process. ID Process numbers are reused, so they only identify a process for the lifetime of that process.	0.1	PERF_COUNTER_RAWCOUNT	4 bytes
Page Faults/sec	The rate of Page Faults by the thread executing in this process. A page fault occurs when a thread refers to a virtual memory page that is not in its working set in main memory. This will not cause the page to be fetched from disk if it is on the standby list and hence already in main memory, or if it is in use by another process with whom the page is shared.	0.1	PERF_COUNTER_COUNTER	4 bytes
Page File Bytes	The current number of bytes this process has used in the paging file(s). Paging files are used to store pages of memory used by the process that are not contained in other files. Paging files are shared by all processes, and lack of space in paging files can prevent other processes from allocating memory.	0.000001	PERF_COUNTER_RAWCOUNT	4 bytes

Object/Counter Name	Description	Default Scale	Counter Type	Counter Size
Process				
Page File Bytes Peak	The maximum number of bytes this process has used in the paging file(s). Paging files are used to store pages of memory used by the process that are not contained in other files. Paging files are shared by all processes, and lack of space in paging files can prevent other processes from allocating memory.	0.000001	PERF_COUNTER_RAWCOUNT	4 bytes
Pool Nonpaged Bytes	The number of bytes in the Nonpaged Pool, a system memory area where space is acquired by operating system components as they accomplish their appointed tasks. Nonpaged Pool pages cannot be paged out to the paging file, but instead remain in main memory as long as they are allocated.	0.00001	PERF_COUNTER_RAWCOUNT	4 bytes
Pool Paged Bytes	The number of bytes in Paged Pool, a system memory area where space is acquired by operating system components as they accomplish their appointed tasks. Paged Pool pages can be paged out to the paging file when not accessed by the system for sustained periods of time.	0.00001	PERF_COUNTER-RAWCOUNT	4 bytes

Priority Base	The current base priority of this process. Threads within a process can raise and lower their own base priority relative to the process's base priority.	1	PERF_COUNTER_RAWCOUNT	4 bytes
Private Bytes	The current number of bytes this process has allocated that cannot be shared with other processes.	0.00001	PERF_COUNTER_RAWCOUNT	4 bytes
Thread Count	The number of threads currently active in this process. An instruction is the basic unit of execution in a processor, and a thread is the object that executes instructions. Every running process has at least one thread.	1	PERF_COUNTER_RAWCOUNT	4 bytes
Virtual Bytes	The current size in bytes of the virtual address space the process is using. Use of virtual address space does not necessarily imply corresponding use of either disk or main memory pages. Virtual space is however finite, and by using too much, the process may limit its ability to load libraries.	0.000001	PERF_COUNTER_RAWCOUNT	4 bytes

Object/Counter Name	Description	Default Scale	Counter Type	Counter Size
Process				
Virtual Bytes Peak	The maximum number of bytes of virtual address space the process has used at any one time. Use of virtual address space does not necessarily imply corresponding use of either disk or main memory pages. Virtual space is however finite, and by using too much, the process may limit its ability to load libraries	0.000001	PERF_COUNTER_RAWCOUNT	4 bytes
Working Set	The current number of bytes in the Working Set of this process. The Working Set is the set of memory pages touched recently by the threads in the process. If free memory in the computer is above a threshold, pages are left in the Working Set of a process even if they are not in use. When free memory falls below a threshold, pages are trimmed from Working Sets. If they are needed they will then be soft-faulted back into the Working Set before they leave main memory.	0.00001	PERF_COUNTER_RAWCOUNT	4 bytes

Working Set Peak	The maximum number of bytes in the Working Set of this process at any point in time. The Working Set is the set of memory pages touched recently by the threads in the process. If free memory in the computer is above a threshold, pages are left in the Working Set of a process even if they are not in use. When free memory falls below a threshold, pages are trimmed from Working Sets. If they are needed they will then be soft-faulted back into the Working Set before they leave main memory.	0.00001	PERF_COUNTER_RAWCOUNT	4 bytes
Process Address Space	**Process Address Space object type displays details about the virtual memory usage and allocation of the selected process.**			
Bytes Free	The total unused virtual address space of this process.	0.0001	PERF_COUNTER_RAWCOUNT	4 bytes
Bytes Image Free	The amount of virtual address space that is not in use or reserved by images within this process.	0.0001	PERF_COUNTER_RAWCOUNT	4 bytes
Bytes Image Reserved	The sum of all virtual memory reserved by images run within this process.	0.0001	PERF_COUNTER_RAWCOUNT	4 bytes

Object/Counter Name	Description	Default Scale	Counter Type	Counter Size
Process Address Space				
Bytes Reserved	The total amount of virtual memory reserved for future use by this process.	0.0001	PERF_COUNTER_RAWCOUNT	4 bytes
ID Process	The unique identifier of this process. ID Process numbers are reused, so they only identify a process for the lifetime of that process.	1	PERF_COUNTER_RAWCOUNT	4 bytes
Image Space Exec Read Only	The virtual address space in use by the images being executed by the process. This is the sum of all the address space with this protection allocated by images run by the selected process. Execute/Read Only memory is memory that can be executed as well as read.	0.00001	PERF_COUNTER_RAWCOUNT	4 bytes
Image Space Exec Read/Write	The virtual address space in use by the images being executed by the process. This is the sum of all the address space with this protection allocated by images run by the selected process. Execute/Read/Write memory is memory that can be executed by programs as well as read and written and modified.	0.00001	PERF_COUNTER_RAWCOUNT	4 bytes

Image Space Exec Write Copy	The virtual address in use by the images being executed by the process. This is the sum of all the address space with this protection allocated by images run by the selected process. Execute Write Copy is memory that can be executed by programs as well as read and written. This type of protection is used when memory needs to be shared between processes. If the sharing processes only read memory, then they will all use the same memory. If a sharing process desires write access, them a copy of this memory will be made for that process.	0.00001	PERF_COUNTER_RAWCOUNT	4 bytes
Image Space Executable	The virtual address space in use by the images being executed by the process. This is the sum of all the address space with this protection allocated by images run by the selected process. Executable memory is memory that can be executed by programs, but may not be read or written. This type of protection is not supported by all processor types.	0.00001	PERF_COUNTER_RAWCOUNT	4 bytes

Object/Counter Name	Description	Default Scale	Counter Type	Counter Size
Process Address Space				
Image Space No Access	The virtual address space in use by the image being executed by the process. This is the sum of all the address space with this protection allocated by images run by the selected process. No Access protection prevents a process from writing to or reading from these pages and will generate an access violation of either is attempted.	0.00001	PERF_COUNTER_RAWCOUNT	4 bytes
Image Space Read Only	The virtual address space in use by the images being executed by the process. This is the sum of all the address space with this protection allocated by images rum by the selected process. Read Only protection prevents the contents of these pages from being modified. Any to write or modify these pages attempts will generate an access violation.	0.00001	PERF_COUNTER_RAWCOUNT	4 bytes
Image Space Read/Write	The virtual address space in use by the images being executed by the process. This is the sum of all the address space with this protection allocated by images run by the selected process. Read/Write protection allows a process to read, modify, and write to these pages.	0.00001	PERF_COUNTER_RAWCOUNT	4 bytes

Image Space Write Copy	The virtual address space in use by the images being executed by the process. This is the sum of all the address space with this protection allocated by images run by the selected process. Write Copy protection is used when memory is shared for reading but not for writing. When processes are reading this memory, they can share the same memory; however, when a sharing process wants to have read/write access to this shared memory, a copy of that memory is made for writing to.	0.00001	PERF_COUNTER_RAWCOUNT	4 bytes
Mapped Space Exec Read Only	Virtual memory that has been mapped to a specific virtual address (or range of virtual addresses) in the process's virtual address space. Execute/Read Only memory is memory that can be executed as well as read.	0.00001	PERF_COUNTER_RAWCOUNT	4 bytes
Mapped Space Exec Read/Write	Virtual memory that has been mapped to a specific virtual address (or range of virtual addresses) in the process's virtual address space. Execute/Read/Write memory is memory that can be executed by programs as well as read and modified.	0.00001	PERF_COUNER_RAWCOUNT	4 bytes

Object/Counter Name	Description	Default Scale	Counter Type	Counter Size
Process Address Space				
Mapped Space Exec Write Copy	Virtual memory that has been mapped to a specific virtual address (or range of virtual addresses) in the process's virtual address space. Execute Write Copy is memory that can be executed by programs as well as read and written. This type of protection is used when memory needs to be shared between processes. If the sharing processes only read the memory, then they will all use the sane memory. If a sharing process desires write access, then a copy of this memory will be made for that process.	0.00001	PERF_COUNTER_RAWCOUNT	4 bytes
Mapped Space Executable	Virtual memory that has been mapped to a specific virtual address (or range of virtual addresses) in the process's virtual address space. Executable memory is memory that can be executed by programs, but may not be read or written. This type of protection is not supported by all processor types.	0.00001	PERF_COUNTER_RAWCOUNT	4 bytes

Mapped Space No Access	Virtual memory that has been mapped to a specific virtual address (or range of virtual addresses) in the process's virtual address space. No Access protection prevents a process from writing to or reading from these pages and will generate an access violation if either is attempted.	0.00001	PERF_COUNTER_RAWCOUNT	4 bytes
Mapped Space Read Only	Virtual memory that has been mapped to a specific virtual address (or range of virtual addresses) in the process's virtual address space. Read Only protection prevent the contents of these pages from being modified. Any attempts to write or modify these pages will generate an access violation.	0.00001	PERF_COUNTER_RAWCOUNT	4 bytes
Mapped Space Read/Write	Virtual memory that has been mapped to a specific virtual address (or range of virtual addresses) in the process's virtual address space. Read/Write protection allows a process to read, modify, and write to these pages.	0.00001	PERF_COUNTER_RAWCOUNT	4 bytes
Mapped Space Write Copy	Virtual memory that has been mapped to a specific virtual address (or range of virtual addresses) in the process's virtual address space. Write Copy protection is used when memory is shared for reading but not for writing. When processes are reading this memory, they can share the same	0.00001	PERF_COUNTER_RAWCOUNT	4 bytes

Object/Counter Name	Description	Default Scale	Counter Type	Counter Size
Process Address Space				
	memory; however, when a sharing process wants to have write access to this shared memory, a copy of that memory is made.			
Reserved Space Exec Read/Write	Reserved Space is virtual memory that has been reserved for future use by a process, but has not been mapped or committed. Execute/Read Only memory is memory that can be executed as well as read.	0.00001	PERF_COUNTER_RAWCOUNT	4 bytes
Reserved Space Exec Read/Write	Reserved Space is virtual memory that has been reserved for future use by a process, but has not been mapped or committed. Execute/Read/Write memory is memory that can be executed by programs as well as read and modified.	0.00001	PERF_COUNTER_RAWCOUNT	4 bytes
Reserved Space Exec Write Copy	Reserved Space is virtual memory that has been reserved for future use by a process, but has not been mapped or committed. Execute Write Copy is memory that can be executed by programs as well as read and written.	0.00001	PERF_COUNTER_RAWCOUNT	4 bytes

	This type of protection is used when memory needs to be shared between processes. If the sharing processes only read the memory, then they will all use the same memory. If a sharing process desires write access, then a copy of this memory will be made for that process.			
Reserved Space Executable	Reserved Space is virtual memory that has been reserved for future use by a process, but has not been mapped or committed. Executable memory is memory that can be executed by programs, but may not be read or written. This type of protection is not supported by all processor types.	0.00001	PERF_COUNTER_RAWCOUNT	4 bytes
Reserved Space No Access	Reserved Space is virtual memory that has been reserved for future use by a process, but has not been mapped or committed. No Access protection prevents a process from writing to or reading from these pages and will generate an access violation if either is attempted.	0.00001	PERF_COUNTER_RAWCOUNT	4 bytes

Object/Counter Name	Description	Default Scale	Counter Type	Counter Size
Process Address Space				
Reserved Space Read Only	Reserved Space is virtual memory that has been reserved for future use by a process, but has not been mapped or committed. Read Only protection prevents the contents of these pages from being modified. Any attempts to write or modify these pages will generate an access violation.	0.00001	PERF_COUNTER_RAWCOUNT	4 bytes
Reserved Space Read/Write	Reserved Space is virtual memory that has been reserved for future use by a process, but has not been mapped or committed. Read/Write protection allows a process to read, modify, and write to these pages.	0.00001	PERF_COUNTER_RAWCOUNT	4 bytes
Reserved Space Write Copy	Reserved Space is virtual memory that has been reserved for future use by a process, but has not been mapped or committed. Write Copy protection is used when memory is shared for reading but not for writing. When processes are reading this memory, they can share the same memory; however, when a sharing process wants to have read/write access to this shared memory, a copy of that memory is made.	0.00001	PERF_COUNTER_RAWCOUNT	4 bytes

Unassigned Space Exec Read Only	Unassigned Space is mapped and committed virtual memory is used by the process that is not attributable to any particular image being executed by that process. Execute/Read Only memory is memory that can be executed as well as read.	0.00001	PERF_COUNTER_RAWCOUNT	4 bytes
Unassigned Space Exec Read/Write	Unassigned Space is mapped and committed virtual memory is used by the process that is not attributable to any particular image being executed by that process. Execute/Read/Write memory is memory that can be executed by programs as well as read and written.	0.00001	PERF_COUNTER_RAWCOUNT	4 bytes
Unassigned Space Exec Write Copy	Unassigned Space is mapped and committed virtual memory is used by the process that is not attributable to any particular image being executed by that process. Execute Write Copy is memory that can be executed by programs as well as read and written. This type of protection is used when memory needs to be shared between processes. If the sharing processes only read the memory, then they will all use the same memory. If a sharing process desires write access, then a copy of this memory will be made for that process.	0.00001	PERF_COUNTER_RAWCOUNT	4 bytes

Object/Counter Name	Description	Default Scale	Counter Type	Counter Size
Process Address Space				
Unassigned Space Executable	Unassigned Space is mapped and committed virtual memory is used by the process that is not attributable to any particular image being executed by that process. Executable memory is memory that can be executed by programs, but may not be read or written. This type of protection is not supported by all processor types.	0.00001	PERF_COUNTER_RAWCOUNT	4 bytes
Unassigned Space No Access	Unassigned Space is mapped and committed virtual memory is used by the process that is not attributable to any particular image being executed by that process. No Access protection prevents a process from writing to or reading from these pages and will generate ac access violation if either is attempted.	0.00001	PERF_COUNTER_RAWCOUNT	4 bytes
Unassigned Space Read Only	Unassigned Space is mapped and committed virtual memory is used by the process that is not attributable to any particular image being executed by that process. Read Only protection prevents the contents of these pages	0.00001	PERF_COUTNER_RAWCOUNT	4 bytes

	form being modified. Any attempts to write or modify these pages will generate an access violation.			
Unassigned Space Read/Write	Unassigned Space is mapped and committed virtual memory is used by the process that is not attributable to any particular image being executed by that process. Read/Write protection allows a process to read, modify, and write to these pages.	0.00001	PERF_COUNTER_RAWCOUNT	4 bytes
Unassigned Space Write Copy	Unassigned Space is mapped and committed virtual memory is used by the process that is not attributable to any particular image being executed by that process. Write Copy protection is used when memory is shared for reading but not for writing. When processes are reading this memory, they can share the same memory; however, when a sharing process wants to have read/write access to this shared memory, a copy of that memory is made for writing to.	0.00001	PERF_COUNTER_RAWCOUNT	4 bytes
Processor	**The Processor object type includes as instance all processors on the computer.**			

Object/Counter Name	Description	Default Scale	Counter Type	Counter Size
Processor				
% Privileged Time	The percentage of processor time spent in Privileged Mode in non-Idle threads. The Windows NT service layer, the Executive routines, and the Windows NT Kernel execute in Privileged Mode. Device drivers for most devices other than graphics adapters and printers also execute in Privileged Mode. Unlike some early operation systems, Windows NT uses process boundaries for subsystem protection in addition to the traditional protection of User and Privileged modes. These subsystem processes provide additional protection. Therefore, some work done by Windows NT on behalf of your application may appear in other subsystem processes is addition to the Privileged Time in your process.	1	PERF_100NSEC_TIMER	8 bytes
% Processor Time	A percentage of the elapsed time that a processor is busy executing a non-Idle thread. It can be viewed as	1	PERF_100NSEC_TIMER_INV	8 bytes

	the fraction of the time spent doing useful work. Each processor is assigned an Idle thread in the Idle process which consumes those unproductive processor cycles not used by any other threads.			
% User Time	The percentage of processor time spent in User Mode in non-Idle threads. All application code and subsystem code execute in User Mode. The graphics engine, graphics device drivers, printer device drivers, and the window manager also execute in User Mode. Code executing in User Mode cannot damage the integrity of the Windows NT Executive, Kernel, and system device drivers running in Kernel Mode. Unlike some early operation systems, Windows NT uses process boundaries for subsystem protection in addition to the traditional protection of User and Privileged modes. These subsystem processes provide additional protection. Therefore, some work done by Windows NT on behalf of your application may appear in other subsystem processes in addition to the Privileged Time in your process.	1	PERF_100NSEC_TIMER	8 bytes

Object/Counter Name	Description	Default Scale	Counter Type	Counter Size
Processor				
Interrupt/sec	The number of device interrupts the processor is experiencing. A device interrupts the processor when it has completed a task or when it otherwise requires attention. Normal thread execution is suspended during interrupts. An interrupt may case the processor to switch to another, higher priority thread. Clock interrupts are frequent and periodic and create a background of interrupt activity.	0.01	PERF_COUNTER_COUNTER	4 bytes
RAS Port	**The RAS object type handles individual ports of the RAS (Remote Access Service) device on a system.**			
Alignment Errors	The total number of Alignment Errors for this connection. Alignment Errors occur when a byte received is different from the byte expected.	1	PERF_COUNTER_RAWCOUNT	4 bytes
Buffer Overrun Errors	The total number of Buffer Overrun Errors for this connection. Buffer Overrun Errors occur when the software cannot handle the rate at which data is received.	1	PERF_COUNTER_RAWCOUNT	4 bytes

Bytes Received	The number of bytes received total for this connection.	1	PERF_COUNTER_RAWCOUNT	4 bytes
Bytes Received/sec	The number of bytes received per second.	1	PERF_COUNTER_COUNTER	4 bytes
Bytes Transmitted	The number of bytes transmitted total for this connection.	1	PERF_COUNTER_RAWCOUNT	4 bytes
Bytes Transmitted/sec	The number of bytes transmitted per second.	1	PERF_COUNTER_COUNTER	4 bytes
CRC Errors	The total number of CRC Errors for this connection. CRC Errors occur when the frame received contains erroneous data.	1	PERF_COUNTER_RAWCOUNT	4 bytes
Frames Received	The number of data frames received total for this connection.	1	PERF_COUNTER_RAWCOUNT	4 bytes
Frames Received/sec	The number of frames received per second.	1	PERF_COUNTER_COUNTER	4 bytes
Frames Transmitted	The number of data frames transmitted total for this connection.	1	PERF_COUNTER_RAWCOUNT	4 bytes
Frames Transmitted/sec	The number of frames transmitted per second.	1	PERF_COUNTER_COUNTER	4 bytes
Percent Compression In	The compression ratio for bytes being received.	1	PERF_COUNTER_RAWCOUNT	4 bytes
Percent Compression Out	The compression ratio for bytes being transmitted.	1	PERF_COUNTER_RAWCOUNT	4 bytes

Object/Counter Name	Description	Default Scale	Counter Type	Counter Size
Processor				
Serial Overrun Errors	The total number of Serial Overrun Errors for this connection. Serial Overrun Errors occur when the hardware cannot handle the rate at which data is received.	1	PERF_COUNTER_RAWCOUNT	4 bytes
Timeout Errors	The total number of Timeout Errors for this connection. Timeout Errors occur when expected data is not received in time.	1	PERF_COUNTER_RAWCOUNT	4 bytes
Total Errors	The total number of CRC, Timeout, Serial Overrun, Alignment, and Buffer Overrun Errors for this connection.	1	PERF_COUNTER_RAWCOUNT	4 bytes
Total Errors/sec	The total number of CRC, Timeout, Serial Overrun, Alignment, and Buffer Overrun Errors per second.	1	PERF_COUNTER_COUNTER	4 bytes
RAS Total	**The RAS Total object type handles all combined ports of the RAS device on your system.**			
Alignment Errors	The total number of Alignment Errors for this connection. Alignment Errors occur when a byte received is different from the byte expected.	1	PERF_COUNTER_RAWCOUNT	4 bytes

Buffer Overrun Errors	The total number of Buffer Overrun Errors for this connection. Buffer Overrun Errors when the software cannot handle the rate at which data is received.	1	PERF_COUNTER_RAWCOUNT	4 bytes
Bytes Received	The number of bytes received total for this connection.	1	PERF_COUNTER_RAWCOUNT	4 bytes
Bytes Received/sec	The number of bytes received per second.	1	PERF_COUNTER_COUNTER	4 bytes
Bytes Transmitted	The number of bytes transmitted total for this connection.	1	PERF_COUNTER_RAWCOUNT	4 bytes
Bytes Transmitted/sec	The number of bytes transmitted per second.	1	PERF_COUNTER_COUNTER	
CRC Errors	The total number of CRC Errors for this connection. CRC Errors occur when the frame received contains erroneous data.	1	PERF_COUNTER_RAWCOUNT	4 bytes
Frames Received	The number of data frames received total for this connection.	1	PERF_COUNTER_RAWCOUNT	4 bytes
Frames Received/sec	The number of frames received per second.	1	PERF_COUNTER_COUNTER	4 bytes
Frames Transmitted	The number of data frames transmitted total for this connection.	1	PERF_COUNTER_RAWCOUNT	4 bytes

Object/Counter Name	Description	Default Scale	Counter Type	Counter Size
RAS Total				
Frames Transmitted/sec	The number of frames transmitted per second.	1	PERF_COUNTER_COUNTER	4 bytes
Percent Compression In	The compression ratio for bytes being received.	1	PERF_COUNTER_RAWCOUNT	4 bytes
Percent Compression Out	The compression ratio for bytes being transmitted.	1	PERF_COUNTER_RAWCOUNT	4 bytes
Serial Overrun Errors	The total number of Serial Overrun Errors for this connection. Serial Overrun Errors occur when the hardware cannot handle the rate at which data is received.	1	PERF_COUNTER_RAWCOUNT	4 bytes
Timeout Errors	The total number of Timeout Errors for this connection. Timeout Errors occur when expected data is not received in time.	1	PERF_COUNTER_RAWCOUNT	4 bytes
Total Connections	The total number of Remote Access connections.	1	PERF_COUNTER_RAWCOUNT	4 bytes
Total Errors	The total number of CRC, Timeout, Serial Overrun, Alignment, and Buffer Overrun Errors for this connection.	1	PERF_COUNTER_RAWCOUNT	4 bytes

Total Errors/sec	The total number of CRC, Timeout, Serial Overrun, Alignment, and Buffer Overrun Errors per second.	1	PERF_COUNTER_COUNTER	4 bytes
Redirector	**The Redirector is the object that manages network connections to other computers that originate from your own computer.**			
Bytes Received/sec	The rate of bytes coming in to the Redirector from the network. It includes all application data as well as network protocol information such as packet headers.	0.0001	PERF_COUNTER_BULK_COUNT	8 bytes
Bytes Total/sec	The rate the Redirector is processing data bytes. This includes all application and file data in addition to protocol information such as packet headers.	0.0001	PERF_COUNTER_BULK_COUNT	8 bytes
Bytes Transmitted/sec	The rate at which bytes are leaving the Redirector to the network. It includes all application and file data in addition to protocol information such as packet headers	0.0001	PERF_COUNTER_BULK_COUNT	8 bytes
Connects Core	The number of connections you have to servers running the original MS-Net SMB protocol, including MS-Net, XENIX, and VAXs.	1	[ERF_COUNTER_RAWCOUNT	4 bytes

Object/Counter Name	Description	Default Scale	Counter Type	Counter Size
Redirector				
Connects Lan Manager 2.0	Counts connections to LAN Manager 2.0 servers, including LMX servers.	1	PERF_COUNTER_RAWCOUNT	4 bytes
Connects Lan Manager 2.1	Counts connections to LAN Manager 2.1 servers, including LMX servers.	1	PERF_COUNTER_RAWCOUNT	4 bytes
Connects Windows NT	Counts the connections to Windows NT computers.	1	PERF_COUNTER_RAWCOUNT	4 bytes
Current Commands	Counts the number of requests to the Redirector that are currently queued for service. If this number is much larger than the number of network adapter cards installed in the computer, then the network(s) and/or the server(s) being accessed are seriously bottlenecked.	1	PERF_COUNTER_RAWCOUNT	4 bytes
File Data Operations/sec	The rate the Redirector is processing data operations. One operation includes many bytes. You can determine the efficiency of this path by dividing the Bytes/sec by this counter to determine the average number of bytes transferred/operation	1	PERF_COUNTER_COUNTER	4 bytes

File Read Operations/sec	The rate at which applications are asking the Redirector for data. Each call to a file application program interface (API) call counts as one operation.	1	PERF_COUNTER_COUNTER	4 bytes
File Write Operations/sec	The rate at which applications are sending data to the Redirector. Each call to a file system or similar Application Program Interface (API) call counts as one operation.	1	PERF_COUNTER_COUNTER	4 bytes
Network Errors/sec	Counts serious unexpected errors that generally indicate the Redirector and one or more Servers are having serious communication difficulties. For example an SMB (Server Message Block) protocol error will generate a Network Error. These result in an entry in the system Event Log, so look there for details.	1	PERF_COUNTER_COUNTER	4 bytes
Packets/sec	The rate the Redirector is processing data packets. One packet includes many bytes. You can determine the efficiency of this path by dividing the Bytes/sec by this counter to determine the average number of bytes transferred/packet. You can also divide this counter by Operations/sec to determine the average number of packets per operation, another measure of efficiency.	0.1	PERF_COUNTER_BULK_COUNT	8 bytes

Object/Counter Name	Description	Default Scale	Counter Type	Counter Size
Redirector				
Packets Received/sec	The rate at which the Redirector is receiving packets (also called SMB's or Server Message Blocks). Network transmissions are divided into packets. The average number of bytes received in a packet can be obtained by dividing Bytes Received/sec by this counter. Some packets received may not contain incoming data, for example an acknowledgment to a write made by the Redirector would count as an incoming packet.	0.1	PERF_COUNTER_BULK_COUNT	8 bytes
Packets Transmitted/sec	The rate at which the Redirector is sending packets (also called SMB's or Server Message Blocks). Network transmissions are divided into packets. The average number of bytes transmitted in a packet can be obtained by dividing Bytes Transmitted/sec by this counter.	0.1	PERF_COUNTER_BULK_COUNT	8 bytes
Read Bytes Cache/sec	The rate at which applications on your computer are accessing the Cache using the Redirector. Some of these data requests may be	0.0001	PERF_COUNTER_BULK_COUNT	8 bytes

	satisfied by merely retrieving the data from the system Cache on your own computer if it happened to be used recently and there was room to keep it in the Cache. Requests that miss the Cache will cause a page fault.			
Read Bytes Network/sec	The rate at which applications are reading data across the network. For one reason or another the data was not in the system Cache, and these bytes actually came across the network. Dividing this number by Bytes Received/sec will indicate the efficiency of data coming in from the network, since all of these bytes are real application data.	0.0001	PERF_COUNTER_BULK_COUNT	8 bytes
Read Bytes Non-Paging/sec	Those bytes read by the Redirector in response to normal file requests by an application when they are redirected to come from another computer. In addition to file requests, this counter includes other methods of reading across the network such as Named Pipes and Transactions. This counter does not count network protocol information, just application data.	0.0001	PERF_COUNTER_BULK_COUNT	8 bytes

Object/Counter Name	Description	Default Scale	Counter Type	Counter Size
Redirector				
Read Bytes Paging/sec	The rate at which the Redirector is attempting to read bytes in response to page faults. Page Faults are caused by loading of modules (such as programs and libraries), by a miss in the Cache (see Read Bytes Cache/sec), or by files directly mapped into the address space of applications.	0.0001	PERF_COUNTER_BULK_COUNT	8 bytes
Read Operations Random/sec	Counts the rate at which, on a file-by-file basis, reads are made that are not sequential. If a read is made using a particular file handle, and then is followed by another read that is not immediately the contiguous next byte, this counter is incremented by one.	0.1	PERF_COUNTER_COUNTER	4 bytes
Read Packets/sec	The rate at which read packets are being placed on the network. Each time a single packet is sent with a request to read data remotely, this counter is incremented by one.	0.1	PERF_COUNTER_COUNTER	4 bytes

Read Packets Small/sec	The rate at which reads less than one-fourth of the server's negotiated buffer size are made by applications. Too many of these could indicate a waste of buffers on the server. This counter is incremented once for each read. It does not count packets.	0.1	PERF_COUNTER_COUNTER	4 bytes
Reads Denied/sec	The rate at which the server is unable to accommodate requests for Raw Reads. When a read is much larger than the server's negotiated buffer size, the Redirector requests a Raw Read which, if granted, would permit the transfer of the data without lots of protocol overhead on each packet. To accomplish this the server must lock out other requests, so the request is denied if the server is really busy.	1	PERF_COUNTER_COUNTER	4 bytes
Reads Large/sec	The rate at which reads over 2 times the server's negotiated buffer size are made by applications. Too many of these could place a strain on server resources. This counter is incremented once for each read. It does not count packets.	1	PERF_COUNTER_COUNTER	4 bytes

Object/Counter Name	Description	Default Scale	Counter Type	Counter Size
Redirector				
Server Disconnects	Counts the number of times a Server has disconnected your Redirector. See also Server Reconnects.	1	PERF_COUNTER_RAWCOUNT	4 bytes
Server Reconnects	Counts the number of times your Redirector has had to reconnect to a server in order to complete a new active request. You can be disconnected by the Server if you remain inactive for too long. Locally even if all your remote files are closed, the Redirector will keep your connections intact for ten minutes. Such inactive connections are called Dormant Connection. Reconnecting is expensive in time.	1	PERF_COUNTER_RAWCOUNT	4 bytes
Server Sessions	Counts the number of active security objects the Redirector is managing. For example, a Logon to a server followed by a network access to the same server will establish one connection, but two sessions.	1	PERF_COUNTER_RAWCOUNT	4 bytes

Server Session Hung	Counts the number of active sessions that are timed out and unable to proceed due to a lack of response from the remote server.	1	PERF_COUNTER_RAWCOUNT	4 bytes
Write Bytes Cache/sec	The rate at which applications on your computer are writing to the Cache using the Redirector. The data may not leave your computer immediately, but may be retained in the Cache for further modification before being written to the network. This saves network traffic. Each write of a byte into the Cache is counted here.	0.0001	PERF_COUNTER_BULK_COUNT	8 bytes
Write Bytes Network/sec	The rate at which your applications are writing data across the network. Either the system Cache was bypassed, as for Named Pipes of Transactions, or else the Cache wrote the bytes to make room for other data. Dividing this counter by Bytes Transmitted/sec will indicate the 'efficiency' of data written to the network, since all of these bytes are real application data.	0.0001	PERF_COUNTER_BULK_COUNT	8 bytes
Write Bytes Non-Paging/sec	The rate of the bytes that are written by the Redirector in response to normal file outputs by an application when they are redirected to go to another computer. In addition to file requests	0.0001	PERF_COUNTER_BULK_COUNT	8 bytes

Object/Counter Name	Description	Default Scale	Counter Type	Counter Size
Redirector				
	this counter includes other methods of writing across the network such as Named Pipes and Transactions. This counter does not count network protocol information, just application data.			
Write Bytes Paging/sec	The rate at which the Redirector is attempting to write bytes changed in the pages being used by applications. The program data changed by modules (such as programs and libraries) that were loaded over the network are 'paged out' when no longer needed. Outer output pages come from the Cache.	0.0001	PERF_COUNTER_BULK_COUNT	8 bytes
Write Operations Random/sec	The rate at which, on a file-by-file basis, writes are made that are not sequential. If a write is made using a particular file handle, and then is followed by another write that is not immediately the next contiguous byte, this counter is incremented by one.	0.1	PERF_COUNTER_COUNTER	4 bytes

Write Packets/sec	The rate at which writes are being sent to the network. Each time a single packet is sent with a request to write remote data, this counter is incremented by one.	0.1	PERF_COUNTER_COUNTER	4 bytes
Writes Denied/sec	The rate at which the server is unable to accommodate requests for Raw Writes. When a write is much larger that the server's negotiated buffer size, the Redirector requests a Raw Write which, if granted, would permit the transfer of the data without lots of protocol overhead on each packet. To accomplish this the server must lock out other requests, so the request is denied if the server is really busy.	1	PERF_COUNTER_COUNTER	4 bytes
Writes Large/sec	The rate at which writes are made by applications that are over 2 times the server's negotiated buffer size. Too many of these could place a strain on server resources. This counter is incremented once for each write; it counts writes, not packets.	1	PERF_COUNTER_COUNTER	4 bytes

Object/Counter Name	Description	Default Scale	Counter Type	Counter Size
Server	**Server is the process that interfaces the services from the local computer to the network services.**			
Blocking Requests Rejected	The number of times the server has rejected blocking SMBs (Server Message Blocks) due to insufficient count of free work items. Indicate whether the maxworkitem or minfreeworkitems server parameters may need tuning.	1	PERF_COUNTER_COUNTER	4 bytes
Bytes Received/sec	The number of bytes the server has received from the network. Indicate how busy the server is.	0.0001P	PERF_COUNTER_BULK_COUNT	8 bytes
Bytes Total/sec	The number of bytes the server has sent to and received from the network. This value provides an overall indication of how busy the server is.	0.0001	PERF_COUNTER_BULK_COUNT	8 bytes
Bytes Transmitted/sec	The number of bytes the server has sent on the network. Indicates how busy the server is.	0.0001	PERF_COUNTER_BULK_COUNT	8 bytes
Context Block Queue Time	The average time, in milliseconds, a work context block sat on the server's FSP queue waiting for the server to act on the request.	1	PERF_AVERAGE_BULK	8 bytes

Context Blocks Queued/sec	The rate at which work context blocks had to be placed on the server's FSP (Free System Page) queue to await server action.	0.1	PERF_COUNTER_COUNTER	4 bytes
Errors Access Permissions	The number of times opens on behalf of clients have failed with STATUS_ ACCESS_DENIED. Can indicate whether somebody is randomly attempting to access files in hopes of getting at something that was not properly protected.	1	PERF_COUNTER_RAWCOUNT	4 bytes
Errors Granted Access	The number of times accesses to file opened successfully were denied. Can indicate attempts to access files without proper access authorization.	1	PERF_COUNTER_RAWCOUNT	4 bytes
Errors Logon	The number of failed attempts to the server. Can indicate whether password-guessing programs are being used to crack the security on the server.	1	PERF_COUNTER_RAWCOUNT	4 bytes
Errors System	The number of times an internal Server error was detected. Unexpected errors usually indicate a problem with the Server.	1	PERF_COUNTER_RAWCOUNT	4 bytes

Object/Counter Name	Description	Default Scale	Counter Type	Counter Size
Server				
File Directory Searches	The number of searches for files currently active in the server. Indicates current server activity.	1	PERF_COUNTER_RAWCOUNT	4 bytes
Files Open	The number of files currently opened in the server. Indicates current server activity.	1	PERF_COUNTER_RAWCOUNT	4 bytes
Files Opened Total	The number of successful open attempts performed by the server of behalf of clients. Useful in determining the amount of file I/O and the overhead for path-based operations.	0.001	PERF_COUNTER_RAWCOUNT	4 bytes
Pool Nonpaged Bytes	The number of bytes of non-pageable computer memory the server is currently using. Can help in determining good values for the MaxNonpagedMemoryUsage parameter.	0.0001	PERF_COUNTER_RAWCOUNT	4 bytes
Pool Nonpaged Failures	The number of times allocations from nonpaged pool have failed. Indicates that the computer's physical memory is too small.	1	PERF_COUNTER_COUNTER	4 bytes

Pool Nonpaged Peak	The maximum number of bytes of nonpaged pool the server has had in use at any one point. Indicates how much physical memory the computer should have.	0.0001	PERF_COUNTER_RAWCOUNT	4 bytes
Pool Paged Bytes	The number of bytes of pageable computer memory the server is currently using. Can help in determining good values for the MaxNonpagedMemoryUsage parameter.	0.0001	PERF_COUNTER_RAWCOUNT	4 bytes
Pool Paged Failures	The number of times allocations from paged pool have failed. Indicates that the computer's physical memory of pagefile is too small.	1	PERF_COUNTER_RAWCOUNT	4 bytes
Pool Paged Peak	The maximum number of bytes of paged pool the server has had allocated. Indicates the proper sizes of the Page File(s) and physical memory.	0.0001	PERF_COUNTER_RAWCOUNT	4 bytes
Server Sessions	The number of sessions currently active in the server. Indicates current server activity.	1	PERF_COUNTER_RAWCOUNT	4 bytes
Sessions Errored Out	The number of sessions that have been closed due to unexpected error conditions. Indicated how frequently network problems are causing dropped sessions on the server.	1	PERF_COUTNER_RAWCOUNT	4 bytes

Object/Counter Name	Description	Default Scale	Counter Type	Counter Size
Server				
Sessions Forced Off	The number of sessions that have been forced to log off. Can indicate how many sessions were forced to log off due to logon time constraints.	1	PERF_COUNTER_RAWCOUNT	4 bytes
Sessions Logged Off	The number of sessions that have terminated normally. Useful in interpreting the Sessions Times Out and Sessions Errored Out statistics.	1	PERF_COUNTER_RAWCOUNT	4 bytes
Sessions Timed Out	The number of sessions that have been closed due to their idle time exceeding the autodisconnect parameter for the server. Shows whether the autodisconnect setting is helping to conserve resources.	1	PERF_COUNTER_RAWCOUNT	4 bytes
Work Item Shortages	The number of times STATUS_DATA_NOT_ACCEPTED was returned at receive indication time. This occurs when no work item is available or can be allocated to service the incoming request. Indicates whether the InitWorkItems of MaxWorkItems parameters may need tuning.	1	PERF_COUNTER_COUNTER	4 bytes

System	**The System object includes those counters that apply to all processors on the computer collectively. These counters collectively represent the activity of all processors on the computer.**			
% Total Privileged Time	The average percentage of time spent in Privileged mode by all the processors. On a multiprocessor system, if all processors are always in Privileged mode this is 100%, if all the processors are 50% in Privileged mode this is 50%, and if one-fourth of the processors are in Privileged mode this is 25%. When a Windows NT system service is called, the service will often run in Privileged Mode in order to gain access to system-private data. Such data is protected from access by threads executing in User Mode. Calls to the system may be explicit, or they may be implicit such as when a page fault or an interrupt occurs. Unlike some early operating systems, Windows NT uses process boundaries for subsystem protection in addition to the traditional protection of User and Privileged modes. These	1	PERF_100NSEC_TIMER	8 bytes

Object/Counter Name	Description	Default Scale	Counter Type	Counter Size
System				
	subsystem processes provide additional protection. Therefore, some work done by Windows NT on behalf of an application may appear in other subsystem processes in addition to the Privileged Time in the application process.			
% Total Processor Time	The average percentage of time that all the processors on the system are busy executing non-idle threads. On a multiprocessor system, if all processors are always busy this is 100%, if all processors are 50% busy this is 50%, and if one-fourth of the processors are busy this is 25%. It can be viewed as the fraction of the time spent doing useful work. Each processor is assigned an Idle thread in the Idle process which consumes those unproductive processor cycles not used by any other threads.	1	PERF_100NSEC_TIMER_INV	8 bytes

% Total User Time	The average percentage of time in User mode by all processors. On a multiprocessor system, if all processors are always in User mode this is 100%, if all the processors are 50% in User mode this is 50%, and if one-fourth of the processors are in User mode this is 25%. Applications execute in User Mode, as do subsystems like the window manager and the graphics engine. Code executing in User Mode cannot damage the integrity of the Windows NT Executive, Kernel, and device drivers running in Kernel Mode. Unlike some early operating systems, Windows NT uses process boundaries for subsystem protection in addition to the traditional protection of User and Privileged modes. These subsystem processes provide additional protection. Therefore, some work done by Windows NT on behalf of an application may appear in other subsystem processes in addition to the Privileged Time in the application process.	1	PERF_100NSEC_TIMER	8 bytes
Alignment Fixups/sec	The rate of alignment faults fixed by the system.	1	PERF_COUNTER_COUNTER	4 bytes

Object/Counter Name	Description	Default Scale	Counter Type	Counter Size
System				
Context Switches/sec	The rate of switches form one thread to another. Thread switches can occur either inside of a single process or across processes. A thread switch may be caused either by one thread asking another for information, or by a thread being preempted by another, higher-priority thread becoming ready to run. Unlike some early operating systems, Windows NT uses process boundaries for subsystem protection in addition to the traditional protection of User and Privileged modes. These subsystem processes provide additional protection. Therefore, some work done by Windows NT on behalf of an application may appear in other subsystem processes in addition to the Privileged Time in the application process. Switching to the subsystem process causes one Context Switch in the application thread. Switching back causes another Context Switch in the subsystem thread.	0.01	PERF__COUNTER_COUNTER	4 bytes

Exception Dispatches/sec Index	The rate of processor exceptions dispatched by the system.	0	PERF_COUNTER_COUNTER	4 bytes
File Control Bytes/sec	An aggregate count of the number of bytes transferred for all file system operations that are neither reads nor writes. These operations usually include file system control requests or requests for information about device characteristics or status.	1	PERF_COUNTER_COUNTER	4 bytes
File Data Operations/sec	The rate at which the computer is issuing Read and Write operations to file system devices. It does not include File Control Operations.	1	PERF_COUNTER_COUNTER	4 bytes
File Read Bytes/sec	An aggregate of the bytes transferred for all the file system read operations on the computer.	0.0001	PERF_COUNTER_BULK_COUNT	8 bytes
File Read Operations/sec	An aggregate of all the file system read operations on the computer.	1	PERF_COUNTER_COUNTER	4 bytes
File Write Bytes/sec	An aggregate of the bytes transferred for all the file system write operations on the computer.	0.0001	PERF_COUNTER_BULK_COUNT	8 bytes
File Write Operations/sec	An aggregate of all the file system write operations on the computer.	1	PERF_COUNTER_COUNTER	4 bytes
Floating Emulations/sec	The rate of floating emulations performed by the system.	1	PERF_COUNTER_COUNTER	4 bytes

Object/Counter Name	Description	Default Scale	Counter Type	Counter Size
System				
Processor Queue Length	The instantaneous length of the processor queue in units of threads. This counter is always 0 unless you are also monitoring a thread counter. All processors use a single queue in which thread wait for processor cycles. This length does not include the threads that are currently executing. A sustained processor queue length greater than two generally indicates processor congestion. This is an instantaneous count, not an average over the time interval.	10	PERF_COUNTER_RAWCOUNT	4 bytes
System Calls/sec	The frequency of call to Windows NT system service routines. These routines perform all of the basic scheduling and synchronization of activities on the computer and provide access to non-graphical devices, memory management, and name space management.	0.1	PERF_COUNTER_COUNTER	4 bytes
System Up Time	Total time (in seconds) that the computer has been operational since it was last started.	0.00001	PERF_ELAPSED_TIME	8 bytes

Total Interrupts/sec	The rate the computer is receiving and servicing hardware interrupts. Some devices that may generate interrupts are the system timer, the mouse, data communication lines, network interface cards, and other peripheral devices. This counter provides an indication of how busy these devices are on a computer-wide basis. See also Processor: Interrupt/sec.	0.01	PERF_COUNTER_COUNTER	4 bytes
TCP Object	**The TCP Object Type includes those counters that describe the rate at which TCP Segments are received and sent by a certain process using the TCP protocol. In addition, it describes the number of TCP connections that are in each of the possible TCP connection states.**			
Connection Failures	The number of times TCP connections have made a direct transition to the CLOSED state from the SYN-SENT state or the SYN-RCVD state, plus the number of times TCP connections have made a direct transition to the LISTEN state from the SYN-RCVD state.	1	PERF_COUNTER_RAWCOUNT	4 bytes

Object/Counter Name	Description	Default Scale	Counter Type	Counter Size
TCP Object				
Connections Active	The number of times TCP connections have made a direct transition to the SYN-SENT state from the CLOSED state.	1	PERF_COUNTER_RAWCOUNT	4 bytes
Connections Established	The number of TCP connections for which the current state is either ESTABLISHED or CLOSE-WAIT.	1	PERF_COUNTER_RAWCOUNT	4 bytes
Connections Passive	The number of times TCP connections have made a direct transition to the SYN-RCVD state from the LISTEN state.	1	PERF_COUNTER_RAWCOUNT	4 bytes
Connections Reset	The number of times TCP connections have made a direct transition to the CLOSED state from either the ESTABLISHED state or the CLOSE-WAIT state.	1	PERF_COUNTER_RAWCOUNT	4 bytes
Segments Received/sec	The rate at which segments are received, including those received in error. This count includes segments received on currently established connections.	0.1	PERF_COUNTER_COUNTER	4 bytes
Segments Retransmitted/sec	The rate at which segments are retransmitted, that is, segments transmitted containing one or more previously transmitted bytes.	0.1	PERF_COUNTER_COUNTER	4 bytes

Segments Sent/sec	The rate at which segments are sent, including those on current connections, but excluding those containing only retransmitted bytes.	0.1	PERF_COUNTER_COUNTER	4 bytes
Segments/sec	The rate at which TCP segments are sent or received using the TCP protocol.	0.1	PERF_COUNTER_COUNTER	4 bytes
Telephony Object	**The Telephony Object includes counters for monitoring telephone-related equipment (e.g. telephones, telephone lines, and modems) that use the Windows NT TAPI interface.**			
Active Lines	The number of telephone lines serviced by this computer that are currently active.	1	PERF_COUNTER_RAWCOUNT	4 bytes
Active Telephones	The number of telephone devices that are currently being monitored.	1	PERF_COUNTER_RAWCOUNT	4 bytes
Client Apps	The number of applications that are currently using telephony services.	1	PERF_COUNTER_RAWCOUNT	4 bytes
Current Incoming Calls	Current incoming calls being serviced by this computer.	1	PERF_COUNTER_RAWCOUNT	4 bytes
Current Outgoing Calls	Current outgoing calls being serviced by this computer.	1	PERF_COUNTER_RAWCOUNT	4 bytes
Incoming Calls/sec	The rate of incoming calls answered by this computer.	1	PERF_COUNTER_RAWCOUNT	4 bytes

Object/Counter Name	Description	Default Scale	Counter Type	Counter Size
TCP Object				
Lines	The number of telephone lines serviced by this computer.	1	PERF_COUNTER_RAWCOUNT	4 bytes
Outgoing Calls/sec	The rate of outgoing calls made by this computer.	1	PERF_COUNTER_RAWCOUNT	4 bytes
Telephone Devices	The number of telephone devices serviced by this computer.	1	PERF_COUNTER_RAWCOUNT	4 bytes
Thread Object	**The Thread Object is the entity that actually requests the execution of instructions on a processor. Every running process has at least one thread.**			
% Privileged Time	The percentage of elapsed time that this thread has spent executing code in Privileged Mode. When a Windows NT system service is called, the service will often run in Privileged Node in order to gain access to system-private data. Such data is protected from access by threads executing in User Mode. Calls to the system may be explicit, or they may be implicit such as when a page fault or an interrupt occurs. Unlike some early operating systems, Windows NT uses process	1	PERF_100NSEC_TIMER	8 bytes

	boundaries for subsystem protection in addition to the traditional protection of User and Privileged modes. These subsystem processes provide additional protection. Therefore, some work done by Windows NT on behalf of an application may appear in other subsystem processes in addition to the Privileged Time in the application process.			
% User Time	The percentage of elapsed time that this thread has spent executing code in User Mode. Applications execute in User Mode, as do subsystems like the window manager and the graphics engine. Code executing in User Mode cannot damage the integrity of the Windows NT Executive, Kernel, and device drivers. Unlike some early operating systems, Windows NT uses process boundaries for subsystem protection in addition to the traditional protection of User and Privileged modes. These subsystem processes provide additional protection. Therefore, some work done by Windows NT on behalf of an application may appear in other subsystem processes in addition to the Privileged Time in the application process.	1	PERF_100NSEC_TIMER	8 bytes

Object/Counter Name	Description	Default Scale	Counter Type	Counter Size
Thread Object				
Context Switches/sec	The rate of switches from one thread to another. A thread switch may be caused either by one thread asking another for information, or by a thread being preempted by another, higher-priority thread becoming ready to run. Unlike some early operating systems, Windows NT uses process boundaries for subsystem protection in addition to the traditional protection of User and Privileged modes. These subsystem processes provide additional protection. Therefore, some work done by Windows NT on behalf of an application may appear in other subsystem processes in addition to the Privileged Time in the application process. Switching to the subsystem process causes one Context Switch in the application thread. Switching back causes another Context Switch in the subsystem thread.	0.01	PERF_COUNTER_COUNTER	4 bytes

Elapsed Time	The total elapsed time (in seconds) this thread has been running.	0.0001	PERF_ELAPSED_TIME	8 bytes
ID Process	The unique identifier of this process. ID Process numbers are reused, so they only identify a process for the lifetime of that process.	1	PERF_COUNTER_RAWCOUNT	4 bytes
ID Thread	The unique identifier of this thread. ID Thread numbers are reused, so they only identify a thread for the lifetime of that thread.	1	PERF_COUNTER_RAWCOUNT	4 bytes
Priority Base	The current base priority of this thread. The system may raise the thread's dynamic priority above the base priority if the thread is handling user input, or lower it toward the base priority of the thread if the thread becomes compute-bound.	1	PERF_COUNTER_RAWCOUNT	4 bytes
Priority Current	The current dynamic priority of this thread. The system may raise the thread's dynamic priority above the base priority if the thread is handling user input, or lower it toward the base priority if the thread becomes compute bound.	1	PERF_COUNTER_RAWCOUNT	4 bytes
Start Address	Starting virtual address for this thread.	1	PERF_COUNTER_RAWCOUNT	4 bytes

Object/Counter Name	Description	Default Scale	Counter Type	Counter Size
Thread Object				
Thread State	The current state of the thread. It is 0 for Initialized, 1 for Ready, 2 for running, 3 for Standby, 4 for Terminated, 5 for Wait, 6 for Transition, 7 for Unknown. A Running thread is using a processor; a Standby thread is about to use one. A Ready thread wants to use a processor but is waiting for a processor because none are free. A thread in Transition is waiting for a resource in order to execute, such as waiting for its execution stack to be paged in from disk. A Waiting thread has no use for the processor because it is waiting for a peripheral operation to complete or a resource to become free.	1	PERF_COUNTER_RAWCOUNT	4 bytes
Thread Wait Reason	Thread Wait Reason is only applicable when the thread is in the Wait state (see Thread State). It is 0 or 7 when the thread is waiting for the Executive, 1 or 8 for a Free Page, 2 or 9 for a	1	PERF_COUNTER_RAWCOUNT	4 bytes

	Page In, 3 or 10 for a Pool Allocation, 4 or 11 for an Execution Delay, 5 or 12 for a Suspended condition, 6 or 13 for a User Request, 14 for an Event Pair High, 15 for an Event Pair Low, 16 for an LPC Receive, 17 for an LPC Reply, 18 for Virtual Memory, and 19 for a Page Out (20 and higher are not currently assigned values). Event Pairs are used to communicate with protected subsystems.			
Threads Details	**The Threads Details object contains the thread counters that are time consuming to collect.**			
Datagrams No Port/sec	The rate of Received UDP datagrams for which there was no application at the destination port.	0.1	PERF_COUNTER_COUNTER	4 bytes
Datagrams Received Errors	The number of received UDP datagrams that could not be delivered for reasons other than the lack of an application at the destination port.	1	PERF_COUNTER_RAWCOUNT	4 bytes
Datagrams Received/sec	The rate at which UDP datagrams are delivered to UDP users.	0.1	PERF_COUNTER_COUNTER	4 bytes
Datagrams Sent/sec	The rate at which UDP datagrams are sent from the entity.	0.1	PERF_COUNTER_COUNTER	4 bytes

Object/Counter Name	Description	Default Scale	Counter Type	Counter Size
Threads Details				
Datagrams/sec	The rate at which UDP datagrams are sent or received by the entity.	0.1	PERF_COUNTER_COUNTER	4 bytes
WINS Server	**The WINS Server object type includes counters related to the WINS (Windows Internet Name Service) Server service**			
Failed Queries/sec	The total number of Failed Queries/sec.	1	PERF_COUNTER_BULK_COUNT	4 bytes
Failed Releases/sec	The total number of Failed Releases/sec.	1	PERF_COUNTER_BULK_COUNT	4 bytes
Group Conflicts/sec	The rate at which group registration received by the WINS server resulted in conflicts with records in the database.	1	PERF_COUNTER_BULK_COUNT	4 bytes
Group Registration/sec	The rate at which group registration is received by the WINS server.	1	PERF_COUNTER_BULK_COUNT	4 bytes
Group Renewals/sec	The rate at which group renewals are received by the WINS server.	1	PERF_COUNTER_BULK_COUNT	4 bytes
Queries/sec	The rate at which queries are received by the WINS server.	1	PERF_COUNTER_BULK_COUNT	4 bytes

Releases/sec	The rate at which releases are received by the WINS server.	1	PERF_COUNTER_BULK_COUNT	4 bytes
Successful Queries/sec	The total number of Successful Queries/sec.	1	PERF_COUNTER_BULK_COUNT	4 bytes
Successful Releases/sec	The total number of Successful Releases/sec.	1	PERF_COUNTER_BULK_COUNT	4 bytes
Total Number of Conflicts/sec	The sum of Unique and Group conflicts per second. This is the total rate at which conflicts were seen by the WINS server.	1	PERF_COUNTER_BULK_COUNT	4 bytes
Total Number of Registrations/sec	The sum of the Unique and Group registrations per second. This is the total rate at which registration are received by the WINS server.	1	PERF_COUNTER_BULK_COUNT	4 bytes
Total Number of Renewals/sec	The sum of the Unique and Group renewals per second. This is the total rate at which renewals are received by the WINS server.	1	PERF_COUNTER_BULK_COUNT	4 bytes
Unique Conflicts/sec	The rate at which unique registrations/renewals received by the WINS server resulted in conflicts with records in the database.	1	PERF_COUNTER_BULK_COUNT	4 bytes
Unique Registrations/sec	The rate at which unique registration are received by the WINS server.	1	PERF_COUNTER_BULK_COUNT	4 bytes
Unique Renewals/sec	The rate at which unique renewals are received by the WINS server.	1	PERF_COUNTER_BULK_COUNT	4 bytes

Index

B

C

D

E

F

G

H

I

J

K

L

M

N

O

Q

R

T

U

V

W

X

Z

IDG BOOKS WORLDWIDE, INC.
END-USER LICENSE AGREEMENT

READ THIS. You should carefully read these terms and conditions before opening the software packet(s) included with this book ("Book"). This is a license agreement ("Agreement") between you and IDG Books Worldwide, Inc. ("IDGB"). By opening the accompanying software packet(s), you acknowledge that you have read and accept the following terms and conditions. If you do not agree and do not want to be bound by such terms and conditions, promptly return the Book and the unopened software packet(s) to the place you obtained them for a full refund.

1. **License Grant.** IDGB grants to you (either an individual or entity) a nonexclusive license to use one copy of the enclosed software program(s) (collectively, the "Software") solely for your own personal or business purposes on a single computer (whether a standard computer or a workstation component of a multiuser network). The Software is in use on a computer when it is loaded into temporary memory (RAM) or installed into permanent memory (hard disk, CD-ROM, or other storage device). IDGB reserves all rights not expressly granted herein.
2. **Ownership.** IDGB is the owner of all right, title, and interest, including copyright, in and to the compilation of the Software recorded on the disk(s) or CD-ROM ("Software Media"). Copyright to the individual programs recorded on the Software Media is owned by the author or other authorized copyright owner of each program. Ownership of the Software and all proprietary rights relating thereto remain with IDGB and its licensers.
3. **Restrictions On Use and Transfer.**

   (a) You may only (i) make one copy of the Software for backup or archival purposes, or (ii) transfer the Software to a single hard disk, provided that you keep the original for backup or archival purposes. You may not (i) rent or lease the Software, (ii) copy or reproduce the Software through a LAN or other network system or through any computer subscriber system or bulletin-board system, or (iii) modify, adapt, or create derivative works based on the Software.

   (b) You may not reverse engineer, decompile, or disassemble the Software. You may transfer the Software and user documentation on a permanent basis, provided that the transferee agrees to accept the terms and conditions of this Agreement and you retain no copies. If the Software is an update or has been updated, any transfer must include the most recent update and all prior versions.

4. **Restrictions On Use of Individual Programs.** You must follow the individual requirements and restrictions detailed for each individual program in Appendix A of this Book. These limitations are also contained in the individual license agreements recorded on the Software Media. These limitations may include a requirement that after using the program for a specified period of time, the user must pay a registration fee or discontinue use. By opening the Software packet(s), you will be agreeing to abide by the licenses and restrictions for these individual programs that are detailed in Appendix A and on the Software Media. None of the material on this Software Media or listed in this Book may ever be redistributed, in original or modified form, for commercial purposes.

5. **Limited Warranty.**

   (a) IDGB warrants that the Software and Software Media are free from defects in materials and workmanship under normal use for a period of sixty (60) days from the date of purchase of this Book. If IDGB receives notification within the warranty period of defects in materials or workmanship, IDGB will replace the defective Software Media.

   (b) IDGB AND THE AUTHOR OF THE BOOK DISCLAIM ALL OTHER WARRANTIES, EXPRESS OR IMPLIED, INCLUDING WITHOUT LIMITATION IMPLIED WARRANTIES OF MERCHANTABILITY AND FITNESS FOR A PARTICULAR PURPOSE, WITH RESPECT TO THE SOFTWARE, THE PROGRAMS, THE SOURCE CODE CONTAINED THEREIN, AND/OR THE TECHNIQUES DESCRIBED IN THIS BOOK. IDGB DOES NOT WARRANT THAT THE FUNCTIONS CONTAINED IN THE SOFTWARE WILL MEET YOUR REQUIREMENTS OR THAT THE OPERATION OF THE SOFTWARE WILL BE ERROR FREE.

   (c) This limited warranty gives you specific legal rights, and you may have other rights that vary from jurisdiction to jurisdiction.

6. **Remedies.**

   (a) IDGB's entire liability and your exclusive remedy for defects in materials and workmanship shall be limited to replacement of the Software Media, which may be returned to IDGB with a copy of your receipt at the following address: Software Media Fulfillment Department, Attn.: *Optimizing Windows NT*, IDG Books Worldwide, Inc., 7260 Shadeland Station, Ste. 100, Indianapolis, IN 46256, or call 1-800-762-2974. Please allow three to four weeks for delivery. This Limited Warranty is void if failure of the Software Media has resulted from accident, abuse, or misapplication. Any replacement Software Media will be warranted for the remainder of the original warranty period or thirty (30) days, whichever is longer.

(b) In no event shall IDGB or the author be liable for any damages whatsoever (including without limitation damages for loss of business profits, business interruption, loss of business information, or any other pecuniary loss) arising from the use of or inability to use the Book or the Software, even if IDGB has been advised of the possibility of such damages.

(c) Because some jurisdictions do not allow the exclusion or limitation of liability for consequential or incidental damages, the above limitation or exclusion may not apply to you.

7. **U.S. Government Restricted Rights.** Use, duplication, or disclosure of the Software by the U.S. Government is subject to restrictions stated in paragraph (c)(1)(ii) of the Rights in Technical Data and Computer Software clause of DFARS 252.227-7013, and in subparagraphs (a) through (d) of the Commercial Computer – Restricted Rights clause at FAR 52.227-19, and in similar clauses in the NASA FAR supplement, when applicable.

8. **General.** This Agreement constitutes the entire understanding of the parties and revokes and supersedes all prior agreements, oral or written, between them and may not be modified or amended except in a writing signed by both parties hereto that specifically refers to this Agreement. This Agreement shall take precedence over any other documents that may be in conflict herewith. If any one or more provisions contained in this Agreement are held by any court or tribunal to be invalid, illegal, or otherwise unenforceable, each and every other provision shall remain in full force and effect.

my2cents.idgbooks.com

Register This Book — And Win!

Visit **http://my2cents.idgbooks.com** to register this book and we'll automatically enter you in our monthly prize giveaway. It's also your opportunity to give us feedback: let us know what you thought of this book and how you would like to see other topics covered.

Discover IDG Books Online!

The IDG Books Online Web site is your online resource for tackling technology — at home and at the office.

Ten Productive and Career-Enhancing Things You Can Do at www.idgbooks.com

1. Nab source code for your own programming projects.
2. Download software.
3. Read Web exclusives: special articles and book excerpts by IDG Books Worldwide authors.
4. Take advantage of resources to help you advance your career as a Novell or Microsoft professional.
5. Buy IDG Books Worldwide titles or find a convenient bookstore that carries them.
6. Register your book and win a prize.
7. Chat live online with authors.
8. Sign up for regular e-mail updates about our latest books.
9. Suggest a book you'd like to read or write.
10. Give us your 2¢ about our books and about our Web site.

Not on the Web yet? It's easy to get started with *Discover the Internet*, at local retailers everywhere.

Installation Instructions

To view the contents of the CD-ROM, follow these steps:

1. Insert the CD-ROM into your CD-ROM drive.
2. If you have CD-ROM AutoPlay enabled, your default Web browser will launch and automatically load the CD's main page.
3. To learn more about each piece of software, choose the link to the software and read through the documentation and any specific installation notes for that application.
4. To install the software for a particular platform, click on the Install Software! link for the appropriate machine type (Alpha or Intel). This will start the installation routine or self-extracting installer.
5. For programs that use self-extracting installers, you will first need to extract the installation files to a temporary directory on your hard disk (such as `C:\TEMP`), and then run the main installation program which is extracted to this directory.
6. After clicking on a program's installation link, your browser may ask if you wish to open the file or save it to disk. If this happens, choose Open to launch the installer or self-extracting archive utility.

Follow these alternate steps if you have AutoPlay disabled:

1. Launch your browser manually.
2. Point your browser to the `INDEX.HTML` file in the root directory of the CD-ROM.
3. If you wish to re-enable CD-ROM AutoPlay, change the data for the following registry value from 0 (disabled) to 1 (enabled): `HKEY_LOCAL_MACHINE\SYSTEM\CurrentControlSet\Services\Cdrom\Autorun`.

You must have System Administrator privileges to run most of the programs on this CD-ROM.

See Appendix A for more information about the contents of the CD-ROM.